LEO BAECK INSTITUTE
YEAR BOOK

1998

The first issue of *Die Deborah*, a journal addressed to the "daughters of Israel" which became the most important Jewish German-language periodical in nineteenth-century America.

By courtesy of the American Jewish Archives, Cincinnati

LEO BAECK INSTITUTE

YEAR BOOK
1998

XLIII

SECKER & WARBURG · LONDON
PUBLISHED FOR THE INSTITUTE
LONDON · JERUSALEM · NEW YORK

FOUNDER EDITOR: ROBERT WELTSCH (1956–1978)
EDITOR EMERITUS: ARNOLD PAUCKER (1970–1992)

Editorial office: Leo Baeck Institute
4 Devonshire Street, London W1N 2BH

THE LEO BAECK INSTITUTE
was founded in 1955 for the study of the history and culture of German-speaking Central European Jewry

The Institute is named in honour of the man who was the last representative figure of German Jewry in Germany during the Nazi period

LEO BAECK INSTITUTE

JERUSALEM: 33 Bustanai Street
LONDON: 4 Devonshire Street, W1
NEW YORK: 129 East 73rd Street

© Leo Baeck Institute 1998
Published by Martin Secker & Warburg Limited
Random House, 20 Vauxhall Bridge Road, London SW1V 2SA
ISBN 0 436 22078 4
Photoset by Wilmaset Limited, Birkenhead, Wirral
Printed in Great Britain by Mackays of Chatham PLC

J. A. S. Grenville
EDITOR

Julius Carlebach
ASSOCIATE EDITOR

Shayla Walmsley
Gabriele Rahaman
ASSISTANT EDITORS

ADVISORY BOARD

Great Britain:	Marianne Calmann	London
	David Cesarani	London/Southampton
	Ian Kershaw	Sheffield
	Jeremy Noakes	Exeter
	Peter Pulzer	Oxford
	Bernard Wasserstein	Oxford
Germany:	Werner T. Angress	Berlin
	Wolfgang Benz	Berlin
	Ursula Büttner	Hamburg
	Michael Graetz	Heidelberg
	Arno Herzig	Hamburg
	Stefi Jersch-Wenzel	Berlin
	Monika Richarz	Hamburg
	Reinhard Rürup	Berlin
United States:	Christopher Browning	Tacoma
	Vicki Caron	Brown
	Peter Gay	Yale
	Marion Kaplan	New York
	Hillel J. Kieval	Washington
	Steven Lowenstein	Los Angeles
	Michael A. Meyer	Cincinnati
	Jehuda Reinharz	Brandeis
	Ismar Schorsch	New York
	David Sorkin	Madison
	Fritz Stern	New York
	Guy Stern	Wayne State
Israel:	Steven Aschheim	Jerusalem
	Avraham Barkai	Lehavoth Habashan
	Evyatar Friesel	Jerusalem
	Hagit Lavski	Jerusalem
	Robert Liberles	Beersheva
	Paul Mendes-Flohr	Jerusalem
	Chaim Schatzker	Haifa
	Shulamit Volkov	Tel-Aviv
	Robert S. Wistrich	Jerusalem
	Moshe Zimmermann	Jerusalem

Contents

Preface by John Grenville and Julius Carlebach IX

I. RELIGION AND JEWISH TEACHING

MAREN R. NIEHOFF: Zunz's Concept of *Haggadah* as an Expression of Jewish Spirituality 3
AVI BERNSTEIN-NAHAR: Hermann Cohen's Teaching Concerning Modern Jewish Identity (1904–1918) 25
MARIA T. BAADER: From "the Priestess of the Home" to "the Rabbi's Brilliant Daughter" Concepts of Jewish Womanhood and Progressive Germanness in *Die Deborah* and the *American Israelite*, 1854–1900 47
JACOB HABERMAN: Kaufmann Kohler and his Teacher Samson Raphael Hirsch 67
ANDREAS GOTZMANN: The Dissociation of Religion and Law in Nineteenth-Century German-Jewish Education 103

II. ANTISEMITISM BEFORE NATIONAL SOCIALISM

GÜNTER REGNERI: Salomon Neumann's Statistical Challenge to Treitschke. The Forgotten Episode that Marked the End of the *Berliner Antisemitismusstreit*.. 129
JÜRGEN MATTHÄUS: German *Judenpolitik* in Lithuania during the First World War 155
DAVID T. MURPHY: FAMILIAR ALIENS: GERMAN ANTISEMITISM AND European Geopolitics in the Interwar Era 175

III. JEWS AND THE FATHERLAND IN THE TWENTIETH CENTURY

ELISABETH ALBANIS: Ostracised for Loyalty: Ernst Lissauer's Propaganda Writing and its Reception 195
JONATHAN SKOLNIK: Dissimilation and the Historical Novel: Hermann Sinsheimer's *Maria Nunnez* 225

IV. PERSECUTION AND RESCUE UNDER NATIONAL SOCIALISM

MICHAEL WILDT: Before the "Final Solution". The *Judenpolitik* of the SD 1935–1938.. 241
MOSHE AYALON: "Gegenwaertige Situation": Report on the Living Conditions of the Jews in Germany. A Document and Commentary .. 271
ANNE KLEIN: Conscience, Conflict and Politics. The Rescue of Political Refugees from Southern France to the United States, 1940–1942.. .. 287

V. THE DEBATE ABOUT GERMAN-JEWISH RELATIONSHIPS CONTINUED

STEVEN E. ASCHHEIM: German History and German Jewry: Boundaries, Junctions and Interdependence 315
EVYATAR FRIESEL: Jewish and German-Jewish Historical Views. Problems of a new Synthesis 323

VI. MEMOIR

FRANCIS L. CARSTEN: From Berlin to London 339

VII.   BIBLIOGRAPHY FOR 1997 351

VIII.   LIST OF CONTRIBUTORS 501

IX.   INDEX 505

Illustrations

Die Deborah	Frontispiece
Kaufmann Kohler	between pp. 70–71
Das Land OberOst	between pp. 166–167
Ernst Lissauer	between pp. 198–199
False papers	between pp. 294–295
Emergency Rescue Committee	between pp. 306–307

Preface

We live in a multicultural, ethnically and religiously diverse society. When the immigrants first arrived, the relatively homogeneous societies in which they settled viewed them as aliens, as not "German", "British" or "French". Their difference – real and, far more importantly, imagined – was met with intolerance and in some cases still is. The degree of non-acceptance increased when the immigrant was seen not only as "racially" different, but also as following a different religious faith from the majority. But ethnically and culturally homogeneous societies no longer exist in the West or, indeed, scarcely anywhere in the modern world. What lessons can be learnt from the past that may help to overcome prejudice and encourage progress?

A better understanding of the history of the Jews in the Diaspora has much to contribute. It is not simply a history of religious conflict and persecution, although it is certainly that too. It is also part of the history of multicultural and multi-ethnic societies, the history of relationships, of assimilation, of successes and failures, of toleration and hatred, and of progress and regression. There remains a large gap in the writing of national history, which has not found a way to treat the histories of its minorities as an integral part of a national history. Instead, books and journals focusing on such relationships are regarded as "specialised", of concern to particular interest groups. There are some exceptions to this generalisation. The Holocaust is recognised as the darkest chapter not only of Jewish but of German history: a failure of society.

If anyone excelled in analysing the failure of German society which led to the catastrophe of German Jewry, it was Eva G. Reichmann, the noted historian and sociologist who died on 16th September 1998 at almost 102. In her *magnum opus Hostages of Civilisation* she had demonstrated that it was an immature German nationalism to which a progressive German-Jewish community fell victim. Eva Reichmann, the last survivor of the group which formed the Leo Baeck Institute, was an inspiration to a whole generation of students of German-Jewish history. She is mourned by us all.

There is less popular concern for the centuries of German-Jewish interaction before the Holocaust. This is not a uniquely German problem. In the United States it has taken decades to integrate the history of African-Americans into the mainstream, but today American histories are probably further ahead in this respect than European ones.

The aim of the Leo Baeck Year Book is to make a major contribution to the study of multicultural and ethnic history. Until the Second World War, in Western Europe the Jews were the single most important, and by far the largest, religious minority not *completely* accepted as an indistinguishable segment by these societies, despite the progress made. Obstacles to such acceptance had remained, as they remain even now for many minorities. That is why the scholars who research and who contribute to the Year Book are making such an important contribution in studying the culture of a minority and its social relationships. To many, the Year Book is still a "special interest" publication in one of many corners of academic learning. The fact is that it is not. If it were, it would hardly be flourishing after forty-five years, with a global readership of Jews and non-Jews (the latter by now in the majority).

The cost of producing the Year Book and its important and unique bibliography (both to be offered on CD ROM) is high. In this respect it has the same experience as other academic year books. It receives a subsidy to enable it to widen its readership through libraries and individual subscription. Subscriptions have most notably shown a rapid increase in Germany. To subsidise the Year Book we continue to rely on contributions made by the *Bundesministerium des Innern* and the *Ständige Konferenz der Kultusminister der Länder in der BRD*; through better and more difficult times of state finances, they have unfailingly maintained their support. We also rely on the loyalty of old members and on attracting new members from a younger generation.

The editors would particularly like to thank their two assistant editors, Shayla Walmsley and Gabriele Rahaman. When the Bibliography was short-staffed, the longest-serving assistant editor *emeritus*, Sylvia Gilchrist, set aside her plans to provide essential help, while the editorial staff has again been able to draw on the experience of the editor *emeritus*, Arnold Paucker. Thanks are also due to the two long-standing bibliographers, Barbara Suchy and Annette Pringle, and to Janet Langmaid for the skill and care with which she compiles the General Index.

Julius Carlebach *John Grenville*

Religion and Jewish Teaching

Zunz's Concept of Haggadah as an Expression of Jewish Spirituality[1]

BY MAREN R. NIEHOFF

Rabbinic *Haggadah* played an important role in Zunz's overall concept of Judaism. He saw these traditional stories as a distinctly Jewish form of spirituality which would, he hoped, provide a vibrant alternative to both assimilation and Orthodoxy.[2] The key to Zunz's understanding of *Haggadah* lies in the sixty-one sermons which he delivered in 1820–1821 in Berlin. While Zunz himself attributed considerable importance to his sermons and carefully preserved them, only a few of them have ever been published. Most of them are held in the Jewish National Library in Jerusalem, where they remain unnoticed.[3] Consequently, there developed the mistaken impression that the sermons are both intellectually insignificant and irrelevant to Zunz's scholarship proper.

The sermons are important because they reveal Zunz's intellectual development from his initial position, close to Enlightenment thought, to his mature views, which shaped the *Wissenschaft des Judentums*.[4] This path is not documented elsewhere since Zunz was, during that formative period, too busy as a journalist

---

[1] This paper is based on an article published in Hebrew, in *Tarbiz* 54 (1995), pp. 423–459. It is part of a broader study of ideas of *Haggadah* in the nineteenth century which I hope to present soon in book form. I wish to thank the Department of Manuscripts of the Jewish National and University Library in Jerusalem for help and permission to use unpublished material for this article. I also thank the Leo Baeck Institutes of New York and Jerusalem, and the Memorial Foundation for Jewish Culture, for granting me, respectively, a David Baumgardt Memorial Fellowship and postdoctoral fellowships in support of my research into the notions of *Haggadah* in nineteenth-century German Judaism. I also thank the audiences of the following institutions for their response to lectures based on this article: the Faculty Seminar of the Center for Israel and Jewish Studies, Columbia University; the Leo Baeck Institute, New York; The Jewish Theological Seminary of America, New York; Hochschule für Jüdische Studien, Heidelberg; and Evangelisches Seminar der Universität Tübingen. I thank the following for their helpful comments on a draft of this article: Professors Menahem Cahana, Moshe Idel, Hermann Lichtenberger, Michael A. Meyer, Ismar Schorsch and Daniel Schwartz.

[2] For a description of the dilemma of the Jew in modern Germany, see especially Michael A. Meyer, *The Origins of the Modern Jew. Jewish Identity and European Culture in Germany, 1749–1824*, Detroit 1967.

[3] Only Alexander Altmann seems to have investigated Zunz's sermons in his 'Zur Frühgeschichte der jüdischen Predigt in Deutschland. Leopold Zunz als Prediger', in *LBI Year Book VI* (1961), pp. 3–59.

[4] Leopold Zunz became familiar with the values of the Enlightenment at the Samsonsche Freischule in Wolfenbüttel, which he describes in *Zunz Buch*, Zunz Archive C13, 14–24 (also partly published in Fritz Bamberger, *Das Buch Zunz. Künftigen ehrlichen Leuten gewidmet*, Berlin 1932). See also Leopold Zunz, *Samuel Meyer Ehrenberg. Inspektor der Samsonschen Freischule zu Wolfenbüttel*, Braunschweig 1854, especially pp. 20–23.

and as the head of a school to express himself in other academic work. The framework of a sermon moreover suggested to Zunz a freer and more speculative style than he would have allowed himself in a scholarly work.

The sermons enable us to distinguish three phases in Zunz's intellectual development up to 1832. In the first phase, in 1817, his position is marked by groping explorations in the fields of homiletics and academics. While Zunz, the preacher, sees himself as a kind of prophet inculcating the ethics of the Enlightenment, the author of *Etwas über die rabbinische Literatur* outlines an ambitious plan for the encyclopedic study of Judaism, which still lacks an historicist dimension. The second phase, the period of the sermons between 1820–1821, is marked by a transition from his Enlightenment position to an historico-phenomenological conceptualisation of Judaism. This new approach is based on notions of Christian theology to which he was introduced by his admired teacher, Wilhelm Markus Leberecht de Wette, and his friend, Johann Gottfried Eichhorn.[5] The sermons indicate that Zunz increasingly conceived prophecy to be the spiritual-national essence of early Judaism. He furthermore defined prophecy as the Torah's abstract ethics as they were transmitted by spiritual exegesis. These views of prophecy largely rested on Johann Gottfried Herder's work, which Zunz at this point embraced to the extent of accepting also its christological biases.[6] Zunz thus thought that the destruction of the Second Temple signified the end both of Jewish nationality and of prophecy, the latter of which is said to have continued only among the nations.[7]

Finally, Zunz's masterpiece, *Die gottesdienstlichen Vorträge der Juden, historisch entwickelt*, published in 1832, integrates his earlier views into a positive appreciation of Judaism throughout the ages. He now argues that rabbinic *Haggadah* expresses the revived spirit of Jewish prophecy, which he traces up to Jewish liberalism of his own time. The dynamics of *Haggadah* are moreover described in terms of the contemporary Romantic discourse, highlighting especially the notions of "organic" and "saga". These developments show that Zunz achieved his historical-spiritual conceptualisation of Judaism on the basis of theology. Indeed, his notion of *Haggadah* as an expression of Jewish spirituality is a response to the challenge of Christian Romanticism.

---

[5]According to the *Zunz Buch*, p. 82, in 1816–1817 Zunz attended de Wette's lectures on the Bible and Pseudepigrapha. He also paid de Wette personal visits. Zunz later thanked him for having introduced him to Bible criticism (letter of 1st July 1838, MGWJ 60 [1916], pp. 258–259) and describes him as his "vertrautester Umgang" at the university (letter of 11th July 1817, published in Nahum Glatzer, *Leopold Zunz. Jude – Deutscher – Europäer. Ein jüdisches Gelehrtenschicksal des 19. Jahrhunderts in Briefen an Freunde*, Tübingen 1964 [Schriftenreihe wissenschaftlicher Abhandlungen des Leo Baeck Instituts 11], p. 86). See also his letters of 12th November 1815, 13th October 1818 and 1st January 1819). Zunz visited Eichhorn in 1818 in Göttingen (*Zunz Buch*, p. 30).

[6]Herder's importance for the young Zunz is indicated, *inter alia*, by Zunz's very early acquisition of his works (*Zunz Buch*, p. 83) and by Adelheid Zunz's mention of her husband's great familiarity with Herder (letters of March 1835, in Glatzer, *Zunz*, p. 178). See also Ismar Schorsch, 'From Wolfenbüttel to Wissenschaft. The Divergent Paths of Isaac Marcus Jost and Leopold Zunz', *LBI Year Book XX* (1977), especially pp. 127–128.

[7]For a parallel example of initial acceptance of Christian customs and their subsequent re-evaluation, see Michael A. Meyer, 'Christian Influence on Early German Reform Judaism', in *Studies in Jewish Bibliography, History and Literature in Honor of I. Edward Kiev*, New York 1971, pp. 289–305.

ZUNZ THE ENTHUSIASTIC PREACHER AND BURGEONING SCHOLAR (1817)

Zunz's intellectual starting point is marked by two early writings which reflect different aspects of his personality: his first sermon, 'Predigt über Religiosität',[8] and his programmatic article *Etwas über die rabbinische Literatur*, published in 1818.[9] Despite the difference in genre and tone, both pieces indicate Zunz's affiliation with the Enlightenment and his lack of historical perspective.

The title of Zunz's sermon echoes the universal spirit of the Enlightenment, according to which rational morality informs all religions. However, addressing the subject of religiosity rather than simply religion, Zunz emphasises the emotions and *Gemüth* – two popular subjects among the Romantically-inspired preachers of the early nineteenth century. For Zunz spiritual authenticity, as opposed to merely external ritual, is particularly important. While generally criticising Orthodoxy, Zunz's sermon – like those of many of his contemporaries – uses some rabbinic sayings in support of universal ethics.[10] It is, moreover, interesting that Zunz clearly identifies with the Prophet Isaiah, whose warnings he reapplies within his own context of moral sentiment.

The article *Etwas über die rabbinische Literatur* reveals another aspect of Zunz's personality. He demanded here that Jewish literature, including rabbinic sources, medieval philosophy and Enlighenment works, be recognised as a subject of academic research. One of its opening sentences has often been interpreted as a sign that Zunz already implemented at this early stage Friedrich Carl von Savigny's Romantic historiography.[11] Zunz demanded that the spirit of Jewish culture should be investigated by a study of its language and literature:

> "He who regards the literature of a nation as the entrance to a comprehensive understanding of its cultural development, truly approaches this temple of the gods with reverence. [He will understand] how the culture's essence takes shape in every moment as the result of the given and the added, namely the internal and the external; [he will furthermore understand] how fate, climate, ethics, religion and chance interact either in a friendly or hostile fashion; and finally [he will understand] how the present emerges as the necessary result of all the past phenomena."[12]

Zunz's lecture notes of the summer semester in 1817 reveal that the above sentences are directly based on Savigny's course on the history of law.[13] Savigny distinguished in this context between authentic *Volkskultur* and accidental features which were added during the course of history. He coined the term "internal

---

[8]In Leopold Zunz, *Gesammelte Schriften von Dr. Zunz*, ed. by Curatorium Zunzstiftung, vol. 1, 1875, pp. 1–31. A copy of this article with handwritten notes by Zunz is preserved in the Zunz Archive, E2.
[9]Leopold Zunz, *Etwas über die rabbinische Literatur*, Berlin 1818.
[10]Regarding his criticism of Orthodoxy, see especially Zunz, 'Geist der Rabbiner' (1819), reprinted by Ludwig Geiger in *Allgemeine Zeitung des Judentums* 80 (1916), pp. 413–414. Regarding the contemporary use of rabbinic sayings, see Maren R. Niehoff, 'Jacob Weil's Contribution to a Modern Concept of *Haggadah*', *LBI Year Book XLI* (1996), pp. 21–50.
[11]See especially Fritz Bamberger, 'Zunz's Conception of History', in *Proceedings of the American Academy for Jewish Research* 11 (1941), pp. 11–25.
[12]Zunz, *Etwas über rabbinische Literatur*, pp. 6–7.
[13]Zunz Archive C12, especially pp. 305–333.

history of law", for the history of the people's spirit as reflected in its institutions, decisions and general behaviour. Zunz, in the above-quoted passage, undoubtedly describes the aims of Jewish research in terms of Savigny's theory. He distinguishes between the external and the internal development of Jewish culture and proposes a clearly historical perspective.

It is equally significant, however, that the rest of Zunz's article does not follow Savigny's phenomenology. Indeed, the disciplines of Jewish research which he proposes neither contribute to a deeper understanding of the spirit of Judaism nor provide the tools to distinguish between characteristic and accidental features. Zunz instead suggests an encyclopedic study of Judaism. He is interested in pure linguistics and grammar, while disregarding Herder's pre-Romantic approach, which saw language as a reflection of culture. Zunz's lack of interest in Herder's theory of language is all the more significant because his teacher, de Wette, had already embraced it in his inaugural lecture at the University of Berlin.[14] A similar picture emerges from his discussion of ethics and theology, both of which he interprets in the universal terms of the Enlightenment. Rather than dwelling on the national dimension of these disciplines, he stresses the individual and pedagogy.

While Zunz does not implement Savigny's historical method, he alludes to another, distinctly Christian, historiography which was subsequently to become important for his work. He suggests that post-biblical Jewish literature is devoid of creative powers and that it reflects the political and spiritual decline of Judaism[15] – a theory which had been used for centuries by Christian theologians to "prove" that the early Church inherited Israel's election.[16]

ZUNZ THE PREACHER INVESTIGATES JUDAISM (1820–1821)

Zunz's sermons cover a formative phase in his intellectual development. They are initially universalistic and Romantic, later reflecting a historico-phenomenological conceptualisation of Judaism. The main feature of this transformation is Zunz's changing view of biblical prophecy. Whereas he initially regards it as a timeless feeling of religiosity, he increasingly views it as a form of ancient spirituality characteristic of the biblical prophets and subsequently also of the exegetes of Scripture.

Zunz's third sermon, 'Begeisterung', was delivered on 3rd June 1820 and deals with the spirit of prophecy in the context of Numbers XI:25–29.[17] The biblical passage describes prophecy in clearly communal and national terms: God causes the prophetic spirit to rest on the seventy elders and Moses hopes that "all the

---

[14]Wilhelm M. L. de Wette, *Aufforderung zum Studium der Hebräischen Sprache und Literatur*, Jena–Leipzig 1805, pp. 13-25.
[15]Zunz, *Etwas über rabbinische Literatur*, p. 3.
[16]Regarding Christian biases in modern German research on ancient Judaism, see also Christhard Hoffmann, *Juden und Judentum im Werk deutscher Althistoriker des 19. und 20. Jahrhunderts*, Leiden 1988, pp. 9–11.
[17]Leopold Zunz, *Predigten*, Berlin 1923, pp. 3–14. The manuscript has not been preserved.

Lord's people be prophets". Although Zunz opens his sermon with a general explanation of the biblical scene, thus showing greater historical sensitivity than in his first sermon, he conspicuously mostly ignores the national context. He speaks instead of a universal prophetic feeling, which dwells in everybody and enables the individual to elevate himself above the material condition of his life. Prophetic enthusiasm does not even "acknowledge any difference of religion".[18] Prophecy is not, in other words, particularly connected to Judaism and instead belongs to any religious person. Zunz's emphasis on the individual is particularly significant in view of Herder's essay on the spirit of Hebrew prophecy, which uses precisely the same biblical passage to prove that prophecy is the distinct characteristic of Israel.[19]

Zunz defines prophecy in this sermon as "holy enthusiasm" prompted by God who inspired him (the prophet), and made him get up and teach his brothers the word of God. God's spirit penetrates the enthusiast, whose soul is excited and feels an "enthusiasm for virtue".[20] These terms reflect the ethical principles of the Enlightenment nuanced by a new Romantic tone in Christian theology as developed especially by de Wette. Indeed, Zunz's lecture notes reveal that in 1817 he had already heard de Wette speak about the prophets as "enthusiastic individuals" who are filled with the spirit of God "and outwardly announce divine ideas through enthusiastic speech".[21] Zunz's view of prophecy as an expression of every individual also reflects his teacher's Romantic phenomenology. Parallel to de Wette, Zunz contrasts the enthusiasm for moral spirituality with the "bestiality" of everyday life and stresses the function of man's inner voice: "Should there, however, be no prophet, the unknowable of our inner self can teach us to sense a vocation which does not belong to the world of the senses."[22] Yet in comparison to de Wette's, Zunz's sermon maintains a more moralising tendency. His earlier commitment to the Enlightenment clearly prevents him from sacrificing ethics to emotions.[23]

The draft of Zunz's sermon 'Vom Daseyn Gottes' (28th October 1820) betrays the first signs of a more historical approach.[24] Zunz explains here the different ways by which God's existence can be recognised. After mentioning rationalistic and Romantic arguments, he also refers to history as a teacher of theology. He stresses that he does not mean political but religious history, namely "God's finger" in human affairs. The notion of divine providence thus becomes his first

---

[18] *Ibid.*, p. 7: "... kennt nicht den Unterschied der Glaubensgenossen und der Umstände".
[19] Johann G. Herder, 'Vom Geist der ebräischen Poesie', in *Herders Werke*, ed. by Theodor Matthias, vol. 3, Leipzig–Vienna 1903, p. 265.
[20] The quotations are from pp. 12, 8, 5 and 7 respectively.
[21] Zunz Archive C12, pp. 173–174.
[22] Leopold Zunz, 'Begeisterung', p. 7: "Ist aber kein Prophet da, so kann uns das Unergründliche unseres Innern belehren, eine Bestimmung zu ahnen, die keine Sinnenwelt erfüllt"; the previous quotation is from *ibid.*, p. 5; cf. Wilhelm M.L. de Wette, *Biblische Dogmatik*, Berlin 1818 (1st edn. 1813), pp. 13–20.
[23] See also Zunz's tenth sermon, which is entitled 'Licht' and refers to the radiance of knowledge and morality (Zunz Archive D9).
[24] Zunz Archive D9.

framework for an historico-spiritual conceptualisation of Judaism. Zunz's theological orientation is particularly noteworthy because his friends at the *Culturverein* had already applied secular Hegelian models to the study of Judaism in 1818.

Zunz's increasingly historical outlook crystalises in the discussions of prophecy in his subsequent sermons. His sermon on the 'Sendung der Propheten' (30th December 1820) represents an important turning point in this development.[25] He focuses here on Moses's central role in shaping biblical ethics and describes the figure and his achievements in terms of Herder's theology. He introduces Moses as a "man of God" and a "divine man" – titles which had become common after Herder's essay on Moses.[26] Zunz then points to the enormous gap which supposedly existed between Moses and his people, "who lived in a dark and shameful period". This gap between the divine messenger and his people was a prominent theme in contemporary Christian scholarship, which sought to show that Moses's mission was not met by Israel and had therefore passed on to Christianity. Indeed, Zunz describes Moses as a lonely fighter for spiritual ethics, who begins a line of prophets who will later continue his task despite many adversaries:

> "Therefore he took a numerous people on his shoulders, so that this people should be elevated through him – therefore he fasted, worked and lived in the desert, therefore he gave up the pleasures of life for innumerable hardships, therefore he fought, struggled, taught, and suffered; therefore he dies (lonely) on the threshold of his career, so that (the great) perishes in his (greater) work, so that a seed of happiness and virtue will issue from his deeds, and so that men like him will rise (after him) to proclaim God."[27]

In the course of his sermon Zunz identifies three groups against which Moses's fight is directed: the innocent who lack knowledge of virtue, the scribes (*Schriftgelehrten*) or – according to Zunz's amendment – the Pharisees, who "do not forget to extinguish the little light still left among the people" and, finally, the superstitious.[28] These three groups are said to oppose divine ethics and to corrupt the people. Moses's struggle against them is described in particularly dramatic and Romantic terms:

> "And the divinely inspired – how will he in the desert entreat let his eyes wander without consolation and turn upwards to heaven his yearning heart, which searches in vain upon the earth, imploring from heaven salvation for corrupted human beings, [from there] knowledge for the deaf, light for the blind the dazzled, recovery for the diseased, and but in the mourning solitude to which his grief drove him, God reveals

---

[25] *Ibid.*
[26] Herder, *Poesie*, pp. 242ff.
[27] Leopold Zunz, 'Sendung des Propheten', p. 2: "Denn darum wars dass er ein zahlreiches Volk auf seine Schultern lud, dass dieses Volk s.[ich] d.[urch] ihn erheb.[en] solle – darum hat er gefastet u. gemacht u. in Wüsten gelebt, darum d.[ie] Freuden des Lebens hingegeben für zahllose Plagen, darum gekämpft, gestritten, gelehrt u. geduldet, darum ist er an der Grenze d.[er] Laufbahn (einsam) gestorben, dass (der grosse) in sein.[em] grösseren Werke untergehe, dass aus sein.[en] Thaten die Saat u. Glückseligk.[eit] hervorgehe u. e.[ine] Tugend, u. dass Männer wie er (nach ihm) aufstehen, um Gott zu verkünden."
[28] *Ibid.*, pp. 3–4.

Himself with enthusiasm, and there ~~he decides~~ (God makes him take) decisions to return to his brethren, to teach them and be active, ~~and if this is not for the living generation, may it be for the coming~~ (and not to forget the innocent and the minors on account of the sinners). Yet the nobility ~~of his new appointment~~ of such a mission, while inspiring him, also makes him despair."[29]

The two passages describe Moses's prophetic mission. Two themes are prominent: the struggle of the lonely leader and the degree of the people's sinfulness. The great number of amendments which Zunz added to these passages indicate both the sensitivity of these subjects and the process of Zunz's thinking. The first theme – the struggle of the individual against society – was highly popular in the literature of the *Sturm und Drang*, which recognised it as an expression of genius.[30] Zunz stresses the solitude of Moses, who flees alone into the desert. An hypostasising nuance is added when solitude is described as a companion who sympathises with the hero's suffering. The sentimental tone here exceeds earlier dramatic descriptions of Moses, such as Jacob Weil's.[31]

Zunz's emendations, moreover, reveal his wavering concerning the degree of emphasis to be given to Moses's individuality. In the first passage, the word "lonely" is added to the description of Moses's death. In the second passage changes are introduced regarding Moses's decision to assume leadership. According to the initial wording, Moses himself takes the decision, while the final version has God commanding him to do so. This change indicates a transition from a more Romantic orientation towards greater faithfulness to the biblical story.

Zunz illuminates his hero's mood and personal development. Moses is described as being filled with pain, excited about his mission, and as roaming around in his tireless search for truth and salvation. Moses's ascetic tendencies are also highlighted: he fasts, renounces material pleasures and takes upon himself a considerable amount of suffering in order to fulfil his prophetic mission. Later in the sermon it becomes clear that Zunz considers suffering a distinct characteristic of the prophets. In light of these extraordinary pains it is surprising indeed that Zunz relates positively to Moses's premature death. After briefly mentioning that Moses's task had not yet been fulfilled, he justifies his death by the fact that he thus prepared the way for his successors.

Zunz's emphasis on Moses's suffering and his positive interpretation of his early death both become understandable in light of Herder's work. Herder

---

[29] *Ibid.*, p. 7: "Und der Gotterfüllte ... wie wird er in der Wüste ~~dem flehen~~ trostlos umherschauen u. das sehnsüchtige Herz, das auf der Erde vergebens sucht, zu dem Himmel hinaufwenden, von da Rettung zu erflehen den sinkenden Menschen, Erkenntnis den Tauben, Licht den~~bl~~verblendeten, Genesung den Erkrankten, ~~und aber in der trauernden Einsamkeit, wohin der Schmerz ihn gejagt, da offenbart s.[ich] ihm d.[er] Herr in Begeisterung, und dafasst er~~ (heisst ihn) Entschlüsse (fassen) wiederumzukehren z.[u] sein.[en] Brüdern, z.[u] lehren u. z. wirken, u. ~~ist für d.[as] lebende nicht, sei es für d.[as] werdende Geschlecht~~) und über die Sünder nicht die Schuldlosen und Unmündigen zu vergessen). Aber die Hoheit ~~seines Amtes~~ solchen Auftrages, dieselbe ihn begeistert, die macht ihn ~~wieder~~ zugleich verzagt."

[30] See especially Gerhard Kaiser, *Aufklärung, Empfindsamkeit, Sturm und Drang*, Munich 1979 (3rd edn.), pp. 177–193; Ferdinand J. Schneider, *Die Deutsche Dichtung der Geniezeit*, Stuttgart 1952, pp. 1–44.

[31] See Nichoff, 'Jacob Weil's Contribution', pp. 27-31.

stresses Moses's hardship and defines suffering as an inherent feature of prophecy. He even presents the prophets as personifications of suffering – a feature which is apparently meant to foreshadow the life of Jesus. Herder moreover expresses considerable satisfaction about the timing of Moses's death, claiming that it was "wise and good that he did not see the completion [of his mission]".[32] He suggests that Moses in this way avoided participation in wars, which would have compromised his reputation and high standard of ethics.

The second theme is the nature and fate of Israel. Zunz regards Israel as an opponent of Moses because it does not sufficiently support his prophetic mission and spiritual elevation. The emendations to the text of the sermon indicate Zunz's hesitations concerning the degree of both the people's sinfulness and Moses's success in enlightening them. The first passage suggests that Moses failed in his own generation and died with hopes for a better future. There is even an allusion that the future fulfilment of Moses's mission might actually have been its original intent. At the beginning of the second passage Zunz refers in the same style to Moses's failure, implying that his programme is meant for a future generation. This idea is, however, replaced by the plea "not to forget the innocent and minors on account of the sinners". Zunz thus remembers that the whole people is not lost and that some might indeed have been prepared for Moses's mission. The same tendency is implied in his replacement of the word "blind" by "dazzled". Zunz begins with the assumption of the people's complete and irreversable corruption, and later concedes that they may have only been temporarily blinded.

Despite these stylistic changes it remains obvious that Zunz criticises the people for its materialism and refusal to accept Moses's mission. This overall negative evaluation is also based on Herder's views of Moses as a transitory figure with only partial success. Herder calls the people in this context "barbaric and stubborn". He moreover claims that the subsequent prophets achieved the full completion of Moses's mission, which is now redefined as love of God.[33] It is noteworthy that Zunz accepts Herder's views, including their Christian biases, to a far greater extent than his young predecessor Jacob Weil. Although the latter also discussed Moses's lonely leadership, he avoided Christian concepts and stressed instead that Moses succeeded so completely that all subsequent generations are judged by the degree of their loyalty to his laws.

Zunz moreover presents Moses's prophecy as spiritual leadership characteristic of early Judaism. While he mentions Moses's exemplary and influential actions, his legislative and literary activities are not discussed, despite their weight in Herder's and Weil's treatments of Moses. This significant omission reflects Zunz's lack of appreciation for Scripture. He still conceives Judaism to be a religion in the Enlightenment sense, namely as a system of universal and abstract ethics rather than as a religion of the Book.

---

[32]Herder, *Poesie*, p. 248.
[33]*Ibid.*, p. 242.

The sermon 'Sendung der Propheten' further points to the direction of Zunz's subsequent intellectual development. Dealing with factors opposing prophecy, Zunz mentions the priests, whom he presents in the following harsh words: "priestly despotism shouts: curse him [the prophet], he liberates the enchained spirit".[34] Zunz thus identifies prophecy with free spirituality, while the priests symbolise the petrification of Judaism.[35] This extreme picture is also based on Herder, who contrasted Aaron with Moses as two types of religiosity. Whereas Moses stands for authentic religion and ethics, Aaron represents false religiosity, enticing the people to external and petty forms of worship.

At the end of the sermon Zunz points to subsequent generations, about which he is rather optimistic:

> "But the situation is not so bleak, my faithful ones, take comfort, it is not so bleak! When ~~the prophet~~ the divinely inspired has triumphantly gone through all the doubts and struggles and is now devoted to God, he proclaims the truth and the Eternal One is in covenant with him. Truth victoriously proceeds through the centuries and countries. No period is so miserable that the truth cannot ~~meet~~ find some receptive souls. No period so ill that it is unable to bear any enthusiasm and devotion."[36]

In his concluding remarks Zunz refers not only to the generations immediately following Moses, but also to his own time. It emerges that he now regards prophecy as a phenomenon of moral enthusiasm which is historically rooted in the figure of Moses but which continues to inspire every subsequent generation. Zunz hopes that the original prophecy will be fulfilled in the near future.

Zunz's sermons between 'Sendung der Propheten' and 'Simchat Torah' (9th March 1822) reveal his increasing tendency towards an historico-textual conceptualisation of Judaism. In his sermon on 'Die Widersacher der Wahrheit' (20th January 1821) he already speaks about the study of the biblical text. Truth is no longer regarded as a universal idea of rational ethics, but is now said to "teach the law" and to involve specific commandments to be learned by studying.

In his important sermon on the 'Krummer und grader Wandel' (19th May 1821) Zunz speaks for the first time about the "education of humanity" – a phrase which had become famous through Gotthold Ephraim Lessing's essay of that title. Moses Mendelssohn had significantly rejected Lessing's Christian historiography, according to which Judaism represents the infant stage of human religiosity, while Christianity is the more advanced stage which replaced the

---

[34]Zunz, 'Sendung des Propheten', p. 8: "... verflucht ihn, ruft der Priesterdespotismus, er befreit den gefesselten Geist."
[35]In other sermons, such as 'Der Priesterdienst vor Gott' and 'Pflichten des Lehramtes', Zunz presents the priests as spiritual leaders. In this context, however, he uses them as typologies without any reference to ancient Judaism.
[36]Zunz, 'Sendung des Propheten', pp. 13–14: "Aber so arm ist es nicht, m.[eine] Tr.[euen], tröstet Euch, so ist es nicht! Wenn d.[er] Prophet Gotterfüllte d.[urch] alle Zweifel und Kämpfe siegreich hindurchgegangen und nun in Gott ergeben die Wahrheit verkündet, so ist d.[er] Ewige mit ihm im Bunde, u. durch die Länder u. Jahrhunderte schreitet die Wahrheit fort. Keine Zeit ist so verarmt, dass d.[ie] Wahrheit nicht in ihr empfängliche Gemüter ~~antreff~~ auffinden könnte ... keine so krank dass sie gar nichts mehr von Begeisterung u. Aufschwung z.[u] ertrag.[en] vermöchte".

childhood of man.[37] Mendelssohn instead defended the idea of eternal and unchanging religious truths, which are implemented with more or less success in different places and at different times. Zunz departs from this position, which he himself had earlier embraced, and now accepts the notion of progress. This progress is manifest, he argues, in the transition from the Torah as a crude legal text to the prophets' spiritual-ethical interpretation of it:

> "Thus, my faithful ones, does God educate humanity. He does not explain the greatness of virtue and its splendour and larger context to peoples who are still raw and rude. He instead commands them to act rightfully in specific cases and leaves it to the progress of humanity, and wise visionary prophets of later times to reveal the large context of everything noble and to investigate the way of dispositions, which are the basis of everything good, and to acquire the whole wealth of the spirit and the mind. They alone can acquire truly beautiful deeds, songs of ethical law. Therefore Scripture so often commands action and leaves it to our reflection to discover the way of its implementation. Scripture speaks with such concision and brevity, that the command of duty appears insignificant, although a noble disposition must be presupposed for its implementation. But we should not immerse ourselves (in gaping) at the visible letter (which is finite, so) that we fail to recognise the invisible infinite spirit ruling over it."[38]

In this passage Zunz alludes to the Bible as an example of the simple legal system appropriate for the level of a raw and undeveloped people. He agrees in this respect with Eichhorn, who had, on the basis of Herder, argued that the Pentateuch was a "document on the education of the human mind from its first youth onwards". Eichhorn even describes Israel with the same adjective as Zunz, namely as "raw".[39] More importantly, Zunz defines the progress of humanity in terms of a movement towards spiritual exegesis, which makes explicit the underlying moral principles rather than dealing with the details of behaviour. He attributes central importance to the later prophets, who are for him the real

---

[37] Moses Mendelssohn, 'Jerusalem. Oder Über die Religiöse Macht im Judenthum', in *Moses Mendelssohns Gesammelte Schriften nach Originaldrucken und Handschriften*, ed. by G.B. Mendelssohn, vol. 3, Leipzig 1843 (1st edn. 1783), pp. 317–318. See also Alexander Altmann, *Moses Mendelssohn. A Biographical Study*, London 1973, pp. 540–542; Hans Leibeschütz, *Das Judentum im deutschen Geschichtsbild von Hegel bis Max Weber*, Tübingen 1967 (Schriftenreihe wissenschaftlicher Abhandlungen des Leo Baeck Instituts 17), pp. 113–117.

[38] Leopold Zunz, 'Krummer und gerader Wandel', Zunz Archive D9 (No. 27), p. 2: "Und so (meine Tr.[euen]) erzieht Gott das Menschengeschlecht. Den Völkern die noch roh und lieder sind, setzt er die Grösse der Tugend und ihre Herrlichkeit und ihr.[en] grossen Zusammenhang nocht nicht auseinander, sondern befiehlt ihr recht zu handeln in bestimmten Fällen, und überlässt es dem Fortschreiten der Menschheit, und weisen schauenden Propheten späterer Zeit, den grossen Zusammenhang alles Edlen aufzufinden, die Bahn der Gesinnungen, die jeder guten That zur Grundlage dienen z.[u] erforschen, und den ganzen Reichthum im Geist u. Gemüth zu erwerben, für den man allein wahrhaft schöne Handlungen, Lieder des Sittengesetzes erkaufen kann. Daher gebietet die Schrift so oft mit den Handlungen und überlässt es unserem Nachdenken den Weg zu deren Ausführung aufzuspüren. Sie spricht so kurz u. einfach, dass das Pflichtgebot ein kleines erscheint, wenngleich eine grosse Gesinnung es zu üben vorrausgesetzt werden muss. Aber wir sollen uns nicht in dem (Angaffen) des sichtbaren Wortes (das endlich ist, so versenken, dass wir) den unsichtbaren, unendlichen Geist verkennen, der über ihm waltet."

[39] Johann G. Eichhorn, *Einleitung in das Alte Testament*, Reutlingen 1790 (2nd rev. edn.), vol. 3, p. 118. The previous quote is to be found in *ibid.*, vol. 2, p. 334.

educators of humanity. These prophets are here, for the first time, seen as interpreters of texts, which they allegedly strip of their "infantile" garments.

The Christian background of this view emerges also from Zunz's amendment of the expression "wise prophets" to "visionary prophets", the latter implying in the Christian context the anticipation of Jesus. Zunz's concept of the prophets as educators of humanity is based on theological notions which had become commonplace after Herder. The latter stated in his essay on the spirit of Hebrew poetry that the later prophets were no longer heroes of action as Moses had been. Instead they were *literati* who guided humanity, by way of spiritual-moral exegesis of Scripture, towards the Christian era.[40] Eichhorn embraced this view in his later works and insisted that Jesus had been the "greatest teacher of humanity", which required no further educators.[41]

At this stage, Zunz relied uncritically upon Christian theology, which he later abandoned. This is presumably also the reason for his harsh criticism of the *Halakhah*. After his scornful reference to the literal meaning of Scripture – "we should not immerse ourselves in gaping at the visible letter" – Zunz defines the upright person as someone who interprets Scripture spiritually. The literal *halakhic* meaning, by contrast, is identified as unauthentic pretentiousness:

> "Trusting in virtue and zealous for truth, he is everywhere concerned about the right meaning, not for pretended fulfilment of the law. He discovers the thought in the words, the hidden spirit in visible action – only the truth evokes his inner peace."[42]

Zunz presents here the spiritual interpretation of Scripture as an earnest zeal for the truth, while *Halakhah* is seen as utter hypocrisy. In another sermon Zunz moreover interprets the Golden Calf as the "sin of adhering to the literal sense of Scripture", particularly the *halakhic Peshat*.[43] Significantly, this interpretation parallels Herder's understanding of this biblical episode. He, too, regarded it as a story about the sin of "sticking" to *Halakhah* and the literal meaning of the text.[44]

Despite these Christian biases, Zunz's concept of prophecy as developed in his sermons provides the basis for his later notion of rabbinic *Haggadah* as an expression of Jewish spirituality. When he subsequently transforms the elements of Christian Romanticism into a distinctly Jewish theology, he transfers to *Haggadah* precisely those features which he had previously identified with the biblical prophets. In order to understand this transition fully, two further issues need to be illuminated: the national dimension of prophecy and the immediate impetus for the change in Zunz's views.

Explanations of both issues can be found in the sermon on Simchat Torah

---

[40]Herder, *Poesie*, pp. 248ff.
[41]Eichhorn, *Einleitung*, vol. 3, p. 18.
[42]Zunz, 'Krummer und gerader Wandel', pp. 13–14: "Ausgerüstet mit dem Zutrauen zum Guten und mit Eifer für Wahrheit ist es ihm überall um den rechtlichen Sinn, nicht um scheinbare Gesetzesbeobachtung zu thun. Aus dem Worte findet er den Gedanken heraus, aus dem sichtbaren Thun den verborgenen Geist, nur Wahrheit beruhigt ihn...."
[43]Leopold Zunz, 'Das goldene Kalb', Zunz Archive D11, Sermon No. 49.
[44]Herder, *Poesie*, p. 242.

(19th October 1821). This sermon deals with the significance of Scripture for both Jews and humanity at large. The spiritual prophetic interpretation of the Bible is said to express the national spirit of Israel. Zunz insists at the same time that the Torah was revealed to three successive groups, which correspond to three stages in the development of mankind: the Jewish people, the individual Jew, and humanity. The function of the Torah for the Jews, both as a people and as individuals, was, according to Zunz, already fulfilled in the past. Since then Scripture is said to have passed on to the nations. Zunz, moreover, stresses that Jewish nationality ceased after the destruction of the Second Temple. The spirit of the prophets, no longer specifically associated with Israel, became the universal property of humanity. Zunz concludes his sermon on a political note, stressing that now all the nations, including the Jews and the Germans, share the same task of implementing prophetic ethics.

Initially, Zunz says the following about the national role of prophecy:

> "Our investigation has no longer to do with the near individual and his petty inclinations, but with the distant, mighty mass, who – unconscious of itself – walks a particular path. Before our eyes every people develops a different talent, a force, and shows a particular vocation of its existence. The Lord wished that Israel should also have and fulfil such a vocation, so that it might develop a history in the midst of the apparently perplexing events and disturbances and attacks – a history which would be fruitful and instructive for Israel and others. What did the Lord do? He revealed Himself in the law and gave our forefathers appropriate institutions, which were so harmonious and perfectly complementary that they raised Israel's value, serving and supporting her progress and vocation."[45]

In this passage Zunz uses theological and historico-Romantic notions to define national character. Relying on the idea of Israel's election, he refers to the special vocation which distinguishes it from that of other nations. He moreover applies the Romantic idea of organic and unconscious features of a nation to the discussion of Judaism. It is implied that a people's destiny is shaped by its diverse talents and particular forces. National character is thus a concept which stresses unity in the different cultural activities and organisations of a people. Israel's institutions therefore reflect its eternal nature:

> "These institutions are became the pillar of her [Israel's] public life, are carried the colours of her moral (abilities) and (served as) a means to (help) fulfil her vocation. Such laws however are divine which educate the people towards that which it should be and which is appropriate to its country, custom, mentality, well-being and the secret plan of its existence. Such laws therefore serve the people's happiness. Yet

---

[45]Leopold Zunz, Sermon on Simchat Torah (untitled), Zunz Archive D10 (No. 39), p. 5: "Nicht mehr mit dem nahen Einzelnen und seinen kleinlichen Neigungen, sondern mit der fernen gewaltigen Masse, die ihrer selbst unbewusst, einen bestimmten Weg zurücklegt hat unsere Betrachtung zu thun – und jedes Volk entwickelt vor uns ein anderes Talent, eine Kraft, und verräth gleichsam einen bestimmten Beruf seines Daseyns. Der Herr aber wollte dass auch Israel einen solchen Beruf haben und erfüllen solle, dass es mitten durch die verwirrend scheinenden Ereignisse und Störungen und Angriffe und Irrthümer eine Geschichte entwickle die ihm und anderen fruchtbar und lehrreich sei. Was that der Herr? Er offenbarte sich im Gesetz und gab unseren Vorfahren Einrichtungen, so ihm angemessen waren, so harmonisch und wunderbar in einander griffen, so ihm seines Daseyns Werth erhöheten, so seinem Fortschreiten und seiner Bestimmung dienlich waren."

wherever arbitrariness and folly intervene thievishly and force something alien upon nations, so that their inner lives become confused and insecure, their movements irregular, their aspirations unclear and their public activity lazy – in that place rules the non-divine."[46]

In this passage, too, Zunz combines theological and Romantic arguments in order to explain the notion of a people's secret plan. He argues that the "finger of God" is visible in institutions linked to the people's inner vocation. In the case of Israel, Scripture provides this divine framework for the nation. It is noteworthy that Zunz stresses Romantic notions at the expense of moral idealism. Instead of speaking about the educational function of national institutions which would elevate the people's ethics, he highlights the harmony which should prevail between a nation's "moral ability" and its institutions. This position reflects the priorities of Savigny's school, which had already been integrated into theological scholarship.

Zunz adds another important idea to his definition of Israel's vocation. He links the notion of national character to prophecy, arguing that the prophets were the guardians of Israel's national spirit:

> "For this reason the law was interwoven with the teaching of the prophets which was who were continually calling to mind the past, the supra-terrestrial and the general. They were the living interpreters of the living older laws, the opponents of the priests who stuck to the form, and the teachers in what was the people's vocation."[47]

Zunz defines prophecy here as both the spiritual-ethical interpretation of Scripture and the expression of Israel's national spirit. This definition is based on a sharp distinction between prophecy and law. *Halakhah* is seen as anachronistic and permanently in danger of petrification, while prophecy is the vibrant spirit keeping the essence of Judaism alive. In this way, Zunz identifies the prophets as authentic Jews. The priests, by contrast, depart from Israel's true vocation. These ideas can yet again be traced to Herder, who defined prophecy as the distinguishing characteristic of Israel.

Zunz's transference of the features of biblical prophecy to rabbinic *Haggadah* is connected to the destruction of the Second Temple and the supposed cessation of Israel's national spirit. Zunz argues here for a complete rupture, ignoring subsequent Jewish developments such as *Haggadah*:

---

[46] *Ibid.*, pp. 5–6: "Diese Einrichtungen sind wurden die Stütze seines öffentlichen Lebens, sind trugen die Farben seines ihrer sittlichen (Fähigkeiten) und (dienten als) Mittel seinem ihrem Beruf erfüllen (zu helfen). Gesetze aber, die ein Volk zu dem, was es sein soll, geschult machen, die seinem Lande, seiner Sitte, seiner Sinnesart, seinem Wohle, und dem geheimen Plan seines Daseyns angemessen sind, die sind göttlich und eben darum zu des Volkes Glückseligkeit. Da aber, wo Willkür und Unvernunft räuberisch eingreifen und fremdartiges den Völkern aufzwingen, das ihr inneres Leben verworren, unsicher, ihr Gang unstet, ihr Streben unklar und ihre öffentliche Thätigkeit faul wird, da freilich waltet das Ungöttliche."

[47] *Ibid.*, p. 7: "Darum zogen als stete lebendige Mahner(in) an das Vergangene, an das Überirdische und an das allgemeine, die Lehre der Propheten durch das Gesetz, sie waren die lebendigen Erklärer des lebendigen älteren Gesetzes, die Gegner der an der Form klebenden Priester, und Lehrer in dem, was des Volkes Beruf war."

"The eternal God is our lawgiver! Therefore His law is also eternal; when Israel as a people still had a vocation, the law helped fulfil that vocation, but today when it has merged with the nations and we have actually become part of the German fatherland, the law is still above us, reminding us of the eternal God and His word. But it reminds not only us, no, but also all the nations who read it and grew fond of it."[48]

According to Zunz, after the destruction of the Temple Jewish nationality was replaced by the national identity of each Jew's place of residence – his new "fatherland". He subsequently stresses the topical relevance of this notion when he says that "we and the other inhabitants of our fatherland share the same vocation so that we are no longer foreigners linked to an ancient period, an old extinguished period whose aims have died".[49] Zunz moreover insists on the equality of all who love Scripture. Indeed, the universal mission of the Torah is described as the "highest goal of the Holy Scriptures". It follows that Zunz at this point prefers the "maturity" of humanity to its "childhood".

Finally, Zunz alludes to the possibility of extending the span of historical prophecy and transferring its features to subsequent forms of Judaism. He thus says that "for a hundred years this force [of biblical prophecy] can be asleep hidden from the eye. But it is not lost and as long as the divine law is alive, it is active and brings happiness".[50] This notion of the hidden continuity of the prophetic spirit lays the foundation for Zunz's subsequent argument that rabbinic *Haggadah* revived this spirit in its specifically Jewish dimension.

ZUNZ'S STUDY OF JEWISH SERMONS (1832)

Zunz's mature work integrates the elements of his earlier sermons into an overall positive appreciation of Judaism throughout the ages – an appreciation which might, to some extent, have been influenced by his friendship with Salomon Jehudah Rapoport. Zunz's *magnum opus* covers the history of the Jewish sermon from its inception until his own day. It aims to trace the modern sermon back to ancient Jewish models.[51] Zunz stresses in this context that the synagogue and the sermon were the only national institutions which survived the destruction of the Temple and thus decisively influenced the continuation of Judaism as a particu-

---

[48]*Ibid.*, p. 11: "Der Ewige ist unser Gesetzgeber! Darum ist a.[uch] sein Gesetz ein ewiges, für die Zeit wo Israel als ein Volk einen Beruf hatte, half das Gesetz diesen Beruf erfüllen, und für heut, wo es in die Völker aufgegangen und namentlich ein Teil geworden ist des deutschen Vaterlandes, stehet das Gesetz noch über uns, an den Ewigen und sein Wort stets mahnend, nicht nur uns, nein, alle Völker, die es gelesen und liebgewonnen."
[49]*Ibid.*, p. 13.
[50]*Ibid.*
[51]Leopold Zunz, *Die gottesdienstlichen Vorträge der Juden. Ein Beitrag zur Alterthumskunde und biblischen Kritik, zur Literatur- und Religionsgeschichte*, Frankfurt am Main 1892, 2nd edn. revised according to Zunz's handwritten notes, especially 'Introduction' and pp. 470–471 and pp. 490–495. Zunz expected his scholarship to have an impact on the contemporary discussion on the modern sermon (Zunz, *Zunz Buch*, p. 77). See also Ismar Schorsch, 'The Emergence of Historical Consciousness in Modern Judaism', *LBI Year Book XXVIII* (1983), pp. 413–437; Michael A. Meyer, 'Jewish Religious Reform and *Wissenschaft des Judentums*. The Positions of Zunz, Geiger and Frankel', *LBI Year Book XVI* (1971), pp. 19–41.

Zunz's Concept of Haggadah

lar religion. Zunz now defines post-biblical Judaism as a culture which thrived on the dialectical dynamics between the text of Scripture and the prophetic spirit of the sermons. Central importance is attributed to *Haggadah*, which is – as the "spoken word' '– seen as the progressive and prophetic element in Judaism. Zunz defines *Haggadah*, in distinctly Romantic terms, as "organic" literature which expresses the spirit of the Jewish people. He distinguishes, moreover, between the main forms of *Haggadah* and describes its place within the overall history of Jewish literature.

Zunz gradually approached the subject of rabbinic literature in his three consecutive essays in the *Zeitschrift für die Wissenschaft des Judentums* (1823) and in a lecture, 'On the Historical Development of Jewish Spiritual Activity', delivered in 1823 at the *Verein für Cultur und Wissenschaft der Juden*.[52] In light of these groping steps his achievements in the book are particularly impressive. Zunz no longer speaks in a general and somewhat opaque manner about the spiritual essence of Judaism. He no longer limits himself to the highly popular period of medieval Spain. He instead presents a comprehensive view of Judaism in all its manifestations and developments. His entries in the *Zunz Buch* indicate that he wrote an outline of this book as early as 1825. The plan then focused on the different disciplines of Jewish scholarship, only one chapter being devoted to the research of rabbinic *Haggadah*. In August 1829 Zunz decided to devote the book to the Sermons of the Jews.

Zunz's book is based on the assumption of a distinct similarity between the homiletics of the synagogue and the homiletics of the "school of the prophets". He initially re-states his view of the prophets, who are described as "enthusiastic" individuals who speak with a "thundering voice". As in the sermons, their exegesis is said to convey ethical spirituality:

> "Finally, the contradictions, obscurities and gaps of these books Scripture must have required explanation even prior to translation. In a different context, the same was the case for the prophets. Their sayings counted as instructions of the right way of life; their speech reflected the spiritual contents of the national law; their thundering word woke the sleeping conscience of the community and the individual; the whole welfare of the nation depended on the weighty legacy of those envoys of God. While the law represented the guideline for the present, the prophetic flashes illuminated the future. It was therefore natural and necessary that those instructing parts of the public service, which was already composed of the reading of Scripture and its translation, complemented by a third element: interpretations, instructions, speeches and extemporary lectures."[53]

This passage echoes Zunz's earlier description of the prophets as educators of the people who convey the ethical principles of the Torah. Zunz further suggests a link between prophetic and rabbinic homiletics, the prophets representing the prototype of Bible exegetes later emulated by the rabbis. In this context Zunz stresses the contribution of the prophets to the early development of *Midrash* and points especially to the exegetical role of the *Haftarah* and Ezekiel's *halakhic*

---

[52]Leopold Zunz, *Über den historischen Gang der jüdischen Geistesthätigkeit*, Zunz Archive D4.
[53]Zunz, *Gottesdienstliche Vorträge*, pp. 12–13.

expansions. Criticising the view that the *Haftarah* readings were established simply in order to circumvent the religious limitations imposed by the Seleucids, Zunz argues that they responded to the popular demand for prophetic commentary on Scripture.[54]

Zunz subsequently shows how rabbinic *Haggadah* expresses the prophetic spirit in a similar type of free, spiritual and moral exegesis. He insists that rabbinic *Haggadah* does not only appear to the scholar as the "sister" of prophecy, but that the *haggadists* themselves meant to "establish an institution which aspired to be the successor of free prophecy".[55] Zunz's argument is based on three claims: 1) *Haggadah* is essentially a free discourse which parallels the prophets' enthusiastic speeches; 2) *Haggadah* shares the prophets' ethical principles; and 3) *Haggadah* has "organic" characteristics and therefore expresses the people's spirit in the same way as the prophets had done.

Rabbinic *Haggadah*, Zunz argues, consists essentially of free discourse and sermons, which developed both in the synagogue and on social occasions connected to synagogue life.[56] Zunz's preparatory notes for his book reveal that his emphasis on the social context of the sermons is based on the research of the Dutch Hebraist Campegius Vitringa, whose work he probably knew through de Wette.[57] It is significant, moreover, that in comparison to Rapoport Zunz gives considerably less attention to the *halakhic* context of the synagogue sermons and highlights instead their rhetorical dimension.[58] He thus explains that the Amora spoke with a "stronger and more pleasant voice" and provides details of the setting of the sermon: the audience, including women and the underprivileged, came in large crowds from afar; they were sitting on the ground, often in front of the president's house, with the women in a separate area. Zunz insists that nobody dared to disturb the sermon, which could consequently be delivered in an atmosphere of courtesy – an atmosphere which Zunz highly appreciated in the service of his own time.

The *Haggadah* is said to have been the only means of education available to the people, who were largely illiterate. He explains that "wit, rhetorical expertise and *midrashic* learning became available to the people through the teacher who lectured in public". The simple language and straightforward style of the sermons, Zunz argues, naturally reflect the people's character.[59] Zunz attributes to *Haggadah* a far more crucial role in the life of the people than Rapoport does.

---

[54]*Ibid.*, pp. 6 and 345.

[55]*Ibid.*, p. 341.

[56]*Ibid.*, p. 346: "Das Hauptmoment ist die *Haggadah*, das 'Gesagte', und darum heisst der Vorgang selber, auch wenn er halachische Materien umfasst, *Haggadah*." On p. 355 Zunz even speaks of "hagadisches Gesetzesstudium".

[57]Zunz's preparatory notes for the book are preserved in Zunz Archiv D18. Vitringa wrote his dissertation of over 1000 pages in Latin and published it under the title *De Synagoga Vetere* (1685). Zunz relied particularly on pp. 669–711 and pp. 948–1015. De Wette cites Vitringa in De Wette, *Dogmatics*, p. 55.

[58]Zunz, *Gottesdienstliche Vorträge*, pp. 349ff. Like Weil, Zunz moreover tends to limit the field of *Halakhah* to the spiritual regulations of the holidays. Compare Salomon J. Rapoport, *Erekh Milim*, vol. 1, Prague 1852, p. 6.

[59]Zunz, *Gottesdienstliche Vorträge*, pp. 367–367. The previous quotation can be found in *ibid.*, p. 355.

Zunz's Concept of Haggadah

The latter mainly considers *Haggadah* as a rhetorical means employed by the elitist rabbis in order to maintain the attention of the audience, while Zunz suggests a profound link between *Haggadah* and the spirit of the people. He even suggests that the simple people had an active part in the creation of *haggadic* traditions.[60]

The free and enthusiastic style of the *Haggadah* is another important feature mentioned by Zunz. He regards *Haggadah* to be so free that – like prophecy – it cannot be subordinated to rhetorical devices or specific subjects. The *haggadists* "so to speak transmit the echo of prophetic enthusiasm".[61] Zunz regrets that the oral *Haggadah* had been increasingly committed to writing. In contrast to Rapoport he does not regard this as a natural process, but rather as a loss of spiritual vibrancy. He argues that the committment of *Haggadah* to writing did not suit the people and was accompanied by numerous hesitations and anxieties. Zunz's concern reflects the values of contemporary Romantic theologians, who spoke in identical terms about biblical prophecy.

Zunz identifies the contents of rabbinic *Haggadah* with prophetic ethics. Following his earlier sermons, he now stresses that both the rabbis and the prophets express Judaism's authentic principles of ethics:

> "We return now to the original dwelling places of the Jews in Asia. In former times religious free speech had a forceful life there. Today nobody tells the princes and the nations the truth as the prophets did, and only a few love their homeland as ardently and as self-denyingly. They wished for the rule of the people, but simultaneously worked for the rule of justice and virtue; they advocated the consolidation of faith but also its progress. And the same holds true for the *haggadists*. The eternal pole towards which their sermons were orientated is the glorious victory of the Jews and Judaism over suffering and adversity and evil in the world. The *Haggadah* brings heaven closer to the community while elevating man towards heaven, and functions in this vocation as both a praise of God and a comfort for Israel. Therefore the most important contents of the sermons are: religious truths, ethics, talks about just retribution, inculcation of the law as a witness of nationality, descriptions of Israel's former and past glory, scenes and sagas from Jewish history, parallels between divine and Israelite institutions, praises of the Holy Land, uplifting stories and solace of all kinds."[62]

This passage presents the *haggadists* as the prophets' spiritual heirs. Both are said to teach authentic Judaism, namely ethics, justice and consolation. Both strike the right balance between faithfulness to tradition and innovation. Prophets and *haggadists* thus study the Torah and preserve the past, while also criticising the present and working for a better future. Like the prophets, the *haggadists* specifically address the individual, whom they encourage to find authentic faith. In comparison to his sermons, Zunz here highlights more the national dimension of the prophetic spirit. While he had earlier suggested that prophecy expresses the people's spirit, he now mentions love for the land of Israel, commemoration of Israel's glory and the hope for Judaism's ultimate victory. This new tone presum-

---

[60] *Ibid.*, p. 353.
[61] *Ibid.*, p. 341.
[62] *Ibid.*, p. 362.

ably derives from the disappointments he experienced after his sermons were written, namely the collapse of the *Verein für Cultur und Wissenschaft des Judentums*, the conversion of some of his friends, and the conservative reaction in German politics. In light of these difficulties his emphasis shifts towards the national consolation provided by the prophets and the *haggadists*.

Following this passage, Zunz discusses the "strange" and anthropomorphic *Haggadah* which does not meet the ideal requirements of his ethical-spiritual definition. Both the term "strange *Haggadah*" and its explanation echo Rapoport's discussion. Like his friend, whose manuscript he had available when writing his own book, Zunz suggests that these anomalous forms of *Haggadah* were prompted only by pedagogic necessities and do not reflect the deeper nature of rabbinic literature.[63] In one important aspect, however, Zunz departs from Rapoport's views. He avoids the late dating of "strange *Haggadah*" and suggests instead, in a Romantic tone, that these traditions echo the "spirit of the East" with its typical anthropomorphisms.

Zunz describes in detail how rabbinic *Haggadah* addresses the individual while also reflecting the spirit of the whole people. He relies on the Romantic model of a living organism, which harmoniously integrates all of its different members:

> "Law and Freedom in the state correspond to what the head and the heart are in the individual: the head as much as the law has to draft the fixed cold rules, freedom and the heart make its application and exceptions possible. The constitution and the priesthood preserved in the Hebrew state the law and the Ark of the Covenant which are the visible pillars of nationality, while the prophets preserved the fire of freedom and the original principle, which was not physically transmitted from generation to generation, but was ignited in each generation directly from the flame of enthusiasm. When Jewish nationality after the loss of independence was centred anew in the Holy Scriptures, *Midrash* became its representative... It soon developed in two distinct directions: *Halakhah*, the organ of the law [*Organ des Gesetzes*] and *Haggadah*, the organ of freedom [*Organ der Freiheit*]."[64]

Zunz describes here the cultural function of *Haggadah* and suggests that it is the hidden spirit of Jewish nationality. *Haggadah* preserves the fire of religious enthusiasm, the foundational idea of Judaism and its inner force and authenticity. Zunz moreover identifies the *Haggadah* with the freedom which softens the stringency of *Halakhah* by taking into consideration the exceptional circumstances of life. *Haggadah* thus symbolises free will and the superiority of ethics over law and custom. This view is also echoed in his preference of Palestinian *Midrash* over the Babylonian Talmud, which he criticises for too much *Pilpul*.[65] Zunz nevertheless insists on the necessity of both aspects of Judaism and describes their connection in Romantic terms:

> "But both institutions, prophecy and *Haggadah*, existed as unconditional expressions of national life: the same patriotism and confidence in God hovers in both of them; the same uncompromising courage and the power of the same hope for a future redemp-

---

[63]*Ibid.*, pp. 363 and 116; cf. Rapoport, *Erekh*, pp. 9ff.
[64]Zunz, *Gottesdienstliche Vorträge*, p. 334.
[65]*Ibid.*, pp. 320–321.

tion sustain both the prophets and the *haggadist* heroes. As prophecy was not useless rhetoric or arbitrary literary work, neiher should *Haggadah*, which has an overwhelming impact on the nation's deepest veins and all the pulses of its development, be considered thus. The products of *Midrash* are instead expressions of an activity which is grounded in the life, the ideas and the interests of the Jewish people, who had in a certain sense always actively participated therein. The outstanding works of both *Halakhah* and *Haggadah*, parallel to the law and the prophets, are therefore national writings, in the face of which later generations voluntarily almost eliminated their independence. Thus they became the property of everybody: as the results of a thousand years of history, as memorials of the nation's life, as products of its excellent minds. The inner necessity of *Midrash* was its main force [*Die innere Nothwendigkeit des Midrasch war die Triebfeder*]."[66]

Zunz explains in this passage the role of the different institutions of national life and the nature of their relationship to each other. He uses the Romantic metaphor of a living organism to describe all expressions of national life as interwoven and mutually dependent. Unlike later Romantics, such as Heinrich Heine and Michael Sachs, however, he stresses that the *Haggadah*, despite its more playful freedom, is not just aesthetic poetics but fulfils a decisive role in the Jewish nation.[67] Indeed, *Haggadah* functions like the heart and is therefore vital for the whole body, which develops according to the rhythm of its pulse. Zunz moreover suggests that all Jews, despite their variety, are like one body functioning in perfect harmony. *Haggadah* and *Halakhah* thus complement each other, following the dynamics of an inner necessity. *Haggadah* appeals therefore not only to the imagination of the individual, but also to the spirituality of the whole people:

"Every saying of the *Haggadah*, ... though usually the opinion of an individual and marked by the seal of time, conforms nevertheless to a general, organically develped fundamental law [*ein organisch ausgebildetes Grundgesetz*], which depends on religion and history."[68]

Finally, Zunz's distinction between different categories of *Haggadah* deserves some attention. It is not only the first modern survey of the different fields of *Haggadah*, but also reveals the parameters of Zunz's definition of *Haggadah*. The following four categories are specified by Zunz: ethical and historical *Haggadah*, secret lore, and "specific" or exegetical *Haggadah*. The first category dates back to the Enlightenment and refers mainly to the classical tractates *Avot, Derech Eretz* etc. Jacob Weil focused exclusively on this type of *Haggadah*. Zunz gives it less emphasis and also provides a historical framework for its appreciation by pointing to its roots in such works as Ben Sira and the Wisdom of Solomon. This historical perspective reflects Zunz's scholarly orientation and expresses his belief in the continuity of the prophetic spirit.

Exegetical *Haggadah* is the vaguest of Zunz's categories. Since Zunz thought that all *Haggadah* derives from exegesis, it is not clear whether the term "exegeti-

---

[66]*Ibid.*, pp. 334–335.
[67]On Heine's and Sachs's view of *Haggadah* see Maren R. Niehoff, 'Heine und die Jüdische Tradition', in *Ich Narr des Glücks. Heinrich Heine 1797–1856. Bilder einer Ausstellung*, ed. by J. A. Kruse, Düsseldorf 1997.
[68]Zunz, *Gottesdienstliche Vorträge*, p. 324.

cal *Haggadah*" is meant to embrace all *Haggadah* or whether it refers to a specific sub-class. This lack of clarity should not, however, obscure the seminal importance of Zunz's emphasis on the exegetical dimension of *Haggadah*. It indicates his departure from the universal, timeless principles of the Enlightenment, which leads to his greater appreciation of tradition and historical development. The importance of Zunz's innovation becomes clear in light of the fact that it is acknowledged and revived even today.

The remaining two categories of *Haggadah* are particularly interesting. It is highly significant that Zunz includes in his definition of *Haggadah* secret lore or *Kabbalah*.[69] Indeed for him, Jewish mysticism began as a regular process of *Midrash* on the first chapters of Genesis and Ezekiel. Yet he also discusses such works of *Hekhalot* literature as the *Sefer Hayashar* and the *Alphabet of Rabbi Akiva*. He relates to all of them in a distinctly positive, even respectful way. These works of the irrational tradition of Judaism are appreciated by Zunz both because he regards them as an extention of the *midrashic* principle and because he believes that the mystical interest in the creation of the world was inspired by scientific curiosity. The latter explanation might appear as a rationalisation of the irrational. It remains clear, however, that Zunz's position, subsequently continued by Adolf Jellinek, Michael Sachs and Gustav Landauer, was far more positive and complex than that of which Gerschom Scholem later accused the *Wissenschaft des Judentums*.[70]

The category of "historical *Haggadah*" is given most attention by Zunz.[71] It is perhaps his most important discovery and complements his theoretical discussions of the national character of *Haggadah*. He means by "historical *Haggadah*" a folk-story or saga which reflects Jewish history and the ethics and experience of the Jewish people. Zunz here uses a term which had become increasingly fashionable after the publication of the the Grimm brothers' *Deutsche Sagen* (1816–1818). Indeed, the second volume of the Grimms' collection is devoted to "historical stories". The editors, who, like Zunz, had heard Savigny's lectures, explain that these stories reflect a distinctly ethical inclination and reflect the authentic spirit of the German people.[72] The Grimm brothers stressed the oral roots of their tales and claimed that they collected them in the countryside, listening, often under rather adventurous circumstances, to local storytellers and simple folk. This trend in contemporary German literature obviously suited Zunz very well. He also followed the Grimms' emphatic assertion that these sagas do not belong to

---

[69] *Ibid.*, pp. 165–179.

[70] On Scholem's attitude towards *Wissenschaft des Judentums* and his own concept of scholarship, see especially Gerschom Scholem, 'Wissenschaft vom Judentum Einst und Jetzt', in *Bulletin des Leo Baeck Instituts*, No. 9 (1960), pp. 10–20; David Meyr, *Reinventing the Past*, Oxford 1996, and references therein.

[71] Zunz, *Gottesdienstliche Vorträge*, pp. 125–156.

[72] Jacob Grimm heard in 1803, in Marburg, the same lecture on Roman law which Zunz was to hear in Berlin. Grimm felt that they "made an immense impression" on him, "decisively influencing my whole life and studies". Grimm even became Savigny's assistant. See Hermann Gerstner, *Die Brüder Grimm. Ihr Leben und Werk*, 1952, especially p. 5.

Zunz's Concept of Haggadah

the field of poetic entertainment but possess great intellectual value because they instruct the people and preserve their past.

From the end of the eighteenth century onwards theological scholarship, too, relied on the notions of saga and folk-tale. Eichhorn's "mythological school" in particular regarded biblical stories as types of myth or saga which had developed on the basis of ancient events, thus reflecting the infancy of humanity.[73] Eichhorn insisted on the historical kernel of biblical myths and assumed that in the process of their transmission important events were increasingly embellished. Saga is defined as an orally transmitted myth.

Zunz's description of *Haggadah* as saga clearly echoes contemporary discussions in the fields of literature and theology. He highlights particular aspects of the term and adapts it to Judaism. Initially he defines a saga as a folk-tale based on an historical kernel. The story of Judith is an example of such a narrative process: "It is possible that a popular festival was celebrated in a small Palestinian town in memory of a woman's heroism; and after the true occasion was forgotten and replaced by a heavily embellished saga, a legend in honour of Judith was invented probably even before the destruction of the Temple."[74]

Zunz describes the emergence of a saga, stressing the function of the people and the Holy Days, which he considered, with contemporary scholarship, to be formative factors in shaping national memory. Zunz presents the national remembrance as a process which is transformed from a personal account of an important historical event to an increasingly embellished story. In the end, when the historical kernel is already forgotten, the fanciful dimensions are said to increase and become dominant. Despite this imaginative dimension, saga is continuously distinguished from myth, which Zunz defines as a story which never had a historical basis. This definition of saga is then specifically applied to Judaism. Zunz argues now that Scripture itself must also be considered as a "true kernel" which distinguishes saga from myth. Any story based on the Bible cannot therefore be mythological. Conversely, Zunz makes the pioneering suggestion that some passages from Ezekiel and Daniel must be considered from a literary (rather than a theological) point of view and must thus be identified as sagas.

The saga reflects, according to Zunz, the spirit of the people so well that the book Josippon, which is largely based on non-Jewish sources "contains after all only little of the spirit of ancient *Haggadah*".[75] The character of *Haggadah*, its ethics and confidence in God, are transmitted by three kinds of historical *Haggadah*: stories about national events, or miracles, or highly respected persons. Zunz stresses that these different stories all serve the same purpose of strengthening the people's faith and national identity. While Zunz suggests the same idea of *haggadic* cohesion as he had earlier done in the context of the organic nature of *Haggadah*, his statements lack the Romantic tone. This differ-

---

[73] Johann P. Gabler (ed.), *Johann Gottfried Eichhorns Urgeschichte herausgegeben mit Einleitungen und Anmerkungen*, Nuremberg 1790; Christian Hartlich and Walter Sachs, *Der Ursprung des Mythosbegriffes in der Modernen Bibelwissenschaft*, Tübingen 1952.
[74] Zunz, *Gottesdienstliche Vorträge*, p. 132.
[75] *Ibid.*, p. 155.

ence probably derives from their different contexts: while saga is discussed from a strictly literary perspective, the prophetic spirit is associated with highly Romantic notions.

SUMMARY AND CONCLUSION

We have examined Zunz's notion of rabbinic *Haggadah* in his first *magnum opus* in light of his earlier intellectual development. His concept of *Haggadah* as an expression of Jewish spirituality can be traced back to his theological views, which had been influenced by his teacher de Wette. The early sermons of Zunz himself, which have thus far remained unpublished, reveal the basic elements which he later synthesised into a new concept. They show that initially Zunz fully embraced Herder's notion of biblical prophecy as spiritual exegesis and as reflection of the people's character. He also absorbed Herder's criticism of the priesthood, including his harsh view of the *Halakhah* and the literal meaning of Scripture. He moreover thought, with Herder, that specifically Jewish spirituality had ceased with the destruction of the Second Temple.

In his later book on the sermons Zunz develops his innovative and distinctly positive approach to rabbinic *Haggadah*. He now regards it as an expression of the continued spirit of prophecy, which reflects the special essence of Jewish culture. He explains the nature and structure of *Haggadah* by reference to Romantic literary models of the contemporary discourse. The most important of these terms are organic mechanism and saga. Zunz also highlights the oral sources of *Haggadah*, which are considered to account for its authentic and vibrant spirituality. Whether or not one agrees with these conceptualisations of *Haggadah*, one has to acknowledge that Zunz was the first to place *Haggadah* at the very centre of the modern Jewish experience. He also laid the foundation for scholarship on *Haggadah* which reverberates even in today's works.

Hermann Cohen's Teaching Concerning Modern Jewish Identity (1904–1918)

BY AVI BERNSTEIN-NAHAR

Two recent developments suggest that the time has arrived to begin a reappraisal of the Jewish writings of Hermann Cohen.[1] The first concerns Cohen the philosopher. Beginning in the early 1980s with the publication of Alasdair MacIntyre's *tour de force*, *After Virtue*,[2] a new and broad interest has begun to develop within academia in just the kind of philosophical project in which Hermann Cohen was engaged.[3] For Cohen, as well as for MacIntyre and a growing number of contemporary philosophers and theologians, modern philosophy's most urgent task is the revival of a "moral psychology" which can be applied to issues of contempor-

---

[1] "[T]he unique heart of the subject/matter/cause." Hermann Cohen, 'Die Errichtung von Lehrstühlen für Ethik und Religionsphilosophie an den jüdisch-theologischen Lehranstalten', in *Jüdische Schriften*, ed. by Franz Rosenzweig, 3 vols., Berlin 1924, vol. I, p. 122; In Cohen's context, this term resonates with the sense of the human subject, *der Mensch*, as well as the divine subject, the prime moral cause which, according to Cohen's teaching concerning divine attributes, reflects the true subjectivity of *der Mensch*. See Alexander Altmann, 'The Divine Attributes', in *Judaism*, 15 (1966), pp. 40–60. Cohen identifies the term *Herz* with the Hebrew word *Lev*, and the notion of character, the seat of the virtues and the locus of control in *der Mensch*. See especially Cohen, 'Innere Beziehungen der Kantischen Philosophie zum Judentum', in *Jüdische Schriften I*, pp. 284–306 and 'Gesinnung', in *Jüdische Schriften I*, pp. 196–211. This article is limited to a consideration of Cohen's systematic teaching concerning Jewish identity. The latter commences only in 1904 in connection with the publication of Cohen's general philosophical anthropology, *Ethik des reinen Willens*, Hildesheim 1981 (1st edn., Berlin 1907, hereafter *Ethik*). Cf. note 8. I would like to thank Professor Arnold Eisen of Stanford University for commenting on an earlier version of this essay. I would also like to thank the following institutions for their support during the research and writing of this essay: the Lady Davis Fellowship Trust, the National Foundation for Jewish Culture, and the Memorial Foundation for Jewish Culture.

[2] Alasdair MacIntyre, *After Virtue*, Notre Dame 1984.

[3] Cf. Cohen's own description of his work: "Die systematische Philosophie ist die Lehre von der Einheit des Menschen in seinen Erzeugungsweisen der Kultur", in *Begriff der Religion im System der Philosophie*, Giessen 1915, p. 136 (hereafter *Begriff*); On the view of Cohen's project as moral psychology, see Gerd Wolandt, 'Einleitung', in Hermann Cohen, *Ästhetik des reinen Gefühls*, Hildesheim 1982 (1st edn., Berlin 1912), pp. VII, XVI, note 2; Ernst Cassirer, 'Hermann Cohen. Worte gesprochen an seinem Grabe am 7. April 1918', in Helmut Holzhey, *Hermann Cohen*, Frankfurt am Main 1994, pp. 67–74; Steven Schwarzschild, 'The Title of Hermann Cohen's *Religion of Reason*', in Hermann Cohen, *Religion of Reason*, Atlanta 1995, p.18, note 40 (hereafter *Religion*).

ary ethical and religious concern.[4] Foremost among the latter for the mature Cohen stands the question of German-Jewish identity.

The second consideration concerns Jewish studies in the university as we approach the end of the twentieth century. Hermann Cohen, after a hiatus of over fifty years, is again being given a modest hearing in the academic world.[5] Jewish studies programmes are now for the first time commonplace in the finest American universities, and many include both modern Jewish philosophy and Hermann Cohen in their curriculum. Moreover, an English translation of Cohen's *magnum opus, Religion der Vernunft aus den Quellen des Judentums*, which was out of print for many years, has just been reissued, making Cohen more easily accessible to the scholarly community. In short, the man once regarded as the intellectual leader of German Jewry is again being heard in the halls of academe, and a reconsideration of his work is a pressing task.

In this paper I focus on Cohen's mature Jewish writings. In my view, these represent Cohen's most successful effort to apply his moral psychology to the question of German-Jewish identity. Over the course of his last thirteen years, Cohen developed a subtle explanation of modern German-Jewish identity whose most basic terms (*social type, literary tradition, narrative, community, virtue*) are drawn from that psychology. An examination of these writings will show just how preoccupied Cohen was with the basic issues of modern identity that continue to concern both modern Jews and the broader academic community even today.

INTRODUCTION

In 1915, in the twilight of his career, Hermann Cohen published a short monograph on religion. The work's stated aim was entirely conventional. It would carve out space for yet another concept within the Marburg philosopher's systematic thought. Its closing pages, however, represent a genuine departure from the everyday business of writing philosophy. Here Cohen reflected on the significance of his conception of religion for "the naive consciousness of people in so far as it has not ripened into systematic philosophy".[6]

Cohen's contention represents a noteworthy moment of reflection for an intellectual as committed as Cohen was to the professional practice of philosophy. Though his own audience consisted mainly of professional philosophers and theologians, Cohen cast his glance in a different direction. True, his chosen medium

---

[4]Cohen's moral psychology is outlined most prominently in *Ethik* (throughout), *Begriff*, pp. 108–140, and *Religion*, pp. 400–462. Alasdair MacIntyre emphasises the urgency of reviving moral psychology in 'Moral Philosophy. What Next?', in *Revisions*, Notre Dame 1983, especially p. 9. Continuing interest in MacIntyre's project is reflected in John Horton and Susan Mendus (eds.), *After MacIntyre*, Cambridge 1994.
[5]Eugene Borowitz dates the beginning of the declining interest in Cohen's Marburg Neo-Kantianism from the end of the First World War. See Borowitz, 'Reason', in *Contemporary Jewish Religious Thought*, New York 1987, p. 751.
[6]*Begriff*, p. 137.

was philosophical, but the religious crisis which concerned him in 1915 required a different literary style and a different audience.

> "If the thought is admissible that humanity's education into the knowledge of systematic philosophy is the problem of a not very close future, then for this reason a nearer task may not be put off ... the concept of the unique God in its logical and ethical clarity is to be secured as the main focus and essence of religious instruction inside the education of the nation. Just this concentration of the religious doctrine of monotheism and of the religious instruction in the elementary school ... will in the first place truly establish ethical culture as part of interaction and intercommunication amongst the people."[7]

At the apex of his career as a philosopher, Cohen's most passionate call is reserved not for new disciples to carry on his philosophical legacy but for a new God-centred doctrine and a cadre of teachers to disseminate it.

Yet Cohen's remarks should not be understood as a renunciation of the philosophical muse, nor even as a call for others to take up a doctrinal task to which he was unsuited. The opposite is demonstrably the case. No doctrine could be acceptable to Cohen which did not follow from his systematic thought, as *Begriff der Religion* itself tries to argue. Furthermore, Cohen had already been engaged for some time in precisely the task for which he now solicited support. Indeed, between 1904 and 1917, in the scholarly and semi-popular Jewish press, Cohen wrote numerous articles promoting a particular self-understanding for the modern Jew. It is this doctrine which has captured our attention as Cohen's teaching concerning Jewish identity.

In the inaugural article of the revived *Monatsschrift für Geschichte und Wissenschaft des Judentums* of 1904, Cohen launched the opening salvo of his new campaign. On the face of it, 'Die Errichtung von Lehrstühlen für Ethik und Religionsphilosophie an den jüdisch-theologischen Lehranstalten'[8] embodies a modest partisan proposal for organisational reform. A devotee of philosophy urges the scholarly community of Jews to restore the philosopher to a leading position within the Jewish seminary. If we examine the details of Cohen's article, however, we uncover ambitions far grander than those inscribed in the title. Indeed, in 'Errichtung von Lehrstühlen' we find a scholarly programme for the reconstruction of the modern Jew. This programme would remain a beacon for Cohen's work in the Jewish community from this time onwards.

The general argument of 'Errichtung von Lehrstühlen' is easy to recapitulate. If rightly conceived, Judaism is well-suited to contribute to the *Kultur* of the modern state, and to inform the ethical commitments (*Sittlichkeit*) of its citizens. However, Judaism's potential contribution has been eclipsed in the modern period by the inadequate training of Jewish theologians. They are accustomed

---

[7]*Ibid.*, pp. 138–139.
[8]The article, 'Die Errichtung von Lehrstühlen für Ethik und Religionsphilosophie an den jüdisch-theologischen Lehranstalten', appears in *Jüdische Schriften II*, pp. 108–125. It is worth noting that this article appears in 1904, also the date in which Cohen's *Ethik* makes its first appearance. As the latter is the *locus classicus* of his moral psychology, it can be no coincidence that Cohen offers his most programmatic statement for the reconstruction of German-Jewish identity in the very same year.

to weighing Judaism's significance for the general *Kultur* exclusively in terms of the superficial details of its ethical teachings. For Cohen, however,

> "If only the external content of its ethical teaching is heeded, Judaism cannot be fully appreciated according to the significance which it has and maintains for culture; if the link of its ethical teaching with its idea of God is pushed into the background...ethical Judaism loses its main focus and the foundation upon which the specific character of its ethical teaching is based."[9]

Only the establishment of chairs for ethics and philosophy of religion at Jewish seminaries can provide what remains lacking in the seminary curriculum. Only a new sort of Jewish scholar-philosopher can re-focus Jewry's attention on the true source of its *Kultur*, its God.

According to Cohen, Jewish institutions of higher learning stand at an historical turning point. Modern *Kultur* forces an unprecedented division of labour upon the framework of Jewish life, destroying the institutional arrangements which have enabled Judaism's sophisticated articulation and dissemination in the past. In a previous epoch, Jewish communities did not need to provide a special institutional base for *Wissenschaft des Judentums*. The confession (*das Bekenntnis*) of Judaism and its *Wissenschaft* were one and the same. A community needed only to concern itself with the service of God to ensure that this relation between religion and *Wissenschaft* was maintained. Such service would always in principle have included "the widespread and profound study of the Torah". Furthermore, the rabbinate functioned as "the central office for the teaching of the sciences of religion...The rabbi was the scholar of the Science of Judaism [*Wissenschaft des Judentums*]".[10]

This delicate balance of teaching and life has now been thoroughly destroyed, according to Cohen. New demands have impinged upon rabbis and *wissenschaftlich* methods of research have become more specialised. The rabbi is no longer likely to be a "universal personality", able to master practical and theoretical challenges alike. At this historical moment, then, the Jewish community faces a new task. It must establish new institutions that are equipped to restore Judaism's equilibrium with *Wissenschaft*. In this context the question must be faced squarely: why have not chairs in ethics and philosophy been established in Jewish theological seminaries to this end?[11]

The question becomes all the more urgent, say, if we consider the specific demands made on religion by *Wissenschaft* in the modern period. Religion studied under the aegis of *die Geisteswissenschaften* must submit to the systematic test of ethics.

> "The conviction inflames the confessor of Judaism – that his teaching concerning belief is his teaching concerning ethics and his teaching concerning ethics is his teaching concerning belief. The ceremonies do not form a counter to this; they

[9]Cohen, 'Errichtung von Lehrstühlen', p. 109.
[10]*Ibid.*, p. 113.
[11]*Ibid.*

belong to the applied ethical teaching; they are supposed to be of use for the fortification of the ethical life. This is the meaning and purpose of all divine services."[12]

With the new demand of *Wissenschaft* on the Jew so very clear, how could Jewish communities have refrained for so long from placing those scholars with expertise in ethics into leading roles in their educational institutions?

The *jüdische Aufklärung* has cast up the real obstacle to restoring *Wissenschaft* to its former place in the Jewish community, according to Cohen. "One only need consider the well-known, typical phrase, which the Jewish Enlightenment made into a household word, [namely] that we have no doctrines at all."[13] Of course doctrinal argument was never entirely absent from the Jewish community of the nineteenth century.[14] Given the presuppositions of the *Aufklärung*, however, the philosophical articulation of doctrine could not take root, and the philosophically inclined were confined to the periphery of Jewish life.

The *jüdische Aufklärung* misunderstood the importance of doctrine. Consequently, it obscured the proper role of Jewish sources and their exposition in the modern Jewish community. Since, for modern Judaism, "the fundamental teachings of belief and of ethics hang together", doctrines must in fact become ethical "concepts for teaching" Jewish belief. In order to propagate a modern Judaism and a modern Jewish identity, Jewish sources must be studied with the intention of developing such doctrines. Moreover, for both the formulation of doctrine and the reading of sources we require the philosopher's guidance: "the progressive development and continued existence of Judaism is conditioned by its philosophical grounding."[15]

Such is Cohen's general case for philosophy's leadership role in the Jewish theological seminary. But 'Errichtung von Lehrstühlen' goes one step further. Cohen also paints a picture of the Jew who would be shaped by education in the new mould. Indeed, the definition of this new type, "the Modernist, the scientific character [*der Neue, die wissenschaftliche Gesinnung*]", is at the heart of this educational proposal. While an idea of God is the *foundation* of Jewish doctrine for Cohen, and its *exposition* falls within the domain of "the pure scientific ethics [*die reine wissenschaftliche Ethik*]",[16] the principle *subject* of Jewish doctrine is not God, but *der Mensch*. The task that Cohen envisions for the Jewish philosopher is "the determination of the individual human", the construction of a doctrine concerning Jewish identity.[17]

---

[12]*Ibid.*, p. 114.
[13]*Ibid.*
[14]Cohen mentions Ludwig Salomon Steinheim, Samuel Hirsch and Salomon Formstecher.
[15]Cohen, 'Errichtung von Lehrstühlen', pp. 114–115.
[16]"Wenn wir der jüdischen Glaubenslehre ein erneutes, verjüngtes Studium zuwenden werden, so wird sich die Überzeugung erwecken lassen, daß die jüdische Gottesidee in einem lebendigen Zusammenhange mit der reinen wissenschaftlichen Ethik steht; daß die Ethik eine Torso bleibt, wenn der Gottesbegriff von ihr abgetrennt wird. Diese Einsicht zu begründen ist Sache der Philosophie, der philosophischen Ethik", *ibid.*, p. 121.
[17]"[D]ie Bestimmung des Menschen", *ibid.*, p. 115. The extended discussion of doctrine, the teaching concerning Jewish identity, begins on p. 122 ("unsere Anregung"). There Cohen locates his

In the final pages of 'Errichtung von Lehrstühlen' Cohen brings his proposal to its climax with a description of the exemplary modern Jew. These pages contain passages by Cohen as passionate as his writing is elsewhere arid and plodding.[18] Since their language is at the very heart of my argument, I will quote from them at length. Cohen here assumes the vocation to which he continued to call his academic fellows, Jew and non-Jew alike, as late as 1915: a pedagogy of identity based on belief in a unique God.

> "To be a Jew means to avow, as the foundation of existence, as the anchor of the world, the God who is uniquely one. This is the kernel of the matter [*Sache*]; it is also the unique heart of the subject [*das einzige Herz der Sache*]."

> "One should not deceive oneself as to whether the Jewish subject [*Sache*] may or could have or would have yet another centre of gravity [*Herzpunkt*]. Here any comparison of hypotheses or evaluation of motives is bad. Israel's claim to historical existence stands and falls with its God who is uniquely one. Whosoever is not illuminated with this fundamental thought can possess both ethically and spiritually a great deal of the Jewish style; but his being lacks its grounding [*Schwerpunkt*]."

> "Thus the existence of the Jew will become ambiguous, unstable, anchorless, whenever this guiding light does not shine forth from all of his thinking, feeling and action; [namely] that he believes with his entire soul in the God of history, as revealed by the prophets. The God of Israel has been revealed in the messianic idea; he is the God of world history. This is the root of our belief; and it is the source of our ethics."[19]

To be such a Jew – a believer in the God of history, faithful to the messianic idea – would require distinctive characteristics and particular forms of community, in Cohen's view. However, the greatest share of responsibility for such a revolution in Jewish life would depend on the quality of leadership emanating from the seminary of the new century and the scholarship that it would support. The crucial role would be played by a new kind of Jewish philosopher, master of systematic and historical philosophy.

> "This illumination and grounding of the idea of God, however, requires an independent, complete man as the advocate of his speciality [*Vertreter seines Fachs*]. To that end exhaustive studies of the sources of the history of philosophy are required; and at the same time a professional mastery of systematic philosophy; for ethics [a product of historical philosophy] must be grounded in logic [a product of systematic philosophy]."[20]

Upon the post-*Aufklärung* Jewish philosopher would devolve a scholarly agenda whose aim is the service of God. There should be no doubt whom Cohen has in mind to lead this movement of a Jewish *avant-garde*. The description of "God's

---

proposal in the tradition of Maimonides's *Attributenlehre*. On this point, compare Cohen's essay 'Charakteristik der Ethik Maimunis', in *Jüdische Schriften III*, pp. 221–289.

[18] The editor of *Haschiloah*, justifying the decision to publish a full Hebrew translation of Cohen's lecture, upon which 'Errichtung' is based, comments: "... We feel an obligation to ourselves to translate it in full because there is great merit not only in its content, but also in its wonderful and sublime style." (My translation–A. B.-N.). See *Haschiloah*, vol. XIII (1904), p. 356.

[19] Cohen, 'Errichtung von Lehrstühlen', pp. 122–123.

[20] *Ibid.*, p. 123.

advocate [*der Mann*]" is neatly tailored to suit its author. Cohen's writing is simultaneously systematic and historical. His systematic philosophy founds ethics upon logic. 'Errichtung von Lehrstühlen', the architecture for his teaching concerning Jewish identity, establishes the mode in which Cohen will construct much of his *Jüdische Schriften* from this point forward. Self-presentation and the doctrine of Jewish identity are combined.

Guided by the new scholarship, the modern Jew should approach Jewish sources with the conviction that their study in a *wissenschaftlich* mode is imperative for "a new renaissance of religious thinking and life in Judaism". Cohen singles out medieval Jewish philosophy as a particularly important well-spring for this renewal of Jewish religious life. In these sources, "the statutes are secondary to the ideas [i.e. of God's attributes]". With the aid of philosophical study, the modern Jew can come to see the observance of rabbinic commands as an opportunity for self-improvement, the emulation of God's attributes. Furthermore, the sermon can serve just as well as the scholarly paper for the dissemination of this approach within the community.[21]

This renewed appreciation for Jewish sources, and reinvigorated commitment to Jewish practice, would yield fruit both within and beyond the Jewish community. Within the community, new bonds would arise between "die Alten ... und die Neuen", Jews still living in the orbit of rabbinic law and modern Jews who had outgrown it.[22] Devotion to Jewish literary sources and performance of divine commands would unite them, according to Cohen, however much their understandings of the same might diverge.

> "And if this scientific enthusiasm will speak out from the works and deeds of the moderns, then at the same time this scientific disposition [*Gesinnung*] will show itself as the truly religious one. Before such seriousness of conviction of belief in the ideas [i.e. of God] the most prejudiced ancient will feel respect; and this respect will bind the ancients and the moderns among us more truthfully, powerfully, intimately than the emotion of common suffering, or even the illusion of a racial community, which is an alien drop of blood in the prophetic bloodstream of the messianic Jew."[23]

Amidst discord, Jews of differing commitments had always shared a common text. Modernity need not rob them of it now, if the modern Jew would be willing "to extend a hand in the advancement of the literary good".[24]

The emergence of a modern religious Jew with a *wissenschaftlich* constitution would also pay dividends in the world beyond the Jewish community, according to Cohen. A modern Judaism, steered by *Wissenschaft des Judentums*, would command the recognition and respect of the surrounding culture. "Then no more forbearance for our seperateness would be needed; tolerance will become a

---

[21] *Ibid.*, pp. 124–125.
[22] "Die Alten hüten und pflegen das rabbinische Schrifttum, dessen innerem Leben die Neuen entwachsen sind." Cohen, 'Errichtung von Lehrstühlen', p. 124.
[23] *Ibid.*, pp. 125.
[24] *Ibid.*, p. 124: "Mögen sie [die Neuen] daher in der Förderung des literarischen Gutes den Alten die Hand reichen; daß die Kenntnis und das Studium, das ganze innerliche Studium des rabbinischen Schrifttums nicht aufhöre in Israel; daß die Quellen nicht versiegen, aus denen sich in der ganzen bisherigen Geschichte stets von neuem das jüdische Leben und Denken gekräftigt, gerüstet, beseelt hat."

consequence of the academic culture [*theoretische Kultur*]."[25] Jewish particularity could be robustly affirmed by the non-Jew and disaffected Jew alike.

In the penultimate paragraph of his proposal, Cohen raises hopes for *die Neuen* to their absolute zenith. Might the new scholar-Jew be a prophet, who could lead his people back to the promised land?[26] Cohen has already told his readers that, in making his proposal, he stands on the shoulders of Maimonides. Might Cohen himself be yet another link in the chain which extends from Maimonides, through the biblical prophets, back to Moses? Might another modern Jew achieve such a status with the assistance of Cohen's instruction? These questions are left for the reader to answer.

All the achievements Cohen envisions for the modern Jew depend on the progress of a single institution, *Wissenschaft des Judentums*. Moreover, its success depends on the leadership of a new sort of Jew, one whose constitution Cohen describes at length in the years that followed the publication of 'Errichtung von Lehrstühlen'. Cohen gives the centrality of *Wissenschaft des Judentums* and the Jewish philosopher the emphasis of his final words.

> "Therefore, the independent, professional advocacy of ethics and philosophy of religion must form the focus of our teaching system [*Lehrwesens*]; as it must also be the central point for all our efforts for the progress of the Science of Judaism."[27]

I. SOCIAL TYPE[28]

In May 1914, Cohen toured Eastern Europe, stopping to lecture in St. Petersburg, Moscow, Riga, Vilna and Warsaw[29]. If Cohen's recollections of this time are to be trusted, however, his principal agenda was first and foremost not the dissemination of his philosophical system, but the export of *Wissenschaft des Judentums* from its native home in Germany. Cohen's recollections are contained in an article of 1916 entitled 'Der polnische Jude'. With German politicians considering a blockade of their border to prevent Jewish immigration from the East, Cohen speaks out in favour of a renewed commitment to an East-West interchange, but only – it might seem – for the good of the unfortunate Polish Jew. In Arthur Cohen's estimation, the Polish Jew in this essay is portrayed for

---

[25] *Ibid.*, p. 124.
[26] *Ibid.*, p. 125. Cohen asks: "Konnte doch sogar das Wort entstehen, welches Maimonides mit dem Unvergleichlichen, mit Mose, verknüpft. So tief hat man die Erneuerung gewürdigt, welche der 'Führer der Verirrten' dem Judentum geschaffen hat." The "expression" at issue here is not only a philosophical work, i.e. *Guide for the Perplexed*, but also prophecy. Cohen implies here that Maimonides, like Moses, was a prophet.
[27] *Ibid.*
[28] Cohen makes plentiful use of typological language. See e.g., note 97 below and Cohen, 'Der polnische Jude', in *Jüdische Schriften II*, pp. 166–167: "Das ist das große Beispiel, die vorbildliche Bedeutung, die der deutsche Jude für die Zukunft des Judentums, und zwar des Judentums der ganzen Welt in seiner religiösen Entwicklung darstellt." The use of social types in reflection on modern identity is also associated with the revival of "moral psychology" today. See, for example, MacIntyre, *After Virtue*, pp. 27–35; Robert Bellah *et. al.*, *Habits of the Heart*, New York 1985.
[29] Cohen, 'Der polnische Jude', p. 167.

the reader "as somehow a stunted flower...to be rescued by the higher *Kultur* of German Jewry".[30]

If in reading 'Der polnische Jude', however, we pay special attention to the paradigmatic social type of Jew that Cohen champions, Cohen's cultural politics are cast in a somewhat different light. Moreover, this social type is an important *locus* for Cohen's teaching concerning Jewish identity. According to this teaching, the Jew of the future will take shape as a result of East-West reciprocity.[31] It is true, of course, that German *Wissenschaft des Judentums* will play the formative role in the education of this modern person. Nevertheless, both the *deutscher Jude* and the *Ostjude* will give shape to the social type to be enshrined in the developing *Kultur* of European Judaism. Both are essential, according to Cohen's teaching.

The *Kultur* of the *Ostjude* forms a special problem for Cohen. In a word, the *Ostjude* lacks a model for "a religiously truthful/authentic life".[32] Such a life, whatever else it might entail for a Jew, must include exacting ideals for ethical and political conduct, fulfilment of some (though not all) of the "ritual" obligations of rabbinic Judaism, and immersion in the study of the Jewish literary tradition.[33] To become acquainted with such a Jew, contends Cohen, the *Ostjude* can only look towards German-Jewry's institutions of *Wissenschaft* and the ideology of religious liberalism.

> "This is the great example, the pattern of significance, which the German Jew represents for the future of Judaism, and indeed of the Judaism of the whole world in its religious development ...We have managed to harmonise the conception of our history, as well as the progress of our rituals [*Kultus*] with the most central driving forces of our religious tradition and at the same time with those of the common culture. No insightful person can doubt that our independent piety [*freie Religiosität*] is a deep source [*Herzkraft*] for our concept of culture [*Kulturgesinnung*] and especially also for our general politics."[34]

The Eastern Jew has lacked the opportunity to acquire a truly modern Jewish spirituality. Cohen does not doubt, however, that this Jew possesses the means for such development, if given the proper education. Indeed, the primary impetus for his lecture tour, reports Cohen, was to assist in the institutionalisation of *Wissenschaft des Judentums* in the places of contemporary Jewish learning and

---

[30] Arthur Cohen, *The Jew*, Alabama 1980, p. 52. Cf. Steven E. Aschheim, *Brothers and Strangers. The East European Jew in German and German Jewish Consciousness, 1800–1923*, Madison 1982, p. 177: "German Judaism [for Cohen in 'Der polnische Jude'] remained the historical ideal – an ideal worth emulating by Eastern Jews...Once again it became apparent that Eastern Jews had to be remade in German Jewry's spiritual image."
[31] "Aller Segen im Kulturleben aber beruht auf Wechselwirkung." Cohen, 'Der polnische Jude', p. 170.
[32] "Wahrhaftes Leben der Religiosität muß bei dem Kulturmenschen bedingt sein durch den lebendigen Zusammenhang mit religiöser Wissenschaft und religiöser Bildung." *Ibid.*, p. 167. On the translation of *Wahrhaftigkeit*, cf. Jacques Derrida, 'Interpretations at War. Kant, the Jew, the German', in *New Literary History*, 22 (1991), pp. 63–64.
[33] On ethical conduct, cf. sections II & III of this article. On ritual, see Cohen, 'Der polnische Jude', pp. 166–167. On the study of the literary tradition, see *ibid.*, p. 164 and section II.
[34] *Ibid.*, pp. 166–167.

scholarship. No Jew, whether from East or West, could achieve a truthful life of piety without *Wissenschaft* and self-cultivation (*Bildung*).[35]

If his essay had drawn to a close with these remarks, perhaps we would have been impelled towards the conclusion that Cohen was a German-Jewish chauvinist, unable to see beyond the perceived merits of his own social type in order to recognise the merits of another. In fact the paragraphs which follow on the heels of these remarks take Cohen's argument in a very different direction. The *freier Jude*, the social type which Cohen so prizes, represents not an empirical achievement of the current generation of German Jews but rather an ideal which – according to Cohen's description – they have embraced, and an end towards which they should strive. Progress in embodying this ideal, however, cannot be assured. Indeed, Cohen intimates that the German Jew is ill-equipped to realise his goal.

Redemption may be forthcoming from the East, however. "We need not altogether despair about it," Cohen insists. "The Eastern Jew himself will bring us salvation if henceforth, and perhaps in greater numbers than before, they were to go on immigrating to our provinces...." If the German Jew requires the *Ostjude* in his midst in order to flourish, it is because only a symbiosis of the two might result in a new Jew, a closer approximation to the ideal, the *freier Jude*.[36] "Indeed, all blessings in cultural life are based upon reciprocity."[37]

The German Jew, for his part, must instruct his Eastern compatriot in the ways of the *freier Jude*, in ethics and politics, and in rituals, as well as in *Wissenschaft*. As a result the *Ostjude* will learn to comport himself according to rigorous standards of personal behaviour and will merit (if not receive) political emancipation. Furthermore, he will come to understand his religion, both its ritual and its doctrines, according to the strictest standards of *wissenschaftlich* philosophy.[38] The new free and independent self-awareness which such education would bring in its train would shine as the crowning achievement of Jewish emancipation.[39]

The *Ostjude*, however, must also shape the future character of Western Jewry. Indeed, he is the very prerequisite for the possibility of the *freier Jude*.[40] Without

---

[35] *Ibid.* The language of these paragraphs is significant for my argument. Categories such as *Einheit*, *Herzkraft*, *Gesinnung*, and *Sache* all point to Cohen's teaching concerning Jewish identity.

[36] I assume that Cohen, being politic, chooses not to be quite so explicit as I am here.

[37] Cohen, 'Der polnische Jude', p. 170.

[38] It should not be lost on the reader that this philosophy, i.e. of the unique God, is Cohen's. "Er soll einsehen lernen, daß die wahre, die wissenschaftliche Philosophie, die nicht den Dilettantismus der Phantasie hegt, sondern mit den Wissenschaften methodisch verwachsen ist, den Glauben an den einzigen Gott zu rechtfertigen vermag", *ibid.* For some suggested religious reforms, see p. 171. It would be a mistake to see an uncomplicated cultural imperialism in this instruction, even leaving aside the reciprocity that Cohen demands in terms of cross-cultural exchange. Cohen here suggests that the Polish Jew learn from the German one "für sein eigenes persönliches, wie für das Gemeindeleben, in *Selbständigkeit und nach seiner Eigenart* anzubauen." (Italics mine–A. B.-N.). For a related point, see p. 168.

[39] *Ibid.*, p. 171: "... die Vollendung des geschichtlichen Sinnes aller Judenemanziption ist es, welche sonach im Selbstbewußtsein des Juden zur Reife kommen würde."

[40] *Ibid.*, pp. 168, 171. For an explanation of Cohen's use of the logical category *Ursprung* (origin) in terms of *Ermöglichungsbedingungen* (enabling conditions), see Helmut Holzhey, 'Einleitung des Her-

his number being replenished from the East, the German Jew cannot withstand the assimilatory pressures of his environment. The moral resources required to be a good Jew are readily available in the Jewish tradition, as they have always been. However, assimilation into the cultural mainstream has undone the German Jew's ability to be nourished and refreshed by the Jewish tradition, its rituals and literary sources. In this historical moment, only an influx of Eastern Jewry can provide the necessary medicine: the powers and capacities *native* to the *freier Jude*.[41] The power most fundamental to this ideal type of Jew, in Cohen's estimation, is command of the Jewish literary tradition.[42]

If the German Jew is to regain his bearings, it will be due to a reorientation to the literary sources inspired by the Jew from the East.[43] These literary sources are the ultimate root of the modern Jew's intellectual and ethical power.[44] For the *freier Jude*, the ideal social type which Cohen imagines for the German Jew, Judaism's literary sources are a constituent of his very being, and a force at work throughout his life. "The spiritual energy of the Jews has its ultimate source in the literary treasures of the Jewish religion."[45]

II. LITERARY TRADITION[46]

Cohen, we have seen, envisions a modern Jew dedicated to the study of literary sources, e.g. the Hebrew Bible, rabbinic literature, and medieval Jewish philosophy. In a short article first appearing in the *Gemeindeblatt der Jüdischen Gemeinde zu*

---

ausgebers', in Hermann Cohen, *Logik der reinen Erkenntnis*, Hildesheim 1977, (1st edn. of *Logik*, Berlin 1902) p. IX.

[41] 'Der polnische Jude', p. 171. Cohen uses the term *Autochthonie* to commend what is called here the native powers and capacities of the Eastern Jew. The native powers of the autochthon from Eastern Europe are necessary but not sufficient for the *Neuer*, the *freier Jude*.

[42] On the character of the *Ostjude*, see especially *ibid.*, p. 169: "Mit seiner schier übermenschlichen Dulderkraft, die er erprobt hat, wird er unserer idealen Sittlichkeit, unserer Opferfreudigkeit für übersinnliche Aufgaben einen neuen Schwung geben"; and p. 171: "Ihr Leiden hat den Ostjuden ein geschichtliches Vorrecht zuerteilt. Es hat ihnen mit dem Witz und dem Humor eine Ursprünglichkeit bewahrt, die eine Art von Autochthonie ist." In Cohen's teaching, this capacity for suffering is constituted in the Jew in at least two ways: in the constitutive narrative considered in section. III; and through the virtues (cf. section V).

[43] *Ibid.*, pp. 169–170. (Compare section II on Jewish literary tradition.)

[44] "Die jüdische Intelligenz, wie die Sittlichkeit der Juden, wurzelt aber nicht allein in Mose und den Propheten nebst den Psalmen, sondern nicht minder auch in der mündlichen Lehre, in Talmud und Midrasch, wie endlich auch in den Religionsphilosophen des Mittelalters." *Ibid.*, p. 169.

[45] *Ibid.*, p. 164. Social types other than the *freier Jude* also make appearances in Cohen's Jewish writings. For examples, see the apostate-philosopher in 'Gedanken über Jugendlektüre', *ibid.*, p. 127 and in 'Mahnung des Alters an die Jugend', *ibid.*, pp.177–180; the apostate-scholar in 'Errichtung von Lehrstühlen', *ibid.,* pp. 120–121; and the Jewish dissident in 'Eine Pflicht der Selbstachtung', *ibid.*, pp. 173–174. Significantly, these types can all be understood as deformations of Cohen's exemplar, the *freier Jude*.

[46] Cohen most often uses the phrase "literarische Quellen" in connection with the subject matter discussed here. This phrase, whose precise connotation cannot be taken up in the confines of this essay, has significant affinities with the the English "literary tradition", as it is discussed in contemporary moral psychology. Cf. MacIntyre, *After Virtue*, pp. 204–226.

Berlin in February 1911, he offers a concise expression of the grounds for such commitment. The essay is entitled 'Die Liebe zur Religion' and Cohen suggests the fundamental reason for studying Jewish sources is love.[47]

That a Jew might be commanded to love God is relatively uncontroversial. Cohen need only allude to the commandment of Deuteronomy VI:5: "Thou shalt love the Lord thy God with all thy heart, and with all thy soul, and with all thy might." The character of this love, however, its source and its object, is a good deal less straightforward. This problem provides the pretext for Cohen's essay.

'Die Liebe' is an important *locus* for Cohen's teaching. The modern observance of Deuteronomy VI:5, according to 'Die Liebe', requires the cultivation of a particular Jewish identity, a "historico-ethical personality". Love of God, Cohen argues, is knowledge of God, appropriately mediated by the Jewish literary tradition. Moreover, the character of this literary mediation is the critical element for the Jew's loving-knowledge of God. For Cohen, the literary sources conspire to provide a knowledge of God's attributes (*Eigenschaften Gottes*), not God's essence (*seines Wesen*). In turn, God's attributes provide the model for ethical behaviour. In Cohen's view, therefore, loving-knowledge of God points the modern Jew to his particular vocation as an ethical person. Ultimately, then, loving-knowledge of God constitutes self-knowledge, knowledge of one's own personality and of the kind of Jew one should be.

It is easy to be misled by Cohen's choice of words in this appeal. The command in Deuteronomy is to love "God". Why, then, does Cohen insist on the love of "religion" and in what could such "love" consist? Moreover, his ostensible subject is love of "religion" rather than of "Judaism". Will the love of any (monotheistic) religion do? Finally, in the context in which Cohen is writing, love is *prima facie* a passion. Why, then, does Cohen understand it primarily as a cognitive relation, even if between lover and beloved? Does any element of passion in the relationship remain?

The command to study Torah immediately follows Deuteronomy's command to love God, Cohen points out:

> "And these words, which I command thee this day, shall be in thy heart: and thou shalt teach them diligently to thy children, and shalt talk of them when thou sittest in thy house, and when thou walkest by the way, and when thou liest down, and when thou risest up."

In the spirit of this literary connection, claims Cohen, Judaism has forged an enduring link between the love of God and the knowledge of Torah. Moreover, Torah is an important Jewish expression of religion.[48] For a Jew, in a significant respect, to love religion is to know Torah.

Deuteronomy makes no mention of Judaism, nor of religion, however. Might the modern Jew properly love God while renouncing "religion" altogether? Could Cohen's contemporaries make a principled decision to study primarily

---

[47] Cohen, 'Die Liebe zur Religion', p. 142.
[48] "Die Liebe zu Gott ist die Liebe zur Religion, die Gottes Schöpfung in der Geschichte und in der Vernunft der Menschen ist", *ibid*.

literature beyond the bounds of Jewish tradition, even with the intention of observing the commandment to love "the Lord thy God"? Neither of these choices would be desirable for his readership, urges Cohen.

No one, neither Jew nor non-Jew, can renounce religion, he claims.[49] Religion, and especially the literature found within it, stands as a constitutive element in the make-up of the modern person. Not only what we study but how we study it makes a crucial difference to who we are. Refraining from outward acts of religious behaviour cannot disentangle a person from the *problem* of religion.[50] Accordingly, failure to engage in the sophisticated study of the literary sources does not divest the Jew of a relation to them. On the contrary, such a lack of commitment makes the Jew's relation to "literary sources" all the more problematic, conferring upon the religiously illiterate Jew a retrograde *ersatz* religion as a result.[51]

Furthermore, German Jews have a particular need to steel themselves with the study of the Jewish literary tradition. German Jews, argues Cohen, live in a state of political siege, constantly attacked on account of their "confession". If they try to observe their religion without a "vital love" for it, they will inevitably fail. Moreover, the source of the failure will be readily identifiable: a conspicuous flaw in the German-Jewish character. Indeed, without a thorough grounding in the literary sources, German Jews will eventually abdicate their historical vocation entirely. Ultimately, claims Cohen, they will sacrifice their very right to existence as Jews.[52]

But in what does love's "vitality" consist, if not in a flame of human passion? For Cohen, love is a fit description for the appropriate relation of the Jew to God and to Torah, but only in a highly specific sense. As we have noted, the proper love of God is, for Cohen, a kind of knowledge, not a conventional emotion. "*Love is knowledge*. Affective states cannot be trusted, not even that of love."[53] An affective state rightly animates the *freier Jude* in relation to God, but a *concept*, not a passion, is its cause.

The concept of *Ehre*,[54] not the passion of Eros, stands behind the Jew's loving-attachment to God.[55] Cohen did not explain this point at any length in 'Die

---

[49]*Ibid.*, p. 142–143: "Jeder Kulturmensch hat seine eigene Religion. Er hat sie von seiner eigenen sozialen und persönlichen Entwicklung empfangen, und er kann sich ihrer gar nicht entledigen. Er kann sie verleugnen und äußerlich verlassen, aber sie bleibt ein wie immer latentes Moment in seiner seelischen und geistigen Verfassung."
[50]For a discussion of the Jew who tries to deny the "problem of religion", see Cohen's discussion of the "dissident" in 'Eine Pflicht der Selbstachtung', *Jüdische Schriften II*, pp. 172–175.
[51]Cohen, 'Die Liebe zur Religion', pp. 142–143.
[52]*Ibid.*, pp. 143–144.
[53]*Ibid.*, pp. 144–145: "*Liebe ist Erkenntnis*. Auf die Affekte ist kein Verlaß, auch auf den der Liebe nicht." Italics in the original.
[54]*Die Ehre* is the disposition to act honourably towards others as well as to be deserving of honour. It is both activity and goal. Cohen, *Ethik*, p. 490.
[55]Cohen, 'Die Liebe zur Religion', p. 145. Cohen does not mention Eros explicitly as the competing motivation for love, here understood as cognition. Rather, in 'Die Liebe zur Religion', Cohen calls the competing motive "die Pietät ... eine starke Kraft". However, Eros is for Cohen an unnamed concern here in relation to the love that his religion commends. It is the force in human consciousness in opposition to which he offers the notion of love as cognition. See, e.g., *Ethik*, pp. 480–481.

Liebe', but he had already addressed it in significant detail in his *Ethik* in 1904. The Jew who leads an authentic religious life must successfully cultivate certain affective states, foremost among them being honour.[56] To be honourable in this regard is inseparable from an ethical and political vision of enormous significance to Cohen: to respect the equality of all persons, to promote their full inclusion in the nation-state and, finally, to advocate a federation of nation-states of *Kultur* in pursuit of peace.[57]

The Jew's vocation in the pursuit of this new horizon is to draw near to God by pursuing the truth. This vocation is founded on the affinity of a God who is spirit, a truth which is spiritual, and a knowing spirit who is the *freier Jude*. Cohen makes no effort to plumb the depths of these affinities in the course of 'Die Liebe'. He does note here, however, the prerequisite for any realisation of such a vocation, namely, self-cultivation through the study of Jewish sources.[58] A knowing spirit is hardly a natural property of the Jew; on the contrary, the intellectual power of the Jew, the capacity to draw near to the divine, is utterly dependent on the disciplined development of such a spirit in one's self. Accordingly, no trend among modern Jewry more undermines its historical vocation than Jewry's increasing unfamiliarity with its literary sources, and with the sophisticated means for their study.

> "We cannot be so very injured by political and social oppression and, indeed, not so badly by defection [from the Jewish community] as when we no longer apply our intellectual power to our religious sources in academic research and in education for self-cultivation. No amount of historical pride, of love for one's own tribe, can replace the power which alone acquaintance with the sources of religion forms for the living confession...
>
> Not all Jews have to become scholars of Judaism. This profound fundamental demand of ancient Judaism can perhaps not continue to be maintained. The modern world, however, distinguishes education for personal self-cultivation from science. Education for one's own self-cultivation is the adhesive which binds academic research and the commercial vocations. Such an education in the literature and history of our religion must become a common good, a religious, a cultural obligation of our co-religionists."[59]

Cohen makes no effort in these pages to elaborate further on the character of the required study. For greater detail the reader must turn to Cohen's more philosophical writings, 'Charakteristik der Ethik Maimuni' and *Religion der Vernunft aus den Quellen des Judentums*.[60] To one familiar with these works, however, the character of study to which Cohen alludes in 'Die Liebe' is apparent. If the modern

---

[56] Contemporary moral psychology has revived the issue that Cohen takes up here, the relation of passions to affective states. See MacIntyre, 'Moral Philosophy', p. 9; Peter Berger, 'On the Obsolescence of the Concept of Honor', in *Revisions*, pp. 172–181; Lee Yearley, *Menscius and Aquinas*, Albany 1990, pp. 95–113.

[57] *Ethik* , pp. 490–497. The origin of Cohen's concept of honour appears to be *Kavod*, an attribute of God found in the Hebrew Bible. See *Ethik*, p. 491.

[58] "Die geschichtliche Ehre ist ein hoher Begriff, aber er muß seinen klaren, unerschöpflichen Quell haben in der wissenschaftlichen Erkenntnis, oder wenigstens in der Einsicht von den literarischen Werten unserer Religion." Cohen, 'Die Liebe zur Religion', p. 145.

[59] *Ibid.*, p. 146.

[60] Cited in notes 3 and 17 above.

student of the Jewish literary tradition takes the venerable approach of a seeker of God's attributes, the sources will reward him or her with a paradigm for the human self.[61] "The love for our religion is the love for our historico-ethical personality." Love of religion, love of the literary sources, is knowledge of them. Truly to know these sources is to know oneself.[62]

III. NARRATIVE[63]

For Cohen, however, Jewish literary sources point not only to God's attributes but also to a *narrative* of Jewish existence and, with this, to the very constitution of the modern Jew.[64] Cohen makes this case in 1915 in the closing pages of his *Begriff der Religion*. A proper understanding of the narrative inscribed in the fifty-third chapter of Isaiah, Cohen suggests, provides us with knowledge of the Jewish people, both individually and as a collective. In this source Israel is revealed as the "Servant of God".[65]

The text of Isaiah LIII which concerns Cohen here reads as follows:

> "He had no form nor comeliness, that we should look upon him, nor beauty that we should delight in him ... But he was wounded because of our transgressions, he was crushed because of our iniquities; the chastisement of our welfare was upon him ... Yet it pleased the Eternal to crush him by disease; to see if his soul would offer itself as a guilt offering ... Of the travail of his soul he shall see to the full, even My servant, who by his knowledge did justify the Righteous One to the many, and their iniquities did he bear."[66]

According to Cohen, these verses illuminate the condition of the Jew by clarifying the nature of the human person. Indeed, on Cohen's reading, the modern Jew, properly moulded by Isaiah's prophetic outlook, is the human person, a representative of the ends towards which all persons should strive. Jewish particularity is not undone in the Jews' embodiment of a human narrative, however. Throughout his exegesis Cohen maintains the ambivalence of Israel's significance. Israel's vocation is always at once to inhabit its own story in particular and to represent the human narrative in general.[67]

---

[61] See Altmann, pp. 40–60.
[62] Cohen, 'Die Liebe zur Religion', p. 147: "Die Liebe zu ihr [unsere Religion] ist die Liebe zu unserer geschichtlich-sittlichen Persönlichkeit."
[63] This is my rendering of "die Geschichte" in this context, i.e. in *Begriff*, pp. 131–133. Narrative is a basic term in the discussion of contemporary moral psychology. See MacIntyre, *After Virtue*, pp. 187–203; Charles Taylor, *Sources of the Self*, Cambridge, MA 1989, pp. 25–53; Jerome Bruner, 'The Narrative Construction of Reality', in *Critical Inquiry*, 18 (Autumn 1991), pp. 1–21.
[64] *Begriff*, p. 131. The distinction between God's attributes and the Jews' narrative is useful here, but the categories are not mutually exclusive. The Messiah, which serves as a *telos* for the *Mensch* in accord with this narrative, is itself an attribute of God. See 'Die Bedeutung des Judentums für den religiösen Fortschritt der Menschheit', *Jüdische Schriften I*, p. 31.
[65] *Begriff*, pp. 126–133; see also *Religion*, pp. 308–313 and pp. 328–335.
[66] The translation is Simon Kaplan's. *Religion*, pp. 283–285. Cohen goes to great lengths to argue that the servant's "guilt-offering" in no way absolves anyone of personal responsibility for sin. See *Begriff*, p. 130 and *Religion*, pp. 332–334.
[67] This ambivalence is particularly prominent in *Religion*, pp. 311–313.

"Suffering," Cohen argues, "belongs to the essence of the human person".[68] Israel, portrayed by Isaiah as the suffering servant of God, stands in opposition to every effort to establish an *exclusively* aesthetic, ethical or cognitive human ideal. The *Mensch* was intended to be neither (first and foremost) beautiful, nor pleased, but to suffer in the pursuit of God's ends. Neither intellectual virtue nor personal integrity, in themselves desirable, can supplant suffering as a feature of the fully flourishing person. Only in suffering does Man begin to internalise his true identity. "Indeed, now it comes to light that the greatest deficiency and weakness in the person is rather his greatest wealth and his most powerful source for life, and that only by means of this supposed blemish does he in truth become an integrated whole [*Einheit*]."[69]

In this context, we must remember, personal identity is not a quality given to an individual by nature. On the contrary, it is an achievement of individual consciousness and collective *Kultur*. Cohen's language is characteristically precise. *Einheit* – identity – signifies a person's success at incorporating diverse capacities and interests, and becoming an integrated "unit".[70] Such success is primarily a function of individual ability to act reflexively to cultivate the self, integrating it into a whole whose parts function well and harmoniously. In this effort, personal suffering is invaluable. Suffering is a school for self-possession and self-control, potentially increasing one's powers to strive towards the good, and to persevere in the face of opposition.[71] In this context, the image of Israel as the suffering servant in Isaiah LIII is distinguished as a valuable cultural resource.[72]

Ultimately, Israel's mission is to disseminate a teaching concerning identity to all Jews and to all peoples. *Kultur*, collective cognitive, ethical, aesthetic and religious advancement, is the mission of all nations both to their members and to one another.[73] In this effort the Jew must conceive his personal and collective history to be a tale of suffering in the service of God. Suffering, Cohen cautions, is never an end in itself, however. On the contrary, consciousness of the lachrymose character of Jewish existence plays its legitimate role only as a yeast for the rise of an identity proper to the modern Jew.[74]

---

[68] *Begriff*, p. 126: "...das Leiden gehört zum Wesen des Menschen."

[69] *Ibid.*, p. 131. Cohen's mention of "seine Einheit in Wahrheit" may allude to the role of *die Wahrhaftigkeit*, truthfulness and authenticity, in the development of Jewish identity.

[70] "Unit" captures the mathematical-logical connotation of *Einheit* for Cohen. Terms such as *Einheit*, *Mehrheit*, and *Totalität*, whose logical connotations are developed by Cohen in his *Ethik*, serve for him as building blocks for a logic of identity.

[71] *Begriff*, p. 132.

[72] Cohen notes the traditional identification of the servant with Israel, *ibid.*, p. 126, and in *Religion*, pp. 305, 311.

[73] *Begriff*, pp. 131–132.

[74] *Ibid.*, p. 133: "...kann das Leiden nimmermehr Selbstzweck, sondern nur Mittel der Einheit des Bewusstseins sein...." The conception of Jewish history in Isaiah LIII is not the only constitutive narrative of Jewish existence. A person finds his or her *telos* not only in the image of a suffering Messiah, but also in that of a labouring Faust, *ibid.*, pp. 132–133.

IV. COMMUNITY[75]

The individual, we noted above, achieves an identity by virtue of individual striving and communal membership. In his 1916 article 'Die Zugehörigkeit zur Gemeinde', Cohen elaborates on the role of the latter in the constitution of the individual Jew.[76] Responsibility for one's Jewish identity requires membership in the community. Even dissenters from established forms of religious belief and expression can and should find a place within it.

Cohen's essay is directed to the growing number of German Jews who were exercising their option to leave the community. In 'Zugehörigkeit' he searches for an adequate ideological *explanation* for this developing crisis in communal allegiance. Cohen rejects the suggestion that an economic motive, avoidance of the communal tax, might sufficiently explain the crisis. A social phenomenon such as this separation, insists Cohen, has its basis in ideas. Behind the phenomenon of attrition from the community stand Jewish assertions of individual freedom and claims concerning the demands of conscience and conviction.

These ideas do not pass muster with Cohen.[77] To be sure, freedom of conscience and sincerity of conviction do deserve a priority within the life of the modern Jew. Their preservation would never require departure from the community, however. "With such arguments," suggests Cohen, a person "avoids the difficulty which is raised in all questions of political, societal, and historical existence for the individual in relation to totalities, from which the individual has emerged and in which alone his individuality can be maintained". The Jewish community, which Cohen refers to here as a "totality",[78] is the very condition that makes possible the Jewish individual. Cohen makes a point of logic designed to disarm the Romantic individualist, who sees himself beholden to no group for personal identity. He insists that one could not even distinguish an individual *as Jewish* who did not belong (in a logical sense) to a Jewish community. The individualist can try to "avoid" the difficulties raised by his (logical) membership in a community by withdrawing his (official) membership. He cannot, however, truly leave the Jewish community without ceasing to be a Jew.[79]

Cohen's partisanship is obvious in this analysis. He skilfully shifted his discussion from rights to responsibilities, from freedom's privileges to its obligations.

---

[75] This is my rendering of "Gemeinde". Until 1876, affiliation with the *Gemeinde* was compulsory, and all its members were subject to taxation. Only in that year did resignation, without the implication of apostasy, become possible. Cf. note 78. "Community" is a basic term in the contemporary discussion of moral psychology. See Taylor, *Sources*, pp. 35–40; Charles Taylor, 'Introduction', in *Human Agency and Language*, Cambridge 1985, p. 8; *idem*, 'What is human agency?', and 'Self-interpreting animals', in *ibid.*, pp. 28–50; MacIntyre, *After Virtue*, p. 194.

[76] Cohen, 'Die Zugehörigkeit zur Gemeinde', *Jüdische Schriften II*, pp. 156–161.

[77] *Ibid.*, p. 158.

[78] The Jewish *Gemeinde* is for Cohen a "relative totality [*relative Gesamtheit*]" since only the human community can be the absolute totality for an individual, *ibid*. Nevertheless, a religious community like the *Gemeinde* is distinguished from other communities (for example, Socialist collectives, fraternal organisations) for containing within it "all cultural totalities", i.e. logic, ethics, and aesthetics, *ibid.*, p. 161.

[79] *Ibid.*, pp. 158–159.

Did Cohen step beyond partisanship and into polemic? At first glance, one might be inclined to read 'Zugehörigkeit' that way. Cohen should have been aiming quite specifically to persuade his readers of their obligations to the *Gemeinde*, but he appears to have taken aim at a more general target that was suspiciously easy to hit. Jews must belong to a Jewish community (*Gemeinschaft*)[80] in order to remain Jews, urged Cohen. Are we to assume that he was naive as to other existing forms of Jewish community? Why did Cohen think that Jews had an obligation to remain affiliated specifically with the *Gemeinde*?

Cohen's line of argument is in fact a product neither of naïveté nor of polemic. For Cohen, the *Gemeinde* has a unique claim to the status of Jewish community, even in the face of conscientious dissent. It "stands behind" the individual to a degree which sets it apart from any other.[81] The *Gemeinde*, as a product of mishnaic legislation and the heritage of the medieval *Kehillah*, is an enduring agent in Jewish history, a living, corporate personality.[82] Just as the modern Jew must be responsible for his own identity, so he must be responsible for the identity of the *Gemeinde*. Indeed, for Cohen, responsibility for the *Gemeinde* is a form of responsibility for the Jewish self.

Cultivation of the self and activism in the community are expressions of the very same impulse to self-responsibility.[83] We have already noted that, for Cohen, the *Mensch* serves as a *telos* for Jewish identity. What follows from this is made explicit in 'Zugehörigkeit'. *Menschlichkeit* cannot be realised by the individual acting alone. It is achieved by individuals only in concert, acting together as an organised corporate unit.[84] In the context of this teaching, Cohen affirms that the *Gemeinde* is "the living, the unique corporate unit of the Jewish religion...which again forms one of the most important agents of his [the Jew's] particular sociological existence".[85] The community is an expression of the individual's Jewish self. The Jew who ceases to labour to shape it has "debased himself" for a very low price.[86]

---

[80] Cohen could appear to be engaging in a polemical sleight of hand in shifting from the terms *Gemeinde* to *Gemeinschaft* just as he makes his logical claim. See *ibid.*, p. 158. As suggested below, however, I take Cohen's argument here to carry the full weight of his conviction.

[81] "...Gemeinschaft...die vor allem andern – auf seinen Beistand angewiesen ist", *ibid.*

[82] *Ibid.*, pp. 156, 159. Cohen states, for instance, (p. 159) that the *Gemeinde* "die lebendige, die einzige Einheit der jüdischen Religion ist...". And Cohen refers (p. 160) to the *Gemeinde* as an "Organ der Geschichte".

[83] *Ibid.*, p. 159. Cohen asks, for instance: "Oder wäre die Verantwortlichkeit der Gesamtheit gegenüber etwa nur ein äußeres Band, und gehörte sie nicht vielmehr als eine intime Schuld in das Soll und Haben der persönlichen Freiheit?"

[84] Cf. *Begriff*, p. 127: "Am Individuum läßt sich überhaupt der Begriff des Menschen nicht erkennen." For Cohen there is an analogy between the individual as a corporate unit and the community as such. Hence the term *Einheit* is applied to the identity of both. A description of the identity of such a community, namely, how it functions as a harmonious and integrated unit, can be found in the opening paragraphs of Cohen, 'Die Zugehörigkeit zur Gemeinde', pp. 156–157. In the closing paragraphs, Cohen asserts that the *Gemeinde* "alone bears the responsibility for the progress of the fundamental ethical ideas of Jewish religion". Hence the *Gemeinde*, as a collective Jewish subject, is ultimately responsible for cultivating God's attributes, which serve as the model for "the fundamental ethical ideas of Jewish religion". (Cf. section II).

[85] *Ibid.*, p. 159, "die lebendige, die einzige Einheit der jüdischen Religion...die hinwiederum eines der wichtigsten Medien seines eigenen soziologischen Daseins bildet".

[86] *Ibid.* "Zu dieser Freiheit erniedrigt er sich...."

For mere "subjective freedom",[87] he has forsaken a path to genuine, responsible freedom, one among his most important avenues for self-cultivation as a Jew.[88]

Communal responsibility does not require collective conformity, however. In concluding 'Zugehörigkeit', Cohen directly addresses "those Jews who do not want to feel, to know and to confess their ethical connection with Judaism".[89] Emulate those millions of Protestants, pleads Cohen, who refuse to give up identification with the Church, their corporate identity, even when they dissent from official Church doctrine.[90] They contest that doctrine, and construct one more adequate to their beliefs while remaining firmly within the Church. Many Jews who contemplate departure from the *Gemeinde* could exhibit similiar tenacity, and with integrity, intimates Cohen. Indeed, the road has already been paved.[91]

No responsible Jew would leave the community without a vigorous inquiry into those modes of identification which might continue to sustain him there, in Cohen's view. But, precisely this sort of inquiry has been lacking. "You are not familiar with this religion of the prophets!"[92] According to Cohen, the "religion of the prophets" promises a conception of Jewish belief and practice likely to appeal to many Jews who leave the *Gemeinde*. Their failure to discover it is tragic; indeed, their ignorance undermines the very values that they claim to cherish most. Conscience cannot be exercised without broad knowledge of the tradition at which one ostensibly takes offence. Spiritual convictions cannot truly be tested without a vision of the full range of spiritual alternatives within one's community of origin.

Leaving the community is an unnecessary and avoidable self-mutilation, according to Cohen. Modernity offers no substitute for the kind of agency afforded by the *Gemeinde* . What other organ stands ready to shape the collective energies of the German-Jewish population into a useful whole? For Cohen, the destruction of the *Gemeinde* to which continued exodus contributes would eviscerate the German-Jewish self.[93]

V. EXPLAINING MODERN JEWISH IDENTITY: VIRTUE AND SELF-RESPONSIBILITY[94]

In an address published just months before his death,[95] Cohen finally grapples directly with a pre-eminent question of the period we have been reviewing: why

---

[87] *Ibid.*, p. 158.
[88] Cf. *ibid.*, p. 160: "... an der Gemeinde hängt unser religiöses Selbstbewußtsein."
[89] *Ibid.*, "jene Juden, die ihren sittlichen Zusammenhang mit dem Judentum nicht bekennen, nicht erkennen und fühlen wollen".
[90] *Ibid.*, "Sie wollten die ideale Einheit ihres religiösen Fundamentes nicht aufgeben".
[91] Here, as elsewhere, Cohen's teaching is both doctrine and self-presentation.
[92] Cohen, 'Die Zugehörigkeit zur Gemeinde', p. 160: "Ihr kennt sie nicht, diese Religion der Propheten!"
[93] *Ibid.*
[94] Here *Tugend* is rendered as "virtue". Virtue is a basic term in the contemporary discussion concerning moral psychology. See Charles Taylor, 'Justice After Virtue', in Horton and Mendus, pp. 16–43; Taylor, *Sources of the Self*, pp. 53–111; *idem*, 'Neutrality in Political Science', in *Philosophy and the Human Sciences*, Cambridge 1985, pp. 58–90, especially pp. 81–90; MacIntyre, *After Virtue*.
[95] 'Mahnung des Alters an die Jugend' was published in December 1917.

is the Jewish community afflicted with so severe a crisis of identity? Typically, Cohen gauges the state of the community in relation to the self-understanding of its potential educational leadership: Jewish philosophers. The rate with which they are disaffiliating from Judaism provides Cohen with the occasion for his remarks about the challenge facing his contemporaries generally. In order to restore the proper self-conception to contemporary Jews, its educational leadership must find its way back to a truthful piety (*wahrhaftige Religiosität*). Moreover, to such a piety there is only one mode of recourse: the path mapped out by the virtues of truthfulness and modesty (*Wahrhaftigkeit* and *Bescheidenheit*).

According to Cohen, the comment of a professor of philosophy of Jewish extraction is "characteristic" for a large portion of modern Jewry: only Christianity is a modern religion; "already for hundreds of years Judaism has been lifeless and fossilised".[96] Moreover, this view is reflected more generally in the behaviour of Jews in the philosophy profession in Germany as a whole.[97] By Cohen's estimation, the number of persons of Jewish origin on philosophy faculties at German universities who had converted to Christianity is so large that they form the general rule.[98]

This sociological "fact" – the identification of a characteristic or type among contemporary Jewish philosophers – frames a problem of *explanation* for Cohen in 'Mahnung', and drives its logic as a whole.[99] How is it, asks Cohen, that "our religious education and tradition in the family, in the synagogue and the school, possess so little power to attract in comparison with the driving forces of the public sphere?"[100] To a certain extent cultural context provides the sought-after explanation.[101] The revival of Hegel and Romanticism have extended credibility to specious forms of Christian theosophy, lending respectability to the claim that conversion is a matter of philosophical conviction. A truly satisfying explanation of this phenomenon, however, requires attention to factors beyond the external context of contemporary Jewish existence. Without invoking our own contemporary religious constitution and way of life as explanatory factors, claims Cohen, "this terrible fact cannot be explained".[102]

Consequently, Cohen develops an *internalist* explanation to supplement the *externalist* one to which he is prepared to concede only circumscribed authority.

---

[96]Cohen, 'Mahnung des Alters', p. 177.
[97]Cohen refers to the "Spezialgeschichte der philosophischen Professur", *ibid.*, p. 179. This term, together with "charakteristisch", "statistische Tatsache" and "statistische Bedeutung", signifies Cohen's typological thinking. See *ibid.*, pp. 177, 178, 180.
[98]*Ibid.*, pp. 177–178. Whether Cohen means the rule among the set of persons of Jewish parentage or among the set of philosophy professors is not clear from the context.
[99]"Erwägen wir den Sinn und die Ursache dieser statistischen Tatsache," *ibid.*, p. 178.
[100]*Ibid.*, p. 179.
[101]"In diesem Zusammenhange der Zeitgeschichte, dem allgemeinen Zuge zur Romantik gewinnen wir einigermaßen eine Verständnis für die traurige Tatsache in der Spezialgeschichte der philosophischen Professur", *ibid.*
[102]*Ibid.*, p. 180: "Wahrlich, wir können uns darüber nicht hinwegtäuschen, daß nicht allein die Zeitlage uns so schlecht gemacht haben kann, sondern daß auch in unserer dermaligen religiösen Verfassung und Lebensführung sehr schwere Fehler begangen worden sein müssen, ohne die jene furchtbare Tatsache nicht erklärlich wird."

Truly powerful cultural forces do impinge on the Jewish individual and community from the outside, as it were, and contribute to the present crisis. However, the internal, cognitive life of the Jew also has a share in the dominant popular self-understanding which has emerged, as do educational institutions within the Jewish community. These factors also need to be counted in any adequate explanation of contemporary self-understanding.

The crisis of German-Jewish identity is in large part a product of educational breakdown, a failure to appreciate the link between a philosophical education and attachment to the Jewish community.[103] In the modern period, Jews will only remain loyal to their tradition if they are convinced of its cultural value, claims Cohen. In elaborating on this point we can distil a syllogism that expresses the fundamental argument of his entire internalist explanation of Jewish identity: modern Jewish identity depends on a conviction of the cultural value of Judaism. Conviction of the cultural value of Judaism depends on an understanding of the Jewish belief in the unique God (*der einzige Gott*). *Ergo*, modern Jewish identity depends on a philosophical education with respect to the truth of belief in the unique God.[104]

Cohen does not describe the educational curriculum required to instil the necessary conviction of Judaism's cultural value (a subject we have encountered in any case above). Instead, he describes the sort of Jew who would probably exemplify such a conviction. He is the truthful and modest Jew – the Jew who, for instance, can subscribe with true understanding and without presumption to the proposition that God is unique (*Gott ist Einzig*). The truthful Jew understands the nature of God and what God demands. The truthful Jew also understands the enormity of the gap that exists between himself and the God whom he has come to know. The distinction between truthfulness and modesty, then, is only apparent according to Cohen's conception. A genuine appreciation of God, open to the truthful person, would necessarily include a sense of the fragility and fallibility of this cognitive achievement, an expression of modesty as well.[105]

Cohen's explanation of modern Jewish identity in terms of the virtues supplements his appeal to the force of historical context. The virtues, Cohen intimates, are explanatory tools in one's *geisteswissenschaftlich* tool kit. Analysis in terms of the virtues brings the Jew's religious constitution and way of life to light. Moreover, it serves to capture that measure of responsibility which the German Jew truly bears for himself. When used *in conjunction* with appeal to *external* factors, according to Cohen, the virtues are adequate to explain the crisis of German-Jewish identity, and the potential remedial force of his reconstructive programme.

In 1917, after thirteen years of pursuing the programme he first outlined in 'Errichtung' for the education of the modern Jew, Cohen still finds German

---

[103]For instance, "die natürliche psychische Brücke zwischen dem theoretischen Bewußtsein ... und der gesamten Gefühlsgruppe...", *ibid*.
[104]*Ibid.*, pp. 181–182.
[105]I have drawn on *Religion*, pp. 424–425, in exploring the link between the virtues, truthfulness and modesty, and Cohen's explanation of Jewish identity.

Jewry standing at a very great remove from the promise of the new *Wissenschaft*. The faults which Cohen finds are many. German Jewry is without sufficient interest in the literary sources which could nourish them, especially the prophetic tradition; they are unwilling to play their role as suffering servant for the sake of a higher good; and they are quick to abandon the *Gemeinde*, the agent of their collective subjectivity. While Cohen does acknowledge the role of unfavourable forces operating upon the modern Jew, the bulk of his energies are devoted to placing responsibility for the Jews' condition on the Jew himself. In Cohen's estimation the crisis of Jewish identity afflicting his community stems from institutional shortfall: the failure of the organs of *Wissenschaft des Judentums* – its seminaries, its professors, its journals, and its educated elite – to find new ways to educate towards fulfilment of the Jews' ancient obligation to imitate God.

The end of Cohen's life did not bring anything like the realisation of his programme. His efforts did help place another coherent vision in circulation as modern Jewry turned the corner to the new century, however. Writing in December 1917, Cohen did not falter in his conviction. God, the unique exemplar of human subjectivity, remained at "the very heart of the subject [*das einzige Herz der Sache*]". Moreover, the modern Jew could draw ever nearer to the exemplar if only he or she were schooled in the virtues proper to a truthful and modest life. From the perspective of Cohen's *Wissenschaft*, then, virtue was also at the heart of the subject – the authentic modern German-Jewish identity.

From "the Priestess of the Home" to "the Rabbi's Brilliant Daughter". Concepts of Jewish Womanhood and Progressive Germanness in Die Deborah and the American Israelite, 1854–1900

BY MARIA T. BAADER

"German Israelites! So little is done in this country for the instruction and the intellectual entertainment of the ladies that we believe *Die Deborah* will be welcome to everybody.... [It will form] the connecting link in the chain of Judaism between America and Germany; it will give important service to those who do not read English and it will be welcome to everybody who venerates Judaism and who loves his mother tongue."[1]

With these words Rabbi Isaac Mayer Wise introduced *Die Deborah*, a journal specifically addressed to the "daughters of Israel".[2] In 1854, Wise had begun publishing the English-language weekly *The Israelite* (after 1874 the *American Israelite*). A year later, he supplemented the publication with the German-language journal *Die Deborah*, which became the most important Jewish German-language periodical in nineteenth-century America. In *Die Deborah*, as well as in the *American Israelite*, Jewish immigrants from German-speaking countries negotiated their identities in a multi-faceted process in which German concepts of embourgeoisement, Reform visions of a modernised Judaism, and the endeavour to acculturate into American society converged. Discussions about women's role in German, Jewish, and American society figured prominently in both journals. In these discussions German cultural patterns informed the trajectory from enlightened Jewish womanhood of the 1850s to the New Jewish Woman in late nineteenth-century America.

---

[1]*Die Deborah*, vol. I (24th August 1855), p. 1. Until 1865, the title reads *Deborah* and thereafter *Die Deborah*. I use the form *Die Deborah* throughout this paper. Translations are mine, if not otherwise indicated. I thank Arthur Goren, who first drew my attention to *Die Deborah*, and who continuously supported this project. I am also grateful to Dianne Ashton, Lisa DiCaprio, Hasia Diner, Karla Goldman, Marion Kaplan, Arthur Kiron, Stanley Nadel, Susan Oren, Kerstin Otto, Nils Römer, and the members of the German Women's History Study Group; as well as to Philip Miller at the library of the Hebrew Union College in New York, and Abraham Peck at the American Jewish Archives in Cincinnati.
[2]Subtitle of *Die Deborah*, 1855–1859.

It is by no means self-evident that Jewish immigrants from German-speaking countries identified themselves as Germans. In the early nineteenth century, Jews had begun to integrate and to acculturate into German society and more specifically, into the emerging German middle class; and David Sorkin has suggested that a German-Jewish bourgeois subculture was in place by 1840.[3] However, the majority of the emigrants belonged to the poorer segments of rural Jewry in the German states and many came from places such as Poznan and Hungary, or Bohemia, like Isaac Mayer Wise himself.[4] Scholars of American Jewish history are divided on the issue of whether Jewish immigrants in nineteenth-century America could be considered German and whether their social and cultural life took place within, or was separate from, the Gentile German communities in the United States.[5] Certainly we have to be careful in drawing overall conclusions from publications that appeared in strongholds of German culture in nineteenth-century America, such as the *American Israelite* and *Die Deborah* from Cincinnati. However, examination of the Jewish immigrants who did identify themselves as Germans reveals that they did not perceive being German in America as belonging to an ethnic group. Rather the German identity of the Jews, as expressed in the *American Israelite* and in *Die Deborah*, was cultural, class-specific, and connected to the German concept of *Bildung*.[6] For Jews in early and mid-nineteenth-century Germany, *Bildung* led to social acceptance in the expanding bourgeois cultural *milieu*. In Germany and in the areas of Central Europe where the middle classes were linguistically and culturally German, *Bildung* was an indicator of social achievement. Jews began to acculturate into the middle classes by embracing the concept. *Bildung* stood for social mobility and ultimately,

---

[3]David Sorkin, *The Transformation of German Jewry, 1780–1840*, Oxford 1987.
[4]Avraham Barkai, 'German-Jewish Migrations in the Nineteenth Century 1830–1910', in *LBI Year Book* XXX (1985), pp. 301–318; Hasia R. Diner, *A Time for Gathering. The Second Migration 1820–1880*, Baltimore–London 1992.
[5]Rudolf Glanz and Stanley Nadel have argued that Jewish immigrants from Germany associated with the German Gentile community and were part of the German cultural milieu in America. According to Michael A. Meyer, the Jews who came from Germany from the mid-nineteenth century on brought with them a fair amount of "cultural baggage" and at least for some time retained a specific German-Jewish identity. Naomi Cohen ascribes a "dual ethnicity" to the Jewish immigrants but she does not explore the German cultural and social context in America. Hasia Diner refutes the notion of the predominantly German character of Jewish immigrants and their association with non-Jewish Germans. In contrast to Diner, Avraham Barkai views German-Jewish immigrants in nineteenth-century America as a branch of German Jewry. Avraham Barkai, *Branching Out. German-Jewish Immigration to the United States, 1820–1914*, New York–London 1993; Naomi W. Cohen, *Encounter With Emancipation. The German Jews in the United States, 1830–1914*, Philadelphia 1984; Diner, *A Time for Gathering*; Rudolf Glanz. 'Jews in Relation to the Cultural Milieu of the Germans in America up to the Eighteen Eighties', in *Jewish Social Studies*, 17 (1955), pp. 203–255; Michael A. Meyer, 'German-Jewish Identity in Nineteenth-Century America', in Jacob Katz (ed.), *Toward Modernity. The European Jewish Model*, New Brunswick, NJ 1987 (Publication of the Leo Baeck Institute), pp. 247–265, here p. 249; Stanley Nadel, 'Jewish Race and German Soul in Nineteenth-Century America', in *American Jewish History*, 57 (1987), pp. 6–25.
[6]On *Bildung* see Reinhart Koselleck, 'Einleitung – Zur anthropologischen und semantischen Struktur der Bildung', in *idem* (ed.), *Bildungsbürgertum im 19. Jahrhundert*, vol. 2, *Bildungsgüter und Bildungswissen*, Stuttgart 1990, pp. 11–46; Rudolf Vierhaus, 'Bildung', in Otto Brunner, Werner Conze and Reinhart Koselleck (eds.), *Geschichtliche Grundbegriffe. Historisches Lexikon zur politisch-sozialen Sprache in Deutschland*, vol. 1, Stuttgart 1972, pp. 508–549.

German Jews hoped, it would be honoured with emancipation.[7] Thus, Jews who left Germany and other parts of Europe and settled in America in the mid-nineteenth century thought of being German as being bourgeois, respectable and successful, as well as educated, refined, and morally distinguished. They adopted this prestigious identity even though in the countries from which they emigrated their social background may have been much more modest.

Concepts of bourgeois family life and well-defined ideas on men's and women's gender traits played an important role in nineteenth-century bourgeois culture in Germany and in other parts of Europe, as well as in the United States.[8] What has been called the "cult of true womanhood" postulated that the female virtues of piety, purity, submissiveness and domesticity represented the all-important pillars of morality in a changing and increasingly materialistic world.[9] Thus religion, and especially religious feeling, came to be considered a feminine domain, a development that was not without consequences for modern Judaism.[10] In fact Paula Hyman notes that by the second half of the nineteenth century an ideology had emerged that "placed women at the heart of Jewish identity".[11] However, scholarship has so far paid only cursory attention to the tendencies within the German-Jewish Reform movement that emphasised women's centrality in nineteenth-century bourgeois Judaism. One of the earliest innovations of Reformed Judaism was the introduction of confirmation ceremonies for girls as well as boys.[12] In 1837, Abraham Geiger argued for

---

[7]Marion A. Kaplan, *The Making of the Jewish Middle Class. Women, Family, and Identity in Imperial Germany*, New York–Oxford 1991, pp. 8–10; George L. Mosse, 'German Jews and Liberalism in Retrospect. Introduction to Year Book XXXII', in *LBI Year Book* XXXII (1987), pp. xiii–xxv; idem, 'Jewish Emancipation Between *Bildung* and Respectability', in Jehuda Reinharz and Walter Schatzberg (eds.), *The Jewish Response to German Culture. From the Enlightenment to the Second World War*, Hanover–London 1985; George L. Mosse, 'The Secularization of Jewish Theology', in *idem, Masses and Man. Nationalist and Fascist Perceptions of Reality*, New York 1980. Regarding the economic position of the German-Jewish migrants, note also that bourgeois German culture united otherwise socially heterogenous groups. See Jürgen Kocka, 'Bürgertum und Bürgerlichkeit als Probleme der deutschen Geschichte vom späten 18. zum frühen 20. Jahrhundert', in idem (ed.), *Bürger und Bürgerlichkeit im 19. Jahrhundert*, Göttingen 1987, pp. 21–63.

[8]Leonore Davidoff and Catherine Hall, *Family Fortunes. Men and Women of the English Middle Class, 1780–1850*, Chicago 1987; Ute Frevert, 'Bürgerliche Meisterdenker und das Geschlechterverhältnis. Konzepte, Erfahrungen, Visionen an der Wende vom 18. zum 19. Jahrhundert', in idem (ed.), *Bürgerinnen und Bürger. Geschlechterverhältnisse im 19. Jahrhundert*, Göttingen 1988, pp. 17–48; Karin Hausen, 'Die Polarisierungen der "Geschlechtscharaktere" – Eine Spiegelung der Dissoziation von Erwerbs- und Familienleben', in Werner Conze (ed.), *Sozialgeschichte der Familie in der Neuzeit Europas. Neue Forschungen*, Stuttgart 1976, pp. 363–393; Barbara Welter, *Dimity Convictions. The American Woman in the Nineteenth Century*, Athens, OH 1976.

[9]Welter, pp. 21–41.

[10]Ann Douglas, *The Feminization of American Culture*, New York 1977; Hugh McLeod, 'Weibliche Frömmigkeit – männlicher Unglaube? Religion und Kirche im bürgerlichen 19. Jahrhundert', in Frevert, pp. 134–156.

[11]Paula E. Hyman, 'The Modern Jewish Family. Image and Reality', in David Kraemer (ed.), *The Jewish Family. Metaphor and Memory*, New York–Oxford 1989, p. 190. See also Paula E. Hyman, *Gender and Assimilation in Modern Jewish History. Roles and Representation of Women*, Seattle–London 1995; Kaplan, *Making of the Jewish Middle Class*.

[12]Leopold Zunz, *Die gottesdienstlichen Vorträge der Juden, historisch entwickelt. Ein Beitrag zur Altertumskunde und biblischen Kritik, zur Literatur- und Religionsgeschichte*, Berlin 1832, p. 457; see also Mordechai Eliav, 'Die Mädchenerziehung im Zeitalter der Aufklärung und der Emanzipation', in Julius Carlebach

complete equality of Jewish women before the law and in public worship, and at the 1846 rabbinical conference a commission submitted a like-minded report which, however, was not discussed.[13] There is evidence, too, that Jewish women attended the rabbinical conferences.[14] In the *Sulamith* (1806–1846), the first Jewish periodical in the German language, the *maskil* and early Reformer David Fraenkel established a special connection between feminine gender traits and Jewish religiosity. The journal promoted the religious and intellectual self-improvement of women as part of its efforts to raise Jewish family and synagogue life to the standards of German middle-class culture.[15]

All of these elements were played out in *Die Deborah* and in the *American Israelite*, where Isaac Mayer Wise placed women at a strategic point in his endeavour for Jewish Reform. Wise's journals, in fact, provide a fascinating window into how issues of *Bildung*, social mobility, German identity, modernisation of Judaism and gender interconnect in nineteenth-century German-Jewish history. In addition, an analysis of *Die Deborah* and the *American Israelite* gives important insights into how German Jews integrated into American society and also allows us to trace a distinct German-Jewish path to American feminism. After outlining the broad features of *Die Deborah* and the *American Israelite*, this essay first discusses the German identity of the Jews who expressed themselves in the journals. I will then examine how Jewish women's alleged moral distinction, religious faithfulness and cultural progress allowed *Die Deborah* and the *American Israelite* to welcome women's entry into the professions.

I. THE DEBORAH

Nineteenth-century Cincinnati, where the *American Israelite* and *Die Deborah* were published, was heavily populated by German and German-Jewish immigrants.[16] Under the leadership of Rabbi Isaac Mayer Wise, the city developed into the centre of the American Reform movement, which became the dominant form of Judaism until, at the turn of the century, more traditional, Eastern European Jews started to outnumber the earlier German-Jewish immigrants.[17] While *Die Deborah* and the *American Israelite* clearly reflect

---

(ed.), *Zur Geschichte der jüdischen Frau in Deutschland*, Berlin 1993, p. 105; Mordechai Eliav, *Ha-Hinukh ha-Yehudi be-Germaniyah bi-yemei ha-haskalah veha-emantsipatsyah*, Jerusalem 1960, pp. 257–270.

[13] W. Gunther Plaut, *The Rise of Reform Judaism. A Sourcebook of its European Origins*, New York 1963, pp. 253–255; Michael A. Meyer, *Response to Modernity. A History of the Reform Movement in Judaism*, New York–Oxford 1988, p. 140.

[14] *Der Treue Zionswächter*, vol. I, No. 21 (1845), p. 185.

[15] See *Sulamith*, vol. I, No. 1 (1806), pp. 38–40, 160–165, 215–222, and 374–386; vol. I, No. 2 (1807), pp. 300–322 and 373–396; vol. III, No. 1 (1810), pp. 183–201; vol. III, No. 2 (1811), pp. 177–194, 300–322, and 373–396.

[16] For demographic background see Stephen Mostov, *A "Jerusalem" on the Ohio. The Social and Economic History of Cincinnati's Jewish Community, 1840–1875*, Ph.D. Diss., Brandeis University 1981.

[17] Wise was born in 1819 in a Bohemian village near the Saxonian and Bavarian borders. At the age of twenty one, he came to the United States, where he officiated as a rabbi in Albany, New York, and later in Cincinnati, Ohio. James G. Heller, *Isaac M. Wise. His Life, Work and Thought*, New York 1965; Sefton Temkin, *Isaac Mayer Wise. Shaping American Judaism*, Oxford 1992; Isaac M. Wise,

the cultural setting of Cincinnati, the distribution of the journals reached far beyond the locality. The *Israelite* was the most widespread Jewish newspaper in pre-Civil War America.[18] It is likely that *Die Deborah*, which could be purchased together with the *Israelite* as well as separately, also enjoyed, for at least some of the almost five decades of its existence, a fair amount of popularity. In March 1855, Isaac Mayer Wise first announced his intention of publishing *Die Deborah*. Within four months he had collected 700 subscriptions. In August 1856, *Die Deborah* had 2,000 subscribers.[19] Among the nearly one hundred German-Jewish newspapers launched in the United States, *Die Deborah* can be considered the most successful and the most enduring.[20] Until he died in 1900, Wise edited the *American Israelite*, as well as *Die Deborah*, with the exception of short periods, when the rabbis Max Lilienthal and Solomon Hirsch Sonneschein took over editorial functions. From 1900 to 1902, *Die Deborah* appeared at longer intervals and finally disbanded.

The first issue of the *Israelite* appeared on 15th July, 1854 in Cincinnati, with the subtitle *A weekly periodical devoted to the Religion, History and Literature of the Israelites*. In its platform Wise declared "war against error, superstition, prejudice, ignorance, arrogance, hypocrisy and bigotry". The *Israelite*, he wrote, will "favour enlightenment, education, [and] moderate and rational progress". The paper was intended to be a religious, "but not a sectarian or sectional one".[21] In fact, in the *American Israelite* and later in *Die Deborah*, Wise propagated his vision of cultural betterment in general and of Reform Judaism in particular. After the founding of *Die Deborah*, explicitly German issues and news from Germany tended to be concentrated in the German-language paper. However, the *American Israelite*, assuming a readership conversant with German, printed German phrases without translation, included German-language advertisements, and reported on German theatre performances, May Days and Schiller festivals. The articles in the *American Israelite* and *Die Deborah* were not translations of each other and yet both journals covered major Jewish events such as rabbinical conferences and published contributions on religious, cultural, and educational questions. A reader could be sensibly informed on national and international Jewish issues by reading either of the journals and could read both journals without encountering extensive repetition.

Reminiscences, edited by David Philipson, Cincinnati 1901. For a discussion of the inconsistencies in Wise's autobiography see Leon A. Jick, *The Americanization of the Synagogue 1820–1870*, Hanover, NH 1976, pp. 121–122 and 217–218.

[18]Rudolf Glanz, 'Where the Jewish Press Was Distributed in Pre-Civil War America', in *Western States Jewish Historical Quarterly*, 5 (1972), pp. 1–14.

[19]*Israelite*, vol. I (2nd March 1855), p. 271; (6th July 1855), p. 412; *Die Deborah*, vol. II, (22nd August 1856), p. 1. In his memoirs, Wise claimed that *Die Deborah* never had more than 800 subscribers. I suggest, however, that the information in vol. II of *Die Deborah* is more accurate. See also note 18. Wise, p. 293.

[20]Barkai, *Branching Out*, pp. 109 and 172–173. Arthur Goren counts only sixteen German-Jewish periodicals. Arthur A. Goren, 'The Jewish Press', in Sally M. Miller (ed.), *The Ethnic Press in the United States. A Historical Analysis and Handbook*, New York–London 1987, p. 204. It seems that many of the journals counted by Barkai were extremely short-lived enterprises.

[21]*Israelite*, vol. I (15th July 1854), p. 4.

Although other American Jewish periodicals such as the *Asmonean* had previously featured articles on Jewish women and their place in society, *Die Deborah* was the first Jewish journal in the United States to address women publicly. However, in the first decades of its existence, *Die Deborah* only occasionally featured poetry and other contributions by women. This changed later, when Jewish women published in *Die Deborah* and in the *American Israelite* along with men. In the United States, women had edited periodicals, written religious tracts, and published other literature since the 1820s.[22] Jewish women such as Rebecca Gratz (1781–1869) of Philadelphia and Penina Moïse (1797–1880) of Charleston also had made names for themselves as authors.[23] Both Gratz and Moïse were well-educated women from highly acculturated families and they expressed their ideas of Jewishness and womanhood within the cultural framework of American Protestantism. The model they provided may have inspired Isaac Mayer Wise and other Jewish men from Central Europe when they set out to address women publicly and to discuss Jewish women's role in their communities. However, *Die Deborah* clearly owed its main impetus to German cultural influences and to the German-Jewish Reform movement.

Wise called his journal *Die Deborah* after the biblical prophetess and judge. The precedent for naming a Jewish periodical after a female biblical figure was set by the *maskilim* David Fraenkel and Joseph Wolf with their journal *Sulamith*. The *Sulamith* was the first periodical of the German Reform movement – in fact, the first significant German-language Jewish journal printed in Latin characters.[24] When Wolf explained the journal's title to his readers, he laid out the periodical's Reform programme. He hailed the biblical Sulamith as the saviour of the community of Israel in a time of distress. According to Wolf, only a woman could perform this task; only a woman could be the "gentle goddess of peace, [namely] reason".[25] In fact, in the *Sulamith*, Fraenkel, Wolf, and other reformers consistently turned to women as readers. They postulated that Jewish women had a special affinity with religion and morality and they declared Jewish women's task of infusing their homes and their children with enlightened religion indispensable for a Reformed Jewish lifestyle.[26] Other German-language Jewish Reform journals also addressed women in their titles: the *Jahrbuch für Israeliten und Israelitinnen* (Yearbook for Male and Female Israelites),

---

[22] Nancy Woloch, *Women and the American Experience*, 2nd edn., New York 1994, pp. 131–132.

[23] Sondra Henry and Emily Taitz (eds.), *Written Out of History. Our Jewish Foremothers*, 3rd edn., Sunnyside, NY 1988, pp. 218–228; Anne C. Rose, *Voices of the Marketplace. American Thought and Culture 1830–1860*, New York 1995, pp. 138–139; Diane Ashton, *Rebecca Gratz. Women and Judaism in Antebellum America*, Detroit 1988.

[24] Besides periodicals in Hebrew, the *Jüdisches Lexikon* from 1930 lists *Der Große Schauplatz*, published from 1751 on in Neuwied, and the *Dyhernfurther Privilegierte Zeitung*, published from 1771 to 1772 in German but printed in Hebrew characters. Georg Herlitz and Bruno Kirschner, *Jüdisches Lexikon. Ein encyklopädisches Handbuch des jüdischen Wissens in vier Bänden*, vol. IV/1, Berlin 1930, pp. 1105, IV. See also 'Periodicals', in Isidore Singer (ed.), *The Jewish Encyclopedia*, vol. IX, New York 1916, pp. 616–640.

[25] Joseph Wolf, 'Erklärung der Titelvignette', in *Sulamith*, vol. I, No. 1 (1806), pp. 160–165, here p. 163. Interestingly, Wolf does not refer to the Sulamith in Song of Songs, but to an anonymous female figure in Samuel II: 20.

[26] See note 15.

Jewish Womanhood

published in 1811 in Prague, and *Der deutsche Jugendfreund. Eine Wochenschrift für die Jugend beiderlei Geschlechts* (The German Friend of Youth. A Weekly for Youth of Both Sexes), edited from 1818 on by the Berlin Reformer Jeremias Heinemann.[27] Even a periodical called *Deborah*, aimed at female readers, appeared in Prague in 1865, a decade later than the American *Die Deborah*.[28]

Die Deborah was never exclusively a women's journal. In fact, the gender ratio of *Die Deborah*'s readership remains uncertain. From the outset, the journal served the larger needs of a German-speaking community. However, central to *Die Deborah* was a focus on women's alleged predisposition for religious feeling, morality and *Bildung*, and the conviction that women should be encouraged to exert their unique capacities for the sake of an enlightened Judaism and a progressive society. When, towards the end of the nineteenth century, Jewish readers increasingly turned to English-language publications, the importance of *Die Deborah* declined. Attention to women's issues, however, did not fade with the German-language periodical. Instead, the *American Israelite* took over the role of discussing women's place in the Jewish family, in the Jewish community, and in American society at large. Thus, on the one hand, by the 1880s *Die Deborah* had ceased to be a journal specifically directed at women.[29] In the *American Israelite*, on the other hand, *Die Deborah*'s ideas of the religious, moral, and cultural excellence of German-Jewish women found their expression in an agenda of moderate feminism.

When the *American Israelite* started a "Ladies Department" in 1886, which later became the "Ladies Column", women had begun to contribute in significant numbers to the *American Israelite*, as well as to *Die Deborah*. From the 1890s onwards, the *American Israelite* also featured a "Children's Corner". By then everything pointed to the more important role of the English-language journal. Advertisements and notes on job and housing vacancies appeared in the *American Israelite* in much larger numbers than in *Die Deborah*. After a last controversy over intermarriage in 1884, *Die Deborah* no longer featured major debates between rabbinical scholars and other Jewish notables.[30] Contributions in the *American Israelite* also included fewer theological disputations than in earlier years, but the journal abounded in announcements on engagements, weddings and anniversaries all over the country; news from most distant American Jewish congre-

---

[27]'Periodicals', in Singer, p. 624; Jacob Toury, 'Jewish Periodicals in Germany, 1817–1837', in *Qesher*, 11 (1992), pp. 7–8.

[28]Full title: *Deborah (Die Biene). Ein Volksblatt zur Belehrung für Israeliten, zunächst das weibliche Geschlecht* (Deborah [The Bee]. A Popular Paper for the Instruction of the Israelites, Especially the Female Sex). In the United States, a few Jewish journals appeared that were named after female biblical figures: *Rebecka*, edited by Ferdinand Sarner, Syracuse, NY 1864; *Rebekka*, German supplement to the *Voice of Israel*, edited by Isaac S. Nathan, San Francisco 1874; *Sulamith*, German supplement to the *Jewish Tribune*, edited by S.H. Sonneschein, St. Louis 1881. Robert Singermann (ed.), *Judaica Americana. A Bibliography of Publications to 1900*, 2 vols., New York–London 1990, vol. 2, *Jewish serials published in the United States*, pp. 438, 439, and 444. I am indebted to Arthur Kiron for this information.

[29]From 1859 *Die Deborah*'s subtitle read *Allgemeine Zeitung des amerikanischen Judentums*.

[30]*Die Deborah*, vol. XXIX (23rd May 1884); p. 5, (13th June 1884); pp. 5–6, (20th June 1884), pp. 5–6; vol. XXX (4th July 1884); p. 6, (18th July 1884), p. 6.

gations, charity associations, reading and sewing clubs and their varied meetings and resolutions; and obituaries and miscellaneous reports on events of Jewish interest. The main function of the *American Israelite* at this time was that of an extensive bulletin board. This indicated the *American Israelite*'s relevance and popularity and accordingly, the "woman question", too, was to a large extent debated in the *American Israelite* rather than in *Die Deborah*.

Die Deborah, after two or three decades of existence, had lost its vital function for German-Jewish immigrants, and their American-born children could seemingly do without a German-language press. When, in the last years of the nineteenth century, Wise explained why he continued to publish *Die Deborah* even though its shrinking readership could no longer support the costs of the publication, he stated that *Die Deborah* still formed an important link with Germany.[31] In fact, *Die Deborah* was directed not only towards German-speaking Jewry in America but it also addressed Jews, as well as non-Jews, in Europe, particularly in Germany. On the one hand, Wise and other authors in *Die Deborah* were committed to cultivating their ties with German culture and *Bildung*. On the other hand, the German-Jewish immigrants wanted to inform the German public of the achievements of German Jews in a new continent which offered them politically more favourable conditions. Thus, in 1855, Wise exhorted his American readers to purchase subscriptions of *Die Deborah* for family and friends in Germany. In the same editorial, he stated that he had already received "some hundred" subscriptions from Germany.[32] Although the identity and the motives of these subscribers cannot be established, a glance at the Jewish periodicals published in mid-nineteenth-century Germany shows that the Jewish community indeed followed the development of the Jewish settlement in the United States with interest.[33] The lawyer Emil Lehmann of Dresden, possibly a subscriber to *Die Deborah*, sent his greetings for the 1894 jubilee edition of the journal. His article, entitled 'Faithfully German and Jewish', praised "the journal that, over a period of four decades, cultivated, furthered, ignited and proclaimed German spirit and Jewish soul on American soil".[34] In fact, even towards the end of the century, the journal continued to closely report political events in Germany, especially those of concern to Jews. Many contributions still celebrated the German-Jewish symbiosis, such as the poem 'Yom Kippur at Metz 1870', which – twenty five years after the event – glorified the Franco-German war.[35] These

---

[31] *Ibid.*, vol. XLIV (7th July 1898), p. 5; vol. XLV (6th July 1899), p. 4.

[32] *Ibid.*, vol. I (24th August 1855), p. 1. In the years 1855–1856, such statements were included in the publisher's notes on a regular basis. They can also be found in later years; see also *Israelite*, vol. II, (7th September 1855), p. 70. In the 1880s, subscription fees in *Die Deborah* and in the *American Israelite* included a special one for Europe. Wise also announced a special edition of a *Die Deborah für Deutschland* without advertisements and European news and he recorded individual subscriptions, but it remains uncertain whether such an edition of *Die Deborah* ever appeared. See *Die Deborah*, vol. I (6th June, 11th July, and 8th August 1856), pp. 344, 384, and 416 and other issues; *Israelite*, vol. III, (19th September 1856), p. 83.

[33] For the early part of the nineteenth century see Lothar Kahn, 'Early German-Jewish Writers and the Image of America (1820–1840)', in *LBI Year Book XXXI* (1986), pp. 407–439.

[34] *Die Deborah*, vol. XL (12th July 1894), p. 3.

[35] *Ibid.*, vol. XLI (3rd October 1895), p. 1.

articles surely expressed the feelings of a group of older immigrants. Other contributions read today as mere curiosities, such as an advertisement that offered seeds of the "Bismarck cucumber" which was "cultivated exclusively on the estate of the Chancellor".[36] *Die Deborah* held on to the beloved concept of "the old home country" and, in the 1890s, still affirmed that Jews in America "breathe free German spirit" (*sic*).[37] However, the dynamic aspects of the "free German spirit" had found their expression in English in the *American Israelite*. The analysis of both periodicals suggests that the concepts of German universalism and progressiveness expressed in *Die Deborah* facilitated the integration of the Jewish immigrants into the American middle class as this development manifested itself in the *American Israelite*. In particular, the ideas of women's sublime and indispensable role in a German culture of *Bildung*, in a reformed Judaism, and in an enlightened society, paved the way to an understanding of Jewish women's identities that could include professional careers.

II. PROGRESSIVE GERMANNESS

What was the character of the German identity that informed the trajectory from the enlightened Jewish woman of the 1850s to the New Woman of 1900? Recently, Hasia Diner has questioned the Germanness of Jewish immigrants from Germany and other Central European countries during the nineteenth century. She argues that many of the so-called German Jews came from Poland, Bohemia, Moravia, Galicia, Alsace, and some from Russia and Lithuania. Furthermore, according to Diner, even those who came from the German countries proper "ought not to be viewed as the bearers of the culture of Goethe and Schiller" because their origins were in the lower strata of Jewish society and they had received little formal education before they migrated.[38] In fact, although in American Jewish history the Jewish immigration before 1880 had been labelled "German", an analysis of the content and the meaning of Jewish immigrants' German identity is lacking. When scholars acknowledge the Germanness of American Jews, they tend to refer to it as an ethnic identity.[39] The Germanness that Jewish immigrants expressed in *Die Deborah*, however, was not ethnic but cultural. For the contributors and readers of *Die Deborah* and the *American Israelite*, to be German meant believing in German *Bildung*; in the supposedly high standards of German education; in a "scientific" world view; in bourgeois civility; and in political progress. Those who published in *Die Deborah* and the *American Israelite* may not have come from Germany – in fact, Germany had not yet been unified – but had left regions that belonged to the German *Kulturkreis*. The "Germany" they embraced stood for a cultural, social and political programme rather than for a geographical and political reality. In the same vein, most of the

---

[36]*Ibid.*, vol. XLI (19th March 1896), p. 3.
[37]*Ibid.*, vol. XLII (2nd July 1896), p. 4.
[38]Diner, *A Time for Gathering; idem*, 'A Time For Gathering. The Second Migration', in *American Jewish History*, 81 (1993), pp. 22–33, here p. 30.
[39]See Cohen.

immigrants, and probably most of *Die Deborah*'s contributors and readers, had not belonged to the middle classes when they left Europe. Nevertheless, they were familiar with the German concept of *Bildung* that held the promise of upward mobility, integration and respectability. The determination to become socially and culturally middle-class underlay the universalist and progressive vision that the contributors to *Die Deborah* expressed when they proclaimed their affection for Germany and German culture.

The contributions to *Die Deborah* attest to the prominent role rabbis as well as other Jewish immigrants played in German cultural life beyond the Jewish community. In fact, the journal paid ample attention to German theatre and other cultural events in which Jewish mixed with non-Jewish German-Americans. Apart from synagogue sermons, *Die Deborah* printed speeches delivered in literary, singing and *Turn* (gymnastics) societies, such as the one given by Rabbi Samuel Falk in 1857 at the annual celebration of the German literary society in Albany. In his address, Falk pondered "the ideal and lofty" purpose of the society consecrated to "German literature, German language, German *Bildung*, German society".[40] He praised German as "our mother tongue, in which we think and feel". According to Falk, the German language was not only cultivated because of sentimental reasons, but also because it conveyed an incomparable spirit of freedom, a true sense of society and a tradition of *Bildung* that transcended American standards. "As long as German blood runs in [their] veins," declaimed Falk, Germans would not forget these noble values.[41] For the seventh annual celebration of the secular German club *Allemania*, which was held under the motto "Our fatherland! To the old one our loving respect, to the new one our strength", Wise delivered an address. He agreed with Falk that German was the beloved mother tongue but added that he had never had a fatherland. Neither Palestine, nor Germany or Bohemia, could represent for him what the "new fatherland", America, did.[42]

Some contributors were ambivalent towards Germany-as-fatherland and all of them denounced what they perceived to be the political backwardness of German authorities. The Jews who expressed themselves in *Die Deborah* however, believed in the superiority of German *Bildung* and of German culture. The frequent debates on education and schooling provided occasions for elaborating such views. In 1856 *Die Deborah* published a series of contributions that critically examined the American custom of holding public school exhibitions after the yearly examinations.[43] The only letter to the editor that vindicated such exhibitions praised the American school system for preparing its pupils for their professional careers. Even the author of this letter conceded, however, that American schools failed to promote "the harmonious development of all capacities" and neglected "inner education". Thus precisely those aspects that are

---

[40] *Die Deborah*, vol. II (19th June 1857), pp. 346–347. Wise claimed to have founded this German literary society in 1848, purportedly the first one in the United States. Wise, p. 106.
[41] *Ibid.*, p. 346.
[42] *Ibid.*, vol. III (18th December 1857), pp. 139–141.
[43] *Ibid.*, vol. II (21st November 1856), pp. 107–108; (28th November 1856), pp. 115–116; (5th December 1856), pp. 123–124; (2nd January 1857), pp. 157–158.

peculiar to the German concept of *Bildung* were perceived to be lacking in American schools.[44] Another article in *Die Deborah* criticised elementary schools in Cincinnati for their supposedly low standards, and the author supported separate Jewish elementary schools while at the same time asserting that "we Germans [are] loyal patriots, thoroughly Americanised citizens".[45] For the men, and later also for the women, who expressed themselves in *Die Deborah*, being German, being Jewish and being American were not contradictory. They understood their Germanness as a heritage of scientific progress and democratic idealism that could be fulfilled in America – in fact, it could be fulfilled more fully there than in Germany itself. America was, for them, the political realisation of the true "German spirit".

In July 1866 *Die Deborah* featured on its title page a "German-American national anthem" that Max Eberhardt had composed for the paper. In martial phrases, the poem praised the struggles of "German men" on the shore of the "free country" and it ended with the exclamation "Hail to you! America!"[46] Enthusiasm for German cultural values and American citizenship was present throughout the journal. *Die Deborah* interpreted the Schiller celebration of the *Allemania* club in Cincinnati as a protest "against all reactionary tendencies of the princes, aristocrats and hierarchs [sic] of Germany".[47] It went without saying, *Die Deborah* noted, that "the free German citizens of America", including the Israelites, loved and venerated the poet Schiller, whose heart was with "all the joys and sorrows of humanity".[48] A certain A. Rosenberg delivered the main address for the celebration and Rabbi Lilienthal composed the lyric drama that was performed.

As the historian Kathleen Neils Conzen has suggested in her study on nineteenth-century German ethnicity in America, German immigrants defined German nationalism in "almost exclusively cultural terms" and largely avoided religious symbolism.[49] With the Schiller festivals, German-Americans celebrated Schiller's notion of cosmopolitanism and freedom which the immigrants believed they had found in America. In the Germans' understanding, holding on to the spiritual treasures of German culture truly qualified them to be American citizens.[50] In fact, for both Jewish and non-Jewish Germans, German culture was not only considered compatible with American values; it was also seen as a means to elevate and enhance a weak American character. In an address at a Fourth of July *Turnfest* in Cleveland, "Dr. Mayer" elaborated on the interdependence of freedom and *Bildung*. "This country is free," Mayer stated, "by its

---

[44]*Ibid.*, vol. II (5th December 1856), p. 123.
[45]*Ibid.*, vol XI (14th July 1865), p. 6.
[46]*Ibid.*, vol. XII (6th July 1866), p. 1.
[47]*Ibid.*, vol. V (18th November 1859), p.78.
[48]*Ibid.*
[49]Kathleen Neils Conzen, 'Ethnicity as Festive Culture. Nineteenth-Century German America on Parade', in Werner Sollors (ed.), *The Invention of Ethnicity*, New York–Oxford 1989, pp. 44–76, here p. 70. See also George L. Mosse, *The Nationalization of the Masses. Political Symbolism and Mass Movements in Germany from the Napoleonic Wars Through the Third Reich*, New York 1975, p. 89.
[50]Conzen, pp. 55–58.

constitution, but not by its *Bildung*. It is missing strength of character, loyalty, [and] moral dignity". Therefore, according to Mayer, "the German element [is] saving the Republic".[51] The German idea of "free civic life", in fact, was distinct from Anglo-American concepts of freedom. Rather than having a basis in a catalogue of a citizen's prerogatives, such as a Bill of Rights, the German vision of freedom was connected instead to ideas of moral entitlement. It was *Bildung* that qualified an individual for membership in a free society.[52] At the Schiller festivals in Europe, as well as abroad, Germans celebrated this symbiotic blend of *Bildung* and freedom. By venerating the poet Schiller, they denounced the privileges of the corporate society in Europe.[53]

As the reports and speeches published in *Die Deborah* and in the *American Israelite* show leading Reform rabbis, including Wise himself, actively participated in Schiller festivals and other distinctly German celebrations in America. However, historians often portray Wise as a propagator of "Americanisation" and his contemporaries apparently suspected him of also wanting to abandon German culture and customs.[54]

Wise addressed this apparent contradiction in an article in *Die Deborah*, in which he defended himself against the charge of being an enemy of "German language and literature".[55] He explained why he was against the "Germanisation of the synagogue". The German language, Wise wrote, was not only dear to him for sentimental and nostalgic reasons, but also because German was the language of the "progress of Judaism". According to Wise, progress meant unity and universalism, not particularism and separatism. While in Germany modern German culture served to overcome medieval obstructions, and integrated the Jews so that they could fulfil "their messianic mission" for humanity, German isolationism in America would be retrogressive.[56] In Wise's conception, "Americanisation" was the fulfilment of German universalism. As was the case for Gentile German immigrants, German identity stood for "personal integration and missionizing American society" and thereby made itself obsolete. Non-Jewish Germans were said to acculturate rapidly.[57] Accordingly, if Jews from Germany or parts of Europe where the German cultural influences were strong acculturated quickly to American society, this fact does not necessarily point to their weak attachment to German culture. On the contrary, their absorption of German culture may actually have accelerated the process of "Americanisation"

---

[51]*Die Deborah*, vol. XXI (1st August 1873), p. 2. "Dr. Mayer" was probably the physician Nathan Mayer, author of novels for *Die Deborah* and the *American Israelite*. See Diner, *A Time for Gathering*, p. 212.

[52]Leonard Krieger, *The German Idea of Freedom. History of a Political Idea from the Reformation to 1871*, Chicago–London 1957; Sorkin, esp. p. 150.

[53]Mosse, *Nationalization of the Masses*, p. 87.

[54]Barkai, *Branching Out*, pp. 169–172; Jick, pp. 155–157; Meyer, *Response to Modernity*, pp. 235, 253–255.

[55]*Die Deborah*, vol. XII (30th November 1866), p. 82.

[56]Idem. Two years later, Wise made the same argument again in only slightly different words: *Die Deborah*, vol. XIV (9th October 1868), p. 54. On the Reform movement and the messianic mission of Judaism see Meyer, *Response to Modernity*, pp. 137–138.

[57]Conzen, pp. 51 and 76.

rather than have delayed it. As Wise explicitly stated, to be German meant, for Jews in the United States, to integrate into American society.

An analysis of *Die Deborah* indicates that for the Jews who contributed to and who read *Die Deborah*, German was more than a language acquired for the most basic communication in a German Gentile environment or in order to deal with German-speaking authorities, as Diner suggests.[58] Admittedly, the fact that Isaac Mayer Wise directed *Die Deborah* at women does not necessarily mean that German had thoroughly penetrated the family. To recently arrived Jewish families with only a rudimentary command of German and speaking and reading Judeo-German or Yiddish, German would have been more accessible than English. To publish a journal "in jargon", however, was out of the question for the Jews who expressed themselves in *Die Deborah* and in the *American Israelite*.[59] Many Jewish immigrants from Central Europe may not have grown up with German as their mother tongue, as for instance Wise himself, who learned high German only when he prepared for the rabbinate.[60] In fact, Diner reports that even immigrants from German countries proper, having often had only a few years of elementary schooling and belonging to the poorer elements of German Jewry, "found German difficult to handle".[61] I suggest, however, that the "Germanness" of Jewish men and women from Germany, as well as from Eastern Europe, should be understood not so much as a completed process of cultural adaptation but rather as a project of embourgeoisement and emancipation. Jewish immigrants who themselves had only a superficial grasp of German may nevertheless have adopted the view that German *should* be the language of an enlightened and refined family and that it was the language of *Bildung* for the upwardly mobile. Since the days of Moses Mendelssohn, German *Bildung* and *Sittlichkeit* (morality) had been regarded as the key to Jewish emancipation and respectability.[62] *Die Deborah* must be considered part of this endeavour. In *Die Deborah*, Jewish immigrants who, for the most part, had not been middle class when they emigrated, expressed their aspiration for upward mobility in cultural terms. While only a minority of Jews from Germany and Central Europe may have brought a substantial German education to America, there seems to have been a greater number of men and women for whom, by the 1850s, German *Bildung* and German culture represented progress and social distinction.

---

[58]Diner, *A Time for Gathering*, p. 222.
[59]For the discussion on Yiddish and German in mid-nineteenth-century Germany see Peter Freimark, 'Language Behaviour and Assimilation. The Situation of the Jews in Northern Germany in the First Half of the Nineteenth Century', in *LBI Year Book XXIV* (1979), pp. 157–177; Steven M. Lowenstein, 'The Yiddish Written Word in Nineteenth-Century Germany', in *LBI Year Book XXIV* (1979), pp. 179–196; Anton Rée, *Die Sprachverhältnisse der heutigen Juden, im Interesse der Gegenwart und mit besondrer Rücksicht auf Volkserziehung*, Hamburg 1844.
[60]Heller, pp. 92–93.
[61]Diner, *A Time for Gathering*, pp. 222.
[62]Mosse, *Jewish Emancipation*.

III. ENLIGHTENED GERMAN-JEWISH WOMANHOOD

The addresses and speeches at German and German-Jewish banquets, charitable associations, literary clubs, and singing societies published in *Die Deborah* were directed at an audience of both men and women and often included a special toast to the virtuous women. Without the participation of "the dear mother and the faithful daughter" as dancers, actresses, musicians and singers, an orator at the *Allemania* club proclaimed, the *Allemania* would not be as dignified, beautiful and great as it was.[63] The presence of women was considered spiritually uplifting. Accordingly, the *American Israelite* exhorted its readers to "Educate your daughters!" so that they could become brilliant authors, musicians, and teachers.[64] Education for women was, in fact, of major concern to the Jewish men who contributed to *Die Deborah* and to the *American Israelite*. In 1856, Isaac Mayer Wise launched a campaign to found a high school for girls. The public schools were poor, Wise wrote, the Catholic schools out of the question, and the American private schools, to which the "German mothers" sent their daughters in lieu of an alternative, lacked "system, efficiency, and serious *Bildung*" and served only to drill the young women to be "superficial Parlour Ladies".[65] Wise believed that girls deserved and in fact needed adequate secular and religious instruction as much as boys, but for different reasons. Authors in *Die Deborah* and in the *American Israelite* warned that girls had a pernicious predisposition to pride and vanity. The educational goal in their case consisted primarily in a moral training that would enable young women to withstand the seductions of materialism and atheism. With this educational grounding, they would not only remain within the fold, but would also infuse their children with morality.[66] This assumption was emphasised in an article from the German *Monatsschrift für Geschichte und Wissenschaft des Judenthums* which *Die Deborah* reprinted in September 1858. The author reported favourably on the recently founded school for Jewish religion in Berlin and stated that in this institution girls "absorbed the warmth for Judaism and later diffused it in their domestic life".[67] Accordingly, an important barrier against the further estrangement of Jewish children from their religion had been established. Some weeks later, Max Lilienthal replaced Wise as editor of *Die Deborah* and, in his inaugural editorial, hailed "the mothers and daughters of Israel" as "the priestesses on the domestic altar ... who have to educate the young generation in the faith of their fathers".[68]

In 1861, the theme of Jewish women playing a decisive role in securing their families' faithfulness towards Judaism reappeared. A certain I. Wechsler from Portsmouth, Ohio blamed women's supposedly meagre religious zeal for the

---

[63] *Die Deborah*, vol. I (11th January 1856), pp. 166–167; vol. II (7th November 1865), p. 91; vol. III (13th November, 18th December, and 25th December 1857), pp. 101, 139–141, 150.
[64] *Israelite*, vol. XI (21st October 1864), pp. 130–131.
[65] *Die Deborah*, vol. I (18th January 1856), pp. 241–242. See also articles on the high school for girls in vol. I (7th and 14th March 1856), pp. 17 and 56.
[66] *Die Deborah*, vol. III (28th August 1857), pp. 11 ff; *Israelite*, vol. V (30th July 1858), p. 30.
[67] *Die Deborah*, vol. IV (3rd September 1858), pp. 22–23.
[68] *Ibid.*, vol. IV (26th November 1858), p. 113.

spreading materialism, empty synagogues, and declining domestic devotion he saw among Jews. Since, according to Wechsler, man by himself did not possess the virtues which would reverse this pernicious trend, Wechsler urged Jewish women to restore the piety of the house by exercising their "blessed influence".[69] Articles expressing similar ideas on women's duties appeared repeatedly in *Die Deborah*. Rabbis Adolf Lowy of New York, William Deutsch, the founder of Western Hebrew College in St. Louis, and A. Elkin of Philadelphia warned that the religious instruction children received at school was inadequate if it was not supported by the moral influence of the home.[70] Contemporary bourgeois society prescribed a higher sense of morality and religiosity for women than for men, and assigned women the domestic sphere as the realm in which to preserve and cultivate their families' virtue and devotion. Thus, by definition, women were implicated in any supposed decay in morals or religiosity. When a declining interest in Jewish matters was detected, Jewish women were said to have failed in their allotted task.[71]

A contribution in *Die Deborah*, probably written by Wise, details how a Jewish mother was supposed to fulfil her duties. The mother should encourage her children to be charitable, grateful, truthful, gentle, orderly and punctual, and she should always set a good example by her own conduct. She should accustom her children to attending the synagogue and should read to them from the Bible or religious tracts. According to Wise, such behaviour was apt to preserve "the venerable customs of Judaism".[72] Clearly, what *Die Deborah* propagated as the virtues of Jewish family life were class-specific bourgeois values that had little to do with traditional Jewish housekeeping. Religion was, according to Wise, "an educational system for humanity". The Reform Judaism that Wise advocated was permeated with the German ideals of *Bildung* and freedom. "God," Wise insisted, "commands: Be just, virtuous, pure and faithful! God commands – be rational and free!"[73] In this largely cultural understanding of religion, women, according to Wise's interpretation of the biblical Song of Songs, symbolised the "perfect form" as well as the "perfect human spirit [*Menschengeist*]". In ancient Israel, he continued, women personified "virtue, purity, kindness, wisdom, and beauty", just as they did in Greek and Roman societies, where Homer and Virgil celebrated women's sublimity.[74] In *Die Deborah* and in the *American Israelite*, the concepts of religion, morality, and refined culture were inseparable from each other and they were gendered feminine.

Die Deborah glorified German culture, women and Judaism in the same tone.

---

[69]*Ibid.*, vol. VII (9th August 1861), p. 22; vol. VIII (27th March 1863), p. 150.
[70]*Ibid.*, vol. XII (26th April 1867), p. 166; vol. XIII (14th February 1868), p. 126; vol. XX (17th January 1873), p. 2.
[71]Cf. Marion A. Kaplan, 'Priestess and Hausfrau. Women and Tradition in the German-Jewish Family', in Steven M. Cohen and Paula E. Hyman (eds.), *The Jewish Family. Myths and Reality*, New York 1986, pp. 62–81. The idea of women's responsibility for an alleged crisis in Jewish religiosity can be found in the *Sulamith*, vol. I, No. 1 (1806), pp. 485 and 487.
[72]*Die Deborah*, vol. XIV (18th December 1868), p. 94.
[73]*Ibid.*, vol. I (28th December 1855), p. 145.
[74]*Ibid.*, vol. I (24th August 1855), p. 1; vol. II (6th March 1857), p. 229.

The terms "German mother" and "Jewish mother" were almost interchangeable. They signified moral dignity, cultural refinement and true faithfulness, whereas the term "American mother" was rarely used and did not carry such connotations. This ideal of German-Jewish womanhood figured prominently in the series on women in Jewish history, especially of the biblical period, which *Die Deborah* featured from the first page of its first issue throughout the years of its existence.[75] To some extent, these series responded to Christian voices that viewed the supposedly unworthy and antiquated position of women in the Jewish religion as a sign of Judaism's obsolescence. Or as one commentator put it, "It was the author of Christianity that brought her [the woman] out of this Egyptian bondage and put her on an equal basis with the other sex in civil and religious rites".[76] Wise explicitly referred to such criticism and rejected it. According to him, in the Hebrew Bible "woman held a high, respected and worthy position. In many glorious attributes, she even outshone man".[77] Thus, the "Heroines" series in *Die Deborah* and in the *American Israelite* glorified biblical figures such as Miriam, Deborah, Hannah, Ruth and Naomi. If Moses was a "man of God [*Gottesmann*]", then Miriam, his sister, was a "woman of God [*Gottesfrau*]", who displayed "true female piety".[78] Although these statements need to be read in the context of Reform Judaism's conflict with American Protestantism, *Die Deborah*'s concepts of female piety and German-Jewish motherhood can be traced back to the earliest publications of the German Reform movement at the beginning of the nineteenth century.

With the biographies of women in biblical Israel, however, Isaac Mayer Wise took up a tradition that dates back at least to the sixteenth century. Biblical and *midrashic* tales of the matriarchs played an important role in the *tekhines* and in other pre-modern Yiddish-language literature for Jewish women. Accounts of the female characters in the Bible informed Jewish women's spirituality and Jewish women have sometimes used the images of their foremothers to give value to their own religious practices.[79] In nineteenth-century England, Grace Aguilar published her enormously successful book *Women of Israel*, in which she presented the women of the Hebrew Bible as models of feminine Victorian religiosity. While Aguilar vindicated Judaism, her writings also conveyed "a sense of Jewish women's moral and spiritual power".[80] The series on women in Jewish

---

[75]*Die Deborah*, vol. I (24th and 31st August, 7th, 14th, and 21st September 1855), pp. 1–2, 10–11, 18, 26, 33–34; vol. II (6th and 7th March 1857), pp. 228–229 and 236–237; vol. IX (26th February and 14th March 1864), pp. 138 and 146; vol. XII (1st, 8th, 15th, and 22nd March, and 3rd and 19th April 1867), pp. 138, 139, 142, 146, 155, and 162–163; vol. XXXII (20th July 1888), pp. 5–6, (27th July 1888), p. 4, (3rd August 1888), p. 5, (24th August 1888), pp. 4–5, (2nd November 1888), p. 4, (14th December 1888), p. 5, (21st December 1888), pp. 4–5; vol. XLV (9th November 1899), p. 5.
[76]Quoted after Diner, *A Time for Gathering*, p. 181.
[77]*Die Deborah*, vol. II (6th March 1857), p. 223.
[78]*Ibid.*, vol. I (24th August 1855), p. 2.
[79]Ellen Umansky and Dianne Ashton (eds.), *Four Centuries of Jewish Women's Spirituality. A Sourcebook*, Boston 1992; Chava Weissler, 'Images of the Matriarchs in Yiddish Supplicatory Prayers', in *Bulletin of the Center for the Study of World Religions*, vol. XIV, No. 1 (1988), pp. 44–51.
[80]Dianne Ashton, 'Grace Aguilar and the Matriarchal Theme in Jewish Women's Spirituality', in Maurie Sacks (ed.), *Active Voices. Women in Jewish Culture*, Urbana–Chicago 1995, pp. 79–93, here p. 80.

history in *Die Deborah* resemble Aguilar's work in both respects and, like Aguilar, Wise stressed the motherly, tender and caring qualities of biblical women. Occasionally, however, Wise's accounts also focused on less feminine characteristics of women such as Deborah, the judge and prophetess, who led her people in military campaigns. When Jewish women fought, in biblical times, for the cause of their people with swords in their hands, Wise concluded, their place in worship must have been equal to that of men. Thus, Judaism needed to be purged of its "oriental" and medieval influences in order to restore the original place of women in the synagogue.[81] In fact, from their beginnings, *Die Deborah* and the *Israelite* forcefully propagated a greater role for women in Jewish worship. Liebman Adler, cantor in Detroit, even argued for the full religious emancipation of Jewish women. According to Adler, women should lay *tefillin*, they should be counted in the *minyan*, and they should be called to read Torah.[82] Such ideas put Adler a hundred years ahead of his time.

More moderately, Isaac Mayer Wise propagated women's right to hold independent synagogue memberships and to serve as communal leaders. Ironically, it was a woman known as a feminist, a writer and an activist in the Jewish Sunday School movement, the German-born Minna Kleeberg, who criticised Wise for going too far too fast.[83] Woman's most holy profession, according to Kleeberg, was to be "a mother in Israel" in the home as well as in the community. As the sun promotes the growth of a tree, Kleeberg continued, "women quietly and secretly influence every fibre of public life".[84] Therefore, women needed adequate education, respect and basic rights rather than leadership positions. Kleeberg propagated a temperate form of feminism according to which women should be enabled to exercise a benevolent influence on society without having public standing. Isaac Mayer Wise, although he insisted on a more public role for women within the Jewish community and cited the biblical Deborah in his argument for equality of women in the synagogue, nevertheless opposed the claims of the American suffragist movement. In an article in *Die Deborah*, the author, presumably Wise himself, expatiated on why full citizenship was of no use to women. Since women spend the major part of their lives absorbed by their duties as mothers and wives, Wise argued, women could hardly hold the public offices to which some of them now aspired. Those ladies who forgot their "natural profession" and fought for women's rights were "mannish women", "abnormal and partly repulsive in appearance," he postulated. According to Wise, it was a "crime" to expose a woman to the "falseness, envy, malice and fraud" of this world and thereby destroy "the only poetry in this prosaic life, domestic happiness". However, he declared, the social position of women needed to be improved. In order to fulfil the legacy of the great heroines of Jewish history, such as Miriam or Deborah, and in order to overcome the

---

[81] *Die Deborah*, vol. II (13th March 1857), pp. 236–237.
[82] *Ibid.*, vol. II (23rd and 30th January 1857), pp. 179–181 and 186–187.
[83] Linda Gordon Kuzmack, *Woman's Cause. The Jewish Woman's Movement in England and the United States, 1881–1933*, Columbus, OH 1990, p. 26; Jacob R. Marcus, *The American Jewish Woman, 1654–1980*, New York 1981, pp. 34–35.
[84] *Die Deborah*, vol. XII (3rd April 1867), p. 154.

female passion for pomp and splendour, the Jewish woman needed education – real knowledge that taught her "higher ideals". She thereby gained women's rights and women's privileges.[85]

In the first decades of the existence of *Die Deborah* and the *Israelite*, almost every contribution to the journal concurred with Wise that the position of Jewish women and the education of Jewish girls needed improvement. However, it was highly controversial how far the emancipation of women should go; whether it was advisable for girls to leave the home to be educated and what the appropriate boundaries for women's supposedly benevolent influence were.[86] Whatever the views the overwhelmingly male authors expressed in *Die Deborah* and in the *Israelite* about the adequate boundaries of women's activities, all contributions ascribed to women a central place in Judaism and in a truly civilised society. Both journals expressed great pride in Jewish women's cultural excellence – understood according to German parameters of freedom, *Bildung*, respectability, morality, and enlightened Judaism.

IV. THE NEW WOMAN

Throughout the nineteenth century, motherhood, domesticity, and religiosity continued to represent the central points of reference for what *Die Deborah* and the *American Israelite* upheld as the ideal of the Jewish woman. However, the emphasis on women's education and the high esteem for women's contributions in a progressive society and in Reform Judaism let both journals welcome what, towards the end of the century, was called the "New Woman". The New Woman was the personification of a new generation of young American women who, before and also within marriage, took advantage of expanding employment opportunities for women.[87] Economically independent and sometimes even belonging to the small elite of college graduates, they often engaged in social welfare work.[88] As contributions to *Die Deborah* and the *American Israelite* had previously supported women's participation in the cultural and religious sphere, they now encouraged women to apply their supposedly uniquely feminine capacities in the professional and even in the political world. In an article in 1887, in which Wise went so far as to revise his opinion and to approve of women's

---

[85] *Ibid.*, vol. XV (6th May 1870), p. 2.
[86] Scholars have alternately stressed *Die Deborah*'s and the *American Israelite*'s tendencies to restrict or enlarge women's sphere. See Charlotte Baum, Paula Hyman, and Sonya Michel, *The Jewish Woman in America*, New York 1976, pp. 29–33; Barkai, *Branching Out*, pp. 152–153; Kuzmack, *Woman's Cause*, pp. 22–27; Marcus, pp. 57–58; Kerstin Otto, *The Image of Women in Isaac M. Wise's* Die Deborah, *1855–1874*, MA. diss., University of Cincinnati 1993, see esp. p. 72.
[87] Angela Howard Zophy (ed.), *Handbook of American Women's History*, New York 1990, p. 432.
[88] Before 1900, young women in colleges did not form more than 3% of their age cohort. Although information on the relations in the Jewish population is not available, the percentage may be considerably higher, due to the solid middle class position of a great part of the Jewish population. Patricia Alberg Graham, 'Expansion and Exclusion. A History of Women in American Higher Education', in *Signs*, vol. III, No. 4 (1978), p. 760; Barbara Miller Solomon, *In the Company of Educated Women. A History of Women and Higher Education in America*, New Haven–London 1985, p. 64.

suffrage, he stated that now, "a woman's enlarged sympathies take in the interests of the whole community".[89]

By the 1890s, Jewish women were expressing themselves in considerable numbers in *Die Deborah* and in the *American Israelite*; in 1893 and they also founded their own nation-wide organisation, the *National Council of Jewish Women* (NCJW), which had its roots in the secular women's club movement and in moderate feminism.[90] The NCJW was actively supported by some of the most prominent Reform rabbis, such as Isaac Mayer Wise and Emil Hirsch. Due to what they perceived as a growing crisis of Jewish religiosity, these male Jewish leaders were pleased that, according to the statutes of the NCJW, the first purpose of the organisation was "to serve the best interests of Judaism".[91] The rabbis looked to women as the saviours of Judaism and, accordingly, many contributions to *Die Deborah* and the *American Israelite* treated the NCJW with great sympathy. Correspondingly, a talk which Jenny Mannheimer delivered at the Jewish Women's Religious Congress of the Chicago World Fair, where the NCJW was founded, followed a train of thought which, earlier, overwhelmingly male contributors had expressed in *Die Deborah* and in the *American Israelite*. Deducing women's place in society from Jewish history, Mannheimer set forth three types of women in Judaism: the mothers, the prophetesses and "a group of energetic women, who by their example showed how to solve with quiet dignity the problem of the proper sphere of woman's activity".[92] These women were judges and queens, learned women who gave public lectures, and ordinary women who took their affairs in their own hands. Mannheimer concluded that women in ancient Israel fully enjoyed equality of rights and therefore, she implied, the expansion of Jewish women's realm of activity was in the spirit of Judaism.

Previously, rabbis and other authors in *Die Deborah* and the *American Israelite* had cited Jewish women from the biblical and later periods when they argued for a greater role for women in the synagogue. In a series on women in Jewish history and in other articles, they praised the high cultural and religious standing of the woman in the Jewish tradition. After the 1880s, the slightly defensive tone of earlier contributions was abandoned and articles in *Die Deborah* and the *American Israelite* emphasised the superiority of Judaism over other cultures. In his discussion of "the woman question", Rabbi Adolph Moses of Louisville stated that only Judaism, "being from its very beginning and its nature a religion of justice and charity", was free from the "prevailing barbarism" that

---

[89] *American Israelite*, vol. XXXIII (4th March 1887), p. 2.
[90] Faith Rogow, *Gone to Another Meeting. The National Council of Jewish Women, 1893–1993*, Tuscaloosa–London 1993.
[91] Deborah Grand Golomb, 'The 1893 Congress of Jewish Women. Evolution or Revolution in American Jewish Women's History', in *American Jewish History*, 70 (1980), pp. 52–67; Rogow, pp. 32 and 49–51; Beth S. Wenger, 'Jewish Women and Voluntarism. Beyond the Myth of Enablers', in *American Jewish History*, 79 (1989), pp. 16–36, esp. p. 33.
[92] *American Israelite*, vol. XL (14th Sept. 1893), p.3. This talk had been written by Jenny Mannheimer's mother, Louise Mannheimer, who presided over the German Women's Club in Rochester and the Cincinnati section of the NCJW. See Rogow, pp. 63 and 231–232.

treated women as "mere beasts of burden or objects of lust". It was in present-day America, however, that the Jewish religion could entirely fulfil its potential since, according to Moses, America "redeemed woman from the state of legal, social and intellectual inferiority" in which all societies – the Greco-Roman as much as the ancient German and contemporary European culture – used to hold women.[93]

In 1894, Isaac Mayer Wise reported on a lecture by Rabbi Henry Berkowitz, who was to be among the rabbis to speak at the NCJW's first triennial.[94] According to Wise, Berkowitz claimed that the Jewish woman in biblical Israel differed from "the shallow society belle of ancient days" which predominated in other cultures. Her "industry, thrift, charity, ... wifely ambition, ... motherly tenderness, ... gentle dignity and quiet strength of character" set the pattern "for the new ambitions, new hopes, new undertakings that enlist the active womanhood of today.... The changed conditions of recent years," the author continued, liberated women "from the life of emptiness.... [Now] every woman must redeem herself from ignorant life. It has been a great victory, which has opened to her all the doors of the schools, universities and professions".[95] Thus today, Wise reported, a woman had all the prerogatives to fulfil her mission according to the Jewish tradition and to extend her charitable work to society at large. Wise, Berkowitz, Mannheimer, Moses, and other contributors to the *American Israelite* and *Die Deborah*, plainly argued that the educated and emancipated woman was a Jewish ideal that could finally be realised in America. In fact, articles in both journals applauded women in almost every course of study and every profession. Wise encouraged women to become rabbis and to occupy the pulpit, and he complimented two young women who successfully ran a typewriting office.[96] Rabbi Adolph Moses defended, in the *American Israelite*, the "inalienable right of a woman" to have access to the Louisville School of Pharmacy and "to try to earn her bread as a druggist";[97] Louise Mannheimer, more moderately, exhorted women to apply their talents in philanthropy and as teachers of religion.[98] Articles in *Die Deborah* and in the *American Israelite* argued not only that women had the right to expand their activities beyond the domestic realm and to enter schools and professions, but that, due to women's unique moral and maternal gender traits, it was their duty to do so. This line of argument has been called "maternal feminism".[99] For Isaac Mayer Wise and other authors in the

---

[93]*American Israelite*, vol. XXXII (21st August 1885), p. 6; vol. XXXIX (2nd March 1893), p. 4. As a rabbinical student, Adolph (then Adolf) Moses served as volunteer in Garibaldi's army, which fought for national unification and Jewish emancipation in Italy. See Ismar Elbogen, *A Century of Jewish Life*, Philadelphia 1945, p. 29.
[94]Rogow, p. 254.
[95]*American Israelite*, vol. XLI (26th July 1894), p. 1.
[96]*Ibid.*, vol. XXXVII (27th November 1890), p. 4; vol. XXXIX (24th November 1892), p. 4; vol. XL (16th November 1893), p. 1.
[97]*Ibid.*, vol. XXXII (28th August 1885), p.8.
[98]*Die Deborah*, vol. XL (23th August 1894), p. 7.
[99]Ann Taylor Allen, *Feminism and Motherhood in Germany 1800–1914*, New Brunswick, NJ 1991; Catherine Prelinger, *Charity, Challenge, and Change. Religious Dimensions of the Mid-Nineteenth-Century Women's Movement in Germany*, New York–London 1987.

American Israelite and in *Die Deborah*, the belief in Jewish women's moral distinction and religious faithfulness went hand in hand with German concepts of cultural and political progress. In the last decades of the nineteenth century, these notions led to the claim that Jewish women's participation in wider society expressed the spiritual and social elevation of Jewish womanhood according to a Judaism restored to its original, progressive principles.

The ideal of enlightened modesty and unsophisticated purity that Wise had preached for women in the 1860s was hopelessly outmoded by the 1890s. The women who were addressed and who expressed themselves in the *American Israelite* and in *Die Deborah* in the last decade of the nineteenth century were, by then, comfortably middle class. That their families had achieved what many of them had only aspired to in Europe manifested itself in many ways. Concern with beauty and fashion, formerly criticised, occupied a new, prominent place. Advertisements invited "the ladies ... to the finest hair store[s]"; face lotions against freckles and soaps for soft, white hands were recommended; articles advised women on "how to become thin", on when and where jewels should be worn, and on the appropriate ways to entertain guests; other contributions discussed methods of "entering society", and pointed out the pitfalls of being a "parvenu".[100] This social mobility, according to *Die Deborah* and the *American Israelite*, brought new risks. An article in the *American Israelite*, reprinted from the *New York World*, stated that "the decline of the kitchen" and its replacement by "an anomalous monster – cuisine" equalled "the abolition of the family altar".[101] Contributors to the *American Israelite* and *Die Deborah* repeatedly reminded their readers that neither housework nor children's education could be fully delegated to servants without causing serious damage to home and family.[102] As in the early years of the journals, writers emphasised that Jewish women were responsible for the moral and religious upbringing of their children, but now they added that the children's manners, especially table manners, also required the close supervision of the mother.[103] The overwhelming majority of contributions in the *American Israelite*'s "Ladies Column" continued to feature cooking recipes and to emphasise women's domestic duties.

Some of these contributions expressed concern about the family life of Jewish middle-class women who could afford to free themselves from many of their domestic responsibilities in order to pursue professional or social interests. On the one hand, in the 1890s the *American Israelite* and *Die Deborah* catered to college-educated women and defended women's entrance into the professions. On the other hand, however, the question of whether education and career endangered a woman's ultimate profession as mother, wife and mistress of a home was intensely debated in the journals. This discussion in the first place addressed the issue of marriage prospects for highly educated women. While

---

[100] *American Israelite*, vol. XXXIX (23th February 1893), p. 8; vol. XLIII (5th November 1896), p. 8; vol. XXXVII (16th April 1891), p.8; vol. XLII (21 November 1895), p. 8.
[101] *Ibid.*, vol. XL (19th April 1894), p. 8. See also *ibid.*, vol. XLII (2nd April 1896), p. 8.
[102] *Ibid.*, vol. XLII (23rd January 1896), p. 8.
[103] *Ibid.*, vol. XLII (October 1895), p. 8.

some contributions in the *American Israelite* and in *Die Deborah* emphasised how important a girl's education and professional training was in case she "had to forgo her natural profession", many others argued that a woman's education served to enhance married life.[104] The *American Israelite* reprinted an article by the British feminist Josephine Butler which stated that "girls should certainly be equipped to earn their own living" and that "they should never be taught to look to marriage as necessity", since too much "romantic feeling" could make a woman morbid. According to Butler, "the more independent young women are, the more they will be able to find real happiness in marriage".[105] Josephine Butler was not the only feminist to appear on the pages of the *American Israelite* and *Die Deborah*. From as early as 1861, Wise reported the speeches of the suffragist Ernestine Rose. In an obituary for Rose, Wise stated that she "deserved a monument in honour of the good work done". Wise's commendation of Rose is even more remarkable since Rose, although of Jewish descent, was only marginally active in the Jewish community.[106]

The modern type of woman was first identified in the *American Israelite* as the "New Woman" in 1894 by way of a reprint from the English *Cornhill Magazine*. The article was an attack on independent and self-confident women. The author branded the New Woman's supposed "unbounded self-satisfaction", her "aggressive air of independence", her lack of respect for her parents, and her hostility towards men. A man may be impressed by "the treasures of her intellect", declared the unknown author, but certainly would not marry her.[107] Another contribution warned that the change in women's roles led to "the decline of religious belief"; an article taken from *Madame*, the London publication, declared that "the smart woman ... will devastate a home".[108] All of these articles were reprints from other publications and were usually introduced with the comment that the opinions expressed in the articles, although somewhat overstated, needed to be considered.[109]

The attacks against the New Woman that the *American Israelite* reprinted evidently belonged to the wave of anti-feminist hostility in the 1890s.[110] Under the public pressure that associated the New Woman with radical feminism, the NCJW gave up the use of the term.[111] However, the *American Israelite* came to the defence of the New Woman. An article on the front page of the *American Israelite*, signed M.H.S., Cincinnati, declared that the negative characteristics often attributed to the New Woman were much exaggerated. "After the preliminary caricatures have departed," M.H.S. stated, everybody could recognise that "the

---

[104]*Die Deborah*, vol. XXXVI (26th February 1891), p.7.
[105]*American Israelite*, vol. XL (26th October 1893), p. 8.
[106]*American Israelite*, vol. XXXIX (6th October 1892), p. 4. See also Baum, pp. 40–42; Kuzmack, *Woman's Cause*, pp. 22–24.
[107]*American Israelite*, vol. XLI (13th December 1894), p. 8.
[108]*Ibid.*, vol. XLII (11th July 1895), p. 8; vol. XLIII (12th November 1896), p.8.
[109]*Ibid.*, vol. XLI (13th December 1894), p. 8; vol. XLII (11th July 1895), p. 8; vol. XLIV (26th August 1897), p. 8.
[110]Carroll Smith-Rosenberg, *Disorderly Conduct. Visions of Gender in Victorian America*, New York 1985, p. 265.
[111]Rogow, p. 94.

world is better for her [the New Woman] having been in it. ... The truly great new women" excelled in philanthropy and "labored for the cause of humanity".[112] Another contribution in the *American Israelite*, typical for the journal, refuted the opinion that college girls were lost for marriage and asserted that educated women became "happy wives and mothers, all the happier because they have used their well-trained minds in deciding upon the men they should accept for husbands and in bringing up their little ones".[113] Articles in the *American Israelite* not only praised the New Jewish Woman for her engagement in social well-being and in charity, but also rejected the newly medicalised charge that women who left their proper sphere were prone to disease. It opened its columns to women doctors such as Mary Putnam Jacobi, who challenged male preconceptions of female fragility.[114] An anonymous Philadelphia doctor, quoted in the "Ladies Column" of the *American Israelite*, countered that women fell ill with morbidity, melancholy, and nervousness if "they haven't enough to occupy their minds and their hands".[115] In fact, contributions to *Die Deborah* and the *American Israelite* expressed their concern that the lifestyle that women of leisure and "society belles" led put domestic happiness and piety at risk and that it caused "women's" diseases. The best remedy against such indispositions of women, articles in both journals argued, was a meaningful occupation.

Such an occupation, however, asserted Jewish women in *Die Deborah* and in the *American Israelite*, did not lead them to repudiate their mothers' world. Julia Moch from Gallipolis, Ohio stated that the New Woman had proved that she was fit to go "out into the world to do man's work ...; she is free to choose her own vocation, her own sphere of action, her own companionship, her own rewards". Nevertheless, according to Moch, the New Woman knew by her own free choice and her better insight that the most fulfilling and rewarding duty of a woman was to be a wife and mother.[116] This statement was similar in tone and content to contributions in the *American Jewess*, the first journal in America to be edited by a Jewish woman.[117] The *American Jewess*, on the one hand, campaigned for national and Jewish communal suffrage, defended single and professional women, and advocated equality of opportunity. On the other hand, the journal affirmed that women's highest goal was marriage and motherhood and that "a

---

[112]*American Israelite*, vol. XLIII (9th July 1896), p. 1.
[113]*Ibid.*, vol. XLIII (18th February 1897), p. 8. See also *ibid.*, vol. XLII (27th February 1896), p. 8.
[114]*Ibid.*, vol. XLIV (23rd December 1897), p. 8; Smith-Rosenberg, p. 262.
[115]*American Israelite*, vol. XL (23rd December 1893), p. 8.
[116]*Ibid.*, vol. XLIII (2nd July 1896), p. 7.
[117]The *American Jewess* (1895–1899) was published by the feminist Rosa Sonneschein who, until her divorce in 1893, had been the wife of Rabbi Solomon Hirsch Sonneschein, a close friend and co-worker of Isaac Mayer Wise. See Linda Gordon Kuzmack, *The Emergence of The Jewish Women's Movement in England and the United States, 1881–1933. A Comparative Study*, Ph.D. Diss., George Washington University 1986, pp. 289–308; Jack Nusan Porter, 'Rosa Sonneschein [sic] and *The American Jewess*. The First Independent English Language Jewish Women's Journal in the United States', in *American Jewish History*, 68 (1978), pp. 57–63; *idem*, 'Rosa Sonneschein and *The American Jewess* Revisited. New Historical Information on an Early American Zionist and Jewish Feminist', in *American Jewish Archives*, 32 (1980), pp. 125–131; Jane Heather Rothstein, *Rosa Sonneschein, the American Jewess, and American Jewish Women's Activism in the 1890s*, MA. Diss., Case Reserve University 1996. I thank Jane Rothstein for sharing an earlier version of her thesis with me.

woman's finest role was as the pillar of her family". In this combination, the *American Jewess, Die Deborah*, and the *American Israelite* did not differ from non-Jewish women's magazines such as *The Ladies' Home Journal, Woman's Home Companion, Good Housekeeping* and *The Homemaker*.[118] Although a high percentage of college-educated women remained unmarried or married late – a fact that gave rise to great public concern – even the suffragist press of the late nineteenth and early twentieth centuries propagated an image of the New Woman that was less threatening.[119] Articles and novels in periodicals such as *Woman's Journal* and *Woman's Citizen* saw the "essence of the New Woman" in professional women who were successful doctors, civic workers, brilliant speakers, and yet simultaneously happily married and beautiful.[120] Similar descriptions can be found in *Die Deborah* and in the *American Israelite*, where the authors particularly emphasised the women's Jewish or German-Jewish origin and pointed to the pioneering role they played in their professions.[121] Authors in *Die Deborah* and in the *American Israelite* took great pride in Jewish women who, in their eyes, put the concept of German progressiveness into practice and excelled in professional and cultural life. In this perception, the public role of these women by no means infringed on the respectability of a Jewish family: on the contrary, their *Bildung* and their high moral standing reflected well on the Jewish community. A last example may illustrate the new ideal of Jewish womanhood as it was advanced by the *American Israelite* and by *Die Deborah*. An article on Rosalie Loew appeared on the front page of the *American Israelite* in 1898, entitled 'The Rabbi's Brilliant Daughter'. Rosalie Loew was praised for her excellence as a lawyer. Even senior male colleagues came to her for advice. At the same time Loew's "female qualities" were useful in her work for the Legal Aid Society. Moreover, the *American Israelite* stated, "in spite of her professional quality, she [was] very womanly" and she fulfilled her domestic duties.[122]

---

[118]Selma Berrol, 'Class or Ethnicity. The Americanized German Jewish Woman and Her Middle Class Sisters in 1895', in *Jewish Social Studies*, vol. XLVII, Nos. 3–4 (Summer–Fall 1985), pp. 21–32, here p. 25.

[119]Joyce Antler, ' "After College, What?" New Graduates and the Family Claim', in *American Quarterly*, 32 (1980), pp. 409–434; Sheila M. Rothman, *Woman's Proper Place. A History of Changing Ideals and Practices, 1870 to the Present*, New York 1978, pp. 46–47; Roberta Wein, 'Women's Colleges and Domesticity, 1875–1918', in *History of Education Quarterly*, 13 (1973), pp. 31–47.

[120]Patricia Smith Butcher, *Education for Equality. Women's Rights Periodicals and Women's Higher Education 1849–1920*, New York 1989, pp. 84–85.

[121]*American Israelite*, vol. XLIV (23rd June 1898), p. 7; *Die Deborah*, vol. XLII (4th February 1897), p. 3. There seem to have been a few Jewish women doctors before 1890. However, it remains uncertain whether Jewish women pioneered as professionals in equivalent, higher or lower numbers than their representation in the general population or in the middle class. Lois W. Banner, *Women in Modern America. A Brief History*, 2nd edn., San Diego 1984, pp. 34–36; Barbara J. Harris, *Beyond Her Sphere. Women and the Professions in American History*, Westport, CT 1978, pp. 104–116; Miller Solomon, pp. 130–133; Marcus, pp. 32–33.

[122]*American Israelite*, vol. XLIV (19th May 1898), p. 1. A similar article on Rosalie Loew appeared in the *American Jewess*, vol. II (June 1896), pp. 474–475.

V. CONCLUSION

By the end of the nineteenth century, the *American Israelite* and *Die Deborah* were propagating an ideal of the Jewish woman that united feminine domesticity with professional success. Although notions of women's primary roles as mothers, wives, and propagators of morality and religiosity were not suspended, contributions to both journals argued solidly feminist positions on women's education and women's professional activities. In mid-nineteenth-century America, only very few Jewish women had been involved in the early American women's rights movement which, interconnected with evangelism, temperance and abolitionism, had a strong Christian character.[123] Furthermore, early American feminism was not part of the heritage of most Jewish women who belonged to an immigrant community.[124] The feminist stance that Jewish men and women took in the *American Israelite* and in *Die Deborah* towards the end of the nineteenth century developed instead out of the concepts of German-Jewish womanhood that *Die Deborah* advocated in the early decades of its existence. In *Die Deborah*, the belief in *Bildung* – the harmonious formation of the intellect and the character – was paired with a democratic and progressive vision of a society in which women represented the pinnacle of creation. *Die Deborah* and the *American Israelite* from their inception advanced a rhetoric of high esteem for Jewish women's religious role and for their accomplishments in the history of their people. Wise and other Jewish men, among them a substantial number of Reform rabbis, portrayed Jewish mothers and wives as national heroines and Judaism as essentially progressive. This alleged cultural excellence and political progressiveness was expressed in a persistent concern for religious and secular education for Jewish women, as well as in the attempt to emancipate women in the synagogue. Certainly, the greater role of women in the American synagogue was also due to pressures from a Christian society that considered women's participation in worship part of a graceful service.[125] Strikingly however, the synagogue was not the central focus when contributors to *Die Deborah* and the *American Israelite* debated women's issues. More prominently, the journals expounded on the Jewish woman's role as mother of Jewish children and "priestess of the home". Her religious, moral and cultural distinction was considered essential for the survival of Judaism as well as for the bourgeois respectability of a Jewish family. Accordingly, religious education and the secular schooling of young women was at the heart of *Die Deborah*'s enterprise. The *Bildung* of the women in their families was an integral part of the project of embourgeoisement for Jewish immigrants, most

---

[123]Kuzmack, *Woman's Cause*, p. 23; Alice S. Rossi, *The Feminist Papers. From Adam to Beauvoir*, New York 1973, pp. 141–281.

[124]An estimated 15,000 Jews had been in the United States in 1848, while in 1880 they numbered 240,000–280,000. Barkai, *Branching Out*, p. 9; Cohen, *Encounter With Emancipation*, p. 13; Diner, *A Time for Gathering*, p. 56.

[125]Karla Goldman, *Beyond the Gallery. The Place of Women in the Development of American Judaism*, Ph.D. Diss., Harvard University 1993; Jick; Robert Liberles, 'Conflict over Reforms. The Case of Congregation Beth Elohim, Charleston, South Carolina', in Jack Wertheimer (ed.), *The American Synagogue. A Sanctuary Transformed*, Cambridge, MA 1987, pp. 274–296.

of whom were not middle class at the time of their departure from Germany or were from countries where German cultural influences were strong.

The immigrants who expressed themselves in *Die Deborah* and in the *American Israelite* had adopted a German identity that was not ethnic or insular. On the contrary, their universalist conception of Germanness promoted acculturation into American society. Thus, in the 1890s, Wise and other contributors to the *American Israelite* and to *Die Deborah* encouraged Jewish women in America to enter colleges and professions. Not only did the periodicals reject the current notion that an educated woman would abandon marriage and motherhood, but the Jewish woman professional also represented the fulfilment of the Jewish immigrants' social aspirations. In the *American Israelite* and in *Die Deborah*, the New Jewish Woman, "the rabbi's brilliant daughter", was the embodiment of progressive Germanness, dignified Jewishness and successful integration into the American middle class.

Kaufmann Kohler and his Teacher Samson Raphael Hirsch

BY JACOB HABERMAN

The publication in 1836 of the *Neunzehn Briefe über Judentum* by Samson (ben) Raphael Hirsch (1808–1888), followed a year later by his *Horeb*, a compendium of Jewish laws and observances with particular emphasis on their underlying ideas, caused a sensation among German-Jewish intellectuals.[1] We need mention only three aspiring scholars who were to become outstanding in their fields. Hermann Cohen (1842–1918), later famous as a Neo-Kantian and Jewish philosopher, was a rabbinical student at the *Jüdisch-Theologisches Seminar* in Breslau when he read the *Neunzehn Briefe*. After reading them he wrote a personal and private letter to the author in an attempt to mediate a dispute between Zacharias Frankel, the director of the seminary, and Hirsch. The letter, in which Cohen defended the personal piety of his teacher Frankel against animadversions on his conduct, was publicised and printed by Hirsch (without authorisation) in his journal *Jeschurun*. This was Cohen's first published writing. A few years later, Cohen felt called upon to explain to an old friend that his departure from the seminary and his change of career was not caused by anything that Hirsch had written or said.[2] Moritz Steinschneider (1816–1907), the future father of modern Jewish bibliography and then a twenty-one year-old student, wrote to the rabbi of his home town, Hirsch B. Fassel, to inquire whether Hirsch's formulation of Jewish law in *Horeb* was accurate and would sustain criticism. In a series of seven letters, Fassel gave a generally favourable review of the work which the young Steinschneider published, together with a preface under

---

[1]Nachman Syrkin (1868–1924), the first ideologist and leader of Socialist Zionism, went so far as to say that he considered the *Neunzehn Briefe* the most important Jewish book of modern times: Hans Liebeschütz and Arnold Paucker (eds.), *Das Judentum in der Deutschen Umwelt 1800–1850. Studien zur Frühgeschichte der Emanzipation*, Tübingen 1977 (Schriftenreihe wissenschaftlicher Abhandlungen des Leo Baeck Instituts 35) p. 307, n. 56. This essay is dedicated to Rabbi Seymour Brickman. I am most grateful to Professors David Ellenson, David Weiss Halivni, Leonard S. Kravitz, and Mr. Henry Resnick for reading the manuscript and making many helpful suggestions and critical comments. I am especially indebted to my elder son, Sinclair Curtis Haberman, for the genuine help he provided in the crystallisation of the ideas presented in this essay. I owe special thanks to Evelyn Hubbard, Joann Abrams Rosoff and Judge Arthur Birnbaum, who corrected the manuscript and prepared it for publication.

[2]*Hermann Cohens Jüdische Schriften*, ed. by Franz Rosenzweig, 3 vols., Berlin 1924, vol. 1, pp. xxi and 331; Hermann Cohen, *Briefe*, ed. by Bertha and Bruno Strauss, Berlin 1939, pp. 11ff: letter to Eduard Steinthal, and see the editors' comments in the Introduction, pp. 6f.

the pseudonym M.S. Charbonah, a Hebrew translation of his name.[3] Heinrich Graetz (1817–1891), the future Jewish historian *par excellence*, was brought back to Orthodox Judaism by reading the newly published *Neunzehn Briefe* after having undergone a religious crisis.[4]

In the case of all three individuals, the influence of Hirsch was a mere passing episode in their lives. Of the three, Hirsch's impact was greatest on Graetz, who spent the years 1837–1840 as Hirsch's assistant and companion. In 1846, when Graetz published his doctoral dissertation *Gnostizismus und Judenthum*, he dedicated it "to Samson Raphael Hirsch, the spirited champion of historic Judaism, the unforgettable teacher, the fatherly friend, in love and gratitude". But several years later when, at the opening of the Breslau Seminary in 1854, Zacharias Frankel, Hirsch's old adversary, appointed Graetz teacher of Jewish history, they became estranged. The break became complete when Hirsch severely criticised Graetz's *Geschichte der Juden* in a series of a dozen essays appearing in volumes II-IV (1855–1858) of his journal *Jeschurun*.[5] By that time Graetz had become a fervent adherent of positive-historical, or, as we would now say, Conservative Judaism, standing for an entirely different concept of the tradition from that espoused by Hirsch. In the preface to volume 5 (1860) of his *Geschichte*, Graetz alluded to Hirsch as "a heresy-hunting hermit (*ketzerriechender Klausner*)".

Kaufmann Kohler (1843–1926) was a student of Hirsch's for about eighteen months when Hirsch was the rabbi of the separatist *Israelitische Religionsgesellschaft* in Frankfurt am Main in the mid-1860s. Although the mature Kohler became the foremost exponent of classical Reform Judaism and held much more radical views on the Jewish religion than Graetz, he remained under the lifelong spell of Hirsch, whom he revered as a man of faith. In his personal reminiscences of his early life, Kohler wrote:

> "The man who exerted the greatest influence upon my young life and imbued me with the divine ardor of true idealism was none other than the representative of what was called Neo-Orthodoxy, Samson Raphael Hirsch ... Whether he spoke in the pulpit or expounded the Scripture to large audiences, or led us through discussions of the Talmud, there was a striking originality and the fascinating power of

---

[3] M. S. Charbonah [H. B. Fassel] *Horeb Beesyon. Briefe eines jüdischen Gelehrten und Rabbinen über das Werk 'Horeb' von S.R. Hirsch*, Leipzig 1839. See Alexander Marx, *Essays in Jewish Biography*, Philadelphia 1948, pp. 118f.; and Tobias Tal, *Samson Raphael Hirsch*, Amsterdam 1914, p. 11. Hirsch's sharp rejoinder is contained in his *Postscripta*, Altona 1840. The two Hebrew words in the title of Fassel's book are taken from Isaiah XXV:5 and mean "drought on parched ground", an allusion to the name of Hirsch's work. Perhaps Hirsch felt that Fassel was damning him with faint praise and patronising him. In 1847 Fassel competed unsuccessfully against Hirsch for the position of Chief Rabbi of Moravia.

[4] See Heinrich [Hirsch] Graetz, *Tagebuch und Briefe*, ed. and annotated by Reuven Michael, Tübingen 1977 (Schriftenreihe wissenschaftlicher Abhandlungen des Leo Baeck Instituts 34), pp. 25–26, 54–58, 61–63 and 91–93. See also Markus Brann, 'Aus H. Graetzens Lehr- und Wanderjahren', in *Monatsschrift für Geschichte und Wissenschaft des Judentums*, vol. 62 (1918), pp. 257f.; and the 'Memoir of the Author' by Philipp Bloch, appended to vol. VI (Index volume) of the English translation of Graetz's *History of the Jews*, Philadelphia 1898, pp. 11–22.

[5] See S. R. Hirsch, *Gesammelte Schriften*, ed. by Naphtali Hirsch, Frankfurt am Main 1910, vol. 5, pp. 318–509. The articles have recently been translated into English. See S.R. Hirsch, *The Collected Writings*, vol. 5, New York–Jerusalem, 1988, pp. 3–206.

genius in his grasp of the subject. His method of reading and explaining the Scripture or the Talmud was quite different from the usual way; he made us find the meaning of the passage independently, though his own system of thought was peculiar. His was a strange combination of Hebrew lore and German culture, which culminated in his concept of the 'Jisroel-Mensch', that is of a humanity which finds its highest expression in loyal, traditional Judaism. Every Saturday night in my letter to my dear ones at home I gave a faithful synopsis of the sermon I heard in the morning and the impressive teachings laid down in the *Horeb* and the other works by Hirsch became part and parcel of my innermost life."[6]

It is difficult to overestimate the tremendous influence which Hirsch exercised on the young Kohler. Kohler's admiration for Hirsch was to remain with him even after he left the ranks of the Orthodox. Years later, in 1921, in the course of a memorial address for the financier and philanthropist Jacob H. Schiff, Kohler said: "It was no small matter for Jacob H. Schiff to be trained in the Religious School of Samson Raphael Hirsch, the great leader of Neo-Orthodoxy, the lofty-minded idealist among conservative Rabbis, whose mighty spiritual influence as a teacher still abides also with me to this day."[7]

In 1908, on the occasion of the celebration of the centenary of Hirsch's birth, Kohler, who had become the president of the Hebrew Union College, the seminary for the training of Reform rabbis, paid the following beautiful tribute to his illustrious teacher before the Central Conference of American (Reform) Rabbis:

"I gladly offer on this occasion my tribute of regard and admiration for him whom I proudly call my teacher, and to whom I am indebted for the very best part of my innermost life. It may sound paradoxical, and yet it is true, that without knowing it, Samson Raphael Hirsch liberated me from the thraldom of blind authority worship and led me imperceptibly away from the old mode of thinking, or rather of not thinking, into the realms of free reason and research. His method of harmonizing modern culture, with ancient thought, however fanciful, fascinated me. His lofty idealism impressed me. He made me, the Yeshibah Bachur from Mayence and Altona, a modern man. The spirit of his teachings electrified me and became a life long influence to me. Samson Raphael Hirsch was imbued with the spirit of cultured humanity. In all his sermons and writings he deplored the narrowness of the Ghetto view, which estranged Jews from the world in which and for which they should live and work... His teachings were a bold attempt at a revival of Orthodoxy. He tried to galvanize its dry bones by the power of his fertile, resourceful and vigorous mind."[8]

This essay investigates the paradox to which Kohler himself refers, namely, that the foremost exponent of classical Reform Judaism was inspired by the unyielding champion of Neo-Orthodoxy. I shall begin by examining six points on which Hirsch sided with the Reformers against the old-line Orthodoxy. I shall next explore some of the options which resulted from the confrontation of Judaism with emancipation. This encounter widened the spectrum of Jewish

---

[6]Kaufmann Kohler, 'Personal Reminiscences of My Early Life', in idem, *Studies, Addresses and Personal Papers*, New York 1931, p. 475.
[7]*Ibid.*, p. 530.
[8]*Yearbook of the Central Conference of American Rabbis*, vol. 18 (1908), pp. 211–212.

reactions and placed Kohler and Hirsch closer on the continuum of the various responses. I shall then consider how Hirsch's approach to Jewish learning influenced the scholarly method of Kohler. It will be noted that Kohler was very much like Hirsch in temperament and in his reaction to criticism. The essay concludes with a critical evaluation of Kohler and his work. It is hoped that this comparative study will shed light on the personalities of both men.

The first three issues of agreement between Kohler and Hirsch can be dealt with briefly. During the winter of 1899–1900 Dr. Gustav Karpeles delivered a series of lectures before the *Verein für jüdische Geschichte und Literatur* in Berlin, on Jews and Judaism in the nineteenth century. In one of the lectures he stated that, to an unbiased observer raised above party issues, three great achievements of Reform Judaism cannot be denied: a well-regulated synagogue service; sermons delivered in the language of the land; and systematic religious instruction. "One cannot estimate these achievements too highly," says Karpeles, "for after a period of utter degeneration, Judaism, through them, was brought back to introspection and a self-conscious purpose".[9] Hirsch adopted all three of these "reforms". His attire during services was patterned after the Reform rabbis, whose ceremonial robes resembled the vestments of the Christian clergy. He introduced a choir which sang compositions based on the German *Lied* and which were sometimes patterned on Protestant hymns. Hirsch regularly preached in German. Of his inaugural sermon in Oldenburg, delivered on Rosh Hashanah 1831, Rosenbloom writes: "Its style and content resembled that used by Reform rabbis who patterned themselves after their Christian counterparts."[10] Finally, Hirsch placed such a high priority on the modernisation of Jewish education and educational reforms that, in Frankfurt, he advocated the building of a new religious school before the construction of a synagogue.

The other three points on which Hirsch agreed with the Reformers were: the need for secular education; the theory of the Jewish mission; and the belief that the Jews are a religious community and not a nation. These issues need to be examined in greater detail.

Kohler relates that in the strictly Orthodox circles in which he was raised a secular education was regarded as an irresistible solvent of traditional Judaism, if not the first step towards apostasy. "What the [Book of] Proverbs say[s] of the evil woman: 'None that go unto her return again [II:19]', and 'Numerous are those slain by her [VII:26]' was, in all seriousness, applied to university educa-

---

[9]Gustav Karpeles, *Jews and Judaism in the Nineteenth Century*, transl. by Henrietta Szold and Adele Szold, Philadelphia 1905, p. 42.

[10]Noah H. Rosenbloom, *Tradition in an Age of Reform. The Religious Philosophy of Samson Raphael Hirsch*, Philadelphia 1976, p. 65. A popular historian of Orthodox Jewry acknowledges that some of the concessions that Hirsch made to the spirit of his age evoked opposition and that "in certain circles inside and outside Germany Hirsch was regarded as a reformer": Hermann Schwab, *History of Orthodox Jewry in Germany*, transl. by Irene Birnbaum, London 1950, p. 88. In Breslau, around the same time the municipal authorities directed Abraham Geiger, the leading Reform rabbi, to remain true to Jewish tradition and not to wear clerical robes in imitation of Christian custom. See Max Wiener, *Abraham Geiger and Liberal Judaism*, Philadelphia 1962, pp. 28ff.

tion."[11] From the point of view of the ultra-Orthodox, Hirsch would have been considered unfit to serve as a rabbi since he had matriculated at a university. In the famous Geiger-Titkin affair at Breslau in 1840, the venerable *Oberrabbiner* of the community, Solomon Titkin, said in reference to Abraham Geiger, the intellectual leader of the Reform movement who had been appointed his assistant, that anyone who had set foot in a university was *ipso facto* disqualified from becoming a rabbi. In fact it is to the eternal credit of Geiger that he was instrumental in allowing Jewish students at German *Gymnasien* to be excused from writing on the Sabbath while most contemporary Orthodox rabbis limited themselves to simply opposing attendance at any secular school.[12] Elsewhere Kohler remarks that it was said of his (and Hirsch's) teacher, the renowned talmudist Jacob Ettlinger, who had attended a university but remained strictly Orthodox, that Satan made him go to the university and come forth immune and loyal so as to lure all other modern rabbis to pursue those studies which would cause their disloyalty to traditional Judaism.[13]

Hirsch's ideal of *Torah im derech eretz* (Torah and secular culture) has often been misunderstood and misconstrued by revisionist interpreters, including some of his own descendants. They argue that the union of Torah and secular culture was not Hirsch's goal, but was intended merely as a temporary stop-gap (*hora'at sha'ah*) to save German Jewry from total assimilation. Hirsch's writings belie such an interpretation. One has only to read the essays explaining his educational ideals, attached to the annual reports of his school from 1865–1875, to see that he placed religious and secular studies on the same footing, giving them an equal role in the education of the child.[14] In this attitude he differed not only from contemporary Eastern European rabbis, but also from his Orthodox colleagues in Germany. The latter justified the need for a secular education because it prepared students for an occupation which helped them to earn a livelihood after graduation, but such studies were considered subordinate or ancillary to religious instruction. The difference between Hirsch and other Orthodox German rabbis of the time is well illustrated in his controversy with Rabbi Seligmann Bamberger of Würzburg. Hirsch complained that Bamberger was not in total agreement with the principle of *Torah im derech eretz*. Bamberger denied this; he too believed in the principle, but in the more traditional sense of "Torah study along with a worldly occupation" (M. Abot 2:2). Bamberger did not want the principle to be misinterpreted because he did not believe in the equal status of religious and secular education. He did not want secular education at the expense of Torah study; it must always be subordinated to the latter. He offered several examples of its correct interpretation. "I want teachers of religion to

---

[11] Max J. Kohler, 'Biographical Sketch of Dr. K. Kohler', in *Studies in Jewish Literature Issued in Honor of Professor Kaufmann Kohler, Ph.D.*, Berlin 1913, p. 4. In the Talmud (be-Abodah Zarah 17a), the verse from Proverbs II:19 is applied to those who have succumbed to heresy (*minuth*).
[12] See Felix Perles, *Jüdische Skizzen*, Leipzig 1912, p. 45.
[13] Kohler, 'Personal Reminiscences', p. 474.
[14] Many are reprinted in English in *Judaism Eternal*, ed. and transl. by Isidor Grunfeld, vol. 1, London 1956, pp. 155–220. See also, Mordechai Breuer, *The Torah Im Derech Eretz of Samson Raphael Hirsch*, Jerusalem 1970.

acquire a scientific, secular education," he said, "but I would not want this to happen at the expense of their religious studies. The latter must be protected and safeguarded, within the sphere proper for such teachers, in its full vigor against any abridgment or detraction. I want to see schools established in which scientific, secular disciplines, too, will be taught, but I do not want this to happen at the expense of religious instruction. For this reason, these schools must give particular care and attention to the trees of life represented by religion".[15]

Hirsch had a strong emotional attachment to Germany, its culture, its civilisation, and its literature. In 1859 he delivered an address in his school, on the centenary of the birth of Friedrich von Schiller, in which he extolled the poet as a role model, praised his ethical teachings, and said that Jews could learn about the idea of freedom from him.[16] He did all this despite the fact that Christian divines refused to take part in any celebrations in honour of the poet because of his known opposition to all organised religion. Hirsch's congregants regularly attended concerts, theatres and the opera – activities which were normally eschewed by the Orthodox.

Concerning the "mission of Israel" there is little to choose between Hirsch and the Reformers. One could transpose sentences, even paragraphs, from Hirsch's Reform opponents and interchange them with Hirsch's words and not notice any *hiatus* or break in the continuity of thought. The following excerpt from paragraph 613 in *Horeb* could well have come from a sermon of some uncompromising champion of Reform Judaism, such as Kohler's father-in-law, David Einhorn, or from Kohler himself.

> "What the priest is to his people, so should Israel be to the whole of mankind. When, in the choice of Abraham, the foundation-stone of this people was laid, God, Who did it, pronounced its significance: 'and in thee shall all families of the earth be blessed' (Gen. XII: 3), and explained the blessing that came from this choice:'... seeing that Abraham shall surely become a great and mighty nation, and all the nations of the earth shall be blessed in him? For I know him, that he will command his children and his household after him, and they shall keep the way of the Lord, to do justice and judgment' (Gen. XVIII: 18) – meaning that Abraham's descendants should follow with love and justice in the ways of God and by this silent example become a blessed monument to God and humanity among the peoples of the earth, so that they should be 'a kingdom of priests and a holy nation' (Exod. XIX: 6). As the priest among the people, so should they among mankind uphold the vision of God and humanity and by so doing be a holy nation, raised above every injustice, profaneness and hardheartedness, as becomes the bearers of such a message. Brothers and sisters, if only we lived up to such a noble vocation!"

The final point of agreement between Hirsch and the Reformers is that they viewed the Jews not as a national or political community (*ethnos*) but as a religious body (*ecclesia*). This last point presents certain difficulties. Whereas on the

---

[15]See the letter from Bamberger to Hirsch dated 7th May 1877, reprinted in S.R. Hirsch, *Gesammelte Schriften*, ed. by Naphtali Hirsch, vol. 4, Frankfurt am Main 1908, pp. 540f. (pp. 516–542); English translation in vol. 6 of Hirsch's *Collected Writings*, New York–Jerusalem 1990, p. 251.

[16]'Worte am Vorabend der Schillerfeier, November 9, 1859', in S.R. Hirsch, *Gesammelte Schriften*, vol. 6, ed. by Naphtali Hirsch, Frankfurt am Main 1912, pp. 308–321; also printed separately.

other points discussed no Eastern European Orthodox rabbi would have agreed with Hirsch and the Reformers, the matter is different in this case, as the following incident illustrates. Towards the end of the First World War, when for a short period it seemed possible that Germany might gain control of Poland, the German government sent the biblical scholar and Orientalist professor Alfred Jeremias (1864–1935) to Poland to make a first-hand study of the more than three million Eastern European Jews who might find themselves within German territorial boundaries. After the war he wrote a report about his experiences and findings. Jeremias makes clear that his study is limited to a characterisation of the pure authentic Eastern European Orthodox Judaism unaffected by modern Western modes. He states specifically that he has excluded Liberal or Reform Judaism from consideration. His considered conclusion is that the unifying element uniting Jews everywhere is not a future Temple, not Palestine, but the Torah. He mentions that, as an observer, he attended a convention of rabbis meeting in Warsaw. Turning to a group of the rabbis, he called attention to the striking utterance of the prophet Hosea (III:4): "For the Israelites shall live for a long time without king or leader, without sacrifice or sacred pillar, without ephod or teraphim" – Jeremias wanted to know the attitude of these Jewish leaders to political Zionism. Thereupon one of them solemnly raised the Torah scroll and said: "But Professor, we do have our country – a portable country."[17]

What Hirsch asserted is not very different from what the rabbi in Warsaw said. "From where the Torah emanates, there is my Zion."[18] This non-nationalistic "love of Zion" is also echoed by Kohler, who sees in Jerusalem not an earthly city but a metaphysical *idea* of the religious metropolis of the world. "The law is to go forth from Zion and the word of the Lord from Jerusalem, as a spiritual, not a geographical center."[19]

Hirsch and Kohler were, of course, aware of the fact that Judaism was not a religion pure and simple, and that it also possessed national features. Kohler expressly says at the beginning of his *Jewish Theology*: "Religion and race form an inseparable whole in Judaism."[20] But when it furthered their "mission"

---

[17]A. Jeremias, *Jüdische Frömmigkeit*, Leipzig 1927, p. 11. G. van der Leeuw (1890–1950), the Dutch authority on the phenomenology of religion, quotes this statement and waxes lyrical over it: "That is legal piety at its highest power; the written word of the law replaces everything: celebration and sacred space, the 'how' and the 'where'. The 'what' of the divine word, fixed for all time, suffices in the actuality of obedience and love", *Religion in Essence and Manifestation*, Princeton 1986, chapters 64, 5, p. 446.

[18]Quoted by Saemy Japhet in *Historia Judaica*, vol. 10 (October 1948), p. 106. It has been perceptively observed that in a sense Hirsch is even more negative in his evaluation of the national element in Judaism than the Reformers. Whereas the latter acknowledge the importance of nationalism in the biblical period, but argue that it was superseded by the providentially designed dispersion of the Jews, Hirsch minimises the national element even in ancient times. See Max Wiener, *Jüdische Religion im Zeitalter der Emanzipation*, Berlin 1933, pp. 72f. For passages in Hirsch's commentary on the Pentateuch and the Book of Psalms which extol the mission-theory or deprecate nationalism see, e.g., Genesis XII:7; Exodus VI:3; Leviticus XXVI:13; Deuteronomy IV:26, XXIX:27, XXXI:29; Psalms XXII:27.

[19]Kohler, *Jewish Theology*, New York 1968 (first published 1918) p. 365.
[20]*Ibid.*, p. 7.

theory, or when they wanted to stress their patriotism, they deemed Judaism to be exclusively a religion. Thus the Pittsburgh Platform of Reform principles (1885), which was authored by Kohler, explicitly states, "We consider ourselves no longer a nation, but a religious community".[21] Nearly fifty years earlier, Hirsch had asserted that Israel had to give up its national homeland for the sake of its religious mission: "It was forced to leave the happy soil which had seduced it from its allegiance to the Most High."[22]

The problem is that it is very difficult to pin the authors down. What is asserted in one context is qualified almost out of existence in another. What can be shown is that at times they overshoot the bounds of legitimate argument and not only engage in special pleading, but have recourse to misinterpretation and mistranslation of sacred texts. In chapter 96 of *Horeb*, Hirsch considers the 'Duties of the Subject and of the Citizen", and inculcates as divinely ordained duties on Jews in whatever land they dwell, *inter alia*:

> "...not only to fulfil all the duties which the laws of that land explicitly lay down, but over and above that, to do with thought, word and deed everything that can contribute to the weal of that nation.... to give honestly and joyously all that the community demands for the common good from the individual in the way of treasure, energy and wisdom; and to sacrifice even life itself when the Fatherland calls its sons to its defense.... to be loyal to the State with heart and mind ... to guard the honor of the State with love and pride, to strive with enthusiasm wherever and whenever you can so that the nation's institutions shall prosper ... And this duty is an unconditional duty and not dependent upon whether the State is kindly intentioned towards you or is harsh. Even though they deny your right to be a human being and to develop a lawful human life upon the soil which bore you — *you* shall not neglect your duty."

As an epigraph to the chapter, Hirsch quotes from the letter of the prophet Jeremiah to the Babylonian Jewish community found in the twenty-ninth chapter of his book. The quotation ends with verse seven, which Hirsch translates as follows: "And seek the welfare of the city to which I [i.e., God] have led [*geführt*] you, and pray to the Lord on its behalf; for in its welfare you will find your welfare etc." (Jeremiah XXIX:7). But the prophet does not say, "to which I have led you"; he says, "to which I have exiled [(*higléthi*] you".[23] The "etc." conveniently enables Hirsch to gloss over verse ten, which promises the restoration of the exiles to their homeland after seventy years. Certainly Jeremiah never advocated that his brethren familiarise themselves with the Babylonian *Kultur*, join the Babylonian army, and sacrifice their wealth and life for the greater glory of the Babylonian "fatherland". This lesson from *Horeb* was not lost on Kohler. Shortly after the entry of the United States into the First World War, Kohler, as president of the Hebrew Union College, addressed the student body

---

[21]Fifth Principle. See W. Gunther Plaut, *The Growth of Reform Judaism. American and European Sources Until 1948*, New York 1965, p. 34.

[22]Samson Raphael Hirsch, *Neunzehn Briefe über Judentum*, Altona 1836; English version, *The Nineteen Letters of Ben Uziel*, transl. by Bernard Drachman, New York 1899, reprinted with the same pagination in 1942, p. 79, Ninth Letter. I have made some slight verbal changes in Drachman's translation here and elsewhere. Page references in this essay are to the New York edition.

[23]The mistranslation is surreptitiously corrected in the English version without note or explanation.

at the opening exercises of the academic year on 29th September 1917. In this address he quite properly stressed the Jews' loyalty and devotion to the land in which they lived. In speaking of this loyalty to one's country he quotes the "significant monition" of the prophet Jeremiah to his brethren: "Seek the peace and welfare of the city *in which you will live*, and pray for it, for in its peace you will have peace."[24] But Kohler knew better; on page 320 of *Jewish Theology* he translates the italicised phrase correctly as "whither I have caused you to be carried away captive".

The points of agreement between Hirsch and the Reformers help to take the edge off the paradox of how the staunchly Orthodox Hirsch could have remained an abiding influence on Kohler. In many respects Hirsch, in his formative years, met the Reformers more than half way. His early friendship with Abraham Geiger, the most learned of the Reform rabbis, has often been commented upon. What is remarkable is that this friendship continued even after Geiger openly expounded his advanced views in his sermons at the *Philanthropin*, the Jewish school in Frankfurt. Hirsch severed relations with Geiger only after the latter severely criticised the *Neunzehn Briefe*. It was, therefore, for personal rather than religious reasons that their friendship came to an end.[25] And while Hirsch was generally meticulous in his observance of Jewish law, while serving in his first rabbinical position in Oldenburg, he abolished the *Kol Nidre* prayer for the annulment of religious vows on Yom Kippur, fearing that the prayer might be misinterpreted by antisemites as giving the Jews a licence to break their promises and obligations. He shared the contempt of the Reformers for "the Polish-Jewish teachers", and the late Professor Isaac Heinemann expresses surprise that Hirsch had an engraving made in Oldenburg which shows him in his rabbinical gown with white bands, without a beard and with uncovered head – something inconceivable for a traditional Eastern European rabbi. What is even more remarkable is that Hirsch asked Rabbi David Hoffmann to remove his headgear when he came to visit Hirsch in his home.[26]

The best characterisation of Hirsch, at the time he developed his theology, is that given by himself in the last of the *Neunzehn Briefe*. "In an age when the contrasts stand so sharply over against each other, and when the truth is on neither side, in such an age the man *who belongs to no party*, who has only the cause in his heart, and serves it alone, cannot... expect approval or agreement on any side."[27]

---

[24]Kohler, *A Living Faith*, ed. by Samuel S. Cohon, Cincinnati 1948, p. 157.
[25]See Robert Liberles, *Religious Conflict in Social Context. The Resurgence of Orthodox Judaism in Frankfurt am Main, 1837–1877*, Westport, CT 1985, pp. 121–124 and the literature there cited.
[26]Isaac Heinemann, 'Samson Raphael Hirsch', *Historica Judaica*, vol. 13 (April 1951), pp. 29–54; "Kol Nidre", pp. 42f.; "uncovered head", pp. 46f.; "Polish teacher", *Nineteen Letters*, beginning; David Hoffmann, *Mellamed Leho'il*, Responsa, Part II, "Yoreh Deah", No. 56, Frankfurt am Main 1927, p. 51. Regarding the abolition of Kol Nidre, Kurt Wilhelm correctly observes that this action indicates that "as District Rabbi in Oldenburg he [Hirsch] had compromised with reformist tendencies", Kurt Wilhelm, 'The Jewish Community in the Post-Emancipation Period', in *LBI Year Book II* (1957), p. 64.
[27]*The Nineteen Letters*, pp. 212f., emphasis added.

Hirsch's analysis of what ails the Judaism of his time does not differ markedly from that of the moderate Reformers.

> "Where is the Jew who knows himself, who is cognisant of the import and meaning of his destiny, of the import and meaning of his Mission? Where are the sons of Israel in whose breast echo the tones of the harp of David and the words of the prophets, and whose mind – but, ah! I should be silent concerning the mind – comprehends the extent of the Israel-duty? And what wrong and mischievous notions exist concerning the principles, ordinances, and teachings of Judaism? Even that which is known externally and superficially, how little is it known as regards its wondrously profound inner meaning! For instance, the *Edoth* duties, so useful and indispensable through the lessons they teach, are looked upon by some as mere mechanical *opus operatum*, or as talismanic jugglery for the prevention of physical evils or the erection of mystic supramundane worlds. Others again look upon the holiest laws of righteousness as matters outside of Judaism, not, as they should regard them, indissolubly interwoven with its very fabric. As for those highly important laws of Judaism, which strengthen us to do battle with the sensual lusts of appetite and passion, of indulgence and ease, how little are they understood, how often denounced as cruel privation beyond the power of human nature to endure; how can they otherwise than succumb in this unequal combat, since their victory is gained by the spirit, and that is either absent or woefully deficient? This inner conception is lacking comprehension of Judaism, of the significance of its historic destiny and teachings, and, therefore, love for it has no soil upon which to grow. How extreme the resultant danger is can be conceived when we consider that this love is our only counterbalance against internal and external temptation, and the attainment of this love our aim and our only salvation."[28]

Nor does Hirsch's remedy differ essentially from that of the Reformers. "You will at once discern," Hirsch makes his spokesman say in the *Neunzehn Briefe*, "how numerous are the steps which we must still make, and how great the distance yet to be climbed before we can reach the glorious summit of our aspiration and our hope. Therefore, may our motto be – Reform. Let us strive with all our power, with all the good and noble qualities of our character to reach this height of ideal perfection – Reform!"[29]

The paradox of how a theologian so seemingly different from Kohler as Hirsch could have been a significant and pervasive influence in Kohler's life can be appreciated by considering the effect of the emancipation of the Jews. The impact cannot be overestimated. The physicist and historian of science Thomas S. Kuhn originated the theory of "paradigms" to account for the development of scientific theories. By "paradigm" Kuhn means a set of broad assumptions constituting an entire constellation of beliefs, values, techniques and so on, shared by a given community. A scientific revolution consists of the process whereby one paradigm replaces another. Although Kuhn himself hesitates to take his paradigm concept from the natural to the social sciences, in recent years his analyses have been extended by others to the social sciences and even to theology. Hans Küng, the Catholic Swiss theologian, applied the

---

[28] *Ibid.*, pp. 171–173. The *Edoth* are testimonial symbolic precepts having an educational function; Grunfeld, Introduction to *Horeb*, p. lix.
[29] *Nineteen Letters*, p. 170.

theory of paradigm shifts to Jewish history.[30] One epoch-making change was the emancipation and Enlightenment of Jewry. Emancipation transformed the Jews from a distinct group, concentrated in urban ghettos and living a social and intellectual life essentially different from that of the surrounding population. It integrated them into the general population amongst which they lived. Jewish reactions to the process of emancipation were varied. If we consider only the different religious responses, Hirsch and Kohler are far apart, but if we consider the entire spectrum of responses, including assimilation, conversion, secularism, Marxism, atheism, and modern naturalism, the two appear much closer. One observer has noted that the most prominent Jews in the post-emancipation period – Albert Einstein, Henri Bergson, Sigmund Freud, Emile Durkheim, Jacques Derrida and others – never joined a synagogue or paid any attention to the Torah lifestyle. "They found bourgeois Reform as parochial as traditional Orthodoxy."[31]

At the universities of Munich and Berlin, Kohler was shocked to discover that Hirsch's excursions into linguistics were without a solid foundation, and that his exegetical system was based on a fanciful interpretation of biblical Hebrew words. It is said that Samuel Rolles Driver, the Regius Professor of Hebrew at Oxford University, always commenced his initial lecture on the Hebrew language with the words, "Gentlemen, this is the language which God spoke." But what was for Canon Driver a picturesque way of speaking was taken quite literally by Hirsch. In his study of Arabic philology it became apparent to Kohler that Hirsch's naive exegetical system was mistaken and the belief that Hebrew was the original language of the human race was wrong. Hirsch, however, based much of his theology on that assumption. "My Arabic studies under Prof. Mueller in Munich," Kohler writes, "at once undermined the exegetical system of S.R. Hirsch, built upon the assumption that Hebrew was the original language, and the philosophical and historical lectures I attended knocked the bottom out of his whole theology".[32] In his perplexity, Kohler travelled to Frankfurt to lay his doubts and scruples before his revered teacher and to seek reassurance. To his surprise, Hirsch announced: "My dear Kohler, he who wants to journey around the world must also pass the torrid zone; proceed and you will come back safely."[33] Two things may be noted about this remarkable answer. First, although Hirsch has often been criticised for his reply, I do not know how a wise spiritual counsellor could deal with an honest perplexed doubter more satisfactorily. Secondly, while Jewish homiletic literature does speak of Hebrew as the original language of mankind, this folkloristic belief was

---

[30]Thomas S. Kuhn, *The Structure of Scientific Revolutions*, 2nd edn., Chicago 1970, p. 175. Kuhn expresses his concern about extending his concept to the social sciences as follows: "It remains an open question what parts of social science have yet acquired such paradigms at all", *ibid.*, p. 15. Cf. Gary Gutting (ed.), *Paradigms and Revolutions. Appraisals and Applications of Thomas S. Kuhn's Philosophy of Science*, Notre Dame–London 1980; Hans Küng, *Judaism Between Yesterday and Tomorrow*, New York 1992.
[31]Sherwin T. Wine, *Humanistic Judaism*, Buffalo 1978, p. 1.
[32]Kohler, 'Personal Reminiscences', p. 476.
[33]*Ibid.*

never made *de fide* by the synagogue.[34] The romantic etymologising, without regard to other Semitic languages and their development, is a personal idiosyncrasy of Hirsch's. Professor Barry Levy of McGill University, who is himself an ordained Orthodox rabbi from the R. Isaac Elchananan Theological Seminary and formerly an instructor in Bible at Yeshiva University, writes in a caustic critique: "Hirsch's linguistic ingenuity is sometimes remarkable and was obviously supplemented by a creative mind and (for some people) appealing doctrines, but it is totally unacceptable to any scientific appreciation of the dynamics of language. Indeed, it has much in common with some of the very approaches that many of the medieval [Jewish] linguists and commentators attacked as unfounded. Such fanciful philology is legitimate, only as another form of *midrash*, which, like the *midrashim* of old, is unrestrained by any limits of grammar or lexicography and can do almost anything to the Bible text in the name of religious [edification]."[35] Heinrich Leberecht Fleischer, the eminent nineteenth-century Orientalist, called Hirsch the "Kabbalist of philology" and characterised his fantastic exegesis as a "fraud in etymology [*Etymologien Schwindel*]".[36]

Kohler proceeded, but he never did come back. Instead, he underwent a spiritual crisis. "I passed days and weeks of indescribable woe and despondency; the heavens seemed to fall down upon me and crush me."[37] Kohler's older contemporary, the poet and critic Matthew Arnold, caught this mood well in his poetry as he reflects on the ebbing and withdrawal of the 'Sea of Faith', which leaves the poet

> "... as on a darkling plain
> Swept with confused alarms of struggle and flight,
> Where ignorant armies clash by night".

Kohler found himself, like Arnold,

> "Wandering between two worlds, one dead,
> The other powerless to be born,
> With nowhere yet to rest my head...".

It is frequently asserted that Kohler soon found himself in the opposing camp as a disciple of Abraham Geiger. This is at best a half-truth. Certainly, in later

---

[34] Genesis Rabbah XVIII:4 and Rashi on Gen. II:23. Hirsch's view is found in his Commentary on Gen. XI:7. See also I. Grunfeld's Introduction to the English translation by I. Levy of Hirsch's *Commentary on the Pentateuch*, New York 1959, pp. xiii–xvi.

[35] B. Barry Levy, 'Our Torah, Your Torah, and their Torah', in *Truth and Compassion. Essays on Judaism and Religion in Memory of Rabbi Dr. Solomon Frank*, ed. by Howard Joseph et al., Waterloo 1983, pp. 137–189 (here p. 148).

[36] Fleischer in a letter to Geiger in *Jüdische Zeitschrift für Wissenschaft und Leben*, vol. 10, (1872), pp. 158–159, quoted by Max Heller in *Yearbook of the Central Conference of American Rabbis*, vol. 18 (1908), p. 188, n. 28. But while Fleischer refers to Hirsch as the head of the "Sprachkabbalisten" he uses, in the place cited, the characterisation "phantastische Etymologisirung" (fantastic etymologising) and not "Etymologien Schwindel". Similarly, Max Wiener speaking of Hirsch's fanciful philology says: "One can disregard the audacity of the haggadist Hirsch, who here found a very wide arena for his whims." Wiener, *Jüdische Religion im Zeitalter der Emanzipation*, p. 76.

[37] Kohler, 'Personal Reminiscences', p. 476.

years, Kohler looked up to Geiger as the master builder of modern Judaism who "gave the Reform movement its scientific basis [and] its historical foundation".[38] Geiger welcomed Kohler as a promising scholar in his *Zeitschrift* and in private letters. At Geiger's suggestion, Kohler continued with the idea of preparing himself for an academic career. But his heart was not in mere literary enterprises; he "felt... little at home in the camel-charged atmosphere of Arabic desert poetry".[39] Geiger then counselled him to go to America, "the land of promise for progressive Judaism", and asked his friends in the New World to use their good offices to find a rabbinical position for Kohler. Geiger did help him and Kohler was grateful, but he never considered himself Geiger's disciple, nor was he as inspired by him as he was by Samson Raphael Hirsch. Kohler had to work out his problems by himself and to develop his own ideal of progressive Liberal Judaism. He writes:

> "Samson Raphael Hirsch, the glowing exponent of Jewish orthodoxy in its boldest type in our age, had become my ideal and idol, when, lo! philological and philosophical studies roused my mind from the slumber of child-like belief in the letter, and cast bitter doubts in my soul. I longed for light, for truth – for a truth which satisfied not merely the mind, but also the heart's craving. *In vain did I seek spiritual support, a firm and clear basis, from Geiger, the great historian and critic. None of the Reformers would fan the flame of enthusiasm for our faith into full blaze again.* Professor Steinthal... had dissolved for me the whole life and law of Moses, the Bible, religious belief into myth and fable. And yet, I was no skeptic nor [*sic*] agnostic. In my heart of hearts, I had remained a Jew, a Jewish theologian of positive faith."[40]

Kohler's declaration is highly significant. He was not a sceptic nor a scoffer who wanted to break the shackles of Jewish tradition. He was not an ethical universalist and a citizen of the world. Kohler wanted to perpetuate Judaism, but he understood that blind authority-worship was not possible for educated people and he was looking for a rational faith. But he loved Judaism and was emotionally attached to it. In the Bible and Jewish tradition, he wanted to separate the kernel from the husk, the grain from the chaff, and the spirit from the temporary form. He expressly states that in this endeavour he was not influenced by Geiger or any other Reform thinker.[41] But surely his theology did not drop down from heaven ready-made like manna. From where, then, did it originate? At the risk of the charge of speculation, for there is no hard documentary evidence, I would like to suggest that during his days of "anxiety and trial" Kohler reviewed Hirsch's views on Judaism. With a discerning eye, he determined what was alive and what

---

[38] K. Kohler, *Hebrew Union College and Other Addresses*, Cincinnati 1916, p. 83.
[39] Kohler, 'Personal Reminiscences', p. 479; letter to Dr. Samuel Adler, dated 6th April 1869, in *Hebrew Union College Annual*, vol. 2 (1924), p. 429.
[40] Kohler, *A Living Faith*, p. 200 (emphasis added).
[41] Kohler does acknowledge that just before leaving for the New World he attended the sessions of the Reform Jewish Synod in Leipzig. Its president, Moritz Lazarus (1824–1903), a layman, made a deep and lasting impression on him. The inspiring closing address which Lazarus delivered on 4th July 1869 fired Kohler's spirit. "While others listened to him as if a prophet had spoken," he wrote many years later, "I heard the voice of a new revelation... It was the inspiration of a lifetime". Kohler, *A Living Faith*, pp. 199f. But by that time Kohler had already worked out the essentials of his theological system.

was not in Hirsch's theology. From that he built his own thought on what he considered tenable in Hirsch's religious philosophy.

Hirsch's views on Jewish scholarship fall into two parts: (1) his criticism of the historico-critical Jewish new learning (*Wissenschaft des Judentums*) which developed in Hirsch's youth in the first half of the nineteenth century, and (2) his positive views on Jewish learning and how it should grow from the Jewish tradition itself, free from external influence. Hirsch attacked "Jewish science [*Wissenschaft des Judentums*]" for its essentially "museumish" approach. He charged its practitioners with having produced "not a physiology of living Judaism, but a pathological anatomy of a dead and dying Judaism". He accused them of dealing pretentiously with trivia and externalities: "they have hardly ventured to touch the supposed corpse itself, but only its garments and wrappings – on what field the flax grew from which the linen was woven, what sheep bore the wool from which the pall was prepared, and in what year was born the nurse of the woman who spun the thread for both". The goals of *Wissenschaft* were mainly negative; it had not revitalised Judaism and it sought to undermine tradition and to put the seal of scholarship on ignorant heresy. The critical method of Talmud study purported to show that "the later authorities did not understand the earlier nor the latest the later, that the *Gemara* did not understand the *Mishnah*, nor the Babylonian Talmud the Jerusalem, nor the commentaries and *Posekim* [decisors or legal authorities] either of them, and so insinuating that the basis on which living Judaism rested at the present day and on which the Jew who was still a Jew staked his very life and fortune and that of his children was nothing but one deception built on another by guides stricken with blindness and ignorance. "Jewish learning ought to be the fertile soil of Jewish life, and so long as it was such it occupied the first place in actual life; but their learning is the dust from the tombs of decomposed corpses blown about over the barren steppes of the present." Those who do not pray, study prayer. "How many of those who write about *Selichoth*, *Yozeroth*, and *Piyyutim* actually go to *Selichoth*; how many of them do not in fact banish *Yozeroth* and *Piyyutim* from the liturgy? How many of those who write biographies and histories of Rabbi Jochanan ben Zakkai, of Rabbi Eliezer ben Hyrkanos, Rabbon Gamliel, of Rabbi Akiba, of Rabbi Joshua ben Chanaya, etc., does the practicing Jew still see following the traditions which these teachers have transmitted to us, washing their hands for instance before eating bread?"[42] What is vitally

---

[42]. Although Hirsch's tone is polemical and he allowed himself some strategic over-emphases for effect, his critique is essentially sound. See Ismar Schorsch, 'Scholarship in the Service of Reform', in *LBI Year Book XXXV* (1990), pp. 73–101, especially the sections devoted to Geiger (pp. 83–91) and Joshua Heschel Schorr (1818–1885), the Galician radical scholar (pp. 97–99); and Joseph Klausner's introduction to the Hebrew translation of Geiger's *Urschrift und Übersetzungen der Bibel* which first appeared in 1857 (Jerusalem 1949). Although this magisterial and monumental work retains its value even after a century and a half, we must add that it does have a hidden agenda: the undermining of traditional Judaism and of belief in the divine origin of the Bible. Hirsch early recognised that Geiger was determined to raze traditional Judaism to its very foundation and build a new religion called Reformed Judaism on its ruins. That this was indeed Geiger's intention is made clear in his contemporaneous correspondence with Joseph Derenbourg (1811–1895) which,

important and needed is "a science of Jewish ideas of nature and history, and, in the light of these truths which have been handed down by Judaism, to judge from the Jewish standpoint the events of the present, and the struggles and expectations of the people, along with the principles and views which guide them".[43]

According to Hirsch, the proper method for the study of Judaism is that of the scientist. What distinguishes modern science and scientific method is its empirical attitude: it does not try to construe *a priori* that which can be grasped by the senses, and it does not build up from some preconceived notions of arbitrarily posited truths that can be brought within the scope of observation. The scientist starts from observation and experiment and is not satisfied until the subsequent generalisations have, as far as possible, been verified. Hirsch boldly challenges his audience to test Judaism in the same way. "In order to understand Judaism, we must be able to judge from within its sphere and ask ourselves, 'what will human beings be who recognize the contents of this book as a basis and rule of life given to them by God?' ... Only when you have thus comprehended Judaism from itself, as it represents itself to be, and have then found it untenable and unworthy of acceptance, may you, if you wish, cast upon it the stone of obloquy."[44]

The keystone of Hirsch's philosophy of religion is his extended comparison of the two revelations of God.

> "Two revelations are open before us; nature and the Torah. In nature all phenomena stand before us as indisputable facts, and we can only endeavor *a posteriori* to ascertain the law of each and the connection of all. The right method is to verify our assumptions by the known facts, and the highest attainable degree of certainty is to be able to say, "The facts agree with our assumption" – that is, all the phenomena observed can be explained according to our theory. A single contradictory phenomenon will make our theory untenable. If, however, all efforts should fail in disclosing the inner law and connection of phenomena revealed to us as facts in nature, the facts remain, nevertheless, undeniable, and cannot be reasoned away. The same principles must be applied to the investigation of the Torah. In the Torah, even as in nature, God is the ultimate cause. In the Torah, even as in nature, no fact may be denied, even though the reason and the connection may not be understood. In nature, the phenomena are recognized as facts, though their cause and relationship to each other may not be understood, and are independent of our investigation. So, too, the ordinances of

---

however, was only published posthumously in 1896. See the excerpts of the correspondence translated by Wiener in *Abraham Geiger and Liberal Judaism*, pp. 83–96, especially the letter dated 6th November 1836; cf. Solomon Schechter, 'Abraham Geiger', in *Studies in Judaism*, vol. 3, (1924), pp. 47–83.

[43] All quotations from Hirsch in this paragraph are taken from Grunfeld (ed.), *Judaism Eternal*, vol. II, pp. 282–290, and are found in an essay entitled 'How Can We Carry Jewish Learning into Practical Life?', pp. 274–290. A century later many charges in Hirsch's indictment were also voiced by Gershom Scholem in his harsh critique of *Wissenschaft* in *Explications and Implications. Writing on Jewish Heritage and Renaissance* (in Hebrew), Tel Aviv 1975, pp. 285–403, first published in *Luah Ha'ares* (1944–45, pp. 112–194). A toned down version of Scholem's critique may be found in his essay, 'The Science of Judaism. Then and Now', in *idem.*, *The Messianic Idea in Judaism*, New York 1971, pp. 304–313.

[44] *Nineteen Letters*, p. 14.

the Torah remain the law even if we do not comprehend the reason and the purpose of a single one."[45]

Kohler shared a good deal of Hirsch's indictment of *Wissenschaft*. He endorsed the charge that the new learning lacked vitality and imagination, and that it was antiquarian and pedantic. Its pioneering founder, the renowned Leopold Zunz, he discovered to be a "morose misanthrope" who was inaccessible, especially to theological students. The scholarly study of Judaism was regarded by Zunz as a "swan song rather than as the dawn of a new era in Jewish life" and he was convinced that by the beginning of the twentieth century a Hebrew book would be well-nigh impossible to obtain.[46] Kohler profited little from Moritz Steinschneider's lectures, which offered him "only the husks of Jewish learning, lists of names and dates of authors and of manuscripts, with all sorts of attacks on other bibliographers".[47] Dr. Steinschneider once pointed to a hoard of medieval Hebrew manuscripts on his desk and exclaimed: "Only one task remains, to give a decent burial to the remains of Judaism."[48] Years later Kohler confessed: "I feel I cannot be a scholar unless I can be a Jew at the same time. To me truth should be clear, lucid, objective; nevertheless it ought at the same time to have the warm pulse of life, or else it is no truth for me; it is no truth for man. We must have that truth which touches the heart as well as the mind; not a matter of reason only, but also of the soul."[49]

Kohler's doctoral dissertation, *Der Segen Jakobs*, his first published work, appeared in 1867. Using the critical biblical scholarship method, Kohler examines the forty-ninth chapter of Genesis, the Blessing of Jacob, trying to discover the period in which it was probably written and the conditions which it reflects. Kohler seeks to demonstrate that the prophetic element is not limited to one period of Jewish history, but is already reflected in the Pentateuch and forms part of the continuous evolution of Judaism. Perhaps the most striking and interesting aspect of his dissertation is the introduction, in which Kohler discusses the spiritual needs of his own age and plans for a living religion which would adapt the past to the needs of the present.

> "In the name of religion, everything that is old and traditional is called holy, while all that is new is as such condemned, as well as all progress. In the name of religion, men are not allowed to think, to gain spiritual independence and maturity. That foolish

---

[45] *Ibid.*, pp. 194f. (abridged). That the doctrine of two revelations (nature and the Torah) is an overarching principle in Hirsch's thought is shown by Samuel A. Hirsch, 'Ein Wort über S.R. Hirsch's wissenschaftliche Methode', in *Der Israelit*, S.R. Hirsch Anniversary Issue, 1908, pp. 33–34; *idem, A Book of Essays*, London 1905, pp. 196ff. See, also, Pinhas Paul Grünewald, *Pédagogie, Esthétique et Ticoun Olam. Redressement du Monde Samson Raphael Hirsch*, Berne 1986, pp. 40ff. Louis Ginzberg, in his lecture 'The Religion of the Pharisee', delivered before the Harvard Divinity School, paraphrases this concept of two revelations without mentioning Hirsch, as if it were typical of Pharisaic thought at the time of Jesus. See Louis Ginzberg, *Students, Scholars, and Saints*, Philadelphia 1928, pp. 104f.

[46] See Luitpold Wallach, *Liberty and Letters. The Thoughts of Leopold Zunz*, London 1959, Publication of the Leo Baeck Institute, pp. 18f.

[47] . Kohler, 'Personal Reminiscences', p. 477.

[48] . Quoted by Gotthold Weil, *Jüdische Rundschau XII*, No. 6 (8th February 1907), p. 54.

[49] Kohler, *Yearbook of the Central Conference of American Rabbis*, vol. 13 (1903), p. 137.

principle has served to transplant crass ignorance and pollution to Jewish soil, also; a principle, the harshness and cruelty of which is felt in its full force by him only who, through love of truth and in the service of faith and by a sense of deep union with Judaism, has struggled for freedom of thought and has had to pay for it dearly step by step."[50]

Complete sincerity in one's religious quest, Kohler argues, is indispensable to a meaningful religion. "Is it not imperative," he asks, "that children be taught nothing in the name of religion which, the next hour, would be contradicted or nullified by the teacher of the natural sciences?" "Shall we by our attitude, help to make religion ridiculous, or undermine it?"[51] Kohler believes that Judaism is not a static religion fixed for all time by the revelation at Sinai, but an ever-growing dynamic faith driven forward by the evolutionary process. "Religion," he urges, "is eternal".

> "Man will never be able to dispense with it. It can never be displaced by cold philosophic statements or ethical abstractions. Mankind can never dispense with the higher unity of action and thought, of will and duty, yes, with the idea of a Deity which has given to the free will its ethical laws and to the world of the sense its natural laws, no matter what different forms the Deity might take on in the conception of the individual. Religion, however, must try to adopt the form in which it can best serve the struggle of the age towards truth, unity, and ethical freedom, and thus connect the traditions of the past with the ideals of the future. And what are the ideals of the future of mankind, if not those which Judaism, or to speak more generally, Prophetism, put forth more than twenty-five hundred years ago, namely, that the time would come when men, united by a love of peace and truth, would regard and love one another as the children of one God?"[52]

The ideas mentioned by Kohler in the introduction to his doctoral dissertation remained the abiding themes of his life's work. In the last quotation, we note a clear difference between Kohler and his teacher, Hirsch, regarding the two revelations of God. Hirsch had argued that God's ordinances must be accepted in their entirety as undeniable phenomena; they are laws for us, even if we do not comprehend their reason and purpose. All of them are equally divine. The ritual, as well as the ethical, laws are introduced by the declaration, "And the Lord spoke unto Moses, saying . . .". The commandments "You shall love your neighbour as yourself" and "Do not wear a garment that contains a mixture of wool and linen" stand side by side in the same paragraph in the nineteenth chapter of Leviticus. In *Horeb* (§454) Hirsch ends a discussion of the rationale of the dietary laws with the following statement:

> "All these meditations are speculations and perhaps flow from lack of insight into the essential nature of things. However that may be, one thing is certain: high above all human speculation stands the Torah, the law of Israel's life, eternal and immutable like the laws by which the planets move in the sky and the grain of seed grows in the soil. The same God Who laid down the law which Nature of necessity follows, also

---

[50]Kohler, *Der Segen Jakobs*, transl. by H.G. Enelow, Berlin 1867, p. IV; 'A Biographical Essay', in idem., *The Origin of the Synagogue and the Church*, New York 1929, p. xi.
[51]*Ibid.*
[52]*Ibid.*, pp. Vf.; Enelow, pp. xif.

pronounced the law which Israel is asked to follow of its own free will. And just as the laws of Nature are unchangeable – despite any opinion man may hold – so all speculations on the laws of the Torah can only be an enlightenment of our own minds, but never the cause of their validity; for the *causa causarum* of the laws of Nature as well as of the laws of the Torah is ... God."[53]

Kohler limits the divine inspiration to the *ethical* laws which ideally govern mankind. He does this because his studies in comparative religion and anthropology had convinced him that circumcision, the dietary laws, and the sacrificial cult were not distinctively and essentially Jewish. All these rites in the biblical legislation were adapted from neighbouring peoples, although given a higher and more spiritual meaning by the divine Lawgiver. There was little development of Kohler's views in later life. In the 'Pittsburgh Platform' (1885) of the American Reform rabbis, written by Kohler, principles three and four deny the validity of the Mosaic legislation.

> "We accept as binding only its moral laws, and maintain only such ceremonies as elevate and sanctify our lives, but reject all such as are not adapted to the views and habits of modern civilization.... We hold that all such Mosaic and rabbinical laws as regulate diet, priestly purity and dress originated in ages and under the influences of ideas entirely foreign to our present mental and spiritual state. They fail to impress the modern Jew with a spirit of priestly holiness; their observance in our days is apt rather to obstruct than to further modern spiritual elevation."[54]

The foregoing illustrates how Kohler arrived at a diametrically opposite position from that of Hirsch on Jewish ritual observance while attempting to leave the framework of Hirsch's argument intact. A bolder thinker might have pointed out that Hirsch's whole argument is based on a logical equivocation of the word "law". In the one case "law" is used in a *descriptive* way to express the regularity of natural phenomena, while in the second case it is used in a *prescriptive* way to characterise the principles of religious conduct and morality ("law and order") promulgated by a supernatural Being. One cannot "break" or violate a law of nature as one can the commandments of the Torah.[55]

But we must not be too harsh with a twenty-three year old doctoral candidate. Kohler, in later life at least, attempted to construct a science of Jewish morality and nature. Hirsch indeed spoke of a "selbstbegreifend" Judaism, that is, one which is "understood from within itself", but there is not one solitary work during his lifetime which he acknowledged as meeting his standards. Hirsch was unalterably opposed to the *Wissenschaft des Judentums*, the new scholarly study of

---

[53] Ellipsis in the original.
[54] Quoted in Plaut, *The Growth of Reform Judaism*, p. 34.
[55] The force of this criticism may perhaps be somewhat mitigated if we consider Hirsch as having anticipated the phenomenalist doctrine of "bracketing". Husserl and the phenomenalists would have us bracket the existence of the objective, external world and suspend judgment about the existence of the things around us. The botanist, for example, takes the existence of trees for granted and studies their characteristics. So too, the Jew should take the Torah as God's own revealed word, irrespective of the origin, evolution and transmission of the biblical text, and examine into what sort of person it moulds those who govern their way of life by its commandments.

Judaism as it developed in the nineteenth century, particularly as it applied to the scientific and historical development of the *Halakhah*. When Zacharias Frankel published his *Darke ha-Mishnah* (1859), Hirsch fiercely attacked him. In the course of savaging his work, Hirsch coined the famous slogan: "Better a Jew without *Wissenschaft* than *Wissenschaft* without Judaism [*Lieber Jude ohne Wissenschaft als Wissenschaft ohne Judentum*]."[56] He objected not only to studies of the *Wissenschaft* type written by Reform scholars such as Geiger, but also to works by such staunch defenders of Orthodoxy as David Hoffmann and other faculty members of the Hildesheimer Orthodox *Rabbinerseminar* in Berlin. In reality, Hirsch wanted to insulate the Torah from any sort of criticism by claiming that its ordinances and laws, written and oral, are phenomena which are a given and cannot be questioned.[57] But this approach is the very opposite of the scientist's procedure. A very powerful weapon in the scientist's arsenal is the putting forward of alternative hypotheses. It is very rare for science to find a situation in which there is an obvious explanation of a given phenomenon; usually there are several competing possible explanations, and the scientist has to weigh the merits of the alternative explanations. To take a particular explanation for a starting point, to count it as a fact, is an abuse of scientific method. Granted that the ordinances and laws of the Torah must be accepted as undeniable phenomena, but they are capable of diverse explanations – those of the higher critics no less than those of fundamentalists like Hirsch. It is true as a historical fact that until the Enlightenment the vast majority of Jews believed in the verbal revelation of the Torah to Moses on Mount Sinai, but one cannot conclude from this that the concept of the Torah as binding as law is necessarily included as a phenomenon of authentic Jewish life. Elementary logic demands that we separate the fact of an explanation from the allegation of fact as to its truth, that is, its validity, and to assume its validity is only one (not the *only*) possible explanation of that fact as an historical record. (If Hirsch's argument were sound we could substitute "astrology" for "the Torah" and transpose the argument to establish the truth of astrology.)[58]

---

[56] Hirsch, *Gesammelte Schriften*, vol. 6, p. 393; *Collected Writings* vol. 5, p. 287. This catchword shows that Hirsch viewed *Wissenschaft* and Judaism as mutually exclusive.
[57] See Marx, *Essays in Jewish Biography*, pp. 204–206; Mordechai Eliav (ed.), *Rabbiner Esriel Hildesheimer Briefe*, Jerusalem 1965, Veröffentlichung des Leo Baeck Instituts, Letter 74, pp. 210f.; Mordechai Breuer, *Modernity Within Tradition. The Social History of Orthodox Jewry in Imperial Germany*, transl. by Elizabeth Petuchowski, New York 1992, pp. 185ff.; *idem*, 'Three Orthodox Approaches to *Wissenschaft*' (in Hebrew), in Shaul Israeli, *et al.* (eds.), *Sefer Yovel li-Kevod Morenu ha-Gaon Rabbi Yosef Dov ha-Levi Soloveitchik*, Jerusalem 1984, vol. 2, pp. 856–865, here p. 860. Hoffmann's son-in-law, Alexander Marx (*Essays in Jewish Biography*, p. 188) remarks that already as a fledgling scholar Hoffmann noted that sometimes the *Midrashim* understood the *Mishnah* in a sense opposed to the explanation in the Babylonian Talmud. See, also, the excellent summary and discussion in David Ellenson, *Rabbi Esriel Hildesheimer and the Creation of Modern Jewish Orthodoxy*, Tuscaloosa, 1990, pp. 149–156, and the literature there cited.
[58] In this paragraph I am indebted to the brilliant criticism of Abraham Wolf, in *Jewish Quarterly Review*, vol. 18 (1906), p. 177. On Wolf's contribution to Jewish scholarship see Jacob Haberman, 'Abraham Wolf: A Forgotten Jewish Reform Thinker', in *Jewish Quarterly Review*, vol. 81 (1991), pp. 267–304.

Kohler's work on the *Jewish Encyclopedia* (1901–1906), on which he was the most influential member of the editorial board and served as head of the Department of Theology and Philosophy, helped to mature his thinking. He had been invited to serve as early as 1899 and he was instrumental in enlisting other scholars, such as Louis Ginzberg, to become contributors.[59] In all he wrote 288 articles for the *Encyclopedia*, including all the main entries in his department up to and including the eighth volume, after which he had to curtail his activities as he left New York, where the editorial office was located, to assume the presidency of the Hebrew Union College in Cincinnati. The need to cooperate with other scholars representing different viewpoints helped to reduce party politics greatly. It transformed Kohler from a vociferous pamphleteer to a disciplined, serious scholar. From the time he began working for the *Encyclopedia* there is a marked change in his tone. Christianity, rather than Orthodox Judaism, becomes the foil for Kohler's advanced views. In 1885 he had delivered a series of five pulpit discussions which were later published under the title of the first of the series, 'Backward or Forward?' In them Kohler is scathing and merciless in his attacks on the Orthodox position. "Must we still be cowed down by fear of the thunders of Sinai?" he asks in a rhetorical outburst, and he describes Orthodox Judaism as "a bucketful of stale water carried along from the Sinai wilderness" and as "fanatical, inconsistent, and anachronistical"; and he asserts with authority that "Orientalism on our Free American Soil will not stand the test of time". He demands "a Bible purified from all its offensive and obnoxious elements", and grumbles that "we dwelt too long on the rubbish of the past".[60] With these specimens (which could readily be multiplied) contrast Kohler's appeal for Jewish

---

[59] Ginzberg wrote a total of 406 articles for the *Encyclopedia*, mainly in the first two volumes. One Sunday he had to see Kohler urgently in connection with some business relating to his work. He was told at the *Encyclopedia* office that Kohler was conducting services at Temple Beth-El. Ginzberg went to the Temple and waited until the service was over. Kohler, spying him in the audience and being surprised to find him there, greeted him jocularly with the question from the *Midrash*: "What is a priest [who must not defile himself by coming into contact with the dead] doing in a cemetery?" Ginzberg's riposte was sabre-sharp: "The graves of Gentiles do not defile" (cf.bBM 114b). It must have pained Kohler greatly to see that Ginzberg was reading him out of the Jewish community. See David Druck, *Louis Ginzberg* (in Hebrew), New York 1933; pp. 61f.; Eli Ginzberg, in *Keeper of the Law. Louis Ginzberg*, Philadelphia 1966, pp. 68f., presents a milder version of the incident. Kohler inaugurated the transfer of Sabbath services to Sunday in 1875 when he was minister of Chicago Sinai Congregation. This congregation has maintained this policy to the present day. (Kohler's successor, Emil G. Hirsch, quipped that he was the only Sabbath observer among Chicago's rabbis since his temple was closed on Saturdays.) Kohler later reversed his position on this ill-conceived religious innovation, claiming that the renewal of anti-Jewish feelings in the world prevented him from continuing to support the Sabbath transfer. See Kerry M. Olitsky, 'The Sunday-Sabbath Movement in American Reform Judaism: Strategy or Evolution?', in *American Jewish Archives*, vol. 34 (April 1982), pp. 75–88, especially pp. 78f. See also *Jewish Theology*, p. 459. The most detailed examination of Kohler's changing opinions regarding Sunday services at different stages in his career may be found in Robert J. Marx, *Kaufmann Kohler as a Reformer*, Cincinnati 1951, pp. 30–35, 62–65, 71–81.

[60] Kohler, 'Backward or Forward?', in *Studies, Addresses, and Personal Papers*, pp. 201–235; "thunders of Sinai", *ibid.*; p. 206; "bucketful of stale water"; "fanatical, inconsistent", p. 217; "Orientalism", *ibid.*; "Bible purified", p. 218; "rubbish of the past", p. 219.

unity and for an end to religious strife delivered before the Central Conference of American Rabbis at their 1898 convention in Atlantic City:

> "The time for strife and party division is over. We need consolidation. My message is: A United Israel! Let all differences of opinion be waived. Let all wrangling and bickering between Reform and Orthodoxy, between Conservative and Radical, between East and West, in pulpit and press, cease once for all! ... Mark well! there is no plural in the verb *Sh'ma* – hear; no plural to the noun Israel.... I am the very last to deprecate Orthodoxy. It is the soil out of which we have drawn sap and marrow. Orthodox Judaism is the mother that has nursed us with her life-blood, and even if she shows the wrinkles of old age, we will never forget to pay her homage and reverence her in due humility."[61]

The eminent historian of ideas Isaiah Berlin has argued persuasively, in his lecture for the Agnelli Foundation entitled 'The Pursuit of the Ideal', that certain ultimate values by which people live cannot be harmonised or combined because they are incompatible with one another. For example, liberty and equality; justice and mercy; and knowledge and happiness can collide. Maximum liberty for the wolves cannot be combined with maximum liberty for the sheep. A woman who discovers that she has breast cancer is not made happy by her knowledge.[62] The naturalist and literary critic Joseph Wood Krutch pointed out that love (both intellectual and romantic) is not compatible with true knowledge. The attitude of calm and dispassionate detachment of the disengaged, neutral scholar (which is essential to clear understanding) conflicts with the passionate religious enthusiasm of the committed believer (which is necessary to the conviction that an ideal object has supreme worth). Krutch, therefore, concludes that "Ours is a lost cause".[63] The student of religion will sympathise with the plaint of Thomas à Kempis: "I had rather feel compunction than know its definition." In practice such a student will either sacrifice enthusiasm to understanding or understanding to enthusiasm. Ernest Renan (1823–1892), the French Orientalist whom Kohler greatly admired, said that, to study a religion, it is first necessary to have believed it (otherwise we should not be able to understand how it has charmed and satisfied the human conscience); but, in the second place, to believe it no longer in an absolute manner, for absolute faith is incompatible with objective study.[64] The mature Kohler was more successful than most writers on religion in dealing with this conflict between fundamental values.

---

[61] Kohler, *A Living Faith*, pp. 9, 11.
[62] Isaiah Berlin, 'The Pursuit of the Ideal', in *idem*, *The Crooked Timber of Humanity*, New York 1991, pp. 1–19, especially pp. 12ff.
[63] Joseph Wood Krutch, *The Modern Temper*, New York 1929, especially chaps. III, IV, V, and p. 249. Krutch's criticism of the analysis of love in terms of physiological conditions is reminiscent of Hirsch's criticism of *Wissenschaft*. The lover is described as suffering from a "fixation" and when he holds his sweetheart's hand the two must be portrayed, from the physiological standpoint, in the words of Aldous Huxley, as "quietly sweating, palm to palm", pp. 98f.
[64] Ernest Renan, *Vie de Jésus* (1863), Introduction *ad fin*. Renan was too much of a sceptic and scoffer to carry out his own programme. After he resigned from his priestly vocation and left the Catholic Church, Renan was once asked whether he had become a Protestant. "I have lost my faith, not my reason," he is alleged to have replied. Kohler's tribute to Renan is found in *A Living Faith*, pp. 185–191.

The procedure followed by Kohler (and others) in the *Jewish Encyclopedia* was to have important topics discussed from both the critical view and the traditional perspective. In order to distinguish the treatment of the Bible in the *Encyclopedia* from the treatment in parallel reference works issued at about the same time, such as the *Encyclopaedia Biblica* edited by T.K. Cheyne and J. Sutherland Black (four volumes, 1899–1903) and Hastings's *Dictionary of the Bible* (five volumes, 1898–1902), there was a triple treatment of biblical articles: (a) biblical data, giving without comment or separation of "sources" the statement of the text; (b) rabbinical literature, giving the interpretation placed upon biblical facts by the Talmud, *Midrash*, and the commentaries of the most famous Jewish traditional expositors; and (c) critical view, stating concisely the opinions held by the "higher criticism" as to the sources and validity of biblical statements, and the process by which they came to assume their present form.

In the earlier volumes, Kohler often presented both the traditional and the critical view. In the article 'Dietary laws', for example, Kohler wrote both 'From the Traditional Point of View' and 'Considered Historically and from the Critico-Historical and Reform Point of View'. The coverage of the Orthodox viewpoint is fair and accurate, and *parti pris* and apologetics are kept in bounds. Yet, as Shuly Rubin Schwartz has shown, in her fine study of the *Jewish Encyclopedia*, the impression is subtly conveyed that Orthodox Judaism is what Jews *used to believe* and that Reform Judaism of the kind espoused by Kohler is what modern Jews *currently believe*. Religious ceremonial practices are often glowingly described, but in the past tense in order to historicise their significance and minimise their present day importance and function.[65] What concerns us especially in this context is that Kohler, in his study of Jewish theology, was able to combine a detached critical analysis of the Jewish tradition with a passionate and enthusiastic avowal of Reform Judaism, and to weave the two into a positive *credo* which he felt would be meaningful and fulfilling to the modern Jew. It is this aspect of Kohler's work that makes it significant and meaningful to the student of Jewish thought.

Kohler was one of the few Jewish scholars of the nineteenth and early twentieth centuries, besides Geiger, to encourage the modern critical approach to the Bible. Even at the Jewish Theological Seminary of America which trains rabbis for the Conservative Movement, the critical approach to the Pentateuch was not taught to rabbinical candidates until the latter part of the Finkelstein era in the late 1960s. Solomon Schechter had cleverly equated biblical criticism with "Higher Anti-Semitism" and Louis Finkelstein remarked on more than one occasion that "what was good enough for Schechter", as regards the avoidance of higher criticism, was good enough for Finkelstein. Only Kohler pointed out that, without the scholarly apparatus of modern biblical criticism, the Scriptures remain a book with seven seals. "Such brilliant phraseology as is the label 'Higher Anti-Semitism' given to the Higher Criticism," he asserted shortly after assuming the

---

[65]Shuly Rubin Schwartz, *The Emergence of Jewish Scholarship in America. The Publication of the 'Jewish Encyclopedia'*, Cincinnati 1991, p. 159.

presidency of the Hebrew Union College, "may captivate many – *baahizat enayyim* – by its seeming truth, but it cannot stand the test of scrutiny.... We cannot escape the conclusions of Higher Criticism.... What geology did for us in laying bare the different strata of the earth telling of the various epochs of creation, Higher Criticism does in disclosing the various stages of the growth of truth of the divine revelation".[66]

Kohler's article 'Judaism' in the *Jewish Encyclopedia* reads like an outline of his *Jewish Theology*, which itself is a revision of the German compendium on this subject, *Grundriss einer systematischen Theologie des Judentums auf geschichtlicher Grundlage*, which appeared under the auspices of the *Gesellschaft zur Förderung der Wissenschaft des Judentums* (Society for the Promotion of the Science of Judaism). The German version of *Jewish Theology* appeared in 1910 and the English edition was published by the Macmillan Company in 1918. This volume is Kohler's *magnum opus*, into which he poured the sifted results of a lifetime of thought and teaching. The work is a systematic Jewish theology on an historical basis. Kohler described the procedure which he followed in preparing his study of theology:

> "I treat each subject in paragraphs, beginning with Biblical times, coming then to the Talmudic, and proceeding to our own era. In conclusion I state our [Reform] beliefs. I wish to state this, that at no time in my book will it be said that such and such is the absolute creed. I give the historical development of every doctrine.... In my opinion the Jewish religion has never been static ... but has ever been and still is the result of a dynamic process of growth and development ... Judaism is a religion of *historical* growth which, far from claiming to be the final truth, is ever regenerated anew at each turning point in history."[67]

Kohler had a commanding familiarity with the primary sources and the secondary literature on the subject of Jewish theology, as well as a good knowledge of contemporary German Protestant theology and scholarship. He was less familiar with the relevant philosophical literature, and ignores leading American writers on religion and philosophy such as William James (1842–1910), Josiah Royce (1855–1916) and George Santayana (1863–1952). As he comes to the end of his discussion of each theme, the historical interest gives way to the systematic and Kohler generally concludes each chapter in his book by presenting a glowing and passionate account of the "viewpoint" (a favourite word of Kohler's) of Reform Judaism.

---

[66] See S. David Sperling, *Students of the Covenant. A History of Jewish Biblical Scholarship in North America*, Atlanta 1992, p. 44, and p. 62, n. 96. See also, the veiled reference to conditions at the Jewish Theological Seminary of America in Mordecai M. Kaplan, *Judaism as a Civilization*, New York 1934; reprinted Philadelphia 1981, p. 549, n. 6. For Schechter's equation of biblical criticism with "higher anti-semitism", see *idem, Seminary Addresses and Other Papers*, Cincinnati 1915, pp. 36–37 (pp. 35–39). This address was delivered at a banquet given in honour of Kaufmann Kohler on 26th March 1903. Kohler's reply is found in his essay 'The Four Ells of the Halakah, and the Requirements of a Modern Jewish Theological School', in *Hebrew Union College Annual*, 1904, pp. 8–25, especially pp. 10, 12–13.
[67] Kohler in *Yearbook of the Central Conference of American Rabbis*, vol. 18, (1908), p. 112; *idem, Jewish Theology*, p. 4.

"Closer acquaintance with the religious and philosophical systems of modern times," Kohler writes at the beginning of his *Jewish Theology*, "has created a new demand for a Jewish theology by which the Jew can comprehend his own religious truths in the light of modern thought, and at the same time defend them against the aggressive attitude of the ruling religious sects".[68] In this regard he at times polemicises against some Christian theologians, such as Albert Ritschl of Göttingen, and sometimes effectively avails himself of the work of radical Christian and anti-Christian theologians for his apologetic purposes. For example, the Christian devil, God's enemy, is contrasted with the Satan of Jewish folklore, God's prosecuting attorney. It is quite possible, Kohler argues, to be a Jew without believing in Satan, but a Christian must accord a prominent place to the devil in his scheme of salvation. Kohler refers to David Friedrich Strauss's work on dogmatics, *Die christliche Glaubenslehre*, in which the author observes acutely that the New Testament interprets "the redemptive work of Christ" in terms of the overthrow of the devil and his cohorts, minions and servants.

> "The whole (Christian) idea of the Messiah and his kingdom must necessarily have as its counterpart a kingdom of demons with a personal ruler at its head; without this it is no more possible than the north pole of the magnet would be without the south pole. If Christ has come to destroy the works of the Devil, there would be no need for him to come, unless there were a Devil. On the other hand, if the Devil is to be considered merely the personification of evil, a Christ who would be only the personification of the ideal, but not a real personality, would suffice equally."[69]

A detailed analysis of Kohler's *Jewish Theology* would require a separate essay. For our purpose this is unnecessary because Hirsch and Kohler differ less in theology than in the discipline of the observance of the *Halakhah*, Jewish religious law, as the embodiment of the Jewish way of life. The most significant theological difference between Hirsch and Kohler lies in their divergent conception of revelation.

Kohler correctly summarises Hirsch's view as follows: "Orthodox Judaism accepted as a fundamental doctrine that both the Mosaic law and its Rabbinical interpretation were given by God to Moses on Mt. Sinai."(p. 46) Kohler rejects this viewpoint because he claims that it is undermined and contradicted by our knowledge of history, biblical criticism, comparative religion, and the modern religious consciousness itself. Before considering Kohler's alternative view, let us briefly consider how Hirsch defends his view. Hirsch uses a bold "either/or" argument: Either the statement, "And God spoke to Moses saying", with which all the laws of the Torah commences is literally true, or else the whole tradition is a fraud by which the priestly caste wanted to impose its views on the people for its own benefit. The choice must be made. This is the only alternative: there is no other course open.[70] I have not found this argument in Jewish writers before

---

[68] *Ibid.* p. 3.
[69] *Ibid.*, p. 195, quoting David Friedrich Strauss, *Die christliche Glaubenslehre*, vol. II (1841, reprinted 1984), p. 15. (Kohler incorrectly gives the reference as page 18.)
[70] Hirsch, *Judaism Eternal*, vol. 2, pp. 216f.

Hirsch, but the Scholastics used a similar argument to justify the Incarnation. On a popular level it remained beloved of Christian apologists such as C.S. Lewis (*Mere Christianity*, chapter 3). Jesus *ben* Miriam (who was called the Christ), so the argument runs, could not have been merely a great moral teacher. *Aut deus aut malus homo* – either God or a bad man. Jesus put forward such stupendous, transcendental claims that he must have been either the eternal Son of God, or else the greatest fraud that ever lived (or something even worse, the devil). Jesus was mad, bad or God.

Kohler is quite definite in his rejection of Hirsch's view of revelation, but less clear in formulating his own position. He says: "Our modern historical view ... rejects altogether the assumption of a supernatural origin of either the written or the oral Torah, and insists that the subject of prophecy, revelation, and inspiration in general be studied in the light of psychology and ethnology, of general history and comparative religion" (p. 24). Kohler asserts that the term "revelation" traditionally signifies two different things: God's self-revelation, and the revelation of His will. "The former appealed to the child-like belief of the biblical age, which took no offence at anthropomorphic ideas such as the descent of God from heaven to earth, His appearing to men in some visible form, or any other miracle; the latter appears to be more acceptable to those of advanced religious views" (p. 34, emphasis added). It only *appears* more acceptable because there is a higher stage still when "the prophet receives the divine truth in the form of pure thoughts and with complete self-consciousness" (p. 36). As the conception of God becomes purer, revelation begins to disappear. "As the Deity rose more and more above the realm of the visible, the newly conceived truth was realised as coming to the sacred writer through the spirit of God or an angel. *Inspiration* took the place of *revelation*" (p. 39, Kohler's italics). Finally, in the highest stage, we get rid of revelation and inspiration altogether "as the supernatural element disappears gradually and passes over into sober, self-conscious thought, in which the writer no longer thinks of God as the Ego speaking through him, but as an outside Power spoken of in the third person" (p. 39). But then how can Kohler maintain (on the same page, no less) that "It is an indisputable fact of history that the Jewish people, on account of its peculiar religious bent, was predestined to be the people of revelation"?

Kohler does not seem to be able to make up his mind whether revelation is a good thing or a bad thing. He vacillates. At times he seems to endorse the concept of progressive revelation: "The divine revelation in Israel was by no means a single act, but a process of development, and its various stages correspond to the degrees of culture of the people" (p. 36). The "story" of the giving of the law at Sinai represents "the consecration of the Jewish people at the outset of their [*sic*] history to be a nation of prophets and priests ... from a larger point of view, we see here the dramatized form of the truth of Israel's *election* by divine providence for its historic religious mission" (p. 37, Kohler's italics). Joseph Blau's comment is very much to the point: "It seems strange that Kohler should have boggled at the idea of the revealing of the law at Mount Sinai and have been willing to accept without hesitation the idea of the revealing of a religious mission at that time and place."[71]

The difficulty raised by Blau is not limited to the above instance, however important, but pervades Kohler's whole theological system. Kohler is in the same position as the bigot in Hermann Cohen's story. The great philosopher pointed out that the self-same antisemite may prove "logically" that Jesus of Nazareth is a myth and never existed, and may yet prove "historically" that the Jews crucified him. We smile, because we recognise at once that if Jesus was not a real historical figure no one could have killed him, so that no individual Jew or group of Jews could be "Christ-killers", much less deicides. Similarly, while Kohler views Noah and Abraham not as historical characters but as figures of legend such as Aeneas or Hercules, he tells us at the same time that God made such-and-such a covenant with each of them. Take, for example, Chapter VIII of *Jewish Theology*, on "God's Covenant". At the outset we are told that "Judaism has one specific term for religion, representing the moral relation between God and man, namely, *Brith*, covenant. The covenant was concluded by God with the patriarchs and with Israel by means of sacrificial blood, according to the primitive custom by which tribes or individuals' become 'blood brothers', when they were both sprinkled with the sacrificial blood or both drank of it" (p. 48). Kohler then summarises the covenants made with Noah, and later with Abraham, and continues: "the covenant made with Abraham was only precursor of the covenant concluded with Israel through Moses on Mt. Sinai, by which the Jewish people were [*sic*] consecrated to be the eternal guardians of the divine covenant with mankind, until the time when it shall encompass all the nations" (p. 49). Kohler is here playing fast and loose with scientific method to obtain divine sanction for his pet "mission" theory which must be established, if at all, on other grounds.

In reality, evolution and historical development take the place of revelation in Kohler's theology. In speaking of the process of growth in Judaism, Kohler uses the telling phrase "evolution is the master key". He points out that "the law of evolution (which rules religion as well as other domains of life) exerts its power also in regard to ceremonies".[72] But the argument cuts both ways because no one can predict the course of evolution. If human thought is radically historical, one must conceive the possibility that the viewpoint of classical Reform may very well be upset in turn and that a full restoration of Orthopraxy, if not Orthodoxy, may take place.

---

[71] See Joseph L. Blau, Introduction to Kohler, *Jewish Theology*, p. XXX. Cf. Professor Messer who sardonically remarks that the concept of God "covenanting" with an historical people, Israel, the "martyr priest" of pure monotheism, identified through the ages by its "enduring Spirit," a living "kernel" protected by the changing "shells" of tradition, and "revealing" to it moral laws and intellectual ideas, demands a giant leap of faith. See Ellen Messer, 'Franz Boas and Kaufmann Kohler. Anthropology and Reform Judaism', in *Jewish Social Studies*, vol. XLVIII (Spring 1986), p. 140, n.24.

[72] Kohler, *Studies, Addresses and Personal Papers*, p. 431; Kohler, 'Ceremonies', in the *Jewish Encyclopedia*, vol. 3, p. 656.

In *Jewish Theology*, Kohler advocates the discarding of the dietary laws, the wearing of the *tallit* (prayer shawl) and the *tefillin* (phylacteries), and recommends the abolition or radical transformation of many characteristic Jewish ceremonies and institutions. He argues that the wearing of the *tallit* and *tefillin* because of their "talismanic character" are superfluous for the "modern Jew" (pp. 453–455).

George Foot Moore (1851–1931), the great Harvard authority on comparative religion and Judaism in the first centuries of the common era, is reported to have said on reading Kohler's *Jewish Theology* that Reform Judaism is Judaism without Judaœn, having discarded the specific elements which constituted classical Judaism. The remark is penetrating, if ungracious. Since Kohler had jettisoned the sum total of the commandments, rituals, rules of conduct, and ceremonials which constitute the Jewish way of life – what the medieval philosopher-theologians call the *misvot ma'asiyot* – he had to accentuate differences between Reform Judaism and liberal Christianity and mount a vociferous attack on Christianity. Cyrus Adler, who succeeded Schechter as president of the Jewish Theological Seminary, noted that in *Jewish Theology* Kohler "has gone out of his way to attack Christianity, and that his language is at least unnecessarily vigorous. In some aspects he is not as tolerant of Christianity as were medieval Jewish scholars".[73]

Let us consider a few of these problematic passages in Kohler's *Jewish Theology*. "The Jewish people, unlike any other civilization of antiquity, entered history with proud claim that it possessed a truth destined to become some day the property of mankind, and its three thousand years of history have verified this claim." (p. 9) "Judaism sets forth its doctrine of God's unity and life's holiness in a far superior form than does Christianity" (p. 17). "Ultimately there can be but the one religion [Judaism]" (p. 51). "This [Jewish] conception of grace is far deeper and worthier of God than is that of Pauline Christianity." "The great advantage of Judaism over other religious systems lies in its unified view of life" (p. 189). "The belief in the election of Israel rests on the conviction that the Jewish people has a certain superiority over other peoples in being especially qualified to be the messenger and champion of religious truth.... It is due to hereditary virtues and to tendencies of mind and spirit which equip Israel for its calling" (pp. 325, 328). Israel is "the triumphant Messiah of the nations" (p. 445). Even in a book written for Hebrew School children he states categorically: "The Jewish religion is intended to be the religion of the whole human race."[74]

Not only in his younger days, but even in his Frankfurt period when he became more rigid, Hirsch was more guarded in his utterances and more sensitive to the feelings of non-Jews. One does not find in his writings the self-righteous sense of superiority, the triumphalism and the haughtiness that is so offensive in Kohler. Unlike Kohler, Hirsch is not obsessed with Christianity and sees no necessity to

---

[73]Letter from Adler to Louis Marshall, dated 19th August 1918, in Cyrus Adler, *Selected Letters*, ed. by Ira Robinson, Philadelphia 1985, vol. 1, pp. 394f.
[74]Kohler, *Manual of Religious Instruction*, New York 1887, p. 11.

descant negatively on it. One example will serve to illustrate this. The Talmud (bSuk 55b) already points out that on Sukkot, the Festival of Tabernacles, seventy bullocks were offered up in the Temple in Jerusalem, corresponding to all the then known nations of the world, to expiate their sins. Hirsch goes much further than this. In his commentary on the book of Numbers which first appeared in 1876, he interprets the significance of the decreasing number of bullocks sacrificed on each successive day of the festival as follows. The fact that on the Festival of Tabernacles the additional offerings consist of *two* rams and *fourteen* lambs (in addition to the bullocks), as compared to *one* ram and *seven* lambs on the other festivals, indicates that this is a dual offering, half for the Israelites and half for the nations of the world. The thirteen bullocks offered at the altar on the first day of Sukkot should similarly be regarded not as one entity, but as the sum of *two* groups, one of seven and one of six. The first group represents the people of Israel and the second, other nations. But this contrast is diminishing day by day. It starts with six to seven, on the second day it is already five to seven, then four to seven etc. However much it diminishes, Israel and the nations must retain their separate missions; Israel is to observe all the manifold laws given on Mount Sinai, and the nations are to observe the seven Noahide laws; the basic rules of morality, including the prohibitions against murder, incest, adultery and robbery, and the need to establish a proper system of justice. "Israel and the nations, the nations and Israel," says Hirsch, "remain two separate great factors in leading the world for the purpose of humanity, *both equally near and equally precious to God in His direction of world-history*". But in the fullness of time, with the coming of the Messiah and the redemption of history, Hirsch strongly intimates, there will be no religions, but only religion in its universal significance, and the other communions will come together with Israel, or Israel with them. Hirsch concludes his daring comments by quoting Zechariah XIV:9, which the pious Jew recites thrice daily in the *Alenu* prayer: "The Lord shall be King over all the earth; on that day the Lord shall be One and His name One."[75]

At times Kohler's apologetics leads him to make problematic or indefensible assertions. In discussing God's redeeming love, Kohler informs us that the prophet Hosea considered God's "gracious and all-forgiving love his highest quality" (p. 115). "The Rabbis came to regard *love* as the innermost part of God's being," he tells us (p. 129) and we are led to believe that the rabbis were not wrong. But then Kohler reminds himself that Christianity asserts that the highest moral attribute in God and man is love (*agape*). Kohler therefore feels that he must adversely criticise and find fault with love and set up a rival *summum bonum*, which for him is either "justice" or "holiness". To dethrone love from its supremacy and make it appear inferior to justice, Kohler engages in some special pleading: "Judaism does not proclaim love, absolute and unrestricted, as

---

[75]Hirsch, commentary on Numbers XXIX:13; the quotation is from p. 494 of the English translation (emphasis added); *idem, Commentary on the Siddur*, Jerusalem–New York, 1969, pp. 600–605. It is noteworthy that this interpretation dates from a late period in Hirsch's life when he is often regarded as being rigid and inflexible. In the later editions of the *Horeb* (p. 638, additional note) Hirsch still admits that the significance of the decreasing sacrifices is not clear to him.

the divine principle of life. That is left to the Church, whose history almost to this day records ever so many acts of lovelessness. Love is unworthy of God, unless it is guided by justice" (p. 130). "The highest principle of ethics in Judaism, the cardinal point in the government of the world, is not love but justice. Love has the tendency to undermine the right and effeminize society" (pp. 121f). Unfortunately for Kohler, the divine Lawgiver in the Holiness Code (Leviticus XIX:18) says, "You shall love your neighbour as yourself"; he does not say: "You shall be just to your neighbour, but you shall not love him, for if you love him, you will undermine his right and effeminize him." Again, in order to differentiate classical Reform Judaism from Pauline Christianity, Kohler proposes the argumentative thesis that "Paul's opposition to the Law includes the moral law, and even the Decalogue" (p. 437), which certainly would be hotly contested by most Christian theologians. Paul's position seems to be that although Christians are not bound by the 613 commandments of the Torah, and although the Jewish ceremonial law is fulfilled in the new covenant, the essence of the *moral* law as expressed in the Ten Commandments must be obeyed by all. In a key passage in Romans (XIII:9–10), Paul quotes the Decalogue and writes: "The commandments, 'Thou shalt not commit adultery', 'Thou shalt not murder', 'Thou shalt not steal', 'Thou shalt not covet' and all other commandments are summed up in this one rule, 'Thou shalt love thy neighbour as thyself.' Love does no wrong to a neighbour; therefore love is the fulfilment of the Law."[76] Kohler is forced into an untenable stance since he had argued earlier that modern knowledge and historical consciousness constrain the modern Jew to adopt the position of the prophets that "the *real* Torah is the unwritten *moral law* which underlies the percepts of both the written law and its oral interpretation" (p. 46, emphasis added). That this is indeed the prophetic view is at best a disputed assumption.

Finally, I should like to suggest that Kohler may have viewed himself as the Reform counterpart of Hirsch in the New World. Kohler concludes a sketch of his personal reminiscences with the following sentence: "Looking back upon my years of preparation and my years of activity as American Rabbi, I feel like saying in the words of Scripture: 'I have wrestled wrestlings for God, and have prevailed'." The quotation is from the exclamation of Rachel at the birth of Naphtali, found in Genesis XXX:8; the key word in Hebrew, *naphtule* (wrestlings), is a word-play on that name. Hirsch called one of his early works *Naphtulei Naphtali. Erste Mitteilungen aus Naphtalis Briefwechsel* (Altona 1838), and the wise counsellor in the *Neunzehn Briefe*, Hirsch's *alter ego*, is called Naphtali. Hirsch had a good reason for choosing this verse. In the blessing of Jacob in Genesis (which we may remember was the subject of Kohler's doctoral dissertation) Naphtali is

---

[76]Paul is not necessarily engaging in an anti-Jewish polemic here. See Israel Abrahams, 'The Greatest Commandment', in *Studies in Pharisaism and the Gospels. First Series*, Cambridge 1917, pp. 18–29; see also George Foot Moore, *Judaism in the First Centuries of the Christian Era*, Cambridge 1927, vol. II, p. 85 and the literature there cited. It has been shown that even after his conversion, Paul often followed the rules of conduct and morality prescribed by the *Halakhah*. See Samuel Belkin, 'The Problem of Paul's Background', in *Journal of Biblical Literature*, vol. 54, (1935), pp. 41–60, and the endorsement of this position by the New Testament authority in Edgar J. Goodspeed, *An Introduction to the New Testament*, Chicago 1937, p. 50, note.

called "a fleet deer", which in German is a *Hirsch*. (Naphtali Hirsch is a popular composite first name among German Jews.) Possibly it is just a coincidence that Kohler chose this verse, and possibly he chose it to signify that he was a champion of Reform. But there are other similarities. When Kohler went to his teacher Hirsch for help with his religious doubts, the master assured him that he would get over them in the course of time, that they were merely "the torrid zone" in one's journey through life. Kohler himself never expressed any reservations about this answer, although some of his followers found it less than satisfactory. Many years later Kohler offered similar advice to a young scholar he knew well. Shortly after Kohler's death, Adolph S. Oko (1883–1944), the librarian of the Hebrew Union College, wrote a moving personal tribute of love and friendship as a eulogy to his master. Although of unusual intelligence and ability, Oko was in many ways the opposite of Kohler: an atheist, a Spinozist, and a womaniser.[77] In a transparently autobiographical passage Oko says: "I recall here as an instance the friendship that existed between Dr. Kohler and a man of the most opposite opinions, and his junior by forty years. Dr. Kohler surely must have thought that the friend had gone far astray – but he never reproached him. 'Remain true to yourself,' the old man once admonished the younger."[78]

Kohler's theological system is only of historical interest today,[79] but Kohler the man deserves to be remembered for the intense Jewish spirit that animates all of his work and for his relentless pursuit of truth according to his own lights. In the year that Kohler died a great philosopher wrote a book on religion. In it the author, Alfred North Whitehead, says of the essence of religion: "Religion is force of belief cleansing the inward parts. For this reason the primary religious virtue is sincerity, a penetrating sincerity."[80] This text could well serve as an epitaph for Kaufmann Kohler.

---

[77]See *Hebrew Union College. Jewish Institute of Religion At One Hundred Years*, ed. by Samuel E. Karff, Cincinnati 1976, pp. 73, 118f.
[78]Adolph S. Oko, 'Kaufmann Kohler', in *Menorah Journal*, vol. 12, (1926), pp. 513–521, here p. 520. Kohler was born in 1843, Oko exactly forty years later, in 1883.
[79]A trenchant critique of the classic Reform theology espoused by Kohler, especially the mission theory, by a trained philosopher who was his younger contemporary, will be found in the following essays of Horace M. Kallen:, 'On the Import of "Universal Judaism"', 1910; 'Judaism, Hebraism, Zionism', 1910; 'Judaism by Proxy', 1916, all reprinted in *idem, Judaism at Bay*, New York 1932.
[80]Alfred North Whitehead, *Religion in the Making*, New York 1926, p. 15.

Kaufmann Kohler

By courtesy of the American Jewish Archives, Cincinatti.

The Dissociation of Religion and Law in Nineteenth-Century German-Jewish Education

BY ANDREAS GOTZMANN

One of the most remarkable details in the socio-cultural transformation of German-Jewish society at the turn of the eighteenth century was the creation of a new education and, with it, a specific religious schoolbook literature. Although there had already been government efforts in the eighteenth century to establish and enforce a general educational system for growing parts of the non-Jewish population, for example in the Prussian states, the result of these efforts had been meagre. The granting of more rights to Jewish inhabitants included, however, the creation and regulation of a new educational system for Jewish youth.[1] This innovation not only reflected one of the central ideals of the Enlightenment – to educate and to grant at least basic knowledge to broader segments of the population; it also represented the conviction that a cultural-religious minority such as the Jews could only be integrated into the greater bonds of citizenship and nation if it left certain parts of its supposedly "alien" and "corrupt" cultural tradition behind. Gaining citizenship almost invariably

[1] I wish to express my warm thanks to Petra Lindner, Frank Laurence and Alan Barnes for their meticulous proofreading and stylistic advice. Hans-Günther Thien, *Schule, Staat und Lehrerschaft. Zur historischen Genese bürgerlicher Erziehung in Deutschland und England (1790–1918)*, Frankfurt 1984, pp. 29ff; Hans-Georg Herrlitz, Wulf Hopf and Hartmut Titze, *Deutsche Schulgeschichte von 1800 bis zur Gegenwart. Eine Einführung*, Königstein 1981, pp. 14ff; Moritz Güdemann, *Quellenschrift zur Geschichte des Unterrichts und der Erziehung bei den deutschen Juden. Von den ältesten Zeiten bis auf Mendelssohn*, Berlin 1891 (repr. 1968); *Geschichte des Erziehungswesens und der Cultur der abendländischen Juden während des Mittelalters und der neueren Zeit*, 3 vols., Vienna 1880–1888, 2nd edn.(repr. 1966). Simcha Assaf, *Meqorot le Toldot ha-Khinukh b Yisrael*, 4 vols., Tel Aviv 1925, vol. 1, 1948; Mordechai Eliav, *HaKhinukh ha Yehudi beGermania be Yeme haHaskala wehaEmanzipatia*, Jerusalem 1960; Isidore Fishman, *The History of Jewish Education in Central Europe. From the End of the 16th to the End of the 18th Century*, London 1944; Zvi Scharfstein, *Toldot haKhinukh be Yisrael beDorot haAkharonim*, New York 1945, vol. 1; D. Weinstein and M. Yizhar (eds.), *Modern Jewish Educational Thought*, Chicago 1964; Zvi Erich Kurzweil, *Modern Trends in Jewish Education*, New York–London 1964; *Hauptströmungen jüdischer Pädagogik in Deutschland von der Aufklärung bis zum Nationalsozialismus*, Frankfurt am Main 1987; Julius Carlebach, 'Der Säkularisationsprozeß in der Erziehung', in H. Liebeschütz and A. Paucker (eds.), *Das Judentum in der deutschen Umwelt, 1800–1850*, Tübingen 1977, pp. 55–93 (Schriftenreihe wissenschaftlicher Abhandlungen des Leo Baeck Instituts 35); Ezriel Shokhet, *Im Khilufe Tekufot. Reshit haHaskala b Yahadut Germania*, Jerusalem 1960, pp. 123ff. There are numerous regional studies: outstanding are Claudia Prestel, *Jüdisches Schul- und Erziehungswesen in Bayern 1804–1933. Tradition und Modernisierung im Zeitalter der Emanzipation*, Munich 1989 (Schriftenreihe der Historisches Kommission bei der Bayerischen Akademie der Wissenschaften 36); Dorothee Schimpf, *Emanzipation und Bildungswesen im Kurfürstentum Hessen 1807–1866. Jüdische Identität zwischen Selbstbehauptung und Assimilationsdruck*, Wiesbaden 1994 (Veröffentlichungen der Kommission für die Geschichte der Juden in Hessen 13).

meant – to a greater or lesser extent – assimilation into German culture, a vague construct of common norms that would obviate ethno-cultural differences. This conviction had a definite influence on the new Jewish education. The external pressure to create an educational system, planned and supervised in one way or another by the state, coincided with the pedagogic ideas and projects developed by the German *Haskalah*.[2] Consequently, we already find a new and comparatively broad schoolbook-literature in the first decades of the nineteenth century. Counting only textbooks that were meant for religious education and that were published within the borders of the later German *Reich*, there were more than 100 publications.[3] These included books for the study of the Hebrew language, schoolbooks with biblical – rarely also rabbinic – text excerpts, and compendia especially designed to teach the tenets of the Jewish religion.[4]

This study concentrates on the latter compendia, which were called *Religionskatechismen*, a term taken over from their Christian model. In nineteenth-century Germany this genre saw more than sixty publications focused specifically on the courses in Jewish religion. The number of books analysed is further restricted to those which gained a definite standing and some significant use in the field of this new kind of literature as indicated, among other criteria, by Jewish or government recommendations or directives that they be used in classes. The analysis also includes books which were widely used or which represent the educational views of the main religious trends of nineteenth-century

---

[2] Reinhard Rürup, *Emanzipation und Antisemitismus. Studien zur 'Judenfrage' der bürgerlichen Gesellschaft*, Frankfurt am Main 1987, pp. 17ff; Jacob Katz, *Aus dem Ghetto in die bürgerliche Gesellschaft. Jüdische Emanzipation 1770–1870*, Frankfurt am Main 1986, pp. 188f; David Sorkin, *The Transformation of German Jewry, 1780–1840*, New York 1987, pp. 45ff.

[3] The numbers given by several authors differ according to their definition of the contents of the books: see B. Straßburger, *Geschichte der Erziehung und des Unterrichts bei den Israeliten. Von der vortalmudischen Zeit bis auf die Gegenwart. Mit einem Anhang. Bibliographie der jüdischen Pädagogik*, Breslau 1885; Sigismund Maybaum, *Methodik des jüdischen Religionsunterrichts*, Breslau 1896, p. 4; Hermann Levy, *Lehrbuch und Jugendbuch um jüdisches Erziehungswesen des 19. Jhs. in Deutschland. Versuch einer entwicklungsgeschichtlichen Darstellung nach Inhalt und Methode*, Diss., University of Cologne 1933; Eliav, *HaKhinukh haYehudi*, p. 262; Salomon Plessner, *Dat Moshe wYehudit. Oder jüdisch-mosaischer Religionsunterricht für die israelitische Jugend. Ein für den öffentlichen, auch Privat- und Selbstunterricht sich eignendes Lehrbuch der Hauptreligionswahrheiten und Lehren des Judenthums*, Berlin 5599 (= 1838).

[4] Jacob J. Petuchowski, 'Manuals and Catechisms of the Jewish Religion in the Early Period of Emancipation', in Alexander Altmann (ed.), *Studies in Nineteenth Century Intellectual History*, Cambridge, MA. 1964, pp. 47–64. Petuchowski deals mainly with the anti-talmudic position and the inclusion of contemporary philosophical trends in education. In so doing he also comments on the general development of a delegalisation of Jewish religion (p. 63). After Eliav's short survey of this literature (Eliav, *HaKhinukh haYehudi*, pp. 243ff., 262ff.), Petuchowski's article was the first analysis of the religious concept, the "religio laici" as he calls the philosophy represented by these books. Altogether, Petuchowski's view of the redifinition of religious culture supports the ideas presented here. While he chose a rather heterogenous pool of books, including some from the *Haskalah* and several from Austria, I am restricting myself – with one exception – to the literature created in nineteenth-century Germany. After this article was written, a history of Jewish *Jugendbücher* was published that concentrates on the development of this new literature and of its pedagogics. This very interesting work confirms the general development of pedagogic views and the turn towards a new concept of Orthodox teaching by the school of Samson Raphael Hirsch. Gabriele von Glasenapp and Michael Nagel, *Das jüdische Jugendbuch. Von der Aufklärung bis zum dritten Reich*, Stuttgart 1996.

German-Jewish culture.[5] Thus the number of publications surveyed for this study is about half the total of works of this kind, of which about twenty are discussed.

This study deals with the change and transfer of the *Halakhah* as a crucial cultural constituent of pre-emancipation Jewish culture through this religious literature. How did the Jewish authors of these books evaluate and describe Jewish religious law and religion? Did they care about transferring the knowledge of this central factor of pre-emancipation Judaism to the next generation?[6] Then, if the legal tradition was thought to be a central aspect for Jewish life in the nineteenth century, how did the authors present it?

---

[5]According to Petuchowski, *ibid.*, p. 47, these books were written in connection with the new rite of confirmation. This is true for only a few of the books: Anonymous (Joseph Maier), *Lehrbuch der israelitischen Religion zum Gebrauche der Synagogen und israelitischen Schulen im Königreiche Württemberg. Auf Veranstaltung der Kgl. israelitischen Oberbehörde*, Stuttgart 1837, p. x. The prescription of any single book for all schools was usually avoided, in recognition of existing religious differences: Josef Johlson, *Alume Yosef. Erster Theil, welcher den Unterricht in der Mosaischen Religion für die Israelitische Jugend beiderlei Geschlechts enthält. Nebst einem Anhange von den Ceremonialgesetzen und Gebräuchen*, Frankfurt am Main 1814; Eliav, *HaKhinukh ha Yehudi*, p. 254; Anonymous (Alexander Behr), *Hauptlehren der mosaischen Religion für den Unterricht der Jugend. Verfaßt unter Aufsicht und Leitung des Ober-Rabbiners zu Würzburg Abraham Bing und anerkannt von angesehenen Rabbinern*, Munich 1834, p. ix. In Baden only selected books were used. From 1881 on, the *Oberrat der Israeliten* prescribed certain books; e.g. H. Sondheimer, *Geschichtlicher Religionsunterricht. 1. Abt.: Biblisch-geschichtl. Religionsunterricht. Von . . ., Bezirksrabbiner in Heidelberg, Ritter des Zähringischen Löwenordens, 17. Aufl.*, Lahr 1899; *2. Abt.: Jüdisch-geschichtlicher Religionsunterricht, 9. Aufl.*, Lahr 1898; see the extra page at the beginning of the book in StA Koblenz, 441/26149, fol.191ff. The Christian minister who inspected the religious courses was upset about the low level; Johlson's textbook, used then, was "completely unsuitable". Benjamin Hirsch Auerbach, *Torat Emet – Torat Emet. Lehrbuch der israelitischen Religion nach den Quellen bearbeitet. Zum Gebrauche in den obersten Klassen der Religionsschulen, mit sehr wichtigen erläuternden Anmerkungen für Eltern, Lehrer, angehende Theologen. Von . . ., Ghzgl. Hessischen Stadt- und Landrabbinern zu Darmstadt. Approbirt von den Großherzogl. Hessischen Rabbinern zu Bingen, Friedberg, Mainz, Michelstadt, Offenbach, Worms, von den Kgl. Preuss. Israelitischen Consistorien zu Bonn und Crefeld, und von fünf und dreißig anderen israelitischen Geistlichen des Auslandes*, Darmstadt 1839; Ludwig Stern, *Amude haGola. Oder die Vorschriften der Thora welche Israel in der Zerstreuung zu beobachten hat. Ein Lehrbuch der Religion für Schule und Familie. Von . . ., Direktor der israel. Schule in Würzburg*, Frankfurt am Main 1882; Maier, p. xiii. Although it claims to have been accepted by all rabbis in Württemberg, no names were published. See *Israelitische Annalen*, No. 35, 1839, p. 278; Peter Beer, *Handbuch der mosaischen Religion. Für studierende oder sonst höherer Bildung geniessende Jünglinge. Von . . ., Öffentlicher Lehrer der Moral der israelitischen Jugend an der Gymnasial- und Hauptschule zu Prague, 2. Curs, 2 Abt.*, Prague 1818; Moses Büdinger, *More le Tora. Oder Leitfaden bei dem Unterrichte in der israelitischen Religion für Knaben und Mädchen in Schulen und beim Privatunterricht. Von . . ., Erster Lehrer an der israelitischen Schul- und Schullehrer-Bildungsanstalt zu Cassel*, Cassel 1830; Benjamin Hochstädter, *Die biblisch reine Glaubens- und Pflichtenlehre des Judenthums gegenüber den Un- und Aberglauben. Von . . ., Bezirksrabbiner und israel. Seminar-Direktor zu Bad Ems im Hzgt. Nassau, 2 Hefte*, Ems 1862–1864; Israel Schwartz, *Emunat Israel. Lehrbuch der israelitischen Religion zum Unterrichte für die Jugend. 1. und 2. Cursus. Mit punctierten hebräischen Belegstellen und vielen Anmerkungen versehen*, Bamberg 1853; Samuel Holdheim, *HaEmuna wehaDea. Jüdische Glaubens- und Sittenlehre. Leitfaden beim Religionsunterricht der jüdischen Jugend. Zunächst für die Religionsschule der jüdischen Reformgemeinde zu Berlin*, Berlin 1857; Leopold Stein, *Tora uMizva – Tora uMizwa. Lehre und Gebot. Israelitisches Religionsbuch. Zunächst für Confirmanden, dann für gereiftere Schüler überhaupt. 2. vielfach verbesserte Aufl.*, Frankfurt am Main 1858; Stern, *Amude haGola*.

[6]Petuchowski, pp. 52ff., underlined the anti-talmudic – that is, anti-legal – tendency of this literature. The difficult term "traditional" refers only to a construct of pre-emancipation German-Jewish culture. About the construction of such a concept, see Andreas Gotzmann, *Jüdisches Recht im kulturellen Prozeß. Die Wahrnehmung der Halacha im Deutschland des 19. Jahrhunderts*, Tübingen 1997 (Schriftenreihe wissenschaftlicher Abhandlungen des Leo Baeck Instituts 53), pp. 13, 22ff.

This study concentrates on the inclusion and the development of a new vision of religion. The great majority of German Jews had already internalised the idea of a religious sphere separated from a civic realm by the end of the eighteenth century. This had taken place regardless of the *halakhic* religious ideal of an holistic legal system. Although this division of the perception of reality was still feeble, the privileges granted to the Jewish communities by the states had led to a new conception of religious culture which defined some legal entities as religious and others not. This general development towards a bourgeois society had a special effect on Judaism because it crushed its foundation: the definition of all aspects of life according to the *Halakhah* as God-given law. The intrusion of this new concept of religion into German-Jewish culture had not been an active process initially, but rather an enforced duplication of external structures. With the first changes in the legal situation at the beginning of the nineteenth century this underlying concept was eagerly activated. The main concern of this essay is the role education played, by redefining and implanting a new model of Judaism as a Jewish confession and a definite part of bourgeois culture for the successive generations.[7]

While most studies of the transformation of German-Jewish culture and identity in the nineteenth century have focussed on the inclusion of general philosophical views, this essay is concerned with the dynamics of change. How was the inherited cultural concept altered, and what effect did this have on the different religious groups? The broadening of the traditional legal definition will be shown by the mutation of some vital characteristics of the *halakhical* system. Furthermore, we will have to deal with the dynamics of the growing "historicisation" of the rabbinic tradition. Further description of specific *halakhic* contents and their representation in these compendia will be left aside.

If one takes the maintenance and development of cultural tradition as a continuous but ever-evolving process, the question must be: did the Jewish pedagogues think that religious law formed a central part of Jewish culture, which had to be imparted by school education? If so, how did the authors of these textbooks (re-)define it? This analysis concentrates solely on religious schoolbooks because they provide us with insights other data and sources that have already been discussed cannot give.[8] Compared with these, the curricula of Jewish schools or educational programmes, for example, show an ideal of education rather than what was actually transmitted in class. As we know from Orthodox schools, even their

---

[7] Gotzmann, *Jüdisches Recht*, chap. 1.
[8] For example, StA Koblenz, 441/9807, fol.13ff.: 'Bericht des Schulinspektors u. Superintendenten Oertel (24.11.1840)'; 441/9808, fol. 86ff: timetable of the Jewish teacher Salomon Tiefenbronner (Monzigen), 16th August 1860. This accounts also for Jewish examinations of the schools: Hauptstaatsarchiv Wiesbaden, 211/79981, fol. 270–279; visitations of the district rabbi Dr. Hochstädter (Bad Ems) (30th June 1860). These comparatively extensive reports deal with nothing more than the general subjects, adding brief remarks about the quality of the lessons and the ability of the students to read Hebrew. Leo Trepp, *Die Oldenburger Judenschaft. Bild und Vorbild jüdischen Seins und Werdens in Deutschland*, Oldenburg 1973 (Oldenburger Studien 8), pp. 169–189. The definite gap between the pedagogical programmes as they were presented in curricula and the reality of the actual lessons has already been pointed out by Mordechai Breuer in 'Khazon uMeziut beKhinukh haOrthodoxy shebeGermania beMea ha-19.', in *Bar-Ilan Year Book*, Nos. 16–17 (1979), pp. 317–335.

Dissociation of Religion and Law

programmatic call for intensive Hebrew lessons and the teaching of the basics of the traditional literature could not initially be answered because the number of compulsory subjects would not leave enough time for such intensive studies.[9] Other sources that more directly represent the course contents (*Lehrinhalte*) as actually taught – such as reports of school visits – bear certain restrictions. For example, they were mainly written by non-Jewish officials and therefore fail to show the Jewish perspective. In addition to this, these reports quite often reflect anti-Jewish stereotypes. Even if we were to take all these difficulties into account, these reports would barely provide any more information than the subjects taught and an evaluation of the qualities teachers and students showed. Furthermore, it would be very hard to achieve a broader view of general developments from these individual reports. Here the broad scope of the textbooks gives not only a more immediate insight into the re-evaluation of the traditional *halakhic* concept by pedagogues in the nineteenth century; it actually represents the ideas implanted in the new generations of pupils.

Indeed, the textbooks show the subject matter that was actually taught. This can be concluded from familiar complaints pedagogues voiced throughout the nineteenth century. The religious catechisms were used to teach Jewish religion by means of maxims and other such set sentences for rote learning. Teachers were supposed to present this material, and students were required to learn it, in exact wording or – according to the more lenient pedagogic tendencies in the second half of the century – to recapitulate these texts in their own words. Contemporary information tells us that lessons in religion meant, almost exclusively, nothing more than this. Even the innovative, progressive call for a somewhat more flexible method of teaching only demanded some variation of the texts by the teacher and, as an exception, some further explanations of it.[10] In general the teacher was supposed neither to rearrange the given contents nor to mediate them in any individual way. Even Salomon Plessner from Berlin, an Orthodox teacher who heavily criticised this educational concept, calling the catechisms "a literature demolishing the greater whole by narrowing the infinite in order to educate but half-Jews", would not deviate from this path.[11] The schoolbook he wrote in 1838 preserved the very form he criticised. Plessner only went so far as to allow the individual teacher to meet this deficiency by occasional variations of the given maxims or by providing some supplemental information.

This example shows that mere memorising of the written maxims was increas-

---

[9]For a cursory analysis of the re-evaluation of such structures see Eliav, *HaKhinukh haYehudi*, pp. 241–246; Salomon Herxheimer, *Yesode haTora. Israelitische Glaubens- und Pflichtenlehre für Schule und Haus*, Hannöverisch-Münden 1831 cited in Magdeburg, pp. v–vii.

[10]Büdinger, *More leTora*, Introduction; *More leMorim. Anweisungen für den Lehrer, wie der israelitische Religionsunterricht zu ertheilen und der Leitfaden More leMorim dabei anzuwenden sei*, Kassel 1833; Herxheimer, p. vff; Maybaum, *Methodik*, pp. 60, 62. But see Maier, p. xii; Stein, *Tora uMizva*, Introduction; Jakob Stoll, *Die Methodik des jüdischen Religions-Unterrichts, 1. Heft*, Frankfurt am Main 1916, pp. 61ff. Obviously, at this time any teaching method that allowed students to answer textbook questions in their own words would have seemed extraordinary.

[11]Plessner, pp. ii, xxxiii: "das große Ganze zerstückelnde Kompendien und Catechismen, in die wir jetzt das Unendliche einengen, um Halbjuden zu bilden." But see Breuer, *Jüdische Orthodoxie im Kaiserreich 1871–1918. Sozialgeschichte einer religiösen Minderheit*, Frankfurt am Main 1986, p. 98.

ingly seen as a useless nuisance for the pupil. However, this criticism related primarily to the method of teaching and not to the content of religious education. The schoolbooks kept this specific form of a fixed and restricted transmission of knowledge throughout the century.

As late as 1899 another author excused himself because, as a teacher, he also used the very same teaching practice that he rejected as a pedagogue. He merely added laconically that new methods of teaching would at least give the teacher the opportunity to show the students he knew more than the book.[12] So it seems that, in the nineteenth century, the prevailing theory of education and, in practice, the method of teaching agreed upon the efficacy of repetitive memorising of textbook lines – which, from a modern point of view, scarcely stands up as an adequate way to educate children. This seems even more serious because the authors used quite an abstract, philosophical language.[13] Thus, as there seems to have been a rather close correspondence between what textbooks recommended to teachers and the way classes were actually taught, an analysis of these collected books might provide insight into the information and ideas about the Jewish religion schoolchildren came to have.[14]

The structure of this genre is as fixed as its contents. The authors used forms which had already been fostered by such authors of the Jewish Enlightenment as Naphtali Herz Wessely, Herz Homberg and David Friedländer, and by early Reformers like Peter Beer.[15] The catechisms took over traditional structures such as the Decalogue, the Principles of Jewish Religion formulated by Maimonides and Albo, the 613 *mizvot* and the differentiation between laws and prohibitions (*mizvot ase welo taase*). The authors frequently combined several traditional categories such as these to gain a more refined and complex descriptive

---

[12]Sondheimer, preface to the first edition, p. vii: Thus the teacher could at least "den Schülern zeigen, daß er mehr weiß als das Lehrbuch". For the similar trend in general education see Lieberkühn, Philip Julius, *Kleine Schriften*, Gedike, L.F.G.E. (ed.), Züllichau–Freystadt 1791, pp. 95–6; K.Fischer, *Geschichte des Volksschullehrerstandes*, 2 vols., Hannover 1892 (repr. 1969), vol. 2, pp. 230f; Straßburger, p. 265; Herrlitz *et al.*, p. 59.

[13]For example Auerbach, p. 61: "Der Tod ist eine Anordnung des Naturgesetzes (in dem nur Notwendigkeit und keine Freiheit herrscht); die Seele steht aber nicht unter dem Naturgesetze, sondern unter dem Sittengesetz (sie hat sittliche Freiheit). Daher kann sie das Naturgesetz der Verwüstung und Zerstörung nichts angehen." Here an admittedly difficult religious idea (the immortality of the soul) is explained with the use of several other philosophical terms.

[14]Towards the middle of the century the complaints grew, especially in conservative and Orthodox circles, that the schools could only provide a larger framework, whereas the family has the greatest influence on religious behaviour. Neither the scale of religious teaching, nor the often highly philosophical contents, nor the fixed educational form succeeded in maintaining religious behaviour. Although education already applied to girls, the educational scope was far more restricted. M. Eliav, 'Die Mädchenerziehung im Zeitalter der Aufklärung und der Emancipation', in Julius Carlebach (ed.), *Zur Geschichte der jüdischen Frau in Deutschland*, Berlin 1993, pp. 97–111.

[15]The authors themselves point to older ethical treatises like that of Rödelheim. Eleasar Susman, *Mikra Mephorash*, Amsterdam 1749; S. Maybaum, *Abraham Jagels Katechismus Lekach-tob. Ein Beitrag zur Geschichte des jüdischen Religionsunterrichts*. Separatdruck zum 10. Bericht der Lehranstalt f.d. Wissenschaft des Judentums, Berlin 1892, p. 17; M. M. Faierstein, 'The Liebes Brief. A Critique of Jewish Society in Germany (1749)', in *LBI Year Book* XXVII (1982), pp. 219–241; 'Brief exists only as a manuscript. S. Stein, 'Liebliche Tefilloh. A Judaeo-German Prayerbook Printed in 1709', in *LBI Year Book* XV (1970) pp. 41–72. Regardless of such very questionable predecessors, these textbooks depend heavily on Christian catechisms. Petuchowski, pp. 47ff.

pattern.[16] Although most of these structures had a definite *halakhic* meaning, it was this legal character which was frequently pushed aside. It is astonishing that this accounts not only for textbooks of the Reform Movement but for Orthodox ones as well. With regard to these "traditional" structures used to describe the religious heritage, the compendia show a general tendency that can be traced back to non-Jewish traditions: the division of Jewish religion into two opposed aspects. By the intrusion of such a binary concept these well-known categorisations, handed down by rabbinic tradition, were reconstructed. One distinguished for instance a *Glaubenslehre*, meaning the moral teachings of religion, from a *Pflichtenlehre*, the practical religious obligations that were quite often identified as the *Halakhah* itself.[17] It was this dual view of Jewish religion that lead to a questioning of the traditional holistic concept of the *Halakhah*. The conception of divine law as the general normative structure, evolving in a closed self-referential way and defining and enclosing all aspects of life and culture, could not endure restriction to some specific aspects of the life cycle and the mental world. At the same time its theonomy claimed that all the diverse laws are equivalent and equally binding.

Some authors used this scheme in a more traditional way – to differentiate the legal concept itself, for example, by defining "religious" teachings that were part of the Jewish religious tradition alone and general "human" norms of morality. Their combination formed the corpus of Jewish religion. This model could be compared to the *halakhic* construct of the Noahide laws. Accordingly one could argue that here the *halakhic* concept was kept intact. However, such patterns were rare, whereas almost all compendia, even those from an Orthodox background, show the general tendency to use this dual structure for a differentiation between non-juridical categories and those that were increasingly seen as truly juridical ones.

This redefinition confronted "philosophical beliefs" with "religious laws", a new and – from a pre-emancipation point of view – unusual way to describe Judaism.[18] Yet the most startling innovation lay in a further step: at least since the Enlightenment non-Jewish thinkers had seen the philosophical and moral norms as the very core of religion, an outlook that strongly influenced the Jewish intellectuals of the nineteenth century. The Jewish pedagogues integrated this idea, interpreting it by means of the redefinition of the new dual concept according to authoritative structures provided by the rabbinic tradition. Those structures were, for example, the *halakhic* differentiations which had been used even in previous centuries as descriptive patterns. The required textbook for Württemberg, anonymously published in 1837 by the Reform-orientated Chief Rabbi Joseph Maier, puts the religious teachings – concerning knowledge about

---

[16]Levi, pp. 25ff; Eliav, *HaKhinukh ha Yehudi*, pp. 260ff., 241–246. A model for this literature was Herz Homberg, *Ben Jakir. Ueber Glaubenswahrheiten und Sittenlehre für die israelitische Jugend in Fragen und Antworten gerichtet*, Vienna 1815. Often the Rambam's 13 *Iqarim* were used. See Holdheim, p. 25; Stein, *Tora uMizvah*; combines them with the Decalogue. For differing patterns, see Büdinger, *More le Tora*, pp. 50f; Herxheimer, pp. 6, 34; Johlson, p. 7; Maier, pp. 2–4, 63, 73. Behr, pp. 8ff., 18ff.

[17]Eliav, *HaKhinukh ha Yehudi*, pp. 241f.

[18]Johlson, suppl. Büdinger, *More le Tora*, pp. 86–87; Herxheimer, p. 69; Beer, *Handbuch*, 1. Curs, 1821, p. 108.

God and about man's destination – on one side and the teachings of the religious obligations – regulating the form of the individual religiosity – on the other. Only the latter category was thought to have a legal character; the conservative Reformer Maier reassured his readers that it nevertheless remained a definite part of religion itself.[19] The same structure for yielding to a more conservative perspective is reflected by Maier's conceptualisation of the Jewish Law as obligation towards God, as "religious reminders", as he calls the ritual laws, and as "other obligations". Although these rather feeble categories were in fact taken from a *halakhic* context, the concept of religious law was ambiguously restricted to a certain part of the religious norms. Yet in a hesitating step back, these legal aspects were again confirmed as important and even constitutive parts of Jewish religion. But if one follows Maier's conservative and not very concise concept, his redefinition aimed at a restricted legal entity, the so-called *Ceremonialgesetze*. In the end, these laws governing religious ritual would be defined as the legal components of Jewish religion.

Although there is a wide range of different and frequently inconsistent ways to describe, *ergo* how to redefine, Jewish religion, the main traits of this process of delegalisation are clear. The distinction between "legal" aspects of Judaism, generally rejected as being of a religious nature, and its favoured "ethical" religious contents was a general trend that can be found in the works of all religious convictions. As the example of Maier's book has already shown, descriptive *halakhic* categories like a-logical laws (*khuqim*) and logical ones (*mishpatim*) were filled with new meanings, conferring thereby their juridical character on a vague entity commonly defined as ceremonial, or *Ritualgesetze*, the laws of religious ritual. This term originates from the external definition of the religious law of the Jews and other religious denominations. With this legal entity the state authorities defined the sphere of religious practice and decisions they accepted as concommitant with the freedom of action granted to some groups that deviated from the state religion. Fenced by the privileges of residence, they were not seen as a part of the state's legal authority but as a part of the mostly feeble autonomy of these religious minorities. Apart from adopting a term that bore specific connotations, such as the restriction to "religious" decisions, the very term *ritual* evoked the contemporary Christian discussion that discredited the religious ritual as a meaningless, useless act. In contrast to this, the true believer was called upon to act and communicate directly with God, perceiving the religious conviction and the moral fitness or embetterment of the individual as the core of religion. At the same time the prescribed fulfilment of ritual acts was rejected as a true devotion to God. The authors of the Jewish textbooks were to an astonishing extent influenced by these Christian discussions, which were enhanced by much older stereotypes of Judaism as the paradigmatic "legal unreligion". Jewish pedagogues integrated them into their thinking and, moreover, into the educational transfer of cultural norms.[20]

---

[19]Maier, pp. 16, 73, 75 and 121.
[20]Sander Gilman, *Jewish Self-Hatred. Anti-Semitism and the Hidden Language of the Jews*, Baltimore 1986, pp. 84ff.

Paradoxically, this external legal concept of *Ceremonialgesetz* had helped Jewish communities in the eighteenth century to practise Jewish Law.[21] The general acknowledgment of an autonomous legal tradition left at least the ritual and specific contents of the *Halakhah*, as "religious" decisions, to the jurisdiction of the rabbinates. It had also helped to keep the *halakhic* ideal, which regarded the fulfilment of all existing regulations of the religious law as the truest form of religiosity, intact. For example, the disposition of monetary matters, which coincided to a great extent with the external definition of non-religious legislation, was left by contemporary *halakhic* decision to private settlement and even to non-Jewish jurisdiction. This procedure only legalised a practice that was already enforced by the government.[22] Now the religious schoolbooks turned to the opposite direction and redefined just this domain of the *Ceremonialgesetz*, granted as autonomous "religious" jurisdiction, primarily as a legal, and therefore not as a religious, entity. This change, too, came from the integration of the Christian conception of contemporary Judaism, which considered the rabbinic tradition as an a-religious distortion of the meaning of the Holy Scriptures. In this conception the central negation of the common religious tradition was invoked by the dominant legal character of the rabbinic tradition.[23] The Jewish pedagogues rejected this prejudice, implying that the legal side was not the central religious content of Jewish religion. With this apologetic move they adopted the widespread contemporary definition of religion as a system of ethical values, aimed at the moral betterment of the individual. This attempt – that is, to redefine Jewish religion directly or indirectly according to external views – was intended to be a positive reaction against the perception of Judaism as an "a-religious religion of law". Apologetically retracing the external shifts of meaning, the authors were able to use the Christian legal concept of *Ceremonialgesetz* to redefine their own cultural tradition of a divine law. The construction of restricted legal categories within a wider concept of religion allowed the pedagogues to abandon religious acts that they increasingly perceived to be senseless or as cultural discriminatory signs (e.g. *tefillin*, *mezuzot* or *zizit*). The inclination to give way to external pressure for cultural accommodation was determined by the wish to gain equal rights and to change the negative image of the Jew. In particular, the religious Reformers sought to redefine a "truly religious" realm within the Jewish tradition or – in their words – to clean off the distorting peel of centuries of oppression.

During these processes the definition of the *Halakhah* became increasingly vague, its contours blurred by the ambiguous conceptual shifts, and its scope reduced considerably. The standard thereby applied was again indebted to contemporary notions about law. Hence matters of civil law, or of such important *halakhic* prescriptions as family law, were promptly eliminated. Accordingly, even early textbooks do not mention such *halakhic* entities as civil or monetary

---

[21]Gotzmann, *Jüdisches Recht*, pp. 25ff.
[22]Gil Graff, *Separation of Church and State. Dina de Malkhuta Dina in Jewish Law, 1750–1848*, Alabama 1985.
[23]Gilman, *Self-Hatred*, pp. 84ff; Johann David Michaelis, *Mosaisches Recht*, 6 vols., Frankfurt am Main 1770–1775, e.g. vol. 5, 1774, pp. 8f.

laws. Quite soon only those remnants of traditional *Halakhah* were left which were esteemed as legal ordinances and yet at the same time as religious parts of Judaism. Usually these were seen – even according to the contemporary standard – as an integral part of religion, as was the religious ritual. But at the same time the conviction grew that these could not be the proper form and expression of religiosity.

Here definite differences between Orthodox, Conservative, and Reform-orientated books can be found. At the start of the century one of the earliest Reformers, Josef Johlson, the renowned teacher at the Philanthropin in Frankfurt am Main, had defined the *Ceremonialgesetze* – understood as the legal parts of religion – as the *Halakhah* in its totality.[24] He retained this rather conservative view only because of the influence the Orthodox Chief Rabbi of Frankfurt, Hirsch Horwitz, exacted over the edition of this schoolbook. Compared to this projection of the new term onto the inherited tradition, most of the later Reformers regarded the *Ceremonialgesetze* as laws governing the religious act alone. The other legal aspects of the *Halakhah* were almost entirely consigned to oblivion.[25] Even within the realm of religious ritual, most of these authors did not mention basic laws such as those of *kashrut* or even the obligation to put on *tefillin*, not to mention such sensitive subjects as *halitza*, *nidda*, betrothal or divorce. They were avoided mainly because of the anti-legal concept of religion the authors so cherished.[26] The refusal to describe even this limited legal category properly, although it was nothing more than a small reminder of the *Halakhah* of pre-emancipatory times, deprived the next generation of this tradition or – according to the conviction of most of the authors – freed it from a distorted idea of religion.

This heterogeneous process of dissociating Jewish religion from the legal conception by separating it from its legal background through the redefinition of its legal structures is clearly visible in the further development of the religious textbooks. In fact, most of the books tended to omit the legal aspects altogether. After the first, less secure efforts to find a new literary form and to formulate the general idea, the vast majority of Reform authors did not even mention the restricted area of *Ceremonialgesetze*. By 1814 Josef Johlson had only added a short appendix on the legal aspects of Judaism to his book because the rabbinate forced him to do

---

[24] Johlson, suppl.
[25] See above. Holdheim, pp. 107ff., uses this term to describe especially laws regarding rituals, but sticks to the *halakhic* categorisation e.g. by adding the *mizvot schetaluyot baarez* to this entity. Plessner, pp. xxi, 136, sees the ritual as an "outward form of worship". Schwarz, pp. v, 77, keeps the holistic construct intact.
[26] The early Reform books that had to uphold a conservative appearance nevertheless included such parts, but it should be noted that they were definitely set aside. This accounts for Johlson's book but also for an earlier work of Peter Beer, *Das Judenthum*, 2. vols., Prague 1810, pp. 76–152; Gotzmann, *Jüdisches Recht*, pp. 247f; Sander Gilman, *The Jew's Body*, New York 1991, pp. 93ff., 157f. Typically, a more detailed description of the act of divorce is only mentioned by the neo-Orthodox Stern, pp. 199, 257, 524. He wanted his book to be something like a *Kizzur Shulkhan Arukh*, and therefore added an index about the rituals of everyday life. Stein, *Tora uMizva*, p. 28, mentions without further comment the *khaliza*. *Kashrut* is mentioned by: Maier, pp. 121ff; Holdheim, pp. 114 § 351; and by Orthodox authors like Plessner, p. 145, p. 210; Auerbach, pp. 7ff. § 12; Stern, p. 238. Even Reformers complained about the lack of "Jewish content" *Orient, Literatur Blatt*, No.11, 1847, Sp. 161–163.

so.[27] And Peter Beer, another influential Reformer from the earliest days, pleaded for the elimination of all the antiquated juridical and ceremonial factors from the lessons. In contrast to this, the more conservative schoolbook from Württemberg, which has already been mentioned, does speak of some legal aspects. However, at the same time it states that it is impossible to explain these rituals because of the juridical casuistry which would be necessary. That should be kept out of the textbooks once and for all.[28]

Most of the conservative, and certainly the radical, books followed this scheme and only some of the Orthodox textbooks differ from it. In the textbook of the renowned Rabbi Benjamin Hirsch Auerbach, a devoted fighter for the Orthodox cause, no separate legal category is mentioned at all, implying that all the set maxims are enclosed in the whole of the *Halakhah*. And Ludwig Stern, a follower of Samson Raphael Hirsch, the leading figure of Frankfurt Neo-Orthodoxy, explicitly avoids the usual differentiation between legal and religious parts, keeping the holistic view of the *halakhic* system as the religious one intact. His book, published in 1882, must be seen as a concise and vigorous rejection of the anti-legal educational trend that dominated the entire nineteenth century.[29] Stern also mentions a basic factor most authors omitted, namely that all laws were deemed to be of the same value and validity, regardless of their classification. But most authors failed to establish this constitutive factor, or left out on purpose a basic principle which had been self-evident in traditional Judaism. Before the end of the eighteenth century one presumed that the differences between all these categories were merely descriptive ones and did not influence the legal condition of the laws. To omit this detail was rather typical for the Reform authors of course. The religious Reform had begun quite early to associate the contemporary description and evaluation of certain laws with their validity.[30] But even Orthodox teachers such as Salomon Plessner from Berlin, used the category of *Ceremonialgesetze* to describe the legal obligations of religious life. Plessner nevertheless tried to avoid the total division between legal and religious contents suggested thereby. Other Orthodox authors such as Israel Schwarz, the head of the Jewish School in Würzburg, the southern centre of Orthodoxy, held the conviction that a schoolbook should not be a *Shulkhan Aruch*. Its only purpose should be to teach the main principles of belief and religious obligations. Even if Schwarz avoids the presentation of a concise two-fold structure as well, he

---

[27] Johlson, p. vi; Holdheim, p. viii. This part was just meant for the teacher, as an explanation for the abolition of certain rituals by the *Berliner Reformgemeinde*.

[28] Beer, *Handbuch der mosaischen Religion*, p. vi: "antiquirten Judiciösen und Ceremoniösen." For Maier, p. ix, this would need a legal casuistry, which should "ein für allemal aus einem Lehrbuch für das Volk ausgeschlossen bleiben". Stein, *Tora uMizva*, p. 28, discriminates between "Sitten- and Ceremonialgesetz". Ludwig Philippson, *Die israelitische Religionslehre. Ausführlich dargestellt*, 3 vols. (4 Abth.), Leipzig 1861–1865 (earlier he published *Kleiner Katechismus der israelitischen Religion*, Leipzig 1843 and 1858), leaves it aside, as does Hochstädter, p. i. Josef Aub, *Grundlage zu einem wissenschaftlichen Unterrichte in der mosaischen Religion*, Mainz 1865, only mentions the holidays.

[29] Stern, *Amude HaGola*.

[30] A few books provide some hints: Beer, *Handbuch*, 1821, pp. 95, 102, 108–109; Behr, p. 6; Büdinger, *More le Tora*, pp. 50f; Stein, *Tora uMizva*, p. 28. Aub, p. 3 is a definite exception because he theoretically reunites the two-fold of *Sitten- und Glaubenslehre* again in the corpus of the law.

nevertheless relies strongly on the very same differentiation shown in Reform-orientated books. Furthermore, Schwarz contents himself with only citing some outstanding rituals.[31]

While these discrepancies between the religious convictions are not astonishing, and are, in any case, sometimes quite vague, the predominance of the concept of religion as a philosophical, ethical system rather than a juridical one is visible even in Orthodox books. Probably the authors neither intended nor recognised this conceptual change. For the bulk of them, the contemporary definition was self-evident, and the depiction of religion in legal categories, as by differentiations between laws and prohibitions (*mizvot ase welo taase*) or between logical and a-logical laws (*mizvot sekhelyot weshemayot/mishpatim wekhuqim*), appeared to be unable to grasp Jewish religion in its totality. Therefore they eagerly used the dual concept as well, or at least referred to traditional categories, such as the 13 *Ikarim* of Maimonides, which were usually seen as "philosophical" maxims and therefore suited this anti-legal tendency. This conceptual shift incorporated a dynamic in itself: the predominance of philosophical aspects pushed the juridical cultural concept aside. In particular, Orthodox authors who wanted to strengthen the acceptance of the Jewish Law had to avoid this inner dynamic. Therefore some of them repeatedly reminded pupils of the basic factor of the theonome law: that religion has to be seen as a whole, all of its parts being equally binding and of the same value.[32] They did not consider that this idea of divine law was already endangered by the fundamental distinction between legal and religious parts. Once the new dual concept of religion was evoked, it could not be easily neutralised. Furthermore, even the Orthodox authors had absorbed the basic evaluation of religion as being, above all, a moral and not a legal system. They therefore recurrently fell back into argumentative structures which were directly connected to the dual concept. Orthodox pedagogues used, for example, "philosophical" arguments to show the meaning of so-called a-logical laws such as *kashrut*. This trend also tended to blur the differences between Orthodox and Reform-orientated books, which were quite often scarcely visible.[33] From a pedagogical point of view one could perhaps appraise these "relapses" as quite understandable because they served the expectations of the readers and thereby made the subject matter easily accessible. Endowing legal contents with a "philosophical" meaning, because this would be more appropriate and acceptable concealed, however, the characteristic of the religious law: the theonomy of its multivalent regulations, which forbids the equation of the

---

[31] Plessner, pp. xxi, 136; Schwarz, p. v: "das Religionsbuch ist kein Schulchan Aruch und hat nur die alleinige Aufgabe: die Grundprinzipien der Glaubens- und Pflichtenlehre in eindringlichen Worten dem Schüler mitzutheilen". Gabriele von Glasenapp, 'Von der Neo-Orthodoxie bis zum Dritten Reich', in Nagel and Glasenapp, *Jüdische Jugendbuch*, pp. 79–94.

[32] Auerbach, p. 66; Schwarz, p. 60; Plessner, p. 34; Stern, p. 5. For the term "religious law" see Andreas Gotzmann, 'Religiöses Recht', in Dieter Haller and Thomas Hauschild (eds.), *Einführung in die Kulturanthropologie*, Stuttgart 1997.

[33] E.g. *kashrut*: Maier, pp. 121–123; Holdheim, p. 114 § 351; Plessner, p. 145, p. 210; Auerbach, p. 66. But note the programatic neo-Orthodox standing of Schwarz, p. 140: "Nicht etwa, damit du körperlich nicht erkrankst, [...] sondern weil diese [...], deine Seele als Israelit verunreinigen."

meaning of specific laws with their validity. Once encouraged, this association could only be destroyed by direct reference to this very characteristic of *Halakhah*. Therefore Salomon Plessner, one of the few to do so, urgently insisted: the teacher should not forget to tell his pupils that all ceremonial laws are based on higher meanings and on God's inconceivable benevolence, uncovering their true meaning sooner or later. Again according to Plessner, the teacher should and could provide nothing more than the most reasonable and "closest" meaning of a certain law.[34] This typical restriction conceals the specific character of the religious obligations.

The integration of such ideas into the consciousness of the Jewish population had definite advantages for the Reformers because it favoured their intention of wiping out legal prescriptions and ritual obligations often regarded as corrupt. Nevertheless, at the same time even this Reformatory trend was additionally weakened by the intrinsically conservative character of the German-Jewish Reform Movement. The way in which the new dual concept was furnished with authority likewise bore its own dynamic. The early Reform textbooks of Peter Beer, which were a model for many other publications, show, for example, the shift in the concept of religious law. To endow his own construct with the necessary authority, which according to most of the Reformers only the rabbinic tradition could provide, Beer used those accepted descriptive patterns of the *Halakhah* employed by other authors. However, applying such legal classifications to delegalise the religious tradition raised some difficulties: after differentiating between the religious obligations and the moral teachings of religion, Beer identifies, in a supposedly more traditional Orthodox *halakhic* outlook, the religious teachings with the legal contents of religion.[35] Yet this reunion is again broken up when he defines them as *Ceremoniales*, as the legal portions of religion kept apart from its philosophical contents. As some details of Peter Beer's description of Jewish religion show, his rigorous distinction between "philosophical" and "juridical" factors did not work out. This was mainly due to the fact that he used *halakhic* categories which had always been quite arbitrary. Therefore he was not able to free certain obligations, redefined as exclusively "religious" ones, from their underlying legal character. That is why we find religious acts such as the prayer categorised as "philosophical" – and this respectively meant "religious" or "non-juridical", although the prayer obviously displayed – even according to Beer – legal aspects, for example fixed prayer-times.[36] Here the de-legalisation of Jewish religion was opposed by the dynamic created by Beer's use of basically legal classifications as an authoritative structure.

In contrast to the problems Reform thinkers had with their conservative

---

[34]Plessner, pp. xxiif.: "vergesse der Lehrer dem Schüler nicht zu bemerken, daß jedem Zeremonialgesetz noch höhere Ursachen und ein unbegreifliches Wohlwollen Gottes zu Grunde liegen, das früher oder später uns kund werde, während die obgedachten Schriften, nur die nächstliegende und jedem einleuchtende Ursache anzugeben gesucht haben."
[35]Beer, *Handbuch*, vol. 2, 1818, pp. 130–136; vol. 1, 1821, pp. 95, 102, 108, 109 and 155.
[36]Beer, *Handbuch*, 1821, p. 114. But these remnants of the legal character could be reduced even more, e.g. Maier, p. 99.

inclination towards the inherited legal tradition as a legitimising structure, the anti-legal trend as such already forced severe conflicts on Orthodox pedagogues, as has been shown above. The great majority of them, however, did not even realise that they were caught in a double-bind.

Although the restraints and dynamics of this conceptual change are complex, and the way the textbooks treat these reorientations are heterogeneous, the fundamental changes were the same. Apart from the two basic conceptual changes, vital characteristics of the religious law were either radically transformed or not taught at all. If we take a close look at the way in which some of the most central aspects of the Jewish Law were transmitted, the processes become clearer. Such basics are, for example, its theonomy; its two-fold structure of a Written and an Oral Tradition; its central myth of authorisation; and the Chain of Tradition (*shalshelet haqabbala*), which connects contemporary legal decisions to the revelation of the law at Mount Sinai. Any change, let alone negation, of one of these vital aspects would undermine the integrity of the entire religio-legal tradition. Hence the issue of how they were transmitted, or whether they remained integral to education at all, takes on a special significance.

Even a cursory glance at the religious compendia shows that most of the books do not even mention these fundamentals of the pre-emancipatory cultural concept. Those which did were far from presenting a concise description to their readers. In his 1818 higher education textbook, Peter Beer mentions the existence of the Oral Tradition only as historical evidence for the authenticity of the Holy Scriptures, the Written Tradition. Although this affiliation lends some authority to the Oral Tradition, the connection between the two strands and the divinity of the oral one is not mentioned. A closer look at Beer's textbook for primary school classes shows that this was not an erroneous omission. Nor did the author consider these to be self-evident facts. Here Beer limits the divine revelation to the Bible and, the Written Tradition, and confines the delivery of the law explicitly to the Decalogue.[37] This implies that later developments such as the rabbinic tradition are not God-given but are only human interpretations of divine Law. This had been a common argument of Reform thinkers since the Enlightenment. Later Reform-orientated authors such as Benjamin Hochstädter or the retired Chief Rabbi of Frankfurt, Leopold Stein, followed this concept.[38] On the other hand, more moderate Reformers like Rabbi Salomon Herxheimer emphasised the obligation to fulfil the divine law. In Herxheimer's textbook the existence of an Oral Tradition could only be indirectly concluded from those laws, which he mentions as handed down directly by Moses and lacking any reference to the Pentateuch (*hilkhot lemoshe misinai*).[39] It is however highly improbable that a pupil could have

---

[37] See note 35.
[38] Hochstädter, 1. Heft, p. i; the supplement about the "Mosaischen Gesetzgebung" never appeared, see *ibid.*, 2. Heft, 1864; L. Stein, *Tora uMizva*, p. 28, *Torath-Chaijim. Das israelitische Religionsgesetz. Anleitung wie der Israelite der Gegenwart nach den Erfordernissen der Religion und der Zeit sein Leben religionsgesetzlich zu ordnen habe. In zwei Abtheilungen, 1. Abt: Religionsgeschichtlich, 2. Abt: Religionsgesetzlich*, Strasburg 1877.
[39] Herxheimer, pp. 27–28, 33.

made this abstract connection, which requires some knowledge of the *halakhic* system.

Mentioning some aspects of the *Halakhah*, while omitting and forsaking its greater design, was a common practice of the Reform textbooks. This ambiguous proceeding helped to maintain the connection to the older rabbinic tradition and thus served to authorise the innovations. This method was a special nuisance for Orthodox contemporaries. After the first decades of the nineteenth century, Orthodoxy had ceased to acknowledge these links to the legal heritage, which the Reformers had forged as serious attempts to deal with the common tradition. On the contrary, these efforts seemed merely to veil the fundamental differences between the two religious convictions. For this reason the Orthodox *Landesrabbiner* of Darmstadt, Benjamin Hirsch Auerbach, criticised the repeated ambivalences of Reform schoolbooks, which stated on the one hand that the divine law is normative, while failing, on the other hand, to mention the prescriptions.

How heated these controversies became can be seen by the turmoil which Auerbach's own description of the revelation and of the two-fold tradition provoked.[40] He had differentiated between certain stages of the legal tradition by stating that those laws transmitted by the Oral Tradition and accepted by all of Israel were not to be seen as divine law by biblical prohibition.[41] Contemporaries misunderstood this description of some specific ordinances of the Jewish Law to be a negation of the theonomy of the Oral Tradition because it separated the legal interpretations of the rabbinic tradition from the act of revelation. But Auerbach had meant only those decrees which had ordained as a fence around the law (*gadarim/siagim*). Indeed, according to the rabbinic tradition these enactments gained their validity not as God-given law but by their broad and unrefuted acceptance as a guard of the Law. Nevertheless, Auerbach's readers had gained the impression that now even an Orthodox rabbi admitted that not all the parts of the *Halakhah* were to be seen as of divine origin. Such a statement – typical for the Reform movement – was understood to mean that a law adjudicated by man at a specific time and for a specific purpose could be altered as soon as the circumstances under which the decision had been enforced were changed, or even when its "meaning" did not meet the contemporary conception of religiosity. The idea that he was negating the theonomy of some parts of the *Halakhah* forced Auerbach to react vehemently against this misinterpretation. This incident of the year 1835 shows the sensitivity developed by the Jewish public developed towards the implications of even such meticulous legal distinctions. At the same time this "misunderstanding" shows once more how close the argumentative structures between the Orthodoxy and the Reform were. This was, partly caused on the one hand, by the integration of the common "modern"

---

[40]See the preface on a separate leaf as a part of the supplement, Univ. Lib., Frankfurt am Main, Sign. Jud. 4425, pp. 2–5; 9 § 13; *Israelitische Annalen*, No. 33, 1839, pp. 262f.

[41]*Ibid.*, p. 12f. § 16. The laws, registered by the Oral Tradition, "und von ganz Israel angenommenen Verordnungen unserer Gesetzgeber, nicht als göttliche Gesetze gelten können, weil die Schrift dies verbietet, nichts desto weniger aber, als Mittel zur Erhaltung und Befestigung der göttlichen Gebote, für uns heilig sind". See the supplement with a reply to the article published in *Didaskalia* (9th August 1835).

ideas and, partly on the other, by the Reformers' dependence on the traditional concept.

It can easily be seen that the pedagogues' perception of religion was also constantly influenced by the heated debates about reforms. The interpretations and ideas formulated by the Reform movement became increasingly established so that even the Orthodox had at least to recognise them as central points of discussion. The way in which Orthodox authors dealt with these changes is illuminating. In 1838 Plessner, a pupil of the well-known guardian of the pre-emancipation rabbinic tradition Akiva Eger, described the difficult contradiction of a stable God-given law, which is perfect by definition, and its ongoing interpretative change in a way quite typical for Reformers. He asked: should there not have been further causes for the Oral Tradition? Among many others motives, the foremost seemed to him the impossibility of writing down all possible legal cases. The interpretation of the basic commandments must be left to the future decisions of the rabbis.[42] Although this is – from an Orthodox and also from a system-analytical point of view – a correct description, it could also be read as a historicisation of the development of the *Halakhah*. And this was typical of the Reformers' approach to the rabbinic tradition because it legitimised the possibility for change. Plessner, therefore, had to strengthen his Orthodox conviction elsewhere in his book, re-emphasising the divine character of the Jewish Law as a revelation that reaches from the giving of the Law on Mount Sinai down to the present day.[43] If one reads the two passages together, the author actually presents the structural paradox of Jewish Law as a self-evident fact, negating its development and accepting at the same time its interpretive expansion. It documents his unbroken rootedness in pre-emancipation views. At the same time Plessner writes this explicitly in confrontation with the ideas of the Reform movement, for example when he defines the question of belief not – as one might think – as the question whether one believes in God's existence, but as the belief in the two-fold tradition. He states this controversial point thereby as a central norm of the Orthodox creed.[44]

Yet Plessner's outlook proved an exception. Other Orthodox authors tried to avoid the contradictions enclosed in the concept of a divine law. Indeed, Israel Schwarz leaves the differentiation between distinct levels of the law aside to show the equivalence of all parts of the religio-legal system.[45] But he thereby produces a harmonised picture of the concept of the Jewish Law which must have reminded the contemporary reader of Reform-orientated descriptions.

---

[42]*Ibid.*, pp. x, 8, 11, especially p. 37, No. 150: "Sollten nicht noch andere Gründe die Mündliche Überlieferung veranlaßt haben? Unter anderen mehreren dürfte vorzüglich der sein, daß unmöglich alle vorkommenden Fälle niedergeschrieben werden können, man muß solche erst von der Zukunft erwarten und die Entscheidung dem jedesmaligen Richter ... überlassen."

[43]*Ibid.*, pp. 41f., 70.

[44]*Ibid.* p. 128.

[45]Schwarz, 2. Curs, pp. 8, 34f. The second edition was published with the title *Glaube und Pflicht. Lehrbuch der israelitischen Religion. 2. umgearb. verm. Aufl.*, Bamberg 1857; Behr, p. 9; Stern, pp. 1ff., 8ff. For Reform textbooks see David Leimdörfer, *Kurzgefaßte Religionslehre der Israeliten nach den Lehrbüchern von Herxheimer und Büdinger. Bearb. von ..., Prediger der Synagogengemeinde Nordhausen*, Nordhausen 1876, p. 9.

Dissociation of Religion and Law

Thus only the Decalogue is singled out as a prototypical codex of law which confirms the sanctity of the divine act of law-giving.[46] The textbooks of the Reform influenced Schwarz's description of the legal heritage so deeply that the basic intention to counter their representation of Judaism was contradicted by his own simplifying description. Thus his compendium shows a seemingly more consistent system at the expense of omitting such important structures as the question of development and stability of the *Halakhah*. This must have confronted his pupils only with further unsettling questions.

At the same time some compendia mention, for example, the existence of the two strands of tradition without providing any further information.[47] The great bulk of books, however, does not mention such basic structures at all. And, moreover, few of the Orthodox authors gave further detailed information about Jewish religious life. If we take a look at some other basic structures of the religious law, we are able to estimate the extent to which the Reformers were obliged to the legal heritage. Josef Johlson, whose textbook had been supervised by the Orthodox rabbinate, deviated only in some points from the Orthodox scheme. Hence Hirsch Horwitz merely added annotations to Johlson's description of the everlasting validity of the Jewish Law. Johlson had limited it to laws which were legitimised by the moral norms of the law of nature or by the Written Tradition. Notwithstanding the insertion of a non-*halakhic* legal category, this definition questioned almost all of the rabbinic legal interpretations. Therefore Horwitz annotated that not only were the laws of the Oral and the Written Tradition definitely binding but also the rabbinic decrees guarding the law.[48]

It seems quite astonishing that Horwitz did not insist on a complete change of this passage. His leniency can only be explained if one remembers that many parts of Johlson's book did conform with the rabbinic tradition as defended by Orthodoxy. The obvious Reform tendency of this textbook did not seriously offend the traditional Orthodox rabbinate which would otherwise have refused its approbation. It had been the questioning of the legal tradition or, more precisely, the programmatic changes of the *halakhic* concept that provoked the opposition of the religious authority. Yet, to other contemporaries, the confusing ambivalence between Reform and Orthodox points of view was not acceptable at all.[49] Johlson himself found it much more difficult than the rabbinate to reconcile their conservative demands with his own Reform intentions. Hence his book includes statements about the absolute normativity of the Written Tradition

---

[46]Schwarz, 2. Curs, p. 30. Plessner, p. xxxii, points to the integrity of the actual Jewish Law which develops "although" it was founded together with the Written Tradition.

[47]For Orthodox and Reform differences see above.

[48]Johlson, pp. 5f; Horwitz's annotation only makes sense compared to Johlson's maxim No. 15, and not to No. 14 as the text states; *ibid.*, p. 52, No. 103. The few annotations of Horwitz's were constantly – and perhaps not by chance alone – misprinted, commenting on wrong points.

[49]See Auerbach, separate preface. In 1841 even a Christian supervisor of Jewish education called the book unsuitable; StA Koblenz, 441/26149, fol. 191–193. Friedrich Wilhelm Carové, *Ueber Emancipation der Juden, Philosophie des Judenthums und Jüdische Reformprojekte zu Berlin und Frankfurt am Main*, Siegen–Wiesbaden 1845, pp. 97f.

alone, as well as some about the validity of the rabbinic decrees.[50] At the beginning the Reform movement had to harmonise its propaganda with its precarious standing in the communal organisations, not to speak of its small support in the Jewish population. Nevertheless, the signs towards a social change, the difficult political situation, and – to a certain extent – the leniency of the rabbinate at least towards non-legal questions left them a sizeable space of action which was eagerly used to redefine the concept of Judaism as an ethical confession.

Other earlier textbooks, such as the one for Württemberg, show similar discrepancies. Here the ambiguous process towards a re-evaluation of the legal tradition is well underway. While the Oral Tradition is again presented as of divine origin, the new dual concept already dominates. Its anonymous author, the Jewish state official and *Oberrabbiner* Joseph Maier, differentiates between the teachings of morals and belief, all directly connected to the Written Tradition, and the *Ceremonialgesetze*, tied to the Oral Tradition. In contrast to the idea of a greater unity of both strands of tradition, Maier goes on to distinguish them in a way that had been typical for the German *Haskalah*. The biblical tradition is displayed as the original, pure and unobstructed tradition.[51] The moral laws of the Pentateuch are seen as true remnants of the divine revelation, their meaning so obvious that they would not need any further interpretation. Here the validity of rabbinic interpretation, revealing the very sense of the biblical laws, is questioned. Nevertheless, Maier restricts the significance of talmudic laws even more: only their unanimous acceptance or their "correct" deduction from the Written Tradition could make them acceptable as divine decrees for future generations.[52] Although these categorisations again use *halakhic* structures, they distort and redefine their accepted meaning by putting the main emphasis on the biblical tradition.[53] Here the connection between these structural categories and the validity of the laws described is already made. Even though Maier began to desacralise the legal tradition, he did not draw any further conclusions, remaining ambiguously conservative.[54] He wanted to satisfy all religious convictions, which meant in those days the almost exclusively Orthodox rural population of Württemberg. But the Reform trend of his book is nevertheless quite visible. Maier neither presents the *halakhic* concept as a consistent one, nor does he mention the divinity or the obligatory validity of the legal tradition. Orthodox critics again judged this book somewhat conciliatory. It seems as if the general disposition of the Reform to negate the concept of

---

[50] Johlson, pp. 64, 88; Paul Arnsberg, *Die Geschichte der Frankfurter Juden seit der Französischen Revolution*, vol. 1, Darmstadt 1983, p. 223; Horwitz also supported the establishment of an hour of devotion at the *Philanthropin*, where Johlson worked as a teacher. These informal prayers were the starting point for the Reform service in the Frankfurt community. Eliav, *HaKhinukh ha Yehudi*, pp. 116ff.

[51] Moshe Pelli, *The Age of Haskalah. Studies in Hebrew Literature of the Enlightenment in Germany*, Leiden 1979 (Studies in Judaism in Modern Times 5), pp. 78–80, 126.

[52] Maier, pp. viif., 125. See the review in *Israelitische Annalen*, No. 8, 1841, p. 57.

[53] The author speaks here of the laws defined as "*mideorayta*" or as "*miderabbanan*".

[54] Such inconsistencies can also be seen in his differentiation between the two strands of tradition, while he limits the revelation itself to the Decalogue. On the other hand he equates law with religion several times. He accepts too that even the smallest religious custom has its own value, if only to limit its binding force to its connection to the biblical Tradition. *Ibid.*, pp. 4, 63, 67f.

a divine law was not identified; as in the case of Josef Johlson, only the definite negation of essential *halakhic* structures evoked criticism.[55] Although at the beginning of the century the authors of the Reform movement were forced to maintain the appearance of a conservative standing, they showed quite early on not only a tendency but a full-fledged a-legal, anti-rabbinic concept that helped to change the cultural representation of Jewish religion. On the other hand the Reform, in general, never discarded its conservative bonds to the legal conception of Judaism because its system depended strongly upon the inherited legal system as an authoritative referential structure.

These changes in the general concept of religion and in the rabbinic tradition were further advanced by the insertion of a new critical norm. As is often mentioned, the process of desacralisation in the nineteenth century was based on the integration of a new concept of history. During the *Haskalah* such a new idea had already intruded upon theological-philosophical views, as seen in Moses Mendelssohn's philosophical outline of his concept of revelation. To the idea of truth, legitimised by the law of nature, he added the so-called historical truth (*Geschichtswahrheiten*), defining it as the divine revelation of an Oral and a Written Tradition.[56] Here the historical aspect upheld the rabbinic concept, appearing as an integral part of it.[57] In contrast to this still-consistent evaluation of the tradition, doubts, for instance about the historical facticity of the act of revelation, grew rapidly. With the new conception of the historical-critical school, a process of desacralisation of the religious tradition began. The director of the *Lehrerseminar* in Kassel, Moses Büdinger, refers in his textbook to the act of revelation and the Chain of Tradition from Moses to Jehuda HaNasi. But he uses it neither solely as a cultural myth nor as an historical fact. The traditional construct is actually enwrapped by a historised concept: for Büdinger, the Jewish people only gradually accepted the Talmud as the Oral Tradition. Compared to Mendelssohn, he applies this new historical conception to re-evaluate the traditional pattern and not to reassure it. By this slight change of the traditional construct, Büdinger achieves the separation of the act of revelation from the rise of the rabbinic tradition, de-sacralising the sanctity of the latter.[58]

The description of the revelation given by one of the most radical Reformers, Samuel Holdheim, twenty-seven years later in his textbook for the *Berliner Reform-*

---

[55] E.g. Schwarz, 1. Curs, p. v.

[56] Moses Mendelssohn, *Jerusalem, Oder über die religiöse Macht und Judentum* (1783), in *idem, Gesammelte Schriften*, Stuttgart 1983, vol. 8, pp. 156–160, here p. 191.

[57] This argumentative support was taken over by Orthodox, sometimes also by Reform-orientated, authors; Schwarz, vol. 2, p. 36; Johlson, pp. 5f, 29 and 32f.

[58] Büdinger, *More le Tora*, p. 44. Even Orthodox authors (except Behr and Stern) who accepted the act of revelation as an historical event, concentrate on such legitimisations. Plessner, pp. xvi, 70, 77; Auerbach, pp. 5 § 9 and 7ff; Maier, pp. 4–7. See the close adherence of textbooks for Jewish history to traditional presentations of history: M. Elkan, *Leitfaden beim Unterricht der Geschichte der Israeliten von den frühesten Zeiten bis auf unsere Tage. Nebst einem kurzen Abriß der Geographie Palästinas für israelitische Schulen. 5. verb. und mit einer Zeittafel versehene Aufl.*, Oeynhausen–Leipzig 1861, pp. 65ff; Elias Willstätter, *Allgemeine Geschichte des Israelitischen Volkes. Von der Entstehung desselben bis auf unsere Zeit. Ein kurzer Abriß nach den vorliegenden Quellen und größern Werken der Geschichte für die ersten Klassen israelitischer Elementarschulen und zum Selbststudium bearbeitet*, Karlsruhe 1836, pp. 22–25.

gemeinde displays, in contrast, the *Ceremonialgesetze* merely as one further step in the ongoing development of Jewish religion. Holdheim abandons thereby the theonomy of the Oral Tradition, as well as the idea of two tightly connected strands of tradition.[59] Talmudic law is now seen merely as the legal interpretation of the Holy Scriptures at the time of the Second Temple. Although Holdheim accepts that these explanations were inspired by the religiosity of their interpreters, he concludes that the authority of the Talmud is grounded only in its free acceptance by Jewish communities, which judged it according to its adequacy and ability to further religious life.[60] Holdheim thus makes use of the same construction drawn up by Büdinger; however, he elaborates the consequences of the new historical concept. This intrusion of a critical measure to evaluate the given symbols enables Holdheim to reduce the Talmud to its factual significance, which means to its historical, instead of a dogmatic authority. In contrast to the majority of authors, Holdheim displays his methodology and intentions quite frankly, accepting the Written Tradition as God-given while he consciously evaluates the Oral Tradition according to a framework of historical references. This historicisation enables him to conclude that even in his own time the rabbinic laws had to be judged according to their religious adequacy.[61] Although almost all of the rabbinic tradition loses its sanctity, Holdheim's radical concept succeeds in developing a concise new religious system.

A comparable radical historicisation can be seen in Ludwig Philippson's religious textbook intended for adult education. He too appraises the rabbinic tradition as merely a further step in an ongoing historical process. Although Philippson tries to keep the sanctity of the Written legacy intact, the revelation of the Oral Tradition is not even accepted as an historical event. Like Holdheim, he uses a modern concept of history as a pivot to redefine the religious normative system.[62]

Only few catechisms go beyond this limited point of desacralisation. Only the moderate Reform rabbi Josef Aub attacks even the sphere of the Written Tradition vehemently, by defining the Pentateuch as a text corpus that had only gradually evolved. On the other hand, he legitimises the Oral Tradition by stating that every interpretation that keeps the spirit of the Written Tradition is to be seen as a fresh bud sprouting from an old root.[63] Again the historicisation elevates the idea of a revelation, passed on to the latest interpreters of the Law. Now it is the idea of an inspired formation of the law that lends authority to the rabbinic legislation. Moreover, Aub is the only author to integrate the results of the new-fledged text-critic in his textbook, referring, for example, to lost text-traditions paralleling the talmudic heritage.[64] Certainly he had to limit this process

---

[59]Holdheim, pp. viii-3, point 1.
[60]*Ibid.*, pp. 121ff. He is one of the few contemporary thinkers who perceived the *Shalshelet haQabbala* in its function as a cultural *mythomoteur*; Samuel Holdheim, *Ueber die Autonomie der Rabbinen und das Princip der jüdischen Ehe. Ein Beitrag zur Verständigung über einige das Judenthum betreffende Zeitfragen. 2. verm. Aufl.*, Schwerin 1847, p. 70.
[61]Holdheim, *Autonomie*, pp. viiif., 124f.
[62]*Ibid.*, p. 121.
[63]Philippson, 1861, vol. I, pp. 62, 94.
[64]Aub, pp. 15ff., 23–25; *Sabbath-Blatt*, No. 26, 1844, p. 101: "Man thut dem Thalmud Unrecht: das Gesetz (*Halacha*) hat er gläubig entwickelt."

Dissociation of Religion and Law

of displacement too, otherwise the religious tradition would have lost its sacred character entirely. Therefore Aub defines the Decalogue as the very legal code originally revealed by God. By the simultaneous revalorisation of the Written Tradition as the foundation of a common universal morality, Aub counterbalances the secularisation of great parts of the rabbinic tradition.[65]

The method of a critical historicisation also concentrated on the rabbinic tradition, which meant the legal heritage.[66] The restructuring of the religio-cultural tradition by a process of desacralisation furthered the conception of Jewish religion as a non-legal system. This was at least the definite trend of the Reform-orientated books.[67] Here the differences between Orthodox and Reform textbooks are only obvious when structural specifics of the *Halakhah*, such as the question of the ever-enduring validity of the law, are concerned.[68] For the Orthodox authors, this was a prerequisite of their creed, which had to be upheld in their books. Hence Orthodox books differ less in the inclusion of a critical-historical concept than by the ways this notion was transmitted.[69] If we take a look at more sensible questions, such as the possibilities of the traditional *Halakhah* to change or even to abolish laws, only two of the six Orthodox compendia analysed here dared to mention the *halakhic* possibilities for changing laws. The reason for this astonishing self-limitation was the Reformers' demand for a restriction of the law and their specific way of reinterpreting the traditional possibilities for a "legal" change. Yet knowledge about the ways of change, accepted by the Orthodoxy, could have proven a definite stronghold against the Reform's claim to confirm Orthodox *Halakhah* by its reinterpretation.[70]

Only one of the Orthodox authors, however, refers to the argument, established by Moses Mendelssohn, that it would need a new revelation to change the law. Again, only Salomon Plessner risks mention of the traditional legal criteria for change, for instance the possibility of advocating a change for a fixed time, without any interpretative legitimation for such ordinances (*horaat hashaa*). At the same time, this forced him to teach the restrictions of such a legal act, principally that the court had to meet certain qualifications, such as being confined to the possibilities and the regulations of the *Halakhah* itself.[71] Thus he not only mediated the idea of an autopoietic formation of the religious law but also supplied the pupil with the Orthodox norm to judge the innovations of the Reform.

Compared to these difficulties in establishing a concise Orthodox standpoint,

---

[65] Aub, pp. 25f.
[66] Ismar Schorsch, *From Text to Context. The Turn to History in Modern Judaism*, New England 1994, especially chapter 10, pp. 177–204. Schorsch depends on a concept of history fundamentally different from the one presented here.
[67] David Ellenson and Richard Jacobs, 'Scholarship and Faith. David Hoffman and his Relationship to Wissenschaft des Judentums', in *Modern Judaism*, vol. 8, No. 1 (1988), pp. 27–40.
[68] Aub, pp. 15ff. and Sondheimer, 1. Abt., pp. 40f.; 2. Abt., pp. 33f.
[69] Cf. Behr, pp. 5, 21 and Leimdörfer, p. 13.
[70] Plessner, p. 106; Stern, p. 154.
[71] Auerbach, pp. 7ff. § 11. The other authors are Plessner, Stern and Behr; and, as a conservative author, Leimdörfer. Plessner, p. 38, No. 152, p. 39, Nos. 153f.

the Reformers could use these *halakhic* criteria far more easily to support their own position. Like many of his Reform colleagues, Salomon Herxheimer told his readers that the givers-of-law may abolish or decree laws, if social changes make it unavoidable.[72] This short sentence contains the Reformers' critical argument: that the unchangeable law had actually been changed in the past. The proof of a constitutive and not, as the Orthodox saw it, an interpretative character of a substantial part of the rabbinic legislation legitimised the call for a change in the law, for on the basis of this *halakhic* prescription the accommodation of the law to the changing social situation appeared as a "legal" action according to the traditional *Halakhah*.[73] Here, one of the foremost arguments for Reform was transferred to subsequent generations in a convincing way.

If we take into account everything mentioned here, the standpoint of Orthodoxy was – compared to the compendia of the Reform – rather weak.[74] The changes in

---

[72] Herxheimer, pp. 27f., No. 87.

[73] E.g. Maier, p. 14: "diese durch die Zeitbedürfnisse gebotenen Anordnungen und Gebräuche von den Lehrern nicht für göttliche Gesetze ausgegeben wurden, so kann dieses für keine Uebertretung jenes Verbots gehalten werden". Beer, *Handbuch*, 2. Curs, 1. Abt., 1818, p. 68: "auch bey ihrer Einführung Zeit und Umstände berücksichtigt worden sind, und sie daher den erweiterten Einsichten, den Zeiten und Umständen gemäß verändert werden müssen" Aub, pp. 22f.

[74] This can be measured by the rate of re-edition. Herxheimer's *Yesode haTora* was one of the most popular books; the editions were: Hannöverisch-Münden 1:1831, Bernburg 3:1840, 4:1841, 5–7:1843–5, 8:1849, 9:1851, 11:1856, Leipzig 12:1860, 14–17:1863–7, 18–24:1868–74, 26–27:1877, 28:1880, 29:1883, 30:1886, 31:1889, 32:1893, 34:1897, 35:1904. (Sources on the use of these books are: LBI Archives NY; Joseph Coll. Perles; AR 4993, Gemeinde München; Kgl. Regierung von Oberbayern, Kammer des Innern an Perles, Munich, 18th May 1890; reply 15th June 1890. Mordechai Eliav, 'Jüdische Erziehung in Deutschland im Zeitalter der Aufklärung und der Emancipation', in *Bulletin des Leo Baeck Instituts*, No. 11 (1960), pp. 213ff., p. 258; Levi, pp. 32f.) Johlson's book was published four times in Frankfurt am Main (1:1814, 2:1819, 3:1829), and together with other writings (4:1837–42, 1857 and 1865) in further editions in Vienna. Levi, pp. 25–26. Isaac Marcus Jost, *Neuere Geschichte der Israeliten, 3. Abt*, Breslau 1820, p. 36: Carové, p. 139: *Sulamith*, 6:1819–1821, vol. I, 5. Heft, p. 304; Eliav, 'Erziehung', pp. 118, 197, 244, esp. p. 254; Levi, pp. 25–26; gives different dates, as does Straßburger, p. 278. The copy of Johlson's book 1814 edition did not appear under the title *Shorshe haDat* (Part 1), but as *Alume Yosef*, (Part 1). Plessner, p. xxxvi, confirms the data given by the *Gesamtverzeichnis der gedruckte Schriften* (GV). Büdinger's *More leMorim* was only published in 1830; but his *More leTora* saw several editions: 1:1830, 3:1837, 4:1843, 5:1851, 6:1862, 7:1872; Eliav, 'Erziehung', 1960, pp. 253–255; Lewin, Adolf, *Geschichte der badischen Juden seit der Regierung Karl Friedrichs (1738–1909)*, Karlsruhe 1909, p. 256; Berthold Rosenthal, *Heimatgeschichte der badischen Juden seit ihrem Auftreten bis zur Gegenwart*, Bühl 1927, pp. 348–349. Cf. *Israelitische Annalen*, No. 1, 1840, p. 9. The Württemberger book was also used outside Württemberg; Prestel, p. 192. Philippson's copious book was not used in elementary schools. The book written by the preacher at the *Hamburger Tempel*, Dr. Leimdörfer, was not widely used. The books of Leopold Stein were read far more. Holdheim's book was restricted to the school of the Berlin Reform Community. Aub's *Grundlage für den wiss. Unterricht* was published in Mainz 1:1865 and Leipzig 2:1874. Alexander Behr's book, with its approbation by Abraham Bing and with its printing costs paid for by the state, was comparatively widely known in Bavaria; later its place was taken by Orthodox works, e.g. Nathan Bamberger's '*Leitfaden für den Religionsunterricht*', which was, according to the GV, published only once in Munich in 1826. (Prestel, p. 192; Jost, p. 3; Abt., 1820, p. 36. *Israelitische Annalen*, No. 25, 1841, p. 198; No. 2, 1841, pp. 11ff. Anonymous, *Die Reformation der Juden und das D. Behr'sche Lehrbuch. Ein wohlgemeintes Wort an die Judenschaft – besonders in Bayern, von einem Kosmopoliten aus Bayern*, Nuremburg–Altdorf 1827, pp. 17–179.) Plessner's book was mostly confined to Berlin; only Auerbach's *Torat Emet*, with its numerous approbations, was apparently used even outside Hessen; Darmstadt (1:1839, 2:1853 and 3:1893) in Giessen. (StA Koblenz; Best.441, No. 26149, pp. 191ff.

the cultural representation of the *Halakhah*, with its intrusion of a new dual concept of Jewish religion and was typical redefinition of its as an ethical rather than a legal system, *Halakhah* for all the religious groups of the nineteenth century. These basic changes already proved to be a definite advantage for the Reform cause. Only if we take the general trend into consideration, namely to historicise the religious tradition according to a new, increasingly text-critical standard and, furthermore, to redefine basic factors of the *halakhic* system, do we sometimes find even significant differences. But here the Reform not only had a better standing, it also used the new possibilities in a much more dynamic way than the Orthodox authors ever could have done.[75] They had to accommodate the general problem of finding a new way to teach religion as a subject among many others. At the same time they had to resist those general trends that characterised the conceptual changes to which they yielded. While these changes furthered the cause of the Reform, the quest for a delegalisation of Judaism was fundamentally opposed to the Orthodox perception of the importance of the religious law. Yet the unconscious integration of these general conceptual changes contradicted their own views and the claims of an Orthodox position. The Orthodox pedagogues also wanted to master the vehement socio-cultural change imposed on the Jewish population in the nineteenth century. Thus they had to harmonise the redefinition of the legal heritage – a process they evaluated as keeping the traditional concept unchanged – with the strain caused by the integration of new norms that led to a general change of the concept of religion as a whole. Their pedagogic presentations of the *Halakhah* therefore often resembled the arguments of the Reformers. Even when it came to specific, distinct conceptions, the difficulties in outlining a concise and unique Orthodox programme were numerous.

Compared to this, the transfer of a new model of Jewish religion advocated by the Reform was not only innovative but also much more effective. From the start, this new form of education had been presented in a consistent way. Thus the Reform movement won considerable ground in subsequent generations, while its factual position in the communal structures, not to speak of its general acceptance by the Jewish population, was still far from strong. Thus the process of the establishment of the Reform movement was decisively supported by the new religious education. This system-analytical conclusion is supported by the vast number and the wide use of Reform textbooks. While the number of Reform-orientated school projects was limited and paralleled by less well-researched

---

On Plessner see Mordechai Breuer, 'Emancipation and the Rabbis', in *Niv HaMidraschia*, vols. 13– 14 (1978–9), p. 33; Eliav, 'Erziehung', 1960, p. 294; *Allgemeine Zeitung des Judenthums*, 2:1838, No. 83, p. 338, and *ibid., Lit. u. homil. Beiblatt*, 1:1838, No. 24, pp. 413–414; Jost, 3. Abt., 1820, pp. 157ff; Sigismund Stern, *Geschichte des Judenthums von Mendelssohn bis auf die heutige Zeit. Nebst einer einleitenden Ueberschau der älteren Religions- und Culturgeschichte. Neue Ausgabe*, Breslau 1870, p. 253.) For Schwarz's and Stern's books see Prestel, p. 192 and Levi, pp. 34–345. Their influence was restricted to the centre of Bavarian Orthodoxy.

[75]E.g. Johlson, p. 56, No. 113; see also the annotations on pp. 5–6, 103, 106; Herxheimer, pp. 27–28, No. 87. Beer, *Handbuch*, 2. Curs, 1818, p. 68. Hochstädter, 1. Heft, 2. Abt., p. 33; Maier, p. 14; Aub, pp. 22f.

Orthodox institutions, the use of these compendia inside and outside the Jewish schools guaranteed a wide influence for the respective teachings. One could therefore assume that the reorientation towards a confessional and de-legalised concept of Jewish religion was already implanted in Jewish youth and was widespread when the number of Jewish children attending Jewish schools and receiving a religious education dwindled towards the end of the nineteenth century.[76]

---

[76]For the general development of education in the nineteenth century see Detlef K. Müller, *Sozialstruktur und Schulsystem. Aspekte zum Strukturwandel des Schulwesens im 19. Jh. Gekürzte Studienausgabe*, Göttingen 1981, pp. 105f; Herrlitz *et al.*, pp. 54–5; Fischer, 1969, vol. 2, pp. 230f; Thomas Nipperdey, *Deutsche Geschichte 1800–1866. Bürgerwelt und starker Staat*, Munich 1987, pp. 463–468; Leschinsky, Achim and Röder; Peter Martin, *Schule im historischen Prozeß. Zum Wechselverhältnis von institutioneller Erziehung und gesellschaftlicher Entwicklung*, Stuttgart 1976, pp. 137–139. For Jewish developments, see Eliav, 'Erziehung', 1960, pp. 213, 323–324, 334ff; until 1839 55% of the Jewish children attended Jewish schools; by 1867 the figure had dropped to 25%; by around 1858 two-thirds of all Jewish children in Berlin were outside the "Jewish educational system". But one should not be misled by these striking percentages. Many of those children probably attended private lessons, Sorkin, p. 130. Not all states enforced a religious education, Jakob Toury, *Soziale und politische Geschichte der Juden in Deutschland 1847–1871*, Düsseldorf 1977, pp. 166ff; A. Michaelis, *Die Rechtsverhältnisse der Juden in Preußen*, Berlin 1910, p. 257; Adolf Kober, '150 Years of Religious Instruction', in *LBI Year Book II* (1957), p. 103. For an evaluation of the education, see Breuer, *Khazon uMeziut*, pp. 317–335, StA Koblenz; Best. 441, No. 9807, pp. 13ff; Trepp, pp. 169–189.

Antisemitism Before National Socialism

Salomon Neumann's Statistical Challenge to Treitschke: The Forgotten Episode that Marked the End of the "Berliner Antisemitismusstreit"

BY GÜNTER REGNERI

"But year after year multitudes of over-ambitious trouser-selling youths pour over our Eastern frontier from the inexhaustible Polish cradle. Their children and children's children will one day dominate Germany's stock exchanges and newspapers. This immigration increases perceptibly." (Heinrich von Treitschke, November 1879)[1]

"This question of Jewish immigration has been dealt with since in the most detailed way. One of our best statisticians, Herr Neumann, has written a special little pamphlet on it. I would really ask you to refer to it, should the issue be discussed again. I would be pleased to provide you with a copy." (Rudolf Virchow, 20th November 1880, addressing the members of the *Preußisches Abgeordnetenhaus*)[2]

"The Jewish mass immigration ... has not only turned Herr H. v. T[reitschke] into a prophet but also into a statistician. This would not have been necessary for his faithful followers. The vision [of mass immigration] only had to be proved statistically because of the sceptics and because modern consciousness is impressed by the harmony of knowledge and belief." (Salomon Neumann, May 1881)[3]

In November 1879, the historian Heinrich von Treitschke published an article in his periodical *Preußische Jahrbücher* which initiated the *Berliner Antisemitismusstreit*. Treitschke claimed that for decades there had been Jewish mass immigration from the East which threatened the future of Germany. This was a key element

---

[1] "...über unsere Ostgrenze aber dringt Jahr für Jahr aus der unerschöpflichen polnischen Wiege eine Schaar strebsamer hosenverkaufender Jünglinge herein, deren Kinder und Kindeskinder dereinst Deutschlands Börsen und Zeitungen beherrschen sollen; die Einwanderung wächst zusehends...", Heinrich von Treitschke, 'Unsere Aussichten', in *Preußische Jahrbücher*, vol. 44 (1879), pp. 572–573.

[2] "Diese Frage der Judeneinwanderung ist in allereingehendster Weise seitdem erörtert worden. Einer unserer besten Statistiker, Herr Neumann, hat darüber eine besondere kleine Broschüre geschrieben, die ich doch bitten möchte, wenn diese Sache mal wieder zur Verhandlung kommt, zum Geenstand einer Betrachtung zu machen; ich stelle gern ein Exemplar davon zur Verfügung," Rudolf Virchow in *Die Judenfrage vor dem Preußischen Landtage. Wortgetreuer Abdruck der Verhandlungen im Abgeordnetenhause am 20. und 22. November 1880*, Berlin 1880, p. 28.

[3] "Die jüdische Masseneinwanderung ... hat Herrn H. v. T[reitschke] nicht bloß zu einem Propheten, sondern auch zu einem Statistiker gemacht. Für seine gläubie Gemeinde wäre es nicht nothwendig gewesen. Nur um der Skeptiker willen und weil die Harmonie von Glauben und Wissen dem modernen Bewußtsein imponirt, mußte die Vision auch statistisch bezeugt werden." Salomon Neumann, *Nachschrift zur Fabel von der jüdischen Masseneinwanderung, enthaltend: I: Antwort an Herrn Adolf Wagner; II. Herr Heinrich v. Treitschke und seine jüdische Masseneinwanderung; III. Die Antwort des königl. preußischen statistischen Bureaus*, Berlin 1881, p. 11.

in the antisemitic debate. In contrast to other critics, the Jewish physician and statistician Salomon Neumann focused his response solely on this element of antisemitic agitation. His pamphlet, *Die Fabel von der jüdischen Masseneinwanderung. Ein Kapitel aus der preußischen Statistik*, published in the summer of 1880, presented sophisticated demographic research on the Jewish population in Prussia which proved Treitschke's claim to be wrong.[4] However, Treitschke ignored Neumann's study until Theodor Mommsen, another famous historian, forced him to recognise it publicly. When Treitschke reviewed Neumann's study in *Preußische Jahrbücher* in February 1881, it marked the end of the *Berliner Antisemitismusstreit*.[5]

Modern research describes the *Berliner Antisemitismusstreit* in great detail.[6] Nevertheless, the impact of the *Fabel von der jüdischen Masseneinwanderung* on the outcome of this public debate has been largely overlooked.[7] More research on Neumann is, on the whole, badly needed.[8] This neglect is partly due to the diffi-

---

[4] Salomon Neumann, *Die Fabel von der jüdischen Masseneinwanderung. Ein Kapitel aus der preußischen Statistik*, Berlin 1880.

[5] Heinrich von Treitschke, 'Die jüdische Einwanderung in Deutschland', in *Preußische Jahrbücher*, vol. 47 (1881), pp. 109–110.

[6] The debate, or at least special aspects of it, are dealt with in Arthur Rosenberg, 'Treitschke und die Juden. Zur Soziologie der deutschen akademischen Reaktion', in *Die Gesellschaft. Internationale Revue für Sozialisus und Politik*, 7, vol. 2, (1930), pp. 78–83; Reuwen Michael, 'Graetz contra Treitschke', in *Bulletin des Leo Baeck Instituts*, 4, No. 16 (1961), pp. 301–322; Michel A. Meyer, 'Great Debate on Antisemitism. Jewish Reaction to New Hostility in Germany 1879–1881', in *LBI Year Book XI* (1966), pp. 137–170; Hans Liebeschütz, *Das Judentum im deutschen Geschichtsbild von Hegel bis Max Weber*, Tübingen 1967 (Schriftenreihe wissenschaftlicher Abhandlungen des Leo Baeck Instituts 17), pp. 157–219; Ian Hacking, *The Taming of Chance*, Cambridge 1990, pp. 189–199; Christhard Hoffmann, 'Der Berliner Antisemitismusstreit 1879/81', in *Geschichte in Wissenschaft und Unterricht*, vol. 46 (1995), pp. 167–178. A substantial collection of essays and letters on the controversy is published in Walter Boehlich (ed.), *Der Berliner Antisemitismusstreit*, Frankfurt am Main 1988.

[7] Only Hacking deals with the issue of statistics in the *Berliner Antisemitismusstreit*, focusing on the dispute Neumann had with the *Königlich Preußisches Statistisches Bureau*. With this exception, only Liebeschütz refers to Neumann's study, in a footnote and without further detail; see Liebeschütz, p. 185, note 49. Boehlich does not even mention the *Fabel von der jüdischen Masseneinwanderung* in the bibliography although he publishes Treitschke's review article of it.

[8] Secondary literature on Neumann is mostly of a commemorative kind: Richard Böckh, 'Salomon Neumann, geboren am 22. October 1819', in *Statistisches Jahrbuch der Stadt Berlin*, vol. 24 (1899), pp. iii-vii; Hermann Cohen, 'Salomon Neumann. Rede bei der Gedächtnisfeier der Lehranstalt für die Wissenschaft des Judentums', in *Allgemeine Zeitung des Judentums*, vol. 72 , No. 44 (30th October 1908), pp. 519–524; Rudolf Lehnhoff, 'Salomon Neumann', in *Medizinische Reform. Wochenschrift für Soziale Medizin, Hygiene und Sozialstatistik*, 16 (1908), pp. 477–478; Julius Leopold Pagel, 'Salomon Neumann (Gestorben 20. September 1908)', in *Deutsche Medizinische Presse*, 12 (1908), pp. 148–149; Heinrich Silbergleit, 'Vorwort', in *Statistisches Jahrbuch der Stadt Berlin*, vol. 31 (1909), pp.iii-xiii; Ismar Elbogen, 'Salomon Neumann', in *Jüdisches Lexikon*, vol. IV/1, Berlin 1930, pp. 469–470; Elsbeth Meyer-Neumann, 'S. Neumanns Wirksamkeit auf dem Gebiete der Sozialhygiene', in *Sozialhygienische Mitteilungen*, 17 (1933), pp. 14–19. The only biography of Neumann focusses on his activities in public health issues. It also provides an extensive bibliography and three of Neumann's own texts: Karl-Heinz Karbe, *Salomon Neumann 1819 -1908. Wegbereiter sozialmedizinischen Denkens. Ausgewählte Texte*, Leipzig 1983. See also Gerhard Baader, 'Salomon Neumann', in Wilhelm Treue and Rolf Winau (eds.), *Berliner Lebensbilder. Mediziner*, Berlin 1987, pp. 151–174. Two recent publications acknowledging Neumann's social and political activities in Berlin should be mentioned: Ragnhild Münch, *Gesundheitswesen im 18. und 19. Jahrhundert. Das Berliner Beispiel*, Berlin 1995; Ludovica Scarpa, *Gemeinwohl und lokale Macht. Honoratioren und Armenwesen in der Berliner Luisenstadt im 19. Jahrhundert*, Munich 1995.

culty of gaining access to research materials. A substantial personal *Nachlaß* of Salomon Neumann does not exist. Sources can be found in different archives all over the world. Until 1990 it was thought that the *Sammlung Neumann* had disappeared. It had been part of the *Gesamtarchiv der deutschen Juden* until the *Reichssicherheitshauptamt* confiscated it in 1933. In 1945, the Red Army transferred the archives of the *Reichssicherheitshauptamt* to Moscow, where they became part of the classified collection of the former Central State Archive, now renamed the Centre for Conservation and Restoration of Documents. The 383 folders of the *Sammlung Neumann* hold mainly newspaper cuttings, pamphlets and other material on antisemitism.[9] The Central Archives for the History of the Jewish People (CAHJP) in Jerusalem possess a small *Nachlaß Sanitätsrat Dr. Salomon Neumann*. This consists of only one file of letters from a number of Jewish communities to Neumann from August 1894, as well as newspaper cuttings and some statistical information on the Jews of Prussia.[10] The archive of the Leo Baeck Institute in New York possesses a small collection of secondary sources relating to Neumann. There are items concerning the *Salomon-Neumann-Stiftung zur Pflege der Wissenschaft des Judentums*, as well as genealogical documents of the Neumann-Oppenheim families.[11] Fritz Stern has discovered odd letters of Neumann, in the course of his research on Bleichröder, in archives in France and the USA.[12] Karl-Heinz Karbe used the collections of former GDR archives for his detailed research on Neumann's role in the *Berliner Gesundheitspflegeverein*. Today, these collections are integrated in the *Geheimes Preußisches Staatsarchiv Berlin-Dahlem* and the *Bundesarchiv, Außenstelle Potsdam*. There are also the files of the *Berliner Stadtverordnetenversammlung* which are kept in the *Landesarchiv Berlin* and which could shed new light on Neumann's forty-six years of political activities in this institution. Nevertheless, the question remains why a main protagonist of the *Berliner Antisemitismusstreit* has, so far, been overlooked.

SALOMON NEUMANN – A BIOGRAPHICAL INTRODUCTION

During his lifetime, the Berlin physician, statistician and city councillor Salomon Neumann was a well-known figure. Neumann, the son of a Jewish shopkeeper, was born on 22nd October 1819 in the Pomeranian town of Pyritz. After he had been both to *cheder* and to the local primary school, he was sent to a *Gymnasium* in Frankfurt an der Oder. In 1838 he obtained his *Abitur* from the *Friedrich-Wilhelm-Gymnasium* in Berlin. In the same year, he enrolled as a medical student at the

---

[9] Tsentr Konservatsii i Restavratii Dokumentov, Moscow, *Assets of German Provenance*, Sign. 1194, *Gesamtarchiv der deutschen Juden (Sammlung Neumann)*.

[10] CAHJP, P/52, *Nachlass Sanitätsrat Dr. Salomon Neumann*.

[11] See Fred Grubel (ed.), *Catalog of the Archival Collections of the Leo Baeck Institute*, Tübingen 1990 (Schriftenreihe wissenschaftlicher Abhandlungen des Leo Baeck Instituts 47), pp. 111, 334.

[12] The letters held in the Bleichröder Archive in the Baker Library at Harvard University and the Archive of the *Alliance Israélite* in Paris are related to Neumann's activities in the *Comité für die rumänischen Juden* and the *Berliner Lokalkomitee der Alliance Israélite Universelle* (A.I.U.). See Fritz Stern, *Gold and Iron. Bismarck, Bleichröder and the Building of the German Empire*, New York 1977, p. 370 note 64 and p. 373 note 73.

University of Berlin. In 1841 he transferred to the University of Halle-Wittenberg, where he graduated in July 1842. Only a few months later, he was awarded the title of Dr. med. for his thesis on diseases of the intestines. He completed his medical training in various hospitals in Vienna and Paris before returning to Berlin, and in 1845 he acquired a licence to practise as a general practitioner and obstetrician.

His setting up in practice had an immediate political impact. Neumann refused to swear the "Jewish oath" as an oath of office because he felt that the compulsory oath contradicted the *Edikt* of 11th March 1812, which granted civil rights to the Jews of Prussia. According to Elbogen, Neumann's refusal led to the abolition of this discriminatory regulation.[13] Very soon, Neumann became politically involved in a *freie Association*. Regarding the medical profession, he wrote in 1847 that it was a society "which directs the free activities of the individual towards a universal goal, and in which the solitary forces of weak egoists will unite in a great and purposeful power by means of which one can strive for the certain and dependable achievement of the common good".[14]

The "Social Question" was one of the major issues that concerned Neumann all through his life. He lived according to the maxim "It is one's duty to help the poor," as Hermann Cohen remembered.[15] Neumann was confronted with poverty every day. He worked part-time as one of the thirty badly-paid Poor Law practitioners and witnessed the lack of medical supplies for the working poor in Berlin. Since 1800, the city had experienced a sharp increase in population. In 1845 roughly 45% of the 400,000 inhabitants of Berlin were regarded as poor and, in order to be entitled to medical treatment by a Poor Law practitioner, the poor had to register as paupers at the *Armendirektion*, thus giving up their civil rights. It was regarding this issue that the physician Neumann published for the first time. With the publication of *Die öffentliche Gesundheitspflege und das Eigenthum* in 1847, he joined in the *Medizinalreformdebatte*. Until then, questions of social standing and rank had dominated the debate. Neumann made it clear that questions of medical reform were inseparably linked to the issue of poverty. He was not alone in this opinion. Other democratically-minded physicians, such as Rudolf Virchow and Rudolf Leubuscher, also demanded substantial reforms. Standards of living and the health of the working classes could only be improved by political and social reform, in conjunction with better, that is, scientific, training of medical personnel and a new attitude towards the poor.[16]

When the Revolution reached Berlin in 1848, a substantial medical reform

---

[13] See Elbogen, p. 469.
[14] "...welche die freie Thätigkeit des Einzelnen nach dem allgemeinen Ziele hinlenkt, welche die isolirten Kräfte schwächlicher Egoisten zu einer großen und inhaltsvollen Macht vereinigt, mittels welcher die Erfüllung des allgemeinen Zweckes sicher und zuverlässsig angestrebt werden kann", Salomon Neumann, 'Die öffentliche Gesundheitspflege und das Eigenthum (Berlin 1847)', quoted in Karbe, p. 108.
[15] Cohen, p. 521.
[16] On *Medizinalreform*, see Erwin H. Ackerknecht, 'Beiträge zur Geschichte der Medizinalreform von 1848', in *Sudhoffs Archiv für Geschichte der Medizin*, 25 (1932) pp. 61–109 and pp. 113–183. On the development of medical services in Berlin, see Münch; also Rolf Winau, *Medizin in Berlin*, Berlin 1987.

Salomon Neumann and the Berliner Antisemitismusstreit 133

seemed likely. Virchow and Leubuscher published the *Medicinische Reform*, which soon became the organ of the radical faction of the medical reform movement. Neumann was a regular contributor to the periodical. He was also involved in the meetings of the *Generalversammlung der Berliner Ärzte*, for which he drafted a public health bill. Even before both the Revolution and the medical reform movement failed, Neumann had taken the first practical steps to improve the living conditions of the working classes. Between 1849 and 1853 he was the driving force behind the *Gesundheitspflegeverein des Berliner Bezirks der Arbeiterverbrüderung* and for the first time he was able to successfully implement his ideas of social medicine and of an association of physicians. In contrast to the rigid and mandatory health insurance of the local authority, the *Gewerkskrankenverein*, the *Gesundheitspflegeverein* was an autonomous part of the labour movement, aiming not only to provide treatment but also to prevent disease.[17]

The *Gesundheitspflegeverein* was important for Neumann in another respect. Since the mid-1840s, Neumann had taken a strong interest in statistics. He had argued that the health situation could only be improved if both state and medical personnel had sufficient information. In 1849 he published a study on health statistics which was based on official data.[18] His aim was to show the correlation between the financial situation of the different classes in society and their overall medical condition. Statistics provided the method for doing this "scientifically". In his post as physician of the *Berliner Gesundheitspflegeverein* Neumann was able to go one step further. He began to collect his own data for the basis of a future statistical study of different trades, publishing his findings in quarterly reports. He soon became known as a sophisticated statistician and was asked to develop a new concept for the census of 1861. He promoted a supervised system of self-calculation; he also created questionnaires which broadened the range of data collected in the census he later organised. As a result, the city knew for the first time the exact number of its inhabitants – important not least in terms of fiscal contributions. The 1861 census also provided crucial information about the social situation in Berlin, for example in the housing sector. This made the social policy of local government more effective in subsequent years.[19]

Up to the 1850s, Berlin statistics were strikingly backward. It was Neumann who could take credit for making Berlin a model for international statisticians. Many Prussian cities used Neumann's ideas in the census of 1864, and although Berlin had the newly-founded *Statistisches Bureau*, Neumann once again supervised the 1864 census. In the following decades he was a member of the municipal statistical committee, which consisted of members of both the city council and the municipal authority, and which supervised the *Statistisches Bureau*. Neumann's achievements regarding local statistics were publicly honoured on his eightieth

---

[17]On the *Gesundheitspflegeverein*, see Karbe.
[18]Salomon Neumann, *Zur medicinischen Statistik des preußischen Staates. Nach den Acten des statistischen Bureau's für das Jahr 1846*, Berlin 1849.
[19]See *Die Berliner Volks-Zählung vom 3. December 1861. Bericht der städtischen Central-Commission für die Volks-Zählung über die Mitwirkung der Commune an der Zählung-Ausführung und deren Resultate. Erster Theil: Die Ausführung der Zählung sowie die Erläuterung der Zählung-Resultate*, Berlin 1863.

birthday, when the senior municipal statistician, Richard Böckh, presented him with an offprint of the commemorative preface to the twenty-fourth volume of the *Statistisches Jahrbuch der Stadt Berlin*.[20]

Between 1859 and 1905 Neumann served continuously as an elected city councillor in Berlin. In the beginning he belonged to a group of Liberals which included the prominent figure of Virchow. In his later years Neumann also became a friend of Paul Singer, who brought him closer to *Sozialdemokratie*, although he never joined the party. Neumann influenced local politics greatly in many areas. In 1899, in celebration of his fortieth year as a member of the *Berliner Stadtverordnetenversammlung*, he was made a councillor of the city. When he resigned after forty-six years because of ill health, he was one of the longest ever serving city councillors of Berlin. His daughter summarised the issues for which he was lobbying:

> "He took particular interest in introducing sewers, abolishing gutters, banning basement flats, erecting covered markets, building the town hall, constructing schools and hospitals, in improving street lighting, the transport system, the water supply (such as the Tegel waterworks) and street cleaning, in bringing businesses into public ownership and laying out parks in previously neglected quarters of the city."[21]

Neumann's political involvement can only be understood in conjunction with his strong Jewish awareness. He never denied his identity, and conversion to Christianity, especially for the sake of a career, was out of the question. In 1853 Carl von Hinckeldey, Berlin's chief of police, offered him the post of statistician within his administration, on condition that Neumann convert; Neumann vehemently refused. He suffered Hinckeldey's revenge shortly afterwards when he was denied the chance to take the examination for the relatively well-paid and respected post of municipal medical officer. According to reports from police headquarters, Neumann was politically unreliable. Strangely enough, Berlin police headquarters – although then under another chief of police – proposed Neumann for the honorary title of *Sanitätsrat*, which was granted in 1870. He was involved in Jewish organisations on both the local and international level and he was one of the founders of the *Hochschule für die Wissenschaft des Judentums*. From 1895 he was chairman of its board of trustees. When, in 1907, the *Hochschule* finally moved into its own building in the *Artilleriestraße*, now *Tucholskystraße*, the opening ceremony took place on Neumann's eighty-seventh birthday. He was declared "honorary member for life" but could not attend the ceremony because he was already bedridden.[22]

In 1864 Neumann founded the *Zunz-Stiftung* and ten years later he proposed the publication of the complete works of Leopold Zunz. On an international level Neumann was involved with the *Alliance Israélite Universelle* (A.I.U.). In 1869, he became chairman of the local committee of the A.I.U. in Berlin. Three

---

[20]See Silbergleit, Foreword, p. xi. On the history of the *Statistisches Bureau*, see Heinrich Silbergleit, *Das Statistische Amt der Stadt Berlin 1862–1912*, Berlin 1912; Statistisches Landesamt Berlin (ed.), *100 Jahre Berliner Statistik*, Berlin 1962.
[21]Meyer-Neumann, p. 19.
[22]See *Allgemeine Zeitung des Judentums*, vol. 71, No. 43 (25th October 1907), suppl. *Der Gemeindebote*, p. 1.

years later, Neumann became a member of its central committee. He confronted antisemitism in Germany from at least 1880, when he published the *Fabel von der jüdischen Masseneinwanderung*. He also supported an official response organised by committees of prominent personalities. He was one of the founders of the *Jüdisches Comité vom 1. Dezember 1880* which came into being on the initiative of Moritz Lazarus. Again in 1893, shortly before the general election to the *Reichstag*, Neumann was involved in establishing the *Comité zur Abwehr antisemitischer Angriffe*. The huge amount of material on antisemitism Neumann collected, which now lies in a Moscow archive, is probably related to his involvement in this organisation.[23]

After the death of his wife in 1903, Neumann suffered from deteriorating health, which made it impossible for him to appear in public any longer. He resigned as city councillor in the autumn of 1905. Soon afterwards, the newly-founded *Gesellschaft für soziale Medizin, Hygiene und Medizinalstatistik* declared Neumann the society's only honorary member. In 1906 the *Salomon-Neumann-Stiftung zur Pflege der Wissenschaft des Judentums* was founded. Felix Liebermann, a well-known legal historian and brother of the painter Max, became the foundation's first chairman. During the Nazi period, Leo Baeck was its last. The office of the *Chef der Sicherheitspolizei und des SD* ordered its compulsory incorporation into the *Reichsvereinigung der Juden in Deutschland in 1940*.[24] Salomon Neumann died on 20th September 1908 and his funeral two days later, at the Jewish cemetery in Berlin-Weißensee, was very well attended.

THE BEGINNING OF THE *BERLINER ANTISEMITISMUSSTREIT*
1879 TO 1880

The *Berliner Antisemitismusstreit* was a public debate initiated by Heinrich von Treitschke, the famous Berlin historian. In November 1879 he published the essay 'Unsere Aussichten' in the *Preußische Jahrbücher*, of which he was chief editor. In this essay he coined the phrase "The Jews are our misfortune" and it marked the beginning of a whole series of antisemitic articles. The first three articles, produced between November 1879 and January 1880, were re-published in February 1880 as a booklet, *Ein Wort über unser Judenthum*.[25] No other antisemitic pamphlet received so much public attention, but it also attracted much criticism from respected public figures.

Most of Treitschke's critics were Jewish intellectuals, rabbis, university lecturers and politicians. At the beginning of the debate, the few non-Jewish critics were not very prominent. Heinrich Graetz, the historian of Judaism, whom Treitschke attacked fiercely in 'Unsere Aussichten', reacted in early December.

---

[23] On the *Comité zur Abwehr antisemitischer Angriffe*, see Ismar Schorsch, *Jewish Reactions to German Anti-Semitism 1870–1914*, New York 1972, pp. 113–115. On the *Jüdisches Comité vom 1. Dezember 1880*, see Moritz Lazarus, *Unser Standpunkt*, Berlin 1881; Schorsch, pp. 59–65; Sanford Ragins, *Jewish Responses to Antisemitism in Germany, 1870–1914. A Study in the History of Ideas*, Cincinnati 1980, pp. 33–35.
[24] Archives of the Leo Baeck Institute, S. Neumann Collection, item 4/2.
[25] An enlarged fourth edition was published in 1881.

His open letter, entitled 'Erwiderung an Herrn von Treitschke', was printed by the Breslau newspaper *Schlesische Presse* on 7th December 1879. This prompted an even stronger attack from Treitschke in the December issue of the *Preußische Jahrbücher*, 'Herr Graetz und sein Judenthum'.

With the article 'Noch einige Bemerkungen zur Judenfrage' and the brief report 'Zur Judenfrage' in the issues of January and February 1880 of the *Preußische Jahrbücher*, Treitschke responded to some of his critics but published no more antisemitic articles for several months. In the spring of 1880, therefore, it seemed that the controversy was gradually subsiding.

This first wave of the *Berliner Antisemitismusstreit* succeeded in making antisemitism culturally acceptable among the educated classes of German society. As Shulamit Volkov put it: "It has been rightly claimed that Treitschke made antisemitism '*salonfähig*' in bourgeois society and openly introduced it into German universities."[26] A key element in Treitschke's antisemitic argumentation was the claim of a Jewish mass immigration from the East. Early critics doubted such a mass immigration. To support his claim, Treitschke referred to certain demographic reports. From this point on, statistics played a part in many contributions to the *Berliner Antisemitismusstreit*, but the first and only response to Treitschke based solely on the immigration argument was the *Fabel von der jüdischen Masseneinwanderung* by Salomon Neumann.

THE "IMMIGRATION" DEBATE

The *Berliner Antisemitismusstreit* was the academic mirror-image of the *christlich-soziale* Stoecker movement and the *Antisemiten-Petition* that was supported by roughly 265,000 people throughout Germany. Both movements demanded measures to stop the alleged Jewish mass immigration. So when, in November 1879, Treitschke claimed that masses of trouser-selling young Jews were pouring in from the East, he brought this antisemitic claim to a new audience rather than invented it.[27]

This claim was, as already indicated, contested immediately. On 7th December 1879 Heinrich Graetz replied:

> "Your claim of an immigration of trouser-selling Polish Jewish youths is also incorrect. Statisticians will demonstrate how few Jews from the East are at present settling in Germany. In Galicia, Jews are actually enjoying full and unconditional equality and do not feel like migrating; their intelligent sons are frequently promoted into the officers' ranks; Russia does not allow a single youth liable for military service to cross the border. So where are these trouser-selling youths coming from?"[28]

---

[26]Shulamit Volkov, 'Antisemitism as a Cultural Code. Reflections on the History and Historiography of Antisemitism in Imperial Germany', in *LBI Year Book XXIII* (1978), p. 42.

[27]On Stoecker and the Antisemites' Petition, see Peter Pulzer, *The Rise of Political Anti-Semitism in Germany and Austria*, London 1988, pp. 83–97; Günter Brakelmann et al., *Protestantismus und Politik. Werk und Wirkung Adolf Stoeckers*, Hamburg 1982.

[28]Heinrich Graetz ,'Erwiderung an Herrn von Treitschke', quoted in Boehlich, p 30.

In his leader of 9th December 1879 the editor of the *Allgemeine Zeitung des Judenthums* also denied that there was significant Jewish immigration. He stated that according to official statistical tables, the growth of the Jewish population in Germany was due to natural increase rather than to the number of immigrants which was extremely small.[29]

In his counterattack on Graetz, 'Herr Graetz und sein Judenthum' of December 1879, Treitschke took up the statistical argument. By showing figures of Jewish populations in different Western European countries he tried to prove that the number of German Jews was extraordinarily high. He then produced three different sets of figures for Prussia. According to the data of the statistical office, the Jewish population numbered 123,921 in 1816; by 1846 the figure had risen to some 214,857, and in 1875 to some 339,790. The Jewish population had nearly tripled and, for Treitschke, "this could only be explained if one assumed a strong Jewish immigration, and this in fact can be shown in figures for the period when the religious affiliation of the immigrants was still officially published".[30]

The latter was actually false, since there had never been gross immigration statistics showing religious affiliation. Furthermore, Treitschke made an unfair comparison, since Prussia had grown massively both in territory and in population. The occupation of Hanover, Hesse and Schleswig-Holstein in 1866 had increased the Jewish population of Prussia by roughly 50,000. As Neumann explained later, these new provinces contributed more than 16% to the Jewish population of Prussia.[31]

On 2nd December 1879 Moritz Lazarus gave a speech to the general assembly of the *Hochschule für die Wissenschaft des Judentums* entitled 'Was ist national?'. In the speech he focused on the elements that give a nation its identity, stressing that it was language and culture that constituted a people or a nation rather than religion or descent. In early January 1880 he published this speech as a booklet with an appendix on Jewish migration.[32] In the appendix Lazarus remarked that the fear of a Jewish mass immigration had its historical precedent in the 1850s. In 1859 Salomon Neumann had already published a study on this issue.[33] He was able to prove that there, until 1843, there has only been a Jewish net immigration, after which there had been a net emigration of Jewish people. Although there had been no similar study of migration since 1855, merely comparing population change and natural increase rates showed a Jewish net emigration for this period as well. Lazarus submitted percentage figures for Jews in the total population during this period. The figure for 1875 showed a low of 1.322%, compared with the peak of 1.377% in 1861. Although the minority Jewish population showed a higher fertility rate than the population as a whole, it nevertheless did

---

[29] *Allgemeine Zeitung des Judenthums*, vol. 43, No. 50 (9th December 1879), p. 786.
[30] Heinrich von Treitschke, 'Herr Graetz und sein Judenthum', in *Preußische Jahrbücher*, vol. 44 (1879), p. 662.
[31] See Neumann, *Nachschrift*, p. 20, Table II.
[32] Moritz Lazarus, *Was ist national?*, Berlin 1880.
[33] Neumann's study was published in Ph. Wertheim (ed.), *Kalender und Jahrbuch für die jüdischen Gemeinden Preußens*, vol. 3 (1859). The *Preußische Staatsbibliothek* in Berlin lists the *Kalender* as a casualty of the Second World War. It must be assumed that no other copy of it exists.

not increase in the same proportion as the latter. This cast strong doubts on Treitschke's claim of a Jewish mass immigration.

Treitschke, however, did not comment on the statistical details Lazarus provided. In 'Noch einige Bemerkungen zur Judenfrage' he only referred to the question of national identity.[34] This showed his selective approach to criticism. It also made it clear that statistical evidence *per se* could not influence the discourse. One could argue that neither Graetz nor Lazarus were authorities in the field of statistics, but that does not explain why another non-expert, Treitschke, could deny or ignore statistical evidence and still claim a mass immigration, without loss of integrity.

SALOMON NEUMANN'S *FABEL VON DER JÜDISCHEN MASSENEINWANDERUNG*

In the summer of 1880 Salomon Neumann published the *Fabel von der jüdischen Masseneinwanderung* as a response to Treitschke. It took him until July to complete his demographic study. His publishing house, Leonhard Simion, also printed the *Statistische Jahrbücher der Stadt Berlin*. The aim of the *Fabel* was to use statistics to scientifically disprove the popularly-held belief of a Jewish mass immigration. The first edition was forty-three pages long. The main part consisted of six chapters and a substantial postscript. Five tables in the appendix supported the explanations in the main text. When the first edition was finally published, antisemitic agitation was relatively slight. A second edition, published in November 1880, was only slightly altered, but Neumann had added a sixth table giving gross migration figures, mainly in order to illustrate the third chapter. Finally in the spring of 1881, after the end of the *Berliner Antisemitismusstreit*, Neumann published a twenty-two-page *Nachschrift zur Fabel von der jüdischen Masseneinwanderung*. It contained his responses to the criticism he had received concerning the first two editions. The *Nachschrift* was also published together with the *Fabel von der jüdischen Masseneinwanderung* in its third edition, now containing sixty-six pages.

The *Fabel von der jüdischen Masseneinwanderung* was not aimed at the broader public. In its structure and argumentation it was directed at middle-class intellectuals but Neumann still faced the difficulty of presenting demographic data as a text and with tables to make them comprehensible to laymen in the field of statistics. Yet he wanted to avoid subjective judgements or interpretations. This rationale resulted in shifting all commentaries into the postscript. Thus the tables of the appendix served not only to illustrate but also to verify Neumann's research.

Neumann had to overcome certain difficulties. Firstly, there were no specific statistics available on Jewish immigration to Prussia, and Neumann had to extrapolate these figures from the official census data. In the first two and in the last

---

[34]See Heinrich von Treitschke, 'Noch einige Bemerkungen zur Judenfrage', in *Preußische Jahrbücher*, vol. 45 (1880), p. 92.

chapters of the main part of the *Fabel von der jüdischen Masseneinwanderung* Neumann used only data of this kind. These chapters were the most readily comprehensible and they came close to Neumann's wish to be objective. Chapters three to five seemed to be more artificial and were harder to understand. In these chapters Neumann combined different statistics to obtain absolute figures for the rates of immigration, divided into different religious denominations. A second difficulty was caused by a change of policy within the *Königlich Preußisches Statistisches Bureau*. In the census of 1875 the statistical office had not collated denominational data. Instead they calculated the parochial figures from the population register. Since one could not obtain net migration data from these figures, Neumann had to restrict his study to the last census with a religious count, the 1871 one. The third problem was to produce comparable data with regard to the massive territorial gains of Prussia in the nineteenth century. The acquisition of Lichtenstein in the 1830s and Hohenzollern in the 1850s increased the number of Prussian Jews by only some 1,500, so Neumann disregarded them. The impact of the annexation of Hanover, Hesse and Schleswig-Holstein, as mentioned above, was immense. Neumann decided to restrict the study to the *alte Landesteile* of Prussia. The population figures for the period of 1867 to 1871, therefore, excluded the newly-acquired Prussian provinces.

Neumann used only official data, analysing and evaluating the censuses of 1822 to 1871 and the respective vital statistics. He also used the *Statistik der kontrollierten Wanderung*. This type of statistic had been introduced in Prussia only in 1844. Although it provided gross migration figures, the figures did not specify religious denomination. The percentage of Jewish migration had to be estimated. A comparison with the change in the balance of the population made it clear that the *Statistik der kontrollierten Wanderung* was incomplete, and that it showed incorrect figures. Thus, Neumann stated, the use of figures for population change was "the best and indeed the only method to quantify growth and decline caused by migration".[35] Neumann explained this particular demographic method at the beginning of the first chapter:

> "In the calulation of population the increase of population from one census to the next is compared with the excess of births over deaths. If the increase is higher than this natural increase, the growth in the balance denotes net population increase caused by immigration. If the increase is lower than the natural increase, the decline in the balance denotes net population loss caused by emigration. So it is not the figure of gross immigration or emigration that is shown in the calculation but rather the surplus of one over the other."[36]

---

[35] Neumann, *Fabel*, p. 15.
[36] "In den Bevölkerungsbilanzen wird der zwischen zwei Volkszählungen stattgehabte Bevölkerungszuwachs verglichen mit dem Geburtenüberschuß während der Zählungsperiode. Ist der Zuwachs größer als der Geburtenüberschuß, so beziffert das plus in der Bevölkerungsbilanz Bevölkerungszunahme durch Mehreinwanderung; ist der Zuwachs kleiner als der Geburtenüberschuß, so beziffert das minus in der Bevölkerungsbilanz Bevölkerungsabnahme durch Mehrauswanderung. Nicht also die Ein- oder Auswanderung an sich, sondern der Überschuß der einen über die andere wird in der Bilanz gemessen", Neumann, *Fabel*, p. 5.

STRUCTURE AND CONTENT OF THE *FABEL VON DER JÜDISCHEN MASSENEINWANDERUNG*

The first two chapters of the *Fabel von der jüdischen Masseneinwanderung* deal solely with figures from censuses and the vital statistics. In his first chapter on the immigration and emigration of Jews in Prussia from 1822 to 1871, Neumann analysed the increase of population in conjunction with net migration. He compared the figures of the total population with that of the Jewish section of the population.

Acknowledging the lower standards of early Prussian censuses, Neumann subdivided the fifty-nine-year-long period into one section covering 1822–1840 and another section covering 1840–1871. Tables A and B of the appendix illustrated the text of this chapter. Table A showed the figures for the total population and its Jewish section according to the censuses and natural increases. It also showed, by comparing the difference between the two, the net migration. Table B showed the percentage of change.

For the period 1822 to 1840, Neumann stated that a similar increase in the Prussian population and in its Jewish section was caused by immigration of about 6.4% and 6.61% respectively. The fact that the Jewish proportion of the total population had increased since 1822 was due to higher fertility rather than to immigration. Neumann analysed the second period, from 1840 to 1871, more thoroughly. He observed that this period was "characterised by a predominance of net emigration".[37] The Jewish population had lost half a percent of its number, three times as much as the total population. Since 1843 it had experienced growing net emigration. Overall, the Prussian population had lost a total of 432,287 people. Applied to the figures of 1840 this indicated a share of 2.9%. The Jewish sub-group, in contrast, had lost 18% or a total of 35,106 people. As a result, for the whole period of 1822 to 1871:

> "First of all: if and when the Prussian population increased through immigration at all, the ratio between Jewish and total immigration was exactly the same as the ratio between Jews and the population as a whole, no more and no less. Moreover, immigration plays absolutely no part in the greater increase of the Jewish population. Secondly, since then and insofar as the growth in the Prussian population is hampered by emigration, the Jewish population has suffered a relatively stronger decline than the population as a whole."[38]

Methodologically absolutely correctly, Neumann drew attention to the difference between cross-border migration and internal migration. In the second chapter on the migratory movement of the Jewish population within Prussia and their emigration with regard to the provinces and districts of the state, he

---

[37] Neumann, *Fabel*, p.7.
[38] "Erstens: solange und so weit die preußische Bevölkerung überhaupt durch Einwanderung sich vermehrt hat, war die jüdische Bevölkerung an der Einwanderung genau in demselben Verhältnisse, wie die Gesamtbevölkerung, nicht mehr und nicht weniger, betheiligt. An der stärkeren Vermehrung der jüdischen Bevölkerung dagegen ist die Einwanderung absolut unbetheiligt. Zweitens: seitdem und soweit die preußische Bevölkerung in ihrer Vermehrung durch Auswanderung gehemmt wird, hat die jüdische Bevölkerung in ihrer Vermehrung eine verhältnißmäßig viel stärkere Beeinträchtigung erlitten, als die Gesamtbevölkerung", Neumann, *Fabel*, p. 9.

thus dealt with demographic calculations. Neumann covered the period from 1856 to 1871 and illustrated it with Table C of the appendix, showing the figures for the nine provinces plus the city of Berlin.[39] All nine provinces of the Prussian state were areas of Jewish emigration and only the city of Berlin was a destination area. From 1856 to 1871 a net number of 41,907 Jews had left the provinces. The province of Poznan alone contributed 63.5% of these "outmigrants". This proved wrong the claim of antisemites that Poznan was a destination area for Jewish migrants. Only the city of Berlin showed an increase in population from migration: 19,012 of the 36,015 Berlin Jews had migrated to Berlin since 1856. Using listings of the *Statistisches Bureau der Stadt Berlin* Neumann demonstrated that the increase of the Jewish population was predominately due to migrants from other Prussian provinces. The balance of roughly 42,000 "outmigrants" from the provinces and around 19,000 "inmigrants" in Berlin was the minimum figure of gross emigration. In other words, 23,000 Jews had left Prussia altogether since 1856. Other German states such as Bavaria showed a similar Jewish migratory pattern. The main destination for German-Jewish emigration was the United States.

In chapter three, on the question of Jewish immigration, Neumann explained that, due to the lack of complete gross migration figures, Jewish immigration figures had to be estimated from the official statistical tables. Main sources were again the summaries of population change. In conjunction with the incomplete *Statistik der kontrollierten Wanderung* an estimate was made of up to 250,000 immigrants of all denominations to Prussia for the period 1844 to 1871.[40] To extract a Jewish proportion from this total immigration figure, Neumann used a factor of 1.3%. This was roughly the percentage of the Jewish sub-group in the Prussian population. He substantiated this with the constantly higher emigration ratio of the Jewish population. As a result he calculated around 3,250 Jewish immigrants over a period of twenty-seven years.[41] It was methodologically dubious to assume that the denominational proportion of the Prussian population would also match that of the immigrants. The figure was clearly underestimated and should have been four times as high. The results of a special immigration table of the census of 1880 showed this and Neumann acknowledged it in his own second demographic study, *Zur Statistik der Juden in Preussen*.[42] It should be noted that none of Neumann's critics attacked him on this methodlogical shortcoming. Despite

---

[39] Neumann did not subdivide the twin province of Prussia into East Prussia and West Prussia because it was not common practice. Nevertheless, in his second demographic study he subdivided them into both provinces and districts. See Salomon Neumann, *Zur Statistik der Juden in Preussen. Zweiter Beitrag aus den amtlichen Veröffentlichungen*, Berlin 1884, Tables II–VII.

[40] Neumann, *Fabel*, p. 16. The census of 1871 registered 182,000 foreign-born inhabitants in Prussia. This was the most likely figure. Nevertheless, Neumann increased the figure to 320,000 in the following editions. Neumann, *Fabel von der jüdischen Masseneinwanderung . . . .*, 3rd edn., Berlin 1881 (subsequently quoted as Neumann, 3rd edn.), p. 18.

[41] See Neumann, *Fabel*, p. 16. In the following editions he excluded the period of 1844 to 1846. Once again he obtained a figure of 250,000. In contrast to the first edition his factor of 1.4% provided a result of 3,500 Jewish immigrants. Unfortunately, he did not give an explicit reason for this exclusion. See Neumann, 3rd edn., p. 18.

[42] See Neumann, *Statistik der Juden*, pp. 16–20.

142   *Günter Regneri*

Neumann's mistake in this case, it must be noted that he was right to call mass immigration a *Fabel*. A figure of some 14,000 Jewish immigrants from Russia and Austria within roughly one generation was hardly massive.

In the same chapter Neumann also dealt with the question of whether immigration and emigration necessarily occurred simultaneously. He answered this question strictly in the negative, referring to the accounts of population change and the *Statistik der kontrollierten Wanderung*. Both ruled out a simultaneous massive immigration and emigration.

In the fourth chapter, on the hypothesis of a Jewish mass immigration over the Eastern borders of Prussia, as well as in the fifth, on the denomination of both foreign-born inhabitants and foreign nationals, Neumann analysed the proportions of foreign-born residents to the Prussian population as a whole. The basis for his calculation was the census of 1871. On 1st December 1871, the day of the census, 182,162 foreign-born, non-German inhabitants, regardless of their denomination, were counted in Prussia. Most of them lived in the border provinces in the west, the north and the east and 72,453 of them lived in the eastern provinces of Prussia, Poznan and Silesia. Only 18,922 of them were foreign nationals. For Neumann these figures, compared with a total population of roughly twenty million, showed clearly "to what extent a foreign non-German element is added to the population at all. For the three Eastern provinces the comparison shows that in their population such an element of foreign nationality is only very marginal".[43] The percentage of foreign-born inhabitants in the Prussian population was 0.74%; in the provinces of Silesia and Prussia it was slightly higher, with respectively 0.96% and 0.83%, although in the province of Poznan it was below the overall rate of only 0.66%. In contrast to these provinces, relatively more foreign-born inhabitants lived in the northern province of Schleswig, as well as in the Rhine province in the west. The Rhine province tallied 1.24% foreign-born and Schleswig 2.6%. Seen in this light "not the East but rather the West was the right place to speak of a 'massiveness' ".[44]

In the fifth chapter Neumann compared the figures of foreign-born individuals with the Jewish population in the three eastern provinces. Referring to the detailed survey in a table of the appendix, he concluded:

> "The statistical swoop throughout the 150 districts of the Eastern provinces found no massive immigration anywhere. In the few, single places where foreign immigration was noticeable to a somewhat larger degree, Jews were either not present or else they did not constitute a significant proportion of the foreigners... And finally, in the not insignificant number of districts and particularly municipalities with a proportionately unusually high Jewish population, there was barely any trace of foreign immigration."[45]

---

[43]"... in welcher Ausdehnung überhaupt ein fremdes, nichtdeutsches Element der heimischen Bevölkerung beigemischt ist, und für die drei östlichen Provinzen ergiebt der Vergleich, daß in ihrer Bevölkerung ein solches Element fremder Nationalität verhältnismäßig sehr schwach vertreten ist", Neumann, *Fabel*, p. 18.
[44]*Ibid.*, p. 18.
[45]"Die statistische Razzia – kreuz und quer durch die 150 Kreise der östlichen Provinzen unternommen – ist nirgends auf eine massenhafte Einwanderung gestoßen. Wo an einigen wenigen, vereinzel-

Salomon Neumann and the Berliner Antisemitismusstreit 143

Having explained that the Jewish population had not increased because of immigration, it was logical for Neumann to emphasise its natural increase. He listed the figures of population changes in conjunction with the natural increase. The percentage of Jews in the Prussian population had risen from 1.241% in 1822 to 1.341% in 1849. It then reached its peak in 1861 with 1.377%, before falling to 1.334% in 1867. In 1871 it had risen again to 1.344%, thus almost matching the figure for districts in 1849. This proportional increase was due to a continuously higher Jewish fertility rate compared with that of the total population. However, the natural increase of the Jewish population showed a relative decline since 1858, bringing it more into line with that of the population as a whole. The slight proportional increase in the period 1867 to 1871 was, according to Neumann, caused by the exceptionally high net emigration rate of the Prussian population.

In the postscript, Neumann did not submit new data. Instead he reviewed a publication of the *Königlich Preußisches Statistisches Bureau* on the migration issue. In 1879, the office had published a *Rückblick auf die Bewegung der Bevölkerung im preußischen Staate* in its official series *Preußische Statistik*.[46] The editor of the volume was a certain A. Freiherr von Fiercks. Neumann accused him of prejudice against the Jewish population. In his inconsistent essay, Fiercks identified four reasons for the increase in the Jewish population, each contradicting the others. At first he stated that the large increase in the Jewish population was "partly the result of the Jewish longevity, partly (in earlier times) the consequence of immigration".[47] A few pages later he declared that the Jewish population increased "mainly by immigration, and to be precise from the Russian Empire and Austro-Hungary".[48] However, further down the same page and once again a few pages later, he stressed the impact of the extraordinary lower mortality rate.[49] Neumann regarded this as a subjective judgement refuted by official data: statistical evidence proved that immigration was not the cause of the Jewish population increase. Statisticians should abstain from such "subjective", personally prejudiced, comments. Furthermore, the statistical office was wrong to legitimise such comments by publishing them in a volume of *Preußische Statistik*. In conclusion, he demanded an impartial role for the statistical office: "Informing the public is the duty of statistics and of official statistics even more. It is ... imperative at any time."[50]

---

ten Punkten fremde Einwanderung in etwas stärkerem Grade bemerkbar war, waren die Juden überhaupt nicht vorhanden, oder waren an dem fremden Elemente keinesfalls in irgend welchem besonderen Grade beteiligt.... In einer nicht geringen Zahl von Kreisen endlich, und insbesondere von Gemeinden, mit einer unverhältnismäßig starken jüdischen Bevölkerung ist von fremder Einwanderung kaum die leiseste Spur vorhanden", Neumann, *Fabel*, p. 21.

[46] *Preußische Statistik (Amtliches Quellenwerk)*, vol. 48A: *Rückblick auf die Bewegung der Bevölkerung im preußischen Staate während des Zeitraums vom Jahre 1816 bis zum Jahre 1874*, ed. by. A. Frh. von Fiercks, Berlin 1879.
[47] *Ibid.*, p. 22.
[48] *Ibid.*, p. 27.
[49] See *ibid.*, pp. 27, 29.
[50] Neumann, *Fabel*, p. 31.

PATTERNS OF ARGUMENTATION

The axiom of scientific objectivity runs like a thread through the *Fabel von der jüdischen Masseneinwanderung* and its *Nachschrift*. Neumann believed this was fundamental for a debate with an educated opponent. Although he believed statistics should be used for political ends, he opposed any attempt to predetermine statistical results to draw up state policy. For Neumann statistical observation had to be scientifically founded and measurable. And this was, of course, important for the question of how statistics classified the Jewish population. Demographic surveys on Jews were only legitimate within a framework of statistics on denomination. Thus Neumann questioned the basis of all ethnic statistics.[51] He also believed the racial category was unscientific because it was impossible to enumerate. The use of this category in volume 48A of *Preußische Statistik* deeply concerned him. He saw it as an acknowledgement of racial differentiation by the official statisticians:

> "Here, a Jewish race is juxtaposed with a German race for the first time in Prussian statistics. Hitherto, in all statistical surveys on nationalities in the Prussian state Jews are categorised as Germans. Of course, all these surveys are based on the mother tongue and language spoken in the family."[52]

Prussia (as well as the German Empire) was by no means an ethnically homogenous state. Ten percent of all Prussian citizens alone were Poles, and there was also a considerable number of Danes, Dutch and Belgians. The statisticians categorised them as national minorities, based on the language spoken. Jews, therefore, were not a national minority. If they did not speak high German they spoke Yiddish; a language statisticians regarded as a German dialect. In statistical terms, Jewishness did not appear as a nationality, only as a denomination. Race as a category contradicted this long-held statistical practice.

Another important issue for Neumann was the accurate distinction between internal and transnational migration. This distinction enabled Neumann to refute Treitschke's claim of a Jewish mass immigration while not denying an internal migratory movement that had Berlin as its main destination area. Any inaccuracy in dealing with these different categories of migration jeopardised scientific objectivity.

Accurate categorisation also had a political dimension. Emigration had effects on foreign policy, whereas internal migration only affected domestic policies in that all migrants were citizens. In constitutional terms no specific group of internal migrants could be denied their civil rights, including the right of free movement.

Neumann fiercely disputed the term "polnische Juden". This linguistic conflation of two different population groups was a battle cry of the new nationalist

---

[51]*Ibid.*, p.14.
[52]"Zum ersten Male wird hier in der preußischen Statistik die jüdische Raçe der deutschen gegenübergestellt. In allen bisherigen statistischen Untersuchungen über die Nationalitäten im preußischen Staate, die allerdings alle die Mutter- und Familiensprache zu ihrer Grundlage haben, sind die Juden als Deutsche gezählt worden," *ibid.*, pp. 30–31.

movement which propagated an ethnically homogeneous population. In statistical terms the connection made no sense. Poles were a national minority distinguishable by their language and were predominantly Catholic. If they possessed no Prussian citizenship, the statistics did not count them as Poles but as foreign nationals, that is, as Russians or Austrians. Jews were not counted as a national minority, and their religious denomination separated them from the Poles as well. In political terms, however, the term "Polish Jews" served an important purpose. Poles were denounced as *Reichsfeinde* and thus had to suffer severe discrimination. Through the linguistic connection the image of *Reichsfeinde* rubbed off on the Jewish population in the eastern provinces.

THE IMPACT OF THE *FABEL VON DER JÜDISCHEN MASSENEINWANDERUNG* ON THE *BERLINER ANTISEMITISMUSSTREIT*

The *Berliner Antisemitismusstreit* was in a trough when the *Fabel von der jüdischen Masseneinwanderung* was first published in the summer of 1880. In contrast to Graetz and Lazarus, Neumann was eminent in the field of statistics. However, his study had no immediate impact on the debate simply because Treitschke ignored it. The reason why Neumann could not force Treitschke to acknowledge his statistical findings was his relatively inferior status in academic terms. To turn the debate around, another protagonist was needed whose authority matched that of Treitschke. The man who fulfilled this task was Theodor Mommsen.[53]

Just before the elections to the Berlin *Stadtverordnetenversammlung* in the autumn of 1880 the debate flared up again. The united antisemites of the Stoecker movement and the conservatives managed to prevent the re-election of the Liberal Jewish chairman of the city council, Straßmann. Now Theodor Mommsen took a stand in the controversy. He signed the Declaration of Notables that was published in different Berlin newspapers between the 12th and 14th November 1880. The second wave of the *Berliner Antisemitismusstreit* actually started with a newspaper clash between Treitschke and Mommsen. In an open letter to the *Nationalzeitung*, published on 19th November 1880, the latter made it clear that the declaration was aimed at Treitschke. Treitschke responded with a letter to the *Post*, which was published two days later. He denied all the accusations made in the declaration and pronounced that Mommsen's response might "perhaps intimidate a few weak souls, but he does not contribute in any way to calming public agitation".[54] Such arrogant behaviour had proved successful in dealing with Treitschke's predominately Jewish critics. Now the course of the *Berliner Antisemitismusstreit* changed considerably. Treitschke was to learn that Mommsen was

---

[53]On Mommsen's position on Jewry and antisemitism, see Liebeschütz, pp. 192–205; Christhard Hoffmann, *Juden und Judentum im Werk deutscher Althistoriker des 19. und 20. Jahrhunderts*, Leiden 1988, pp. 87–132.
[54]Heinrich von Treitschke, 'Eine Erwiderung', quoted in Boehlich, p. 211.

even more influential than he was himself when the latter managed to isolate him politically within the senior staff of the University of Berlin.

In November 1880, Neumann published the second edition of the *Fabel von der jüdischen Masseneinwanderung*. In the preface he wrote: "The second ... edition is published at a time when the catchword 'Jewish mass immigration' is once again heard across all the battle-lines of Jew-baiting. Again it is conjured up as a spectre for the masses."[55] Not only did the antisemitic agitation reach its climax, the *Fabel von der jüdischen Masseneinwanderung* also reached the zenith of its popularity. On 12th November 1880 the *Vossische Zeitung* told its readers that Neumann's study had "destroyed the foundation-stone of the notorious Jew-baiting Petition".[56] Only a few days later, on 20th November 1880, Rudolf Virchow used the *Fabel von der jüdischen Masseneinwanderung* to support his arguments in a debate on the "Jewish Question" in the *Preußisches Abgeordnetenhaus*. He accused the conservatives of stirring up the masses with the threat of an alleged immigration, although Neumann had shown that this immigration did not exist. On the second day of the debate, on 22nd November 1880, the representative for Breslau, Alexander Meyer, also referred to the *Fabel von der jüdischen Masseneinwanderung*.[57]

Mommsen published *Auch ein Wort über unser Judenthum* in November 1880. His main attack was against Treitschke's view that the German nation needed internal and external enemies to define itself. Mommsen also demanded the acknowledgement of the *Fabel von der jüdischen Masseneinwanderung*:

> "The crux of Herr von Treitschke's articles is the Jewish mass immigration across the Eastern border. It is well known that Herr Neumann has shown this to be a complete fabrication by using statistics in a compelling way. Herr von Treitschke says – and this is also well-known – that he retracts nothing. Another convinced antisemite, by contrast, Herr Adolf Wagner, who had proclaimed the same opinion, has frankly admitted that he was wrong on this issue."[58]

Treitschke was now on the defensive. In December 1880 he published an 'Erwiderung an Herrn Th. Mommsen' in his *Preußische Jahrbücher*. He tried to gloss over the arrogant remarks he had made in his open letter to the *Post* and also made a statement concerning the *Fabel von der jüdischen Masseneinwanderung*:

> "Herr Mommsen accuses me of not retracting my claims about Jewish mass immigration. I simply counter that I do not know the book by Neumann which he is recommending. Since he is recommending it, I shall read it and, if I am convinced by the

---

[55] Salomon Neumann, 'Zur zweiten Auflage', quoted in Neumann, 3rd edn., p. 3.
[56] *Vossische Zeitung*, No. 315 (12th November 1880), section 2, p. 2.
[57] *Die Judenfrage vor dem Preußischen Landtage*, pp. 28 and 45. Heckling from the benches of the *Zentrumsfraktion* showed that Neumann's study was already well known in these circles.
[58] "Daß die jüdische Masseneinwanderung über die Ostgrenze, welche Hr. v. Treitschke an die Spitze seiner Judenartikel gestellt hat, eine reine Erfindung ist, hat Hr. Neumann bekanntlich an Hand der Statistik in schlagender Weise dargethan, und, wenn Hr. v. Treitschke, wie ebenfalls bekannt, von dem, was er gesagt hat, kein Wort zurücknimmt, so hat dafür Hr. Adolf Wagner, auch ein entschiedener Antisemit, der dieselbe Meinung ausgesprochen hatte, unumwunden zugestanden, daß er hierin geirrt habe." Theodor Mommsen, 'Auch ein Wort über unser Judenthum (1880)', quoted in Boehlich, p. 215.

argument, then these *Jahrbücher* will not hesitate to correct this claim which is, in fact, not central to the dispute."[59]

This announcement was remarkable. The *Fabel von der jüdischen Masseneinwanderung* was already wel known, even in antisemitic circles. Adolf Wagner, a professor of political economics at the University of Berlin, had already reviewed the book in his *Zeitschrift für die gesammte Staatswissenschaft*.[60] He acknowledged that there was no significant Jewish immigration from Russia and Austria. For "cultural reasons", however, Wagner preferred to use the term "immigration" when in fact internal migration was at issue.[61] Treitschke had commented on the November debate, in which Neumann's study had been mentioned twice, in his article 'Zur inneren Lage am Jahresschlusse' in the December issue of the *Preußische Jahrbücher*.[62] Treitschke pretended not to have read a book concerning a major issue of *his* dispute which had been widely discussed in public.

Eventually, in January 1881, Treitschke published a review in the *Preußische Jahrbücher*. This article on 'Die jüdische Einwanderung in Deutschland' was the last one he wrote in the *Berliner Antisemitismusstreit*. Treitschke had to admit that he was wrong on the issue, although he did not do so unreservedly. In his review he confirmed Neumann's findings of a Jewish net emigration since 1843. In his own defence he referred to non-Prussian demography that was allegedly more complete on the issue of immigration. The Saxon metropolis of Leipzig, he claimed, had seen an extraordinary immigration of Jews from Eastern Europe and he supplied selected figures on the Eastern European birthplaces of the Leipzig Jews. His definition of Eastern Europe included not only Russia and Austria but also the Prussian provinces of Silesia and Poznan.[63] It was clearly a rearguard action to avoid losing his argument on the issue.

This review marked the end of the *Berliner Antisemitismusstreit*. During the course of the debate Treitschke had only responded to a tiny number of critics: the Jewish historians Heinrich Graetz and Harry Breslau; the psychologist Moritz Lazarus; the philosopher Hermann Cohen; the convert priest Paulus Cassel; Theodor Mommsen; and – last but not least – Salomon Neumann. It is evident that Neumann's part in the controversy was fundamentally linked to Mommsen. The latter attacked Treitschke on the politically weighted issue of nationality, and he forced him to take the statistical argument seriously that

---

[59]"Herr Mommsen wirft mir vor, daß ich meine Behauptungen über die jüdische Einwanderung nicht zurückgenommen habe. Ich erwidere einfach, daß ich das von ihm empfohlene Neumann'sche Buch nicht kenne. Da er die Schrift empfiehlt, so werde ich sie lesen; und sollte ich ihre Beweisführung stichhaltig finden, so werden diese Jahrbücher nicht anstehen, eine Behauptung, die mit dem Kerne der Streitfrage wenig zu thun hat, zu berichtigen." Heinrich von Treitschke, 'Erwiderung an Herrn Th. Mommsen', in *Preußische Jahrbücher*, vol. 46 (1880), p. 662.
[60]Adolf Wagner, 'Dr. S. Neumann, die Fabel von der jüdischen Masseneinwanderung', in *Zeitschrift für die gesammte Staatswissenschaft*, 36 (1880), pp. 777–783.
[61]*Ibid.*, p. 780.
[62]Heinrich von Treitschke, 'Zur inneren Lage am Jahresschlusse', in *Preußische Jahrbücher*, vol. 46 (1880), p. 644
[63]See Treitschke, 'Jüdische Einwanderung in Deutschland'.

Treitschke himself had introduced into the debate. Neumann's task was to defeat Treitschke using empirical data. In the scientific area of statistics Treitschke could not win the argument against Neumann. At that point his only option, in order to avoid losing face, was a retreat from the debate.

AFTER THE END OF THE *BERLINER ANTISEMITISMUSSTREIT*

After the *Berliner Antisemitismusstreit* ended in January 1881, the antisemitic propaganda concerning a Jewish mass immigration did not stop. Neumann published the *Nachschrift*, as well as the third edition of the *Fabel von der jüdischen Masseneinwanderung*, in the spring of 1881. He reproached Treitschke for his statistical shortcomings and also dealt with the responses of the political economist Adolf Wagner and, once again, with the *Königlich Preußisches Statistisches Bureau*. Neumann was disappointed by the refusal of the statistical office to openly admit that one of its official publications contained unscientific and contradictory statements on Jewish immigration.[64]

Treitschke did not comment again on the issue of Jewish immigration for more than two years. Only when Eugen von Bergmann's study *Zur Geschichte der Entwickelung deutscher, polnischer, und jüdischer Bevölkerung in der Provinz Posen seit 1824* was published in 1883 did he take up the issue again. In a two-page note Bergmann published extensive migratory figures for the Silesian city of Breslau and the province of East Prussia, and launched a polemic against Mommsen and Neumann. Treitschke reviewed the book in the *Preußische Jahrbücher* in an article entitled 'Die jüdische Einwanderung in Preußen'. He gleefully revoked his statements of January 1881.[65] A closer look at Bergmann's study, however, does not show the refutation of the *Fabel von der jüdischen Masseneinwanderung*. His references to Breslau and East Prussia proved superficial. His figures, added up, showed no extensive immigration at all. Methodologically the book showed certain avoidable weaknesses. Bergmann, as he admitted, did not distinguish between internal and external migration: "The terms emigration and immigration are here – contrary to common usage – used in a specific way to include the so-called in-migration and out-migration (i. e. the migration from one area of the Prussian state to another)."[66]

Bergmann spoke of three nations living in the province of Poznan – Germans, Poles and Jews – but he was not able to provide statistical evidence for his classification. Therefore he had "to use primarily denominational figures instead of those for the nationalities".[67] In contrast to Neumann he used not only official statistics but also the demographic calculations of Friedrich Julius Neumann, a professor of political economics at Tübingen University. Nevertheless, his study

---

[64]See Neumann, *Nachschrift*.
[65]See Heinrich von Treitschke, 'Die jüdische Einwanderung in Preußen', in *Preußische Jahrbücher*, vol. 52 (1883), pp. 534–538.
[66]Eugen von Bergmann, *Zur Geschichte der Entwicklung deutscher, polnischer, und jüdischer Bevölkerung in der Provinz Posen seit 1824*, Tübingen 1883, p. 313, note 170.
[67]Bergmann, p. 28.

showed only those results Salomon Neumann had already published: a Jewish out-migration from Poznan to Berlin. When describing the Prussian population in general, Bergmann employed the already discredited volume 48A of the *Preußische Statistik*. Despite – or even because of – its deficiency, antisemites used it as "scientific proof" of a Jewish mass immigration.

In the long run the *Fabel von der jüdischen Masseneinwanderung* could not neutralise the antisemitic claim of Jewish mass immigration. It was only in the specific environment of the second wave of the *Berliner Antisemitismusstreit* that its scientific argumentation became powerful enough to help end the debate.

RUDOLF VIRCHOW AND THE ANTHROPOLOGICAL MASS SURVEY OF GERMAN SCHOOLCHILDREN

A comparison with another attempt at eliminating unscientific antisemitic ideology from scientific and political discourse proves revealing. In the mid-1880s, Rudolf Virchow challenged the pseudo-scientific claims of antisemites in the field of anthropology. Like Neumann he used a statistically-backed, rational argumentation to do so, publishing sophisticated results of an anthropological mass survey of German schoolchildren. This survey, he believed, would end "the controversy regarding the existence of pure Aryans and Jews".[68]

Virchow was one of the most eminent German scientists and a highly respected politician.[69] His life connected with Neumann's at many points. Virchow was slightly younger than Neumann and, like him, came from the Prussian province of Pomerania. He was born in 1821 in the small town of Schievelbein. After studying medicine at the Berlin military academy, the *Pépinière*, he became a houseman at the Berlin *Charité*, where he took his examinations in 1843 and his *habilitation* in 1847. Virchow actively participated in the Revolution in Berlin, and from June 1848 to July 1849 he was joint editor of the *Medicinische Reform*. "Many of the ideas which Virchow aggressively and often successfully promoted and put into action in 1848, had been conceived and felicitously worded by Salomon Neumann."[70] Accused of "democratic tendencies", Virchow lost his job at the *Charité* at Easter 1849. He went to Würzburg, where he was offered a professorship of medicine at the university. There he developed his concept of cellular pathology, which revolutionised medical science by replacing the old concept of humoral pathology. In 1856 he was invited to the *Friedrich-Wilhelms-Universität* in Berlin, where he set up an institute of pathology. His friend

---

[68] George L. Mosse, *Toward the Final Solution. A History of European Racism*, 2nd edn., Madison 1985, p. 92.
[69] On Virchow's involvement in politics, see Erwin H. Ackerknecht, *Rudolf Virchow. Arzt, Politiker, Anthropologe*, Stuttgart 1957; Arnold Bauer, *Rudolf Virchow – der politische Arzt*, Berlin 1982; Anja Thybusch, *Rudolf Virchow. Parlamentarische Tätigkeit und Gesundheitspolitik im Reichstag und Preußischen Abgeordnetenhaus*, Ph.D. diss., University of Kiel 1989.
[70] Wladimir Eliasberg, 'Rudolf Virchow and his Friends Heinrich Schliemann and Salomon Neumann', in *Proceedings of the Rudolf Virchow Medical Society in the City of New York*, vol. XXVI (1967), p. 67.

Neumann urged him to stand for a seat in the *Berliner Stadtverordnetenversammlung*. They were both elected in 1859 for the first time and Virchow kept his seat until he died. Together with Neumann he was a member of the municipal statistical committee. In 1861 he founded the *Deutsche Fortschrittspartei* and was elected to the *Preußisches Abgeordnetenhaus*, where he represented his Berlin constituency for forty-one years and defended his seat repeatedly against the antisemite Adolf Stoecker. During the debate on the "Jewish Question" in the *Preußisches Abgeordnetenhaus* in November 1880, it was Virchow who rejected the claim of a Jewish mass immigration, referring to the *Fabel von der jüdischen Masseneinwanderung*. From 1880 to 1893 he was a member of the Reichstag. He died as a result of an accident in 1902.

At the end of the nineteenth century Virchow's influence in German anthropology was even more important than in German medical science. In 1870 he was one of the founders of the *Berliner Anthropologische Gesellschaft*. A year later he initiated an anthropological mass survey covering more than 6.7 million German pupils, including around 75,000 Jewish children. With the exception of the city of Hamburg, where the education authorities did not allow the survey to be conducted for constitutional reasons, it covered all German schoolchildren. Virchow developed a questionnaire to be filled in by the teachers. It contained all possible combinations of hair, skin and eye colours and asked for the age of the pupils surveyed.

The complete results, with detailed statistical tables for the different German regions, were published in 1886.[71] By that time the initial trigger for the survey, a publication by the French anthropologist De Quatrefages, had lost its importance. Now the "Jewish Question" was again high on the agenda. Thus it was understandable that Virchow showed the results of the Jewish pupils separately. It became evident that the idea of predominantly blond and blue-eyed German people was a myth. In not a single region were Germans "racially pure". Only 31.8% proved to be blond, blue-eyed and fair skinned (*Blonde*). 14.05% had dark hair and eyes and brownish skin (*Brünette*). Every second pupil (54.15%) was of a mixed type. The pure blond type was to be found more often in northern Germany, whereas in certain parts of Bavaria their share was only 18.44%. Although the Jewish pupils, who made up 1.11% of all observed, had fewer *Blonde* (only 11.17%) but a higher number of *Brünette* (42.0%), Virchow insisted that this did not affect the composition of the German schoolchildren significantly. Excluding the Jewish children only reduced the share of *Brünette* of German pupils to 13.73%.[72] In the following years, Virchow used the findings of the survey – and of course his authority – to slow down the spread of the racial myth within German anthropology.[73] Nevertheless, Virchow could not stop unscientific racial theories spreading within the general public. Antisemites were determined not to accept his findings. Since they could not contest the

---

[71] Rudolf Virchow, 'Gesamtbericht über die von der deutschen anthropologischen Gesellschaft veranlassten Erhebungen über Farbe der Haut, der Haare und der Augen der Schulkinder in Deutschland', in *Archiv für Anthropologie*, vol. 16 (January 1886), pp. 275–475.
[72] See Virchow, 'Gesamtbericht', pp. 298–300.
[73] See Ackerknecht, *Rudolf Virchow*, p. 195.

results of the survey by scientific methods they claimed that Virchow "was either a slave of the Jews and part of the Jewish world conspiracy, or indeed himself of Jewish blood".[74]

The similarities between Virchow's and Neumann's efforts to combat antisemitic ideologies are striking. They both tried to influence the public debate by providing scientific, statistical evidence. Both Virchow and Neumann believed this way of arguing to be successful. In reality they only succeeded in influencing public debate where the scientific argumentation was connected to an important event or authority in the *Berliner Antisemitisusstreit* and in the *Deutsche Anthropologische Gesellschaft*. Neither Neumann nor the very famous and highly respected Virchow were able to refute unscientific racist and antisemitic ideologies within the broader public.

"JEWISH MASS IMMIGRATION" IN DEMOGRAPHY AND POLITICS

The demography of Prussia up to 1880 shows that the influx of foreigners was marginal. At the time of the *Berliner Antisemitismusstreit*, the number of non-German foreign nationals of all denominations was actually declining, both in absolute and in relative terms. Their number fell from 120,993 (0.47% of the total population) in 1875 to 98,959 (0.36%).[75] Any significant immigration of Jews from the East only happened after the pogroms that followed the assassination of Tsar Alexander II in 1881. Yet the vast majority of these migrants passed through Germany rather than settling.[76] German authorities and police were also determined to prevent illegal immigration into Germany.

The conservative classes and the Bismarck administration deliberately created the spectre of an immigration threat. The official Prussian statisticians acted as auxiliary troops on their behalf. The introduction of special tables on nationality and descent within the publication of the official results of the census of 1st December 1880 points in that direction. As we have seen, the number of foreign nationals was less than 100,000, a figure that clearly disproved the claim of a mass immigration. Reluctant to lose the argument, the *Königlich Preußisches Statistisches Bureau* emphasised the number of 217,511 foreign-born inhabitants in Prussia. Further, they added two tables showing the birthplaces of the Jewish population in the Eastern provinces and selected cities. The overall figure of foreign-born Jews in Prussia was given as 15,940. Applied to a total population of 27 million, Jewish immigrants made up less than 0.06%, of whom 11,512 were born in

---

[74]Mosse, pp. 92–93.

[75]*Preußische Statistik (Amtliches Quellenwerk)*, vol. 66, *Die definitiven Ergebnisse der Volkszählung vom 1. December 1880 im Preußischen Staate*, Berlin 1983, pp. 44–45. The same development was to be seen in the rest of the German Empire. From 1875 to 1880 the number of foreigners fell from 290,799 to 276,057. See *Das Deutsche Reich in gesundheitlicher und demographischer Beziehung*, ed. by Kaiserlichen Gesundheitsamte und vom Kaiserlichen statistischen Amte, Berlin 1912, p. 33.

[76]On the issue of transitional migration, see Michael Just, 'Transitland Kaiserreich. Ost und südosteuropäische Massenauswanderung über deutsche Häfen', in Klaus J. Bade (ed.), *Deutsche im Ausland – Fremde in Deutschland. Migration in Geschichte und Gegenwart*, Munich 1992, pp. 295–302.

Russia and 2,816 in Austria.[77] The table did not specify how many of the foreign-born Jews had already obtained Prussian or any other German citizenship. Neither was it specified how many had a legal residence permit. In his second statistical study, *Zur Statistik der Juden in Preussen*, Neumann criticised the new figures. He accused the official statisticians of creating a new *Judentabelle* mainly for discriminatory purposes.

> "The new table was undoubtedly ... aimed to illustrate the entire Jewish immigration from Russia to Prussia and therefore its title covers the four Eastern provinces. It has thereby incidentally enlarged their territory. Not only are the cities of Berlin and Frankfurt am Main incorporated in the diagram but also the nine Russian Jews in the town of Stolp, just in order not to miss a single Russian Jew."[78]

Soon Neumann's fears proved correct. In 1884, the year his second study was published, 667 Russian nationals of mainly Jewish denomination were expelled from Berlin. In 1885 and 1886 Prussia expelled nearly 32,000 Russian and Austrian citizens, of whom 9000 were Jews.[79] This action must be seen in conjunction with an increasingly anti-Polish, anti-Russian and anti-Jewish naturalisation policy. Since 1871 the Prussian government had impeded the naturalisation of Russian immigrants. After 1881 the Prussian Home Office rejected almost every Jewish application solely on the grounds that the applicants were Jews.[80] As a result, Jewish immigrants continued to have the legal status of foreigners. In other words, the Prussian administration deliberately created a "problem" of Jewish immigration.

Historians often claims that Treitschke had increasing Jewish immigration in mind when he initiated the *Berliner Antisemitismusstreit*. Neubach gives a good example: "The journal *Die Grenzboten* certainly exaggerates, when it calls the Jewish immigration a 'new exodus', but, like Treitschke, it is undoubtedly right, if it rejects Neumann's statement that the mass immigration is a fable."[81] As I have shown, this opinion is not supported by historical evidence. The antisemitic call to restrict Jewish mass immigration was *not* a response to real migratory movement. On the contrary, the "mass migrations began when German Jews themselves felt under attack".[82]

---

[77] See *Preußische Statistik*, vol. 66, pp. 128–132, lxxx.

[78] "Die neue Tabelle war unzweifelhaft ... dazu bestimmt, die gesamte jüdische Einwanderung aus Rußland in Preussen zu veranschaulichen und deshalb lautet auch ihre Überschrift für die vier östlichen Provinzen; sie hat indess so zu sagen nebenbei ihr Territorium erweitert. Um sich keinen russischen Juden entgehen zu lassen, ist nicht nur Berlin und Frankfurt am Main, sondern auch die Stadt Stolp mit ihren 9 russischen Juden in die Darstellung hineingezogen", Salomon Neumann, *Statistik der Juden*, p. 18.

[79] On mass expulsions from Prussia, see Helmut Neubach, *Die Massenausweisungen von Polen und Juden aus Preussen 1885/86. Ein Beitrag zu Bismarcks Polenpolitik und zur Geschichte des deutsch-polnischen Verhältnisses*, Wiesbaden 1967.

[80] On the administrative measures against Jews see Wertheimer, pp. 42–74, especially pp. 54–60 on the issue of naturalisation.

[81] Neubach, p. 12. For a similar opinion see Jack Wertheimer, *Unwelcome Strangers. East European Jews in Imperial Germany*, New York 1987, p. 27; Inge Blank, ' "...nirgends eine Heimat, aber Gräber auf jedem Friedhof". Ostjuden in Kaiserreich und Weimarer Republik', in Bade, p. 325.

[82] Steven E. Aschheim, *Brothers and Strangers. The East European Jew in German and German Jewish Consciousness, 1800–1923*, Madison 1982, p.34.

Salomon Neumann and the Berliner Antisemitismusstreit

Neubach's mistake, however, gives one probable explanation for the "invisibility" of Neumann in the historiographic reception of the *Berliner Antisemitismusstreit*. In his view, the *Fabel von der jüdischen Masseneinwanderung* appears merely apologetic or even wrong in its contents and is not worthy of recognition in an academic study. A second explanation can be found in the political division of German Jewry at the turn of the century. Neumann represented the liberal, acculturated faction of German Jewry. He always rejected national or Zionist ambitions. When the *Verein für jüdische Statistik* was founded in 1903, Neumann stayed away. Twenty years earlier, he had criticised Treitschke, Wagner, Bergmann and others for the introduction of scientifically unjustifiable categories, for instance "Jewish nation" or "Jewish race", into the field of statistics. Since the *Verein für jüdische Statistik* applied these categories, Neumann could not be involved. *Vice versa*, the most important institution of Jewish statistics seldom referred to Neumann's demographic studies on Prussian Jewry.

German Judenpolitik *in Lithuania During the First World War*

BY JÜRGEN MATTHÄUS

"I don't know whether you are familiar enough with history to know that in 1914 and 1915 the Jews of Poland perceived the Germans as liberators and that they went over into the German camp with flying flags and beating drums, but that they said later: rather Russian than Prusso-German."[1]

When the leader of the *Centralverein* made this statement at a meeting of politicians, administrators and representatives of German-Jewish groups in early 1919, the negative consequences of German *Judenpolitik* in occupied Eastern Europe were, at least for insiders, plain to see. In the inter-war years, the image faded but after the Holocaust, the problem of continuity in German history loomed large. Some scholars have analysed the growth of German antisemitism during the First World War – from the rising tide of right-wing publications via official measures like the *Judenzählung* in the German army and the *Grenzsperre* against Eastern Jews to large-scale annexation projects like the *Grenzstreifen*-plan involving the evacuation of Polish Jews, as well as the *Kaiserreich*'s attempt to attain a global position of power.[2] However, so far little is known about the formal and informal elements of German occupation policy in the East in general and German patterns of conduct towards the Eastern Jews in particular.[3] Relying on documents from

---

[1] Dr. Eugen Fuchs, in a meeting at the German Foreign Office, 31st March 1919, regarding the *Judenfrage*; Archives of the United States Holocaust Memorial Museum, Washington D.C., RG-14.011M, reel 9, No.1722 (microfilm copy of an original held at the Sächsisches Hauptstaatsarchiv Dresden, Varia. Juden betr. 1910–19). This article reflects the opinion of the author. It does not necessarily reflect the opinions of the US Holocaust Memorial Council, nor the US Holocaust Memorial Museum. My thanks go to Nechama Tec for her valuable comments on this paper.

[2] See Immanuel Greiss, *Der polnische Grenzstreifen 1914–1918. Ein Beitrag zur deutschen Kriegszielpolitik im Ersten Weltkrieg*, Lübeck 1960; Fritz Fischer, *Griff nach der Weltmacht. Die Kriegszielpolitik des Kaiserlichen Deutschland 1914/18*, Düsseldorf 1964; Egmont Zechlin and Hans Joachim Bieber, *Die deutsche Politik und die Juden im Ersten Weltkrieg*, Göttingen 1969; Trude Maurer, *Ostjuden in Deutschland 1918–1933*, Hamburg 1986; Wolfgang Jochmann, 'Die Ausbreitung des Antisemitismus in Deutschland 1914–1923', in Werner E. Mosse and Arnold Paucker (eds.), *Deutsches Judentum in Krieg und Revolution*, Tübingen 1971 (Schriftenreihe Wissenschaftlicher Abhandlungen des Leo Baeck Instituts 25), pp. 409–510.

[3] Zosa Szajkowski, in 'Jewish Relief in Eastern Europe', in *LBI Year Book X* (1965), pp. 24–56, covers not only relief efforts on behalf of the *Ostjuden* but also aspects of German policy. Lilli Lewerenz, *Die deutsche Politik im Baltikum 1914–1918*, Ph.D. diss., University of Hamburg 1959, deals primarily with top-level German policy and remains rather inaccessible. Still useful are the studies by Werner Basler, *Deutschlands Annexionspolitik in Polen und im Baltikum, 1914–1918*, Berlin 1962, and Gerd Linde,

Lithuanian archives, this article seeks to reconstruct the major characteristics of *Judenpolitik* in Lithuania and its place in twentieth-century German history.[4]

I.

In order to adequately understand our topic, it has to be analysed from within the wider perspective of German occupation policy. The administrative apparatus of the *Oberbefehlshaber Ost (OberOst)*, which covered Lithuania as well as other parts of the Baltics and the Bialystok-Grodno region of Eastern Poland, emerged in autumn 1915 after the German army, led by Fieldmarshal Paul von Hindenburg, had forced the Russian troops to withdraw from their Western *gouvernements*. Schaulen and Libau (in Latvia) had already been occupied by early May 1915; Kovno fell to the Germans on 18th August; Grodno on 3rd September; and Vilna on 19th September.[5] By the late summer of 1915, a vast strip of land with a population of about three million had come under the control of the German army.

Hindenburg and his Chief of Staff Erich Ludendorff had ambitious aims: first, for the duration of the war, to exploit the occupied territory for the economic benefit of Germany's soldiers and the *Reich*; second, to create, in the long run, a *cordon sanitaire* in anticipation of what General Ludendorff called the "second Punic war" in the event that Germany's defeated enemies should again attempt to usurp the *Reich*'s dominant position in Europe. Ideas and projects which had long taken shape in right-wing circles regarding Eastern Europe's potential for German expansionism provided the general framework for practical policy. The slogan of national liberation and self-determination, restricted to peoples living under Russian rule, was to play a key role in camouflaging the conqueror's concept of *Weltmacht*.[6]

Die deutsche Politik in Litauen im Ersten Weltkrieg, Wiesbaden 1965. For a more recent general account see Maurer, pp. 34–44, and, for a detailed study based on Lithuanian files, Abba Strazhas, *Deutsche Ostpolitik im Ersten Weltkrieg. Der Fall OberOst 1915–1917*, Wiesbaden 1993; idem, 'Kolonial'nyi re.im germanskich imperialistov v Litve v gody pervoj mirovoj vojny', in *Voprosy Istorii* 12 (1958); idem, 'Bor'ba litovskogo naroda protiv germanskich kolonizatorov i ich posobnikov v 1915–1917 gg', ibid., 10 (1959).

[4]The documents presented here are from the Historical Archive of Lithuania (subsequently HAL), and the Lithuanian Academy of Science, Manuscript Division (subsequently LAS), both in Vilna. Material held on the topic in German archives is restricted to a few collections of Prussian or *Reich* agencies such as the *Haushaltsausschuß* of the *Reichstag*, and some personal papers. (See the list of sources in Basler and Linde who extensively use the *Verwaltungsberichte* of the administrative chiefs in *OberOst*, now held at the Geheimes Staatsarchiv Preussischer Kulturbesitz Berlin–Dahlem, P135/6209–6213.) The most important contemporary Jewish accounts can be found in the files of the *Zionistische Zentralbüro* and the *Nachlässe* Bodenheimer and Friedemann in the Central Zionist Archives, Jerusalem, which were used by Szajkowski and Strazhas.

[5]See *Das Land OberOst. Deutsche Arbeit in den Verwaltungsgebieten Kurland, Litauen und Bialystok-Grodno. Herausgegeben im Auftrage des Oberbefehlshabers Ost. Bearbeitet von der Presseabteilung OberOst*, Stuttgart 1917, pp. 5–8; Linde, pp. 18–20. The spelling of place-names and regions follows that used in contemporary German documents.

[6]See Geiss, pp. 13–22; Linde, pp. 9–17; Fischer, pp. 758–772; Michael Burleigh, *Germany Turns Eastward. A Study of* Ostforschung *in the Third Reich*, Cambridge–New York 1988, pp. 3–22.

While other areas in the Baltic, especially Kurland with its predominantly German elite, had been earmarked very early on in the war for annexation,[7] the German plans for Lithuania remained vague regarding the exact methods of subordination. After the Russian Revolution, leading officials of the *Reich* favoured a kind of informal rule which would have left little room for a truly independent state to emerge.[8] In order to prepare for the post-war redrafting of the European map and "to protect Germany from the flood that in the first months of the war spilled over the Eastern border of our Fatherland", a unique administrative structure was established in the occupied and broadly defined "border region [*Grenzmark*] separating the Western European world from Greater Russia".[9] In this way civilian affairs were ruled without the influence of non-military – and, indeed, non-*OberOst* – agencies.

Frequent changes kept this administrative structure in constant flux. Any attempt at reconstructing the hierarchy of German offices presented the same insurmountable problems as clearly defining the tasks of agencies involved in the control of local and Jewish affairs. Various branches of the German occupation apparatus – the *Etappeninspektionen* of the armies, the offices in the *OberOst*-general staff or centralised offices with specific functions – were involved, thus creating a considerable degree of bureaucratic rivalry and confusion.[10] In August 1917, an Office for Jewish Affairs (*Dezernat für Jüdische Angelegenheiten*) led by a member of the *Komitee für den Osten*, Dr. Hermann Struck, an artist and reserve officer, was created in the apparatus of the *OberOst* as a gesture of goodwill towards German-Jewish organisations.[11] Matters of day-to-day policy towards the civil population, including the Jews, were, for most of the duration of the German occupation, determined by the *Deutsche Verwaltung für Litauen* (established in September 1915 as the administrative arm of the military under Lieutenant-Colonel Prince Franz Joseph Isenburg-Birstein) and especially by *Kreis*- and *Stadthauptmänner*, who were, like their superior army officers, often members of the reserve.[12]

---

[7]See Basler, pp. 240–263.
[8]For a detailed account of German political planning regarding Lithuania see Linde.
[9]*Das Land OberOst*, p. 9.
[10]For examples regarding police-matters see *Kreishauptmann* (subsequently KH) in Rossienie, *Verwaltungsbericht* (subsequently VB); for the second quarter of 1917, HAL 641-1-53, fol. 146; idem, VB, 26th September 1917, *ibid.*, fol. 166; idem, VB, 29th December 1917, *ibid.*, fol. 189.
[11]*Geschäftsverteilungsplan der Verwaltungsabteilungen beim Stabe OberOst (Oberquartiermeister)*, 15th August 1917, LAS F9–3118. Struck's office was subdivided into sections dealing with *Allgemeine jüdische Angelegenheiten*, *Jüdische Presse und Zensur* and *Jüdische Arbeiterfragen*. In August 1918, Struck was transferred to the central administration of the *Militärverwaltung Litauen* (*OberOst, Sammelbefehl* No.42, 24th August 1918; *Sammelbefehl* No.43, 31st August 1918, LAS F23–24/1). For a critical assessment of Struck's work see Abba Strazhas, 'Die Tätigkeit des Dezernats für jüdische Angelegenheiten in der "Deutschen Militärverwaltung OberOst"', in Andrew Ezergailis and Gert von Pistohlkors (eds.), *Die Baltischen Provinzen Russlands zwischen den Revolutionen von 1905 und 1917*, Cologne–Vienna 1982, pp. 315–329.
[12]The *Deutsche Verwaltung* was run by a central office first in Tilsit, then from June 1916 in Kovno, and from March 1917 in Vilna. In early 1918, Isenburg-Birstein was succeeded by Theodor von Heppe (see *Verwaltungsübersicht*, 22nd April 1916, HAL 641-1-883a, fol. 128f.; *Militärverwaltung Litauen*, *Geschäftsübersicht*, 1st April 1917, HAL 641-1-1061, fol. 2–5; Strazhas, *Ostpolitik*, pp. 108–115;

In early 1918, a staff of roughly 12,000 Germans controlled an area of nearly 87,000 square kilometres which stretched from Bialystok via Kovno to Vilna and was inhabited by more than 2.5 million people.[13] To ensure that the German version of law and order would be upheld, local officials relied on the *Korpsgendarmerie* (a special *OberOst* police force consisting of ten to fifteen men per district, who were recruited from military ranks and led by one or two career policemen), as well as on the *Feldgendarmerie* of the military.[14] Despite a constant shortage of personnel, the Germans did not appoint officials from the population except at the most subordinate level of the administration, usually in the form of the *Starosten*.[15]

II.

The German officials of the *Deutsche Verwaltung*, in their attempt to keep peace and order behind the front-line troops – essential for the systematic use of the area during and after the war – saw local conditions through the lens of the German officer who was – *ex officio* as well as by self-definition – a member of the social elite and a firm believer in the "German mission". These men were intrigued by the the highly heterogeneous ethnic composition of the population. In contrast to Kurland, where there was a powerful and articulate group of *Deutschbalten*, the Germans in Lithuania were of marginal importance.[16] Even in places where Lithuanians remained in the majority, Poles, Jews, Russians and Belorussians still formed quantitatively significant groups or communities to the point where, as in Vilna, they vastly outnumbered Lithuanians.[17]

Linde, pp. 31–34). The interrelation between the *OberOst*, the *Etappeninspektionen* and the *Deutsche Verwaltung* remained unclear (see *Chef der Militärverwaltung Litauen* Abt.C1, 30th August 1917, and *OberOst* Abt.V, 21st August 1917, LAS F23–1, fol. 334–336). In late 1915, the central administration of the *Deutsche Verwaltung in Litauen* consisted of three divisions (*Zentral-, Landwirtschafts- and Forstabteilung*) with a total of 22 *Referate*; territorially, the area was subdivided into 14 districts (*Kreise*) (*Übersicht über den Verwaltungsbereich*, LAS F23–24/2; see also *Verwaltungsübersicht*, 22nd April 1916, HAL 641–1–883a, fol. 128f.; *Geschäftsübersicht*, 1st April 1917, HAL 641–1–1061, fol. 2–5). Reports had to be submitted by each *Kreishauptmann* monthly, and quarterly from early 1917, covering twenty-four topics, from general administration to the mood of the population (see *Chef der Deutschen Verwaltung für Litauen* Abt. C8, 25th October 1916, LAS F23–1, fol. 184).

[13] See *Militärverwaltung Litauen, Angaben nach dem Stande von März 1918*, LAS F23–26; *OberOst* Abt.VP, *Bevölkerung des Gebiets der militärischen Landesverwaltung Ob.Ost*, n.d., HAL 641–1–967a.

[14] See *Verordnungsblatt der Deutschen Verwaltung für Litauen*, No.1, 26th October 1915, HAL 641–1–978; *Befehl- und Verordnungsblatt des OberOst*, No.17, 29th March 1916, p. 162, HAL 641–1–883a; *Dienstverhältnisse im Gendarmeriekorps des OberOst, Dienstanweisung B*, 30th March 1916; *Dienstanweisung A*, 23rd March 1916, LAS F9–3118.

[15] In March 1918 there was one German *Beamter* per 16 square kilometres and per 500 inhabitants in Northern Lithuania. In addition to the 3,700 *Beamte* for economic purposes, 1,250 gendarmes and 4,100 soldiers were needed, adding up to the comparatively high ratio of one German official per about 200 locals (see *Militärverwaltung Litauen, Angaben nach dem Stande von März 1918*, LAS F23–26).

[16] Basler, p. 241. Plans by *OberOst* to create a relief organisation for *Auslandsdeutsche* similar to those run by Jews, Poles and Lithuanians failed in the summer of 1917 (see HAL 641–1–728, fol. 12f., 26).

[17] See *Das Land OberOst*, pp. 433–435 (appendix to *Völkerverteilung im besetzten Gebiet, 1897*); Dr. Dalberg, 'Die Völker Litauens',in *Zeitung der 10. Armee*, No. 23, 27th January 1916. *OberOst* Abt.VP, n.d.,

German Judenpolitik in Lithuania 159

The reports of the *Kreishauptmänner* indicate how the representatives of the Fatherland felt in this "hubbub of races".[18] Clearly, preference was given to the Germans already living in the area and those to come; yet it remained unclear how this preference was to be transformed into practical policy. From Rossienie it was reported that, instead of fostering one localised settlement of Germans, "a permeation [*Durchsetzung*] of many rural communities with capable German farmers" would not only quicken the pace of Germanisation (*Verdeutschung*) but would also serve economic purposes.[19] To another *Kreishauptmann* it seemed likely that in the future, "i.e. after the incorporation of the area into the *Reich*", compensation would have to be paid for any foreign-owned property deemed to be important for "reasons of colonisation, military aims or population policy [*bevölkerungspolitische Zwecke*]".[20] Despite a moratorium on land-sales, some Germans were already making plans for creating their own "living-space" in the East and approached the *Deutsche Verwaltung* with requests for allocations of land and farms – even in the last stage of the war. [21]

Measures which sought too openly to establish long-term German rule came to be dismissed by at least some of the officials in charge. Although the majority of Lithuanians had, according to German sources, no interest in, nor any understanding of, political questions,[22] there was a limit to German freedom of action. From Skaudwile, *Kreishauptmann* Matuschka reported that, as the Lithuanians saw in the Germans their "natural ally in the fight for their *Volkstum*", it was all the more important not to endanger this element of trust by "forcible Germanisation" or by any policy evoking the impression that protestant Prussia was – as in the province of Poznan – fighting the Catholic Church. Matuschka's superior, *Verwaltungschef* Isenburg-Birstein, shared this opinion, although some months earlier he had himself proposed a plan for the Germanisation of Lithuania.[23]

The other ethnic groups in the population had, in the German mind, one thing in common: their relative inferiority, which manifested itself in low cultural, social and hygienic standards, as well as in total political immaturity. Instead of individuals, the Germans saw only national stereotypes. The occupied area thus

---

Bevölkerung des Gebiets der militärischen Landesverwaltung Ob.Ost, gives the following population figures for Lithuania: Latvians 16,826 (0.6% of the total population); Lithuanians 1,255,521 (49.8%); Poles 720,202 (28.6%); Jews 302,810 (12.1); Russians 34,255 (1.4); Belorussians 159,278 (6.3%); and Germans 28,862 (1.2%).

[18]*Das Land OberOst*, p. 56 (*Hexenkessel der Rassen*).
[19]KH in Rossienie, VB, 29th August 1916, HAL 641-1-53, fol. 68.
[20]KH in Kielmy, VB, 28th March 1916, HAL 641-1-306, fol. 45.
[21]See Abt.I D 1, HAL 641-1-697a, file on *Ansiedlungsbewerber, Ansiedlungsbestreben*, August–November 1918, 176 fols., including requests from Freiherr Magnus von Braun (father of the rocket scientist Wernher von Braun) and others who were working in the *Deutsche Verwaltung*. See also KH in Rossienie, VB, 13th July 1916, HAL 641-1-53, fol. 58.
[22]See e.g. KH in Skaudwile, VB for the third quarter of 1917, HAL 641-1-306, fol. 149; KH in Johanischkele, VB, 31st March 1918, HAL 641-1-389, fol. 142.
[23]KH in Skaudwile, VB for the second quarter of 1917, HAL 641-1-306, fol. 131f. For Isenburg-Birstein's memorandum of September 1916, see Zechlin, pp. 230f.

became a kind of animated ethnographic museum.[24] The alleged backwardness of the locals served not only as a constant excuse for keeping them out of political affairs; it also gave German rule over the area the appearance of a colonising mission equal to that undertaken centuries before by the Teutonic knights.[25] Even in late 1917, at a time when the contradictions in German occupation policy had become all too obvious, propagandists of the *Deutsche Verwaltung* insisted that the *Reich* had brought "the spirit of order and peaceful work even to enemy territory".[26]

The *Deutsche Verwaltung* tried to present its activities as a decisive effort to overcome the effects of the systematic pre-war Russian policy of neglect and of random destruction during the retreat. Over and over again it was stressed that the most basic elements of a constructive policy had been missing when the Germans arrived, either as a result of traditional backwardness or of Russian war-policy.[27] All authority had crumbled with the withdrawal of the Russian administration; significant parts of the population had been forcefully evacuated, especially Jews;[28] valuable assets had been destroyed so that essential tasks such as bringing in the harvest could not be carried out. Self-interest coupled with traditional role-perception motivated the German soldier, after conquering the country, to reconstruct what lay in ruins.[29]

The most graphic sign of Germanisation was the flooding of the area with a deluge of orders and decrees. Beginning in December 1915, *OberOst* published a weekly *Befehls- und Verordnungsblatt* for local use and, from October 1916, a special information leaflet (*Korrespondenz B*) for use inside the *Reich*.[30] The 8th and 10th army and their rear inspectorates came up with their own set of daily or weekly orders (*Tages-, Etappen-* and *Kommandanturbefehle*). Isenburg-Birstein's office put out weekly *Verwaltungsbefehle* (from December 1915), as well as a *Verordnungsblatt*

---

[24] KH in Juschinty, VB, 15th July 1916, HAL 641–1–359, fol. 13f: "Der Litauer ist i.a. vertrauensvoll und willfährig, der echte Russe auch bei Unterwürfigkeit nicht vertrauenswürdig, der Pole immer zweideutig, der Jude stets klug auf den eigenen Vorteil bedacht, oft deshalb ergeben und brauchbar, öfter gewagt ungehorsam mit allen Verstellungskünsten."

[25] See KH in Johanischkele, VB, 31st March 1918, HAL 641–1–389, fol. 142; KH in Rossienie, VB, 30th January 1916, HAL 641–1–53, fol. 34; *idem*, VB, 29th December 1917, *ibid*., fol. 198f., 211; *Stadthauptmann* in Kovno, VB, 5th April 1918, HAL 641–1–584, fol. 107.

[26] "Zwei Jahre Verwaltung Ob.Ost', in *Korrespondenz B*, No.64 (5th November 1917).

[26] See e.g. 'Ob.Ost', in *Korrespondenz B*, No.1 (11th October 1916); "*Die deutsche Verwaltung*", *ibid*., No.22, 7th March 1917; *Das Land OberOst*, p. 81; Erich Ludendorff, *Meine Kriegserinnerungen 1914–1918*, Berlin 1920, pp. 146f.

[27] See Strazhas, *Ostpolitik*, pp. 79–81. One of the central tasks of German administrative agencies was to gather reliable data on the ethnic as well as religious composition of the population (see *Gendarmerie-Dienstanweisung* A, 23rd March 1916, LAS F9–3118; *OberOst* Abt.V, *Sammelbefehl* No.1, 17th November 1917, LAS F23–24/1; and various references in the *Verwaltungsberichte* of the *Kreis-* and *Stadthauptmänner*).

[29] "Wir sahen uns einer fremden Bevölkerung gegenüber, die aus verschiedenen sich gegenseitig befehdenden Stämmen zusammengesetzt war, uns sprachlich nicht verstand und größtenteils innerlich ablehnte. Der Geist treuer und selbstloser Pflichterfüllung, das Erbteil hundertjähriger preußischer Zucht und deutscher Tradition, beseelte alle", Ludendorff, p. 148.

[30] From late 1917 until August 1918, *OberOst* also published a weekly *Sammelbefehl*. The *Korrespondenz B* (from mid-1918 called *Baltisch-Litauische Mitteilungen* and later *Litauische Mitteilungen*) was issued by the press division of *OberOst*. Arnold Zweig belonged to the editorial staff.

German Judenpolitik in Lithuania 161

(from July 1916 as a special addendum to the *Kownoer Zeitung*). Sometimes this was too much, even by German standards.[31] The local population was left bewildered at the flurry of orders regulating nearly every aspect of daily life. In his recollections about the time of the German occupation of Vilna, Joseph Buloff, a Jewish actor, quotes some examples together with the impressions of those affected:

> " 'Whoever owns a horse must cut the hair from its tail and mane and present it to this and that collection center.' And a bit later the same day: 'Along with the cut hair, the owner must also present the horse.' From this, it became apparent that the Germans were not at all *verrückt* but simply out to drive the city crazy."[32]

From the beginning, German administrators faced a dilemma: to reconcile the short- and long-term aims of German occupation policy with the various means adopted. No doubt existed as to the necessity for economic exploitation; there were different ways, however, to achieve this aim. Whereas the *Deutsche Verwaltung* had a vital interest in establishing a planned, well-ordered administrative routine, the military favoured a hand-to-mouth approach. Requisitioning of horses, food and other supplies for the troops, sometimes even resulting in the mistreatment of reluctant owners, as well as the practice of not paying for products taken from the local population, continued irrespective of orders from superiors. Although these short-sighted measures were perceived by administrators to be counterproductive and dangerous, there was little they could do.[33] In addition, different agencies were in competition for scarce assets. Each ton of grain sent to the *Reich* reduced the already depleted local food supply; every man drafted into a labour unit not only added to the dissatisfaction of the population but also made him unavailable for the district's labour market, even though workers were constantly in high demand, especially during the harvest.[34]

Even in the early phase of the German occupation, the *Reich*'s representatives experienced severe problems. In rural areas, and especially in districts with forests, the *Kreishauptmänner* reported "great masses of armed hordes, partly made up from escaped POWs".[35] Over time they were joined by others who had reason to escape from the sphere of German rule – persons called up for compulsory labour, impoverished refugees from towns and cities, and political activists,

---

[31] See KH in Kupischky, VB, 11th July 1916, HAL 641–1–572, fol. 27; KH in Rossienie, VB, 31st March 1917, HAL 641–1–53, fol. 146; KH in Kielmy, VB for the first quarter of 1917, HAL 641–1–306, fol. 106; *idem*, VB for October 1917 to March 1918, *ibid.*, fol. 179f.; *Chef der Deutschen Verwaltung für Litauen* Abt.C6, 9th September 1916, HAL 641–1–879, fol. 12.

[32] Joseph Buloff, *From the Old Marketplace*, Cambridge 1991, p. 263. I am indebted to Solon Beinfeld for referring me to this memoir.

[33] See KH in Rossienie, VB, 31st December 1916, HAL 641–1–88; KH in Johanischkele, VB, 6th December 1915, HAL 641–1–389, fol. 3–5; *idem*, VB, 6th January 1916, *ibid.*, fol. 13; Linde, pp. 57–59.

[34] For complaints by the *Kreishauptmänner* about the negative effects of the compulsory labour brigades see KH in Rossienie, VB, 26th September 1917, HAL 641–1–53, fol. 178; KH in Wiezajcie, VB for the second quarter of 1917, HAL 641–1–515, fols. 211, 214.

[35] KH in Rossienie, VB, 29th April 1916, HAL 641–1–53, fol. 49. Possession of firearms by locals was punishable by death. See *Verordnungsblatt der Deutschen Verwaltung für Litauen*, No. 1 (26th October 1915), *Verordnung über die polizeiliche Gewalt der Zivilverwaltungsbehörden*.

as well as common criminals.[36] Although these groups, in many cases, had other than political motives, they primarily targeted German institutions and officials, including those of the local population who collaborated with them. Shops, storage rooms and farms were plundered; policemen and others were disarmed, beaten up and sometimes murdered.[37] The Germans had difficulty coming to terms with this phenomenon, which struck at the root of their policy. In order to stress that those hiding in the forests were not to be regarded as freedom fighters but as criminals, they were referred to as *"Banden"*, the overall problem thus becoming *"das Bandenunwesen"*.[38]

In this triple aim of exploiting, pacifying and – in the long run – incorporating the occupied territory there was, despite the vague promise of a brighter future under German protection, only limited room for considering the fate of the local population. The *Reich* had already committed itself to some extent, however, by propagating the idea that its soldiers had come to the rescue of those oppressed by Tsarism – a perception shared by German and, from a different perspective, Eastern Jews.[39] With a *Kulturnation* moving in, the days of the Pale of Settlement and state-sponsored pogroms seemed to be over; yet it remained unclear what German rule would bring in their place.

III.

The most striking experience for the Germans was contact with the Eastern Jews. Their perception was dominated by the impact of wartime destitution, as well as by deep-seated stereotypes about the aimless and timeless Ahasverus reminiscent of medieval ghettos. German-Jewish soldiers often encountered key elements of Jewishness in their Eastern brethren which had long been lost in Western Europe.[40] Their Christian comrades usually lacked the open-mindedness to see anything but filth, corruption and decay. In March 1916, the *Kreishauptmann* in Birshi reported: "Jews live everywhere in considerable numbers – a cancerous sore on the land."[41] Contemporary publications were filled with sarcastic comments on the faulty argot of local Jews ("a garbled

---

[36] For a detailed account of partisan warfare in Lithuania see Strazhas, *Ostpolitik*, pp. 13–70; see also Linde, pp. 37–39 and Basler, pp. 266f., 281f.

[37] See KH in Rossienie, VB for the second quarter of 1917, HAL 641-1-53, fol. 146f.; KH in Birshi, VB for the third quarter of 1916, HAL 641-1-52, fol. 119.

[38] See e.g. KH in Rossienie, VB, 29th August 1916, HAL 641-1-53, fol. 67.

[39] Although the famous public appeal by the German High Command "to the Jews of Poland" in late August 1914 did not address Jews in other areas, it clearly had an impact in Lithuania too. See Zechlin, pp. 124f., and Strazhas, *Ostpolitik*, pp. 79f..

[40] See Zosa Szajkowski, 'The Struggle for Yiddish during World War I. The Attitude of German Jewry', in *LBI Year Book IX* (1964), pp. 155f.; Steven E. Aschheim, *Brothers and Strangers. The East European Jew in German and German Jewish Consciousness, 1800–1923*, Madison 1982, pp. 139–156.

[41] "Juden sind in beträchtlicher Zahl überall wohnhaft – ein Krebsschaden des Landes." (KH in Birshi, VB, 12th March 1916, HAL 641-1-52, fol. 5). According to a census completed in early 1917, out of a total population of 40,235 there were only 522 Jews in the district of Birshi (*idem*, VB for the second quarter of 1917, *ibid.*, fol. 206).

Middle High German mixed with numerous Slavic expressions") and on their repulsive habits.[42]

Mingling with the locals in general, but with the Jews in particular, was regarded as dangerous both for political and for sanitary reasons. Typhus and other diseases seemed to lurk in every house, despite intense efforts by the German administration to improve sanitary conditions. *Kreishauptmann* Matuschka reported from Kielmy in late January 1916 that "the uncleanliness, particularly of the Jewish population ... is of such a degree that strong action has to be taken".[43] Orders were given regarding the regular removal of garbage and faeces; bath-houses were established – using, wherever available and after agreement with the rabbi, existing Jewish ritual baths; and delousing was made compulsory, in some areas for Jews and the urban population only.[44]

The popular *Zeitung der 10. Armee*, published in Vilna and widely read even outside German military circles, favoured literary descriptions of urban scenes, including explicit vignettes such as this one printed in the first issue of the newspaper in December 1915:

> "Filthy Jews, with full beards in the lightest red to the darkest black, stand in their ragged kaftans amongst pale women and young girls. Dirty children crouch on wooden stairways. Unwashed, uncombed they are all – and over all of them the smell that gives the whole city its atmosphere pervades."[45]

Another, supposedly humorous, account of shopping in Vilna was published in January 1916. It featured Jewish merchants who advertised their wares "with screeching voices" and "repugnant praise", as well as Jewish youngsters who "will never get used to proper work and will later, just like their parents, enter into dubious businesses".[46] Forever remaining a "strange people", they evoked among most Germans a feeling of revulsion or, at best, disgusted pity.[47]

Even where the German press claimed to enlighten, it tended to reinforce existing prejudices. The author of an article on the culture of the Eastern Jews admitted that there was

> "a certain kind of strangeness in the language and habits, and, by German standards, unbearable uncleanliness which, however, is of no greater degree than that of the rest of the population of similar social standing; an often apparent disposition towards dishonesty and to what we call haggling spirit [*Schachergeist*], and finally the not infre-

---

[42] *Das Land OberOst*, p. 19; also KH in Kielmy, VB, 24th January 1916, HAL 641-1-306, fol. 26. For the psychological aspects of the encounter see Pamela Maclean, 'Control and Cleanliness. German-Jewish Relations in Occupied Eastern Europe during the First World War', in *War and Society*, vol.6 No. 7 (September 1988), pp. 47-69.
[43] KH in Kielmy, VB, 24th January 1916, HAL 641-1-306, fol. 25.
[44] See e.g. KH in Skaudwile, VB for the first quarter of 1917, HAL 641-1-306, fol. 107; *idem*, VB for the second quarter of 1917, *ibid.*, fol. 121-123.
[45] Curt Pabst, 'Örtliche Nachrichten. Im Abenddämmern', in *Zeitung der 10. Armee*, No. 1 (9th December 1915).
[46] 'Zwischen Wilja und Düna: Strassenhandel', in *Zeitung der 10. Armee*, No. 17 (13th January 1916); see a similar account in No. 22 (25th January 1916).
[47] See Walter Wolff, 'Judentypen aus der Etappe', in *Korrespondenz B*, No. 30 (30th May 1917).

quent desire to achieve certain aims by bribing officials – these are the phenomena which jump out at you and which combine to give a rather unfavourable overall picture".[48]

Amid the "everyday pictures of dirt and neglect" in the cities, the ghetto stood out. In this "embodiment of the Orient, transferred to the North" the stench and noise was as "appalling as the behaviour of the numerous merchants pestering the passers-by to buy their indescribable products and to listen to their impossible German".[49]

The perception that the cramped and desolate living conditions of the Jews were the result of Russian policy did not alter the prevailing negative image.[50] In that respect, Germans found a positive side to Tsarism since it had prevented the Lithuanian administration from falling into Jewish hands.[51] The conquerors saw themselves forced into a similar role, in spite of their reluctance. In March 1916 the *Kreishauptmann* in Birshi reported that the local Jews "create most of the work as they constantly apply for travel permits etc., and it is they who cause the authorities to react to breaches in the regulations on trade and especially price limitation".[52] If they complained to the authorities about requisitions and abuse, despite their sometimes limited knowledge of the German language they were rebuked or became the object of ridicule.[53]

IV.

The ideological stereotyping that was an important part of the baggage of German officialdom almost invariably influenced the latter's practical policy towards Jews as well as non-Jews in the occupied area. Patterns of prejudice, however, were not the only factors influencing occupation policy. For the German administration, the local population was as economically indispensable, especially given the poor state of the labour market, as it was culturally backward and politically burdensome. In order to meet the expectations created by the German promise to liberate the peoples that had suffered discrimination by Tsarist Russia, *Reich* officials enacted a number of reforms aimed at improving the status of the local population in general and of the Jews in particular. The German administration created an efficient court system which was widely used by the population despite its high fees. It also improved the conditions of roads,

---

[48] Ismar Freund, 'Die Ostjuden im Spiegel ihrer Religionsquellen', in *Zeitung der 10. Armee*, No. 23 (27th January 1916, *Beilage*). See also *idem*, 'Die Ostjuden im Spiegel ihrer Geschichte', *ibid.*, No. 25 (1st February 1916, *Beilage*).
[49] *Das Land OberOst*, pp. 46–50. For other German complaints about Jewish uncleanliness see 'Besuch in Wilna', in *Zeitung der 10. Armee*, No. 30 (12th February 1916); KH in Wiezajcie, VB, 15th July 1916, HAL 641–1–515, fol. 113.
[50] Dr. Dalberg, 'Die Völker Litauens', in *Zeitung der 10. Armee*, No. 23 (27th January 1916).
[51] 'Zwei Kulturen', in *Zeitung der 10. Armee*, No. 26 (3rd February 1916).
[52] KH in Birshi, VB, 12th March 1916, HAL 641–1–52, fol. 35.
[53] See *Das Land OberOst*, pp. 70f.

schools and print media.⁵⁴ Regarding the Jews, settlement restrictions were lifted, special taxes abolished and opportunities created for the development of Jewish culture. In many cases these measures seem to have been initiated by German Jews. While the *Feldrabbiner* in the *OberOst*-armies — one of whom was Leo Baeck — tried to mediate between the authorities and local Jews, organisations like the *Komitee für den Osten* or the *Hilfsverein der deutschen Juden* provided material support and intervened through their Berlin offices.⁵⁵

The benevolence displayed, or tolerated, by the German administration had limitations when more important issues on the German agenda were at stake. Concerned about revenue, some officials had second thoughts about abolishing the Russian poll-tax on Jews. The practice of setting aside wheat flour for the baking of *matzot* was criticised as aggravating the growing food crisis.⁵⁶ In mid-October 1916, Leopold von Bayern, who had succeeded Hindenburg as *OberOst* in late August 1916, issued an order in which Germans were reminded that the experience of living among a people critical of German rule should not lead to a reversal of measures taken in the interest of army and Fatherland. The needs governing German action were never to be influenced by the wishes or complaints of the local population.⁵⁷

The *Deutsche Verwaltung* camouflaged its mixture of patronising interventionism and real disregard for the basic interests of the people of Lithuania as driven by necessity and by genuinely impartial discipline. The main administrative regulations (*Verwaltungsordnung*) formally guiding the actions of German officials which, after months of intense deliberations, were published in late June 1916, comprised ninety-one paragraphs in thirty-five pages. They dealt with issues such as administrative structuring and accounting and contained only three paragraphs on the local population.

After a general description of the basic aim of German rule, "to create and sustain a well-ordered political and economic situation" within which "the interests of the German army and *Reich* always have priority over those of the occupied country", Lithuanians were advised "to obey immediately and willingly the reg-

---

⁵⁴See Linde, pp. 34–37, 39–52. The Historical Archive in Vilna has an extensive holding of German court files, especially from the *Friedensgerichte* (fond 644: 307 files; fond 642: 329 files; fond 643: 2,998 files).

⁵⁵See Szajkowski, *Jewish Relief*; Strazhas, *Tätigkeit*; Ludendorff, p. 154. In the first year of the German occupation, the *Feldrabbiner* in the *OberOst*-area (Dr. Winter in Bialystok, Dr. Rosenack in Kovno, Dr. Levi in Vilna, Dr. Hanover in Schaulen and Dr. Baeck in Nowo-Alexandrowsk; see *Tagesbefehl der Etappen-Inspektion der 10. Armee, Regelung der Seelsorge*, 29th December 1917, HAL 641–1–964, fol. 159–161) were *ex officio* in contact with the local Jews. See appeal in Yiddish by Dr. Rosenack to the local rabbis to report cases of contageous diseases to the German authorities, 23rd January 1916, HAL 641–1–879, fol. 15. In late 1916, they seemed to be dispensable and were ordered to restrict themselves to ministering to German-Jewish soldiers; see letter by AOK 10 to Dr. Levi, 1st October 1916, LAW F23–1–, fol. 160f.

⁵⁶See KH in Kurschany, VB for the fourth quarter of 1915, HAL 641–1–622, fol. 45; KH in Rossienie, VB, 31st March 1917, HAL 641–1–53, fol. 134. The provision of *matzo*-flour was cited to after the war as an indication of the constructive nature of German policy in the *OberOst*-area. See Ludendorff, p. 159; Zechlin, p. 227.

⁵⁷*OberOst* Abt.V, 14th October 1916, *Betrifft: Behandlung der Landeseinwohner*, LAS F23–1, fol. 173–174.

ulations and orders of German agencies". While these agencies were obliged not to issue any unfair orders, locals had no explicit right to complain; punishment for non-compliance included fines or incarceration for up to five years. If called upon to assist the German administration, they could neither decline nor quit and they were not entitled to payment – a policy which severely dampened their enthusiasm and willingness to cooperate.

The *Verwaltungsordnung* contained an expression of German good-will combined with a threat: "The different ethnic groups [*Völkerstämme*] in the area are to be treated equally by German agencies. To indulge in any activities threatening to disturb the ethnic peace [*völkische Frieden*] in the local population is prohibited."[58] Subordinated as it was to the central aim of keeping control over the area, "ethnic peace" remained open to interpretation. It was the Jews who came to be perceived by German officials as a threat to the existing or desired equilibrium. The *Kreishauptmann* in Kielmy, Count Matuschka, estimated in his first report of mid-September 1915 that his district had about 40,000 inhabitants, including 34–35,000 Lithuanians, 5–6,000 Jews, 500 Russians and 400 Germans. According to Matuschka, the Jews' primary income came from trade and money-lending, thus "holding the entire rural population in a state of financial dependence". The statement by the *Kreishauptmann* "that it does damage to the public esteem of German agencies if the Jew – who is often hated and despised by Poles and Lithuanians alike for other reasons – is used as a German auxiliary" received a favourable reply in the margin ("sehr richtig") from his superior in Tilsit. Matuschka saw a real danger that Lithuanians would equate the local Jew with the German and would thus transfer Gentile hatred of the former to the latter.[59]

The element of occupation policy that most affected Lithuanian Jews was the German attempt to restructure the economy. Assuming that control of local trade was the key to the solution of many problems, the *Reich*'s representatives quickly and effectively monopolised the exchange of goods. In so doing they followed – and in some cases preceded – the pattern adopted in the *Reich* proper as a consequence of the war situation. Ethnic preferences, however, influenced the deliberate German attempt to control trade. Jews were to be excluded from trade; the most efficient way to achieve this was to establish cooperative societies (*Genossenschaften* or *Konsumvereine*).[60]

---

[58] *Befehls- und Verordnungsblatt des Oberbefehlshabers Ost*, No. 34 (26th June 1916), *Verwaltungsordnung für das Etappengebiet im Befehlsbereich des OberOst*, pp. 269–304, HAL 641–1–967. In the semi-official *Korrespondenz B*, this passage was hailed as a guarantee for "die Gleichheit aller Völkerstämme und die Freiheit für jeden, seine Kultur zu wahren", in *Die deutsche Verwaltung, Beilage zur KB*, No.22 (7th March 1917).
[59] KH in Kielmy, VB, 19th September 1915, HAL 641–1–306, fol. 2–4.
[60] KH in Wiezajcie, VB for the first quarter of 1917, HAL 641–1–515, fol. 185: "Um die Bevölkerung daran zu gewöhnen, ihren Bedarf anderwärts als bei den jüdischen Händlern zu decken, sind im Kreise fünf amtliche Verkaufsstellen eingerichtet worden, die in der Lage sind, ihre Waren billiger zu verkaufen, als der jüdische Händler." See also *Chef der Militärverwaltung für Litauen*, 30th July 1917, HAL 641–1–728, fol. 407, advising the *Kreisämter* to sell wood "möglichst unter Umgehung der einheimischen jüdischen Händler". See also KH in Retowo, VB for August/September 1915, HAL 641–1–360, fol. 17, prohibiting horse-trading by Jews in the district.

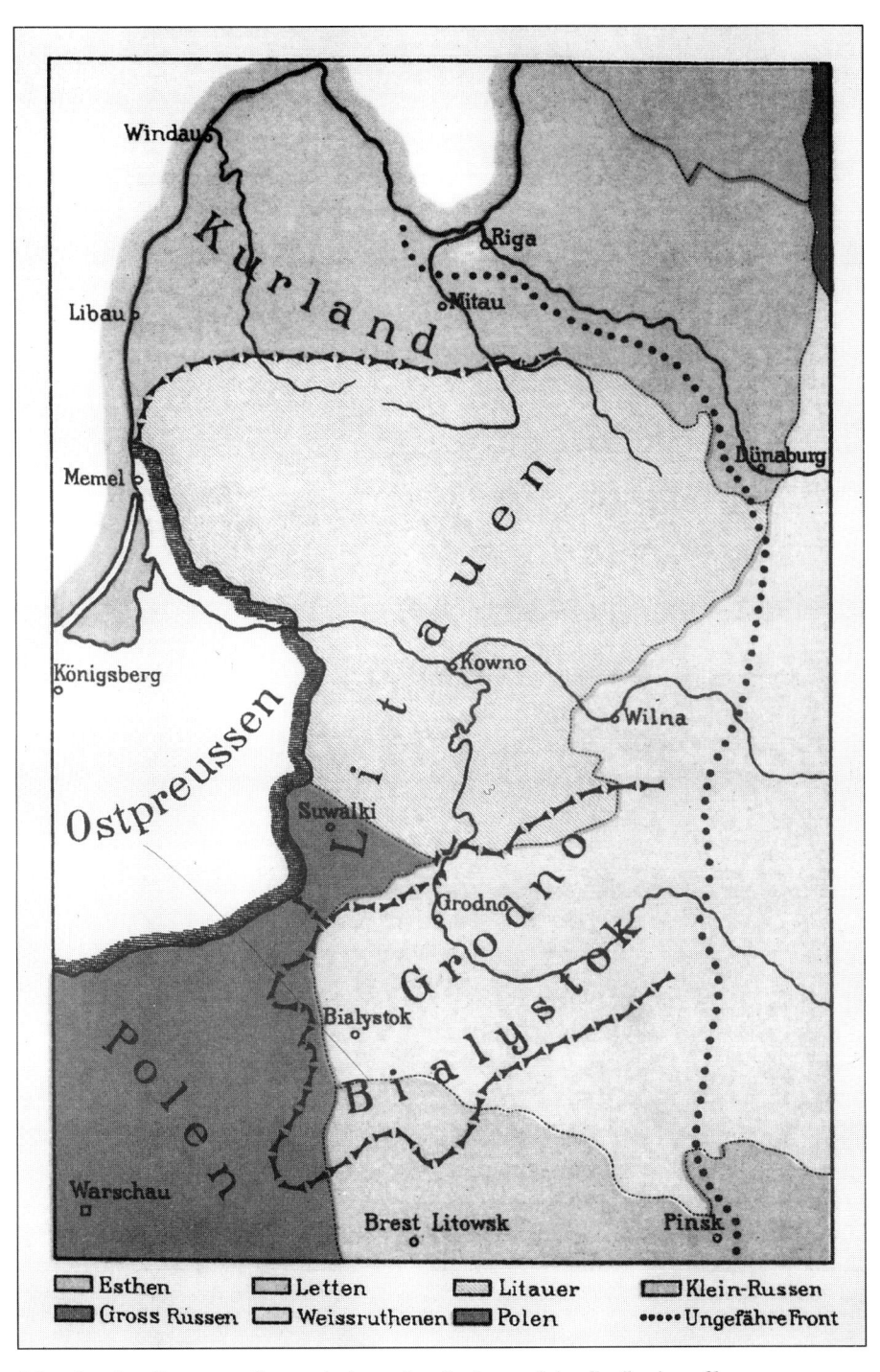

Map showing German military adminstrative districts and the distribution of language groups in Latvia, Lithuania and Bialystok-Grodno during the First World War.

From Das Land OberOst. Deutsche Arbeit in den Verwaltungsgebeiten Kurland, Lithauen und Bailystok-Grodno. Herausgegeben in Auftrage des Oberbefehlshabers Ost. Bearbeitet von der Pressabteilung OberOst, Stuttgart 1917.

Although the concept of cooperative societies was not new – some had already been created in the area before the war – under German rule it became inextricably linked with *Judenpolitik* in Lithuania. Here as elsewhere, trade had been traditionally in the hands of Jews. In its trade policy, in contrast to other policies, the German administration was willing to work for what it regarded as the benefit of the majority of the local population, stressing its "intention to save the rural population from exploitation by the Jews".[61] The Germans were not blind to the serious disadvantages of cooperative societes: they were neither very cost-effective nor did they fulfil the promise of providing benefits for their members, thus aggravating the frustration of the population. They offered, however, the tempting prospect of squeezing Jewish merchants out of business.[62]

Massive problems had to be overcome in order to change established patterns of trade. Some of the priests, who had been instructed about the importance of the *Konsumvereine* for the exclusion of Jewish traders, stressed that the Lithuanians, although they despised the Jew, had been used to him for centuries. It would take considerable time and effort for the trade societies to take firm enough roots "to push out the Jewish middlemen, especially as the Jew can often deliver for lower prices than the *Konsumvereine*, due to smuggling which cannot be suppressed totally".[63]

The consequences of an economic policy that focused on German rather than local needs occasionally surfaced in official reports. Irrespective of how well the state-sponsored trade societies were doing, the monopolisation of a great number of products in a situation of chronic scarcity led to diminishing sources of income for those who had to compete with the *Genossenschaften*. Reporting on the success of the *Konsumvereine* in his district, the *Kreishauptmann* in Rossienie mentioned the "drawback" that "the Jewish merchants have been robbed of nearly all business opportunities and that, in order to make a living, they are increasingly forced into illegal activities".[64] Consequently, the Jews had to engage in black marketeering and smuggling – a development frequently reported by German officials but not always seen as rooted in the *Reich*'s official economic policy.[65]

The dreaded but, given the German preference, unavoidable "proletarianisa-

---

[61] Paper given by KH in Wiezajcie, *Chef der Deutschen Verwaltung für Litauen, Verwaltungsbefehl* XVIII, 10th June 1916, *Anlage* I, p. 3, HAL 641–1–883a.
[62] *Ibid.*, pp. 3–6.
[63] KH in Skaudwile, VB, 27th August 1916, HAL 641–1–306, fol. 74. See also paper given by KH in Wiezajcie, *Chef der Deutschen Verwaltung für Litauen, Verwaltungsbefehl* XVIII, 10th June 1916, *Anlage* I, p. 5, HAL 641–1–883a; KH in Kurschany, VB, 14th July 1916, HAL 641–1–622, fol. 122.
[64] KH in Rossienie, VB, 31st March 1917, HAL 641–1–53, fol. 138.
[65] See KH in Kielmy, VB, 11th July 1916, HAL 641–1–306, fol. 66; KH in Johanischkele, VB, 6th January 1916, HAL 641–1–389, fol. 14; KH in Rossienie, VB, 30th January 1916, HAL 641–1–53, fol. 31; *idem*, VB, 31st March 1917, *ibid.*, fol. 134; *idem*, VB, 26th September 1917, *ibid.*, fol. 180; *idem*, VB, 29th December 1917, *ibid.*, fol. 189, 208, 210; KH in Birshi, VB, 12th March 1916, HAL 641–1–52, fol. 35; KH in Retowo, VB, 15th September 1915, HAL 641–1–360, fol. 17, 22, 32; KH in Wiezajcie, VB for the second quarter of 1917, HAL 641–1–515, fol. 221; KH in Kurschany, VB, 5th April 1918, HAL 641–1–622, fol. 232f.; *Chef der Geheimpolizei, Polizeibericht* 17, 14th October 1915, LAS F23–17, fol. 197; *idem*, *Polizeibericht*, 5th August 1915, *ibid.*, fol. 215; *idem*, *Polizeibericht*, 16th October 1915, *ibid.*, fol. 222.

tion" of the Jews[66] progressed rapidly. In early 1917 the *Kreishauptmann* in Skaudwile reported:

"... Jewish merchants, forced by the prevailing need, have started to rent land and thus, fortunately, to contribute their money and some of their horses towards supplying food for the people, even though the physical work is always done by Lithuanians."[67]

Other ways out of destitution and despair, for example emigration to the United States (until its entry into the war) were still open, but were in practice blocked for the majority.[68] The only means of alleviating the "dire need" of the Jewish population, especially in larger towns and cities, was through the donations received more or less regularly from organisations like the *Hilfsverein der deutschen Juden* or the American Jewish Joint Distribution Committee, although the Germans ordered these funds to be distributed to non-Jews too.[69] Thus what for the local Jews were strategies of survival seemed to the Germans to be signs of cunning, deception and dishonesty. This perfectly fitted into their prevailing image of "the Jew".[70]

V.

Given the constraints of the war situation, in combination with the primacy of hegemonic aims, the German effort to harmonise propaganda with actual policy turned out to be an attempt to square the circle. The more radical the measures adopted to help Germany win the war, the less credit its agencies had with the locals. The argument that hard times required stern measures, and that

---

[66]KH in Kurschany, VB, 12th September 1915, HAL 641-1-622, fol. 10; *idem*, VB, 28th March 1916, *ibid.*, fol. 90.

[67]KH in Skaudwile, VB for the first quarter of 1917, HAL 641-1-306, fol. 110. Isenburg-Birstein commented on this finding with a "gut" in the margin. For similar accounts of the loss of income-base suffered by merchants in general and Jews in particular as a result of German policy, see KH in Rossienie, VB, 29th April 1916, HAL 641-1-53, fol. 53; *idem*, VB, 31st December 1916, *ibid.*, fol. 97.

[68]See KH in Rossienie, VB, 31st December 1916, HAL 641-1-53, fol. 91f. On a similar report from the KH in Juschinty, VB, 19th October 1916, HAL 641-1-359, fol. 25, which mentioned the desire of the Jewish population to emigrate to the USA, *Verwaltungschef* Isenburg-Birstein noted "nur los".

[69]Order by *Deutsche Verwaltung für Litauen*, 1st December 1915, LAS F23-1, fol. 89. See also KH in Skaudwile, VB for the first quarter of 1918, HAL 641-1-306, fol. 201; KH in Rossienie, VB, 31st December 1916, HAL 641-1-53, fol. 99; *idem*, VB, 26th September 1917, *ibid.*, fol. 189; *Stadthauptmann* in Kowno, VB, 2nd July 1917, HAL 641-1-584, fol. 58; *idem*, VB for April to September 1917, *ibid.*, fol. 76; KH in Wiezajcie, VB for the second quarter of 1917, HAL 641-1-515, fol. 240; KH in Kurschany, VB, 31st December 1916, HAL 641-1-622, fol. 153; *idem*, VB, 2nd July 1917, *ibid.*, fol. 182; *idem*, VB for April to September 1917, *ibid.*, fol. 197; *idem*, VB for October 1917 to March 1918, *ibid.*, fol. 234; *Verordnungsblatt der Deutschen Verwaltung für Litauen*, No.11, 28th May 1916, HAL 641-1-883a. For the support given by Jewish organisations see Szajkowski, *Jewish Relief*.

[70]KH in Wiezajcie, VB for the last quarter of 1917, HAL 641-1-515, fol. 266: "Schwerer noch als der Litauer ist der stets unzufriedene Jude zu behandeln. Während jener sich, wenn auch widerwillig, in die harte Notwendigkeit schließlich schickt ... sucht der Jude sich immer wieder durch alle möglichen Ausflüchte und unwahre Behauptungen seinen Verpflichtungen zu entziehen, wobei ihm seine Kenntnis der deutschen Sprache sehr zustatten kommt." See also OberOst Abt.V, 1st December 1915, LAS F23-1, fol. 89; *Stadthauptmann* in Kowno, VB, 5th April 1918, HAL 641-1-584, fol. 107; KH in Kurschany, VB, 29th February 1916, HAL 641-1-622, fol. 75.

in Germany, too, people were suffering from the war, wore off after a while, although news about conditions in Russian territory across the frontline, where things seemed to be even worse, tended to work in favour of the Germans.[71] Making use of unpaid local officials or appointing Lithuanian figureheads could be no substitute for real political or economic reform.[72] Incorporating locals into the *Deutsche Verwaltung* primarily offered the prospect of relieving the chronic personnel problem and of opening a "valve for regulating the public mood".[73] Far-reaching reforms were out of the question: the population seemed unfit to take even partial control over their own affairs. Instead, people in Lithuania were reminded that during the war only those who did not obstruct German interests could expect to be treated well.[74]

Because of the multitude of problems German officials faced in administering the occupied territory, they had a vital interest in presenting themselves as safeguards to prevent the situation from getting worse in the future. Lithuania, so the prevailing argument went, needed a powerful neighbour to protect it. The budding Lithuanian nation appeared to be under threat from various external and internal sources: from a victorious Tsarist Russia reinstating its pre-war imperialist policy; from the Bolshevik Revolution, which promised to overturn existing rights of ownership; from the Poles in the country eager to swallow large parts of Lithuania; and, last but not least, from the local Jews who seemed capable, as well as determined, to take over key areas of Lithuanian political, economic and cultural life.[75] The *Reich* was willing to offer what Lithuania was unable to provide for itself: a guarantee of its continued existence.

Political participation, although a central issue since the Russian Revolution, was just one, and not the most immediate, problem facing the local population. Gradually, German efforts to mobilise Lithuanian workers manifested themselves in increasingly repressive measures. In addition to the conscription of labourers by the administration and the military for local or short-term purposes, from mid-1916 onwards compulsory labour battalions were established. They soon became notorious for their intolerable conditions and ultimately comprised more than 50,000 workers.[76] The Germans opened "workhouses" for the "work-shy" and for "dissolute women", as well as camps

---

[71]See e.g. KH in Rossienie, VB, 29th December 1917, HAL 641-1-53, fol. 199.
[72]See KH in Wiezajcie, VB for the second quarter of 1917, HAL 641-1-515, fol. 248. On the German attempt to use the idea of Lithuanian independence for their own purposes, *inter alia* by creating *Landesräte*, see Linde, pp. 69-93; Strazhas, *Ostpolitik*, pp. 108ff.
[73]KH in Wiezajcie, VB for the last quarter of 1917, HAL 641-1-515, fol. 250f., 266. See also KH in Rossienie, VB, 31st March 1917, HAL 641-1-53, fol. 141; KH in Johanischkele, VB, 1st October 1917, HAL 641-1-389, fol. 116; KH in Skaudwile, VB for the first quarter of 1917, HAL 641-1-306, fol. 117; *idem*, VB for the second quarter of 1917, *ibid.*, fol. 131.
[74]See *Befehls- und Verordnungsblatt des OberOst*, No.18, 7th April 1916, p. 166, HAL 641-1-883a.
[75]KH in Wiezajcie, VB for October 1917 to March 1918, HAL 641-1-515, fol. 288: "Der einsichtige Litauer sagt sich, daß Litauen ohne starke deutsche Unterstützung sich als Nation nicht halten kann, sondern den Polen oder Juden anheimfällt."
[76]See e.g. KH in Johanischkele, VB, 1st October 1917, HAL 641-1-389, fol. 110; KH in Rossienie, VB, 31st March 1917, HAL 641-1-53, fol. 142; Linde, pp. 62-64.

for those called up for compulsory labour,[77] thus forcing a growing number of the destitute to escape into the forests. While the local population obviously suffered from the *Banden*, in a situation in which the occupying power could not guarantee security, there was immense pressure to assist them. This was sometimes a consequence of circumstances perceived by German officials, but was more often used as a subterfuge for retaliation.[78] German statistics reflect the randomness of the measures adopted to "pacify" the area, because the majority of those arrested by the *Gendarmerie* were not in fact "bandits".[79]

As *Arbeiterkolonnen, Zivilarbeiterbataillone* and *Zivilgefangenenlager* thrived all over the area, acts of non-compliance and open resistance by locals increased, thus bringing the dilemma of German policy into sharper focus. Deserters from work units, if caught, turned out to be a burden on the prison system as they had to be fed and transferred back to their places of work. Although the officials of the *Deutsche Verwaltung* favoured fines in order to avoid food shortages, an increasing number of people who had violated one of the countless German regulations found themselves imprisoned in miserable conditions.[80] Collective punishment was also practised, especially in the fight against the *Bandenunwesen*, in which local police had more success than the larger military units brought in from outside.[81] Administrators were advised by their superiors that punitive measures should take "the low cultural level of the population" into account: "To judge and to punish *merely* according to the letter of the law and to German concepts is not practical."[82]

Sometimes German officials had scruples about taking measures against

---

[77] KH in Johanischkele, VB, 1st July 1917, HAL 641–1–389, fol. 102; *idem*, VB, 1st October 1917, *ibid.*, fol. 109.

[78] In his report on a large-scale operation in Rossienie in late 1916, the commanding general, Freiherr von Roeder, noted that it "had been proven beyond doubt that the Russians [i.e. the *Banden*] are to a large degree assisted by the local population" and called for "rigorous measures" against civilians, HAL 641–1–53, fol. 106. See also *Chef der Deutschen Verwaltung für Litauen, Verwaltungsbefehl* XVIII, 10th June 1916, p. 6, HAL 641–1–883a; *Tagesbefehl der Etappen-Inspektion der 10. Armee, Verordnung betr. das Bandenunwesen*, 9th December 1917, HAL 641–1–964. For accounts of the terror exerted by the *Banden* on the local population see KH in Rossienie, VB, 31st March 1917, *ibid.*, fol. 125; *idem*, VB for the second quarter of 1917, *ibid.*, fol. 146; KH in Kupischki, VB, 30th December 1916, HAL 641–1–572, fol. 43; *idem*, VB for fourth quarter of 1917, *ibid.*, fol. 110.

[79] According to the KH in Johanischkele (VB, 31st March 1918, HAL 641–1–389, fol. 131), the *Korpsgendarmerie* had arrested "28 bandits, 102 escaped Russian POWs, 30 escaped civil workers, 219 other persons under military jurisdiction, 214 other persons" between October 1917 and March 1918. See also *Stadthauptmann* in Kowno, VB, 5th April 1918, HAL 641–1–584, fol. 95.

[80] See Strazhas, *Ostpolitik*, pp. 35–38, who seems to exaggerate the number of death sentences and deaths in prison. For a sample of cases investigated by the *Deutsche Verwaltung*, see HAL 641–1–705 (*Strafvollstreckungs-Papiere*).

[81] See KH in Rossienie, VB, 31st March 1917, HAL 641–1–53, fol. 126; *idem*, VB, 26th September 1917, *ibid.*, fol. 179; KH in Skaudwile, VB for the first quarter of 1918, HAL 641–1–306, fol. 179–181; KH in Johanischkele, VB, 28th September 1916, HAL 641–1–389, fol. 63; *idem*, VB, 31st March 1918, *ibid.*, fol. 130; KH in Rossienie, VB, 31st December 1916, HAL 641–1–53, fol. 86–88 (enclosed is Inspekteur der Mil.Bez.Inspektion Generalmajor Freiherr von Roeder, *Bericht über die militärischen Maßnahmen in den Kreisen Rossienie und Georgenburg*, 31st December 1916, *ibid.*, fol. 103–106, which states that, after a month-long military operation involving more than a thousand German soldiers, only 62 persons had been arrested).

[82] *Chef der Deutschen Verwaltung für Litauen* to *Kreisämter* reporting order by AOK 8, 29th January 1917, LAS F23–1, fol. 92 (emphasis in the original).

people who had been separated from their families, deceived by their employers, and who were desperate from hunger and clothed in rags.[83] However, in dealing with matters of national interest, the German sense of duty often prevailed: "A considerable number of Jews from the district of Saldogischki have been suddenly deported [*abgeschoben*] to Schadow. This ... is not pleasant but it seems to have been inevitable."[84] From Kupischki, *Kreishauptmann* Tafel complained about refugees from Vilna: "While these primarily Jewish parasites are regarded as a plague [*Landplage*], families deported from the area of military operations have turned out to be a useful, capable labour resource."[85] In at least one case in the area of Suwalki-Vilna those about to be deported were kept together in a camp-like facility called *Konzentrationslager*.[86]

Along with the rest of the population, Jews were drafted into compulsory labour units. However, the Germans treated them differently from the local Gentiles, and judged their work by different standards. If their performance was poor, this was not seen as a result of the present situation, but of "a century-old disuse" of physical abilities.[87] Attempts were made to accommodate the needs of Jewish workers: labour brigades were advised to provide kosher food and to allow Jews to honour their holidays; exclusively Jewish labour units were formed from which pupils of *cheder*-schools were exempt.[88] However, it seemed impossible to overcome biological impediments. From Wiezajcie, the *Kreishauptmann* complained about an "almost totally useless labour force [*fast völlig wertloses Arbeitermaterial*]", consisting mainly of Jews who "in addition to being unproductive consumers [*unnütze Mitesser*], pose a serious threat as transmitters of typhus".[89]

While large amounts of agricultural and forestry products were shipped off to the *Reich*, the food situation in the area went from bad to worse.[90] Some of the *Kreishauptmänner* made no effort to hide the fact that mortality rates were

---

[83] See KH in Johanischkele, VB, 1st January 1917, HAL 641–1–389, fol. 107; KH in Rossienie, VB, 26th September 1917, HAL 641–1–53, fol. 166, 178f.; *idem*, VB, 31st December 1916, *ibid.*, fol. 100.

[84] KH in Schadow, VB, 29th September 1916, HAL 641–1–233, fol. 78. See also KH in Kielmy, VB, 11th July 1916, HAL 641–1–306, fol. 59; KH in Johanischkele, VB, 1st January 1917, HAL 641–1–389, fol. 107.

[85] KH in Kupischki, VB for the second quarter of 1917, HAL 641–1–572, fol. 91.

[86] *Chef der Deutschen Verwaltung* Wilna/Suwalki Abt.VIII 2327, 13th September 1916 regarding "*Konzentrationslager* Pogulanka", HAL 641–1–728, fol. 687f. To eradicate the effects of pre-war Tsarist settlement policy, it seemed advisable to remove the Russian minority from the population. See KH in Skaudwile, VB for the second quarter of 1917, HAL 641–1–306, fol. 132; *idem*, VB for the first quarter of 1918, *ibid.*, fol. 181; KH in Johanischkele, VB, 12th July 1916, HAL 641–1–389, fol. 56.

[87] KH in Rossienie, VB for the second quarter of 1917, HAL 641–1–53, fol. 157; similar KH in Kupischki, VB for the second quarter of 1917, HAL 641–1–572, fol. 80.

[88] See *OberOst* Abt.V, 14th October 1916, LAS F23–1, fol. 173f.; *Korrespondenz B* No.54, 2nd October 1917; *OberOst* Abt.V, *Betr.: Behandlung der Landeseinwohner*, 14th October 1916, LAS F24–1, fol. 173f.

[89] KH in Wiezajcie, VB for October 1917 to March 1918, HAL 641–1–515, fol. 285.

[90] KH in Rossienie, VB, 31st March 1917, HAL 641–1–53, fol. 133f.; *idem*, VB, 26th September 1917, fol. 176; *idem*, VB, 29th December 1917, *ibid.*, fol. 205; KH in Janischki, VB, 28th December 1916, HAL 641–1–374, fol. 83; *Stadthauptmann* in Kovno, VB, 2nd July 1917, HAL 641–1–584, fol. 65; *idem*, VB for period April to September 1917, *ibid.*, fol. 79; KH in Wiezajcie, VB, 1st April 1916, HAL 641–1–515, fol. 86.

significantly higher under German occupation than before the war.[91] The figures compiled by the *Deutsche Verwaltung* itself spoke for themselves: in Skaudwile, during the winter of 1917–1918, there had been 1,572 deaths compared with 1,304 births (including seventy-nine still-born babies) out of a population of roughly 66,000.[92] Local Jews, as well as Jewish organisations outside Lithuania, participated in joint efforts to alleviate the hardships created by German measures.[93] From Vilna the authors of a petition protesting against a further rise in the price of bread stated that the death-rate had reached eighty one per thousand inhabitants, while before the war it had been twenty one per thousand.[94] The semi-official *Korrespondenz B* of *OberOst* tried to dismiss such figures as a gross exaggeration.[95]

Despite claims to the contrary, German rule in occupied Lithuania, in fact far from total, had important (and for the people affected, primarily negative) ramifications.[96] Ludendorff mentions "diesen litauischen Wirrwarr"; to *Verwaltungschef* Heppe, the administrative apparatus created by his predecessor, Isenburg-Birstein, seemed like a "Wasserkopf".[97] As far as economic exploitation – the prime objective of German policy – is concerned, it remains questionable whether the benefits outweighed the costs.[98] For the administration, as well as for the police and for the military deployed in the area, preserving law and order turned out to be impossible, despite the fact that from December 1917 captured members of the *Banden* faced the death sentence.[99] By then even the puppet-agencies appointed by the Germans to keep up the appearance of Lithuanian self-determination revolted against being abused for the *Reich*'s benefit.[100]

---

[91] See KH in Skaudwile, VB for the second quarter of 1917, HAL 641–1–306, fol. 124; *Stadthauptmann* in Kowno, VB, 2nd July 1917, HAL 641–1–584, fol. 44; *idem*, VB, 31st December 1917, *ibid.*, fol. 82; *idem*, VB, 5th April 1918, *ibid.*, fol. 97.

[92] KH in Skaudwile, VB for the first quarter of 1918, HAL 641–1–306, fol. 187f. (For deaths and births in this *Kreis* in 1917 see also *ibid.*, fol. 209f.).

[93] See petition *"an Seine Königliche Hoheit den OberOst"*, 9th November 1916, signed by 16 representatives of various groups, including the *Oberrabbiner* of Vilna and the presidents of the Jewish relief committees, the Jewish merchants and the Jewish artisans, LAS F23–45, fol. 4–6. For German-Jewish initiatives see Szajkowski, *Jewish Relief*.

[94] Undated petition (probably mid-1917) signed by five Catholic, Lithuanian, Belorussian and Jewish (Rubinstein, Rosenbaum) representatives, LAS F9–3270, fol. 64f.

[95] Die Sterblichkeit in Vilna, in *Korrespondenz B*, No.56 (7th October 1917).

[96] "Die Repräsentanten der deutschen Autorität übten ihre Tyrannei bis in die kleinste Gemeinde aus." Camille Rivas, *La Lituanie sous le joug allemand 1915–1918. Le plan annexioniste allemand en Lituanie*, Lausanne 1919, p. 157; cf. Basler, p. 268.

[97] Ludendorff, p. 428; Linde, p. 68.

[98] The 10 to 20 million Marks listed as profits made by the *Deutsche Verwaltung* (see, for example, *Zusammenstellung der Verwaltungsausgaben 1916/17*, HAL 641–1–971, fol. 88f.; *Verwaltungshauptkassenabschlüsse* for 1917/18, HAL 641–1–697b) look impressive but do not contain the real costs of the administrative apparatus, which remained hidden in the overall army budget. As early as April 1916 the finance department of *OberOst* had dropped the ambition to make a profit and hoped "als Ergebnis ihrer sparsamen und angestrengten Tätigkeit nicht einen Fehlbetrag von mehreren hundert Millionen Mark figurieren zu sehen". Memorandum by Captain Tiesler, chief of *OberOst Finanzabteilung*, April 1916, HAL 641–1–883.

[99] *Tagesbefehl der Etappen-Inspektion der 10. Armee. Verordnung betr. das Bandenunwesen*, 9th December 1917, HAL 641–1–964.

[100] See Basler, pp. 279f., 302; Linde, pp. 94–110.

In villages, towns and cities, the people had lost all trust in a power which, at the beginning of the occupation, had claimed to liberate them from the Russian yoke.

For the Jews, Germany's defeat removed not only most of the pressure of monopolised trade but also Gentile inhibitions against antisemitic agitation.[101] A German informer in Krottingen reported as early as August 1915 that a local priest had tried to provoke the murder of Jews who had helped the German army.[102] In the district of Olita, where the long-suppressed frustration of the Lithuanians found its expression in early November 1918 in violent acts against German officials, the local Jews seemed an equally natural target. After incitement by a priest, Jewish houses were plundered and damaged.[103] This merely foreshadowed what the future held in store. It is not surprising, therefore, that in the inter-war years and especially after the Holocaust, Lithuanian Jews tended to regard the time of the German occupation during the First World War as a period of relative security and Prussian benevolence.

VI.

In Lithuania, German officials implemented a *Judenpolitik* based on pre-existing stereotypes and political exigencies, within an institutional framework designed to exploit and pacify the country. The results were as mixed as the origins. On the one hand, it presented an attack on the Jewish means of subsistence, an attack legitimised by an economic rationale. On the other hand, it included elements of "positive discrimination" which reinforced the German and Lithuanian aversion to Jews. However, this predominantly negative German *Judenpolitik* in Lithuania was neither a state-sponsored attempt to destroy Jewish existence nor an effort to transform individual or group-related antisemitism into political practice.

Despite the shortage of comparative studies on German occupation policies in the two world wars,[104] the evidence presented here offers some insight into the problem of continuity. Indeed, the negative elements of First World War *Judenpolitik* in the German-occupied parts of Russia re-emerged during Operation Barbarossa. Their significance, however, was greatly diminished by the "Final Solution of the Jewish Question" that followed. Moreover, those responsible for occupation policy in the Second World War rarely made reference to the *Kaiser-*

---

[101] Whether Lithuanian antisemitism was a new phenomenon resulting directly from German occupation policy, as claimed by Strazhas, *Ostpolitik*, p. 90; idem, *Dezernat*, pp. 316f., and Zechlin, p. 234, seems doubtful, given the complex mechanisms and long-standing traditions of ideological stigmatisation. See Dina Porat, 'The Holocaust in Lithuania. Some unique aspects', in David Cesarani (ed.), *The Final Solution. Origins and Implementation*, London New York 1994, pp. 159–174.

[102] *Chef der Geheimpolizei, Polizeibericht*, 5th August 1915, LAS F23–17, fol. 215, p. 2. The German secret police had advised its agents to recruit "primarily Germans and Jews" as local subagents. See instructions by *Chef der Geheimpolizei*, 16th July 1915, *ibid.*, fol. 167, p. 2.

[103] Protocol on the events in the district of Olita, 22nd November 1918, LAS F23–1, fol. 358–363. For early accounts of hostility towards the Jews see the reports by the *Geheimpolizei* dated August 1915, LAS F23–17, fol. 36, 211.

[104] See Gerhart Hass, 'Weltmachtziele – Europastrategie – Besatzungspolitik. Aspekte einer vergleichenden Okkupationsforschung', in *1999. Zeitschrift für Sozialgeschichte des 20. und 21. Jahrhunderts* 2 (1992), pp. 12–30.

reich's attempt to establish German power in Eastern Europe. Only in some areas did it seem appropriate to draw a direct line from Ludendorff to Hitler. For example, in 1941 an article in the Nazi journal *Jomsburg* identified the "parallel between military strategic and settlement-related thinking [*Nebeneinander von militärstrategischem und siedlungspolitischem Denken*]" prevailing in the *OberOst*-area, especially in regard to Kurland, as a point of reference for the Third *Reich*'s occupation policy in Eastern Europe.[105] In West German historiography up to the Fischer debate of the early 1960s, events during the First World War were presented as unconnected to the Nazis' grab for *Weltmacht*. Ironically but not surprisingly, those who, prior to 1945, had seen the First World War as a precedent for Hitler's *Lebensraum*-policy, insisted during the Cold War on the absence of historical continuity. After the war Robert Stupperich, the author of the 1941 article in *Jomsburg*, became professor and director of a centre for Eastern European research at the University of Münster, where he helped publish studies emphasising the comparatively benevolent nature of German rule in the *OberOst*-area.[106]

There can be no doubt that in the First World War, concepts like ethnic homogeneity, *Lebensraum* and *Bandenkampf* already guided German occupation policy. In contrast to what followed Germany's attack on the Soviet Union in the summer of 1941, this policy had not resulted in genocide during the First World War because of a number of interrelated factors – mainly factors linked to the actual historical situation. This calls for extensive analysis.[107] In addition to crucial differences between the political systems of the *Kaiserreich* and the Third *Reich*, both the German image of the Jew and the treatment of the "Jewish Question" underwent significant changes during the inter-war years. In Hitler's Germany the Jews were regarded as enemies of the healthy racial state and as the personification of Bolshevism. To the *Kaiser*'s representatives they appeared as one of many backward, repulsive and potentially troublesome groups. At that time, with the exception of the attempted restructuring of the economy, German *Judenpolitik* was incoherent and lacked a clear focus. In contrast, the Third *Reich*'s anti-Jewish policy developed in a gradual process, driven to a large extent by the eagerness of subordinates to implement what they regarded as the wish of the *Führer*.

---

[105] Robert Stupperich, 'Siedlungspläne im Gebiet des Oberbefehlshabers Ost (Militärverwaltung Litauen und Kurland) während des Weltkrieges', in *Jomsburg* 5 (1941), pp. 348–367; see also Basler, pp. 244f. and Rolf-Dieter Müller, *Hitlers Ostkrieg und die deutsche Siedlungspolitik. Die Zusammenarbeit von Wehrmacht, Wirtschaft und SS*, Frankfurt am Main 1991, p. 11. The importance of economic and demographic planning as a factor leading to the Holocaust is stressed by Götz Aly and Susanne Heim, *Vordenker der Vernichtung. Auschwitz und die deutschen Pläne für eine neue europäische Ordnung*, Hamburg 1991.

[106] See Linde, p. xiii.

[107] The thesis presented by Daniel J. Goldhagen, *Hitler's Willing Executioners. Ordinary Germans and the Holocaust*, New York 1996, of a long tradition of German "eliminationist antisemitism" poses the question why Germany did not perpetrate a Holocaust prior to the Nazis' coming to power. See the critical review by Christopher R. Browning, 'Daniel Goldhagen's Willing Executioners', in *History & Memory* vol. 8, No. 1 (Spring–Summer 1996), pp. 88–108.

Familiar Aliens:
German Antisemitism and European Geopolitics in the Inter-War Era

BY DAVID T. MURPHY

Historical efforts to trace the sources of the Holocaust have come nearly full circle in the half-century since the end of the Third *Reich*. Beginning with a dominant historical paradigm, which in the immediate post-war era located the origins of Nazi genocide in what seemed its most obvious site – the character of popular German antisemitism, Western historians who concerned themselves with the specific mechanics of the war against the Jews moved for a time toward so-called "functionalist" and other interpretative models which tended to minimise the direct role of Jew-hating.[1] These works rejected, implicitly or explicitly, the presumption that there was an immediate chain of events and decisions leading from the general cause of German antisemitism to the specific effect of the death camp. The results of more recent historical research, however, suggest that the serpent has at last swallowed its tail. Scholars writing since the early 1990s, including Christopher Browning, Norbert Kampe, Paul Lawrence Rose and, most contro-

---

[1]In the mid-1960s, for example, a work such as Peter Pulzer's *The Rise of Political Anti-Semitism in Imperial Germany and Austria*, New York 1964, p. 219, could talk of the "increasing pervasion of [German] social life" by antisemitism in the twentieth century. See, too, the conclusions of Eva G. Reichmann, 'Diskussionen über die Judenfrage, 1930–1932', in Werner E. Mosse and Arnold Paucker (eds.), *Entscheidungsjahr 1932. Zur Judenfrage in der Endphase der Weimarer Republik*, Tübingen 1965 (Schriftenreihe wissenschaftlicher Abhandlungen des Leo Baeck Instituts 13), pp. 503–534. On the other hand, by the 1970s a wave of local studies inspired by William Sheridan Allen's work was suggesting that antisemitism was not particularly significant as a reason for ordinary, non-Nazi Germans to support Nazi leadership or policies. See, for example, Jeremy Noakes, *The Nazi Party in Lower Saxony, 1921–1933*, Oxford 1971, pp. 208–210; Geoffrey Pridham, *Hitler's Rise to Power. The Nazi Movement in Bavaria, 1923–1933*, New York 1974; and, more recently, Walter Rinderle and Bernard Norling, *The Nazi Impact on a German Village*, Lexington, KY 1993, pp. 210–213. Many influential interpretations of the Holocaust from the 1970s to the 1990s, those of the so-called "functionalist" school whose best-known exponents are probably Karl Schleunes and the late Martin Broszat, interpreted the system of death camps as a makeshift response to German conquests in Eastern Europe. While not ignoring antisemitism, it was not central to this interpretation of the Nazi extermination of the Jews of Eastern Europe. See Martin Broszat, 'Hitler und die Genesis der "Endlösung". Aus Anlass der Thesen von David Irving', in *Vierteljahrshefte für Zeitgeschichte*, 25 (1977), pp. 739–775, and Karl Schleunes, *The Twisted Road to Auschwitz. Nazi Policy toward German Jews, 1933–1939*, Urbana 1970. For a perceptive overview of so-called "intentionalist" and "functionalist" interpretations of the Holocaust, see Michael R. Marrus, *The Holocaust in History*, Hanover, NH 1987, pp. 34–46.

versially, Daniel Goldhagen, have in various ways turned the attention of historians who study the Holocaust back to reflection upon the particular nature of German attitudes toward the Jews in the first half of the twentieth century.[2]

The effort to return antisemitism to the centre of our understanding of the Holocaust, however, confronts contemporary historians with a number of responsibilities and challenges. Some of these are fairly obvious. Before all else, for instance, the revived focus upon antisemitism requires careful, renewed attention to the details of the German public discourse on Jews in the years prior to and during the Holocaust. The public language of the Weimar and Nazi eras, examined in many settings, is the key to locating those specific images and perceptions of the Jews which might have served to legitimate in the popular mind policies which were directed toward the eradication of a Jewish presence in Germany.

Less obvious, perhaps, is the fact that such an attempt to gauge the unique dimensions of German antisemitism, and to place that antisemitism accurately in the German public consciousness of the inter-war years, demands a deliberately comparative perspective. Efforts to locate the sources of the Holocaust by focusing exclusively upon the dynamics of antisemitism within Germany alone are not likely to be very revealing. No one, after all, contends that antisemitism during the first half of the twentieth century was a phenomenon unique to Germany. Nearly everyone, on the other hand, concedes that the Holocaust was a uniquely German historical event. This simple reality challenges historians to transcend the bounds of German history, to seek through comparison answers to the question of what, if anything, distinguished German understandings of Jewishness in the pre-war era from popular understanding of Jewishness elsewhere. In other words, historians have to determine, in as precise a manner as possible, the exact ways in which German ideas about the Jews differed from those of the English, French, Americans or others on the eve of the Holocaust.

Insight into such popular German understanding might be teased from any number of threads in the vibrant warp of Weimar Germany's public intellectual life. One might examine the dramatic and controversial transformation of ideas about gender and sexuality, for example, or the revealing Weimar cinematic discourse on Jewry. One of the most promising venues for such an examination of ideas about Jews and Judaism in the period, however, might be found in the mix of geography, ethnography and political science which became widely known during the inter-war years, both in Germany and throughout the West, as "geopolitics".

Geopolitical thought was rooted in the waning years of the nineteenth century, when the global might of the Western industrialised nations (and of Japan as

---

[2]Christopher R. Browning, *Ordinary Men. Reserve Police Battalion 101 and the Final Solution in Poland*, New York 1992; Daniel Jonah Goldhagen, *Hitler's Willing Executioners. Ordinary Germans and the Holocaust*, New York 1996; Norbert Kampe, *Studenten und "Judenfrage" im deutschen Kaiserreich. Die Entstehung einer akademischen Trägerschicht des Antisemitismus*, Göttingen 1988; Paul Lawrence Rose, *Revolutionary Antisemitism in Germany from Kant to Wagner*, Princeton 1990. See also the essays collected in John Milfull (ed.), *Why Germany? National Socialist Anti-Semitism and the European Context*, Providence–Oxford 1993.

well, where geopolitics enjoyed a brief popularity) was at its zenith.[3] The ideological contours of geopolitical thinking were initially surveyed by Americans such as naval captain Alfred Thayer Mahan, whose *Influence of Sea Power upon History* found a striking resonance among an international audience at the turn of the century, and Britons such as the geographer Halford Mackinder, who argued that the continental "heartland" of Eurasia was the key to global power.[4] Mahan, particularly, was received with enthusiasm among the political and military elites of the Wilhelminian *Kaiserreich*, where geopolitical thinking initially emerged as an academic offshoot of geography.[5] The ubiquitous Friedrich Ratzel, a journalist, scientist and academic gadfly whose interests and writings ranged from geography to zoology to current politics and other topics, was the most influential promoter of geopolitical ideas in Germany in the decades prior to the First World War.[6]

The language of pre-war geopolitics in Germany, as in France, Italy and the Anglo-American world, was preoccupied with power politics and international competition. The First World War and its aftermath, however, transformed German geopolitical thought. The trauma of unexpected defeat, the almost surrealistic brutality of the war-time experience, which helped in the inter-war era to "normalise the unspeakable", and the profound intellectual disorientation produced by the political and social turbulence of the Weimar era, combined to turn German geopolitical thinkers in new directions.[7] The enormity of the political upheaval produced by the war, particularly in Eastern Europe, where Germany succeeded temporarily in restructuring the political geography of the entire region, encouraged German academic geographers to turn away from their pre-war interests in physical and mathematical geography and to attend

---

[3] An appraisal of the impact of geopolitics in late nineteenth- and early twentieth-century Japan can be found in Keiichi Takeuchi, 'The Japanese Imperial Tradition, Western Imperialism and Modern Japanese Geography', in Anne Godlewska and Neil Smith (eds.), *Geography and Empire*, Oxford 1994, pp. 188–206.
[4] A useful brief survey of the genesis of geopolitics can be found in S. D. Brunn and K. A. Mingst, 'Geopolitics', in Michael Pacione (ed.), *Progress in Political Geography*, London 1985, pp. 41–76. This essay also perpetuates some widespread distortions about the career of Karl Haushofer, however, including the assertion (p. 43) that Haushofer ran an "Institute für Geopolitik" (*sic*) in Munich during the war.
[5] Alfred Thayer Mahan, *The Influence of Sea Power upon History, 1660–1783*, Boston 1890, was translated into German within a few years at the insistence of Alfred Tirpitz and the *Reichsmarineamt*, which then distributed thousands of complimentary copies of the work to generate support for fleet construction. See Christian Graf von Krockow, *Die Deutschen in ihrem Jahrhundert 1890–1990*, Reinbek bei Hamburg 1990, p. 400.
[6] On the origins and development of geopolitics in Germany, see Geert Bakker, *Duitse Geopolitiek, 1919–1945: een imperialistische ideologie*, Utrecht 1967, pp. 170–178; Michel Korinman, *Quand l'Allemagne pensait le monde: grandeur et décadence d'une géopolitique*, Paris 1990; David T. Murphy, *The Heroic Earth. Geopolitical Thought in Weimar Germany, 1918–1933*, Kent, OH–London 1997; and Woodruff D. Smith, *Politics and the Sciences of Culture in Germany 1840–1920*, New York 1991. See the discussion of Ratzel as a geopolitical thinker in Heinz Gollwitzer, *Geschichte des weltpolitischen Denkens*, vol. II, *Zeitalter des Imperialismus und der Weltkriege*, Göttingen 1982, pp. 59–60.
[7] R. Weiss's characterisation of the war as an event which "normalises the unspeakable" is cited in Omer Bartov, *Murder in Our Midst. The Holocaust, Industrial Killing, and Representation*, New York–Oxford 1996, p. 49.

to more subjective branches of their discipline, such as political and cultural geography. "The monstrous experiences during the war," observed the geographer Karl Rathjens in 1927, "have weakened the distinct pre-war emphasis on geomorphological questions".[8] Geopolitical writers and teachers broadened the scope of their interests, creating a hybrid quasi-discipline which comprised elements of many fields. While geopolitics continued to denote a kind of topical and contemporary variant of simple political geography in the states to Germany's west, the German school of geopolitics began to diverge from the geopolitical thought of other western states in the post-war era, creating a new field with a number of distinctive characteristics.

The attention of German geopolitics after the war was drawn more and more insistently to the relationship between geography and race; environment and culture; national migrations; and social transformation. The intellectual *Eintopf* which German geopoliticians concocted from snippets of many related fields – anthropology, history, political science, statistics and ethnography, among others – then found its way, by the late 1920s and early 1930s, into German schools, newspapers, political propaganda and other venues.[9] For some of its practitioners, these geopolitical preoccupations led seemingly naturally to reflection upon the history and the characteristic traits of the Jews as a people, both within the borders of Germany and throughout Eastern Europe. The particular dimensions of German inter-war geopolitical thought offer historians an especially useful perspective on antisemitism, particularly as geopolitical thinking was most emphatically not confined to Germany in the inter-war years. Instead, it claimed the attention of a considerable academic audience in England, France and the USA during the same years, providing a potentially revealing field for the comparative examination of the geopolitical discourse on Jews across Western societies.

This discourse was characterised within Germany by an unarticulated tension which permeated the geopolitical perspective on the Jews, a tension

---

[8]Karl Rathjens, 'Das Hamburgische Weltwirtschaftsarchiv und seine Bedeutung für die Geographie', in *Petermanns Geographische Mitteilungen*, 73 (1927), p. 161.
[9]By the early 1930s, concepts and theories associated with "geopolitics" in Germany could reach an educated public through many institutional conduits. Seminars on geopolitics were a part of university life at places like the University of Göttingen, for example, where the geopolitical theorist Hans-Julius Schepers led a *"geopolitische Arbeitsgemeinschaft"* as part of the university's programme in international law. See *Georg-August Universität zu Göttingen. Verzeichnis der Vorlesungen, Sommerhalbjahr 1933*, Göttingen 1933, p. 12, and the letters on the library resources pertaining to geopolitics in Universitätsarchiv Göttingen, XVI.II.C.c.1., Mappe II, Bl. 21. Erich Obst at the Technical University of Hannover, Johann Wilhelm Mannhardt at the University of Marburg and many others worked to make geopolitical ideas part of the curriculum at their institutions. Popular school textbooks such as Paul Wagner, *Erdkunde für höhere Lehranstalten. Nach der Erdkunde von Fischer-Geistbeck unter Anlehnung an die neuen Lehrpläne*, Munich 1926, or Alexander Supan, *Leitlinien der allgemeinen politischen Geographie*, Berlin 1922, had a heavy geopolitical content. Political activists on the Right and the Left also used geopolitical concepts to justify German political claims in Eastern Europe. For their use in a right-wing political weekly, see (Anonymous), 'Ostpolitische Thesen', in *Standarte*, 14th September 1929, p. 865. On the Left, geopolitical ideas were often used to make demands for the restoration of German colonies overseas. See Max Cohen, 'Kolonialwirtschaft ist notwendig', in *Sozialistische Monatshefte*, 34 (1928), pp. 1042–1046.

deriving from the juxtaposition of two seemingly contradictory perceptions of the position of Jews in German social and cultural life. The leading German geopolitical writers of the inter-war era – Karl Haushofer, Walther Vogel, Otto Maull, Richard Hennig, Friedrich Burgdörfer and many others – adopted in the first place an implicit but nonetheless characteristic and frequently evidenced dual perspective on the on the role of the Jews in German society.[10] The critic or historian who seeks violent antisemitism in these writings will usually be disappointed. Until well into the Nazi era, beginning most noticeably in the late 1930s, this literature did not target Jews as objects of overt hatred, scorn or slander. Instead one finds frequent, casual allusions to Jews and Jewish history in relation to discussions of central geopolitical theories. The narrative voice of these writers' works presumes that its audience is both familiar with the Jewish presence in German society and that it is so aware that the Jews present a problem for this society that the fact itself requires little explicit articulation. In a backhanded way, this assumption of German familiarity with a problematic Jewishness implies a sort of intimacy which might be said to admit the Jews within the bounds of German society. At the same time, however, such familiarity is accompanied by a subtle but clear and disquieting effort to distance Jews from "genuine" German society, an attempt to persuade the reader that in fact the Jew is, after all, an alien. And not an alien, furthermore, whose presence is to be carelessly tolerated. Rather, Jews represent a potentially destructive alien presence, one whose familiarity, even ubiquity, cannot hide the fact that he lacks a truly "organic" relationship to the German geographical space.

Consider, for example, the features of the Jews as they appear in one of the canonical works of inter-war German geopolitics, Otto Maull's *Politische Geographie*, published in 1925.[11] Maull was one of the most academically reputable of the geopoliticians, a professor of geography at Frankfurt am Main, a co-founder of the influential *Zeitschrift für Geopolitik*, and by no stretch of the imagination a

---

[10]Haushofer is by far the best-known geopolitical theorist and is frequently given the dubious credit for having introduced Adolf Hitler to the term *Lebensraum*, through their mutual acquaintance Rudolf Hess. See Hans-Adolf Jacobsen, *Karl Haushofer. Leben und Werk*, Bd. I, Boppard am Rhein. 1979, pp. 240–241. However, the focus on Haushofer as the embodiment of German geopolitical thought can also lead to serious distortions. Vogel, Maull and Hennig, for example, all academic geographers or historians during the Weimar era (Vogel at Berlin, Maull at Frankfurt and Hennig at Düsseldorf) wrote influential geopolitical works of a substantially different nature from that which Haushofer represented. Burgdörfer, a committed supporter of the Nazis and Party member from 1937, was the director of the *Statistisches Reichsamt* during the late 1930s. His many publications on race and demography were a vital contribution to the development of a quasi-scientific racism as a central component of inter-war geopolitics. For example, see Friedrich Burgdörfer, 'Stadt oder Land? Berechnungen und Betrachtungen zum Problem der deutschen Verstädterung', in *Zeitschrift für Geopolitik* (hereafter *ZfG*), 10 (1933), pp. 105–113; also *idem, Volk ohne Jugend. Geburtenschwund und Überalterung des deutschen Volkskörpers. Ein Problem der Volkswirtschaft–der Sozialpolitik–der nationalen Zukunft*, Berlin 1932. On his career and Nazi Party affiliation, see Berlin Document Center, Personalakten Burgdörfer. An informative discussion of Haushofer's typically opaque utterances concerning Jews and Judaism is to be found in Dan Diner, '"Grundbuch des Planeten". Zur Geopolitik Karl Haushofers', in *Vierteljahrshefte für Zeitgeschichte*, 32 (1984), pp. 6–10.
[11]Otto Maull, *Politische Geographie*, Berlin 1925.

person who would be deemed a conventional antisemite.[12] In Maull's book, an exhaustive and magisterial theoretical exposition of some 750 pages which exerted a potent formative influence on a generation of geopoliticians, the Jew is a figure who is both peripheral and yet curiously recurrent. He is exhibited again and again, always in passing, as an example of mostly dysfunctional social or cultural responses to the influence of geography. The Jew, for example, is adduced as evidence in support of the assertion that some groups which possess a unique and clearly defined ethnographic identity have nonetheless historically remained "stateless peoples". Such groups, though they may own land as individuals, have never achieved as a nation "the synthesis between people and space [*Volk und Raum*] necessary to a state".[13] Later, the Jew vindicates Maull's observations concerning the dire effects of the loss of the *Staatsidee*, or commitment to a national political vision, for peoples who have lost or never had "state organisms" of their own. The Jews of European Russia are cited by Maull's narrative as an instructive example of the tendency inherent in certain linguistic subgroups towards rejection of the dominant *Staatsidee* of their political nation, leading Maull to argue that American and German suspicion of the war-time loyalties of immigrant Jews from Eastern Europe was perfectly natural, given what he portrayed as their disruptive impact upon society and politics in Tsarist Russia.[14] None of this, obviously, bears any direct resemblance to the more extreme forms of Nazi-era antisemitism. Maull's attitudes toward the concept of "race" were quite complex, and he openly scorned many of the crucial tenets of biological racist theories. And yet the accumulated impact of his frequent, offhand exhibition of the Jews as exemplars of destructive cultural responses to geopolitical influences cannot but leave the uncritical reader of Maull's work with the impression of a Jewish "problem".[15]

Works of history, geography and political science written by geopolitical theorists throughout the Weimar and early National Socialist eras persistently follow this pattern. Only very rarely do these geopolitical narratives engage the Jews and their history in any direct or systematic fashion. Instead, Jews appear in various guises as examples of negative trends in the relationship between landscape or geography on the one hand and ethnicity or race on the other. One writer contrasts the ancient Hebrews unfavourably with the ancient Phoenicians, who overcame the continental heritage of their "plains origins" to construct a seagoing empire, an evolution which the Jews of antiquity never achieved. Another writes about the threat of downward population pressure exerted upon ethnic

---

[12] The history of the magazine and an appraisal of its influence (its peak circulation was around 5,000) are available in Karl-Heinz Harbeck, *Die "Zeitschrift für Geopolitik" 1924–1944*, Ph.D. diss., University of Kiel 1963.

[13] Maull, p. 67.

[14] *Ibid.*, pp. 109, 413.

[15] While at times embracing the importance of race – "Die Rassengrundlage ist letzten Endes nichts anderes als der Urgrund alles politischen Seins" – Maull also ridicules simplistic racial theories – "Von einer 'germanischen' und 'slawischen', von einer 'arischen' und 'jüdischen' Rasse reden ist ebenso, als wenn man von einer 'kurzschädeligen Grammatik oder blonden Syntax' reden wollte", *ibid.*, p. 370.

groups by the modern migration to urban landscapes, using demographic trends among German Jews as her example of "extinction through urbanisation". Another laments the "unnatural" impact of Jews on the geographical landscape since they are supposedly given as a people to destructive migrations and urbanisation, as well as spreading nonorganically derived political doctrines such as those of Karl Marx ("What mischief this single Hebrew has brought upon the world!"). Still another warned in the mid-1920s of the dissolution wrought in national unity by *"nationalfremd"* elements, arguing that, in the case of Germany specifically, the divisive doctrine of Socialism "is disseminated in the first degree by members of a nationally foreign people [*Volkstum*], that is, by Jewry".[16]

The ideological ancestry of this pseudo-scientific and subtly antisemitic subtheme of German geopolitics (for it would be a distortion to present Jews as a thematic preoccupation of the geopoliticians) is clear and, in most respects, fairly well known. It blended theories from the last days of the Enlightenment with concepts which were radically modern. The geopolitical depiction of Jews as foreign elements in the German *Nationalkörper* grew in part out of a tradition of environmentalist racialism which reached back as far as Immanuel Kant, particularly in his lectures on physical geography delivered in 1765, and in essays such as 'Von den verschiedenen Racen der Menschen'. While it would be grossly misleading to present Kant as some kind of early modern biological racist, his theories that the origins of physical variations among human beings lay in their geographical environment, and his speculation that this might also exert a formative influence upon non-physical traits, lent the patina of German humanism to a fateful trend.[17] This climatic and environmentalist determinism was kept alive in the *Kaiserreich* and was transmitted directly into modern German geopolitical thought by theorists such as Ratzel, whose key geopolitical work, *Politische Geographie* (1897), had just before the turn of the century adopted a modified environmental determinism regarding the supposedly characteristic qualities of peoples and ethnic groups.[18] Geopolitical writers who sought to

---

[16] Adolf Grabowsky, *Staat und Raum. Grundlagen räumlichen Denkens in der Weltpolitik*, Berlin 1928, pp. 23 and 26; Elisabeth Pfeil, 'Die deutschen Juden als Beispiel für das Aussterben bei Verstädterung', in *ZfG*, 10 (1933), p. 113; Karl Haushofer to Kurt Vowinckel, 1st April 1943, in Jacobsen, Bd. II, p. 553; Walther Vogel, *Das neue Europa und seine historisch-geographischen Grundlagen*, Bonn 1925, p. 100. Curiously, though he laments an imagined cultural prominence of Jews in Germany – the German-Jewish "Herscherrolle ist unerträglich" – Vogel on the other hand lauds the Jews as "movers and shakers of the often somewhat phlegmatic Germans", a view of the German character which had been common for decades at least, *ibid.*, p. 101. See, for example, almost precisely the same appraisal of the nature of Germans written over half a century earlier, in Johannes Scherr, *Illustrierte Deutsche Kultur- und Sittengeschichte*, Bd. II, Berlin 1870 (reprinted Berlin 1984), p. 287; or, Rudolf Hess's rather surprising assertion that the infusion of non-Germanic blood sometimes produced "the best Germans". See his letter to Karl Haushofer's wife Martha, 17th December 1921, in Jacobsen, Bd. II, pp. 6–7.

[17] See, for example, the notes on "Physische Geographie" in 'Nachricht von der Einrichtung seiner Vorlesungen in dem Winterhalbjahre von 1765–1766', in Preussische Akademie der Wissenschaften (ed.), *Kants Werke. Akademie-Textausgabe*, Bd. II, Berlin 1968, pp. 312–313; also, 'Von den verschiedenen Racen der Menschen', *ibid.*, pp. 427–443; also, Immanuel Kant, 'Physische Geographie', in *Klassische Texte der Physischen Geographie in Faksimile*, Bd. II, Amsterdam 1975, pp. 1–7.

[18] Friedrich Ratzel, *Politische Geographie*, 3rd edn., Munich 1923, pp. 155, 404–427. The work first appeared in 1897.

portray Jews as fundamentally alien due to the non-German origins of Jews and Judaism, to characterise "*Judentum*" as a kind of "Asiaticness [*Asiatentum*] contrary to the autochthonous western soul", were merely developing one of many elements in the theoretical heritage of their pseudo-science.[19]

Portions of the intellectual pedigree of the geopolitical suspicion of Jews were thus quite old. At the same time, however, a much more modern language focused upon the interaction of two elements — race and *Raum* — infusing inter-war German geopolitics with a very modern biological racism which had been barely evident in the field before the war.[20] The intellectual *milieu* of which Ratzel's political geography was a part included both the speculative ethnography of fantasists like Houston Stewart Chamberlain and the pre-war racist biology of Alfred Ploetz and the *Archiv für Rassen- und Gesellschaftsbiologie*.[21] In the intellectual hothouse of the Weimar Republic, these aspects of Wilhelminian academic life mingled to produce strange fruits indeed. While Kant, Ratzel and others had speculated (rather than asserted) that some cultural traits might have a link to environmentally-generated, physical racial differences, post-war geopoliticians increasingly emphasised the centrality of biologically-transmitted racial traits to the interaction between race and *Raum*.[22] "All human development goes back in the final analysis to two things," as one put it, "to the race, which creates, and to the environment, which supplies the potential for creation".[23] By the late 1930s, such deterministic environmentalist racism had become a staple of geopolitics and history in Germany, one which was widely used to trace the historical development of the German *Reich*: "Without *Raum* no race, without race no *Reich*, whose development, flowering and passing can be handed on by history. As the *Raum* has etched its deep runes in the character of the race, so the *Raum*, as an organic component of the essence of the national life form, stamps its impression upon the manifestations

---

[19] Hans Mühlestein, 'Deutschland in der Ost-West Spannung', in *ZfG*, 3 (1927), pp. 6–7.

[20] An excellent illustration of the shift in the geopolitical understanding of the importance of race can be seen in the work of Alfred Hettner, editor in the 1920s of the *Geographische Zeitschrift*. In his book *Das europäische Rußland. Eine Studie zur Geographie der Menschen*, Leipzig 1905, Hettner emphasised culture, not race, as the chief human factor modifying the impact of geography upon societies (see p. 57 and p. 87, for example). On the other hand, in a post-war work such as his *Die Geographie. Ihre Geschichte, ihr Wesen und ihre Methoden*, Breslau 1927, he places a new emphasis upon race (see the discussion beginning on p. 144, for example).

[21] See the antisemitic phrenology of Chamberlain, as well as his interpretation of the causes and impact of Jewish dispersal, which is similar to some subsequent geopolitical writing, in Houston Stewart Chamberlain, *Die Grundlagen des neunzehnten Jahrhunderts. Erste Hälfte*, 13th edn., Munich 1919, pp. 426–427 and 536–537. The work first appeared in 1898. For valuable commentary on Chamberlain's place in European antisemitism, as well as an informative discussion of biological racism in Germany before the war, with details on Alfred Ploetz and his journal, see George L. Mosse, *Toward the Final Solution. A History of European Racism*, New York 1978, pp. 79–81 and 105–108.

[22] In this, of course, geopolitics simply conformed with the generally growing impact of racial theories in the German and Western intellectual worlds. See also the discussion of racist and racialist thought with regard to the "Jewish Question" in Rose, pp. 124–125.

[23] Alois Fischer, 'Neue Untersuchungen über Rasse und Volkstum, II', in *ZfG*, 3 (1926), p. 952.

of that life form."[24] Racial biology and geographical space, as another put it, "had to make the German people what they are today".[25]

As this abbreviated examination of uses of the idea of "race" in German geographical and geopolitical writing suggests, the meaning and significance of race experienced a considerable evolution in Germany between the late nineteenth century and the early 1920s, an evolution hastened by the violence and brutality of the First World War. The speculation about the nature of environmentally-generated differences between human populations which had characterised the work of a social scientist such as Ratzel, or which may still be noted in the writings of turn-of-the-century pioneers of demography such as Max Haushofer, were increasingly replaced by the strident certainties of eugenicists and colonial enthusiasts.[26] As Detlev Peukert has observed, researchers in the human and social sciences began to assign value to individuals and groups on the basis of the alleged genetic endowment inherent in members of "races".[27] The geographic profession was as susceptible as other fields to the infiltration of racial theories, initially through such sub-disciplines as cultural geography and political geography, which functioned as the progenitors of the post-war German geopolitical discourse.[28]

Little historical imagination is necessary to predict accurately where the amplified strain of racism in post-war geopolitical thought would leave the Jews in the geopolitical vision of Germany once the nation came under the sway of National Socialism. Increasingly, geopolitical writers took the position that it was no longer enough merely to ensure that Germany had sufficient geographical space, or *Lebensraum*: it was just as important to see that the human content of this space possessed the proper racial characteristics.[29] One can thumb through the pages of the *Zeitschrift für Geopolitik* from the late 1930s and early 1940s almost at random, for example, and find increasingly overt, geopolitically-derived argu-

---

[24]Hans-Julius Schepers, *Stoffe und Gestalten der deutschen Geschichte*, Bd. II, Heft 1, *Geopolitische Geschichtsschreibung*, Berlin 1937, p. 3.

[25]Louis von Kohl, *Ursprung und Wandlung Deutschlands. Grundlagen zu einer deutschen Geopolitik*, Berlin 1932, p. 5: "... what the German people is today, with its strengths and weaknesses, with its good and its bad, that it had to be. There was no other way in which it could go. The racial composition of the population and the formation of the soil, the type of climate, its position in the middle of Europe, had to make the German people that which it is today."

[26]Haushofer's largely forgotten pioneering demographic work was concerned primarily with determining population policies designed to improve material living standards. See for example, Max Haushofer, *Bevölkerungslehre*, Leipzig 1904, pp. 111–114.

[27]Detlev J. K. Peukert, 'The Genesis of the "Final Solution" from the Spirit of Science', in David F. Crew (ed.), *Nazism and German Society 1933–1945*, London 1994, p. 279.

[28]An informative discussion of this process may be found in Mechthild Rössler, *"Wissenschaft und Lebensraum". Geographische Ostforschung im Nationalsozialismus*, Berlin 1990, pp. 49–63. See also the review of the evolution of racist thought in the second chapter of Michael Burleigh and Wolfgang Wippermann, *The Racial State. Germany 1933–1945*, Cambridge 1991, pp. 23–43.

[29]"Hand in Hand mit der Propagierung der Lebensraumtheorie ging die Diskriminierung der anderen Völker mit Hilfe der Rassentheorie." Hellmut Harke, 'Die Legende vom mangelnden Lebensraum', in Claus Remer (ed.), *Auf den Spuren der "Ostforschung". Wissenschaftliche Zeitschrift der Karl-Marx-Universität Leipzig, Gesellschafts- und Sprachwissenschaftliche Reihe*, Sonderband I, Leipzig 1962, p. 61.

ments for the view that the Jew does not belong in a healthy German society. In considering whether Palestine, Manchuria (where the Soviet Union experimented with the creation of a Jewish autonomous region) or Madagascar was the most suitable site for Jewish resettlement in 1940 (the necessity of Jewish expatriation itself is presumed), for example, one of the magazine's contributors captured the geopolitical viewpoint quite succinctly: "Because of their strongly-marked racial peculiarity, proven through many centuries of residence among outsiders, which hinders their assimilation among the host people, the Jews, thanks to their growing population, have become increasingly viewed as a foreign body [*Fremdkörper*] by the nations among whom they live."[30] Similar sentiments, sometimes put in considerably more direct form, are found throughout the pages of the *Zeitschrift für Geopolitik* during the war.[31]

When German geopoliticians between the wars replaced culture with race as the main variable mediating the impact of geography upon human populations, they articulated a geo-racial vision of national identity which gradually but clearly tended towards expulsion of the Jews from a place in the *Nationalkörper*.[32] This geo-racial vision was entirely congenial to the National-Socialist regime, of course, and Jews begin to appear in geopolitical literature with greater frequency, and as a progressively more malignant influence after January 1933. The influx of Jews into Eastern Europe in the late medieval and early modern eras, for example, now explained the subsequent retreat of the German cultural and racial presence from that region in more recent centuries, a retreat which created a vacuum "whose heirs would in many places become the Eastern Jews".[33] It was the Jew, with his inorganic relationship to the region's geography, who was made responsible for the "uprooting" of Germanic culture in the Eastern European *Raum*, and who threatened to hasten the decay of that culture in Germany itself.[34] Geopolitical and *völkisch* writers increasingly, in their own words, "grasped the *Raum* and its inner articulation" to warn their fellow Germans, "Woe to the community which is too strongly irradiated by a foreign race!"[35]

---

[30] F.W. Borgman, 'Palästina, Birobidjan oder Madagaskar? Eine geopolitische Untersuchung', in *ZfG*, 16 (1939), p. 1.

[31] See for example, P.H. Seraphim, 'Die Wanderungsbewegung des jüdischen Volkes. II', in *ZfG*, 17 (1940), p. 43: "It obviously can not be in the interest of the German people and *Reich* to allow a Jewish population of such numerical significance and even greater economic importance to remain in the German Eastern districts which must first of all be ethnically strengthened (*in den völkisch erst zu befestigenden deutschen Ostgebieten*)". The "German Eastern districts" here discussed were in Poland prior to September 1939.

[32] A pre-war geopolitician such as Ratzel, for example, had been quite sceptical of the value of the concept of "race" as a means of interpreting or explaining the links between social and cultural development on the one hand and geography on the other. See his critical comments on *völkisch* and racialist thought cited in Gollwitzer, p. 59.

[33] Hans Roeseler, 'Die Ausbreitung der Deutschen in der Welt', in Karl Haushofer and Hans Roeseler (eds.), *Das Werden des Deutschen Volkes. Von der Vielfalt der Stämme zur Einheit der Nation*, Berlin 1940, p. 513.

[34] Peter-Heinz Seraphim, *Das Judentum im osteuropäischen Raum*, cited in Götz Aly and Susanne Heim, *Vordenker der Vernichtung. Auschwitz und die deutschen Pläne für eine neue europäische Ordnung*, 2nd edn., Frankfurt am Main 1993, p. 98.

[35] Adolf Helbok, *Grundlagen der Volksgeschichte Deutschlands und Frankreichs. Vergleichende Studien zur deutschen Rassen- Kultur- und Staatsgeschichte*, Berlin 1935, pp. 10–11.

The National-Socialist effort to bring all aspects of German public life under the control of their party, the so-called *Gleichschaltung*, was especially successful within the geographical sciences, due in part to their already highly developed sensitivity to the racial questions which preoccupied the Nazis.[36] Naturally, this intensified the engagement of German geopolitical writers with the question of the place of the Jews in German society. Within three months of the Nazi accession to power, the *Arbeitsgemeinschaft für Geopolitik*, a loose consortium of journalists, academics and others concerned with heightening the geopolitical awareness of the German people, had petitioned the education authorities in each German state to pay particular attention to the geopolitical consideration of "the state as a life form" and the significance of "population science" in relationship to geopolitical factors.[37] Over the next few years, geopolitical theorists exhorted their fellows in ever more vehement tones to incorporate the "significance of racial factors" into their practice of geopolitical analysis.[38] By the onset of the war in 1939, German geopolitical writers responded by adopting the clichés of National-Socialist antisemitism, including warnings against the "Jewish-capitalist" conspiracy to weaken German self-determination and admonitions to take heed of the dire geopolitical consequences of racial mixing from the example of the "niggerisation (*Verniggerung*)" of a declining France.[39]

It is not difficult, then, to find a good deal of evidence to prove that a pervasive, muted biological and environmentalist antisemitism infused German geopolitical writing before the advent of the Third *Reich*. This strain of geopolitical thinking, furthermore, intensified demonstrably between 1933 and 1945. Like antisemitism, however, geopolitics was a supranational ideology, an academic fashion that was embraced in all the Western states before the First World War and during the inter-war period. As Hans Weigert pointed out during the Second World War, Karl Haushofer derived his own geopolitical convictions from the works of a German (Ratzel), an Englishman (Mackinder) and a Swede, Rudolf Kjellen, who is generally credited with having coined the word "geopolitics" in 1899.[40] While the geopolitical project of analysing relations between states from a spatial perspective probably found its most enthusiastic devotees in Germany, geopolitics was practised in various forms in the states to Germany's west, as well as in the United States, Italy

---

[36] For an account of the profession and its educational policies under Nazism, see Henning Heske, ... *und morgen die ganze Welt. Erdkundeunterricht im Nationalsozialismus*, Giessen 1988, pp. 35ff.
[37] Arbeitsgemeinschaft für Geopolitik (ed.), 'Denkschrift: Geopolitik als nationale Staatswissenschaft', in *ZfG*, 10 (1933), pp. 301–302. On the *Arbeitsgemeinschaft*, its purposes, and the assessment of its founder that it was a failure, see Jacobsen, Bd. I, pp. 248–250, and Bd. II, pp. 152–154.
[38] Louis von Kohl, 'Biopolitik und Geopolitik als Grundlagen einer Naturwissenschaft vom Staate', in *ZfG*, 10 (1933), p. 308.
[39] Arbeitsgemeinschaft für Geopolitik (ed.), *Geopolitische Geschichtslehre und Volkserziehung*, Heidelberg 1939, pp. 24, 44. One could also cite the satisfaction at the decline in the population of "foreign elements", particularly the Jews, in such works as *Erdumfassender Bericht über die Bevölkerungsentwicklung 1937–1941. Schriften zur Geopolitik*, Heft 21, Heidelberg 1941, pp. 9–10.
[40] Hans W. Weigert, *Generals and Geographers. The Twilight of Geopolitics*, London–New York 1942, p. 24. For the first use of the term "geopolitics", see Rudolf Kjellen, 'Studier öfver Sveriges politiska gränser', in *Ymer*, IX (1899), pp. 283–332.

and Russia.[41] Was the racist antisemitism of geopolitics in Germany in fact unique to the Germans, and did it contribute to what some scholars have characterised as a phobic antisemitism, a "hallucinatory, lethal view" of the Jews which prepared the way for German acquiescence and participation in the Holocaust?[42]

The answers to these two questions, respectively, are Yes, definitely and Yes, probably. German geopolitical rhetoric between the wars was distinguished from other Western geopolitical traditions not by its racism, which was endemic in various forms throughout the West, but by the extent of its general concern with issues of race and by its specific racial preoccupation with Jews. The concept of race appeared less frequently as a factor in the geopolitical writings of Germany's Western neighbours, including the United States, than it did in those of the Germans. Moreover, when race was treated in these other geopolitical traditions at that time, there was a tendency to concentrate on topics concerning the supposed three great human families of white, black and yellow.[43] But there is not even a great deal of this omnipresent form of early twentieth-century Western racialism to be sifted out of the geopolitical traditions of England, France or the United States at the time. Certainly, the comments and writings of Mackinder or J. A. Hobson, who is sometimes included among *fin-de-siècle* English geopolitical thinkers, occasionally betrayed racist and antisemitic attitudes.[44] Outside Germany, however, the mandarins of Western geomancy – Mackinder, Derwent Whittlesey, James Fairgrieve or Nicholas Spykman in the Anglo-American world, and Albert Demangeon or Paul Vidal de la Blache in France – were so intently focused upon military preparedness, maritime competition and the international conflict over access to vital resources that race rarely figured in their prognostications, and Jewry

---

[41] Giorgio Roletto and Ernesto Massi, founders of *Geopolitica*, the Italian counterpart to the *Zeitschrift für Geopolitik*, can be seen as representative of the Italian school of colonialist geopolitics in the interwar era. For an appraisal of their ideas see Lucio Gambi, 'Geography and Imperialism in Italy. From the Unity of the Nation to the "New" Roman Empire", in Godlewska and Smith (eds.), pp. 74–91. A good example of a Russian geopolitical perspective can be seen in Oskar von Niedermayer and Juri Semjonow, *Sowjet-Russland*, Berlin 1934.

[42] Daniel Goldhagen, 'The Evil of Banality', in *The New Republic*, 13 (1992), p. 52. (Review of Christopher Browning, *Ordinary Men. Police Reserve Battalion 101 and the Final Solution in Poland*, New York 1992.)

[43] For example, the lengthy discussion of the impact of environment upon the development of racial characteristics to be found on pages 278–282 of Paul Vidal de la Blache and Emanuel de Martonne, *Principes de géographie humaine*, Paris 1922, although subscribing to environmental determinism, has nothing to say about the Jews, but discusses Christianity, Islam and the "Semitic" peoples of Northern Africa. Similarly, although Albert Demangeon, in *Le déclin de l'Europe*, Paris 1920, discusses black-white relations (pp. 264–265, for example), he has little to say on questions regarding the Jews.

[44] Mackinder in a number of speeches expressed a colonialist, "white man's burden" form of racism, arguing that the European global hegemony of his era was justified by the supposed civilising mission of the "white races". Hobson unquestionably subscribed to a conspiracy theory of Jewish financial capital, but his thinking was never a part of the mainstream of English geopolitical thought. See the discussion of both thinkers in Gerry Kearns, 'Fin de siècle geopolitics. Mackinder, Hobson and theories of global closure', in Peter J. Taylor (ed.), *Political Geography of the Twentieth Century. A Global Analysis*, London 1993, pp. 23–25.

almost never.[45] The most influential work of geopolitics published anywhere in the West between the wars, Halford Mackinder's *Democratic Ideals and Reality*, has in almost three hundred pages nothing to say about race as a concept, and treats the Jews once, describing in a single paragraph the prospects for a future Jewish homeland in Palestine.[46]

Direct comparisons project the distinctive language and concerns of the German school of geopolitics with particular clarity. One of the most widely-read works of the English school of geopolitics during the inter-war period, James Fairgrieve's *Geography and World Power*, diverges in significant respects from a German work of equal influence in its own land of origin, Ratzel's *Politische Geographie*. Both works subscribed to a similar environmental determinism: "We have seen that men may advance or fall behind because the geographical conditions affecting their bodies react on their minds," as Fairgrieve put it – but their racial preoccupations differ.[47] A comparison of index entries in Fairgrieve's work, for example, suggests that blacks and Catholics came more readily to mind as examples of geopolitical trends: eight entries appear under the heading "Negroes", and seven under that of "Catholics", while "Judaism" appears twice. Fairgrieve's only more-than-passing reference to Jews and their history discusses the eclipse of the weak kingdom of the Hebrews by the ancient Assyrians and Egyptians.[48] For Ratzel, while Jews are no obsession (they appear four times in his index), they receive more extended and ambivalent treatment as exemplars than they are accorded by Fairgrieve. The tenacity of the Jews in their faith, for example, (which one might suppose would be viewed as a positive trait) is adduced paradoxically as evidence that any state which aspires to permanence must have what the Jews did not, a firm grounding in the soil.[49] What Ratzel sees as the cultural malleability of the Jews is cited later on as one of the sources of the "Jewish Diaspora, already mighty by the time of the Roman Empire".[50]

An equally revealing contrast can be discerned between two later, approximately contemporaneous geopolitical works, both concerned with the relationship of geography to defence, but one English and the other German: David Henry Cole's *Imperial Military Geography. General Characteristics of the Empire in*

---

[45] A perusal of the following (admittedly far from comprehensive) list of Anglo-American-French works contemporaneous with the German geopolitical writings under consideration found no discussions of Jews or Judaism: Albert Demangeon, *Le Rhin*, Paris 1935; De la Blache and Martonne; James Fairgrieve, *Geography and World Power*, New York 1917, a work which was translated into German by Karl Haushofer's wife, Martha; Nicholas John Spykman, *The Geography of the Peace*, ed. by Helen R. Nicholl, New York 1944; Derwent Whittlesey, *The Earth and the State. A Study of Political Geography*, New York 1944.

[46] Halford J. Mackinder, *Democratic Ideals and Reality. A Study in the Politics of Reconstruction*, New York 1962, pp. 173–174. The book first appeared in 1919: "The Jew, for many centuries shut up in the ghetto, and shut out of most honorable positions in society, developed in an unbalanced manner and became hateful to the average Christian by reason of his excellent, no less than his deficient, qualities."

[47] Fairgrieve, p. 117.

[48] *Ibid.*, p. 45: "Leaning first to one and then to another of the two great empires, the kingdom of the Hebrews was finally crushed in the struggle between them."

[49] Ratzel, p. 28.

[50] *Ibid.*, p. 166.

Relation to Defence (1924), and Ewald Banse's Raum und Volk im Weltkriege (1934). Cole's very popular work (nine editions in fourteen years) anticipates Banse's in many ways. Like Banse, the Englishman is concerned with the impact of new weapons technologies upon defence. Like Banse, he adopts a deliberately spatial and geographical perspective from which to consider military history, resource competition and the sources of political friction within the international system. The differences between the two works are as glaringly apparent as are these thematic similarities, however. Apart from mentioning Britain's imperial reliance upon non-white troops in some regions, for instance, Cole has nothing whatsoever to say about race, let alone about Jews or Judaism. On the other hand, race takes an early and prominent role in Banse's discussion of the strategic dilemmas which confronted Germany during both the World War and the 1930s, and he considers the Jews directly as an example of a problematic racial subgroup. In a sub-chapter devoted to "Race, Nation and Temperament", for example, Banse argues that the failure of the Austro-Hungarian armies in the Great War was due in part to their being composed of "completely different and warring races which hated and despised each other", and among whom the Jews assumed a prominent place.[51] Any point-by-point comparison fails, however, to convey the striking difference in tone which characterised the two works – dispassionate and academic, on the one hand, and detached apocalyptic, racialist and Social Darwinist on the other.

The difference in the authors' voices displayed in these two works carried over into many other works in both schools of geopolitics, particularly after 1933. Even at the most basic level of definitions, the language of the German geopolitical tradition between the wars differed markedly from that of the other Western nations. For a Swede like Kjellen, for example, geopolitics was, quite simply "The theory of the state as a geographic organism or phenomenon in space, i.e., land, territory, area, or most especially, as nation".[52] For the American geographer Richard Hartshorne, writing in 1935, geopolitics meant "the application of the knowledge and techniques of political geography to the problems of international relations".[53] Contrast the relative clarity and directness of these definitions with that offered by Ewald Banse in the *Lexikon der Geographie*, first published in 1923 but reissued in 1933 (when "The time of the German rebirth has arrived," as the editor stated in the introduction to the second edition) with the following under its entry for "*Geopolitik*": "Geopolitics, a term coined during the World War utilised the laws of political geography in politics, which obviously does not yet have a clearly delineated content. The foundations of existence are embodied in each state in its political idea. Geopolitics must clearly discern this, and pursue it in unerring, clever fashion, discerning also the degree to which it is capable of development, and so far as this expresses itself territorially thereby leading to

---

[51] David Henry Cole, *Imperial Military Geography. General Characteristics of the Empire in Relation to Defence*, 9th edn., London 1937; Ewald Banse, *Germany Prepares for War. A Nazi Theory of "National Defense"* (original title *Raum und Volk im Weltkriege*), transl. by Alan Harris, New York 1934, p. 52.
[52] Rudolf Kjellen, *Der Staat als Lebensform*, transl. by Margarethe Langfeldt, Leipzig 1917, p. 46.
[53] Hartshorne cited in Brunn and Mingst, p. 48.

conflict with other political bodies. The possibility of executing sound geopolitics is strongly influenced by conditions of geographical situation and spatial extent, by racial and nationality questions (ethnopolitics), by economic, social and domestic political circumstances, and not least by the propaganda of the press."[54]

The racialism of the German school of geopolitics, therefore, especially in its specific manifestation in the attention devoted to the Jews, does distinguish German geopolitics from Western geopolitics in general. And, the inter-war German geopolitical gloss upon the meaning of Judaism may be justly characterised as antisemitic. It remains difficult, however, to answer the question of the role of all this in preparing the ground for the Holocaust in anything like a definitive fashion. Jews were far from being a central thematic concern for German geopoliticians. Is the tendency of geopolitical writers to occasionally exhibit the Jews as substantiating evidence of geopolitical maladaptation in the *Nationalkörper* really the ancestor of, or even a real conributor to, Adolf Hitler's racist obscenities? Is casting the Jews as the largely undeserving beneficiaries of German cultural pioneering in eastern Europe somehow related to casting the Jews as Hitler's "maggot in a rotting corpse"?[55]

Unfortunately, the answer to this question is probably Yes. It is extremely unlikely that any of the authors here cited to demonstrate German geopolitical devaluation of Jews would have confirmed Hans Frank's insistence that the Jews were a lower species of life.[56] Few would have been likely to argue with Prof. Dr. Franz Alfred Six, SS *Untersturmführer* and professor of law at the university at Königsberg, however, when he declared in 1943 that the "racial-*völkisch* consciousness", conditioned by "the Germanic race and the Greater German *Raum*", called for the creation of a new "Germanic *Gemeinschaft*" in East-Central Europe.[57] There is no question that the turn of German geography, and to a certain extent German history, towards exclusionary theories of race and national formation under the Nazis clearly provided an intellectual underpinning for the extermination of the Jews. It seems clear that this process of exclusion was facilitated and endowed with the apparent sanction of scientific scholarship by the language of German geopolitics during the inter-war era.[58]

---

[54] Ewald Banse (ed.), *Lexikon der Geographie*, Bd. I, Leipzig 1933, p. 495. Contributors to the work included Haushofer, Hugo Hassinger and others.
[55] Cited in Robert Jay Lifton, *The Nazi Doctors. Medical Killing and the Psychology of Genocide*, New York 1986, p. 16.
[56] Cited in Raul Hilberg, *The Destruction of the European Jews*, Chicago 1967, p. 12.
[57] Cited in Léon Poliakov and Josef Wulf (eds.), *Das Dritte Reich und seine Denker. Dokumente*, Berlin 1959, p. 380. Six was not at all unique in incorporating geopolitical concepts into his understanding of law. This was common throughout Germany during the Nazi era, as in the cases of the seminar for international law at Göttingen already noted, or in the work of theorists of international law such as Carl Schmitt or Otto Koellreutter, a prolific author and member of the *Akademie für Deutsches Recht*. See, for example, the passages on "Staatslehre und Geopolitik" in Otto Koellreutter, *Grundriss der Allgemeinen Staatslehre*, Tübingen 1933, pp. 29 ff, and on Schmitt, Peter Gowan, 'The Return of Carl Schmitt', in *Debatte*, 2 (1994), pp. 82–127.
[58] To obtain a sense of the geopolitical contribution to these fields, see the discussion of *Volks- und Raumgeschichte* and *Raumforschung und Raumordnung* in Willi Oberkrome, *Volksgeschichte. Methodische Innovation und völkische Ideologisierung in der deutschen Geschichtswissenschaft 1918–1945*, Göttingen 1993, pp. 91–98 and 108–111.

As always, when considering the impact of ideas, it is not easy to come to conclusions which may be empirically tested concerning the influence of geopolitical thought either in Germany or in the other states here examined. A good deal of evidence suggests, however, that geopolitical ideas enjoyed a higher profile in Germany in these years than they did in other Western nations. Among Germany's academic geographers, geopolitics was something of an unloved stepchild.[59] No German universities established academic chairs for geopolitical instruction or research, for example. On the other hand, German geopolitical thinkers had their own successful journal, a considerable presence in textbooks, and connections in the early 1930s to a network of journalists and scholars in the so-called *Arbeitsgemeinschaft für Geopolitik*.[60] Secondary schools in Prussia were issued curriculum guidelines in 1925 which required that students be familiarised with "the system of state in its dependence upon its position and the natural attributes of its *Lebensraum*". The same guidelines explicitly stipulated that such instruction was to culminate in "discussion of world economic and geopolitical problems".[61]

Somewhere in this period, too, Hitler himself acquired *Lebensraum* and other geopolitical jargon, and at least some of his soldiers who marched into Russia in 1941, according to their later accounts, explained what they were doing by reference to *Geopolitik*.[62] The German student at work in his school library, the German newspaper reader riding the underground home from work, the casual observer of German politics, all seem to have been more likely to come across geopolitical ideas than their American, English or French counterparts, and an important component of those geopolitical ideas was a subtle, exclusionist antisemitism. As the descent into the abyss continued under Adolf Hitler, the apologetic role of geopolitics in the propaganda justifying National-Socialist imperialism and the use of what was euphemistically called "*Volkstumspolitik*" to prepare the newly-conquered German *Lebensraum* became ever more prominent.[63]

[59] An academic geographer such as Alfred Hettner, for example, could be scathing in his condemnation of the pretences and the "more obscuring than clarifying terminology" of geopolitics. See Alfred Hettner in *Geographische Zeitschrift*, 34 (1928), p. 308. (Review of Adolf Grabowsky, *Deutschland und das Weltbild der Gegenwart*, Berlin 1928).
[60] Haushofer's academic and media connections were extensive. On the short-lived *Arbeitsgemeinschaft für Geopolitik* see Jacobsen, Bd. II, pp. 152–153, and on media connections for geopolitical thinkers, Bd. I, pp. 181–182.
[61] *Richtlinien für die Lehrpläne der höheren Schulen Preußens. Amtliche Ausgabe*, Berlin 1925, pp. 19, 22; also, the suggestions in 'Erdkundlicher Unterricht in den höheren Lehranstalten', in *Zentralblatt für die gesamte Unterrichts-Verwaltung in Preußen*, 66 (5th May 1924), p. 12. Both of the above are in *Geheimes Staatsarchiv Preussischer Kulturbesitz*, Berlin–Dahlem. Instruction in Prussia was by no means more "geopoliticised" than in other German states at the time. See the comparative tables in Fritz Klute, 'Die Lehrpläne der Geographie an den höheren Schulen', in *Geographischer Anzeiger*, 28 (1927), pp. 351–359. Geographical propaganda in German education in this regard is discussed in Heske, pp. 35–36.
[62] Heinz-Werner Hübner, who served at the start of the Russian campaign, recalled later that one soldier, explaining to his comrades the need for the invasion, "lectured on geopolitics". See Heinz-Werner Hübner, 'Vom Feldzug zum Krieg', in *Die Zeit*, 14th June 1991, p. 12.
[63] The observations of Lothar Gruchmann on the role of geopolitics are still apt: see *idem*, *Nationalsozialistische Grossraumordnung. Die Konstruktion einer "deutschen Monroe-Doktrin"*, Stuttgart 1962, pp. 9–22. See too the discussion of the use of the *Lebensraum* ideology in Militärgeschichtliches Forschungsamt (ed.), *Das Deutsche Reich und der Zweite Weltkrieg*, Bd. 5, Stuttgart 1988, pp. 133–135.

Many years ago, George Mosse wrote that "German antisemitism is a part of German intellectual history. It does not stand outside it".[64] Mosse was undoubtedly right, but he might have expanded on the obvious implications of his observation to note that just as antisemitism is part of the larger whole of German intellectual history, so that intellectual tradition is also a part of a larger totality. The quiet, gradual relegation of the Jew to the status of problematic German at best and corrosive foreign presence at worst, which was evident in German geopolitical writing between the wars, represented one strand of a complex intellectual tradition which had disastrous political and social conseqences. The unobtrusive utilisation of the Jew as an obvious case of dangerous geo-racial trends carried with it an implication that author and audience shared an unspoken awareness of the Jews as a "problem". The casual geopolitical familiarity with problematic Jewishness ironically served to emphasise the status of the Jew as an unauthentic German, as an outsider, "other", or alien. In the Western geopolitical language of the period, this familiar alien was a distinctively German creation. It is difficult not to conclude that this distinctive creation, established as a part of the mental furniture of many Germans through the "science" of geopolitics, helped to create the distinctive fate which this familiar alien was later compelled to endure.

---

[64]George L. Mosse, *Germans and Jews. The Right, the Left, and the Search for a " Third Force" in Pre-Nazi Germany*, New York 1970, p. 60.

Jews and the Fatherland in the Twentieth Century

Ostracised for Loyalty:
Ernst Lissauer's Propaganda Writing and its Reception*

BY ELISABETH ALBANIS

"Was schiert uns Russe und Franzos',
Schuß wider Schuß und Stoß um Stoß!
Wir lieben sie nicht,
Wir hassen sie nicht,
Wir schützen Weichsel und Wasgaupaß,-
Wir haben nur einen einzigen Haß,
Wir lieben vereint, wir hassen vereint,
Wir haben nur einen einzigen Feind:
Den ihr alle wißt, den ihr alle wißt,
Er sitzt geduckt hinter der grauen Flut,
Voll Neid, voll Wut, voll Schläue, voll List.
Vernehmt das Wort, sagt nach das Wort,
Es wälze sich durch ganz Deutschland fort:
Wir wollen nicht lassen von unserm Haß,
Wir haben alle nur einen Haß,
Wir lieben vereint, wir hassen vereint,
Wir haben alle nur einen Feind:
England."[1]

This verse from Ernst Lissauer's poem *Haßgesang gegen England* could be seen in the room displaying war propaganda at the exhibition on First World War art and modernity, *Die letzten Tage der Menschheit*, in the *Altes Museum* in Berlin from 10th June to 28th August 1994.[2] It was the exhibition's only specimen of textual propaganda and shows that although Lissauer may be largely forgotten, his poem is not.

No other German war publication was as well known and as widely distributed

---

*I am indebted to Dr. Anna Carrdus, Dr. Gabriele Rahaman and Dr. Diane Spielmann for editorial and archival assistance. For encouragement and advice in the course of writing this paper I am deeply grateful to my supervisor Professor Peter Pulzer as well as to Dr. David Rechter and Dr. Edmund Thomas.

[1] Ernst Lissauer, 'Haßgesang gegen England', in *Worte in die Zeit. Flugblätter 1914 von Ernst Lissauer*, 1. Blatt, Göttingen 1914.

[2] The exhibition was organised by the *Deutsches Historisches Museum*, the *Staatlichen Museen zu Berlin – Preußischer Kulturbesitz*, the National Gallery and Barbican Art Gallery, in conjunction with the Imperial War Museum, London. The English title of the exhibition was "The Avant-Garde and the Great War. A Bitter Truth. Last Days of Mankind. Images of World War I".

as the *Haßgesang*. Its author was associated throughout his life with this poem, and no effort on his part could dissociate him from it.[3] This powerful poem, which "threw back at him the curse of exclusion",[4] certainly struck a nerve when it was first published in September 1914:

> "The poem exploded like a bomb in a munitions depot. Possibly no other poem in Germany, not even the 'Watch on the Rhine', spread as quickly as this notorious 'Hymn of Hate'. The Kaiser was most enthusiastic and bestowed the Order of the Red Eagle upon Lissauer; the poem was reprinted in all the newspapers; teachers read it out to their pupils; officers at the front recited it to their soldiers, until everyone knew the litany of hate by heart."[5]

The poem's impact, both in Germany and abroad, was immense. It was translated into other languages and regional dialects, its first verse was printed on postcards, and parts of it were used as the titles of official leaflets. Lissauer's biographer, Guido Brand, claims that the poem, translated into three languages, was even distributed to neutral countries through the business correspondence of banks and merchant houses. In addition, it was sent to all regiments by order of the Bavarian Crown Prince.[6] In 1935 Lissauer received the Honorary Cross for War Services (*Ehrenkreuz für Kriegsteilnehmer*).[7] The certificate was issued "in the

---

[3]"Ernst Lissauer's *Haßgesang gegen England* had become frowned upon by the middle of the war and it became the tragi-comedy of the author that these otherwise forceful and honest verses, which had made him an instant celebrity, subsequently took their revenge on him; he could not rid himself of that odium all his life. Possibly less so because he was a Jew." Robert Faesi, *Erlebnisse. Ergebnisse. Erinnerungen*, Zürich 1963, p. 206.
[4]Guido K. Brand, *Ernst Lissauer*, Stuttgart–Berlin 1923, p. 71.
[5]Stefan Zweig, *The World of Yesterday*, 3rd English edn., London 1944, p. 180.
[6]Brand, p. 70. It seems that there has been some misunderstanding over this point. Brand's mention of the Bavarian command caused some to believe that Lissauer himself served in the Bavarian army. Accordingly, the *Mitteilungen* of the *Verein zur Abwehr des Antisemitismus* described Lissauer as "a soldier of the Bavarian Infantry Regiment": *Mitteilungen*, No. 19 (3rd December 1914), Art. 'Kriegslyrik.' This is, of course, not the case. From November 1916 he served in the Home Guard (*Landsturm*) in Hungary and from the end of 1917 in the Press Office of the War Ministry. I am grateful to Erik Lindner for providing me with the quotations from the *Mitteilungen* and the *Hammer* (this note, and n. 55 below) and for first pointing out that Lissauer was believed to have served in the Bavarian army.
[7]This point requires some explanation. The certificate entitling Lissauer to collect his Honorary Cross was issued in the name of the "*Führer* and *Reichskanzler*" on 12th July 1935. One would expect military awards for service in the First World War not to have been issued to Jews after 1933 but closer investigation into the nature of the *Ehrenkreuz* shows that the award, founded by Field Marshal von Hindenburg on 13th July 1934, was intended for all participants in the war, as well as for the widows and parents of the fallen. "Participants in the war" are defined as every *Reichsdeutscher* who fought on the side of the German or on the side of Germany's allies. The second decree, which was passed only a month later, stated that it was now to be issued in the "name of the *Führer* and *Reichskanzler*". By November 1936 the Honorary Cross had been issued to over eight million Germans, not counting those Germans who were in the *Wehrmacht*, resided in the Saar region or anywhere else outside the German Empire including, at that time, of course, Austria, where Lissauer resided. Kurt-Gerhard Klietmann (ed.), *Deutsche Auszeichnungen*, vol. II, *Deutsches Reich 1871–1945*, Berlin 1971, pp. 27f. I am grateful to Dr. Tutenberg of the Militärbibliothek, Dresden, for his assistance. Particularly fascinating in this connection are Professor W.T. Angress's recollections, which seem to confirm that Jews and non-Jews alike were entitled to receive the *Ehrenkreuz* if they fulfilled the requirements of the decree mentioned above: "Some time in late 1934 or early 1935 my father came home one day and displayed his *Ehrenkreuz* for service during World War I which he had just picked up at the local *Meldestelle*. ... [P]rior to the 'Nuremberg laws', anybody, regardless of descent, who could prove

name of the *Führer* and *Reichskanzler*" on 12th July and bears the issue number 58/3 190 K.

The five entries for Lissauer in the exhibition catalogue refer to him as a German writer, little known prior to the publication of the notorious *Haßgesang*. No reference is made to Lissauer's Jewish heritage. Lissauer's identity, however, is an important factor in the context of his nationalist writings. His Jewishness is significant because it influenced his stance as a German not because "only a Jew could have written the Haßgesang," as Houston Stewart Chamberlain wrote polemically in his *Neue Kriegsaufsätze*,[8] but because Lissauer's determination not to let his Jewish heritage diminish his commitment to Germany is a distinguishing characteristic of his writings. His fierce and uncompromisingly assimilationist stance caused him to glorify the notion of an undivided nation.

In the twenty years before the First World War, and even more so during the course of the war, questions were raised regarding the position of Jews in Germany. Until the late 1880s there had been a widespread expectation among both Jews and Gentiles that subscription to legal emancipation would lead automatically to social emancipation and integration. It is arguable, however, that from the 1880s German Jews began to realise that living as a Jew in Germany created conflicts which could not be eradicated by legal emancipation alone. The question became whether non-Jews could accept that Jews were a distinct kind of German.

Those who took the principal initiative in re-defining and re-emphasising the validity of the emancipation contract were politicians and individuals who, if not politicians themselves, acted through political channels such as the *Centralverein deutscher Staatsbürger jüdischen Glaubens* and the *Verein zur Abwehr des Antisemitismus*. It is likely, however, that reasonably educated German Jews would also have looked to a writer rather than to politicians for a role model.

Lissauer is known to have held an extreme assimilationist view during the pre-war period. He became, during the war, a figure of some controversy because an increasing number of Jews and non-Jews were not prepared to accept such a stance. This led him, as far as one can tell, to abandon his political affiliation with *Deutschtum*, although he continued to regard himself as a German writer. In this transformation of his identity he might, therefore, be taken to represent a section of German-speaking Jewry whose security as Germans had also been undermined by the war.

The question is whether Lissauer's political stance, as expressed in his pre-war writings, is consistent with the *Haßgesang*, which was not a mere momentary slip caused by the poet sharing in the general enthusiasm for war. This essay will attempt to answer this question by discussing, first, Lissauer's pre-war and wartime writings, especially those whose themes affected his relationship with

---

that he had served somewhere during World War I as a soldier, could pick up the *Ehrenkreuz für Kriegsteilnehmer*." I am very grateful to Professor Angress and Dr. Arnold Paucker for sharing their profound personal knowledge of this question with me.

[8]Houston Stewart Chamberlain, *Neue Kriegsaufsätze*, Munich 1915, p. 8.

Germany, the importance of a unified nation and the conscious promotion of an historical memory; second, how the war intensified Lissauer's call for national unity, culminating in the creation of a universal *Feindbild* in his *Haßgesang gegen England*, the poem's reception at home and abroad, and its impact on the debate on the "racial disposition" for hatred among Jews; third, Lissauer's self-awareness as a writer and its effect on his self-prescribed mission of letting his writings work as a national unifying force. The essay will also examine the contrast between Lissauer's motivation in his intellectual war service and that of Thomas Mann. Fourth, an analysis of the shift that took place in Lissauer's identity from a commitment to German culture to a commitment to Jewishness will show that Lissauer's change of allegiance cannot only be linked to the setback he experienced in 1915 because of negative reactions to the *Haßgesang*, as Lissauer portrays it in his autobiographical account *Bemerkungen zum Leben*. Finally, the essay will examine Lissauer's struggle with, and acceptance of, his dual identity as illuminated by his poems.

Born in 1882 in Berlin into a family which, as co-founders of the *Berliner Reformgemeinde*,[9] had opted for the de-hebraisation of Judaism and assimilation with German culture, Lissauer was brought up "as a German".[10] Stefan Zweig, who planned to edit a lyrical anthology with Lissauer in 1912,[11] described him as "perhaps the most Prussian or Prussian-assimilated Jew I knew".[12] In his *Autobiographische Skizze*, written during the war, Lissauer himself described the relationship between his Germanness and Jewishness: "In my upbringing my parents did not stress the Jewish element in the least. I have always felt myself to be primarily a German, without suppressing my Jewishness."[13] In 1933, Lissauer used a somewhat harsher tone to describe the attitude of his parents, grandparents and school friends towards Jewish people, especially those of Eastern European origin. Even the word "Jew" was not permitted to be used in his parents' house in the presence of young girls, but had to be substituted by the terms "Armenians" or "Abyssinians". Lissauer might well have grown up a Protestant had his father carried out his intention to have him baptised before the age of fourteen. Since he failed to do so, the choice was, by law, left to Ernst himself, who refused to convert – not because he wanted to maintain his Jewish faith, but because institutionalised religion had no meaning for him.[14] Lissauer's biographer confirms that Judaism had little influence on the poet:

---

[9]Michael A. Meyer, *The Origins of the Modern Jew. Jewish Identity and European Culture in Germany, 1749–1824*, Detroit 1967, pp. 81–83 and 134–135; Ludwig Geiger, *Geschichte der Juden*, vol. II, p. 221. Cf. Ernst Lissauer, 'Bemerkungen über mein Leben' (1933), in 'Bemerkungen über mein Leben: Zu den Aufzeichnungen des Dichters Ernst Lissauer aus dem Jahre 1933', in *Bulletin des Leo Baeck Instituts*, Nos. 17–20 (1962), pp. 286–301, here p. 290.

[10]Renate Heuer, in *Neue Deutsche Biographie*, vol. XIV, Berlin 1985, pp. 690–691. Note that Ernst Lissauer had mistakenly been referred to as an "Austrian writer". Knut Beck et al. (eds.), *Stefan Zweig. Briefe 1897–1914*, Frankfurt am Main 1995, p. 504.

[11]Cf. Stefan Zweig's letter to Julius Bab, dated 22nd June 1912, in Beck et al., pp. 258 and 504.

[12]Zweig, p. 267.

[13]Ernst Lissauer, *Autobiographische Skizze*, (*Sonderdruck Literarisches Echo*), (1917/18), Leo Baeck Institute Archives, New York.

[14]Lissauer, 'Bemerkungen über mein Leben', pp. 297–299.

Ernst Lissauer

From the Archives of the Leo Baeck Institute, New York.

"Lissauer never made a secret of his Jewishness and never made attempts to curtail or hide it. It had no special significance in his upbringing, but continued to grow beside his Germanness without his having to fight the same battles as those who, living in a host country, are made intellectually and spiritually restless by ancient tradition. Zionism is as alien to him as the renunciation of his birth, and certain spiritual tendencies, which over time became ever clearer, led him away from Judaism and Christianity."[15]

Brand's book was an attempt to distance himself, by "de-judaising" Lissauer's writings, from the anti-Jewish interpretation of literary history. As a result, although Brand's book was a direct rejection of *völkisch* literary history and probably an implicit criticism of Adolf Bartels,[16] it targeted only the indiscriminate rejection of cultural contributions by Jews, not antisemitism as a movement. In the latter, Lissauer was regarded as the exception, who did not fit into the category of those Jews influenced by their dual heritage. Ludwig Geiger had asked Lissauer in either late 1914 or early 1915: "Permit me a frank question: were you or are you still a Jew?"[17] To which Lissauer responded:

"I come from a Jewish family and converted neither to nor from Judaism. To what extent any ancestors still have an influence on me, I do not know; in my consciousness I am rooted in Germanness. I have always openly admitted my Jewishness and I also took part in the debate initiated by Moritz Goldstein in *Der Kunstwart* in 1912."[18]

In his denial of the need for conversion Lissauer emphasised that Judaism was not decisive enough a factor to require renunciation. Yet the very fact that Lissauer felt compelled to state that he did not conceal his Jewish heritage makes it clear that he was not entirely indifferent to how the Jewish community perceived him.

---

[15]Brand, p. 16.
[16]It becomes very evident that Lissauer's biographer was strongly opposed to so-called *deutsch-völkisch* literary interpretation and, in particular, to Adolf Bartels's book on literary history. Brand devotes a separate chapter to that kind of literary criticism in Germany, the sole purpose of which was to use literature as a political expression of racial theories. The most prominent representative of this kind of literary criticism he saw in Adolf Bartels, of whom he wrote:

"Der gewiegteste, wortvollste, zettelkatalogreichste Propagandist des gepachteten Deutschtums ist Adolf Bartels, der stolz darauf ist, ...eine antisemitische Literaturgeschichte geschrieben zu haben ... Den Begriff 'deutsch-völkisch' führt er in die Literaturgeschichte als ein Maßstab des Dichter- und Schriftstellertums ein, er ergänzt ihn nach und nach mit dem gehässigen Gegenbegriff 'jüdisch'. Er ist ein Verdächtiger par excellence und Spürhund nach jüdischen Müttern und Vätern. Er wittert in Grammatik jüdische Gesinnung, in Stoffwahl jüdische Vorliebe. Wie oft er danebengreift: darüber müßte ein besonderes Buch geschrieben werden, wenn es der Mühe wert wäre."

Guido K. Brand, *Werden und Wandlung. Eine Geschichte der deutschen Literatur von 1880 bis heute*, Berlin 1933, p. 227.
[17]Letter from Ludwig Geiger to Ernst Lissauer, Berlin, n.d., in Ernst Lissauer, Diary 16, Nov. 1914–April 1915, LBI Archives, New York. Ludwig Geiger (1848–1919) was a literary historian and editor of the *Allgemeine Zeitung des Judentums*. I am grateful to Dr. Lutz Sartor for his help in deciphering Geiger's letter.
[18]Lissauer, draft for an answer to Ludwig Geiger, LBI Archives, New York.

COMMEMORATION, NATIONAL UNITY AND THE EVOCATION OF TRADITION

Lissauer was well known as an author before the publication of the *Haßgesang* in 1914. He had published a volume of poems entitled *Der Acker* in 1907, followed by a second volume, *Der Strom*, in 1912 and had used much of his writing to express his strong and undivided affiliation to Germany. This was less due, as Egmont Zechlin argues, to an intrinsically Jewish sensitivity to "the secret currents of time" than to a strong identification with German nationalist ideals and aims.[19] Werner Mosse argues that Lissauer's works also conveyed the coming of war.[20] Indeed, Lissauer's diaries show a strong preoccupation with Anglo-German relations, in particular with the arms race.[21] Lissauer was concerned about Germany's future welfare and independence. He had already foreseen Anglo-German confrontation in 1912 and kept a close watch on Britain's political movements.[22] He followed the speeches made by British politicians with suspicion and from his review of Rudolf Schröder's book *Deutsche Oden*, it is clear that his concerns were consistent with the classic pre-war antagonism between the established naval power, Britain, and an Imperial Germany aspiring to world-power status.[23]

> "... The poet is worried about the future of Germany, her position on the European continent, the weakness of our foreign policy and the growing strength of our opponents; and he is full of concern about whether the Germany of export and industry, the Germany of recently acquired wealth, is prepared to brave the dangers and fight the battles which may be necessary for the sake of her future."[24]

Lissauer's review covers most of Germany's contemporary political concerns, including the emphasis on common ground between all Germans, the strengthening of the bonds of unity of interests, Germany's position in the hierarchy of states, the striving for a stronger presence in foreign politics, the oft-quoted "place in the sun" called for by Chancellor von Bülow, and the search for new markets and spheres of influence.[25]

Lissauer repeatedly evokes a sense of history and remembrance in his writings. He strives to uphold and continue tradition and calls for greater unity within the German nation. Of these themes the latter was the strongest, especially at the outbreak and during the first year of the war.

---

[19]Egmont Zechlin, *Die deutsche Politik und die Juden im ersten Weltkrieg*, Göttingen 1969, p. 97.
[20]Werner E. Mosse, 'Die Krise der europäischen Bourgeoisie und das deutsche Judentum', in *Deutsches Judentum in Krieg und Revolution 1916–1923*, Tübingen 1971 (Schriftenreihe wissenschaftlicher Abhandlungen des Leo Baeck Instituts 25), p. 6.
[21]Cf. Ernst Lissauer, Diary 13 (June 1912–June 1913), LBI Archives, New York.
[22]*Ibid.*, pp. 21–41.
[23]Cf. Jonathan Steinberg, *Yesterday's Deterrent. Tirpitz and the Birth of the German Battle Fleet*, Ipswich 1965.
[24]'Ernst Lissauer über Rudolf Alexander Schröder, "Deutsche Oden", Leipzig', in 'Lyrisches', in *Das Literarische Echo. Halbmonatsschrift für Literaturfreunde*, vol. XVI, No. 12 (15th March 1914), p. 862.
[25]"With his name [Bernhard von Bülow] is associated above all the expansionist German '*Weltpolitik*'. Bülow did not invent this policy. But he summed it up in a catchy formula and rapidly gained decisive influence on the 'world-political' actions of the Imperial government." Gerd Fesser, *Reichskanzler Bernhard Fürst von Bülow. Eine Biographie*, Berlin 1991, p. 155.

The *Haßgesang*, the most famous but also the most reviled of Lissauer's poems, occupied a pivotal role in the poet's life and may therefore serve here as the prism through which to observe how Lissauer, as a German Jew, experienced a conflict in his commitment to national ideas.

Before the publication of the *Haßgesang*, Lissauer's nationalism was expressed most unambiguously in the *Kunstwart* debate sparked by Goldstein's *Deutsch-Jüdischer Parnass*. In Lissauer's view there were only two alternatives for a Jew in Germany:

> "Only two things are possible: either to emigrate, or to become German. But then [you have] to dig yourself in, to root yourself with all your might, with all your sinews and all your muscles to educate yourself as a German, and to make the tasks and endeavours of the Germans your own."[26]

Lissauer had a passion for Prussia and ascribed this to his sensibility for the monumental architecture in Berlin, such as the *Gendarmenmarkt*, the Schiller monument, the monument to Frederick the Great and the Brandenburg Gate, and for patriotic youth literature. Oscar Höcker's *Preussens Wehr – Preussens Ehr* and Franz Otto's *Der grosse König und sein Rekrut* inspired the fourteen-year-old: "My enthusiasm for 1813 and my indignation about French oppression were set alight by that fourth volume."[27] He maintained his enthusiasm until the centenary of the *Völkerschlacht* when, in his collection of poetry entitled *1813*, he dealt with the German liberation from French occupation. In these poems, which already contain aspects of what was later to be used in propaganda, Lissauer rejected the idea of submitting to foreign rule for reasons of safety and convenience. In this poem the temptation to give in to the French and betray the Prussian will to victory and power is violently resisted by blond and blue-eyed people who, possessing prophetic qualities, see hope for Germany and her freedom in the future. In one poem from *1813*, entitled *Windsaersage I. Die Notzeit* (Times of Distress), which describes an emergency meeting among Silesian, Pomeranian and Brandenburg farmers whose fields and tools have been devastated and destroyed by the French, a Prussian peasant speaks out against accepting French rule:

> " '...Eine Hilfe ist auf Erden: Französisch werden!'
> Aber ein Mann aus der preußischen Heide
> Hieb ihm die Faust in den redenden Mund:
> 'Da hast Du ein Maulvoll Getreide
> Für die Wegfahrt in den rheinischen Bund.
> Wir wollen lieber preußisch verhungern
> Als uns französisch mästen!' "[28]

---

[26]Lissauer, in 'Sprechsaal. Deutschtum und Judentum', in *Der Kunstwart*, vol. XXV, No. 13 (April 1912), p. 12. See also Zweig, p. 267, on Lissauer's commitment to Germanness and German language and culture in particular: "Deutschland war ihm die Welt, und je deutscher etwas war, um so mehr begeisterte es ihn. Niemand kannte besser die deutsche Lyrik, niemand war verliebter, verzauberter in die deutsche Sprache – wie viele Juden, deren Familien erst spät in die deutsche Kultur getreten, war er gläubiger an Deutschland als der gläubigste Deutsche."

[27]Lissauer, 'Bemerkungen über mein Leben', p. 293.

[28]Ernst Lissauer, *Windsaersage I. Die Notzeit, 1813. Ein Cyklus*, Jena 1913.

It is also no coincidence, given that Lissauer ascribed the original source of resistance to French rule to a leader of Scandinavian origin, that in Lissauer's historical play *Yorck*, written between 1916 and 1921, it is a Norwegian professor who stirs up the students at the University of Breslau to urge war against France.[29]

Lissauer knew and exploited the many parallels between 1813 and 1914. Friedrich Wilhelm III's *Aufruf an mein Volk* (Appeal to my People) served to unite the anti-Napoleonic forces, which resulted six months later in Prussia's victory over France. In 1813, a year after the edict that brought Jews in Prussia a step closer to civil equality with non-Jews, men fought as Prussians and Germans.[30]

> "On 16th March 1813 the King issued an 'Appeal to my People'. Even though not absolutely everyone responded to that appeal, many volunteers – including many Jews – signed up with the Free Corps or the Militia or the Home Guard. Hopes of reform and hatred of the French had created at least among the educated bourgeoisie a consciousness of communal spirit and the idea of national autonomy."[31]

Wilhelm II's speech some hundred years later, known as the civic truce (*Burgfrieden*), in which he disregarded party differences in order to create a common front ("I see no parties any longer; I see only Germans"), had the same function.[32] In his New Year's Eve essay entitled *1914/15*, Lissauer, too, harked back to General Blücher's heroic leadership in the winter campaign of 1814 to create the impression that none of what was happening at the Western front in 1914 was new, and that German troops had previously been victorious against the French:

> "Let us turn back in time. The Prussian army under Field Marshal Blücher pursued the French, and when their sentry saw the valley of the silvery Rhine, they jubilantly greeted the watery border with cheers. Now, again, our troops are pushing their way to the West towards another great river; it has not as yet been bridged, but we are all hoping for the crossing of the Marne, which another Blücher will force. It is with this in mind that we remember the New Year's Eve of a hundred years ago."[33]

In this essay the invocation of a new era at the outbreak of the war on the one hand, and the occasion of New Year's Eve on the other, form a significant parallel. The "eve of peace", 31st July 1914, is evoked as a minutely described countdown to the making of world history with the Germans in the forefront. Above all, the war signifies the strengthening of the bond of each individual with the whole. The feeling that fate has unified the nation must never be forgotten, as Lissauer implores his readers:

---

[29]Ernst Lissauer, *Yorck. Schauspiel in 5 Akten und einem Vorspiel*, Berlin 1921, pp. 85 ff.
[30]*Edikt betreffend die bürgerlichen Verhältnisse der Juden in dem Preußischen Staate*, Berlin (11th March 1812), in 'Gesetz-Sammlung für die Königlich Preußischen Staaten', vol. III, Berlin 1812, in G. Korff and W. Ranke, *Preußen. Versuch einer Bilanz*, Hamburg 1981, p. 295. For a more in-depth discussion of the legal-historical background of the Emancipation Edict of 1812 and Jewish participation in the so-called *Befreiungskriege*, see the recent study by Erik Lindner, *Patriotismus deutscher Juden von der napoleonischen ra bis zum Kaiserreich*, Frankfurt am Main 1997, pp. 48–104.
[31]*Edikt*, in Korff and Ranke, *Preußen*, p. 300.
[32]'Eröffnungssitzung. Dienstag den 4. August 1914 im Weißen Saale des Königlichen Schlosses zu Berlin. Verhandlungen des Reichstags. Dreizehnte Legislaturperiode. Zweite Session. 1914. Band 306', in *Stenographische Berichte*, Berlin 1916.
[33]Ernst Lissauer, *Worte zur* [...], 1914/15, LBI Archives, New York.

> "Especially to us, who stayed at home, may the end of this year be an occasion to remember ... because this much is certain: ... this great war signifies a great distinction for our nation. The strengthening of the responsibility of every individual towards the community, the feeling that, despite all differences of party and class, we are bound together by a common fate – this must never be forgotten: it has to be said over and over again.... We are placed in a great connectedness."[34]

This New Year's Eve essay is an example of the uses of remembrance, history and the call for unity. That Lissauer consciously exploited historical themes to stir his readers also becomes apparent in the introductory line of his short essay on Frederick the Great: "1813 is to us the paradigm of an immense national upsurge; the situation of Prussia in the Seven Years War resembles our own in several respects; everyone is struck by the similarity...."[35] In these writings Lissauer created an impression of tradition and of continuity and this notion of continuity carried with it an idea of obligation and a need to complete the process of history. Thus Lissauer sought to connect Germany's previous wars with the war of 1914. He referred to war as an educational force which brought back long-forgotten values such as discipline and obedience, as well as unconditional surrender to the *patria*. As a celebration of the heroic element in man, Lissauer imagines protagonists of the past as present in 1914:

> "And the heroes awake. Frederick the Great suddenly appears among us, as the nightmare of the European coalition, which haunted Bismarck's dreams, presses upon the Empire ... with redoubled intensity we perceive Luther, Bach, Goethe, Beethoven, Schiller as being human symbols of our threatened nationhood. Bismarck ... is with us, with greater power than ever."[36]

The mythic quality Lissauer ascribes to the war reinforces the identification with Germany's history. By evoking the assistance of the *Generalstab der Geister*, Lissauer militarises culture and places war and religion in proximity.[37] The ennoblement of war and its portrayal as an educational force also served to legitimatise the nation's past. In *Pfingstgesänge* war is depicted as a long-awaited blessing and as a yearned-for natural event, like rain after a drought. The pentecostal fire awakens the earth and creates a bond between genius and historical figures. The fusion of Homer with St. Francis of Assisi, and of Luther with Beethoven, signifies the unifying power of war.[38]

In *Kriegspredigt* (War Sermon) Lissauer refers to war as an iron blessing (*Segen*) and as steel salvation (*Heil*) and chides those who remain frivolously uninvolved in wartime. He appeals to those not in active service to contribute to the war

---
[34]*Ibid.*
[35]Ernst Lissauer, 'Über Friedrich den Großen', in *Flugblätter 1914/15*, 3. Blatt, Göttingen 1914/15.
[36]Ernst Lissauer, 'Krieg', in *ibid.*
[37]See also Lissauer, 'Führer', in *Worte in die Zeit*, 1. Blatt, Göttingen 1914. Lissauer's biographer explains the curious combination of field marshals and religious leaders as inspirations of national identity and a victorious attitude as follows: "Luther und Yorck, Bach und Savonarola? Religion und Krieg? Nicht der Unterschied ihrer Taten und die Richtung ihres Wirkens ist es, sondern die Gemeinsamkeit ihrer Sendung." Brand, p. 80.
[38]Ernst Lissauer, 'Pfingsten der Erde' and 'Die Ausgiessung', in *Die ewigen Pfingsten. Gesichte und Gesänge*, Jena 1919, pp. 7–10.

effort by whatever means they can and goes to great lengths to eliminate any undermining of the *Burgfrieden*. In this context Lissauer actually refers to jokes being made about Jewish soldiers at the frontline:

> "In pretentious glitzy bars comedians appear on stage and tell jokes about Jews fighting in the field ...: 'A Yid goes to the camp doctor,' they say. In times like these, someone actually gets up and says: 'A Yid goes to the camp doctor'. And there really are people sitting at these fake marble tables who cheer and jeer at this.... Those at the front get their brains blown out, and at home there are some who roar with laughter at Jewish jokes. No decent person should enter establishments where jokes are made about Jewish soldiers or where the civic truce is disturbed by public jokes about Jews. No decent human being should do this, be they Jew or Christian."[39]

The view that the war of 1914 stood in a tradition of great German wars was shared by others. S. Silberstein wrote: "This is the third uprising in Germany that we have experienced; 'a cord of three strands is not quickly broken,' as Qoheleth says (Ecclesiastes IV:12)."[40] Ludwig Geiger dedicated an entire book to the topic of German-Jewish participation in the war. *Die deutschen Juden und der Krieg* is an historical account of the development of Prussian legislation that enabled Jews to join the Prussian army and participate in wars. Geiger divided his book into sections relating to the wars of 1813–1815, 1870–1871, and the period 1871–1915. He draws the same parallel between the wars of 1813–1815, the king's proclamation, and the war of 1914, concluding that Jewish participation in 1914 was not a singular phenomenon, but rather a tradition that started with the legislation of 1812 that allowed Jews to become soldiers.[41] But the frequent historical connotations in Lissauer's writing remain more an instrument and setting for the main message, namely that of national unity. Lissauer's primary concern in the New Year's Eve essay undoubtedly lies in the formula: "We are bound together by a common fate – this must never be forgotten: it has to be said over and over again."[42]

In the same period, Lissauer's poem *Bekenntnis* (Confession) appeared. The poem presents a more personal account of his relationship with Germany.

> "Ich fühl's Natur, daß Du mich auserhöhst,
> Mit Schärfe durchbeizt, mit Klarheit durchbadest du mich.
> Ich öffne mich beseligt, und gelöst
> Entsteigt mir selber das erneute Ich.
>
> Drum liegen mir in Deutschlands Westen, Süden, Norden
> Viel Heimatörter eingesprengt.
> Sie wurden mir nicht durch Geburt geschenkt,
> Durch liebend Schauen sind sie mein geworden...."[43]

---

[39]Ernst Lissauer, 'Kriegspredigt', *Gegenwart*, No. 50, p.788, LBI Archives, New York
[40]S. Silberstein, 'Ohne Unterschied von Geburt und Religion', in *Monatsschrift für Geschichte und Wissenschaft des Judentums*, 23 (1915), p. 103.
[41]Ludwig Geiger, 'Die deutschen Juden und der Krieg', in *Kriegspolitische Einzelschriften*, vol. III, 1915, p. 22.
[42]Lissauer, *Worte zur* [...], 1914/15, LBI Archives, New York
[43]Ernst Lissauer, *Bekenntnis*, read in public for the first time before the Literarische Gesellschaft zu Hamburg on 8th December 1914, in Diary 16, p. 46, LBI Archives, New York

If in this and in the following poems the poetic "I" may be taken to represent the poet himself, we may draw certain conclusions about Lissauer. In *Bekenntnis* it is immediately apparent that Lissauer recognises all directions of the compass except the east. This omission is not a trivial coincidence, but a deliberate dissociation from Eastern European Jewry. In an entry in his diary at the beginning of 1915, Lissauer wrote that "Galicia should not be supported".[44] In the *Kunstwart* debate of 1912 he had already made it clear that Jews from Eastern Europe were associated with an image which assimilated German Jews had to avoid if they wanted to achieve lasting acceptance in Germany. Another striking statement in the poem is contained in the lines: "Sie wurden mir nicht durch Geburt geschenkt, / Durch liebend Schauen sind sie mein geworden." Here Lissauer regards his relationship with Germany not as natural and to be taken for granted, but rather as something to be acquired through conscious effort. The poem attests that German Jews were not assumed to belong "innately". In another poem from the lyrical volume *Der Strom*, Lissauer, with obvious reference to the biblical nativity scene, sees himself as one of the three wise men seeking salvation (*Heil*) in Germany:

"Ich bin ein König aus Morgenland,
Ich wandre nach einem Stern,
Irgend in Deutschland, fern,
Über einem Haus ist er entbrannt." [45]

In another poem, *Nachgefühl*, he seems to anticipate his own fall from grace following the reaction to the *Haßgesang*. The poet imagines that he was initially part of an all-embracing cosmic harmony, but is then expelled and condemned to roam the cosmos endlessly:

"Oft ist es mir, ich war vormals ein Stern unter Sternen,
In das Gesetz der Himmel eingeschlossen von bannender Kraft,
Aber gelöst aus der seligen Hast,
In Fall
Durch das All,
Reise ich rastlos von Fernen zu Fernen."[46]

The absence of firm ground is also depicted in a poem entitled *Vergangenheit*.[47] The poem *Ich wohne in meinem Leid* describes Lissauer's sense of isolation through the metaphor of living on an island.[48] However, Lissauer also wrote a poem which could be interpreted as an affirmation of a multi-faceted identity. In *Manchmal bindet Gott Stücke Welt* he describes people as glass vessels filled with "fragments of world" resembling a bunch of wild flowers.[49] Similarly, he describes loneliness not always in terms of painful isolation, but also as a confident encounter of the self with the world at large.[50]

---

[44]*Ibid.*, p. 54.
[45]Lissauer, 'Das Heil', in *Der Strom*, 1912, p. 51.
[46]Lissauer, 'Nachgefühl', in *Der Strom*, p. 49.
[47]*Ibid.*, p. 48.
[48]*Ibid.*, p. 42.
[49]*Ibid.*, p. 21.
[50]Lissauer, 'Spruchband', 'Seele 1', 'Seele 2', in *Der Strom*, pp. 12 and 10f.

THE *HASSGESANG* AND ITS RECEPTION

The degree to which the reaction to the publication of the *Haßgesang* influenced Lissauer's shift from German to Jewish affiliation becomes clear from his *Lebenstafel* (*Curriculum Vitae*). In this work Lissauer divides his life into the periods before and after the *Haßgesang*, clearly regarding his war poem as a turning point in his life and career and seeing the reaction to it as shaping his own identity and recognition as a writer.[51]

Lissauer's *Bemerkungen zum Leben* is the the main source from which to gauge the effect the reception of the *Haßgesang* had on the poet's increasing affiliation with Judaism. (This manuscript, which he dictated to his wife in 1923, is the basis of, but not identical with, *Bemerkungen über mein Leben* published in 1933.)[52] Domestic reactions to the *Haßgesang* came from the press, political debates and private opinion. These can be divided into Jewish and non-Jewish opinion, in which non-Jewish moral arguments were derived from Christian values. There were also reactions from abroad, mainly from France, Italy, the United States and, not surprisingly, Britain. All of these contributed to a shift in Lissauer's self-perception.

Despite its initial immense success and popularity, the *Haßgesang* soon found opponents within Germany. The poem, which was first published in 1914, found its way into some schoolbooks, but was subsequently classified as "liable to corrupt the young [*jugendgefährdend*]". In a debate that took place in the Prussian Chamber of Deputies, the Social Democrat Konrad Haenisch warned that the declamation of the *Haßgesang* in schools would lead to a "corrupting" and "deplorable atmosphere of long-term hatred in our youth" and advocated that the poem be banned from schoolbooks. The open display of generation-long hatred, it was argued, did nothing for an education of mutual understanding between nations and encouraged youths to glorify violence.[53] These fears were also discussed in the press. An article in the *Berliner Tageblatt*, not directly aimed at Lissauer but presumably motivated by the discussion of his controversial poem, warned parents not to give their children military toys for Christmas. The article's main concern was the transmission of hatred from one generation to another.

> "It is not as difficult to keep the war away from the Christmas parlour as some parents might think. We should not let ourselves be misled into letting national hatred and national revenge, although they are necessary in deadly battle, sound the keynote of our Christmas celebrations. Whoever gives their child presents such as jumping-jacks in the shape of caricatured Englishmen or Russians, offends not only against the future of our youth, but against the future of our whole human race."[54]

---

[51]Lissauer, Handschriftliche Lebenstafel, MS, n.d., LBI Archives, New York.
[52]Lissauer, 'Bemerkungen über mein Leben (1933)'. See note 9.
[53]*Auszug aus den Stenographischen Berichten über die Verhandlungen des preußischen Abgeordneten-Hauses der XXII. Legislaturperiode*, 2. Session, 1914–1915, pp. 8635f.
[54]*Berliner Tageblatt*, 14th November 1914, quoted by J. Wohlgemuth, *Der Weltkrieg im Lichte des Judentums*, Berlin 1915, p. 53.

The antisemitic *Hammer* saw in the poem an expression of sentiments "as un-German as possible".

The debate about the *Haßgesang* soon became a discussion of racial predisposition for revenge and hatred, for which, in antisemitic opinion, Jews were supposed to have a particular aptitude.[55] Consequently, Jewish reviewers of the poem distanced themselves from Lissauer in order to dissociate themselves from the idea of fostering hatred and revenge. Disturbed by the negative reactions he encountered, Lissauer wrote:

> "It has been said that only a Jew can hate so passionately; but a hymn of hate which is infinitely inferior to mine in passion and poetic ability is the song 'Germania to her children' by the Prussian *Junker* Heinrich von Kleist, and Bismarck said: 'I hated all night long'. These and other follies, misunderstandings, errors and calumnies have surrounded the *H. g. E.* and its author and have even to this day not completely disappeared. If there had been any obsession with glory, with public approval, or with influence on the masses in me, it has by now been burned out."[56]

Others felt that restraint was not called for at a time when the nation was in danger and that writers demonstrated their integrity by expressing popular sentiment. In a letter to the *Berliner Tageblatt*, Marie von Bülow, the widow of the musician Hans Guido von Bülow,[57] defended Lissauer's "slip of the tongue":

> "[The *Haßgesang* expresses] a very honest sentiment which has been and is shared by millions in Germany;[58] and especially the fact that it is being performed in every recital hall ... is proof of this and must not be interpreted as arbitrary speculation by the author. What, then, is the poem saying? Nothing but what has been stated and explained anew every day in articles of any kind in any newspaper for the last year ... And why should the poet not be allowed to express what everyone is feeling?"[59]

The sudden criticism induced Lissauer, in 1915, to write a letter of justification to the press. He drafted at least two letters for his public defence. Both stress that he had written the poem under "the sudden impulse" of Britain's declaration of war against Germany. The poem was not directed against individual Englishmen, he explained, but rather against England as a political entity. His two drafts differ in tone. Whereas in what appears to be the earlier draft Lissauer hastens to justify the context in which his war poem arose, he makes concessions in the latter, and probably final, draft with regard to its use as school material;

---

[55]"As for the expression of a fanatical hatred, Herr Lissauer's talent for that cannot be disputed, as his race is in this respect generally extraordinarily gifted. What must be alienating in this is that Herr Lissauer reproaches the English with certain characteristics which are also very particular to another race, such as mercantile spirit and avarice." *Hammer*, No. 300 (December 1914), p. 668, Art. 'Undeutsche Verse-Macherei'.
[56]Lissauer, *Bemerkungen zum Leben*, MS, pp. 81f, LBI Archives, New York.
[57]Marie von Bülow, daughter of the Director of the Austrian Ministry of Defence (*Landesverteidigungsministerium*) was an actress at the court theatre and married Hans von Bülow after his divorce from Cosima Flavigny. *Neue Deutsche Biographie*, vol. II, Berlin 1955, p. 734.
[58]Likewise, Victor Klemperer recalls that the *Haßgesang* contained "eine Entrüstung und eine Leidenschaft, die wir 1914 alle als echt empfanden und alle gleichermaßen fühlten". Victor Klemperer, *Curriculum Vitae. Erinnerungen, 1881–1918*, ed. by Walter Nowojski, Berlin 1996, vol. I, pp. 280–281.
[59]The original letter of 11th August 1915, in Ernst Lissauer, Diary 17 (16th June 1915 – 24th August 1915), pp. 119f, LBI Archives, New York.

and whereas in his first draft Lissauer claimed that he had simply expressed in his poem the existing "general view" of Britain, he amended that phrase in his final draft to "widely held view":

> "Dear Editor,
> ... The *Haßgesang* was penned on a sudden passionate impulse ... under the impression of the [British] declaration of war. When I wrote it, I did not know that I was expressing a widely held view [*weit verbreitete Empfindung*; in the earlier version: *allgemeine Empfindung*, "general view" – E.A.]; this I only learned through its success. I have not done the slightest thing to promote this success. Of what kind the 'advantages' are, which I supposedly meant to achieve with the poem, is not clear to me: I expected neither its success nor the present attacks. I note all this with reluctance and only in order to present my 'advantages' in the right perspective.... The *Haßgesang* is a political poem and is not directed against the individual Englishman, but against England as a political collective, against the English will to exterminate Germany."[60]

The arguments Lissauer employs in these letters resurface in later articles and in *Bemerkungen zum Leben*. In these he argues that the poem merely acted as a catalyst and only expressed a personal sentiment which reflected the existing attitude towards England:

> "Like *1813*, my poem [*Haßgesang*] sprang from a personal feeling, and it was, like every poem, meant to communicate this feeling to other people and, like all war poetry, it was meant to transmit strength and stability. It has been claimed that the poem produced anti-English feelings, but in truth it was through its mere existence that anti-English feelings became detectable."[61]

Lissauer's diary shows that he was indeed preoccupied with the question of England's role in the constellation of nations at war. On 30th July 1914 he rejoices: "I am glad that Austria has taken the field: as a human being I feel satisfied that patience has finally come to an end." Reflecting on the likely consequences of Austria's mobilisation, he continues:

> "I am worried because, contrary to my certain hopes, England will not remain neutral. The situation would therefore look like this:
> Intervention of Russia causes the
>   ,,   ,, Germany ,, ,,
>   ,,   ,, France   ,, ,,
>   ,,   ,, England."[62]

Lissauer felt that he had become the embodiment of hatred:

> "The attacks against me increased. The *Haßgesang* was said in the same breath as that silly nonsense 'May God punish England', so that later some people believed that I had invented this phrase.... Since one could not write anything against the leading politicians and generals, outbursts of hatred, envy and at times even [genuine] outrage poured over me; in the imagination of the public I ... became a figure of evil. The radical weeklies testified to my avarice and resentment.... In the imagina-

---

[60]Lissauer's drafted reply to the article 'Gegen den Haßgesang', LBI Archives, New York.
[61]Lissauer, *Bemerkungen*, MS, p. 81.
[62]Lissauer, Diary 15, 30th July 1914, LBI Archives, New York.

tion of the average intellectual I ... never stopped inciting hatred. Recently, in this year of 1923, I learned that a Liberal representative said in a meeting in 1918 that the war was lost due to Mr L.'s *Haßgesang!*"[63]

Reactions from the Jewish press were not confined to hinting, with some satisfaction, that the best-known war poem was written by a German Jew, as, for instance, Ludwig Geiger did.[64] This is not to say, however, that all German Jews welcomed the war and saw in it the overcoming of the last obstacle to achieving complete emancipation and social equality. There were, of course, also dissidents among German Jews and, as Rivka Horvitz has shown, some of these "on account of their deeply Jewish orientation" did not support "fighting 'a war which is not ours' ".[65] Yet one of those listed by Horvitz as articulating dissent, Gustav Landauer, was probably motivated by political conviction rather than by Jewish orientation.[66] Efforts were also made to dissociate the Jewish community from the frequently expressed view that Jews in particular were capable of such war-mongering publications and therefore that Lissauer, who had unintentionally come to be seen as the representative of Jewish attitudes, had to be kept at a distance. This was achieved in one of two ways: either by demonstrating that Lissauer wrote primarily on inoffensive themes or by seeking to prove that it was not the "Jewish element" in Lissauer which induced him to write the *Haßgesang*. The latter line of argument inevitably led to a discussion of the extent to which race influenced the artistic expression of an individual. The journal *Ost und West* countered attacks which claimed that Jews, as an "oppressed people", had an "innate capacity for hatred" by reminding its readers that there were some "very Christian and very Germanic ladies" who justified hatred of Germany's enemies although stirring up hatred was irreconcilable with the ethos of their faith.[67] Poems of hate were also inspired by Christian beliefs. Will Vesper and Hans Schmidt Kestner both confronted the Christian edict to "love thine enemy",[68] and Vesper proclaimed hatred directed against the enemy as the fruit of the highest form of love.

Lissauer's poem unleashed a discussion of the compatibility of Jewish and Christian beliefs with hatred, in which neither side wanted to be seen as the disturber of the peace. The discussion was conducted on theological, as well as on ethical and plainly racial grounds, but questions of race prompted the strongest Jewish defence, as, for instance, against this passage in *Die Grenzboten* by an author writing under the pseudonym "Paphnutius":

> "Many who have been affected by Lissauer's *Haßgesang* in all its mercilessness might have experienced the same as this author did, namely a wave of emotion arising, it

---

[63]Lissauer, *Bemerkungen*, MS, pp. 76–79.
[64]Geiger, 'Die deutschen Juden und der Krieg', p. 74, quoted in Zechlin, p. 97.
[65]Rivka Horwitz, 'Voices of opposition to the First World War among Jewish thinkers', in *LBI Year Book XXXIII* (1988), pp. 233–259, here p. 236.
[66]See also Adam M. Weisberger, *The Jewish Ethic and the Spirit of Socialism*, New York 1997, pp. 158–164, especially p. 161, although I cannot agree with the overall conclusions of Weisberger's study.
[67]Anon., 'Der ewige Haß', in *Ost und West*, Heft 4/5, April/May, 1916, p. 194.
[68]Will Vesper, 'Liebe oder Haß?', in J. Bab (ed.), 'Die Kriegslyrik von heute', *Das literarische Echo*, 1st October 1914, p. 7.

seems, from a world so alien that one is at a loss as to how to respond or even to reject [such emotions]."[69]

What makes this passage offensive and potentially dangerous is only apparent at second glance: the source of Jewish hatred is so quintessentially alien to the non-Jewish mind that it evades reason and comprehension. Consequently, the possibility for mutual understanding becomes so remote that non-Jews cannot even conceive of rejecting the origin of Jewish hatred. By this deliberate and ostentatious lack of comprehension "Paphnutius" pushed German Jews back into a corner of foreignness, removing all possibility of integrating Jewish life into German society, and shifting responsibility for hate, revenge and war onto Jews. Lissauer, then, became something of a pariah for the Jewish community as well. Eager to prove that Lissauer was not a "proper" Jew and that his writings were not influenced by his Jewish heritage, the author of the article in *Ost und West* claimed that, whilst Lissauer's "blood" was responsible for the talent that made him a poet, it was not responsible for the content of his writing.

> "But we Jews are even worse off. All those strict and righteous guardians of virtue to whom the *Haßgesang* was like the blast of a wave of alien emotions, now chide him, a Jew. The inner creative power, the core of the talent, derives from the parental home, the "blood". What he says is not Jewish."[70]

Joseph Wohlgemuth criticised the identification of hatred with Jewish tradition on a theological and ethical level. His book *Der Weltkrieg im Lichte des Judentums* discusses the war and its significance for the observant Jew. In a chapter entitled "Das grosse Hassen", Wohlgemuth differentiates between just and unjust hatreds, and, without naming Lissauer, warns of the irrationality and perniciousness of any malicious campaign against England.

The sensitivity with which the public in Germany reacted to Lissauer's *Haßgesang* might have been partly rooted in the contemporary notion that Germany had been the "most hated" nation even before the war started, and that Lissauer's aggressive war poem only confirmed to other nations that she was worthy of hatred. The philosopher Max Scheler, for example, described in a lecture entitled *Die Ursachen des Deutschenhasses* how hatred of Germans made the war possible in the first place. He claimed that such hatred was not a phenomenon of the war, but rather that it was centred on Germany's culture, art, science and very being (*Wesen*). German nationalism, he argued, did not spring from the core of German being (*Wesen*), but was, rather, a defence mechanism created by French nationalism.[71] Furthermore, Germany was an object of hatred, according to Scheler, because she appeared to be dominated by a hypercritical Jewish spirit (*Geist*) seeking disintegration everywhere. There is no evidence to suggest that Scheler's lecture was particularly motivated by the negative attention Lissauer

---

[69] *Ibid*. Unfortunately, I have not been able to identify the author who used this pseudonym.
[70] Anon., 'Der ewige Haß', in p. 195.
[71] Max Scheler, *Die Ursachen des Deutschenhasses. Eine nationalpädagogische Erörterung*, Leipzig 1917, pp. 37f. (originally a lecture given on 20th November 1916 in Frankfurt am Main as part of a series at the invitation of the *Kulturbund Deutscher Gelehrter und Künstler*). I am grateful to Professor Edgar Feuchtwanger for pointing me to the writings of Max Scheler.

had attracted to Germany, but his argument that Jews appeared to be disproportionately influential to the outside observer because they worked in the liberal professions, which had "indeed an influence on shaping the image of the German *Wesen* abroad",[72] shows his specific concern for the international reputation German Jews such as Lissauer could create for their country.

Barbara Suchy has argued that Lissauer's *Haßgesang* was "regarded as an appropriate proof of the national trustworthiness of German Jews" and "as being in accordance with the depths of the German *Volksseele*" by the *Verein zur Abwehr des Antisemitismus*, although it was never published in the *Verein's* publication, the *Mitteilungen*.[73] Suchy's interpretation of Lissauer's *Haßgesang*, based on Stefan Zweig's memoirs, as an "overcompensation for deep insecurity and an inferiority complex" does not, perhaps, do sufficient justice to Lissauer's stance before the war and the writing of the *Haßgesang*. The *Haßgesang* was not a "plunge" into "a contest of patriotism", but was in fact consistent with Lissauer's previous writings. The "overcompensation" argument neglects the more plausible possibility of Lissauer's genuine identification with German nationalist values. The assumption that "deep insecurity" and an "inferiority complex" lay at the root of Lissauer's ostentatious lyrical call to arms appears unsubstantiated in the light both of his previous works and of his open acknowledgement of his Jewish background.

According to Egmont Zechlin, Lissauer and his poem were regarded as representative of the "state of consciousness of the German middle class" by high-ranking foreign observers such as the then US ambassador to Berlin, James W. Gerard.[74] In a curious pamphlet published a year earlier than his memoirs in 1918, Gerard allegedly recalled: "A well-known general declared to his troops that there was nothing like getting up in the morning, after having passed a night in thought and dreams of hate." He added: "Paper money was overprinted with the words, 'Gott strafe England', to which, after the United States entered the war in 1917, was added the phrase '- und Amerika'." Gerard then quoted the first verse of the *Haßgesang* by "a well-known poet", namely Ernst Lissauer.[75] In Italy Lissauer's poem was included in an anthology of German war lyrics covering three wars. There, however, Lissauer is referred to as a previously unknown poet.[76] Through the recently published memoirs of Victor Klemperer, who was a lecturer at Naples in 1914–1915, we know, however, that Lissauer made it into the Christmas issue of *Il Messaggero*, where he was described as "the famous and terrible poet Ernesto Lissauer".[77] Klemperer recalls discussing Lissauer's poem in Italy with two Americans who were appalled by its "ante-

---

[72] Scheler, p. 115.
[73] Barbara Suchy, 'The Verein zur Abwehr des Antisemitismus (II). From the First World War to its Dissolution in 1933', in *LBI Year Book XXX* (1985), pp. 67–103, here p. 72.
[74] Zechlin, p. 97 and note 77.
[75] 'My four years in Germany. The Serial Extraordinary comprising 10 single reel instalments produced under the personal supervision of James W. Gerard, late American Ambassador in Berlin', the Electra Palace, Queen Street, Oxford, July 29th to August 3rd 1918, Instalment Five. This is the only reference to paper money being printed with this slogan and may be a fabrication.
[76] Anton Giulio Bragaglia, *I Tedeschi. Le Canzoni di Guerra. 1813–1870–1915*, Bari 1915, pp. 184–185.
[77] Klemperer, vol. II, p. 252.

diluvian sentiment", which induced Klemperer to defend Lissauer as having expressed in his poem his own – Klemperer's – and everyone else's feelings.[78] In another conversation with a Jewish officer at the front, the criticism was directed not against the content of Lissauer's poem but against his false and obsequious intention to copy a popular song by Hugo Zuckermann:

> "... a folk song by Zuckermann,[79] a hymn of hate against England by Lissauer, that goes against the grain, that curries favour too clumsily, that is wholly insincere."[80]

Foreign reactions to Lissauer's poem also took the shape of poetic acts of reprisal, as for example in Jules de Marthold's *Chant de Haine*, written as his *Réponse à Berlin*. This poem was saturated with such contempt that it omitted the detested word "German" until the final verse, where it refers to teaching young children to hate so that the grain of poison can grow into suffocating branches.[81]

Among Elizabeth Marsland's discoveries of lyric war *curiosa* is a small Australian publication in the form of a Christmas card "though the words 'Season's Greetings' on the cover hardly seem commensurate with the malevolence of the contents – a translation of Ernst Lissauer's notorious 'Haßgesang' ... and an equally belligerent poem in response".[82] In Britain several English translations of the *Haßgesang* existed to be used as anti-German war propaganda.[83] The *New York Times* published a translation of Lissauer's *Haßgesang* with the title *England The Only Foe*, and a discussion of the poem followed in the *New York Evening Post* in 1915.[84] In 1916 Charles Clarke published a translation of Houston Stewart Chamberlain's *Kriegsaufsätze* with a scathing introduction by Lewis Melville on the man who "fouled the nest" at such a time, citing as Chamberlain's worst *faux pas* that "he echoes the refrain of Herr Lissauer's infamous (but to British folk amusing) 'Hymn of Hate' ".[85]

LISSAUER'S SELF-AWARENESS AS A WRITER

> Und ward mir nicht gegeben, mitzuschlagen,
> Gewehr und Säbel in stürmender Hand,
> Sei mir vergönnt, ein kämpfend Wort zu sagen.
> O nimm auch diese Gabe an, mein Land![86]

It is illuminating to study the reactions of intellectuals to the outbreak of the war. Lissauer was certainly no exception in that the war brought to a climax a conflict

---

[78] *Ibid.*
[79] Hugo Zuckermann (1881–1915), who wrote 'Österreichisches Reiterlied'.
[80] Klemperer, vol. II, p. 362.
[81] Jules de Marthold, *Chant de Haine. Réponse à Berlin*, Paris 1915.
[82] Arthur A. Adams, 'My Friend, Remember! Lines Written on Reading Lissauer's Chant of Hate', Sydney 1915, in Elizabeth A. Marsland, *The Nation's Cause. French, English and German Poetry of the First World War*, London–New York 1991, pp. 7–8.
[83] Marsland, p. 246, note 92.
[84] Gilbert Hirsch on Lissauer and the *Haßgesang*, in the *New York Evening Post*, (23rd October 1915), LBI Archives, New York.
[85] *The Ravings of a Renegade. Being the War Essays of Houston Stewart Chamberlain*, transl. by Charles H. Clarke with an introduction by Lewis Melville, London, n.d. [Bodleian acquisition stamp shows April 1916], pp. 7f.
[86] Lissauer, *Worte in die Zeit. Flugblätter 1914*, 1. Blatt, Göttingen 1914.

in him between the call to duty and a paralysis caused by contemplation of its possible consequences:

> "This night again sleepless till dawn
> in the morning still no decision
> I am incapable of any thought or of any feelings but those concerning the war".[87]

Lissauer writes here in an uncharacteristically *staccato* style. But the events did not jolt him into action, or even induce him to rejoice in patriotic fervour. Overwhelmed by the outbreak of the war – the noise, the chaos, and the inevitable casualties – he sinks into doubt-ridden inertia:

> "The tremendous events which lie in store press upon me like Alpine ranges . . .; the possibility of losing Otto; I feel that the war is necessary, that behind its catalyst and apparently purely economic rivalries lie greater reasons."[88]

The same mixture of disbelief, foreboding and relief is expressed by Thomas Mann in a letter to his brother Heinrich. "I am still always as if in a dream – and yet one must now be ashamed of not having thought it possible and not having seen that the catastrophe had to come. What a visitation!" he writes, shaken by the advent of war and the disruption it caused even to the tranquillity of Bad Tölz, his Bavarian retreat. After speculating on how the war would disrupt his own life, he dismisses those reflections as petty, personal considerations, conceding with a grand gesture the wider significance of the war. He then attempts to revel in what to him and his contemporaries seemed – justifiably so to be – an historic turning-point.

> "Must one not be grateful for the wholly unexpected, for being allowed to experience such great things? My main feeling is one of immense curiosity – and, I admit it, the deepest sympathy for this hated, fateful and mysterious Germany."[89]

One day in August 1914, on his way to sign up as a volunteer for non-combatant service, Lissauer encountered Friedrich Naumann, who, as Lissauer recounted in his diary, gives his blessing to the poet's endeavour.[90] Since he always sought external recognition, approval from Naumann, a well-known Liberal, must have relieved Lissauer, who no doubt felt ambivalent about the discrepancy between his bloodthirsty literature and the fact that he himself was not taking a more active part in the war.

From Lissauer's letter of defence, written for the press, in which he expressed his regret about being unfit to serve, it becomes clear that he, like many other intellectuals of his time, regarded writing to support the war effort as his duty to society.

---

[87] Lissauer, Diary 15, 31st July 1914, LBI Archives, New York.
[88] *Ibid.*
[89] Thomas Mann to Heinrich Mann, 7th August 1914, in *Thomas Mann. Briefe 1889–1936*, ed. by Erika Mann, Frankfurt am Main 1961, pp. 111–112.
[90] Lissauer, Diary 15, before 25th August 1914, LBI Archives, New York.

"That so far I have been considered unfit to go into the field pains me; but unfitness for physical military service cannot suspend the duty to do military service of an intellectual kind."[91]

Lissauer portrayed writing the *Haßgesang* as a compensation for his inability to take part in combat and by no means as a "slip of the tongue". He also applied to others his view that the quality of a writer was measurable above all by his dedication to his country, as we have already seen from his review of Rudolf Alexander Schröder's book of poetry, *Deutsche Oden*. These sentiments were echoed two years later in his *Autobiographische Skizze*:

> "... the wholly unexpected success of the poem [*Haßgesang*] delighted me all the more as I am not fit for military service and saw in my war poetry and essays a kind of intellectual military service, especially as I have never thought of the poet as being detached, but rather as being implicated and committed."[92]

Lissauer's ideas on the duty of the poet to society and the nation are expressed in his book *Von der Sendung des Dichters* (On the Mission of the Poet). In this collection of essays he states that there is "no art without purpose".[93] The book deals with the "suprapersonal task" of the poet, "which is at the same time a duty of the highest degree".[94] Of immediate relevance to Lissauer's self-perception as a German nationalist is a passage in which he prescribes for himself the role of "mouthpiece of the nation":

> "By expressing his personal experience the poet speaks for many: and he will be the more important, the more people he speaks for in the long term ... the poet is a representative, as it were a deputy, of many people, of a social rank, a class, or a nation, a representative of the human collective. He is the mouthpiece of a multitude.... Representatives are of course only possible if there is a culture in existence ... an intellectual atmosphere which welds many individuals to the great unity of the nation."[95]

This essay, which Lissauer claimed he had conceived in 1910, and which was published in 1922, was actually published in 1915.[96] It can be safely assumed that the essay was originally written in defence of the *Haßgesang*, but then put forward as a general treatise on the mission of the poet written before the war. It is, therefore, an important document for the interpretation of Lissauer's self-perception and his sense of mission during the war. As for the quotation itself, Lissauer's idea of culture was that it should be a catalyst for national unity. Accordingly, the poet was the representative of the national will, as well as the provider of the unifying element. Germans cited by Lissauer as having held this perception of the purpose of their work include Luther and Frederick the Great. Luther's trans-

---

[91] Lissauer's draft for an answer to the article 'Gegen den Haßgesang', 1915, MS, LBI.
[92] Lissauer, *Autobiographische Skizze*.
[93] Ernst Lissauer, *Von der Sendung des Dichters. Aufsätze. Kritische Schriften*, vol. I: *Zweckfreie Kunst*, Jena 1922, p. 20.
[94] *Ibid.*, Introduction, p. 3.
[95] Lissauer, *Von der Sendung des Dichters, I. Teil der Kritischen Schriften*, pp. 21f.
[96] In Lissauer's estate the date 6th December 1915 is written next to the title *Von der Sendung des Dichters*, LBI Archives, New York.

lation of the Bible is described as a "nation-creating event".[97] Lissauer seeks to establish the position of the poet as an indispensable part of the nation, without which it could not exist as a unified body. In a newspaper article published in 1915, Lissauer characterises the poet's role not only as the mouthpiece of the nation, but also as the sensor of its innermost nature. The nation is defined in this context as an organically grown entity bound by a common language, which is regarded by the poet as his possession and tool. It is significant for the history of the formation and reception of Lissauer's war writings and the *Haßgesang* in particular that in this article Lissauer makes the poet not only the mouthpiece of the nation's sentiments but also as its manipulator, working in the background to rouse the people's emotions. The poet

> "... does not want to have an effect on their knowing judgment, but on their perceiving instinct, their inflammable passion; without them knowing it, he wants to transform them, and he may not even know himself that he wants this".[98]

In contrast to his letter defending the *Haßgesang* as an expression of what was already felt by the nation, here Lissauer attributes responsibility to writers of propaganda literature for planting hatred and the the idea of war into the collective consciousness of the nation. Lissauer did not, however, regard the author as responsible for the impact of war poetry on the nation:

> "A poem which causes such effects is not harmless. But it was harmless, politically harmless, to elevate this poem to a political battle-cry. As a poet who expressed himself, it was not my job to consider consequences; today, ... taught by experience, I would calculate the political effect of a political poem."[99]

Lissauer's view of writing as a form of military service was motivated by his conception both of the poet's mission and responsibility and of literature as a unifying force. As expressed in his New Year's remembrance essay, the paramount role of literature was to eliminate the divisions in society that prevent identification with a common aim. Lissauer's promotion of the abandonment of political and religious differences again seems to reflect a deeper, socially and psychologically, rooted desire to amalgamate his own identity with the German nation for the purpose of avoiding an assessment of his own loyalties. The text projects this notion onto an anonymous group:

> "It is a great good fortune for many that, for a while, they cannot be individuals any more, and it is the highest task of literature to prevent these centripetal forces from being lost again after the centrifugal ones have been dominant for so long."[100]

Lissauer believed that the "centripetal forces" of literature gave writers an opportunity for intellectual war service. "These times, and the future to which they give birth, create an opportunity for the writer, in taking up his pen, to be once more a man of action."[101] In *Der Krieg und der Schriftsteller* he argued that an

---
[97]Lissauer, *Von der Sendung des Dichters. II. Teil der Kritischen Schriften*, p. 67.
[98]Lissauer, 'Von der Sendung des Dichters', in *Deutsche Allgemeine Zeitung*, (6th December 1915), LBI Archives, New York.
[99]Lissauer, 'Bemerkungen zum Leben', MS, p. 80.
[100]Ernst Lissauer, 'Der Krieg und der Schriftsteller', LBI Archives, New York.
[101]*Ibid*.

interaction existed between the nation and literature. Literature, he declared, should express the thoughts of the nation; especially in times of crisis, the mental clarity of a writer was required as a catalyst for the sentiments of the nation engaged in physical struggle. Lissauer concluded that the writer was a public figure who functioned as an "intellectual organiser of society [*geistiger Ordner der Gesellschaft*]". He saw himself as someone who bore responsibility for the "dignity of public opinion" and acted as a "national pastor [*nationaler Seelsorger*]", whose duty it was to keep mind and temper under control.[102]

The "spirit of 1914" affected many German writers and intellectuals who shared the common perception of Germany as a sleepy giant who had finally risen to strive for her place in the hierarchy of states. Their technique was, as in Mann's *Friedrich und die grosse Koalition*, one of historical allegory, comparing Frederick the Great's invasion of Saxony with the invasion of Belgium by German troops.[103] They had in common the belief that German culture was destined to restore a doomed era, which they perceived as threatened by social and industrial progress, and to produce a reconciliation of culture with militarism, resulting in a powerful and no longer scorned *Kulturnation*. Prominent proponents of this stance are Rudolf Borchardt[104] and Thomas Mann, the latter particularly in his essay *Gedanken im Kriege*.[105] Borchardt, in his essay *Der Krieg und die deutsche Selbsteinkehr*, in which he argued that culture was a German invention, untranslatable into any other language, claimed that the war would confirm Germany's strength in her "otherness" and isolation, and, moreover, that she could not only be certain of victory, but deserved it for her monopoly of virtue and for having been chosen by God.

Thomas Mann took up the gauntlet of intellectual war service in *Betrachtungen eines Unpolitischen*, and Lissauer cites him as an example of an author whose writings reflected German militarism. It was the ambiguity of being both an artist and a *bourgeois* which forced Mann into the conflict between, on the one hand, the conviction that it was through intellectual contributions that he best served Germany and her war effort and, on the other, his feeling of numbness and awe at the heroism of those who made a physical contribution to "real life".[106] According to Golo Mann, his father struggled through the war years behind his desk with paper and pen wearing a military jacket.[107] While Thomas Mann, however, regarded his literary version of military service as

---

[102]*Ibid.*
[103]Thomas Mann, 'Friedrich und die grosse Koalition. Ein Abriß für den Tag und für die Stunde' (1915), in *Gesamte Werke*, 2nd edn., Frankfurt am Main 1974, vol. X, pp. 76 ff., especially p. 79. Contemporaries were, of course, aware of the parallels in the essay. See for example Moritz Heimann, 'Politisches von einem Dichter', in *Frankfurter Zeitung*, vol. LX (24th December 1915).
[104]Cf. Rudolf Borchardt, 'Der Krieg und die deutsche Selbsteinkehr', in *Prosa V*, Stuttgart 1979, pp. 217–264.
[105]Thomas Mann, 'Gedanken im Kriege' (1914), in *Gesamte Werke*, vol. XIII, pp. 527ff.
[106]Elisabeth Albanis, *Thomas Mann and the First World War*, diss., Cambridge University 1991, p. 73.
[107]Golo Mann, *Erinnerungen und Gedanken. Eine Jugend in Deutschland*, 2nd edn., Frankfurt am Main 1986; idem, *Reminiscences and Reflections. Growing up in Germany*, transl. by Krishna Winston, London 1990, p. 25.

"the work of a galley slave [*Galeerenfron*]", Lissauer's dedication was more reminiscent of Ernst Bertram, the "godfather" of the *Betrachtungen*.[108] The general importance of some form of involvement in the war effort, with actual fighting regarded as being the first and foremost contribution, becomes apparent, for example, from the correspondence of the writer Richard Dehmel to his colleagues and his publisher Samuel Fischer.[109] That writing was usually considered to be an inferior substitute for front-line service might provide some explanation of why wartime literary efforts were sometimes uncharacteristically extreme in their sentiments. For many writers, what was at stake in this war was the "future intellectual [*geistige*] domination of the whole world" by means of German *Wesensart*.[110] What offended them in Lissauer's poem was, therefore, not the sentiment but the extreme nature of it.

In 1915 Lissauer was awarded the Order of the Red Eagle (*Roter Adlerorden 4. Klasse*), along with several other writers, including Richard Dehmel and Rudolf Alexander Schröder.[111] He refers to this honour in the *Bemerkungen*:

"The medal which I received in January 1915 has also given me pleasure, precisely because I, a Jewish writer living in complete isolation without any connections, forced the ruling circles to award it to me without any effort on my part, but simply because of merit."[112]

This picture of an isolated Jewish writer who has triumphed in forcing the establishment to honour his work is striking evidence of Lissauer's post-war self-justification, and especially of his retrospective emphasis on his Jewishness. The projection of his Jewish identity as motivation for his supposed detachment from German cultural honours is significant because it shows how Lissauer attached qualities to Jewish identity which were synonymous with an "anti-establishment" attitude. More importantly for this study, it shows how the distinctive shift from the "firmly-rooted" German writer in 1912 to the "completely isolated Jewish writer" in 1923 was projected retrospectively to 1915. That Lissauer should only have been delighted at success stemming from the *Haßgesang* in connection with his identity as a Jewish writer also contradicts the passage quoted earlier from the *Autobiographische Skizze*.

---

[108]The extent to which Ernst Bertram assisted in the *Betrachtungen* can be read in Inge Jens (ed.), *Thomas Mann an Ernst Bertram. Briefe aus den Jahren 1910–55* (in association with the Schiller-Nationalmuseum), Pfullingen 1960; Katia Mann, *Meine ungeschriebenen Memoiren*, Tübingen 1974.
[109]Cf. Samuel Fischer to Richard Dehmel, 14th January 1915 and 10th February 1915, in Dierk Rodewald and Corinna Fiedler (eds.), *Samuel Fischer. Hedwig Fischer. Briefwechsel mit Autoren*, Frankfurt am Main 1989, p. 40.
[110]Helmut Fries, 'Deutsche Schriftsteller im Ersten Weltkrieg', in Wolfgang Michalka (ed.), *Der Erste Weltkrieg. Wirkung. Wahrnehmung. Analyse*, Munich–Zurich 1994, p. 831.
[111]"The *Literarisches Echo* announced on 1st March 1915 (17. Jg., 11 H., Sp. 705) that 'the Order of the Red Eagle, 4th class, with the royal crown, was issued to the following writers: Gerhart Hauptmann, Caesar Flaischlen, Ernst Lissauer, Rudolf Presber, Richard Dehmel, Walter Flex, Ferdinand Avenarius...'" Rodewald and Fiedler, p. 848. Cf. Zweig, p. 268; Thalheim et al. (eds.), *Geschichte der Deutschen Literatur*, p. 310.
[112]Lissauer, 'Bemerkungen', MS, pp. 75f. Note that Lissauer subsequently added "jüdischer" before "Schriftsteller". The text originally read: "...Freude gemacht, weil [er ohne] [crossed out] ich, ein völlig isoliert lebender Schriftsteller, ohne alle Verbindungen, ihn erhielt."

Lissauer was deemed fit to join the war effort in 1916 and was conscripted to join the armed forces, having worked in a prisoners' bakery in Silesia. With the assistance of General von Seeckt,[113] Lissauer succeeded in being posted as second editor of the *Deutsche Karpathenzeitung*.[114] In 1917 Lissauer observed a "deep gap, a hostility" between his comrades and the officers at the front. This he ascribed to a rumour that no more shooting was to take place from 1st October 1917. After the peace of Brest-Litovsk, Lissauer was sent to Berlin, to the Press Office of the War Ministry.[115] But even before taking up his official post he was given a forum for his propaganda in a regular leaflet called *Worte in die Zeit*. Seeckt's letter of conscription explicitly referred to Lissauer as the "spirit that evoked the deeds of our ancestors of a hundred years ago" and as the author of the "immortal expression" of the *Haßgesang*.[116] From the letter it is clear that Lissauer and his war propaganda were not universally dismissed. In fact, it seems that a double standard was applied to the author and the reception of his writings. While the poem was publicly opposed in order to counter the identification of Germany as a warmongering nation, on the political and military level Lissauer's lyrical reprisals were encouraged and exploited. Although the critical responses of the press and the debate over the poem's unsuitability for young people give the impression that Lissauer's talent was not appreciated, the government still made use of Lissauer's propaganda skills.

Historians today cannot avoid attributing a prophetic uncanniness to a poem Lissauer wrote in 1918. Reflecting on the sacrifices, deaths and the state of disorder in Germany, he asks:

> "Ist uns kein Führer gesendet?
> Geht ein Volk dahin wie das Gras?
> Wacht auf! Deutschland verendet,
> Am Rande der Geschichte, ein Aas, –
>
> Kommt kein Retter alsbald,
> Von Gram hochgewühlt,
> Der aufbirst in Gewalt,
> Einer, der fühlt und befiehlt...."[117]

LISSAUER'S SHIFT IN ALLEGIANCE

The question of whether Lissauer's growing Jewish identity in 1915 was a reaction to the negative reception of his poem or to the realisation that nothing was to be gained by insisting on a fervent German nationalist stance is almost impossible to answer, especially if one has to rely on the autobiographical

---

[113]"Generalstabschef der Heeresfront Erzherzog Josef zu der das Karpathen-Corps gehörte." Lissauer, 'Bemerkungen', MS, p. 86.
[114]*Ibid.*, p. 84.
[115]*Ibid.*, pp. 89f.
[116]Letter from v. Seeckt to Lissauer, 3rd January 1917, LBI Archives, New York.
[117]Ernst Lissauer, 'Um Deutschland', in *Vossische Zeitung*, (29th December 1918), LBI Archives, New York.

account written after the war, so obviously tailored to justify his wartime writings. The other question, of what Lissauer's shift to a Jewish identity meant – namely an admission of a long concealed and deeply felt affiliation or an opportunistic seizure of something which could hardly be more remote from his previous German nationalism – is equally difficult to answer. Historians, after all, cannot peer into the unfathomable depths of individual souls. To a certain extent Lissauer is a good example of the rivalry between the value of literary and non-literary sources. While his personal accounts and poems express a language of conflict and inner change, his non-literary writings remained consistently pro-German during the war.

The main sources for Lissauer's changing attitude to the *Haßgesang*, and for his simultaneous or subsequent inclination to Jewishness, are the *Bemerkungen zum Leben* and his poetry. However, the majority of poems which deal with his dilemma of allegiance to Germany while searching for a place in Jewish tradition were written after the war, some of the poems as late as 1933. The second of Lissauer's autobiographical documents, a 1923 manuscript in the handwriting of his wife, was entitled *Bemerkungen zum Leben;* its motivation seems to have been to provide an apologetic account of the lack of recognition following the rejection of the *Haßgesang*. The other, published under the title *Bemerkungen über mein Leben*, however, was, according to its preface, sparked by a different theme:

> "I have tried to live and to shape that indissoluble unity of Jewishness and Germanness ... which is today regarded as impossible. But I believe I have created a work with which the German people must come to terms."[118]

Lissauer thus confronted the Germans with a question echoed by Ernst Simon in his speech to mark the opening of the Leo Baeck Institute in Jerusalem in May 1955. This is the question of what German Jewry consisted of and it demands a detailed answer.[119]

According to *Bemerkungen zum Leben* the gradual shift in Lissauer's identity from committed German nationalist to conscious Jew began in 1915, the year in which he experienced the first negative reactions to the *Haßgesang*. It was only then that Lissauer wrote his first psalms, apparently "in a sudden impulse, and in a state of trance".[120] In his published autobiographical account Lissauer ascribed even more importance to his spiritual state when dictating the psalms to his wife.[121] They were not published at the time because of "domestic difficulties", by which he meant the mental illness of his wife, and because of the attacks he was subjected to as a result of the publication of the *Haßgesang*.[122] Ten years later he indicated

---

[118]Lissauer, 'Bemerkungen über mein Leben', p. 287.
[119]Ernst Simon, 'Das geistige Erbe des deutschen Judentums', in Christoph Schulte (ed.), *Deutschtum und Judentum*, Stuttgart 1993, p. 162.
[120]Lissauer, 'Bemerkungen', MS, p. 83. In the preface to the psalms Lissauer speaks of God speaking through him, which might be understood as Lissauer's "state of trance". Ernst Lissauer, 'Vorklang', in *Die ewigen Pfingsten. Gesichte und Gesänge*, Jena 1919, p. 59.
[121]Lissauer, 'Bemerkungen über mein Leben', p. 299.
[122]Lissauer, 'Bemerkungen', MS, pp. 83f.

that he had by then (1915) grown tired of the war and the image of God contained in the psalms seemed to glorify hatred.[123] It should be emphasised, however, that the psalms do not deal with specifically Jewish themes and that it is therefore difficult to see how they indicate Lissauer's change of identity. The God in Lissauer's psalms is neither a Jewish nor a Christian God, but rather a German God or a God of cultural inspiration, "the God of Beethoven and of Michelangelo".[124] The themes of Lissauer's psalms revolve around experiencing God through suffering, the need to isolate oneself in order to understand God's will and, interestingly, the necessity of rejecting the notion of plurality in favour of the idea of a single, complete entity.[125] These themes are of interest regarding Lissauer's state of mind in 1915, but it would not be accurate to project Jewish spirituality onto them. Lissauer had by then come to realise that there were painful limits to his ability to become an integral part of German society by expressing his affiliation to German culture in his poetry, and his psalms bear witness to his sense of rejection. In another passage he speaks of a process of alienation from as early as 1913.[126] According to the *Bemerkungen zum Leben*, only a part of himself responded to the success of the poem:

> "Altogether the poem has made me five to six thousand Marks as I only accepted [royalties] for reproduction on postcards, wall displays, etc. In my innermost depths, I realise today, I did not experience the success of the poem at all. I envisaged the idea of something whole, with which I wanted to influence German intellectual life. It was not I who enjoyed the success, but only a minute fraction of myself... Nonetheless, this poem did not remain without an effect on my inner self. I looked on it as a sign of strength, that this work could, without my doing anything, have such an effect and travel around the whole globe, and I wish that I could compose such a work out of my innermost, timeless, cosmic, religious endeavour."[127]

Lissauer does not explicitly state that it was the non-Jewish, German part of his person which rejoiced in its success, but this is suggested by two further statements. First, Lissauer writes that he wanted to have an effect on German culture as a whole, implying that he had to hold back an important part of himself; and, second, that he wished he could achieve such an impact by his innermost religious striving, implying again that poetry deriving from Jewish sentiments could not have achieved such fame.

LISSAUER'S POETRY: A LEGACY OF DUAL IDENTITY

A powerful testimony to Lissauer's shift to Jewishness is provided by his later poems, which can only be dealt with briefly here. In these, Lissauer examines

---

[123] Lissauer, 'Bemerkungen über mein Leben', p. 300.
[124] Lissauer, 'Anruf', in *Die ewigen Pfingsten*, p. 60.
[125] Lissauer, 'Der Psalm von den Bekennern', p. 61; 'Gott spricht: Du sollst Dir um Dich bauen eine weite Stille', p. 66; 'Gott spricht: Du sollst fliehen das Viele', p. 65; 'Gott spricht: Ich bin nicht gerecht', p. 71, in *Die ewigen Pfingsten*, pp. 61–71.
[126] Lissauer, 'Bemerkungen', MS, p. 89.
[127] *Ibid.*, pp. 74f.

his Jewish origins, his acculturation to German culture, his apparent integration, and his fall, which he described as a condemnation. These poems describe a search for his position before himself, society and God. Whereas in his pre-war poems Lissauer evoked the notion of unity, these later poems speak of disintegration, loss, polarity and distance from the self;[128] and whereas he formerly looked outwards, describing historical events and persons, he now looks inwards.

Two examples of the poetry dealing with his identity must suffice here. The better known one is the poem *O Volk, mein Volk*, which will be dealt with later.[129] The second is an untitled and apparently unpublished poem begun in 1933 and completed in 1935:

> "Vielleicht im Weltall schweifen freigelassene Geister,
> Wiederzukehren als Mann oder Weib,
> Vielleicht war ich vormals[130] ein deutscher Meister,
> Der niederfuhr in eines Juden Leib.
> Vielleicht steht irgend noch ein Kruzifix,
> Das ich damals aus Lärchenholz schnitzte.
> Ein Jude, dessen Blut von meinem Hieb verspritzte,
> Verfluchte mich, gebrochnen Blicks."[131]

However unfamiliar we may find Lissauer's choice of metaphors today, they tell of the extent to which he felt it necessary to justify his denial of his Jewishness. By attributing the reasons for his overriding affiliation to Germanness to a kind of reincarnation of a German soul in the body of a Jew, he is in effect stating that he had no choice but to be German. The remarkable message of the poem speaks not only of random forces which condemned him, formerly a German *Meister*, to lead the life of a Jew, but also of a "Jewish curse". This curse, in the words of the poem, is uttered by a Jew whom the "I" of the poem had persecuted and violated. It does not require any particular psychological expertise to recognise that the poem expresses feelings of guilt. The persistent denial of his Jewish background, the call for complete assimilation, his contempt for Eastern European Jewry in the name of *Deutschtum*, when, as he was aware, "... at the same moment as Gandhi wants to abolish contempt of the pariah, new pariahs are being created in Germany",[132] all caused Lissauer severe anguish and guilt.

The better known poem *O Volk, mein Volk* shows how Lissauer was forced by the rejection he had experienced, which weighed on him like a *Bannfluch*,[133] to confront the conflict between his German and Jewish identities and involuntarily, but inevitably, to betray one of his identities:

---

[128] In the poem "Ein Mensch ruft zu Gott", for example, the lyric persona changes into an observer of the self: "Du Mensch, der da hört auf meinen Namen."
[129] For instance, the first verse of this poem is used by Klara Pomeranz Carmely as a motto for her book *Das Identitätsproblem jüdischer Autoren im deutschen Sprachraum. Von der Jahrhundertwende bis zu Hitler*, Königstein Taunus 1981.
[130] Originally this read "vorzeit".
[131] Lissauer, Diary 51, LBI Archives, New York.
[132] *Ibid*.
[133] Brand, p. 71.

> "O Volk, mein Volk! Welch Volk ist denn nun mein?
> Wie eine Kiepe voll Geschichtsgestein
> Schleppe ich zweier Völker Last.
> Dem Deutschen Jude, deutsch getarnt,
> Dem Juden deutsch, treulos an Israel, –
> Hört ihr die Klapper, welch weithin warnt?
> Aussätzig von der beiden Völker Fehl!
> Dumpf um mich bläst Jahrtausendwind,
>
> Ich kauere hoch am wilden Zeitenpaß
> Und kratze mir den grauen Grind
> Der Weltgeschichte, siech von Völkerhaß."[134]

This poem is a striking example of Lissauer's conflict with regard to his identity. An earlier poem of his, *Seele 3*, describes the inner self as a source of strength in the face of disappointment; *O Volk, mein Volk*, the opening refrain of which is reminiscent of the style of the Psalms, expresses an inner struggle. In *O Volk* Lissauer speaks of his Germanness as a "disguise". The image of the "wandering Jew" is intensified by the accessory of a "rattle", a medieval device used by those who were infected with an incurable disease. The symptom of the disease, here described with the Middle-High German word *Grind*, meaning a grey, scaly rash, in this context brought about by hatred, is the unacceptability of either element of his identity. In the poem, both Germans and Jews have an historical legacy which makes them unacceptable to others. This self-ostracism culminates in the image of someone crouching with the burden of all nations' hatred heaped on his shoulders.

CONCLUSION

The war brought many German Jews into direct confrontation with the dilemma of their German and Jewish identities, and it left them with a stronger Jewish identity or at least made them examine their Jewishness more closely. Ernst Lissauer had not previously acknowledged the existence of a German-Jewish dilemma and he developed a personal awareness of it for the first time during the war. Formerly, he had been so uncompromisingly assimilationist that he even challenged the possibility of Jews living *qua* Jews in Germany, and it was only through his own experience of rejection that he was suddenly confronted with precisely this problem.

Contemporary glorification of Prussia and Prussian history, and with it the perpetuation of *Feindbilder* in Europe's nation states, had made a lasting impact on the impressionable student Lissauer.[135] This factor, coupled with an upbringing that focused on playing a full part in German life and rejecting any possible interference from the Jewish element, contributed to his refusal to acknowledge

---

[134]Lissauer, 'O Volk, mein Volk!' (1933), in *Zeitenwende. Gedichte 1932/36. Neue Dichtung*, vol. 3, Vienna–Leipzig 1936, p. 23.

[135]Egmont Zechlin even saw in the *Haßgesang* and its powerful creation of an image of the enemy an anticipation of totalitarian thinking. Zechlin, p. 97.

diversity in German society. At first he avoided the problem of dual identity because he perceived it as a potential obstacle to achieving public recognition. Recognition was a key element in Lissauer's life and work, and finds its expression in the idea that he had to acquire his Germanness, rather than assuming that he belonged to German culture and society by birthright or, indeed, that he constituted part of it in the sense described by the editor of the *Bemerkungen*: "[I]t is the tragedy of the Jew that he always wants to prove his legitimacy on foreign soil and in foreign pastures by overdoing it."[136] The perception of the fragility of his position in German life led to his excessively pronounced stance and his devaluation of what appeared to be a threat to Germany, namely France, England and Eastern European Jewry. In taking this position he overstepped boundaries, especially after the first wave of enthusiasm had subsided and the realities of the cruelties of war demanded an explanation from those found responsible for its course. His attempts to use the heat of the moment to unite the nation around the *Feindbild* he created resulted in his ostracism.

Lissauer was associated with the *Haßgesang* for a long time . The poem was labelled by Chamberlain, on the one hand, as "something only a Jew could have written" and, on the other hand, as the expression of German aggression. Yet both Jews and Germans distanced themselves from its overt message on the grounds that it was neither in the Jewish nor in the Christian tradition to foster hatred. Since no group, either at home or abroad, either German or Jewish, saw the *Haßgesang* as representative of their culture, Lissauer was left with sole responsibility for the reception of the poem and subsequently became isolated.[137] This ostracism breached Lissauer's German identity. He was forced to try to reestablish his credibility as a representative of German culture, and did so by defending his writing as a momentary slip in his reaction to the British declaration of war.

The experience of rejection brought Lissauer into direct confrontation with his Jewishness, and several Jewish themes emerged in his later writings. Although Lissauer portrayed his shift to Jewish spirituality as having taken place as early as 1913, nothing in his writings supports this. It may be argued that Lissauer discovered Jewish culture as a new literary form for himself, but it was not until the 1930s, when he lived in Vienna, that he emphatically turned to Judaism. Although his last autobiographical account seems to suggest that it had been his aim, throughout his life and work, to reconcile the German and Jewish cultures, this appears to be a projection of his stance in the mid-1920s and 1930s onto earlier periods of his life. His Jewish identity before then had been a private affair.

Ernst Lissauer's work reflects the changes in identity of a Jew living in Germany. Such transformations in self-awareness were not merely internal phenomena of a single author's literary persona, but responses to the changing reali-

---

[136]Lissauer, 'Bemerkungen über mein Leben', p. 286.
[137]This seemed to have remained so until the late 1930s, as the rector of the University of Hamburg, Hans Friedrich Blunck, remembers in his memoirs: "Ernst Lissauer, much idolised and much hated ... does not have it easy because, as with Hofmannsthal, the Jewish press rejected him because of his conservative stance and the conservative one because of his Jewish descent." Hans Friedrich Blunck, *Unwegsame Zeiten. Lebensbericht*, vol. 2, Mannheim 1952, pp. 47–48.

ties of the conditions of his time. Lissauer believed that his writing had a direct political purpose, being a kind of substitute for military service. A change in the political context writers were placed in the aftermath of the First World War may, therefore, also be significant for understanding the evolving self-perception of German Jews.

Dissimilation and the Historical Novel: Hermann Sinsheimer's Maria Nunnez

BY JONATHAN SKOLNIK

The German-language historical novel experienced a tremendous boom from the end of the Great War to the fall of the Nazi regime. In the 1930s, historical fiction was extremely popular across the political spectrum: it was one of the most beloved genres of the German Right and the literary form *par excellence* of exiled writers.[1] Perhaps because they fall outside of the established research paradigms of "exile literature", "National-Socialist literature", or the "literature of the inner emigration", works by Jewish writers published in Hitler's Germany have not received comparable critical treatment.[2] Thus, a remarkable historical novel has not received the attention it merits: Hermann Sinsheimer's *Maria Nunnez. Eine jüdische Überlieferung*, published in 1934.[3] Sinsheimer's tale of a young *conversa* in sixteenth-century Portugal resonates with the political and cultural crisis faced by German Jewry in the 1930s. *Maria Nunnez* is a novel which both reacts to the Nazis' antisemitic cultural policies and creatively confronts the legacy of nineteenth-century German Jewry from beyond a profound historical *caesura*.

Sinsheimer, born in Freinsheim in 1883, is an unjustly neglected figure in German, and especially German-Jewish, cultural history.[4] A theatre critic, essayist and novelist, Sinsheimer directed the Munich *Kammerspiele* in 1916–1917 and wrote prolifically for a number of journals. In 1920 he published memoirs of his small-town Jewish childhood in a volume co-edited with Lion

---

[1]The literature is extensive. See Frank Westenfelder, *Genese, Problematik und Wirkung nationalsozialistischer Literatur am Beispiel des historischen Romans zwischen 1890 und 1945*, Frankfurt am Main 1988, p. 203, and Hans Dahlke, *Geschichtsroman und Literaturkritik im Exil*, Berlin 1976.
[2]Cf. Henry Wasserman, *Bibliographie des jüdischen Schrifttums in Deutschland, 1933–1943*, Munich–New York 1989. Bearbeitet für das Leo Baeck Institut, Jerusalem.
[3]Hermann Sinsheimer, *Maria Nunnez. Eine jüdische Überlieferung*, Berlin 1934. I would like to express my gratitude to Prof. Yosef H. Yerushalmi for bringing Sinsheimer to my attention.
[4]Gert Weber and Rolf Paulus (eds.), *Hermann Sinsheimer. Schriftsteller zwischen Heimat und Exil*, Landau/Pfalz 1986, have assembled an anthology and an incomplete bibliography, but their short introduction only sketches his long and varied career. Cf. his autobiography: Hermann Sinsheimer, *Gelebt im Paradies*, Munich 1953. Lisa Lampert's *After Eden, Out of Zion*, diss. University of California, Berkeley 1996, analyses Sinsheimer's *Shylock*. Cf. Hermann Sinsheimer, *Shylock. The History of a Character*, New York 1963 (reprint.). On his role in the *Kulturbund*, see *Geschlossene Vorstellung. Der jüdische Kulturbund in Deutschland 1933–1941*, ed. by the Akademie der Künste, Berlin 1992, pp. 59, 72. On Sinsheimer's political positions in the 1930s, see Herbert Freeden, *Die jüdische Presse im Dritten Reich*, Frankfurt am Main 1987, pp. 90, 100 and 113.

Feuchtwanger.[5] Sinsheimer was the chief editor of *Simplicissimus* (1923–1929), and edited the *Berliner Tageblatt*'s *feuilleton* from 1930 until 1933. After 1933 he became a convinced Zionist and wrote for the *CV-Zeitung*, *Jüdische Rundschau*, and other newspapers. He was also active in the *Kulturbund deutscher Juden*, where he became a leading advocate for Jewish content in its activities. In 1936–1937 he worked on his study of *Shylock*, first published in England in 1947, and it is primarily as a Shakespeare scholar that he is remembered. Believing that it was too late in life for him to begin anew in Palestine, Sinsheimer emigrated to Britain in 1939, and died there in 1950.[6]

Sinsheimer's *Maria Nunnez* is an historical novel about Sephardim. The story begins in Portugal in the 1590s. Maria Nunnez Homem, a beautiful young *conversa*, is inflamed by the faith of her ancestors and flees persecution in Iberia for freedom in Amsterdam with her uncle Jacob Tirado, the poet Jakob Israel Belmonte, and several other relatives. All are historical figures. In the novel, their ship is seized by the English Navy and the Portuguese Jews are taken to London as prisoners. A young English captain falls in love with Maria. Queen Elizabeth I hears of Maria, who has become a subject of popular fascination, and summons her to appear at court. The queen offers the group refuge. But "shunning all the pomp of England" and rejecting her Christian suitor, Maria pleads for and wins her release, in order to help found the Jewish community in Amsterdam.[7] The episode involving the queen is probably not historical.

Sinsheimer was not alone in choosing a chapter from Sephardic history as the subject for his novel. In the 1930s, the historical novel was fertile ground for Jewish authors, and a cluster of fictional works set in the era of the Spanish Inquisition and expulsion appeared.[8] Popular works of history, such as those by Valeriu Marcu or Yitzhak (Fritz) Baer, might also be considered in this context. As Yosef Yerushalmi notes, these German-Jewish authors used the historical parallel with the Spanish expulsion to place the contemporary crisis of the Hitler regime's first years in a normative historical framework.[9]

This "return to history" did not go unchallenged as an appropriate literary strategy to counter the Nazi threat, and Kurt Hiller's polemical attack on histor-

---

[5]Hermann Sinsheimer, Lion Feuchtwanger, Fritz Cassirer and Paul Schlesinger, *An den Wassern von Babylon*, Munich 1920.
[6]Cf. Hermann Sinsheimer, *Gelebt im Paradies*, pp. 279ff.
[7]Cecil Roth, *A History of the Jews in England*, Oxford 1941, p. 142. Roth, following the historian Sigmund Seeligman, dismisses the story as a legend but notes that it contains elements of truth. This view is shared by David S. Katz, *The Jews in the History of England, 1485–1850*, Oxford 1994, p. 102.
[8]Cf. Josef Kastein, *Uriel da Costa*, Berlin 1932; Hermann Kesten, *Ferdinand und Isabella*, Amsterdam 1936; and Fritz Heymann, *Marannenchronik*, reprinted as *Tod oder Taufe. Die Vertreibung der Juden aus Spanien und Portugal im Zeitalter der Inquisition*, ed. and with an introduction by Julius H. Schoeps, Frankfurt 1988. Although Heymann's work was published only posthumously in lecture form, Hermann Kesten's comments in his introduction to the second edition of Heymann's *Der Chevalier van Geldern*, Cologne 1963 (reprint. Publication of the Leo Baeck Institute), pp. x–xii, lead the author to believe that he may have conceived of the project as historical fiction.
[9]Yosef H. Yerushalmi, *"Diener von Königen und nicht Diener von Dienern." Einige Aspekte der politischen Geschichte der Juden*, Munich 1995, pp. 47–48.

ical novelists' alleged "flight from the present" is interesting from the perspective of the realignment of Jewish identity in exile from Nazi Germany:

"We are Germans. (As much as we are proletarians or Europeans or humanists.) For us, therefore, the core problem of the day is: How to clean out the German Augean stables? [...] Is it right] to write books about Machiavelli or Ignatius of Loyola or Moses Mendelssohn today. There are still a few Isabellas about whom a novel has yet to be written; and Rameses IV too, and Pippin the Middling.... The day after tomorrow Hitler will be emperor of Europe because today you are eagerly and cravenly fleeing from the demands of the present...."[10]

Sinsheimer's *Maria Nunnez*, far from an escape from the exigencies of the moment, is implicitly an active political engagement to which the author attributed Zionist motives. In his memoirs, Sinsheimer notes that the novel marked an important transformation: an author deeply immersed in German theatre now enthusiastically embraced Jewish history and Jewish culture as a productive response to a legacy of attempted integration that now appeared to have irrevocably failed.[11]

In choosing the historical novel as a medium for his new cultural politics, Sinsheimer tapped a rich German-Jewish literary tradition. From the 1820s to the 1930s historical fiction was a preferred genre for many Jewish writers.[12] Berthold Auerbach and Heinrich Heine both wrote historical novels on Jewish subjects during their youthful engagements with Jewish cultural causes. In the mid-nineteenth century, rabbi and publisher Ludwig Philippson became a major proponent of historical fiction, extolling the medium's pedagogical potential in the pages of the *Allgemeine Zeitung des Judenthums* and writing several novels himself.[13] By mid-century, a full-fledged minority literature had emerged, with works by such now-forgotten authors as Ludwig and Phöbus Philippson, Isaac Ascher Francolm and Moses Wassermann. The German-Jewish historical novel remained important in the twentieth century and formed part of a renewal of a self-contained Jewish culture in Weimar Germany.[14]

The nineteenth-century German-Jewish historical novel was, for the most part, liberal in its tendency,[15] with Orthodox writers such as Marcus Lehmann adopting the genre decades after both Auerbach's and Phöbus Philippson's first novels were published in 1837. Sephardic themes were overrepresented and Ismar Schorsch has described these historical novels as contributions to a preva-

---

[10]Kurt Hiller, *Profile. Prosa aus einem Jahrzehnt*, Paris 1938, p. 236. All translations are by the present author unless otherwise stated. For more of Kurt Hiller on Jewish questions, see his reply to the Arnold Zweig-Kurt Tucholsky exchange of 1936: 'Tucholsky und der Selbsthass', *idem*, pp. 85–89.
[11]Cf. Sinsheimer, *Gelebt im Paradies*, pp. 279ff.
[12]The German-Jewish historical novel has gone largely unrecognised as a sub-genre. Cf. Hugo Aust's recent survey, *Der historische Roman*, Stuttgart 1994. Exceptions are Lothar Kahn (with Donald D. Hook), *Between Two Worlds. A Cultural History of German-Jewish Writers*, Ames 1993; Hans Otto Horch, *Auf der Suche nach der jüdischen Erzählliteratur*, Frankfurt am Main 1985; Nitsa Ben-Ar, *Romance with the Past* (in Hebrew), Tel Aviv 1997. See also Walter Jacob, 'A bibliography of Novels and Short Stories by German Jewish Authors 1800–1914', in *Studies in Bibliography and Booklore*, Cincinnati, vol. VI, 1962–1964, pp. 75–92, and the author's forthcoming study.
[13]Horch, pp. 144–164.
[14]Michael Brenner, *The Renaissance of Jewish Culture in Weimar Germany*, New Haven–London 1996, pp. 129–152.
[15]Lothar Kahn, p. 62.

lent "myth of Sephardic supremacy", as works of literature which created a noble, "usable past" to serve an apologist agenda that excluded *Ostjuden*.[16] It is against this background that Hermann Sinsheimer's *Maria Nunnez* should be understood.

Sixty-seven years prior to Sinsheimer's novel, Ludwig Philippson had published *Jakob Tirado*, an historical novel on the same subject.[17] Philippson's 1867 novel narrates the same legend of Maria, Queen Elizabeth, and the English captain, although the novel's focus is centred on the figures of Tirado and the poet Belmonte. Nowhere is the difference between the two historical novels as pronounced as in the tone in which Maria asks Queen Elizabeth for permission to leave England. In the nineteenth-century novel, Maria respectfully declines the queen's offer to use her power to obscure "the deficiencies of her family tree", thereby allowing her to marry the noble captain. It would be wrong, Maria argues in Philippson's novel, to pursue rank and status when she, "of lowly birth", has to answer to a different calling.[18] The Maria Nunnez of 1934, by contrast, implores the queen:

> "This alien soil burns my feet, this soil which is no homeland, the pressure of this soil which impedes me from acknowledging the God of my fathers."[19]

The same literary genre would now illustrate drastically changed historical relations. Philippson's Maria is concerned with behaving according to correct social and moral codes. Sinsheimer's heroine, on the other hand, thirsts for religious and national wholeness. *Maria Nunnez* has adopted the nationalistic rhetoric of "soil [*Boden*]" and "homeland [*Heimat*]". The Amsterdam which the Portuguese Jews want to reach is now understood more as a space where a free Jewish life can take root than as a model of European tolerance. The historical novel about the Sephardim, the same literary means by which nineteenth-century German Jews sought to write themselves into German and universal history, would now be a medium for Jews to write themselves out of this history. Sinsheimer turns what was a potent didactic and apologist instrument in the service of integration on itself. Could the historical novel written just before the founding of the *Reich* and the granting of equal rights to Jewish citizens be called a novel of *assimilation*, and the work composed just after the *Machtergreifung* of 1933 a novel of *dissimilation*? With *Maria Nunnez* is Sinsheimer, an author steeped in the German theatrical tradition, writing the final acts of the tragi-comedy that the generation of the Philippsons had begun?[20]

---

[16]Ismar Schorsch, 'The Myth of Sephardic Supremacy', in *LBI Year Book XXXIV* (1989), reprinted in Ismar Schorsch, *From Text to Context. The Turn to History in Modern Judaism*, Hanover–London 1994, pp. 71–92.
[17]Ludwig Philippson, *Jakob Tirado*, Leipzig 1867.
[18]*Ibid.*, pp. 316–318.
[19]"Mir brennt unter den Sohlen der Boden der Fremde, der Boden, der keine Heimat ist, der Zwang dieses Bodens, der mich hindert, mich zum Gott meiner Väter zu bekennen." Sinsheimer, *Maria Nunnez*, p. 202.
[20]For Sinsheimer's conception of German-Jewish history as tragi-comedy, see both his preface to *Shylock*, pp. 17–20, where he describes his radical alienation from Germany and *Gelebt im Paradies*, pp. 279ff., where his treatment by publishers in post-war Germany, who rejected his *Shylock* as irrelevant for the "deutsche Problematik", is described as "der satirische Mummenschanz, der nach uraltem Rezept der Tragödie auf dem Fuß zu folgen pflegt".

David Sorkin has persuasively argued that the paradigms of "assimilation" and "emancipation", enmeshed as they are in the historical polemics of the *Centralverein deutscher Staatsbürger jüdischen Glaubens* (C.V.) and the *Zionistische Vereinigung für Deutschland*, are outdated for a contemporary historiography.[21] He notes that for many historians these concepts are unable to convey how German Jews actively shaped themselves and their environment, and her calls for alternative conceptual categories that can encompass both social and cultural phenomena. It is in this spirit that the term "dissimilation" has attracted the attention of a number of scholars.

Dennis B. Klein used "dissimilation" in his critique of Peter Gay to describe the limits of Jewish integration in Central Europe, the self-conscious affirmation of cultural distinctiveness by a small but significant minority of Jews.[22] Shulamit Volkov first employed the term to describe the dynamics at work in assimilation as an ongoing process, with immigrant Eastern Jews reminding German Jews of their own status as relative newcomers on the assimilation ladder.[23] More recently, Volkov expanded her use of "dissimilation" as a relative term to "assimilation" to connote the fluid synthesis of integration and isolation which characterised Jewish life in nineteenth-century Germany.[24] Using the term in Volkov's earlier sense, Gavriel Rosenfeld opted for "dissimilation" in his study of art criticism in the journal *Ost und West* to illustrate how German and Eastern European Jews participated in a Jewish cultural renaissance.[25] David Sorkin views the term as a symptom of the assimilation paradigm's inadequacy.[26] In my view, "dissimilation" is a highly charged concept that is most productive for historiography when understood as part of an historical discourse.

"Dissimilation", a term borrowed from linguistics, was used by Franz Rosenzweig to describe a dialectical process in Jewish history not far removed from Volkov's model.[27] It was also applied to German-Jewish history in less lofty circumstances – by Lutz Lenders in the *Völkischer Beobachter*.[28] Lenders's polemic repeated the standard charges that Reform Judaism and German-Jewish cultural integration were merely "tasteless ... artificial ... masquerades", and

---

[21]David Sorkin, 'Emancipation and Assimilation. Two Concepts and their Application to German-Jewish History', in *LBI Year Book XXXV* (1990), pp. 17–33.

[22]Dennis B. Klein, 'Assimilation and Dissimilation. Peter Gay's *Freud, Jews, and other Germans*' in *New German Critique* 19 (Winter 1980), pp. 151–165.

[23]Shulamit Volkov, 'The Dynamics of Dissimilation. *Ostjuden* and German Jews', in Jehuda Reinharz and Walter Schatzberg (eds.), *The Jewish Response to German Culture. From the Enlightenment to the Second World War*, Hanover 1985, pp. 195–211.

[24]Shulamit Volkov, *Die Juden in Deutschland 1780–1918*, Munich 1994, pp. 53–56. Volkov uses "dissimilation" as a conceptual category concomitant with "acculturation", one that has found favour with reviewers. Cf. Arno Herzig in *Aschkenas*, 5.Jg./Heft 2 (1995), pp. 526–528.

[25]Gavriel Rosenfeld, 'Defining "Jewish Art" in *Ost und West*, 1901–8. A Study', in *LBI Year Book XXXIX* (1994), pp. 83, 86.

[26]Sorkin, 'Emancipation', p. 28.

[27]Franz Rosenzweig, *Gesammelte Schriften I. Briefe und Tagebücher*, ed. by Rachel Rosenzweig, Edith Rosenzweig-Scheinmann and Bernhard Casper, vol. 2: 1918–1929, Den Haag 1979, p. 770 (Entry of 3rd April 1922).

[28]Lutz Lenders, 'Zum Problem der Dissimilation', *Völkischer Beobachter*, 25th April 1934.

argued that "dissimilation", by which he meant the extirpation of Jews from German culture, could not be legislated for by National Socialists, but must come from Jews themselves. He suggested that this would be most effectively accomplished through cultural means. Lenders's article found a positive reception in the *Jüdische Rundschau*.[29] Alfred Hirschberg of the *CV-Zeitung* was outraged, and responded with a lengthy article.[30] His conclusions predictably argue that Jews sharing his newspaper's point of view prefer to effect a "Jewish regeneration" restricted to the cultural-religious sphere, while at the same time "remaining German". Hirschberg's premises, which show an awareness that cultural questions can never be discussed independently of the power relations within which they are embedded, are more interesting. They show his very different sense of the "totality of life" that *CV-Zeitung* readers strove for, and his historical sense that "dissimilation" could not be projected back onto German-Jewish history and retroactively undo the synthesis of Jewish ethics and Enlightenment ideals. Less than four months later, a review of Sinsheimer's new novel appeared in the pages of the same paper.[31]

Maria Nunnez was published by Philo Verlag, founded by Ludwig Holländer in 1919. When Gabriel Riesser's descendents objected to the use of his original name for the firm, the press of the *C.V.* chose the Greek-speaking Jewish philosopher as the figurehead for an institution that was to be the organ of an exemplary cultural synthesis of *Deutschtum und Judentum*.[32] A 1927 catalogue gives a picture of Philo's pre-1933 programme: roughly two-thirds of the titles represent the C.V.'s "*Aufklärungsarbeit*" of countering antisemitic slander, while the rest is a mix of books on history, religion (including Franz Rosenzweig's *Zweistromland*), and a very small number of *belles-lettres*, such as *Berühmte jüdische Frauen in Vergangenheit und Gegenwart*.

Sinsheimer's *Maria Nunnez* was part of a redefinition of the cultural programme of this mainstream Jewish publisher. Ingrid Belke notes the great disappointment that the Nazis' rise to power must have caused Jews of the Philo Verlag *milieu*.[33] The publisher, rather than continue the pre-1933 programme in which apologetic literature predominated, now engaged in a productive transformation of Jewish culture. Whereas some may have viewed (and still view) the

---

[29]Cf. *Jüdische Rundschau*, 27th April 1934.
[30]Alfred Hirschberg 'Dissimilation oder Assimilation?', in *CV-Zeitung*, 3rd May 1934.
[31]Jakob Picard, (review of *Maria Nunnez*) in *CV-Zeitung*, 30th August 1934. Picard's positive review argued that Sinsheimer's use of Jewish history and Kafka's modernist prose of "ethical strictness and special melody" were two examples of a "Jewish art" which compared favorably with the fashionable works of successful contemporary authors. The *Jüdische Rundschau*'s cultural pages, preoccupied for weeks with the death of Bialik, did not carry a lengthy review, but *Maria Nunnez* was included in a list of books recommended as *Hanukkah* presents (27th November 1934).
[32]'Philo Verlag', in Isaac Landman (ed.), *Universal Jewish Encyclopedia*, New York 1969, vol. 8, pp. 496–497. Philo Verlag's offices were destroyed on 10th November 1938 and its managing editor, Lucia Jacoby, was deported and killed. Thus it would prove difficult to write its history on the scale of Volker Dahm's study of Schocken Verlag, *Das jüdische Buch im dritten Reich*, Frankfurt am Main 1979. For another outline of its rich and varied history, see Ingrid Belke, *Marbacher Magazin* 25 (1983).
[33]Belke.

continued attempt at a definition of Jewish art in this period as artificial, a delivery of weapons into the hands of antisemites,[34] Philo Verlag supported projects such as Franz Landsberger's *Einführung in die jüdische Kunst*[35] in order to fulfil a perennial need to define oneself in all social and cultural spheres, in this case in drastic historical circumstances. These, of course, worsened, and Philo Verlag responded with its popular lexicon (*Philo-Lexikon. Handbuch des jüdischen Wissens*) as well as other books for youth and, ultimately, with its *Philo-Atlas. Handbuch für die jüdische Auswanderung*, to aid emigration to Palestine. Printed on 8th November 1938, it was the last Jewish book to be published in Nazi Germany.

Sinsheimer's *Maria Nunnez* participates in the contemporary debates about assimilation, "dissimilation", and the search for a space in which Jews and Jewish culture can exist, insofar as these dynamics are enacted by the characters and explored by the narrator in the novel. The fact that Sinsheimer's Portuguese *conversos* appear to be thinly-veiled historical stand-ins for Germans of Jewish origin in the 1930s was not lost on contemporary critics.[36] The historical analogy is successful not because Sinsheimer's characters are mere mouthpieces for an ideology of return, but because the novel's didactic moments are balanced by the psychological depth of the character portraits. Maria's father, a prosperous merchant, is a figure in conflict. Although he is "Christian and Portuguese like his father and grandfather before him, and completely Spanish for centuries", Maria's father has an ominous sense that the Jews' fate will be his, too.[37] But he is troubled by his daughter's newly-found Jewish religious fervour and this leads to generational strife:

> "Finally, that is to say towards the end of 1593, the atmosphere in the Homem household became almost unbearable. Maria demanded that nothing except Jewish questions be discussed, and this was received with approval from some quarters, disapproval from others. Her father became increasingly laconic. He spoke less about Judaism than about the refined means with which the Inquisition sought to unmask secret Judaising."[38]

Sinsheimer shows more understanding for the complexity of his Portuguese *conversos* than does Philippson. In *Jakob Tirado*, Maria says flatly to her English admirer shortly after they meet, "Duke, I am a Jewess. I want to be one and must be one".[39] Sinsheimer's Maria, by contrast, is confused by her conflicting emotions. Elsewhere *Maria Nunnez* is effective not because it aims at historical verisimilitude based on elaborate, "realistic" costumes with accurate detail, but rather because, like a good play, it relies on the skill of the actors to create illusion.

---

[34] Cf. Eike Geisel, 'Das jüdische Museum in Berlin 1933–1938', in *Tel-Aviver Jahrbücher für Deutsche Geschichte* 14 (1985), pp. 277ff.
[35] Berlin 1935.
[36] The Dutch poet Albert Vigoleis Thelen's review (9th December 1934, reprinted in Thelen, *Die Literatur in der Fremde*, Bonn 1996, pp. 52–54) highlighted the novel's implicit analogy with the situation of Jews in Nazi Germany.
[37] Sinsheimer, *Maria Nunnez*, pp. 6–7.
[38] *Ibid*, pp. 17–18. Sinsheimer's work exhibits deep sensitivity for generational dynamics. Cf. his earlier novel *Peter Wildangers Sohn*, Munich 1919.
[39] Philippson, *Jakob Tirado*, p. 207.

The sheer weight of the date of publication, however, "alienates" at every turn,[40] and the historical examples of racism, expulsion, flight, and cultural regeneration are unmasked as operative social givens.

The German-Jewish historical novel was an important literary arena in which a minority defined and redefined its relation to the great collective singular history and to German culture. In the hands of a Ludwig Philippson, the historical novel could be a pulpit from which the virtues of social integration of the Jews in Germany, based on universal Enlightenment values, could be extolled. In the last pages of *Jakob Tirado*, where the intellectual and monetary riches brought by the Jews to their new Dutch homeland are enumerated, Tirado's spirit is said to radiate throughout Europe, encouraging all the peoples in their fight against "fanaticism and superstition".[41] In the book's opening panorama of Brussels, with its statue of Egmont, the landscape of Jewish history is, by implication, merged with Goethe's historical drama. The first chapters of Philippson's novel detail Tirado's involvement in a failed plot against the hated Duke of Alba. This provides the motivation for his flight to Amsterdam via Portugal and London. Tirado becomes involved in the conspiracy, writes Philippson, not so much to avenge the wrongs done to his people by the Inquisition but to "free humanity from this plague".[42] Philippson's use of Goethe's *Egmont* as an intertext marries a minority "popular" literary genre to the highest ideals of the *Kulturnation*.

The theatre critic Hermann Sinsheimer obviously could not resist hinting at a parallel with German classical drama in his own historical novel. As in Schiller's *Maria Stuart*, the dramatic high point in Sinsheimer's novel comes as Maria and Queen Elizabeth finally meet. But other than borrowing Schiller's characterisation of a temperamental Elizabeth who confronts a prisoner named Maria, *Maria Nunnez* has little in common with *Maria Stuart*. Sinsheimer's novel has an ironic tone and the story has a happy end. The result of the encounter between Elizabeth and Maria in Sinsheimer's novel is that the queen grants the young Jewish girl's request and is so impressed by her that she takes her for a ride in the royal carriage. In the midst of historical catastrophe, Sinsheimer fancifully twists a scenario from German tragedy into a comedy as his Maria exits stage right to freedom.

Sinsheimer's *Maria Nunnez* inverts the focus of Philippson's *Jakob Tirado* on multiple levels. On the surface, the 1934 novel effects a reversal of ethnic clichés: Philippson's Maria is a blue-eyed beauty, while Sinsheimer emphasises her jet black hair. More importantly, whereas Philippson's novel is centred on a mature man, Sinsheimer's text directs the reader's attention to the problems of an adolescent girl. As Paula Hyman notes, the bourgeois society into which Jews were integrating encoded religion as "feminine" and Jewish women were often blamed for a decline in Jewish knowledge.[43] *Maria Nunnez*, with its *telos* of re-establishing an integrated Jewish life, celebrates the religious fervour of a young girl who has the

---

[40]Sinsheimer was an early champion of Brecht's theatre. Cf. his review of *Trommeln in der Nacht*, reprinted in Weber and Paulus, *Hermann Sinsheimer*, pp. 80–81.
[41]Philippson, *Jakob Tirado*, p. 372.
[42]*Ibid*, p. 52.
[43]Paula Hyman, *Gender and Assimilation in Modern Jewish History*, Seattle 1995, pp. 48–49.

power to mobilise a community. *Jakob Tirado*'s pedagogical paradigm is reversed: whereas Philippson's Maria listens passively as she is instructed by the older male figure in the history of anti-Jewish persecutions, Sinsheimer's figure is a motivating force for her family's return to Judaism and their decision to emigrate.

Maria's return to the religion of her ancestors does not, however, occur in a vacuum. While the enforcers of the Inquisition lurk everywhere to uncover and deliver "Judaisers" to the *auto-da-fé*, the Portuguese *conversos* are said to have preserved traces of their Jewishness. Sinsheimer's novel is subtitled *Eine jüdische Überlieferung*. *Überlieferung* is a recurring motif in the novel and is used to describe oral tradition in the form of stories passed down to daughters and sons. *Maria Nunnez* reveals a changed relationship to history. Historical consciousness has become multivalent in the novel of dissimilation. History, and not religion, language or culture, has become the sole tie linking the converted Jews with Judaism:

> "Thus, the family enviroment was Christian.... Jewish ritual had been forgotten because the baptised fathers had not passed it on [*überliefert*] to their children. Not so with the handing down [*Überlieferung*] of the great Jewish past ... to tell the children about the past had become a half pious, half routine exercise amoung the Marranos."[44]

This custom of instructing children in Jewish history (and it is, to be sure, history as *Verfallsgeschichte* and martyrology) is treated ambivalently in *Maria Nunnez*. On the one hand, it is the source from which Maria's return is nourished; on the other hand, it constitutes part of the incomplete Jewish life against which the young girl rebels.

Sinsheimer's narrator remarks that the only type of Judaism that the *conversos* are able to pass on is a religion elevated above all ritual, with "mythic power" and "historical mission".[45] Perhaps it is in this sense that Sinsheimer understood his own novel – as an appeal for Jewish solidarity on the most basic level. Although the narrator praises Maria's positive return to Judaism at every opportunity, the novel refrains from depicting the concrete form of an "authentic" Judaism. The sense of an inherent Jewishness which Maria's father shares with other Portuguese "New Christians" is described as a "great, grey cloud of their ineradicable Jewish destiny [*große, graue Wolke ihrer unausrottbaren jüdischen Bestimmung*]".[46] This is as much an image of vagueness and foreboding as one of a

---

[44]"Das Milieu der Familie also war christlich.... Der Ritus des Judentums war verloren gegangen, weil die getauften Väter ihn den Kindern nicht überliefert hatten. Dahingegen war die Überlieferung der großen jüdischen Vergangenheit, ... davon den Kindern zu berichten, war zu einer halb pietätvollen, halb auch nur gewohnheitsmäßigen Übung unter den Marranen gewordenen." Sinsheimer, *Maria Nunnez*, pp. 10–11.
[45]*Ibid.*
[46]*Ibid.*, pp. 7, 190–193. Cf. Paul Celan, *Gesammelte Werke*, Frankfurt am Main 1983, vol. I, p. 227: "große, graue/wie alles Verlorene nahe/Schwestergestalt." The strength of a refusal to positively depict a social utopia is offset by the political vacuum it creates. In a 1936 article, Sinsheimer advocated a political programme based on the affirmation of religious Orthodoxy for believers based on faith and for non-believers based on an "unbedingte Treue zum Judentum als Volk", H.S., 'Treue zum Judentum', in *Israelitisches Familienblatt*, No. 23, p. 1, reprinted in Weber and Paulus, pp. 119–121.

latent "authentic" Judaism. *Bestimmung* could connote either Israel's divinely ordained destiny or the Inquisition's diabolically ordered designation; *unausrottbar* suggests that extermination is understood to be a real posibility. Thus Maria's father, representative of the older generation, eventually gives cautious support to his daughter's plans for escape and religious renewal, but asserts that he wants to die in Portugal. Maria, on the other hand, absorbs as much as she can of the Jewish elements in Christianity, "with all of the enthusiasm of an adolescent seeking out something forbidden".[47] On board the ship from Lisbon, Tirado takes Maria and the others to a secret room where a Hebrew bible has been hidden. None of the group can read Hebrew but they all ritually kiss the text and then hold hands. The travellers' destination of Amsterdam, and the details of their new religious life there, are neither described in any substance nor invested with heavy-handed ideological pronouncements as in *Jakob Tirado*.

The German-Jewish search for a usable Jewish past in the nineteenth century, and the quest for an "authentic" Jewish culture in the early twentieth, led to various appropriations of the Sephardic and Eastern European legacies: a "myth of Sephardic supremacy" in the former period and a "cult of the *Ostjuden*" in the latter.[48] *Maria Nunnez* subverts the nineteenth-century paradigm at this level as well. Philippson's Jakob Tirado, upon arrival in Amsterdam, advises the young Alonso to travel to Emden to meet the Ashkenazi Rabbi Uri, who can instruct the youth in *Kabbalah*, which Tirado shuns ("My spirit demands something else ... clarity of thought," he says).[49] By contrast, Sinsheimer's Rabbi Uri is referred to as "an Eastern Jewish scholar [*ein Schriftgelehrter aus der Judenschaft des Ostens*]" who instructs the whole community in rites that are not specified, in keeping with the narrative's reluctance to give shape to an "authentic" culture.[50] If Sinsheimer idealises the Sephardic wanderings in his next published work, *Rabbi, Golem, Kaiser*,[51] it is because of his concept of a dialectic force in Jewish history between wandering and sedentary periods,[52] which may have been the impulse behind his stage adaptation of *Mendele Mokher Sforim* entitled *Benjamin, wohin?*[53]

In *Maria Nunnez*, a mixed picture is given of the prospects for a new life in England for the Portuguese Jews. Jakob Tirado meets Rodrigo Lopez, a Portuguese *converso* who was (in history as well as fiction) Queen Elizabeth's doctor. In Sinsheimer's novel, Tirado and Lopez have a heated argument over the wisdom of undertaking yet another journey and making a new beginning just to live as Jews. Dr. Lopez argues that Tirado and the others would do better to stay in England and become Puritans who, he says, are great friends of the Old Testament and would surely accept Jews. Tirado counters that Lopez was neither

---

[47]Sinsheimer, *ibid*, p. 16.
[48]See, for example, Schorsch *passim*, and Brenner, pp. 129–152.
[49]Philippson, *Jakob Tirado*, p. 342.
[50]Sinsheimer, *Maria Nunnez*, pp. 228–229.
[51]Hermann Sinsheimer, *Rabbi, Golem, Kaiser*, Berlin 1935.
[52]Cf. Sinsheimer's view of "settled" German Jewry in his autobiographical *An den Wassern von Babylon*.
[53]The play premiered in Berlin on 15th December 1938. Cf. *Geschlossene Vorstellung*, p. 72.

Catholic, nor Jew, nor Protestant; neither English nor Portuguese; and that one could not live in this way. The narrator then introduces a report of Lopez's historical fate: he is implicated in a conspiracy and hanged, castrated, drawn, quartered and decapitated, the traditional penalty for traitors.[54] Sinsheimer's narrator sides with Tirado: "A martyr? A suicide! The open torment of his death was no less than the secret torment of his life."[55]

The poet Belmonte's odds for a life in England are better. He establishes contact with local poets, with whom he can communicate in Latin, and realises that he could easily feel at home in this liberal cosmopolitan enviroment. Both character and novel opt instead for an artform which is implicitly politically engaged. Unlike Philippson's novel, which puts German nature poetry into the mouth of the historical poet,[56] *Maria Nunnez* gives the reader actual snippets of Belmonte's poetry only as it is quoted by the other characters or described by the narrator. Sinsheimer prudently refrains from illustrating an "authentic" Jewish art, while model inspirational or political interpretations of Belmonte's poetry are made by the other characters.

Sinsheimer's theatrical flair proved extremely productive for his treatment of questions of assimilation and identity. His revision of the German-Jewish historical novel is loaded with Shakespearean clichés – mistaken identity and cross-dressing.[57] As the Portuguese Jews sail towards Amsterdam, they are attacked by the English Navy and taken to England as (well-treated) prisoners who inspire the curiosity of the populace. An English captain, who uncannily resembles Maria's uncle Jakob Tirado, falls in love with the girl whose budding femininity is apparent despite her boy's clothes, which she dons for the sea voyage to freedom. Maria, at first extraordinarily shy and unable to speak to the captain, eventually develops an irrepressible sexual attraction to her uncle's non-Jewish look-alike. Whereas the Jewish men seek to impose their authority to keep the lovers apart, the adolescent girl, in due course, comes to her own conclusion that a genuine exchange cannot occur in a world of unequal power relations, for she is, after all, the captain's prisoner. Summoned to appear before Queen Elizabeth, Maria, allowed to choose from an assortment of elegant feminine apparel, chooses a simple grey dress to emphasise her true social position as a prisoner and refugee, and celebrates a double "revelation" as a woman and a Jew. Maria pleads convincingly for her people's liberation and the Jews are allowed to continue on to Amsterdam, where Maria ultimately marries a cousin with the same first name as her brother. Although *Maria Nunnez* enacts the re-establishment of strictly controlled bourgeois gender roles, readers, of course, may ask

---

[54]Cf. Katz, p. 96.

[55]Sinsheimer, *Maria Nunnez*, p. 166.

[56]"Seid gegrüßt, ihr Meereswellen/Kreisend um der Erde Saum!/Euer Stürzen, euer Schwellen/ Webet einen ew'gen Traum." Philippson, *Jakob Tirado*, p. 146. Sinsheimer's Belmonte remarks "wo Gott selbst gedichtet hat, müsse der Dichter verstummen". Sinsheimer, *Maria Nunnez*, p. 58.

[57]For perspectives on cross-dressing and gender, sexuality, and religion, see Marjorie Garber, *Vested Interests. Cross-Dressing and Cultural Anxiety*, New York 1992. Garber discusses literary representations of cross-dressed Jews centered around the antisemitic trope of the feminised Jewish male.

what new power relations will be established in the new community, and the novel retains a critical element that inhibits its slide into complete *kitsch*.

This episode of cross-dressing is entirely absent from Ludwig Philippson's 1867 novel. It is likely that Sinsheimer kept abreast of current scholarship. In the 1920s, the German-born Dutch-Jewish historian Sigmund Seeligman discovered a letter sent from London by the Dutch *Staten-Generaal*'s agent in 1597 detailing the capture of a Portuguese ship carrying Jewish refugees, including "a 'noble lady' dressed in male attire".[58]

In Sinsheimer's novel, the case of a girl who disguises her sexual and religious identity becomes the perfect means by which the discussion of "assimilation" and "dissimilation" can be wrested from the legions of Lutz Lenders, who railed against Jewish cultural integration as a "tasteless masquerade". Sinsheimer's Maria chooses her own costumes with a mature sense of the networks of power and domination within which culture is articulated. The cross-dressing episode unmasks "dissimilation" as being itself a masquerade, yet one which is an historical necessity. For Maria, to remain in Portugal is to risk death at the hands of the Inquisition. To seek refuge in England would only mean a new costume, the fiery red dress with which the queen provides her for the carriage ride. This, however, lets her appear merely as an object of curiosity to the people of the court:

> "... it was a Jewish picture that they draped with a gown, it was the rejoicing cry and call of a race near to and blessed by God, which they draped with the colour of a fabric."[59]

For the voyage to Amsterdam, Maria once again wears men's clothes. She does not want to be recognised and believes this to be the best way to leave her past behind. Her previous attempt at disguise was easily seen through by the English captain and the reader might assume that, had she remained in Lisbon, the Inquisition would have "unmasked" her as well. Sinsheimer's *Maria Nunnez* recognises that a mere costume change cannot effect a cultural transformation. Yet, dressed once again as a "little ship's officer", Maria Nunnez retains a modicum of authority in the process.

With its pronounced anti-integrationist tendency, Sinsheimer's *Maria Nunnez* can surely be termed a novel of dissimilation. Yet the narrative will not be backed into a corner where Jewish "authenticity" must be depicted, and Sinsheimer's characters drift in the realm of "what is still not Jewish, but no longer Christian", while taking concrete steps in their struggle for a space in which this in-between can find its own way. By rewriting Philippson's historical novel, Sinsheimer creatively confronts the nineteenth-century German-Jewish cultural legacy on its own terms, paradoxically perpetuating the very genre it undermines. Although

---

[58] Cf. Sigmund Seeligmann, *Bibliographie en Historie. Bijdrage tot de Geschiedenis der eerste Sephardim in Amsterdam*, Amsterdam 1927, pp. 16–19, cited in Jonathan Israel, 'Manuel Lopez Pereira of Amsterdam, Antwerp, and Madrid. Jew, New Christian, and Advisor to the Conde-Duque de Olivares', in *Studia Rosenthaliana*, vol. 19, No. 2 (October 1985), p. 112.

[59] "... es war ein jüdisches Bild, das sie mit einem Kleid behingen, es war der jubelnde Aufschrei und Ruf einer gottnahen und gottseligen Rasse, den sie mit der Farbe eines Stoffes behingen". Sinsheimer, *Maria Nunnez*, p. 213.

"dissimilation" was now a Nazi *Schlagwort* and the return to Jewish culture was now imposed, Sinsheimer's *Maria Nunnez* articulates dissimilation with dignity. Conscious of both the Zionists' grasp of the necessity for a Jewish withdrawal from Germany and Alfred Hirschberg's understanding that, though they might now wield power, the nationalists could not undo history, the novel pays homage to a German-Jewish culture which was at that point no longer possible.

*Persecution and Rescue
Under National Socialism*

Before the "Final Solution":
The Judenpolitik of the SD, 1935–1938*

BY MICHAEL WILDT

On 24th May 1934 *Abteilung* IV 2 of the SS-*Sicherheitsamt* sent a memorandum to its director, Reinhard Heydrich, entitled "On dealing with the Jewish Question", which contained the following:

> "The aim of *Judenpolitik* must be the emigration of all Jews. In order to sustain the present flow of emigration, a certain gradient is essential. This gradient is dependent on the space available outside Germany and on internal circumstances. There is great danger that the gradient will diminish, that Jewish emigration might stagnate and remain fixed at the present interim point. This would have the consequence that emigration as a final aim would be forgotten by Jews and Germans alike or that it would disappear as an unrealisable, distant goal. Instead of the emigration problem, a minorities problem might arise and the present interim state could become legally and psychologically permanent....
>
> The Jews are to have their opportunities to live in this country reduced – and not only in economic terms. Germany has to be a country without a future for Jews, in which the older generation will die off in their remaining positions, but in which young Jews are unable to live so that the attraction of emigration is constantly kept alive. The use of mob antisemitism [*Radau-Antisemitismus*] is to be rejected. One does not fight rats with guns but with poison and gas. The damage incurred by crude methods, especially the effect on our foreign policy, is disproportionate to the local success rate."[1]

Of course this statement did not anticipate the murder of Jews by gassing but it equated the Jews with vermin to be destroyed by pest control. This comparison is frequently found in Hitler's *Mein Kampf*.[2] It shows how dehumanised Jews had become in the thinking of the *Sicherheitsdienst* (SD) and that their "eradication" was not to remain a metaphorical demand.[3] While it was the duty of the *Geheime*

---

*This essay was translated by Gabriele Rahaman.
[1] Memorandum of the SD-*Amt* IV 2 addressed to Heydrich, 24th May 1934; Zentrum für die Aufbewahrung historisch-dokumentarischer Sammlungen (Osobyin), Moscow (hereafter Osobyi Archive Moscow), 501/1/18; reprinted in Michael Wildt (ed.), *Die Judenpolitik des SD, 1935–1938. Eine Dokumentation*, Munich 1995, pp. 66–69.
[2] Cf. Eberhard Jäckel, *Hitlers Weltanschauung*, enlarged and rev. edn., Stuttgart 1981, pp. 69–71.
[3] A similarly differentiated, as well as lucid, view of the idea of a *"judenrein"* Germany is presented by Donald L. Niewyk, 'Solving the "Jewish Problem" – Continuity and Change in German Antisemitism 1871–1945', in *LBI Year Book XXXV* (1990), pp. 335–370; regarding "annihilation antisemitism" see also Daniel Goldhagen's controversial *Hitler's Willing Executioners. Ordinary Germans and the Holocaust*, New York 1996, pp.49–80.

Staatspolizei (*Gestapo*) to carry out the persecution of Jews, and while other authorities of the *Reich* were working on the "exclusion of Jews from the economy", and *Radau-Antisemiten* in the NSDAP were stirring up feelings through acts of violence, the *Judenreferat* of the SD developed the basis of a "sober" but no less radical policy against the Jews which explicitly included humiliation, expropriation, maltreatment and expulsion. In the 1930s the systematic mass murder of European Jews was still beyond the horizon of the SD, but genocide was already inherent in its mentality and in the rationale of its policies.

The academic debate, conducted in Germany in particular, as to which factors led to the decision to murder the European Jews,[4] always assumes as a matter of course that the outbreak of war was the decisive date for the start of the "Final Solution", whereas the period between the passing of the Nuremberg Laws in 1935 and the November Pogrom of 1938 is considered by some historians as a "quiet" phase in the persecution of the Jews.[5] It seems that only when Eichmann started work in Vienna in 1938 did the SD and the *Gestapo* appear on the scene and subsequently assumed increasing control over the persecution of the Jews. This historiographical perspective not only omits the routine physical violence which Jews were subjected to from the early 1930s onwards,[6] but also fails to answer the question why it was the SD and the *Gestapo* which succeeded in gaining acceptance for their concept of the "solution to the 'Jewish Question'".[7] What was it about the SD and its *Judenreferat* – such a marginal and numerically insignificant organisation within the National-Socialist power structure at the beginning of the 1930s – which led it from the periphery to the centre of power within a few years?

Until recently historians could not answer this question because few documents relating to the SD-*Judenreferat* had survived and those which did presented very sparse information.[8] Archives in Moscow, however, which recently became accessible to the academic world, have brought to light the holdings of the former *Reichssicherheitshauptamt* (RSHA) which had been stored in *chateaux* and which were captured by the advancing Red Army at the end of the war and subsequently kept in Moscow. The Centre for the Preservation of Historical-Documentary Collections in Moscow, better known as the 'Osobyi' Archive, holds a

---

[4]Cf. particularly Eberhard Jäckel and Jürgen Rohwer (eds.), *Der Mord an den Juden im Zweiten Weltkrieg. Entschlußbildung und Verwirklichung*, Stuttgart 1985; Ulrich Herbert (ed.), *Nationalsozialistische Vernichtungspolitik 1939–1945. Neue Forschungen und Kontroversen*, Frankfurt am Main 1988.

[5]See e.g. Uwe Dietrich Adam, *Judenpolitik im Dritten Reich*, Düsseldorf 1972, p. 153; Michael Burleigh and Wolfgang Wippermann, *The Racial State. Germany 1933–1945*, Cambridge 1991, pp. 84–85; Avraham Barkai defines these years more correctly as "the illusion of a 'closed season (*Schonzeit*)' "; Avraham Barkai, *Vom Boykott zur 'Entjudung'. Der wirtschaftliche Existenzkampf der Juden im Dritten Reich 1933–1943*, Frankfurt am Main 1988, p.65; cf Saul Friedländer's brilliant *Nazi Germany and the Jews*, vol. I, *The Years of Persecution, 1933–1939*, London 1997.

[6]Cf. Michael Wildt, 'Violence Against Jews in Germany, 1933–1939', in David Bankier (ed.), *German Society's Responses to Nazi Anti-Jewish Policy*, Jerusalem 1998.

[7]Only recently the Austrian historian Hans Safrian wrote about the "Eichmann-Men": Hans Safrian, *Die Eichmann-Männer*, Vienna 1993.

[8]Klaus Drobisch's essay 'Die Judenreferate des Geheimen Staatspolizeiamtes und des Sicherheitsdienstes der SS 1933 bis 1939', in *Jahrbuch für Antisemitismusforschung*, 2, Frankfurt am Main–New York 1992, pp. 230–254, is solely based on the limited material held by the *Bundesarchiv*.

particularly large number of German files.[9] This archive became known to the public through a series of articles entitled 'Five Days in the Special Archive. Behind Lock and Key', published by the Russian journalist E. Maximova at the beginning of 1990 in *Isvestija*. According to her research, in the summer of 1945 the commander of the 59th division of the Soviet army reported the discovery of a large number of German documents in Silesia. The RSHA had actually started to relocate the documents in 1943 in order to save them from bomb damage. The documents were first taken to Schloß Fürstenstein in Waldenburg in Lower Silesia, but as that location turned out to be unsuitable, the removal of all documents to Schloß Wölfelsdorf in the district of Habelschwerdt was planned but not implemented. In 1945 these documents – originating from different locations and containing many files from other institutions of the *Reich* in Berlin – were captured and taken to Moscow by the Red Army. For reasons hitherto unknown, the Soviet Union did not make documents from these holdings available either during the Nuremberg Trials or for the purpose of historical research. It seems certain, however, that the Soviet Secret Service combed through these files for the names of possible collaborators with the German occupying forces.

To date there is no "official" history of this archive and the reason for the secrecy in which its existence was kept is merely speculative. From some records and various notes in the *Findbücher* one may conclude, however, that at the end of the 1950s and the beginning of the 1960s the German Democratic Republic (GDR) gained access to these holdings; some of the original documents were brought back to Germany and subsequently distributed among various archives in the GDR, according to criteria which are unclear. The interest of the GDR representatives focused mainly on the political persecution of Communists and Socialists, in other words on documents confiscated by the *Gestapo* from the files of the KPD and SPD. In addition, the *Ministerium für Staatssicherheit* in the GDR received photocopies of documents from the holdings of the Osobyi Archive which had been assigned to *Hauptabteilung* IX 11, the department responsible for documents from the National-Socialist period, and which in turn were transferred to the *Bundesarchiv* after the re-unification of Germany. Today these documents are held in the *Bundesarchiv Zwischenarchiv Dahlwitz-Hoppegarten*, but with no indication of their provenance. Photocopied documents from the Moscow Osobyi Archive can also be found in the *Zentrale Stelle der Landesjustizverwaltung zur Aufklärung von NS Verbrechen* in Ludwigsburg, which received many files from the Soviet Union in the 1970s – again, however, without indication of provenance.

Only after the opening of the Osobyi Archive to international academic research at the beginning of the 1990s did the extent and nature of the German documents in these holdings become apparent. Among them are a considerable number of documents from former ministries of the *Reich*, including the *Reichswirtschaftsministerium* and the *Reichsinnenministerium*; files from the political police

---

[9]The most comprehensive overview is to be found in Götz Aly and Susanne Heim, *Das Zentrale Staatsarchiv in Moskau ('Sonderarchiv'). Rekonstruktion und Bestandsverzeichnis verschollen geglaubten Schriftguts aus der NS-Zeit*, ed. by Hans Böckler Stiftung, Düsseldorf 1992.

in occupied Eastern European countries; documents from the *Gestapo* in Berlin and other regional offices; and files captured in conquered Europe, including a large number of personal dossiers compiled in the 1930s by the French political police and confiscated by German troops after the occupation of France. A large number of letters from German soldiers killed in action[10] and documents relating to German prisoners of war are held by the Osobyi Archive, together with many personal *Nachlässe* from both Germany and Austria. A significant part of the holdings consists of substantial documentation, some of which dates from the turn of the century, relating to German-Jewish and Freemasons' organisations, which was confiscated by the *Gestapo* after these organisations were banned. As Avraham Barkai recently explained, the history of organisations such as the *Centralverein deutscher Staatsbürger jüdischen Glaubens* (C.V.) can only be reconstructed with the help of files which were previously believed to have been lost.[11]

The "Fond 500 Reichssicherheitshauptamt" is of central importance among the holdings in the Moscow Osobyi Archive. It contains approximately 3,000 files, relating above all to the RSHA. (The title given to these files by the Russians is, incidentally, incorrect, since many were started before the RSHA was set up in 1939.) It is these files in particular which show that the SD-*Judenreferat* was an active organisation, in no way merely restricted to the collection of information.[12] There was no difference between the SD and other National-Socialist institutions as far as their antisemitic, racist attitude, based on biological assumptions, was concerned. But the programme of the SD-*Judenreferat* was more radical and more consistent from the start than competing policy proposals. In contrast to the emotional antisemitism and incitements to hatred embodied by *Der Stürmer*, the SD invested in an objective, rational and statistically precise approach to studying the "Jewish Question". The *Judenreferat* concerned itself with current German-Jewish organisations and marked the differences between them; this then formed the basis for *Gestapo* power tactics *vis-à-vis* Jewish organisations in Germany between 1935 and 1938. These methods were nevertheless radical: the "final aim of Jewish emigration", already emphasised in the early document of May 1934, was nothing less than the expulsion of German Jews from their homeland by terrorist means – their destination was immaterial.

When, in 1931, *Reichsführer* SS Heinrich Himmler ordered Reinhard Heydrich, then a retired naval officer, to set up a secret service for the SS, the department initially consisted only of Heydrich, sharing an office and without a typewriter.[13]

---

[10]In 1991 the first volume based on this material and expressly citing the Osobyi Archive as a source was published: Anatoly Golvchansky *et al.* (eds.), *"Ich will raus aus diesem Wahnsinn." Deutsche Briefe von der Ostfront 1941–1945*, Wuppertal–Moscow 1991.

[11]Cf. Avraham Barkai, 'Der CV im Jahre 1933. Neu aufgefundene Dokumente im Moskauer "Sonderarchiv"', in *Tel Aviver Jahrbuch für deutsche Geschichte*, 23 (1994), pp. 233–246.

[12]Cf. the informative essay by Susanne Heim, '"Deutschland muß ihnen ein Land ohne Zukunft sein". Die Zwangsemigration der Juden 1933–1938', in *Arbeitsmigration und Flucht*, Berlin 1993, (Beiträge zur nationalsozialistischen Gesundheits- und Sozialpolitik 11), pp. 48–81.

[13]Shlomo Aronson, *Reinhard Heydrich und die Frühgeschichte von Gestapo und SD*, Stuttgart 1971, p. 58.

Three years later the SD had approximately 150 members, of whom most, however, were not full-time employees.[14] The number of informants was, of course, higher, but compared with the *Gestapo*, whose *Geheimes Staatspolizeiamt* (*Gestapa*) in Berlin consisted of 600 officials and other employees in the spring of 1934 in addition to the approximately 2,000 officials working for the Prussian *Staatspolizei*,[15] the number of employees in the SD appeared very low.

During the *Machtergreifung*, the persecution of political opponents, above all Communists and Social Democrats, was a priority for the *Gestapo* and the "Jewish Question" played a more subordinate role during these months. The *Gestapo* played no major role in the boycott of Jewish businesses on 1st April 1933, nor in the subsequent antisemitic legislation which led to the dismissal of thousands of Jewish *Beamten* and other employees from public office.[16] In the *Gestapo*'s job allocation plan of June 1933, the same department was responsible for Jews, "riots, explosives, assassinations, foreigners, emigrants, and Freemasons".[17] The political police saw the "Jewish Question" only in terms of *Greulpropaganda* and of the political connections the emigrants may have had to the opposition in Germany.

At this time the SD's main task was to support the increase of Himmler's sphere of influence as commander of the political police beyond the borders of Bavaria.[18] After his appointment as head of the Prussian *Gestapo* in 1934, the various political forces in the German *Reich* were concentrated in the hands of the *Reichsführer* SS; after the bloody purge of the SA at the end of June 1934, in which the SD was also involved,[19] the latter's role could be re-defined. On 9th November 1933 Himmler had given the SD the status of an SS-*Amt* and had made Heydrich its chief. The earliest information about the organisational structure of the SD dates from this time.[20] The office in Munich was subdivided into the *Stabsabteilung* and the *Zentral-Abteilung* Z, which handled correspondence and registration, as well as into the following departments: *Abteilung* I, responsible for personnel and general organisation; *Abteilung* II, responsible for administration; *Abteilung* III, responsible for information on home affairs; *Abteilung* IV, responsible for counter espionage and external affairs; and *Abteilung* V, dealing with matters

---

[14]George C. Browder, 'The Numerical Strength of the *Sicherheitsdienst des* RFSS', in *Historical Social Research/Historische Sozialforschung*, No. 28, October 1993, pp. 30–41.

[15]Regarding these figures cf. Johannes Tuchel and Reinhold Schattenfroh, *Zentrale des Terrors. Prinz-Albrecht-Straße 8: Das Hauptquartier der Gestapo*, Berlin 1987, p. 80; Christoph Graf, *Politische Polizei zwischen Demokratie und Diktatur. Die Entwicklung der preußischen Politischen Polizei vom Staatsschutzorgan zum Geheimen Staatspolizeiamt des Dritten Reiches*, Berlin 1983, pp. 176–177.

[16]Graf gives some examples to show that, although the *Gestapo* was not totally uninvolved, the boycott campaign as well as the April legislation had been initiated and organised by other authorities of the National-Socialist regime; cf. *ibid.*, p. 238.

[17]'Geschäftsverteilungsplan Gestapa', 19th June 1933; Bundesarchiv (hereafter BA), R 58/840, *Blätter* 2–6; cf. also Drobisch, *Judenreferate*, pp. 232–239.

[18]George C. Browder, *Hitler's Enforcers. The Gestapo and the SS Security Service in the Nazi Revolution*, New York–Oxford 1996, pp. 105–152.

[19]Concerning the participation of the SD in acts of murder, see Ulrich Herbert, *Best. Biographische Studien über Radikalismus, Weltanschauung und Vernunft, 1903–1989*, Bonn 1996, pp. 143–147.

[20]George C. Browder, 'Die Anfänge des SD. Dokumente aus der Organisationsgeschichte des Sicherheitsdienstes des Reichsführers SS', in *Vierteljahrshefte für Zeitgeschichte*, 27 (1979), pp. 299–317.

relating to Freemasons. A subdivision of *Abteilung* IV, *Unterabteilung* IV 2 which dealt with "Jews, pacifists, atrocity propaganda, emigrants abroad", was first headed by (retired) Major Walter Ilges and then, from 1935, by Leopold Itz Edler von Mildenstein.[21]

The variety of subjects covered by the SD-*Referat* IV 2 shows, as with the *Gestapa*, that at this time the "Jewish Question" was still closely connected to the prejudice that Jews from abroad would act to damage the German *Reich*. Nevertheless at this same time the SD came out with a clear and wide-ranging programme regarding *Judenpolitik*. In the memorandum of May 1934 quoted at the beginning of this essay, the *Judenreferat* demanded, as the basis for dealing with Jewish organisations, that the Zionists who openly promoted emigration to Palestine should be given preferential treatment over the "assimilationist" organisations which remained Germany-orientated. This view was also adopted in the following months by the *Gestapo*. As late as March 1934 the *Bayrische Politische Polizei* (BPP) had given permission to the *Reichsbund jüdischer Frontsoldaten*,[22] which was of nationalist orientation, as well as to various other Jewish youth organisations, to operate again under certain conditions.[23] Ten months later, in January 1935, the BPP changed its mind and instructed its local offices "to treat members of Zionist youth organisations with less severity than is necessary when dealing with the so-called German-Jewish organisations (assimilationists)".[24] The policy of differentiated treatment in the persecution of Jewish organisations became standard police practice as the following report by the *Gestapa-Judenreferat* of November 1934 shows:

"It [is] the aim of the *Staatspolizei* to support Zionism and its emigration policy as fully as possible. The German assimilationists are being restricted in their activities as

---

[21] Leopold Itz Edler von Mildenstein, born 1902 in Prague, was a civil engineer. He joined the NSDAP in 1929 and the SS in 1933. From 1934 he worked for the SD. Because of his position as correspondent for the *Berliner Börsenzeitung*, his frequent trips abroad and many personal contacts, he was regarded as an expert on the Orient. His many pro-Zionist articles – so Mildenstein claimed after the war – brought him to Heydrich's attention. At the invitation of Zionist organisations, he had indeed travelled through Palestine, and in the autumn of 1934 he had published his very sympathetic impressions of Zionism in Goebbels's journal *Der Angriff*, in a series of articles entitled 'A Nazi travels to Palestine'. Cf. Tom Segev, *The Seventh Million. The Israelis and the Holocaust*, transl. by Haim Watzman, New York 1993, p. 30. Mildenstein was in charge of the *Judenreferat* from the beginning of 1935 to the summer of 1936 and subsequently worked in the Foreign Press Department of the *Reichspropagandaministerium*.

Walter Ilges, born in 1870 in Breslau, studied *Germanistik* and tried to make a living as a writer after the First World War. As one of the *"alte Kämpfer"* who joined the NSDAP before 1934, Ilges found employment in the SD, where he remained until 1936. He died in 1941.

[22] Founded in 1919, the *Reichsbund jüdischer Frontsoldaten* (R.j.F.) had more than 30,000 members in the 1920s. In 1933 the leadership of the R.j.F. believed that it could keep its independence by expressing its loyalty to the new political masters, but it quickly began to realise that National Socialist policies were particularly directed against Jews with nationalistic views. In October 1936 the R.j.F. was banned from any political activities. Cf. Ulrich Dunker, *Der Reichsbund jüdischer Frontsoldaten 1919–1938*, Düsseldorf 1977, pp. 113–177.

[23] 'Rundverfügung BPP', 20th March 1934, signed by Heydrich; reprinted in Hans Mommsen, 'Der nationalsozialistische Polizeistaat und die Judenverfolgung vor 1938', in *Vierteljahrshefte für Zeitgeschichte*, 10 (1962), pp. 68–87, here pp. 77–78.

[24] 'Rundverfügung BPP', 28th January 1935, reprinted in *ibid.*, pp. 78–79.

much as possible in order to force them into the Zionist camp.... The enforced isolation of the Jews, combined with restrictions on emigration, contains the inherent danger that those staying behind in Germany may demand to be treated as a national minority. It should, therefore, be the strategy of every authority involved to be aware of the conflicts between the various groups and to exploit and deepen them through differentiated treatment. Every authority concerned should, in particular, concentrate their efforts in recognising the Zionist organisations and in supporting their training and emigration endeavours; at the same time the activities of German-Jewish groups should be restricted in order to force them to abandon the idea of remaining in Germany."[25]

Thus the *Gestapa* and the SD were united in their fundamental assessment of the "Jewish Question" and the SD had early on formulated and consistently expanded the idea that emigration was the only strategy promising success in the National-Socialist sense. In the following years members of the SD dealing with the "Jewish Question" were not to be diverted from this aim and judged every antisemitic measure introduced by the regime according to whether it supported the expulsion of Jews from Germany or not. The institutional niche in which the SD found itself at the beginning of the National-Socialist regime offered sufficient scope – apart from day-to-day persecution which was the task of the *Gestapo* – for collecting information; for observing political events, economic conditions and social developments; and for drafting plans for the "solution of the Jewish Question".

In 1935 dissatisfaction at party grassroots level with the "sluggish progress" of the persecution of Jews, stirred up by Streicher's rabble-rousing newspaper *Der Stürmer*, began to be vented in local acts of violence. In Stettin SA members and *Hitlerjugend* obstructed business in Jewish-owned shops; in the Bavarian town of Fischach (near Augsburg) members of the local SA pasted antisemitic posters on the synagogue and maltreated the community leader; in Bad Tölz Jewish holiday-makers were forced to leave; in Arnswalde (West Prussia) the manager of the local branch of the *Reichsbank* was publicly slandered as a traitor for shopping in Jewish-owned shops in a show-case article of *Der Stürmer*.[26] In Gemen (Westphalia) Austrian National Socialists forced their way into a synagogue during a service and threw stones at the congregation. In the summer of 1935, pogrom-type actions were also carried out in Berlin against Jewish-owned businesses. A report of August 1935 from the *Staatspolizeistelle* in Berlin to the *Reichs- und Preußisches Innenministerium* states:

> " 'Incidents' usually occurred in the following manner: in the evening young people gathered in large numbers outside ice-cream parlours and vociferously demanded their closure; customers and Aryan personnel were threatened and even physically attacked; goods bought in the shop were knocked out of shoppers' hands as they left. Furthermore, slogans like 'Don't buy from Jews' were shouted in unison in order to prevent the public from entering the ice-cream parlours. In many instances owners

---

[25]Report 'Gegenwärtiger Stand der Judenfrage', *Gestapa* II 1 B 2, November 1934; Osobyi Archive Moscow, 501/1/18, Bl. 49–56.
[26]Friedlander, pp. 125–128, 137–139.

were ordered to close their shops at once in order to avoid eviction or vandalism. After the shops were closed, boycott notices, together with pages from *Der Stürmer*, were pasted on them. Such activities continued throughout the night. Boycott notices and posters were also pasted on other Jewish businesses and many were defaced with paint; the pavements, too, were painted with antisemitic slogans. Waterglass was often used as glue for the posters because of its acid reaction with glass, which made the glass in shop windows opaque and therefore useless. In numerous cases shop windows were also broken during the night."[27]

At first these activities were carried out by the *Hitlerjugend*, but later more and more adults joined in. According to the report by the *Gestapo* in Berlin, the police tried to "nip such demonstrations in the bud" and even had "particularly vulnerable shops" guarded by policemen. But this put the police in a difficult situation, because their actions were "misunderstood by the majority of the population" as the report regretfully states. The police officers were greeted with shouts of "Jewish lackeys".[28]

In the report about the riots he sent to the *Reichskanzlei* on Himmler's orders, Heydrich exploited this show of "public anger" unleashed by sections of the party by demanding stricter laws and harsher actions against the Jews: "The reports about antisemitic demonstrations, which continue to arrive from all parts of the *Reich*, show that there is widespread growing dissatisfaction with the hitherto inconsistent application of measures against the Jews. Those among the German people who are racially conscious believe that the measures so far tacitly taken against the Jews have been insufficient and demand altogether harsher actions."[29]

The SD-*Judenreferat* wrote in August that a "solution of the Jewish Question through acts of terrorism" was not attainable:

"A concerted approach to the Jewish problem is almost impossible as long as clear legislation is missing. This lack has created the conditions for such repeatedly condemned independent actions. The people [*Volk*] who – on the one hand – wish to see the Jews driven out of Germany in accordance with their National-Socialist *Weltanschauung* see – on the other hand – no action taken by the responsible authorities; it

---

[27] Staatspolizeistelle Berlin an das Reichs- und preußische Ministerium des Innern, 22nd August 1935, in Osobyi Archive Moscow 500/1/379, Bl. 108–113.

[28] *Ibid*. Apparently this kind of rowdy behaviour originated in the lower ranks of the party, because the *Gauleitung* threatened all members of the NSDAP, SA, SS and HJ who participated in such actions with expulsion from the party. The police had instructions to take immediate action and report the ringleaders to the *Gauleitung*. These instructions, however, were not primarily concerned with the protection of Jewish citizens but with public order and the threat to the monopoly of state power. On 30th July a meeting took place in the office of the *Polizeivizepräsident* at the Berlin *Rathaus*, with the mayor and representatives of the *Gestapo*, the NSDAP-*Gauleitung* and the SA participating; this meeting decided on a whole range of communal antisemitic measures, in order to (as the minutes state) "effectively fight the Jews in Berlin without public demonstrations and independent actions"; Gestapa II 1 B 2 to Heydrich, 31st July 1935, in Osobyi Archive Moscow, 500/1/379, Bl. 51–53.

[29] Heydrich to *Reichskanzlei*, 16th July 1935; quoted in Werner Jochmann, 'Die deutsche Bevölkerung und die nationalsozialistische Judenpolitik bis zur Verkündung der Nürnberger Gesetze', in *idem*, *Gesellschaftskrise und Judenfeindschaft in Deutschland 1870–1945*, Hamburg 1988, pp. 236–254, here pp. 245–246.

SD Judenpolitik 1935–1938

is an unfortunate fact that the example set by some party functionaries and their families in their personal life in relation to Jews and Jewish business does not always conform with the wishes and demands of the ordinary party member. [...] It should be remembered in this context that there is legal uncertainty regarding mixed marriages and *Rassenschande*. Registrars who act according to their conscience and refuse to marry such couples are often forced by the courts to do so. On the other hand those registrars who wish deliberately to go against National-Socialist beliefs can claim the support of official decrees. Effective laws should therefore be passed which show the people that the Jewish Question is being regulated by law from above."[30]

The SD stressed above all the urgent need for legislation on nationality, freedom of movement and the marking of "Aryan" businesses. This criticism did not arise from concern for human lives but from concern for the preservation of a state monopoly of power. The SD and the *Gestapo* had an interest in radicalising *Judenpolitik*. They tolerated terrorist activities by the SA and the HJ to a certain extent but made it clear at the same time that the executive power of the police and the "solution of the Jewish Question" should remain in the hands of higher state and party authorities.

In order to coordinate future operations, *Reichswirtschaftsminister* Schacht sent out invitations to a top-level meeting on 20th August in which, apart from himself, *Reichsinnenminister* Frick and *Reichsjustizminister* Gürtner took part, as well as Reinhard Heydrich and senior ministerial officials.[31] Schacht demanded at the meeting that "the present lack of legislation and unlawful activities must come to an end". The demand that Jews should not even be sold food was, according to Schacht, "barbarism of the worst kind". Despite such strong words he was by no means against antisemitic measures. The *Gestapa* reporter quotes the *Reichsinnenminister* as follows:

"I have lived with Jews for thirty years and I have taken their money for many years – not the other way round. The methods employed at the moment are, however, intolerable. A system must introduce order into the present chaos, and until such a system has been implemented, all other measures have to cease."[32]

Neither Schacht nor Frick had such a "system" they could have put forward at that meeting. Frick simply repeated that the "Jewish Question" had to be solved

---

[30]Report by SD-Hauptamt JI 6 (Juden), 17th August 1935, in Osobyi Archive Moscow, 500/3/316, Bl. 1–3; reprinted in Wildt, (ed.), *Judenpolitik des SD, 1935–1938*, pp. 69–70.

[31]There are several reports of this conference of 20th August 1935, of which the *Reichskanzlei* minutes of 22nd August 1935, Nürnberger Dokument NG-4067, is the most frequently cited in academic literature. Because of this, researchers have failed to notice that Heydrich, too, was one of the participants in this conference. The *Gestapa* report, which will be cited later, has not been used before to the best of the author's knowledge. *Gestapa* II 1 B 2, "Bericht über die am 20.8.35 im Reichswirtschaftsministerium stattgehabte Besprechung über die praktische Lösung der Judenfrage", 20th August 1935 in Osobyi Archive Moscow 500/1/379, Bl. 75–85.

[32]Schacht's attitude towards Jews always followed the National-Socialist leadership. Although he believed that Jewish business activities should not be drastically restricted, he readily agreed with the relegation of Jews to second-class citizenship and the curtailment of their civil rights. Adam's claim that only Schacht's resignation as *Reichswirtschaftsminister* in August 1937 made the decisive change of direction in National-Socialist antisemitic policy possible, is disputed by Albert Fischer, *Hjalmar Schacht und Deutschlands "Judenfrage". Der "Wirtschaftsdiktator" und die Vertreibung der Juden aus der deutschen Wirtschaft*, Cologne 1995, p. 208.

in a legal way. The extent to which this top-level meeting digressed into practical detail is shown by the remark from a *Gestapo* official that a "large part of the discussion" centred on the question "whether individual communities should be allowed to put up antisemitic posters when relevant regulations have been passed by the authorities in those communities". Heydrich spoke at the end of the meeting. He lamented that the police were "always the ones to suffer" and that the current situation could only be remedied by legislative measures which would achieve the goal of eradicating Jewish influence step by step, and that secondly, thorough political and ideological training and education of both party members and the people was needed. In concrete terms Heydrich demanded a ban on so-called "mixed marriages", the legal prosecution of *Rassenschande*, special legislation for Jews, and restriction of the freedom of mobility, especially migration to large cities.[33]

The top-level meeting of ministerial officials on 20th August contradicts the view that the Nuremberg laws were put together hastily and without much preparation.[34] It shows only too clearly how broad a consensus existed on future legislation, even before the Nuremberg Party Rally, between the ministerial offices, the NSDAP, the *Gestapo* and the SD. The *Reichsbürgergesetz* (nationality law), the *Blutschutzgesetz* (race law) and, above all, subsequent regulations to implement these laws largely fulfilled the demands made by the *Reichswirtschaftsministerium*. Although there may even have been some Jews who considered the Nuremberg Laws to be measures which created a certain kind of security in terms of the aims of the National-Socialist state:

> "... It is without doubt that, from a historical perspective, the social isolation and moral branding of Jews – enacted or actually sealed by this legislation and based on purely biological criteria – prepared the way psychologically for the more radical measures of persecution undertaken later by members of the party leadership for whom these laws were merely a stepping stone in their *Judenpolitik*."[35]

---

[33] Heydrich did not restrict himself to verbal proposals. In a letter to the conference participants at the beginning of September he formulated his demands in detail: Heydrich to the participants of a top-level meeting in the *Reichswissenschaftsministerium*, 9th September 1935, in Osobyi Archive Moscow, 500/1/379, Bl. 115–120; reprinted in Wildt, (ed.), *Judenpolitik des SD, 1935–1938*, pp. 70–73.

[34] Lösener, the *Rassereferent* of the *Innenministerium*, stressed, almost in his own defence, how rapidly and hastily the Nuremberg Laws had been passed: Bernhard Lösener, 'Als Rassereferent im Reichsministerium des Innern', in *Vierteljahrshefte für Zeitgeschichte*, 9 (1961), pp. 261–313. Uwe Dietrich Adam agreed with this interpretation and called the Nuremberg Laws a "sudden stroke [*überraschenden Schlag*]": Adam, *Judenpolitik*, p. 125. Two historians objected to this view early on: Reinhard Rürup, 'Das Ende der Emanzipation. Die antijüdische Politik in Deutschland von der "Machtergreifung" bis zum Zweiten Weltkrieg', in *Die Juden im nationalsozialistischen Deutschland/The Jews in Nazi Germany, 1933–1943*, ed. by Arnold Paucker with Sylvia Gilchrist and Barbara Suchy, Tübingen 1986 (Schriftenreihe wissenschaftlicher Abhandlungen des Leo Baeck Instituts 45), pp. 97–114; and Jochmann, 'Die deutsche Bevölkerung und die nationalsozialistische Judenpolitik'. Jochmann stressed that the Nuremberg Laws had been "planned over a long period and were meticulously prepared" (p. 247). For the "spirit" of the Nuremberg Laws see Cornelia Essner, 'Die Alchemie des Rassenbegriffs und die "Nürnberger Gesetze"', in *Jahrbuch für Antisemitismusforschung* 4, Frankfurt am Main–New York 1995, pp. 201–225.

[35] Helmut Krausnick, 'Judenverfolgung', in Hans Buchheim *et al.*, *Anatomie des SS-Staates*, Olten and Freiburg im Breisgau 1965, vol. II,, pp. 283–448, here p. 324.

SD Judenpolitik 1935–1938

The radicals in the NSDAP, as well as those in the SS and SD, understood the mechanisms that had brought success in 1935: "Public anger unleashed" had begun to break down bureaucratic resistance and could be used to justify harsher state action. 1936 was the year in which the *Gestapo* and SD regrouped in order to improve and reorganise their efforts. On Heydrich's orders the SD was restructured on 15th January 1936. The old organisation was superseded by a *Stabskanzlei*, which dealt with administration and personnel, while *Amt* II was responsible for investigating "enemies of the National-Socialist *Weltanschauung*" and *Amt* III was responsible for counter-espionage. Within *Amt* II, in the *Zentralabteilung* II 1 for the evaluation of "*Weltanschauung*", the *Abteilung* II 112 dealt with "Judentum" and was led by Kurt Schröder[36] after the previous director, von Mildenstein, left in the summer of 1936. Adolf Eichmann, who had fled to Germany following the Austrian prohibition of the NSDAP in June 1933, stayed first in Lechfeld and then in Dachau, where he joined the SD in 1934. In the autumn of that year he was ordered to transfer to the SD-*Amt* in Berlin. At first he worked in the so-called Freemason museum and then, at the beginning of 1935, transferred to Mildenstein's department (at the latter's request), where he stayed until 1938. Among the four directors – Mildenstein, Schröder, Dieter Wisliceny and Herbert Hagen – Eichmann, who dealt with the "Zionist" section, represented the continuous element in the SD-*Judenreferat*, particularly since his area of expertise, Zionist organisations, was at the centre of SD-policy.

In the spring of 1937 the staff of *Abteilung* II 1 2 was again reorganised and expanded. Among the newcomers were Theodor Dannecker,[37] former *Judenreferent* at the SD-*Oberabschnitt Südwest* and now adviser on "assimilationists"; Wisliceny,[38] who headed the department from April 1937; and Hagen[39] who finally took over the leadership of the *Judenreferat* in the late autumn of 1937. This constituted the staff which shaped the policies of the *SD-Judenreferat*. Apart from Dannecker, none had previously distinguished himself as a "*Judenexperte*";

---

[36]Kurt Schröder, the son of a farmer, was born in 1904 in Hohendorf/Thüringen. After an apprenticeship in banking he studied at the *Handelshochschule* in Frankfurt am Main. He joined the NSDAP in May 1933 and the SS in June the same year; from 1934 onwards he worked for the SD-*Oberabschnitt Rhein*. In 1935 he was transferred to the *Hauptamt für Volkswohlfahrt* and subsequently joined the SD *Hauptamt* where he headed *Abteilung* II 112 until March 1937. He then worked as economic adviser at the SD-*Leitabschnitt Berlin* and as late as 1944 he was drafted into an *Einsatzgruppe*.

[37]Theodor Dannecker, born 1913 in Tübingen, trained as a textile merchant. From 1934 he was a member of the *SS-Wachtruppe* first at *Columbia-Haus* in Berlin, then with *SS-Wachverband "Brandenburg"*. He was dismissed in May 1935 over a misdemeanour but soon after, in June 1935, he was employed by the SD-*Oberabschnitt Südwest*. In the spring of 1937 he moved to the SD-*Hauptamt Abteilung* II 112; cf. Claudia Steur, *Theodor Dannecker. Ein Funktionär der Endlösung*, Ph.D. diss., Essen 1997.

[38]Dieter Wisliceny, born in 1911 in Regulowken (East Prussia), briefly studied theology, worked in a design office, became unemployed and joined the NSDAP and SA in June 1931. In 1933 or 1934 he became a member of Göring's *Stabswache*. In June 1934 he joined the SS and SD. Initially he was a consultant in the SD-*Hauptamt* responsible for matters relating to Freemasons, then in April 1937 he was put in charge of *Abteilung* II 112 until his transfer to the SD Danzig in November 1937.

[39]Herbert Hagen, born in 1913 in Neumünster, joined the SD in 1934, unable to afford university, unsuccessful in pursuing an officer's career, and having dropped out of an apprenticeship in business. Initially he worked in the press department, but in the spring of 1937 he joined the *Zentralabteilung* II1 together with Six, and at the end of 1937 he took over the management of *Abteilung* II 112.

they all gained their reputation as *"Spezialisten"* through their work in the department.

The SD-*Zentrale* paid particular attention to the training of regional advisers. During a training conference in March 1936 reports from the *Oberabschnitten* suggested that the regional *Judenreferate* were considerably underdeveloped in the eyes of the SD-*Hauptamt*. Apart from the SD in Chemnitz and Hanover, the advisers were dealing with many subject areas in addition to that of Jewry. In Stuttgart two men were responsible for matters relating to Freemasons, Jews, libraries, border questions and emigration. In Düsseldorf the *"Judensachbearbeiter"* had been in his post for only six weeks, in Munich for only two weeks. In Breslau one assistant adviser was in charge of matters relating to Marxism, churches, national opposition and Jews, and even in Berlin only one single adviser was responsible for matters relating to "Jews, atrocity propaganda, homosexuality" and the spying activities of the *Deutsche Arbeitsfront* (DAF). In the SD-*Referate*, which were in general staffed with few employees, it was common to find two or more functions being carried out by one person. The example of the adviser on *Juden* and *Mittelbewegung* in Halle an der Saale, who, in his main occupation, was a doorman, may have been extreme but it was quite typical.[40]

A large number of the training conference participants were transferred in subsequent months, so the conference had a long-term effect only in those areas where *Referenten* retained their area of responsibility. The centrally organised training in Berlin was therefore all the more important. About the eight *Oberabschnittsreferenten* ordered to attend a training course in *Abteilung* II 112 of the SD-*Hauptamt* in August 1936, Eichmann wrote:

> "...most of them therefore arrived here with a very superficial knowledge of the matter and the few days set aside for the training course were spent in giving them a thorough introduction. *Abteilung* II 112 can without doubt claim one success already, namely success in shaping the minds of *Oberabschnittsreferenten* in conformity with the views of the SD-*Hauptamt* on factual and ideological questions."[41]

In April 1937, Wisliceny and Hagen formulated the specific profile the SD wanted *Judenreferenten* to have in their "Richtlinien und Forderungen an die Oberabschnitte":

> "The specialist working in *Abteilung II 112* in the *Oberabschnitten* and *Unterabschnitten* should not be an intellectual theoretician. It is not absolutely necessary for him to be a graduate, either. But he must be agile and active in his external duty and at the same time clear thinking and sober in his approach to given tasks. Those who merely

---

[40] Osobyi Archive Moscow, 500/3/320, Bl. 171–187.

[41] Adolf Eichmann, "Bericht über den Erfolg der Schulung der Oberabschnittsreferenten", 1st September 1936, in Osobyi Archive Moscow, 500/3/320, Bl. 197–198. ("Die meisten kamen daher mit nur oberflächlichen Kenntnissen hier an, und es wurden die wenigen, für die Schulung zur Verfügung stehenden Tage dazu benutzt, sie von Grund auf in die Materie einzuführen. Als Erfolg kann die Abteilung II 112 zweifellos jetzt schon buchen, daß es ihr gelungen ist, die gewünschte Gleichrichtung der OA.-Referenten in weltanschaulicher und sachlicher Hinsicht im Sinne des Hauptamtes sicherzustellen.")

'wrestle' with the Jewish Problem in intellectual terms are unfit for work in the SD-*Oberabschnitten* and *Unterabschnitten*."[42]

Objectivity and commitment were desired, rather than intellectual ability or academic detachment. When Himmler, in January 1937, in a speech on the nature and work of the SS and the police, allocated only general tasks to the SD and stated that it should not be interested in "individual details of an executive nature" but exclusively in the "great ideological questions",[43] he failed to describe the real nature of their operation.

In order to come closer to the declared goals of "pushing back Jewish influence in all areas of public life" and of the "promotion of Jewish emigration", SD departments were asked to compile statistics on the effects of antisemitic legislation, that is the effect of the dismissal of Jewish doctors, judges, teachers and other professions, as well as of Jewish emigration. Subsequently the goal was set even higher: because no precise data existed about the Jewish population at the beginning of 1937, the SD-*Hauptamt* demanded exact figures from the *Oberabschnitte* for the local Jewish population. Although only a few of the *Oberabschnitte* were able to meet the mid-January deadline,[44] the central office extended the project even further and forcefully pushed for the compilation of a comprehensive register of Jews. At the beginning of April, the SD-*Hauptampt* sent a request by telex to Berlin asking for lists of all Jews working in enterprises of national importance.[45] On 12th April a conference of the *Abteilungsleiter* II 11 took place in Berlin; among other topics, the question of a register for Jews was discussed.[46] On 1st June, Eichmann put forward extensive proposals regarding the "registration of all Jews and their descendants living in Germany".[47] According to Eichmann, such a register was essential to evaluate the effect of the racial laws on the one hand, but also, on the other hand, because state authorities were inactive and no census was planned for the near future. Eichmann therefore proposed a tripartite division of work: the *Unterabschnitte* were to keep the basic register and were to report "Jews of significance for the *Oberabschnitte*" to the *Oberabschnitte* and the "Jews important to the *Reich*" to the SD-*Hauptamt* in order to establish specialised registers. Franz Six, the head of IIa, agreed to this proposal and gave his permission for the relevant party authorities to be contacted.

On 1st July the plan was presented to Heydrich for approval. He agreed in principle to the establishment of a register of Jews, but voiced misgivings about

---

[42]Dieter Wisliceny and Herbert Hagen "Richtlinien und Forderungen an die Oberabschnitte", 21st April 1937; BA, R 58/544, Bl. 31–40; reprinted in Wildt, (ed.), *Judenpolitik des SD, 1935–1938*, pp. 110–115.
[43]Heinrich Himmler, 'Wesen und Aufgabe der SS und der Polizei', (Nationalpolitischer Lehrgang der Wehrmacht vom Januar 1937), in *Internationaler Militärgerichtshof (IMG), Der Prozeß gegen die Hauptkriegsverbrecher*, 42 vols., Nuremberg 1948, vol. 29, pp. 222–224 (1992[A]-PS).
[44]Correspondence between SD-*Hauptamt* and *Oberabschnitten*, January 1937, in Osobyi Archive Moscow, 500/1/495, Bl. 66–67.
[45]Note from Hagen, 22nd July 1937, in Sonderarchiv Moscow, 500/1/495, Bl. 86–88.
[46]SD-Hauptamt to SD-Oberabschnitte, Geheime Kommandosache, 20th May 1937, in Osobyi Archive Moscow, 500/1/495, Blatt 83.
[47]Note by Eichmann, 1st June 1937, in Osobyi Archive Moscow, 500/1/495, Bl. 53–56.

the financing of the project; he instructed Six to discuss this problem with *Staatssekretär* Wilhelm Stuckart of the *Reichsinnenministerium* and also requested the SD to apply to the *Reichsstelle für Sippenforschung* to obtain a copy of their register of Jews.[48] At the same time, other authorities within the regime were engaged in similar plans. At the end of May, the SD-*Hauptamt* informed the *Oberabschnitte* that the *Rassenpolitisches Amt* of the NSDAP was planning to set up a register of Jews with the help of party organisations.[49] At the beginning of July, Kurt Daluege, the head of the *Ordnungspolizei*, reported to his superior Heinrich Himmler that a number of meetings had taken place between *Ministerialrat* Krause of the *Reichsinnenministerium* and representatives of the *Ordnungspolizei* and the *Sicherheitspolizei*. They were all in agreement that "it is difficult to establish with certainty Jewish racial affiliation through police registration procedures".[50] Krause had therefore proposed a special census of Jews to be carried out within the framework of the national census planned for 1938. This census was to incorporate the categories of religious affiliation and "racial origin [*blutsmäßige Abstammung*]".[51]

On 12th July, when Wisliceny met the *Gestapa-Referenten* Haselbacher and Flesch, the framework for action had fundamentally changed. State authorities had already agreed a procedure with the *Ordnungspolizei* which amounted to a census being carried out by the *Statistisches Reichsamt*. Haselbacher was therefore of the opinion that it was "pointless [*unzweckmäßig*]", for an immediate survey to be conducted by the party and the SD, stating that: "The census would be conducted before the SD index of Jews could be finalised".[52] In order to make a start, Haselbacher suggested that the SD should take over the membership lists of Jewish organisations held by the *Gestapa*, and that they should be kept up-to-date by the *Unterabschnitte*. Abteilung II 112 had failed in its ambitious goal of creating a comprehensive register of Jews for the whole *Reich* by means of the SD-*Oberabschnitte*. The SD was still operating too far away from the centre of power to be able to push through its own programme against the resistance of the *Ordnungspolizei* and ministerial bureaucracy. Even Heydrich's support, which was in any case somewhat half-hearted, was not sufficient. In spite of all this, the SD could at least claim one success: the take-over of one complete section of the holdings kept by the *Gestapo* – the membership lists of Jewish organisations. The SD had also shown that it had concepts of its own and was sufficiently confident to undertake projects of the magnitude of the complete register of Jews in the *Reich*.

---

[48]Aktennotiz Six, 2nd July 1937, in Osobyi Archive Moscow, 500/1/495, Bl. 6.

[49]SD-Hauptamt to SD-Oberabschnitte, 20th May 1937, in Osobyi Archive Moscow, 500/1/495, Bl. 83.

[50]Chef der Ordnungspolizei to the RFSSuChdDP (Reichsführer-SS und Chef der Deutschen Polizei), 3rd July 1937, in Osobyi Archive Moscow, 500/1/495, Bl. 81: "die Zugehörigkeit zur jüdischen Rasse im polizeilichen Meldeverfahren nicht in erschöpfender Weise feststellen läßt."

[51]Regarding the Jewish census statistics of the 1939 census cf. Götz Aly and Karl Heinz Roth, *Die restlose Erfassung. Volkszählen, Identifizieren, Aussondern im Nationalsozialismus*, Berlin 1984, pp. 55–79.

[52]Wisliceny to Six, 12th July 1937, in Osobyi Archive Moscow, 500/1/495, Bl. 8–9. ("Noch ehe die Judenkartei des SD fertig sein könne, käme die Volkszählung.")

SD Judenpolitik 1935–1938

In a more limited regional framework the SD proved that it was capable, in conjunction with the *Gestapo*, of practical activity, in spite of the fact that it held no official executive functions. After a majority of eligible voters in Upper Silesia had opted in March 1921 to remain with Germany and after the region had been divided, Germany and Poland, under the auspices of the League of Nations, had come to an agreement in May 1922 to protect minorities – an agreement which was to be in force for fifteen years. After the expiration of an additional two-month protection period, this agreement ended on 15th July 1937. Thus, according to Adolf Eichmann in his "Disposition für die Judenbearbeitung im Gebiet des SD-OA [*Oberabschnitt*] Südost" of 10th May 1937, "there existed an opportunity in Upper Silesia, too, to deal with the Jewish Problem in its entirety",[53] since all the discriminatory laws against Jews would now come into force there as well. Eichmann suggested registering all Jews, arresting all leading officials of Jewish organisations immediately, and banning all Jewish organisations. Special attention was to be paid to attempts on the part of Jews to sell land and property to Poles. The rapid action programme (*Sofortprogramm*) formulated by Eichmann, authorised by Six and signed by Heydrich, was sent to the SD-*OA Südost* in Breslau at the end of May. The programme provided for the appropriate executive responsibilities in concrete terms. Eichmann himself was ordered to go to Breslau at the end of May to supervise the implementation of these instructions.[54]

In the autumn of 1937 the SD also initiated the dismissal of Jews of foreign origin who were employed by Jewish organisations in Germany. At the meeeting of the SD-*Oberabschnitte Judenreferenten* on 1st November 1937 in Berlin, Adolf Eichmann raised the spectre of the Jew as spy. International Jewish organisations, he claimed, only "appeared to be a chaotic and somewhat haphazard conglomeration". In reality, he stated, despite their disunity, they were united in a concerted effort to fight National-Socialist Germany. He tried to convince the assembled SD-*Referenten* that these organisations would increasingly use foreign employees for this purpose.[55] The demand "for the removal of Jews of foreign nationality and stateless persons from the boards of political Jewish organisations" was, therefore, one of the "directives" issued to the regional SD-*Judenreferenten* in November 1937. In co-operation with the local

---

[53] Adolf Eichmann, "Disposition für die Judenbearbeitung im Gebiet des SD-OA Südost", 10th May 1937, in Osobyi Archive Moscow, 500/1/403, Bl. 45–48.

[55] The assumption that Eichmann, until his move to Vienna in 1938, was "mainly concerned with theoretical research on the 'enemy *Judentum*' " is still held today; see Gabriele Anderl, ' "Zentralstellen für jüdische Auswanderung" in Wien, Berlin und Prag – ein Vergleich', in *Tel Aviver Jahrbuch für deutsche Geschichte*, 23 (1994), pp. 275–299, here p. 276. One should, instead, regard Eichmann as an engaged member of the SD, ready for action and keen to work for the organisation, from as early as 1937. This can be seen particularly in his trip to Palestine in the autumn of 1937 and the special responsibilities given to him by the SD leadership (by Six in particular), which went far beyond those usually given to consultants. Not without reason was Eichmann promoted to the rank of *Untersturmführer* in November 1937, thereby becoming a member of the SS-*Führerkorps*.

[55] Adolf Eichmann, 'Das Weltjudentum: Politische Aktivität und Auswirkung seiner Tätigkeit auf die in Deutschland ansässigen Juden', in Osobyi Archive Moscow, 500/3/322, Bl. 193–209, reprinted in Wildt, (ed.), *Judenpolitik des SD, 1935–1938*, pp. 133–139.

Gestapo, the SD-*Abschnitte* were to summon the leadership of the Jewish organisations in different regions and instruct them to dismiss all their foreign personnel by 31st December 1937.[56] It was in Berlin that this collaboration between the SD and the *Gestapo* worked most smoothly. As early as the beginning of November Eichmann was able to report to Six that five of the nine foreign Jews employed by the *Hilfsverein der Juden in Deutschland* had been dismissed. Of twenty-eight such employees in the *Zionistische Vereinigung*, nineteen had been dismissed, in the *Reichsvertretung* four out of five, in the *Jüdische Gemeinde Berlin* 136 out of 244. Since the SD intended to dissolve the *Centralverein* in the near future, the two foreign nationals working there were "to remain in their posts for the time being".[57] In the provinces persecution moved more slowly than the headquarters in Berlin would have liked, and occasionally local *Gestapo* offices had reservations about SD initiatives. The State Police in Zwickau and Dresden, for instance, refused to take measures against foreign nationals, because they had received no such orders from their superiors and because of the fear that the dismissed Jewish employees could become a burden to the welfare system. In Leipzig the *Gestapo* did not press for dismissals, but instead were content with resignations from positions on the boards of Jewish organisations. In such cases the *Geheimes Staatspolizeiamt* in Berlin had to send special directives to the regional offices to show approval for the SD initiative.[58] It seems, however, that following intervention by the Czech General Consulate in Berlin and a subsequent enquiry by the Foreign Office, the SD and the *Gestapo* conceded that the *Aktion* was not directed against Czech nationals in particular or against foreign nationals in general.[59] This intervention saved a few dozen Czech nationals from dismissal for a short time, but it did not prevent the dismissals in the long run. The SD was not deterred from its initiative, in spite of the awareness that these independent actions were repeatedly causing them administrative and institutional difficulties. On the contrary, its increasing self-confidence during this time is marked not only by wanting to devise "solutions" to the "Jewish Problem" but also by the desire to implement them.

As far as the *Gestapo* was concerned, this conceptual initiative by the SD led to a shift in the latter's favour. Heydrich's so-called *Funktionsbefehl* (operational order) of 1st July 1937, which was supposed to clarify once and for all the relationship between the *Gestapo* and the SD, offered an opportunity to increase the SD's area of competence. According to Heydrich's decree, the SD was to take charge of "all general and fundamental questions concerning Jews (whenever *Staatspolizei* executive measures do not apply)", while the *Gestapo* was to deal

---

[56]"Arbeitsanweisungen für das Sachgebiet II 112", in Osobyi Archive Moscow, 500/1/506, Bl. 104–110, reprinted in Wildt, (ed.), *Judenpolitik des SD, 1935–1938*, pp. 156–160.

[57]Eichmann to Six, 4th November 1937, in Osobyi Archive Moscow, 500/1/499a, Bl. 78–81. In fact the *Centralverein* was dissolved only at the beginning of 1939.

[58]SD-OA Elbe to SD-Hauptamt, 2nd May 1938, note by Hagen, 4th May 1938, as well as a copy of the *Gestapo* order, in Osobyi Archive Moscow, 500/1/459a, Bl. 100–103.

[59]Eichmann to Geheimes Staatspolizeiamt, 4th February 1938, in Osobyi Archive Moscow, 500/1/290, Bl. 211–212, and note by Hagen on a discussion with the *Judenreferat* of the *Gestapa*, 12th May 1938; *ibid.*, 500/1/499a, Bl. 84.

with "all single incidents (where *Staatspolizei* executive measures do apply)".[60] The claim to be principally responsible for the "Jewish Question" was the topic of a discussion between Six and Wisliceny, Eichmann and Hagen and the *Gestapa-Judenreferent* Assessor Flesch on 17th June 1937 at the SD-*Hauptamt*.[61] Six proposed that a member of the SD should check through all the *Gestapa* files relating to the "Jewish Question". Flesch agreed, and a few days later Hagen reported to the *Gestapa*. According to his report, the general files of the *Gestapa* were subdivided into internal and foreign files whereby the foreign files consisted of a rather arbitrary collection of documents.[62] The *Gestapareferent* himself agreed that all foreign files were to be handed over to the SD for systematic registration. Although an index of persons existed at the *Gestapa*, this did not by any means cover all members of Jewish organisations and furthermore, it was organised cumulatively, which meant that a new index card was only added after an incident had occurred. The membership lists of Jewish organisations, first ordered by the *Gestapa* in October 1935 and expanded every quarter, had not been evaluated before this time. Now these lists were handed over to the SD. A few days later, Heydrich's deputy and administrative head of the *Gestapa*, Werner Best, gave the order for all files of the *Gestapa-Judenreferat* to be handed over to the SD, including as Wisliceny reported to Six, "not only closed files but mainly current matters which in future are to be administered by the SD".[63] The SD thereby not only obtained important information, but without its involvement few initiatives, enquiries or legislative measures with regard to *Judenpolitik* could be taken.

It was therefore only natural that *Abteilung* II 112 derived through the SD "a certain intellectual leadership role".[64] The fact that Werner Best, who had as director of organisation in 1934–1935 greatly influenced the rebuilding of the SD,[65] gave orders in his capacity as deputy director of the *Gestapa* to hand over all files to the SD, pointed to the internal division of labour the leadership of the *Sicherheitspolizei* had in mind. To hand the administration of *Judenpolitik* to the SD meant to strengthen the political police simultaneously as an executive power and as an instrument of terror. The *Gestapo* and SD remained a united force vis-à-vis the Jews. But since the SD had proved its conceptual initiative in earlier years, now the main institutional planning for *Judenpolitik* within the security system was also transferred to it.

---

[60]"Gemeinsame Anordnung für den Sicherheitsdienst des Reichsführer-SS und die Geheime Staatspolizei" by the head of the SD-*Hauptamt* and the *Sicherheitspolizei*, 1st July 1937; BA, R 58/239, Bl. 198–203.

[61]Minutes of meeting by Hagen, 19th June 1937, in Osobyi Archive Moscow, 500/3/315, Bl. 139–141.

[62]Report by Hagen about co-operation between II 112 and *Gestapa* II B 4 of 29th June 1937, in Osobyi Archive Moscow, 500/3/315, Bl. 155–159; reprinted in Wildt, (ed.), *Judenpolitik des SD, 1935–1938*, pp. 115–118.

[63]Wisliceny to Six, 20th July 1937, in Osobyi Archive Moscow, 500/3/, Bl. 152–154. The progress report of *Abteilung* II 112 from 6th July to 5th October 1937 mentions approximately 2,000 files which had been received from the *Gestapa*, BA, R 58/991, Bl. 83–87.

[64]Wisliceny, "Richtlinien und Forderungen an die Oberabschnitte", 21st April 1937; BA, R 58/544, Bl. 31–40.

[65]Cf. Herbert, *Best*, pp. 141–150.

Central to SD-policy was the expulsion of the Jews. Even in the document of May 1934 Jewish emigration had been posited as "the final goal", and subsequent reports and comments by the SD-*Judenreferat* always focused on this point, judging every political move according to whether or not it brought this goal nearer. In January 1937 the SD was in possession of a large manuscript entitled "On the Jewish Problem",[66] the principal demand of which was to "rid Germany of Jews [*Entjudung Deutschlands*]". The memorandum encompassed the National-Socialist fear that Jewish emigrants might start a new world conspiracy in other countries but immediately made the following qualifications: "Such a solution could only consist of emigration to areas at a low level of civilisation – in order to prevent the Jews from acquiring new wealth." In a comprehensive selection process potential countries on a "low cultural level" were examined. The final list included Ecuador, Columbia, Venezuela and Palestine. Even before the decision-makers of the National-Socialist state had come to see the expulsion of the Jews as the "solution to the Jewish problem", the author of this memorandum had envisaged the next step, namely, the settlement of Jews in inhospitable areas. The subsequent Madagascar Plan – which already incorporated the aspect of annihilation – was based on such ideas, since the planners were conscious of the fact that this island offered no chance of survival to millions of people.[67]

However, numerous difficulties stood in the way of the expulsion of Jewish Germans from Germany. The number of countries prepared to accept German Jews was not exactly large. Strict immigration quotas limited opportunities to either well-trained artisans or to those with sufficient capital to buy an immigration visa. Even emigration to Palestine was much curtailed by the British Mandate, which established the categories of "immigrants disposing of means or income" (Category A) and "immigrants whose employment is secured (workers)" (Category C). 36 per cent of the 52,000 Jews who emigrated from Germany to Palestine between 1933 and 1942 obtained certificate A1, which specified that holders should bring at least £1,000 sterling with them; a further 32.6 per cent were workers holding certificate C.[68] But despite this, Palestine was the only area in the world which, according to the Balfour Declaration of 1917, was explicitly designated as a "national home for the Jewish people". Palestine did indeed accept more German-Jewish emigrants between 1933 and 1936 than any other country. It therefore played a central role in the calculations of the SD .

---

[66]Memorandum "Zum Judenproblem", January 1937, BA, R 58/956, Bl. 2–19; reprinted in Wildt, (ed.), *Judenpolitik des SD, 1935–1938*, pp. 95–105.

[67]For the Madagascar Plan, see Christopher R. Browning, *The Final Solution and the German Foreign Office. A Study of Referat D III of Abteilung Deutschland 1940–43*, New York 1978, pp. 35–43; Leni Yahil, 'Madagascar – Phantom of a Solution for the Jewish Question', in George L. Mosse and Bela Vego (eds.), *Jews and Non-Jews in Eastern Europe 1918–1945*, New York 1974, pp. 315–334; Magnus Brechtken, *"Madagascar für die Juden." Antisemitische Idee und politische Praxis, 1885–1945*, Munich 1997.

[68]Herbert A. Strauss, 'Jewish Emigration from Germany. Nazi Policies and Jewish Responses (II)', in *LBI Year Book XXVI* (1981), pp. 343–347.

SD Judenpolitik 1935–1938

At a very early stage the *Gestapo* and the SD had tried to use Zionist agitation for their own ends. By treating Jewish organisations differently, for example by strongly limiting those which advocated assimilation and giving greater scope to Zionist associations, they not only played off Jewish organisations against each other but also hoped, above all, to come much closer to their goal of expelling all Jews from Germany.[69] As Dieter Wisliceny and Herbert Hagen formulated in their "Guidelines and Demands for the *Oberabschnitte*", dated the end of April 1937, "the solution to the Jewish Question can only be achieved by the complete removal of Jews from Germany". The question of Palestine therefore demanded all the attention of the SD "since, in the final analysis, the solution of the Jewish Question in Germany depends upon it".[70] The British plan to divide Palestine into a Jewish and an Arab state was therefore also of interest to the SD. In a comprehensive memorandum of 17th July 1937, Wisliceny posed the question, "What is to become of Palestine?"[71] and he personally attended the twentieth Zionist Congress in Zurich at the end of July 1937 in order to inform himself first hand about the Zionist attitude towards the British plan for dividing the territory.[72]

In the autumn of 1937, in a seemingly bizarre but quite seriously intended undertaking, the SD tried its own initiative to speed up Zionist emigration. Using Dr. Franz Reichert, chief of the German News Service in Jerusalem and an SD-informer, as an intermediary, the *Judenreferat* made contact with a certain Feivel Polkes (or Feibl Folkes). Polkes, who was a member of the Zionist military organisation *Haganah*, provided Reichert with information about Jewish and Arab activities.[73] Between 26th February and 2nd March 1937, with Reichert's assistance, a visit to Berlin was arranged for Polkes, who was travelling through Europe as the representative of *Haganah* at the beginning of 1937. Travelling costs and the stay in Berlin were paid for by the SD.[74] During this visit Polkes met Eichmann on several occasions and, although Eichmann's SD membership remained secret, Polkes was certainly aware that a National Socialist in an official capacity was sitting opposite him. Polkes explained the position of the Zionists in Palestine and offered further information if the National Socialists were prepared to make Jewish emigration from Germany to Palestine easier. In particular, he claimed to have background information on the assassination of

---

[69]Regarding the sensitive relationship between National Socialism and Zionism, cf. Francis R. Nicosia, 'The End of Emancipation and the Illusion of Preferential Treatment: German Zionism, 1933–1938', in *LBI Year Book XXXVI* (1991), pp. 243–265; *idem*, 'Ein nützlicher Feind. Zionismus im nationalsozialistischen Deutschland 1933–1939', in *Vierteljahrshefte für Zeitgeschichte*, 37 (1989), pp. 367–400; and more recently Yehuda Bauer, *Jews for Sale? Nazi-Jewish Negotiations, 1933–1945*, New Haven–London 1994.
[70]"Richtlinien und Forderungen an die Oberabschnitte", 21st April 1937; BA, R 58/544, Bl. 31–40.
[71]Wisliceny, "Was wird aus Palästina?", 15th July 1937, reprinted in The Beate Klarsfeld Foundation (ed.), *Centre de Documentation Juive Contemporaine, Recueil de Documents du Service des Affaires juives, le II-112, du Sicherheitsdienst SD (1937–1949)*, by Serge Klarsfeld, New York 1980, pp. 76–84.
[72]Progress Report II 112, 6th July to 5th October 1937, BA, R 58/991, Bl. 83–87.
[73]Feivel Polkes, born in Poland in 1900, emigrated to Palestine in 1920, where he became a member of the underground army *Haganah*; report by Hagen to Heydrich about Polkes, Geheime Kommandosache, 17th June 1937; BA, R 58/954, Bl. 42–46.
[74]*Ibid.*

Wilhelm Gustloff, the Swiss *Landesgruppenleiter* of the NSDAP. On 2nd March Polkes departed after inviting Eichmann to continue their discussions in Palestine. The report on Polkes's visit was presented to Heydrich personally, who decided that Eichmann was to accept the invitation and travel with Hagen to the Near East. Heydrich made it clear, however, that he would take no official responsibility and that the political risk of this trip was to be carried exclusively by Schellenberg, as the *Abwehrbeauftragter* (security officer) of the SD, and by Six, as the *Zentralabteilungsleiter*.[75]

On 26th September 1937 Eichmann and Hagen started out on their journey. Travelling via Poland and Romania, and from there by ship via Stambul and Piräus, they reached Haifa on 2nd October. They were unable to make contact with Polkes. The steamer continued to Alexandria the following day, and on 7th October the two *Judenexperten* reached Cairo. There they met the DNB-representative for Egypt, Gentz, and an acquaintance of Reichert's, the businessman Wilhelm Bormann, whom they had previously met in Haifa. They also had discussions with other German officials and visited the German School in Alexandria.[76] This trip gave the two SD agents ample opportunity to make general observations and to form opinions about the politics, the economy and culture of the countries they visited and, as expected, the "Jewish Question" played a major part. They became aware that the widespread German belief that Arab "opposition to Jews is based on racial hatred, is false. This is wrong; it is, rather, a social question, fear of losing their own business. As far as the Egyptians are concerned, the Jewish Question is solved the moment Jews retreat from any businesses that native Arabs regard as theirs". The "Jewish Problem" therefore became particularly important in Palestine, as it was mainly seen in terms of land ownership.[77]

The meeting with Polkes finally took place on 10th and 11th October. However, the information Polkes was offering was extremely meagre. On the assassination attempt on Gustloff he was unable to give any concrete facts, and merely promised to make further inquiries. As far as emigration to Palestine was concerned, he denounced newly arrived German emigrants as "work-shy" and as constantly planning to leave the country again. He nevertheless maintained that "national-Jewish circles" (Zionists) "were pleased with Germany's radical Jewish policies ... because they ensured the growth of the Jewish population in Palestine to such an extent that it was fairly certain that in the near future Jews would outnumber Arabs in Palestine".[78]

It is difficult to establish the position Polkes held within the *Haganah*. According to a later note by the *Haganah* leader Shaul Avigur, the contact between Polkes and Eichmann had been a "passing, insignificant episode".[79] His

---

[75]Memo Six, 4th September 1937; BA, R 58/623.
[76]"Bericht über die Palästina-Ägyptenreise von SS-Hptscharf. Eichmann und SS-O'Scharf. Hagen", 4th November 1937; BA, R 58/954, Bl. 11–64.
[77]*Ibid.*, Bl. 28: "... Gegnerschaft gegen die Juden um einen Rassenhaß handele. Das ist falsch; vielmehr ist es eine soziale Frage, die Angst um das eigene Geschäft. Die Judenfrage hört also in dem Augenblick auf, ein Problem für den einheimischen Ägypter zu sein, in dem sich der Jude aus dem Geschäft heraushält, das der einheimische Araber für sich beansprucht."
[78]*Ibid.*, Bl. 40–42
[79]Cited in Segev, p. 31, note.

contacts with the SD, it seems, were damaging to Polkes. In a note dated 7th March 1938 Eichmann reported that, according to Bormann, who served the SD as an informer, Polkes was relieved of all his responsibilities within the *Haganah* because of his connection with Reichert.[80] Indeed, the contact between the SD and Polkes can only be described as close. According to a report by Hagen and Eichmann he received – *via* Dr. Reichert – £15 a month, for which he even wrote receipts, enabling the SD to exert unique pressure on him.[81]

Hagen and Eichmann were not able to obtain visas for Palestine a second time. They left Egypt on 19th October 1937 without having achieved their objective. Despite the lengthy report of over fifty pages which Hagen and Eichmann produced, it was clear that their trip had failed. The unauthorised action undertaken by the SD had not fulfilled the expectations of the *Zentrale* in any way. No concrete agreements had been reached with the Zionists concerning the emigration of German Jews, nor had the Gustloff murder case been solved. The lesson the SD learned from this failed venture, and which Eichmann followed strictly to the letter in his later position as *Referatsleiter* in the RSHA, was unequivocal: the problem of emigration could not be solved by pursuing a separate "foreign policy" but only through co-ordinated action in conjunction with the police and the ministerial authorities.

Possibly the SD's own steadfast course in pursuing the Palestine option was also shaken in the short-term by its own foreign travel experiences at the end of 1937. In January 1937 the *Auswärtiges Amt* warned that a Jewish state in Palestine would strengthen Jewish influence in the world to an unforeseen extent and that Jerusalem would become the centre of Jewry just as Moscow had become the centre of Communism.[82] At the beginning of June, *Außenminister* Konstantin von Neurath informed the German Embassy in London that "the establishment of a Jewish state or any form of government under Jewish leadership within the British Mandate is not in the German interest".[83] The memorandum sent to all diplomatic missions on 22nd June 1937 went one step further, emphasising that – in contrast to the previous policy which had supported Jewish emigration – it was now in "the greater German interest to pursue the fragmentation and dispersal of Jewry, as the Jewish Question is not solved for Germany when there are no longer any members of the Jewish race remaining on German soil".[84] Wisliceny, in his article 'What is to Become of Palestine?', had already voiced concern that the SD could not remain indifferent to the establishment of a Jewish state in Palestine. In the report on their Palestine trip, Hagen and Eichmann rejected one of Polkes's

---

[80]Note by Eichmann, 7th March 1938, reprinted in *Centre de Documentation Juive Contemporaine*, pp. 214–215.

[81]"Bericht über die Palästina-Ägyptenreise", 4th November 1937; BA, R 58/954, Bl. 61.

[82]Nicosia, *Nützlicher Feind*, pp. 388–389. For the ever-growing and thereby undermining demands German authorities made on the *Haavara* agreement from 1936/1937 onwards, see Bauer, *Jews for Sale?*, pp. 24–29.

[83]*Akten zur Deutschen Auswärtigen Politik 1918–1945*, Serie D (1937–1945), vol. 5, No. 561.

[84]*Ibid.*, No. 564: "... ein größeres deutsches Interesse daran, die Zersplitterung des Judentums aufrecht zu erhalten. Denn die Judenfrage wird nicht für Deutschland gelöst, wenn kein Angehöriger der jüdischen Rasse mehr auf deutschem Boden seßhaft ist."

proposals to expand the *Haavara* transfer by allowing 50,000 Jews per year to emigrate to Palestine. They further stated that the SD did not intend "to allow Jewish capital to flow abroad, but primarily to encourage impoverished Jews to emigrate". Another aspect of allowing large-scale emigration would be that it would mainly strengthen Jewry in Palestine and as "the *Reich*'s chief interest was to prevent an independent Jewish state in Palestine, this subject was no longer up for discussion".[85] Even in his short report to Heydrich, entitled 'On Jewry', of 12th November 1937, Hagen supported the position of the Foreign Office, rejecting the establishment of an independent Jewish state.[86]

Hitler himself ended all further discussion. According to a note by the *Wirtschaftspolitische Abteilung* of the Foreign Office dated January 1938, Hitler restated his position to Alfred Rosenberg that the emigration of Jews to Palestine should be speeded up and the *Haavara* agreement be kept.[87] This meant the SD was once again in accord with the top leadership. Interference from the Foreign Office evaporated, especially as German fears about the establishment of a Jewish state in the Near East were dispelled by the end of 1937. The reasons for this were the continued resistance to the British Peel Plan, and clashes between Jews and Arabs which put an end to the recommendations of the British Royal Commission to partition the territory. In spite of Eichmann's and Hagen's failed visit to the Near East, the SD had shown itself to be sufficiently self-confident not only to propose an independent (from all other *Reich* authorities) solution to the Palestine emigration problem but also to attempt to put such a proposal into practice. The SD's demand to participate at ministerial level in the discussions on Jewish policies was taken into consideration. When, at the beginning of October 1937, the *Reichsinnenministerium* issued invitations to another conference on the Palestine problem, the SD was asked to participate, along with the *Auswärtiges Amt*, the *Reichswirtschaftsministerium* and the *Parteikanzlei*.[88]

Although from a National-Socialist viewpoint antisemitic policies appeared to have been successful, they had reached a dead end five years after Hitler's coming to power. Government departments had successfully pushed ahead with the legal exclusion of Jews from public life; special legislation for Jews had been drafted and implemented in ever finer detail. The expulsion of Jews from the economy had had considerable success; "Aryanisation" of Jewish businesses had made great progress. The economic legislation of April 1938 removed the basis for existence from thousands of small Jewish traders and businesses which had survived until then. With this the National-Socialists had largely excluded the Jews from the community of the German nation and had further deprived them of their property and wealth; as a result the impoverished Jews lost the ability to

---

[85] "Bericht über die Palästina-Ägyptenreise", 4th November 1937; BA, R 58/954, Bl. 143–144.
[86] "Kurzbericht für C. über das Judentum", 12th November 1937; BA, R 58/544, Bl. 107–110.
[87] Cf. Bauer, *Jews for Sale?*, p. 27. Nicosia, *Nützlicher Feind*, pp. 392–393, cites further evidence for Hitler's decision.
[88] *Ibid.*, p. 392.

leave the country of their own free will, since they lacked the capital that potential immigration countries demanded. Only the young or very wealthy could hope for a fresh start abroad.

Comments by Eichmann and Hagen point to the fact that the SD was no longer inclined to solve the perceived "Jewish Problem" by "orderly emigration", especially as German willingness to enforce Jewish emigration by sheer terror was growing immensely. At the beginning of May 1938 members of an NSDAP-*Ortsgruppe* in Berlin had overnight damaged and defaced local Jewish shops and the synagogue. In other parts of Berlin shop windows were broken, and on 17th June violence against Jewish businesses broke out all over Berlin, clearly on the order of the *Gauleiter*, Goebbels . Even some looting occurred.[89] In June Jewish shops were daubed with paint in Magdeburg;[90] in Frankfurt am Main shop windows were broken, synagogues were damaged and Jewish shopowners were even physically attacked.[91] Although the SD and the *Gestapo* officially distanced themselves from such terrorist acts, they did so less because they rejected the violence than because these "rowdy antisemitic" pogroms interfered with the SD programme of expulsion. Characteristically, however, the police exploited the existing pogrom climate. In June 1938 the *Gestapo* arrested 1,500 "asocial" Jews, most of whom were transported to Buchenwald concentration camp. At the same time the police arrested more than 10,000 persons classified as "social misfits" and "work shy", who were also sent to concentration camps.[92]

In Austria the SD had its first opportunity to put its antisemitic policy into practice. At the beginning of November 1937 Hitler confided to his closest military leaders that he was determined to go to war, his first aim being the "lightning defeat" of Czechoslovakia and Austria. On 12th March 1938 German troops marched into Austria. The previous night, Austrians in Vienna and elsewhere had already given vent to their antisemitic feelings. Jewish shops were looted, and Jews were arbitrarily arrested, banished from their homes and maltreated. Personal gain from such actions was a daily occurrence.[93] Immediately after the invasion a *Sonderkommando* of *Referat* II 112 began its work in Vienna. Herbert Hagen had been in Austria since 12th March. Eichmann joined him on 16th March.[94] The initial task of the *Sonderkommando* was to arrest Jewish officials – using a previously compiled list – and to confiscate documents

---

[89]Report from Abteilung II 112 to Heydrich, 30th June 1938, in Osobyi Archive Moscow, 500/1/645, Bl. 33 37.

[90]Telex from SD Leipzig to SD-Hauptamt, 22nd June 1938, in Osobyi Archive Moscow, 500/1/645, Bl. 10.

[91]SD-OA Fulda-Werra to SD-Hauptamt, 23rd June 1938, in Osobyi Archive Moscow, 500/1/645, Bl. 11; cf. Friedländer, pp. 261–263.

[92]Cf. Wolfgang Ayaß, '"Ein Gebot der nationalen Arbeitsdisziplin". Die Aktion "Arbeitsscheu Reich" 1938', in *Feinderklärung und Prävention*, Berlin 1988 (Beiträge zur nationalsozialistischen Gesundheits- und Sozialpolitik 6), pp. 43–74.

[93]Cf. Hans Safrian and Hans Witek, *Und keiner war dabei. Dokumente des alltäglichen Antisemitismus in Wien 1938*, Vienna 1988.

[94]Progress Report II 112, 1st January–30th June 1938; BA, R 58/991, Bl. 106–121.

and files from Jewish organisations and from private individuals.[95] In a situation where grassroots antisemitism was met with indecisive action from above, Eichmann single-mindedly tried to centralise all National-Socialist *Judenpolitik* in his department. In mid-April – after Hagen's return to Berlin – Eichmann compiled a list of those Jewish organisations which were to be allowed to reopen in order to promote forced emigration. He blackmailed the *Israelitische Kultusgemeinde* into handing over one hundred thousand *Reichsmark*, thus demonstrating that the SD, using sufficient criminal energy, was successful in managing to get the Jews to pay for their own expulsion, in contrast to the complicated currency debates taking place in other ministerial departments. Eichmann demanded "an emigration figure of 20,000 impoverished Jews for the period of 1st May 1938 to 1st May 1939".[96] This number was vastly exceeded. Heydrich claimed at the conference of 12th November, held in the *Reichsluftfahrtministerium*, that by the end of October about 50,000 Jews had been expelled from Austria. More recent research shows that about half of the approximately 190,000 Austrian Jews had left their country by May 1939.[97]

Eichmann's office, only the *Abteilung* II 112 of the SD-*Oberabschnitt Österreich*, was promoted to *Zentralstelle für jüdische Auswanderung* (Central Office for Jewish Emigration) in August 1938 by *Reichskommissar* Bürckel; however, the SD chief for Austria, Stahlecker, remained in overall charge.[98] The aim of centralising *Judenpolitik* in the hands of the SD had been achieved to a great extent in Austria. The interest the SD-*Hauptamt* showed in this new institution was correspondingly great. After inspecting the *Zentralstelle für jüdische Auswanderung* in Vienna at the end of November 1938, Hagen reported to Heydrich in November 1938, summarising once again the advantages of the *Zentralstelle*:

"The establishment of the *Zentralstelle* guarantees the speedy issue of emigration visas to Jews, usually within 8 days. Furthermore, the *Zentralstelle* knows the exact numbers of those who wish to emigrate, their professions, wealth etc., which will enable it to assemble the necessary emigration transportation as soon as the *Israelitische Kultusgemeinde Wien* has obtained sufficient immigration permits [...]. According to our assesment approximately 25,000 Jews have so far been made to emigrate by the *Zentralstelle* so that the overall number of Jews having left Austria is now approximately 50,000. The establishment of the *Zentralstelle* does not put an extra financial burden on the SD *Oberabschnitt Donau* because it and its employees are self-financed

---

[95] In May 1938 a special *Österreich-Auswertungskommando* (ÖAK) was formed, which in the following months evaluated the many boxes of documents that had been transported to Berlin; BA, R 59/991, *passim*.

[96] Eichmann to Hagen, 8th May 1938; BA, R 58/982, Bl. 20.

[97] Jonny Moser, 'Österreich', in Wolfgang Benz (ed.), *Dimension des Völkermords. Die Zahl der jüdischen Opfer des Nationalsozialismus*, Munich 1991, pp. 67–93; here p. 68. The thousands of people forcefully and illegally deported, mainly to Switzerland, by the SA and the SS should not be forgotten; cf. Jacob Toury, 'Ein Auftakt zur "Endlösung"': Judenaustreibungen über nichtslawische Reichsgrenzen 1933–1939', in *Das Unrechtsregime. Internationale Forschung über den Nationalszoialismus*, ed. by Ursula Büttner with Werner Johe and Angelika Voß, vol. 2, Hamburg 1986, pp. 164–169.

[98] For the *Wiener Zentralstelle*, see Jonny Moser, 'Die Zentralstelle für jüdische Auswanderung', in Kurt Schmid and Robert Streibel (eds.), *Der Pogrom 1938*, Vienna 1990; also Safrian, *Eichmann-Männer*, pp. 36–46; Friedländer, pp. 241–248.

SD Judenpolitik 1935–1938   265

by the tax levied on every Jewish emigrant. In view of the success rate of the *Zentralstelle* regarding Jewish emigration, it is recommended – with reference to the recent proposal of 13th January 1938 concerning the establishment of an emigration office – that the possibility of such an office is considered for the whole of the *Reich* as well."[99]

Hagen's report landed on Heydrich's desk at a critical time. On 10th November, one day after the pogrom of the night of the 9th-10th and two days before the conference at the *Reichsluftfahrtministerium*, Heydrich made a handwritten note in the report to the effect that the SD should, in co-operation with the *Gestapa*, make a corresponding proposal for the *Altreich* and the *Sudetenland*. Eichmann's *Zentralstelle für jüdische Auswanderung* in Vienna became the model for Berlin and Prague.

The annexation of Austria had, in the meantime, aggravated the "Jewish Question" by adding approximately one hundred thousand additional Jews to the *Großdeutsches Reich*. At the beginning of 1938 the SD had to admit that

> "The opportunities for emigration are being drastically reduced by international measures so that one can hardly speak of organised emigration anymore – with the exception, to some extent, of the *Ostmark*. Even if the necessary support from foreign Jewish organisations is forthcoming, and the foreign exchange is made available by the *Reich*, this question will not be solved so easily in the future. Only two countries can be considered for a larger Jewish immigration, namely Palestine and – for the next calendar year – the United States".[100]

The international conference in the French spa of Evian-les-Bains at Lake Geneva, which took place in July 1938 at the request of US President Roosevelt with the purpose of improving emigration opportunities for German Jews in the face of increasingly aggressive National-Socialist antisemitic policies, revealed that hardly any country was willing to increase its immigration quotas. The Australian delegate explained frankly that his country did not have a "real racial problem" and did not wish to introduce one either.[101] In his report on the conference Hagen came to the conclusion that "the period in which emigration policy could be exclusively determined by Germany is now over" and that future emigration opportunities would be severely restricted.[102]

In this context the Pogrom of November 1938 served as both culmination and turning point.[103] It had not been initiated either by the SD or by the *Gestapo*, but it resulted in considerably more power for both. Goebbels, who had instigated the

---

[99]Herbert Hagen, "Bericht über die Zentralstelle für jüdische Auswanderung in Wien", November 1938, in Osobyi Archive Moscow, 500/1/625, Bl. 87–89; reprinted in Wildt, (ed.), *Judenpolitik des SD, 1935–1938*, pp. 193–194.

[100]Monthly Progress Report II 112, August 1938, in Osobyi Archive Moscow, 500/3/316, Bl. 240–245.

[101]Quoted from Ralph Weingarten, *Die Hilfeleistung der westlichen Welt bei der Endlösung der Judenfrage. Das "Intergovernmental Committee on Political Refugees" (IGC) 1938–1939*, Berne–Frankfurt am Main 1981, p. 64; regarding the Evian Conference see *ibid.*, pp. 47–87.

[102]Report by Hagen on the Evian Conference 29th July 1938, in Osobyi Archive Moscow, 500/1/649, Bl. 122–123.

[103]Cf. Ulrich Herbert, 'Von der "Reichkristallnacht" zum "Holocaust". Der 9. November und das Ende des "Radauantisemitismus"', in idem, *Arbeit, Volkstum, Weltanschauung. Über Fremde und Deutsche im 20. Jahrhundert*, Frankfurt am Main 1995, pp. 59–77.

Pogrom on the evening of 9th November, and all the other *Radau-Antisemiten* in the party, hoped that this action would allow them to set the tone again with regard to Jewish policies. Himmler and Heydrich only found out about the Pogrom late that night, but used the unleashed violence for their own purpose by ordering the police to arrest over 20,000 mainly wealthy Jews and to incarcerate them in concentration camps in order to force them to pay large sums of money and then emigrate. The Pogrom brought German Jews abruptly face to face with the increase in violence against them and how even murder in the street did not arouse much resistance in the German populace. For the *Radau-Antisemiten* the Pogrom was a political disaster: millions of marks of damage to the economy, severe international reactions, and apparently no support from the German population for the excesses of violence.[104] Göring, like Himmler and Heydrich an opponent of the Pogrom, openly confessed at the beginning of December to leaders of the party: "I am extremely angry about the whole affair and flew into a rage because it caused such a racket and did so much economic damage [*daß ich über die ganze Geschichte maßlos erbost bin, weil mir das wirtschatftlich soviel Klamauk und Schaden gemacht hat*]".[105] According to Göring, the only value of the Pogrom had been that it was now clear to the world and to German Jews that there was no longer a place for Jews in Germany.

At this turning point in National-Socialist policy against the Jews, in November 1938 the SD appeared to have all the knowledge and experience needed to show a way out of this self-created *impasse*, especially as time was running out. The SD concept of forced emigration appeared to be the "solution to the Jewish Question". It seemed reasonable, therefore, that Heydrich asked Eichmann to join them from Vienna and attend the conference in the *Reichsluftfahrtministerium* on 12th November in order to obtain first-hand information.[106] At the conference Heydrich introduced the Vienna *Zentralstelle* as a model institution which had successfully expelled 50,000 Jews since the annexation, whereas over the same period only 19,000 Jews had been expelled from the *Altreich*.[107] Göring voiced a few objections with respect to the difference between deportation and emigration, as well as raising the foreign exchange question, which Heydrich was able to counter by pointing out that the Jews themselves would cover the expenses for the less well-off emigrants. Göring gave his consent and a few weeks later announced the establishment of a *Zentralstelle* for Jewish emigrants, based on the Viennese model, with Heydrich in charge.[108]

---

[104]David Bankier, *The Germans and the Final Solution. Public Opinion and Nazism*, Oxford–Cambridge 1992, pp. 85–88.
[105]Speech by Göring of 6th December 1938, reprinted in Susanne Heim and Götz Aly, 'Staatliche Ordnung und "organische Lösung". Die Rede Hermann Görings "Über die Judenfrage" vom 6. Dezember 1938', in *Jahrbuch für Antisemitismusforschung* 2 (1992), pp. 378–404, here p. 395.
[106]SD-Hauptamt to SD-Führer Donau, Telegramme, 11th November 1938; BA, R 58/486, Bl. 28; also the incomplete shorthand notes on the conference, in *IMG*, vol. 28, pp. 499–540 (Document 1816–PS).
[107]*Ibid.*, pp. 532–533.
[108]For the *Berliner Zentralstelle* see Anderl, ' "Zentralstellen für jüdische Auswanderung" ', pp. 275–288.

The programme of expulsion was expressly supported by Hitler. At the beginning of December 1938 Göring informed *Gauleiter, Oberpräsidenten and Reichsstatthalter* alike that, on Hitler's orders, the foremost principle had to be the following: "All our thinking and our actions have to be guided by the idea to rid ourselves of the Jews as effectively and quickly as possible, to force emigration with the utmost vigour and to remove all possible obstacles to emigration."[109] Göring still claimed overall responsibility regarding the "Jewish Question", but the power to act had already been passed to the *Sicherheitspolizei* and the SD.

The murder and violent excess of 9th and 10th November 1938 forced tens of thousands of German Jews to flee the country. Between 126,000 and 129,000 Jews had left Hitler's Germany by the end of 1937; in 1938 33,000–40,000 fled; and in 1939 a further 75,000–80,000 left the country.[110] Those who stayed behind were deprived of their last possessions and, without jobs and impoverished, were ultimately used as forced labour. On 30th January 1939 Hitler threatened the Jews that in case of war, the result would not be the "bolshevisation of the world" but the "extermination of the Jewish race in Europe". In March 1939, in violation of the Munich Agreement, Germany occupied the rest of the Czech Republic. Six months later Germany attacked Poland. On the brink of war the "solution to the Jewish Question" was increasingly seen in terms of physical extermination.

The men of *Abteilung* II 112 of the *SD-Hauptamt*, which had merged in September 1939 with the RSHA, were directly involved in the planning and organisation of the Holocaust. When there was no territory left into which the Jews could be expelled, they radicalised the "solution to the Jewish Question" into the "Final Solution". Throughout Europe they served as *Judenexperten* in order to deport European Jewry to the extermination camps in Eastern Europe. From 1940 to 1943 Dieter Wisliceny acted as so-called *Judenberater* to the Slovak government and in 1943–1944 he took part in the deportation of Jews from Salonika and Hungary. Captured by the Americans in 1945, he was extradited to Czechoslovakia where, in February 1948, he was tried and executed for being an accessory to mass murder. As *Judenberater* to the commander of the *Sicherheitspolizei* and the SD from 1940–1942 in occupied France, Theodor Danneker was responsible for the first deportations to Auschwitz. He was one of the RHSA "deportation experts" employed all over Europe: in Italy in 1942, in Bulgaria in 1943, in 1944 in Hungary and finally again in Italy. He committed suicide in 1945 while in American custody.

---

[109]Speech by Göring of 6th December 1938, cited in Heim and Aly, *Staatliche Ordnung*, p. 384; For Hitler's instructions following the November Pogrom see also Adam, *Judenpolitik*, pp. 216–219. ("An der Spitze aller unserer Überlegungen und Maßnahmen steht der Sinn, die Juden so rasch und so effektiv wie möglich ins Ausland abzuschieben, die Auswanderung mit allem Nachdruck zu forcieren, und hierbei all das wegzunehmen, was die Auswanderung hindert.")

[110]Ino Arndt and Heinz Boberach, 'Deutsches Reich', in Benz, *Dimension des Völkermords*, pp. 23–65, here p. 34.

Herbert Hagen also went to France in 1940 and ran the *Außenstelle* of the *Sicherheitspolizei* in Bordeaux. He became personal aid to the *Höhere* SS-*und Polizeiführer* and was also heavily involved in the deportation of French Jews. In 1945 he was imprisoned by the British and was released in 1948. In 1955 a French military court sentenced him *in absentia* to hard labour for life; in 1980 the *Landgericht Köln* sentenced him to twelve-years' imprisonment for being an accessory to murder. After having built up the *Zentralstellen* in Vienna and Prague, Adolf Eichmann was promoted to *Sonderreferent* for the "evacuation of the Eastern provinces" in *Amt* IV of the RSHA, which later became *Referat* IV B 4, which was responsible for mass deportations to extermination camps. Caught by the Americans, Eichmann became a prisoner of war, but managed to escape before he could be identified. For a while he went underground in the area around Alt-Aussee in Austria and emigrated in 1950, with the help of Roman Catholic clergymen and papers issued by the Red Cross, via Italy to Argentina, where he was arrested in 1960 by the Israeli Secret Service. He was tried in Jerusalem for crimes against the Jewish people and crimes against humanity, was sentenced to death, and was executed on 1st June 1962.

Among the many authorities of the National-Socialist regime working on programmes for the "solution to the Jewish Question", the SD was successful in putting its proposals into practice. From 1934 onwards its officers had concentrated on comprehending and recording the "Jewish Question" from a biological-racial perspective in a practical, rational and statistically exact way, thus distinguishing itself from '*Radau-Antisemitismus*' without, however, acting any less radically. The advantage the SD had as an institution was its close link with the political police which, by expanding its power base, was put more and more into an executive position. The SD thus gained information and areas of competence which would otherwise have remained closed to it. The position of *Abteilung* II 112 of the SD-*Hauptamt* within the power structure of the National-Socialist system was, in reality, not as peripheral as it appears at first glance.

From 1935 onwards, the division of labour between the SD and the *Gestapo* was not the only factor in its success *vis-à-vis Judenpolitik*. This was mainly due to its early development of, and faithfulness to, the option of forced emigration which, at a particular historical juncture, when all other avenues were blocked, seemed to offer a "solution to the Jewish Question". Last but not least, the policy of the SD-*Judenabteilung* always was, in its basic orientation, in agreement with Hitler, who, notwithstanding tactical considerations, regarded the "removal of the Jews" as the cornerstone of his policy.

The rationality and objectivity which the SD claimed for its *Judenpolitik* failed in its purpose, because the biological racism inherent in the basic assumption that the Jews were damaging the German nation and must therefore be "removed" led, in a complex industrialised society, to a variety of obstacles which the agents of the SD were unable to assess pragmatically. The extirpation of the Jews from Germany (*Entjudung Deutschlands*) was to be achieved at any price. It was not the confusion about responsibilities among the various National-Socialist authorities that made the most radical solution the smallest common denominator, but rather it was the goal and the practice of the protagonists themselves that created the *impasse* that then had to be overcome by even more radical measures. The '*Judenexperten*' of the SD were not forced into radicalisation by the existing structure: they themselves radicalised the policy.[111]

The SD never perceived the handling of the "great ideological questions [*großen weltanschaulichen Fragen*]" in exclusively theoretical terms or merely as a responsibility of the intelligence service. The "scientific" and meticulous way in which, from 1935 to 1938, the SD-*Judenreferat* amassed information about those who were to be expelled was always connected to political practice. The SD's understanding of itself can only be conceptualised as a combination of ideology and power, *Weltanschauung* and practice. No "formalised set of values devoid of content" (Hans Mommsen) triumphed here; it was not merely the "spirit of efficiency" (Hans Buchheim) that reigned; and even such an intelligent observer as Hannah Arendt erred in describing these men as "terrifying and terribly normal".[112]

The SD did not see itself as a merely technocratic organisation based on a division of labour which was given functional responsibilities as part of a larger system. It rather perceived itself as an elite which not only supplied better analyses but also delivered more successful political concepts. *Weltanschauung* had no value unless it could be put into practice. Objectivity and rationality became totally radicalised in its goal of a centralised organisation and an absolute command structure, combined with unbridled destructiveness. These perpetrators were not small wheels in an extermination mechanism. They themselves constructed the machinery that made the murder of millions possible.

---

[111]This argument can also be found in the policy of expulsion of Jews and Poles from the Wartheland in 1939–1940 by the RSHA, as Götz Aly demonstrated recently; see Götz Aly, "*Endlösung*". *Völkerverschiebung und der Mord an den europäischen Juden*, Frankfurt am Main 1995, *passim*. The self-created problems of *NS-Judenpolitik* have already been emphasised by Karl A. Schleunes, *The Twisted Road to Auschwitz. Nazi Policy toward German Jews, 1933–1939*, Urbana, IL 1970.
[112]Hannah Arendt, *Eichmann in Jerusalem. A Report on the Banality of Evil*, London 1963, p. 253.

"*Gegenwaertige Situation*": Report on the Living Conditions of the Jews in Germany. A Document* and Commentary

BY MOSHE AYALON

GEGENWAERTIGE SITUATION

I.

Zur Auswanderung gehoeren drei Dinge:
(1) die juedischen Menschen, die auswandern koennen und wollen,
(2) Laender, nach denen diese Menschen auswandern koennen (Einwanderungslaender),
(3) Geld.

Zu (1): Vorhanden ist von diesen drei Voraussetzungen bisher nur die Erste. Die juedischen Menschen sind auswanderungswillig; Deutschland duldete bisher die Auswanderung, ja es fordert sie sogar. Es gibt, im Gegensatz zu frueheren Jahren, keine juedischen Menschen mehr in Deutschland, die glauben, in Deutschland auf die Dauer leben zu koennen und die dort weiter leben wollen. Soweit die juedischen Menschen in Deutschland nicht so alt oder so krank sind, dass sie die Hoffnung haben, dort noch sterben zu duerfen, draengen sie ohne Ausnahme zur moeglichst beschleunigten Auswanderung. Dieser Drang wird von der Staatsfuehrung durch einen unerhoerten Druck unterstuetzt. Dieser Druck geht nach zweierlei Richtungen: erstens werden den Juden systematisch die Lebensmoeglichkeiten in Deutschland abgeschnitten, ausser den angestellten Rabbinern und juedischen Funktionaeren gibt es nur noch ganz wenige Juden, die in Deutschland ihr Brot verdienen koennen. Soweit die Juden Vermoegen haben, wird es durch staendige Eingriffe gemindert; ausserdem koennen die Juden ueber ihr Vermoegen nicht frei verfuegen, da Verkaeufe von Grundstuecken und Wertpapieren von der staatlichen Genehmigung abhaengig sind, die nur schwer erhalten werden kann.

Neben diesem mittelbaren Druck, den die Staatsfuehrung zum Zwecke der Auswanderung ausuebt, steht der unmittelbare. Noch heute befinden sich viele Menschen in den Konzentrationslagern, die nur unter der Bedingung sofortiger

---
*The author wishes to thank the Central Zionist Archives, Jerusalem, for permission to reproduce this document.

Auswanderung von dort entlassen werden koennen. Soweit die Menschen Ende vorigen Jahres aus den Lagern entlassen wurden und bisher noch nicht ausgewandert worden sind, werden sie zur Polizei vorgeladen und es wird ihnen mitgeteilt, dass sie mit ihrer erneuten Verbringung in die Lager zu rechnen haben, sofern sie nicht spaetestens innerhalb weniger Wochen doch das Land verlassen. Viele Leute haben sich taeglich bei der Polizei zu melden und Bericht ueber den Fortgang ihrer Auswanderung zu geben. Aus dem Reich, aber auch aus Berlin, ist eine erhebliche Anzahl von Faellen bekannt geworden, in denen man die Leute zwang, sich drei Mal am Tage, morgens, mittags und abends, auf der Polizei einzufinden.

Zu (2) und (3): Sind somit die Menschen, die zur Auswanderung draengen und auswandern sollen, vorhanden, so fehlt es indessen an den Voraussetzungen zu (2) und (3). Verhandlungen wegen der finanziellen Voraussetzungen werden von dem Evian Committee gepflogen und auch mit der deutschen Regierung gefuehrt. Soweit diese Verhandlungen darauf hinauslaufen, das in Deutschland noch vorhandene juedische Vermoegen der Auswanderung der Juden aus Deutschland nutzbar zu machen, bedarf es der Hervorhebung, dass diese Verhandlungen nutzlos, ja schaedlich sein muessen, wenn nicht gleichzeitig oder gar vorher die Einwanderungslaender gefunden werden, nach denen die Juden auswandern koennen. Erst wenn man feststellt, welche Laender bereit sind, juedische Menschen aus Deutschland aufzunehmen und unter welchen Bedingungen dies geschehen kann, erst dann wird man wissen, welche Mittel fuer jedes einzelne Einwanderungsland erforderlich sind, um die Juden dorthin zu bringen, und sie dort sesshaft zu machen. Fehlt es aber an den Einwanderungslaendern, so besteht die Gefahr, dass die Verhandlungen ueber die finanziellen Voraussetzungen mit der deutschen Regierung lediglich dazu fuehren, dieser Regierung das Stichwort zu liefern, um die juedischen Vermoegen in Deutschland, soweit sie ueberhaupt noch vorhanden sind, unter dem Gesichtspunkt der Auswanderungs-Finanzierung sicherzustellen. Das wuerde bedeuten, dass die Juden zwar mangels Vorhandensein von Einwanderungslaendern nicht aus Deutschland heraus kommen, dass ihnen aber die letzten Mittel entzogen werden, die sie fuer ihren Lebensunterhalt in Deutschland benoetigen.

II.

Zur Zeit ist von Deutschland aus gesehen die Auswanderungs-Lage derart, dass es praktisch neue Einwanderungslaender ueberhaupt nicht gibt. Die Auswanderung nach U.S.A. vollzieht sich staendig innerhalb der Quote, neue Moeglichkeiten "beyond the quota" stehen bisher nicht zur Verfuegung, obwohl es eine ungeheure Erleichterung des Problems waere, wenn U.S.A. Kinder und alte Menschen, die keine Konkurrenz fuer den Arbeitsmarkt darstellen, ausserhalb der Quote aufnehmen wuerde, vorausgesetzt, dass fuer den Unterhalt sowie fuer die Erziehung der Kinder in U.S.A. gesorgt ist, was weitgehendst der Fall sein duerfte.

Die Palaestina-Einwanderung macht wegen der augenblicklich schwierigen politischen Lage die groessten Schwierigkeiten, wie sie sich in Zukunft gestalten wird, laesst sich nicht voraussehen.

Australien uebernimmt bisher nur 5,000 Menschen jaehrlich, aus ganz Mitteleuropa, was gegenueber der Groesse des Kontinents eine verschwindende Zahl ist.

Im uebrigen ist die Welt fuer die juedische Einwanderung praktisch gesperrt, insbesondere sind die europaeischen Laender mit Emigranten vollgestopft. Durch die neueste Entwicklung in der Tschecho-Slovakei wird das europaeische Fluechtlings-Problem noch schwieriger, als es bereits vorher war.

Der einzige Ort, wohin heute Juden ohne Visum und ohne Permit gelangen koennen, ist Shanghai. Es bedarf nicht erst der Betonung, wie unerwuenscht diese Anhaeufung von Tausenden von Juden in Shanghai ist, da dort fuer diese Zahl in absehbarer Zeit eine Lebensmoeglichkeit nicht besteht. Man kann auch der Auffassung sein, das es wuerdiger fuer einen Juden ist, in Mitteleuropa den Maertyrer-Tod zu erleiden, als in Shanghai zu Grund zu gehen. Das erste ist ein "Kiddusch Haschem", das Zweite ist lediglich eine Fehlleitung juedischer Auswanderungspolitik. Man wird auch unbedingt gewisse Gruppen von Menschen von Shanghai fernhalten muessen, z.B. keine jungen Maedchen oder junge Frauen in die Hafen-Quartiere von Shanghai senden. Und trotz all dieser Hemmungen steht eines fest: Die Auswanderung nach Shanghai kann nicht voellig unterbunden werden, solange es ueberhaupt keine anderen Orte in der Welt gibt, wo die Juden, die in unmittelbarer Lebensgefahr sind, in verhaeltnismaessig kurzer Zeit hingebracht werden koennen. So ablehnend die deutsch-juedischen Organisationen gerade wegen ihrer Verantwortung fuer das weitere Schicksal der juedischen Menschen dieser Auswanderung von Haus aus gegenueberstehen, so kommen doch immer wieder Faelle vor, – und zwar hunderte von Faellen –, wo diese Menschen, deren Leben in den Konzentrationslagern unmittelbar bedroht ist, mit Hilfe ihrer Angehoerigen auf die Auswanderung nach Shanghai draengen, weil ihnen jeder Platz in der Welt besser zu sein duengt [sic], als der weitere Aufenthalt in Deutschland.

Es kommt noch hinzu, dass die Auswanderung nach Shanghai von der deutschen Regierung gefoerdert wird, ja die Geheime Staatspolizei hat wiederholt versucht, sie auch gegen den Willen der juedischen Organisationen zu erzwingen. Mehrmals haben Reisebureaus mit Unterstuetzung der GESTAPO Sonderschiffe gemietet und juedische Gemeinden angewiesen, die ihnen ueberlassenen Plaetze nach Shanghai mit juedischen Auwanderern zu fuellen; insbesondere verlangt die GESTAPO, dass die Wohfahrtsempfaenger mit diesen Schiffen nach Shanghai fahren, die Kosten sollen die Gemeinden bezahlen, soweit sie dazu nicht in der Lage sind, wird den vermoegenden juedischen Leuten der Gemeinde oder in der Provinz aufgegeben, eine Sonderabgabe von ihren Vermoegen zu leisten, damit die Passagekosten fuer die armen Juden gedeckt werden. Es ist mit Hilfe der zentralen deutschen Stellen bisher gelungen, diese Sonderaktionen abzustoppen, jedoch nur unter der Bedingung, dass die Auswanderung nach Shanghai in die Auswanderungsplanung aufgenommen wird, weil es ja tatsaechlich kein anderes Auswanderungsziel augenblicklich gibt. Die juedischen

Zentral-Organisationen koennen sich dieser polizeilichen Bedingung nicht entziehen, weil sie selber die in Not befindlichen Menschen unbedingt herausbringen muessen und auch ihnen ein anderes Einwanderungsziel nicht zur Verfuegung steht. Wenn die juedischen zentralen Organisationen die Entsendung von besonderen Judenschiffen bisher nach Moeglichkeit verhindert haben, so geschah das aus dem Grunde, weil (siehe Beispiel Suedafrika) die Ankunft von juedischen Sonderschiffen in Shanghai moeglicherweise doch die sofortige Schliessung der juedischen Einwanderung zur Folge haben wuerde, was im Interesse von etwaigen juedischen Notfaellen in Deutschland auch nach Auffassung der juedischen Organisationen denkbar unerwuenscht waere. Es besteht vielleicht die Hoffnung darauf, dass die in Shanghai sich ansammelnden juedischen Menschen zum Teil spaeter einmal die Moeglichkeit haben werden, in das Innere von China weiter zu wandern, sofern sich die Verhaeltnisse in Ostasien einigermassen geklaert haben. Soweit dies nicht moeglich ist, wird nur ein Teil von Shanghai aufgenommen werden koennen, all die Uebrigen muessen spaeter in der Welt andere Auswanderungsmoeglichkeiten suchen.

So ist fuer Tausende von Juden der Shanghai-Aufenthalt dem Aufenthalt in einem Transit-Camp vergleichbar. Genau so, wie der Aufenthalt in diesen Transit-Camps von den juedischen Organisationen im Ausland finanziell gedeckt wird, wird die finanzielle Unterstuetzung des juedischen Committees in Shanghai durch den JOINT bei der gegenwaertigen Lage der Dinge nicht aufhoeren duerfen. Dass die hierfuer zur Verfuegung gestellten Mittel sparsamst verwendet werden muessen, versteht sich von selbst. In allen Faellen, in denen mit Hilfe der juedischen Organisationen in Deutschland Menschen nach Shanghai zur Auswanderung gebracht werden, wird das Shanghai Committee sofort verstaendigt, falls diese Auswanderer Geldmittel mitbringen, damit nicht die dort ankommenden Menschen ohne Zwang die Hilfe des Committees in Anspruch nehmen. Dasselbe ist mit Frau van Tyjn in Amsterdam vereinbart worden.

III.

Finanzlage: In finanzieller Beziehung hat sich die Lage der auswandernden, wie der in Deutschland verbliebenen Juden in den letzten Monaten stark verschaerft.
(1) Die Reichsfluchtsteuer betraegt nach wie vor 25% des Vermoegens des auswandernden Juden.
(2) Die Milliarden-Busse betraegt weitere 20%, dabei verdient Hervorhebung, dass diese Busse erhoben wird nach dem Stand des Vermoegens vom 27. April 1938 (Goering Erklaerung) und dass nur zu einem Teil die erhebliche Verminderung und Entwertung des Vermoegens beruecksichtigt wird, die in der Zwischenzeit eingetreten ist. Um hier ein charakteristisches Beispiel zu nennen, braucht nur auf die Abgabe von Schmuck, Gold, Silber, Edelsteinen verwiesen zu werden.
(3) Bis Ende dieses Monats haben saemtliche Juden ihren gesamten Besitz an die staatlichen Pfandleihen abzuliefern, soweit er aus Edelmetallen, Platin, Gold, Silber, Schmuck oder Edelsteinen besteht. Hierzu gehoert das gesamte Tafelsil-

ber, alle persoenlichen Gebrauchsgegenstaende, soweit sie aus edlen Metallen sind, religioese Geraete (Kiddusch Becher, Leuchter etc.), auch wenn sie schon hunderte von Jahren im Besitze der betreffenden Familie sind.

Verguetet wird dafuer von den Pfandleihestellen ein Spottpreis fuer den reinen Metallwert; der wirkliche Wert betraegt natuerlich weit mehr als das Zehnfache. Behalten darf der Einzelne lediglich die goldenen Trauringe, eine silberne Uhr, 2 Messer, 2 Gabeln, 2 Loeffel. Fuer die Zahlung der Milliarden-Busse ist dieser ganze Besitz bei Berechnung des Vermoegens noch mitgeschaetzt worden und wird auch weiter der Abgabe zu Grunde gelegt, waehrend in Wirklichkeit die juedischen Menschen diesen Teil ihres Vermoegens garnicht mehr besitzen. Dies hat fuer die Auswanderung folgenden merkwuerdigen Zustand zur Folge:

An Stelle der goldenen Uhr oder der silbernen Bestecke, die abgeliefert werden muessen, muessen sich die Auswandernden eine silberne Uhr oder Stahluhr kaufen oder Bestecke aus Stahl und dergleichen, weil sie ja schliesslich nicht mit den Fingern essen und auch ohne eine Uhr schwer auskommen koennen. Wandern diese Menschen jetzt aus, so wird festgestellt, was sie nach dem Jahre 1933 angeschafft haben; fuer diese neuangeschafften Gegenstaende muessen sie eine Abgabe an die Golddiskont-Bank zahlen, die oertlich verschieden ist, in Berlin 100% und mehr ausmacht und in manchen sueddeutschen Orten bis 500% des Kaufpreises heraufgeht. Das bedeutet, dass der jetzt auswandernde Jude, dem seine Uhr oder seine Bestecke weggenommen wurden, den doppelten oder sechsfachen Preis dafuer zu zahlen hat, wenn er mit den ihm erlaubten Gegenstaenden auswandern will.

(2) Auch der neueingefuehrte ausserordentliche juedische Auswanderer Beitrag, durch den die auswandernden vermoegenden Juden die Auswanderung der armen Juden finanzieren sollen, wird, wie die Milliarden-Busse, nach dem Vermoegen berechnet, das der Auswandernde im Jahre 1938 hatte. Umgerechnet auf das heutige stark verminderte Vermoegen bedeutet das eine weitere ganz erhebliche Konfiskation fuer die auswandernden Juden. Hoffentlich wird dieser Betrag auch spaeter tatsaechlich fuer die Auswanderung armer Juden verwendet.

(3) Die verschiedenen Staedte sind dazu uebergegangen, von den juedischen Gemeinden zu verlangen, dass sie die oeffentlichen Wohlfahrtslasten fuer die Juden uebernehmen, die sich nicht selber ernaehren koennen. Nach der gesetzlichen Grundlage soll die oeffentliche Wohlfahrt nur da einsetzen, sofern die juedischen Gemeinden nicht in der Lage sind, die armen Juden selber zu unterhalten. Die juedischen Gemeinden haben darauf hingewiesen, dass sie bei der jetztigen Lage der Steuereinnahme nicht dazu in der Lage sind, diese Lasten zu uebernehmen. Ihnen wurde daraufhin mitgeteilt, dass es nicht darauf ankaeme, ob die juedischen Gemeinden genuegend Vermoegen besitzen, vielmehr muessten dann aber die vermoegenden Juden der Gemeinde zusammentreten und einen Teil ihres Vermoegens abgeben, um die armen Juden mit zu ernaehren (Haftungsgemeinschaft der Juden fuer einander, vergl. das Vorbild in Danzig). Eine zentrale Regelung ist bisher noch nicht erfolgt. Es verdient Hervorhebung, dass in Berlin gluecklicherweise dieser Zustand bisher noch nicht eingetreten ist.

IV.

Gewaltsame Eingriffe und Verhaftungen groesseren Stiles sind seit Beginn dieses Jahres im Bezirk des Altreiches nicht eingetreten. Gleichwohl steht ein grosser Teil der noch nicht ausgewanderten juedischen Bevoelkerung unter der Androhung der Verhaftung und der Verbringung in das Konzentrationslager fuer den Fall, dass die Auswanderung nicht bald stattfindet. Aus den oeffentlichen Theatern, Kinos, Restaurants etc. sind die Juden voellig verbannt. Auch in Geschaeften, selbst in Lebensmittel-Geschaeften, haeufen sich die Ankuendigungen, "dass an Juden keine Ware abgegeben wird" oder "dass Juden unerwuenscht sind".

Gottesdienste koennen im ausreichenden Umfange nicht gehalten werden. Die meistens in kleineren Saelen stattfindenden Gottesdienste sind durchweg ueberfuellt und genuegen bei weitem nicht den Beduerfnissen. Zum Teil versucht man Abhilfe dadurch, dass man mehrere Gottesdienste hintereinander abhaelt. Die niedergebrannten Synagogen in Berlin, z.B. Fasanenstrasse, Prinzregentenstrasse, Franzensbaderstrasse werden nicht aufgebaut. Es ist allerdings in Berlin gestattet worden, in zwei der bisher geschlossenen Synagogen (Oranienburgerstrasse und Levetzowstrasse) Pesach-Gottesdienst abzuhalten. Dass damit zu den Feiertagen das Beduerfnis bei weitem nicht gedeckt werden kann, leuchtet ein.

* * *

Early in 1939, Dr. Julius Seligsohn, a member of the executive of the *Reichsvereinigung der Juden in Deutschland*, wrote a revealing account of the living conditions of the Jews in Germany, with particular emphasis on the problem of emigration. The report contains an apparently strange remark concerning emigration to Shanghai: "One can also be of the opinion that it is more honourable for a Jew to die as a martyr in Central Europe than to perish [*zu Grunde gehen*] in Shanghai. The first is *Kiddush Hashem*, the second is simply a misled Jewish emigration policy."[1] Before turning to the document and to the remark about Shanghai, it is important to look at the life of its author, as far as we know it.

Julius Seligsohn was born in Berlin in 1890. His family originally came from Posen, where it was well-regarded. In Berlin, it was considered one of the Jewish aristocratic families. From an early age on Julius showed an interest and involvement in Jewish and intellectual life. He studied law and political science. During the First World War he served as an officer in the German army, and was awarded medals for valour. After finishing his studies he became a lawyer and was also active in Jewish welfare organisations and in the Jewish community of Berlin.[2]

---

[1]"Gegenwaertige Situation", Central Zionist Archives, A140/126 (hereafter: The Report.) The *Reichsvereinigung* at that time underwent an organisational change and consolidation as the successor of the *Reichsvertretung der Juden in Deutschland*. See Jacob Toury, 'From Forced Emigration to Expulsion', in *Yad Vashem Studies*, XVII (1986), pp. 84–85. Official English translation of the citation in: NARS, RG 59/840 Ref. No. 1510.

[2]Leo Baeck, 'In Memory of Two of our Dead', in *LBI Year Book I* (1956), pp. 55–56; E.G. Loewenthal (ed.), *Bewährung im Untergang. Ein Gedenkbuch*, Stuttgart 1965, p. 157.

When the *Reichsvertretung der Deutschen Juden* was founded in 1933, Seligsohn became one of its leading personalities. This *Reichsvertretung* was reorganised shortly after its foundation and was renamed *Neue Reichsvertretung der Deutschen Juden*. An official statement of this change was made in September 1933. The leading personalities of the former organisation had been akin to a working executive or an umbrella organisation of delegates of the Jewish associations in the various German provinces (*Länder*), whereas in the new organisation the emphasis was put on personalities who would meet for practical consultations. Besides the chairman, Rabbi Dr. Leo Baeck, there were eight other members, among them Seligsohn. The aim was to construct an executive body which could come to decisions without being deterred by local political or communal interests. Nevertheless, the members were chosen from the main orientations and groups which existed among the Jews in Germany: the *Centralverein* (C.V.), Zionists (ZVfD), the General League of Jewish Frontline Soldiers (RJF), the Liberals, and the Religious Party.[3] Seligsohn was also a member of the Presidial Executive of the Relief Organisation of German Jews (*Zentralausschuss der deutschen Juden für Hilfe und Aufbau*), which was originally founded in 1901 as *Hilfsverein der deutschen Juden* and which changed its functions to meet current needs in April 1933. As chairman of the *Hachsharah* (Emigration Training Farm) at Gross-Breesen for Jewish youngsters interested in emigrating to countries other than Palestine, Seligsohn co-operated with the director, the well-known educator and psychologist Curt Bondy, in his attempts to settle the trainees overseas.[4]

In October 1940, when about 5000 Jews from the Palatinate and the Province of Baden were deported to Southern France, the *Reichsvertretung* of the Jews in Germany sent a circular to the Jewish communities in Germany requesting that they fast and pray for those deported. The *Gestapo* discovered that Seligsohn was the author of the letter, and he was sent to the concentration camp at Oranienburg, where he died on 28th February 1942.[5]

From its foundation, Seligsohn was involved in many of the vital activities of the *Reichsvertretung*. At the end of 1933 or the beginning of 1934, he prepared a petition to the German leader. This document was examined and corrected by Leo Baeck, Otto Hirsch and Siegfried Moses, and, signed by Leo Baeck, was handed, in January 1934, to the Chancellery of the *Führer* and to the German government. There were four main requests:

a) To end economic discrimination of the Jews. (Jews had already been removed from key positions in the economy.)

b) Not to exclude Jews from certain fields of occupation and to enable them also to work in agriculture, foresting, as artisans and the like, all in order to correct the one-sided structure of their activities.

---

[3]H. Tramer, *In Zwei Welten*, Tel Aviv 1962, p. 103.
[4]Werner T. Angress, *Between Fear and Hope. Jewish Youth in the Third Reich*, New York 1988, pp. 44, 59, 181.
[5]Loewenthal, pp. 155,157.

c) Government assistance in emigration and professional education towards it.
d) To stop the anti-Jewish discrimination and slander.[6]

Seligsohn was a man with a positive personality, a strong spirit and personal courage, and he stood upright before the German authorities. On an occasion the time of which has not been definitively established, he proclaimed the need to take up a strong position *vis-a-vis* the authorities, saying: "Today I delivered an ultimatum. They wanted to confirm the emigration of old people only, and I told [them] that if young people can not emigrate, the old ones will stay here too, because there would be no one to care for them abroad."[7] Leo Baeck described Seligsohn as a man "who could think clearly and calmly", with a sense of humour and reality, deep personal religious convictions, and as a person who gave advice and overcame many obstacles. Baeck himself was arrested in 1935 because he wrote a prayer to be read in the synagogues, which encouraged pride in being a Jew in front of human beings, but humiliation before God. Seligsohn arranged a hearing before a high-ranking Nazi, and through this courageous deed, with the aid of involvement from abroad, Baeck was released.[8] Seligsohn's main activities were in the areas of travel, finance, administration, advice and in planning emigration. He therefore travelled abroad a great deal to find suitable localities for immigration.

During these travels, he stayed away only long enough to conclude the necessary arrangements, because he felt he had a duty to be in Germany. This sense of duty caused him also to return from the Netherlands in November 1938 when the Pogrom broke out. After the murder of vom Rath, third secretary at the German Embassy in Paris, members of the *Reichsvertretung* feared retaliation, and asked the British authorities to send an official whose influence might help to avoid the outbreak of a pogrom. The British minister of foreign affairs, Lord Halifax, opposed such a delegation, but through the initiative of British Jews, Sir Michael Bruce went to Berlin. There he met with German-Jewish leaders, including Seligsohn. The latter asked him to express his concern to Sir George Ogilvie-Forbes, the adviser at the British Embassy, and to ask him to meet Hitler and express dissatisfaction about possible occurrences. Sir George refused because of Halifax's objection.[9] Soon after the Pogrom, Seligsohn arranged for the emigration of his wife and two daughters to the United States. He himself refused to join them, explaining: "In war time, women and children must remain behind, and that means New York. I myself must stay in Berlin, because the front-line is here."[10]

His last act of courage, as far as we know, was to compose the circular to the

---

[6]A. Margalioth, *Bein Hazala L'Avadon. Eyunim B' Toldoth Yehudei Germania 1932–1938*, (*Between Rescue and Annihilation. Studies in the History of German Jewry 1932–1938*), Yad Vashem, The Institute of Contemporary Jewry, and the Leo Baeck Institute, Jerusalem 1990, p. 198. The document is reprinted in Tramer, pp. 124–127.
[7]Loewenthal, p.157.
[8]Baeck, pp. 55–56.
[9]Lionel Kochan, *Pogrom. 10 November 1938*, London 1957, pp. 44–45, note 1.
[10]Loewenthal, p. 157.

Jewish communities in Germany after the deportations from the Palatinate and Baden to Southern France in October 1940.

We do not know for whom the report was written in early 1939. It is not likely that, according to Toury,[11] the author wrote it as a memorandum for the *Reichsvereinigung*, as the latter was under constant observation by the *Gestapo* and some of the expressions used were certainly not meant to be seen by that authority. It is more likely that it was written for the American Jewish Joint Distribution Committee (JDC), which carried a substantial part of the financial burden needed to sustain the Jews in Germany and to aid their emigration. This report contains some seemingly strange expressions. The report deals mainly with emigration and points out three conditions:

"1) the existence of Jewish persons, who are able to, and want to, emigrate;
2) countries to which they can emigrate; and
3) money."

As to the first condition, the author dealt with this question at the beginning of the report: "In contrast to former years, there are no Jewish persons in Germany who believe in the possibility of living in Germany forever, and who also wish to continue living there."[12]

Concerning the "Jewish people" mentioned, Seligsohn apparently meant the Jewish community in general and not the exceptions who thought that by keeping a low profile they could weather the storm and survive, or other individuals who collaborated with the *Gestapo*, either by coercion or in the hope that they would be saved. They too were Jews but not what he called "jüdischen Menschen". He explained the wish to emigrate through examples of direct and indirect pressure brought to bear on the Jews by the Nazi government. The indirect pressure caused economic stagnation and deterioration by depriving Jews of their sources of income, blocking their bank accounts and forbidding free use of their own money. Direct pressure was brought on detainees in concentration camps who would be released only on condition of immediate emigration, and those already released were threatened with being sent back there if they did not leave within a short time. Of the latter, Seligsohn used the expression ". . . noch nicht ausgewandert worden sind" [not yet having been emigrated] – meaning that the emigration was compelled by external forces. As to the second condition, countries to which they could emigrate, and the third condition, money, Seligsohn opposed the suggestion that a special committee at the Evian Conference should negotiate the financial conditions with the German government, and argued, in his report, that first, there would have to be found countries which would agree to the immigration of Jews and only then, and after learning the conditions, should the negotiations start. Negotiating with the German government about financial conditions before finding harbouring countries would also endanger residual Jewish capital, which would be confiscated on the

---

[11]Toury, see note 1.
[12]The Report, p. 1.

pretext of financing the emigration. On the other hand Jews would not be permitted to leave because in fact there were no harbouring countries. As a result there would be no financial means to sustain bare life.

II.

At the beginning of 1939 Jews in Germany were anxious and living with a sense of heavy foreboding. Only a few weeks had passed since the frightful Pogrom of November 1938, when many thousands were thrown into concentration camps. Nearly one hundred Jews perished there, and hundreds more died soon after their release, as a result of maltreatment or torture suffered in the camps. Jews in Germany wanted only to flee the country but it was very difficult to find countries willing to accept and absorb them. The United States issued entrance visas according to the yearly quota it had issued many years before and with no consideration for the special adversities faced by Jews in Germany. Many obstacles were placed by the British government in the way of those wishing to emigrate to Palestine, and even Australia limited the annual quota of immigrants to five thousand for the whole of Central Europe. The only place available for free immigration, with no need for entrance visas or permits of any kind, was Shanghai,[13] about which Seligsohn offered the opinion of preferring a martyr's death in Central Europe to perishing in Shanghai.

This seems difficult to understand, especially in the light of the plight of the Jews in Germany, and especially as the author, in the same document, wrote the following: "... Since the beginning of this year [1939] no violent outbreaks or mass arrests took place in the old *Reich*. In spite of this, a great part of the Jewish population which has not yet emigrated is in danger of being arrested and sent to the concentration camp if the emigration does not take place soon".[14] In retrospect we know that Jews who emigrated to Shanghai came to no harm and certainly did not perish. Until the outbreak of the Second World War, some 17,000–18,000 Jews arrived there, including approximately 1000 Yeshiva students from Poland, who made their long journey via Siberia and Kobe in Japan and from there were transferred to Shanghai. Among those immigrants were also some 1,500 "non-Aryan" Christians. As if to mock destiny, the only case of violent deaths in Shanghai occurred as the result of an American bombing attack on 17th July 1945, when thirty-one Jewish refugees were killed and about 250 wounded.[15]

The report also stated that the German government required, and the *Gestapo* even tried to force, Jewish organisations to arrange emigration to Shanghai. We know of advanced negotiations in Hamburg to buy two motorised sailing vessels for that purpose, but at the outbreak of the war they were confiscated by the

---

[13]*Ibid.*, p. 3.
[14]*Ibid.*, p. 7.
[15]David Kranzler, *Japanese, Nazis and Jews. The Jewish Refugee Community of Shanghai, 1938–1945*, New York 1976, p. 554

German navy. Dr. Max Plaut, head of the Jewish community of Hamburg, recounted after the war that he had been active in this affair and had approved of the action but that it was opposed by the *Reichsvereinigung*.[16] At Breslau, the *Gestapo* initiated proceedings to lease a ship for sailing to Shanghai and the heads of the Jewish community there had been ordered to negotiate this matter, but it seems that the higher echelons of the *Gestapo*, the *Reichssicherheitshauptamt* or the government, were not pleased with this local initiative and the assignment was not carried out.[17] A memorandum written on 17th March 1939 at the JDC's main office in New York pointed out the difficulty of settling immigrants in Shanghai, and asked the Jewish *Hilfsverein* in Germany to stop the emigration. In its reply, via the JDC's office in Paris, the *Hilfsverein* explained that it was impossible to stop Jews emigrating where they could, and, what was more, "...we are convinced that for the majority of the emigrants, their lot in Shanghai would be much better – in spite of all the disadvantages of this situation – than in Germany if they remained there".[18]

The question remains, however: how could it have been possible to equate rescue and the suggestion that Jews would "perish" in Shanghai, while referring to the danger of being sent to a concentration camp in Germany as *Kiddush Hashem*. Maimonides explained that if a Jew is killed because he is a Jew, that is *Kiddush Hashem*, and his explanation is accepted as *Halakhah*.[19] It is obvious, then, that a Jew who died from torture or in a concentration camp is considered to have sanctified His Holy Name (*Kiddush Hashem*). On the other hand, it is obvious, by the same *halakhic* decree, that this same Jew must use every possible means to save his life. If he could have emigrated, but instead remained and was killed, this would violate the obligation (*mitzvah*) of self preservation.

What induced Seligsohn to make the equation he did? Knowledge of his personality does not enable us to understand the meaning of his declaration. In trying to understand it we have to look first at the prevailing atmosphere and at the plans and activities of the *Reichsvereinigung*. The declaration must also be seen in the context of the report.

Seligsohn, along with the majority of the executive members of the *Reichsvereinigung*, preferred organised emigration, as he indicates in his report:

"Insofar as the central Jewish organisations did their best to prevent sending off special Jew-ships [*Judenschiffe*], the reason was (see South Africa) that the arrival of special Jewish ships at Shanghai could cause the immediate prohibition of Jewish immigra-

---

[16]Max Plaut, "Die Gemeinde Hamburg"; Yad Vashem 01/54.
[17]Willy Gluskinos, acting head of the Jewish community in Breslau, in a report written in the winter of 1939–1940; Yad Vashem 01/27. Confirmation of this story can be found in the diary of Dr. Willy Cohn. In an entry of 8th February 1939, he writes: "A special ship for Shanghai did not depart. It was a special operation of the *Gestapo* in Breslau, without confirmation from Berlin." Yad Vashem 01/260, p. 2.
[18]Memorandum written on 13th March 1939 by J.C. Hyman to George Backer. American Jewish Joint Distribution Committee: Germany file, doc. 631.
[19]Chaim Strauss, 'Mashma'uth *Kiddush Hashem* Bashoa' (The meaning of *Kiddush Hashem* during the *Shoah*), in Jaakov ben Joseph (ed.), *AGID*, 1980, p. 58.

tion, and even the Jewish organisations are of the opinion that such a step would prejudice the interests of possible Jewish emergency cases in Germany."[20]

Plaut, too, who, as head of the Jewish community in Hamburg, tried to obtain ships, claimed after the war that the *Reichsvereinigung* had been opposed to illegal emigration.[21]

In this document, Seligsohn wrote down his evaluation of anti-Jewish incidents. It seems that his assessment of the future of Jews in Germany was based on this, and he concluded that the chances for survival of Jews in Germany – at least in the Old *Reich* – were no worse than the chances of survival in Shanghai.

Mass annihilation of German Jews began about eighteen months later, after the beginning of their mass deportation to the East in October 1941, and it became known even later. At the time the memorandum was written, there could not have been the slightest idea of the violent end almost all of the deportees would meet. Meanwhile, most of the Jews in Germany belonged to a Jewish community and lived in an environment and atmosphere they were used to, and in which they participated. They met in synagogues and prayer halls and listened to lectures about Judaism. In the cities, there were still the manifold activities of the Jewish *Kulturbund*. The Jewish welfare organisations took care of the necessities of life, even if only with scarce supplies. Consequently, if a Jew died in Germany as a result of being a Jew, his death would be a *Kiddush Hashem*. It might even be possible that Seligsohn meant this expression to apply also to a Jew who in Germany could still lead a Jewish life, in the sense of observing Jewish religious or social obligations within a Jewish community, and could end his life in a natural way. On the other hand, in Shanghai he would be destined to die as a result of bad living conditions in strange surroundings, with no connection to a Jewish community or to his Jewishness.

It seems, therefore, that Seligsohn thought the chances of staying alive in these two places to be equal, and that only the way of life would be different. This was not the evaluation of a single, even if important, individual but the point of view of the majority of the Jewish leaders in Germany. Until the outbreak of war in September 1939, the *Gestapo* demanded forced mass emigration of the Jews and even aided in illegal border crossings and in obtaining means for transportation. The Jewish organisations were asked to cooperate, but the executive of the *Reichsvereinigung* preferred instead organised and planned emigration so as to stop the practice of a mass exodus which – so they feared – would bring an end to German Jewry.[22]

With this explanation one can understand the meaning of Seligsohn's words. The leaders of the German Jews were alert to the ominous meaning of the persecutions but thought that the structure of Jewry was strong enough to hold out, and only unplanned dispersal would bring an end to what had once been German Jewry. Planned and organised emigration, on the other hand, would

---

[20]The Report, p. 4.
[21]Supp. footnote 16. Dr. Max Plaut lived in Germany and acted as the head of the *Reichsvereinigung* for northwest Germany. In 1944 he was permitted to emigrate to Palestine.
[22]Margalioth, 'Hagirath Yehudei Germania – Tichnun um'ziuth' (Migration of German Jews – Plans and Practice), *Yahadut Zemanenu* 5, Jerusalem 1989, p. 300.

allow German Jewry to hold on to its structure, either by contact with formations of its members in the countries to which they emigrated, or by mutual contact between the new centres, and it is even possible that the leaders hoped for the return of at least a substantial number of the *émigrés* once the horror was over.

From still another angle, Seligsohn's words were not a declaration *per se*, but must be seen in the context of other thoughts he expressed.

The memorandum begins with the statement of the desire of the Jews in Germany to leave. The subsequent sentences deal with the problem of the lack of places willing to allow immigration. The exception was Shanghai, but it would not be advisable to send masses of Jews there because there were no known means for existence.

After that preamble, the author wrote the declaration we are dealing with, and also stated that one could not entirely stop the emigration to Shanghai for Jews whose lives were in direct danger. Generally, German-Jewish organisations did not favour this destination because of their sense of responsibility for the future of the Jewish people.

Seligsohn's sceptical attitude concerning emigration to Shanghai, as against his belief that it could not be stopped entirely for Jews whose life was in danger as long as there were no other destinations available, shows that he and other Jewish leaders in Germany thought the danger to life in Germany to be about the same as in Shanghai. Only direct danger in Germany, and that included in these times, Jews released from concentration camps on condition of immediate emigration, and others who were ordered by the *Gestapo* to do so, would be worse than life in Shanghai. Seligsohn's dilemma emphasises a terrible ambivalence. He still believed in the firm structure of German Jewry, whose creativity had been famous for centuries. The dangers were understood, too, but these were believed to concern Jews as individuals and not German Jewry as a whole. At the beginning of 1939, no-one could foresee the terrible disaster which lay in store. Only the will to preserve that which still existed despite the atmosphere of fear and persecution which was already there, especially from the end of 1938, could lead to the belief that "... it is more honourable for a Jew to die as a martyr in Central Europe than to perish in Shanghai". Against this opinion, in which Seligsohn did not necessarily believe but only expressed its possibility, was another point of view – to our great sorrow shared by not too many – which had understood long before that in Germany there was no future for Jews.

III.

Seligsohn described the economic situation and summarised it thus:[23]

1) Emigration tax was, and remained, 25% of the value of the Jewish emigrant's possessions. We do not know whether the possessions were assessed according to the date of the assessment, or according to their value on 26th April 1938, the

---

[23]The Report, pp. 5–7.

date the new regulation, ordered by Göring in connection with Jewish capital, came into effect.

2) Jewish possessions, of which 20%, later 25%, would have to be paid as punishment for the murder of vom Rath, were also assessed as to their value in April 1938, some six and a half months before that incident, and their devaluation in the meantime was only partly taken into account. In the interim individual Jews had nearly no income and had to live on their capital. Seligsohn also pointed to the decree of 21st February 1939 which ordered Jews to deliver, within two weeks, all of their gold, silver, platinum and jewels.

3) At about that time an additional emigration tax was levied on rich Jews, in order to assist the emigration of the poor. This new tax was also assessed as to its value in April 1938. Seligsohn expressed his hope that the amount of money thus collected would indeed help to further emigration of poorer Jews. An interesting example can be seen in Breslau, where 200 rich members of the Jewish community were ordered to pay 20% of their property for the promotion of emigration. This forced collection resulted in 1,500,000 Reichsmarks deposited in a special account for emigration.[24] The well-known Rabbi Hofmann of Breslau remarked that no rabbi would have succeeded in persuading the rich to provide such a contribution for the poor.[25]

4) In several places Jewish communities were now compelled to carry the burden of public welfare for Jews in need: the municipal institutions for public welfare would assist only where the Jewish communities were not able to do so. As to the argument of the communities that they were unable in their present state to carry this burden, their representatives were told that whether or not they had the needed financial means was of no importance: rich Jews would have to contribute part of their assets in order to support those in need.

IV.

Seligsohn also mentioned that, even though from the beginning of 1939 no violent outbreaks or mass arrests had taken place, the danger remained for a great part of the Jewish population if they failed to emigrate soon.

Concerning prayer services he wrote: "There are not enough places and a solution has been found, partly by arranging services in turn one after another – but this is not enough on holidays." At that time prayer services served not only religious people. The Jewish public in general was looking for opportunities and occasions to come together and be in friendly surroundings.

V.

Seligsohn's description of the life of Jews in Germany at the beginning of 1939 paints a sad and sorrowful picture of difficult living conditions under constant

---

[24] Willy Gluskinos, see note 17.
[25] Moshe Friedlaender, "Breslau from 1933 to 1939", Yad Vashem 01/237.

fear of arrest, and shows the obvious wish to emigrate. His description of the economic situation for Jews in general and for each individual only adds to it.

The report seems to be a very important document of Jewish life in Germany in early 1939, seen through the eyes of a central member of this community. Seligsohn mentioned that "... in Germany there are no more Jewish people who believe in the possibility of living in Germany forever and who also wish to continue living there". Contrary to this statement he expressed his doubt about mass emigration to Shanghai. His doubts seem to have been based on tactical considerations (mass emigration there could cause prohibition of entrance and thus prevent rescue of German Jews in case of emergency), as well as on the grounds of fear of the unknown (as against suffering in a Jewish environment).

At this stage the author could not have foreseen a future of deportations and the murder of nearly all the Jews in Germany who did not succeed in finding and escaping to a harbouring country.

Conscience, Conflict and Politics. The Rescue of Political Refugees from Southern France to the United States, 1940–1942

BY ANNE KLEIN

"And so a defeatist attitude toward the refugee problem, created by the opponents of democracy, becomes a defeatist attitude toward democracy itself."[1]

I.

When the well-known journalist Dorothy Thompson published her analysis of the refugee question in March 1938, she launched a new debate about US immigration policy with a strong appeal to decision-makers to oppose the National-Socialist expulsion of innocent citizens and to take responsibility for the refugee problem in Europe. In France, a centre of German emigration, more than ten thousand refugees were waiting for their visas to the United States. Immediately after the National Socialists annexed Austria, there began a new mass emigration of Jewish people to Czechoslovakia and France. The US administration, however, proved to be unreceptive. At the first international refugee conference in the summer of 1938 in Evian, government representatives confirmed the existing quota regulations and the implementation of restrictive immigration legislation.[2]

As Nazi aggression expanded over Western Europe, and the French army capitulated, the US president and other leading figures were obliged to respond to the pressure of the pro-refugee lobby by initiating measures to rescue the victims of Nazi persecution. The fate of political refugees in southern France, many of whom were interned in concentration camps, aroused particular sympathy in American intellectual circles. Pressure groups formed committees to demand the liberalisation of immigration laws. On 22nd June 1940, Hamilton Fish Armstrong, publisher of the journal *Foreign Affairs* and member of the President's Advisory Committee on Political Refugees (PACPR),[3] presented a list of the

---
[1]Dorothy Thompson, *Refugees. Anarchy or Organisation?*, New York 1938, p. 12; see *idem, Kassandra spricht. Antifaschistische Publizistik 1932–1942*, Leipzig–Weimar 1988, pp. 61–87.
[2]See Salomon Adler-Rudel, 'The Evian Conference on the Refugee Question', in *LBI Year Book XIII* (1968), pp. 236–278; and Ralph Weingarten, *Die Hilfeleistung der westlichen Welt bei der Endlösung der deutschen Judenfrage*, Berne–Frankfurt am Main 1981, p. 59.
[3]The PACPR was established in May 1938 ahead of the Evian Conference. Among its members were Hamilton Fish Armstrong, Paul Baerwald, chairman of the American Joint Distribution Committee, and Joseph F. Rummel, Archbishop of New Orleans and president of the Committee for Catholic

most famous *émigrés* in Europe to the White House. The Jewish Labor Committee, the American Jewish Congress and a group of Orthodox rabbis also telegraphed a list with seven hundred names. A delegation of the American Federation of Labor made a request to the president to expedite the immigration of the listed persons and their families.[4]

To co-ordinate the various activities, the Emergency Rescue Committee (ERC)[5] was constituted on 25th June 1940, three days after the Franco-German armistice, for the purpose of rescuing emigrants who were being persecuted by the Nazis for political or intellectual reasons from southern France.[6] Political refugees were perceived to be in great danger, because Article 19.2 of the armistice treaty stipulated that the Vichy regime was obliged to surrender all German refugees identified by the National-Socialist government.[7] Although Pétain tried to pretend, through juridical interpretations of the Article, to maintain the French tradition of providing a haven for refugees, the Franco-German agreement put an end to political asylum in France.

To organise the migration of those in danger, the administration decided to extend existing immigration regulations by granting emergency visas, thus providing a select group with the opportunity to emigrate to the United States. By promising a fast and non-bureaucratic process, the government backed the PACPR position on granting refuge to asylum-seekers – mostly artists, intellectuals and political activists.[8] The ERC staff in Marseilles was to select those refugees who qualified for an emergency visa and support them in arranging the necessary documents. The complete application had to be sent to New York, where it passed through three stages: first the ERC bureau, then the PACPR, and finally the State Department. Under the regulations of the Emergency Visa Programme, the State Department then decided whether the visa would be granted or not.[9]

Refugees from Germany. This organisation was intended to function as an intermediary between the US administration, refugee relief organisations and the Intergovernmental Comittee for German Refugees (IGCR). The PACPR's task was to advise President Roosevelt on refugee questions. The Committee only became active in the summer of 1940.

[4]David S. Wyman, *Paper Walls. America And The Refugee Crisis 1938–1941*, Massachusetts 1968, p. 139.

[5]The founders of the ERC were German emigrants such as Thomas and Erika Mann, the American Guild for German Cultural Freedom, well-known intellectuals like Alvin Johnson of the New School for Social Research, journalist Dorothy Thompson, and representatives of trades unions and Jewish organisations.

[6]Varian Fry, *Auslieferung auf Verlangen – Die Rettung deutscher Emigranten in Marseilles 1940/41*, Munich–Vienna 1986, first published New York 1945.

[7]Deutsche Bibliothek (ed.), *Deutsche Intellektuelle im Exil. Ihre Akademie und die "American Guild for German Cultural Freedom"*, Frankfurt am Main 1993, p. 429. "German" refugees meant all refugees from Germany, Austria, Czechoslovakia and Poland. See Laura Fermi, *Illustrious Immigrants. The Intellectual Migration from Europe 1930–1941*, Chicago–London 1968, p. 85.

[8] In the United States there existed no law for granting asylum. After the war, the government responded to the refugee problem with the Displaced Persons Act (1948) and the Refugee Relief Act (1952).

[9]DB EB 73/21 Helmut Marciewicz. In the archives of the Deutsche Bibliothek, Frankfurt am Main, there are the dossiers of 183 refugees, 47 women and 136 men, who were supported by the ERC after 1940 (DB EB 73/21). The size and content of the dossiers vary: some of them contain 150 pages,

Varian Fry and the Rescue of Jews

Historical research has treated the rescue of refugees by the ERC in various ways. It has been pointed out that the organisation succeeded in saving over 2000 *exilés* of the European intellectual and political elite from Nazi persecution.[10] Many of those rescued, such as Hannah Arendt, Heinrich Mann and Marc Chagall, greatly influenced the intellectual climate in subsequent years.[11] Little attention has been given to the fact that most of those in danger were saved only because ERC staff members were courageous enough to work in clandestine conditions, using illegal methods of escape.[12] The ERC violated the regulations pertaining to the Emergency Visa Programme, which stipulated that the rescue of refugees should only be carried out within the boundaries of the law. This inevitably lead to a severe conflict with the US administration. When the United States Holocaust Memorial Museum opened in 1993 with an exhibition on the ERC, the museum's director, Yeshayahu Weinberg, emphasised that most of the refugees owed their rescue to the courage and engagement of Varian Fry and his staff: "This story carries a moral and political lesson. In the context of the attitude of the American government at that time, Fry's decision to risk his life in order to save the lives of those destined for persecution and murder is an outstanding act of heroism."[13]

This essay will focus on the tense relationship between the legal rescue programme and illegal escape activities. Its thesis is that the Emergency Visa Programme, as a rescue programme, was in fundamental conflict with a restrictive immigration policy designed to keep refugees out of the country. As the task of Varian Fry and his co-workers was to implement this programme, they were confronted simultaneously with a rescue assignment and restrictive regulations.[14] What decisions did the ERC staff take in the face of these contradictory instruc-

---

others only three. They include personal letters, cables between the two ERC offices, correspondence with other refugee relief organisations and the PACPR, and bureaucratic material such as application forms for emergency visas. In the ERC file can also be found the documents of the International Relief Association (IRA). These organisations worked closely together and were amalgamated in 1942 into the International Rescue and Relief Committee (IRRC). See Aaron Levenstein, *Escape to Freedom – The Story of the International Rescue Committee*, New York 1983.

[10] See Wolfgang D. Elfe, 'Das Emergency Rescue Committee', in John M.v. Spalek and Joseph Strelka eds,, *Deutschsprachige Exilliteratur*, Bern–Munich, 2 vols., 1989; Hans-A. Walter, *Deutsche Exilliteratur*, vol. III, *Internierung, Flucht und Lebensbedingungen im Zweiten Weltkrieg*, Stuttgart 1988, pp. 318–342 and 358–372; Patrik von zur Mühlen, *Fluchtweg Spanien-Portugal. Die deutsche Emigration und der Exodus aus Europa 1933–1945*, Bonn 1992, pp. 48–53 and pp. 183–185.

[11] Varian Fry reports on the literary activities of former ERC clients now living in the United States in his article 'What Has Happened To Them Since', in *Publisher's Weekly*, 147 (23rd June 1945), pp. 2434–2437.

[12] See the reports of staff members Fry, *Auslieferung auf Verlangen*; Daniel Bénédite, *La Filière Marseillaise. Un chemin vers la liberté sous l'occupation*, Paris 1984; Lisa Fittko, *Mein Weg über die Pyrenäen. Erinnerungen 1940–41*, Munich 1989; Mary Jane Gould, *Crossroads Marseilles 1940*, New York 1980.

[13] Newsletter of the United States Holocaust Memorial Museum, November–December 1993, p. 6. Some ERC clients were rescued with the help of emergency visas without encountering any difficulties. See Sigrid Schneider, 'Deutschsprachige Journalisten und Publizisten im New Yorker Exil', in Spalek and Strelka, *Deutschsprachige Exilliteratur*, vol. II, pp. 1257–1299.

[14] The work of all refugee relief organisations was hampered by the restrictions placed on immigration by the United States. See Juliane Wetzel, 'Fluchtpunkt New York. Jüdische Auswanderung aus

tions? Why were they forced to use illegal methods when a visa programme existed? What requirements had to be fulfilled to qualify as an applicant? Did these criteria correspond adequately with the refugees' situation? Or did they place new barriers on emigration? British and American historians researching the political response of the United States to the refugee problem during the Second World War have largely agreed that US immigration policy prevented the effective rescue of Jews and anti-Fascist refugees.[15]

ERC documents[16] and papers from the Varian Fry collection[17] allow a deeper insight into the conflict which emerged from the contradiction between rescue and restriction than in previous research. This paper will focus upon two aspects. On the one hand there is the Emergency Visa Programme, which defined the basic rules for rescue activities. On the other, there is the local context, with its possibilities and conditions for clandestine escape. The war, and increasing xenophobic and antisemitic persecution, forced ERC staff to work fast, but to act with circumspection. Under these circumstances, each decision of the committee in Marseilles was a decision of conscience: for abiding by the law or for helping refugees.[18]

II.

In the context of US immigration policy, the Emergency Visa Programme was a special agreement with specific conditions. Two main points relating to visa applications differed substantially from normal procedure: the applicant did

---

Deutschland in die USA während der NS-Zeit', in Karin Schulz (ed.), *Hoffnung Amerika. Europäische Auswanderung in die Neue Welt*, Bremerhaven 1994, p. 180.

[15] For an overview, see Deborah E. Lipstadt, 'America and the Holocaust', in *Modern Judaism*, 10 (1990), pp. 283–196; Frank W. Brecher, 'The Western Allies and the Holocaust. David Wyman And The Historiography Of America's Response To The Holocaust. Counter-Considerations', in *Holocaust and Genocide Studies*, vol. 5, No. 4, (1990), pp. 423–446. In contrast to the other authors, Brecher emphasises that the United States had neither the responsibility nor the opportunity to rescue refugees. The US response to the refugee question should, in his opinion, be evaluated in its historical context. See Frank W. Brecher, *Reluctant Ally. United States Foreign Policy Toward The Jews From Wilson To Roosevelt*, New York–London 1991. I would also mention the important publications of Herbert A. Strauss on Jewish emigration from Germany during the Nazi regime and of immigration to the United States. See Herbert A. Strauss, *Jewish Immigrants of the Nazi Period in the USA*, vols. 1–6, Munich–New York 1978–1992.

[16] See note 9.

[17] Karen J. Greenberg (ed.), 'The Varian Fry Papers', in Sybil Milton and Henry Friedlander (eds.), *Archives of the Holocaust*, vol. 5, New York 1990.

[18] Methods associated with historical anthropology should be used in research on the phenomenon of rescue. Questions asking for abstract structures, as they are used in historical research, should be broadened into questions which could shed light on the interconnection of ideas, mentalities and motivations on the one hand, and practice on the other. Up to now studies of this topic have been mainly social-psychological. See Samuel P. Oliner and Pearl M. Oliner, *The Altruistic Personality. Rescuers of Jews in Nazi Europe*, New York 1988; Eva Fogelman, *"Wir waren keine Helden." Lebensretter im Angesicht des Holocaust*, Frankfurt am Main–New York 1995. Nechama Tec takes up the question of mentality in her historical study on the rescue of Jews in Poland during the Second World War. See Nechama Tec, *When Light Pierced Darkness. Christian Rescue of Jews in Nazi-Occupied Poland*, New York 1986.

Varian Fry and the Rescue of Jews

not fall under the quota laws, and the visa was granted directly by the State Department. This meant that the number of visas was not initially limited and that the applicant no longer depended on the arbitrary decisions of the consuls.[19] The centralisation of decision-making was accompanied by increased paperwork for the applicant. The following documents had to be submitted:

1. the regular affidavit, guaranteeing the economic autonomy of the applicant;
2. the newly-instituted affidavit of sponsorship, or moral affidavit, in effect a certificate of good conduct, which confirmed the refugee's political reliability. Questions eight, nine and ten of the form C, entitled "Affidavit of Support and Sponsorship on Behalf of Aliens Desiring to Proceed to the United States", concerned the applicant's political activities. Anarchist or Communist affiliations were of special interest, but information about membership of Fascist organisations was not required. The sponsor, who was required to be an American citizen, had to prove that he had never been a member of either a left-wing group or of the Communist Party. These declarations had to be submitted in triplicate, with two copies certified by a notary;
3. a detailed *curriculum vitae* of the applicant, also written by an American citizen, which was decisive in judging the level of danger in which the applicant lived, and whether he or she qualified for representation by the ERC. This statement also provided important information about the applicant's potential contribution to American culture.[20]

The certificates, the moral affidavit and the biographical sketch were all designed to investigate the applicant's political convictions,[21] and thus to prevent the entry of left-wing and Communist *émigrés*. From the beginning of the war in Europe, a new argument characterised the debate on immigration and asylum in the United States: refugees were compared to Trojan horses who, having arrived, would turn out to be subversive enemies of democracy. This propaganda fed restrictionist attitudes in all strata of society. The public was alarmed by the increasing number of foreigners, who were defined by nativist ideology as a danger to American democracy.[22] Public opinion polls showed

---

[19]The Visa Division of the State Department cabled the names of those who had been granted a visa to the consulates in Southern France. A decision could still be made by the consuls to delay the visa procedure. See Walter, *Deutsche Exilliteratur*, vol. II, *Europäisches Appeasement und überseeische Asylpraxis*, Stuttgart 1984, p. 472; Haim Genizi, 'James McDonald and the Roosevelt Administration', in Pinchas Artzi (ed.), *Bar-Ilan Studies in History*, Ramat Gan 1978, pp. 285–306, here p. 297.

[20]DB EB 73/21 Walter Meckauer.

[21]Anna Seghers emphasises, in her report on the escapes from southern France, that enquiries into the political convictions of the refugees had moral implications for single female refugees. "How should a single woman like me get two American sponsors, who would guarantee that I have never embezzled money, condemn the Hitler-Stalin-pact, do not, did not and will never sympathise with the Communists, at no time welcome any strange men into my room, lead, have led and will always lead a moral life?" See Anna Seghers, *Transit*, Darmstadt–Neuwied 1985, p. 107.

[22]For a discussion of the interconnection of prejudices concerning immigration and radicalism, see Herbert A. Strauss and L.P. Liggio, 'Einwanderung und Radikalismus in der politischen Kultur der Vereinigten Staaten von Amerika', in Spalek and Strelka, *Deutschsprachige Exilliteratur*, vol. I, pp. 168–194.

that 71% of those polled believed that the Germans had already started to build up an army of Fifth Columnists. Neighbours came under suspicion of being members of radical movements. In a single day, in May 1940, the FBI received 2,900 allegations of espionage.[23]

Some political representatives, such as Under-Secretary of State Breckinridge Long, stirred up xenophobic sentiment. During 1940, sixty bills were put forward aimed either at restricting immigration or at curtailing the rights of foreigners.[24] The restrictionists argued that "the enemy within" had been responsible for the capitulation of France, because liberal French immigration policies had permitted the subversion of the French government and army by Nazi agents and spies. US spokesmen claimed that German refugees constituted more than half of those in the French army arrested on charges of military espionage.[25]

The US administration had reacted to the National Socialists' rise to power by establishing an investigation committee to observe Fascist activities. When Samuel Dickstein, who had lobbied for the committee to be set up in 1934, demanded a new investigation into the Nazi danger three years later, the House of Representatives rejected it.[26] In 1939, Congress decided to install a Special Committee to Investigate Un-American Activities in the United States.[27] Surveillance was no longer directed against alleged Nazi activities, but was instead aimed directly against left-wing intellectuals, Communists, Socialists, labour leaders and even supporters of the New Deal.[28] Hearings of "revolutionary radicals" supposedly confirmed "dangerous connections"[29] between Communist organisations and liberal circles. The Committee's members shared the conviction that "hostility to the Constitution, overthrow of the government, Communism and Jewry" were closely connected. Jewish refugees and immigrants from all over Europe were stigmatised as "enemies of the American nation".

Previously, restrictive refugee policies and resentment against foreigners had been legitimised by economic and social arguments; now explicitly political arguments shaped the discussion on the refugee question.[30] In May 1940, the administration took its first steps towards putting this new development into political practice: the Immigration and Naturalisation Service, which had

---

[23] Walter, *Europäisches Appeasement*, p. 445.
[24] Richard Breitmann and Alan M. Kraut, *American Refugee Policy and European Jewry, 1933–1945*, Bloomington 1987, p. 275.
[25] During August 1939, 200 German Jews serving in the French army were arrested on suspicion of espionage. See Timothy P. Maga, *America, France, and the European Refugee Problem, 1933–1947*, New York–London 1985, p. 149.
[26] Strauss, *Jewish Immigrants*, p. 273.
[27] This committee was intended to work for a period of only seven months, but was active until 1945.
[28] In 1931, Congressman Martin Dies presented a bill to legalise the ban on Communists immigrating to the US, and the deportation of those who already lived there. The liberals voted against it. See Hans J. Wendler, *Universalität und Nativismus. Das nationale Selbstverständnis der USA im Spiegel der Einwanderungspolitik*, Hamburg 1978, p. 254.
[29] The committee had the power to summon witnesses, and tried to extract confessions of Communist affiliations. See Strauss and Liggio, 'Einwanderung and Radikalismus', p. 179.
[30] Strauss states that, although political reasons were decisive, they were sometimes hidden behind economic arguments. See Strauss, *Jewish Immigrants*, p. 189.

previously formed part of the Labour Department, was transferred to the Justice Department. Labor Secretary Frances Perkins, who had supported demands for the liberalisation of immigration policy, was thus deprived of responsibility for this sensitive area.[31] Perkins herself believed that this was due to a change in attitude within the administration towards the refugee problem.[32] Roosevelt stated at a press conference that it was necessary to legalise measures against saboteurs and spies in order to protect national security.[33] At the same time, Congress passed the Alien Registration Law with a majority of 382 to four.[34] The law, which came into force on 1st July 1940, required that the 4.9 million foreigners living in the United States provide fingerprints and details of their affiliations to political parties and groups. Even newcomers and visitors were subject to this investigation procedure. The law allowed for the deportation of members of Communist and Fascist parties. Advocate Robert Jackson, who was responsible for the Immigration and Naturalisation Service, affirmed that, from then on only refugees who were able to prove a hundred per cent loyalty to American interests would be allowed into the United States.[35] With the new law, the State Department virtually stopped granting visas altogether.

Viewed in this context, the conditions were less than favourable for the successful implementation of the Emergency Visa Programme. The programme aimed primarily to rescue those refugees who had actively opposed Hitler, many of them labour leaders, Communists, social democrats and anti-Fascist artists or intellectuals, and most of them of Jewish origin. The political resentment directed against all anti-Fascist refugees applied particularly to the clients of the ERC. To submit an application for an emergency visa, the sponsors had to provide precise details of the special political persecution of the applicant. A claim based on racial persecution alone was regarded as insufficient.[36] Information about membership of left-wing organisations could have fateful consequences. Various examples show that this applied especially to refugees suspected of sympathies with Communist ideas. Two ERC clients interned in Le Vernet camp in southern France, for example, were refused visas because Vichy officials explained, when asked by Breckinridge Long, that both of them were Trotskyists.[37]

---

[31]Frances Perkins, Eleanor Roosevelt – who was said to be the conscience of her husband – and Dorothy Thompson belonged to a group of women leaders which pressed for women's rights and asylum for refugees within the context of a general human rights policy.
[32]Henry Feingold, *The Politics of Rescue. The Roosevelt Administration and the Holocaust 1938–1945*, Chicago–London 1968, p. 140.
[33]Wyman, p. 187.
[34]The law, known as the Namen-Smith Act, was the legal basis for the conviction of eleven Communists in 1951.
[35]Wyman, p. 188.
[36] The Emergency Visa Program used the definition of political refugee adopted by the League of Nations in 1938. Hannah Arendt shows that, in the face of antisemitic persecution, this definition was highly inadequate. See Hannah Arendt, *The Origins of Totalitarianism*, 2nd edn., London 1958, p. 280.
[37]See Claus-Dieter Krohn, 'Nobody has a right to come to the United States. Die amerikanischen Behörden und das Flüchtlingsproblem nach 1932', in *Exilforschung*, vol. 3 (1985), p. 134.

The reliability of sponsors was also the subject of inquiry, even if this meant a delay of months before visas were granted. Nora Block, who after the war became a judge in the High Court in Kassel, and her sister waited in vain for their visas. Their sister's husband, Leo Gallagher, was an American citizen and was therefore allowed to provide an affidavit on their behalf, but when it became known that he sympathised with the Communists his declaration was not accepted.[38] Both women were refused visas, and after the Germans occupied southern France in 1942 they escaped to Switzerland with the help of friends.

Instructions to administrative staff about enquiring into the political convictions of applicants often led to absurd results. After his return from Marseilles to the United States, Varian Fry reported the following incident: an American vice-consul asks a German Jew from the camp in Gurs what he would do if he was admitted to the United States and was asked to do something against the interests of the Italian or German government. The man answers that he would do what was in the interest of the United States. "'Visa refused,' the vice-consul snaps. 'We don't want anyone in the United States who is going to get mixed up in politics.'"[39]

It is ironic that the Emergency Visa Programme began just at the point when legal measures against foreigners had reached a peak. Closer inspection shows, however, that the programme itself had an ambivalent character. It was not only intended to implement legal rescue but was also the first example of the new refugee policy. In contrast to the usual quota and visitor's visa, for which questions of nationality, health and economic autonomy were of central importance, the emergency visa procedure focused on the political convictions of the applicant. The programme therefore created an image of refugees as potential enemies of American democracy. The State Department could not guarantee, as it had originally promised, a swift and non-bureaucratic implementation of the programme because of the protracted enquiries into the political convictions of applicants and sponsors. At the end of September 1940, the PACPR protested vociferously against the procedure, complaining that only forty of the 567 visa applications submitted to the State Department since the previous August had been dealt with.[40] Subsequent negotiations between the Justice Department, the State Department and the PACPR ended in a compromise. The Emergency Visa Programme continued, but new bureaucratic hurdles were instituted. From now on, all applications were to be submitted to a committee of inquiry. This Interdepartmental Visa Review Committee (IVRC) had to decide, on the sole criterion of national security, whether or not to accept applications. The Justice Department apparently prevented the implementation of even stronger measures. When Breckinridge Long attempted to introduce measures to curtail the right of foreigners to free speech and association, the Justice Department declared such restrictions unconstitutional.[41]

---

[38]Helga Haas-Rietschel and Sabine Hering, *Nora Platiel. Sozialistin, Emigrantin, Politikerin. Eine Biographie*, Cologne 1990, p. 110.
[39]Varian Fry, 'Our Consuls at Work', in *Nation* (2nd May 1941), p. 508.
[40]Wyman, p. 143.
[41]Breckinridge Long was one of the leading anti-Communist and antisemitic restrictionists. See Walter, *Europäisches Appeasement*, p. 476; Feingold, p. 146.

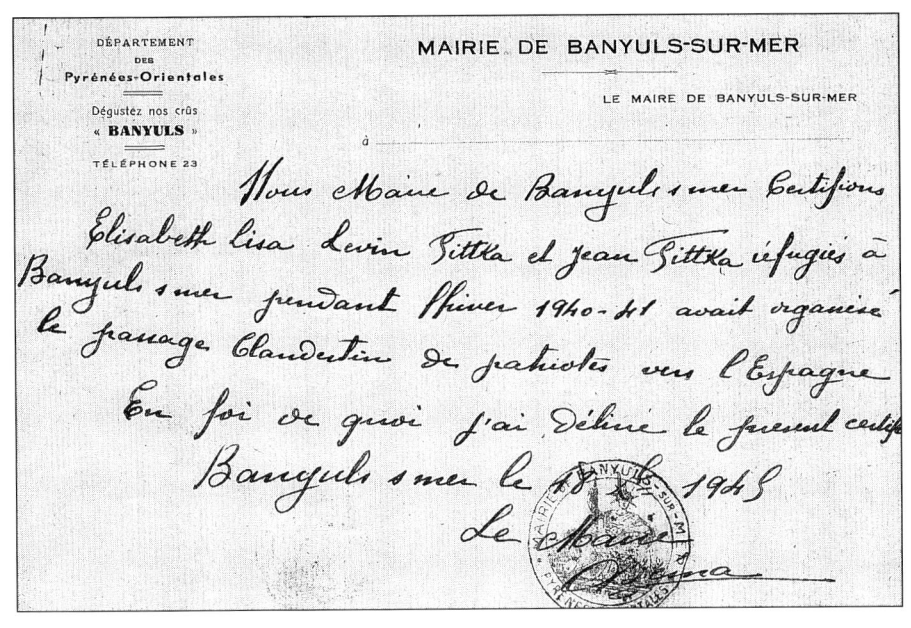

The false papers issued to Lisa Fittko by Marie-Ange Rodrigues, secretary of the Town Hall in Banyuls-sur-Mer, who forged the mayor's signature. The name was changed and the "agency for foreigners" invented.

By courtesy of Lisa Fittko

Members of the American Rescue Centre at the train station in Cerbere.
Daniel Benedite is third from the left.

By courtesy of the Rare Book and Manuscript Library, Columbia University

Members of the Emergency Rescue Committee at the Villa Air-Bel near Marseilles. Seated from left to right are Charles Wolff, Theodora Ungemacht Benedite, Daniel Benedite, Lotta Feibel Ludwig Coppermann, Maurice Verzeano and Jean Gemahling.

By courtesy of the United States Holocaust Memorial Museum Photo Archives, Washington D.C.

Varian Fry in the offices of the American Rescue Centre

By courtesy of the Museum of Modern Art, New York

III.

On 4th August 1940, Varian Fry arrived in Lisbon. He had entered into an agreement with the ERC staff in New York that he would, by the end of August, investigate the possibilities of refugee support in Portugal and southern France, and that he would also arrange the emigration of some of the persecuted mentioned on a "First List".[42] The agreement allowed for a delay of two months for his return. In October he would receive his last salary as an employee of the Foreign Policy Association.[43] The rescue operation was to have finished at this point. In fact, Fry worked feverishly for more than a year for the rescue of refugees from southern France. On 29th August 1941 the Vichy police expelled him as an undesirable alien. Without the support of the US administration and with few financial resources, he had, by the time he was expelled, organised with his staff at Marseilles the emigration of nearly 2,000 refugees.

After the French capitulation, the port at Marseilles became a centre of emigration, transit and internment, because here the refugees could complete all the formalities necessary for emigration.[44] Outside the town was the American consulate, where visa applications for the United States had to be made. The prefect of the department Bouches-du-Rhône was the only prefect authorised by the Vichy government to distribute French exit visas.[45] Each relief agency – and without their support an emigration would not have been successful – had a branch office in Marseilles.

In the second half of 1940, the Vichy regime began to intern those refugees in the Marseilles region who had the slightest chance of acquiring an overseas visa: men in the camp Les Milles, and women and children in four hotels in the city centre.[46] After the Franco-German armistice, German refugees had felt comparatively secure in the south of France. They did not know that soon the newly-established Vichy regime would declare them the pariahs of the new France. Following initial administrative chaos, Vichy established an organised bureaucratic structure with clearly defined antisemitic and xenophobic aims. More than 15,000 French citizens who, as immigrants, had received their citizenship under the recent Blum government, were deprived of their French passports in July 1940.[47] A law passed on 3rd September provided for the internment,

---

[42]The ERC correspondence contains a "First List", a "Dubinsky List" and an "American Federation of Labor List", which were clearly used synonymously. Among trade unionists the subject of whose name should appear on the list and whose not was much discussed. See Jack Jacobs, *Ein Freund in Not. Das jüdische Arbeiterkomitee in New York und die Flüchtlinge aus den deutschsprachigen Ländern, 1933–1945*, Bonn 1993, pp. 11–17.

[43]Greenberg, pp. 1–3, document 1.

[44]Donna Frances Ryan, *Vichy and the Jews. The Example of Marseilles 1939–1944*, Washington 1984. Donna Frances Ryan has expanded her research in the study *The Holocaust and the Jews of Marseilles: The Enforcement of Anti-Semitic Policies in Vichy France*, Washington 1996.

[45]*Ibid.*, p. 96.

[46]André Fontaine, *Le Camp d'Étranger Des Milles 1939–1943*, Aix-en-Provence 1989.

[47]Robert O. Paxton, *Vichy France. Old Guard and New Order 1940–44*, New York 1972, p. 170.

without trial, of all *étrangers indésirables*. The anti-Jewish statute of October the same year provided for the internment of all foreign Jews.[48]

The agreement to surrender political refugees was, from the beginning, one of the most striking examples of political collaboration between France and Germany. The Vichy regime was now empowered to decide who received an emigration visa, and all applications had to be submitted to the Minister of the Interior.[49] Refugees were afraid that German government officials had access to the lists of applicants and could demand that they be handed over. Pétain stated officially that he was interested in the further migration of refugees to the United States, not in delivering them to the Germans.[50] Vichy, however, handed over 5,889 interned refugees and a list of all others to the German *Kundt-Kommission* following an inspection of thirty concentration camps in southern France.[51] The refugee question became one of the main touchstones of co-operation between France and Germany. Between August and December 1940, the ERC was unable to procure any exit visas for its clients.[52] During the first two months after the armistice, the frontier to Spain could be passed by foot or even by car, because it was not kept under surveillance. Once the political situation in Vichy had stabilised, however, refugees could no longer count on the passivity of the French border officials, who now formed armed patrols where once they would have shown the refugees, in a friendly manner, the route to Spain.[53] Without a valid exit visa it was impossible to pass the border patrol.

The French police increasingly interfered in the work of the administrative body. Harry Kriszhaber, a well-known trade unionist, and his wife Maria, were cross-examined by the French police when applying for an exit visa they never received.[54] In addition, a French exit visa was a prerequisite for applying for an emergency visa. If the refugee could not show this visa to the American consul, he or she could not receive an emergency visa.[55] Eleanor Roosevelt, informed by the ERC about this bureaucratic obstacle, turned to Secretary of State Welles, who explained that the administration wanted the ERC and the refugees to avoid violating French laws.[56]

---

[48]The law required all foreign Jews to register at the *préfecture*. Those who registered were later interned; for those who did not, it meant living under illegal conditions. See Denis Peschanski, 'The Statutes on Jews October 3, 1940 and June 2, 1941', in *Yad Vashem Studies XXII* (1992), pp. 65–88.
[49]Ryan, *The Example of Marseilles*, p. 263; Fry, *Auslieferung auf Verlangen*, p. 107.
[50]Maga, p. 190.
[51]Christian Eggers, 'Die Reise der Kundt-Kommission durch die südfranzösischen Lager', in Jacques Grandjonc and Theresia Grundtner (eds.), *Zone der Ungewißheit. Exil und Internierung in Südfrankreich 1933–44*, Reinbek bei Hamburg 1993, pp. 235–248. Herschel Feibel Grynszpan, who had assassinated the German ambassador in Paris, was among those handed over.
[52]Greenberg, p. 4, doc. 2; Fry, *Auslieferung auf Verlangen*, p. 67.
[53]Fry, *Auslieferung auf Verlangen*, p. 148.
[54]DB EB 73/21 Harry Kriszhaber. There existed a special understanding between the German and French police, intended to circumvent the official agreement on the surrender of German emigrants. See Barbara Vormeier, 'Die Lage der deutschen Flüchtlinge in Frankreich. Sommer 1939 bis Juli 1942', in Grandjonc and Grundtner, pp. 217–223.
[55]Maga, p. 185.
[56]If the United States did not react positively to the Vichy regime, neither did it question its legitimacy. See Wyman, p. 142.

These contradictory rules, which blocked the whole emigration process, placed many refugees in a hopeless position. The writer and educator Sofie Lazarsfeld was threatened with internment because her residence permit had expired, but the emigration visa had not been granted.[57] The persecuted lived in a "state of captivity," as one of the refugees phrased it.[58]

Before Fry arrived in Marseilles, Walther Victor had stressed in a letter to friends in the United States the need to find a way out of this *impasse*. At that time Dr. Frank Bohn was on his way to southern France with instructions from the American Federation of Labor, and especially from the Jewish Labor Committee, to support refugees. So far he had not succeeded in organising the departure of those in danger. Victor wrote: "Rapid action is needed, and it is high time that an energetic and active person is sent over here by clipper, who has full power to do everything that is necessary and who can handle the situation efficiently in this extreme emergency."[59]

When Fry arrived in Marseilles he had to deal immediately with the fact that emigration could not be organised legally. The most important task, therefore, was to establish a clandestine escape structure.[60] Other relief organisations worked strictly within legal boundaries, but at that time the ERC was the only group which helped the refugees to leave southern France.[61] News of its activities not only travelled through refugee circles, but also aroused the suspicion of the local police. When the queue in front of Fry's room at the Hotel Splendide became longer and longer shortly after his arrival, the police arrested some of the waiting people and questioned them about his activities.[62] Fry also reported that he was frequently observed by "snoopers", under direct order from the *Sûreté Nationale* in Vichy.[63] To avoid further suspicion, he soon established an officially registered welfare centre for refugees in the Rue Grignan, the *Centre américain de Secours* (CAS).[64] This was a tactical step in a long-term strategy: under the cover of refugee relief, the ERC staff hoped to be able to organise the escape of the refugees with less difficulty.

Police repression was not the only reason for building up a clandestine structure. The legal and bureaucratic boundaries forced staff to work in grey areas of legality. "Rescue through emigration" was not as easily achieved as the committee in New York had thought. The refugee lobby there had endeavoured to create

---

[57]DB EB 73/21 Sofie Lazarsfeld. The situation became more flexible when the American government decided to grant visas for those refugees who could submit an affidavit in lieu of a passport, i.e. a permit to stay in France. See Bénédite, p. 64.
[58]DB EB 73/21 Walther Victor.
[59]*Ibid.*
[60]In a letter to the New York bureau, Fry criticised Bohn's tactic of "confessing". See Fry in Ingrid Warburg-Spinelli, *Erinnerungen. Die Dringlichkeit des Mitleids und die Einsamkeit, nein zu sagen*, Hamburg–Zürich 1991, p. 189.
[61]For example, HICEM opened the bureau a few months later when the French government began to grant exit visas.
[62]Fry, *Auslieferung auf Verlangen*, p. 47.
[63]When Pétain visited Marseilles in December 1940, the ERC staff was arrested for several days. See *ibid.*, pp. 163 and 179.
[64]*Ibid.*, p. 51.

the opportunity for further immigration by pushing through the Emergency Visa Programme. Subsequent events, such as Vichy stopping all exit visas, had not been taken into account.

The refugee lobby had also ignored the complexities of the visa programme itself. Almost no refugee could fulfil the conditions for an emergency visa. Those who possessed a valid passport, a French exit visa, a Spanish and Portuguese transit visa, an American immigration visa, the different affidavits of American citizens, and the proof of a paid passage could consider themselves lucky. In most cases, at least one of the missing documents had to be forged. Almost no-one, for example, possessed a valid passport, although this was a precondition for applying for the other necessary documents. In fact, most of the refugees were stateless. The National-Socialist regime had deprived them of citizenship after their emigration because they were anti-Fascists or Jews, or because their passports had expired and could not be renewed without contacting the German authorities.[65] Although thousands were affected by this measure, the western democracies had no political instrument with which to react. Statelessness, as well as homelessness, as Hannah Arendt wrote, appeared as "an unfortunate exception to an otherwise sane and normal rule".[66] International agreements, such as the League of Nations *Convention concernant le statut des réfugiés provenant d'Allemagne* of 1938,[67] provided identity papers for stateless persons, but there was no guarantee that the United States would acknowledge this passport-substitute.[68] The Spanish authorities also demanded the presentation of national identity papers before granting a transit visa.[69] The ERC therefore had to arrange for identity papers for all those who took the route through Spain and Portugal. Varian Fry contacted the Czech consul in Marseilles, Vladimir Vochoc, who placed many newly printed Czech passports at his disposal. They could hardly be distinguished from the original ones.[70] "If a consular office ever was necessary, it was then," Vladimir Vochoc later wrote in his records.[71] The consuls of Poland

---

[65] By July 1933 the German government had passed into law the revocation of naturalisations and the withdrawal of citizenship from Jews. This was directed against political *émigrés*, but also against Jews from eastern Europe who were naturalised during the Weimar Republic. A contemporary survey is given by Hugo Emmerich and John Rothschild, *Die Rechtslage deutscher Staatsangehöriger im Ausland*, Haarlem 1937.

[66] Arendt, *Origins of Totalitarianism*, pp. 267–268; Isaac Kornfeld, 'The tragedy of people without nationality', in *Contemporary Jewish Record*, vol. II, No. 3 (1939), pp. 42–48.

[67] This agreement shows that refugees were still defined according to national categories even when they were stateless.

[68] The United States was not a member of the League of Nations. In any case, this institution was without any real power because of the contradiction of national sovereignty and transnational policies. See Richard Kohn, *Reflections on Modern History. The Historian and Human Responsibility*, New Jersey 1963, p. 327; Louise W. Holborn, 'The League of Nations and the Refugee Problem', in *Annals of the American Academy of Political and Social Science* (Refugees), No. 203 (May 1939), p. 124.

[69] Sybil Milton and Frederick D. Bogin (eds.), *Archives of the Holocaust*, vol. 10, *American Jewish Joint Distribution Committee*, New York–London 1995, p. 809, document 163.

[70] This shows the fluid frontiers between legality and illegality during that time. Vochoc could not get any more passports from Prague, but in his function as consul he had the right to arrange the printing of Czech passports in France. See Fry, *Auslieferung auf Verlangen*, p. 30.

[71] Archiv der sozialen Demokratie, NL Vladimir Vochoc (transl. by Vera Pikowa).

Varian Fry and the Rescue of Jews 299

and Lithuania acted as courageously as Vochoc by willingly providing national passports for ERC clients. When presenting a Polish passport, refugees even had a good chance of receiving a French exit visa.[72] Because this regulation only applied to men and women over forty-eight years old, the birth date on the passport was changed accordingly.[73] In the most complicated cases, the ERC engaged the Austrian caricaturist Bill Freier, alias Willy Spira, to produce one of his artistic forgeries. The stamp was so perfect that only experts could see that it had been drawn by brush.[74]

The missing exit visa was the biggest obstacle to emigration because it was impossible to replace it with a forgery. The French border patrol would have recognised at once that it was not an original document. There were, therefore, only two options: to bribe the border patrol for one of its exit visas[75] or to cross the border illegally, which seemed to be the more certain way out of France.

IV.

"Escape relief is something quite different from refugee relief."[76] This important distinction is made by Patrik von zur Mühlen in his research on the escape routes of German anti-Fascist emigrants through southern Europe. While refugee relief ameliorates the consequences of exile and asylum-seeking by improving the living conditions of the refugees, escape relief aims to rescue the persecuted by removing them to safety by all possible means. To choose the latter required ERC staff to transgress legal boundaries and to breach their official loyalty to the Vichy regime and to the US administration. They had to use their own values and convictions of human dignity as a maxim for political action. Fry himself thought that it was a mistake to use the term "underground work" to describe escape relief, because what was done did not happen underground but only under a cover, which in itself seemed to be completely above suspicion.[77]

By adopting this attitude towards the refugee problem, the ERC differed completely from other American relief agencies. As Anne Grynberg has shown in her study on the Nîmes Committee, the alliance of relief organisations in southern France was not even prepared to protest openly against the French internment policy and demand the release of the interned.[78] At a meeting in November

---

[72] Milton and Bogin, p. 791, document 158; Fry, *Auslieferung auf Verlangen*, p. 107.
[73] DB EB 73/21 Nathan Thon; Fry, *Auslieferung auf Verlangen*, p. 57. It can be safely assumed that the passports usually hid the real identity of the refugee.
[74] Fry, *Auslieferung auf Verlangen*, p. 65.
[75] Milton and Bogin, p. 809, document 163.
[76] Von zur Mühlen, p. 43.
[77] *Ibid.*, p. 50.
[78] The Nîmes Commitee was the representative organ of 25 French and international, religious and humanitarian relief organisations in southern France. The French-Jewish organisations also supported more radical definitions of refugee relief. OSE (*Oeuvre de Secours aux Enfants*), for example, in 1942 established a rescue structure for Jewish children. See Anne Grynberg, 'Das Nîmes-Komitee oder die Grenzen der Philantropie', in Grandjonc and Grundtner, pp. 474–490; Sabine Zeitoun, *L'OSE du légalisme à la résistance, 1940–1944*, Paris 1988.

1940, Daniel Bénédite, Fry's closest colleague in Marseilles, proposed to the Committee that it publicly accuse Vichy of degrading refugees. If Vichy was not prepared to change the situation, he suggested, the Committee should call upon the US administration to halt all support for the French population. The representatives seemed to be paralysed. Bénédite remembered: "With some exceptions, my 'colleagues' looked at me with disapproval. I am an angry disturber, nearly an obsessive. There is an outcry against my words, which are seen as unfortunate, if not rebellious. They contradict me: 'We would make an enemy of those whom we hope to convince and whose good will is not doubted at all' etc. Donald Lowrie [representative of the Young Men's Christian Association and president of the Nîmes Committee] finishes the discussion with a dry and reproachful 'Monsieur, here is not the place to talk politics'."[79]

There was a consensus among the other relief committees in southern France that refugees should be aided on a humanitarian basis, and that criticism of the political conditions which had created the refugee problem in the first place was to be avoided. The organisations of the Nîmes Committee, for example, offered to take over the care of the camp inmates and the running costs of the internment camps themselves – which the Ministry of the Interior readily accepted.[80] In contrast, the ERC staff rejected the internment system totally, and refused to become willing executioners of a dehumanising policy. They understood that there was no future for refugees on the European continent in the face of racist and antisemitic persecution. From this they drew the conclusion, justified by subsequent events, that the only option was to transfer those in danger beyond the National Socialists' reach.

Shortly after his arrival in Marseilles, Varian Fry began to build up the clandestine structure necessary for organising illegal escapes. He could refer, on the one hand, to commercial underground organisations, and, on the other hand, to social networks of an incipient resistance to the Vichy regime. Many political *émigrés* had already gained experience in underground work, including Lisa and Hans Fittko, who had been engaged in anti-Fascist activities before and after their escape from Nazi Germany.[81] When the couple finally received French and Portuguese transit visas and American emergency visas in September 1940 Lisa Fittko went to the Spanish border to find out how to leave France illegally. Friends had told her that she should contact the mayor of Banyuls-sur-mer, who was said to show solidarity with the refugees in every respect.[82] When Varian Fry learnt that Lisa Fittko had taken Walter Benjamin over the frontier to Spain,[83] he asked her and her husband to work for the ERC committee. The escape route used up to then was perceived to be too danger-

---

[79]Bénédite, p. 140 (transl. by the present author).
[80]Grynberg, 'Das Nîmes-Komitee', p. 474.
[81]See Lisa Fittko, *Solidarität unerwünscht. Erinnerungen 1933–1940*, Munich 1992.
[82]Konrad Scheurmann and Ingrid Scheurmann (eds.), *Für Walter Benjamin. Dokumente, Essays und ein Entwurf*, Frankfurt am Main 1992, p. 146.
[83]After Benjamin was turned back at the Spanish border, he committed suicide in his hotel at Port Bou.

ous, following an article about the escape of Lion Feuchtwanger and his wife, published in the *New York Times* on 6th October, which had divulged the smugglers' path over the Pyrenees.[84] Jeopardising their own lives, the Fittkos decided to provide escape relief for ERC clients using the "F-route".[85] Lisa Fittko later reflected on the decision: "Our task now is to escape this trap. We have to rescue ourselves and we have to try to save one another. Thus we can help to free Europe and the whole world of barbarism."[86]

The little village of Banyuls-sur-mer, near the Spanish border, became a centre of the ERC's escape activities. The population eagerly accepted both the couple and other passing refugees. Mayor Azéma confiscated, in the name of the municipality, a large building and there set up the *Centre d'Hébergement de Banyuls pour les réfugiés*. A French hotelier offered his house as a hiding-place for refugees without registering their names, despite a legal requirement to do so.[87] The success of the rescue efforts depended on local support, the good-will of influential politicians and the help of officials working in the administration. For the rescue workers, this network provided protection against the police and the secret services, which were active at the Franco-Spanish border. The mayor himself issued a sort of identity paper for the Fittkos and offered the couple advice on how to avoid being recognised as foreigners by the border patrol.[88]

From the beginning, the ERC planned the escape network with great care and professionalism. Several factors made this necessary. First, the CAS in Marseilles had to be careful not to be seen to be involved with clandestine activities. Second, the escape workers themselves needed a sheltered space in which they could work without hindrance. Third, the ERC had to ensure the safety of the refugees. The purpose of the support networks was to save the lives of human beings. The committee staff, therefore, had to proceed very carefully to make sure that refugees who had entrusted themselves to an organisation which, in many cases, was their last hope of survival, were not exposed to further danger.

Maurice Verzeanu, who worked at the Marseilles bureau, was the contact person for the Fittkos.[89] In October 1940 he met the couple for the first time, to prepare the next trip over the Pyrenees. Lisa Fittko reported in her diary: "We agreed that the ERC should send us only three persons at a time, because otherwise the risk would be too high. To offer security we will be informed in advance who will come; we already know the refugees they will send us next week. In all cases we will be sent one half of a torn piece of paper and the refugee will carry the other half. This simple old method is still relatively

---

[84]*New York Times*, 6th October 1940.
[85]The letter "F" stood for the couple Fittko and was used as a code by ERC staff. This old smugglers' path had previously been known as *la route Lister*, after General Lister of the Spanish Republican army.
[86]Fittko, *Solidarität unerwünscht*, p. 214.
[87]Greenberg, p. 34, document 7.
[88]Fittko, *Mein Weg über die Pyrenäen*, p. 153.
[89]Maurice Verzeanu was a doctor and a Romanian emigrant. He was originally meant to look after the health of ERC clients. After Beamish (the codename of the German emigrant Albert Hirschmann) had departed, Verzeanu took over the organisation of the illegal escape routes.

reliable."[90] The so-called "invisible staff",[91] an underground network of around ten helpers, accompanied the refugees through southern France to the Spanish border, and provided them with money, hiding places, food and the documents necessary for escape. Among those *"hommes et femmes de confiance"*[92] were French Socialists, and Spanish, Italian and German emigrants, who never appeared in the Marseilles bureau but with whom Verzeanu made special appointments at secret locations.

When, at the beginning of December 1940, Mayor Azéma was replaced by a Pétain appointee, the political climate grew more hostile, and summonses to the gendarmerie and border controls increased. The Fittkos had to take more safety precautions but were nevertheless able, until March 1941, to lead up to eight refugees a week over the border to Spain. The unpredictable behaviour of the refugees was one of the main risks for clandestine work. Many emigrants found it difficult, for example, to obey the committee's instructions to take only a small bag over the mountains in order not to be recognised from a distance as refugees by the border patrol.[93] Other refugees, such as two former secretaries of the SDP executive, under the pressure of secrecy and illegality, suddenly broke down *en route*. Only by virtue of his rigorous authority could Hans Fittko ease the crisis and persuade them to go on.[94] A third group of refugees simply could not imagine using the path over the Pyrenees. Amongst these there were Rudolf Breitscheid and Rudolf Hilferding, former SPD ministers and members of the *Reichstag* during the Weimar Republic. For them, it was unthinkable that statesmen and party representatives should use illegal methods, even if it meant saving their lives. Both were taken to Paris by the French police in February 1941, before being extradited to Germany.[95]

During the first six months of its existence the Marseilles ERC bureau used most of its budget to finance clandestine rescue operations. A large proportion was used to pay for forged passports and safehouses. Bénédite wrote in a confidential letter that four-fifths of the visa costs, a total of 200,000 francs, was spent on forged papers and the same sum on accommodation, food and travel expenses.[96] To maintain the reputation and credibility of the organisation in the US, it was never made official that donations were being used to finance illegal activities. This would have meant a loss of confidence and consequently a loss of support. In the publicity material aimed at encouraging sponsorship of the ERC, the

---

[90]Fittko, *Mein Weg über die Pyrenäen*, p. 136. By comparing Fry's report with that of Lisa Fittko, it becomes obvious that Fry underestimated the role of Lisa Fittko in the refugee rescue, compared to that of her husband.
[91]Fry, *Auslieferung auf Verlangen*, p. 181.
[92]Bénédite, p. 109.
[93]Dr. Hirschfeld, a former member of the Prussian Reichstag, did not want to give away his valuable fur coat, and thus attracted the attention of the border control. See Fittko, *Mein Weg über die Pyrenäen*, pp. 180–182.
[94]*Ibid.*, p. 165.
[95]See *ibid.*, pp. 183–185; Bénédite, pp. 175–188.
[96]The exchange rates from dollar to franc varied enormously. The ERC usually used the black market.

escape operations were not even mentioned.[97] For reasons of security, underground work did not appear in the official book-keeping of the Marseilles bureau. Bénédite wrote: "Everyone knows, of course, that certain refugees left 'on the quiet', but officially we did not help them ... so when we began to fear that our books might be examined, we destroyed these compromising papers."[98] But the staff in New York found it hard to cover for the Marseilles bureau. The New York staff faced pressure from the US government, which demanded strict adherence to the law. After the smugglers' path over the Pyrenees became known, the State Department advised the American embassy in Vichy to withdraw all means of support for the ERC.[99]

When, during Pétain's visit to Marseilles in December, the entire ERC staff was arrested for some days, the New York bureau decided to recall Fry and replace him with the journalist Jay Allen, hoping thereby to force the Committee to keep its operations legal. Faced with this provocation, Varian Fry queried whether there was any common basis for co-operation. In a letter of 21st January 1941, he wrote: "Therefore, if, as Mr. Allen kindly suggests, my name is mud in your eyes, please let me know and I shall sever all connections with you, however remote. If, on the other hand, you think, as I hope and believe you do, that I have done a hard job these last six months, inform him and ask him to resign the 'mission' you gave him."[100]

Fry repeatedly emphasised the autonomy of the Marseilles bureau. Not only had an extraordinary team succeeded in building up a functioning refugee relief operation at a time of severe political instability, but American citizens who lived in southern France had, to a great extent, sponsored the escape work. If the New York bureau was unwilling to support the rescue any longer, the Marseilles bureau would manage without that support. On his departure to France, the ERC at New York had written to Fry "that your personal judgement must, under the circumstances existing, play a large part in the success or failure of your efforts on our behalf",[101] but his unconventional interpretation of "rescue through emigration" was highly criticised within his own organisation. Only a few of the committee members in New York agreed without reservation with his decision to continue the rescue without support from the US administration. Max Ascoli, who was responsible for Italian refugees, was one of those who showed complete commitment to Fry. In a letter to the ERC's executive board, he quoted the words of his friend Lussu at Lisbon: "Fry is extremely courageous. He is bravely and unostentatiously going through an extremely difficult time, because of a series of extralegal actions that the French police half suspect ... If you have in the United States a medal for civilian bravery, Fry deserves it utterly for the way he has been behaving here for months on the edge of the war."[102]

[97]See finance report in the brochure '602 Lives. The First Year of the Emergency Rescue Committee', in Milton and Bogin, pp. 670–678, document 143.
[98]Greenberg, p. 24, document 3.
[99]Fry, *Auslieferung auf Verlangen*, p. 155.
[100]Greenberg, p. 54, document 13.
[101]*Ibid.*, p. 1, document 1.
[102]*Ibid.*, p. 63, document 17.

V.

At the beginning of 1941, when the Vichy regime began to support the refugees' efforts to organise emigration by granting emigration visas, the situation eased. Dr. Frank Kingdon, chairman of the ERC, telegraphed from New York that the purpose of rescue should be given priority over personal conflicts,[103] thus signalling a preliminary peace offer. After all, the Marseilles bureau could now boast the first rescues to have taken place under completely legal conditions. An administrative report shows that under the new regulations many ERC clients now received their exit visas, having applied for them months before.[104] An interdepartmental commission in Vichy had decided in principle that each emigrant was allowed to leave France, with the exception of political refugees whose names appeared on the lists of the French Minister of the Interior.[105] The question of which refugees should be delivered to the Germans had by now clearly been decided between Germany and France.[106] About fifty ERC clients from the Montauban region emigrated successfully. When the Germans occupied northern France, many members and supporters of left-wing emigrant groups and clients of Jewish relief organisations[107] had escaped to this town. With the support of the municipality and of the local population, the refugees established a well functioning self-help structure.[108] There were also useful contacts with political sympathisers in the United States, and before his departure, Varian Fry had been explicitly instructed to look after the refugees in Montauban.[109] Thanks to the ERC connection, the refugees living there were soon able to apply for their various emigration documents.

Harry and Maria Kriszhaber, Austrian-Jewish emigrants and former trade union activists, had applied for an emigration visa on 11th October 1940. Because of the new regulations, in February 1941 the prefect commanded them, in writing, to take part in the next *"départ collectif d'émigrants"* via Martinique[110] At 11 a.m. on the 25th February, at Villebourbon station, they would receive their passports and documents.

Although these refugees had fulfilled all the conditions of the Emergency Visa Programme, the United States reacted with strict controls when they arrived in the US. Up to now American representatives had argued that Vichy was

---

[103] *Ibid.*, p. 57, document 14.
[104] *Ibid.*, p. 8, document 2.
[105] Walter, *Internierung, Flucht und Lebensbedingungen*, pp. 183 and 288.
[106] Ryan, *The Example of Marseilles*, p. 283.
[107] In Montauban Austrian socialists, members of the *Internationaler Sozialistischer Kampfbund* (ISK) and different Communist opposition groups met. Hannah Arendt met her future husband Heinrich Blücher here following her internment at Gurs. See Elisabeth Young-Bruehl, *Hannah Arendt. For Love of the World*, New Haven–London, 1982, p. 156.
[108] Karel Sternberg, a young Czech refugee, represented the Montauban emigrants and later became chairman of the ERC's successor-organisation in New York. See, for Montauban, Henry Jacoby, *Davongekommen, 10 Jahre Exil 1936–1946*, Frankfurt am Main, n.d., pp. 87–89 and 95–113; Reinhard Otto, *Wie haste det jemacht? Lebenslauf von Hanna Grunwald-Eisfelder*, Soltau 1992, p. 30.
[109] Greenberg, document 1, p. 3.
[110] Martinique was a French colony and one of the few possible sea routes in war time.

blocking the emigration of the persecuted; now it became clear that political refugees were not welcome in the United States either.[111] The restrictionist refugee legislation did not offer much scope. On the one hand, the Alien Registration Law required the registration of all foreigners; on the other, the committee established in the framework of the Emergency Visa Programme once more scrutinised the political reliability of the refugees. Both regulations had to be taken into consideration, and because officials were unsure how to proceed, they took the refugees into safekeeping as a first step. The new arrivals were interned in hotels or provisional reception camps.[112] Using special methods of inquiry, officials tried to force them to give statements about their political convictions. Walter Mehring reported as follows in a letter to the ERC on his internment in January 1941: "When I arrived on Saturday I was arrested in this hotel; then, on Monday I was interrogated for five hours. I was accused of not possessing a passport ... not carrying enough money with me.... They asked why I came *via* Martinique rather than from Lisbon, why I denied belonging to a political party although I admitted to writing on political problems (I said: on *kulturpolitische* problems)...."[113]

Only a few months later, Roosevelt signed the Bloom-Van Nuys Bill. Under this law, the US administration arranged for the transfer of the bureaucratic standards of the Emergency Visa Programme to the general visa procedure for normal immigration.

The Emergency Visa Programme served as a model for new restrictions. The programme itself, as far as it concerned further rescue, was stopped.[114] From now on Washington decided on the issue of visas, because this had already proved an effective control in the context of the Emergency Visa Programme. Procedural regulations were also extended to immigration as a whole. Now each applicant had to submit a biographical sketch, the moral affidavit and financial guarantees.[115] In addition, each visa application was submitted to a committee.[116] The staff of the American consulate was explicitly authorised to refuse a visa if there was reason to suspect that the applicant was engaged in activities which endangered national security.

Together with this new law, a regulation was introduced which has become known as the "hostage instruction". A "close relatives" statement was aimed at preventing the immigration of refugees whose relatives still lived under the Axis powers. The official explanation was that the *Gestapo* could force these immigrants to spy against the US by blackmailing them with threats of repression against their relatives in Germany or in the occupied countries. The "close relatives" statement had to be provided in triplicate, with two copies notarised. The

---

[111] On 9th January 1941, the *New York Times* published an article about the mutual blame placed by the US and France for the refugee problem. See *New York Times*, 9th January 1941.
[112] DB EB 73/21 Siegfried Thalheimer; Walter, *Europäisches Appeasement*, p. 484.
[113] DB EB 73/21 Walter Mehring.
[114] Wyman, p. 194.
[115] *Ibid.*, p. 195.
[116] The visa application was submitted to the Primary (Visa) Committee, to the Interdepartmental Visa Review Board and, if necessary, to the Appeals Committee. See Breitmann and Kraut, p. 135.

sponsor had to confirm the place of residence of all of the applicant's close relatives. If the applicant had relatives in Germany or in the occupied countries, he or she was asked how often they were in contact. If a relative had died, this had to be mentioned, along with the date and cause of death.[117]

The ERC staff had learned, in the middle of May 1940,[118] that the "close relatives" regulation had been applied to the first few cases, but none of the ERC members in Marseilles knew with what applicants had to comply, nor which documents had to be submitted under the new regulation.[119] Applications were no longer processed and visas which had already been granted were no longer issued after 1st July 1941. Each refugee had to submit a complete new application according to the current regulations.[120] "This decision is scandalous," complained an ERC supporter.[121] Some refugees who had already complied with regulations and whose visas had been granted were not issued their visas, while others did not know whether their visas would come through at all under the new regulations. Robert Keller and his family remained in France because of a tragic coincidence. Their visas had been granted in New York, but the French postal service had failed to deliver the cable from the American consul in Lyon. The family had still not left France when the new regulations came into force.[122] Alfons Zinner, also a client of the ERC, had been arrested trying to escape through Spain. When his brother anxiously asked what could be done, the ERC could only tell him that his visa for the United States was no longer valid under the new conditions.[123]

Finally, at the end of July, the new forms became available. Käthe Vortriede, waiting in Switzerland for her US visa, was asked by the consul to submit the testimony of two sponsors. The forms were then sent to the State Department for examination. Outraged by this bureaucratic procedure, Käthe Vortriede's son asked the ERC whether this "long-winded action" could not be shortened.[124]

The new regulations constituted an almost insurmountable hurdle for the *émigrés*. To prove they faced political persecution, they often provided evidence not only of their own experience but also of repression against their relatives. The "close relatives" regulation allowed these statements then to be used against the applicant.[125] Almost every emigrant had left behind relatives in Germany or in German-occupied countries. Persecution and escape had torn families apart. Old people, women and invalids who had stayed behind were subsequently deprived of their rights, arrested and deported to the camps. The refugees tried to keep in contact, hoping to meet their relatives again.[126]

---

[117]DB EB 73/21 Willi Wolff, Walter Meckauer, Willy Steiner.
[118]DB EB 73/21 Margarete Wertheim.
[119]DB EB 73/21 Marcel Verzeanu.
[120]DB EB 73/21 Eva Stedeli.
[121]DB EB 73/21 Heinz Michaelis.
[122]DB EB 73/21 Robert Keller.
[123]DB EB 73/21 Alfons Zinner.
[124]DB EB 73/21 Käthe Vortriede.
[125]Wyman, p. 199.
[126]Until the Nazis halted all Jewish emigration from the German *Reich* in October 1941, the *Reichsvereinigung der Juden in Deutschland* tried to organise the emigration of those who still lived in German

Varian Fry and the Rescue of Jews

The "close relatives" regulation condemned the refugees to stay in France. This became increasingly dangerous as the situation in Vichy came to a head. On 21th July 1941 the Vichy regime issued the second anti-Jewish statute, requiring the registration of all Jews within a month. A wave of raids and internments swept over southern France. All efforts to organise further emigration broke down.[127] A few months later, the *Reichssicherheitshauptamt* (RSHA) enacted a decree stating that Jews were no longer allowed to emigrate from Vichy France. The National-Socialist government planned to retain the Spanish transit visa for those Jews who still lived inside Germany, to speed up their emigration.[128] In the face of the imminent deportation of foreign Jews, the difference between leaving and remaining soon became the difference between life and death.

On 29th August 1941, Fry was deported. An expulsion order signed by Rodellec du Porzic, chief of the Marseilles police, stated that this measure was necessary because Fry had helped Jews and anti-Nazis. During interrogation a few weeks before, du Porzic had predicted: "I know that you in the United States still believe in the old idea of human rights. But even you will adopt our point of view one day. This is only a question of time. We have recognised that society is more important than the individual. You will also recognise this."[129] Events, however, had already overtaken du Porzic's prognosis. When the State Department learned that Fry was smuggling refugees out of France, the Secretary of State cabled that the State Department "would not accept activities bypassing the laws of countries with which the United States maintains friendly relations".[130] In the middle of 1941, as the war threatened the western hemisphere, and with interest in rescuing the refugees having reached its lowest point, the US administration tried to push through Fry's departure from Marseilles. He had been in France for eight months without valid papers, because his passport had only been renewed on the assumption of his immediate return to the United States. Eileen Fry, Varian Fry's wife, turned to Eleanor Roosevelt to ask her to support her husband in his rescue efforts in France. But the president's wife, although she had formerly supported the interests of refugees, refused: "I think he will have to come home because he has done things which the government does not feel it can stand behind."[131]

---

areas. Those who had already emigrated were asked to support those who had stayed behind. See Konrad Kwiet, 'Gehen oder Bleiben? Die deutschen Juden am Wendepunkt', in Walter Pehle (ed.), *Der Judenpogrom 1938. Von der "Reichskristallnacht" zum Völkermord*, Frankfurt am Main 1988, p. 139.

[127] Paxton, *Old Guard and New Order*, p. 185.
[128] Ryan, *The Example of Marseilles*, p. 226; Marrus and Paxton, *Vichy and the Jews*, p. 226.
[129] Fry, *Auslieferung auf Verlangen*, p. 261.
[130] *Ibid.*, p. 101.
[131] Greenberg, p. 62, document 16.

VI.

After Fry's expulsion at the end of August 1941, his French colleagues in Marseilles continued working until the French police closed down the bureau on a charge of subversive activity in August 1942.[132] During that time, the staff tried to make the safehouses more secure, and in a cloak-and-dagger operation, took some of the most imperilled refugees over the border to Switzerland. ERC staff in New York supported the applicants in fulfilling the new regulations. Thus at least 300 refugees succeeded in emigrating to the United States.

Because the Emergency Visa Programme had officially ended, and the whole visa procedure was blocked, the ERC staff did not initially know what to do. They therefore tried to obtain more detailed information on some of the cases with the help of Lena Fagan, who had contacts in the Visa Division of the State Department. The ERC first contacted her on 11th August 1941 about the case of Marcel Verzeanu. Almost three weeks had passed since his "close relatives" statement had been submitted, and the visa had not yet been granted.[133]

ERC staff were unsure whether, in outstanding cases, the PACPR should be used or even mentioned. The PACPR had explicitly been responsible for the political refugees in the context of the Emergency Visa Programme. Now, under the new regulations, it appeared unwise to mention the political persecution of the applicant. However, as Lena Fagan stated, it was impossible to influence the proceedings. The Visa Division automatically received a copy of each case submitted to the PACPR, and it was therefore pointless to pretend that the applicant was totally apolitical, although this would have increased his or her chances of obtaining a visa.[134]

The PACPR, which had protested against the halting of the Emergency Visa Programme, tried to establish better visa regulations by talking personally to President Roosevelt. Subsequently, from 1st December 1941, new regulations concerning refused visa applications came into force. Although the administration ignored the PACPR's central demand that the "close relatives" statement be abolished and that the FBI and the secret service be excluded from the committees, each rejected applicant could now appeal against the decision. The applicant's supporters could act as witnesses to speak in favour of the refugee. This regulation applied to all applicants, including those who had been refused their visas on political grounds. Their number increased when the United States entered the war on 7th December 1941, and the administration ordered the examination committee to grant no more visas to so-called "enemy aliens". The Interdepartmental Visa Review Committee was replaced by an even more complex system of committees, with the process now including five stages of appeal.[135]

---

[132]*Ibid.*, p. 96, document 29.
[133]DB EB 73/21 Marcel Verzeanu.
[134]DB EB 73/21 Ludwig Ullmann.
[135]Wyman, p. 201. The title Interdepartmental Advisory Committee was also used. See Mark Wischnitzer, *Visas to Freedom. The History of HIAS*, Cleveland–New York 1985, p. 177.

There is no evidence of a single decision in favour of an applicants. ERC files show that applications became stuck in this labyrinthine system. Walter Meckauer, who had been refused a visa in September 1941 because of the "close relatives" regulation, wrote despairingly to the New York *émigré* newspaper, *Aufbau*, in January 1942: "You know that shortly after the first authorisation the blocking of visas was ordered, and that after having submitted the close relatives statement and waited for those protracted formalities, on 29th September 1941 the ERC transmitted my complete file to the PACPR. From here it should have been passed on to Washington at the end of October, so I hoped to get the definite visa confirmation in December. But then the events of the war intensified and here we are now cut off from everything...."[136] Meanwhile the committees negotiated the case of Walter Meckauer. The Duke of Württemberg, chairman of International Catholic Help for Refugees and one of Meckauer's sponsors, was summoned to be heard in front of the committee. The committee members, especially the representative of the State Department, wanted to know whether Walter Meckauer was a Communist or at least a member of a party with Communist tendencies.[137]

Anna Stein, who appeared as a witness in the case of Walter Kakies, and Helene Caspary, who testified in the case of Otto Weinrich, also reported that the committee was mainly interested in the applicants' political attitudes.[138] The mode of questioning resembled a cross-examination rather than an enquiry, apparently aimed at confusing the witnesses in order to catch them giving false testimony. In the case of Walter Kakies, the committee members faulted his application because evidence of the deaths of his mother and brother was missing. The fact that Kakie's fiancée, who already lived in the United States, had only shortly been divorced from her former husband, also aroused their suspicions.

After the United States had entered the war, ERC clients had almost no hope of receiving a visa. Applicants for an emergency visa remained stigmatised as political activists because the Emergency Visa Programme had provided visas especially for political refugees. Moreover, they were now declared "enemy aliens". The statements of their sponsors were mostly insufficient to overcome doubts about the refugees. In the case of Walter Meckauer, the State Department informed the ERC in August 1942 that new doubts had arisen, and that it was therefore awaiting a report from the consul in Nice.[139] When, in September, the French police raided buildings in the Cote d'Azur, Meckauer was forced to escape to Switzerland, where all trace of him was lost. Klaus Dohrn, who had been arrested during his attempt to escape through Spain, was only released through the intervention of the Catholic Church. In May 1942, he had still not received a visa for the United States. Varian Fry turned to Senator Wagner, who tried to obtain information on the visa procedure directly from the State Depart-

---

[136] DB EB 73/21 Walter Meckauer.
[137] *Ibid.*
[138] DB EB 73/21 Walter Kakies, Otto Weinrich.
[139] DB/EB Walter Meckauer.

ment.[140] Avra Warren, the president of the Visa Division, put him off with the comment that the Dohrn case belonged in the category of "enemy alien" and had to be re-examined by the committees.[141]

The examination procedures continued without reaching positive conclusions. United States policy was directed towards winning the war and not towards saving refugees. To achieve a national consensus on entry into the war, the government ostracised foreigners and stigmatised "the inner enemy". The war-time alliance with the Soviet Union had no effect on severe anti-Communist attitudes in the United States.[142] At the same time, unprecedented open antisemitism heightened tensions in American society.[143]

VII.

The establishment of the Emergency Visa Programme created very few opportunities for potential immigrants. Instead of realising, as it had promised, the fast and unbureaucratic escape of refugees at risk, the programme created new barriers to immigration. Few refugees qualified for a visa, and those who did were unable to prove their political reliability, or their applications became stuck in the labyrinth of committees, or they were declared to be "enemy aliens" because they had left relatives in the German *Reich*, of whom they did not know whether they were still alive or whether they had been killed by the Nazi terror. Time was lost, and it became increasingly difficult to escape from southern France. Varian Fry emphasised in his letters to the New York bureau the necessity of doing everything possible to speed up the granting of visas at the State Department. He demanded: "Tell them [State Department officials] of the suicides ... the increasing poverty of these people.... Tell them of the horrific conditions in the camps, the high death rate ... and tell them that it depends on them whether the European elite can be rescued or not."[144]

In contrast to the ERC staff in New York, which worked on refugees' files and which promoted public campaigns in support of the refugees in southern France, the relief workers at Marseilles were in constant close contact with the refugees. They could not avoid recognising that helping refugees to escape was the only way of preventing them being relinquished to the Germans. The Emergency

---

[140]Senator Wagner had a record of promoting further immigration. In 1939, for example, he had supported the rescue of 20,000 refugee children in the Wagner–Rogers Bill, which failed in Congress.

[141]DB EB 73/21 Klaus Dohrn.

[142]In a letter to Hannah Arendt, Mary McCarthy reported in March 1952 that, during a meeting with Varian Fry, he had spoken heatedly to her of the perceived need "to keep dangerous elements out of our society". He said that he himself had been under observation for nine months although well-known anti-Communists had confirmed in writing that he was politically reliable. See Carol Brightman (ed.), *Between Friends. The Correspondence of Hannah Arendt and Mary McCarthy, 1949–1975*, London 1995, p. 6.

[143]Arthur Miller fictionalised the history of antisemitic hounding in the United States at the end of the Second World War. See Arthur Miller, *Focus*, New York 1945.

[144]Report by Fry, in Warburg-Spinelli, p. 198.

Varian Fry and the Rescue of Jews

Visa Programme, however, did not provide a realistic basis for rescue. The decision to lead refugees out of the country illegally and to provide them with forged papers meant that the ERC staff had to be willing to transgress legal boundaries. In open conflict with the US administration and the Vichy regime, each relief worker was personally at risk. The decisive influence here was apparently not so much the consciousness of resistance[145] as the belief that "solidarity"[146] was an important principle of democratic politics. To take responsibility for persecuted people without regard to nationality, religion or political beliefs was seen as an important factor for international peace and human rights. This conviction led Varian Fry in particular to work tirelessly against time and against the bureaucracy for the rescue of the refugees. He wrote in a letter to the New York staff: "I have nearly become a monomaniac concerning my work. I think of nothing else, dream of nothing else, speak of nothing else ... but I want to stay here because I do not simply believe but I really *know* that I am doing something good in the world and from that I draw a deep satisfaction which I never knew existed."[147]

From today's standpoint, the refugee problem, and asylum as a phenomenon in the historical process before the Holocaust, carries specific importance.[148] Even if it is true that the ERC could not have rescued more refugees, this does not mean the conflict of conscience has passed. It is a cause for concern that the rescue of the few[149] was only possible because some people dared to establish their own moral standards as a yardstick for action. They decided *against* complying with given legal regulations, and *for* civil disobedience. They relied only on their own power of judgement. Only thus could they retain what Hannah Arendt once called "some minimum of humanity in a world grown inhuman".[150]

One purpose of historical research should be to illuminate and appreciate this phenomenon. As a researcher one is confronted with the insoluble problem of not being able to do so with traditional research methods. Questions which enquire into the interconnection of conscience, morals and ethics on the one hand, and political action on the other, are often brushed aside as not of scientific relevance, but as the sociologist Zygmunt Bauman emphasises, the meaning of the Holocaust strongly informs present-day challenges to humanity. He writes: "It does not matter how many people chose moral duty over the rationality of self-preservation – what does matter is that some did."[151]

---

[145]The importance of this form of resistance is emphasised by Jacques Semelin, *Unarmed against Hitler. Civilian resistance in Europe 1939–1945*, Westport, Conn.–London 1993.
[146]Fry, *Auslieferung auf Verlangen*, p. 10.
[147]Report by Fry, in Warburg-Spinelli, p. 200.
[148]See Dan Diner, 'Die Katastrophe vor der Katastrophe. Auswanderung ohne Einwanderung', in Dirk Blasius (ed.), *Zerbrochenene Geschichte. Leben und Selbstverständnis der Juden in Deutschland*, Frankfurt am Main 1991, pp. 138–160.
[149]See Hans Sahl, *Die Wenigen und die Vielen. Roman einer Zeit*, Frankfurt am Main 1959.
[150]Hannah Arendt, *Men in Dark Times*, London 1970, p. 17.
[151]Zygmunt Bauman, *Modernity and the Holocaust*, Cambridge 1989, p. 207.

*The Debate About German-Jewish
Relationships Continued*

German History and German Jewry: Boundaries, Junctions and Interdependence

BY STEVEN E. ASCHHEIM

The following scattered reflections are offered in the form of a quite unsystematic, indeed playful, *Denkschrift*.[1] It is intended as a means of generating and exploring ideas and examining new directions of thought and research, rather than as a polished, fixed product. In a sense it is a preliminary response to the symposium on "German-Jewish History" conducted in the *LBI Year Book XLI* (1996)[2] and a tentative attempt to go beyond the "dead end" to which Shulamit Volkov has drawn our attention by providing some possible contours for the desired "new beginning".[3]

In order to begin this task we have to think through the ways in which Jewish and European history intersect beyond the familiar narratives of apologetic "contribution" history or even the more sophisticated emancipation-assimilation-integration model. Despite their obvious differences, both approaches assume a kind of one-way historical direction in which Jews are remade, absorbed (or not absorbed) into the given, normative external structures – the homogenising centralising nation state, market forms of economy, secularising cultures and so on. This, in many ways, has been the master-narrative around which modern Jewish history, at least in Western and Central Europe, has been constructed. Historians have examined the complex ways in which such transformations have proceeded and analysed the relative successes and failures of such integration.

I am not for the moment questioning either the obvious power and validity or the palpable and continuing fruitfulness of this model but I am interested here in examining some of its (usually unstated) assumptions and suggesting some possible supplementary viewpoints. Whether written from a "liberal" or a "national-Zionist" point of view, this transformative, integrative, modernising

---

[1]The following was presented, with minor changes, at the workshop on "Varieties of Multiculturalism in Modern European History: The Case of the Jews" in Jerusalem (5th–9th January 1997) as part of an ongoing project on "The Integration of Jewish History into Modern European History Curricula".

[2]See the articles by Evyatar Friesel, 'The German-Jewish Encounter as a Historical Problem. A Reconsideration'; Christhard Hoffmann, 'The German-Jewish Encounter and German Historical Culture'; Samuel Moyn, 'German Jewry and the Question of Identity. Historiography and Theory'; Shulamit Volkov, 'Reflections on German-Jewish Historiography. A Dead End or a New Beginning?' in *LBI Yearbook XLI* (1996).

[3]Volkov, pp. 309–320, here p. 320.

model, while certainly not a passive one, is almost always posited in uni-directional, "absorbtive" terms, in which Jews in one way or the other appropriate the majority normative culture. Thus even David Sorkin's brilliant revisionist account, *The Transformation of German Jewry, 1780–1840*, which demonstrates the creative making of a modernised new form of Jewish identity, paradoxically sees its origins in the drive to integration. This appropriative drive and the primary use of German cultural materials to effect this operation, Sorkin argues, rendered that sub-cultural identity, as a new basis for separation, invisible even to its own makers.[4]

How can we begin to think differently about these matters? How can we conceptualise the relationship between "normative" national and "minority" Jewish history? In which ways, for instance, can the new "multi-cultural" sensitivity be brought to bear? Of late, some historians have suggested that its emphases may be helpful in challenging traditional conceptions of the centralised, homogeneous nation-state. By rethinking the making of Europe "in unfamiliar terms such as diasporas, borderlands, and peripheries", John Gillis has recently argued, we will be able to rediscover the remarkably diverse (yet repressed) multi-cultural and multi-ethnic nature of that civilisation.[5] Such an approach may significantly help to challenge and transform accepted perceptions and definitions. Amongst other things it questions the given, static categories of centre and periphery, and seriously problematises notions of set "minority-majority" relations. The young scholar Till van Rahden has persuasively suggested that, in relation to both German and German-Jewish history, a sensitivity to the multi-cultural dimension may lead us to question the "givenness" of a prior, normative German culture into which Jews (and other groups) were to be "fitted".

In this view assimilation is regarded less "as a process in which outsiders increasingly adapt to a stable core culture" than one in which so-called "'minorities' have a hand in defining and redefining 'majority' culture".[6] This holds out the somewhat mischievous possibility of reconceptualising not only German-Jewish but German history itself.[7] Now, instead of (always somewhat perplexedly) registering the (never easy or comfortable) "contributions" and adaptive presence of Jews within German life, and analysing their integration (or otherwise) into what are taken to be pre-existent, static, normative structures, the very creation of crucial aspects of emergent society, for example of German liberalism, market society, Socialism, intellectual culture and so on, would have

---

[4]See David Sorkin, *The Transformation of German Jewry, 1780–1840*, New York 1987, especially pp. 6ff.
[5]John R. Gillis, 'The Future of European History', in *Perspectives. American Historical Association Newsletter* 34, 4 (April 1996), p. 5.
[6]Till van Rahden, 'Mingling, Marrying, and Distancing. Jewish Integration in Wilhelminian Breslau and its Erosion in Early Weimar Germany', in Wolfgang Benz, Arnold Paucker and Peter Pulzer (eds.), *Jüdishes Leben in der Weimarer Republik / Jews in the Weimar Republic*, Tübingen 1998. (Schriftenreihe wissenschaftlicher Abhandlungen des Leo Baeck Instituts 57).
[7]Perhaps for that reason this analysis has been put forward by a young non-Jewish scholar, questioning the wisdom of his historiographical elders. For another analysis of why an increasing number of young German non-Jewish scholars are entering the field, see Hoffmann, pp. 277–290.

to be viewed dynamically as negotiated constructions in which, at critical points, the role of the Jews (whether or not they identified as such) is conceived not simply as contributory but well-nigh *co-constitutive*. As such it puts into question any "essentialising" understandings of a fixed "German" or "Jewish" culture and identity. It emphasises the fact that such complex cultures and identities are contextually and interactively constructed. This is a point to which I will return.

These suggestions can be applied throughout Central and Western Europe but they may be most fruitful in terms of Germany, where not only was the process of emancipation exceptionally protracted and contested but so too were the virtually coincidental processes of nation-building and then construction of a modern culture. From the late eighteenth century on, Jews were an integral part of this (always bitterly contested) moulding process. Ironically, liberal historians have either channelled this co-constitutive and negotiating role into the less threatening "contribution" paradigm or tended to deny it entirely because – translated into different terms – it more or less validates the claim of antisemites dissatisfied with the emergent, modernising transformations of German society. For did not the persistent and peculiarly powerful notion of "*Verjudung*" ("Judaisation"), as it developed throughout the nineteenth century and up to 1945, hold that Jews were increasingly wielding disproportionate influence, occupying pivotal positions of inordinate economic, political and cultural power and that, most dangerously, the Jewish *Geist* was seeping (or had already seeped) through the spiritual pores of the nation to penetrate and undermine the German psyche itself?[8] This notion was not merely the province of hostile antisemites. Germans of many hues expressed such sentiments to one degree or another. Indeed, the young Zionist Moritz Goldstein provoked a scandal amongst liberal Jews when, in 1912, he proclaimed that "We Jews are administering the spiritual property of a nation which denies our right and ability to do so".[9]

What do we do in the face of this dilemma? If we genuinely intend to pursue its co-constitutive foundational track, we will have to take heed of Jacob Katz's repeated observation that precisely because (unlike the liberals) they treated the Jewish dimension with deadly seriousness, antisemitic observations about Jews could at times be as revealing and insightful as their evaluations and intentions were repugnant.[10] In any case, it would not be wise for historians to be affected by either apologetic, liberal particularist blindness or antisemitic hostility. What they should do is rethink the question of the complex nature and structure of interactions and interdependencies. It would be well, for a moment, to examine the possibilities of this approach at a very late, critical moment of

---

[8] For an analysis of this in another context see my '"The Jew Within". The Myth of "Judaization" in Germany', in Jehuda Reinharz and Walter Schatzberg (eds.), *The Jewish Response to German Culture: From the Enlightenment to the Second World War*, Hanover–London 1985, pp. 212–241.
[9] See my 'Assimilation, German Culture and the "Jewish Spirit". The Moritz Goldstein Affair (1912)', in Sander Gilman and Jack Zipes (eds.), *Yale Companion to Jewish Writing and Thought in German Culture, 1096–1996*, New Haven 1997.
[10] See Jacob Katz, *From Prejudice to Destruction. Anti-Semitism, 1700–1933*, Cambridge, MA 1980, and 'Misreadings of Anti-Semitism', *Commentary* 73 (July 1983), pp. 39–44.

German history – the Weimar Republic. After all, many contemporary Germans (as well as subsequent historians) portrayed the Republic in significant, indeed constitutive, ways as "Jewish" and alien to Germans. In the more sublimated phrasing of Peter Gay this was a society in which the outsider had become insider.[11] How can we determine the nature of Weimar's inter-textual cultural inter-dependencies and tensions?

It goes without saying that Weimar Jewish culture, in all its affirmative expressions, is unthinkable outside whatever we may take to be general Weimar culture. In this sense the older "integrative" model retains its validity.[12] The question here, however, is whether the opposite applies: can one conceive of Weimar culture, that short era of explosive and astonishing creativity, without the Jewish presence?[13] If Jews (whether *qua* Jews or not) could co-found, perpetuate and thrive within its ambience it is precisely because it was characterised by freedoms and an openness unprecedented in German history. Indeed, this intensely experimental, *avant garde* and liberal atmosphere has come to define at least part of what we mean by "Weimar culture". "Without the Jews," Walter Laqueur writes, "there would have been no 'Weimar culture' – to this extent the claims of the antisemites, who detested that culture, were justified. They were in the forefront of every new, daring, revolutionary moment".[14]

Laqueur, of course, should have qualified this by mentioning that many non-Jews were also very much in the vanguard of this culture – the names of Bertolt Brecht, Erwin Piscator, Ernst Ludwig Kirchner, Otto Dix, Emil Nolde, Hermann Hesse, Carl von Ossietzky and many others spring immediately to mind. Moreover, it would be wise to mention that there were some important conservative Jewish intellectuals, men of the Right such as Leo Strauss and Karl Wolfskehl, Ernst Kantorowicz and Friedrich Gundolf of the Stefan George circle. Peter Gay is undoubtedly correct when he says that "there were many Modernists who were not Jews, many Jews who were not Modernists. And many Jews who were Modernists were so not because they were Jews". I would also agree with his contention that viewing Modernism from the vantage of the Jewish question "is sheer anti-Semitic tendentiousness, or philo-semitic parochialism...".[15]

But what I am suggesting here is something else: not that Modernism, or

---

[11] Peter Gay, *Weimar Culture. The Outsider as Insider*, New York 1968.

[12] This applies too – perhaps especially – to the post-liberal, radical, apocalyptic sensibility of those intellectual creations (of people like Gershom Scholem, Franz Rosenzweig, Walter Benjamin and Ernst Bloch) that today seem most vital to the vaunted Jewish renaissance and which most quintessentially replicate a mood characteristic of what today we understand by Weimar culture (including such right-wing thinkers as Ernst Jünger, Oswald Spengler and Martin Heidegger). See Steven E. Aschheim, 'German Jews beyond *Bildung* and Liberalism. The Radical Jewish Revival in the Weimar Republic', in *idem, Culture and Catastrophe. German and Jewish Confrontations with National Socialism and other Crises*, New York 1996. See too Michael Brenner, *The Renaissance of Jewish Culture in Weimar Germany*, New Haven 1996.

[13] I owe this formulation to Eugene Sheppard.

[14] Walter Laqueur, *Weimar Culture. A Cultural History*, New York 1976, p. 73.

[15] See the introduction to Peter Gay, *Freud, Germans and Jews. Masters and Victims in Modernist Culture*, New York 1978, p. 21.

more precisely Weimar culture, was "Jewish" but rather that it was jointly constructed by both Jewish and non-Jewish intellectuals (who were not acting in their "Jewish" or "non-Jewish" capacities.) Indeed, in this context the notion of co-constitutionality is not multi-cultural (at least not in the usual sense of the term) but rather highlights the search for, and founding of, a new sensibility in which older ethnic and religious differences are either peripheral or play no role at all.

While the co-constitutive model helps us grasp modes of interaction, we must keep in mind that the dynamics and dialectics of Weimar society were characterised by an equally important negative reaction to this perceived co-constitutionality. It is this tension that defines the era. As Laqueur puts it: "The Jews gave greatness to this culture and at the same time helped to limit its appeal and make it politically impotent."[16] The "core of the current Jewish question," Walter Benjamin painfully observed in November 1923, was the fact that Jews endangered "even the best German cause for which they stand up *publicly*, because their public German expression is necessarily venal (in the deeper sense) ... nowadays a salutary complicity obligates those individuals of noble character among both peoples to keep silent about their ties".[17]

It was precisely the widespread perception of Weimar as a *Judenrepublik*, as essentially alien, cosmopolitan, rootless, and denigrative of the German "spirit",[18] that was also the spur to creating a novel, radical, right-wing, genuinely "German" counter-cultural alternative. There is an intertextual irony here. One generally, and correctly, identifies the rise of modern, self-affirmative *Jewish* cultures (or sub-cultures) in connection with a felt need to counter a sense of debilitating dependency. The Weimar case is the strongest example I can think of that illustrates the opposite: the revolt of a putatively core, normative culture, the assertion of a self-affirmative "German" alternative, to overcome what it took to be a debilitating "Jewish" hegemony. It was exactly against and around these points of co-constitutionality that countermodels of *Deutschtum* were constructed.

Given the preliminary nature of these remarks, let me suggest that in the – still insufficiently examined – area of intellectual confrontation, this ironic process most tantalisingly reveals itself. In one way or another, and at the very highest levels, these clashes – the titanic Heidegger-Cassirer 1929 *Davos* debate on

---

[16]Laqueur, p. 77.

[17]Letter 122 to Florens Christian Rang (18th November 1923), in *The Correspondence of Walter Benjamin 1910–1940*, ed. and annotated by Gershom Scholem and Theodor W. Adorno, transl. by Manfred R. and Evelyn M. Jacobson, Chicago–London 1994. The letter appears on pp. 214–217. The quote appears on p. 215. I thank Zvi Jagendorf for drawing my attention to this reference.

[18]When in 1924 Edmund Husserl, a convert to Protestantism of many years standing, suggested that the long-standing confessional restriction on the chair of Christian philosophy at the University of Freiburg be removed ("the Catholic internationale had been accommodated to a very large extent during the war"), the Catholic scholar Heinrich Finke responded: "This is the kind of thing we have to listen to from an Austrian Jew. I've never in my life been an anti-Semite; but today I find it hard not to think along anti-Semitic lines." See Hugo Ott, *Martin Heidegger. A Political Life*, transl. by Allan Blunden, London 1993, pp. 114–115.

Kant, the confrontations between Martin Buber and various *völkisch* theologians, the subtle polemics between Carl Schmitt and Leo Strauss, whether in explicit or coded form – revolved around this tension and the desire of the non-Jewish intellectuals somehow to reassert a threatened "German" spirit.[19] Perhaps inherent to the very act of co-constitutionality is this (Bloomian) "anxiety of influence", fuelling the desire to proceed from perceived dependency to autonomy. It is a process in which the drive for separation unwittingly reveals a recognition of intimacy and the incapacity to abide it. Paradoxically, these quasi-Freudian categories beautifully capture the convoluted Freud-Jung relationship itself, a relationship that poignantly embodies the complex intertextual, interpersonal aspects of our story: the father-son, teacher-pupil relationship; Jung as the Christian outsider, and Freud bending over backwards to keep him within the fold and thus render analysis more respectable; and then the break, the revolt of the son, the parricide; and the end, in which an angry Freud pinpoints and defines the difference by confiding in their common patient, Sabina Spielrein, "We are and remain Jews...",[20] while Jung insists that he has formulated a creative, healthy "Aryan" psychology as opposed to psychoanalysis, which was sickly, destructive and "Jewish". Freud, Jung proclaimed, "did not know the Teutonic soul".[21] Out of a previous intimacy, the differences are again constructed as "essentialised", incommensurable entities.

Of course, the co-constitutive approach by definition calls into question any "essentialising" understandings of either "German" or "Jewish" culture and identity; and any development of its ideas will have to try to distinguish modes of "co-constitutionality" and identity-formation from the traditional, familiar,

---

[19] Once such an essentialising logic is unleashed, the ironies entailed in this commonplace of German cultural criticism become virtually endless. Martin Heidegger's mammoth and engaged efforts to formulate the outlines of an authentic "German spirit" are well known – although his *explicit* linking of this with the "Jewish Question" is far less so. This becomes apparent in a letter (written to Viktor Schwoerer on 2nd October 1929) in which he states: "... what is at stake here is nothing less than the need to recognize without delay that we face a choice between sustaining our *German* intellectual life through a renewed infusion of genuine, native teachers and educators, or abandoning it once and for all to the growing Jewish influence – in both the wider and the narrower sense...." But obviously the respective German and Jewish "spirits" possessed remarkable flexibility and protean qualities, at times within the same person. Thus while in 1929 Heidegger championed Eduard Baumgarten as the "great white hope of German intellectual life, a bulwark against the rising tide of Jewish influence", by 1933 he described him as "a Jewish protégé". Clearly here was a casuistic tool of political labelling that could easily boomerang against its user. Thus Erich Jaensch, a Nazi philosopher opposed to Heidegger, wrote in a report to the National-Socialist authorities that Heidegger obsessively indulged in the same "hairsplitting distinctions as Talmudic thought", a fact that inevitably attracted Jews to him. If Heidegger were to acquire influence, "our universities and intellectual life will favour those of Jewish stock... These people, even if the non-Aryan blood entered their family a long time ago, will invariably take up this hairsplitting nonsense with alacrity ... their academic careers will prosper accordingly, while our fine young Germans cannot compete because their minds are too healthy and they have too much common sense". See Ott, pp. 378, 379 and 257 respectively.

[20] The quote appears in Yosef Hayim Yerushalmi, *Freud's Moses. Judaism Terminable and Interminable*, New Haven–London 1991, p. 97.

[21] For an English translation of Jung's comments, see Frederic V. Grunfeld, *Prophets Without Honour. A Background to Freud, Kafka, Einstein and their World*, New York 1979, pp. 58–59.

model of "assimilation".[22] It is a viewpoint in which, as Samuel Moyn has recently argued in a stimulatingly instructive paper in these pages, "*Deutschtum* and *Judentum* ... deserve to be seen as constantly evolving and mutually implicated rather than ontologically fixed and polarised categories".[23] But there is a crucial disjunction here between our own historical understanding and preferences and the ways in which many nineteenth- and twentieth-century Germans either saw or wanted to shape their reality. In the first place, the "drive to uniformity" was an overall characteristic of the emergent, centralising nation-state. "Essentialist" thinking may have been an inevitable part of this process in general but given the extremely delayed, always precarious nature of German efforts first to create and then to consolidate a unified national state and identity out of radically fragmented political, religious, regional and class realities, it was at a premium there. The novelty and insecurity of its identity rendered the quest for its realisation ever-more obsessive and exclusionary. The construction of the notion of *Deutschtum*, and the evolving discourse around it, increasingly assumed an essentialist nature precisely because liberalism continued to be regarded largely as a problem rather than a solution and heterogeneity a threat rather than an enrichment.

We should remember that the term "*Deutschtum*" emerges only during the Wars of Liberation[24] and as late as 1860 the Grimms' *Wörterbuch* reports that its usage was mainly ironic.[25] Yet by the end of the century the discourse between these two contrasting hypostatisations – *Deutschtum* and *Judentum* – as warring, radically incommensurate principles, was already in place. German antisemitism is by now too familiar for it to be necessary to give examples of this. What is more interesting is that, given the increasing power of the discourse, Jews too, willy-nilly, became enmeshed in its logic and were forced to conduct the dialogue within this essentialist framework. As Jakob Wassermann put it in 1921, "The German and the Jew: I once dreamed an allegorical dream ... I placed the surface of two mirrors together, and felt as if the human images contained and preserved in the two mirrors would have to fight another tooth and nail".[26] But this was only an extreme expression of a generalised, virtually unavoidable, mode of thought. Not only extreme assimilationists but Orthodox and liberal Jews and Zionists alike were increasingly forced to negotiate within its premises. In seeking to counter, recode or deflect it or even send out an entirely different message they automatically became involved in its inner logic. From that point on, one could argue, the German-Jewish experience was defined by these essentialist categories. If these tensions and hypostatisations form part of the tragedy of German Jewry, they also prompted its unprecedented creativity, its reshaping of various fields of Jewish, German and general self-understanding and knowledge.

---

[22]The need to address this distinction was stressed by Shulamit Volkov at the conference where this paper was originally presented.
[23]Moyn, p. 295.
[24]See Friedrich Kluge, *Etymologisches Wörterbuch*, 17th edn., Berlin 1957, p. 129.
[25]Jacob Grimm and Wilhelm Grimm, *Deutsches Wörterbuch* 2, Leipzig 1860, p. 1053.
[26]Jacob Wassermann, *My Life as German and Jew*, transl. by S.N. Brainin, New York 1933, pp. 220–221.

This is a very large subject but I must come back to the ways this impinges on our problematic here. For all those concerned, even those most unwilling to accept it, there was a lurking understanding that however incommensurable they were supposed to be, *Deutschtum* and *Judentum* were as deeply co-implicated as could possibly be. "German and Jew," Walter Benjamin said, "stand opposite one another like related extremes".[27] This was true even – perhaps especially – for those who were most unwilling to accept this relationship. "Has it not struck you," Adolf Hitler is reported to have said in one of his rambling table conversations, "how the Jew is the exact opposite of the German in every single respect, and yet is as closely akin to him as a blood brother".[28] The discourse tried to cover up but nevertheless often unwillingly betrayed the perceived bond, the recognition of mutual implication as much as it generated identity and role-confusions.

To be sure, the essentialising reduction of identity rendered more plausible numerous "psychologised" definitions of Jewishness (enunciated by any number of diverse people, including Freud, Buber and Rosenzweig) as something deeply internal, invisible yet infinitely powerful, transmitted by unconscious and little understood mysterious forces.[29] Moreover, given the illiberal, threatening framework in which the discourse operated, Jews were forced more and more to state the sense of mutuality and connectedness in tragic, continuingly essentialist ways, unthinkable to Jews in more obviously pluralist cultures. Questioned about his relation to Germanness and Jewishness, Franz Rosenzweig retorted that he refused to answer: "If life were at one stage to torment me and tear me into [these] two pieces ... I would not be able to survive this operation ... I ... ask [you] ... not to torment me with this truly life-threatening question, but to leave me whole."[30]

Nothing better illustrates the degree of German-Jewish integration into German life than this and the later obsessive, horrible impulse to undertake that eradicative operation and make it truly life-destroying.

---

[27]Benjamin, Letter 55 to Gerhard Scholem (22nd October, 1917), in *The Correspondence*, pp. 97–102. The quote appears on p. 98.

[28]Quoted in Max Horkheimer, 'The German Jews' (1961), in his *Critique of Instrumental Reason*, New York 1974, p. 111.

[29]On Freud see especially chapter 5 of Yerushalmi, *Freud's Moses;* on Martin Buber see 'Judaism and the Jews', in his *On Judaism*, ed. by Nahum N. Glatzer, New York 1972, pp. 11–21; on Rosenzweig, see the quote on p. 106 of my *Brothers and Strangers. The East European Jew in German and German-Jewish Consciousness, 1800–1923*, Madison 1982.

[30]Quoted in Karl Löwith, *My Life in Germany before and after 1933*, transl. by Elizabeth King, Urbana, IL 1986, pp. 138–139.

Jewish and German-Jewish Historical Views
Problems of a New Synthesis

BY EVYATAR FRIESEL

Have we reached a dead end in our conceptual views about Jewish and German-Jewish history? Shulamit Volkov, in her thoughtful essay 'Reflections on German-Jewish Historiography. A Dead End or a New Beginning?', believes we have.[1] In the last century, Volkov explains, Jewish and German-Jewish history were considered according to two main approaches: the "liberal" (the term needs careful definition, since it has an internal Jewish significance), and the "national", sometimes also called the Zionist approach. It seems that "national" is the correct term, not in the sense that the Jews are a nationality, but that they are a people.[2] But perhaps I may suggest that instead of using the term "liberal", using "cultural", "Jewish-cultural", or even "liberal-cultural", to define the other approach. The term "liberal", in the sense used by certain sectors of German Jewry, referred more to religious orientation than to Jewish historical awareness.

According to Volkov's analysis, both views, and the complex relationship between them, still dominate Jewish historical work: "We are left, as in the past, with two alternative approaches to Jewish history. Both are products of historical circumstances and critical ideological choices." However, Volkov believes that these are "obsolete ideological constraints", and that we should try to overcome them. A major task of modern Jewish and German-Jewish historiography is to arrive at a new synthesis: "It is time for a new beginning."[3]

A different conclusion is reached by Jonathan Frankel, in a recent essay[4] which is undoubtedly one of the most serious statements on this theme written in recent years. Frankel believes that the era of the "grand generalization" in Jewish historiography has passed: "In the older historiography, the clash between community and assimilation, Eastern and Western European Jewry, centripetal and

---

[1] *LBI Year Book XLI* (1996), pp. 309–320.
[2] The difference between a national and a Zionist approach was in the underlying prognosis: the Zionists had a critical attitude towards present and future Jewish life in the Diaspora. However, regarding the interpretation of the past, there were no significant distinctions between the Jewish-national and the Zionist historians.
[3] *LBI Year Book XLI* (1996), p. 320.
[4] 'Assimilation and the Jews in Nineteenth-Centruy Europe. Towards a New Historiography?', in Jonathan Frankel and Steven J. Zipperstein (eds.), *Assimilation and Community. The Jews in Nineteenth-Century Europe*, Cambridge 1992, pp. 1–37.

centrifugal forces served as the key, the paradigmatic theme." The more recent historiography, he continues, "is no longer informed by a bi-polar world-view". Frankel does not spell out his own opinion regarding the new historiographical situation. He only recognises it, but his recognition is so emphatic that it comes near to being a statement in itself: "... [W]e are left with a sub-world subjected to a multiplicity of conflicting forms interacting in unpredictable ways ... Order has been replaced by flux; one law of motion by a myriad of contexts, and by a multiplicity of responses."[5]

Just because Frankel's essay is so authoritative, the questions left open are all the more stimulating. What were the reasons for the passage from one period in Jewish historiography, the period of the "grand generalization", to another one, in which "order has been replace by flux"? Does he mean that generalisation in Jewish history is no longer desirable? Or that it is no longer possible?

In spite of their differences, it is important to stress how close Volkov and Frankel are in their historical approaches. Both recognise the necessity to integrate the understanding of Jewish history in "general" history: Frankel would certainly accept Volkov's assertion that any understanding on German-Jewish history has to be reached with due concern for general German affairs; or that, correspondingly, it is impossible to write German-Jewish history without embedding it in a general view on Jewish history. Both move effortlessly between the liberal (or cultural) and national approaches to Jewish history (which Frankel implicitly recognises); both acknowledge the great influence of Simon Dubnow on our concepts of Jewish history; both are aware of the problems of the broader, integrative view of Jewish history, and attentive to the great body of descriptive and analytical work, which concentrates on more defined and narrower themes, done in the last decades on German-Jewish and Jewish history. Nevertheless, it is difficult to accept Frankel's implicit position that there is a difference in historical conception between the older, integrationalist, synthesising Jewish historiography and the more recent one, which is "no longer informed by a bi-polar world-view". One is the continuation of the other, and not its dialectical negation. In spite of its great diversity, most of the descriptive-analytical research of recent years has been done in the same general conceptual framework that inspired the older synthesis-orientated Jewish historiography. If we dare to introduce the emotion-laden notion of a "school" in Jewish studies, Frankel and Volkov belong to the same one. It may be added that their far-reaching consensus is shared by a large majority of present-day Jewish historians, this author included. This poses for all of us several questions: what are the historical circumstances that brought about the present situation? Is it possible or even desirable to overcome the dead end that, in Volkov's words, we have reached in our historical concepts, and to look for a new beginning in our broader views on Jewish history?

I shall try to show that the German-Jewish historical paradigm represents one

---

[5]*Ibid.*, pp. 30–31.

of the possible points of departure for our quest, and I will also suggest ideas about the position of research concepts in Jewish history.

JEWISH HISTORICAL SYNTHESIS: HOLLOWING OUT THE CONCEPTS

Shmuel Ettinger, who was fascinated by the issue of intellectual generalisation, used to muse about its mysteries: how was it, he asked, that certain ages in Western culture produced an integrated view of things – in the arts, in culture, in historical concepts – and other ages did not? Ettinger believed that the reason did not lie in any particular academic trend, nor that it depended on the talent and interests of individual historians, but that it was related to the general circumstances of a given period. There are times, Ettinger concluded, for analytic history, and there are times for synthesising history, and mostly it is beyond our comprehension to explain why one or the other is taken up, or why analysis blends into historical synthesis.

A great and sobering example served to corroborate Ettinger's observations: the failure of Salo W. Baron, perhaps the outstanding Jewish historian of our time, to produce a new general view of Jewish history. We all admired Baron's intellectual stature, and were awed by his encyclopaedic knowledge, his originality and his productivity. If there was one person able to produce a new history of the Jewish people in the great tradition of Graetz and Dubnow, it was Salo Baron. Indeed, Baron was labouring on such a work in the 1960s – his monumental *A Social and Religious History of the Jews*, of which eighteen volumes appeared between 1952 and 1983.[6] Nevertheless, even then we felt that Baron would not achieve his goal, not because he was reaching old age, but because something was unclear in his concept of history. The impression was that Baron would run into difficulties when dealing with the modern period because it would then become clear that he was unable to offer a convincing synthesis, a new "grand generalization". Baron never really dealt with the modern era.[7]

What could have been wrong with Baron's concept of history? Perhaps our reflections on German-Jewish historiography may suggest an answer. Volkov's explanation about the two main approaches to Jewish history, the liberal-cultural and the national ones, is especially true with regard to the history of German Jewry, and not only because both concepts were rooted in German political thought (although, as already mentioned, "liberal", in the sense used here had a specific German-Jewish meaning). Perhaps more important than the concepts themselves was the peculiar dichotomy. In spite of the tension between them, the dichotomy created a certain equilibrium, a certain sense of order in

---

[6]Baron aimed to write an enlarged version of the edition in three volumes that had appeared in New York in 1937. For Baron's historical ideas, see his *The Contemporary Relevance of History. A Study in Approaches and Methods*, New York 1986.

[7]His last volumes reached the middle of the seventeenth century, and the only modern material was about the European Sephardim. In the shorter 1937 edition, the modern period was not as thoroughly treated as the chapters dealing with earlier Jewish history.

Jewish life. Later on they came to serve as a point of conceptual reference for the work of most Jewish historians in the twentieth century. Nowhere was the balance between the two approaches better expressed than in the German-Jewish experience. Even though there had also been something close to a liberal-cultural Jewish approach in Eastern Europe, it never reached the social and cultural creativity it attained in Germany, and later in the United States. Salo Baron never felt comfortable with the national and liberal-cultural paradigm of modern Jewish history. The weight he attached to each one of these concepts – liberal-cultural and national – was not the same as that in most of the historical works on Jewish history in his and in our time. For most twentieth-century Jewish historians, the liberal and national views of Jewish life were dynamic concepts. As employed by Baron, they acquired a strangely static quality. Because of this, Baron's direction became unclear: it was difficult to understand what, in his view, were the social or ideological forces shaping modern Jewish life. Apparently, Baron found such forces in the Jewish community. If so, he never explained the transition of "community" from a social concept to an ideological one. Nor did he elucidate how the Jewish community could continue to fulfil its previous tasks in a modern society in which it had lost so much of its power and influence.

Both the national and the liberal-cultural views have undergone a significant change over the last two generations. In the first half of the century, historians usually worked from one or the other perspective. In the last two generations scholars have begun to integrate the two concepts, to regard both as dynamic dimensions in Jewish life. Such a development also involved a new, positive view about Jewish life in the Diaspora, something with which not all Jewish historians of the national-Zionist trend felt comfortable. Still, most of them accepted the new approach, perhaps because it was limited to the interpretation of the past, and did not necessarily involve a change in position regarding the Jewish present. However, even given their views about the present Jewish reality in the second half of the twentieth century, the differences between Jewish historians inspired by liberal-cultural and national concepts of history, have lost much of their significance. It is difficult to agree with the conclusion arrived at by Todd M. Endelman that the "classic Zionist interpretation, with its pessimistic view of the survival of Diaspora communities, is more or less dead in academic circles".[8] Apart from some American-Jewish demographers, whose high professional competence stands in inverse proportion to their cultural sensibility in Jewish matters, I know scarcely any thoughtful Jewish historian who is not uneasy about the situation of the contemporary Diaspora Jewries. Why not turn to some of the concepts of classical cultural Zionism to explain what this Diaspora situation we have in mind is? To use Ahad Ha'am's thesis, the "situation of the Jews" in the Diaspora may be very good, but the "situation of [their] Judaism" is rather worrying.

---

[8]Todd M. Endelman, 'The Legitimization of the Diaspora Experience in Recent Jewish Historiography', in *Modern Judaism*, 11 (1991), p. 205. I wonder if Endelman was referring not to Zionist interpretation but to Zionist *prognosis*.

In any case, Volkov is equally comfortable with both the liberal-cultural and the national historiographical approaches to modern Jewish life and so are many of her colleagues, myself included. While stating that the two approaches have reached a dead end, however, Volkov seems oblivious to the fact that her equitable reference to both represents in itself a new approach to German-Jewish or Jewish history. We should not ignore the novelty of such a position. As recently as 1988 I was criticised in this Year Book by two distinguished colleagues (and dear friends), both specialists in modern German-Jewish history, because I argued that there was much to be positively evaluated in the conceptual approach of the most active of the German-Jewish "liberal" organisations, the *Centralverein deutscher Staatsbürger jüdischen Glaubens*.[9]

However, I dare to go a step further. This conceptional evolution seems to be only a latter-day reflection of a similar development that had happened in Jewish life in general, a process of approximation among the people and organisations belonging to the Zionist and the liberal-cultural directions. In previous work I have tried to describe this evolution in the liberal direction because it seemed to me that the changes there were more interesting and far-reaching than among the Zionists. Again, one of the most typical examples was to be found in German Jewry, namely the analysis of the ideological and organisational changes that had happened in the *Centralverein* during the first decades of the twentieth century. Certainly, the *Centralverein* had not accepted ideological elements that could be termed Jewish-national, but it had adopted some new ideas that were close to the cultural, people-centred views portrayed by Simon Dubnow. In fact, the roots of that development run much deeper. David Sorkin, in his very perceptive work, has shown how subtle sociological processes among German Jews, going back to the period of the *Haskalah*, had laid the foundations for a Jewish sub-culture in Germany, without most German Jews being aware of it or even wanting it.[10] This Jewish sub-culture was the fertile soil in which subsequently grew most of the interesting religious and ideological creations of German Jewry, among them the position of the *Centralverein*.

This evolution in German Jewry was interrupted in 1933. Nevertheless (and here the reader is begged for a measure of tolerance for professional imagination), these developments continued, no longer in Germany but in the United States, through the outstanding representatives of the liberal approach in American Jewry, namely the Reform movement and the American Jewish Committee. Both were created by the German section of American Jewry, and built on social and religious concepts introduced by Jewish immigrants from Germany.[11]

---

[9]'The German-Jewish Centralverein in Historical Perspective' (with Chaim Schatzker and Abraham Margaliot), in Section II of *LBI Year Book XXXIII* (1988), pp. 97–111.

[10]David Sorkin, *The Transformation of German Jewry, 1780–1940*, New York 1987; see also his 'Emancipation and Assimilation. Two Concepts and their Application to German Jewish History', in *LBI Year Book XXXV* (1990), pp. 17–33; and his 'The Impact of Emancipation on German Jewry: a Reconsideration', in Frankel and Zipperstein, pp. 177–198.

[11]See Evyatar Friesel, 'The Political and Ideological Development of the German-Jewish Centralverein before World War I', in *LBI Year Book XXXI* (1986), pp. 121–146; 'The Centralverein and the American Jewish Committee – A Comparative Study', in *LBI Year Book XXXVI* (1991), pp. 97–125.

At that point, I can no longer subscribe to Volkov's opinion regarding the continuing dichotomy between the Zionist and the liberal-cultural stance in present-day Jewish historiography. I believe that in the decades between the mid-sixties and the mid-eighties both views, as well as the social groups who had held them, very much came together. In our contemporary Jewish reality, in which the American Reform movement has become a participant in the Zionist Congress, I fail to perceive significant conceptual differences between Zionists and liberals. The dichotomy has, apparently, disappeared. Indeed, I wonder if the very labels – liberals and Zionists – still apply.

How far does this erosion of the concepts underlying the view of modern Jewish history as an integration of past and present reach? At this point it is befitting to leave the rarified realm of historical paradigms and consider what is happening in real life. After all, it seems senseless to consider historical trends like a paper kite flying freely in the air without an intelligible connection with the situation of the human group whose history is being described. Graetz and Dubnow built their gigantic historical structures looking at the history of the Jews through the lenses of the social and intellectual concepts of their respective times and places. In our generation, too, it is in the light of the realities shaping contemporary Jewish life that an integrated view of recent and older Jewish history will probably emerge. Perhaps such a general view is beyond our present intellectual capacity – as Baron's failure may have shown. If so, at least we should recognise the situation we are in. After all, an historical picture is only the mirror of a human condition; in order to understand historical trends it is the condition that we have to study, not the mirror. It is in the post-Holocaust condition that contemporary Jews are living.

JEWISH HISTORICAL SYNTHESIS: THE COLLAPSE OF THE FRAMEWORK

Our post-Holocaust reality poses questions that, in my opinion, make the quest for a synthetic view of Jewish history extremely difficult. As in other fields of Jewish life, I wonder if our generation has fully digested the consequences of the disaster: in this case, the consequences for a broader conception of Jewish history.

The very mention of the Holocaust presents a problem of scholarly approach. In the quicksand of concepts relating to the Holocaust, the moment one suggests an idea, the ground begins to shift under one's feet – and it seems as if one had proposed something completely different. If one tries to connect the destruction of European Jewry to an integrated view of Jewish history one is soon labelled an historical inevitabilist. Personally, I do not subscribe to interpretations of the Holocaust which are grounded in a sense of historical inevitability. German Jews did not live under the sign of the apocalypse. Neither did other European Jews, not even the most fervent Zionists of the *shlilat-hagalut* orientation. Nevertheless, once an historical cataclysm has occured, it is nonsensical to expect the next generation of historians to carry on as if it had not happened. No historian knows what is going to occur tomorrow, but woe betide him if he ignores what happened yesterday.

We are told, and we tell ourselves, that the situation of the Jews is better today than at any other time in the twentieth century. Seen historically, however, the real question is not whether the situation of the Jews is better or worse today than in the past. The real question is: from a post-Holocaust historical perspective, what has happened to the Jewish-Gentile relationship as a whole?

The destruction of European Jewry during the Second World War put an end to a pattern of Gentile-Jewish co-existence in the Western world that had endured for almost two thousand years. The roots of that relationship (if it may be called that) were religious and were formulated in the first centuries of the common era. With time, that connection also acquired social and cultural dimensions. The relationship was always a coin with two faces, one positive, the other negative. The negative one is what historically has been called hatred of the Jews, or, in modern times, antisemitism. But there was a positive side too, as Salo Baron never ceased to stress in his attempts to create a conceptual balance against the fixation on antisemitism that was (very understandably) characteristic of his generation. Jews, after all, did not only suffer and die during the centuries of life in the Diaspora; they also lived, developed and procreated. The active survival of the Jews may be an historical riddle but it was, and is, a reality. Jews absorbed something from the patterns of life of the Gentile environment and from its spiritual values, mixed them with the age-old traditions of Judaism, and produced new Jewish concepts of life, generation after generation. From an historical perspective, it was a situation that had many shadows and a few spots of light, but, all considered, it represented a framework that made possible the continuing existence of the Jewish people in Europe for about fifteen hundred years – almost the only non-Christian group tolerated in Christian society. That pattern of co-existence prevailed until the modern era. It collapsed at a time when liberty and freedom of thought and belief were proclaimed, at least by some sectors of European society, as new social and political hopes for human society. The crisis, when it came, was the worst possible: the Holocaust. Although the physical extermination of European Jewry was perpetrated by Nazi Germany, the ideological background of the destruction was European, not just German.

It can be argued that a new reality in Gentile-Jewish relations, a positive one, has developed since the destruction of European Jewry, at least in the Western world. True, such a new reality exists, but it is neither well-understood nor clearly formulated, certainly not in Jewish terms. In terms of a Jewish self-definition in the contemporary world, we are still living in the chaos that has resulted from the Holocaust.

Zionist activists claim that the concentration of the Jewish people in the Land of Israel represents an alternative to the Diaspora-based conception of Jewish existence. Does it really? As interesting and successful as Israel may be, it is still far from achieving that degree of stability necessary to inspire a new "grand generalization" of Jewish existence. Regarding its external life, the relationship between Israel and her neighbours in the Middle East has still to be worked out. And internally, Israeli society has not yet developed a convincing *modus vivendi* between its diverse social and religious components.

All in all, then, this is not the time to expect the emergence of a new synthetic view of Jewish history. The spiritual instability that characterises contemporary Jewish life, in Israel and in the Diaspora, is a far-reaching phenomenon that touches the very roots of Jewish self-awareness. This brings us to the analytical work done in the last two generations in Jewish history.

THE PERIOD OF HISTORICAL DESCRIPTION AND ANALYSIS

The collapse of the classical system of Jewish history was one of the reasons why Jewish historians have concentrated on the descriptive-analytical dimension of their calling in the last part of the twentieth century. Undoubtedly, recent analytical research has produced an impressive harvest. The major Jewish communities, organisations and movements; many of the major figures; the main ideas; and the ways in which these ideas have been adopted by the diverse Jewries and adapted to their existential conditions, have all been examined or re-examined. This work has been done through the lens of a highly differentiated spectrum of methodological approaches. The amount of valuable Jewish historical work produced in the last fifty years has created a new understanding of Jewish life in the past as well as in the modern period.

Many are tempted to believe that in time this accumulation of historical knowledge will serve or even produce a new synthesis of Jewish history. The situation, however, is more complex. There has been a fair measure of conceptual agreement underlying the historical approach of most Jewish scholars of the descriptive-analytical tendency, namely, the cultural-national approach to Jewish life and history. For many researchers the emphasis was on "national", for many others it was on "cultural". In almost all cases both elements were present, even if in uneven proportions. Most Jewish historians accepted, consciously or not, some common premises, such as a positive attitude towards Jewish collective life, that is that the Jews are a people, or at least have characteristics of peoplehood, to use the American-Jewish concept; and a positive attitude regarding the Jewish-Gentile cultural and social symbiosis that found diverse expressions in different lands and circumstances. Obviously, each historian and each historical trend added their own emphases and viewpoints to this general approach.

There is an incongruity between the present-day Jewish condition and the views underlying present-day Jewish historiography. Almost all important historical work done in the last few decades follows, knowingly or unknowingly, the conceptual guidelines laid down by Simon Dubnow, and in some cases, by Heinrich Graetz.[12] The problem is that a shadow has been cast over these older Jewish historical syntheses. They were all inspired, in various ways and degrees, by Jewish realities and Jewish hopes that were either destroyed or transformed –

---

[12]This is also true of the very important four-volume work edited by Michael A. Meyer, *Deutsch-Jüdische Geschichte in der Neuzeit*, Munich 1996–1997, Publication of the Leo Baeck Institute. We are presented with what is undoubtedly the best available overall treatment of the theme, but which is still a work written according to traditional conceptual guidelines.

especially by the Holocaust but in a certain measure also by the re-establishment of the old-new Jewish polity, Israel.

Generally speaking, only two groups of historians working on Jewish (or Israeli) themes are outside this historiographical conundrum. One group comprises the so-called "New Historians", whose field of interest is a rather limited one, namely, the political history of Israel and of those Arabs influenced by, or connected with, these developments. They represent an historiographical tendency worthy of attention, but we shall not dwell on it here. The other is the group of German historians working on the history of the Jews in Germany and on related themes.

JEWISH-GERMAN HISTORIOGRAPHY: ELEMENTS OF A FUTURE HISTORICAL CONCEPTION

There is no country, apart from Germany, where we find today so large a group of non-Jewish scholars and scholarly institutions dedicated to, or interested in, Jewish studies. The phenomenon has been duly observed and described.[13] In an illuminating essay published in 1990, Moshe Zimmermann analysed some of the complex trends underlying this development.[14]

The bulk of these studies has been done in the last thirty years or so, concentrating on the history of the Jews in Germany, although not exclusively.[15] Less attention (pehaps unfairly) is paid to a younger generation of German scholars which has been working in recent years on the history of the Jews but also in the broader field of Jewish classical studies, from the Second Temple period, through the Middle Ages and up to modern times. In contrast to the scholars of the older group, who mostly did not know Hebrew – some well-known cases excepted – most of the members of this younger group are not only familiar with the language but many are also capable of working on the difficult classical Hebrew sources. It is not only "external" history (mainly relations between Jews and non-Jews, or non-Jewish attitudes towards Jews) that is explored by this newer body of researchers, but also "internal" Jewish history (for instance, spiritual movements and ideological trends).

---

[13]See Reinhard Rürup (one of the founding fathers of that historical trend), 'An Appraisal of German-Jewish Historiography', in *LBI Year Book XXXV* (1990), pp. XV-XXIV; complemented by Christhard Hoffmann's recent essay 'The German-Jewish Encounter and German Historical Culture', in *LBI Year Book XLI* (1996), pp. 277–290. Michael A. Meyer, in 'Recent Historiography on the Jewish Religion', in *LBI Year Book XXXV* (1990), pp. 3–16, broadens the academic spectrum to religious history, mainly (but not only) in Germany. Additional works are mentioned by Rürup, Meyer, in 'Recent Historiography', and Hoffmann.

[14]Moshe Zimmermann, 'Jewish History and Jewish Historiography. A Challenge to Contemporary German Historiography', in *LBI Year Book XXXV* (1990), pp. 35–52. Zimmermann's essay is all the more interesting because he tries to concentrate on the German historiography separately from works on the Holocaust – an effort he himself admits is problematic, but which is certainly worthwhile for methodological purposes.

[15]To give but one example, Heinz-Dietrich Loewe's *The Tsars and the Jews. Reform, Reaction and Antisemitism in Imperial Russia 1772–1917*, Chur, Switzerland 1993, leaves nothing to be desired in terms of academic excellence.

All indications show that this broad group of German scholars, comprising already two quite distinct generations, will continue to grow. So far, most of their work has been done, probably unwittingly, close to or parallel to the Jewish national-cultural historical tradition. It should not surprise us if sooner or later a new conceptual tendency emerges from this group, in directions yet unknown.

There are clear signs pointing towards such a possibility. As Zimmermann has shown, since its emergence this group has had its own characteristics. The *Historikerstreit* in the late 1980s was an additional hint of the specific questions and tensions moving German scholars on themes relating to the history of the Jews in Germany. And the most important, although very indirect, indication of a possible new way is reflected in the recurrent discussion on the "German" and "Jewish" dimensions of German-Jewish history, and the ever-repeated emphasis on the necessity to pay attention to the German background while working on German-Jewish themes. On the face of it, the whole debate would appear to be irrelevant. It seems a truism that Jewish history in Germany cannot be understood outside the context of German life in general. How is it, then, that for more than forty years there have been so few historians of German Jewry, Jewish or non-Jewish, who have not found it necessary to proclaim the indispensibility of a combined view, and to do so as they were discovering the truth for the first time? From the very beginnings of this Year Book to the most recent volume, the necessity of working on German-Jewish history in the context of general German history has been stressed in dozens of articles.

One cannot avoid wondering if the whole phenomenon does not signal one of those cultural codes in which one thing is said and another is meant. If so, I suggest that behind this apparently methodological question lies a major conceptual issue: who is looking for what in the history of German Jewry? In other words, from a broader perspective, a perspective that one day may rise to the level of a synthetic view, we are dealing not with one history but with two: a Jewish one and a German one. It would mean that the ever-repeated methodological demand is but a mutual signal that each side, recognising that it is bound to the other in ways that cannot be avoided or ignored, is trying to establish – or to demolish – mutual borders.

It is certainly justifiable to consider the Jewish presence in Germany from a purely German angle. Germans who try to comprehend their own history cannot avoid looking into the Jewish moment in Germany. From that point on, it was almost natural that the interests of researchers should expand to other historical periods and the spiritual phenomena of Jewish life. All in all, this may explain the emergence of such an impressive body of German non-Jewish scholars, a phenomenon that is, as already mentioned, exclusively German. At the same time, there is also a Jewish angle to this German history, whose aim is to incorporate the Jewish-German experience as a link in the Jewish historical tradition. It is to be expected – indeed it is happening – that between these two circles engaged in Jewish studies but moved by differenct inspirations, a relationship of collaboration and also of mutual challenge, of creative tension, will develop. Seen from a Jewish angle, such a situation may sooner or later cause established concepts in Jewish historiography to be questioned. In itself this would be a very positive intellectual phenomenon, although not always an easy one. Both sides, however, should be as clear-minded as possible about their terms of reference. No detailed account of all the books and articles written during the past decades in Germany on matters Jewish; no long list of all the research institutions created or programmes of Jewish studies established in Germany; no methodological wizardries or learned lucubrations about the setting of German-Jewish history in a German historical background, can alter the basic fact that we are dealing with a history that has two legitimate, albeit different, angles. The student of Jewish history in Germany who is unable to accept the existence of an intrinsically Jewish point of view on that history has still not learned one of the major lessons emerging from the tragedy of German Jewry.

Those adhering to the Jewish viewpoint can suggest to their German colleagues questions for their work in Jewish history and Jewish studies, but they can hardly give an overall direction. The Jewish circle can act as partner in an intellectual dialogue, but the German circle will have to define for itself what moves it in its labours, and *vice versa*. For the Jewish historian, one of the tasks underlying his or her labours – sometimes explicitly stated, sometimes not – is to ask what element of the German-Jewish experience impresses us as "Jewishly relevant" – in our unavoidably subjective eyes – today. What, from the Jewish episode in Germany, "talks" to us, in the crucially different realities of present-day Jewish life, in our search for an historical perspective?

Considered from such a view, the tragic pertinence of the history of German Jewry is that it represents a closed chapter. It had a beginning, a flowering and an end. It is not the only closed chapter in modern Jewish history: for instance, the Jewish-Socialist *Bund*, in its day one of the most powerful organisations among Eastern European Jews, disappeared too. The peculiar lifestyles of the Jews in the diverse countries of East-Central and Eastern Europe, with their many patterns, each pattern with a core of social and intellectual creativity, are no more. Even the Zionist idea and movement, although they have not disappeared, exist today in a vastly mutated form.

The special historical significance of the German-Jewish episode is that it demonstrated the viability of a new Jewish-Gentile amalgamation of concepts and values in the conditions of the modern world – the very modern, the Western European world – an amalgamation that, from our point of view, was ultimately Jewish. If there was a truly creative dimension in the Jewish life of German Jewry, it lay in that integration of German culture and its social paradigms and Jewish historical beliefs and traditions; it lay in the new Jewish type and new Jewish society that emerged from that encounter. Furthermore, German Jewry created an impressive array of organisations that functioned not only on the communal, but also on a national level, aimed at encompassing all German Jews. These associations were, in principle, "Jewish-secular" – again, a novelty in the sense that the type of Jewish religiosity, or even Jewish religiosity itself, was not a condition for affiliation. This organisational model did not start in Germany, and also found significant expression in other European countries.

The first association of this kind was the Jewish-French *Alliance Israélite Universelle*, founded in 1860, and it can be claimed that the *Alliance* itself had roots further back in Jewish history. In German Jewry, however, this organisational pattern, of the civil-rights type and others, reached a flowering that by far surpassed the *Alliance* and similar Jewish associations in other parts of Europe. It represented a model adopted later on by American Jewry, and there it again developed in new directions.

Seen through our present-day lens, however, the lasting contribution of the German-Jewish experience seems to be the religious conceptual framework it created. This modern religious paradigm continues to be as relevant today as it was in the past. It lives on in American Jewry, and in a more modest form also among other Diaspora Jewries, although in the United States that "liberal" religious position has split long ago in two directions, Conservative and Reform. The American Jewish Reform movement was a direct offspring of its German counterpart; the Conservative movement was not. Nevertheless, both are ideologically (although not religiously) connected with the central stream of the "liberal" German-Jewish religious movement of old.

CONCLUSION

At the end of the twentieth century, Jews are not living in a time propitious for Jewish historical synthesis. Jewish statehood, and especially the Holocaust, have caused internal and external turmoil in Jewish collective life that continues unabated. Considered in secular terms, very little of our historical knowledge squares with the present quests of Jewish life in Israel or in the Diaspora. The Jews are today a people historically old but sociologically young. None of the established, leading Jewish communities of our day has existed for much longer than one or one-and-a-half centuries. Altogether, this is hardly a situation making for much spiritual stability, and hardly a situation leading to a sedate, synthetic view of Jewish history – more a time for descriptive and analytical work concentrating on limited themes.

Does that mean that a synthetic view of Jewish history has become superfluous? If history is an occupation the aim of which is to serve itself, or if it is a gentleman's leisure pursuit, then, indeed, there is no justification for synthesis-aware historical efforts. Some years ago, while teaching at the Hochschule für Jüdische Studien in Heidelberg, I gave a lecture to a group of German-Jewish activists. The theme was Jewish demography, and at some point I made a critical comment about mixed marriages and Jewish assimilation. One of the ladies present (incidentally, a member of the Board of the Jewish community in Berlin) criticised my approach and asked, with considerable emotion: "What is wrong with Jewish assimilation?" If the continuing existence of the Jewish people, I answered, is a desirable and honourable proposition, then Jewish assimilation is undesirable. From the same point of view, efforts to advance the understanding of a Jewish historical consciousness, too, are an honourable point of reference.

Jewish Historical Views

If historical knowledge is supposed to offer the Jewish people some orientation for its collective identity, then the search for a new synthetic view of modern Jewish history, for a "grand generalization", is today more important than ever. Hardly anyone believes nowadays that the aim of the grand historical picture is to establish the broad truth that supposedly governs the unfolding of historical events. Historicism in this classical sense is no longer accepted by historians. However, if ideas such as human cohesion and group consciousness – in our case, Jewish group consciousness – still have a significance, then the grand historical concept has something to offer. In this secular age, in this time of failed ideologies and weakened beliefs, an historical view is one of the few values (and here I ask for tolerance for such a partisan term) capable of suggesting, describing and analysing some of the elements people belonging to a given group do have in common. In that sense, historical consciousness represents an integrating effort – one among several – of a human group to understand itself and to express itself.

An integrated view of the Jewish past can only be achieved from the solid basis of a perception of present-day Jewish life. In our contemporary reality this may not yet be possible. The best we can do is to identify some of the probable elements of such a concept, and even then we cannot guarantee that they, and not other factors that we have not yet recognised, will be part of, or will influence, that general picture that has still to emerge. We will have to look at modern Jewish history through the lens of the destruction of European Jewry, and ask ourselves what it means for past and present Jewish life. In other words, what new paradigm of Jewish-Gentile relations may be feasible, following the collapse of the previous one? We will also have to learn from our recent past which models of Jewish life remain significant in the contemporary Jewish condition. Considered historically, the German-American paradigm, with its diverse religious and organisational expressions, seems to have had more impact than the Eastern European Jewish model – in itself, one of the great creations in Jewish history. This is so because the German-American type offered, and still offers, existential answers to Jewish collective life in a modern minority situation. Last, and certainly not least, we have to ponder the new Jewish polity, the state of Israel. From an historical perspective, the last question is the most complex of all. The knowledge about recent and past Jewish history gives us as yet very few clues how the reality of renewed Jewish political independence, with all its social and cultural consequences, fits into the continuum of Jewish life.

Even if such an an integrated view of Jewish history may be at present beyond our reach, the very recognition of its importance provides parameters for our historical labours in a more limited descriptive and analytical framework, and establishes a direction for our thoughts. Nevertheless, this awareness does not bring us closer to such a new view. A "grand generalization" cannot be forced, nor does it emerge from the compilation of all our historical knowledge. An overall view has to mature slowly and patiently. It needs the stable spiritual soil that develops under the surface, below the social and intellectual upheavals that may be stirring above, in the day-to-day struggles of a human group. One day, a new conception may emerge, for, in Simon Dubnow's unique formulation:

"Each generation in Israel carries within itself the remnants of worlds created and destroyed during the course of the previous history of the Jewish people. The generation, in turn, builds and destroys worlds in its form and image, but in the long run continues to weave the thread that binds all the links of the nation into the chain of generations ... Thus each generation in Israel is more the product of history than it is its creator."[16]

---

[16] Simon Dubnow, 'The Survival of the Jewish People' (1911), in Koppel S. Pinson (ed.), *Dubnow. Nationalism and History*, Philadelphia 1958, p. 326.

Memoir

*From Berlin to London**

BY F. L. CARSTEN

GROWING UP IN BERLIN IN THE 1920s

I was born on 25th June 1911, the second son of the ophthalmologist Paul Carsten and his wife Frida, *née* Born, in a comfortable Jewish upper-middle-class family. My father had a very large practice and owned a small clinic not far from my parents' flat in the "old West" of Berlin. He never went to the synagogue but my mother went with her mother for Rosh Hashanah and Yom Kippur. Judaism was not prominent in our education, which was left almost entirely in the hands of a governess. My parents were rather remote and we saw them mainly at mealtimes. It was all very old-fashioned and Victorian. The flat was typical of bourgeois Berlin: in front were the dining room, salon, gentlemen's room and living room; then came a very long corridor; and at the other end five bedrooms, a maid's room and a bathroom. There was a covered veranda looking out over the Landwehr Canal. There the flags were put out to celebrate the victories of the First World War, of which I only remember the many badly wounded soldiers, some of them in my father's clinic. Later, in the war, my father appeared in uniform with a spiked helmet and sabre, a medical officer in a large military hospital near Berlin. He was a busy man and very taciturn. My mother seemed fully occupied with running the household. My parents were entirely non-political and basically conservative and patriotic. Many years later my mother would still talk about "Unsere Kaiserin (our Empress)".

A short walk from my parents' flat was the large villa in the Tiergartenstraße where my grandmother Jennie lived; her husband, Sigismund Born, had died before I was born. There she lived in style with her only son, my mother's former governess as a companion, several maids, a cook, a resident porter and his wife, a resident gardener and coachman, a stable for horses, hothouses, a winter garden, and a very large garden at the back. Camellias, orange trees and palms were grown in large pots which had to be moved indoors during the cold season. But the coachman and horses were conscripted in the war of 1914 and did not return. The porter and the gardener were too old to be conscripted. My grandmother was not Orthodox but would not eat pork or game. She was surrounded by her children, grandchildren, and nephews and nieces with their children, who came to visit her. In the central hall of the villa stood a bookcase

---

*Before this essay could appear, Professor F. L. Carsten died. We are privileged to have been able to publish the last contribution of a distinguished historian.

which contained my grandfather's library: Thomas Carlyle's *History of Frederick the Great*, Heinrich Sybel's *Die Begründung des Deutschen Reiches unter Wilhelm I* in five volumes, and books on the history of Berlin and Florence. What attracted me most were the many volumes by Gustav Freytag, especially *Die Ahnen*. I was enthralled by the early volumes on the Germanic past, *Ingo und Ingraben*. There were no books on Jewish topics but there were many patriotic German ones.

Under my grandfather, Born & Busse had been a flourishing bank, but after his death the bank was wound up. Only his youngest brother, Uncle Ludwig, continued as a private banker and as the head of the family clan. He lived in a large flat facing the Brandenburg Gate, together with a lady whom he had adopted by a Count Schack, so that she became a countess; they were not married. Uncle Ludwig was not a great banker. During the inflation he sold the Born & Busse house in Berlin's principal banking street for a large sum of paper marks, on the assumption that he would never again get such a good price. In 1933 he also went on record that the Nazis would be quite all right if only they were not so antisemitic. His political information often came from Hjalmar Schacht, the president of the *Reichsbank* (later Hitler's Minister of Economics), whom he knew quite well.

The Borns considered themselves very much part of Berlin's Jewish aristocracy, along with the Liebermanns, the Lachmanns and other prominent families. Another brother of my grandfather, Julius, also a banker, was ennobled in Austria, converted to Catholicism, and his two sons married into the Austrian and Hungarian nobility. The Born family was very wealthy, but a large part of its fortune was lost in the hyperinflation of the early 1920s as the money was largely invested in state securities and Russian railway loans. In the 1920s the front part of the villa was let, for financial reasons, to the Italian Consulate. As children, my brother, my sister and I spent many afternoons and weekends in my grandmother's large garden and, with other children, we even had gymnastic lessons there. Today the site is occupied by the new *Kunstgewerbemuseum* with its many treasures.

My father's parents were much less grand. They owned a well-known clothing house, *Die Goldne Hundertzehn*, in the prominent Leipzigerstraße in the centre of Berlin, so called because the firm occupied number 110. It was mentioned, when it opened, in one of Theodor Fontane's novels, and in the 1890s Fontane celebrated it in a poem which included the firm's name. In a letter of May 1897 he called it his "most favoured literary source", for the firm's advertisements appeared in verse. The two sons of the couple studied medicine and became specialists. The firm disappeared after my grandparents' death.

My father and his brother went to school in the *Wilhelmsgymnasium* near the Potsdamer Platz, and my brother and I were sent to the same school, where I started at the age of seven in 1918. But after only three years the school was amalgamated with another well-known school, the *Französisches Gymnasium*, founded by the Huguenots in the eighteenth century, where the principal teaching was still conducted in French. But my parents considered it too far from our flat – a short walk through the Tiergarten – and decided on the *Mommsen-Gymnasium*, round the corner from my father's clinic. This proved to be a big mistake, for it was an awful school: cold, Prussian and strictly disciplinarian, with many

From Berlin to London

unpleasant teachers. After every break, the smaller boys had to form columns and were conducted to their forms by some of the older pupils. Some of the teachers had been officers and would talk about their war experiences at the front and make anti-French and anti-Polish speeches, in particular at the time of the fighting in Upper Silesia in the early 1920s. The Treaty of Versailles was contemptuously pronounced "Versalj". My form master was a choleric petty tyrant and everybody was afraid of him. The teaching of Latin and Greek was excellent but I hated the whole atmosphere and did the minimum of work.

When I was about fifteen years old my oppositional instincts led me in to an active left-wing Socialist group in the school. The Socialist Pupils' League came into being and joined with similar groups from other schools. Soon we edited a journal, *Der Schulkampf*, in which we wrote on the arbitrary methods of our teachers and their nationalist and reactionary bias. One such issue was published at the time of my leaving examination in the spring of 1929 and caused a phenomenal row, with the result that the leaving certificates were at first withheld and only granted after intervention from above. My parents had strongly objected to my joining the Socialist Pupils' League, and there was another row when I joined nevertheless. From then on I spent all my free time in Socialist meetings and Marxist study groups. As the organisation was led by active Communists it was, for me, but a short way to the Young Communist League (KJVD) which I joined in 1928. Without much knowledge of Marxist theory or the reality of Soviet Russia, I became an enthusiastic young Communist. I was trying to escape a stifling bourgeois atmosphere, and was full of romantic ideas. A lasting memory is that of the monster parade on May Day 1928, when the SPD and KPD joined forces for the last time. Any subsequent joint action was prohibited by the left-wing turn of the Comintern in that year, and the Communist demonstrations on May Day 1929 led to bloody clashes with the police. I greatly admired the Karl Marx School in Neukölln which, under a Socialist headmaster, was progressive and coeducational; we were permitted to attend occasional classes there. The contrast with the *Mommsen-Gymnasium* could not have been sharper. At that time I developed a strong interest in modern art, and particularly in the German Expressionists. The *Kronprinzenpalais* (the former residence of the crown prince) in Unter den Linden, where modern paintings were exhibited, became one of my favourite haunts. I also admired Otto Dix and George Grosz for their iconoclastic attitude.

Although history was my favourite subject at school I decided to read law and economics, thinking vaguely of a political career as a lawyer or journalist. In my politics I was at first absolutely loyal to the ultra-left party line, but during two terms at Heidelberg in 1930–1931, I became a close friend of Richard Löwenthal, who had been expelled from the KPD for "right-wing deviationism", and of his future wife Charlotte. Very slowly I became more critical and noticed that, during the great slump, the membership of the Party consisted almost entirely of the unemployed with the result that it was unable to lead any major working-class action – partly through its own fault, for the constant wild strikes it called led to the dismissal and blacklisting of the activists.

After my return to Berlin in 1931 my criticism grew much stronger. My political activities were still mainly in the KJVD and the 'red' student group which was involved in frequent clashes with the much more numerous Nazi students. On one occasion I came home with a head wound which required four stitches: my parents were horrified. Among the "red" students there was a large percentage of Jewish students, but also many non-Jews, among them the three daughters of the commander-in-chief of the army, General von Hammerstein. Very likely, the rampant German antisemitism drove many young Jews to the left, but at least equally important was the economic misery of the years of the great slump, which affected many students. Many intellectuals joined the KPD. Some Jews were prominent among its leaders, for example Heinz Neumann, the son of a prominent Berlin lawyer. In general, however, "true" proletarians were preferred in the Party's higher ranks. Jewish party members would tend to suppress any pro-Jewish feelings and submerge them in the great fight for the revolution. The Communist attitude towards Jewish groups and organisations, even left-wing ones, was decidedly hostile, whether these were pro-German or Zionist. Both kinds were considered enemies. True Communists were expected to leave the Jewish community (as they were expected to leave the Church), but there was no open antisemitism. In 1930 I went to a huge Hitler meeting in Frankfurt, with its carefully orchestrated propaganda which slowly drew the whole audience in its ban. It was a masterly performance.

With other like-minded comrades I eagerly read the various pamphlets in which Trotsky vehemently attacked the Party line, which prohibited any united front with the Social Democrats. Even cooperation with Social-Democratic students was forbidden. The party line only permitted a "united front from below", which meant the attempt to win over individual Social Democrats to the Communist side, while the SPD leaders and officials were termed "Social Fascists". My rejection of Party tactics grew along these lines and I became more and more miserable. These were the years of the rapid growth of the Nazi Party, which the disunited Socialist movement was unable to oppose. I developed a strong interest in the chequered history of the German labour movement and bought numerous books and pamphlets which became the basis of my collection. They could be obtained for small sums on the many book carts near Berlin University.

THE 'ORG' AND *NEU BEGINNEN*

One day, early in 1932, I sat on a bench in the Tiergarten with Richard Löwenthal, with whom I maintained close contact, and told him of my despair at the sorry state of the KPD. He then informed me of the existence of a secret organisation whose aim it was to reunite the feuding working-class parties. Löwenthal himself was not a member but a close friend of his, Georg Eliasberg, was, and soon afterwards I was recruited to the "Org", which had no name and which was strictly conspiratorial. The members used only cover names: the leader was 'Kurt' (Walter Löwenheim), supported by a small "Circle" of his close political friends who had all been expelled from the KPD for "right-wing" tendencies. In the spring of 1932 I took part in a months-long study group to which a member of the leading Circle lectured on bourgeois and Socialist revolution; bourgeois and Marxist ideologies; the history of the German labour movement; Bolshevism and Soviet Russia; and the way to power and to Socialism (with the Russian NEP as the prototype). With the guiding example of Lenin's *What is to Be Done?*, the aim was to form a secret organisation of 'professional revolutionaries' who would work clandestinely both in the SPD and KPD, occupy leading positions in them and one day reunite the German Socialist movement. How that could be done in the hierarchical KPD, a party in which the slightest deviation from the 'line' was punished by expulsion and which was strictly controlled by Moscow, was not stated. I absorbed this new conception avidly, as it seemed to show a way out of the hopeless situation of the movement, and became a loyal member. The Org did not anticipate the coming of Fascism in Germany. I was fully prepared to leave the KPD but was instructed to stay in the party and gain influence within. This I did by conducting study groups and giving talks. When Hitler was made chancellor in January 1933 I ran a large group in a red working-class district of Berlin on Engels' *The Origin of the Family, Private Property and the State* — a topic far removed from the German reality. At the same time I was forbidden, under Party orders, to make any preparation for the Party to go underground; its normal activities were to continue as if nothing had happened. The illusion would not last many weeks.

Meanwhile I pursued my legal studies without much enthusiasm, but in the end I worked very hard to pass the first state examination. I did this in May 1933 at the *Kammergericht* in Berlin, four months into the Hitler dictatorship, gaining the mark 'satisfactory'. This was the end of my legal career, as 'non-Aryans' were not allowed to continue. So I worked, during the next twelve months, in a bank, the successor of Bleichröeder, which had been famous under Bismarck. Thereafter Eliasberg and I opened a book shop on the Kurfürstendamm, but after a few weeks the *Gestapo* closed the shop because we were not members of the professional Nazi "chamber". My family did not suffer from antisemitic measures: my father's practice continued as before, with high-ranking officers as his patients. Only I was briefly arrested in 1934 because a former student had given my name under pressure to the *Gestapo*. He was a member of the Socialist Workers' Party, with which I had nothing to do, and the official carrying out the arrest, von Plotho, was not interested in any other party. He became a non-paying patient of my father.

With the dissolution of the left-wing parties early in 1933 and the arrest of many members, the Org's policy of working from within became unrealistic and its members were instructed to withdraw quickly. It was now a small underground group, with the great asset of not being known to the *Gestapo*, and continued its activities undisturbed for the time being. This meant recruiting more members, in particular from the former Socialist Youth (SAJ), whose Berlin leaders joined the Org. I worked closely with one of them, Fritz Erler, whom I learned to estimate very highly. In 1933 the Org even acquired a name because in Czechoslovakia Walter Löwenheim published, under the auspices of the exiled leaders of the SPD, a brief version of his idea entitled *Neu beginnen. Faschismus oder*

Sozialismus. He blamed the "bourgeois ideologies" of the left-wing parties for their disastrous defeat and advocated the complete renewal of the Socialist movement under new leaders inside Germany, in other words under the guidance of the underground Org. In effect *Neu Beginnen* was now a left-wing Socialist group, still very small but expanding quickly inside and outside Berlin, especially in Saxony and Thuringia. The pamphlet made a considerable impression in left-wing circles inside and outside Germany. An English translation, *Socialism's New Start. A Secret German Manifesto*, appeared in 1934. Its long-term perspective was much more realistic than the illusions cherished by so many of the leaders and followers of the SPD and KPD.

My own activities in Berlin in 1933–1935 consisted mainly of finding and organising sympathisers among left-wing intellectuals; raising funds and finding flats suitable for meetings of small groups; collecting reports on local conditions; and establishing contacts with other underground groups. I remember meetings with the leaders of the dissolved association of religious Socialists, Protestant clergymen who desired information on events abroad and who were completely isolated. The problem was where all these activities were leading to, for the Nazi regime was clearly firmly established and the *Gestapo* ever present. Whatever we did could not possibly make any impression. In 1935 Löwenheim came to the conclusion that the regime could not be overthrown from inside Germany, and that the underground organisation should be liquidated and its members should emigrate, with only a few "listening posts" left inside Germany. But in Berlin and elsewhere strong opposition developed against this course. There were heated discussions, and a revolt of the majority of the members led to the appointment of a new leadership and a new analysis of the situation conceived by Richard Löwenthal, which was published in several issues of the *Zeitschrift für Sozialismus*, the theoretical journal of the SPD leaders in Prague.

These moves coincided with a wave of arrests, first in Saxony and then in Berlin, because one of the arrested was "persuaded" by the *Gestapo* to divulge what he knew about their contacts in Berlin. The arrests were facilitated by a mass of Org material found in a suitcase which had failed to sink in one of the lakes near Berlin. In 1936 there were several trials for 'treason' and stiff sentences were imposed. In Berlin only a small remnant remained, which was finally liquidated in 1938. Among the arrested was my close friend Georg Eliasberg, who was a member of the new leading group. In his flat a carpenter had hollowed out a door and in this hiding place a copy of the new analysis was hidden. I possessed a key to the flat and at night Gerhard Bry and I went there and retrieved the incriminating documents so that the arrested could plead that the organisation had been dissolved. Eliasberg survived his sentence, was expelled from Germany and later told me that we had saved his life. It became clear that, because of my close association with him, my arrest was only a question of time. I was told to leave Germany and, possessing a legal passport, was able to go to Basle. I told my parents, who were on holiday in Switzerland, that I could not return to Berlin because of Eliasberg's arrest, but without giving them any details. They left Germany legally the following year and went to Rome and later to the United States, where my father continued to practise.

I was now a political refugee without any means of existence and with profession. I first went to London, where I had many political friends. In Paris I met Norbert Elias, who soon afterwards moved to London, and in discussions with him and others, a plan emerged that I should develop my interest in history and work on early Prussian history. I aimed to discover the factors which had caused the peculiar development of Prussia, especially of its nobility, the Junkers, and the secret of the latter's long-lasting power. Early in 1936, I decided to move to Amsterdam, where living was much cheaper and where I could begin work undisturbed. I spent three years in the Netherlands, in close contact with the newly founded International Institute of Social History and with Dutch historians who were interested in my work. One of them, J.G. van Dillen, published my first essays in the *Tijdschrift voor Geschiedenis*, on the 'Jewish Question in the Conflict between the Great Elector of Brandenburg and the Estates', on 'Social Movements in the Pomeranian Towns from the Fourteenth Century to the Reformation', and on the 'Social Basis of Prussia'. Another essay, 'The Peasants' War in East Prussia in 1525', appeared in the *Review* published by the International Institute, and several articles were published in Dutch newspapers. Above all, I collected material for a book on the origins of the East German *Gutsherrschaft*, which formed the basis of Junker power, and of the peasants' serfdom into the nineteenth century – a development so different from that in other parts of Germany. This was possible thanks to the many editions of printed documents sponsored by the House of Hohenzollern: Riedel's *Codex diplomaticus Brandenburgensis* alone has forty-two volumes. The work was to become my Oxford thesis.

At the same time I was still a loyal member of *Neu Beginnen* and, as such, established contact with the International Transport Workers' Federation and its massive and powerful secretary Edo Fimmen, who did what he could to support the German Socialist movement. I also had close contacts with the many Socialist refugees in Amsterdam who were split into warring factions, from Revolutionary Socialists to adherents of the SPD leaders in Prague. In my opinion, we were all social democrats and it was essential to overcome the feuds and quarrels. Together with a few friends I therefore tried to organise a German social-democratic group and was partially successful. The local followers of the exiled Prague leaders, two former SPD *Reichstag* deputies, refused to join, although many others did. It was at the time of the Spanish Civil War and many hoped for the formation of a united front. Erich Kuttner, who had been one of the editors of *Vorwärts*, the SPD daily, went to Spain to speak for the popular front, and others joined the International Brigades; but the Communists, with Russian backing, united against so-called Trotskyists and other 'traitors'. When the Amsterdam KPD group suggested to us that we should meet their Party secretary, Walter Ulbricht, to discuss the formation of a united front, a friend of mine and I went to hear him. In the discussion I mentioned that some of our comrades had disappeared in Spain: what would happen in Germany if the Communists ever came to power there? Ulbricht indignantly demanded names and I gave that of Mark Rein, a German Socialist of Russian origin who had gone to Spain and was kidnapped in Barcelona. Ulbricht promised an enquiry and to let us know the result, but this never happened. Obviously, the Communists did not change their spots. The Moscow trials, then in progress, confirmed my view, as did my close friendship with Boris Sapir, an exiled Menshevik who joined the International Institute of Social History. He had been imprisoned in Russia, an early victim of the Gulag.

OXFORD AND THE WAR YEARS

I might have stayed on in the Netherlands, where I felt very much at home. But after Munich and the German march into Prague the political situation became so threatening that I decided to return to England in April 1939. I intended to try and obtain a scholarship so that I could continue my research. During the spring of 1939 I was busy visiting colleges in Oxford and Cambridge and drafting applications for research grants. I had recommendations from Dutch historians and the list of my publications was useful. Patrick Gordon-Walker of Christ Church (later a member of the Wilson government and a member of the House of Lords) was most helpful; I had met him in Berlin when he visited our group there. I was finally successful and obtained a research scholarship to Wadham College, Oxford worth £120 p.a., and in the autumn I moved to Oxford. Meanwhile the war had broken out and my movements, as an alien, were severely restricted. Wadham was a very small, friendly college: the Warden, Maurice Bowra, and the dons helped me, as did the Regis Professor of Modern History, Maurice Powicke, and many others. I happily settled down in this new atmosphere and was soon active in the Labour Club. It was dominated by active Communists for whom the war was an imperialist war which they very strongly opposed. There were heated discussions in which those supporting the war effort joined hands. Together with Tony Crosland and many others, we broke away from the Labour Club and formed the Democratic Socialist Club, on the executive committee of which I served for two years, together with Crosland, Roy Jenkins and Philip Williams. The weekly discussion meetings of the Cole Group, in G.D.H. Cole's rooms in University College, were full of interest. In spite of the war, Oxford was lively and not much changed.

But the war was to intrude upon my life nevertheless. All "enemy aliens" had to appear before legal tribunals which classified them from A to D, the latter considered pro-Nazi and subject to internment; those in classification A were the proven anti-Nazis. I had to attend a tribunal in March 1940, and the presiding judge complimented me on my political record, which was confirmed by the Labour Party, and I was classified A. In the summer vacation I wanted to work for the war effort and volunteered for the Oxford University forestry camp in the Forest of Dean. But as soon as I got there I was arrested by the Newport police – they were pleased to have found a German spy – and interned with many thousands of refugees, following Churchill's dictum "Collar the lot!" I was first interned at Warth Mill near Manchester, a ghastly disused cotton mill, and later on the Isle of Man in somewhat better conditions. At Warth Mill the few German Social Democrats soon combined to oppose an active KPD cell which made propaganda against the war. There were many German academics from Oxford and prominent anti-Nazis such as the well-known writer Rudolf Olden, who was later drowned when his boat was torpedoed in the Atlantic. I used my enforced idleness to start to learn Polish but did not get very far.

I was only interned for about three months and then released to join the army, for which I had volunteered at Oxford. I was sent to the Pioneer Corps at Ilfracombe in Devon and employed there as a clerk in the NCO School near the harbour – not a very exacting duty. The British officers, remnants from the First World War, were rather puzzled by all the "Germans" around them. My army service lasted only a few months because in mid-winter I caught severe pneumonia which left a shadow on my lungs. I was sent on sick leave and then pronounced unfit for military service and discharged with a weekly pension of ten shillings. I returned to Oxford and finally finished my thesis, 'The Development of the Manorial System – *Grundherrschaft* and *Gutsherrschaft* in Northeastern Germany to the Seventeenth Century'. My principal thesis was that the origin of the *Gutsherrschaft* was due to the widespread desertion of the land after the Black Death and the many other catastrophes of the late Middle Ages, as well as to the decline of the comparatively small towns of the whole area. This enabled the nobles to extend their *demesne* farming at the expense of the peasants, to impose heavy labour services on them and to export their produce directly to western lands. The thesis was examined early in 1942 by G.N. Clark and M. Postan, two professors of economic history. I also obtained the Alexander Prize of the Royal Historical Society for an essay entitled 'Medieval Democracy in the Brandenburg Towns and its Defeat in the Fifteenth Century'.

Oxford was full of interesting people and I became friendly with Norman Baynes, retired professor of Byzantine history in London and a most erudite and charming man, who translated Hitler's speeches into English as his war work. I went to lectures on medieval agrarian history, where I learnt a lot about enclosures, and other lectures on Eastern Europe given by experts from Chatham House such as R.W. Seton-Watson. I lectured to army units in the Oxford region on Nazism and current affairs. Above all, I met my future wife, Ruth Moses, on a rainy day in Cornmarket. After 1945 she was to help me with my publications and was to patiently suffer my long absences in German and Austrian archives. With her liveliness and wide intellectual interests she was an admirable companion.

I now had to find a job, for my small army pension and occasional lectures were insufficient to support myself, and I was still an "enemy alien". I was interviewed at Bush House in London by Sefton Delmer for one of his "clandestine" radio stations, but I disliked the use of "lies and dirt" (as he put it) for propaganda purposes. Later in 1942 Duncan Wilson, later the British ambassador to Belgrade and Moscow, came to see me in Oxford and offered me a post in the Political Warfare Executive (PWE), preparing a handbook on Germany for the use of officers of the army of occupation after the war ended. Naturally I accepted gladly and was instructed to proceed on a certain day to Bletchley, where I would be met. I did this at the arranged time, but there was no one there to meet me. I did not want to loiter suspiciously about the station and asked a porter what

I should do. He told me right away that I should ring Woburn Abbey, which I did and was then collected. The Abbey, belonging to the Duke of Bedford, was in fact the secret headquarters of PWE and the surrounding villages served to house the numerous staff, as well as Delmer's various outfits. My work had nothing to do with propaganda. I was to write chapters on German administration, local government, social services, and Nazi organisations and politics, which were to form, together with other contributions, a *Basic German Handbook* for the subsequent occupation. The only other man who was taken on for this purpose at the same time was Richard Samuel, who had been a teacher at a Berlin *Gymnasium* and was to write on education. A chapter on German history by A.J.P. Taylor was so anti-German that it was rejected at my suggestion; the chapter was finally written by J. Passant. PWE received all the German newspapers and certain journals *via* Stockholm, but had no library to speak of and no files for the pre-war period. I therefore, after a short time, returned to Oxford, where the press-cutting service of Chatham House, then called the Foreign Office Research Department and housed at Balliol, proved invaluable for my purposes. The members of its small German section were extremely helpful and I learned a great deal about Germany. Among the staff at Woburn Abbey were many German political refugees and some old friends of mine. In contrast with Chatham House, PWE could recruit 'enemy aliens' and also used German prisoners of war.

With the end of the heavy air attacks large sections of PWE moved to London and were accommodated in Bush House and Ingersoll House opposite, enabling me to use the British Library. When the (top secret) *Basic German Handbook* was more or less completed – meanwhile Wolfgang Friedmann had joined us to write on the legal system – we had to prepare smaller handbooks on Berlin and parts of the later British zone: Schleswig-Holstein, Hamburg and Bremen, Lower Saxony, Rhineland-Westphalia and Hesse. They included brief histories of the area in question, surveys of the local political and labour movements and, for the Rhineland, of the previous Allied occupation after 1918. We also wrote an *ABC of German Administration and Government*. For this work we were entitled to interrogate German prisoners of war who were brought to London from their camps. For example, there was the question: what were the functions of a *Landrat* and how did he spend his day? A *Landrat* was duly found among the prisoners from Normandy and I spent some hours with him to find out; he was most willing to talk about his work. I lectured at Cobham near London on German local government and administration to British officers who were being trained for administrative tasks in Germany. I also began to lecture on Germany in prisoner-of-war camps in various parts of England. This was a fascinating experience, especially my regular weekly lectures at Wilton Park near Beaconsfield, a camp for anti-Nazi prisoners of war which had been started on the initiative of Waldemar von Knoeringen and was run by Heinz Koeppler. My lectures were mainly on the history of the Weimar Republic and the Nazi period, and many long discussions took place. I had meanwhile been awarded a Senior Demyship at Magdalen College and continued to work on Prussian history in the British Library. I left government service in January 1946 after three busy years, but continued lecturing at Wilton Park and elsewhere. Ruth and I married in 1945 when the war had ended. In 1946 we became British citizens, with strong backing from Oxford, after a detailed investigation by the Home Office.

Meanwhile I tried to get a university post and was interviewed several times. Norbert Elias, with whom I maintained close contact throughout, strongly advised me to try the provinces, but we did not want to leave London. Ruth had a part-time teaching post (paid by the hour) and we had found a charming flat in Highgate on top of an old house. I was finally successful in 1947 and was appointed to a lectureship in modern history at Westfield College, University of London, with a salary of £600 p.a. I had given up politics and become an academic historian. I was at Westfield for fourteen years, first as a lecturer, and later as a reader.

In London I saw George Lichtheim, the eminent writer on Marxism and Socialism, almost daily He moved into the top flat of our Hampstead house when we bought it in 1955 and became a close friend of the family. His suicide in 1972 was a tragedy. Closer still were my relations with Norbert Elias, who lived in London before he moved to Leicester and later to Germany and Holland. He often joined our Swiss holidays and was always ready to advise and comment on my work. But he had certain preconceived ideas to which he clung against all the evidence. He was, for example, convinced that King Frederick William I of Prussia (1713–1740) was a "bourgeois king", like Louis Philippe of France. I even wrote a paper on the reign which showed that Frederick William was a despot but far from bourgeois; Prussia did not yet have a bourgeoisie and no powerful towns, but it did have a very strong nobility which the king tried to press into state service. Norbert remained unconvinced. At the conference in honour of his ninetieth birthday in 1987, he claimed that in the course of time the smaller nationalities were likely to disappear and would be merged with larger nations. I opposed this, pointing to recent examples of small nationalities with which I was familiar. Norbert replied that this showed the difference between the sociologist and the historian: the latter thought only in the short term but the sociologist took the long view. Norbert did not take kindly to criticism but he was a most loyal friend. He had a life full of difficulties, but late in life he received all the recognition and the honours he deserved. His book *Über den Prozess der Zivilisation* (Basle 1939) was a remarkable achievement and later became a bestseller in Germany.

Publications on German-speaking Jewry

A Selected and Annotated Bibliography of Books and Articles 1997

Compiled by

BARBARA SUCHY and ANNETTE PRINGLE

Leo Baeck Institute
4 Devonshire Street
London W1N 2BH

CONTENTS

		Page
I.	HISTORY	
	A. General	353
	Linguistics/Western Yiddish	358
	B. Communal and Regional History	358
	1. Germany	358
	1a. Alsace	373
	2. Austria	374
	3. Central Europe	375
	4. Switzerland	377
II.	RESEARCH AND BIBLIOGRAPHY	
	A. Libraries and Institutes	379
	B. Bibliographies, Catalogues and Reference Books	381
III.	THE NAZI PERIOD	
	A. General	383
	B. Jewish Resistance	406
IV.	POST WAR	
	A. General	407
	B. Education and Teaching. Memorials	411
V.	JUDAISM	
	A. Jewish Learning and Scholars	413
	B. Perception and Identity	418
	C. Jewish Life and Organisations. Genealogy	420
	D. Jewish Art and Music	421
VI.	ZIONISM AND ISRAEL	
VII.	PARTICIPATION IN CULTURAL AND PUBLIC LIFE	
	A. General	424
	B. Individual	429
VIII.	AUTOBIOGRAPHY, MEMOIRS, LETTERS	
IX.	GERMAN-JEWISH RELATIONS	
	A. General	455
	B. German-Israeli Relations	458
	C. Church and Synagogue	459
	D. Antisemitism	460
	E. Noted Germans and Jews	464
X.	FICTION AND POETRY	466
	INDEX	469

BIBLIOGRAPHY 1997

Includes books and articles published in 1997 as well as supplementary books and articles published in 1995 and 1996 and not yet listed in the bibliography.

Preference has been given to entering as many publications as possible and, to this end, cross-references and reviews have been cut somewhat. All titles are, however, fully indexed.

Communal and regional histories are listed either in Section I B (Communal and Regional History), or in Section III (The Nazi Period), depending on their main focus.

Autobiographies and memoirs are listed either in section III (The Nazi Period), or in Section VIII (Autobiography, Memoirs, Letters), again depending on their main focus. (B.S.)

I. HISTORY

A. General

34677. BATTENBERG, FRIEDRICH: *Grenzen und Möglichkeiten der Integration von Juden in der Gesellschaft des Ancien Régime.* [In]: Migration und Integration. Aufnahme und Eingliederung im historischen Wandel. Hrsg. von Mathias Beer [et al.]. Stuttgart: Steiner, 1997. (Stuttgarter Beiträge zur Hist. Verhaltensforschung, Bd. 3.). Pp. 87–110, footnotes.

34678. BATTENBERG, J. FRIEDRICH: *Die Privilegierung von Juden und der Judenschaft im Bereich des Heiligen Römischen Reiches deutscher Nation.* [In]: Das Privileg im europäischen Vergleich. Hrsg. von Barbara Dölemeyer [et al.]. Bd. 1. Frankfurt am Main: Klostermann, 1997. Pp. 139–190, footnotes.

34679. BORUT, JACOB: *Die jüdischen Abwehrvereine zu Beginn der neunziger Jahre des 19. Jahrhunderts.* [In]: Aschkenas, Jg. 7, H. 2, Wien, 1997. Pp. 467–494, footnotes. [On the Cologne branch of the 'Verein zur Abwehr des Antisemitismus', the 'Vereinigung Badischer Israeliten', Karlsruhe, and the 'Comitée zur Abwehr antisemitischer Angriffe', Berlin.]

34680. COHEN, DANIEL J.: *Die Landjudenschaften in Deutschland als Organe jüdischer Selbstverwaltung von der frühen Neuzeit bis ins neunzehnte Jahrhundert.* Eine Quellensammlung. Hrsg. von Daniel J. Cohen. Bd. 1. Jerusalem: Israelische Akad. der Wiss.; Akademie der Wiss. zu Göttingen, 1996. XXXVIII, 732 pp., notes. [At head of title page: Fontes ad Res Judaicas Spectantes. Hebrew title on p. 732. Cont.: Vorwort (Rudolf Vierhaus/Stefi Jersch-Wenzel, V–VIII; on Daniel J. Cohen, his family background and his work). Einleitung. Entwicklung der Landjudenschaften und ihrer Institutionen (XIII–XXV). Dokumente (more than 1,000 docs. from 28 archives and libraries, partly in Hebrew and in Yiddish): I. Rheinland (1–143). II. Mittelrheinland und Hessen (145–732).] [D.J.C., 1921 Altona – Dec. 19, 1989 Jerusalem, archivist of the Central Archives for the History of the Jewish People, Jerusalem.]

34681. DAXELMÜLLER, CHRISTOPH: *Hochzeitskutschen und Romanzen. Zur jüdischen Assimilation in der frühen Neuzeit.* [In]: Bayerisches Jahrbuch für Volkskunde 1996, München, 1996. Pp. 107–120, notes.

34682. *Deutsche jüdische Soldaten.* Von der Epoche der Emanzipation bis zum Zeitalter der Weltkriege. Eine Ausstellung des Militärgeschichtlichen Forschungsamtes in Zusammenarbeit mit dem Moses Mendelssohn Zentrum, Potsdam, und dem Centrum Judaicum, Berlin. Hamburg: E.S. Mittler & Sohn, 1996. IX, 205 [5] pp., illus., notes, bibl. (197–204). [Incl.

memoirs by Jewish soldiers and contribs. by Dietz Bering, Manfred Messerschmidt, Frank Nägler, Ernst-Erich Schmidt, Wolfgang Schmidt, Julius H. Schoeps and Peter Steinbach.]

34683. *Deutsch-jüdische Geschichte in der Neuzeit.* Bd. 1–4. Hrsg. im Auftrag des Leo Baeck Instituts von Michael A. Meyer unter Mitwirkung von Michael Brenner. München: Beck, 1996–1997. (Das Gesamtwerk.) Bd. 1: Tradition und Aufklärung 1600–1780. Von Mordechai Breuer und Michael Graetz. Bd. 2: Emanzipation und Akkulturation 1780–1871. Von Michael Brenner, Stefi Jersch-Wenzel und Michael A. Meyer [see Nos. 33671 and 33644/YB XLII]. Bd. 3 [publ. 1997]: Umstrittene Integration 1871–1918. Von Steven M. Lowenstein, Paul Mendes-Flohr, Peter Pulzer und Monika Richarz. 428 pp., illus., notes (388–399), bibl. (400–411), chronol. tab., index (415–428). [Cont. (Engl. contribs. transl. by Holger Fliessbach): Einführung (Peter Pulzer, 9–12). I. Die Entwicklung der jüdischen Bevölkerung. II. Berufliche und soziale Struktur III. Frauen in Familie und Öffentlichkeit (Monika Richarz, 13–100). IV. Das religiöse Leben. V. Die Gemeinde (Steven M. Lowenstein, 101–149). VI. Rechtliche Gleichstellung und öffentliches Leben. VII. Die Wiederkehr des alten Hasses. VIII. Die Reaktion auf den Antisemitismus (Peter Pulzer, 151–277). IX. Ideologie und Identität. X. Der jüdische Anteil an der deutschen Kultur (Steven M. Lowenstein, 278–332). XI. Neue Richtungen im jüdischen Denken (Paul Mendes-Flohr, 333–355). XII. Der Erste Weltkrieg (Peter Pulzer, 356–380). Schluß (Monika Richarz, 381–384). Bd. 4 [publ. 1997]: Aufbruch und Zerstörung 1918–1945. Von Avraham Barkai und Paul Mendes-Flohr mit einem Epilog von Steven M. Lowenstein. 429 pp., illus., notes (386–393), bibl. (394–409), chronol. tab., index (413–429). [Cont.: Einführung (Paul Mendes-Flohr, 9–11). Erster Teil: 1918–1933. I. Im Schatten des Weltkrieges (Paul Mendes-Flohr, 15–36). II. Bevölkerungsrückgang und wirtschaftliche Stagnation. III. Jüdisches Leben in seiner Umwelt. IV. Die Organisation der jüdischen Gemeinschaft. V. Politische Orientierungen und Krisenbewußtsein (Avraham Barkai, 37–124). VI. Jüdisches Kultur- und Geistesleben. VII. Zwischen Deutschtum und Judentum – Christen und Juden. VIII. Juden innerhalb der deutschen Kultur (Paul Mendes-Flohr, 125–190). Zweiter Teil: 1933–1945. IX. Etappen der Ausgrenzung und Verfolgung bis 1939. X. Jüdisches Leben unter der Verfolgung. XI. Organisationen und Zusammenschluß (Avraham Barkai, 193–271). XII. Jüdisches Kulturleben unter dem Nationalsozialismus (Paul Mendes-Flohr, 272–300). XIII. Selbsthilfe im Dilemma "Gehen oder Bleiben?" XIV. Im mauerlosen Ghetto. XV. Das letzte Kapitel. Schluß (Avraham Barkai (301–371). Epilog: Die deutsch-jüdische Diaspora (Steven M. Lowenstein, 372–381).] [American edn. publ. simultaneously by Columbia Univ. Press, New York (distrib. in UK by Wiley, Chichester; for Vol. 1 see No. 33671/YB XLII): Vol. 2: Emancipation and acculturation 1780–1871 (1997, transl. by Allison Brown). Vol. 3: Integration in dispute 1871–1918 (1997, transl. by Carol A. Devore). Vol. 4: Renewal and destruction 1918–1945 (1998, transl. by William Templer).] [Cf.: Bewahrte Erinnerung. Die vierbändige große "Deutsch-jüdische Geschichte" liegt jetzt komplett vor (Helmut Berding) [in]: Die Zeit, Nr. 47, Hamburg, 14. Nov. 1997, p. 13.]

34684. FREUND, SUSANNE: *Jüdische Bildungsgeschichte zwischen Emanzipation und Ausgrenzung. Das Beispiel der Marks-Haindorf-Stiftung in Münster (1825–1942).* Paderborn: Schöningh, 1997. XI, 403 pp., footnotes, illus., tabs., docs., bibl. (360–395), index (persons, 396–403). (Forschungen zur Regionalgeschichte, Bd. 23.). Zugl.: Münster, Univ., Diss, 1995. [Cf.: Besprechung (Arno Herzig) [in]: Aschkenas, Jg. 8, H. 1, Wien, 1998, pp. 261–263.]

34685. GOTZMANN, ANDREAS: *Jüdisches Recht im kulturellen Prozeß. Die Wahrnehmung der Halacha im Deutschland des 19. Jahrhunderts.* Tübingen: Mohr Siebeck, 1997. X, 434 pp., footnotes, bibl. (407–426), index (names, places, subjects, 427–434). (Schriftenreihe wissenschaftlicher Abhandlungen des Leo Baeck Instituts, 55.)

34686. HAHN, HANS-WERNER: *Zwischen Emanzipation und Restauration. Die Auseinandersetzungen um die preußische Judengesetzgebung zwischen Wiener Kongreß und Judengesetz von 1847.* [In]: Konflikt und Reform: Festschrift für Helmut Berding. Hrsg. von Winfried Speitkamp [et al.]. Göttingen: Vandenhoeck und Ruprecht, 1995. Pp. 183–197.

34687. HAVERKAMP, ALFRED/VOLLRATH, HANNA, eds.: *England and Germany in the High Middle Ages.* Oxford: Oxford Univ. Press, 1996. X, 390 pp. (Studies of the German Historical Institute

London.) [Papers presented at a conference organised by the German Historical Institute in London in 1987. Incl.: The relationship between the Jews of Germany and the King (11th–14th centuries); a European comparison (Alexander Patschovsky, 193–218). Kingship and crusade in twelfth-century Germany (Rudolf Hiestand, 235–265).] [Cf.: Besprechung (Regine Birkmeyer) [in]: Zeitschrift für Geschichtswissenschaft, Jg. 45, H. 7, Berlin, 1997, pp. 656–657.]

34688. HAVERKAMP, ALFRED: *Verfassung, Kultur, Lebensform.* Beiträge zur italienischen, deutschen und jüdischen Geschichte im europäischen Mittelalter. Dem Autor zur Vollendung des 60. Lebensjahres. Hrsg. von Friedhelm Burgard [et al.]. Mainz: v. Zabern, 1997. XIII, 552 pp., frontis., footnotes, index (places, persons, 527–552). (Trierer historische Forschungen.) [Incl.: Die Juden im mittelalterlichen Trier (127–188; first publ. 1979). Die Judenverfolgungen zur Zeit des Schwarzen Todes (223–298; first publ. 1981). Lebensbedingungen der Juden im mittelalterlichen Deutschland (463–484; first publ. 1991).]

34689. *Hebräische Berichte über die Judenverfolgungen während der Kreuzzüge.* Hrsg. von Adolphe Neubauer und Moritz Stern. Ins Deutsche übersetzt von S. Baer. Hildesheim; New York: Olms, 1997. XII, 224 [2] pp., footnotes, index. (Quellen zur Geschichte der Juden in Deutschland, II, Bd. 2.) [Reprint of 1892 edn. publ. in Berlin. Cont. introduction (Moritz Stern), Hebrew text and German translation.]

34690. HERZIG, ARNO: *Jüdische Geschichte in Deutschland* Von den Anfängen bis zur Gegenwart. München: Beck, 1997. 323 pp., notes (278–287), bibl. (288–308), indexes (names; places; subjects, 309–323).

34691. HEUBERGER, RACHEL: *Die Stellung der Frau im Judentum. Tradition und Moderne.* [In]: Edith Stein Jahrbuch 1997. Bd. 3, Würzburg, 1997. Pp. 190–202.

34692. *Juden in Politik und Gesellschaft der 1920er Jahre.* Hrsg. von der Friedrich-Ebert-Stiftung in Verbindung mit dem Inst. für Sozialgeschichte e.V., Braunschweig-Bonn. [Rahmenthema in]: Archiv für Sozialgeschichte, Bd. 37, 1997, Bonn, 1997. Pp. 1–253, notes. [Incl.: Juden als wissenschaftliche "Mandarine" im Kaiserreich und in der Weimarer Republik. Neue Überlegungen zu sozialen Ursachen des Erfolgs jüdischer Naturwissenschaftler (Shulamit Volkov, 1–18). Jüdische Intellektuelle in der deutschen Arbeiterbewegung zwischen den beiden Weltkriegen (Helga Grebing, 19–38). Die Rezeption sozialdemokratischer Politik in jüdischen Zeitschriften der Weimarer Republik 1924–1932 (Martin Liepach, 39–54). Zukunftserwartungen deutscher Juden im ersten Jahr der Weimarer Republik (Moshe Zimmermann, 55–72). A "Most remarkable 'Jewish Sect'"? Jewish identity and the Institute of Social Research in the years of the Weimar Republic (Jack Jacobs, 73–92). "Das ungewohnte Bild jüdischer Wahlversammlungen". Zum Stilwandel innerjüdischer Wahlkämpfe in der Weimarer Republik (Jakob Borut, 93–120). Frauenpolitik oder Parteipolitik? Jüdische Frauen in innerjüdischer Politik in der Weimarer Republik (Claudia Prestel, 121–156). "Wir Westjuden haben jüdisches Stammesbewußtsein, die Ostjuden haben jüdisches Volksbewußtsein". Der deutsch-jüdische Blick auf das polnische Judentum in den beiden ersten Jahrzehnten des 20. Jahrhunderts (Yfaat Weiss, 157–178). "Dem Ostjuden ist Deutschland das Land Goethes und Schillers". Kultur und Politik von ostjüdischen Arbeitern in der Weimarer Republik (Ludger Heid, 179–206). Bilder Berlins als "jüdischer" Stadt. Ein Essay zur Wahrnehmungsgeschichte der deutschen Metropole (Joachim Schlör, 207–229). Partizipation [misprinted in table of contents as 'Emanzipation'] und Isolation. Juden in Politik und Gesellschaft Österreichs in den "langen" 1920er Jahren (Albert Lichtblau, 231–253, tabs.). Engl. and French summaries of essays (303–318). Also two contribs. on Soviet Jewry by Antje Kuchenbecker and Matthias Vetter (255–302).]

34693. KAPLAN, MARION A.: *Jüdisches Bürgertum: Frau, Familie und Identität im Kaiserreich.* [Übers. aus dem Amerikan. von Ingrid Strobl.] Hamburg: Dölling und Galitz, 1997. 404 pp., illus., notes (304–375), bibl. (376–395), indexes (persons; places, 397–404). (Studien zur Jüdischen Geschichte, Bd. 3.) [For American edn., publ. in 1991 with the title 'The making of the Jewish middle class', see No. 27949/YB XXXVII.]

KAPLAN, MARION A.: *The "German-Jewish symbiosis" revisited.* [See in No. 35774.]

34694. KORTÜM, HANS-HENNING: *Menschen und Mentalitäten. Einführung in Vorstellungswelten des Mittelalters.* Berlin: Akademie, 1996. 373 pp., footnotes, indexes (353–373). [Incl. section titled: Annäherungsversuche an Randgruppenmentalitäten: Juden und Prostituierte (pp. 141–156).]

34695. KOREN, CHAJA/KRYMALOWSKI, JEANETTE: *Jewish women over five centuries.* Transl. by Edmund Jephcott. London: Winter-Heyden, 1996. 48 pp., illus., ports. [Incl. many German-Jewish women: Glückel von Hameln, Henriette Hardenberg, Fanny Lewald, Fanny Mendelssohn, Charlotte Salomon, Margarete Susman, Bertha Pappenheim, Gertrud Kolmar. First publ. in German in 1995.]

Krisenwahrnehmungen im Fin de siècle. Jüdische und katholische Bildungseliten in Deutschland und der Schweiz. [See No. 34914.]

34696. KROCHMALNIK, DANIEL: *Scheintod und Emanzipation. Der Beerdigungsstreit in seinem historischen Kontext.* [In]: Trumah, H. 6, Berlin, 1997. Pp. 107–150.

34697. *Liber amicorum necnon et amicarum für Alfred Heit.* Beiträge zur mittelalterlichen Geschichte und geschichtlichen Landeskunde hrsg. von Friedhelm Burgard [et al.]. Trier: THF, 1996. XII, 534 pp., footnotes. (Trierer historische Forschungen, Bd. 28.) [Incl.: "Die Juden waren stets eine Randgruppe". Über eine fragwürdige Prämisse der aktuellen Judenforschung (Gerd Mentgen, 393–412). Further contribs. dealing with Judaica are listed according to subject.]

34698. LINDNER, ERIK: *Patriotismus deutscher Juden von der napoleonischen Ära bis zum Kaiserreich.* Zwischen korporativem Loyalismus und individueller deutsch-jüdischer Identität. Frankfurt am Main; New York: Lang, 1997. 448 pp., illus., footnotes, bibl. (403–448). (Europäische Hochschulschriften: Reihe 3, Geschichte und ihre Hilfswissenschaften, Bd. 726.) Zugl.: Münster, Univ., Diss., 1995.

MAURER, TRUDE: *Die Wahrnehmung der Ostjuden in Deutschland 1910–1933.* [See in No. 34942.]

34699. NAGATA, HIROAKI: *Der Nationalismus und die Assimilation der Juden in Deutschland.* [In]: Cultural history of hegemony: decoding of modern Europe. Ed.: Akira Okamoto. Kyoto: Minerva, 1997. Pp. 289–316. [In Japanese, title transl.]

34700. OBERWEIS, MICHAEL: *Übersetzungsprobleme in den hebräischen Kreuzzugsberichten.* [In]: Aschkenas, Jg. 7, H. 2, Wien, 1997. Pp. 441–452, footnotes.

34701. PRUSSIA. CLARK, CHRISTOPHER: *Jewish conversion in context: a case study from nineteenth-century Prussia.* [In]: German History, Vol. 14, No. 3, London 1996. Pp. 281–296.

34702. PULZER, PETER: *Emancipation and its discontents. The German-Jewish dilemma.* Brighton: Centre for German-Jewish Studies, Univ. of Sussex, 1997. 28 pp., notes.

34703. RICHARZ, MONIKA/RÜRUP, REINHARD, eds.: *Jüdisches Leben auf dem Lande.* Studien zur deutsch-jüdischen Geschichte. Hrsg. von Monika Richarz und Reinhard Rürup. Tübingen: Mohr Siebeck, 1997. XI, 444 pp., footnotes, bibl. (413–422), indexes (persons; places, 427–444). [Papers presented at a conference in Bielefeld, Sept. 14–17, 1992. Cont.: Vorwort (eds., V–VII). Ländliches Judentum als Problem der Forschung (Monika Richarz, 1–8). Aus der Stadt auf das Land? Zur Vertreibung und Neuansiedlung der Juden im Heiligen Römischen Reich (J. Friedrich Battenberg, 9–35). Stadt und Land: Zur "inneren" Situation der süd- und westdeutschen Juden in der Frühneuzeit (Stefan Rohrbacher, 37–58). Die ländliche Wirtschaftstätigkeit der Juden im frühmodernen Deutschland (Michael Toch, 59–67). Jüdische Religion und Kultur in den ländlichen Gemeinden 1600–1800 (Mordechai Breuer, 69–78). Ländliche Siedlungsformen und Wirtschaftstätigkeit der Juden östlich der Elbe (Stefi Jersch-Wenzel, 79–90). Landjuden – Stadtjuden. Die Entwicklung in den preußischen Provinzen Westfalen und Schlesien im 18. und 19. Jahrhundert (Arno Herzig, 91–107). Aus dem Dorf nach Amerika: Jüdische Auswanderung 1820–1914 (Avraham Barkai,

109–120). Die jüdische Landbevölkerung in den Emanzipationsdebatten süd- und südwestdeutscher Landtage (Reinhard Rürup, 121–138). Kommunaler Antisemitismus. Christliche Landgemeinden und Juden zwischen Eder und Werra vom späten 18. bis zur Mitte des 19. Jahrhunderts (Robert von Friedeburg, 139–171). Antisemitismus auf dem Lande: der Fall Hessen 1881–1895 (Jacob Toury, 173–188). Synagogenausstattungen als Dokumente jüdischen Lebens auf dem Lande in Franken und Schwaben im 18. Jahrhundert (Annette Weber, 189–205, unpag. illus.: 10 pp.; on the Photosammlung Harburger, kept in the Central Archives for the History of the Jewish People, Jerusalem). Die Genisot als Geschichtsquelle (Frowald Gil Hüttenmeister, 207–218; incl. a list of Genisot, mostly from Franconia). Jüdisches religiöses Leben in deutschen Dörfern. Regionale Unterschiede im 19. und frühen 20. Jahrhundert (Steven M. Lowenstein, 219–229). Religiöses Leben der Landjuden im westlichen Deutschland während der Weimarer Republik (Jacob Borut, 231–248). Jüdische Familie und kulturelle Kontinuität im Elsaß des 19. Jahrhunderts (Paula E. Hyman, 249–267). Haushalt und Familie auf dem Lande im Spiegel südbadischer Nachlaßakten (Gisela Roming, 269–291). Das jüdische Schulwesen auf dem Lande. Baden und Elsaß im Vergleich 1770–1848 (Uri R. Kaufmann, 293–326). Jüdische Erziehung auf dem Lande seit Beginn der Emanzipation im Königreich Hannover 1831–1866 (Rainer Sabellek, 327–345). "Faule Geschichte"? Über "Landjuden" und deutsche Literatur (Michael Schmidt, 347–371). Verfolgung und Alltagsleben der Landjuden im nationalsozialistischen Deutschland (Christhard Hoffmann, 373–398). Nachrede: Erinnerungen an die Dorfjuden heute (Utz Jeggle, 397–411).]

34704. *Sachor. Zeitschrift für Antisemitismusforschung, jüdische Geschichte und Gegenwart.* Bd. 7 (1997) [with the issue title]: *Deutsche – Juden – Polen: Aspekte einer wechselvollen Beziehung.* Mit Beiträgen von Heike Catrin Bala [et al.]. Verantw. Redakteure: Andrea Löw/Christian Scholz. Essen, 1997. 1 issue, footnotes, bibl. [Incl.: Invasion der "hosenverkaufenden Jünglinge"? Die Diskriminierung der Ostjuden in Monarchie und Republik (Lothar Mertens, 56–59). Kurt Grossmann: Individueller Einsatz für die deutsch-polnische Verständigung (Jens Brockschmidt, 60–62). Incl. also a report on the October 1938 deportation (from Bochum) by Susi Schmerler/Shulamit Nadir (63–66).]

34705. SCHULIN, ERNST: *"Das geschichtlichste Volk". Die Historisierung des Judentums in der deutschen Geschichtswissenschaft des 19. Jahrhundert.* [In]: Ernst Schulin: Arbeit an der Geschichte [see No. 35480]. Pp. 114–191, notes (234–248). [Extended version of previous essays on this topic; hitherto unpubl.]

34706. *Thema: "Juden und Christen zur Zeit der Kreuzzüge".* Auf der Insel Reichenau vom 26.-29. März 1996. Konstanz: Konstanzer Arbeitskreis für Mittelalterliche Geschichte, 1996. 110 pp. (Protokoll über die Arbeitstagung Konstanzer Arbeitskreis für Mittelalterliche Geschichte e.V., Nr. 351.)

34707. THIERFELDER, JÖRG/WÖLFING, WILLI, eds.: *Für ein neues Miteinander von Juden und Christen.* Weinheim: Dt. Studien Verlag, 1996. 332 pp., footnotes. (Schriftenreihe der Päd. Hochschule, Bd. 27.) [Cont. contribs. to a series of lectures at the Heidelberg PH in winter 1995/1996. Selected articles: Von der Vielfalt des Judentums und ihren Wurzeln in Deutschland (Uri R. Kaufmann, 98–113). Das Leben der Juden in der deutschen Kultur (Trude Maurer, 267–286). Die Rolle der Frau im Judentum (Rachel Heuberger, 287–304). Further selected articles are listed according to subject.]

34708. TOCH, MICHAEL: *The formation of a Diaspora: the settlement of Jews in the medieval German 'Reich'.* [In]: Aschkenas, Jg. 7, H. 1, Wien, 1997. Pp. 55–78, footnotes.

34709. TOURY, JACOB: *Deutschlands Stiefkinder.* Ausgewählte Aufsätze zur deutschen und deutschjüdischen Geschichte. Gerlingen: Bleicher, 1997. 232 pp., footnotes. (Schriftenreihe des Instituts für Deutsche Geschichte, Universität Tel Aviv, 18.) [Incl. a preface by Dan Diner and seven contribs., some of them first publ. in German: Das Reichsbanner Schwarz-Rot-Gold – Stiefkind der Republik. Zur Gründungsgeschichte republikanischer Wehren (11–92). Jüdische Aspekte der Reichsbannergründung (93–114). Der Prozeß der Lokal-Emanzipation – Herausbildung jüdischer Bürgerrechte in deutschen Ortschaften (127–158). Zur

Problematik der jüdischen Führungsschichten im deutschsprachigen Raum 1880–1933 (159–190). Gab es ein Krisenbewußtsein unter den Juden während der "Guten Jahre" der Weimarer Republik, 1924–1929? (191–214). Bibliographie der Schriften von Jacob Toury 1940–1995 (Gideon Toury, 215–231).]

34710. ZIMMERMANN, MOSHE: *Die deutschen Juden 1914–1945*. München: Oldenbourg, 1997. 167 pp., bibl. notes (141–160), indexes (persons, subjects, 161–167). (Enzyklopädie deutscher Geschichte, Bd. 43.) [Cf.: Besprechung (Ernst Schulin) [in]: Historische Zeitschrift, Bd. 266, Göttingen, 1998, pp. 800–802.]

Linguistics/Western Yiddish

—— COHEN, DANIEL J.: *Die Landjudenschaften in Deutschland als Organe jüdischer Selbstverwaltung von der frühen Neuzeit bis ins neunzehnte Jahrhundert*. Eine Quellensammlung. [See No. 34680.]

34711. ENGEL, ULRICH/GELLER, EVA: *Das Verb in seinem Umfeld. Die deutsche Standardsprache im Licht des Schwäbischen, des Jiddischen und des Polnischen*. [In]: Deutsch-typologisch. Hrsg. von Ewald Lang [et al.]. Berlin; New York: de Gruyter, 1996. Pp. 384–401.

34712. ISHIDA, MOTOHIRO: *Der sprachliche Verkehr zwischen den jüdischen und den deutschen Gaunern*. [In]: Doitsu Bungaku, No. 99, 1997. Pp. 123–133. [In Japanese, title transl.; with German abstract.]

34713. KLEINE, ANKE: *"Der Gefährte im Paradies". Der 'guote Gêrhart' und die jüdische Überlieferung*. [In]: Jiddistik-Mitteilungen, Nr.17, Trier, April 1997. Pp. 1–17, notes. [Incl. the complete annotated and transcribed text of the Yiddish tale from the late 16th cent.]

34714. KÖNIG, WERNER: *Zur Sprache der Juden in Ichenhausen*. Ein Beitrag zur Rekonstruktion des Jiddischen sowie seiner ehemaligen Funktion in der deutschen dialektalen Alltagssprache. [In]: Sprachgeschichtliche Untersuchungen zum älteren und neueren Deutsch. Festschrift für Hans Wellmann zum 60. Geburtstag. Hrsg. von Werner König. Heidelberg: Winter, 1996. Pp. 175–190.

34715. MÜHLEN, BERNT TURE VON ZUR: *Die jiddische Bibliothek Medem in Paris*. [In]: Börsenblatt für den Deutschen Buchhandel, Nr. 69, Frankfurt am Main, 27. Aug. 1996. Pp. A 335–A 338, illus. [On one of the world's biggest Yiddish libraries founded in 1928; cont. also Western Yiddish titles.]

—— REGENSTEINER, HENRY: *Goethe and Yiddish*. [See No. 35856.]

34716. RÖLL, WALTER: *Die Bibelübersetzung ins Jiddische im 14. und 15. Jahrhundert*. [In]: Die Vermittlung geistlicher Inhalte im deutschen Mittelalter. Hrsg. von Timothy R. Jackson [et al.]. Tübingen: Niemeyer, 1996. Pp. 183–195.

34717. TIMM, ERIKA: *Die jiddische Literatur und die italienische Renaissance*. [In]: Alte Welten – Neue Welten. Akten des IX. Kongresses der Int. Vereinigung für germanische Sprach- und Literaturwissenschaft (IVG). Hrsg.: Michael S. Batts. Bd. 1. Plenarvorträge. Tübingen: Niemeyer, 1996. Pp. 60–75.

B. Communal and regional History.

1. Germany

34718. AACHEN. PETERS, DIETER: *Der jüdische Friedhof in Aachen: Gräberliste 1837–1992*. Aachen: D. Peters, 1997. 39 pp. [Privately printed; available at the Bibliothek Germania Judaica, Cologne.]

Bibliography

34719. ACHERN. PETER, F: *Schicksale. Dokumentation nationalsozialistischer Gewaltherrschaft für einen regionalbezogenen Unterricht.* 77855 Achern: Realschule, [1996]. 80 pp., facsims. [Achern: in Baden.]

34720. ADELSDORF. *Spuren jüdischer Vergangenheit in Adelsdorf.* 91325 Adelsdorf: Arbeitskreis "Jüdische Landgemeinden an Aisch und Ebrach", 1996. 195 pp., illus., facsims., gloss., index (places). [Adelsdorf: nr. Nuremberg.] [Cont. contribs. on the history of Jews in Adelsdorf from its beginnings to the Nazi period; incl. the cemetery in Zeckern, the rabbis and other outstanding personalities, 19th-cent. emigration to the US, and the end of Jewish life in Adelsdorf by Johann Fleischmann, Christiane Kolbet, Michael E. Matuschka, Ulrike Krzywinski, Barbara Ohm, Lucia and Hans Schaub and Gerhard Schönbrunn.]

—— ALTONA. [See Hamburg]

34721. ANKLAM. BECKER, GERHARD: *Zur Geschichte der jüdischen Gemeinde in Anklam.* [In]: Baltische Studien. Pommersche Jahrbücher für Landesgeschichte, N.F., Bd. 83, Marburg, 1997. Pp. 60–68, illus., footnotes. [Anklam: in Vorpommern.]

34722. ARNOLDSWEILER. WYRSCH, RUDOLF A.H.: *Von Abraham Fromm zu Josef Schönfeld. Zwei jüdische Familien in Arnoldsweiler seit 1800 bis zum Holocaust.* [In]: Dürener Geschichtsblätter, Nr. 84. Festschrift zum 100jährigen Jubiläum am 18. November 1997, Düren, 1997. Pp. 467–508, illus., footnotes.

34723. ARNSTADT. TITTELBACH-HELMRICH, WOLFGANG: *Arnstadts jüdische Mitbürger.* Arnstadt: Bartheldruck, 1995. 91 pp., illus., facsims. [Arnstadt: in Thuringia; incl. the Nazi period.]

34724. AUGSBURG. KÜNAST, HANS-JÖRG: *Chajjim Schwarz und Paulus Aemilius: jüdisch-hebräischer Buchdruck in Augsburg (1533–1544).* [In]: Fördern und Bewahren. Studien zur europäischen Kulturgeschichte der frühen Neuzeit. Hrsg. von Helwig Schmidt-Glintzer. Wiesbaden: Harrassowitz, 1996. (Wolfenbütteler Forschungen, 70). Pp. 157–171, footnotes, bibl.

34725. BADEN. *Badische Synagogen aus der Zeit von Großherzog Friedrich I. in zeitgenössischen Photographien.* Hrsg. von Franz-Josef Ziwes. Karlsruhe: G. Braun, 1997. 69 pp., illus., bibl. [Incl.: Badische Synagogen neu entdeckt (ed., 9–12). Jüdische Huldigungsadressen an Großherzog Friedrich I. von Baden (Hansmartin Schwarzmaier, 13–24). Großherzog Friedrich I. und der Antisemitismus in Baden (Lore Schwarzmaier, 25–33). Synagogen im Großherzogtum Baden. Bemerkungen zu Architektur und Stil (Wilfried Rößling, 75–82). Der Synagogenritus in Baden und seine Veränderungen im 19. Jahrhundert (Monika Preuß, 83–92).]

34726. BADEN. KAUFMANN, URI R.: *Quellen zur badischen Geschichte in Jerusalem und Berlin.* [In]: Zeitschrift für die Geschichte des Oberrheins, Bd. 145, Stuttgart, 1997. Pp. 491–499, footnotes. [On parts of the archival collection of the Oberrat der Israeliten Badens in the Central Archives for the History of the Jewish People in Jerusalem and in the Centrum Judaicum in Berlin.]

34727. BADEN. LIEPACH, MARTIN: *Die politische Orientierung der "Landjuden" in Baden am Ende der Weimarer Republik 1928–32.* [In]: Historical Social Research. The official Journal of Quantum and Interquant, Vol. 22, No. 1, 1997. Pp. 88–106.

34728. BADEN-WÜRTTEMBERG. ANTMANN, S. MICHAL/PREUß, MONIKA: *Das Projekt zur Erfassung jüdischer Grabsteine in Baden-Württemberg.* [In]: Denkmalpflege in Baden-Württemberg, Jg. 25, Nr. 4, Stuttgart, 1996. Pp. 231–243, illus., map.

34729. BAVARIA. AMBRONN, KARL-OTTO: *Ein "Registrum der Juden verschribungen" aus der Neumarkter Kanzlei Pfalzgraf Ottos II.* Ein Beitrag zur Geschichte der Juden im Neumarkter Herzogtum, verbunden mit allgemeinen Beobachtungen zur Registerführung der Neumarkter Kanzlei und zur Verwaltungsorganisation des Herzogtums. [In]: Archivalische Zeitschrift, Bd. 80 [with the title]: Festschrift. Walter Jaroschka zum 65. Geburtstag. Hrsg. von Albrecht Liess [et al.], Köln, 1997. Pp. 37–55, footnotes.

34730. BENTHEIM. Kolks, Zeno: *Die Orientation von Kirchen, Moscheen und Synagogen im allgemeinen, und von denen in der Grafschaft Bentheim.* [In]: Bentheimer Jahrbuch 1997, Bad Bentheim, 1996. Pp. 61–68, illus., notes. [On Bentheim and Nordhorn.]

34731. BERGHEIM. Friedt, Heinz Gerd: *Ein jüdischer Arzt des 18. Jahrhunderts in Bergheim/Erft: Dr. med. Moyses Samuel Levi.* [In]: Geschichte in Bergheim. Jahrbuch des Bergheimer Geschichtsvereins, Bd. 4, Bergheim, 1995. Pp. 42–51, footnotes, facsims.

34732. BERGHEIM. Pavel, Ingrid von: *Die beiden jüdischen* [sic] *Synagogen in Bergheim.* [In]: Geschichte in Bergheim. Jahrbuch des Bergheimer Geschichtsvereins, Bd. 6, Bergheim, 1997. Pp. 184–195, illus., footnotes.

34733. BERLEBURG. Riedesel, Karl-Ernst: *Ein Berleburger Judeneid.* [In]: Wittgenstein. Blätter des Wittgensteiner Heimatvereins, Jg. 84, Bd. 60, H. 2, Laasphe, 1996. Pp. 64–68, notes.

34734. BERLIN. *Europäische Sozietätsbewegung und demokratische Tradition. Die europäischen Akademien in der Frühen Neuzeit zwischen Frührenaissance und Spätaufklärung.* Bd. 2. Hrsg. von Klaus Garber [et al.]. Tübingen: Niemeyer, 1996. Pp. 951–1840, footnotes. (Frühe Neuzeit, Studien und Dokumente zur deutschen Literatur und Kultur im europäischen Kontext, Bd. 27.) [Incl.: Die "andere Akademie". Juden, Frauen und Berliner literarische Gesellschaften (Barbara Becker-Cantarino, 1478–1506; deals with Moses Mendelssohn, Markus and Henriette Herz and the emancipation of Jews and women. Lazarus Bendavid und die Akademie zu Berlin (Dominique Bourel, 1454–1462).]

—— BERLIN. Ladwig-Winters, Simone: *Wertheim – ein Warenhausunternehmen und seine Eigentümer.* [See No. 35448.]

—— BERLIN. Levine, Glenn S.: *Yiddish publishing in Berlin and the crisis in Eastern European Jewish culture 1919–1924.* [See No. 35385.]

34735. BERLIN. Littmann-Hotopp, Ingrid: *Bei Dir findet das verlassene Kind Erbarmen. Zur Geschichte des ersten jüdischen Säuglings- und Kleinkinderheims in Deutschland (1907 bis 1942).* Berlin: Hentrich, 1996. 148 pp., illus.

34736. BERLIN. Mattenklott, Gert, ed.: *Berlin: Jüdisches Städtebild.* Hrsg. von Gert Mattenklott. Mit einer stadtgeschichtlichen Einführung von Inka Bertz und 27 Fotografien von Wolfgang Feyerabend. Frankfurt am Main: Jüd. Verlag, 1997. 365 pp., illus. [An anthology of texts by Jewish authors. Incl.: Juden in Berlin (Inka Bertz, 7–39). Berliner Juden literarisch (Gert Mattenklott, 40–55).]

34737. BERLIN. Mittag, Susanne: *Frauen und Salonkultur in Berlin im Zeitalter der Romantik und Restauration. Ein Literaturbericht.* [In]: Mitteldeutsches Jahrbuch, Bd. 3, Weimar, 1996. Pp. 137–150, illus., footnotes. [Review essay, incl. Jewish women of the salons.]

—— BERLIN. Schlör, Joachim: *Bilder Berlins als "jüdischer" Stadt. Ein Essay zur Wahrnehmungsgeschichte der deutschen Metropole.* [See in No. 34692.]

34738. BERLIN. Schütz, Erhard: *Berlin. Jüdische Heimat um Neunzehnhundert?* [In]: Zeitschrift für Germanistik, N.F., Bd. 7, H. 1, Bern, 1997. Pp. 74–90, notes.

34739. BERLIN. Sprengel, Peter: *Populäres jüdisches Theater in Berlin von 1877 bis 1933.* Berlin: Haude & Spener, 1997. 144 pp., illus., facsims.

34740. BERLIN. Taylor, Ronald: *Berlin and its culture: a historical portrait.* New Haven; London: Yale Univ. Press, 1997. XIV, 416 pp., illus., ports., map, notes, bibl. (398–403). [Incl. the Jewish contribution to culture in Berlin, as well persecution and elimination of Jews from professional life under the Nazis.]

34741. BERLIN. Weinland, Martina/Winkler, Kurt: *Das Jüdische Museum im Stadtmuseum Berlin. Eine Dokumentation. The Jewish Museum in the Berlin Municipal Museum. A record.*

Hrsg. vom Verein der Freunde und Förderer des Stadtmuseums e.V. Ed. by the Association of Friends and Supporters of the Municipal Museum. Berlin: Nicolai, 1997. 460 pp., illus., facsims., docs., notes, bibl. (232–238). [Texts partly English, partly German. Chronicles the history of the Jewish Museum and documents the progress of the new building by the architect Daniel Libeskind.]

34742. BERLIN-PRENZLAUER BERG. *Leben mit der Erinnerung. Jüdische Geschichte in Prenzlauer Berg.* Hrsg. vom Kulturamt Prenzlauer Berg, Prenzlauer Berg Museum für Heimatgeschichte und Stadtkultur. Berlin: Hentrich, 1997. 447 pp., illus., tabs., graphs., facsims., notes (381–420), gloss., index (431–438), bibl. [Incl. personal memoirs and articles on social and economic aspects of the Jewish population; also on synagogues, cemeteries and other Jewish institutions by Larissa Dämmig, Matthias Frühauf, Christa Heinrich, Sibylle Hinze, Birgit Jerke, Ulla Jung, Birgit Kirchhöfer, Michael Kreutzer, Christiane E. Müller, Bernt Roder, Regina Scheer and Daniela Zunzer.]

34743. BERLIN-TEMPELHOF. SCHILDE, KURT: *Die Bibliotheca Judaica-Hebraica-Rabbinica von Ephraim Pinczower.* [In]: Marginalien, H. 140 (4, 1995), Wiesbaden, 1995. Pp. 8–20, facsim., notes. [On the Berlin-Tempelhof doctor and book collector E.P. (1873–1930) and the fate of his private library of ca. 22,000 books in 1930.]

34744. BIELEFELD. PETERS, DIETER: *Der jüdische Friedhof in Bielefeld.* Aachen: D. Peters, 1997. 39 pp. [Privately printed; available at the Bibliothek Germania Judaica, Cologne.]

34745. BIELEFELD. RENDA, GERHARD: *Jüdisches Leben in Bielefeld: Zeugnisse, Spuren, Orte.* Bielefeld: Historisches Museum, [1997]. 34 pp., illus., map. (Schriften der Hist. Museen der Stadt Bielefeld, Bd. 9.)

34746. BOCHOLT. WESTERHOFF, EDUARD: *Cosman David Cohen (1753–1823) und seine Nachkommen.* [In]: Die westmünsterländische Textilindustrie und ihre Unternehmer. Hrsg. von Hans-Jürgen Teuteberg. Rheinisch-Westfälische Wirtschaftsbiographien, Bd. 16. Münster: Aschendorf, 1996. Pp. 376–416, illus., footnotes, bibl. [On the Cosman Cohen family in Bocholt and their textile factory.]

34747. BOCHUM. KELLER, MANFRED/WILBERTZ, GISELA, eds.: *Spuren in Stein. Ein Bochumer Friedhof als Spiegel jüdischer Geschichte.* [Hrsg.: Ev. Stadtakademie Bochum]. Essen: Klartext, 1997. 376 pp., illus., facsims., plans, lists, notes. [On the Jewish cemetery in Bochum-Wiemelhausen. Incl. list of names; family trees of 14 families. Selected contribs.: Jüdische Friedhöfe. Geschichte und religiöse Besonderheiten (Manfred Keller, 17–42). Geschichte der jüdischen Friedhöfe in Bochum (Gisela Wilbertz, 43–53). Die Bild-Textdokumentation (82–202; incl. German and Hebrew inscriptions). Auswertungsbericht (Gisela Wilbertz/ Barbara Pörsch, 203–216). Geschichte der jüdischen Gemeinde in Bochum (Gisela Wilbertz, 255–286). Die Bochumer Rabbiner Moritz David und Josef Kliersfeld (Manfred Keller, 316–322). Berufsverbot und Enteignung (Britta Weber, 336–355). Die Anfänge der jüdischen Gemeinde Bochum nach 1945 (Hubert Schneider, 357–367). Entwicklungen in der jüdischen Gemeinde in Bochum zwischen 1945 und 1997 (Udo Arnoldi, 368–372).]

34748. BOLLENDORF. COLLJUNG, PAUL: *Die Juden von Bollendorf – 90 Jahre Zusammenleben.* Dokumentation von der Integration bis zum Exodus jüdischer Mitbürger. [In]: Heimatkalender 1997, Landkreis Bitburg-Prüm, Trier, 1997. Pp. 50–57, illus. [Bollendorf: nr. Trier.]

34749. BUTTENHAUSEN. ZACHER, EBERHARD: *Die Juden von Buttenhausen: Alltag und Brauchtum, Verfolgung und Schicksal.* Leben und Untergang einer jüdischen Minorität in einer württembergischen Landgemeinde. Unter Mitarbeit von Mechthild Kreye. Tübingen: Oberschulamt, 1996. 105 pp. (Materialien zur Landeskunde und Landgeschichte, 13.)

34750. BUTTENWIESEN. NEUNER, FRANZ XAVER: *Das jüdische Begräbnis in Buttenwiesen.* [In]: Jahrbuch des Historischen Vereins Dillingen, D. 98, Dillingen, 1996. Pp. 359–384, illus., map.

34751. CASTROP. SCHOLZ, DIETMAR: *"Wornach . . . der Magistrat des Orths . . . des Impetranten Sohn . . . gehörig zu schützen hat."* Die ersten Juden in Castrop: "Schutzjuden" in der brandenburgisch-preußischen Grafschaft Mark und "gleichberechtigte Bürger" im Großherzogtum Berg (1699–1813). [In]: Vestische Zeitschrift, Bd. 94/95/96, Recklinghausen, 1997. Pp. 257–266.

34752. CELLE. GLATTER, SABINE [et al.]: *Die Bauwerke und Einrichtungen der jüdischen Gemeinde in Celle: Synagoge – Mikwe – Friedhof.* Bielefeld: Verl. für Regionalgeschichte, 1995. 102 pp., illus. (Kleine Schriften zur Celler Stadtgeschichte, Bd. 2.)

34753. COLOGNE. DÖPP, SUSKA: *Jüdische Jugendbewegung in Köln 1906–1938.* Münster: Lit Verlag, 1997. 248 pp., illus., facsims., gloss., docs., footnotes, bibl. (217–239).

34754. COLOGNE. MAGNUS, SHULAMIT S.: *Jewish emancipation in a German city: Cologne, 1798–1871.* Stanford, CA: Stanford Univ. Press, 1997. XII, 336 pp., illus.,tabs., maps, appendixes, notes, bibl. (307–330). (Stanford studies in Jewish history and culture.) [Incl. chaps.: From old regime to revolution. The genesis and development of a community in emancipation, 1798–1814. Sinking roots: the consolidation of Jewish settlement, 1814–35. Jewish integration and the politics of resistance, 1814–35. The business of equality: Rhenish liberals, Jewish bankers, and Jewish rights in Cologne, 1835–50. Profile of the Jewish group in the era of liberal ascendancy, 1835–48."A large Gemeinde like Cologne": a community comes into its own, 1850–71.] [Cf: Jewish emancipation in a German city (Lionel B. Steiman) [in]: Canadian Journal of History, Vol. 32, No. 3, Saskatoon, Dec. 1997, pp. 464–466. Besprechung (Tobias Brinkmann) [in]: Zeitschrift für Geschichtswissenschaft, Jg. 46, H. 1, Berlin, 1998, pp. 78–80.]

34755. DEMMIN. BAUCKMEIER, JOCHEN: *Die Juden in Demmin – Versuch einer Schilderung der Verhältnisse bis 1939.* [In]: Baltische Studien. Pommersche Jahrbücher für Kirchengeschichte, N.F., Bd. 83, Marburg, 1997. Pp. 54–59, illus., footnotes. [Demmin: in Mecklenburg.]

34756. DESSAU. GILL, MANFRED/LÖHNERT, PETER: *Jüdische Chemiker aus Dessau in der Filmfabrik Wolfen.* Ein Beitrag zum Schicksal jüdischer Wissenschaftler und der jüdisch verheirateten Wissenschaftler der Filmfabrik Wolfen in der Zeit des Nationalsozialismus. Dessau: M.-Mendelssohn-Ges., 1997. 99 pp., facsims., docs. (Schriftenreihe der M.-Mendelssohn-Ges., Nr. 5.)

34757. DIEZ. HÖLTKEN, TH.: *Das israelitische Kinderheim in Diez.* [In]: Rhein-Lahnkreis: Heimatjahrbuch, Bad Ems, 1997. Pp. 144–146. [Diez: nr. Limburg.]

34758. DORTMUND. *Heimat Dortmund.* Stadtgeschichte in Bildern und Berichten, 1996. Jg. 11, H. 1, Dortmund, 1996. 1 issue. [Incl. 15 contribs. (pp. 1–44) on the history of the Jews in Dortmund from the middle ages to the present day (incl. cemeteries, memorials) by Mosche Awes, Hans-Wilhelm Bohrisch, Ludger Heid, Fritz Hofmann, Dieter Knippschild, Tim Michalak, Wolfgang Polak, Sigrid Schäfer, Thomas Schilp and Katharina Tiemann.]

34759. DRENSTEINFURT (Westphalia). OMLAND, SABINE: *Zur Geschichte der Juden in Drensteinfurt 1811–1941.* 48231 Warendorf: Private publ. [obtainable via Archiv des Kreises Warendorf], 1997. 368 pp., illus., facsims., geneal. charts, docs., footnotes, bibl. (353–361), index (363–368). [Incl. synagogue, cemetery.]

34760. DRIBURG. BRINKMÜLLER, KARL: *Jüdische Bürger in Bad Driburg: 1900 bis heute.* Dokumentation. Hrsg. von Karl Brinkmöller. Mit einem Beitr. von Waldemar Becker. Bad Driburg: Heimatverein, [1997]. 158 pp., illus., facsims. (Aus der Heimatkunde der Stadt Bad Driburg, 21.) [Driburg: East Westphalia.]

34761. DÜLMEN. PIERENKÄMPER, TONI: *Paul Bendix (1878–1932) und seine Familie.* [In]: Die westmünsterländische Textilindustrie und ihre Unternehmer. Hrsg. von Hans Jürgen Teuteberg. Rheinische Wirtschaftsbiographien, Bd. 16. Münster: Aschendorff, 1996. Pp. 236–252, illus., footnotes, bibl. [On the Bendix family and their textile factory in Dülmen, which existed until 1993.]

34762. DÜREN. *Juden im Kreis Düren*. [Teil 1–4] [In]: Jahrbuch des Kreises Düren 1994–1996/97. Düren, 1993 (pp. 124–134), 1994 (pp. 141–160), 1995 (pp. 79–96), 1997 (pp. 89–112), facsims., docs., notes. [Author of part I: Willi Dovern, of part II: Renate Xhonneux, of part III: Bernd Hahne, of part IV: Ludger Dowe.]

34763. DÜSSELDORF. *Aspekte jüdischen Lebens*. In Düsseldorf und am Niederrhein. Hrsg.: Mahn- und Gedenkstätte. Red. und Bearb.: Angela Genger/Kerstin Griese. Düsseldorf: Der Oberstadtdirektor der Landeshauptstadt Düsseldorf/Mahn- und Gedenkstätte Düsseldorf. 277 pp., illus., facsims., notes. [Cont. (titles partly abbr.): Vorwort [&] Juden in Düsseldorf. Eine Einführung (Angela Genger, 6–47). Juden am Unteren Niederrhein im 19. und 20. Jahrhundert (Jutta Prieur, 24–47). Die Düsseldorfer Rabbiner vom 18. Jahrhundert bis zur Zeit des Nationalsozialismus [&] Synagogen in Düsseldorf [&] Die jüdischen Friedhöfe (Barbara Suchy, 48–87). Zur Geschichte jüdischer Frauen in Düsseldorf (Helen Quandt, 88–105). Jüdische Schulen in Düsseldorf (Frank Sparing, 106–115). Jüdische Jugendgruppen in Düsseldorf (Annette Klerks, 116–129). Makkabi und der jüdische Sport in Düsseldorf (Heiko Zielke, 130–141). Die Zionistische Bewegung in Düsseldorf (Kerstin Griese, 142–155). Ostjuden in Düsseldorf [&] Juden in der Düsseldorfer Wirtschaft (Frank Sparing, 156–175). Jüdische Ärzte in Düsseldorf (Wolfgang Woelk, 176–185). Jüdische Künstler (Sigrid Kleinbongartz, 186–197). Jüdische Musik? (Hildegard Jakobs, 198–207). Adolf Zürndorfer (Karola Regent, 208–211). Siegfried Thalheimer [&] Fritz Heymann (Ingo Piel, 212–226). Die Jüdische Gemeinde Düsseldorf von 1945 bis in die Gegenwart (Alice Feuser-Weyrich, 226–233). Evangelische Kirche und die Juden im Rheinland (Sigrid Lekebusch, 234–241). Katholizismus zwischen traditionellem Antijudaismus und modernem Antisemitismus (Ulrich Brzosa, 242–255). Die Heine-Denkmäler in Düsseldorf (Holger Ehlert, 256–269).]

34764. DÜSSELDORF. *Spuren jüdischen Lebens in Düsseldorf*. Ein Stadtrundgang. Autorinnen: Hannelore Lutz/Andrea Sonnen. Hrsg.: Arbeitskreis der NS-Gedenkstätten NWe.V. Gesellschaft für Christl.-Jüd. Zus.-arbeit in Düsseldorf [et al.]. [Düsseldorf], 1997. [Private print.] 63 pp., illus.

34765. ERFURT. *Die Geschichte der Juden in Erfurt*. Nebst Noten, Urkunden und Inschriften aufgefundener Leichensteine, größtenteils nach primären Quellen bearb. von Adolph Jaraczewsky. Neuauflage der Jüdischen Landesgemeinde Thüringen nachgesetzt nach der alten Vorlage, Erfurt 1868. Erfurt: Verl. u. Druckerei Fortschritt, [1996?]. 120 pp.

34766. FILEHNE. HERZBERG, ARNO: *A town in Eastern Germany. The story of Filehne – a memoir*. [In]: Leo Baeck Institute Year Book XLII, London, 1997. Pp. 327–336, footnotes. [Author, a jurist who lives in the US, describes Jewish life in Filehne (Posen), where he spent his childhood.]

34767. FRANCONIA. *"Denn das Sterben des Menschen hört nie auf . . .": Aspekte jüdischen Lebens in Vergangenheit und Gegenwart*. [Hrsg.: Ulrich Wagner]. Mit Beiträgen von Aron Benario [et al.] Würzburg: Schöningh, 1997. 186 pp., illus. (Schriften des Stadtarchivs Würzburg, H. 11.) [Incl.: "Denn das Sterben des Menschen hört nie auf. . .". Das Leben des Aron Benario von Obernbreit (Aron Benario; Transkription, Vorwort und Stammtafel von Michael Schneeberger, 9–44; memoirs, written between 1883 and 1886). ILBA [Israelitische Lehrer-Bildungsanstalt] – Würzburg. Rückblick eines Absolventen (Simon Berlinger, 45–72, illus.). Jahre der Panik (Mina Schlesinger, 73–90). Die jüdische Gemeinde von Rottenbauer und ihre wechselvolle Geschichte (Joachim Braun, 91–99). Damast, Atlas und Samt. Wege einer Postkarte aus Prag nach Würzburg (Karl Theodor Grashof, 101–112). Das Aufkommen der Hostienfrevellegende und die Judenverfolgung in Franken um 1298 (Friedrich Lotter, 113–130, illus., footnotes). Die "Deggendorfer Gnad". Entstehung und Geschichte einer umstrittenen Hostienwallfahrt (Manfred Eder, 131–156, footnotes). Judenfeindliche Kulte und regionale Identität. Religiöse Verehrung von 'Ritualmord'-Opfern und die Folgen (Georg R. Schroubek, 157–168). Der angebliche Ritualmord von Manau im Jahre 1929 und seine Instrumentalisierung durch die unterfränkische NSDAP (Roland Flade, 169–182, footnotes).]

34768. FRANCONIA. HIMMEL, BARBARA: *Synagogenbau in Oberfranken: dargestellt am Beispiel Kronach.* Bayreuth: [Druckerei Emil Mühl], 1997. 44 pp., illus. (Heimatbeilage Nr. 328 zum Amtlichen Schulanzeiger des Regierungsbezirks Oberfranken.)

34769. FRANCONIA. *Jüdisches Leben in der Fränkischen Schweiz.* Mit Beiträgen von Toni Eckert [et al.]. [Hrsg.: Arbeitskreis Heimatkunde im Fränkische-Schweiz-Verein]. Erlangen: Palm & Enke, 1997. 858 pp., illus., facsims., docs., gloss., bibl. (820–834), index (subjects, 835–858). (Die Fränkische Schweiz – Landschaft und Kultur: Landschaft und Kultur, Bd. 11.) [Incl. the sections: A. Leben auf dem Lande (19–190; contribs. by Reinhold Glas, Walter Tausendpfund and Gerhard Philipp Wolf, 72–78). B. Orte mit größeren jüdischen Gemeinden (191–631; contribs. on Tüchersfeld, Ermreuth (incl. cemetery), Kunreuth, Pretzfeld, Hagenbach, Wannbach, Egloffstein, Aufseß, Heiligenstadt, Mittlerweilersbach, Forchheim by Georg Knörlein, Peter Landendörfer, Rajaa Nadler, Josef Seitz, Walter Tausendpfund, Petra Weiß and Gerhard Philipp Wolf). C. Jüdische Zentren am Rande der Fränkischen Schweiz (632–721; contribs. on Schnaittach and Baiersdorf by Walter Tausendpfund and Gerhard Philipp Wolf; also on Andreas Osiander and Johann Christoph Georg Bodenschatz). D. Exemplarische Persönlichkeiten – Biographische Skizzen (722–770; contribs. by Toni Eckert, Peter Landendörfer, Josef Seitz and Walter Tausendpfund. E. Quellenauszüge (771–805).]

34770. FRANKFURT am Main. *Frankfurter jüdische Erinnerungen.* Ein Lesebuch zur Sozialgeschichte 1864–1951. Hrsg. im Auftrag des Magistrats der Stadt Frankfurt am Main, Dezernat Kultur und Freizeit, von der Kommission zur Erforschung der Geschichte der Frankfurter Juden. Bearb. von Elfi Pracht. Sigmaringen: Thorbecke, 1997. 329 pp., gloss., bibl. (320–326).

—— FRANKFURT am Main. HEUER, RENATE/WOLF, SIEGBERT, eds.: *Die Juden der Frankfurter Universität.* [see No. 35446.]

34771. FRANKFURT am Main. HOPP, ANDREA: *Jüdisches Bürgertum in Frankfurt am Main im 19. Jahrhundert.* Stuttgart: Steiner, 1997. 331 pp., footnotes, bibl. 307–324), index (325–332), illus.: 11 pp. (Frankfurter historische Abhandlungen, Bd. 38.)

34772. FRANKFURT am Main. JÜDISCHES MUSEUM, FRANKFURT AM MAIN: *Jüdisches Museum, Frankfurt am Main.* [Texte: Georg Heuberger [et al.]. Red.: Johannes Wachten. München; New York: Prestel, 1997. 112 pp., illus. (Prestel-Museumsführer.)

34773. FRANKFURT am Main. KLAUSMANN, CHRISTINA: *Politik und Kultur der Frauenbewegung im Kaiserreich.* Das Beispiel Frankfurt am Main. Frankfurt am Main; New York: Campus, 1997. 404 pp., footnotes, tabs., bibl. (378–391), index. [Refers passim to the Jewish activists of the women's movement in Frankfurt am Main; incl. chap. VI: Die Sittlichkeitsdebatte in der Frankfurter Frauenbewegung (151–192; dealing with Bertha Pappenheim, the 'Jüdischer Frauenbund', and its fight against 'white slavery'.]

34774. FRANKFURT am Main. KREFT, GERALD/KOHRING, ROLF: *"Ich bin also sozusagen ein auserwähltes Wesen. . .".* Tilly Edinger (1897–1967), Begründerin der Paläoneurologie in Frankfurt am Main. [In]: Forschung Frankfurt. Wissenschaftsmagazin der Johann Wolfgang Goethe-Universität Frankfurt am Main, Jg. 15, No. 4, Frankfurt am Main, 1997. Pp. 16–24, illus., ports.

34775. FRANKFURT am Main. OTTO, ARNIM: *Juden im Frankfurter Osten 1796–1945.* 2. bearb. Aufl. Offenbach am Main: Arnim Otto Verlag; Ed. Lamond, 1997. 454 pp., illus., facsims., ports., bibl.

34776. FRANKFURT am Main. *Selig Goldschmidt: picture of a life.* (From letters and commemorative pages). Compiled by Meier Selig Goldschmidt. Completed by Robert (Ezriel) Cramer. Jerusalem: Elmar Printers, 1996. 183 pp., illus., facsims. [On the antique dealers 'Fa. J. & S. Goldschmidt, Frankfurt am Main'.]

34777. FÜRTH. GIERSCH, ROBERT: *Archivalienforschung zur Geschichte des sogenannten Gabrielshofes mit der Gabrielssynagoge, Königstraße 57, 90762 Fürth.* [In]: Nachrichten für den jüdischen Bürger Fürths, Fürth, Sept. 1997. Pp. 34–40, illus.

34778. GERA. SIMSOHN, WERNER: *Juden in Gera I: ein geschichtlicher Überblick.* Mit Berichten von Hermann Birnbaum [et al.]. Hrsg. von Erhard Roy Wiehn. Vorwort von Ralf Rauch. Konstanz: Hartung-Gorre, 1997. 286 pp., illus., facsims., bibl. [Incl.: Totenliste: Opfer des Holocaust von Gera (7–9).]

34779. GESEKE. MARX, REINHARD: *Gedicht für einen jüdischen Frontsoldaten.* [In]: Geseker Heimatblätter, Jg. 54, Nr. 403, Geseke, 1996. Pp. 235–236.

34780. GIESSEN. STEIL, DIETER: *Juden im Wirtschaftsleben des Kammerbezirks.* [In]: 125 Jahre Industrie- und Handelskammer Gießen. Wirtschaft in einer Region. Hrsg. von Helmut Berding. Darmstadt: Hessisches Wirtschaftsarchiv, 1997. (Schriften zur hessischen Wirtschafts- und Unternehmensgeschichte, 2.) Pp. 113–140, illus., tabs., notes. [Covers the period 1800 – 1943, deals also with the districts of Gießen, Alsfeld und Lauterbach. Also, by same author: Zur Geschichte der Juden. [In]: 800 Jahre Gießener Geschichte 1197–1997. Hrsg. im Auftrag des Magistrats der Universitätsstadt Gießen von Ludwig Brake und Heinrich Brinkmann. Gießen: Brühlscher Verlag, 1997. Pp. 381–409, illus., notes.]

34781. GLÜCKSTADT. STUDEMUND-HALÉVY, MICHAEL: *Die portugiesisch-spanischen Grabinschriften in Norddeutschland: Glückstadt und Emden.* [In]: Aschkenas, Jg. 7, H. 2, Wien, 1997. Pp. 389–439, footnotes. [See also No. 34787.]

34782. BAD GODESBERG. SCHAMPEL, INGRID: *Die Villa Cahn, eine fast unendliche Geschichte.* [In]: Godesberger Heimatblätter, H. 35, Bad Godesberg, 1997. Pp. 115–121, illus. [On a house built by Edwin Oppler for Albert Cahn, a Bonn banker, in the 1860s.]

34783. GÖTTINGEN. SCHASER, ANGELIKA: *Schutzjuden zwischen Studenten und Bürgerschaft in Göttingen am Ende des 18. Jahrhunderts. Oder: Wie der Herrmannstädter Student Johann Georg Hertel den Schutzjuden Moses Gumbrecht und die Göttinger Bürgerschaft um 2000 Taler betrog.* [In]: Schlaglichter Preußen – Westeuropa. Festschrift für Ilja Mieck zum 65. Geburtstag. Hrsg. von Ursula Fuhrich-Grubert [et al.]. Berlin: Duncker & Humblot, 1997. (Berliner Historische Studien, Bd. 25.). Pp. 349–362, footnotes.

34784. HAGEN. ZABEL, HERMANN: *Ehemalige Hagener in Israel.* [In]: Heimatbuch Hagen und Mark 1996, Jg. 37, Hagen, 1996. Pp. 136–146.

34785. HAMBURG. BRIX, BARBARA: *"Land, mein Land, wie leb' ich tief aus dir". Dr. Walter Bacher – Jude, Sozialdemokrat, Lehrer an der Klosterschule.* Geleitwort von Ruben Herzberg. Hamburg: Gymnasium Klosterschule/Dölling und Galitz, 1997. 69 pp., illus.

34786. HAMBURG. COMMICHAU, GERHARD: *Zur Herkunft und zum Berufsweg hansestädtischer Juristen im 19. Jahrhundert.* [In]: Zeitschrift des Vereins für Hamburgische Geschichte, Bd. 83, Teil 1: Bewahren und Berichten. Festschrift für Hans-Dieter Loose zum 60. Geburtstag hrsg. von Hans Wilhelm Eckardt [et al.], Hamburg, 1997. Pp. 415–426, ports., footnotes. [Incl. Gabriel Riesser and Isaac Wolffson (Hamburg).]

34787. HAMBURG. FAUST, JÜRGEN/STUDEMUND-HALÉVY, MICHAEL: *Betahaim. Sefardische Gräber in Schleswig-Holstein.* Glückstadt: Augustin, 1997. 116 pp., illus., gloss., bibl., index. [Incl. the history of the cemeteries of Glückstadt, Hamburg-Altona, Hamburg-Bahrenfeld. Documents the grave stones (1616–1879) and their inscriptions.]

—— HAMBURG. KASISCHKE-WURM, DANIELA: *Antisemitismus im Spiegel der Hamburger Presse während des Kaiserreiches (1884–1914).* [See No. 35829.]

34788. HAMBURG. OPHIR, BARUCH ZWI: *Über traditionell-gesetzestreue Rabbiner in Hamburg-Altona "AHU") im 19. und 20. Jahrhundert.* [In]: Mitteilungen 31. Hamburger Arbeitskreis für Regionalgeschichte (HAR), Hamburg, Nov. 1997. Pp. 22–32.

34789. HAMBURG. Studemund-Halévy, Michael, ed.: *Die Sefarden in Hamburg. Zur Geschichte einer Minderheit*. Zweiter Teil. Hamburg: Buske, 1997. Pp. 503–940, illus., index. [Incl.: Progressiver Sprachverfall des Portugiesischen unter den Hamburger Sefardim im 17. und 18. Jahrhundert (Benjamin N. Teensma, 503–550). The storied stones of Altona. Biblical imagery on Sefardic tombstones at the Jewish cemetry of Altona-Königstraße, Hamburg (Rochelle Weinstein, 551–660). Some episodes of sefardic history as reflected in epitaphs of the Jewish cemetry in Altona (Marian and Ramon F. Sarraga, 661–720). Alfonso Cassuto und der Portugiesenfriedhof an der Königstraße (Michael Studemund-Halévy, 721–752). Los Salmos de David (Abenar Melo) (Harm den Boer/Monserrat Gómez García, 753–780). The Spanish and Portuguese Golden Age Parnassus in Hamburg: Jeosuah Habilho's 'Coleccion Nueva' (1764) (Kenneth Brown, 781–878). La familia De Lima entre Hamburgo, Curacao y Chile (Günter Böhm, 879–900). Meines Vaters Haus: Ein Interview mit David Shaltiel (901–922). Das Maß seiner Tage: Erinnerungen an David Shaltiel (texts by Gershom Scholem, Erich Lüth, Haim Cohn, Yemima Avidar-Tchernovitz, 923–935). For Vol. 1 see No. 31506/YB XL.]

34790. HAMBURG-WANDSBEK. Bar-Giora Bamberger, Naftali: *Memor-Buch. Die jüdischen Friedhöfe in Wandsbek*. Hamburg: Dölling u. Galitz, 1997. 2 vols.: 742; 179 pp., illus., maps, docs., indexes, bibl. [At head of title: Zum ewigen Gedächtnis. Book title also in Hebrew. Incl. Hebrew inscriptions, German transl. and notes.]

34791. HANOVER. Brunngraber-Malottke, Ruth/Schulze, Peter: *Richard Dammann (1890–1939). Das Portrait eines hannoverschen Wilhelm-Busch-Sammlers*. [In]: Wilhelm-Busch-Jahrbuch 1995, Mitt. der Wilhelm-Busch-Gesellschaft Nr. 61, Hannover, 1996. Pp. 6–14, port., illus. [R.D., 1890 Hanover – 1939 Sao Paulo, co-owner of the private bank 'Gebr. Dammann Bank' founded by his father, 1879.]

34792. HANOVER. Schulze, Peter: *Heimat auf Widerruf. Jüdische Jugend in Hannover um 1930*. [In]: "Mit 17. . .". Jugendliche in Hannover von 1900 bis heute. Begleitheft zur gleichnamigen Ausstellung. Hannover: Hist. Museum Hannover, 1997. (Schriften des Hist. Museums Hannover, H. 12.). Pp. 55–64, illus. [Deals also with numerous Jewish youth and sport organisations.]

34793. HECHINGEN. Vees, Adolf: *Das Hechinger Heimweh. Begegnungen mit Juden*. Hrsg. vom Hohenzollerischen Geschichtsverein [et al.]. Tübingen: Silberburg, 1997. 192 pp., illus. [Cf.: Besprechung (Andreas Mink) [in]: Aufbau, Vol. 64, No. 14, New York, July 3, 1998, p. 5.]

34794. HEIDELBERG. Giovannini, Norbert: *Zwischen Emanzipation und Verfolgung – jüdisches Leben in Heidelberg*. [In]: Für ein neues Miteinander von Juden und Christen [see No. 34707]. Pp. 188–220.

34795. HESSE. Battenberg, Friedrich: *Die verzögerte Emanzipation der Juden in der Grafschaft Erbach*. [In]: Archiv für hessische Geschichte und Altertumskunde, N.F., Bd. 55, Neustadt an der Aisch, 1997. Pp. 63–92, footnotes.

34796. HESSE. Köhler, Gustav Ernst: *Die Judengemeinde von Burkhardsfelden im Busecker Tal*. 2., überarb. und erg. Aufl. Reiskirchen: Heimatgesch. Vereinigung Reiskirchen, 1996. 33 pp. (Schriftenreihe der heimatgesch. Vereinigung Reiskirchen, Nr. 14.)

34797. HESSE. Lange, Thomas, ed.: *"L'chajim". Geschichte der Juden im Landkreis Darmstadt-Dieburg"*. Reinheim: [Landkreis Darmstadt-Dieburg], 1997. 370 pp., illus., facsims., map, bibl. [Incl. (titles partly condensed): Einführung (ed., 1–4). Die jüdische Geschichte des Kreisgebiets vom Mittelalter bis ins 19. Jahrhundert (Eckhart G. Franz, 5–26). Vom Hausierer zum Ladenbesitzer. Zur beruflichen Tätigkeit der Juden im Landkreis Darmstadt-Dieburg [&] Religiöses Leben und Volksfrömmigkeit der Landjuden (Uri R. Kaufmann, 27–60). Alte Synagogen im Landkreis Darmstadt-Dieburg (Eva Reinhold Postina, 61–106). Die jüdischen Friedhöfe im Landkreis Darmstadt-Dieburg (Hartmut Heinemann, 107–138). Judenfeindschaft und Antisemitismus zwischen 1890 und 1933 (Thomas Lange,

139–168). Die Leidensgeschichte der jüdischen Bevölkerung im Gebiet des heutigen Landkreises Darmstadt-Dieburg 1933–1945 mit einem Rückblick auf die zwanziger Jahre (Gerd Steffens, 169–270). Nach 1945 – ein neuer Anfang? (Dieter Kohlmannslehner/Thomas Lange, 271–338). Eine Perspektive für jüdisches Leben heute? (Moritz Neumann, 339–346).]

34798. HESSE. LIEPACH, MARTIN: *Die politische Orientierung der Dorf- und Kleinstadtjuden in Hessen am Ende der Weimarer Republik*. [In]: Archiv für hessische Geschichte und Altertumskunde, N.F., Bd. 55, Neustadt an der Aisch, 1997. Pp. 93–110, notes.

34799. HESSE. NUHN, HEINRICH: *Judenpredigten und Judentaufen*. [In]: Zeitschrift des Vereins für Hessische Geschichte und Landeskunde, Bd. 102, Hofgeismar, 1997. Pp. 89–98, notes. [Deals with a file in the Staatsarchiv Marburg entitled "Rotenburger Judenpredigten" from the 17th cent.]

34800. HETTENLEIDELHEIM. BLUM, KARL: *Die Juden und die beiden jüdischen Friedhöfe in Hettenleidelheim*. Hettenleidelheim: Heimatmuseum – Archiv K. Blum e.V., 1995. 177 pp., illus., facsims. (Eine Schriftenreihe des Heimatmuseums Hettenleidelheim, Bd. 2.) [Hettenleidelheim: Palatinate]

34801. HORN. FAASSEN, DINA VAN: *"Hat die Schutzgelder an die Kammer geschickt"*. *Jüdisches Leben vom Spätmittelalter bis zur Weimarer Republik*. [In]: Stadtgeschichte Horn 1248–1998. Horn-Bad Meinberg: Hütte-Verlag, 1997. Pp. 482–513, illus., facsims., notes (604–607). [Horn: Krs. Lippe; at present part of Horn-Bad Meinberg.]

34802. HUNSRÜCK. ZIEMER, HANS-WERNER: *Die jüdischen Gemeinden im Jahre 1913 in Orten des heutigen Rhein-Hunsrück-Kreises*. [In]: Hunsrücker Heimatblätter, Jg. 35, Nr. 97, Simmern, 1997. Pp. 436–437.

34803. ICHENHAUSEN. HARRIES-SCHUMANN, LISA: *Orthodoxy and reform, revolution and reaction. The Jewish community in Ichenhausen 1813–1861*. [In]: Leo Baeck Institute Year Book XLII, London, 1997. Pp. 29–48, footnotes.

—— ICHENHAUSEN. KÖNIG, WERNER: *Zur Sprache der Juden in Ichenhausen*. Ein Beitrag zur Rekonstruktion des Jiddischen in Ichenhausen sowie seiner ehemaligen Funktion in der deutschen dialektalen Alltagssprache. [See No. 34714.]

34804. ISSUM. KEUCK, THEKLA: *Die Rechtsverhältnisse der Juden im Kurfürstentum Köln im 18. Jahrhundert am Beispiel Issum*. [In]: Geldrischer Heimatkalender 1998, Geldern, 1997. Pp. 49–50, notes.

34805. KASSEL. MEY, EBERHARD: *Zur Integration der Juden in die Kasseler Bürgerschaft – das Beispiel Hirsch Fränkel (1818–1907)*. [In]: Zeitschrift des Vereins für Hessische Geschichte und Landeskunde, Bd. 102, Hofgeismar, 1997. Pp. 167–172, notes. [Deals with the life of the book printer H.F.]

34806. KESTRICH. OFFHAUS, ERNST-UWE: *Aus der Geschichte des Feldatales. Beinahe schon vergessen: ehemalige jüdische Mitbürger von Kestrich*. [In]: Mitteilungen des Oberhessischen Geschichtsvereins Giessen, N.F., Bd. 80, Giessen, 1995. Pp. 243–333. [Incl. family data; also documents the cemetery (without Hebrew inscriptions).]

34807. KIRCHHEIMBOLANDEN. KUKATZKI, BERNHARD: *Jüdische Kultuseinrichtungen in der Verbandsgemeinde Kirchheimbolanden*. Schifferstadt: B. Kukatzki, 1997. 30 pp., illus., facsims., notes, index. [On synagogues, cemeteries and ritual baths in Gauersheim, Ilbesheim, Kirchheimbolanden and Marnheim.]

34808. KIRCHSCHÖNBACH. HASS, NORBERT J.: *Jüdisches Familienbuch der ehemaligen jüdischen Gemeinde zu Kirchschönbach 1814–1875*. [Bamberg]: Norbert J. Haas, [1995]. 45 pp. (Beiträge zur fränkischen Familienforschung, 11.)

34809. KREUZAU. NOLDEN, NIKOLAUS: *Beiträge zur Geschichte von Kreuzau (1794–1988)*. Im Auftrag der Gemeinde Kreuzau hrsg. von Reiner Nolden. Düren: Gemeinde Kreuzau, Der Gemeindedirektor, 1997. 288 pp., illus. [Incl.: Die Juden (54–61).] [Kreuzau: nr. Aachen.]

34810. BAD KREUZNACH. PETERS, DIETER: *Genealogische Daten von jüdischen Friedhöfen im Kreis Bad Kreuznach*. [Bestandsaufnahmen, Gräberlisten, Sterberegister u.a. aus eigenen und fremden Bestandsaufnahmen sowie aus der Dokumentation "Jüdische Grabstätten im Kreis Bad Kreuznach. Teil 1"] [Hrsg.: Kreisverw. Bad Kreuznach]. Aachen: Dieter Peters [privately printed], 1995. 60 pp.

34811. LANGENHAIN. THIEL, HANS: *Juden in Langenhain*. Ein Beitrag zur Geschichte des nassauischen Landjudentums. [In]: Nassauische Annalen, Bd. 108, Wiesbaden, 1997. Pp. 145–168, facsims., footnotes. [Langenhain: since 1972 part of Hofheim am Ts.; also on the cemetery near Wallau.]

34812. LANGSTADT. WITTENBERGER, GEORG: *Der Religionslehrer und Kantor Simon Wetzler (1853–1919)*. [In]: Mainfränkisches Jahrbuch für Geschichte und Kunst, 49, Würzburg, 1997. Pp. 211–219, illus., notes. [On the Wetzler family of Langstadt (at present part of Babenhausen, Hesse). Simon Wetzler was cantor and teacher in Aschaffenburg for 35 years.]

34813. LEIPZIG. REINHOLD, JOSEF: *Die Entstehung einer jüdischen Grossgemeinde*. Vor 150 Jahren konstituierte sich die Israelitische Religionsgemeinde zu Leipzig. [In]: Sächsische Heimatblätter, Jg. 43, H. 3, Dresden, 1997. Pp. 117–141, illus., facsims., maps.

34814. LOWER SAXONY. HERBST, DETLEV: *Jüdisches Leben im Solling. Der Synagogenverband Bodenfelde – Uslar – Lippoldsberg und die Synagogengemeinde Lauenförde*. Mit einer Einführung in die jüdische Religion von Yaacov Ben-Chanan: Die Tora-Anweisung zum richtigen Leben. Uslar: Schlieper, 1997. 291 pp., illus., bibl. (278–289). [Incl. Nazi period.]

34815. LOWER SAXONY. HEUTGER, NICOLAUS: *Jüdische Spuren in Niedersachsen*. Münster: Lit Verlag, 1997. 160, footnotes, index: 9 pp., illus.: 17 pp., bibl.(146–160). (Jüdische Studien, 1.) [Incl. the Nazi period.]

34816. LUCKENWALDE. FREUDENTHAL, JOSEPH: *Chronik der Synagogengemeinde zu Luckenwalde und deren Vorgeschichte*. Zum 50jährigen Jubiläum der Synagogengemeinde 1919. Hrsg. von Detlev Riemer in Zusammenarbeit mit Irene Diekmann. Potsdam: Verl. für Berlin-Brandenburg, 1997. 206 pp., illus. (Beiträge zur Geschichte und Kultur der Juden in Brandenburg, Mecklenburg-Vorpommern, Sachsen-Anhalt, Sachsen und Thüringen, Bd.1.) [Reprint of the 1919 original. Incl. also: Zur Geschichte der Juden in Luckenwalde 1919–1996 (Detlev Riemer). Chronologie und Statistisches. Der Chronist Joseph Freudenthal und seine Familie.]

34817. LÜNEBURG. BOLLGÖHN, SIBYLLE: *Jüdische Familien in Lüneburg*. Erinnerungen. Lüneburg: Geschichtswerkstatt Lüneburg, 1995. 156 pp., illus., ports., facsims., maps. [Deals also with the Nazi period. Incl.: Gedenkteil (124–151; on 42 Lüneburg families).]

34818. MANNHEIM. STORCK, JOACHIM W.: *"Für die Kunst" – Herbert Tannenbaum und sein Kunsthaus*. [In]: Mannheimer Geschichtsblätter, N.F., Bd. 3, Sigmaringen, 1996. Pp. 379–397, illus., footnotes. [H.T., March 7, 1892 Mannheim – Sept. 30, 1958, Frankfurt, art dealer, jurist, owner of an art gallery in Mannheim and from 1949 in New York; emigr. 1937 to the Netherlands, 1947 to the US.]

34819. MECKLENBURG. HIRSCH, HEINZ: *Spuren jüdischen Lebens in Mecklenburg*. 2., überarb. Aufl. Schwerin: Friedrich-Ebert-Stiftung, Landesbüro Mecklenburg-Vorpommern, 1997. 119 pp., map, bibl. (Reihe Geschichte Mecklenburg-Vorpommern, Nr. 6.) [Covers also the Nazi period. For previous edn. see No. 32599/YB XLI.]

34820. MEINERZHAGEN. BARTSCH, KARL-HEINZ: *"Edict wegen der Betteljuden"*. [In]: Meinhardus. Heimatblätter für Stadt und Amt Meinerzhagen 1996. Jg. 30, Meinerzhagen, 1996. Pp. 46–52.

34821. MERZHAUSEN. FRIEDEBURG, ROBERT VON: *Herren, Juden und Pfarrer.* Die 'Samuel-Stelle' (I. Sam. 8, 11 ff. und 1. Sam. 12) und antijüdische Ressentiments im sozialen Konflikt zwischen Pfarrer, Landgemeinde und adliger Herrschaft nach dem Dreißigjährigen Krieg. [In]: Religion und Religiosität im Zeitalter des Barock. Hrsg.: Dieter Breuer [et al.]. Teil 1. Wiesbaden: Harrassowitz, 1995. Pp. 175–189, footnotes. [On Pastor Johannes Hassenpflug in Merzhausen (Hessen-Kassel) and the role of the local "Schutzjuden".]

34822. MESCHEDE. *Jüdische Familien in Meschede.* Hrsg. im Auftrag des Synagogenvereins von Hanneli Kaiser-Löffler [et al.]. Meschede: [privately printed], 1997. 119 pp., illus., facsims., bibl. [Also on the synagogue (Erika Richter) and the cemetery (Wilfried Oertel).] [Meschede: on the Ruhr.]

34823. MILTENBERG. DEBLER, ULRICH: *Die jüdische Gemeinde von Miltenberg.* Aschaffenburg: Geschichts- und Kunstverein, 1995. 160 pp., illus., ports., facsims., notes, plans. (Sonderveröff. aus dem Aschaffenburger Jahrbuch für Geschichte, Landeskunde und Kunst des Untermaingebietes, Bd. 17.) [Incl. the Nazi period.]

34824. MOERS. WIRSBITZKI, BRIGITTA: *Juden in Moers. Eine Minderheit in einer niederrheinischen Kleinstadt bis zum Ende der Weimarer Republik.* Berlin: Köster, 1997. 241 pp., graphs. (Wissenschaftliche Schriftenreihe Geschichte, Bd. 5.) Zugl.: Dortmund, Univ., Diss., 1996.

34825. MONSCHAU. OFFERMANN, TONI: *Juden im Landkreis Monschau.* [In]: Das Monschauer Land, Jahrbuch 1997. Jg. 25, Monschau-Imgenbroich, 1997. Pp. 52–57, notes.

34826. MÜHLEN. *Die alten Häuser von Mühlen.* Geschichten (und Geschichte) aus einem schwäbischen Judendorf. Aufgelesen und zusammengetragen von Manfred Steck. [Hrsg.: Stadtarchiv Horb a.N.]. Horb a.N., 1997. [Privately printed]. 2 vols. (163; 151 pp.), facsims., footnotes, maps. (Mühlener Schriften Bd. 1 & 2).

34827. MÜNSTERMAIFELD. BURGARD, FRIEDHELM: *Zur Geschichte der jüdischen Gemeinde in Münstermaifeld im Spätmittelalter.* [In]: Liber amicorum necnon et amicarum für Alfred Heit [see No. 34697]. Pp. 359–370, footnotes. [Münstermaifeld: nr. Koblenz.]

34828. MUNICH. LARGE, DAVID CLAY: *Where ghosts walked: Munich's road to the Third Reich.* New York: Norton, 1997. XXV, 406 pp., illus., ports., notes (363–394). [Incl. antisemitism and the treatment of Jews.]

34829. NASSAU. BECKER-HAMMERSTEIN, WALTRAUD/BECKER, WERNER: *Julius Israel Nassau. Juden in Nassau an der Lahn im 19. und 20. Jahrhundert.* [In]: Stadt Nassau. Ursprung und Gestaltung. Geschichte und Geschichten. Hrsg.: Stadt Nassau. Nassau: Selbstverlag der Stadt Nassau, 1997. Pp. 62–85, illus., facsims. [Incl. list of Nazi victims.]

34830. NÖRDLINGEN. VOGES, DIETMAR-H.: *Die Anfänge der Nördlinger Judengemeinde im 19. Jahrhundert.* [In]: Hist. Verein für Nördlingen und das Ries. Jahrbuch 28, Nördlingen, 1996. Pp. 295–317.

34831. NUREMBERG. KUßMAUL, SIBYLLE: *Die "Ostjuden" in Nürnberg 1880–1933. Eine Minderheit zwischen Ausweisung und Assimilation.* [In]: Mitteilungen des Vereins für Geschichte der Stadt Nürnberg, Bd. 84, Nürnberg, 1997. Pp. 149–224, illus., facsims., footnotes.

34832. OBEREMMEL. KÖRTELS, WILLI: *Geschichte der Juden von Oberemmel.* Kell am See: Alta Silva, 1996. 64 pp., facsims., notes, bibl. [Oberemmel: nr. Trier.]

34833. OFFENBURG. RUCH, MARTIN: *In ständigem Einsatz. Das Leben Siegfried Schnurmanns.* Jüdische Schicksale aus Offenburg und Südbaden 1907–1997. Mit einem Geleitwort von Nathan Peter Levinson. Hrsg. von Erhard Roy Wiehn. Konstanz: Hartung-Gorre, 1997. 112 pp., illus., facsims. [S. Sch., b. 1907 in Offenburg, escaped from Denmark to Sweden, emigr. 1945 to Palestine, returned to Offenburg in 1951.]

34834. OLDENBURG. Schrape, Joachim: *Quelleninventar zur Oldenburgischen Feuerwehrgeschichte.* Bestandsnachweise aus dem Niedersächsischen Staatsarchiv in Oldenburg und aus den oldenburgischen Kommunalarchiven. [Privately printed: J. Schrape, 1997.] 155 pp., illus., facsims., indexes (persons; places, 137–155). [Available in the Bibliothek Germania Judaica, Cologne.] [Testifying to the strong representation of Jews among the members of the fire brigades in several villages and small towns such as Brake, Harpstedt, Oldenburg, Varel and Vechta.]

34835. ORTENAU. Fliedner, Hans Joachim: *Unser jüdisches Erbe und wir.* Vortrag zum 20jährigen Bestehen des Deutsch-Israelischen Arbeitskreises in Ettenheim am 9. November 1994 [etc.]. [In]: Die Ortenau, Bd. 77, Offenburg/Baden, 1997. Pp. 637–646. [On the cemeteries of Diersburg and Schmieheim, the synagogue in Kippenheim, and on Ludwig Frank.]

34836. PALATINATE. Kaufmann, Uri R.: *Über die jüdische Geschichte der Kurpfalz.* [In]: Kurpfalz. Hrsg. von Alexander Schweickert. Mit Beiträgen von Andreas Czer [et al.]. Stuttgart: Kohlhammer, 1997. (Schriften zur politischen Landeskunde Baden-Württemberg, Bd. 25.). Pp. 165–176, notes.

34837. PALATINATE. Kukatzki, Bernhard: *Die Familiennamen der Grünstadter Juden nach dem napoleonischen Dekret des Jahres 1808.* [Hrsg.: Ges. für Christl.-Jüd. Zusammenarbeit Pfalz]. Landau in der Pfalz: B. Kukatzki, 1997. 22 pp.

34838. PALATINATE. Kukatzki, Bernhard, ed.: *Pfälzisch-jüdischer Alltag im Kaiserreich.* Eine Quellensammlung. Landau/Pfalz: [private print], 1997. 68 pp., facsims., index (places, persons, 66–68).

34839. PALATINATE. *Sachor. Beiträge zur jüdischen Geschichte und Gedenkstättenarbeit in Rheinland-Pfalz.* Jg. 7, H. 13 & Sonderheft. Bad Kreuznach, 1997. 2 issues., illus., facsims., notes, index. [H. 13 incl. contribs. on the Jews of Hahnstätten, Nastätten, Flacht, Miehlen, Hennweiler and Trier by Abraham Frank, Uli Jungblüth, Heinz Monz, Hans-Werner Ziemer; also contribs. on projects, exhibitions and memorials. 'Sonderheft' (with the title: 27.Januar. Tag des Gedenkens an die Opfer des Nationalsozialismus) incl.: Synagogen und Denkmalpflege in Rheinland-Pfalz (Joachim Glatz, 59–71). Haus des Lebens und der Ewigkeit. Betreuung, Pflege und Besuch jüdischer Friedhöfe (Fritz Reuter, 72–75); also reports on projects of 10 schools, on memorials and related topics.]

34840. PIRNA. Jensch, Hugo: *Juden in Pirna.* Mit Berichten von Max Tabaschnik, Ilse Fischer, geb. Engler und Esra Jurmann. Pirna: Kuratorium Gedenkstätte Sonnenstein e.V., 1997. 129 pp., illus., facsims., notes (119–125), bibl. [Incl. the Nazi period.]

34841. POSEN. Kemlein, Sophia: *Die Posener Juden 1815–1848.* Entwicklungsprozesse einer polnischen Judenheit unter preußischer Herrschaft. Hamburg: Dölling und Galitz, 1997. 376 [4] pp., facsims., tabs., maps., footnotes, bibl. (355–376). (Hamburger Veröff. zur Gesch. Mittel- und Osteuropas, Bd. 3.). Zugl.: Hamburg, Univ., Diss., 1995.

34842. POSEN. Makowski, Krysztof: *When on the streets of Posen – apart from Polish – German and Yiddish was heard. Germans and Jews in Posen in the years 1815–1848.* [In Polish, title transl.] [In]: Kronika Miasta Poznania, Poznan, No. 3, 1996. Pp. 48–65.

34843. POSEN. Östreich, Cornelia: *"Des rauhen Winters ungeachtet. . .". Die Auswanderung Posener Juden nach Amerika im 19. Jahrhundert.* Hamburg: Dölling und Galitz, 1997. 398 pp., tabs., maps., footnotes, bibl. (350–386), indexes (places, persons, 387–398). (Hamburger Veröff. zur Gesch. Mittel- und Osteuropas, Bd. 4.). Zugl.: Hamburg, Univ., Diss., 1994.

34844. RECKLINGHAUSEN. Moers, Jürgen: *Jüdische Friedhöfe im Vest.* [In]: Vestischer Kalender 1996, Jg. 67, Buer, 1996. Pp. 210–215. [Also in this issue: 2000 Jahre Schicksalsgemeinschaft Vest Recklinghausen Nordgaliläa/Israel [sic] (Peter Borggraefe, 21–26).]

34845. REGENSBURG. *Das Regensburger Ghetto.* Foto-Impressionen von den Ausgrabungen. Regensburg: Mittelbayrische Druck- u. Verl.-Ges., 1997. 87 pp., illus. [Documents the excavation of the medieval remains of the ghetto.]

34846. REUTLINGEN. KOST, GERHARD: *Christian Gottlieb Bleibtreu. Eine Reutlinger Judentaufe im Jahr 1763.* [In]: Reutlinger Geschichtsblätter, Jg. 1997, N.F. 36, Reutlingen, 1997. Pp. 257–264, footnotes.

34847. REXINGEN. *In Stein gehauen. Lebensspuren auf dem jüdischen Friedhof in Rexingen.* Dokumentation des Friedhofs und des Schicksals der 300 Jahre in Rexingen ansässigen jüdischen Gemeinde. Hrsg. vom Stadtarchiv Horb. Mit Beiträgen von Renate Karoline Adler, Nils-Christian Engel, Gil Hüttenmeister, Nina Michielin, Adolf Sayer. Stuttgart: Theiss, 1997. IX, 424 pp., illus., bibl. (Jüdische Friedhöfe der Stadt Horb, Bd. 1.) [Incl.: Liste der jüdischen Einwohner von Rexingen und anderen Orten, die nach 1933 weggezogen, zugezogen, verstorben, ausgewandert oder die deportiert worden sind (139–163). Gräberdokumentation (189–394).]

34848. RHEINDAHLEN. KAUFMANN, ANDREA: *Juden in Mönchengladbach-Rheindahlen.* [In]: Rheindahlen Almanach, Mönchengladbach, 1997. 1–39 pp., facsims., footnotes.

34849. RHINELAND. CORBACH, DIETER: *Juden im Oberbergischen – Nachbarschaft, Freundschaft, Feindschaft.* [In]: Beiträge zur Oberbergischen Geschichte, Bd. 6, Gummersbach, 1997. Pp. 151–163, illus., facsims. [Mainly on Jews from Nümbrecht and Waldbröl.]

34850. RHINELAND. *Hier wohnte Frau Antonie Giese. Die Geschichte der Juden im Bergischen Land.* Essays und Dokumente. Hrsg. vom Trägerverein Begegnungsstätte Alte Synagoge Wuppertal e.V. Mit Beiträgen von Jochen Bilstein [et al.]. Wuppertal: [Trägerverein Begegnungsstätte Alte Synagoge Wuppertal e.V.], 1997. 146 pp., illus., facsims., docs., bibl. [Incl. : Grussworte: (Ignatz Bubis, Ilse Brusis, 6–7). Essays, documents, personal recollections (partly previously publ.) on Jews and synagogues in Solingen, Nümbrecht, Barmen, Remscheid, Velbert, Wuppertal (incl. Nazi period and today's community) by Jochen Bilstein, Wilhelm Bramann, Wilhelm Crecelius, Leonid Goldberg, Ulrich Föhse, Michael Okroy, Audrey Pomerance, Horst Sassin, Katja Schettler, Ulrike Schrader.]

34851. RHINELAND. PRACHT, ELFI: *Jüdisches Kulturerbe in Nordrhein-Westfalen.* Teil I: Regierungsbezirk Köln. Köln: Bachem, 1997. XV, 650 pp., illus., maps., bibl. (610–625), index (places, 632–648). (Beiträge zu den Kunst- und Baudenkmälern im Rheinland, Bd. 34, 1.)

34852. RIETBERG. *Die Juden der Grafschaft Rietberg.* Beiträge zur Synagogengemeinde Neuenkirchen. Hrsg.: Heimatverein Neuenkirchen und Stadt Rietberg. Mit Beiträgen von Manfred Beine [et al.]. [Fotos: Andreas Hemstege]. Rietberg: Stadt Rietberg, Kulturamt, 1997. 280 pp., illus., facsims. [Incl. (titles partly abbr.): Schicksale jüdischer Familien in Neuenkirchen und Rietberg (Beate Schrewe, 9–49; incl. the Nazi period). Jakob Löb Eltzbacher in Neuenkirchen (Elisabeth Hanschmidt, 50–69). Die Synagoge in Neuenkirchen (Manfred Beine, 70–106). Der jüdische Friedhof in Rietberg-Neuenkirchen (Michael Brocke/Martina Strehlen, 107–277; documentation of 156 gravestones, Hebrew and German inscriptions, transl. and annotated).] [Rietberg: nr. Rheda-Wiedenbrück, Westph.]

34853. SACHSEN-ANHALT. *Geschichte jüdischer Gemeinden in Sachsen-Anhalt.* Versuch einer Erinnerung. Autorengruppe: Bärbel Bugaiski, Ildiko Leubauer, Günter Waesche. Hrsg.: Landesverband Jüdischer Gemeinden Sachsen-Anhalt. Wernigerode: Oemler, 1997. 310 pp., illus., facsims., gloss., bibl. [Incl. historical overviews of more than 50 communities (in alphabetical order).]

34854. SAXONY. HÖPPNER, SOLVEJG/JAHN, MANFRED: *Jüdische Vereine und Organisationen in Chemnitz, Dresden und Leipzig 1918 bis 1933.* Ein Überblick. Dresden: Sächs. Druckerei- u. Verl.-Haus, 1997. 76 pp.

34855. SCHLITZ. SIPPEL, HEINRICH: *Jüdisches Leben in Schlitz*. 50259 Pulheim-Stommeln: Eigenverl. H. Sippel, 1997. 104 pp., illus., facsims., notes (93–97). (Schlitz im Spiegel der Geschichte, H. 28.) [Incl. the Nazi period.] [Schlitz: nr. Fulda.]

34856. SCHMALLENBERG. SCHENK, HANNELORE: *Der Schmallenberger Leo Goldschmidt 1945 als US-Soldat in Deutschland*. [In]: Schmallenberger Heimatblätter, Ausgabe 62, 1995/96. Schmallenberg, 1996. Pp. 58–61.

34857. SCHMITTEN. BUS, E.: *Die Synagoge in Schmitten. Ein verschwundenes Gotteshaus im Usinger Land*. [In]: Jahrbuch Hochtaunuskreis, Jg. 5, Frankfurt am Main, 1997. Pp. 215–221. [Also in this vol.: interview with Marianne Schwab née Rothschild by A. Rieber about her family, orig. from Bad Homburg (223–231).]

34858. SCHOTTEN. ENDERS, HERMANN/HYSKY-DAMBMANN, HENNY: *Geschichte der Juden in der Stadt Schotten*. Schotten: Vogelsberger Kultur- und Geschichtsverein, [1996]. 14 pp., illus.

—— SCHWABEN. KIEßLING, ROLF: *Between expulsion and emancipation: Jewish villages in East Swabia during the early modern period*. [See in No. 34944.]

34859. SCHWÄBISCH HALL. KOHRING, HEINRICH: *Der jüdische Friedhof in Schwäbisch Hall-Steinbach*. Einführung. Hebräische Texte mit Übersetzung, Register. Photos: Marion Reuter. Schwäbisch-Hall: Stadtverwaltung, 1996. 160, 31 pp.

34860. SELTERS. JUNGBLUTH, ULI: *Landjuden in Selters/Ww*. [Westerwald]. [In]: Nassauische Annalen, Bd. 108, Wiesbaden, 1997. Pp. 169–183, illus., footnotes.

34861. SILESIA. HERZIG, ARNO: *Beiträge zur Sozial- und Kulturgeschichte Schlesiens und der Grafschaft Glatz*. Gesammelte Aufsätze zum 60. Geburtstag hrsg. von Johannes Hoffmann, Frank Golczewski, Helmut Neubach. Dortmund: Forschungsstelle Ostmitteleuropa, 1997. XIV, 222 pp., frontis., illus., facsims., footnotes, indexes (places; names, 196–208). [A collection of articles, some previous publ. and revised; new article on a Jewish topic: Landjuden – Stadtjuden in Schlesien und Westfalen (14–36). Incl. also bibl. A. Herzig (212–222).]

34862. SPEICHER. STREIT, WERNER P.: *Simon Salomon – ein jüdischer Bürger aus Speicher*. [In]: Heimatkalender 1995, Landkreis Bitburg-Prüm, Bitburg, 1995. 33–37. [On the poet and writer Simon Salomon (pseud.: Siegbert Salter), 1873 Speicher – 1943 Theresienstadt.]

34863. ST. TÖNIS. SCHMIDT, WILLI: *Zum Gedenken an die jüdische Synagogengemeinde in St. Tönis und ihr Ende unter dem Hakenkreuz*. [In]: St. Töniser Heimatbrief, Nr. 133, St. Tönis, 1995. Pp. 41–43.

34864. STEINBACH. MÜLLER, HANNO: *Juden in Steinbach Kreis Gießen*. Fernwald: Jambu-Verlag, 1995. 61 pp., illus.

34865. TANN. HOHMANN, JOACHIM S., ed.: *Chronik der jüdischen Schule zu Tann (Rhön)*. Mit einer kurzen Geschichte der israelitischen Gemeinde und zeitgenössischen Lichtbildern. Frankfurt am Main; New York: Lang, 1997. 189 pp., illus. [Incl. the school chronicle covering the years 1879 until Nov. 1938 and saved by the last teacher, Rabbi Henry Okolica. Also a list of tombstones of the Jewish cemetery compiled by Max Michel Freudenthal in 1934.]

34866. TAUNUS. ZINK, WOLFGANG: *Hebräischer Gebetsgesang nach Opernmelodien oder deutsche Erbauungschoräle mit gemischtem Chor? Die jüdischen Gemeinden des 19. Jahrhunderts im Main-Taunus-Kreis zwischen Reform und Orthodoxie*. [In]: Zwischen Main und Taunus. Jahrbuch des Main-Taunus-Kreis, Jg. 5, Hofheim a.Ts., 1997. Pp. 19–26.

34867. THURINGIA. LÖWENBRÜCK, ANNA-RUTH/OLBRISCH, GABRIELE: *Juden in Thüringen*. [In]: Karl Schmitt, ed.: Thüringen. Eine politische Landeskunde. Weimar: Böhlau, 1996. Pp. 218–226, notes.

34868. THURINGIA. SCHWIERZ, ISRAEL: *Für das Vaterland starben* [sic]. Denkmäler und Gedenktafeln für jüdische Soldaten in Thüringen. Dokumentation. Aschaffenburg: Ed. Krem-Bardischewski Verl., 1996. 69 pp., illus., index.

34869. TRIER. BURGARD, FRIEDHELM: *Christlicher und jüdischer Geldhandel im Vergleich.* Das Beispiel der geistlichen Herrschaft Trier. [In]: Shylock: Zinsverbot und Geldverleih in jüdischer und christlicher Tradition [see No. 35844]. Pp. 253–260, notes.

—— TRIER. *Das Museum Karl-Marx-Haus.* [See No. 35636.]

34870. TRIER. MONZ, HEINZ: *Die Synagogen an der Weberbach in Trier.* Zur Wiederansiedlung von Menschen jüdischen Glaubens im 18. Jahrhundert. [In]: Kurtrierisches Jahrbuch, Jg. 37, Trier, 1997. Pp. 121–134, footnotes.

34871. TÜBINGEN. BECHTOLDT, HANS-JOACHIM: *Die Promotion des Rabbinatskandidaten Elias Pleßner an der Eberhard-Karls-Universität zu Tübingen im Jahre 1870.* [In]: Aschkenas, Jg. 1, H. 1, Wien, 1997. Pp. 181–204.

34872. WEILBURG/Lahn. HOOS, H.-H.: *Spuren eines politischen Antisemitismus in Weilburg.* Zu Beginn des 20. Jahrhunderts. [In]: Jahrbuch für den Kreis Limburg-Weilburg. Limburg, 1997. Pp. 208–211.

34873. WERL. DREWKE, LOTHAR: *Der jüdische Friedhof Werls und sein steinernes Zeugnis.* [In]: Werl. Gestern, heute, morgen. Jg. 13, Werl, 1996. [Also in this issue: Deine Rechte ist ausgestreckt – Ehemalige jüdische Mitbürger in Werl (Werner Kohn, 87–91).] [Werl: nr. Hamm.]

34874. WESEL. BAMBAUER, KLAUS: *Eine jüdische Hochzeit in Wesel.* [In]: Mitteilungen der Hist. Vereinigung Wesel e.V., H. 74, Wesel, 1995. Pp. 14–16. [Also in this issue by the same author: Eine jüdische Taufe im Jahre 1615 in Wesel (18–21).]

34875. WESTPHALIA. ILISCH, PETER: *"Münzübeltäter" im Bereich der Grafschaft Mark in den Jahren 1699 und 1700.* [In]: Der Märker, Jg. 45, H. 1, Altena, 1996. Pp. 25–28, illus., notes. [Incl. also Jewish money lenders.]

34876. WÜRTTEMBERG. DÄSCHLER-SEILER, SIEGFRIED: *Auf dem Weg in die bürgerliche Gesellschaft. Joseph Maier und die jüdische Volksschule im Königreich Württemberg.* Stuttgart: Klett Cotta, 1997. 471 pp., footnotes, docs., tabs., bibl. (430–471). (Veröffentlichungen des Archivs der Stadt Stuttgart, Bd. 73.) Zugl.: Ludwigsburg, Päd. Hochschule, Diss., 1996. [Deals with Jews in Württemberg and particularly Stuttgart; also on the development in Talheim nr. Heilbronn and Esslingen.] [J. Maier, 1789 Laudenbach – 1873 Stuttgart, Reform rabbi, first ennobled rabbi in Germany.]

34877. WUPPERTAL. SCHRADER, ULRIKE: *Die Juden im Bergischen.* Eine Ausstellung in der Begegnungsstätte "Alte Synagoge" Wuppertal. [In]: Romerike Berge, Jg. 47, H. 1, Burg an der Wupper, 1997. Pp. 13–18.

1a. Alsace

34878. *18e Colloque de la Societé d'Histoire des Israélites d'Alsace et de Lorraine.* Strasbourg, 10 et 11 février 1996. Textes réunis par Anny Bloch. Strasbourg: Soc. d'histoire des Israélites d'Alsace et de Lorraine, 1996. 106 pp. [Incl. an introduction by Freddy Raphael and Anny Bloch (11–14). 12 essays arranged under the sections: Généalogie, famille et noms (essays by Pierre Katz, André Aaron Fraenkel, Günter Boll, 15–28). Vie culturelle, cultuelle et migrations (essays by Daniel Peter, Serge Braun, Jean-Marc Dreyfus, Jean Daltroff, 29–58). Personnages singuliers (essays by N. Bar-Giora Bamberger, André-Marc Haarscher, Freddy Raphael, Geneviève Herberich Marx, 59–76). Les anées 1930–1940 (essays by Léon Strauss, Françoise Job, 77–96). Incl. also a circumcision register (introd. and transl. by Günter Boll, 97–106.]

34879. FLEURY, JEAN: *Contrats de mariage juifs en Moselle avant 1792.* Recensement à usage généalogique de 2021 contrats de mariage notariés. F-75009 Paris (14, rue Saint-Lazare): Cercle de Généalogie Juive, 1997. 256 pp.

34881. FRAENKEL, ANDRÉ AARON: *Mémoire juive en Alsace. Contrats de mariage au XVIIIe siècle (de 1702 à 1791. Classement par ordre alphabétique des sièges de notariats).* Strasbourg: Ed. du Cédrat, 1997. 448 pp., illus., facsims., map.

34882. HAARSCHER, ANDRÉ-MARC: *Berufstätigkeit der Juden in der ehemaligen Grafschaft Hanau-Lichtenberg im 17./18. Jahrhundert.* [In]: Die Ortenau, Bd. 77, 1997, Offenburg/Baden, 1997. Pp. 295–310, facsims., notes.

— HYMAN, PAULA E.: *Jüdische Familie und kulturelle Kontinuität im Elsaß des 19. Jahrhunderts.* [See in No. 34703.]

— KAUFMANN, URI R.: *Das jüdische Schulwesen auf dem Lande. Baden und Elsaß im Vergleich 1770–1848.* [See in No. 34703.]

34883. REGISHEIM. BOLL, GÜNTER: *Die ersten Generationen der Regisheimer Familie Wahl.* [In]: Maajan, H. 44, Zürich, 1997. Pp. 1075–1083.

34884. *D'un territoire à l'autre: les juifs d'Alsace, de Suisse et du Pays de l'Ortenau.* [Issue title of]: XIXe colloque de la Société d'Histoire des Israélites d'Alsace et de Lorraine, Strasbourg, 8 et 9 février 1997 [on tab. of contents: 1996]. Textes réunis par Anny Bloch [et al.]. Strasbourg, 1997. 1 vol. [Incl.: Histoire des juifs dans le sud de l'Ortenau au regard de leurs installations culturelles (Jürgen Stude, 17–30). Les relations entre Juifs alsaciens et suisses entre 1560 et 1910 (Uri R. Kaufmann, 31–38). Les juifs d'Alsace au Moyen Age (Gerd Mentgen, 39–48). Une communauté rurale juive d'Alsace: Zellwiller (Georges Schlosser, 49–58). Mappot Mi-Mackene. L'héritage caché d'une communauté juive éteinte (Günter Boll, 59–66). Scènes de la vie juive à Wintzenheim (Yvonne Levy Picard, 67–74). Les juifs du comté de Hanau-Lichtenberg, fermiers des impôts seigneuriaux (André-Marc Haarscher, 75–86). Juifs d'Alsace et de Lorraine le long du Mississippi: une culture de l'entre-deux (1830–1950) (Anny Bloch, 87–100).]

2. **Austria**

34885. BURGENLAND. EISENSTADT, JÜDISCHES MUSEUM: *Aus den sieben Gemeinden. Ein Lesebuch über Juden im Burgenland.* Hrsg. von Johannes Reiss aus Anlaß des Jubiläums "25 Jahre Österreichisches Jüdisches Museum" in Eisenstadt. Eisenstadt: Österr. Jüdisches Museum, 1997. 255 pp., illus., ports. [Cont. 25 contribs. by historians, ethnologists, writers as well as personal recollections of Jews and non-Jews about Jewish life in Burgenland, i.e.: in Eisenstadt, Mattersburg, Klittsee, Frauenkirchen, Kobersdorf, Deutschkreutz.]

34886. GALICIA. ADAMCZYK, MIECZYSLAW JERZY: *La jeunesse juive dans des écoles secondaires en Galicie autrichienne 1848–1914.* [In]: Revue des études juives, T. 156, Strasbourg, janvier-juin 1997. Pp. 173–189, footnotes. [With French and Engl. summaries.]

34887. GALICIA. MAKOWSKI, KRYSZTOF: *Jewish population and the events of the 'Springtime of Nations' in the Polish lands.* [In]: Jews in defence of the Polish Commonwealth. The materials of the conference in Warsaw, Oct. 17–18, 1993. Ed. by Jerzy Tomaszewski. Warszawa, 1996. Pp. 43–63. [Incl. the Jews of Posen and Galicia during the events of 1948.]

34888. GRAZ. SENEKOWITSCH, MARTIN: *Verbunden mit diesem Lande. Das jüdische Kriegerdenkmal in Graz.* Graz: Militärkommando Steiermark, 1995. 7 pp., illus.

— HOHENEMS. ARNSTEIN, GEORGE E.: *Hohenems: rise and fall, marital ties and migration.* [See No. 35390.]

34889. HOHENEMS. *Ein Viertel Stadt.* Zur Frage des Umgangs mit dem ehemaligen jüdischen Viertel in Hohenems. [Hrsg.: Johannes Inama, Jüdisches Museum Hohenems]. Innsbruck: Studien Verlag, 1997. 112 pp., illus., facsims., notes, maps. [Most contribs. deal with the conservation order on the town's former Jewish quarter and its consequences. Incl.: "Erinnerung ist Erinnerung an etwas Vergessenes". Die Wiederentdeckung der jüdischen Geschichte in einer Kleinstadt der österreichischen Provinz (Eva Grabherr, 13–26). Zur Sozialgeschichte des jüdischen Viertels in Hohenems im 19. Jahrhundert (Hans Gruber, 41–52).]

34890. KREMS. KALCHHAUSER, MARTIN: *Der Kampf um das Vergessen* [sic]. *Der Weg zum Denkmal auf dem jüdischen Friedhof.* [In]: Das Waldviertel, Jg. 45, Krems, 1996. Pp. 212–218, illus. [Also in this issue: Kein Platz für Dr. Seligmann. Der Kremser Alpenverein und seine Geschichte (Robert Streibel, 333–342, illus.).]

—— LICHTBLAU, ALBERT: *Partizipation und Isolation. Juden in Politik und Gesellschaft Österreichs in den "langen" 1920er Jahren.* [See in No. 34692.]

34891. SPITZER, SHLOMO: *Bne Chet. Die österreichischen Juden im Mittelalter.* Eine Sozial- und Kulturgeschichte. Wien: Böhlau, 1997. 281 pp., illus., footnotes.

—— STRASSER, CHRISTIAN: *Carl Zuckmayer. Deutsche Künstler im Salzburger Exil 1933–1938.* [See No. 35700.]

34892. TEUFEL, HELMUT: *"Ein Schüler Mendelssohns". Herz Homberg als jüdischer Propagandist der josephinischen Aufklärung.* [In]: Ambivalenzen der Aufklärung. Festschrift für Ernst Wangermann. Hrsg. von Gerhard Ammerer und Hannes Haas. München: Oldenbourg, 1997.

34893. VIENNA. LANDESMANN, PETER: *Rabbiner in Wien. Ihre Ausbildung, ihre religiösen und nationalen Konflikte.* Wien: Böhlau, 1997. 289 pp., illus.

34894. VIENNA. MITTENZWEI, INGRID: *Das stille Ringen um Emanzipation. Die jüdische Oberschicht Wiens vom Erlaß des Toleranzpatents 1782 bis zum Wiener Kongreß.* [In]: Europa in der Frühen Neuzeit. Festschrift für Günter Mühlpfordt. Hrsg. von Erich Donnert. Band 3: Aufbruch zur Moderne. Böhlau: Weimar, 1997. Pp. 691–705, footnotes.

34895. VIENNA. WISTRICH, ROBERT S.: *Zionism and its religious critics in fin-de-siécle Vienna.* [In]: Jewish History, Vol. 10, No. 1, Haifa, Spring 1996. Pp. 93–111, notes.

34896. *Wandlungen und Brüche. Von Herzls "Welt" zur "Illustrierten Neuen Welt" 1897–1997.* Hrsg. von Joanna Nittenberg in Zusammenarbeit mit Anton Pelinka, Robert S. Wistrich. Wien: Ed. INW, 1997. 416 pp., illus., facsims., bibl. (343–350), notes (351–377). [Cont. historical essays and memoirs arranged under the sections: Herzls "Welt" 1897–1914; incl.: Theodor Herzl – Zwischen Journalismus und Politik (Robert S. Wistrich, 11–18). Herzls Maitresse – Die Gründung der "Welt" (Angelika Montel, 19–66). Das gelobte Land fest im Blick (Julius H. Schoeps, 67–79). Die Neue Welt/Revue 1927–1938; incl.: Zwischen Aufklärung und Nationalismus (Peter Pulzer, 83–90). Robert Stricker und die "Neue Welt" (Silke Hassler, 91–151). Erinnerungen an Berta und Barak (Jakov Lind, 153–158). Neue Welt und Judenstaat 1948–1974; incl.: Antisemitismus und österreichische Politik (Erika Weinzierl, 161–174). Tradition und Neubeginn (Katharina Demel/Brigitte Halbmayr, 175–230). Hermann Hakel und die "Neue Welt" (Evelyn Adunka, 231–256). Von Wien nach Wien (Asher Ben Natan, 243–256). Illustrierte Neue Welt 1974–1997; incl.: Jüdische Identität in Österreich (Anton Pelinka, 259–266). Zwischen Israel und Österreich (Brigitte Halbmayr/Katharina Demel, 267–331). Möglichkeiten jüdischer Artikulation (Doron Rabinovici, 333–340).]

3. Central Europe

34897. BOECKH, KATRIN: *Zum Judentum in Südosteuropa.* [In]: Religion und Gesellschaft in Südosteuropa. Hrsg. von Hans Dieter Döpmann. München: Südosteuropagesellschaft, 1997. (Südoseuropa-Jahrbuch, Bd. 28.). Pp. 87–104, footnotes. [Incl. the Jews in the former Habsburg Monarchy. Refers also to antisemitism.]

34898. BOHEMIA. IGGERS, WILMA: *Zeiten der Gottesferne und der Mattheit. Die Religion im Bewußtsein der böhmischen Juden in der ersten tschechoslowakischen Republik.* Leipzig: Simon-Dubnow-Inst. für jüd. Gesch. und Kultur e.V., 1997. 17 [2] pp., notes.

34899. BOHEMIA. WLASCHEK, RUDOLF M.: *Biographia Judaica Bohemiae.* Bd. 2. Dortmund: Forschungsstelle Ostmitteleuropa, 1997. VIII, 75 pp., bibl. (65–68). (Veröff. der Forschungsstelle Ostmitteleuropa an der Univ. Dortmund, Reihe B, Bd. 59.) [Incl.: Vorwort (Reuven Assor, VII–VIII). Incl. supplement (5 loose pp.), errata and supplementary data to Vol. 1, publ. 1995 (see No. 32674/YB XLI).]

34900. BOHEMIA. WLASCHEK, RUDOLF M.: *Juden in Böhmen.* Beiträge zur Geschichte des europäischen Judentums im 19. und 20. Jahrhundert. 2., vollständig überarbeitete und erweiterte Auflage. München: Oldenbourg, 1997. 311 pp., footnotes, tabs., bibl. (239–281), indexes (persons; places (285–296). (Veröff. des Collegium Carolinum, Bd. 66.) [First edn. publ. 1990; see No. 27123/YB XXXVI.] [Incl. antisemitism, Zionism, Nazi period, exile; also on concentration camps in Bohemia incl. deportation lists.]

34901. BOHEMIA & MORAVIA. FIEDLER, JIRI: *Jewish sights in Bohemia and Moravia.* Introduction by Arno Parík. Prague: Sefer, 1997 [?]. 224 pp., illus., facsims., map, index (places, 213–224). [First edn. 1991. Incl.: From the history of the Jewish communities in Bohemia and Moravia (Arno Parik, 5–26). Ghettos, synagogues and cemeteries (27–40). Guide (41–210; 138 places of Jewish interest, listed alphabetically). Index incl. also former German names.]

34902. CZECHOSLOVAKIA. *Rhapsody to Tchelet Lavan in Czechoslovakia.* Hashomer Hatzair noar tzofi halutzi netzach. [Eds.: Amos Sinai et al.]. Hatzor: Lahav Printing, 1996. 330 pp., illus., ports., facsims., chronol. [An abbr. version of the Hebrew edn. publ. 1993 (575 pp.). On the Hashomer Hatzair in Bohemia (later Czechoslovakia), its precursor 'Jüdischer Wanderbund' from 1912. Incl. activities after the Nazi occupation and in Theresienstadt, as well as post-war projects in Israel and personal recollections.]

34903. CZERNOWITZ. RUDEL, JOSEF NORBERT: *Das waren noch Zeiten. Jüdische Geschichten aus Czernowitz und Bukarest.* Hrsg. von Erhard Roy Wiehn. Konstanz: Hartung-Gorre, 1997. 74 pp., illus., facsims., maps. (Jüdische Biographien und Geschichten.) [Partly autobiographical stories.]

34904. HAUMANN, HEIKO: *Der "wahre Jakob". Frankistischer Messianismus und religiöse Toleranz in Polen.* [In: Querdenken. Dissens und Toleranz im Wandel der Geschichte. Festschrift zum 65. Geburtstag von Hans R. Guggisberg. Hrsg. von Michael Erbe [et al.]. Mannheim: Palatium, 1996. Pp. 441–460, footnotes. [Deals also with the Frankist movement in Austro-Hungary and Germany.]

34905. *Lücken in der Geschichte 1890–1938. Polemischer Geist Mitteleuropas. Deutsche, Juden, Tschechen.* Ausstellungskatalog. Galerie hlavniho mesta Prahy in Zusammenarbeit mit der Národni Galerie v Praze, Museum der österreichischen Kultur und der Ostdeutschen Galerie, 1995. 140 pp. [Incl. a contrib. by Arno Parik on Jewish artists and culture.] [Cf.: Besprechung (Michaela Marek) [in]: Bohemia, Bd. 38, H. 1, München, 1997. Pp. 234–238.]

34906. MORAVIA. SCHNABL, HEDI ARGENT: *I went back to Pohorelice: old gravestones and new friends in a Moravian village.* [In]: The Jewish Quarterly, Vol. 44, No. 1, London, Spring 1997. Pp. 49–50.

34907. PRAGUE. DEMETZ, PETER: *Prague in black and gold: scenes from the life of a European city.* New York: Hill & Wang, 1997. XVIII, 411 pp., illus., notes, bibl. [Deals also with Jewish life in Prague from 905 A.D. to the present day.]

34908. PRAGUE. WAGNEROVÁ, ALENA: *"Im Hauptquartier des Lärms". Die Familie Kafka aus Prag.* Berlin: Bollmann, 1997. 215 [2] pp., illus., family tree. [On three generations of the Kafka family.]

34909. PRESSBURG. TRANCÍK, MARTIN: *Zwischen Alt- und Neuland. Die Geschichte der Buchhändlerfamilie Steiner in Pressburg.* Ein mikrohistorischer Versuch. Bratislava: PT [Radlinského 33], 1996. 272 pp., illus., ports., facsims., notes, bibl. (254–269). [Incl. prefaces by Ulrike Knotz and Ján Albrecht (5–9) and an afterword: Was ist aus uns geworden? (Selma Steinerová, 249–250). On three generations of the Bratislava book-dealer family Steiner; founded in 1847 by Sigmund Steiner, forced into "Aryanisation" in 1940, the bookshop was reopened in 1991. Also on Orthodoxy and Zionism in Pressburg and the leading role of Siegfried Steiner in the local and also national Misrachi 1919–1939.] [Cf.: Besprechung (Richard Popper) [in]: David, Jg. 9, Nr. 34, Wien, Sept. 1997, pp. 45–46.]

34910. *Red star, blue star: the lives and times of Jewish students in communist Hungary (1948–1956).* Comp. by Andrew Handler. Ed. by Susan V. Meschel. Boulder, CO: East European Monographs, No. 487. (distrib. by Columbia Univ. Press, New York), 1997. X, 224 pp. [Narratives by Jewish Holocaust survivors.]

4. Switzerland

— BASEL. *Der Erste Zionistenkongress von 1897 – Ursachen, Bedeutung, Aktualität.* [See No. 35403.]

— BASEL. HEUMANN, PIERRE: *Israel entstand in Basel. Die phantastische Geschichte einer Vision.* [See No. 35414.]

34911. EXILE. HOERSCHELMANN, CLAUDIA: *Exilland Schweiz: Lebensbedingungen und Schicksale österreichischer Flüchtlinge 1938–1945.* Innsbruck: Studienverlag, 1997. 478 pp., illus. (Veröff. des Ludwig-Boltzmann-Instituts für Gesch. und Gesellschaft, 27.)

34912. EXILE. *Mit der Ziehharmonika.* Jg. 14, Nr. 1/Doppelnummer, [with the issue title] *Exil in der Schweiz*, Wien, 1997. 1 issue, illus. [Incl.: Exilland Schweiz: Flucht aus Österreich 1938–1945 (Claudia Hoerschelmann, 9–18, bibl.). Sicherheit mit begrenzter Haftung. Autorinnen und Autoren im Schweizer Exil (Vladimir Vertlib, 22–32, notes). Also contribs. on several exile writers and artists in Switzerland and personal recollections.]

34913. GAST, URIEL: *Von der Kontrolle zur Abwehr. Die eidgenössische Fremdenpolizei im Spannungsfeld von Politik und Wirtschaft 1915–1933.* Zürich: Chronos, 1997. 440 pp. (Veröff. des Archivs für Zeitgeschichte.) [Deals also with Jewish refugees and the attitude of Heinrich Rothmund and Heinrich Häberlin towards granting political asylum to them.] [Cf.: Ausländer- und Asylpolitik vor der Nazizeit (Kurt Müller) [in]: 'NZZ', Nr. 166, Zürich, 21.Juli 1997, p. 23.]

34914. GRAETZ, MICHAEL/MATTIOLI, ARAM, eds.: *Krisenwahrnehmungen im Fin de siècle. Jüdische und katholische Bildungseliten in Deutschland und in der Schweiz.* Zürich: Chronos, 1997. 382 pp., notes. [Incl.: Einleitung (Michael Graetz, 11–16). Bildung und gesellschaftliche Verantwortung. Das soziale Engagement jüdischer Frauen in der Schweiz (Regina Wecker, 119–138). Die russisch-jüdischen Studenten an den Universitäten in Deutschland und der Schweiz – eine "Subkultur" um die Jahrhundertwende (Michael Graetz, 139–154). Diskurse der Diskriminierung: Antisemitismus, Sozialdarwinismus und Rassismus in den schweizerischen Bildungseliten (Jakob Tanner, 323–340). "Hochschule heisst beim Volk der Hirten jetzt bald Judenschule". Die antisemitische Polemik der Basler Zeitschrift "Der Samstag" gegen jüdische Bildungseliten (Albert M. Debrunner, 341–360). Further contribs. are listed according to subject.]

34915. ROSCHEWSKI, HEINZ: *Rothmund und die Juden. Eine historische Fallstudie des Antisemitismus in der schweizerischen Flüchtlingspolitik 1933–1957.* Hrsg. vom Schweizerischen Israelitischen Gemeindebund. Basel: Helbing u. Lichtenhahn, 1997. 87 pp., bibl. (Beiträge zur Geschichte und Kultur der Juden in der Schweiz, Nr. 6.) [Based on the files of Heinrich Rothmund, chief of the Swiss police and responsible for the Swiss refugee policy.] [Cf.: Wertvolle Ergänzung zu

C. Various Countries

34916. ARGENTINE. Pankow, Gottwald: *Das Antiquariat Henschel in Buenos Aires wird 120 Jahre alt.* [In]: Aus dem Antiquariat, 4, [Beilage zum] Börsenblatt des Deutschen Buchhandels, Jg. 164, Frankfurt am Main, 25. April 1997. Pp. A 206–A 208. [On the book-dealing family Henschel, orig. from Hamburg, owners until the forced "Aryanisation" in 1936 of the firm 'Henschel & Müller'.]

34917. ARGENTINE. Saint Sauveur-Henn, Anne: *Un siècle d'émigration allemande vers l'Argentine.* Köln: Böhlau, 1995. 852 pp., illus. (Lateinamerikanische Forschungen, 23.) [With German summary. Deals also with the immigration of German-speaking refugees in the 1930s.] [Cf.: Revue (Anne-Marie Corbin-Schuffels) [in]: Francia, Bd. 24/3 (1997), Sigmaringen, 1998, pp. 329–330.]

34918. AUSTRALIA. Lausch, Hans: *Felix Adalbert Behrend and mathematics in Camp 7, Hay, 1940–41.* [In]: Australian Jewish Historical Society Journal, Vol. 14, Part 1, Nov. 1997. Pp. 110–119. [On Behrend's mathematical activities in the Hay internment camp, Australia.] [F.A.B., 1911 Berlin – 1962 Melbourne, mathematician, emigr. 1934 to UK, then Switzerland, later Prague, 1939 UK, interned and sent to Australia.]

34919. EXILE. König, Karin: *Zuflucht bei den Türken. Die wissenschaftliche deutschsprachige Emigration in der Türkei von 1935 bis 1945.* [In]: Mittelweg 36, Jg. 6, H. 5, Hamburg, 1997. Pp. 69–79, footnotes. [On non-Jewish and Jewish émigrés in Turkey, in particular on Traugott Fuchs, who followed his teacher, Leo Spitzer, into exile.]

—— EXILE. Stephan, Alexander: *Personal and confidential. Geheimdienste, Alfred Döblin und das Exil in Südkalifornien.* [See No. 35510.]

34920. GREAT BRITAIN. Raab Hansen, Jutta: *NS-verfolgte Musiker in England. Spuren deutscher und österreichischer Flüchtlinge in der britischen Musikkultur.* Hamburg: von Bockel, 1996. 530 pp., illus., graphs, footnotes, bibl. (489–514), index (515–529). (Musik im "Dritten Reich" und im Exil, 1.). Zugl.: Hamburg, Univ., Diss., 1995. [Incl. short biographies of 298 musicians (398–478).]

34921. GREAT BRITAIN. Terwey, Susanne: *Kabale und Intrige zum Fin de Siècle – Deutsche und Juden in britischen Phobien.* [In]: Tel Aviver Jahrbuch für deutsche Geschichte, Bd. 26, Gerlingen, 1997. Pp. 479–493, footnotes. [Refers also to Jews from Germany or those with a German-Jewish background.]

34922. KATTOWITZ/KATOWICE. Namyslo, Aleksandra: *Die Rolle und das Wirken der jüdischen Glaubensgemeinde in Kattowitz in den Jahren 1922 bis 1939.* [In]: Oberschlesisches Jahrbuch, Bd. 12, 1996, Berlin, 1997. Pp. 93–105, footnotes. [Kattowitz/Katowice, since 1922 Polish.]

34923. SHANGHAI. Guang, Pan: *The Jews in Shanghai.* Shanghai: Shanghai Pictorial Publ. House, 1995. 90 pp., illus., facsims., maps, docs. [Texts in Chinese and English. Incl. Preface (Pan Guang, Center of Jewish Studies, Shanghai). Haven for Holocaust victims (sic) from Nazi Europe, 22–45).]

34924. SHANGHAI. *Leben im Wartesaal. Exil in Shanghai 1938–1947.* Berlin: Jüdisches Museum im Stadtmuseum Berlin, 1997. 128 pp., illus., facsims., bibl. [Catalogue of exhibition, held in Berlin July 4 – Aug. 24, 1997; incl. contribs. by Georg Armbrüster, Amnon Barzel, Horst Eisfelder, Christine Fischer-Defoy, Christiane Hoss, Petra Löber.]

34925. URUGUAY. Wegner, Sonja: *German-speaking emigrants in Uruguay 1933–1945.* [In]: Leo Baeck Institute Year Book XLII, London, 1997. Pp. 239–271, illus., footnotes.

34926. USA. COHEN, THEODORE: *Walter Jonas Judah and the New York yellow fever epidemic of 1798.* [In]: American Jewish Archives, Vol. 48, No. 1, Cincinnati, OH, Spring/Summer 1996. Pp. 23–34, notes, facsims. [German-Jewish family from Breslau. Also on other German-Jewish doctors in early America.]

34927. USA. FLICKER, TED: *The good American.* First intern. edn. Santa Fe, NM: Shalako, 1997. VI, 452 pp. [Describes German-Jewish existence in America, particularly immigrants from Bavaria, from the middle of the 19th century.]

34928. USA. HEILBUT, ANTHONY: *Exiled in paradise: German refugee artists and intellectuals in America from the 1930s to the present.* Berkeley: Univ. of California Press, 1997. XIV, 524 pp., illus., ports., notes. [Paperback edn. of No. 19895/YB XXIX, publ. in 1983.]

34929. USA. KIRCHHEIMER, GLORIA DEVIDAS/KIRCHHEIMER, MANFRED: *We were so beloved: autobiography of a German-Jewish community.* Foreword by Steven Lowenstein. Afterword by Dan Bar-On. Pittsburg: Univ. of Pittsburg Press, 1997. XX, 367 pp., illus. [History of the German-Jewish community in Washington Heights, New York.]

34930. USA. LAUGWITZ, BURKHARD: *Mit 93 noch aktiv. Die Künstleragentin Thea Dispeker im Gespräch mit Burkhard Laugwitz.* [In]: Das Orchester, Jg. 44, H. 2, Mainz, 1996. Pp. 12–15, illus. [T.D., b. 1902 in Munich, musicologist, emigr. in 1938 to the US, founded in 1947 in New York 'Thea Dispeker Inc. – Artist's Representative', which became one of the country's biggest agencies for singers.]

34931. USA. RIEMER, SHIRLEY: *The German research companion.* Sacramento, CA: Lorelei Press, 1997. 638 pp., illus., geneal. notes, bibl. (623–638). [Deals with emigration to the US from Germany, Austria, Switzerland, incl. Jews in the 1930s.]

34932. USA. SALTER, RONALD: *Deutsche Emigranten in der amerikanischen Buchkunst.* [In]: Marginalien, H. 147 (3, 1997), Wiesbaden, 1997. Pp. 6–24, notes.

34933. USA. URBACH, NELLY/MAUTNER, WILLY: *Hella.* Washington, DC: American Financial Printers, 1996. 139 pp., illus., ports., maps, geneal. tab. [The story of Hella Mautner (1896–1983), b. in Vienna, who went to the US in 1939 and settled in Birmingham, AL.]

II. RESEARCH AND BIBLIOGRAPHY

A. Libraries and Institutes

34934. DEUTSCHE BIBLIOTHEK, FRANKFURT AM MAIN: *Archivalien des Deutschen Exilarchivs 1933–1945.* Bestandsübersicht. Frankfurt am Main: Die Dt. Bibl., Dt. Exilarchiv 1933–1945, 1997. 37 pp.

34935. FORSCHUNGSSTELLE JUDENTUM, THEOLOGISCHE FAKULTÄT LEIPZIG: *Mitteilungen und Beiträge.* 12/13, September 1997. Leipzig: Thomas-Verlag, 1997. 92 pp. [Selected articles are listed according to subject.]

34936. KALISCH, JUDITH. FRITZ BAUER INSTITUT, FRANKFURT AM MAIN: *Holocaust: die Grenzen des Verstehens. Das Fritz Bauer Institut in Frankfurt.* [In]: Tribüne, Jg. 36, H. 142, Frankfurt am Main, 1997. Pp. 33–38.

34937. HESSISCHES HAUPTSTAATSARCHIV WIESBADEN: *Quellen zur Geschichte der Juden im Hessischen Hauptstaatsarchiv Wiesbaden 1806–1866.* Bearbeitet von Hartmut Heinemann. Wiesbaden: Kommission für die Geschichte der Juden in Hessen, 1997. XI, 577 pp., index (names, places, subjects, 447–577). (Quellen zur Geschichte der Juden in hessischen Archiven, 3.)

34938. INSTITUT FÜR GESCHICHTE DER JUDEN IN ÖSTERREICH, ST. PÖLTEN [in Verbindung mit dem] DEUTSCHEN KOORDINIERUNGSRAT DER GESELLSCHAFTEN FÜR CHRISTLICH-JÜDISCHE ZUSAMMENARBEIT]:: *Aschkenas. Zeitschrift für Geschichte und Kultur der Juden.* Hrsg.: Friedrich Battenberg, Hans Otto Horch, Markus J. Wenninger. Red.: Till Schicketanz, Ulli Steinwender. Wien: Böhlau, 1997. Jg. 7, H. 1 & 2. VI, 618 pp., footnotes, index (persons, subjects, 593–614). [H. 1 cont.: Aufsätze (11–172). Kleinere Beiträge (173–204). Rezensionen und Buchanzeigen (205–266). Projektberichte und Veranstaltungshinweise (267–276). H. 2 cont.: Aufsätze (277–440). Kleiner Beiträge (441–494). Rezensionen und Buchanzeigen (495–586). Projektberichte und Veranstaltungshinweise (587–592). Individual contributions are listed according to subject.]

34939. INSTITUT FÜR GESCHICHTE DER JUDEN IN ÖSTERREICH, ST. PÖLTEN.: *Sommerakademie-News.* H. 7. Hrsg.: Institut für Geschichte der Juden in Österreich, St. Pölten. St. Pölten: Inst. f. Gesch. d. Juden in Österreich, 1997. 1 issue. [Cont. information about current research on Jewish history and culture. Issue title: "Synagoge des Satans" – "Gottes erste Liebe": Kirchen und Judentum. Incl.: Sind traditioneller Antijudaismus und Rassenantisemitismus wirklich zwei verschiedene Phänomene der Judenfeindschaft? (Klaus Lohrmann, 4–7).]

34940. LEO BAECK INSTITUTE. LBI NEW YORK. ZUR MÜHLEN, BERNT TURE VON: *Das Leo Baeck Institut in New York.* [In]: Aus dem Antiquariat, 3/1997 [Beilage zum] Börsenblatt für den Deutschen Buchhandel, Jg. 164, Nr. 25, Frankfurt am Main, 27. März 1997. Pp. A 128–129.

34941. LEO BAECK INSTITUTE: *Jüdischer Almanach 1998/5758.* Hrsg. von Jakob Hessing und Alfred Bodenheimer. Frankfurt am Main: Jüdischer Verlag, 1997. 186 pp., illus., notes. [Incl.: Zu diesem Almanach (eds., 7–8;). Jüdische Gemeinden im polnischen Feudalsystem (Adam Teller, 87–99). Short stories by the Israeli writer Jossel Birstein (113–123, port.). Der Erzähler Jossel Birstein (Yona Bachur, 124–125). Essays pertinent to German-Jewish history are listed according to subject.]

34942. LEO BAECK INSTITUTE: *LBI Information.* Nachrichten aus den Leo Baeck Instituten in Jerusalem, London, New York und der Wissenschaftlichen Arbeitsgemeinschaft des LBI in Deutschland. Hrsg. von den Freunden und Förderern des LBI e.V. in Frankfurt am Main. Red.: Georg Heuberger, Mitarbeit: Ursula Thürich. Nr. 7, Frankfurt am Main (Liebigstraße 24): Freunde und Förderer des LBI e.V., 1997. 118 pp., illus. [Incl. reports on publications, conferences, projects and special events of the LBI Institutes and activities of the Wissenschaftliche Arbeitsgemeinschaft des LBI. Selected articles: Grußwort (Michael A. Meyer, 7–10). Eva G. Reichmann zum 100. Geburtstag (Arnold Paucker, 22–24). Nestor der deutsch-jüdischen Geschichtsschreibung – Ehrendoktorwürde für Dr. Arnold Paucker (Julius H. Schoeps, 25–29). Leo Baeck Medaille für Dr. Fred Grubel (Ismar Schorsch, 37–38). Quellen zur Geschichte der Juden in den Archiven der neuen Bundesländer (Manfred Jehle, 59–62). Die Wahrnehmung der Ostjuden in Deutschland 1910–1933 (Trude Maurer, 67–85, footnotes). Koscher und Trefe. Die Veränderung der religiösen Praxis im Deutschland des 19. Jahrhunderts (Andreas Gotzmann, 85–109, footnotes). Obituary Elias Hofmann (113).]

34943. LEO BAECK INSTITUTE: *Leo Baeck Institute Year Book 1997.* Vol. XLII. Ed.: J.A.S. Grenville, assoc. ed.: Julius Carlebach, assist. eds.: Anna Carrdus, Ulla B. Weinberg. London: Secker & Warburg, 1997. X, 501 pp., frontis., illus., bibl. (357–479), general index (485–501). [Cont.: Preface (eds., IX–X). Essays are arranged under the sections: I. Individual and community in the age of emancipation. II. Yiddish studies in the Wilhelminian and Weimar years. III. Self-defence and German-Jewish identities. IV. Persecution and exile during the National-Socialist regime. V. Continuity and new beginnings in the post-war period. VI. Memoirs. Individual contribs. are listed according to subject.]

—— LEO BAECK INSTITUTE, NEW YORK: *Stammbaum.* The Journal of German-Jewish Genealogical Research. [See No. 35390.]

34944. *Shofar* Vol. 15, No. 4 [with the issue title] *Historical memory and the state of Jewish studies in Germany.* Guest editor: Dean Phillip Bell. West Lafayette, IN: Purdue Univ., Summer 1997. 1 issue, footnotes. [Cont. (titles abbr.): Historical memory and the state of Jewish studies in Germany (Dean Phillip Bell, 1–6). Jewish studies in Germany today: reflections from the Fulbright German studies seminar 1996 (Michael Brenner, 7–15). Memory and modern

Jewish history in contemporary Germany (Tobias Brinkmann, 16–23). Judaistik at German universities today (Margarete Schlüter, 25–31). The new construction of Jewish studies at the universities in the former GDR (Christoph Schulte, 32–39). The current state of the study of Jewish history in Westphalia (Diethard Aschoff, 41–58, tabs., maps, appendix). Between expulsion and emancipation: Jewish villages in East Swabia during the early modern period (Rolf Kießling, 59–86). The Center for Research on Antisemitism in Berlin: purposes and primary research foci (Wolfgang Benz, 88–95). The College for Jewish Studies/Hochschule für jüdische Studien Heidelberg (Dean Phillip Bell, 96–99).]

34945. THE WIENER LIBRARY, LONDON BARKOW, BEN: *Alfred Wiener and the making of the Holocaust Library*. London: Vallentine Mitchell; Portland, OR: Cass, 1997. XX, 260 pp., illus. (Parker-Wiener series on Jewish studies.) [Combines a biography of Alfred Wiener with the history of the library and research institution specialising in the history of Nazism and Fascism. Founded by A.W. in Amsterdam in 1933 and moved to London in 1939.] [Cf.: How valuable research source developed depth (Zev Ben-Shlomo) [in]: Jewish Chronicle, London, July 18, 1997.]

34946. ZENTRALARCHIV ZUR ERFORSCHUNG DER GESCHICHTE DER JUDEN IN DEUTSCHLAND. HONIGMANN, PETER: *10 Jahre Zentralarchiv zur Erforschung der Geschichte der Juden in Deutschland*. [In]: Der Archivar, Jg. 50, H. 3, Düsseldorf, 1997. Cols. 585–587.

34947. ZENTRUM FÜR ANTISEMITISMUSFORSCHUNG, BERLIN. *Jahrbuch für Antisemitismusforschung* 6. Hrsg. von Wolfgang Benz für das Zentrum für Antisemitismusforschung der Technischen Universität Berlin. Red.: Werner Bergmann, Johannes Heil. Geschäftsführende Redakteurin: Juliane Wetzel. Frankfurt am Main; New York, 1997. 366 pp., illus., notes. [Incl.: Vorwort (Wolfgang Benz, 9–11). Cont.: (a.o.): five contribs. on Lithuania, Poland, France, one on gypsies, review essays. Contribs. pertaining to antisemitism in German-speaking countries are listed according to subject.]

B. Bibliographies, Catalogues and Reference Books

34948. COHEN, SUSAN SARAH, ed.: *Antisemitism: an annotated bibliography*. Vol. 4. 1988–1990: Part I, 0001–1124. Vol. 5. 1988–1990: Part II, 1125–3078. Vol. 6. 1988–1990: Part III, 3079–4132; with index to vols. 4–6. [Publ. by the Vidal Sassoon International Center for the Study of Antisemitism, the Hebrew University of Jerusalem.] München: Saur, 1997. LV, 367 pp.; X pp., pp. 368–969; X pp., pp. 970–1450. [For Vol. 1 see No. 24162/YB XXXIII; for Vol. 2 see No. 29261/YB XXXVIII; for Vol. 3 see No.31686/YB XL. Incl. Germany and Austria.]

34949. *Enzyklopädie des Nationalsozialismus*. Hrsg. von Wolfgang Benz, Hermann Graml und Hermann Weiß. Mit zahlreichen Abbildungen, Karten und Grafiken. München: Dt. Taschenbuch Verlag, 1997. 900 pp., illus. Orig.-Ausg. [Cont.: Teil I: Handbuch (26 articles, 11–341); selected articles: Verfolgung (Ludwig Eiber, 275–295). Emigration (Maria-Luise Kreuter, 296–308). Teil II: Lexikon (345–815; numerous entries on Jews, persecution, antisemitism, Final Solution, genocide). Teil III: Personenregister mit Kurzbiographien (817–895; incl. numerous Jews.]

34950. EPSTEIN, ERIC JOSEPH/ROSEN, PHILIP: *Dictionary of the Holocaust*. Biography, geography, and terminology. Foreword by Henry R. Huttenbach. Westport, CT: Greenwood Press, 1997. 384 pp.

—— ERLER, HANS/EHRLICH, ERNST LUDWIG/HEID, LUDGER: *"Meinetwegen ist die Welt erschaffen". Das intellektuelle Vermächtnis des deutschsprachigen Judentums*. 58 Portraits. [See No. 35429.]

—— *Handbuch zur "Völkischen Bewegung" 1871–1918*. Hrsg. von Uwe Puschner, Walter Schmitz und Justus H. Ulbricht. [See No. 35823.]

—— HEUER, RENATE/WOLF, SIEGBERT, eds.: *Die Juden der Frankfurter Universität*. [See No. 35446.]

HONNEF, KLAUS/WEYERS, FRANK, eds.: *Und sie haben Deutschland verlassen . . . müssen. Fotografen und ihre Bilder 1928–1997.* [See No. 35434.]

34951. *Judenverfolgung und jüdisches Leben unter den Bedingungen der nationalsozialistischen Gewaltherrschaft: Tondokumente und Rundfunksendungen.* Hrsg. im Auftrag der Arbeitsgemeinschaft der öffentlich-rechtlichen Rundfunkanstalten Deutschlands (ARD) von Gerhard Hirschfeld [et al.]. Bd. 2/2. 1947–1990, zusammengest. und bearb. von Felix Kresing-Wulf unter Mitw. von Eva-Maria Mühlmann. Potsdam: Verl. für Berlin-Brandenburg, 1997. 414 pp., indexes (persons; subjects; places (361–412). (Veröff. des Deutschen Rundfunkarchivs, Bd. 8; Audiovisuelle Quellen zur Gesch. und Kultur des europ. Judentums und zur Gesch. und Wirkung des Holocaust, Bd. 2.) [For vol. 1 see No. 34075/YB XLII.]

34952. *Kiryat Sefer.* Bibliographical Quarterly of the Jewish National and University Library Jerusalem. Vol. 66, No. 3. Bibliography of all the publications in Israel and of Judaica from abroad. Jersualem: The Jewish National and University Library, 1996. Pp. 593–991. [Incl. publications on the history of German-speaking Jewry and antisemitism.]

LEVINE, GLENN S.: *Yiddish publishing in Berlin and the crisis in Eastern Jewish culture 1919–1924.* [See No. 35385.]

34953. *Lexikon deutsch-jüdischer Autoren.* Bd. 5. Carmo – Donat. Redaktionelle Leitung: Renate Heuer. Unter Mitarbeit von Andrea Boelke-Fabian [et al.] München; New Providence: Saur, 1997. LVII, 498 pp. (Archiv Bibliographia Judaica.)

34954. MÜLLER, THOMAS: *Bibliographie deutschsprachiger Fest- und Gedenkschriften zur jüdischen Kultur und Geschichte.* [In]: Liber amicorum necnon et amicarum [see No. 34697]. Pp. 475–487.

34955. *Publications on German-speaking Jewry.* A selected and annotated bibliography of books and articles 1996. Compiled by Barbara Suchy and Annette Pringle. [In]: Leo Baeck Institute Year Book XLII, London, 1997. Pp. 357–479, index (names, places, periodicals, subjects, 453–479). [On p. 347 incorrect title: Post-war publications on German-speaking Jewry.]

RAAB HANSEN, JUTTA: *NS-verfolgte Musiker in England. Spuren deutscher und österreichischer Flüchtlinge in der britischen Musikkultur.* [See No. 34920.]

34956. RENZ, WERNER: *Vernichtungskrieg: Verbrechen der Wehrmacht 1941 bis 1944 und Holocaust.* Auswahlbibliographie. Frankfurt am Main: Stadt Frankfurt am Main, Arbeitsstelle Fritz Bauer Institut, Studien- und Dokumentationszentrum zur Geschichte und Wirkung des Holocaust, 1997. 34 pp.

SÖLLNER, ALFONS: *Bibliographie der "Exilpolitologen".* [See in No. 35439.]

34957. SPALEK, JOHN M./HAWRYLCHAK, SANDRA H., eds.: *Guide to the archival materials of the German-speaking emigration to the United States after 1933.* Vol. 3, Part 1 and 2. München: Saur, 1997. 970 pp. [For earlier edns. see No. 31693/YB XL.]

34958. STAATSARCHIV LUDWIGSBURG: *Israelitische Oberkirchenbehörde im Königreich Württemberg.* Inventar des Bestands E 212 im Staatsarchiv Ludwigsburg. Bearb. von Erwin Biemann, Wolfgang Schmierer und Gerhard Taddey. Stuttgart: [Staatsarchiv Ludwigsburg], 1996. 119 pp., indexes (places; persons; subjects). (Werkhefte der staatl. Archivverw. Baden-Württ., Serie C, Staatsarchiv Ludwigsburg, H. 2.)

WLASCHEK, RUDOLF M.: *Biographia Judaica Bohemiae.* Bd. 2. [See No. 34899.]

34959. *Yale companion to Jewish writing and thought in German culture 1096–1996.* Ed. by Sander L. Gilman and Jack Zipes. New Haven; London: Yale Univ. Press, 1997. XXXIV, 864 pp. [Cont. 118 contribs. covering 11th cent. to the present, arranged chronologically.]

III. THE NAZI PERIOD

A. General

34960. ALSFELD. *Erinnerungslos: Das Eigene und das Fremde als Heimat. Versuch einer Annäherung an das Schicksal der Juden in Alsfeld.* [Hrsg.: Arbeitskreis Stadtzeichner Alsfeld. Bodo Runte-Wried. Texte: Hans Zitko. Übers.: Theite J. Herron]. Alsfeld: AK Stadtzeichner Alsfeld, 1996. 54 pp., illus., facsims. [Catalogue of exhibition (June 1996).]

34961. ANDERL, GABRIELE: *Berthold Storfer: Retter oder Kollaborateur? Skizzen einer umstrittenen Persönlichkeit.* Ein Beitrag zur Geschichte der "sogenannten illegalen Einwanderung" in das britische Mandatsgebiet Palästina. [In]: David, Jg. 9, Nr. 35, Wien, Dez. 1997. Pp. 15–18; 23–24, illus. [Storfer was commissioned in 1939 by Eichmann to organise "illegal transports" to Palestine.]

34962. ASCHOFF, DIETHARD: *"Jeden Tag sahen wir den Tod vor Augen". Der Auschwitzbericht der Recklinghäuserin Mine Winter.* [In]: Vestische Zeitschrift, Bd. 94/95/96, Recklinghausen, 1997. Pp. 321–386, footnotes. [Incl. the report of Mine Beitowitz née Winter (1914 Recklinghausen – 1985 Phoenix, Arizona), written in the 1950s, on Auschwitz, Ravensbrück and the death march.]

34963. AUSCHWITZ. ADLER, SHIMON: *Block 31: The children's block in the family camp at Birkenau.* [In]: Yad Vashem Studies, Vol. 24, Jerusalem, 1994. Pp. 281–316.

34964. AUSCHWITZ. BAUER, YEHUDA: *Anmerkungen zum "Auschwitz-Bericht" von Rudolf Vrba.* [In]: Vierteljahrshefte für Zeitgeschichte, Jg. 45, H. 2, München, April 1997. Pp. 297–307, footnotes. [With English abstract on p. 350; critical comments on an article by Vrba, see No. 34160/YB XLII.]

34965. AUSCHWITZ. KLEE, ERNST: *Auschwitz, die NS-Medizin und ihre Opfer.* Frankfurt am Main: S. Fischer, 1997. 526 pp., illus., docs., indexes (subjects; persons, 501–526). [Also on experiments in Buchenwald and Dachau.]

34966. AUSTRIA. *Bilder des Nationalsozialismus in Linz.* Wissenschaftlich kommentierte Bilddokumentation über die NS-Zeit in Linz. Hrsg. von Fritz Mayrhofern und Walter Schuster. Linz: Archiv der Stadt Linz, 1997. 200 pp., illus., bibl. (187–193). [Incl.: Juden in Linz (Michael John). Das Konzentrationslager Mauthausen und die Außenlager in Linz (Bertrand Perz).]

34967. AUSTRIA. FREUND, FLORIAN/SAFRIAN, HANS: *Expulsion and extermination: the fate of the Austrian Jews, 1938–1945.* Transl. by Dalia Rosenfeld and Gabriel Biemann. Vienna: The Austrian Resistance Archive, 1997. 62 pp., illus., facsims. [Orig. publ. by the Dokumentationsarchiv des österreichischen Widerstandes in 1993 as part of the project "Registration by name: Austrian victims of the Holocaust".]

34968. AUSTRIA. KLAMPER, ELISABETH: *"We'll meet again in Palestine": Aron Menczer's fight to save Jewish children in Nazi Vienna.* Transl. by Michele Kaiser-Cooke. Vienna: Federal Press Service, 1996. 52 pp., illus., ports., notes. bibl. (Austria Documentation.) [A.M., head of Youth Aliyah in Vienna from 1939–1941.]

34969. AUSTRIA. MÜLLER, ALBERT: *Dynamische Adaptierung und "Selbstbehauptung". Die Universität Wien in der NS-Zeit.* [In]: Geschichte und Gesellschaft, Jg. 23, H. 4, Göttingen, 1997. Pp. 592–617, footnotes. [Incl. the expulsion of Jewish faculty and students.]

34970. AUSTRIA. SCHWARZ, PETER: *Tulln ist judenrein! Die Geschichte der Tullner Juden und ihr Schicksal von 1938 bis 1945: Verfolgung – Vertreibung – Vernichtung.* Wien: Löcker, 1997. 376 pp., illus.

34971. BADEN-WÜRTTEMBERG. BRÄUTIGAM, PETRA: *Mittelständische Unternehmer im Nationalsozialismus.* Wirtschaftliche Entwicklungen und soziale Verhaltensweisen in der Schuh- und Lederindustrie Badens und Württembergs. München: Oldenbourg, 1997. 449 pp., tabs., graphs., footnotes, docs., bibl. (411–440), indexes (persons; places; businesses, 441–449). (Nationalsozialismus und Nachkriegszeit in Südwestdeutschland, Bd. 6.) Zugl.: Tübingen, Univ., Diss., 1995. [Deals also with many firms owned by Jews. Incl. the chapts.: Die Zerstörung der wirtschaftlichen Existenz der jüdischen Bevölkerung [&] "Arisierungen" (245–337).]

34972. BANK, RICHARD D.: *Train to nowhere.* [In]: Midstream, Vol. 43, No. 3, New York, April 1997. Pp. 13–14. [Author describes his grandparent's experiences during the November Pogrom in Odenbach (Palatinate), followed by deportation to Theresienstadt.]

34973. BARONDESS, JEREMIAH A.: *Medicine against society: lessons from the Third Reich.* [In]: JAMA, The Journal of the American Medical Association, Vol. 276, No. 20, Chicago, Nov. 27, 1996. Pp. 1657–1661. [Deals with the perversion of medical ethics by the Nazis, medical experiments on Jews, and the practice of Eugenics.]

34974. BECK-KLEIN, GRETE: *Was sonst vergessen wird: von Wien nach Schanghai, England und Minsk.* Jüdische Schicksale 1918 – 1996. Hrsg. von Erhard Roy Wiehn. Konstanz: Hartung-Gorre, 1997. 113 pp., illus.

34975. BENZ, WOLFGANG: *Judenchristen. Zur doppelten Ausgrenzung einer Minderheit im NS-Staat.* [In]: Edith Stein Jahrbuch 1997. Bd. 3, Würzburg, 1997. Pp. 307–318, footnotes.

—— BENZ, WOLFGANG: *Exodus oder Hierbleiben. Die Situation der Juden zur Zeit der NS-Verfolgung in Deutschland.* [See in No. 35264.]

34976. BENZ, WOLFGANG: *Patriot und Paria. Das Leben des Erwin Goldmann zwischen Judentum und Nationalsozialismus.* Eine Dokumentation. Berlin: Metropol, 1997. 180 pp. (Dokumente – Texte – Materialien.) [E.G., Stuttgart dentist; for further details see No. 31853/YB XL.]

34977. BERGEN-BELSEN. *Belsen in history and memory.* Ed. by Jo Reilly, David Cesarani, Tony Kushner, Colin Richmond. London; Portland OR: Cass, 1997. 260 pp., illus., appendix. [First publ. as special issue of Journal of Holocaust Education in 1996, see No. 33967/YB XLII.]

34978. BERGEN-BELSEN. *Hope, victory and liberation: a collection of testimonies.* [In]: Yad Vashem Studies, Vol. 25, Jerusalem, 1996. Pp. 431–475. [Incl. the Bergen-Belsen diary of Aliza Besser, March – May 1945; the testimony of Muriel Doherty, after liberation.]

34979. BERGEN-BELSEN. JÜRGENS, ARNOLD/RAHE, THOMAS: *Zur Statistik des Konzentrationslagers Bergen-Belsen: Quellengrundlagen, methodische Probleme und neue statistische Daten.* [In]: Die frühen Nachkriegsprozesse [see No. 35269]. Pp.128–148, notes.

34980. BERLIN. *"Ich fürchte die Menschen mehr als die Bomben". Aus den Tagebüchern von drei Berliner Frauen 1938–1946.* Hrsg. von Angela Martin und Claudia Schoppmann im Auftrag der Berliner Geschichtswerkstatt e.V. Berlin: Metropol, 1996. 156 pp., illus. (Dokumente, Texte, Materialien, Bd. 19.) [Diaries by two Jews (Erna Becker, who survived because of her mixed marriage, and Cäcilie Lewissohn, who survived in hiding) and one non-Jew (Marta Mierendorff), whose fiancé was Gottfried Salomon, a Jew murdered in Auschwitz in 1944.]

34981. BERLIN. SCHÜLER-SPRINGORUM, STEFANIE: *Elend und Furcht im Dritten Reich. Aus den Akten der Sammelvormundschaft der Jüdischen Gemeinde zu Berlin.* [In]: Zeitschrift für Geschichtswissenschaft, Jg. 45, H. 7, Berlin, 1997. Pp. 617–641, footnotes.

34982. BERENBAUM, MICHAEL: *Witness to the Holocaust.* New York: Harper Collins, 1997. XXXIII, 367 pp., illus., chronol., tabs., notes, author and title index. [Cont. sections: I. The Boycott (1–8). II. The first regulatory assault against Jews (9–15). III. Early efforts at spiritual resistance (16–23; deals mainly with Martin Buber and Leo Baeck). IV. The Nuremberg laws (24–30). V. The conference at Evian (31–39). VI. The November Pogroms (40–68). VII. The beginning of ghettoization (69–77). VIII. The Judenrat (78–101). IX. A mosaic of victims: non-Jewish victims of Nazism (102–111). X. The Einsatzgruppen (112–135). XI. Babi Yar (136–148). XII. The call to arms (149–157). XIII. Hitler's plan to exterminate the Jews (158–171). XIV. The killers: a speech, a memoir, and an interview (172–201). XV. Choiceless choices (202–214). XVI. The end of a Ghetto: deportation from Warsaw (215–232). XVII. The Warsaw Ghetto uprising (233–247). XVIII. What was known in the West (248–294). XIX. Why Auschwitz was not bombed (295–304). XX. Liberation and its aftermath (305–326). XXI. The Nuremberg Trials (327– 357).]

34983. BERNARD, BIRGIT: *Gleichschaltung im Westdeutschen Rundfunk 1993.* [In]: Geschichte im Westen, Jg. 12, H. 2, Köln, 1997. Pp. 186–194, footnotes. [Incl. the expulsion of Jews from the radio station in Cologne.]

34984. BOLKOSKY, SIDNEY: *Of parchment and ink: varieties of survivor* [sic] *religious responses to the Holocaust.* [In]: The Journal of Holocaust Education, Vol. 6, No. 2, London, Autumn 1997. Pp. 1–35, notes. [Incl. abstracts of interviews with survivors.]

34985. BONN. HÖPFNER, HANS-PAUL: *Die vertriebenen Hochschullehrer der Universität Bonn 1933–1945.* [In]: Bonner Geschichtsblätter, Bd. 1993/94, Bonn, 1996. Pp. 447–487, footnotes, ports.

34986. BENDREMER, JUTTA T.: *Women surviving the Holocaust; in spite of the horror.* Lewiston, NY: Edwin Mellen Press, 1997. 118 pp., illus., ports. (Symposium series, Vol. 43.)

34987. BRENNER, RACHEL F.: *Writing as resistance; four women confronting the Holocaust.* University Park: Penn State Univ. Press, 1997. VI, 216 pp., ports., notes, bibl. [Incl. Anne Frank and Edith Stein.]

34988. BRESLAU. JONCA, KAROL: *Deportation of German Jews from Breslau 1941–1944 as described in eyewitness testimonies.* [In]: Yad Vashem Studies, Vol. 25, Jerusalem, 1996. Pp. 275–316. [Also in this issue: The Transit Camp for Breslau Jews at Riebnig in Lower Silesia (1941–1943) (Alfred Konieczny, 317–342).]

34989. CHANNEL ISLANDS. COHEN, FREDERICK E.: *The Jews in the Islands of Jersey, Guernsey and Sark during the German occupation 1940–1945.* [In]: The Journal of Holocaust Education, Vol. 6, No. 1, London, Summer 1997. Pp. 27–81, notes. [Incl. German-Jewish refugees.]

34990. CHURCH. BÜTTNER, URSULA: *"Die Judenfrage wird zur Christenfrage". Die deutsche evangelische Kirche und die Judenverfolgung im Dritten Reich.* [In]: Zeitschrift für Geschichtswissenschaft, Jg. 45, H. 7, Berlin, 1997. Pp. 581–596, footnotes.

34991. CHURCH. OPPEN, ASTA VON: *Der unerhörte Schrei: Dietrich Bonhoeffer und die Judenfrage im Dritten Reich.* Hannover: Lutherisches Verlagshaus, 1996. 128 pp., bibl. (Schalom-Bücher, Bd. 5.)

34992. CHURCH. PASSELECQ, GEORGES/SUCHECKY, BERNARD: *Die unterschlagene Enzyklika. Der Vatikan und die Judenverfolgung.* Aus dem Franz. von Martin Sedlaczek. München: Hanser, 1997. 322 pp., notes, bibl. [Incl. the document, which had never been publ.: Die Einheit des Menschengeschlechts/Humani generis unitas of 1938, written a few months before Pius XI died (Feb. 10, 1939). Orig. title: L'encyclique cachée de Pie XI. Une occasion manquée de l'Eglise face à l'antisémitisme, publ. 1995.] [Cf.: Endloses Versteckspiel. Erstmals publiziert: die vom Vatikan geheimgehaltene Enzyklika gegen Antisemitismus und Judenverfolgung (Hansjakob Stehle) [in]: Die Zeit, Nr. 29, Hamburg, 19. Sept. 1997, p. 22.]

34993. COLOGNE. CORBACH, DIETER: *6.00 ab Messe Köln-Deutz – Deportationen aus Köln 1938 bis 1945.* Geleitwort: Erwin Schild. Vorwort: Dieter Corbach. Übers. ins Engl.: Fritz Bauchwitz [et al.]. Köln: Scriba, 1997. 704 pp., illus., facsims., gloss., plans, docs. (Spuren jüdischen Wirkens, 6.) [Incl. 7,000 names. Text partly in English.]

34994. DENMARK. KIRCHHOFF, HANS: *SS-Gruppenführer Werner Best and the action against Danish Jews – October 1943.* [In]: Yad Vahem Studies, Vol. 24, Jerusalem, 1994. Pp. 195–222.

34995. DESELAERS, MANFRED: *Und Sie hatten nie Gewissensbisse? Die Biografie von Rudolf Höß, Kommandant von Auschwitz, und die Frage nach seiner Verantwortung vor Gott und den Menschen*. Leipzig: Benno, 1997. 424 pp., illus.

34996. *Deutsche Politik im "Protektorat Böhmen und Mähren" unter Reinhard Heydrich 1941–1942*. Eine Dokumentation. Hrsg. von Miroslav Kárny [et al.]. Berlin: Metropol, 1997. 303 pp., docs., footnotes, index. (Nationalsozialistische Besatzungspolitik in Europa 1939–1945, Bd. 2.)

34997. *Deutsches Judentum unter dem Nationalsozialismus*. Band 1: Dokumente zur Geschichte der Reichsvertretung der deutschen Juden 1933–1939. Hrsg., eingeleitet und erläutert von Otto Dov Kulka unter Mitarbeit von Anne Birkenhauser und Esriel Hildesheimer mit einem Vorwort von Eberhard Jäckel. Tübingen: Mohr Siebeck, 1997. XXIV, 614 pp., frontis., footnotes, gloss., bibl. (547–576), index (608–614). (Schriftenreihe wissenschaftlicher Abhandlungen des Leo-Baeck-Instituts, 54.)

34998. DIEHL, KATRIN: *Die jüdische Presse im Dritten Reich. Zwischen Selbstbehauptung und Fremdbestimmung*. Tübingen: Niemeyer, 1997. 362 pp., footnotes, tabs., bibl. (287–344), index (359–361). (Conditio Judaica, 17.) Zugl.: München, Univ., Diss.

34999. DIPPEL, JOHN V.H.: *Die große Illusion. Warum deutsche Juden ihre Heimat nicht verlassen wollten*. Mit einem Vorwort von Alfred Grosser. Aus dem Amerik. von Angelika Beck. Weinheim: Beltz Quadriga, 1997. 538 pp., notes (457–515), bibl. (516–533), index (534–538). [For orig. edn. see No. 33997/YB XLII.] [Cf.: Tödliches Wunschdenken oder realistische Hoffnung? (Eva-Maria Ziege) [in]: Das Parlament, Nr. 42, Bonn, 10. Okt. 1997, p. IV. Deutscher als die Deutschen (Julius H. Schoeps) [in]: Die Zeit, Nr. 43, Hamburg, 17. Okt. 1997, p. 37.]

35000. DORA. NEANDER, JOACHIM: *Das Konzentrationslager "Mittelbau" in der Endphase der nationalsozialistischen Diktatur*. Zur Geschichte des letzten im "Dritten Reich" gegründeten selbständigen Konzentrationslagers unter besonderer Berücksichtigung seiner Auflösungsphase. Clausthal-Zellerfeld: Papierflieger, 1997. XIV, 521 pp., illus., graphs. Zugl.: Bremen, Univ., Diss., 1996.

35001. DRESDEN. LIEBSCH, HEIKE: *"Ein Tier ist nicht rechtloser und gehetzter." Die Verfolgung der jüdischen Bevölkerung Dresdens 1933–1937*. [In]: Im Herzen der Finsternis. Victor Klemperer als Chronist der NS-Zeit. Hrsg. von Hannes Heer [see No. 35597]. Pp. 73–91. [This vol. incl. also: "Man wird keinen von ihnen wiedersehen". Die Vernichtung der Dresdener Juden 1938–1945 (Nora Goldenbogen, 92–109); three further contribs. by Hannes Heer, Wolfgang Kraushaar and Jan Philipp Reemtsma.]

35002. DÜSSELDORF. SUCHY, BARBARA: *Als "Tietz" zum "Kaufhof" wurde und "Carsch" zu "Seifert". Die ersten "Arisierungen" in Düsseldorf*. Teil 2. [In]: Augenblick, Nr. 10/11, Düsseldorf, 1997. Pp. 14–19, illus., facsims., notes. [Also in this issue interviews of and letters by Jews from Düsseldorf (Angela Genger et. al., 3–9, 28–31).]

35003. DÜSSELDORF. WOELK, WOLF: *Jüdische Ärzte in der Stadt und an der Medizinischen Akademie Düsseldorf im Nationalsozialismus (1933–1938)*. [In]: Die Medizinische Akademie Düsseldorf im Nationalsozialismus. Hrsg.: M.G. Esch [et al.]. Essen: Klartext, 1997. (Düsseldorfer Schriften zur neueren Landesgeschichte und zur Geschichte Nordrhein-Westfalens, Bd. 47.). Pp. 55–85, illus., footnotes.

35004. EDVARDSON, CORDELIA: *Burned child seeks the fire: a memoir*. Transl. from the Swedish by Joel Agee. Boston: Beacon Press, 1997. 105 pp. [For details and German edn. with the title 'Gebranntes Kind sucht das Feuer', first publ. 1986, see No. 23251/YB XXXII.]

35005. EICHMANN, ADOLF. AHARONI, ZVI/DIETL, WILHELM: *Operation Eichmann: the truth about the pursuit, capture and trial*. Transl. by Helmut Bögler. London: Arms and Armour Press; New York: Wiley, 1997. 192 pp., illus. [Cf.: The man who snatched Adolf Eichmann (Jim White) [in]: The Guardian, London, July 16, 1997, pp. 8–9. Interview with author who was a

Mossad agent and came to Israel from Germany in 1938 under the name of Hermann Arndt.]

—— *Enzyklopädie des Nationalsozialismus.* [See No. 34949.]

35006. EXILE. BENZ, WOLFGANG/NEISS, MARION, eds.: *Die Erfahrung des Exils: exemplarische Reflexionen.* Berlin: Metropol, 1997. 175 pp. (Bibliothek der Erinnerung, Bd. 3.) [Cont. 8 texts (introduced by short biographies of the authors): Über Shanghai in die USA. Blick zurück nach Deutschland (W. Michael Blumenthal, 9–26). Überwindung des Nationalsozialismus. Literarische und psychoanalytische Annäherungen (Hans Keilson, 27–46). Emigration und Weltbürgertum. Der notwendige Abschied vom nationalen Denken (Felix Posen, 47–64). Politisches Erwachen. Berlin, das Exil und die antifaschistische Bewegung (George L. Mosse, 65–80). Aus dem Asylland ins Exil. Schriftstellerin in der Tschechoslowakei und in Mexiko (Lenka Reinerová, 81–102). Vergebliche Warnung. Bericht über eine Flucht aus Auschwitz (Rudolf Vrba, 103–124). Flucht und Heimkehr. Der lange Weg zu den Berliner Philharmonikern (Hellmut Stern, 125–154). Emigration und Heimat. Erfahrungen und Hoffnungen (Edzard Reuter, 157–175; E.R., German industrialist, son of the Social Democrat Fritz Reuter, who, with his family, found political asylum in Turkey in 1935).]

35007. EXILE. *Fritz H. Landshoff und der Querido-Verlag: 1933–1950.* Mit einer Bibliographie Querido. Bearb.: Hans-Albert Walter. [Hrsg.: Ulrich Ott]. Marbach am Neckar: Dt. Schillerges., 1997. 285 pp., illus. (Marbacher Magazin, 78. Sonderheft.) [Catalogue of exhibition, Bremen, May-June, 1997; incl. Bibl. Querido-Verlag (237–275).]

35008. EXILE. HORN, GERD-RAINER: *Radicalism and moderation within German Social Democracy in underground and exile, 1933–1936.* [In]: German History, Vol. 15, No. 3, Oxford, 1997. Pp. 200–220, notes. [Incl. Jewish Socialists.]

35010. *Fascism and theatre: comparative studies on the aesthetics and politics of performance in Europe, 1925–1945.* Compiled by Günther Berghaus. Oxford: Berghahn, 1996. VI, 315 pp., illus., facsims., notes, bibl. (277–298), name index. [Incl. chap.: Censorship in Nazi Germany: the influence of the Reich's Ministry of Propaganda in German theatre and drama, 1933–1945 (Barbara Pause). Deals with the banning of plays either written by Jews or with Jewish content.]

35011. *FDR and the Holocaust: did the President do all he could to save European Jewry?* New York: Leo Baeck Institute, 1997. 57 pp. (Occasional paper, No. 2.) [A symposium sponsored by the Leo Baeck Institute and held at the Harvard Club in New York in May 1997, with the participation of Henry Feingold, Ambassador William vanden Heuvel, Arthur Schlesinger, Fritz Stern, Sidney Zion.] [Cf.: America, FDR, and the Holocaust (William J. vanden Heuvel) [in]: Society, Vol. 34, No. 6, New Brunswick, NJ, Sept.-Oct. 1997, pp. 54–65.]

35012. FEINGOLD, HENRY L.: *Zionism and the Holocaust: did the World Zionist Movement fail the Jews?* [In]: Jewish Frontier, Vol. 64, No. 1, New York, Jan./Feb. 1997. Pp. 10–12.

35013. FILM. *Medien & Zeit* Jg. 12, H. 3. Wien, 1997. 1 issue, notes. [Incl.: Nazi-Nibelungen. Juden und Germanenbilder im Dritten Reich (Wolfgang Pensold, 4–21). Schatten des Grauens. Zur Problematik von Filmen über den Holocaust (Edith Dörfler, 22–39). Shoah nach Spielberg. Holocaust und Hollywood oder Schindlers Liste (Patrizia Tonin, 40–51). Hitler – ein Karriere, Schindlers Liste und die Tücken der Sozialwissenschaften (Heinz Wassermann, 51–56).]

35014. FILM. SCHULTE-SASSE, LINDA: *Entertaining the Third Reich: illusions of wholeness in Nazi cinema.* Durham, NC: Duke Univ. Press, 1996. XIV, 347 pp., illus., tabs., filmography (331–338), bibl. (319–330). [Incl. chaps.: Two sides of a coin: The "Jew" and the king as social fantasies. Courtier, vampire, or vermin?: Jew Süss's contradictory effort to render the "Jew" other.]

35015. FILM. TEGEL, SUSAN: *Veit Harlan and the origins of 'Jud Süss,' 1938–1939: opportunism in the creation of Nazi anti-Semitic film propaganda.* [In]: Historical Journal of Film, Radio and Television, Vol. 16, No. 4, Dorchester-on-Thames, Oxford, Oct. 1996. Pp. 515–531.

35016. FINAL SOLUTION. HARTOG, L.J.: *Der Befehl zum Judenmord. Hitler, Amerika und die Juden.* [Aus dem Niederl. übers.]. Bodenheim: Syndikat, 1997. 102 pp. [Dutch title: Hoe ontstand de Judenmoort? Hitler, Amerika en de Endlösung; first publ. 1994.]

35017. FINAL SOLUTION. LEY, MICHAEL/SCHOEPS, JULIUS H., eds.: *Der Nationalsozialismus als politische Religion.* Bodenheim: Philo, 1997. 280 pp., notes, index. (Studien zur Geistesgeschichte, Bd. 20.) [Incl.: Anstelle eines Nachworts: Erlösungswahn und Vernichtungswille. Die sogenannte "Endlösung der Judenfrage" als Vision und Programm des Nationalsozialismus (Julius H. Schoeps, 262–271, notes).]

35018. FINAL SOLUTION. MALLMANN, KLAUS-MICHAEL: *Vom Fußvolk der "Endlösung". Ordnungspolizei, Ostkrieg und Judenmord.* [In]: Tel Aviver Jahrbuch für jüdische Geschichte, Bd. 26, 1997, Gerlingen, 1997. Pp. 355–392, notes.

35019. FINAL SOLUTION. STEUR, CLAUDIA: *Theodor Dannecker. Ein Funktionär der "Endlösung".* Essen: Klartext, 1997. 251 pp., illus., docs., footnotes, bibl. (231–244), index (245–251). (Schriften der Bibliothek für Zeitgeschichte – Neue Folge, Bd. 6.)

35020. FINAL SOLUTION. *Werkstatt Geschichte*, H. 18 [with the issue title] *"Endlösung".* Hamburg, 1997. 1 issue. [Incl.: Die Wannsee-Konferenz, das Schicksal der deutschen Juden und Hitlers politische Grundsatzentscheidung, alle Juden Europas zu ermorden (Christian Gerlach, 7–44). Rudolf Höß und die "Endlösung der Judenfage". Drei Argumente gegen die Datierung auf den Sommer 1941 (Karin Orth, 45–58). Gewalt gegen Juden in Deutschland 1933 bis 1939 (Michael Wildt, 59–82). [Cf. (reviews of Christian Gerlach's article): Himmlers Kalender (Michael Weismann) [in]: 'FAZ', Nr. 284, Frankfurt am Main, 6. Dez. 1997, p. 33. Hitlers bösester Befehl (Volker Ullrich) [in]: Die Zeit, Nr. 3, Hamburg, 8.Jan. 1998, p. 29.]

35021. FINAL SOLUTION. *Yad Vashem Studies* Vol. 24, Jerusalem 1994. 1 issue [Incl. 4 essays on the 'Final Solution': The Holocaust and population policy: remarks on the decision on the 'Final Solution' (Susanne Heim/Götz Aly, 45–70). Rationalization and method: Critique of a new approach in understanding the 'Final Solution' (Dan Diner, 71–108; previously publ. in German in: Vierteljahrshefte für Zeitgeschichte, Jg. 40, H. 3, München, 1992, pp. 359–382). On modernization and the rationality of extermination (David Bankier, 109–130). Racism and rational calculation: the role of "utilitarian" strategies of legitimation in the National Socialist "Weltanschauung" (Ulrich Herbert, 131–146; previously publ. in German, see in No. 28278/YB XXXVII).]

35022. FINKELGRUEN, PETER: *Erlkönigs Reich. Die Geschichte einer Täuschung.* Berlin: Rowohlt Berlin Verlag, 1997. 205 pp. [Deals with the author's attempt to reconstruct his own and his family's history. Also by the author (b. in Shanghai in exile): Rückkehr aus Shanghai [in]: Magazin, [Beilage zu] Die Zeit, Nr. 34, Hamburg, 15. Aug. 1997, pp. 2–37, illus.]

35023. FORCED LABOUR. GRUNER, WOLF: *'Terra incognita'? The camps for "Jewish Labor Conscription" (1938–1943) and the German population.* [In]: Yad Vashem Studies, Vol. 24, Jerusalem, 1994. Pp. 1–44. [Previously publ. in German, see in No. 29310/YB XXXVIII.]

35024. FORCED LABOUR. GRUNER, WOLF: *Der Geschlossene Arbeitseinsatz deutscher Juden. Zur Zwangsarbeit als Element der Verfolgung.* Berlin: Metropol, 1997. 384 pp., tabs., footnotes, bibl. (360–370), indexes (372–384)

35025. FORCED LABOUR. GRUNER, WOLF: *Die Organisation von Zwangsarbeit für Juden in Deutschland und im Generalgouvernement 1939–1943: eine vergleichende Bestandsaufnahme.* [In]: Die Festung Glatz und die Verfolgung in der Zeit des Nationalsozialismus. Veröff. der Vorträge des deutsch-poln. Seminars im Sept. 1995 in Glatz/Kłodzko. [Hrsg.: Stiftung Topographie des

Terrors]. Berlin: [Stiftung Topographie des Terrors], [1997?]. Pp. 43–55, footnotes. [Book title also in Polish.]

35026. FORCED LABOUR. GRUNER, WOLF: *Die Arbeitslager für den Zwangseinsatz deutscher und nichtdeutscher Juden im Dritten Reich.* [Part 1–3]. [In]: Gedenkstätten-Rundbrief, Nr. 78–80, Berlin, 1997. Pp. 1–17; 1–17; 27–37.

35027. FRANCE. GOBITZ, GÉRARD: *Les déportations de réfugiés de zone libre en 1942.* Paris: L'Harmattan, 1997. 290 pp.

35028. FRANCE. LORING, MARIANNE: *Flucht aus Frankreich 1940.* Die Vertreibung deutscher Sozialdemokraten aus dem Exil. Hrsg. von Wolfgang Benz. Frankfurt am Main: Fischer Taschenbuch Verlag, 1996. 153 pp., illus., notes. (Die Zeit des Nationalsozialismus. Eine Buchreihe.) Originalausgabe. [Personal recollections of M.L., daughter of Friedrich Stampfer, the former ed. of the Social-Democratic 'Vorwärts', written in 1941 after her escape to the US. Incl.: Fliehen vor Hitler. Einleitende Bemerkungen zum sozialdemokratischen Exil (ed., 9–20). Flucht aus Frankreich (Friedrich Stampfer, 141–145; first publ. in 1957).]

35029. FRANK, ANNE. *Anne Frank: the legacy . . . the promise.* Teacher's resource guide sponsored by the National Conference [and] the Cleveland Play House. Cleveland, OH: The National Conference, 1997. 44 leaves in ring binder, illus., ports., chronol., bibl. [Guide orig. created in conjunction with an int. exhibit, 'Anne Frank in the world, 1929–1945'.] [Cf.: Remembering Anne Frank (Jacob B. Michaelsen) [in]: Judaism, Vol. 46, No. 2, New York, Spring 1997, pp. 120–128.]

35031. FRANK, ANNE. GIES, MIEP: *Anne Frank's legacy.* [In]: Dimensions, Vol. 11, No. 1, New York, 1997. Pp. 24–26, ports. [Speech given by M.G. in June 1996 at a meeting of the Anti-Defamation League, New York. Author helped the Frank family while they were in hiding.]

35032. FRANK, ANNE. MAARSEN, JAQUELINE VAN: *Meine Freundin Anne Frank.* Aus dem Niederl. von Stefanie Schröder. München: Heyne, 1997. 123 pp., illus. Dt. Erstausgabe. [Orig. title 'Anne en Jopie'.]

35033. FRANK, ANNE. MELNICK, RALPH: *The stolen legacy of Anne Frank: Meyer Levin, Lillian Hellman, and the staging of the diary.* New Haven: Yale Univ. Press, 1997. XXII, 268 pp., ports., illus., notes. [Deals with the controversy surrounding the different stage versions of the diary.] [Cf.: A less-than-frank interpretation of Anne's views (Anne Sebba) [in]: Jewish Chronicle, London, Oct. 10, 1997. The afterlife of Anne Frank (Ian Buruma) [in]: The New York Review, New York, Feb. 19, 1998, p. 4–7.]

35034. FRANK, ANNE. REISZ, MATTHEW: *The odour of sanctity: a new look at Anne Frank's diary.* [In]: The Jewish Quarterly, Vol. 44, No. 2, London, Summer 1997. Pp. 41–43, notes.

35035. FRANKFURT am Main. GOHL, BEATE: *Jüdische Wohlfahrtspflege im Nationalsozialismus: Frankfurt am Main 1933–1943.* Frankfurt am Main: Fachhochschulverl., 1997. 99 pp., illus., graphs, facsims., docs.

35036. FRIEDLANDER, HENRY: *Der Weg zum NS-Genozid.* Von der Euthanasie zur Endlösung. Aus dem Amerikanischen von Johanna Friedman, Martin Richter und Barbara Schaden. Berlin: Berlin-Verlag, 1997. 640 pp., notes (477–590), bibl. (591–613), tabs., index (616–640). [For orig. edn. publ. 1995 see No. 32828/YB XLI.]

35037. FRIEDLÄNDER, SAUL: *Nazi Germany and the Jews.* Vol. 1. The years of persecution, 1933–1939. New York: Harper Collins, 1997. XII, 436 pp., illu., notes (335–395), bibl. (397–425). [Simultaneously publ. in French: 'L'Allemagne nazie et les Juifs. Tome 1. Les années de persécutions (1933–1939). Traduit de l'anglais par Marie-France de Paloméra. Paris: Éd. du Seuil, 1997. 422 pp.] [Cf.: Reviews (Judith Rosen) [in]: The Jewish Book World, Vol. 15, No. 2, New York, Fall 1997, pp. 22–23. Survival of the truth (Neil Gregor) [in]: Jewish Chronicle, London, April 18, 1997. The road to Auschwitz (Robert Wistrich) [in]: Commentary, Vol. 104, No. 1, New York, July 1997, pp. 57–59.]

35038. FRIEDMAN, PHILIP: *The fate of the Jewish books during the Nazi era.* [In]: Jewish Book Annual, Vol. 54, New York, 1996–1997. Pp. 81–94. [Incl. book-burning, looted books, and rare books that were sold for profit.]

35039. FRÖNDENBERG. KLEMP, STEFAN: *Geschichte der Judenverfolgung in Fröndenberg.* Fröndenberg: Stadt Fröndenberg, Fachbreich I/Kultur, 1996. 39, [12] pp., illus. (Beiträge zur Ortgeschichte/Fröndenberg, 9.) [Fröndenberg: on the Ruhr, nr. Unna.]

35040. FÜRTH. *Gedenke – Remember: zum Gedenken an die von den Nazis ermordeten 135 Fürther Juden 1933 – 1945.* Hrsg.: Komitee zum Gedenken der Fürther Shoah-Opfer. Recherchen und Zusammenstellung: Gisela Blume. Fürth: Stadtarchiv Fürth, [1997]. 481 pp., 18 pp. [suppl.], illus., ports. Title and introd. in German, English and Hebrew. Supplement entitled: Einweihung des Denkmals für die Fürther Opfer der Shoah.]

35041. GEVE, THOMAS: *Es gibt hier keine Kinder. There are no children here. Auschwitz, Groß-Rosen, Buchenwald.* Zeichnungen eines kindlichen Historikers. Drawings of a child historian. Hrsg. von/ed. by Volkhard Knigge mit einem Geleitwort von/preface by Avner Shalev und Beiträgen von/contributions by Thomas Geve, Volkhard Knigge, Irit Salmon, Sonja Staar. Göttingen: Wallstein, 1997. 151 pp., illus. [Texts in German, English and Hebrew. Cont. the first complete edn. of 79 drawings by Thomas Geve depicting his experiences in the concentration camps. They were made in 1945 in Switzerland after his liberation and are kept in Yad Vashem, Jerusalem.] [Thomas Geve, b. 1929 in North Germany, engineer, in 1943 deported from Berlin to Auschwitz, in 1950 emigr. from London to Israel. For further data see No. 30523/YB XXXIX.]

35042. GLASS, JAMES M.: *Life unworthy of life: racial phobia and mass murder in Hitler's Germany.* New York: Basic Books, 1997. XIX, 252 pp., notes (197–225), bibl. (227–240).

35043. GÖTTINGEN. BRUNS-WÜSTEFELD, ALEX: *Lohnende Geschäfte. Die "Entjudung" der Wirtschaft am Beispiel Göttingens.* Hannover: Fackelträger, 1997. 318 pp., illus., tabs., plan, bibl. (290–295). [Cf.: Besprechung (Jan Lokers) [in]: Niedersächsisches Jahrbuch für Landesgeschichte, Bd. 69, Hannover, 1997, pp. 478–479.]

35044. GÖTTINGEN. WEGELER, CORNELIA: *". . . wir sagen ab der internationalen Gelehrtenrepublik".* Altertumswissenschaft und Nationalsozialismus. Das Göttinger Institut für Altertumskunde 1921–1962. Wien: Böhlau, 1996. 427 pp., illus., docs., notes (277–331), bibl. (398–419), index (421–427). [Deals also with Jewish historians and their fate, esp. in chap. 3.2 entitled: Ausgrenzung, Vertreibung und Verfolgung von Altertumswissenschaftlern an den deutschen Universitäten (141–219).]

35045. GOLDHAGEN, DANIEL JONAH: *Hitler's willing executioners. Ordinary Germans and the Holocaust.* London: Little, Brown and Co., 1996. [For details and German edn. see No. 34043/YB XLII.] [Selected reviews (continuation): Hitlers willige Vollstrecker (Ernst Nolte) [in]: Jahrbuch Extremismus & Demokratie, Jg. 9, Baden-Baden, 1997, pp. 299–303. Besprechung (Eric A. Johnson) [in]: Historische Zeitschrift, Bd. 265, München, 1997, pp. 254–259. Daniel Jonah Goldhagen's "crazy" theory (Norman G. Finkelstein) [in]: New Left Review, London, No. 224, July-August, 1997, pp. 39–49. Die Widerlegung des funktionalistischen Täterbildes. Daniel Goldhagens Beitrag zur Kriminologie des Völkermords (Herbert Jäger) [in]: Mittelweg 36, Jg. 6, H. 1, Hamburg, 1997, pp. 73–85, footnotes. Erkenntnisse, Bekenntnisse und ihre Widersprüche (Martin Kloke) [in]: Geschichte, Erziehung, Politik, Jg. 7, H. 11, Berlin, 1997, pp. 577–582. Besprechung (Konrad Fuchs) [in]: Nassauische Annalen, Bd. 108, Wiesbaden, 1997, pp. 395–399.]

35046. GOLDHAGEN, DANIEL JONAH: *Les bourreaux volontaires de Hitler. Les allemands ordinaires et l'Holocaust.* Traduit de l'américain par P. Martin. Paris: Ed. du Seuil, 1997. 580 pp. [Cf.: Revue (Madeleine et Jean-Louis Steinberg [in]: Revue d'histoire de la Shoah, No. 159, Paris, janvier-avril 1997, pp. 239–242.]

35047. GOLDHAGEN DEBATE. *Arena*. [Section of] Rechtshistorisches Journal 16, Hrsg. von Dieter Simon. Frankfurt am Main: Löwenklau Gesellschaft, 1997. Pp. 601–702. [This section cont. 12 essays or statements about Goldhagen's book 'Hitler's willing executioners. Ordinary Germans and the Holocaust' (see No. 34043/YB XLII) and the ensuing debates: Nichts gehört, nichts gesehen – und nichts gesagt (Dieter Simon, 601–611). Ma quanti sono gli eroi? (Luigi Capogrossi Colognesi, 612–620). Von deutscher Erfindungskraft oder: Die Kollektivschuldthese in der Nachkriegszeit (Norbert Frei, 621–634, footnotes). Seduction or complicity. How guilty were the Germans? (Istvan Deak, 635–641, footnotes). Kollektivschuld (Stephan Wehowsky, 642–647). Assigning responsibility: a note on Daniel Goldhagen's book (Tony Judt, 648–657, footnotes). After Goldhagen: reconsidering responsibility and guilt (Shulamit Volkov, 658–664). Kollektivschuld und Kollektivhaftung (Junichi Murakami, 665–672, footnotes). Kollektivhaftung im Völkerrecht (Stefan Kadelbach, 673–680). Collective guilt? No ... but: (Charles S. Maier, 681–686). Kollektivschuld. Funktionen eines moralischen und juridischen Unbegriffs (Hermann Lübbe, 687–695). Vom deutschen Schicksalskampf (Gerhard Henschel, 696–702).]

35048. GOLDHAGEN DEBATE. Aschheim, Steven E.: *Archetypes and the German-Jewish dialogue: reflections occasioned by the Goldhagen affair*. [In]: German History, Vol. 15, No. 2, Oxford, 1997. Pp. 240–250, notes.

—— GOLDHAGEN DEBATE. Aschheim, Steven: *Post-Holocaust Jewish mirrorings of Germany: Hannah Arendt and Daniel Goldhagen*. [See No. 35756.]

35049. GOLDHAGEN DEBATE. Birn, Ruth Bettina: *Reviewing the Holocaust* [In]: Historical Journal, Vol. 40, No. 1, Cambridge, March 1997. Pp. 195–215, footnotes.]

35050. GOLDHAGEN DEBATE. Bleier, Suzanne M.: *Ein Lehrstück deutscher Vergangenheitsbewältigung. Die Debatte über Daniel Goldhagens Buch*. [In]: Geschichte, Erziehung, Politik, Jg. 7, H. 12, Berlin, 1997. Pp. 641–644.

35051. GOLDHAGEN DEBATE. *Briefe an Goldhagen*. Eingeleitet und beantwortet von Daniel Jonah Goldhagen. Berlin: Siedler, 1997. 251 pp. [Cf.: Besprechung (Johannes Heil) [in]: Zeitschrift für Geschichtswissenschaft, Jg. 45, H. 11, Berlin, 1997, pp. 1048–1049.]

35052. GOLDHAGEN DEBATE. Cohen, Edmund D.: *National character, collective guilt, and original sin – the Goldhagen controversy*. [In]: Free Inquiry, Vol. 17, No. 2, Buffalo, NY, Spring 1997. Pp. 34–39.

35053. GOLDHAGEN DEBATE. Cowell, Alan: *Holocaust writer debates irate historians in Berlin*. [In]: The New York Times, Vol. 145, Sec. 1, New York, Sept. 8, 1996. 21 col.

35054. GOLDHAGEN DEBATE. Deak, Istvan: *Holocaust views: The Goldhagen controversy in retrospect*. [In]: Central European History, Vol. 30, No. 2, Atlantic Highlands, NJ, 1997. Pp. 295–307, notes.

35055. GOLDHAGEN DEBATE. *Die Deutschen – ein Volk von Tätern?* Zur historisch-politischen Debatte um das Buch von Daniel Jonah Goldhagen "Hitlers willige Vollstrecker. Ganz gewöhnliche Deutsche und der Holocaust". Referat und Podiumsdiskussion eines Kolloquiums des Gesprächskreises Geschichte der Friedrich-Ebert-Stiftung und der AG Bonn der Dt.-Isr. Gesellschaft, Bonn, 4. Sept. 1996. Hrsg. von Dieter Dowe unter Mitarbeit von Bernd Jeschonnek. Bonn: Friedrich-Ebert-Stiftung, 1996. 80 pp. (Gesprächskreis Geschichte, 14.)

35056. GOLDHAGEN DEBATE. Graetz, Michael: *Der "Goldhagen-Effekt"*. [In]: Freiburger Rundbrief, N.F., Jg. 4, H. 1, Freiburg, 1997. Pp. 2–6.

35057. GOLDHAGEN DEBATE. Habermas, Jürgen: *Geschichte ist ein Teil von uns*. Warum ein "Demokratiepreis" für Daniel J. Goldhagen? Eine Laudatio. [In]: Die Zeit, Nr. 12, Hamburg, 14. März 1997. P. 13. [Speech at the award ceremony where Goldhagen received a prize from 'Blätter für deutsche und internationale Politik'.]

35058. GOLDHAGEN DEBATE. Hilberg, Raul: *The Goldhagen phenomenon*. [In]: Critical inquiry, Vol. 23, No. 4, Chicago, Summer 1997. Pp. 721–727.

35059. GOLDHAGEN DEBATE. Husson, Édouard: *Une culpabilité ordinaire? Hitler, les Allemands et la Shoah*. Les enjeux de la controverse Goldhagen. Paris: Éd. F.X. de Guibert, 1997. 198 pp.

35061. GOLDHAGEN DEBATE. Küntzel, Matthias/Thörner, Klaus [et al.]: *Goldhagen und die deutsche Linke oder Die Gegenwart des Holocaust*. Berlin: Elefanten Press Verl., 1997. 192 pp., notes, bibl.

35062. GOLDHAGEN DEBATE. Littell, Franklin, ed.: *Hyping the Holocaust: scholars answer Goldhagen*. Merion Station, PA: Merion Westfield Press, 1997. XI, 177 pp, notes. [Cont. 13 contribs. by Yehuda Bauer, G. Jan Colijn, Erich Geldbach, Wolfgang Gerlach, Herbert Hirsch, Peter Hoffmann, Eberhard Jäckel, Franklin H. Littell, Hubert C. Locke, Hans Mommsen, Jacob Neusner, Richard V. Pierard, Didier Pollfeyt, Roger W. Smith.]

35063. GOLDHAGEN DEBATE. Parge, Martina: *Holocaust und autoritärer Charakter*. Amerikanische Studien der vierziger Jahre vor dem Hintergrund der "Goldhagen-Debatte". Wiesbaden: Dt. Univ.-Verl., 1997. VIII, 178 pp., footnotes, bibl. (171–178). (DUV: Sozialwissenschaft.) [Deals with works by Erich Fromm, Richard M. Brickner, Bertram Schaffner et al. in the context of Goldhagen's theses and the ensuing debate.]

35064. GOLDHAGEN DEBATE. Peck, Jeffrey M.: *Being a Jewish American Germanist after Goldhagen: a response to Herbert Lehnert, "Was wir von Goldhagen lernen können."* [In]: German Quarterly, Vol. 70, No. 2, Riverside, CA, Spring 1997. Pp. 168–174. [Response to: Was wir von Goldhagen lernen können (Herbert Lehnert) [in]: German Quarterly, Vol. 70, No. 1, Winter 1997, pp. 57–64.]

35065. GOLDHAGEN DEBATE. Pohl, Dieter: *Die Holocaust-Forschung und Goldhagens Thesen*. [In]: Vierteljahrshefte für Zeitgeschichte, Jg. 45, H. 1, München, Jan. 1997. Pp. 1–48, footnotes. [With English abstract on p. 173.]

35066. GOLDHAGEN DEBATE. Sattler, Stephan: *Der Holocaust, Goldhagen und die Deutschen*. Reflexionen über einen Bucherfolg. [In]: Europäische Rundschau, Jg. 25, Nr. 1, Wien, 1997. Pp. 1–12.

35067. GOLDHAGEN DEBATE. Schneider, Michael: *Die "Goldhagen-Debatte"*. Ein Historikerstreit in der Mediengesellschaft. [In]: Archiv für Sozialgeschichte, Bd. 37, Bonn, 1997. Pp. 460–481. [Publ. also as an offprint by Historisches Forschungszentrum der Friedrich-Ebert-Stiftung (Dieter Dowe, ed.), Bonn, 1997. 31 pp. (Gesprächskreis Geschichte, H. 17.).]

—— GOLDHAGEN DEBATE. Senfft, Heinrich: *Hannah Arendts "Eichmann in Jerusalem" im Licht der Goldhagen-Debatte*. [See No. 35482.]

35068. GOLDHAGEN DEBATE. Thiele, Martina: *Goldhagens willige Mitstreiter – Rückblick auf eine publizistische Kontroverse*. [In]: Deutsche Studien, H. 135/136, Jg. 34, Lüneburg, 1997. Pp. 236–255, notes.

35069. GOLDHAGEN DEBATE. Wehler, Hans-Ulrich: *The Goldhagen controversy: agonizing problems, scholarly failure and the political dimension*. [In]: German History, Vol. 15, No. 1, Oxford, 1997. Pp. 80–91.

35070. GOLDHAGEN DEBATE. Wippermann, Wolfgang: *Wessen Schuld? Vom Historikerstreit zur Goldhagen-Kontroverse*. Berlin: Elefanten Press, 1997. 142 pp., notes.

35071. Ganor, Solly: *Das andere Leben. Kindheit im Holocaust*. Frankfurt am Main: Fischer Taschenbuch Verlag, 1997. 222 pp. [S.G., orig. Zally Genkind, data see No. 32914/YB XLI.]

35072. GRUNER, WOLF: *Die öffentliche Fürsorge und die deutschen Juden 1933–1942. Zur antijüdischen Politik der Städte, des Deutschen Gemeindetages und des Reichsinnenministeriums.* [In]: Zeitschrift für Geschichtswissenschaft, Jg. 45, H. 7, Berlin, 1997. Pp. 597–616, footnotes.

35073. GUTMAN, DAWID: *Schwierige Heimkehr. Leben und Leiden in Ungarn, dann auf der "Exodus" und zurück über Bergen-Belsen nach Tel Aviv.* Jüdische Schicksale 1944–1948. Aus dem Engl. durch Chever Transl., Haifa. Hrsg. von Erhard Roy Wiehn. Konstanz: Hartung-Gorre, 1997. 131pp., illus.

35074. HADDA, WOLFGANG: *Knapp davongekommen: von Breslau nach Schanghai und San Francisco.* Jüdische Schicksale 1920–1947. Hrsg. von Erhard Roy Wiehn. Konstanz: Hartung-Gorre, 1997. 258 pp., illus., facsims.

35075. HAMBURG. BAJOHR, FRANK: *"Arisierung" in Hamburg. Die Verdrängung der jüdischen Unternehmer 1933–1945.* Hamburg: Christians, 1997. 415 pp., footnotes, lists, bibl. (389–404), indexes (persons; businesses). (Hamburger Beiträge zur Sozial-und Zeitgeschichte, Bd. 35.) [Cf.: Korruption und Vetternwirtschaft. Frank Bajohr hat erforscht, wer von der Enteignung jüdischen Eigentums in Hamburg profitierte (Gerhard Paul) [in]: Die Zeit, Nr.10, Hamburg, 26. Feb. 1998, p. 40.]

35076. HAMBURG. LORENZ, INA: *Seefahrts-Hachschara in Hamburg (1935–1938). Lucy Borchardt: "Die einzige jüdische Reederin der Welt".* [In]: Zeitschrift des Vereins für Hamburgische Geschichte, Bd. 83, Teil 1 [with the title]: Bewahren und Berichten. Festschrift für Hans-Dieter Loose zum 60. Geburtstag im Auftrag des Vereinsvorstandes hrsg. von Hans Wilhelm Eckardt und Klaus Richter, Hamburg, 1997. Pp. 445–472, footnotes, tabs.

35077. HAMBURG. SCHWARZ, ANGELA: *Von den Wohnstiften zu den "Judenhäusern".* [In]: Kein abgeschlossenes Kapitel: Hamburg im 3. Reich. Hrsg. von Angelika Ebbinghaus und Karsten Linne. Hamburg: Europ. Verl.-anst., 1997. Pp. 232–247, footnotes.

35078. HAMBURG. SIELEMANN, JÜRGEN: *Fragen und Antworten zur "Reichskristallnacht" in Hamburg.* [In]: Zeitschrift des Vereins für Hamburgische Geschichte, Bd. 83, Teil 1 [with the title]: Bewahren und Berichten. Festschrift für Hans-Dieter Loose zum 60. Geburtstag im Auftrag des Vereinsvorstandes hrsg. von Hans Wilhelm Eckardt und Klaus Richter, Hamburg, 1997. Pp.473–501, illus., footnotes.

35079. HAMBURG. WEINKE, WILFRIED: *Die Verfolgung jüdischer Rechtsanwälte Hamburgs am Beispiel von Dr. Max Eichholz und Herbert Michaelis.* [In]: Kein abgeschlossenes Kapitel: Hamburg im 3. Reich. Hrsg. von Angelika Ebbinghaus und Karsten Linne. Hamburg, Europ. Verl.-anst., 1997. Pp. 248–265, footnotes.

35080. HAMBURG. WEINKE, WILFRIED: *The persecution of Jewish lawyers in Hamburg.* A case study: Max Eichholz and Herbert Michaelis. [In]: Leo Baeck Institute Year Book XLII, London, 1997. Pp. 221–238, footnotes.

35081. HERRLINGEN. SEEMÜLLER, ULRICH: *Das jüdische Altersheim Herrlingen und die Schicksale seiner Bewohner.* Blaustein: Gemeinde Blaustein, [1997?]. 195 pp., illus., ports., maps, graphs., index. [Incl. short biographies.]

35082. HERRMANN, MARGIT: *Erinnerung an Auschwitz und Bergen Belsen.* [In]: Dachauer Hefte, Jg. 13, H. 13, München, 1997. Pp. 62–69. [Personal memoirs; M.H., data see No. 32844/YB XVI.]

35083. HERTZ, DEBORAH: *The genealogy bureaucracy in the Third Reich.* [In]: Jewish History, Vol. 11, No. 2, Haifa, Fall 1997. Pp. 53–78, notes.

35084. HETZEL, MARIUS: *Die Anfechtung der Rassenmischehe in den Jahren 1933–1939.* Die Entwicklung der Rechtsprechung im Dritten Reich: Anpassung und Selbstbehauptung der Gerichte. Tübingen: Mohr Siebeck, 1997. XXII, 233 pp. (Beiträge zur Rechtsgeschichte des 20. Jahrhunderts, 20.). Zugl.: Köln: Univ., Diss.

35085. HISTORIOGRAPHY. Hehl, Ulrich von: *Kampf um die Deutung. Der Nationalsozialismus zwischen "Vergangenheitsbewältigung", Historisierungspostulat und "neuer Unbefangenheit"*. [In]: Historisches Jahrbuch, Jg. 117, Halbbd. 2, München, 1997. Pp. 406–436, footnotes.

35086. HISTORIOGRAPHY. Welzer, Harald: *Verweilen beim Grauen.* Essays zum wissenschaftlichen Umgang mit dem Holocaust. Tübingen: Edition Diskord, 1997. 155 pp. [Cf.: Besprechung (Wolfram Stender) [in]: Mittelweg 36, Jg. 6, H. 6, Hamburg, 1997, pp. 56–58.]

35087. *History and Memory*, Vol. 9, Nos. 1/2 [with the issue title] *Passing into history: Nazism and the Holocaust beyond memory. Essays in honour of Saul Friedländer on his sixty-fifth birthday.* Ed. by Gulie Ne'eman Arad. Bloomington, IN, Fall 1997. 1 issue, notes. [Cont. (titles. abbr.): Paucis Verbis (Gulie Ne'eman Arad, 7–8). On Saul Friedländer (Steven E. Aschheim, 11–46). The uncanny voices of the historian and survivor (James E. Young, 47–58). National Socialism and its historical examination en route into history (Norbert Frei, 59–79). Revisiting the Historians' Debate: mourning and genocide (Dominick Lacapra, 80–112). Metahistorical reflections on the debate between Friedländer and Broszat (Jörn Rüsen, 113–144). Hitler's Reichstag speech of 30 January 1939 (Hans Mommsen, 147–161). German soldiers and the Holocaust (Omer Bartov, 162–188). The architects' debate: architectural discourse and the memory of Nazism in the Federal Republic of Germany, 1977–1997 (Gavriel D. Rosenfeld, 189–225). Holocaust memorialization in America since Bitburg (Anson Rabinbach, 226–255). Nationalism, narcissism, and the Historians' Debate in Germany and Israel (José Brunner, 256–300). Epistemological observations regarding the Holocaust (Dan Diner, 301–320). The relevance of a concept (Philippe Burrin, 321–352). Shared memories, private recollections (Carlo Ginzburg, 353–363). Reflections on 'When memory comes'. (Sidra Dekoven Ezrahi, 364–375). Some thoughts on Kitsch (Eli Friedlander, 376–392). "Against all odds" or the will to survive (Gertrud Koch, 393–408). "Nazi Germany and the Jews": reflections on a beginning, a middle and an open end (Gulie Ne'eman Arad, 409–433).]

35088. HITLER, ADOLF. Lukacs, John: *The Hitler of history*. New York: Knopf (distrib. by Random House), 1997. XIV, 279 pp., footnotes, bibl. note (269–271). [Incl. chap.: The Jews: tragedy and mystery (176–196).]

—— HOLOCAUST. [See also No. 34956.]

35089. HOLOCAUST. Alvarez, Alexander: *Adjusting to genocide: the techniques of neutralization and the Holocaust.* [In]: Social Science History, Vol. 21, No. 2, Durham, NC, Summer 1997. Pp. 139–178, notes, bibl.

—— HOLOCAUST. Diner, Dan: *Zivilisationsbruch, Gegenrationalität, gestaute Zeit – Drei interpretationsleitende Begriffe zum Holocaust.* [See in No. 35429.]

35090. HOLOCAUST. Dresden, Sem: *Holocaust und Literatur.* Aus dem Niederl. übers. von Gregor Seferens und Andreas Ecke. Frankfurt am Main: Jüd. Verlag, 1997. 326 pp., illus., bibl. [Cf.: Kein Gewinn (Katrin Diehl) [in]: Tribüne, Jg. 37, H. 145, Frankfurt am Main, 1998. Pp. 225–226. Besprechung (Mona Körte) [in]: Zeitschrift für Geschichtswissenschaft, Jg. 45, H. 10, Berlin, 1997, pp. 948–949.]

35091. HOLOCAUST. Koch, Martin: *Vor Auschwitz. Zu den ideengeschichtlichen Voraussetzungen der NS-Menschenvernichtung.* [In]: Geschichte-Erziehung-Politik, Jg. 7, H. 6, Berlin, 1996. Pp. 321–325.

35092. HOLOCAUST. Langer, Howard J., ed.: *The history of the Holocaust.* A chronology of quotations. Northvale, NJ: Aronson, 1997. XV, 305 pp., bibl. (281–289). [Anthology of quotations taken from speeches, letters, laws, and official transcripts.]

35093. Hüppauf, Bernd: *Emptying the gaze: framing violence through the viewfinder.* [In]: New German Critique, No. 72, Ithaca, NY, Fall 1997. Pp. 3–44, notes. [Discusses the representation of the Holocaust through footage taken by German soldiers; and also through more recent films.]

35094. HUNGARY. BOLGAR, MARIANNE: *Budapest 1944.* [In]: Midstream, Vol. 43, No. 3, New York, April 1997. Pp. 15–17. [Deals with the deportation of Jews from Hungary.]

35095. HUNGARY. BRAHAM, RANDOLPH L./ POK, ATTILA, eds.: *The Holocaust in Hungary fifty years later.* New York; Rosenthal Institute for Holocaust Studies, City Univ. of New York. Budapest: Institute of History of the Hungarian Academy of Sciences. Boulder, CO: East European Monographs, No. 477 (distrib. by Columbia Univ. Press, New York), 1997. 783 pp., notes. [Bilingual transcript of a 1994 scholars' conference held in Budapest on Hungarian Holocaust history.]

35096. HUNGARY. CESARANI, DAVID, ed.: *Genocide and rescue: the Holocaust in Hungary 1944.* Oxford: Berg, 1997. VII, 220 pp., tabs., notes. [Collection of essays by historians from Hungary, Israel, Britain and the US.]

35097. HUNGARY. DENES, MAGDA: *Castles burning: a child's life in war.* New York: Norton, 1997. 384 pp., illus. [Memoir of a Jewish family's survival in war-time Hungary, seen through the eyes of the author as a child. German edn.: 'Brennende Schlösser: eine jüdische Kindheit'. Deutsch von Michaele Link. München: Bertelsmann, 1997. 443 pp., illus.] [M.D., psychoanalyst (died 1997 aged 62), survived in hiding, went to Cuba and later to the US.]

35098. HUNGARY. TSCHUY, THEO: *Carl Lutz und die Juden von Budapest.* Vorwort von Simon Wiesenthal. Zürich: Verlag NZZ, 1995. 446 pp. [On a Swiss-Vice Consul in Budapest who saved thousands of Jews.]

35099. *Inside the concentration camps: eyewitness accounts of life in Hitler's death camps.* Compiled by Eugène Aroneanu. Transl. by Thomas Whissen. Westport, CT: Praeger, 1996. XXII, 174 pp., illus. [100 eyewitness testimonies, arranged by subject matter.]

35100. ITALY. WALSTON, JAMES: *History and memory of the Italian concentration camps.* [In]: Historical Journal, Vol. 40, No. 1, Cambridge, March 1997. Pp. 169–183, footnotes. [Deals with the relative leniency shown to Jews, put into Italian internment camps, partly to protect them from the Germans. Also discusses Italian war atrocities glossed over in their own historiography of the war.]

35101. JASKOT, PAUL B.: *Anti-Semitic policy in Albert Speer's plans for the rebuilding of Berlin.* [In]: The Art Bulletin, Vol. 78, No. 4, New York, Dec. 1996. Pp. 622–632, illus.

—— *Judenverfolgung und jüdisches Leben unter den Bedingungen der nationalsozialistischen Gewaltherrschaft.* [See No. 34951.]

35102. JÜLICH. *An der Synagoge. Jülich und der Holocaust.* Die Aufarbeitung. Festakt zur Umbenennung der Grünstraße. Zur Erinnerung an die Einwohnung jüdischen Glaubens aus Aldenhoven, Inden, Jülich, Linnich und Titz. Hrsg. von Gabriele Spelthahn [et al.]. Jülich: Verlag des Jülicher Geschichtsvereins 1923 e.V., 1997. 160 pp., illus., footnotes, indexes (places; names, 129–158), bibl. [Incl. lists of names of the deportees.]

35103. JÜLICH. BERS, GÜNTER: *Alltägliche Judenhetze in Jülich (1939).* [In]: Neue Beiträge zur Jülicher Geschichte, Bd. 8, Jülich, 1997. Pp. 129–131, footnotes.

—— JÜRGENS, FRANZ J.: *"Wir waren ja eigentlich Deutsche". Juden berichten von Emigration und Rückkehr.* [See No. 35261.]

35104. KANNER, MIA AMALIA/KUGLER, EVE ROSENZWEIG: *Shattered crystals.* New York; London: C.I.S. Publishers, 1997. 406 pp., illus., gloss. [M.A.K. (b. 1904) recounts her life growing up in Leipzig, flight to France, survival in hiding or in camps, and final reunion with her children in the US.]

35105. KAPLAN, MARION: *The school lives of Jewish children and youth in the Third Reich.* [In]: Jewish History, Vol. 11, No. 2, Haifa, Fall 1997. Pp. 41–52, notes.

35106. KATER, MICHAEL H.: *The twisted muse: musicians and their music in the Third Reich.* New York; Oxford: Oxford Univ. Press, 1997. X, 327 pp., notes. [Incl. chaps.: Nazi anti-semitic policy in the music sector. Jewish musicians under Nazi rule. Jewish flight and exile.]

35107. KELLER, HELGA: *Farbig in Moll. Darmstadt – Berlin 1933–1939.* Darmstadt: Roether, 1996. 239 pp., illus. [Childhood memories of a Jewish girl from Darmstadt.]

35108. KORNREICH GELISSEN, RENA: *Renas Versprechen. Zwei Schwestern überleben Auschwitz.* Aus dem Engl. von Elfriede Peschel. München: Knesebeck, 1996. 327 pp. [Orig. title 'Rena's promise'.]

35109. KRAMER, EDITH: *Hell and rebirth: my experiences during the time of persecution.* [In]: The Journal of Holocaust Education, Vol. 6, No. 2, London, Autumn 1997. Pp. 71–102, notes. [E. K., née Liebeck, (Berlin 1899 – Vienna 1994), doctor, called up in 1942 for forced labour as a medical practitioner in various camps in Poland. 1943 sent to Theresienstadt until liberation.]

35110. KRUSENOTTO, WOLFRAM/PRÉGARDIER, ELISABETH: *"Ich sah den Heiligen Rock und erflehte mir Kraft".* Edith Stein am 10. August 1933 in Trier. Schicksale christlicher Frauen von 1933 bis 1945. Annweiler: Plöger, 1996. 92 pp., illus. [On the fate of Edith Stein and other Catholic women of Jewish descent; also on other Christian women active in the resistance and the rescue of Jews.]

35111. LAMBERTI, MARJORIE: *The Jewish defence in Germany after the National-Socialist seizure of power.* [In]: Leo Baeck Institute Year Book XLII, London, 1997. Pp. 135–147, footnotes. [See also No. 35373.]

35112. LAQUEUR, WALTER: *Faschismus: gestern – heute – morgen.* [Aus dem Engl. von Bernd Rullkötter.]. Berlin: Propyläen, 1997. 368 pp., bibl., index. [Title of orig. Engl. edn.: Fascism. Past, present, future; publ. 1996. Incl. chap. on antisemitism and Holocaust denial (218–224).]

35113. LASKER-WALLFISCH, ANITA: *Ihr sollt die Wahrheit erben. Breslau – Auschwitz – Bergen-Belsen.* Mit einem Vorwort von Klaus Harpprecht. Bonn: Weidle, 1997. 221 pp., frontis., illus. [For orig. English publ. see No. 34086/YB XLII.]

35114. LEICHT, LISBETH FISCHER: *The unsung years: my youth 1930–1945.* London: Minerva, 1997. X, 91 pp., illus., ports., facsims. [Deals with author's childhood in Vienna, emigration by Kindertransport and life with family reunited in England.]

35115. LEIPZIG. GRUBEL, FRED & MECKLENBURG, FRANK: *Leipzig: profile of a Jewish community during the first years of National-Socialist Germany.* [In]: Leo Baeck Institute Year Book XLII, London, 1997. Pp. 155–188, footnotes, tabs.

35116. LEIPZIG. KALTER, JOACHIM: *Eine jüdische Odyssee: Von Leipzig nach Polen abgeschoben und deutsche Lager überlebt.* Ein Bericht 1938–1946 = A Jewish odyssee. Vorwort von Edgar Hilsenrath. Hrsg. von Erhard Roy Wiehn. Konstanz: Hartung-Gorre, 1997. 142 pp., illus. [Text partly English, partly German, partly both English and German.]

35117. LETTOW, FRITZ: *Arzt in den Höllen: Erinnerungen an vier Konzentrationslager.* Mit einem Nachwort von Gerhard Leo. Mit Zeichnungen von Henri Gayot aus dem Konzentrationslager Natzweiler. Berlin: Ed. Ost, 1997. [Cf.: Besprechung (Nikoline Hansen) [in]: Die Mahnung, Jg. 44, Berlin, 1. Sept. 1997, p. 6.] [Fritz Lettow, orig. Fritz Leo, b. 1904 to baptised parents of Jewish descent, as a young Communist imprisoned and forced to work as a physician in the camps of Buchenwald, Sachsenhausen, Natzweiler and Bergen-Belsen.]

35118. LEVI, TRUDE: *Eine Katze namens Adolf.* Aus dem Engl. übers. von Birgit Jessen. Witzenhausen: Ekopan-Verlag, 1997. 190 pp., illus. [For orig. edn. see No. 32920/YB XLI.]

35119. LEY, MICHAEL: *"Zum Schutze des deutschen Blutes...". "Rassenschande"-Gesetze im Nationalsozialismus.* Bodenheim: Philo, 1997. 198 pp.

35120. LINDER, BERT: *Verdammt ohne Urteil: Holocaust Erinnerungen eines Überlebenden.* Graz: Styria, 1997. 328 pp., 16 pp.: illus., ports. [Orig. title: 'Condemned without judgement', New York: S.P.I. Books/Shapolsky Publ., 1995. Personal recollections of an Austrian Jew, b. 1911.]

35121. LODZ (LITZMANNSTADT). *"Les vrais riches" – Notizen am Rande. Ein Tagebuch aus dem Ghetto Lódz (Mai bis August 1944).* Hrsg. von Hanno Loewy und Andrzej Bodek. Leipzig: Reclam, 1997. 165 pp. [Incl.: Vorwort (eds., 5–34; on the Ghetto of Lodz); also the diary in facsimile.]

35122. LOEBL, SUZANNE: *At the mercy of strangers.* Pacifica, CA: Pacifica Press, 1997. 163 pp. [Autobiog. account of survival of a Jewish woman from Hanover, using false papers in Nazi-occupied Belgium.] [Cf.:"Wir hatten es ja nicht schlecht. . .": Ein Gespräch mit Suzanne Loebl [in]: Aufbau, Vol. 64, No. 7, New York, March 27, 1998, p. 17.]

35123. MANNHEIMER, MAX: *Gedanken eines Überlebenden von Auschwitz.* [In]: Edith Stein Jahrbuch 1997. Bd. 3, Würzburg, 1997. Pp. 295–306. [M.M., b. 1920 in Neutitschein (Moravia), painter, deported in 1943 to Theresienstadt, later to Auschwitz and Dachau. Memoirs partly reprinted from Dachauer Hefte, No. 1, 1985; see No. 23249/YB XXXII.]

35124. MARINO, ANDY: *Herschel: the boy who started World War II.* Boston; London: Faber & Faber, 1997. 226 pp., notes, bibl. [On Herschel Grynszpan, the Polish-Jewish boy who assassinated German diplomat Ernst vom Rath, thus providing a pretext for the Pogrom of Nov. 9–10, 1938.]

35125. MASTERS, PETER: *Striking back: a Jewish commando's war against the Nazis.* Novato, CA: Presidio, 1997. XIII, 340 pp., illus., maps. [Story of a young refugee from Vienna joining the 3 Troop, No. 10 commando unit of Jewish refugees in Britain who volunteered for hazardous duty.]

35126. MAUTHAUSEN. BAUMGARTNER, ANDREAS: *Die vergessenen Frauen von Mauthausen.* Die weiblichen Häftlinge des Konzentrationslagers Mauthausen und ihre Geschichte. Wien: Verl. Österreich, 1997. 249 pp., illus., gloss., bibl. (234–242), index. [Incl. Jewish prisoners.]

35127. MAUTHAUSEN. TWERASER, KURT: *Sie sind da, wir sind frei' Vive l'Americansky!* Anmerkungen zur Befreiung der Konzentrationslager in Oberdonau durch amerikanische Soldaten. [In]: DÖW Jahrbuch 1997, Wien, 1997. Pp. 89–110, footnotes. [On Mauthausen and attached camps (Nebenlager) Gusen, Ebensee, Gunskirchen. Incl. an American army report.]

35128. *Medical and psychological effects of concentration camps on Holocaust survivors.* Ed. by Robert M. Krell and Marc I. Sherman. Foreword by Elie Wiesel. New Brunswick, NJ: Transaction Books, 1997. XX, 365 pp., port., bibl. [Volume 4 of this bibliography series on Holocaust and Genocide is dedicated to Dr. Leo Eitinger, one of the first to study the medical impact of concentration camps on Jewish survivors. Bibl. incl. 2,500 items, about 50 of which are extensively annotated.]

35129. MILTON, SYBIL: *Registering civilians and aliens in the Second World War.* [In]: Jewish History, Vol. 11, No. 2, Haifa, Fall 1997. Pp. 79–87, notes. [Incl. the treatment of Jews in Nazi Germany.]

35130. NE'EMAN ARAD, GULIE: *Cooptation of elites: American Jewish reactions to the Nazi menace, 1933.* [In]: Yad Vashem Studies, Vol. 25, Jerusalem, 1996. Pp. 31–64.

35131. NETHERLANDS. MOORE, BOB: *Victims and survivors: Nazi persecution of the Jews in the Netherlands, 1940–1945.* London: Elliot Arnold, 1997. (distrib. in the US by St. Martin's Press, New York). X, 340 pp., map, appendixes, notes, bibl. [Incl. the persecution of German-Jewish refugees.]

Bibliography

35132. NETHERLANDS. ZEE, NANDA VAN DER: *Om erger te voorkomen: de voorgeschiedenis en uitvoering van de vernietiging van het Nederlands jodendom tijdens de Tweede Wereldoorlog.* Amsterdam: Meulenhoff, 1997. 287 pp. [Incl. the German-Jewish refugees.]

35133. NETHERLANDS & BELGIUM. ZELLER, RON/GRIFFIOEN, PIM: *Judenverfolgung in den Niederlanden und in Belgien während des Zweiten Weltkriegs. Eine vergleichende Analyse.* Teil 2. [In]: 1999. Zeitschrift für Sozialgeschichte des 20. und 21. Jahrhunderts, Jg. 12, H. 1, Hamburg, 1997. Pp. 29–48, footnotes. [Part 1 see No. 34169/YB XLI.]

35134. NEUENGAMME. KAIENBURG, HERMANN: *Das Konzentrationslager Neuengamme 1938–1945.* Hrsg.: KZ-Gedenkstätte Neuengamme. Bonn: Dietz, 1997. 368 pp., illus., facsims., notes, (291–307), bibl. (337–344). (Dietz-Taschenbuch.)

35135. NORDHAUSEN. RESCHWAMM, DOROTHEA: *Die Vertreibung und Vernichtung der Juden im Spiegel der Akten des Finanzamtes Nordhausen.* [In]: Geschichte-Erziehung-Politik, Jg. 7, H. 7/8, Berlin, 1996. Pp. 405–413, notes.

35136. NOVEMBER POGROM. FRANKE, MANFRED: *Mordverläufe. 9./10. XI. 1938.* Ein Protokoll von der Angst, von Mißhandlung und Tod, vom Auffinden der Spuren und deren Wiederentdeckung. Mit einem Nachwort von Jörg Drews. Hamburg: Rotbuch, 1997. 347 pp. (Rotbuch-Bibliothek.) [First edn. publ. 1973 (Neuwied: Luchterhand), see No. 11190/YB XIX. On the November pogrom in Hilden.] [Cf.: Eine ganz gewöhnliche Stadt (Elke Schubert) [in]: Die Zeit, Nr. 46, Hamburg, 7.Nov. 1997, p. 21.]

35137. NOVEMBER POGROM. KROPAT, WOLF-ARNO: *"Reichskristallnacht". Der Judenpogrom vom 7. bis 10. November 1938 – Urheber, Täter, Hintergründe.* Mit ausgewählten Dokumenten. Wiesbaden: Kommission für die Geschichte der Juden in Hessen, 1997. 278 pp., docs. (185–237), notes (238–260), bibl. (263–275), index (places, 276–278). (Schriften der Kommission für die Geschichte der Juden in Hessen XV.)

35138. NUREMBERG. KOHL, CHRISTIANE: *Der Jude und das Mädchen. Eine verbotene Freundschaft in Nazideutschland.* Hamburg: Hoffmann und Campe, 1997. 283 pp., illus. [On the romantic friendship between Leo Katzenberg and Irene Scheffler from Nuremberg, followed by denunciation and L.K.'s execution in June 1942.]

35139. NUREMBERG TRIALS. DAVIDSON, EUGENE: *The trial of the Germans; an account of the twenty-two defendents before the International Military Tribunal at Nuremberg.* Columbia: Univ. of Missouri Press, 1997. XI, 636, pp., illus., ports., notes. [First publ. by Macmillan in 1966.]

35140. NUREMBERG TRIALS. KELLERMANN, HENRY J.: *Settling accounts – the Nuremberg trial.* [In]: Leo Baeck Institute Year Book XLII, London 1997. Pp. 337–355, footnotes. [Personal recollections of author (1910 Berlin – 1998 Washington DC), jurist, career diplomat, second-in-command of the US prosecution team at the Nuremberg Trials.]

35141. NUREMBERG TRIALS. *The Nuremberg War Crimes Trial, 1945–46: a documentary history.* Compiled and ed. by Michael R. Marrus. Boston: Bedford Books, 1997. XI, 276 pp., illus., tabs., bibl. 262–268. (The Bedford series in history and culture.) [Cf.: The Nuremberg Trial: fifty years after (Michael R. Marrus) [in]: American Scholar, Washington, Autumn 1997, pp. 563–570.]

35142. NUREMBERG TRIALS. PESCHEL-GUTZEIT, LORE MARIA, ed.: *Das Nürnberger Juristen-Urteil von 1947.* Historischer Zusammenhang und aktuelle Bezüge. Baden-Baden: Nomos, 1996. 299 pp., docs., footnotes. [Cont. the complete transcript of the verdict, translated into German. Incl.: Der Nürnberger Juristenprozeß und seine Rezeption in Deutschland (Klaus Bästlein, 9–35).]

35144. NUREMBERG TRIALS. *Revue d'Histoire de la Shoah*, No. 160 [with the issue title]: *1946–1996. Le procès des médicins à Nuremberg. Éthique, responsabilité civique et crimes contre l'humanité.* No. 160, Paris, mai-août 1997. 1 issue, footnotes, bibl. [Incl. 8 essays related to the medical trial, by Roger Errery, Willy Dressen, Benno Müller-Hill, Bernard Kanovitch, Anis Postel-Vinay, Yves Ternon and Elie Wiesel.]

35145. NUREMBERG TRIALS. RUDDER, ANNEKE DE: *"Warum das ganze Theater?". Der Nürnberger Prozeß in den Augen der Zeitgenossen.* [In]: Jahrbuch für Antisemitismusforschung 6, Frankfurt am Main; New York, 1997. Pp. 218–242, notes.

35146. NUREMBERG TRIALS. SCHMIDT, ULF: *German medical war crimes, medical ethics and post-war justice.* A symposium to mark the 50th anniversary of the Nuremberg Medical Trial, held at the University of Oxford, 14 March, 1997. Symposium report. [In]: German History, Vol. 15, No. 3, Oxford, 1997. Pp. 385–391. [On the Nuremberg Medical Trial, December 1946 – August 1947, the first in the series of twelve special war-crimes trials mounted by the US Military Government of Germany.]

35147. NUREMBERG TRIALS. *Von Nürnberg nach Den Haag. Menschenrechtsverbrechen vor Gericht.* Zur Aktualität des Nürnberger Prozesses. Hrsg. vom Nürnberger Menschenrechtszentrum [et al.]. Mit einer Einleitung von Rainer Huhle. Nürnberg: Nürnb. Menschenrechtszentrum, 1996. 274 pp., notes. [A collection of 13 essays. Incl.: Gespräche mit Kindern von Nazi-Tätern: Eine Rückschau nach sieben Jahren (Dan Bar-On, 139–158).]

35148. NUREMBERG TRIALS. WERLE, GERHARD/WANDRES, THOMAS: *Auschwitz vor Gericht. Das Urteil gegen Dr. Victor Capesius.* Göppingen: Jüd. Museum Göppingen, 1997. 40 pp., illus., facsims., footnotes.

35149. NUREMBERG TRIALS. WEST, REBECCA: *Gewächshaus mit Alpenveilchen.* Im Herzen des Weltfeindes. Nürnberg, Berlin 1946. Aus dem Engl. von Elke und Gundolf Freyermuth. Berlin: Ed. Tiamat, 1995. 156 pp., notes. (Critica Diabolis, 52.) [Report for the 'Daily Telegraph' by R.W., novelist and writer, on the Nuremberg War Crimes' Trials; orig. title: 'Greenhouse with cyclamens'.]

35150. OBERLAENDER, FRANKLIN A.: *"My God, they just have other interests".* [In]: Oral History Review, Vol. 24, No. 1, Berkely, CA, Summer 1997. Pp. 23–53, notes. [Deals with the treatment of 'non-Aryan' Catholics in Nazi German and their response. For German edn. see No. 34203/YB XLII.]

35151. OLPE. *Ich trage die Nummer 104953. Ein letztes Zeugnis.* Werner Jacob, Lenhausen, im Gespräch mit Norbert Otto. Mit einer Einführung zur Geschichte der Juden im Kreis Olpe von Christiane Mirgel und Dieter Tröps und Bildern von Hermann Falke, Olpe: Der Oberkreisdirektor des Kreises Olpe, Kreisarchiv, 1997. 208 pp., illus., facsims., footnotes, bibl.

35152. ORTMEYER, BENJAMIN: *Schulzeit unterm Hitlerbild.* Analysen, Berichte, Dokumente. Frankfurt am Main: Fischer Taschenbuchverlag, 1996. 219 pp., illus., facsims., ports., notes, bibl. (Die Zeit des Nationalsozialismus.) [Deals also with Jewish schoolchildren.]

35153. *Out of the dark: short stories by survivors.* Foreword by Alan Sillitoe. London: Holocaust Survivor's Centre, 1997. 128 pp. [Incl. personal experiences of Austrian, Czech, German, and Hungarian Jews.]

35154. PINE, LISA: *Nazi family policy, 1933–1945.* Oxford: Berg, 1997. XII, 208 pp., illus., footnotes, bibl. (188–204). [Incl. chap.: The Jewish family. Also deals with the persecution of Jews in general.]

35155. RAVENSBRÜCK. ESCHEBACH, INSA [et al.]: *Das Frauenkonzentrationslager Ravensbrück: Quellenlage und Quellenkritik.* Fachtagung vom 29. 5. bis 30. 5. 1997. Dokumentation. Berlin: Freie Univ., 1997. 128 pp., illus.

35156. REES, LAURENCE: *The Nazis: a warning from history.* Foreword by Ian Kershaw. London: BBC; New York: New Press, 1997. 256 pp., illus., ports., bibl. [Publ. as a companion volume to the BBC-TV series; incl. the persecution of the Jews. German edn.: 'Die Nazis. Eine Warnung der Geschichte. Mit einem Vorwort von Ian Kershaw. Rastatt: Diana, 296 pp.]

35157. *Remembering the Holocaust.* Ed. by Michael E. Stevens. Ellen D. Goldlust-Gingrich, Ass. Ed. Madison, WI: State Historical Society of Wisconsin, Center for Documentary History, 1997. VIII, 172 pp., illus., ports. (Voices of the Wisconsin past.) [Based on interviews with Holocaust survivors who settled in Wisconsin, incl. chap. on Germany and Austria, 1–28.]

35158. REEMTSMA, JAN PHILIPP: *Die Memoiren Überlebender.* Eine Literaturgattung des 20. Jahrhunderts. [In]: Mittelweg 36, Jg. 6, H. 4, Hamburg, 1997. Pp. 20–39, footnotes. [Focuses mainly on the memoirs of Ladislaus Szücs, Ruth Klüger and Victor Klemperer.]

35159. RESCUE FOR JEWS. *Assignment rescue: the story of Varian Fry and the Emergency Rescue Committee.* Publ. in connection with an exhibition organized by the United States Holocaust Memorial Museum (June 1993–January 1995) and shown at the Jewish Museum, New York, and the Field Museum, Chicago, in 1997 and 1998. Washington, DC: United States Holocaust Memorial Museum, 1997. 14 pp., illus., ports., maps.

35160. RESCUE FOR JEWS. BEJSKI, MOSHE: *Oskar Schindler and 'Schindler's List'.* [In]: Yad Vashem Studies, Vol. 24, Jerusalem, 1994. Pp. 317–348. [Incl. selected excerpts from the testimonies given by survivors.]

35161. RESCUE FOR JEWS. POLLACK, ILSE: *"Es war wirklich meine Absicht, alle diese Leute zu retten". Ein portugiesischer Paul Grüninger: Aristides de Sousa Mendes.* [In]: Mit der Ziehharmonika, Jg. 14, Nr. 3, Wien, Nov. 1997. Pp. 3–8, illus. [This article is also publ. in 'Der Konsul', see No. 35889. On a Portuguese diplomat, who in June 1940 issued visas to thousands of refugees in Southern France and who was therefore dismissed.]

35162. RESCUE FOR JEWS. SASSIN, HORST R.: *Fritz Gräbe, ein Solinger Bauingenieur im Wolhynischen Holocaust.* [In]: Zeitschrift des Bergischen Geschichtsvereins, Bd. 97, Jg. 1995/96, Neustadt an der Aisch, 1997. Pp. 205–256, port., footnotes. [On F.B.'s rescue of several hundred Jews in the Ukraine.]

35163. RESCUE FOR JEWS. SCHINDLER, EMILIE (WITH ERIKA ROSENBERG): *Where light and shadow meet: a memoir.* Transl. by Dolores M. Koch. New York: Norton, 1997. XII, 162 pp., illus., map. [First publ. in Spain in 1996. Author describes life with Oskar Schindler and the work they did together to save Jews during the war. German edn.: In Schindlers Schatten: Emilie Schindler erzählt ihre Geschichte. Aufgeschrieben von Erika Rosenberg. Aus dem Span. von Elisabeth Brilke. Köln: Kiepenheuer und Witsch, 1997. 176 pp., illus. Deutsche Erstausgabe.]

35164. RESCUE FOR JEWS. SCHMITT, HANS A.: *Quakers and Nazis: inner light in outer darkness.* Columbia: Univ. of Missouri Press, 1997. XIII, 296 pp., illus., ports., notes (221–266), bibl. (267–289). [Incl. Quakers' involvement in saving Jews from Nazi Germany by sponsoring refugees to go to Britain. Also discusses Dutch Quaker school, where Jewish refugee children were shielded.]

35165. RESCUE FOR JEWS. STRAETEN, HERBERT: *Andere Deutsche unter Hitler.* Zeitberichte über Retter vor dem Holocaust. Mit einem Nachwort von Ignatz Bubis. Mainz: v. Hase & Koehler, 1997. X, 191 pp., illus.

35166. ROSENHEIM. MIESBECK, PETER: *Bürgertum und Nationalsozialismus in Rosenheim.* Studien zur politischen Tradition. Rosenheim: Stadt und Landkreis Rosenheim, 1994. 652 pp., illus., tabs., map, docs., footnotes, bibl. (617–638), index (639–652). [Incl.: III. Juden in Rosenheim, pp. 297–326.]

35167. ROSENFELD, ALVIN H., ed.: *Thinking about the Holocaust: after half a century.* Bloomington: Indiana Univ. Press, 1997. X, 329 pp., notes. Cont. (titles abbrev.): Part 1: The Holocaust in historical writings, literature, and cinema. The extermination of the European Jews in historiography (Saul Friedländer, 3–17). The Jew in postwar European literature (Michael André Bernstein, 18–37). Holocaust movies and the politics of collective memory (Ilan Avisar, 38–59). Part 2: The Holocaust, the Zionist movement, and the State of Israel. The

Holocaust and World War II as elements of the Yishuv psyche until 1948 (Anita Shapira, 61–82). The Zionist leadership between the Holocaust and the creation of the State of Israel (Jehuda Reinharz and Evyatar Friesel, 83–117). Part 3: The impact of the Holocaust on American Jewish life and thought (three essays by A.H. Rosenfeld, Michael L. Morgan and Gulie Ne'eman Arad). Part 4: European Jewry in the postwar period: Breaking the "cordon sanitaire" of memory. The Jewish encounter with German society (Frank Stern, 213–232). W.W.II in postwar German memory (Elisabeth Domansky, 233–272). Deportation and memory (Annette Wieviorka, 273–299). The Jews and the spirit of Europe: a morphological approach (Shmuel Trigano, 300–318).]

35168. ROTENBERG, STELLA: *Ungewissen Ursprungs*. Gesammelte Prosa. Hrsg. und mit einem Nachwort versehen von Siglinde Bolbecher. Wien: Verlag der Th.-Kramer-Gesellschaft, 1997. 93 pp. [Cf.: Besprechung (Manfred Chobot) [in]: Mit der Ziehharmonika, Jg. 14, Nr. 4, Wien, Dez. 1997, pp. 16–17.] [Author, b. in Vienna, lives in Leeds. Her stories deal with childhood in Austria, persecution, expulsion and exile.]

35169. ROTH, KARL HEINZ: *"Generalplan Ost" und der Mord an den Juden*. Der "Fernplan der Umsiedlung in den Ostprovinzen" aus dem Reichssicherheitshauptamt vom November 1939. [In]: 1999, Zeitschrift für Sozialgeschichte des 20. und 21. Jahrhunderts, H. 2, Hamburg, 1997. Pp. 50–70, footnotes. [First unabr. publ. of document, introd. by the author's analysis.]

35170. RUBINSTEIN, WILLIAM D.: *The myth of rescue: why the democracies could not have saved more Jews from the Nazis*. London; New York: Routledge, 1997. XIII, 267 pp., tabs., maps, notes (217–256). [Cf.: The truth is painful (Tom Bower) [in]: The Sunday Times, London, June 15, 1997. Could the Allies have saved them? (Norman Stone) [in]: The Guardian, London, July 3, 1997, p. 10. There was nothing we could do. . . (Linda Holt) [in]: The Observer, London, July 13, 1997, p. 18. No exit? (Walter Laqueur) [in]: Commentary, Vol. 104, No. 4, New York, Oct. 1997, pp. 59–62.]

35171. SACHSENHAUSEN. BURGER, ADOLF: *Des Teufels Werkstatt. Die Geldfälscherwerkstatt im KZ Sachsenhausen. Zum Fälschen gezwungen*. Ein Tatsachenbericht. Berlin: Verlag Neues Leben, 1997. 272 pp., illus. [For first edn. (1992, with different publ.) and details see No. 29311/YB XXXVIII.]

35172. SARTON-SARETZKI, EDGAR: *Auf Sie haben wir gewartet*. Red.: Ute Daub. Hanau: CoCon, 1997. 144 pp., illus., notes. [Memoirs of a young boy from Frankfurt am Main, who escaped in April 1939 to England and was later sent to Canada. Author, b. 1922 in Limburg, lives in Canada.]

35173. SCHERMBECK. RANDALL, MARGA L.: *Als sei es gestern geschehen. Jüdische Schicksale aus Schermbeck 1930–1997*. Aus dem Engl. von Iris Landgraf. Hrsg. von Erhard Roy Wiehn. Vorworte von Ignatz Bubis [et. al.]. Konstanz: Hartung-Gorre, 1997. 124, 8 pp., illus., facsims., bibl. (Jüdische Überlebensschicksale.)

35174. SCHINDLER, ANJA: *Ein Idealist. Das Schicksal des Kommunisten Hans Linde*. [In]: Beiträge zur Geschichte der Arbeiterbewegung, Jg. 39, H. 3, Kösching, 1997. Pp. 82–85. [On Hans Linde, orig. Löwisohn, b. 1907 in Breslau, who grew up in Berlin and emigr. via Prague to the Soviet Union, where he was shot in 1937.]

35175. SCHWARZ, FRED: *Züge auf falschem Gleis*. Wien: Verl. Der Apfel, 1996. 352 pp. [Memoirs. Author, b. 1923 in Vienna, emigr. 1938 to the Netherlands, survived deportation to Westerbork, Auschwitz and a forced-labour-camp in Meuselwitz.]

35176. SELLA, DOROTHEA: *Der Ring des Prometheus: Denksteine im Herzen*. Eine auf Wahrheit beruhende Romantrilogie. Jerusalem: Rubin Mass, 1996. 570 pp. [Based on personal recollections 1941–1945. Author, née Sperber, grew up in Czernowitz, survived in the Caucasus region.]

35177. SELB, GÜNTHER: *Ohne Ariernachweis durch das Dritte Reich*. Ein autobiographisches Fragment von 1932 bis 1945. Hrsg. von Norbert Elb. Frankfurt am Main: Haag & Herchen, 1996. 194 pp.

35178. SHAVIT, DAVID: *Hunger for the printed word: books and libraries in Jewish Ghettos of Nazi-occupied Europe*. Jefferson, NC; London: McFarland, 1997. 178 pp., tabs. [Incl. Theresienstadt.]

35179. SIEGERLAND. BARTOLOSCH, THOMAS A.: *Zur "Endlösung der Judenfrage" im Siegerland während der nationalsozialistischen Herrschaft*. [In]: Diagonal, Zeitschrift der Universität-Gesamthochschule Siegen, Jg. 1996, H. 2, Siegen, 1996. Pp. 105–114.

35180. SIEGERLAND. DIETERMANN, KLAUS: *Auschwitz: auf den Spuren Siegerländer und Wittgensteiner Juden*. Dokumentation zur Ausstellung. Siegen: Verlag der Ges. f. Christl.-Jüd. Zusammenarbeit, 1997. 12 pp., illus. (Dokumentation, 10.)

35181. SILBERKLANG, DAVID: *The Allies and the Holocaust: a reappraisal*. [In]: Yad Vashem Studies, Vol. 24, Jersualem, 1994. Pp. 147–176.

35182. SILESIA. JONCA, KAROL: *Die schlesische Toleranz hat nicht geholfen. Der Untergang der schlesischen Juden nach 1933*. [In]: Der gemeinsame Weg, H. 83, Bonn, 1996. Pp. 5–7, illus.

35183. SIM, DORRITH M.: *In my pocket*. Illustrated by Gerald Fitzgerald. New York: Harcourt Brace, 1996. [23] pp., coloured illus. [Children's story of a child's rescue from the Nazis on a Kindertransport and subsequent life in Scotland.]

35184. SOFSKY, WOLFGANG: *The order of terror: the concentration camp*. Transl. by William Templer. Princeton, NJ: Princeton Univ. Press, 1997. VIII, 356 pp., notes, bibl. [For orig. German edn. in 1993 see No. 30643/YB XXXIX.]

35185. SPAIN. ROTHER, BERND: *Franco als Retter der Juden? Zur Entstehung einer Legende*. [In]: Zeitschrift für Geschichtswissenschaft, Jg. 45, H. 2, Berlin, 1997. Pp. 122–146, footnotes.

35186. *Spielberg's Holocaust: critical perspective on Schindler's List*. Edited by Yosefa Loshitzky. Bloomington: Indiana Univ. Press, 1997. VIII, 250 pp., illus., notes. [Based on a symposium held in 1994 at the Univ. of Pennsylvania, Philadelphia; essays debate the representation and popular reception of Spielberg's film.]

35187. SWEDEN. LEVINE, PAUL A.: *Anti-semitism in Sweden's Foreign Office: how important was it?* [In]: Historisk tidskrift, Stockholm, 1996. Pp. 8–27, footnotes. [On the highly restrictive policies of Sweden against Jewish refugees from Nazi Germany.]

35188. SWITZERLAND. *Dimensions: a Journal of Holocaust Studies*. Vol. 11, No. 1 [with the issue title]: *Switzerland's war: the myth of neutrality*. New York: Anti-Defamation League, 1997. 1 issue, illus., facsims., notes. [Incl.: Introd.: Neutrality and duplicity (Dennis B. Klein, 2). Jewish victims of the Holocaust and Swiss banks (David Cesarani, 3–6). Europe's gold: Nazis, neutrals and the Holocaust (Paul B. Miller, 7–14). Co-opting Nazi Germany: neutrality in Europe during World War II (Jonathan Petropoulos, 15–21).

35189. SWITZERLAND. KREIS, GEORG: *Die schweizerische Flüchtlingspolitik der Jahre 1933–1945. Was man wußte und was man noch wissen sollte*. [In]: Schweizerische Zeitschrift für Geschichte, Vol. 47, Nr. 4, Basel, 1997. Pp. 532–551, footnotes. [With French abstract.]

35190. SWITZERLAND. MUSCHG, ADOLF: *Die Teilnahms-Ferne. Wenn Auschwitz in der Schweiz liegt. Über die Nichtanerkennung historischer Schuld und den langen Schlaf der Selbstgerechten*. [In]: Die Zeit, Nr. 7, Hamburg, 7. Feb. 1997. P. 50. [A longer version of this essay was first publ. in 'Tages-Anzeiger', Zurich.]

35191. SWITZERLAND. SEILER, LUKREZIA/WACKER, JEAN-CLAUDE: *"Fast täglich kamen Flüchtlinge". Riehen und Bettingen – zwei Schweizer Grenzdörfer in der Kriegszeit. Erinnerungen an die Jahre 1933–1948*. [Hrsg.: Stiftung z'Rieche.] Riehen: Verlag z'Rieche, 1996. 192 pp., illus., notes, bibl. [Incl.: Vorwort (Ernst Ludwig Ehrlich, 11–13). Based on 39 interviews. Incl. also chaps. on Swiss refugee policy and reports of the Swiss border guards.]

35192. SWITZERLAND (JEWISH ASSETS). BALZLI, BEAT: *Treuhänder des Reichs. Die Schweiz und die Vermögen der Naziopfer: Eine Spurensuche.* Zürich: Werd Verlag, 1997. 340 pp.

35193. SWITZERLAND (JEWISH ASSETS). BOWER, TOM: *Blood money: the Swiss, the Nazis and the looted billions.* London; New York: Macmillan, 1997. XV, 381 pp., illus., ports., notes, bibl. [German edn.: Das Gold der Juden. Die Schweiz und die verschwundenen Nazi-Milliarden. München: Blessing, 1997. 416 pp.] [Cf.: Going for the gold (Matthew Stevenson) [in]: The American Spectator, Vol. 30, No. 5, Bloomington, IN, May 1997. Pp. 25–31.]

35194. SWITZERLAND (JEWISH ASSETS). CASTELMUR, LINUS: *Schweizerisch-alliierte Finanzbeziehungen im Übergang vom Zweiten Weltkrieg. Die deutschen Guthaben in der Schweiz zwischen Zwangsliquidierung und Freigabe.* 2. Aufl. Zürich: Chronos, 1997. 421 pp. [1st edn. 1992.]

35195. SWITZERLAND (JEWISH ASSETS). HUG, PETER: *Die nachrichtenlosen Guthaben von Nazi-Opfern in der Schweiz.* [In]: Schweizerische Zeitschrift für Geschichte, Vol. 47, Nr. 4, Basel, 1997. Pp. 532–551, footnotes. [With French abstract.]

35196. SWITZERLAND (JEWISH ASSETS). KOCH, PETER FERDINAND: *Geheim-Depot Schweiz. Wie Banken am Holocaust verdienen.* Mit einem Kapitel von Richard Chaim Schneider. München: List, 1997. 319 pp., illus., bibl. (299–316).

35197. SWITZERLAND (JEWISH ASSETS). LeBOR, ADAM: *Hitler's secret bankers.* Secaucus, NJ: Birch Lane Press, 1997. 261 pp., illus., notes, bibl. [Documents the relationship between the Swiss banking community and the Nazis. Also describes the activities of the Swiss diplomat, Karl Lutz, who helped Raoul Wallenberg save thousands of Jewish lives in Hungary.]

35198. SWITZERLAND (JEWISH ASSETS). NEW, MITYA, ed.: *Switzerland unwrapped: exposing the myths.* London; New York: I.B. Tauris (distrib. in US by St. Martin's Press), 1997. XIII, 210 pp., notes, bibl. [Anthology of articles based on interviews with prominent Swiss personalities; incl. chaps. on Switzerland and the Jews; Holocaust money and Swiss banks; refugees in Switzerland.] [Cf.: A painful history: under pressure, the Swiss are rethinking their complex role in the Nazi era (Thomas Sancton) [in]: Time, Vol. 149, No. 8, Chicago, Feb. 24, 1997. Pp. 40–42, illus.]

35199. SWITZERLAND (JEWISH ASSETS). SCHRÖDER, DIETER: *Raubgold.* [In]: Mittelweg 36, Jg. 6, H. 4, Hamburg, 1997. Pp. 46–52. [Review essay on several recent publs. dealing with the political and financial involvement of Switzerland in general and Swiss banks in particular with Nazi Germany and with today's claims regarding retained Jewish assets.]

35200. SWITZERLAND (JEWISH ASSETS). *Shadows of World War II. Nazi Gold and Holocaust money – victims as accusers.* A Focus File from the Neue Zürcher Zeitung. Ed.: Alfred Cattani. Transl. from the German by Myron B. Gubitz. Zürich: NZZ, 1997. 70 pp.

35201. SWITZERLAND (JEWISH ASSETS). VINCENT, ISABEL: *Hitler's silent partners; Swiss banks, Nazi gold, and the pursuit of justice.* New York: Morrow, 1997. XII, 351 pp., illus., gloss., notes (316–331), bibl. (332–334). [Based on interviews with 335 survivors. German edn.: Das Gold der verfolgten Juden. München: Diana, 1997. 334 pp.]

35202. SWITZERLAND (JEWISH ASSETS). ZIEGLER, JEAN: *Die Schweiz, das Gold und die Toten.* München: Bertelsmann, 1997. 314 pp., docs., notes. [Also publ. in French: La Suisse, l'or et les morts. Paris: Ed. du Seuil, 1997. 320 pp.]

35203. TEVETH, SHABTAI: *Ben Gurion and the Holocaust.* New York: Harcourt, Brace and Co., 1996. LXIV, 310 pp., map, gloss., chronol., notes (261–289). [Deals with the charges, that Ben-Gurion did not do enough to save Jews.] [Cf.: Review (Abraham J. Edelheit) [in]: Jewish Book World, Vol. 15, No. 2, New York, Fall 1997, pp. 19–21. Blaming the Jews (Hillel Halkin) [in]: Commentary, Vol. 103, No. 1, New York, Jan. 1997, pp. 64–67.]

35204. THERESIENSTADT. *Aufzeichnungen von Federica Spitzer und Ruth Weisz*. Mit einem Beitrag von Wolfgang Benz. Berlin: Metropol, 1997. 172 pp. (Bibliothek der Erinnerung, Bd. 1.) [Incl.: Theresienstadt: Ort der deutschen Geschichte (Wolfgang Benz, 158–172).]

35205. THERESIENSTADT. LEIST, KLAUS: *Philipp Manes: a Theresienstadt chronicle*. [In]: The Journal of Holocaust Education, Vol. 6, No. 2, London, Autumn 1997. Pp. 36–70, notes. [P. M., Elberfeld 1875 – Auschwitz after 1944, writer and photographer. His chronicle of life in Theresienstadt 1942–1944, intended for post-war publication, survived, now deposited in the Wiener Library, London.]

35206. THERESIENSTADT. POLLAK, OLIVER B.: *A medical memoir of Terezin (Theresienstadt) concentration camp by Felix Bachmann, M.D.* [In]: Kosmas: Czechoslovak and Central European Journal, Vol. 12, No. 2, New York, Fall 1997. Pp. 127–155, notes. [F. B., b. Jan. 8, 1881 in Velmede, Westphalia, practised medicine in Berlin and Dresden, dismissed in 1935, was taken to Theresienstadt in 1942, where he worked as a camp doctor. In May 1945, F. B. recorded in English his observations of health problems and medical conditions in the form of four "letters", reprinted here. He later settled in Ohio.]

35207. THERESIENSTADT. SPIES, GERTY: *My years in Theresienstadt. How a women survived the Holocaust*. Transl. by Jutta R. Tragnitz. Amherst, NY: Prometheus Books, 1997. 214 pp., illus. [For orig. German edn. publ. in 1984, see No. 21187/YB XXX.]

35208. THERESIENSTADT. *Terezínská Pametní Kniha*. [In Czech, title transl.: Terezín Memorial Book]. Jewish victims of Nazi deportations from Bohemia and Moravia 1941–1945. Issued by the Terezín Initiative Foundation and the Melantrich Publ. House. Editors: Miroslav Kárný, Director, Zdenek Schindler, Margitá Kárná, Lenka Linhartova, Toman Brod in cooperation with Jaroslava Milotová [et al.]. Praha: Terezínská Iniciativa; Melantrich, 1995. 2 vols., 1559 pp., illus., lists., facsims., tabs. [Cont (in Czech, titles transl.): A word (Vaclav Havel, 7). To the reader of the Terezín Memorial Book (Serge Klarsfeld, 9–10). A guide to the Terezín Memorial Book, 13–17). The genocide of the Czech Jews (Miroslaw Kárný, 19–54). Chronological survey of the deportations transports of Jews from Prague to Lodz and Ujazdów, from Brno to Minsk and all the deportation transports to and from Terezín (63–74). Vocabulary of given names (75–76). Transports according to the date of departure (44–1335). Documentation annex (1337–1348). Alphabetical name index (1349–1559). The vols. cont. the names of 81,397 people. A forthcoming vol. will cont. the names of the deportees from Germany, Austria, the Netherlands and Denmark. In 1996 a guide book was publ. in English: Terezín Memorial Book. Jewish victims of Nazi deportations from Bohemia and Moravia 1941–1945. A guide to the Czech original with a glossary of Czech terms used in the list. Praha: Terezín Initiative; Melantrich, 1996. 128 pp.; incl. also the above-listed articles and the documentation annex transl. into English.]

35209. THURINGIA. WOLF, SIEGFRIED: *Quellen zur Judenverfolgung in Thüringen 1942*. [In]: Geschichte-Erziehung-Politik, Jg. 7, H. 6, Berlin, 1996. Pp. 347–356, facsims., docs.

35210. TRANSNISTRIA. OFER, DALIA: *Life in the ghettos of Transnistria*. [In]: Yad Vashem Studies, Vol. 25, Jerusalem, 1996. Pp. 229–274. [On the internment of Jews from Bukowina, Bessarabia and other parts of Romania in the Southern part of the Ukraine, ceded to Romania in summer 1941 by the Germans; in March 1944 returned to the Soviet Union.]

35212. TÜBINGEN. LANGEWIESCHE, DIETER: *Die Universität Tübingen in der Zeit des Nationalsozialismus: Formen der Selbstgleichschaltung und Selbstbehauptung*. [In]: Geschichte und Gesellschaft, Jg. 23, Göttingen, 1997. Pp. 618–648, footnotes. [Deals also with the racist and antisemitic ideas as expressed by jurists, biologists and theologians during the Nazi period.]

35213. VAT, DAN VAN DER: *The good Nazi: the life and lies of Albert Speer*. Boston: Houghton Mifflin, 1997. 406 pp., illus., ports., notes (370–383), bibl. (386–390). [Discusses also Speer's deliberate cover-up of entries in his war-time diaries concerning the deportation of Jews.]

35214. VARGA, SUSAN: *Ich warte nicht, bis sie mich holen: Odyssee einer jüdischen Familie*. Aus dem Englischen von Ulrike Budde. München: Knesebeck, 1996. 320 pp. [Orig. title 'Heddy and me'. Author, b. 1943, tells the story of her mother's and her own life in Hungary before and during the Second World War, and emigration after the war to Australia.]

35215. VARON, BENNO WEISER: *Mother was a Zionist*. [In]: Midstream, Vol. 43, No. 3, New York, April 1997. Pp. 9–11. [Reminiscences of life in Austria, incl. Nazi period.] [B.W.V., b. 1913 in Czernowitz, writer, journalist, Israeli diplomat, lives in Boston.]

35216. VELEN-RAMSDORF. FASSE, NORBERT: *Katholiken und NS-Herrschaft im Münsterland. Das Amt Velen-Ramsdorf 1918–1945*. Bielefeld: Verlag f. Regionalgesch., 1997. 895 pp., illus., graphs. [Studien zur Regionalgeschichte, Bd. 7) (Schriftenreihe der Gemeinde Velen, Bd. 4.) Zugl.: Essen, Univ., Diss. u.d. Titel: Zwischen Kirchenbank, Kriegerdenkmal und Volksempfaänger, 1996. [Incl.: Chap. VI. Judenverfolgung vor Ort.]

35217. VERSE-HERRMANN, ANGELA: *Die "Arisierungen" in der Land- und Forstwirtschaft 1938–1942*. Stuttgart: Steiner, 1997. 202 pp., footnotes, tabs., bibl.(150–167). (Vierteljahrschrift für Sozial- und Wirtschaftsgeschichte, Beihefte, Nr. 131.) Zugl.: Bonn, Univ., Diss., 1995.

35218. *Vingtième Siècle. Revue d'Histoire*, No. 54 [with the issue title] *Dossier: Sur les camps de concentration du 20e siècle*. Paris, Avril-Juin, 1997. 1 issue. [7 contribs. (with Engl. abstracts, pp. 169–171) by David Cesarani, Michel Fabréguet, Anne Grynberg, Nicolas Werth, Juliane Wetzel, Annette Wieviorka and Barbie Zeliger, some of them dealing with German concentration camps, the internment of Nazi refugees in France and Great Britain and with Jewish Displaced Persons in Germany.]

35219. WEIGEL, SIGRID: *Der Ort von Frauen im Gedächtnis des Holocaust: Symbolisierungen, Zeugenschaft und kollektive Identität*. [In]: Die Philosophin, H. 12, Tübingen, 1995. Pp. 53–62, footnotes.

35220. WEISSGLAS, ISAK: *Steinbruch am Bug. Bericht einer Deportation*. Mit einem Beitrag von Wolfgang Benz. Hrsg von. Ernest Wichner und Herbert Wiesner. Berlin: Literaturhaus Berlin, 1995. 100 pp. (Texte aus dem Literaturhaus Berlin, Bd. 10.) [On the deportation of 5,000 Jews from Czernowitz into a forced labour camp in Transnistria, by the father of the poet Immanuel Weissglas.]

35221. WEISS, YFAAT: *Projektionen vom Weltjudentum. Die Boykottbewegung der 1930er Jahre*. [In]: Tel Aviver Jahrbuch für deutsche Geschichte, Bd. 26, 1997, Gerlingen, 1997. Pp. 151–180, notes.

35222. WEISS, YFAAT: *Zweierlei Mass. Die Emigration deutscher und polnischer Juden nach 1933*. [In]: Jüdischer Almanach 1998, Frankfurt am Main, 1997. Pp. 100–112.

35223. WESTPHALIA. ZYMEK, BERND: *Das "Gesetz gegen die Überfüllung der deutschen Schulen und Hochschulen" und seine Umsetzung in Westfalen, 1933–1935*. [In]: Ambivalenzen der Pädagogik. Zur Bildungsgeschichte der Aufklärung und des 20. Jahrhunderts. Harald Scholtz zum 65. Geburtstag. Hrsg. von Peter Drewek [et al.]. Weinheim: Deutscher Studien Verlag, 1995. Pp. 205–226, notes. [Deals with the implementation of one of the first anti-Jewish laws.]

35224. WIESENTHAL, SIMON: *The sunflower: on the possibilities and limits of forgiveness*. Ed. with introd. by Harry James Cargas and Bonny V. Fetterman. New York: Schocken Books, 1997. XII, 271 pp. [Rev. and expanded edn.; first publ. 1969, see Nos. 7749/YBXV and 8570/YB XVI. Incl. 31 new responses by prominent personalities on the question of forgiveness.]

35225. WILKOMIRSKI, BINJAMIN: *Bruchstücke. Aus einer Kindheit 1939–1948*. Frankfurt am Main: Jüd. Verlag, 1995. 143 pp. ["Memoirs" of an orphan, now found to be fictitious.]

35226. WISTRICH, ROBERT S.: *The aesthetic roots of Nazi antisemitism*. [In]: Midstream, Vol. 43, No. 2, New York, Feb./March 1997. Pp. 13–16.

35227. WOLF, KERSTIN UND FRANK: *Reichsfluchtsteuer und Steuersteckbriefe 1932–1942*. Berlin: Verein Biographische Forschungen und Sozialgeschichte e.V., 1997. 43 pp., facsims., tabs., graphs, lists, docs.

35228. WOLKOWICZ, SHLOMO: *Das Grab bei Zloczow. Geschichte meines Überlebens. Galizien 1939–1945*. Berlin: Wichern, 1996. 159 pp., illus., ports., facsims., maps. [Author spent war in constant flight, partly in hiding. After liberation lived in Austria, emigr. in 1949 to Israel.]

35229. WOOD, E.THOMAS/JANKOWSKI, STANISLAW M.: *Jan Karski. Einer gegen den Holocaust. Als Kurier in geheimer Mission*. Vorwort von Elie Wiesel. Aus dem Amerikan. von Anna Kaiser. Gerlingen: Bleicher, 1997. 359 pp. [For orig. edn. see No. 31867/XL.] [Cf.: Was wußten die Alliierten vom Holocaust? Warten auf die Retter: Von der Hilflosigkeit der Verfolgten und der Ohnmacht des Westens (Karl-Heinz Janßen) [in]: Die Zeit, Nr. 5, Hamburg, 24. Jan. 1997, p. 46; essay on the occasion of the forthcoming German edn. of the book.]

—— ZIMMERMANN, MOSHE: *Die deutschen Juden 1914–1945*. [See No. 34710.]

35230. ZÜRNDORFER, HANNELE: *Verlorene Zeit. Jüdische Kindheit im Dritten Reich*. Bearb. und mit einer Einführung versehen von Rolf Schörken. Düsseldorf: Ges. für Christl.-Jüd. Zusammenarbeit in Düsseldorf [et al.], 1997. 203 pp., illus. [Orig. Engl. edn. publ. 1983, first German edn. 1988; see Nos. 20108/YB XXIX and 25546/YB XXXIV. Recollections of childhood in Düsseldorf; November Pogrom, Kindertransport.] [H.Z.(Carola Regent), b. 1925 in Düsseldorf, author, lives in Scotland.]

B. Jewish Resistance

35231. ABOSCH, HEINZ: *Flucht ohne Heimkehr. Aus dem Leben eines Heimatlosen*. Stuttgart: Radius, 1997. 174 pp. [Cf.: Hoffnung um den Kreis der Erinnerung. Zum Tod von Heinz Abosch (Christoph Kuhn) [in]: Die Mahnung, Jg. 44, Berlin, 1.Juli 1997, p. 6.] [H.A., 1918 Magdeburg – March 1, 1997 Düsseldorf, writer, Socialist, emigr. 1933 to France, active in the Resistance, escaped in 1944 from a deportation train, returned 1956 to Germany.]

35232. *Exilforschung*. Ein internationales Jahrbuch. Bd. 15, 1997: Exil und Widerstand. Hrsg. im Auftrag der Gesellschaft für Exilforschung/Society for Exile Studies von Claus-Dieter Krohn [et al.]. München: Text + Kritik, 1997. 282 pp., notes. (Exilforschung, Bd. 15.) [Selected contribs. relevant to Jewish participation in the Resistance and German-speaking refugees: Propaganda als Widerstand? Die 'Braunbuch'-Kampagne zum Reichstagsbrand 1933 (Claus-Dieter Krohn, 10–32). Frankreichs fremde Patrioten. Deutsche in der Résistance (Klaus-Michael Mallmann, 33–65). Verschwiegene Bündnispartner. Die Union deutscher sozialistischer Organisationen in Großbritannien und die britischen Nachrichtendienste (Ludwig Eiber, 66–87). ". . . alle Repressionen unnachsichtlich ergriffen werden". Die Gestapo und das politische Exil (Gerhard Paul, 120–149). Rettung und Restriktion. US-amerikanische Notvisa für politische Flüchtlinge in Südfrankreich 1940/41 (Anne Klein, 213–232).]

35233. GOCH, STEFAN: *Westdeutsche Trotzkisten im Widerstand gegen den Nationalsozialismus und im Exil*. [In]: IWK, Int. wiss. Korrespondenz zur Geschichte der deutschen Arbeiterbewegung, H. 2, Berlin, 1996. Pp. 143–171, footnotes. [Deals with Socialist groups, among them many Jews, in Gelsenkirchen and neighbouring towns.]

35234. HERZBERG, TUSIA: *Der lachende Sand. Junge jüdische Widerstandskämpfer im Zweiten Weltkrieg*. [Aus dem Hebr. übers. von Ruth Mirecki]. Klagenfurt: Alekto, 1996. 104 pp. (Ed. Mnemosyne, Bd. 5.)

35235. HEUTGER, NICOLAUS: *Im Griff eines Koffers*. [In]: Lutherische Monatshefte, H. 9, Hamburg, Sept. 1997. Pp. 36–38. [On Jewish resistance.]

35236. PAUCKER, ARNOLD: "... bis 1970 völlig vernachlässigt". Gedanken zur Geschichtsschreibung des Widerstands der deutschen Juden gegen den Faschismus. [In]: Informationen. Studienkreis deutscher Widerstand, Jg. 22, Nr. 46, Frankfurt am Main, Nov. 1997. Pp. 13–14, notes.

35237. ROSENTHAL, DAVID: Jewish resistance in W.W.II. [In]: Jewish Frontier, No. 7, New York, Nov./Dec. 1997. Pp. 26–28.

35238. SANDVOß, HANS-RAINER: Widerstand in Kreuzberg. Hrsg.: Gedenkstätte deutscher Widerstand. Berlin: Gedenkstätte dt. Widerstand, 1996. 288 pp., ports., illus., facsims. (Schriftenreihe über den Widerstand in Berlin von 1933 bis 1945, Bd. 10.) [Deals also with Jews in the Resistance; incl. the chap.: Verfolgung der Juden/Hilfe für Untergetauchte (246–269.]

35239. STROBL, INGRID: Fräulein sprechen gut deutsch. Österreichische jüdische Exilantinnen in der Résistance. [In]: Tribüne, Jg. 36, H. 141, Frankfurt am Main, 1997. Pp. 128–140.

—— TEPPICH, FRITZ: Der rote Pfadfinder. Der abenteuerliche Weg eines Berliner Juden durch das 20. Jahrhundert. [See No. 35748.]

35240. URBAN-FAHR, SUSANNE: Juden im Widerstand gegen die Shoah. [In]: Edith Stein Jahrbuch 1997. Bd. 3, Würzburg, 1997. Pp. 319–325, footnotes, bibl.

IV. POST WORLD WAR II

A. General

35241. ANGRESS, WERNER T.: Kurzreferat: Ein Zeitzeuge berichtet aus amerikanischer Sicht. [In]: Rainer Schröder, ed.: 8. Mai 1945 – Befreiung oder Kapitulation? Berlin, Berlin Verlag, 1997. (Berliner Juristische Universitätsschriften, Grundlagen des Recht, Bd. 4.). Pp. 45–50. [Personal memoirs of the Berlin-born historian Werner T. Angress, who witnessed the end of World War II as an American soldier in Germany.]

35242. ANTISEMITISM. BERGMANN, WERNER/ERB, RAINER: Anti-Semitism in Germany: the post-Nazi epoch since 1945. Transl. by Belinda Cooper and Allison Brown. New Brunswick, NJ: Transaction (distrib. in UK: Book Representation and Distrib, Hadleigh), 1997. IX, 385 pp., illus., tabs., appendixes, notes, bibl. (359–379). [For orig. German edn. see No. 28899/YB XXXVII.]

35243. AUSTRIA. BODEMAN, MICHAL: Theatre of memory: Austria. [In]: American Jewish Year Book. Vol. 97, New York, 1997. Pp. 353–360. [Reports on the Jewish community in Austria, also on antisemitism. Incl. reports on the Czech Republic and Hungary, 361–382.]

—— BALA, HEIKE KATRIN/SCHOLZ, CHRISTIAN, eds.: "Deutsch-jüdisches Verhältnis"? Fragen, Betrachtungen, Analysen. Mit Beiträgen von Ignatz Bubis [et al.]. [See No. 35757.]

35244. BAUMEL, JUDITH TYDOR: DPs, mothers and pioneers: women in the She'erit Hapletah. [In]: Jewish History, Vol. 11, No. 2, Haifa, Fall 1997. Pp. 99–110, notes. [Deals with Jewish women in DP camps in Germany betwen 1945–1948.]

35245. BAUMEL, JUDITH: Kibbutz Buchenwald: survivors and pioneers. New Brunswick, NJ: Rutgers Univ. Press, 1997. XII, 194 pp., illus., ports., gloss. notes, bibl. (179–187). [First post-war Zionist training farm founded by survivors of Buchenwald. See also No. 34181/YB XLII.]

35246. BERLIN. RODDEN, JOHN G.: Bridge over broken glass? Crisscrossing history in Germany's sole Jewish high school. [In]: The Midwest Quarterly, Vol. 39, No. 1, Pittsburg, Autumn 1997. Pp. 44–55. [Now the only Jewish high school in Germany, established in 1778 in Berlin. Closed by the Nazis in 1942, the school reopened in August of 1993, and now has approx. 20% non-Jewish students.]

35247. BERLIN. *Von Aizenberg bis Zaidelman. Jüdische Zuwanderer aus Osteuropa in Berlin und die Jüdische Gemeinde heute.* [Hrsg.:Die Ausländerbeauftragte des Senats. Text: Judith Kessler.] Berlin: Die Ausländerbeauftrage des Senats, 1997. 79 pp., illus.

35248. BONN. REY, MANFRED VAN: *Kontinuität und Wandel. 16 Jahre Begegnungswoche der Stadt Bonn mit ihren ehemaligen verfolgten jüdischen Bürgerinnen und Bürgern.* [In]: Bonner Geschichtsblätter, Bd. 1993/94, Bonn, 1996. Pp. 531–544, footnotes.

35249. BRENNER, MICHAEL: *After the Holocaust: rebuilding Jewish life in postwar Germany.* Transl. by Barbara Harshav. Princeton, NJ: Princeton Univ. Press, 1997. X, 196 pp., illus., ports., map, notes (173–185), appendix: bibl. essay. [On the lives of Jews who remained in Germany immediately following the Second World War; based on 15 interviews with prominent personalities of today's Jewish community.]

35250. BUBIS, NAOMI/MEHLER, SHARON: *Shtika. Versuch, das Tabu zu brechen.* Frankfurt am Main: Suhrkamp Taschenbuch Verlag, 1996. 240 pp. Erstausgabe. [On the silence between parents and children in families of Shoah-survivors.]

35251. CARLEBACH, JULIUS/BRÄMER, ANDREAS: *Continuity or new beginning? Isaac Emil Lichtigfeld, rabbi in Frankfurt am Main and Hesse, 1954–1967.* [In]: Leo Baeck Institute Year Book XLII, London, 1997. Pp. 275–302, footnotes.

35252. CHURCH. FOSCHEPOTH, JOSEF: *Die Rolle der Kirchen und ihr Verhältnis zu den Juden.* [In]: Freiburger Rundbrief, N.F., Jg. 4, H. 1, Freiburg, 1997. Pp. 32–40, footnotes.

35253. DISCHEREIT, ESTHER: *Ein sehr junges Mädchen trifft Nelly Sachs.* [In]: Jüdischer Almanach 1998, Frankfurt am Main, 1997. Pp. 9–16. [On the impact on the author (and her mother) of Nelly Sachs's being awarded the 'Friedenspreis des Deutschen Buchhandels' in 1956.]

35254. *Enteignet durch die Bundesrepublik Deutschland. Der Fall Mendelssohn-Bartholdy.* Eine Dokumentation. Hrsg. von Julius H. Schoeps. Bodenheim: Philo, 1997. 191 pp., docs.

35255. FRANKFURT AM MAIN. RAPAPORT, LYNN: *Jews in Germany after the Holocaust: memory, identity and Jewish-German relations.* Cambridge; New York: Cambridge Univ. Press, 1997. XI, 325 pp., appendix, notes (269–293), bibl. (294–317). [Sociological study of the postwar Jewish community in Frankfurt, based on over 100 interviews with participants between the ages of 25 and 39.]

—— GOTTWALD, ASTRID: *Jews in Germany. Israeli perceptions in the 1950s.* [See No. 35786.]

35256. GRÖZINGER, ELVIRA: *Report on Jewish communities in Central Europe: Federal Republic of Germany.* [In]: American Jewish Year Book. Vol. 97, New York, 1997. Pp. 329–352. [Incl. antisemitism, Holocaust denial.]

35257. HAFNER, KATIE: *The house at the bridge: a story of modern Germany.* New York: Scribner, 1995. 256 pp., illus., map, bibl. (241–243). [Story of the heirs of the Wallich family and their fight to reclaim their former house in Potsdam.]

35258. HERF, JEFFREY: *Divided memories; the Nazi past in the two Germanys.* Cambridge, MA: Harvard Univ. Press, 1997. XI, 527 pp., illus., ports., bibl. [Deals with post-war antisemitism, particularly in East Germany, 1949–1953, purges of (mainly Jewish) Communists and the aftermath.] [Cf.: Eyes to the Reich (Linda Holt) [in]: The Observer, London, Jan. 4, 1998. Review essay (Y. Michal Bodemann) [in]: Mittelweg 36, Jg. 7, H. 2, Hamburg, 1998, Pp. 46–49.]

35259. ILLICHMANN, JUTTA: *Die DDR und die Juden.* Die deutschlandpolitische Instrumentalisierung von Juden und Judentum durch die Partei- und Staatsführung der SBZ/DDR von 1945 bis 1990. Frankfurt am Main; New York: Lang, 1997. 370 pp. (Europäische Hochschulschriften: Reihe 31, Politikwissenschaft, Bd. 336.) Zugl.: Bonn, Univ., Diss., 1997. [Deals also with restitution.]

35260. *Juden im heutigen Deutschland.* Podiumsdiskussion mit Ignatz Bubis [et al.]. Moderation: Micha Brumlik. [In]: Für ein neues Miteinander von Juden und Christen [see No. 34707]. Pp. 49–76.

35261. JÜRGENS, FRANZ J.: *"Wir waren ja eigentlich Deutsche". Juden berichten von Emigration und Rückkehr.* Berlin: Aufbau Taschenbuch Verlag, 1997. 248 pp. [Cont. 15 accounts based on interviews with former emigrants now living in Germany.]

35262. KAUFMAN, JONATHAN: *A hole in the heart of the world: being Jewish in Eastern Europe.* New York: Viking, 1997. VI, 328 pp., illus., ports., notes, bibl. (321–328). [Author follows the lives of three generations of five families from 1938 to the present. Incl. also East Germany.]

35263. KUSCHEL, ANDREA: *"Die Flügel erwachsen den Nachgeborenen nur aus der Phantasie".* Zur jungen jüdischen Literatur in Deutschland und Österreich. [In]: GrauZone, H. 13, Freiburg, 1997. Pp. 6–9. [In this isssue also an interview with and an article on Doron Rabinovici (Tim Schomacker), and a text by Robert Schindel.]

35264. LOWER SAXONY. OBENAUS, HERBERT, ed.: *Im Schatten des Holocaust. Jüdisches Leben in Niedersachsen nach 1945.* [Hrsg.: Arbeitskreis Geschichte des Landes Niedersachsen (nach 1945).] Hannover: Hahn, 1997. 283 pp., footnotes. (Veröffentlichungen der Historischen Kommission für Niedersachsen und Bremen, 38; Quellen und Untersuchungen zur Geschichte Niedersachsen nach 1945, Bd. 12.) [Incl. (some titles abbr.): Einleitung (ed., 9–24). Exodus oder Hierbleiben. Die Situation der Juden zur Zeit der NS-Verfolgung in Deutschland (Wolfgang Benz, 25–42). Das Zentralkomitee der befreiten Juden in Bergen-Belsen (Juliane Wetzel, 43–54). Jewish Committee und Jüdische Gemeinde Hannover (Anke Quast, 55–74). Die ersten jüdischen Organisationen in Hamburg nach der Schoah (Ursula Büttner, 75–82). Das Land Niedersachsen und die jüdischen Displaced Persons (Herbert Obenaus, 83–118). Die Lager der jüdischen Displaced Persons im besetzten Deutschland (Jacqueline Giere, 119–130). Das "Kazet-Theater" im jüdischen "Displaced Persons"-Lager Bergen-Belsen, 1945–1947 (Nicholas Yantian, 131–164). Die Funktion des Zionismus in den jüdischen Gemeinden in Deutschland nach 1945 (Antje Clara Naujoks, 165–196). Die Anfänge der Landesverbände der jüdischen Gemeinden in der britischen Zone (Hagit Lavsky, 199–234). Jüdische "Volkstrümmer" im Nachkriegsdeutschland. Ein ungeschriebenes Kapitel deutsch-jüdischer-israelischer Beziehungen (Frank Stern, 235–254). Der lange Weg zum neuen deutschen Judentum (Y. Michal Bodemann, 255–281).]

35265. MERTENS, LOTHAR: *Davidstern unter Hammer und Zirkel. Die Jüdischen Gemeinden in der SBZ/DDR und ihre Behandlung durch Partei und Staat 1945 -1990.* Hildesheim; New York: Olms, 1997. 492 pp., chronol., 387–395), graphs., footnotes, bibl. (399–486), index (487–492). (Haskala, Bd.18.) Zugl.: Bochum, Univ., Habil.-Schr., 1996.

35266. MÜNCH, PETER L.: *Zwischen "Liquidation" und Wiederaufbau. Die deutschen Juden, der Staat Israel und die internationalen jüdischen Organisationen in der Phase der Wiedergutmachungsverhandlungen.* [In]: Historische Mitteilungen, Jg. 10, H. 1, Stuttgart, 1997. Pp. 81–111, footnotes.

35267. MYERS, MARGARETE L.: *Jewish Displaced Persons. Reconstructing individual and community in the US Zone of occupied Germany.* [In]: Leo Baeck Institute Year Book XLII, London, 1997. Pp. 303–324, footnotes.

35268. PROSECUTION OF NAZI CRIMES. BOBERACH, HEINZ: *Die Verfolgung von Verbrechen gegen die Menschlichkeit durch deutsche Gerichte in Nordrhein-Westfalen 1946 bis 1949.* [In]: Geschichte im Westen, Jg. 12, Köln, 1997. Pp. 7–23, footnotes.

35269. PROSECUTION OF NAZI CRIMES. *Die frühen Nachkriegsprozesse.* [Hrsg.: KZ-Gedenkstätte Neuengamme. Red.: Kurt Buck [et al.]. Bremen, Ed. Temmen, 1997. 233 pp., notes. (Beiträge zur Geschichte der nationalsozialistischen Verfolgung in Norddeutschland, Heft. 3.) [Incl. seven contribs. by Herbert Diercks, Gregor Espelage, Insa Eschebach, Norman Paech, Joachim Perels, Hermann Kaienburg and Alexandra-Eileen Wenck (12–109). Further contribs. are listed according to subject.]

35270. PROSECUTION OF NAZI CRIMES. STEINBACH, PETER: *NS-Prozesse nach 1945*. Auseinandersetzung mit der Vergangenheit – Konfrontation mit der Wirklichkeit. [In]: Dachauer Hefte, Jg. 13, H. 13, München, 1997. Pp. 3–26, footnotes.

35271. RESTITUTION. KISKER, K.P./BISCHOF, H.H., eds.: *Koblenzer Handbuch des Entschädigungsrechts*. Baden-Baden: Nomos, 1996. 280 pp., subject index (271–280).

35272. RESTITUTION. TIMM, ANGELIKA: *Jewish claims against East Germany: moral obligations and pragmatic policy*. Budapest: Central European Univ. Press, 1997. XI, 279 pp., appendix, list of interviews, notes (244–262), bibl. (263–279), index. [On the history of the Jews in the German Democratic Republic and the Jewish negotiations with the GDR regarding restitution. Also on antisemitism against the background of the officially propagated ideology of antifacism.]

35273. ROSENTHAL, DAVID: *The first Zionist Congress after the Holocaust: reminiscences of a delegate*. [In]: Jewish Frontier, Vol. 64, No. 2, New York, March/April 1997. Pp. 7–9. [Author was the delegate from the British Occupied Zone in Germany to the Basel Congress.]

35274. *Rückkehr und Aufbau nach 1945. Deutsche Remigranten im öffentlichen Leben Nachkriegsdeutschlands*. Hrsg. von Claus-Dieter Krohn und Patrik von zur Mühlen. Marburg: Metropolis, 1997. 360 pp., footnotes, index (355–360). (Schriften der Herbert-und Elsbeth-Weichmann-Stiftung.) [Cont. 16 essays, most of them dealing passim with Jewish remigrés resp. remigrés of Jewish descent; incl. (titles abbr.): Remigranten in der westdeutschen Nachkriegsgesellschaft (Claus-Dieter Krohn, 7–22). Die Region als erste Wirkungsstätte von Remigranten (Marita Krauss, 23–38). Motive, Hindernisse und Wege von Remigranten (Hans Georg Lehmann, 39–70). Remigranten im Bundestag und in den Länderparlamenten (Jan Foitzik, 71–90). Impulse sozialdemokratischer Remigranten auf die Modernisierung der SPD (Hartmut Mehringer, 91–110). Zur Rolle gewerkschaftlicher Remigranten in der Bundesrepublik der 1950er Jahre (Julia Angster, 111–138). Emigranten im kulturellen Wiederaufbau. Die Europäische Verlagsanstalt (Klaus Körner, 139–156). Politische Remigranten in Berlin (Siegfried Heimann, 189–210). Das Saarland nach 1945 (Gerhard Paul, 211–252). Die Gründung der westdeutschen Politikwissenschaft (Alfons Söllner, 253–274). Remigranten in der Publizistik im Nachkriegsdeutschland (Marita Biller, 275–288). Die Remigration von Juristen und der Aufbau der Justiz in der britischen und amerikanischen Besatzungszone (Ulrike Jordan, 305–320). Zur Rolle des Politikwissenschaftlers Hans Simons in Deutschland nach 1945 (Edmund Spevack, 321–338).]

35275. TRESS, MADELEINE: *Foreigners or Jews? The Soviet Jewish refugee population in Germany and the United States*. [In]: East European Jewish Affairs, Vol. 27, No. 2, London, Winter 1997. Pp. 21–38, footnotes, tabs.

35276. *Überlebt und unterwegs. Jüdische Displaced Persons im Nachkriegsdeutschland*. Hrsg.: Fritz Bauer Institut. Frankfurt am Main; New York, 1997. 381 pp., illus., notes. (Fritz Bauer Institut, Jahrbuch 1997 zur Geschichte und Wirkung des Holocaust.) [Selected articles (titles partly abbr.): Einleitung (Jacqueline Giere, 13–26). Erinnerung und Identität der She'erith Hepletah (Abraham Peck, 27–50). Die polnischen Holocaust-Überlebenden. Zwischen Assimilation und Emigration (Andreas Hofmann, 51–70). These are the People. Zu Abraham J. Klausners Film über das Zentralkomitee der befreiten Juden in der amerikanischen Zone (Ronny Loewy, 119–128; on a film produced 1945/1946). Die Begegnung zwischen dem Jischuw und den Überlebenden des Holocaust (Anita Shapira, 129–144). Israel und die Holocaust-Überlebenden (Idith Zertal, 145–152). Jüdische Displaced Persons im deutschen Alltag. Eine Regionalstudie 1945–1950 (Angelika Eder, 163–188; on Landsberg am Lech). Durchgangsstation Berlin (Angelika Königseder, 189–206). Brichah: Fluchtwege durch Österreich (Thomas Albrich, 207–228). Jüdische DPs in historischem Kontext (Dan Diner, 229–248). Talmuddrucke im Nachkriegsdeutschland (Peter Honigmann, 249–266). Zur Traditionsvermittlung jüdischer DP-Familien in Deutschland (Lena Inowlocki, 267–288). Further essays are listed according to subject.]

35277. *Unter Vorbehalt. Rückkehr aus der Emigration nach 1945.* Hrsg. vom Verein EL-DE-Haus Köln, bearb. von Wolfgang Blaschke, Karola Fings und Cordula Lissner. Köln: Emons, 1997. 246 pp., illus., facsims., notes, bibl. [Cont. essays, 8 interviews of and reports on more than 30 other Jewish and non-Jewish remigrés, mostly from Cologne, Bonn and Düsseldorf. Selected essays: Migration in Deutschland 1945–1955 (Volker Ackermann, 13–21). Rückkehr als Politikum – Remigration aus Israel (Karola Fings, 22–32). Rückkehr aus dem Exil an die Universität – Überlegungen zu Lebens- und Organisationsentscheidungen (Frank Golczewski, 33–43). Remigranten und Lizenzpresse (Fritz Bilz/Wolfgang Blaschke, 44–50).]

35278. WETZEL, JULIANE: *Neue Gemeinden – alte Bilder. Von den Schwierigkeiten der Deutung jüdischer Nachkriegsgeschichte in Deutschland.* [In]: Shylock: Zinsverbot und Geldverleih in jüdischer und christlicher Tradition [see No. 35844]. Pp. 253–260, notes.

B. Education and Teaching. Memorials

35279. AUSCHWITZ. RIES, HENRY: *Auschwitz – Prüfstein des deutschen Gewissens.* Berlin: Aufbau, 1997. 95 pp., illus. [On the memorial in Auschwitz, its recent development and its visitors.]

35280. BAR-ON, DAN/BRENDLER, KONRAD/HARE, PAUL A., eds.: *"Da ist etwas kaputtgegangen an den Wurzeln. . .".* Identitätsformation deutscher und israelischer Jugendlicher im Schatten des Holocaust. Frankfurt am Main; New York: Campus, 1997. 306 pp., footnotes. [Selected essays: Wie lassen sich deutsche und israelische Jugendliche zum Thema Holocaust ansprechen? (Dan Bar-On, 9–20). Den Holocaust 'durcharbeiten'? Ergebnisse einer vergleichenden Untersuchung an deutschen und israelischen Studierenden (Dan Bar-On, A. Paul Hare, Manfred Brusten, Friedhelm Beiner, 21–52). The section entitled 'Deutsch-israelische Begegnungen' (191–286) cont. 4 contribs. by Konrad Brendler, Dan Bar-On, Dafna Fromer, Tal Ostrovsky, A. Paul Hare and Julia Chaitin analysing two German-Israeli study group projects.]

35281. BERLIN. *Colloquium. Denkmal für die ermordeten Juden Europas. Dokumentation.* [Bearb.: Ekkehard Klausa]. Berlin: Senatsverw. für Wiss., Forschung und Kultur, Referat V A., 1997. 178 pp., illus. [Incl. speeches, comments and other statements on the Holocaust memorial project.]

35282. BERLIN. HAEHN, ULRIKE/SCHILDE, KURT: *". . . eines Tages waren sie weg." Versteckt in Tiergarten – eine Jugendgruppe auf den Spuren jüdischer Verfolgter.* [In]: Geschichte, Erziehung, Politik, Jg. 8, H. 5, Berlin, 1997. Pp. 279–286.

35283. BERLIN. WENK, SILKE: *Identifikation mit den Opfern und Sakralisierung des Mordes.* Symptomatische Fehlleistungen des Berliner Denkmalprojekts für die ermordeten Juden. [In]: Jahrbuch 1997 zur Geschichte und Wirkung des Holocaust [see No. 35276]. Pp. 341–376, notes.

35284. BERLIN. YOUNG, JAMES E.: *Germany's problems with its Holocaust memorial: a way out of the quagmire?* [In]: The Chronicle of Higher Education, Vol. 44, No. 10, Washington, Oct. 31, 1997. Pp. B4–B6, illus. [Also on this topic: War and memory: dealing with the past causes unending debate (Nomi Morris) [in]: Maclean's, Vol. 110, No. 41, Toronto, Oct. 13, 1997. Pp. 36–27, illus.]

35285. BODEMANN, Y. MICHAL: *Gedächtnisnegativ. Genealogie und Strategien deutscher Erinnerung an Auschwitz.* [In]: Soziologie der Gewalt. Sonderheft. Kölner Zeitschrift für Soziologie und Sozialpsychologie, hrsg. von Trutz von Trotha. Opladen, 1997. Pp. 357–379. [With Engl. summary.]

35286. *Der Deutschunterricht.* Jg. 49, H. 4/1997 [with the issue title] *Kinder und Holocaust.* Hrsg.: Jochen Vogt. Seelze, 1997. 1 issue. [Incl.: Jüdische Identitätsprobleme und ein Strukturgesetz der Holocaust-Memoiren. Ein Unterrichtsvorschlag für Sekundarstufe II (Barbara Bauer, 5–19). Geschichten eines Adjektivs. Was man mit einem kleinen Text von Anna Seghers machen kann (Jochen Vogt, 20–27). Das gerettete Kind. Die "Universalisierung" der Anne Frank (Hanno Loewy, 28–39). Bewusstseinsbildung an Erzählungen über den Holocaust? "Konfrontationen": Der Versuch, ein amerikanisches Curriculum für deutsche Schulen zu adaptieren (Gottfried Kössler, 40–49). "Rosa Weiss wollte wissen. . .". Ansätze und Strategien zur didaktischen Vermittlung des Themas Holocaust (Sigrid Thielking, 50–57). Strategien des Erinnerns. Zur "Erziehung nach Auschwitz" im Literaturunterricht der neunziger Jahre (Clemens Kammler, 58–69). Erinnerung als Konstruktion. Ansätze zum Gedenken an die Shoah (Michael Hofmann, 79–81). Incl. also bibl. notes, and book reviews relevant to this topic.]

35287. DORSTEN. EICHMANN, JOHANNA S./RIDDER, THOMAS: *Das Jüdische Museum Westfalen.* . . . In Dorsten will vor allem für Aufklärung sorgen. [sic] [In]: Jahrbuch Westfalen 1997, Münster, 1997. Pp. 42–51, illus.

35288. ESENS. *Erinnern, nicht verdrängen: zehn Jahre Oekumenischer Arbeitskreis Juden und Christen in Esens e.V. (1987–1997).* Dokumentation, Auswahl und Bearb. der Text- und Bildbeiträge im Auftr. des Oek. Arbeitskreises: Gerd Rokahr. Esens: Der Arbeitskreis, 1997. 118 pp., illus., ports., facsims. [On title page: Rückblick auf einen Versuch, gegenseitiges Kennenlernen und Verstehenlernen durch christlich-jüdische Begegnung zu fördern, Kontakte zwischen Juden und Christen zu vertiefen, sie neu zu knüpfen.]

35289. FRANK, ANNE. KOPF, HEDDA ROSNER: *Understanding Anne Frank's 'The diary of a young girl'.* A student casebook to issues, sources, and historical documents. Westport, CT: The Greenwood Press, 1997. XIV, 272, illus., map. [Supplements the diary with a variety of historical docs., incl. an account of the Frank family's life in Germany, eye-witness accounts of Anne's last seven months in the camps.]

35290. FRANKFURT am Main. LIEPACH, MARTIN: *"Auf den Spuren jüdischen Lebens in Frankfurt" – Erfahrungen eines Geschichtsprojekts.* [In]: Geschichte in Wissenschaft und Unterricht, Jg. 47, H. 11, Seelze, Nov. 1996. Pp. 673–689.

35291. GILBERT, MARTIN: *Holocaust journey: travelling in search of the past.* London: Weidenfeld & Nicolson; New York: Columbia Univ. Press, 1997. XVI, 480 pp., illus., maps, bibl. (453–456). [Describes a two-week tour taken in the summer of 1996 by author and a group of his students across Germany, the Czech Republic and Poland to the sites of the Holocaust.]

35292. HEYL, MATTHIAS: *Erziehung nach Auschwitz. Eine Bestandsaufnahme: Deutschland, Niederlande, Israel, USA.* Hamburg: Krämer, 1997. 435 pp., tabs. Zugl.: Hamburg, Univ., Diss., 1997. [On the Shoah in education and commemoration.]

35293. KANTER, SHAUNA: *Taking 'Legacy' to Germany: a daughter follows in her father's footsteps.* [In]: The Jewish Quarterly, Vol. 44, No. 4, London, Winter 1997/98. Pp. 55–57, illus. [London-based writer, director, wrote the play 'Legacy' depicting her father's role in saving Jews from Nazi-Germany. Author also discusses her experiences with German students when staging her play in Hanover.]

35294. KORN, SALOMON: *Holocaust-Gedenken: Ein deutsches Dilemma.* [In]: Aus Politik und Zeitgeschichte, [Beilage von] Das Parlament, Bonn, 17. Jan. 1997. Pp. 23–30, footnotes. [Mainly on the Berlin Holocaust memorial project and its artistic and sociological aspects.]

35295. KOTZIN, C. R.: *Hearing the voices: the 27th annual scholars' conference on the Holocaust and the churches, 2–4 March 1997.* Teaching the Holocaust to future generations. [In]: The Journal of Holocaust Education, Vol. 6, No. 1, London, Summer 1997. Pp. 87–97, notes. [Report on conference in Florida with 400 scholars, educators, members of the clergy, examining issues of the Holocaust in tandem with the churches' struggle and failure to confront Nazi antisemitism and the Final Solution.]

35296. KUHLS, HEIKE: *Erinnern lernen? Pädagogische Arbeit in Gedenkstätten.* Münster: Agenda, 1996. 109 pp., illus., footnotes, bibl. (100–109).

35297. NORTH-RHINE WESTPHALIA. *Begegnungen mit jüdischer Kultur in Nordrhein-Westfalen: Organisationen, Bildungseinrichtungen und Initiativen.* Netzwerk – Geschichte und Leben der Juden in Nordrhein-Westfalen e.V., Projekt "Kommunikation und Vernetzung". [Red.: Carlo Gentile]. Köln: Martin-Buber-Institut für Judaistik der Univ. zu Köln, 1997. 61 pp.

35298. OFFE, SABINE: *Sites of rememberance? Jewish museums in contemporary Germany.* [In]: Jewish Social Studies, Vol. 3, No. 2, Bloomington, IN, Winter 1997. Pp. [77]-[89].

35299. PATEL, CHRISTINE/NIEF, ROSEMARIE: *The presence of the Holocaust in the present, Berlin, 26 and 27 January 1997.* [In]: The Journal of Holocaust Education, Vol. 6, No. 1, London, Summer 1997. Pp. 82–85. [Report on a conference in Berlin about presenting the history of the Holocaust to descendants of victims and of perpetrators.]

35300. RUSSELL, JUDITH: *From memory to history: the place of the Holocaust in the twenty-first century.* [In]: The Journal of Holocaust Education, Vol. 6, No. 1, London, Summer 1997. Pp. 98–100. [Report on conference sponsored by the Institute for Jewish Policy Research and the Imperial War Museum, London.]

35301. SACHSENHAUSEN. MORSCH, GÜNTER: *Von der Erinnerung zum Monument.* Die Entstehungsgeschichte der nationalen Mahn- und Gedenkstätte Sachsenhausen. [In]: Gedenkstätten-Rundbrief Nr. 77, Berlin, 1997. Pp. 1–15, illus.

35302. SIEGEN. DIETERMANN, KLAUS: *Synagoge – Luftschutzbunker – Museum. Aktives Museum Südwestfalen.* Ein Dokumentations- und Lernort für regionale Zeitgeschichte in Siegen. [In]: Siegener Beiträge. Jahrbuch für regionale Geschichte 2/1997. Siegen, 1997. 160–166, illus., notes.

35303. STEINBACH, LOTHAR: *Der Holocaust und die Erinnerung.* [In]: Für ein neues Miteinander von Juden und Christen [see in No. 34707]. Pp. 221–248. [Also in this book (dealing with education and commemoration): Wer sind wir? Vom Mut zum Lernen mit dem Judentum (Albrecht Lohrbächer, 305–323).]

35304. STEINBACH, PETER: *Die Vergegenwärtigung von Vergangenem. Zum Spannungsverhältnis zwischen individueller Erinnerung und öffentlichem Gedenken.* [In]: Aus Politik und Zeitgeschichte. [Beilage zu] Das Parlament, Bonn, 17. Jan. 1997. Pp. 1–13.

35305. WILCOCK, EVELYN: *Teaching the Holocaust to children of mixed marriage: issues in delivery and reception.* [In]: The Journal of Holocaust Education, Vol. 6, No. 1, London, Summer 1997. Pp. 1–26, notes.

35306. WOLFFSOHN, MICHAEL: *Von der äußerlichen zur verinnerlichten "Vergangenheitsbewältigung". Gedanken und Fakten zu Erinnerungen.* [In]: Aus Politik und Zeitgeschichte, [Beilage zu] Das Parlament, Bonn, 17. Jan. 1997. Pp. 14–22, footnotes.

35307. WÜRTTEMBERG. *Möglichkeiten des Erinnerns: Orte jüdischen Lebens und nationalsozialistischen Unrechts im Zollernalbkreis und im Kreis Rottweil.* Hechingen, 1997. 85 pp., illus.

35308. YOUNG, JAMES E.: *Formen des Erinnerns. Gedenkstätten des Holocaust.* Aus dem Engl. von Meta Gartner. Wien: Passagen, 1997. 504 pp., illus., bibl. (487–502). Deutsche Erstausgabe. (Passagen Zeitgeschehen.) [Orig. title: The texture of memory; first publ. 1993, see No. 30764/YB XXXIX.]

V. JUDAISM

A. Jewish Learning and Scholars

35309. BAECK, LEO: *Werke.* Hrsg. im Auftrag des Leo Baeck Instituts New York von Albert H. Friedlander [et al.]. Bd. 2. Dieses Volk: jüdische Existenz. Hrsg. von Albert H. Friedlander und Bertold Klappert. Bd. 3. Wege im Judentum: Aufsätze und Reden. Hrsg. von Werner

Licharz. Gütersloh: Gütersl. Verlagshaus. Bd. 2, 1996. 373 pp; Bd. 3, 1997. 319 pp. (Originalausgabe.)

35310. BAECK, LEO. BUDDE, GERDA: *Leo Baeck – Predigen aus Berufung*. [In]: Trumah, H. 6, Berlin, 1997. Pp. 151–170.

35311. BAECK, LEO. LEVINSON, N. PETER: *Leo Baeck. Zum 40. Todestag im November 1996*. [In]: Udim, Rabbinerkonferenz, Bd. 18, Stuttgart, 1997. Pp. 81–90.

35312. BAECK, LEO. PANGRITZ, ANDREAS: *Mystery and commandment in Leo Baeck and Dietrich Bonhoeffer*. [In]: European Judaism, Vol. 30, No. 2, London, Autumn 1997. Pp. 44–57, notes.

35313. BAECK, LEO. SCHINE, ROBERT: *Die Tochterreligion: Das Christentum im Werk Leo Baecks*. Vortrag anläßlich des Festaktes "Elektronische Präsenz des Leo-Baeck-Instituts in Deutschland". [In]: Forschungsstelle Judentum, Mitteilungen und Beiträge 12/13, Leipzig, 1997. Pp. 4–18, footnotes.

35314. BRÄMER, ANDREAS: *"Wissenschaft des Judentums" und "Historische Rechtschule"*. Zwei Briefe Zacharias Frankels an Carl Josef Anton Mittermaier. [In]: Aschkenas, Jg. 7, H. 1, Wien, 1997. Pp. 173–180.

35315. BUBER, MARTIN. FRIEDMAN, MAURICE, ed.: *Martin Buber and the human sciences*. Albany: State Univ. of New York Press, 1996. XVII, 415 pp. [Collection of essays by various authors on different aspects of Buber's philosophy.]

35316. BUBER, MARTIN. HÖRNER, HORST: *Die Pädagogik Martin Bubers anhand seiner Briefe*. [In]: Für ein neues Miteinander von Juden und Christen [see No. 34707]. Pp. 249–266.

35317. BUBER, MARTIN. LEVINSON, N. PETER: *Das Werk Martin Bubers*. [In]: Udim, Rabbinerkonferenz, Bd. 18, Stuttgart, 5785 – 1997. Pp. 91–101.

35318. BUBER, MARTIN. WACHINGER, LORENZ: *Einsame Zwiesprache? Martin Bubers kritische Begegnung mit dem Christentum*. [In]: Edith Stein Jahrbuch 1997. Bd. 3, Würzburg, 1997. Pp. 156–164.

35319. CARLEBACH, JULIUS: *Die jüdische Religion*. [In]: Für ein neues Miteinander von Juden und Christen [see No. 34707]. Pp. 15–24.

35320. COHN-SHERBOK, DAN: *Fifty key Jewish thinkers*. New York: Routledge, 1997. XIII, 132 pp., map., chronol. [Incl. Achad Ha-Am, Leo Baeck, Martin Buber, Hermann Cohen, Emil Fackenheim, Abraham Geiger, Heinrich Graetz, Theodor Herzl, Abraham Joshua Heschel, Moses Hess, Samson Raphael Hirsch, Moses Mendelssohn, Franz Rosenzweig, Salomon Ludwig Steinheim a.o.]

35321. DAVIDOWICZ, KLAUS S.: *Jenseits des Ghettotores – Moses Mendelssohn und Samson Raphael Hirsch*. [In]: Edith Stein Jahrbuch 1997. Bd. 3, Würzburg, 1997. Pp. 134–142, footnotes.

35322. ELIAV, MORDECHAI/HILDESHEIMER, ESRIEL ERICH: *The Jewish Rabbinical Seminary in Berlin 1873–1938: the background of its establishment and its students over the years*. [In Hebrew, title transl.] Jerusalem: Leo Baeck Institute, 1996. 125 pp., illus., ports., bibl. (117–125). [Incl. list of 630 students who attended the 'Hildesheimersches Rabbinerseminar' between 1873 and 1938.]

35323. FACKENHEIM, EMIL L./JOSPE, RAPHAEL, eds.: *Jewish philosophy and the Academy*. International Center for University Teaching of Jewish Civilization. Madison, NJ: Fairleigh Dickinson Univ. Press; London: Associated Univ. Presses 1996. 255 pp. [Contains the following chaps. by Emil L. Fackenheim: Jewish philosophy and the Academy. Philosophical considerations and the teaching of the Holocaust. The Jewish return into history: philosophical fragments on the State of Israel. A retrospective of my thought. Other essays of German-Jewish interest (titles abbr.): Abraham Ibn Ezra and Moses Mendelssohn (Raphael Jospe). Levinas,

Rosenzweig, and the phenomenologies of Husserl and Heidegger (Richard A. Cohen). A note concerning Rosenzweig and Levinas on totality (Johanan E. Bauer). Teaching Leo Strauss as a Jewish and a general philosopher. Response to Emil Fackenheim (Steven T. Katz and Ze'ev Mankowitz).]

35324. FRIEDLANDER ALBERT H.. *In honorem: Albert H. Friedlander*. A celebration of his 70th birthday. [In]: European Judaism, Vol. 30, No. 2, Autumn 1997. Pp. 4–84. [Incl.: Interview with Albert H. Friedlander. Albert H. Friedlander profile: CV and partial bibl. (Esther Seidel, 4–17, notes). Also contribs. by Elie Wiesel, Bertold Klappert, Andreas Pangritz, Ekkehard W. Stegemann, and Walter Homolka; some articles are listed elsewhere.]

35325. FRIEDLANDER, ALBERT H.. Stegemann, Ekkehard W./Marcus, Marcel, eds.: *"Das Leben leise wieder lernen". Jüdisches und christliches Selbstverständnis nach der Schoah*. Festschrift für Albert H. Friedlander zum siebzigsten Geburtstag. Mit Beiträgen von Eberhard Bethge [et al.]. Stuttgart: Kohlhammer, 1997. 288 pp., frontis., notes., bibl. A.H. Friedlander (281–287). [Incl. 28 contribs. on A.H. Friedlander, Christian-Jewish encounters, Jewish theological issues and Leo Baeck.]

35326. GRAETZ, HEINRICH. Schlüter, Margarete: *Heinrich Graetzens "Konstruktion der Jüdischen Geschichte" – ein Gegenentwurf zum "Begriff einer Wissenschaft des Judenthums"?* [In]: Frankfurter Judaistische Beiträge, Jg. 24, Frankfurt am Main, Okt. 1997. Pp. 107–128, footnotes.

35328. HESCHEL, ABRAHAM JOSHUA. Heschel, Susannah, ed.: *Moral grandeur and spiritual audacity: essays*. New York: Farrar, Straus & Giroux, 1996. XXX, 428 pp., bibl. [First collection of his essays.]

35329. Hildesheimer, Meir: *The German language and secular studies: attitudes towards them in the thought of the Hatam Sofer and his disciples*. [In]: Proceedings of the American Academy for Jewish Research, Vol. 62, New York, 1996. Pp. 129–163, notes. [Hatam Sofer (R. Moses Sofer), 1763–1839, leader of Orthodox Jewry and Rabbi of Pressburg.]

35330. HIRSCH, SAMUEL. Brand, Gregor: *Samuel Hirsch: Der hochbegabte Nachfahre eines Hunsrücker Viehhändlers*. [In]: Kreis Bernkastel-Wittlich, Jahrbuch 1998, Wittlich, 1997. Pp. 365–367, notes. [On the scholar and Reform rabbi S.H., 1815 Thalfang – 1889 USA, rabbi in Dessau, the Grand Duchy of Luxemburg and, after 1866, in Philadelphia.]

35331. Jacob, Benno: *Das Buch Exodus*. Hrsg. im Auftrag des Leo Baeck Instituts von Shlomo Mayer unter Mitwirkung von Joachim Hahn und Almuth Jürgensen. Stuttgart: Calwer, 1997. XXV, 1098 pp. [First publ. of the magnum opus of one of the most outstanding biblical scholars of his time, written between 1935 and 1940. Incl.: Vorwort (Shlomo Mayer, VII–IX). "Dies wunderbare Buch". Zur deutschen Ausgabe des Exoduskommentars von Benno Jacob (Bernd Janowski/Almuth Jürgensen, XI–XXV). Benno Jacob – Eine Rekonstruktion (Julius Carlebach, XIX–XXV; on B.J.'s life). Bibliographisches Verzeichnis der Veröffentlichungen Benno Jacobs (Almuth Jürgensen, 1090–1098).] [B.J., 1862 Breslau – 1945 London, rabbi, biblical scholar.]

35332. Jonas, Hans: *Aktuelle ethische Probleme aus jüdischer Sicht*. [In]: Scheidewege. Jahresschrift für skeptisches Denken. Jg. 24, 1994/95. Baiersbronn, 1995. Pp. 3–15. [First publ. of essay written c. 1967 (transl. into German by R. Löw).]

35333. Kieval, Hillel J.: *Pursuing the Golem of Prague: Jewish culture and the invention of a tradition*. [In]: Modern Judaism, Vol. 17, No. 1, Baltimore, February 1997. Pp. 1–23, notes.

35334. Löwy, Michael: *Erlösung und Utopie. Jüdischer Messianismus und libertäres Denken*. Eine Wahlverwandtschaft. Aus dem Franz. von Dieter Kurz. Berlin: Karin Kramer, 1997. 303 pp., footnotes, bibl. Deutsche Erstausgabe. [Orig. publ. in 1988 with the title 'Redemption et utopie. Le judaisme libertaire en Europe centrale'. Incl. Martin Buber, Franz Rosenzweig,

Gershom Scholem, Franz Kafka, Walter Benjamin, Gustav Landauer, Ernst Bloch, Erich Fromm and others.]

35335. MAYBAUM, IGNAZ. *In memoriam: Ignaz Maybaum: (A commemoration of his 100th birthday).* [In]: European Judaism, Vol. 30, No. 2, London, Autumn 1997. Pp. 86–94, notes. [Two articles. by Michael Leigh and Albert H. Friedlander.]

35336. MENDELSSOHN, MOSES. HILFRICH-KUNJAPPU, CAROLA: *Facing cross-culturality. On cultures, scriptures and the face in Moses Mendelssohn's Jerusalem and Roland Barthes' Empire of the Signs*. [In]: Zwischen den Kulturen. Theorie und Praxis des interkulturellen Dialogs. Hrsg. von Carola Hilfrich-Kunjappu und Stéphane Mosès. Tübingen: Niemeyer, 1997. (Conditio Judaica, 20.). Pp. 127–142, footnotes.

35337. MENDELSSOHN, MOSES. KAPLAN, LAURENCE: *Supplementary notes on the medieval Jewish sources of Mendelssohn's 'Jerusalem'*. [In]: The Jewish Quarterly Review, Vol. 87, Nos. 3–4, Philadelphia, Jan.-April 1997. Pp. 339–342.

35338. MENDELSSOHN, MOSES. KRONAUER, ULRICH: *Moses Mendelssohns Glück der Grönländer.* [In]: Jüdischer Almanach 1998. Frankfurt am Main, 1997. Pp. 32–44. [On the problem of proselytising as seen by Mendelssohn and his contemporaries.]

35339. MENDELSSOHN, MOSES. LAUSCH, HANS: *Moses Mendelssohn: "Wir müssen uns auf Wahrscheinlichkeiten stützen"*. [In]: Acta Leopoldina, Nr. 27, Halle, 1997. Pp. 201–213, footnotes.

35340. MENDELSSOHN, MOSES. PORSTMANN, GISBERT: *Moses Mendelssohn. Porträts und Bilddokumente.* Stuttgart-Bad Cannstadt: Frommann-Holzboog, 1997. 401 pp., illus., ports., notes (351–375), index (382–392). Gesammelte Schriften. Jubiläumsausgabe, Bd. 24.) [Incl. portraits of Mendelssohn and his contemporaries; also pictures of landscapes and towns related to his life and work.]

35341. MENDES-FLOHR, PAUL: *Images of knowledge in modern Jewish thought*. [In]: Trumah, H. 6, Berlin, 1997. Pp. 93–106.

35342. SCHOLEM, GERSHOM. *The Germanic Review*, Vol. 72, No. 1 [with the issue title] *Gershom Scholem*. Ed. and with introd. by Willi Goetschel and Nils Roemer. Washington, DC, Winter 1997. 1 issue, notes. [Cont. (titles abbr.): Gershom Scholem: between mysticism and scholarship (Joseph Dan, 4–22). Gershom Scholem's studies of Jewish mysticism (Nils Roemer, 23–41). Gershom Scholem und die moderne Literatur (Thomas Sparr, 42–56). Gershom Scholem, Hannah Arendt, and the scandal of Jewish particularity (David Suchoff, 57–76). Review essay: Scholem's diaries, letters, and new literature on his work (Willi Goetschel, 77–92).]

35343. SCHOLEM, GERSHOM: *Judaica 6. Die Wissenschaft vom Judentum*. Hrsg., aus dem Hebr. und mit einem Nachwort versehen von Peter Schäfer in Zusammenarbeit mit Gerold Necker und Ulrike Hirschfelder. Frankfurt am Main: Suhrkamp, 1997. 110 pp. [Incl.: Überlegungen über die Wissenschaft vom Judentum (1994). Brief an Chajim Nachman Bialik (1925).] [Cf.: Selbstmörder, Totengräber und Alleinerben. Als die Rebellion zur Nachfolge degenerierte: Gershom Scholems polemische Überlegungen zur Wissenschaft des Judentums (Christoph Schulte) [in]: 'FAZ', Nr. 39, Frankfurt am Main, 16. Feb. 1998, p. 39.]

35344. SCHOLEM, GERSHOM. STEGEMANN, EKKEHARD W.: *Gershom Scholem: between exile and redemption*. [In]: European Judaism, Vol. 30, No. 2, London, Autumn 1997. Pp. 59–71, notes.

35345. SONNENFELD, CHAIM JOSEF. PIETSCH, WALTER: *Über die Wurzeln der Ultra-Orthodoxie im ungarischen Judentum.* Gestalt und Wirken von Rabbi Chaim Josef Sonnenfeld (geb. 1849 in Verbó/Ungarn, gest. 1932 in Jerusalem). [In]: Aschkenas, Jg. 7, H. 2, Wien, 1997. Pp. 453–466, footnotes.

35346. STRAUSS, LEO: *Jewish philosophy and the crisis of modernity: essays and lectures in modern Jewish thought.* Ed. and with an introd. by Kenneth Hart Green. Albany: State Univ. of New York Press, 1997. XVII, 505 pp. (SUNY series in the Jewish writings of Leo Strauss.)

35347. STRAUSS, LEO. NOVAK, DAVID, ed.: *Leo Strauss and Judaism: Jerusalem and Athens critically revisited.* Lanham, MD: Rowman & Littlefield, 1996. XVI, 200 pp., bibl. [Papers presented at a conference held at the University of Virginia in Charlottesville, Oct. 10–11, 1993.]

35348. STRAUSS, LEO. PLAX, MARTIN J.: *The appeal of Leo Strauss.* [In]: Midstream, Vol. 43, No. 6, New York, Aug./Sept. 1997. Pp. 11–14, notes.

35349. STRAUSS, LEO. SMITH, GREGORY BRUCE: *Who was Leo Strauss?* [In]: American Scholar, Washington DC, Winter 1997. Pp. 95–104.

35350. *Vom Jenseits. Jüdisches Denken in der europäischen Geistesgeschichte.* Hrsg. von Eveline Goodman-Thau. Berlin: Akademie Verlag, 1997. 249 pp., footnotes, index (239–245). [A collection of 13 papers given at a conference in Oldenburg, March 5–7, 1995. Selected essays: Die Lehre von der Unsterblichkeit der Seele in der Religionsphilosophie der Aufklärung (Daniel Krochmalnik, 79–108; refers also to Mendelssohn's views). Transzendenz und Utopie in Blochs Atheismus im Christentum (Horst Folkers, 109–128). Patriotismus und ethischer Unsterblichkeitsglaube: Hermann Cohen (Micha Brumlik, 129–143). Ewigkeit und Wahrheit. Die Messianische Erkenntnistheorie Rosenzweigs (Yehoyada Amir, 143–168). Transzendenz und Verantwortung. Margarete Susman im Dialog mit Nietzsche und der Tora (Ingeborg Nordmann, 169–178). Freud und das Jenseits (Rudolf Heinz, 215–224). Die Juden und das Geheimnis: Das Über-Leben des jüdischen Volkes (Manfred Voigts, 225–238).]

35351. WECHSLER, HILE. MORGENSTERN, MATTHIAS: *Hile Wechsler als Mystiker der jüdischen Einheit.* [In]: Frankfurter Judaistische Beiträge, Jg. 24, Frankfurt am Main, Okt. 1997. Pp. 51–106, footnotes. [Mosche Pinchas Elchanan Chajim "Hile" Wechsler (1843–1894), Orthodox talmudic scholar from Schwalbach, Franconia.]

35352. WEINBERG, DAVID H.: *Between tradition and modernity: Haim Zhitlowski, Simon Dubnow, Ahad Ha-Am, and the shaping of modern Jewish identity.* New York: Holmes and Meier, 1996. X, 385 pp., notes (304–351), bibl. (352–369).

35353. WERBLOWSKY, R.J. ZWI: *Magie, Mystik, Messianismus.* Vergleichende Studien zur Religionsgeschichte des Judentums und des Christentums. Hrsg. von Gary Smith in Zusammenarbeit mit Hermann Simon und Andreas Nachama. Hildesheim; New York: Olms, 1997. 272 pp., frontisp., bibl. (249–262), index (267–272). (Haskala, Bd. 3.) [Incl.: Über R.J. Zwi Werblowsky (Gary Smith, 7–12).]

35354. WISSENSCHAFT DES JUDENTUMS. MENDES-FLOHR, PAUL: *Wissenschaft des Judentums at the Fin-de-siècle.* [In]: Krisenwahrnehmungen im Fin de siécle. Jüdische und katholische Bildungseliten in Deutschland und der Schweiz [see No. 34914]. Pp. 67–82, footnotes.

35355. WISSENSCHAFT DES JUDENTUMS. SCHULIN, ERNST: *Zur Geschichte der Wissenschaft des Judentums.* [In]: Storia della Storiografia, No. 30, Milano, 1996. Pp. 135–139. [Review essay.]

35356. WISSENSCHAFT DES JUDENTUMS. SCHULTE, CHRISTOPH: *Über den Begriff einer Wissenschaft des Judentums. Die ursprüngliche Konzeption der Wissenschaft des Judentums und ihre Aktualität nach 175 Jahren.* [In]: Aschkenas, Jg. 7, H. 2, Wien, 1997. Pp. 277–302, footnotes.

35357. ZAFREN, HERBERT C.: *From Hochschule to Judaica Conservancy Foundation: the Guttmann affair.* [In]: Jewish Book Annual, Vol. 54, New York, 1996–1997. Pp. 44–65, appendix, notes. [Deals with the controversy about the attempt to auction rare Jewish mss. and books from the Berlin Hochschule für die Wissenschaft des Judentums brought to the US by Dr. Alexander Guttmann.]

B. Perception and Identity

35358. CELAN, PAUL. KOELLE, LYDIA: *Paul Celans pneumatisches Judentum: Gott-Rede und menschliche Existenz nach der Shoah.* Mainz: Matthias-Grünewald-Verlag, 1997. 434 pp., footnotes, bibl. (407–434). (Theologie und Literatur, 7: Religion und Ästhetik.) Zugl.: Bonn, Univ., Diss., 1995. [Deals with Celan's perceptions of 'Jewish' and his forms of expressing it, which he himself called 'pneumatic'.]

—— DÖBLIN, ALFRED. EUGSTER-ULMER, ROGER: *Döblins Konvertierung zum Christentum: Eine Verführung durch die Tropik der Sprache?* [See No. 35510.]

35359. FREEMAN, THOMAS: *Jewish identity and the Holocaust in Robert Schindel's 'Gebürtig'.* [In]: Modern Austrian Literature, Vol. 30, No. 1, Riverside, CA, 1997. Pp. 117–126, notes. [Deals with the Jewish "self-hatred" expressed in R. Sch.'s novel (see No. 30068/YBXXXVIII); also discusses responses to the book by German students.]

35360. GELLER, JAY: *Le péché contre le sang. La syphilis et la construction de l'identité juive.* Trad. de l'anglais par N. Robatel. [In]: Revue germanique internationale 5, Evry Cedex, 1996. Pp. 141–164.

—— GILLMAN, ABIGAIL E.: *Hofmannsthal's Jewish pantomime.* [See No. 35583.]

35361. GILMAN, SANDER L.: *You are what you eat. Fantasies of Jews, purity, and slaughter at the fin de siècle.* [In]: Zwischen den Kulturen. Theorie und Praxis des interkulturellen Dialogs. Hrsg. von Carola Hilfrich-Kunjappu und Stéphane Mosès. Tübingen: Niemeyer, 1997. (Conditio Judaica, 20.). Pp. 143–154, footnotes.

35362. GILMAN, SANDER L.: *Die Rolle von Zeugnis und Glauben im Prozess bei Franz Kafka und Arnold Zweig.* [In]: Zeitschrift für deutsche Philologie, Bd. 116, Berlin, 1997. Pp. 254–271, footnotes. [With German and English abstract. On the meaning of "Jewish" as perceived by both authors at the turn of the century.]

35363. GILMAN, SANDER L.: *Salome, Syphilis, Sarah Bernhardt und die "Moderne Jüdin".* [In]: Zeitschrift für Religions- und Geistesgeschichte, Jg. 49, H. 2, Leiden, 1997. Pp. 160–183, footnotes.

35364. GOLDSTEIN, MORITZ: *Texte zur jüdischen Selbstwahrnehmung aus dem Nachlaß.* Mit einer Einführung hrsg. von Elisabeth Albanis. [In]: Aschkenas, Jg. 7, H. 1, Wien, 1997. Pp. 79–136, footnotes.

35365. GOLEC, JANUSZ: *Jüdische Identitätssuche in Aaron Bernsteins Ghettogeschichte und Leopold Komperts Roman "Am Pflug".* [In]: Convivium. Germanistisches Jahrbuch Polen, Bonn, 1997. Pp. 167–180, footnotes.

35366. HERZOG, ANDREAS: *Zur Modernitätskritik und universalistischen Aspekten der "Jüdische Renaissance" in der deutschsprachigen Literatur zwischen Jahrhundertwende und 1918.* [In]: Trans, Zeitschrift für Kulturwissenschaften, Nr. 2, [Internet Periodical], Nov. 1997. 9 pp., notes. [On "German-Jewish" literature.]

35367. HERZOG, ANDREAS: *Die Mission des Übernationalen. Zur Judentumskonzeption einiger deutschsprachiger Schriftsteller.* [In]: Das jüdische Echo, Vol. 45, Wien, 1996. Pp. 155–161, illus., notes. [Deals with Alfred Wolfenstein, Lion Feuchtwanger, Albert Ehrenstein and Joseph Roth.]

35368. HIRSCH, WALTRAUD. *Eine unbescheidene Charakterologie. Geistige Differenz von Judentum und Christentum: Otto Weiningers Lehre vom bestimmten Charakter.* Frankfurt am Main: Lang, 1997. 414 pp., footnotes., docs., facsims., bibl. (355–413). (Tübinger Beiträge zur Religionswissenschaft, Bd.3.) Zugl.: Tübingen, Univ., Diss., 1995. [Incl. also letters and other documents related to O.W.'s life and work.]

35369. JOHN, HEIDE: *Jüdischer Selbsthaß. Ein psychopathologisches Phänomen.* [In]: Tribüne, Jg. 36, H. 142, Frankfurt am Main, 1997. Pp. 145–158.

35370. *Jüdische Selbstwahrnehmung. La prise de conscience de l'identité juive.* Hrsg. von Hans Otto Horch, Charlotte Wardi. Tübingen: Niemeyer, 1997. 292 pp., footnotes, index (285–292). (Conditio Judaica, 19.) [Papers given at a conference in Luxembourg, Oct. 2–6, 1994. Cont.: Vorwort (eds., IX–XIII). Conférence d'ouverture (Claude Vigée, 1–13; on growing up as a Jew in Alsace). Zum Problem der jüdischen Identität (Heinrich Simon, 16–25). Die Faszination des Hasses. Das Verhältnis von Juden und Christen in Deutschland. Ein Versuch (Hans Keilson, 27–43). Die jüdische Orthodoxie in Deutschland zwischen Westen und Osten (Mordechai Breuer, 45–54). Dezisionismus – Zionismus – Thedaismus. Zum Potential eines genuin jüdischen Aufbruchs (Gerhard Biller, 55–76). Du refus au ressourcement. Problèmes identitaires juifs en France (1894–1939) (Jacques Eladan, 77–81). Varianten jüdischer Selbstwahrnehmung in Ungarn (Péter Varga, 83–98). Der Wandel weiblichen Selbstverständnisses in den Lebenszeugnissen jüdischer Frauen (Monika Richarz, 99–110). Zum Selbstverständnis jüdischer Jugend in der Weimarer Republik und unter der nationalsozialistischen Diktatur (Arnold Paucker, 111–128). Jüdische Selbstwahrnehmung. Zum Selbstverständnis des deutsch-jüdischen Großbürgertums (Werner E. Mosse, 129–135). 'Between class and nation'. Jewish workers in Amsterdam, London and Paris, 1880–1914 (Karin Hofmeester, 137–147). Jewish self-perception as shown in English literature and art (Pauline Paucker, 149–160). Proust et la judéité: les destins croisés de Swann et de Bloch (Henri Raczymow, 161–167). Dreyfus in Deutschland. Zur Rezeption der Dreyfus-Affäre (Thomas Sparr, 169–180). Jüdische Expressionisten: Identität im Aufbruch – Leben "im Aufschub" (Hanni Mittelmann, 181–194). "Geborene Schauspieler" – Das jüdische Theater des Ostens und die Theaterdebatte im deutschen Judentum (Hans-Peter Bayerdörfer, 195–215). Hermann Cohen – Kantische Vernunft und jüdisches Selbstbewußtsein (Christoph Miething, 217–229). Edmond Fleg – témoin engagé de son temps (Emmanuel Bulz, 231–238). André Spire et la conscience juive (Marie-Brunette Spire, 239–249). Joseph Bloch (1871–1936). Ein Vorkämpfer der deutsch-französischen Freundschaft im Zeitalter des Rationalismus (Walter Grab, 251–262). "Deines Tores Gold schmilzt an meiner Sehnsucht." Else Lasker-Schülers Hebräische Balladen (Norbert Oellers, 263–274; first publ. 1995). Einige Bemerkungen zur Bedeutung der Sprache bei Kafka, dem Juden (Tuvia Rübner, 275–284).]

35371. LAMPE, EVELYN: *"Aus ihren eigenen Eingeweiden erzeigt die bürgerliche Gesellschaft fortwährend den Juden"*. Antijüdische Stereotypen in Karl Marx' 'Zur Judenfrage'. [In]: Historische Stereotypenforschung. Methodische Überlegungen und empirische Befunde. Hrsg. von Hans Henning Hahn. Oldenburg: Bis, 1995. (Oldenburger Schriften zur Geschichtswissenschaft, H. 2.) Pp. 116–129.

35372. LE RIDER, JACQUES: *Jüdische Identität in Freuds 'Der Mann Moses und die monotheistische Religion'*. [In]: Literatur und Kritik, H. 317, Salzburg, 1997. Pp. 25–32.

35373. NIEWYK, DONALD L.: *Self-defence and German-Jewish identities.* Comments on the papers by Michael Berkowitz, Francis R. Nicosia and Marjorie Lamberti. [In]: Leo Baeck Institute Year Book XLII, London, 1997. Pp. 149–153. [Discusses the papers presented at the Annual Meeting of the American Historical Association in Atlanta, GA, Jan. 5, 1996; see Nos. 35111, 35401, 35419.]

35374. RIEKER, YVONNE: *Kindheiten. Identitätsmuster im deutsch-jüdischen Bürgertum und unter ostjüdischen Einwanderern 1871–1933.* Hildesheim; New York: Olms, 1997. 161 pp., footnotes, bibl. (139–160), index. (Haskala, Bd. 17.) Zugl.: Potsdam, Univ., Diss., 1995. [Analyses 84 publ. memoirs and 34 interviews.]

35375. ROHRWASSER, MICHAEL: *"Der Schädel des Negerhäuptlings Makaua". Das Thema des Antisemitismus im Werk Rudolf Franks.* [In]: Convivium. Germanistisches Jahrbuch Polen 1997, Bonn, 1997. Pp. 181–198, footnotes. [R.F., Mainz 1886 – Basel 1979, writer, stage director, emigr. to Austria in 1936, to Switzerland 1938.]

35376. SAUERLAND, KAROL: *"Das ostjüdische Antlitz" in den Augen von Gustav Landauer, Arnold Zweig, Alfred Döblin und Joseph Roth.* [In]: Convivium, Germanistisches Jahrbuch Polen, Bonn, 1996. Pp. 107–132, footnotes.

35377. SHAPIRO, SUSAN E.: *The uncanny Jew: a brief history of an image.* [In]: Judaism, Vol. 46, No. 1, New York, Winter 1997. Pp. 63–78. [Deals with the depiction of the 'uncanny Jew' in the works of Eduard Gans, Heinrich Heine, Moses Mendelssohn; also on Karl Gutzkow's view of the Jews as a tragic race in terms of a prolonged but outdated existence.]

35378. TREUFUß-SCHALENBECK, BIANCA: *Varianten jüdischer Identitätsentwürfe im Spiegel der Wohnkultur von Emigrantinnen und Emigranten.* Tiefensemiotische und biosoziologische Beobachtungen anhand realer und fiktionaler Räume. [In]: Staffagen. Diskurs über Sprache und Geschichte. Hrsg.: Hermann Schäflich [et al.]. Königswinter: Philo-Klio, 1997. Pp. 17–39.

C. Jewish Life and Organisations. Genealogy

35379. BECHTEL, DELPHINE: *Cultural transfers between "Ostjuden" and "Westjuden". German-Jewish intellectuals and Yiddish culture 1897–1930.* [In]: Leo Baeck Institute Year Book XLII, London, 1997. Pp. 67–83, footnotes. [Deals with the reception of Yiddish literature among German-Jewish writers and intellectuals.]

35380. BRENNER, DAVID A.: *"Making Jargon respectable". Leo Winz, Ost und West and the reception of Yiddish theatre in pre-Hitler Germany.* [In]: Leo Baeck Institute Year Book XLII, London, 1997. Pp. 51–66, footnotes. [Focuses on Berlin Yiddish theatre productions as reflected in 'Ost und West', publ. by Leo Winz.]

35381. GOLDMANN, CHRISTINA: *Selbstbesinnung und Opposition: der Centralverein deutscher Staatsbürger jüdischen Glaubens im Vergleich mit der Reichsvertretung der deutschen Juden 1928–1935.* Trier: MA-Thesis [Typescript], 1996. III, 215 pp., docs., bibl. (185–203). [Available at the Bibliothek Germania Judaica, Cologne.]

—— GOTZMANN, ANDREAS: *Koscher und Trefe. Die Veränderungen der religiösen Praxis im Deutschland des 19. Jahrhunderts.* [See in No. 34942.]

35382. HACOHEN, RAN: *Die Bibel kehrt heim. "Biblische Geschichte" für Kinder.* [In]: Kinder- und Jugendliteraturforschung 1996/97. Hrsg. von Hans-Heino Ewers [et al.]. Stuttgart: Metzler, 1997. Pp. 9–21, footnotes, bibl. [On the beginnings of children's Hebrew biblical reading books with Aron Wolfsohn's 'Abtalion' (1790) and David Samosc's 'Nahar me-Eden' (1837).]

35383. *Jews and Medicine, religion, culture, science.* Ed. by Natalia Berger. Based on the exhibit at Beth Hatefutsoth, the Nahum Goldmann Museum of the Jewish Diaspora. Philadelphia: The Jewish Publication Society, 1997. 275 pp., chiefly illus., ports., facsims., engravings, notes. [Incl. the Nazi era.]

35384. KASPER-HOLTKOTTE, CILLI: *Jüdischer Kultus in napoleonischer Zeit: Aufbau und Organisation der Konsistorialbezirke Krefeld, Koblenz/Bonn, Trier und Mainz.* Wien: Böhlau, 1997. 146 pp. (Aschkenas, Beih. 2.)

35385. LEVINE, GLENN S.: *Yiddish publishing in Berlin and the crisis in Eastern European Jewish culture 1919–1924.* [In]: Leo Baeck Institute Year Book XLII, London, 1997. Pp. 85–108, footnotes, tabs. [Incl. appendixes: numbers of Yiddish titles by publishers and year, classification of titles and bibliography of Yiddish books and periodicals publ. 1919–1931.]

35386. *Maajan – Die Quelle.* Zeitschrift für jüdische Familienforschung. Organ der Hamburger Gesellschaft für jüdische Genealogie [und der] Schweizerischen Vereinigung für jüdische Genealogie. Jg. 11, H. 41–45, 1997. 4 issues. [H. 44 incl.: Auf den Spuren des Malers Ferdinand Heilbut (Helga Heilbut, 1113–1115). H. 45 incl.: Sefardische Grabinschriften aus Norddeutschland als genealogische Quelle (Michael Studemund-Halévy, 1173–1177). For further contrib. see No. 34883.]

35387. *Mappot. "Gesegnet, der da kommt!" Das Band der jüdischen Tradition/Mappot. "Blessed be who comes!" The band of Jewish tradition.* Hrsg. von Annette Weber, Evelyn Friedlander [et al.].

[Verantw.: The Hidden Legacy Foundation, London; Prähist. Staatssammlung, München]. Transl.: Evelyn Friedlander [et al.]. Osnabrück: Secolo, 1997. 223 pp., illus., bibl. [Text in English and German; on Tora Mantles from Germany.]

35388. PLAUT, ELIZABETH S.: *The Guggenheim/Wormser family: a genealogical 300-year memoir.* Hoboken, NJ: KTAV Publ. House, 1996. X, 237 pp., geneal. tabs., bibl. [Families orig. came from Aldingen, Württemberg, and Worms, and settled in America in Pittsburgh, San Francisco, and Petersburg, VA.]

35389. *Quellen zur Alltagsgeschichte der Deutschen 1871–1914.* Hrsg. von Jans Flemming [et al.]. Darmstadt: Wiss. Buchges., 1997. XLVI, 272 pp., footnotes, indexes (253–272). [Incl. the section: 4. Jüdische Identität, Assimilation, Antisemitismus (82–91).]

35390. *Stammbaum.* The Journal of German-Jewish Genealogical Research. Issue 11 & 12. New York: Leo Baeck Institute, June & Dec. 1997. [Issue 11 (32 pp.). Guest editor: George E. Arnstein. Incl.: Hohenems: rise and fall, marital ties and migration (George E. Arnstein, 1–7). Issue 12 (32 pp.). Guest editor George E. Arnstein. Incl.: Dropping names: Jente Hameln and her distinguished descendants (E. Irene Newhouse, 1–7). First issue publ. in Winter 1992–93 with the title 'Stammbaum. Ahnenforschung in Aschkenas. The Newsletter of German-Jewish Genealogical Research' in Winter Springs, FL, by Harry Katzman. Issue No. 10 publ. Dec. 1996. From June 1997 (Issue 11) affiliated with the LBI New York. Cont. contribs. on German-Jewish genealogy, archival collections, bibliographical information, book reviews and reports on conferences and special events.]

35391. STEPPE, HILDE: "... *Den Kranken zum Troste und dem Judenthum zur Ehre...*". *Zur Geschichte der jüdischen Krankenpflege in Deutschland.* Frankfurt am Main: Mabuse, 1997. 396 pp., illus., bibl. (317–362), docs. (365–392). (Reihe Wissenschaft, Bd. 34.) [Cf.: Besprechung (Hubert Kolling) [in]: Zeitschrift für Geschichtswissenschaft, Jg. 46, H. 5, Berlin, 1998, pp. 453–455.]

35392. ZUNTZ (ZUNZ) FAMILY. LEHMANN-BRUNE, MARLIES: *Der Koffer des Karl Zuntz. Fünf Jahrhunderte einer jüdischen Familie.* Düsseldorf: Droste, 1997. 279 pp., illus., facsims., family trees, bibl. (266–274), index. [On a family originating from Zons, Rheinland; incl. Leopold Zunz; the coffee company Berlin-Bonn 'A. Zuntz sel. Wwe.'; Nathan Zuntz.]

D. Jewish Art and Music

35393. MEEK, HAROLD A.: *Die Synagoge.* Ins Deutsche übertragen von Sieglinde Denzel [et al.]. München: Knesebeck, 1996. 240 pp., illus., bibl. [Orig. publ. in 1995. On synagogal art and architecture. Incl. synagogues in Germany.]

35394. SCHUBERT, URSULA: *Hebräische Buchmalerei von der Gotik bis zum Barock.* [In]: David, Jg. 9, Nr. 33, Wien, Juni 1997. Pp. 3–5, illus.

35395. SILBERMANN, ALPHONS: *Von Juden oder für Juden. Über jüdische Musik.* [In]: Tribüne, Jg. 36, H. 144, Frankfurt am Main, 1997. Pp. 166–168.

35396. STAVISKY, NELLIE/EVETTS, DEBORAH: *The conservation and rebinding of the 'New Amsterdam' Esslingen Mahzor.* [In]: Studia Rosenthaliana, Vol. 31, No. 1/2, Assen, 1997. Pp. 152–167, footnotes. [On the earliest Hebrew manuscript in Germany, dating from 1290.]

35397. *Die Von Geldern Haggadah und Heinrich Heines "Der Rabbi von Bacherach".* Hrsg. von Emile G.L. Schrijver und Falk Wiesemann. Mit Beirägen von Gert Kaiser [et al.]. Wien: Brandstätter, 1997. 80 pp, facsims.: 26 pp., illus., notes. [Incl.: Vorwort (Gert Kaiser, 7–10). Geleitwort der Herausgeber (Emile G.L. Schrijver/Falk Wiesemann, 11–12). Die religionsgeschichtliche Bedeutung der Pessach-Haggadah (Edward van Voolen, 13–18). Die 'Von Geldern Haggadah' – Odysse eines jüdischen Kunstwerks (Falk Wiesemann, 19–27; on the tracing of a Haggadah, once owned by Heine's ancestors, to its present owner in the US). Die 'Von Geldern Haggadah' und die jüdische Buchillustration des 18. Jahrhunderts (Emile G.L. Schrijver, 28–36). Der Ursprung der deutsch-jüdischen Literatur in Heinrich Heines 'Der

Rabbi von Bacherach' (Bernd Witte, 37–48). 'Der Rabbi von Bacherach'. (Ein Fragment.) (Heinrich Heine, 49–64). 'Die Pesach-Hagada'. Übersetzung aus dem Hebräischen (1839) (65–80). Die Von Geldern Haggadah (26 pp.; the complete facsimile reproduction of the Haggadah manuscript of Moses Leib from Trebitsch, Vienna, early 18th cent.).] [Cf.: Besprechung (Abraham Frank) [in]: 'MB', Jg. 66, Nr. 135, Tel Aviv, März-April 1998, pp. 1–2. Das Heil auf den Kopf gestellt. Heinrich Heine und die Pessach-Haggadah seines Urgroßvaters (Jakob Hessing) [in]: 'FAZ', Nr. 262, Frankfurt am Main, 11. Nov. 1997, p. 42.]

VI. ZIONISM AND ISRAEL

35398. AUERBACH, ELIAS: *Pionier der Verwirklichung*. [Hebrew title, transl.]. Jerusalem: Leo Baeck Institute Jerusalem, 1997. 364 pp., illus. [Orig. publ. in German in 1969, see No. 7861/YB XV.] [E.A., physician, data see No. 26702/YB XXXV.]

35399. BAUMEL, JUDITH TYDOR: *Bridging myth and reality: the absorption of She'erit Hapletah in Eretz Yisrael, 1945–1948*. [In]: Middle Eastern Studies, Vol. 33, No. 2, London, April 1997. Pp. 362–372. [Tells the story of how members of Kibbutz Buchenwald came to Israel and joined Kibbutz Afikim in the Jordan Valley.]

35400. BERKOWITZ, MICHAEL: *Zion's cities. Projections of urbanism and German-Jewish self-consciousness, 1909–1933*. [In]: Leo Baeck Institute Year Book XLII, London, 1997. Pp. 11–121, illus., footnotes. [See also No. 35373.]

35401. BERKOWITZ, MICHAEL: *Western Jewry and the Zionist project, 1914–1933*. Cambridge; New York: Cambridge Univ. Press, 1997. XVI, 305, illus., notes (201–265), bibl. (266–291). [Incl. German-Jewish attitudes to and involvement with early Zionism, incl. settlements, youth movements (Blau-Weiss); also Einstein's role and interest.]

35402. BODENHEIMER, ALFRED: *Zwischen Sehnsucht und Rückkehr. Exil und Eretz Israel – eine Geschichte in Texten*. [In]: Jüdischer Almanach 1998, Frankfurt am Main, 1997. Pp. 126–137.

35403. *Der Erste Zionistenkongress von 1897 – Ursachen, Bedeutung, Aktualität*. Hrsg. von Heiko Haumann. In Zusammenarbeit mit Peter Haber [et al.]. Basel; New York: Karger, 1997. XII, 402 pp., illus., facsims., footnotes, gloss., bibl. 385–395), index (396–400). [Also publ. in English with the title 'The First Zionist Congress in 1897 – causes, significance, topicality'. Cont. more than 90 contribs. arranged under the following sections: Einführung (2–23). Voraussetzungen und Anfänge des Zionismus (24–126). Der Erste Zionistenkongress von 1897 in Basel (128–165). Porträts zionistischer Persönlichkeiten (166–174). Juden in Basel und in der Region: Ihre Lage und die Anfänge des Zionismus (176–242; also on Jews in Alsace and Baden). Die Folgen des Ersten Zionistenkongresses bis zur Staatsgründung Israels (244–334). Die Aktualität des Zionismus – ein Ausblick (335–374).]

35404. GOLDSTEIN, SANDRA: *Intellektuelle Utopien. Arthur Koestler und der Zionismus*. [In]: Jüdischer Almanach 1998, Frankfurt am Main, 1997. Pp. 158–169, port.

35405. GOODMAN-THAU, EVELINE: *"Immer bleibe ein Mensch". Ein Gespräch mit Chaim Cohn*. [In]: Jüdischer Almanach 1998, Frankfurt am Main, 1997. Pp. 170–185. [Chaim (orig. Hermann) Cohn, former Justice Minister and High Court Judge in Israel, b. 1911 in Lübeck, went to Palestine in 1930. His book 'Der Prozeß und Tod Jesu aus jüdischer Sicht' was publ. (in German) in 1997.]

35406. HACKESCHMIDT, JÖRG: *Von Kurt Blumenfeld zu Norbert Elias. Die Erfindung einer jüdischen Nation*. Hamburg: Europäische Verlagsanstalt, 1997. 374 pp., notes (275–326), appendix (327–342), bibl. (343–369), index (370–374). [Deals with the Blau-Weiß, Kurt Blumenfeld and Felix Rosenblüth; the early involvement with the Zionist movement, youth culture and their leading intellectual advocates: Norbert Elias, Martin Bandmann, Leo Löwenthal, Erich Fromm, Hans Jonas, Leo Strauss and others from the First World War to 1925.] [See also No. 35522.] [Cf.: Besprechung (Anne Chr. Nagel) [in]: Zeitschrift für Geschichtswissenschaft, Jg. 46, Nr. 5, Berlin, 1998, pp. 465–467.]

35407. HAUMANN, HEIKO, ed.: *The First Zionist Congress in 1897 – causes, significance, topicality*. '. . . In Basel I have founded the Jewish State'. Basel: S. Karger, 1997. XII, 402 pp., illus., notes.

35408. HERZL, THEODOR. ALMOG, SHMUEL: *Herzl writes home*. [In]: Jewish History, Vol. 11, No. 2, Haifa, Fall 1997. Pp. 111–115. [Deals with Herzl's letters and diaries.]

35409. HERZL, THEODOR. HEID, LUDGER: *"Wenn ihr wollt, ist es kein Märchen"*. *Theodor Herzl – Wegbereiter des politischen Zionismus*. [In]: Tribüne, Jg. 36, H. 142, Frankfurt am Main, 1997. Pp. 134–144. [Also, by same author: Der schönste Mann. Ein Portrait des Dandys und Kämpfers Theodor Herzl [in] Die Zeit, Nr. 36, Hamburg, 29. Aug. 1997, p. 50.]

35410. HERZL, THEODOR. HEID, LUDGER: *Theodor Herzl – Wegbereiter des Zionismus: "Wenn Ihr wollt, ist es kein Märchen"*. [In]: Damals, H. 6, Stuttgart, 1996. Pp. 20–25, illus.

35411. HERZL, THEODOR. SABLER, WOLFGANG: *Theodor Herzl – Das Neue Ghetto*. Antisemitismus und Dramaturgie. [In]: Aspekte des politischen Theaters und Dramas von Calderón bis Georg Seidel. Hrsg. von Horst Turk [et al.]. Bern: Lang, 1996. Pp. 229–254.

35412. HERZL, THEODOR. SCHOEPS, JULIUS H.: *Theodor Herzl and the Zionist dream*. [American edn. under the title: *Theodor Herzl: a biography*.] Transl. from the German by Annemarie and Francis Clark. London: Thames and Hudson; New York: Wiley, 1997. 223 pp., 354 illus., ports., facsims., maps, bibl. (215–227). [For orig. German edn. see No. 33232/YB XLI.] [Cf.: How Herzl took the lead: causes and concequences of the first Congress of Zionism in Basle (David Vital) [in]: TLS, London, Aug. 29, 1997, pp. 15–16. Herzl's dream (Melvin I. Urofsky) [in]: Midstream, Vol. 53, No. 9, New York, Dec. 1997, pp. 7–10, notes.]

35413. HERZL, THEODOR. *Theodor Herzl: if you will it, it is not a dream*. New York: Yeshiva Univ. Museum, 1997. 108 pp., illus., ports., facsims. [Catalogue publ. in connection with the exhibition held at the Yeshiva Univ. Museum, April 6, 1997 – July 31, 1998, to commemorate the centenary of the first Zionist Congress and the 50th anniversary of the establishment of the State of Israel.] [Cf.: Theodor Herzl: between journalism and politics (Robert S. Wistrich) [in]: Midstream, Vol. 43, No. 4, New York, May 1997, pp. 21–24, notes. Herzl's devotees and detractors: a gallery of profiles (Joseph Adler) [in]: Midstream, Vol. 43, No. 5, New York, June/July 1997, pp. 27–30.]

—— HEUER, RENATE/WUTHENOW, RALPH-RAINER, eds.: *Antisemitismus – Zionismus – Antizionismus 1850–1940*. [See No. 35826.]

35414. HEUMANN, PIERRE: *Israel entstand in Basel. Die phantastische Geschichte einer Vision*. Zürich: Weltwoche, 1997. 238 pp., illus., bibl. (232–238). [On the First Zionist Congress in Basle 1897 and why the congress did not take place in Munich.]

35415. *Israelitisches Wochenblatt* Jg. 34, Nr. 34 [with the issue title] *100 Jahre Zionismus*. Basel, 22. Aug. 1997. 1 issue. [Incl. contribs. on Theodor Herzl, Zionism and the First Zionist Congress, Zionist women participating at the Congress, Theodor Hertzka, Nathan Birnbaum, Isaac Breuer, Jewish opposition to Zionism, Eastern Jews in Basle, Ahron Marcus by Yizhak Ahren, Alfred Bodenheimer, Dieter Frei, Roland Gradwohl, Heiko Haumann, Pierre Heumann, Patrik Kury, Marcel Marcus, Samuel Scheps, Bettina Zeugin.]

35416. KELEMEN, PAUL: *In the name of Socialism: Zionism and European Social Democracy in the inter-war years*. [In]: International Review of Social History, Vol. 41, part 1, Cambridge, April 1996. Pp. 331–350, footnotes. [Deals with the increase in the number of Jewish refugees from Nazi persecution and the effects on the interaction between Social Democrats and Zionists, also in Germany.]

35417. LOEWY, ERNST: *Jugend in Palästina. Briefe an die Eltern 1925–1938.* Hrsg. von Brita Eckert. Berlin: Metropol, 1997. 243 pp., illus., gloss., bibl. (Bibliothek der Erinnerung, Bd. 4.) [Incl.: Einführung (ed., 7–31; on the author and his family; also on Palestine and Youth Aliya. Nachwort (Ernst Loewy, 220–228).] [Cf.: Besprechung (Hans Otto Horch) [in]: Aschkenas, Jg. 8, H. 1. Wien, 1998, pp. 225–226.] [E. L., data see No. 33506/YB XVI.]

35418. NA'AMAN, SHLOMO: *Marxismus und Zionismus.* Gerlingen: Bleicher, 1997. 259 pp., frontis., footnotes, index. (Schriftenreihe des Instituts für Deutsche Geschichte, Univ. Tel-Aviv, 17.). [Author, who died in 1993, analyses the attitude of Karl Marx, Marxism and Leninism towards Judaism and the "Jewish Question" as seen from a Marxist and especially from a Socialist-Zionist viewpoint. The unfinished book was completed and edited by Shulamit Volkov.] [Cf.: Besprechung (Arno Herzig) [in]: Aschkenas, Jg. 8, H. 1, Wien, 1998, pp. 249–251.]

35419. NICOSIA, FRANCIS R.: *Resistance and self-defence. Zionism and antisemitism in inter-war Germany.* [In]: Leo Baeck Institute Year Book XLII, London, 1997. Pp. 123–134, footnotes. [See also No. 35373.]

35420. NORDAU, MAX. PENSLAR, DEREK JONATHAN: *From 'conventional lies' to convential myths: Max Nordau's approach to Zionism* [In]: History of European Ideas, Vol. 2, No. 3, London, 1996. Pp. 217–226, notes.

35421. STONE, LILO: *German Zionists in Palestine before 1933.* [In]: Journal of Contemporary History, Vol. 32, No. 2, London, 1997. Pp. 171–186, notes.

——— *Wandlungen und Brüche. Von Herzls "Welt" zur Illustrierten Neuen Welt" 1897–1997.* [See No. 34896.]

35422. WARHAFTIG, MYRA: *Sie legten den Grundstein. Leben und Wirken deutschsprachiger jüdischer Architekten in Palästina 1918–1948.* Tübingen: Wasmuth, 1996. 394 pp., illus. [Portraits of 47 architects. Incl. short biographies of another 67.]

——— WISTRICH, ROBERT S.: *Zionism and its religious critics in fin-de-siècle Vienna.* [See No. 34859.]

35423. WISTRICH, ROBERT: *Israel and the Holocaust trauma.* [In]: Jewish History, Vol. 11, No. 2, Haifa, Fall 1997. Pp. 13–20, notes.

35424. WUNSCH, BEATE/JAEGER, ACHIM/HORCH, HANS OTTO: *"Die Macht der vollendeten Thatsachen". Die deutsch-jüdische Presse und der Erste Basler Zionistenkongreß.* [In]: Jüdischer Almanach 1998, Frankfurt am Main, 1997. Pp. 138–157.

VII. PARTICIPATION IN CULTURAL AND PUBLIC LIFE

A. General

35425. FISCHER, GERHARD/HAMANN, CHRISTOPH [et al.]: *Die Eule läßt Federn. Das Ullstein-Haus 1926–1986.* Drucker, Setzer, Journalisten. In Zusammenarbeit mit der Industriegewerkschaft Medien, Bezirk Berlin. Berlin: Trafo Verlag, 1997 [?]. 279 pp. [First part of book deals with the Ullstein family and the frequent antisemitic attacks on the publishing and printing house and its numerous Jewish journalists.] [Cf.: Besprechung (Kurt Schilde) [in]: IWK, Int. wiss. Korrespondenz zur Gesch. der deutschen Arbeiterbewegung, H. 2, Berlin, 1997, pp. 293–294.]

35426. BEHR, SHULAMITH: *Jewish women and Expressionism: artists, patrons and dealers.* [In]: Issues in the Theory and Practice of Architecture, Art and Design, Vol. 7, London, 1997. Pp. 99–114, illus., notes. [On Olga Oppenheimer, Elsa Lasker-Schüler, Rosa Schapire, Rosy Fischer.]

35427. BODOFF, LIPPMAN: *The Court Jew in the modern world.* [In]: Midstream, Vol. 43, No. 7, New York, Oct. 1997. Pp. 6–9. [Incl. Mayer Amschel Rothschild and Joseph Süss Oppenheimer.]

35428. CALIMANI, RICCARDO: *I destini e le avventure dell'Intellettuale ebreo*. Milano: Mondadori, 1997. 768 pp. [On Jewish intellectuals in Vienna, Prague, Triest and Berlin.]

35429. ERLER, HANS/EHRLICH, ERNST LUDWIG/HEID, LUDGER, eds.: *"Meinetwegen ist die Welt erschaffen". Das intellektuelle Vermächtnis des deutschsprachigen Judentums*. 58 Porträts. Frankfurt am Main; New York: Campus, 1997. 555 pp., notes, index. [Cont. (titles abbr.): Einführung (Hans Erler, 11–22). Martin Buber (Ernst Ludwig Ehrlich, 25–40). Sigmund Freud (Hanna Gekle, 41–52). Leo Baeck (Edna Brocke, 53–58). Franz Rosenzweig (Paul Mendes-Flohr, 59–65). Ludwig Wittgenstein (Fritz Wallner, 66–71). Regina Jonas (Rachel Monika Herwig, 72–77). Hans Jonas (Franz Josef Wetz, 78–83). Karl Popper (Manfred Geier, 87–101). Hermann Cohen (Margret Heitmann (102–111). Edmund Husserl (Karl Schuhmann, 112–117). Margarete Susman (Ingeborg Nordmann, 118–121). Ernst Bloch (Jan Robert Bloch, 122–128). Helmut Plessner (Khosrow Nosratian, 129–135). Jeanne Hersch (Annemarie Pieper, 136–140). Erich Fromm (Rainer Funk, 143–164). Iwan Bloch (Erwin J. Haeberle, 165–172). Magnus Hirschfeld (Rainer Herrn, 173–178). Melanie Klein (Elisabeth Vorspohl, 179–184). Helene Deutsch (Inge Stephan, 185–190). Margarete Berent (Hiltrud Häntzschel, 191–196). René A. Spitz (Gerd Biermann, 197–202), Alice Rühle-Gerstel (Norbert Abels, 203–211). Charlotte Wolff (Gisela Bleibtreu-Ehrenberg, 212–218). Wilhelm Reich (Bernd A. Laska, 219–222). Hans Weil (Hildegard Feidel-Mertz, 223–228). Erik H. Erikson (Peter Conzen, 229–233). Gisela Konopka (Hildegard Feidel-Mertz, 234–238). Theodor W. Adorno (Hauke Runkhorst, 241–257). Siegfried Kracauer (Gertrud Koch, 258–261). Walter Benjamin (Peter Kleeberger, 262–267). Karl Mannheim (Heinz Abels, 268–275). Max Horkheimer (Oskar Negt, 276–278). Eva Gabriele Reichmann (Arnold Paucker, 279–284). Herbert Marcuse (Micha Brumlik, 285–290). Hugo Preuss (Dian Schefold, 294–310). Eduard Bernstein (Helga Grebing, 311–314). Helene Simon (Hans Pfaffenberger, 315–323). Hugo Sinzheimer (Hans-Peter Benöhr, 324–332). Hans Kelsen (Robert Walter, 333–339). Toni (Tony) Sender (Anette Hild-Berg, 340–344). Hermann Heller (Christoph Müller, 345–361). Robert M.W. Kempner (Ingo Müller, 362–368). Franz Oppenheimer (Dieter Haselbach, 371–393). Rudolf Hilferding (Alfred Pfabigan, 394–400). Ludwig von Mises (Karl Milford, 401–407). Emil Lederer (Hans Ulrich Esslinger, 408–414). Friedrich Pollock (Peter Kalmbach, 415–419). Adolph Lowe (Harald Hagemann, 420–425). Hannah Arendt (Wolfgang Heuer, 429–445). Albert Einstein (Ulrich Charpa, 446–453). Jeannette Wolff (Ludger Heid, 454–462). Käthe Leichter (Marina Sassenberg, 463–468). Norbert Elias (Michael Schröter, 469–474). Ernst Fraenkel (Gerhard Göhler, 475–485). Franz L. Neumann (Andreas Fisahn, 486–491). Günther Anders (Elke Schubert, 492–497). Robert Jungk (Hans Holzinger, 498–504). Gerda Lerner (Barbara Schaeffer-Hegel, 505–512). Statt eines Nachworts: Zivilisationsbruch, Gegenrationalität, gestaute Zeit – Drei interpretationsleitende Begriffe zum Holocaust (Dan Diner, 513–520). Politik und Angst – Konkrete Utopie für das 21. Jahrhundert (Hans Erler, 521–525).]

35430. EXILE. *Ariadne*. Almanach des Archivs der deutschen Frauenbewegung. Heft 32 [with the issue title] *Exil – Emigration*, Kassel, Nov. 1997. 1 issue, illus., facsims., notes. [Incl.: Bleiben oder Gehen? Die Diskussion um Auswanderung im Jüdischen Frauenbund in den Jahren 1933 bis 1938 (Gudrun Maierhof, 8–14). "Frieden ohne Freiheit ist ein Schwindel". Anita Augspurg und Lida Gustava Heymann – Leben und Politk im Exil (Amira Gelblum, 26–32). Dokumentation. Asylrecht: Ninth Congress of the 'Women's International League for Peace and Freedom', Luhacovice, 1937 (33). Die "dritte Generation" der Frauenbewegung. Pädagoginnen und Sozialarbeiterinnen im Exil (Hildegard Feidel-Mertz (36–43). Von Berlin ins Exil nach Barcelona. Etta Federn (1883–1951) und die archosyndikalistische Frauenbewegung in Deutschland und Spanien zwischen 1920 und 1938 (Marianne Kröger, 44–50). Dokumentation. Anna Seghers: Frauen in der Emigration (51–53). Das Exil als Falle. Vier Frauen auf der Flucht vor Hitler und Stalin (Sabine Hering, 54–59).]

35431. EXILE. *Exil*. Forschung, Erkenntnisse, Ergebnisse. Jg. 1997, Nr. 1 & 2. Hrsg. von Edita Koch und Frithjof Trapp. Frankfurt am Main: E. Koch (Postfach 170234), 1997. 2 issues, 105; 106 pp., notes. [No. 1 incl.: Gertrud Kolmar und Nelly Sachs im Kontext (Gudrun Jäger, 5–17). Stationen aus dem Leben Hilde Reachs, Sekretärin von Thomas Mann (Katja Schettler, 18–32). Der existenzialistische Grundzug im Werk Anna Seghers

(Frithjof Trapp, 33–44). Eine Stimme aus Böhmen – Der Prager Autor Ludwig Winder (Christiane Spirek, 45–55). Raphael und Heinrich Löwenfeld (Thomas Müller, 72–85). Nachwirkungen des Exiles: Skandinavien (Einhart Lorenz, 86–97). No. 2 (publ. 1998) incl. (selected essays): Ansprache zur Entgegennahme des Hans-Sahl-Preises 1997 (Anja Lundholm, 5–10; publ. also in: europäische ideen, H. 107, Berlin, 1997, pp. 18–23 with the title 'Das Land ohne Heimat lag hinter mir', followed by: Laudatio auf Anja Lundholm (Freya Klier, 23–26). Revolution als Text und Intertext: Alfred Döblins 'November 1918' (Anne Kuhlmann, 26–35). Grete Weil: "Und bin nach Deutschland zurückgegangen, in das Mörderland" (Laureen Nussbaum, 36–42). "Schrecken ohne Ende". Eingaben deutscher NKWD-Häftlinge an Stalin u.a. (Reinhard Müller, 63–78; docs.: 79–88). "Als Emigrant hat man Geduld gelernt" – Bürokratie und Remigration nach 1945 (Marita Krauss, 89–105).]

35432. EXILE. *Der Exodus aus Nazideutschland und die Folgen. Jüdische Wissenschaftler im Exil*. Hrsg. von Marianne Hassler und Jürgen Wertheimer. Mit Beiträgen von Armin Hermann [et al.]. Tübingen: Attempto, 1997. 347 pp., illus., notes. [Based on lectures held at Tübingen University 1994/1995. Cont. (titles abbr.): Einleitung (Jürgen Wertheimer, 11–15). Einsteins Emigration (Armin Hermann, 19–31). Lise Meitner (Fritz Krafft, 32–58). James Franck (Heinz Maier-Leibnitz, 59–70). William Stern (Werner Deutsch, 73–90). Der Fall Georg Friedrich Nicolai (Lewinstein) an der Friedrich-Wilhelms-Universität Berlin 1919–1922 (Joachim Lerchenmüller, 91–123). The application of Kurt Lewin's social psychology to intergroup conflict today (Miriam Lewin, 124–141). Günther Anders (Konrad Paul Liessmann, 142–156). Der Exodus und die Folgen für die Psychologie (Helmut E. Lück, 157–176). Max Wertheimer (Viktor Sarris, 177–190). Ein kurzer Überblick über die psychologischen Schulen vor dem Zweiten Weltkrieg (Michael Wertheimer, 191–206). Vertreibung und Akkulturation deutscher Wirtschaftswissenschaftler nach 1933 am Beispiel Adolph Lowes (Claus-Dieter Krohn, 209–227). Die Emigration der Frankfurter Schule (Gunzelin Schmid Noerr, 228–245). Gerechtigkeit zwischen den Generationen (Micha Brumlik (246–263; on Walter Benjamin). Paul Celans Inskription der Vernichtung (Stéphane Mosès, 264–273). Ernst Cassirer und Karl Bühler (Brigitte Schlieben-Lange, 274–285). Theodor Lessing (Julius H. Schoeps, 286–303). Wissenschaftsemigration und German Studies (Hinrich C. Seeba, 304–324). Hannah Arendt (Jürgen Wertheimer, 325–341).]

35433. EXILE. *Grafici in ballingschap. Henri Friedlaender en Paul Urban. Duitse grafisch vormgevers en het Nederlandse exil 1932–1950*. Einl.: Kurt Löb. Amsterdam: Universiteitsbibliotheek, 1997. 36 pp., illus.

35434. EXILE. HONNEF, KLAUS/WEYERS, FRANK, eds.: *Und sie haben Deutschland verlassen . . . müssen. Fotografen und ihre Bilder 1928–1997*. Red.: Frank Weyers [et al.]. Köln: PROAG; Berlin: Bugrim, 1997. 536 pp., 603 illus. [Catalogue of exhibition in Rheinisches Landesmuseum, Bonn, May 15 – Aug. 24, 1997. Incl.: "Fremde in der Welt" (Klaus Honnef, 12–22). "Wendepunkte". Thesen und Fakten zu einer Fotografie im "Exil" (Frank Weyers, 23–28). Incl. also biographical dictionary of 212 photographers, most of them Jews or of Jewish descent.]

35435. EXILE. INGRISCH, DORIS: *"Wenn es Wirklichkeitssinn gibt, muß es auch Möglichkeitssinn geben"*. Über die Vertreibung historischer Möglichkeiten anhand exemplarischer Lebensgeschichten von Intellektuellen im Exil. [In]: Wiener Geschichtsblätter, Jg. 52, Wien, 1997. Pp. 14–35, footnotes. [Gender-based analysis; emphasises the disadvantages of female as against male intellectuals.]

35436. EXILE. LÖB, KURT: *Exil-Gestalten. Deutsche Buchgestalter in den Niederlanden 1932–1950*. Arnhem: Gouda Quint, 1996. 341 pp., illus., bibl. [On Henri Friedlaender and Paul Urban by K.L., himself an émigré book designer.] [Cf.: Henri Friedlaender und Paul Urban – das vergessene Exilschaffen zweier deutscher Buchgestalter in den Niederlanden (Ulrich Faure) [in]: Aus dem Antiquariat, 11 [Beilage zum] Börsenblatt für den Deutschen Buchhandel Nr. 95, Frankfurt am Main, 26. Nov. 1996. Pp. A 481–483.] [See also obit. Henri Friedlaender – in memoriam (Stephen Lubell) [in]: Gutenberg-Jahrbuch, Jg. 72, Mainz, 1997. Pp. 348–349, port.; H.F., 1904 Lyon – Nov. 1997, Jerusalem, typographer, type designer and teacher.]

35437. EXILE. RITCHIE, J.M.: *German exiles. British Perspectives.* New York; Frankfurt am Main: Lang, 1997. X, 334 pp., notes, index (319–334). (Exil-Studien/Exile Studies, Vol. 6.) [Cont. 16 essays dealing with the history of Jewish and non-Jewish refugees from Nazism to Britain and with individual émigré writers. Incl. two hitherto unpubl. articles: Theatre in exile in Great Britain (96–128). Voices from the outside: how exile writers saw National Socialism (294–315).]

35438. EXILE. SCHOPF, WOLFGANG: *Mit Heine, im Exil. Heinrich Heine in der deutschsprachigen Exilpresse 1933 bis 1945.* Hrsg. und kommentiert von Wolfgang Schopf. Frankfurt am Main: Verlag Neue Kritik, 1997. 167 pp., footnotes, index.

35439. EXILE. SÖLLNER, ALFONS: *Deutsche Politikwissenschaftler in der Emigration.* Studien zu ihrer Akkulturation und Wirkungsgeschichte. Mit einer Bibliographie. Opladen: Westdt. Verl., 1996. VII, 356 pp., footnotes, bibl. [On 64 political scientists; incl.: Bibliographie der "Exil-Politologen" (291–356).]

35440. EXILE . *Exiles and emigres: the flight of European artists from Hitler.* Compiled by Stephanie Barron with Sabine Eckmann. Contributions by Matthew Affron [et al.]. New York: H.N. Abrams; Los Angeles: Los Angeles County Museum of Art, 1997. 432 pp., illus., ports., maps., notes, bibl. (408–413). [Catalogue of an exhibition organised by the Los Angeles County Museum of Art, Feb. 23–May 11, 1997. German edn.: 'Exil. Flucht und Emigration europäischer Künstler 1933–1945'. München; New York: Prestel, 1997.]

35441. EXILE LITERATURE. BERTHOLD, WERNER: *Exilliteratur und Exilforschung.* Ausgewählte Aufsätze, Vorträge und Rezensionen. Mit einer Einleitung von Wolfgang Frühwald. Wiesbaden: Harrowitz, 1996. 211 pp. (Gesellschaft für das Buch, Bd. 3.) [Publ. for the author's 75th birthday.]

35442. FRANK, KLAUS D.: *Das Dialogische.* [In]: Scheidewege. Jahresschrift für skeptisches Denken, Jg. 25, 1995/96. Baiersbronn, 1996. Pp. 115–125. [On Martin Buber, Rosa Luxemburg and Paul Celan.]

35443. FREUND, RENÉ: *Land der Träumer. Zwischen Größe und Größenwahn – verkannte Österreicher und ihre Utopien.* Wien: Picus, 1996. 224 pp., illus. [Incl. (a.o.): Jakob Lorber, Bertha Eckstein-Diner alias Sir Galahad, Eugenie Schwarzwald, Wilhelm Reich.]

35444. FUHRMANN, HORST: *"Sind eben alles Menschen gewesen". Gelehrtenleben im 19. und 20. Jahrhundert.* Dargestellt am Beispiel der Monumenta Germaniae Historica und ihrer Mitarbeiter. Unter Mitarbeit von Markus Wesche. München: Beck, 1996. 218 pp., illus., docs., notes (163–200). [Deals also with several Jewish scholars and their fate: a.o. Wilhelm Levison, Ernst Perels, Harry Bresslau and Philipp Jaffé.]

—— HACKESCHMIDT, JÖRG: *Von Kurt Blumenfeld zu Norbert Elias. Die Erfindung einer jüdischen Nation.* [See No. 35406.]

35445. HÄNTZSCHEL, HILTRUD/BUßMANN, HADUMOD, eds.: *Bedrohlich gescheit. Ein Jahrhundert Frauen und Wissenschaft in Bayern.* München: Beck, 1997. 356 pp., illus., ports., facsims., tabs., notes (293–325), bibl. (327–341), chronol. (343–345), index (351–356). [Cont. 19 essays, many of them dealing a.o. with Jewish women. Selected essays: Frauen jüdischer Herkunft an bayerischen Universitäten. Zum Zusammenhang von Religion, Geschlecht und 'Rasse' (Hiltrud Häntzschel, 105–136). "Eine neue Form der Bindung und der Freiheit". Die Juristin Margarete Berent (1887–1965) (Hiltrud Häntzschel, 231–235). "Ein voll erfülltes Frauenleben". Die Ärztin, Mutter und Zionistin Rahel Straus (1880–1963) (Marita Krauss, 236–241). "Amerika gab ihr, was ihr ihr Heimatland immer verwehrt hatte". Die Philologin Eva Fiesel (1801–1937) (Hiltrud Häntzschel, 242–247).]

35446. HEUER, RENATE/WOLF, SIEGBERT, eds.: *Die Juden der Frankfurter Universität.* Unter Mitarbeit von Holger Kiehnel und Barbara Seib. Mit einem Vorwort von Notker Hammerstein.

Frankfurt am Main; New York: Campus, 1997. 504 pp., ports. (Campus Judaica, 6.) [Alphabetically arranged short biographies incl. individual bibliographies.]

35447. KREIMEIER, KLAUS: *The UFA story: a history of Germany's greatest film company, 1918–1945*. Transl. by Robert and Rita Kimber. New York: Hill & Wang, 1996. VIII, 451 pp., illus., notes and sources (393–418). [Incl. many Jewish actors and directors, Max Reinhardt, Erich Pommer a.o. Also discusses the expulsion of Jews under the Nazis.] [Cf.: Review essay (Peter Gay) [in]: Dimensions, Vol. 11, No. 1, New York, 1997, pp. 35–37.]

35448. LADWIG-WINTERS, SIMONE: *Wertheim – ein Warenhausunternehmen und seine Eigentümer*. Ein Beispiel der Entwicklung der Berliner Warenhäuser bis zur "Arisierung". Münster: Lit-Verlag, 1997. 491 pp., tabs. (Anpassung – Selbstbehauptung – Widerstand, Bd. 8.) Zugl.: Berlin, Freie Univ., Diss., 1996.

35449. LADWIG-WINTERS, SIMONE: *Wertheim. Geschichte eines Warenhauses*. Berlin: Be.Bra-Verlag, 1997. 160 pp., illus., geneal. tab., bibl., index.

35450. LESSING, THEODOR. NEKULA, MAREK: *Theodor Lessing und Max Brod. Eine mißlungene Begegnung*. [In]: Brücken. Germanistisches Jahrbuch Tschechien – Slowakei, Jg. 10, N.F. 5, Berlin, 1997. Pp. 115–122.

35451. LORENZ, DAGMAR C.G.: *Keepers of the motherland: German texts by Jewish women writers*. Lincoln: Univ. of Nebraska Press, 1997. XXII, 402 pp., notes (329–353), bibl. (355–384), general index, title index. [Anthology, spanning the period from pre-Emancipation to the present.]

35452. LÜER, EDWIN: *Zeit und Zeitung. Über eine Parallele zwischen Ernst Weiß, Leo Perutz und Thomas Mann*. [In]: Brücken, Germanistisches Jahrbuch Tschechien – Slowakei, Jg. 10, N.F.5, Berlin, 1997. Pp. 107–114.

35453. MARTENS, LORNA: *Shadow lines: Austrian literature from Freud to Kafka*. Lincoln; London: Univ. of Nebraska Press, 1996. XII, 291 pp., notes, bibl.

35454. MENDELSSOHN FAMILY. *Mendelssohn Studien*. Beiträge zur neueren deutschen Kultur- und Wirtschaftsgeschichte, Bd. 10. Zum 150. Todestag von Felix Mendelssohn Bartholdy und seiner Schwester Fanny Hensel. Hrsg. für die Mendelssohn-Gesellschaft von Rudolf Elvers und Hans-Günter Klein. 258 pp., frontis., ports., footnotes, index. [Cont. (titles partly abbr.):: Wilhelm Hensel: Fanny und Felix im Porträt (Cécile Lowenthal-Hensel, 9–24). Die Briefe von Carl Friedrich Zelter an Felix Mendelssohn Bartholdy (Thomas Schmidt-Beste, 25–56). Felix Mendelssohn Bartoldy als Lehrer und Freund von Eduard Franck (Andreas Feuchte, 57–76). Autographe von Felix Mendelssohn Bartholdy in Italien (Pietro Zappalà, 77–96). Der fingierte Brief Ludwig van Beethovens an Fanny Mendelssohn Bartholdy (Rudolf Elvers, 97–100). Sieben Charakterstücke op. 7 von Felix Mendelssohn Bartholdy (Wolfgang Dinglinger, 101–130). Mendelssohn and Byron: Two songs almost without words (Monika Hennemann, 131–156). Felix Mendelssohn Bartholdy, Ferdinand David und Johann Sebastian Bach: Mendelssohns Bach-Auffassung im Spiegel der Wiederentdeckung der "Chaconne" (John Michael Cooper, 157–180). Verzeichnis der im Autograph überlieferten Werke Felix Mendelssohn Bartholdys im Besitz der Staatsbibliothek zu Berlin (181–214). Sechs Briefe von Fanny Hensel an Franz Hauser (Renate Hellwig-Unruh, 215–226). In welcher Form soll man Fanny Hensels "Choleramusik" aufführen? (Annegret Huber, 227–246). "Martens Mühle soll leben" (Natalie Nowack, 247–250; on the former country house of the Mendelssohn family near Hamburg).]

35455. *Die Professionalisierung der Frau*. Bildung, Ausbildung und Beruf von Frauen in historischer Perspektive. Hrsg. von Bettina Wahrig-Schmidt. Lübeck: DrägerDruck, 1997. 220 pp., illus., notes. [Incl. 3 essays on Jewish women: Marta Fraenkel – Ärztin, Museumspädagogin und "Public Health Officer" (Susanne Aschenbrenner, 103–112). Dr. Selma Meyer (1881–1958). Erste Professorin für das Fach Kinderheilkunde in Deutschland (Peter Voswinckel, 113–126). "Vita actica" – Beruf und Öffentlichkeit: Zwei Zentren in Hannah Arendts Leben und Denken (Bettina Wahrig-Schmidt, 208–218).]

Bibliography

35456. RABINBACH, ANSON: *In the shadow of catastrophe: German intellectuals between apocalypse and enlightenment.* Berkeley: Univ. of California Press, 1997. VIII, 263 pp., notes (209–253). [Incl.: Between apocalypse and enlightenment: Benjamin, Bloch, and modern German-Jewish Messianism (27–65). The cunning of unreason: mimesis and the construction of antisemitism in Horkheimer and Adorno's 'Dialectic of enlightenment'(166–198). Also incl. chaps. on Heidegger and Jaspers and the question of German guilt.]

35457. RAULFF, ULRICH: *Von der Privatbibliothek des Gelehrten zum Forschungsinstitut. Aby Warburg, Ernst Cassirer und die neue Kulturwissenschaft.* [In]: Geschichte und Gesellschaft, Jg. 23, H. 4, Göttingen, 1997. Pp. 28–43, footnotes.

35458. REICH-RANICKI, MARCEL: *Die verkehrte Krone. Über Juden in der deutschen Literatur.* [In]: Edith Stein Jahrbuch 1997. Bd. 3, Würzburg, 1997. Pp. 203–215. [Lecture held on the occasion of the 15th anniversary of the Hochschule für Jüdische Studien, Heidelberg, Jan. 1995.]

—— *Rückkehr und Aufbau nach 1945. Deutsche Remigranten im öffentlichen Leben Nachkriegsdeutschlands.* [See No. 35274.]

35459. TODOROW, ALMUT: *Das Feuilleton der 'Frankfurter Zeitung' in der Weimarer Republik. Zur Grundlegung einer rhetorischen Medienforschung.* Tübingen: Niemeyer, 1996. IX, 355 pp., 1 Mikrofiche. (Rhetorik-Forschungen, Bd. 8.). Zugl.: Tübingen, Univ., Habil.-Schr., 1994. [Deals a.o. with Siegfried Kracauer, Theodor W. Adorno, Walter Benjamin, Günther Anders (Stern) and numerous other Jewish contributors to the 'Frankfurter Zeitung'.]

35460. TRAVERSO, ENZIO: *Les juifs et la culture allemande. Le problème des générations intellectuels.* [In]: Revue germanique internationale 5, Evry Cedex, 1996. Pp. 15–30.

35461. URBAN-FAHR, SUSANNE: *Von Büchern und Menschen: Jüdische Verlage in Deutschland.* [In] Edith Stein Jahrbuch 1997. Bd. 3, Würzburg, 1997. Pp. 326–346, footnotes.

35462. WEISBERGER, ADAM M.: *The Jewish ethic and the spirit of socialism.* New York: Lang, 1997. XIII, 270 pp., port., notes, bibl. (209–256), index. (Studies in German Jewish history, Vol. 1.) [Incl. biogr. profiles of Eduard Bernstein, Gustav Landauer, and Ernst Toller.]

35463. WIXFORTH, HARALD/ZIEGLER, DIETER: *Deutsche Privatbanken und Privatbankiers im 20. Jahrhundert.* [In]: Geschichte und Gesellschaft, Jg. 23, H. 4, Göttingen, 1997. Pp. 205–235, footnotes, tabs. [Deals also with banks founded and owned by Jews and "Aryanisation".]

B. Individual

35464. ADLER, JANKEL. STAMM, RAINER: *Verfemt und vergessen – Der Maler Jankel Adler.* [In]: Romerike Berge, Jg. 46, H. 2, Burg an der Wupper, 1996. Pp. 17–20, illus.

35465. ADLER, VICTOR. MEYSELS, LUCIAN O.: *Victor Adler. Die Biographie.* Wien: Amalthea in F.A. Herbig, 1997. 286 pp. [V.A. (1852–1918), doctor, politician, leader of Austrian Socialists.]

35466. ADORNO, THEODOR W.: *"Ob nach Auschwitz noch sich leben lasse".* Ein philosophisches Lesebuch. Hrsg. von Rolf Tiedemann. Frankfurt am Main: Suhrkamp, 1997. 569 pp. [A collection of articles, some of them on antisemitism, "Vergangenheitsbewältigung", Gustav Mahler, Heinrich Heine, Franz Kafka.]

35467. ALTENBERG, PETER. BARKER, ANDREW/LENSING, LEO A.: *Peter Altenberg: Rezept die Welt zu sehen.* Kritische Essays, Briefe an Karl Kraus, Dokumente zur Rezeption, Titelregister der Bücher. Wien: Braumüller, 1995. 437 pp., illus., notes (389–426), index (427–437). (Untersuchungen zur österreichischen Literatur des 20. Jahrhunderts, Bd. 11.) [Incl. several sections dealing with Altenberg's Jewish background, his name change, his conversion and other aspects of his life.]

35468. ALTENBERG, PETER. SCOTT, MARILYN: *A zoo story: Peter Altenberg's 'Ashantee' (1897)*. [In]: Modern Austrian Literature, Vol. 30, No. 2, Riverside, CA, 1997. Pp. 48–64, notes.

35469. AMERY, JEAN. FIERO, PETRA S.: *Schreiben gegen das Schweigen: Grenzerfahrungen in Jean Amérys autobiographischem Werk*. Hildesheim; New York: Olms, 1997. 187 pp., footnotes, bibl. (174–183), index (184–187). Zugl.: Diss. [Incl.: biographical essay (10–23): Zusammenhang von Zeitgeschichte, gelebter Erfahrung und Sprache in Amérys essayistisch-autobiographischem Werk.]

35470. AMERY, JEAN. HEIDELBERGER-LEONARD, IRENE: *Jean Amérys 'Meisterliche Wanderjahre'*. [In]: Jahrbuch 1997 zur Geschichte und Wirkung des Holocaust [see No. 35276]. Pp. 289–302, notes.

35471. AMERY, JEAN. SCHEIT, GERHARD: *Am Ende der Metaphern. Über die singuläre Position von Jean Amérys 'Ressentiments' in den 60er Jahren*. [In]: Mittelweg 36, Jg. 36, H. 4, Hamburg, 1997. Pp. 4–17, footnotes. [Analyses Améry's book 'Jenseits von Schuld und Sühne', first publ. in 1966, of which 'Ressentiments' is one essay.]

35472. AMERY, JEAN. STEINER, STEPHAN, ed.: *Jean Améry (Hans Maier)*. Mit einem biographischen Bildessay und einer Bibliographie. Frankfurt am Main: Stroemfeld/Nexus, 1996. 303 pp., illus. [A collection of essays.] [Cf.: Besprechung (Margit Reiter) [in]: Mittelweg 36, Jg. 6, H. 6, Hamburg, 1997, pp. 60–62).]

35473. APPELFELD, AHARON. *A small old Jew with glasses: Aharon Appelfeld in conversation with Michael Mardi*. [In]: The Jewish Quarterly, Vol. 44, No. 2, London, Summer 1997. Pp. 47–49, port.

35474. ARENDT, HANNAH. DINER, DAN: *On the banal and evil in her Holocaust narrative*. [In]: New German Critique, No. 71, Ithaca, NY, Spring-Summer 1997. Pp. 177–190, notes.

35475. ARENDT, HANNAH. ETTINGER, ELZBIETA: *Hannah Arendt – Martin Heidegger*. Eine Geschichte. Aus dem Amerik. von Brigitte Stein. München: Piper, 1997. 141 pp. [For orig. edn. (1995) and details see No. 33601/YB XLI.]

35476. ARENDT, HANNAH. GANZFRIED, DANIEL/HEFT, SEBASTIAN, eds.: *Hannah Arendt. Nach dem Totalitarismus*. Hamburg: Europäische Verlagsanstalt, 1997. 195 pp., notes. (EVA Wissenschaft.) [Cont. 13 essays by Margaret Canovan, Wolfgang Engler, Wolfgang Heuer, Heinz Kleger, Claude Lefort, Urs Marti, Ingeborg Nordmann, Anne-Marie Roviello, Richard Sennett, Hans Saner, Christina Thürmer-Rohr, Sigrid Weigel and Kerry H. Whiteside. Papers were presented at the 'Hannah Arendt Tage 1996' in Zurich.]

35477. ARENDT, HANNAH. HERMES, CLAUDIA: *In den Reißwolf der Geschichte? Wiederbegegnung mit 'Eichmann in Jerusalem'*. [In]: Tribüne, Jg. 36, H.143, Frankfurt am Main, 1997. Pp. 69–76. [Deals with the reception of H.A.'s book in Israel, Germany and elsewhere; also on an international conference on this topic in Potsdam (1997), organised by the 'Einstein-Forum'. On the conference also: Hannah Arendts "Eichmann in Jerusalem". Eine Tagung zur Historiographie des Holocaust (Ulrike Weckel) [in]: WerkstattGeschichte, H. 18, Hamburg, 1997. Pp. 101–106.]

35478. ARENDT, HANNAH. LUDZ, URSULA, ed.: *Hannah Arendt: Ich will verstehen*. Selbstauskünfte zu Leben und Werk. Mit einer vollständigen Bibliographie hrsg. von Ursula Ludz. München: Piper, 1996. 333 pp.

35479. ARENDT, HANNAH. RING, JENNIFER: *The political consequences of thinking: gender and Judaism in the work of Hannah Arendt*. Albany: State Univ. of New York Press, 1997. XIII, 358 pp., appendix, notes (297–336), bibl. (337–348). (SUNY series in political theory.) [Discusses a number of Arendt's writings on Jewish or Holocaust themes, incl. the Eichmann controversy.]

Bibliography

35480. ARENDT, HANNAH. SCHULIN, ERNST: *Hannah Arendt als Historikerin.* [In]: Ernst Schulin: Arbeit an der Geschichte. Etappen der Historisierung auf dem Weg in die Moderne. Frankfurt am Main; New York: Campus, 1997. (Edition Pandora, Bd. 35.) Pp. 192–211, notes (255–257). [First publ. 1992.]

35481. ARENDT, HANNAH. SEIFERT, DORTHE: *Biographie als Freundschaft. Hannah Arendt und Rahel Levin Varnhagen.* [In]: Jüdischer Almanach 1998. Frankfurt am Main, 1997. Pp. 17–31.

35482. ARENDT, HANNAH. SENFFT, HEINRICH: *Hannah Arendts "Eichmann in Jerusalem" im Licht der Goldhagen-Debatte.* [In]: 1999. Zeitschrift für Sozialgeschichte des 20. und 21. Jahrhunderts, Jg. 12, H. 3, Hamburg, 55–75, footnotes.

35483. ARENDT, HANNAH. *"Treue als Zeichen der Wahrheit". Hannah Arendt: Werk und Wirkung.* Dokumentationsband zum Symposium. [Beiträge des internationalen Symposiums vom 12.-15. November 1995]. Hrsg.: Alte Synagoge. [Red.: Karl-Heinz Klein-Rusteberg. Essen: Klartext-Verlag, 1997. 159 pp., footnotes. [Cont. contribs. by Edna Brocke, Seyla Benhabib, Margaret Canovan, Dan Diner, Paolo Flores d'Arcais, Antonia Grunenberg, Jerome Kohn, Ursula Ludz, Bernd Neumann, Karol Sauerland and Thomas Sparr. Incl.: Hannah Arendt – jüdisches Selbstverständnis im Schatten der Eichmann-Kontroverse (Dan Diner, 109–120).]

35484. ASPLER, ALFRED. EXENBERGER, HERBERT: *Alfred Apsler (A. A-r.; A-r). Pädagoge – Schriftsteller – Volksbildner.* [In]: Mit der Ziehharmonika, Jg. 14, Nr. 3, Wien, 1997. Pp. 14–17, port., bibl. [A.A., 1907 Vienna – 1982 US (?), teacher, journalist, writer, emigr. 1938 via Switzerland to the US.]

35485. AUERBACH, ERICH. BAUER, MARKUS/JUNG, ANDREAS: *Wahrnehmen, lesen, deuten. Leben und Werk des Marburger Romanisten Erich Auerbach.* [In]: Alma Mater Philippina, Marburg, WS 1997/98. Pp. 31–33, port. [See also No. 35705.]

35486. BALLIN, ALBERT. RITTER, GERHARD A.: *Der Kaiser und sein Reeder. Albert Ballin, die HAPAG und das Verhältnis von Wirtschaft und Politik im Kaiserreich und in den ersten Jahren der Weimarer Republik.* [In]: Zeitschrift für Unternehmensgeschichte, Jg. 42, Nr. 2, München, 1997. Pp. 137–162, footnotes. [Incl. Engl. abstract.]

35487. BECKER, JUREK. BECKER, JUREK: *Ende des Größenwahns.* Aufsätze, Vorträge. Frankfurt am Main, 1996. 247 pp. [Incl. several autobiographical texts.] [J.B., Sept. 30, 1937 Lodz – March 14, 1997, Berlin, author, details see No. 33305/YB XLI.] [Obits: Anstiftung zum Verrat (Fritz J. Raddatz) [in]: Die Zeit, Nr. 13, Hamburg, 21. März 1997, p. 56. Der augenzwinkernde Humanist (Shoshana Decker) [in]: Tribüne, Jg. 36, H. 142, Frankfurt am Main, 1997, p. 70–72. ". . . schreibend die Realität zu ertragen". Über Jurek Becker (Susanne Wedekind) [in]: Mit der Ziehharmonika, Jg. 14, Nr. 4, Wien, Dez. 1997, pp. 13–18. Ein Kind des Ghettos (Stan Schneider) [in]: Allg. Jüd. Wochenzeitung, Jg. 52, Nr. 6, Bonn, 20. März 1997, p. 7. Die Furcht des Geschichten-Erzählers (Hanns-Josef Ortheil) [in]: 'NZZ', Nr. 63, Zürich, 17. März 1997, p. 20. Unbestechlichkeit und Menschennähe (Jochen Hieber) [in]: 'FAZ', Nr. 64, Frankfurt am Main, 17. März 1997, p. 31. Erinnerung an Jurek Becker (Tilo Medek) [in]: europäische ideen, H. 104, Berlin, 1997, pp. 38–39.]

35488. BECKER, JUREK. DUBROWSKA, MALGORZATA: *Jurek und sein Judentum.* [In]: Convivium, Germanistisches Jahrbuch Polen, Bonn, 1996. Pp. 179–190.

35489. BENJAMIN, WALTER. ROCHLITZ, RAINER: *The disenchantment of art: the philosophy of Walter Benjamin.* Transl. by Jane Marie Todd. New York: Guildford Press, 1996. VI, 298 pp., notes, bibl. (277–284). [First publ. in French in 1992 by Editions Gallimard.]

35490. BENJAMIN, WALTER. *Walter Benjamin: theoretical questions.* Ed. by David S. Ferris. Stanford, CA: Stanford University Press, 1996. XII, 246 pp., bibl. [Nine essays based on papers presented at a conference on W.B. on October 18–19, 1991, at the Whitney Humanities Center, Yale Univ.]

35491. BENJAMIN, WALTER. *Walter Benjamin and the demands of history*. Ed. by Michael P. Steinberg. Ithaca, NY: Cornell Univ. Press, 1996. VI, 252 pp., illus., bibl. [Collection of essays.]

35492. BERG, JIMMY. JARKA, HORST, ed.: *Von der Ringstrasse zur 72nd Street: Jimmy Bergs Chansons aus dem Wien der dreissiger Jahre und dem New Yorker Exil*. Bern; New York: Lang, 1997. XI, 318 pp., illus. (Austrian Culture, Vol. 17.) [Incl. German and English texts, chansons, couplets and a biographical introduction.] [J.B., (1908–1988), popular composer and lyricist, emigr. 1938 to New York.]

35493. BETTELHEIM, BRUNO. POLLAK, RICHARD: *The creation of Dr. B*. A biography of Bruno Bettelheim. New York: Simon & Schuster, 1997. 478 pp., illus., ports., facsims., bibl. (448–452).

35494. BLAU, MARIETTA. GALISON, PETER L.: *Marietta Blau: between Nazis and Nuclei*. [In]: Physics Today, Vol. 50, Washington DC, Nov. 1997. Pp. 42–48, illus., facsims., notes. [M.B., 1894 Vienna – 1969 Vienna, physicist, pioneer in the field of nuclear emulsions, emigr. 1938 via Norway to the US, returned to Vienna in 1960.]

35495. BLOCH, ERNST. *Bloch-Almanach*. H.16/1997 [with the issue title]: *Zum 20. Todestag von Ernst Bloch*. Hrsg. von Karlheinz Weigand. Mössingen-Talheim, 1997. 1 issue. [Selected essays (dealing with Bloch's biography): Ernst Bloch, un Weimarien en exil (Gérard Raulet, 71–94). The ambiguous quest: Ernst Bloch's early love (John K. Dickinson, 157–188); on his relationship to women in general and Else von Stritzki in particular). Eine unbekannte Bloch-Korrespondenz. Ein Bericht (Jürgen Jahn, 199–210; on Bloch's correspondence with Wieland Herzfelde 1938–1949.]

35496. BLOCH, ERNST: *Fabelnd Denken*. Essayistische Prosa aus der 'Frankfurter Zeitung'. Reihe: Promenade. Hrsg. von Gert Ueding. Tübingen: Klöpfer & Meyer, 1997. 176 pp.

35497. BLUMENFELD, ERWIN. EWING, WILLIAM A.: *Blumenfeld, a fetish for beauty: sein Gesamtwerk 1897–1969*. In Zusammenarbeit mit Marina Schinz. [Übers. aus dem Engl.: Alexander Sahm et al.]. Kilchberg b. Zürich: Ed. Stemmle, 1996. 256 pp., illus. [E.B., (1897 – 1969), photographer, lived in the 1920s in Amsterdam, in the 1930s in France, imprisoned in French and Moroccan internment camps, escaped 1941 to the US.]

35498. BROD, MAX. BLOOM, CECIL: *Max Brod, polymath*. [In]: Midstream, Vol. 43, No. 1, New York, Jan. 1997. Pp. 7–9, notes.

35499. CANETTI, ELIAS: *Aufzeichnungen 1992–1993*. München: Hanser, 1996. 96 [3] pp. [Cf.: Niederträchtige Gegenwart. Elias Canettis nachgelassene 'Aufzeichnungen 1992–1993' (Dieter Hildebrandt) [in]: Die Zeit, Nr. 46, Hamburg, 8.Nov. 1996, p. 4.]

35500. CANETTI, ELIAS. *"Ein Dichter braucht Ahnen". Elias Canetti und die europäische Tradition*. Akten des Pariser Symposiums/Actes du Colloque de Paris 16.-18.11.1995. Hrsg. von/Ed. par Gerald Stieg und/et Jean-Marie Valentin. Frankfurt am Main; New York: Lang, 1997. 314 pp., frontis., notes. [19 essays, incl.: Canetti und das Judentum (Martin Bollacher, 37–48).]

35501. CAUER, WILHELM. CAUER, EMIL/MATHIS, WOLFGANG: *Wilhelm Cauer (1900–1945)*. [In]: Archiv für Elektronik und Übertragungstechnik, Vol. 49, No. 5/6, Stuttgart, 1995. Pp. 243–251, port., notes. [W.C., June 24, 1900 Berlin – 1945 Berlin (of Jewish descent), physicist.]

35502. CELAN, PAUL. BÖTTIGER, PAUL: *Orte Paul Celans*. Wien: Zsolnay, 1996. 175 pp. [Cf.: Der Mythos vom reinen Text: 'Orte Paul Celans', eine Spurensuche von Helmut Böttiger (Andreas Breitenstein) [in]: 'NZZ', Nr. 250, Zürich, 26./27. Okt. 1996, p. 65.]

35503. CELAN, PAUL. DEL CARO, ADRIAN: *The early poetry of Paul Celan: "In the beginning was the word"*. Baton Rouge: Louisiana State Univ. Press, 1997. 228 pp.

Bibliography

35504. CELAN, PAUL. FELSTINER, JOHN: *Paul Celan. Eine Biographie.* Aus dem Amerik. übers. von Holger Fliessbach. München: Beck, 1997. 380 pp., illus. [For orig. edn. see No. 33325/YB XLI.] [Cf.: Der Biograph will Vormund sein (Lorenz Jäger) [in]: 'FAZ', Nr. 71, Frankfurt am Main, 25. März 1997, p. L 16. Das wahre, entheiligte Wort. John Felstiners Versuch einer Biographie Paul Celans (Jean Bollack) [in]: 'NZZ', Nr. 176, Zürich, 2./3. Aug. 1997, p. 59.]

35505. CELAN, PAUL. *"Fremde Nähe". Celan als Übersetzer.* Eine Ausstellung des Deutschen Literaturarchivs in Verbindung mit dem Präsidialamt der Stadt Zürich im Schiller-Nationalmuseum Marbach am Neckar und im Stadthaus Zürich. [Ausstellung und Katalog: Axel Gellhaus et al.] Marbach am Neckar: Dt. Schillergesellschaft, 1997. 607 pp., illus., index (593–604). (Marbacher Kataloge, 50.)

35506. CELAN, PAUL. *Ingeborg Bachmann und Paul Celan. Poetische Korrespondenzen.* Vierzehn Beiträge. Hrsg. von Bernhard Böschenstein und Sigrid Weigel. Frankfurt am Main: Suhrkamp, 1997. 269 pp., notes. [A collection of essays dealing with B.'s and C.'s relation and their works.]

—— CELAN, PAUL. KOELLE, LYDIA: *Paul Celans pneumatisches Judentum: Gottrede und menschliche Existenz nach der Shoah.* [See No. 35358.]

35507. COHEN, HERMANN. BLOM, PHILIPP: *Hermann Cohen – Geist und Leben.* [In]: Jüdischer Almanach 1998. Frankfurt am Main, 1997. Pp. 59–71, notes. [Also in this issue: Hermann Cohens Kantianischer Maimonides (David Bollag, 72–78, notes).]

35508. COHEN, HERMANN. POMA, ANDREA: *The critical philosophy of Hermann Cohen.* Transl. by John Denton. Albany: State Univ. of New York Press, 1997. 320 pp., notes, bibl. 267–316. (SUNY series in Jewish philosophy.) [First publ. in Italian in 1988.]

35509. DÖBLIN, ALFRED. ARNOLD, ARMIN: *Alfred Döblin.* Berlin: Morgenbuch-Verl., 1996. 94 pp., frontis., bibl. (87–93). (Köpfe des 20. Jahrhunderts.)

35510. DÖBLIN, ALFRED. *Internationales Alfred-Döblin-Kolloquium Leiden 1995.* Hrsg. von Gabriele Sander. Bern; New York: Lang, 1997. 285 pp., footnotes. [Cont. 17 contribs. and bibl. of publications on Döblin since 1990 (ed., 259–284). Selected essays: Personal and confidential. Geheimdienste, Alfred Döblin und das Exil in Südkalifornien (Alexander Stephan, 181–210, docs., facsims.). Döblins Konvertierung zum Christentum: Eine Verführung durch die Tropik der Sprache? (Roger Eugster-Ulmer, 211–226).]

35511. DOMIN, HILDE. LERMEN, BIRGIT/BRAUN, MICHAEL: *Hilde Domin: "Hand in Hand mit der Sprache".* Bonn: Bouvier, 1997. 199 pp., illus. (Lebensspuren, 1.)

35512. EHRENBERG, HANS. BRAKELMANN, GÜNTER: *Hans Ehrenberg. Ein judenchristliches Schicksal in Deutschland.* Bd. 1. Leben, Denken und Wirken 1883–1932. Waltrop: Spenner, 1997. 364 pp. (Schriften der Hans-Ehrenberg-Gesellschaft, Bd. 3.) [Cf.: Durch die Eisenhütte des Herrn. In den Glaubenskämpfen der Weimarer Republik schmiedete Hans Ehrenberg die Waffe des revolutionären Christentums (Friedrich Wilhelm Graf) [in]: 'FAZ', Nr. 49, Frankfurt am Main, 27. Feb. 1998, p. 42.]

35513. EINSTEIN, ALBERT. CALAPRICE, ALICE, ed.: *Einstein sagt.* München: Piper, 1997. 280 pp., illus. [Incl. a preface by Freeman Dyson. A collection of Einstein quotes, compiled with the assistance of the Collected Papers of Albert Einstein at Boston Univ., as well as numerous Einstein biographies, reflecting various aspects of his personality and life.]

35514. EINSTEIN, ALBERT. FISCHER, ERNST PETER: *Einstein – ein Genie und sein überfordertes Publikum.* Heidelberg: Springer, 1996. XIV, 243 pp., illus., notes, graphs., index (subjects, persons). [On E.'s life and work; reveals several stories about E. to be myth.]

35515. EINSTEIN, ALBERT. FÖLSING, ALBRECHT: *Albert Einstein: a biography.* Transl. from the German by Ewald Osers. New York: Viking, 1997. XIII, 882, illus., chronol., notes, bibl., index of persons. [For German edn. see No.30994/YB XXXIX.] [Cf.: The contradictory genius (Alan Lightman) [in]: New York Review of Books, New York, April 10, 1997, pp. 14–19, port.]

35516. EINSTEIN, ALBERT. FRANKE, ALMUT/FRANKE, FABIAN: *Paul Langevin und Albert Einstein – eine Freundschaft zwischen Relativitätstheorie und politischer Realität.* [In]: Berichte zur Wissenschaftsgeschichte, H. 20, Weinheim, 1997. Pp. 199–215.

35517. EINSTEIN, ALBERT. GOLDMAN, ROBERT N.: *Einstein's God: Albert Einstein's quest as a scientist and as a Jew to replace a forsaken God.* Northvale, NJ: Aronson, 1997. XVIII, 166 pp., illus., bibl. (155–156).

35518. EINSTEIN, ALBERT. HERMANN, ARMIN: *Albert Einstein (1879–1955)*. [In]: Edith Stein Jahrbuch 1997. Bd. 3, Würzburg, 1997. Pp. 165–172.

35519. EINSTEIN, ALBERT. SCHULZ, FRIEDRICH/SCHWARZ, EBERHARD: *"Entzückt von der herben Schönheit des Fischlandes. . .".* Albert Einsteins Aufenthalte in der Ostseeregion. Kückenshagen: Scheunen-Verlag, 1995. 24 pp., illus. (Kleine Schriften des Heimatvereins, H.1.)

35520. EISNER, KURT. EISNER, FREYA, ed.: *Kurt Eisner. Zwischen Kapitalismus und Kommunismus.* Frankfurt am Main: Suhrkamp, 1997. 311 pp., docs.

35521. EISNER, KURT. ROSENFELD, GAVRIEL D.: *Monuments and the politics of memory: commemorating Kurt Eisner and the Bavarian revolutions 1918–1919 in postwar Munich.* [In]: Central European History, Vol. 30, No. 2, Atlantic Highlands, NJ, 1997. Pp. 221–251, illus., notes. [Incl. post-First World War antisemitic attitudes towards Eisner shown in the destruction of Eisner plaques and monuments by Nazis.]

35522. ELIAS, NORBERT. HACKESCHMIDT, JÖRG: *"Die Kulturkraft des Kreises". Norbert Elias als Vordenker der zionistischen Jugendbewegung. Zwei unbekannte Briefe aus den Jahren 1920 und 1921.* [In]: Berliner Journal für Soziologie, Jg. 7, H. 2, Opladen, 1997. Pp. 147–168. [Also in this issue: Soziologisches Sehen – Denkstationen des jungen Elias: Breslau, Heidelberg, Frankfurt (Reinhard Blomert, 169–198).] [See also No. 35406.]

35523. ELIAS, NORBERT. KORTE, HERMANN: *Über Norbert Elias. Das Werden eines Menschenwissenschaftlers.* Opladen: Leske und Buderich, 1997. 200 pp., illus., bibl. (187–200). [Also by this author: Auch ein Prozess der Zivilisation. Der Lebensweg des Menschenwissenschaftlers Norbert Elias [in]: 'NZZ', Nr. 141, Zürich, 21./22. Juni 1997, p. 65–66. Two further contribs. on N.E. in this issue of 'NZZ': Menschenwissenschaft ohne Mensch (Uwe Justus Wenzel, p. 65). Wahrheiten in der Geschichte. Norbert Elias' wissenschaftliche Intention (Peter-Ulrich Merz-Benz, p. 66).]

35524. ELIAS, NORBERT. RUSSELL, STEVEN: *Jewish identity and civilizing processes.* Foreword by Stephen Mennell. London: Macmillian, 1996. XII, 181 pp., notes, bibl. (159–172). [On N. Elias; incl (titles abbr.): The 'underground history' of Europe: Elias's central thesis (1–19). Elias and European Jewry prior to emancipation (20–39). Political and legal aspects of Jewish emancipation (40–61). Personal dimensions of Jewish emancipation (62–86). Elias and the German cultural crisis I, II (87–131). Norbert Elias and the German-Jewish synthesis (132–153).]

35525. ELKANA, ELI. *Eli Elkana. Dr. Georg Michelsohn.* Auszüge aus seinen Werken. Versuch einer Biographie. Ausgewählt, zusammengestellt und mit einer biographischen Abhandlung versehen von Werner Grossert. Dessau: Moses-Mendelssohn-Gesellschaft Dessau e.V., 1995. 160 pp., frontis., illus. [G.M., pseud. Eli Elkana, 1876 Königsberg – 1968 Ramat Gan, dentist, Social Democrat, poet, lived in Dessau, emigr. 1933 via Prague to Palestine.]

35526. ENGELMANN, PAUL. SCHNEIDER, URSULA A.: *Paul Engelmann – Architektur, Judentum und Moderne zwischen Wien, Olmütz und Israel.* [In]: Aschkenas, Jg. 7, H. 1, Wien, 1997. Pp. 155–172, illus., footnotes. [Also on P.E.: Ein Engel im Schatten. Paul Engelmann und das mitteleuropäische Erbe – ein internationales Symposium im Brenner-Archiv in Innsbruck (Hans Rochelt) [in]: Illustrierte Neue Welt, Nr. 4, Wien, April 1997, p. 18.]

35527. ETTLINGER, KARL. Hock, Sabine: *Karlchens Erfolg und Verfolgung.* Die Lebensgeschichte des Schriftstellers Karl Ettlinger (1882 – 1939). Nidderau: Verl. Michaela Naumann, 1997. 152 pp., illus. (Ettlinger-Lesbuch 3.) [K.E., 1882 Frankfurt am Main – 1939 Berlin, humorist, editor.]

35528. FEUCHTWANGER, LION. Rehrmann, Norbert: *"Ein sagenhafter Ort der Begegnung".* Lion Feuchtwangers Roman "Die Jüdin von Toledo" im Spiegel von Kulturgeschichte und Literaturwissenschaft. Berlin: Ed. Tranvía, 1997. 108 pp., bibl. (100–107). (Tranvía Essay, Bd. 1.)

35529. FREUD, SIGMUND. Ferris, Paul: *Dr. Freud: a life.* London: Sinclair-Stevenson, 1997. XIII, 464 pp., illus., ports., notes (409–446), bibl. (447–452). [Incl. Freud's relationship with Judaism.]

35530. FREUNDLICH, ELISABETH. Hertling, Viktoria: *Exil und Post-Exil: Elisabeth Freundlichs Erinnerungsbuch 'Die fahrenden Jahre'.* [In]: Modern Austrian Literature, Vol. 30, No. 1, Riverside, CA, 1997. Pp. 102–116, notes. [Discusses Freundlich's life and years in exile and the memoirs she wrote about her experiences. For details see No. 29884/YB XXXVIII.]

35531. FRIEDMANN, FRIEDRICH GEORG. *Leben und Werk von Friedrich G. Friedmann.* Drei Vorträge im Rahmen eines Symposiums der Jüdischen Kulturwochen 1995 am 16. Nov. 1995 an der Universität Augsburg. Von Manfred Hinz, Herbert Ammon und Adam Zak. Augsburg: Rektor der Univ., 1997. 79 pp., illus. (Augsburger Universitätsreden, 30.) [F.G.F., b. March 14, 1912 in Augsburg, cultural anthropologist, Americanist, emigr. 1933 to Italy, 1939 to the UK, 1940 to the US.]

35532. FÜRTH, HENRIETTE. Epple, Angelika: *Henriette Fürth und die Frauenbewegung im deutschen Kaiserreich.* Eine Sozialbiographie. Pfaffenweiler: Centaurus, 1996. 202 pp., footnotes, bibl. (181–201). (Forum Frauengeschichte, Bd. 17.)

35533. GANS, EDUARD. Braun, Johann: *Judentum, Jurisprudenz und Philosophie. Bilder aus dem Leben des Juristen Eduard Gans (1797–1839).* Baden-Baden: Nomos, 1997. 254 pp., bibl. (225–248). [A collection of nine essays, two of them hitherto unpubl.; three essays deal with the 'Verein für Cultur und Wissenschaft der Juden', Gans's relationship to Heinrich Heine and with the emancipation of the Prussian Jews.]

35534. GANS, EDUARD. Waszek, Norbert: *L'histoire du droit selon Edouard Gans.* Une critique hégélienne de F.C. von Savigny. [In]: Recht zwischen Natur und Geschichte/Le droit entre nature et histoire. Deutsch-französisches Symposion vom 24. bis 26. November 1994 an der Universität Cergy-Pontoise. Hrsg. von François Kervégan und Heinz Mohnhaupt. Frankfurt am Main: Klostermann, 1997. Pp. 257–280, footnotes.

35535. GLÜCKEL VON HAMELN. Jancke, G.: *Die Sichronot (Memoiren) der jüdischen Kauffrau Glückel von Hameln zwischen Autobiographie, Geschichtsschreibung und religiösem Leben. Geschlecht, Religion und Ich in der Frühen Neuzeit.* [In]: Autobiographien von Frauen. Beiträge zu ihrer Geschichte. Hrsg. von Magdalene Heuser. Tübingen: Niemeyer, 1996. (Untersuchungen zur deutschen Literaturgeschichte, Bd. 85.).

35536. Goldschmitt, Hermann Levi: *"Der Rest bleibt".* Aufsätze zum Judentum. Hrsg. von Willi Goetschel. [Deutsche Erstausgabe] Wien: Passagen, 1997. 341 pp. (Werkausgabe in neun Bänden; Passagen Philosophie.) [Essays on Judaism and on Jewish philosophers; also on modern scholars and writers: Moses Mendelssohn, Goethe, Simon Dubnow, Franz Werfel, Jakob Wassermann, Stefan Zweig, Franz Kafka, Thomas Mann.] [H.L. G., 1914 Berlin – March 29, 1998, Zurich, philosopher, founder and director of the Jüdisches Lehrhaus Zürich, emigr. 1938 to Switzerland.]

35537. GOLDSCHMIDT, HERMANN LEVIN. ADUNKA, EVELYN: *"Der letzte deutsche Jude" – über Hermann Levin Goldschmidt.* [In]: Mit der Ziehharmonika, Jg. 14, Nr. 1/Doppelnummer, Wien, 1997. Pp. 33–38, port., facsims., notes.

35538. GROSSMANN, KURT R.. MERTENS, LOTHAR: *Unermüdlicher Kämpfer für Frieden und Menschenrechte. Leben und Wirken von Kurt R. Grossmann.* Berlin: Duncker & Humblot, 1997. 473 [2] pp., frontis., footnotes. [Kurt Richard G., May 21, 1897 Berlin-Charlottenburg – March 2, 1972 St. Petersburg/Florida, Jewish activist, General Secretary of the 'Deutsche Liga für Menschenrechte' (1926–1933), emigr. 1933 to Czechoslovakia, 1938 via France to the US.]

35539. HABER, FRITZ. SZÖLLÖSI-JANZE, MARGIT: *Berater, Agent, Interessent? Fritz Haber, die BASF und die staatliche Stickstoffpolitik im Ersten Weltkrieg.* [In]: Berichte zur Wissenschaftsgeschichte, 19, Weinheim, 1996. Pp. 105–117, footnotes. [Incl. Engl. summary.]

35540. HEINE, HEINRICH: *Historisch-kritische Gesamtausgabe der Werke.* In Verbindung mit dem Heinrich-Heine-Institut hrsg. von Manfred Windfuhr im Auftr. der Landeshauptstadt Düsseldorf. Bd. 16: Nachträge und Korrekturen. Register. Bearb. von Marianne Tilch, Bernd Füllner und Karin Füllner. Hamburg: Hoffmann und Campe, 1997. 840 pp. [Last vol. of the 'Düsseldorfer Heine-Ausgabe' (DHA) begun in 1973. Incl.: Nachwort des Herausgebers (837–840).]

35541. HEINE, HEINRICH. BETZ, ALBRECHT: *Der Charme des Ruhestörers.* Heine-Studien. Aachen: Rimbaud, 1997. 95 pp. (Ästhetik und Politik, 2.)

35542. HEINE, HEINRICH. BRIEGLEB, KLAUS: *Bei den Wassern Babels. Heinrich Heine, jüdischer Schriftsteller in der Moderne.* München: Dt. Taschenbuch Verl., 1997. 439 pp., illus., notes (414–434). Orig.-Ausg.

—— HEINE, HEINRICH. *Die Von Geldern Haggadah und Heinrich Heines "Der Rabbi von Bacherach".* Hrsg. von Emile G.L. Schrijver und Falk Wiesemann. [See No. 35397.]

35543. HEINE, HEINRICH. GÖRNER, RÜDIGER: *Wunder Heine. Versuch aus gegebenem Anlaß.* [In]: Schweizer Monatshefte, Jg. 77/78, H. 12/1, Zürich, Dez. 1997. Pp. 11–16, notes. [Review essay on recent publications.]

35544. HEINE, HEINRICH. GRONAU, DIETRICH: *Heinrich Heine: "nichts als ein Dichter".* München: Heyne, 1997. 237 pp. Orig.-Ausg.

—— HEINE, HEINRICH. GUTMANN, THOMAS: *Im Namen Heinrich Heines.* Der Streit um die Benennung der Universität Düsseldorf 1965–1988. [See No. 35766.]

35545. HEINE, HEINRICH. *Harry Heine stud. juris in Bonn 1819/20.* Zum ersten Studienjahr Heinrich Heines (1797–1856) und zur Bonner Stammbuchblätterfolge von ca. 1820 des stud.med. Joseph Neunzig (1797–1877). Begleitbuch zur Ausstellung. Hrsg. von Ingrid Bodsch. Bearb. und mit Beitr. von Ingrid Bodsch, Inge Hermstrüwer, Norbert Schloßmacher, Marianne Tilch. Bonn: Stadtmuseum Bonn, 1997. 232 pp., illus., facsims. [Exhibition held May 17 – July 13, 1997. Incl. also the student Isaac Coppenhagen.]

35546. HEINE, HEINRICH. HAUSCHILD, JAN-CHRISTOPH/WERNER, MICHAEL: *"Der Zweck des Lebens ist das Leben selbst". Heinrich Heine – eine Biographie.* Köln: Kiepenheuer & Witsch, 1997. 696 pp., bibl. notes (641–665), chronol. (673–686), index (687–696). [Cf.: Wie frei war der Freie Schriftsteller H.H. wirklich? Eine neue Monumental-Biographie gibt ernüchternde Auskunft (Benedikt Erenz) [in]: Die Zeit, Nr. 51, Hamburg, 12. Dez. 1997, p. 51.]

35547. HEINE, HEINRICH. *Heinrich Heine und die Romantik. Heinrich Heine and Romanticism.* Erträge eines Symposiums an der Pennsylvania State University (21.-23. September 1995). Hrsg. von Markus Winkler. Tübingen: Niemeyer, 1997. XIII, 232 pp., footnotes, index. [Incl. 13 essays, some of them dealing with Jewish aspects, by: Diana I. Behler, Jürgen Brummack,

Robert C. Holub, Gerhart Hoffmeister, Kurt Kloocke, Joseph A. Kruse, Jeffrey L. Sammons, Azade Seyhan, Hans-Jürgen Schrader, Ulrich Stadler, and Markus Winkler.]

35548. HEINE, HEINRICH. *Heinrich Heine: poet, critic, exile.* Exhibit at the Leo Baeck Institute, New York in conjunction with the conference at Deutsches Haus, Columbia Univ., "Heinrich Heine's Con/Texts", Nov. 5–Dec. 30, 1997. New York: Leo Baeck Institute, 1997. 12 pp., ports.

35549. HEINE, HEINRICH. HESSING, JAKOB: *Totgeborene Zeit. Zum 200. Geburtstag Heinrich Heines.* [In]: Jüdischer Almanach 1998. Frankfurt am Main, 1997. Pp. 45–58.

35550. HEINE, HEINRICH. HÖHN, GERHARD: *Heine-Handbuch. Zeit, Person, Werk.* Zweite, aktualisierte und erweiterte Auflage. Stuttgart: Metzler, 1997. XV, 570 pp., notes, bibl., (515–551), indexes (subjects; names, 552–570). [First edn. publ. in 1987.]

35551. HEINE, HEINRICH. *Ich Narr des Glücks.* Heinrich Heine 1797–1856. Bilder einer Ausstellung. Hrsg. von Joseph A. Kruse unter Mitwirkung von Ulrike Reuter und Martin Hollender. Stuttgart: Metzler, 1997. XVII, 584 pp., illus., notes, bibl. [Catalogue book to exhibition in Düsseldorf, May 11–July 20, 1997. Incl.: Einleitung. 200 Jahre Heinrich Heine: Wirkung, Ruhm und Kontroversen (Joseph A. Kruse, 3–12. Selected contribs. dealing with biographical and Jewish aspects of Heine and his work: Die Lage der Juden in Deutschland zur Zeit Heines (Edith Lutz, 31–36). Deutscher Dichter jüdischer Herkunft (Robert C. Holub, 44–50). "Eichendorff und Heine sind typische Gegensätze". Wie man den guten Deutschen gegen den bösen Deutschen ausspielt (Martin Hollender, 86–95; on Joseph von Eichendorff as compared to Heine). Heinrich Heine. Exil – mitten in Europa (Helmut Koopmann, 175–180). Der neue Koloß. Vom deutsch-französisch-jüdischen Dichter der Freiheit Heinrich Heine über die amerikanisch-jüdische Dichterin Emma Lazarus zur französisch-amerikanischen Freiheitsstatue (Jeffrey L. Sammons, 241–244). Verschiedene Konversionen? (Wilhelm Gössmann, 307–312). Heine und die jüdische Tradition (Maren R. Niehoff, 318–324). Scheuers Liste und Guntrums Fetzen. Zwei Lebenszeugnisse aus Heines Düsseldorfer Zeit (Jan-Christoph Hauschild, 444–453). Rollenspiel in Variationen. Heinrich Heine und seine Mutter (Ursula Roth, 454–466). Was bleibt. Lebensspuren Heinrich Heines (Jan-Christoph Hauschild/Michael Werner, 536–540).]

35552. HEINE, HEINRICH. JUSTIS, DIANA LYNN: *The feminine in Heine's life and oeuvre: self and other.* New York; Bern: Lang, 1997. 256 pp. (North American studies in nineteenth-century German literature, Vol. 19.) [A psychological analysis of Heine's attitude towards women, real and imagined.]

35553. HEINE, HEINRICH. KLÜGER, RUTH: *"Mein Herz ist liebend wie das Licht": Der romantische Aufklärer Heinrich Heine.* [In]: Heine-Jahrbuch 1997, Jg. 36. Stuttgart, 1997. Pp. 248–254. [Lecture on the occasion of the bestowment of the 'Ehrengabe der Heinrich-Heine-Gesellschaft 1997'. Also in this vol.: Laudatio auf Ruth Klüger (Johannes Rau, 255–261). Lecture also repr. in 'Mit der Ziehharmonika', Jg. 14, Nr. 2, Wien, Aug. 1997. Pp. 9–11.]

35554. HEINE, HEINRICH. KREUTZER, LEO: *Träumen, Tanzen, Trommeln. Heinrich Heines Zukunft.* Frankfurt am Main: Suhrkamp, 1997. 138 pp.

35555. HEINE, HEINRICH. KRUSE, JOSEPH A.: *Heine-Zeit.* Stuttgart: Metzler, 1997. VIII, 401 pp., notes. [A biography, dealing also with H.'s family history, his occupation with literature, his relationship towards Judaism and Christianity, France and the French Revolution and several aspects of the Heine reception; incl. the chaps.: Immermann und Heine (313–320). Assimilation oder jüdisches Selbstbewußtsein (348–361). Richard Wagners Heine (363–380). Heine trifft Brecht (381–395).]

35556. HEINE, HEINRICH. LÄMKE, ORTWIN: *Heines Begriff der Geschichte. Der Journalist Heinrich Heine und die Julimonarchie.* Stuttgart: Metzler, 1997. X, 180 pp. (Heine-Studien.)

35557. HEINE, HEINRICH. LAPIDE, PINCHAS: *Heinrich Heine, der fromme Ketzer. Jüdisch beschnitten – evangelisch getauft – katholisch getraut.* [In]: Edith Stein Jahrbuch 1997. Bd. 3, Würzburg, 1997. Pp. 143–155.

35558. HEINE, HEINRICH. LIEDTKE, CHRISTIAN: *Heinrich Heine.* Reinbek: Rowohlt, 1997. 174 pp., illus. (Rowohlt Monographien, 50535.)

35559. HEINE, HEINRICH. LUTZ, EDITH: *Der 'Verein für Cultur und Wissenschaft der Juden' und sein Mitglied H. Heine.* Stuttgart: Metzler, 1997. 323 pp., footnotes, bibl. (307–323). (Heine-Studien.) [Cf.: Bespr. (Jochanan Trilse-Finkelstein) [in]: Heine-Jahrbuch 1997, Stuttgart, 1997, pp. 267–270.]

35560. HEINE, HEINRICH. MORAWE, BODO: *Heines 'Französische Zustände'. Über die Fortschritte des Republikanismus und die anmarschierende Weltliteratur.* Heidelberg: Winter, 1997. 109 pp. (Beihefte zum Euphorion, 28.)

35561. HEINE, HEINRICH. PAWEL, ERNST: *Heinrich Heines letzte Jahre in Paris.* Aus dem Engl. von Regina Schmidt-Ott. Berlin: Berlin-Verlag, 1997. 239 pp. [For orig. edn. see No. 33377/YB XLI.]

35562. HEINE, HEINRICH. RADDATZ, FRITZ J.: *Taubenherz und Geierschnabel. Heinrich Heine.* Eine Biographie. Weinheim: Beltz Quadriga, 1997. 391 pp., illus., notes, bibl., index.

35563. HEINE, HEINRICH. REGENSTEINER, HENRY: *A note on Theodor Herzl's "Heine and love".* [In]: Midstream, Vol. 43, No. 7, New York, Oct. 1997. Pp. 35–36. [On Herzl's essay "Heine und die Liebe" written for Heine's centenary in 1887.]

35564. HEINE, HEINRICH. REICH-RANICKI, MARCEL: *Der Fall Heine.* Stuttgart: Deutsche Verlags-Anstalt, 1997. 128 pp., notes and bibl. Reich-Ranicki (115–128). [Cont. 5 essays; 3 of them were previously publ. elsewhere.]

⸻ HEINE, HEINRICH. SCHOPF, WOLFGANG, ed.: *Mit Heine, im Exil. Heinrich Heine in der deutschsprachigen Exilpresse 1933–1945.* [See No. 35438.]

35565. HEINE, HEINRICH. SELDEN, CAMILLE: *Heinrich Heines letzte Tage.* Bodenheim: Philo, 1997. 106 pp. [Incl.: Camille Selden – "Une femme d'une autre époque" (Wolf-Daniel Hartwich, 85–106); on Heine's "Mouche", Elise von/de Kri(e)nitz (pseud. Camille Selden), whose memoirs were first publ. in 1884.]

35566. HEINE, HEINRICH. STARKE, MATTHIAS: *Heinrich Heines Auffassungen von der Geschichte und der Revolution als impulsgebenden Elementen des Prosaschaffens im französischen Exil (1831–1848).* Aachen: Shaker, 1997. 291 pp., notes (205–272), bibl. (273–291). (Sprache & Kultur). Zugl.: Leipzig, Päd. Hochsch., Diss., 1992.

35567. HEINE, HEINRICH. STAUF, RENATE: *Der problematische Europäer. Heinrich Heine im Konflikt zwischen Nationenkritik und gesellschaftlicher Utopie.* Heidelberg: Winter, 1997. 517 pp. (Beiträge zur neueren Literaturgeschichte, Folge 3, Bd. 154.) Zugl.: Berlin, Techn. Univ., Habil.-Schr., 1996.

35568. HEINE, HEINRICH. TRILSE-FINKELSTEIN, JOCHANAN: *Gelebter Widerspruch.* Heinrich Heine Biographie. Berlin: Aufbau, 1997. 420 pp., frontis., chronol. tab., bibl., index.

35569. HEINE, HEINRICH. URBAHN DE JAUREGUI, HEIDI: *Freiheit eines Dichtergeistes. Heinrich Heine, die Kunst, die Politik.* [In]: Neue deutsche Literatur, Jg.45, H. 6, Berlin, Nov./Dez. 1997. Pp. 37–51.

35570. HEINE, HEINRICH. WINDFUHR, MANFRED: *Rätsel Heine. Autorprofil – Werk – Wirkung.* Heidelberg: Winter, 1997. 439 pp. (Reihe Siegen, Bd. 133: Germ. Abt.)

35571. HEINE, HEINRICH. Xu, Pei: *Frauenbilder der Romantik*. Düsseldorf: Grupello, 1997. 180 pp., footnotes, bibl. Zugl.: Düss., Univ., Diss., 1996. [Incl.: Heinrich Heine (1797–1856), pp. 141–164; on Heine's perception of women.]

35572. HEINE, HEINRICH. Ziegler, Edda: *Heinrich Heine: Leben, Werk, Wirkung*. Zürich: Artemis, 1997. 255 pp., illus., facsims., ports., bibl. [New edn.; first publ. 1993, see No. 31037/YB XXXIX.]

35573. HENSEL, FANNY [MENDELSSOHN]. Helmig, Martina, ed.: *Fanny Hensel, geb. Mendelssohn Bartholdy*. Das Werk. München: Ed. Text und Kritik, 1997. 189 pp., illus., music, bibl. [A collection of essays. Incl. 8 letters of Wilhelm Hensel to Fanny written in 1829; also list of compositions and discography (178–183).]

35574. HENSEL, FANNY [MENDELSSOHN]. Olivier, Antje: *Mendelssohns Schwester Fanny Hensel*. Musikerin, Komponistin, Dirigentin. Düsseldorf: Droste, 1997. 222 pp., illus., chronol. tab., bibl. [Incl. list of F.H.'s publ. compositions.]

35575. HERMLIN, STEPHAN. Völker, Klaus: *Wir sind das ganze Werk der Zeit*. Erinnerung an Stephan Hermlin. [In]: neue deutsche literatur, Jg. 45, H. 516, Berlin, Nov./Dez. 1997. Pp. 5–26. [Cf.: Dichtung in eigener Sache (Karl Corino) [in]: Die Zeit, Nr. 41, Hamburg, 4. Okt. 1996, pp. 9–11. Der Mann ohne Goldhelm (Fritz J. Raddatz) [in]: Die Zeit, Nr. 43, Hamburg, 18. Okt. 1996, p. 63. Obits.: Zeuge und Zeugnis. Zum Tod von Stephan Hermlin (Fritz J. Raddatz) [in]: Die Zeit, Nr. 16, Hamburg, 11. April 1997, p. 44. Zum Tode von Stephan Hermlin [in]: europäische ideen, H. 104, Berlin, 1997, pp. 26–29. Der letzte Kommunist. Zum Tode des Dichters Stephan Hermlin (Frank Schirrmacher) [in]: 'FAZ', Nr. 81, Frankfurt am Main, 8. April 1997, p. 33.] [St.H. (orig. Rudolf Leder), April 13, 1915 Chemnitz – April 1997 Berlin, writer.]

35576. HERTZ, HENRIETTE. Schwabe, Günter: *Henriette Hertz (1846–1913)*. [In]: Rheinische Lebensbilder, Bd. 17. Hrsg. von Franz-Josef Heyen. Köln: Rheinland-Verl., 1997. Pp. 141–166, illus., notes. [H.H., donor of the Palazzo Zuccari for the Bibliotheca Hertziana in Rome, lived from the 1860s in London with her friends Ludwig and Frida Mond.]

35577. HERZFELDE, WIELAND. Faure, Ulrich: *Wieland Herzfelde zum 100. Geburtstag*. [In]: Aus dem Antiquariat 4 [Beilage zum] Börsenblatt für den Deutschen Buchhandel, Nr. 34, Frankfurt am Main, 26. April 1996. Pp. A 149–A 160. [Incl. a chronol. of H.'s life and of the history of the Malik-Verlag.] [Also on Herzfelde: "Ich bedarf keiner Biografie". Anmerkungen zu Briefen Wieland Herzfeldes (Erika Pick) [in]: Marginalien, H. 147 (3, 1997), Wiesbaden, 1997. Pp. 6–24, notes.]

35578. HERZKA, ELSE FREISTADT. Uehli Stauffer, Beatrice: *Mein Leben leben: Else Freistadt Herzka 1899–1953*. Zwischen Leidenschaft, Psychologie und Exil. Wien: Passagen, 1995. 314 pp., ports., facsims., notes, bibl. (Passagen Zeitgeschehen.) Zugl.: Zürich, Univ., Diss., 1993/94. [Incl.: Nachwort (Heinz Stefan Herzka, 255–263).] [E.F.H., née Freistadt, June 3, 1899 Vienna – Nov. 24, 1953 Zurich, psychologist, co-worker and friend of Alfred Adler, emigr. 1938 to Switzerland.]

35579. HERZL, THEODOR. Steinhardt, Milton J.: *Herzl and Freud*. [In]: Midstream, Vol. 43, No. 9, New York, Dec. 1997. Pp. 11–12. [Discusses similarities and differences in their respective backgrounds.]

35580. HEYMANN, LIDA GUSTAVA. Himmelsbach, Christiane: *"Verlass ist nur auf unsere eigene Kraft!": Lida Gustava Heymann, eine Kämpferin für die Frauenrechte*. Oldenburg: Bis, 1996. 117 pp., bibl. [See also in No. 35430.]

35581. HIRSCH, HELMUT. Hollender, Martin: *Der "unerwünschte" Remigrant. Zum 90. Geburtstag von Helmut Hirsch*. [In]: IWK, Int. wiss. Korrespondenz zur Gesch. der dt. Arbeiterbewegung, H. 3, Berlin, 1997. Pp. 421–428, footnotes. [Also on this occasion: "Verdrängung ist eine ganz normale Sache". Der jüdische Historiker Helmut Hirsch wird 90 (name of author not given) [in]: Aufbau, Vol. 63, No. 18, New York, Aug. 29, 1997, p. 15.] [H.H., historian, data see No. 33506/YB XVI.]

35582. HIRSCHMAN, ALBERT O.: *Selbstbefragung und Erkenntnis*. Aus dem Amerik. von Hanne Herkommer. München: Hanser, 1996. 280 pp., notes (259–276), index. [Cf.: Nachdenken über Zeiten des Übergangs: Albert O. Hirschmans selbstkritische Reflexionen (Warnfried Dettling) [in]: Die Zeit, Nr. 46, Hamburg, 8. Nov. 1996, p. 21.] [Orig title: 'A propensity to self-subversion', first publ. in 1995. A collection of essays written after 1986; incl. (part 2): Über das Selbst. Autobiographische "fragments".] [A.O.H. (formerly Hirschmann), b. 1915 in Berlin, economist, emigr. 1933 to France, then to Italy and Spain, where he fought in the Civil War; emigr. 1941 to the US.]

35583. HOFMANNSTHAL, HUGO VON. GILLMAN, ABIGAIL E.: *Hofmannsthal's Jewish pantomime*. [In]: Deutsche Vierteljahrsschrift für Literaturwissenschaft und Geistesgeschichte, Jg. 71, Bd. 71, Stuttgart, 1997. Pp. 437–460, footnotes. [On 'Der Schüler' (1901). Author challenges the tendency to dissociate Hofmannsthal's ouevre from Jewish concerns. Incl. English and German abstracts.]

35584. HORKHEIMER, MAX. WENZEL, UWE JUSTUS: *Sehnsucht nach dem ganz Anderen. Annäherungen an Max Horkheimer*. [In]: Politisches Denken. Jahrbuch 1995/96. Stuttgart, 1996. Pp. 125–131.

35585. JACOBSOHN, EDITH. FLECHTMANN, FRANK: *"Mein schöner Verlag, Williams & Co."* Erinnerungen an Edith Jacobsohn. [In]: Marginalien, H. 142 (2, 1996), Wiesbaden, 1996. Pp. 11–34, facsims., notes. [E. J., née Schiffer, b. 1891 in Berlin, translator, publisher, wife of Siegfried Jacobsohn, founded a publishing house, mainly for children's literature: Williams & Co.]

35586. KAFKA, FRANZ. COHN, DORRIT: *Kafka and Hofmannsthal*. [In]: Modern Austrian Literature, Vol. 30, No. 1, Riverside, CA, 1997. Pp. 1–17, notes.

35587. KAFKA, FRANZ. *Das Phänomen Franz Kafka*. Vorträge des Symposions der Österreichischen Franz Kafka-Gesellschaft in Klosterneuburg im Jahr 1995. Hrsg.: Wolfgang Kraus [et al.]. Prag: Vitalis, 1997. 176 pp., notes. (Schriftenreihe der Franz Kafka-Gesellschaft, 7.) [13 essays dealing with the Kafka reception and aspects of K.'s life and works.]

35588. KAFKA, FRANZ. SCHWARZ, HOWARD: *The strange case of Franz Kafka*. [In]: Midstream, Vol. 43, No. 6, New York, Aug./Sept. 1997. Pp. 34–37.

—— KAFKA, FRANZ. WAGNEROVA, ALENA: *"Im Hauptquartier des Lärms". Die Familie Kafka in Prag*. [See No. 34908.]

35589. KAHN, ROBERT LUDWIG. BECKSCHULTE, KLAUS: *"Ich hasse die Sprache, die ich liebe": das Leben und Werk von Robert Ludwig Kahn*. München: Tuduv, 1996. 330 pp., illus. (Kulturgeschichtl. Forschungen, Bd. 20). Zugl.: München, Univ., Diss., 1995. [R.L.K., Nuremberg, April 22, 1923 – Houston (Texas), March 1970 (suicide), Prof. of German, emigr. in 1939 to the UK, 1948 to Canada, later to the US.]

35590. KALMAR, FRITZ: *Das Herz europaschwer. Heimwehgeschichten aus Südamerika*. Mit einem Nachwort von Ursula Seeber. Wien: Picus, 1997. 192 pp. (Österreichische Exilbibliothek.) [Cf.: Auch das Heimweh hat seine Geschichte. Ein Porträt des Juristen, Theaterleiters und Autors Fritz Kalmar (Werner Hörtner) [in]: Mit der Ziehharmonika, Jg. 14, Nr. 4, Wien, Dez. 1997, pp. 10–13.] [F.K., b. 1911 in Vienna, emigr. 1938 to Bolivia, since 1953 lives in Uruguay.]

35591. KANTOROWICZ, ERNST. BENSON, ROBERT L./FRIED, JOHANNES, eds.: *Ernst Kantorowicz. Erträge der Doppeltagung. Institute for Advanced Study, Princeton; Johann Wolfgang Goethe-Universität, Frankfurt*. Stuttgart: Steiner, 1997. 296 pp., port., footnotes, index (289–296). [Incl. one text by E.K. and 16 essays on various aspects of K.'s life and work by David Abulafia, Hans Belting, Robert L. Benson, Charles Davis, Marion Dönhoff, Johannes Fried, Jean-Philippe Genet, Ralph E. Giesey, Eckhart Grünewald, Carl Landauer, Robert E. Lerner, Otto Gerhard Oexle, Peter Schöttler and Ihor Sevcenko.] [E.K., 1895 Posen – 1963 Princeton, NJ, historian.]

35592. KANTOROWICZ, ERNST H.. FUHRMANN, HORST: *Ernst Kantorowicz: der gedeutete Geschichtsdeuter.* [In]: Überall ist Mittelalter. Von der Gegenwart einer vergangenen Zeit [see No. 35799]. Pp. 252–270, port., notes (302–303).

35593. KATZ, JACOB. KEDAR, BENJAMIN ZE'EV: *Soziologische Geschichtsschreibung. Jacob Katz als Schüler Karl Mannheims.* [In]: Jüdischer Almanach 1998, Frankfurt am Main, 1997. Pp. 79–86, notes. [Based on the author's lecture given at the Hebrew University in Jerusalem on the occasion of J.K.'s 90th birthday. For data J.K. see No. 33498/YB XLI.]

35594. KERR, ALFRED: *Wo liegt Berlin? Briefe aus der Reichshauptstadt 1895–1900.* Hrsg. von Günther Rühle. Berlin: Aufbau, 1997. 767 pp., frontis., notes (666–739), index (753–767). [Incl. 134 of 191 texts, publ. in the liberal 'Breslauer Zeitung' and summaries of the unpubl. ones.] [Cf.: In Frack und Lack und Claque (Ulrich Weinzierl) [in]: 'FAZ', Nr. 238, Frankfurt am Main, 14.Okt. 1997, p. L 14. Ein Dandy in Berlin (Michael Skasa) [in]: Die Zeit, Nr. 43, Hamburg, 17. Okt. 1997, p. 14.]

35595. KISCH, EGON ERWIN. PATKA, MARCUS G.: *Egon Erwin Kisch. Stationen im Leben eines streitbaren Autors.* Wien: Böhlau, 1997. 565 pp., illus., footnotes, bibl. (441–533), index. (Literatur in der Geschichte, Geschichte in der Literatur, Bd. 41.) [Incl. bibl. E.E. Kisch (409–440).]

35596. KLEMPERER, VICTOR. DIRSCHAUER, JOHANNES: *Tagebuch gegen den Untergang. Zur Faszination Victor Klemperers.* Gießen: Psychosozialer Verlag, 1997. 229 pp., illus.

35597. KLEMPERER, VICTOR. *Im Herzen der Finsternis. Victor Klemperer als Chronist der NS-Zeit.* Hrsg. von Hannes Heer. Berlin: Aufbau, 1997. 220 pp. [Incl. 5 contribs. on various aspects of Victor Klemperer and his diaries by Heide Gerstenberger, Bernd Greiner, Michael Nerlich, Susanne zur Nieden, Yvonne Rieker, and Michael Wildt. Further contribs. are listed according to subject.]

35598. KLEMPERER, VICTOR. TRAVERSO, PAOLA: *Victor Klemperers Deutschlandbild – ein jüdisches Tagebuch?* [In]: Tel Aviver Jahrbuch für deutsche Geschichte, Bd. 26, 1997, Gerlingen, 1997. Pp. 307–344, notes. [Also by the same author: Gott behüte mich vor den Freunden. Wie Victor Klemperer durch seine Rezensenten vereinnahmt wird – ein Nachtrag [in]: Die Zeit, Nr. 49, Hamburg, 28. Nov. 1997, p. 66.]

35599. KOLMAR, GERTRUD. *A Jewish mother from Berlin: a novel; Susanna: a novella.* Transl. from the German by Brigitte M. Goldstein. New York: Holmes & Meier, 1997. 202 pp. (Modern German voices series.)

35600. KORNGOLD, ERICH WOLFGANG. DUCHEN, JESSICA: *Erich Wolfgang Korngold.* London: Phaidon Press, 1996. 239 pp., illus., scores, bibl. (220–231). (20th-century composers.) [Incl. discogr.] [Cf.: Wunderkind wider Willen (Jörn Rohwer) [in]: Die Zeit, Nr. 24, Hamburg, 6. Juni 1997, p. 46; on the occasion of the 100th anniversary of K.'s birth.] [E.W.K., May 29, 1897 Brünn – Nov. 29, 1957 Hollywood, composer, emigr. to the US in 1936.]

35601. KRACAUER, SIEGFRIED: *Frankfurter Turmhäuser. Ausgewählte Feuilletons 1906 bis 1930.* Hrsg. von Andreas Volk. Zürich: Ed. Epoca, 1997. 335 pp., illus. [An anthology of texts written for the 'Frankfurter Zeitung'.] [Cf.: Alles rollt (Volker Breidecker) [in]: 'FAZ', Nr. 266, Frankfurt am Main, 15. Nov. 1997, Beilage.

35602. KRAFT, WERNER. *Werner Kraft: 1896–1991.* Mit Briefen, Gedichten und Prosatexten sowie Auszügen aus seinen Tagebüchern. Bearb. von Jörg Drews. Mit Beiträgen und Texten von Thomas Blume [et al.]. Ausgew. von Volker Kahmen. Marbach am Neckar: Dt. Schillergesellschaft, 1996. 191 pp. [16 pp.: Beilage], illus. (Marbacher Magazin, 75.).

Beiheft (1996): Werner Kraft: Eines schönen Tages. Gedichte und Prosa. 69 pp., illus. (Marbacher Magazin, 75, Beih.) [W.K., data see No. 31068/YB XXXI.]

35603. KRAMER, EDITH. ZWIAUER, CHARLOTTE, ed.: *Edith Kramer. Malerin und Kunsttherapeutin zwischen den Welten.* Wien: Picus, 1997. 148 pp., illus. [E.K., b. Vienna 1916, emigr. 1938 to the US.]

35604. KUH, EMIL. STREITFELD, ERWIN: *"Der Umgang mit einem großen Manne ist wie das Wohnen in der Nähe eines feuerspeienden Berges". Friedrich Hebbel und Emil Kuh. Phasen ihrer Beziehung.* [In]: Hebbel-Jahrbuch 52/1997, Heide in Holstein, 1997. Pp. 85–107, notes. [E.K., writer, data see No. 27784/YB XXXVI.]

35605. LANDAUER, GUSTAV. *Gustav Landauer im Gespräch.* Symposium zum 125. Geburtstag. Hrsg. von Hanna Delf und Gert Mattenklott. Tübingen: Niemeyer, 1997. IX, 288 pp., footnotes, index (283–288). (Conditio Judaica, 18.) [Cont. section 1: Frühe literarische Imaginationen (essays by Lorenz Jäger and Thomas Regehly, 1–24). Section 2: Literaturhistorische Ortsbestimmungen (essays by Bernd Witte, Rolf Kauffeldt, Gert Mattenklott, Hanna Delf, Michael Löwy (25–104). Section 3 entitled Beziehungen cont.: (titles partly abbr.): Gustav Landauer und der Mathematiker Felix Hausdorff (Egbert Brieskorn, 105–128). Gustav Landauers Programm des anarchistischen Föderalismus in Paul Tillichs kulturtheologischem Entwurf von 1919 (Erdmann Sturm, 129–148). Der Dramatiker Georg Kaiser und sein Freund und Kritiker Gustav Landauer (Michael Matzigkeit, 149–164). Der Psychoanalytiker Karl Landauer und seine Beziehung zu Gustav Landauer (Hans-Joachim Rothe, 165–180). Section 4 entitled Politische Versuche cont.: Der Vordenker der Ökolibertären (Peter Glotz, 181–190). Die Siedlung: der Beginn des Sozialismus (Bernhard Braun, 191–202). Gustav Landauer und die Münchener Räterepublik (Norbert Seitz, 203–214). Gustav Landauer und die internationale anarchistische Bewegung (Rudolf de Jong, 215–234). Gustav Landauer im Friedrichshagener Jahrzehnt und die Rezeption seines Gemeinschaftsideals nach dem 1. Weltkrieg (Gertrude Cepl-Kaufmann, 235–278).]

35606. LANDAUER, GUSTAV: *Zeit und Geist.* Kulturkritische Schriften 1890–1919. Hrsg. von Rolf Kauffeldt und Michael Matzigkeit. München: Boer, 1997. 373 pp., illus., docs., facsims., bibl. (363–370), index (371–379).

35607. LANDAUER, GUSTAV: *Dichter, Ketzer, Aussenseiter.* Essays und Reden zu Literatur, Philosophie, Judentum. Hrsg. von Hanna Delf. Berlin: Akademie Verlag, 1997. LVIII, 290 pp., index. (281–290). (Werkausgabe/Gustav Landauer, Bd. 3.)

35608. LANDSHUT, SIEGFRIED. NICOLAYSEN, RAINER: *Siegfried Landshut. Die Wiederentdeckung der Politik.* Eine Biographie. Frankfurt am Main: Jüdischer Verlag, 1997. 678 pp., illus., bibl. (incl. bibl. S. Landshut, 572–618). [1897 Straßburg – 1968 Hamburg, professor of sociology and political science; for further data see No. 32227/YB XL.]

35609. LANG, FRITZ. MCGILLIGAN, PATRICK: *Fritz Lang: the nature of the beast.* London: Faber & Faber; New York: St. Martin's Press, 1997. 548 pp., illus., ports., notes (505–535). [Biography.] [Cf.: Dial M for monocled mythomaniac (Gilbert Adair) [in]: Sunday Times, London, July 13, 1997.]

35610. LASKER-SCHÜLER, ELSE. BODENHEIMER, ALFRED: *"Die Traurigkeit überlassen Sie mir". Else Lasker-Schülers Briefe an Emil Raas.* [In]: Zeitschrift für deutsche Philologie, Bd. 116, Berlin, 1997. Pp. 588–602, footnotes. [With German and English abstract. The hitherto unpubl. letters were addressed to the solicitor E.R. in Bern 1933–1945.]

35611. LASKER-SCHÜLER, ELSE. BODENHEIMER, ALFRED: *'Gottes Lächeln, Mephistos Pferdefuß'. Fährten einer poetischen Theologie bei Else Lasker-Schüler.* [In]: Aschkenas, Jg. 7, H. 1, Wien, 1997. Pp. 137–154, footnotes.

35612. LASKER-SCHÜLER, ELSE. SANDERS-BRAHMS, HELMA: *Gottfried Benn und Else Lasker-Schüler. Giselher und Prinz Jussuf.* Berlin: Rowohlt, 1997. 191 pp., illus. (Paare.) [On the intense, though brief love affair between the two poets which began in 1912.]

35613. LASKER-SCHÜLER, ELSE. STAMM, RAINER: *Else Lasker-Schüler und Heinrich Maria Davringhausen.* [In]: Marginalien, H. 140 (4, 1995), Wiesbaden, 1995. Pp. 20–27, illus., notes. [On L.-Sch.'s painter friend, whom she met in Berlin in 1916.]

35614. LASKER-SCHÜLER, ELSE. STAMM, RAINER: *Else Lasker-Schüker erzählt Märchen – Spuren eines verschollenen Bildes.* [In]: Romerike Berge, Jg. 46, H. 4, Burg an der Wupper, 1996. Pp. 23–26, illus. [On a lost oil-painting of the poetess (1913) by Walther Bötticher.]

35615. LASKER-SCHÜLER, ELSE: *Else Lasker-Schüler. Werke und Briefe.* Kritische Ausgabe. Bd. I, 1: Gedichte. Bd. 1, 2: Anmerkungen. bearb. von Karl Jürgen Skrodzki unter Mitarbeit von Norbert Oellers. Im Auftrag des Franz Rosenzweig-Zentrums [et al.] hrsg. von Norbert Oellers, Heinz Rölleke und Itta Shedletzky. 2 vols. Frankfurt am Main: Jüd. Verlag, 1996. 423; 614 pp. [Cf.: Trockener Südwind der Philologie (Thomas Rietzschel) [in]: 'FAZ', Nr. 295, Frankfurt am Main, 18. Dez. 1996, p. 42. Vom Nachklang der Schöpfung. Endlich erhält die große Dichterin Else Lasker-Schüler eine historisch-kritische Werkausgabe (Stefan Koldehoff) [in]: Die Zeit, Nr. 46, Hamburg, 7. Nov. 1997, p. 67.]

35616. LASKER-SCHÜLER, ELSE: *Gesammelte Werke in drei Bänden.* Hrsg. von Friedhelm Kemp und Werner Kraft. Frankfurt am Main: Suhrkamp, 1996. 3 vols. [Vol. 1: Gedichte 1902–1943. 438 pp.; Vol. 2: Prosa und Schauspiele. 1231 pp.; Vol. 3: Verse und Prosa aus dem Nachlaß. 177 pp.]

35617. LASSALLE, FERDINAND. ADLER, JOSEPH: *Ferdinand Lassalle: life and times of a practical idealist.* [In]: Jewish Frontier, No. 7, New York, Nov./Dec. 1997. Pp. 19–24.

35618. LESSING, THEODOR: *"Wir machen nicht mit". Schriften gegen den Nationalsozialismus und zur Judenfrage.* Hrsg. von Jörg Wollenberg. Mit Beiträgen und Zeichnungen von Walter Grab und Alfred Hrdlicka. Bremen: Donat, 1997. 312 pp. (Ausgewählte Schriften, Bd. 2.) [Vol. 1 of this edn.: Bildung ist Schönheit. Autobiographische Zeugnisse und Schriften zur Bildungsreform. Hrsg. und eingel. von Jörg Wollenberg und unter Mitwirkung von Ruth Schwabe und Helmut Donat. Mit einem Geleitwort von Dietrich Heimann uund einem Nachwort von Ursula und Peter Hansen. 1995. 263, XII pp., illus. (Ausgewählte Schriften, Bd. 1.)]

35619. LEWALD, FANNY. *A year of revolutions: Fanny Lewald's recollections of 1848.* Transl., ed. and annot. by Hanna Ballin Lewis. Oxford; Providence, RI: Berghahn Books, 1997. VIII, 164 pp., footnotes, bibl. (156–160). [Incl. almost all the 1856 edn. of F.L.'s 'Erinnerungen aus dem Jahre 1848'.]

35620. LEWY, FRITZ. BERNARD, BIRGIT: *Essen. Cincinnati. Zur Biographie des Graphikers und Bühnenbildners Fritz Lewy (1893–1950).* [In]: Geschichte im Westen, Jg. 12, Köln, 1997. Pp. 150–174, footnotes.

35621. LIEBERMANN, MAX. *Max Liebermann. Der Realist und die Phantasie.* [Hrsg.: Hamburger Kunsthalle. Katalog-Red.: Birte Frenssen]. Hamburg: Dölling und Galitz, 1997. 272 pp., frontis., illus., bibl. [Catalogue of exhibition held in Hamburg, Nov. 7, 1997 – Jan. 25, 1998. Incl.: Liebermann und sein Judentum (Hermann Simon, 41–48, notes).]

35622. LIEBERMANN, MAX. SCHOLZ, DIETER: *Max Liebermann und Karl Scheffler.* [In]: Jahrbuch Berliner Museen 1997, Berlin, 1997. Pp. 158–167, illus., notes.

35623. LIEBERMANN, MAX. *Was vom Leben übrig bleibt, sind Bilder und Geschichten.* Max Liebermann zum 150. Geburtstag. Rekonstruktion der Gedächtnisausstellung des Berliner Jüdischen Museums von 1936. Hrsg.: Hermann Simon, Stiftung "Neue Synagoge Berlin – Centrum Judaicum" in Zusammenarbeit mit dem Museumspädagogischen Dienst Berlin. Berlin: Stiftung "Neue Synagoge Berlin – Centrum Judaicum"/Max-Liebermann-Gesellschaft e.V./Museumspädagogischer Dienst, 1997. 272 pp., frontis., illus., facsims., notes, index. [Selected essays (titles partly abbr.): Max Liebermann und das Berliner Jüdische Museum (Hermann Simon, 8–17). Zur Geschichte der Familie Liebermann (Miriam A. Dytman, 47–66). Zur Rezeption des Jüdischen im Werk von Max Liebermann (Chana C. Schütz, 67–79; also by this author: Max Liebermann in Eretz Jisrael, 133–145). Max Liebermann als Präsident der Preußischen Akademie der Künste 1920–1932 (Silvia Diekmann/Norbert Kampe, 80–94). Über den Aufstieg des Antisemitismus von der Ideologie zur Staatsdoktrin zu Lebzeiten Max Liebermanns (Thomas Friedrich, 95–117). Zeitgenössische Berichte zu Max Liebermann (146–166).]

35624. LIPPMANN, HEINZ. HERMS, MICHAEL: *Heinz Lippmann. Porträt eines Stellvertreters.* Mit einem Vorwort von Hermann Weber. Berlin: Dietz, 1996 pp., illus., bibl. [H.L. (1921–1974), son of a Jewish father, journalist, deported to Auschwitz and Buchenwald, joined the KPD after liberation and became for a time a political functionary in the GDR.]

35625. LOEB, JAMES. BURGMAIR, WOLFGANG/WEBER, MATTHIAS M.: *". . . daß er sich nirgends wohler als in Murnau fühle. . .". James Loeb als Förderer der Wissenschaft und philanthropischer Mäzen.* [In]: Jahrbuch 1997. Schriften des Historischen Vereins Murnau am Staffelsee e.V., Jg. 18, H. 18, 82418 Murnau, [1997]. Pp. 76–128, frontis., notes (119–126), bibl. [J.L., 1867 New York – 1933 Hochried/Murnau, American-born son of German-Jewish parents, philanthropist, lived from 1905 in Murnau and Munich.]

35626. LÖWENSTEIN, OTTO. LINDNER, ERIK: *Die Wilhelmstraße als Ziel. Ein Verleger im Kaiserreich: Dr. Otto Löwenstein und der Berliner Carl Heymanns Verlag.* [In]: Buchhandelsgeschichte, 1997/1. [Beilage zum] Börsenblatt für den Deutschen Buchhandel, Jg. 164, Nr. 24, Frankfurt am Main, 25. März 1997. Pp. B 19–B 28, illus., notes.

35627. LÖWITH, KARL. *100 Jahre Karl Löwith.* [Special section in]: Heidelberger Jahrbücher, Bd. 41, Heidelberg; New York, 1997. Pp. 263–296. [Incl. contribs. by Eugen Biser, Dominic Kaegi, Peter Ulmer, Wolfgang Wieland.] [Also on this occasion: Widerstand und Ergebung. Vor hundert Jahren wurde Karl Löwith geboren (Uwe Justus Wenzel) [in]: 'NZZ', Nr. 8, Zürich, 11./12. Jan. 1997, p. 66, port.]

35628. LOWE, ADOLPH. KROHN, CLAUS-DIETER: *Der philosophische Ökonom. Zur intellektuellen Biographie Adolph Lowes.* Marburg: Metropolis, 1996. 229 [12] pp., illus., bibl. (231–236). [A.L. (orig. Löwe), (1893–1995), economist, sociologist, emigr. 1933 to UK, 1940 to US.]

35629. LOWENFELD, HENRY. MÜLLER, THOMAS: *Leben und Werk von Henry Lowenfeld (1900–1985).* [In]: Zeitschrift zur Geschichte der Psychoanalyse, Jg. 8, H. 16, Tübingen, 1995. Pp. 56–65. [H.L., orig. Heinrich Julius Löwenfeld, psychoanalyst.]

35630. LUXEMBURG, ROSA. SHEPARDSON, DONALD E.: *Rosa Luxemburg and the noble dream.* New York; Bern: Lang, 1996. 171 pp., notes, bibl. (154–161), index.

35631. MAHLER, GUSTAV. CARR, JONATHAN: *The real Mahler.* London: Constable; Woodstock, NY: Overlook Press, 1997. XIII, 254 pp., illus., scores, facsims., maps, chronol., bibl. [Title of the American edn.: Mahler, a biography. German edn.: Gustav Mahler. Biographie. Aus dem Engl. übers. von Hermann Kusterer. München: List, 1997. 352 pp., illus.; incl.: Werkverzeichnis (339–344).]

35632. MARMOREK, OSKAR. KRISTAN, MARKUS: *Oskar Marmorek, Architekt und Zionist 1863–1909.* Mit einem Beitrag von Samuel D. Albert. Wien: Böhlau, 1996. 290 pp., illus., graphs, bibl. (272–283). (Veröff. der Albertina, Bd. 40.) [O.M., 1863 Galicia – 1909 Vienna (suicide), architect and close friend of Herzl.]

35633. MARX, KARL. GLATZER, ALBERT: *Marx and the Jews – a paradox of sorts.* [In]: Midstream, Vol. 43, No. 4, New York, May 1997. Pp. 10–13, notes. [Describes Marx's ambivalent feelings towards Jews and his own background.]

35634. MARX, KARL. HULL, GORDON: *The Jewish question revisited. Marx, Derrida and ethnic nationalism.* [In]: Philosophy & Social Criticism, Vol. 23, No. 2, London; Thousand Oaks, CA,

1997. Pp. 47–77, footnotes. [Analyses contemporary theories of Nationalism against Marx's early writings.]

35635. MARX, KARL. MONZ, HEINZ: *Karl Marx (1818–1883)*. [In]: Rheinische Lebensbilder, Bd. 17. Hrsg. von Franz-Josef Heyen. Köln: Rheinland-Verl., 1997. Pp. 101–119, illus., notes.

35636. MARX, KARL. *Das Museum Karl-Marx-Haus. Ein Begleitbuch zur ständigen Ausstellung im Geburtshaus von Karl Marx, Trier*. [Text: Heribert Lambert, Boris Olschewski]. Trier: Karl-Marx-Haus, 1997. 106 pp., illus.

35637. MAUTHNER, FRITZ. LEINFELLNER, ELISABETH/SCHLEICHERT, HUBERT, eds.: *Fritz Mauthner: das Werk eines kritischen Denkers*. Wien: Böhlau, 1995. 177 pp.

35638. MEITNER, LISE. CRAWFORD, ELISABETH/SIME, RUTH LEWIN/WALKER, MARK: *A Nobel tale of postwar injustice*. [In]: Physics Today, Vol. 50, No. 9, Washington DC, Sept. 1997. Pp. 26–32, illus., notes. [Based on recently released Swedish documents, the authors reveal why Lise Meitner did not receive the 1946 physics Nobel Prize.]

35639. MENDELSOHN, ERICH. JAMES, KATHLEEN: *Erich Mendelsohn and the architecture of German modernism*. Cambridge; New York; Cambridge Univ. Press, 1997. XVII, 328 pp., illus.

35640. MENDELSOHN, ERICH. NITZANSHIFTAN, A.: *Contested Zionism – alternative modernism: Erich Mendelsohn and the Tel Aviv Chug in Mandate Palestine*. [In]: Architectural History, No. 39, Cambridge, MA, 1996. Pp. 147–180, notes. [E. M. data see No. 29819/YB XXXVII.]

35641. MENDELSSOHN, FELIX. RICHTER, BRIGITTE: *Frauen um Felix Mendelssohn Bartholdy. In Texten und Bildern vorgestellt*. Frankfurt am Main: Insel, 1997. 141 pp., illus. (Insel-Bücherei, Nr. 1178.)

35642. MENDELSSOHN, FELIX & HENSEL, FANNY. *Das verborgene Band. Felix Mendelssohn Bartholdy und seine Schwester Fanny Hensel. Ausstellung der Musikabteilung der Staatsbibliothek zu Berlin – Preußischer Kulturbesitz zum 150. Todestag der beiden Geschwister 15. Mai bis 12. Juli 1997*. [Katalog: Hans-Günther Klein]. Wiesbaden: Reichert, 1997. 251 pp., ports., illus., facsims., family tree, bibl. [Incl.: Werk-Verzeichnis Felix Mendelssohn Bartholdy and Fanny Hensel (241–245).] [Cf.: Will dich küssen, Bruder mein. Liebe, Musik und Tod der Geschwister Felix und Fanny Mendelssohn Bartholdy (Eleonore Büning) [in]: 'FAZ', Nr. 129, Frankfurt am Main, 7. Juni 1997, [Beilage]; essay on the occasion of the exhibition.]

35643. MOSSE FAMILY. KRAUS, ELISABETH: *Jüdische Stiftungstätigkeit: Das Beispiel der Familie Mosse in Berlin*. [In]: Zeitschrift für Geschichtswissenschaft, Jg. 45, H. 2, Berlin, 1997. Pp. 101–121, footnotes.

35644. MOSSE, MARCUS. KRAUS, ELISABETH: *Marcus Mosse. A Jew in the Prussian province of Posen*. [In]: Leo Baeck Institute Year Book XLII, London, 1997. Pp. 3–28, footnotes. [M.M., 1808–1865, father of Rudolf and Albert Mosse.]

35645. NORDAU, MAX. SCHULTE, CHRISTOPH: *Psychopathologie des Fin de siècle. Der Kulturkritiker, Arzt und Zionist Max Nordau*. Frankfurt am Main: Fischer Taschenbuch Verlag, 1997. 399 pp. [Cf.: Besprechung (Jörg Hackeschmidt) [in]: Zeitschrift für Geschichtswissenschaft, Jg. 46, H. 2, Berlin, 1998, pp. 177–178. "Entartung" und Zionismus. der vergessene Max Nordau (Ladislau Löb) [in]: 'NZZ', Nr. 95, Zürich, 25./26. April 1998, p. 69.]

35646. NORDAU, MAX. WISTRICH, ROBERT S.: *Max Nordau, degeneration and the fin-de-siècle*. [In]: Krisenwahrnehmungen im Fin de siècle. Jüdische und katholische Bildungseliten in Deutschland und in der Schweiz [see No. 34914]. Pp. 83–100, footnotes.

35647. OFFENBACH, JACQUES. FISCHER, RALPH: *On Jacques Offenbach's childhood*. [Engl. edn. by Robert L. Folstein] Bad Ems: Verein für Geschichte/Denkmal- und Landschaftspflege e.V.,

1997. 45 pp., illus., music. (Bad Emser Hefte, Nr. 169.) [German edn.: Aus Jacques Offenbachs Kindertagen.]

35648. OPPENHEIMER, FRANZ. *Franz Oppenheimer und Adolph Lowe. Zwei Wirtschaftswissenschaftler der Frankfurter Universität.* Hrsg. von Volker Caspari und Bertram Schefold. Marburg: Metropolis, 1996. 320 pp., illus., bibl. [Contribs. partly German, partly Engl.]

35649. ORLIK, EMIL. *Emil Orlik: Leben und Werk 1870 – 1932. Prag – Wien – Paris.* Hrsg.: Eugen Otto. Mit Textbeiträgen von Birgit Ahrens [et al.]. Wien: Brandstätter, 1997. 176 pp., illus., bibl. (168–173). [Exhibition catalogue. Incl. a chap. dealing with the family history of the banker and industrialist Max von Gomperz, friend and supporter of Orlik. Cf.: Empfänglich für Impression und Expression. Wiederbegegnung mit dem Werk Emil Orliks (Hansres Jacobi) [in]: 'NZZ', Nr. 5, Zürich, 8. Jan. 1998, p. 40.] [E.O., Prague 1870 – 1932 Berlin, painter, book illustrator.]

35650. ORLIK, EMIL. RYCHLIK, OTMAR, ed.: *Emil Orlik – Prag, Wien, Berlin.* Mit Beiträgen von Gerhard Eberstaller [et al.]. Wien: Sonderzahl, 1997. 148 pp.

35651. ORLIK, EMIL. RYCHLIK, OTMAR, ed.: *Emil Orlik an Marie von Gomperz.* Briefe 1902–1932. Wien: Sonderzahl, 1997. 204 pp. [Incl. the correspondence with O.'s friend, the wife of the banker Max von Gomperz, a generous benefactor for many years.]

35652. POMMER, ERIC (ERICH). HARDT, URSULA: *From Caligari to California: Eric Pommer's life in the international film wars.* Oxford; Providence, RI: Berghahn Books, 1996. VI, 256 pp., illus., tabs., appendixes, filmography, footnotes, bibl. (245–253). [E.P., 1889 Hildesheim – 1966 California, film producer, emigr. to the US, via France and London, where he co-founded Mayflower Picture Corp. After the war restarted the German film industry.]

35653. POPPER, KARL. WATKINS, JOHN: *Karl Popper: a memoir.* [In]: American Scholar, Washington, DC, Spring 1997. Pp. 205–224. [K. P., philosopher; author was his student. For data and obits. see No. 32255/YB XL.]

35654. RATHENAU, WALTHER. HEIMBÖCKEL, DIETER: *Widersprüchlicher Universalist: Der Industrielle, Politiker und Schriftsteller Walther Rathenau.* [In]: Schweizer Monatshefte, Jg. 77, H. 11, Zürich, Nov. 1997. Pp. 12–15.

35655. RATHENAU, WALTHER. LÖFFLER, HANS F.: *Walther Rathenau, ein Europäer im Kaiserreich.* Berlin: Berlin Verlag Arno Spitz, 1997. 202 pp., bibl., index.

35656. RATHENAU, WALTHER. THEEL, ROBERT: *"Der Snob Rathenau". Carl Sternheims Parvenü Christian Maske als dramatische Verschlüsselung des wilhelminischen Industriellen, Philosophen und Zeitkritikers Walther Rathenau ('Der Snob', 1913).* [In]: Literaturwissenschaftliches Jahrbuch, NF, Bd. 37, Berlin, 1996. Pp. 229–259, footnotes. [Incl. abstract, pp. 230–231.]

35657. REICH, WILHELM. WEINZIERL, ULRICH: *Der universelle Orgasmus. Pionier der Sozialpsychologie, bedeutender Therapeut und spintisierender Naturforscher. Vor hundert Jahren wurde Wilhelm Reich geboren.* [In]: 'FAZ', Nr. 69, Frankfurt am Main, 22. März 1997, Beilage. Also on this occasion: Nur ein "impetuöser Steckenpferdreiter"? Zum 100. Geburtstag des Psychoanalytikers Wilhelm Reich (Sabine Richebächer) [in]: 'NZZ', Nr. 68, Zürich, 22./23. März 1997. P. 70, port.]

35658. ROSENZWEIG, FRANZ. LUX, RÜDIGER: *Franz Rosenzweig: "Ich bleibe also Jude".* [In]: Mitteilungen und Beiträge, Forschungsstelle Judentum, 12/13, Leipzig, 1997. Pp. 19–35, footnotes.

35659. ROTH, JOSEPH. COHEN, ROBERT: *Männergewalt, Gewalt, Weimarer Republik: Rechtsextremismus im Frühwerk Joseph Roths und in Ernst Ottwalds 'Ruhe und Ordnung'.* [In]: Modern Austrian Literature, Vol. 30, No. 1, Riverside, CA, 1997. Pp. 48–68, notes. [Discusses Roth's concept of the emerging Right-wing movements and antisemitism.]

35660. ROTH, JOSEPH. Kuzmics, Helmut: *Von der Habsburgermonarchie zu 'Österreich'. Reichspatriotismus, 'habsburgischer Mythos' und Nationalismus in den Romanen von Joseph Roth.* [In]: Archiv für Kulturgeschichte, Bd. 79, H. 1, Köln, Pp. 105–122, footnotes.

35661. ROTH, JOSEPH. Schuhmacher, Klaus: *Joseph Roth in Leipzig.* [In]: Interkulturelle Perspektiven. Germanistische Beiträge. Hrsg. von Norbert Honsza, Wroclaw: Wydawnictwo Uniw. Wrocl., 1997. (Germanica Wratislaviensia, CXIX; Acta Univ. Wratislaviensis No. 1887.). Pp. 17–27.

35662. Roth, Joseph: *Briefe aus Deutschland.* Hrsg. von Ralph Schock. Blieskastel: Gollenstein, 1997. 175 pp. [Reports from the Saar, publ. in 1927 in the 'Frankfurter Zeitung'.]

35663. ROTHFELS, HANS. Neugebauer, Wolfgang: *Hans Rothfels als politischer Historiker der Zwischenkriegszeit.* [In]: Ambivalenzen der Pädagogik. Zur Bildungsgeschichte der Aufklärung und des 20.Jahrhunderts. Harald Scholtz zum 65. Geburtstag. Hrsg. von Peter Drewek [et al.]. Weinheim: Dt. Studien Verlag, 1995. Pp. 169–184, notes. [H.R., 1891 Kassel – 1976 Tübingen, 1926–1935 professor in Königsberg, emigr. 1939 from Berlin via England to the US, from 1951 professor at Tübingen university.]

35664. ROTHSCHILD, MEYER AMSCHEL. Elon, Amos: *Le premier des Rothschild. Meyer Amschel fondateur de la dynastie.* Paris: Éd. Calmann-Lévy, 1997. 223 pp. [For Engl. orig. edn. see No. 34488/YB XLII.]

35665. SACHS, NELLY. Rudnick, Ursula: *Reconstructing God-language: the poetry of Nelly Sachs.* [In]: European Judaism, Vol. 30, No. 2, London, Autumn 1997. Pp. 131–150, notes.

35666. SALOMON, CHARLOTTE. Schmetterling, Astrid: *Tracing the life (or theatre?) of Charlotte Salomon.* [In]: Issues in the Theory and Practice of Architecture, Art and Design, Vol. 7, London, 1997. Pp. 115–128, illus., notes. [Ch. S., 1917 Berlin – 1943 Auschwitz.]

35667. SCHEYER, GALKA. *Die Blaue Vier. Feininger, Jawlensky, Kandinsky, Klee in der Neuen Welt.* Hrsg. von Vivian Endicott Barnett und Josef Helfenstein mit Beiträgen von Vivian Endicott Barnett [et al.]. Köln: Dumont, 1997. 367 pp., illus., facsims., chron., index. [Catalogue book of exhibition held in Bern, Dec. 5, 1997 – March 1, 1998 and Düsseldorf, March 28, 1998 – June 28, 1998. Focuses on the role of Galka Scheyer as the friend, promoter and art-dealer of the four painters, for whose work she tried to establish a market in the US between 1925 and 1945. Selected essays: Die Gründung der Blauen Vier und ihre Präsentation in New York (Vivian Endicott Barnett, 15–28). Minister, Kindermädchen, Little Friend: Galka Scheyer und Die Blaue Vier (Christina Houstian, 29–50). Kleine Kreise und brüchige Bündnisse: Galka Scheyer und amerikanische Sammler (Naomi Sawelson-Gorse, 51–62). "Ich habe meine Kunst in ihre Hände gelegt": Emmy Scheyer und Alexej von Jawlensky – eine Freundschaft (Angelica Jawlensky, 63–78). Die letzten Jahre der Blauen Vier, 1933–1945 (Vivian Endicott Barnett, 263–272). "Es ist ein langsamer Weg." John Cage und Galka Scheyer (Maria Müller, 273–278). Galka Scheyer und das Norton Simon Museum (Sara Campbell, 279–290). Die Blaue Vier – Briefe (Karin Zaugg, 291–321).] [Galka (orig. Emmy) Scheyer, April 15, 1889 Braunschweig – Dec. 13, 1945 Hollywood, painter, art teacher, art dealer, lived from 1924 in the US.]

35668. SCHLEGEL, DOROTHEA. Horn, Gisela: *Frauenaufbruch. Das Beispiel Dorothea Mendelssohn-Veit-Schlegel (1764–1839).* [In]: Edith Stein Jahrbuch, Bd. 2, Würzburg, 1996. Pp. 152–164, footnotes.

35669. SCHLESINGER, MORITZ. Unger, Hartmut: *Zwischen Ideologie und Improvisation. Moritz Schlesinger und die Rußlandpolitik der SPD 1918–1922.* Frankfurt am Main; New York: Lang, 1995. 306 pp. (Europäische Hochschulschriften, Reihe III: Geschichte und ihre Hilfswissenschaften, Bd. 694.) [M.S. 1886 Magdeburg – 1974 Washington DC, diplomat, Consul-General, expert on Russia and the Baltic States, emigr. 1939 to the US.]

35670. SCHNITZLER, ARTHUR. FLIEDL, KONSTANZE: *Arthur Schnitzler: Poetik der Erinnerung.* Wien: Böhlau, 1997. 567 pp., bibl. (503–562), index. (Literatur in der Geschichte, Geschichte in der Literatur, Bd. 42.)

35671. SCHNITZLER, ARTHUR. KAWOHL, BIRGIT: *Arthur Schnitzler.* Personalbibliographie 1977–1994. Gießen: Kletsmeier, 1996. 80 pp.

35672. SCHNITZLER, ARTHUR. MÜLLER-SEIDEL, WALTER: *Arztbilder im Wandel. Zum literarischen Werk Arthur Schnitzlers.* Vorgetragen am 3. November 1995. München: Bayerische Akademie der Wissenschaften, Philos.-Hist. Klasse, Sitzungsberichte, Jg. 1997, H. 6, 82 pp., footnotes.

35673. SCHNITZLER, ARTHUR. PLENER, PETER: *". . . und ich bin beruhigt weil ichs notire." Arthur Schnitzlers Tagebücher am Fin de siècle.* [In]: Germanistische Mitteilungen, Jg. 45/46, Brüssel, 1997. Pp. 15–34.

35674. SCHNITZLER, ARTHUR. SCHEIBLE, HARTMUT: *Liebe und Liberalismus. Über Arthur Schnitzler.* Bielefeld: Aisthesis, 1996. 199 pp., footnotes.

35675. SCHNITZLER, ARTHUR. WISELEY, ANDREW C.: *Arthur Schnitzler and the discourse of honor and dueling.* New York; Bern: Lang, 1996. XI, 278 pp. (Austrian culture, Vol. 20.) [Deals with the importance of honour to Schnitzler and also shows the extent to which the issues of class, gender and race sustained the dueling ethic.]

35676. SCHOEPS, HANS-JOACHIM. KROLL, FRANK-LOTHAR: *Hans-Joachim Schoeps (1909–1980), Historiker.* [In]: Fränkische Lebensbilder. Bd. 16. Hrsg. von Alfred Wendehorst. Neustadt: Degener, 1996. Pp. 287–306, notes.. 1996.

35677. SCHOLEM, GERSHOM. NIEWÖHNER, FRIEDRICH: *Der wahre Glaube ist verborgen. Ein schwieriger Prophet: Gershom Scholem zwischen Kabbala und Zionismus.* [In]: 'FAZ', Nr. 278, Frankfurt am Main, 29. Nov. 1997, Beilage.

35678. SCHWARZSCHILD, LEOPOLD. BEHMER, MARKUS: *Von der Schwierigkeit, gegen Illusionen zu kämpfen. Der Publizist Leopold Schwarzschild. Leben und Werk vom Kaiserreich bis zur Flucht aus Europa.* Münster: Lit, 1997. 721 pp., ports., bibl. (663–709), indexes. (Kommunikationsgeschichte, Bd. 2.) Zugl.: München, Univ., Diss., 1996. [Incl. Verzeichnis der Veröffentlichungen Leopold Schwarzschilds (614–662).] [L.Sch., 1891 Frankfurt am Main – 1950 Santa Margherita, Italy, journalist, 1919–1933 editor of 'Das Tagebuch', emigr. in 1933 to Paris, where he edited 'Das Neue Tage-Buch', escaped in 1940 to the US, returned to Europe in 1950.]

35679. SEGHERS, ANNA. HALLER-NEVERMANN, MARIE: *Jude und Judentum im Werk Anna Seghers'. Untersuchungen zur Bedeutung jüdischer Traditionen und zur Thematisierung des Antisemitismus in den Romanen und Erzählungen von Anna Seghers.* Frankfurt am Main: Lang, 1997. 279 pp., footnotes, bibl. (259–279). (Europäische Hochschulschriften: Reihe 1, Deutsche Sprache und Literatur, Bd. 1612.). Zugl.: Berlin, Freie Univ., Diss., 1996. [Cf.: Besprechung (Hans Otto Horch) [in]: Aschkenas, Jg. 8, H. 1, Wien, 1998, pp. 217–218.]

35680. SIMMEL, GEORG. LICHTBLAU, KLAUS: *Georg Simmel.* Frankfurt am Main; New York: Campus, 1997. 182 pp. (Reihe Campus Einführungen.)

35681. SINGER, PAUL. REUTER, URSULA: *Paul Singer im Visier der politischen Polizei (1878–1913).* [In]: Beiträge zur Geschichte der Arbeiterbewegung, Jg. 39, H. 1, Kösching, 1997. Pp. 75–86, notes. [P.S. (1844–1911), Socialist, leader of Berlin SPD.]

35682. SOYFER, JURA: *It's up to us! Collected works by Jura Soyfer.* Selected and transl. by Horst Jarka. Riverside, CA: Ariadne Press, 1996. 593 pp., illus. [J. S., writer, data see No. 28778/YB XXXVII.]

35683. SPERBER, MANES. CORBIN-SCHUFFELS, ANNE-MARIE: *Manès Sperber und Die Umschau.* [In]: Geschichte und Gegenwart, Jg. 16, H. 3, Graz, 1997. Pp. 167–178, footnotes. [Examines Sperber's activities during his exile years in Paris and, after 1945, in the French Occupation Zone, where he was commissioned to publish a journal aiming for German re-education.]

35684. STEIN, EDITH. *Edith Stein Jahrbuch 1997.* Bd. 3. [With the issue title] *Das Judentum.* Würzburg: Echter, 1997. 414 pp., footnotes. [Incl.: Judentum und Martyrium. Das Zeugnis Edith Steins in jüdischer Prospektive (Daniel Krochmalnik, 50–63). Section V, entitled Edith-Stein-Forschung, cont.: Die Frau im Denken Edith Steins. In Auseinandersetzung mit Sigmund Freud (Rachel Feldhay Brenner, 349–366). Emmanuel Levinas und Edith Stein (Andreas Uwe Müller, 367–384). Die Familie Stein in Lublinitz (Maria Amata Neyer, 385–402, facsims.). Das Werk Edith Steins in Polen. Bibliographische Hinweise (Janina Adamska und Zdzislaw Florek, 403–406). Edith Stein im Kölner und Echter Karmel zur Zeit der Judenverfolgung (Waltraud Herbstrith (407–410). Further essays are listed according to subject.]

35685. STEINBERGER, NATHAN. STEINBERGER, NATHAN/BROGGINI, BARBARA: *Berlin – Moskau – Kolyma und zurück. Ein Gespräch über Stalinismus und Antisemitismus.* Mit einem Vorwort von Jakob Moneta. Gespräch zwischen Nathan Steinberger und Barbara Broggini. Berlin: Ed. ID-Archiv, 1996. 142 pp. [N. St., b. 1910, professor of agriculture, Communist, emigr. to the Soviet Union in the early 1930s, 1937 imprisoned, then in a Gulag 1938–1946, returned to Berlin (East) in 1956, where he taught at the Humboldt Univ.]

35686. STEINER, FRANZ BAERMANN. MACK, MICHAEL: *Franz Baermann Steiners Auseinandersetzung mit dem Nationalsozialismus.* [In]: Mit der Ziehharmonika, Jg. 14, Nr. 3, Wien, Nov. 1997. Pp. 17–21, port., notes. [F.B.St., 1909 Prague – 1952 Oxford, poet, social anthropologist, went to London in 1936, returned to Prague 1937, emigr. to the UK in 1938.]

35687. STERN, FRITZ. *Fritz Stern at 70.* Ed. by Marion F. Deshmukh and Jerry Z. Muller. Washington, DC: German Historical Institute, 1997. 82 pp., ports. (Occasional papers, 19.) [F.St., b. 1926 in Breslau, historian, professor emeritus at Columbia Univ. Papers from a meeting held April 26, 1996, by the German Historical Institute, Washingtin, DC, to honour Fritz Stern.]

35688. STERN, JAKOB. STERN, JAKOB: *Vom Rabbiner zum Atheisten. Ausgewählte religionskritische Schriften.* Hrsg. von Heiner Jestrabak. Aschaffenburg: IBDK Verlag, 1997. 140 pp., gloss. [Incl.: Jakob Stern oder: Vom Weg eines württembergischen Rabbiners zum Philosophen des Atheismus (ed. & Marvin Chlada, 7–23). Jakob Stern. Nachruf in 'Die Neue Zeit' vom 14.4.1911 (Clara Zetkin, 24–30).] [Jakob (orig. Isaak) St., May 28, 1843 Niederstetten – April 1, 1911 Stuttgart (suicide), writer, journalist, Socialist functionary, gave up his position as a rabbi in Buttenhausen in 1880 and became an atheist.]

35689. STRUCK, HERMANN. RUSEL, JANE: *Hermann Struck – das Leben und das graphische Werk eines jüdischen Künstlers.* Frankfurt am Main; New York: Lang, 1997. 628 pp., illus. (Judentum und Umwelt, Bd. 66.) Zugl.: Mainz, Univ., Diss., 1995.

35690. TETZNER, LISA. BOLIUS, GISELA: *Lisa Tetzner: Leben und Werk.* Frankfurt am Main: dipa-Verl., 1997. 287 pp. (Jugend und Medien.) Zugl.: Berlin, Freie Univ., Diss. [L.T., 1894 Zittau – 1963 Carona, Switzerland, teacher of voice technique, author of children's books, emigr. 1933 to Switzerland.]

35691. TOLLER, ERNST. HEMPEL-KÜTER, CHRISTA/MÜLLER, HANS-HARALD: *Ernst Toller: Auf der Suche nach dem geistigen Führer.* Ein Beitrag zur Rekonstruktion der 'Politisierung' der literarischen Intelligenz im Ersten Weltkrieg. [In]: Literatur, Politik und soziale Prozesse. Studien zur deutschen Literatur von der Aufklärung bis zur Weimarer Republik. 8. Sonderheft, Int. Archiv für Sozialgesch. der deutschen Literatur. Tübingen, 1997. Pp. 78–106, footnotes.

35692. TORBERG, FRIEDRICH. KLEIN, WALLACE G.: *Remembering Friedrich Torberg 1943–1979. A personal recollection.* [In]: Modern Austrian Literature, Vol. 30, No. 2, Riverside, CA, 1997. Pp. 117–129, notes. [Describes the personal and professional relationship that developed through correspondence between a former soldier-student of F. T., when T. was instructor in the German Studies Section of the Army Specialized Training Program at the Univ. of California.]

35693. TORBERG, FRIEDRICH. TICHY, FRANK: *Friedrich Torberg. Ein Leben in Widersprüchen.* Salzburg: Müller, 1995. 303 pp., illus., notes (272–303).

35694. TUCHOLSKY, KURT. KING, IAN: *Ein Suchender, kein Denkmal: an analysis of research on Kurt Tucholsky.* [In]: German Life and Letters, Vol. 50, No. 1, Oxford, Jan. 1997. Pp. 35–52, footnotes.

35695. VARNHAGEN, RAHEL. ARENDT, HANNAH: *Rahel Varnhagen: the life of a Jewess.* First complete edn., ed. and with introd. by Liliane Weissberg; transl. by Richard and Clara Winston. Baltimore: Johns Hopkins Univ. Press, 1997. XII, 388 pp., frontis., illus., facsims., notes, bibl. comp. by H.A. (369–372), bibl. (373–380). [1st publ. in English 1957 by the LBI, in German 1959. This 9th edn. was publ. in cooperation with the LBI New York.]

35696. VARNHAGEN, RAHEL. HUNDT, IRINA: *Die Muse der Hegelschen Gegenakademie. Zum 225. Geburtstag Rahel Varnhagens.* [In]: Zeitschrift für Geschichtswissenschaft, Jg. 44, H. 5, Berlin, 1996. Pp. 408–420, footnotes.

35697. WARBURG, ABY M. ROECK, BERND: *Der junge Aby Warburg.* München: Beck, 1997. 120 pp., illus., notes.

35698. WIESENTHAL, SIMON. PICK, HELLA: *Simon Wiesenthal. Eine Biographie.* Deutsch von Susanne Klockmann. Reinbek: Rowohlt, 1997. 507 pp., illus., bibl. (487–495), index (497–506). [For English orig. edn. see No. 34513/YB XLII.] [Cf.: Eine geistreiche, mitunter rechtfertigende Biographie Simon Wiesenthals (Nachum Orland) [in]: 'FAZ', Nr. 257, Frankfurt am Main, 5. Nov. 1997, p. 11.]

35699. ZUCKMAYER, CARL. NICKEL, GUNTHER: *Zuckmayer und Brecht.* [In]: Jahrbuch der Deutschen Schillergesellschaft, Jg. 41, Stuttgart, 1997. Pp. 428–459, footnotes.

35700. ZUCKMAYER, CARL. STRASSER, CHRISTIAN: *Carl Zuckmayer. Deutsche Künstler im Salzburger Exil 1933–1938.* Wien: Böhlau, 1996. 335 pp., 20 pp.: illus. (Schriftenreihe des Forschungsinstitutes für pol.-hist. Studien der Dr.-Wilfried-Haslauer-Bibliothek, Bd. 5.) [Deals with Zuckmayer's country home "Wiesmühl", where both exiled anti-Nazis and Nazis enjoyed Z.'s generous hospitality.]

35701. ZWEIG, ARNOLD: *Dialektik der Alpen. Fortschritt und Hemmnis. Emigrationsbericht oder Warum wir nach Palästina gingen.* Berlin: Aufbau, 1997. 516 pp., notes (410–453), index (487–509). (Arnold Zweig; Berliner Ausgabe, Essays/4.) [Incl.: Entstehung und Textgeschichte (Julia Bernhard, 454–483).] [Cf.: In der Gralsburg hausen die Räuber (Günther Rühle) [in]: 'FAZ', Nr. 256, Frankfurt am Main, 4. Nov.1997, p. L 11.] [Incl. two hitherto unpubl. essays written 1939–1940 in Palestine, resp. 1948 in Czechoslovakia.]

VIII. AUTOBIOGRAPHIES, MEMOIRS, LETTERS

35703. ADORNO, THEODOR W.: *Briefe und Briefwechsel. Bd. 2. Briefwechsel 1925–1935. Theodor W. Adorno, Alban Berg.* Hrsg. von Henri Lonitz. Frankfurt am Main: Suhrkamp, 1997. 384 pp. (Briefe und Briefwechsel, Bd. 2.) [Cf.: Der Prophet bei Berg. Adornos Wortschwall hielt ihn schließlich über Wasser: Im Briefwechsel tauschten sie Sturmwarnungen vor der Zukunft aus (Wolfgang Rihm) [in]: 'FAZ', Nr. 70, Frankfurt am Main, 24. März 1998, p. L 27.]

35704. ARONSFELD, C.C.: *Wanderer from my birth*. London: Janus, 1997. 324 pp. [C.C.A., b. in a village in Posen in 1910, grew up in Berlin, went to England in 1933. In 1938 worked in Amsterdam in the Jewish Central Information Office with Alfred Wiener. In 1939 moved with this office (which later became the Wiener Library) to London and after A. Wiener's death became Acting Director; also edited the Wiener Library Bulletin for some 20 years. In 1965 became a senior research officer at the Institute of Jewish Affairs. See also No. 34945.]

35705. AUERBACH, ERICH. *Erich Auerbachs Briefe an Martin Hellweg (1939–1950)*. Edition und historisch-philologischer Kommentar hrsg. von Martin Vialon. Basel: Francke, 1996. 159 pp., facsims., notes, bibl. (141–156), index. [Incl. 11 letters written to his former student from Turkey and the US.] [E.A., professor of Romance languages, data see No. 30963/XXXIX.] [See also No. 34485.]

35706. BENJAMIN, WALTER: *Gesammelte Briefe*. Hrsg. vom Theodor-W.-Adorno-Archiv. Bd. 3. 1925–1930. Hrsg. von Christoph Gödde und Henri Lonitz. Frankfurt am Main: Suhrkamp, 1997. 594 pp.

35707. BINDER, OTTO: *Wien – retour. Bericht an die Nachkommen*. Wien: Böhlau, 1997. 189 pp., illus. [Memoirs of an Austrian-Jewish Social Democrat, b. 1910 in Vienna; emigr. 1939 to Sweden, returned 1949 to Vienna. Memoirs cover the years 1914–1949.]

35708. BÖRNSTEIN, HEINRICH: *Memoirs of a nobody: the Missouri years of an Austrian radical, 1849–1866*. Transl. and ed. by Steven Rowan. St. Louis: Missouri Historical Society Press (distrib. by Wayne State Univ. Press, Detroit), 1997. XIX, 412 pp., illus. [H.B. (1805–1892, Vienna). Memoirs were orig. publ. in 1884 and incl. a chapter on the author's relationship with Heine.]

35709. EPSTEIN, HELEN: *Where she came from: a daughter's search for her mother's history*. Boston: Little Brown, 1997. 322 pp., illus., ports. [Author tells story of the three generations of Central European, German-speaking women who preceded her. The second part of the book deals primarily with her mother's experiences in Czechoslovakia under the Nazis.] [Cf.: Myth turning reality (Monica Strauss) [in]: Aufbau, Vol. 64, No. 8, New York, April 10, 1998, p. 12.]

35710. FRANKL, VIKTOR EMIL: *Recollections: an autobiography*. Transl. by Joseph and Judith Fabry. Foreword by Joseph Fabry. New York: Plenum; Insight Books, 1997. 143 pp., illus. [V.F., b. 1905 in Vienna, psychoanalyst, correspondent of Freud. German edn. appeared in 1995.]

35711. FRIEDLAENDER, SOPHIE/JARECKI, HILDE: *Sophie & Hilde. Ein gemeinsames Leben in Freundschaft und Beruf*. [Cover title: Ein Zwillingsbuch]. Hrsg. von Bruno Schonig. Berlin: Hentrich, 1996. 220 pp., illus. [Autobiographies of two educationalists who worked in Berlin in the 1930s (incl. Landschulheim Caputh) and later in England.] [S.F., b. Jan. 17, 1905 in Hamburg, teacher; H.J., Aug. 31, 1911 Berlin – May 10, 1995, London, social worker, teacher.]

35712. FRIESEL, EVYATAR: *Ballade des äußeren Lebens*. Memoiren. Aus dem Amerik. von Dafna Mach. Leipzig: Leipz. Univ.-Verlag, 1997. 260 pp. [For orig. edn. and data see No. 34535/YB XLII.]

35713. FURST, PETER: *Don Quixote in exile*. Evanston, IL: Northwestern Univ. Press, 1996. 208 pp., (Jewish lives.) [Author's autobiogr. account of emigrating from Berlin in 1934, his exile years, in Spain, the Dominican Republic, then US.]

35714. GENIN, SALOMEA: *Shayndl and Salomea: from Lemberg to Berlin*. Transl. by Brigitte Goldstein. Afterword by Wolfgang Benz. Evanston, IL: Northwestern Univ. Press, 1997. XI, 138 pp., illus. [For German edn. in 1992 and annot. see No. 29889/YB XXXVIII.]

35715. GLATZER, NAHUM NORBERT. *The memoirs of Nahum N. Glatzer*. Ed. and presented by Michael Fishbane and Judith Glatzer Wechsler. Cincinnati: Hebrew Union College Press; New York:

Leo Baeck Institute, 1997. 151 pp., illus., ports., gloss., notes. (Jewish perspective, 6.) [N. G., 1903 Lemberg – 1990 Boston, historian, Judaist, for more data see No. 27490/YB XXXVI.]

35716. GROSSER, ALFRED: *Une vie de Français*. Paris: Ed. Flammarion, 1997. 219 pp. [Memoirs; first chap. deals with the author's upbringing in Frankfurt and exile years in France. For data A. Grosser see No. 31202/YB XXXIX.]

35717. HAUSER, MARTIN: *Wege jüdischer Selbstbehauptung*. Tagebuchaufzeichnungen 1929–1967. 4., erw. Aufl. Bonn: Landeszentrale für politische Bildung, 1997. 336 pp., map; facsims. [For previous edns. and data M.H. see No. 29894/YB XXXVIII.]

35718. HEYM, STEFAN: *Der Winter unsers Mißvergnügens*. Aus den Aufzeichnungen des OV Diversant. München: Goldmann, 1996. 221 pp. (Orig.-Ausg.) [Cf.: Die konspirative Durchsuchung des Papierkorbs. Stefan Heym hat mit seinen Tagebüchern ein Kapitel der DDR-Literaturgeschichte geschrieben (Fritz J. Raddatz) [in]: Die Zeit, Nr. 24, Hamburg, 7. Juni 1996, p. 44.]

35719. JAHODA, MARIE: *"Ich habe die Welt nicht verändert"*. *Lebenserinerungen einer Pionierin der Sozialforschung*. Hrsg. von Steffani Engler und Brigitte Hasenjürgen. Manuskript aus dem Engl. übers. von Hella Beister. Frankfurt am Main; New York: Campus, 1997. 206 pp., illus. [Incl. a bibl. M. Jahoda.] [Cf.: Besprechung (Michael Neumann) [in]: Mittelweg 36, Jg. 7, H. 1, Hamburg, 1998, pp. 50–53.]

35720. KADEN, LALLA: *The first act of my life*. 1997. 287 pp., illus. [Privately printed., available at the LBI in New York and in London.]

35721. KAELTER, WOLLI (WITH GORDON COHN): *From Danzig: an American rabbi's journey*. Malibu, CA: Pangloss Press, 1997. XVIII, 297 pp., illus., ports. [W.K., b. Danzig 1914, went to America in 1935, became Rabbi in Cincinnati, then Long Beach, CA.]

35722. KIMMELMAN, MIRA RYCZKE: *Echoes from the Holocaust*. A memoir. Knoxville: Univ. of Tennessee Press, 1997. XXIV, 176 pp., illus., maps. [Memoir of a young woman from Danzig, incl. pre-Nazi life in Danzig, war-time experiences and life after liberation.]

35723. KLEMPERER, VICTOR: *Und so ist alles schwankend*. Tagebücher Juni bis Dezember 1945. Hrsg. von Günter Jäckel unter Mitarbeit von Hadwig Klemperer. Berlin: Aufbau Taschenbuch Verlag, 1997. 255 pp., notes (225–244). [Incl. a letter from K. to Hans Hirche, a former Wehrmacht officer, answering a request for a character reference. For earlier, abr. edn. (1995) see No. 33501/YB XLI.]

35724. KONOPKA, GISELA: *Mit Mut und Liebe. Eine Jugend im Kampf gegen Ungerechtigkeit und Terror*. Aus dem Amerik. übers. von Luisel Eidenmüller. Hrsg. und mit einem Nachwort versehen von Hildegard Feidel-Mertz. Weinheim: Deutscher Studienverlag, 1996. 283 pp. [Autobiography, first publ. in the US in 1988 with the title 'Courage and love'; see also ed.'s essay on G.K in No. 35429.] [G.K., b. 1910 in Berlin, Socialist, educationalist.]

35725. KOVALY, HEDA M.: *Under a cruel star: a life in Prague, 1941–1968*. Transl. by Francis and Helen Epstein. New York: Holmes and Meier, 1997. 192 pp. [First publ. in 1986, memoir describes Jewish life and suffering under the Nazis and Communists.]

35726. KRACAUER, SIEGFRIED/PANOFSKY, ERWIN: *Briefwechsel 1941–1966*. Hrsg. und mit einem Nachwort versehen von Volker Breidecker. Mit einem Anhang: Siegfried Kracauer: "Under the spell of the living Warburg tradition". Berlin: Akademie-Verl., 1996. XI, 257 pp., illus., notes, index. (Schriften des Warburg-Archivs im Kunstgeschichtl. Seminar der Univ. Hamburg, Bd. 4.) [Incl. also other correspondence with the Warburg Institute.]

35727. KRAFT, WERNER: *Spiegelung der Jugend*. Mit einem Nachwort von Jörg Drews. [Neuausgabe]. Frankfurt am Main: Fischer Taschenbuch Verlag, 1996. 144 pp. [Autobiography, depicting the author's life until his emigr. to Palestine in 1934.] [W.K., 1896 Braunschweig – 1991 Jerusalem, poet, writer.]

35728. KUNERT, GÜNTER: *Erwachsenenspiele*. Erinnerungen. München: Hanser, 1997. 446 pp. [Author, b. 1929 as the son of a Jewish mother, deals also with his family's experience during the Nazi period.]

35729. LEVIN VARNHAGEN, RAHEL: *Briefwechsel mit Pauline Wiesel*. Hrsg. von Barbara Hahn unter Mitarbeit von Birgit Bosold. München: Beck, 1997. 767 pp., illus. (Edition Rahel Levin Varnhagen.) [First complete edn. of 257 letters of R. Varnhagen and her best friend P.W. written between the 1790s and 1833; incl. also correspondence between P.W. and Karl August Varnhagen, 1815–1847.]

35730. LIND, JAKOV: *Selbstporträt*. Aus dem Engl. von Jakov Lind und Günther Danehl. Wien: Picus, 1997. 194 pp. (Österreichische Exilbibliothek.) [Orig. title 'Counting my steps'. First part of author's autobiography covering the years 1927–1945. Second and third parts were also publ. in German in 1997 by the same publisher: 'Nahaufnahme'. Aus dem Engl. von Jakov Lind und Günther Danehl (156 pp.; orig. title: 'A further autobiography'; covering the years 1945–1954). 'Im Gegenwind'. Aus dem Engl. von Jakov Lind und Jacqueline Cuss (215 pp.; orig. title: 'Crossing'; covering the years 1954–1991).] [J.L., b. 1927 in Vienna, writer, fled 1938 to the Netherlands, survived with false papers, after liberation lived in Palestine and several European countries before settling in London.] [Cf.: "Ich sollte eine Autobiografie schreiben, die ich nicht schreiben wollte". Zu Jakov Linds Lebens- bzw. Exiltrilogie (Primus-Heinz Kucher) [in]: Mit der Ziehharmonika, Jg. 15, Nr. 1, März 1998, pp. 61–62.]

35731. MAYER, HANS: *Reisen nach Jerusalem. Erfahrungen 1968 bis 1995*. Frankfurt am Main: Suhrkamp, 1997. 173 pp. [10 essays; incl.: Das Gesetz und das Endspiel. Arnold Schönbergs Oper 'Moses und Aron' (73–92). Deutsche und Juden am Ende des Jahrhunderts (151–173).]. [Cf.: Und Moses war am Ende ganz allein (Friedmar Appel) [in]: 'FAZ', Nr. 71, Frankfurt am Main, 25. März 1997, p. L 12. Der Außenseiter und die Integration. Gelebte Literatur in den Wirren des Jahrhunderts: Zum neunzigsten Geburtstag von Hans Mayer (Lorenz Jäger) [in]: 'FAZ', Nr. 66, 19. März 1997, p. 37.]

35732. MENDELSSOHN [BARTHOLDY], FANNY & FELIX: *"Die Musik will gar nicht rutschen ohne Dich"*. Briefwechsel 1821 bis 1846. Hrsg. von Eva Weissweiler. Berlin: Propyläen, 1997. 494 pp., illus., bibl. (480–482). [Cf.: Du bist der Haupthahn (Eckart Kleßmann) [in]: 'FAZ', Nr. 280, Frankfurt am Main, 2. Dez. 1997, p. L 8.]

35733. MENDELSSOHN BARTHOLDY, FELIX: *Briefe von Felix Mendelssohn Bartholdy*. Bd. 1. Reisebriefe aus den Jahren 1830 bis 1832, hrsg. von Paul Mendelssohn Bartholdy. Vers. mit einem Vorwort von Beatrix Borchard. [Faks.-Dr. der Ausg. Leipzig, Mendelssohn, 1861]. Bd. 2. Aus den Jahren 1833 bis 1847, hrsg. von Paul Mendelssohn Bartholdy in Berlin und Carl Mendelssohn Bartholdy in Heidelberg. Nebst einem Verz. der sämmtlichen musikalischen Compositionen von Felix Mendelssohn Bartholdy, zsgest. von Julius Reitz. [Faks.-Dr. der Ausg. Leipzig, Mendelssohn, 1863] Hrsg. im Auftrag des Moses-Mendelssohn-Zentrums für Europäisch-Jüdische Studien von Julius H. Schoeps]. Potsdam: Verlag für Berlin-Brandenburg, 1997. 2 vols., XX, 340; VI, 420 pp., scores.

35734. MENDELSSOHN BARTHOLDY, FELIX & CÉCILE: *Das Tagebuch der Hochzeitsreise*. Hrsg. von Peter Ward Jones. Mainz: Atlantis Musikbuch-Verlag, 1997. 250 pp., notes, illus., scores. [Diary, kept in the Bodleian Library, Oxford, written and illustrated in 1837 by Felix M. and his wife Cécile, née Jeanrenaud.]

35735. MOSES, JULIUS. FRICKE, DIETER: *Jüdisches Leben in Berlin und Tel Aviv 1933 bis 1939. Der Briefwechsel des ehemaligen Reichstagsabgeordneten Dr. Julius Moses*. Hamburg: von Bockel, 1997. 632 pp., footnotes, bibl. (605–624), index (625–632). [Incl. 185 letters exchanged between Julius Moses in Berlin and the family of his son Erwin Moses in Tel Aviv; also a chap. 'Biographie und Familiengeschichte' (with family tree, 21–69).] [J.M., July 2, 1868 Posen – Sept. 24, 1942 Theresienstadt, pediatrician, Social Democrat, (not to be confused with Dr. Julius Moses, physician and Zionist from Mannheim).]

454   *Bibliography*

35736. ORFALI, STEPHANIE BRAUN: *A Jewish girl finds new roots.* Berkeley, CA: Ronin Publ., 1997. 96 pp., illus., ports. [S. O., b. 1911 in Nuremberg, d. 1994. Went to the US in 1957 via Palestine and Brazil. Posthumously publ. collection of autobiographical stories and poems, intended as a sequel to 'A Jewish girl in the Weimar Republic', 1987, see No. 24726/YB XXXIII.]

35737. PICARD, LEO: *Vom Bodensee nach Erez Israel – Pionierarbeit für Geologie und Grundwasser seit 1924.* Hrsg. von Erhard Roy Wiehn. Konstanz: Hartung-Gorre, 1996. 290 pp., illus., bibl. (285–288). [L.P., June 3, 1900 Wangen/Lake Constance – April 4, 1997 Kfar Saba (Israel), geologist, emigr. 1924 to Palestine.]

35738. REISS, ERICH: *Lieber Bennito: Briefe an Gottfried Benn 1846–1951.* Hrsg. von Helmut Keintel. Warmbronn: Verl. Ulrich Keichel, 1995. 34 pp. [E.R., 1887 Berlin – May 8, 1995 New York, publisher, emigr. in 1940 via Sweden to the US, married to Lotte Jacobi.]

35739. RIEMER, JEHUDA: *Common bonds, different fates. Extracts from the correspondence of Georg Bernhard and Fritz Naphtali 1933–1937.* [In]: Leo Baeck Institute Year Book XLII, London, 1997. 189–220, footnotes. [Cont. an introduction and 11 letters (in German) held in the Deutsche Bibliothek, Deutsches Exilarchiv 1933–1945.]

35740. ROBERTS, STEPHEN: *A youth in Vienna, a life in America.* A memoir. Vienna: Austria Publ., 1996. 213 pp., illus., ports. [Author b. 1914 in Nussdorf, Vienna, describes his life in pre-war Austria and then subsequent life in America.]

35741. SIODMAK, CURT: *Unter Wolfsmenschen.* Bd. 1. Europa. Bd. 2. Amerika. Bonn: Weidle, 1995. 271 pp., illus.; 1997. 323 pp., illus. [Autobiography.] [Cf.: Curt Siodmak in neuem Licht (Lars-Olav Beier) [in] 'FAZ', Nr. 44, Frankfurt am Main, 18. Feb. 1998, p. 44.] [C. Siodmak, b. 1902 in Dresden, scriptwriter, emigr. 1933 to Switzerland, 1937 to the US.]

35742. SPIRA, BIL: *Die Legende vom Zeichner.* Autobiographie. Hrsg. von Konstantin Kaiser in Zusammenarbeit mit Vladimir Vertlib. Wien: Döcker, 1997. 251 pp., illus. (Antifaschistische Literatur und Exilliteratur, 17.) [Cf.: Wien – Paris: mit Umwegen und Zwischenstationen. Über den Zeichner, Cartoonisten, Bühnenbildner und Redakteur Bil Spira (Vladimir Vertlib) [in]: Mit der Ziehharmonika, Jg. 14, Nr. 2, Wien, Aug. 1997, pp. 22–24, illus.] [B. (orig. Wilhelm; pseud. Willy Freier) Spira, b. 1913 in Vienna, artist, cartoonist, emigr. to France 1938, imprisoned in French internment and German concentration camps, lives in France.]

35743. STEINER, GEORGE: *Errata: an examined life.* London: Weidenfeld & Nicholson; New Haven, CT: Yale Univ. Press 1997, 1998. 186 pp., 206 pp. [Autobiography.] [G. S., b. 1929 in Paris into a Viennese Jewish family, man of letters, writer, literary critic, educated at Chicago, Harvard, Oxford; taught at Princeton, Cambridge and Geneva.]

35744. STEINHEIM, SALOMON LUDWIG/STEINHEIM, JOHANNA: *Briefe.* Hrsg. von Jutta Dick und Julius H. Schoeps. Hildesheim; New York: Olms, 1996. 446 pp., illus., bibl. (433–437). (Haskala, Bd.9.)

35745. STRAUSS, HERBERT A.: *Über dem Abgrund. Eine jüdische Jugend in Deutschland 1918–1943.* Aus dem Amerik. von Bettina Abarbanell. Frankfurt; New York, 1997. 309 pp., notes. [H.St., b. 1918 in Würzburg into an Orthodox family, prof. emer. of history and former director of the Zentrum für Antisemitismusforschung, Berlin; one of the last students of the Hochschule für die Wissenschaft des Judentums in Berlin; after forced labour went into hiding and escaped to Switzerland in 1943. Lives in the US.]

35746. STRAUSS, LOTTE: *Über den grünen Hügel. Erinnerungen an Deutschland.* [Aus dem Amerikan. übers. von Irmtrud und Irmhild Wojak]. Berlin: Metropol, 1997. 211 pp. (Bibliothek der Erinnerung, Bd. 2.) [Author, b. 1913 in Salzkotten, recalls childhood years in Wolfenbüttel, life in Berlin, during the Nazi period for some time in hiding, and her escape to Switzerland in May 1943; see also the memoirs of L. St.'s husband Herbert Strauss, No. 35747.]

35747. SULZBACH, HERBERT: *With the German guns: four years on the Western front 1914–1918*. With an introd. by Terence Prittie. Transl. from the German by Richard Thonger. Barnsley: Cooper, 1997. 256 pp., illus., ports. [War diaries, orig. edn. in 1973 see No. 11753/YB XIX.]

35748. TEPPICH, FRITZ: *Der rote Pfadfinder. Der abenteuerliche Weg eines Berliner Juden durch das 20. Jahrhundert*. Berlin: Elefanten, 1996. 311 pp. [Cf.: Besprechung (Werner Berthold) [in]: Beiträge zur Geschichte der Arbeiterbewegung, Jg. 39, H. 2, Kösching, 1997, pp. 119–120.] [F. Teppich, b. 1918 in Berlin into an affluent Jewish family, Communist activist, journalist, fought in the Spanish Civil War, interned in France, fled to Portugal. Returned to Berlin (East) in 1946, since 1966 in West Berlin.]

35749. WACO, LAURA: *Von zu Hause wird nichts erzählt*. Eine jüdische Geschichte aus Deutschland. München: Kirchheim, 1996. 280 pp. [Memoirs; author was born in 1947 in Freising to Polish Holocaust survivors who became DPs in Germany. Emigr. to Canada in the 1960s.]

35750. WALK, JOSEPH: *As yesterday. Essays and reminiscences*. [In Hebrew, with English title]. [Ed.: Leo Baeck Institute; Bar-Ilan University; The Faculty of Jewish Studies; The Samuel Braun Chair for the History of the Jews of Prussia]. Jerusalem: Shashar Publ., 1997. 377 pp. [For a German edn. of W.'s essays and memoirs and data see No. 34559/YB XLII.]

35751. WITTGENSTEIN, LUDWIG. *Wittgenstein Familienbriefe*. Hrsg. von Brian McGuinness [et al.] Wien: Hölder-Pichler-Tempsky, 1996. 215 pp., illus., facsims., index (209–214). (Schriftenreihe der Wittgenstein-Gesellschaft, Bd. 23.)

35752. WITTGENSTEIN, LUDWIG: *Denkbewegungen*. Tagebücher. 1930–1932, 1936–1937 (MS 183). Hrsg. von Ilse Somavilla. Teil 1: Normalisierte Fassung. Teil 2: Diplomatische Fassung. 2 vols. Innsbruck: Haymon, 1997. 159; 243 pp., facsims.: 4 pp. [Cf.: Geschenk der Sprache, Dank an das Leben. Neue Tagebücher von Ludwig Wittgenstein (Dieter Thoma) [in]: Die Zeit, Nr. 43, Hamburg, 17. Okt. 1997, p. 48.]

35753. WOLF, MARKUS (with ANNE MCELVOY): *Man without a face: the memoirs of a spymaster*. London: Cape, 1997. XII, 367 pp., illus. [M.W., head of the East German secret service for 30 years, data see No. 28843/YB XXXVII.]

35754. WOLFF, THEODOR: *Theodor Wolff – der Chronist. Krieg, Revolution und Frieden im Tagebuch 1914–1919*. Hrsg. von Bernd Sösemann. Düsseldorf: Econ, 1997. 440 pp., illus., bibl. (Reihe der Stiftung Pressehaus NRZ.) [Excerpts from Wolffs's diaries.]

IX. GERMAN-JEWISH RELATIONS

A. General

35755. ALY, GÖTZ: *Macht – Geist – Wahn. Kontinuitäten deutschen Denkens*. Berlin: Argon, 1997. 220 pp. [A collection of essays analysing German patterns of "Vergangenheitsbewältigung". Incl.: Rückwärtsgewandte Propheten (on the historians Theodor Schieder and Werner Conze, 153–183). Also on the book by Goldhagen (see No. 35045) and on the plans for the Berlin Holocaust memorial.]

35756. ASCHHEIM, STEVEN: *Post-Holocaust Jewish mirrorings of Germany: Hannah Arendt and Daniel Goldhagen*. [In]: Tel Aviver Jahrbuch für deutsche Geschichte, Bd. 26, 1997, Gerlingen 1997. Pp. 334–354, notes.

35757. BALA, HEIKE CATRIN/SCHOLZ, CHRISTIAN, eds.: *"Deutsch-Jüdisches Verhältnis"? Fragen, Betrachtungen, Analysen*. Mit Beiträgen von Ignatz Bubis [et al.]. Essen: Klartexte, 1997. 158 pp. [Incl. (titles partly abbr.): Vorwort (Hans Mommsen, 9–12). "Deutsch-Jüdisches Verhältnis"? Eine Einleitung (Christian Scholz, 13–24). Das Selbstverständnis der Juden und Jüdinnen in der Bundesrepublik Deutschland und der Zentralrat der Juden (Ignatz Bubis, 25–34). Deutschland und Israel. Last der Vergangenheit – Herausforderung an die Zukunft (Angelika Timm, 35–50). Über das Verschwinden von Auschwitz (Detlev Claussen, 51–72).

Philosemitismus in Deutschland (Frank Stern, 73–88). Die Juden und die deutsche Kultur (Enzio Traverso, 89–196). Jüdische Frauen in Deutschland (Jutta Dick/Marina Sassenberg, 107–124). Die Rolle von Juden und Jüdinnen in der deutschen Arbeiterbewegung (Jakob Moneta, 125–142). Auswahlbibliographie (Heike Catrin Bala/Christian Scholz, 143–156).]

35758. BAYERDÖRFER, HANS-PETER: *Shylock auf der deutschen Bühne nach der Shoah*. [In]: Shylock: Zinsverbot und Geldverleih in jüdischer und christlicher Tradition [see No. 35844]. Pp. 261–280, notes.

35759. BENUSSAN, GÉRARD: *Juifs et allemands. La croisée du langage*. [In]: Revue germanique internationale 5, Evry Cedex, 1996. Pp. 7–14.

35760. COUDERT, ALLISON P.: *Christliche Hebraisten des 17. Jahrhunderts. Philosemiten oder Antisemiten?* Zu Johann Jacob Schudt, Johann Christoph Wagenseil und Franciscus Mercurius von Helmont. [In]: Morgenglantz, Jg. 6, Bern, 1996. Pp. 99–132.

35761. ERSPAMER, PETER R.: *The elusiveness of tolerance: the "Jewish question" from Lessing to the Napoleonic Wars*. Chapel Hill: Univ. of North Carolina Press, 1997. XI, 189 pp., notes (157–176), bibl. (177–186). (Univ. of North Carolina studies in the Germanic languages and literatures, No. 117.) [Orig. publ. as Univ. of Wisconsin Diss., 1992.]

35762. FRIEDLER, EGON: *The "good" Jew in Germany*. [In]: Midstream, Vol. 43, No. 6, New York, Aug./Sept. 1997. Pp. 25–26. [Deals with the Jew as a philosemitic stereotype in today's Germany, and discusses the preoccupation of local communities with writing the history of their Jews.]

35763. GRAF, JOHANNES, ed.: *Judaeus conversus. Christlich-jüdische Konvertitenautobiographien des 18. Jahrhunderts*. Im Anschluß an Vorarbeiten von Michael Schmidt und unter Mitwirkung von Elisabeth Emter. Frankfurt am Main; New York: Lang, 1997. 410 pp., footnotes, bibl. (404–410). [Incl. texts of two converted Jews (Gottfried Selig and Friedrich Heinrich Selig (117–370); also bibl. of conversion reports and autobiographies (387–397).] [Cf.: Besprechung (Eckhard von Nordheim) [in]: Aschkenas, Jg. 8, H. 1, Wien, 1998, pp. 206–207.

35764. GRAF, JOHANNES: *Judentaufen in der Literatur der Spätaufklärung*. [In]: Internationales Archiv für Sozialgeschichte der Literatur, Bd. 22, H. 1, Tübingen, 1997. Pp. 19–42.

35765. GRUBER, RUTH ELLEN: *Letter from Flensburg: Germany's Klezmer craze*. [In]: The New Leader, Vol. 80, No. 6, New York, April 7, 1997. Pp. 9–11.

35766. GUTMANN, THOMAS: *Im Namen Heinrich Heines. Der Streit um die Benennung der Universität Düsseldorf 1965–1988*. Düsseldorf: Droste, 1997. VIII, 216 pp., footnotes, bibl. (203–213), index. [On the debates concerning the change of name of the University of Düsseldorf, resulting finally in 'Heinrich-Heine-Universität' in 1988.]

35767. HERZ, THOMAS/SCHWAB-TRAPP, MICHAEL: *Umkämpfte Vergangenheit. Diskurse über den Nationalsozialismus seit 1945*. Opladen: Westdeutscher Verlag, 1997. 286 pp., notes. [A collection of 10 essays analysing the course of German "Vergangenheitsbewältigung"; incl. historians' debate, "Fall Globke", Kohl's visit to Israel, Fassbinder debate.]

35768. HOMOLKA, WALTER/SEIDEL, ESTHER, eds.: *Nicht durch Geburt allein: Übertritt zum Judentum*. München: Knesebeck, 1995. 300 pp., gloss., bibl. [Essays (some previously publ.) on individual and collective conversions to Judaism and personal testimonies of converts by Lionel Blue, Christine Brinck, Henryk M. Broder, Hadassah Davis, Albert H. Friedlander, Ilan Hameiri, Helga Hegewisch, Dirk & Rachel Monika Herweg, Walter Homolka, Pinchas Lapide, Dorothea Magonet, Sibylle Sarah Niemoeller-von Sell, Walter Jacob, and Esther Seidel.]

35769. KNOCH-MUND, GABY: *Disputationsliteratur als Instrument antijüdischer Polemik. Leben und Werk des Marcus Lombardus, eines Grenzgängers zwischen Judentum und Christentum im Zeitalter des deutschen Humanismus*. Tübingen: Francke, 1997. X, 490 pp., illus., footnotes, bibl.(420–478), indexes (479–490). [On Marcus Lombardus, a Jew b. in Verona at the beginning of the 15th century who converted to Christianity; lived from the 1560s in German-speaking lands. Incl. edition of manuscript of his 'Eine schöne kurtzweilige vnnd vast nutzliche disputation zwischenn ainem Iuden vnnd Christenn'.]

35770. KRAUSS, MARITA: *Die Rückkehr der "Hitlerfrischler"*. Die Rezeption von Exil und Remigration in Deutschland als Spiegel der gesellschaftlichen Entwicklung nach 1945. [In]: Geschichte in Wissenschaft und Unterricht, Jg. 48, H. 3, Seelze, 1997. Pp. 151–160, footnotes.

35771. KRETZENBACHER, LEOPOLD: *Zum Skorpion als Judenzeichen zwischen Bayern und der Steiermark*. [In]: Bayerisches Jahrbuch für Volkskunde 1997, München, 1997. Pp. 99–113, illus., notes. [On the scorpion found in medieval paintings.]

35772. LORENZ, DAGMAR C.G.: *Die schöne Jüdin in Stifters 'Abdias' und Grillparzers 'Die Jüdin von Toledo'*. [In]: Jahrbuch der Grillparzer-Gesellschaft, Folge 3, Bd. 19 (1996), Wien, 1996. Pp. 125–139, notes.

—— MAYER, HANS: *Deutsche und Juden am Ende des Jahrhunderts*. [See in No. 35731.]

35773. *New German Critique*, No. 71 [with the issue title]: *Memories of Germany*. Ithaca, NY: Cornell Univ., Spring-Summer 1997. 1 issue, notes. [Incl. (titles abbr.): The place of the Second World War in German memory and history (Michael Geyer, transl. by M. Latham, 5–40). Watching 'Schindler's List' (Geoff Eley and Atina Grossmann, 41–62). Toward a radical politics of remembrance in Alain Resnais's 'Night and Fog' (Andrew Hebard, 87–113; deals with the removal of the film from the Cannes Film Festival on the insistence of the German Government and the protest in Germany against this decision.). In the shadow of the towers: an ethnography of a German-Israeli student exchange program (Andrew Stuart Bergerson, 141–176; between students of Hildesheim and Haifa).]

35774. *New German Critique*, No. 70 [with the issue title] *Germans and Jews*. Ithaca, NY: Cornell Univ., Winter 1997. 1 issue, notes. [Cont. (titles abbr.): "Männer aus der Fremde": Walter Benjamin and the "German-Jewish parnassus" (Irving Wohlfahrt, 3–85). A glimpse into the workshop of the Buber-Rosenzweig Bible translation (Leora Batnitzky, 87–116). Nazism, culture and 'The origins of totalitarianism': Hannah Arendt and the discourse of evil (Steven E. Aschheim, 117–139). Race, hybridity, and identity in Elisabeth Langgässer's 'Der Gang durch das Ried' (Cathy Gelbin, 141–160). The issue of Heimat in contemporary German-Jewish writing (Anat Feinberg, 161–181). The "German-Jewish symbiosis" revisited (Marion A. Kaplan, 183–190).]

35775. O'DOHERTY, PAUL: *The portrayal of Jews in GDR prose fiction*. Amsterdam; Atlanta, GA: Rodopi, 1997. 348 pp., bibl. (275–339). (Amsterdamer Publikationen zur Sprache und Literatur, 126.) [Discusses literature on Jewish themes by Jewish and non-Jewish authors, incl. Stefan Heym, Stephan Hermlin, Anna Seghers, Arnold Zweig; also deals with the history of the Jewish community in the GDR.]

35776. OEXLE, OTTO GERHARD: *Zweierlei Kultur. Zur Erinnerungskultur deutscher Geisteswissenschaftler nach 1945*. [In]: Rechtshistorisches Journal, Jg. 16, Frankfurt am Main, 1997. Pp. 358–390. [Analyses how and to what extent German scholars dealt, after 1945, with the Nazi regime and its crimes, esp. against the Jews.]

35777. RIORDAN, COLIN: *The sins of the children: Peter Schneider, Allan Massie and the legacy of Auschwitz*. [In]: Journal of European Studies, Vol. 27, No. 108, Chalfont St. Giles, 1997. Pp. 161–180, notes. [Compares the novels of a German and a Scottish writer, Sch.'s 'Vati' and A. M.'s 'Sins of the father', the one postulating a Mengele-like case, the other an Eichmann-like case as specific examples of "Väterliteratur".]

35778. SCHNEIDER, RICHARD CHAIM: *Fetisch Holocaust. Die Judenvernichtung – verdrängt und vermarktet*. München: Kindler, 1997. 286 pp. [The first part deals with the reception of Daniel J. Goldhagen's book (see No. 35045) in Germany, the second part with the debate about the Berlin

Holocaust memorial plans, the Holocaust 'industry' and other topics related to "Vergangenheitsbewältigung"; also on their impact on society in Israel, Germany and the US.]

35779. SCHULTZ, UWE, ed.: *Grosse Prozesse: Recht und Gerechtigkeit in der Geschichte*. München: Beck, 1996. 461 pp. [Incl.: Das Finanzgenie und sein Industrieimperium. Der Fall des 'Eisenbahnkönigs' Bethel Henri Strousberg (Rüdiger vom Bruch, 250–260, notes: 438). Homosexualität, aristokratische Kultur und Weltpolitik. Die Herausforderung des wilhelminischen Establishments durch Maximilian Harden 1906–1908 (Wolfgang J. Mommsen, 279–288, notes: 439–440). Der Nürnberger Prozeß. Grundlage eines neuen Völkerrechts? (Ernst Benda, 340–350, notes: 443). Bürger als Mörder und die Unfähigkeit zur Einsicht. Der Auschwitz-Prozeß (Wolfgang Benz, 382–391, notes: 445).]

35780. WOLFFSOHN, MICHAEL: *Meine Juden – Eure Juden*. München: Piper, 1997. 293 pp. [On tensions, inhibitions and hypocrisies prevailing in the German-Jewish relations.]

35781. ZÖLLER, SONJA: *Abraham und Melchisedech in Deutschland oder: Von Religionsgesprächen, Unbelehrbarkeit und Toleranz. Zur Rezeption der beiden Juden des Giovanni Boccaccios "Decamerone" in der deutschen Schwankliteratur des 16. Jahrhunderts*. [In]: Aschkenas, Jg. 7, H. 2, Wien, 1997. Pp. 303–340, footnotes.

35782. BRADLEY, ERNESTINE SCHLANT: *The language of silence: West German literature and the Holocaust*. New York: Leo Baeck Institute, 1997. 15 pp. (Occasional Paper No. 1.) [Lecture delivered in March 1997 as part of the Leo Baeck Institute Lecture Series.]

B. German-Israeli Relations

— BAR-ON, DAN/BRENDLER, KONRAD/HARE, PAUL A., eds.: *"Da ist etwas kaputtgegangen an den Wurzeln. . .".* Identitätsformation deutscher und israelischer Jugendlicher im Schatten des Holocaust. [See No. 35280.]

35784. BAR-ON, DAN: *The presence of Germany – Jewish and Israeli self-images of the other*. [In]: Tel Aviver Jahrbuch für deutsche Geschichte, Bd. 26, 1997, Gerlingen, 1997. Pp. 393–410, notes.

35785. BARZEL, NEIMA: *Dignity, hatred and memory – reparations from Germany: the debates in the 1950s*. [In]: Yad Vashem Studies, Vol. 24, Jerusalem, 1994. Pp. 247–280. [On the debates in Israel concerning the acceptance or refusal of reparations and restitution.]

35786. GOTTWALD, ASTRID: *Jews in Germany – Israeli perceptions in the 1950s*. [In]: Tel Aviver Jahrbuch für deutsche Geschichte, Bd. 26, 1997, Gerlingen, 1997. Pp. 455–478, notes.

35787. JELINEK, YESHAYAHU A., ed.: *Zwischen Moral und Realpolitik. Deutsch-israelische Beziehungen 1945–1965*. Eine Dokumentensammlung. Gerlingen: Bleicher, 1997. 688 pp. (Schriftenreihe des Instituts für Deutsche Geschichte der Universität Tel Aviv, Bd. 16.)

35788. KLOKE, MARTIN: *Israel und die Apokalypse. Wahrnehmungen und Projektionen christlicher Fundamentalisten in Deutschland*. [In]: Jahrbuch für Antisemitismusforschung 6, Frankfurt am Main; New York, 1997. Pp. 266–284, notes.

35789. PRIMOR, AVI: *". . . mit Ausnahme Deutschlands". Als Botschafter Israels in Deutschland*. Berlin: Ullstein, 1997. 272 pp. [One chapter (Schlußstrich unter die Vergangenheit?) repr. in: 'Allgemeine', Jg. 52, Nr. 9, Bonn, 2. Mai 1997.] [A. P. b. in Palestine to a German-Jewish mother, tells about his experiences; incl. German "Vergangenheitsbewältigung" and the Goldhagen debate.] [Cf.: Kein angepaßter Diplomat (Willi Jasper) [in]: Die Zeit, Nr. 18, Hamburg, 25. April 1997. Pp. 16.]

35790. *Räumt die Steine hinweg . . .* Themenheft. [Hrsg.: Dt. Koordinierungsrat der Ges. für Christl.-Jüd. Zus.-arb.]. Red.: Eva M. Schulz-Jander [et al.]. Bad Nauheim: Koordinierungsrat, [1997]. 119 pp., illus. (Themenheft; Dt. Koordinierungsrat der Ges. für Christl.-Jüd. Zus.-arb., 1997.) [Some contribs. focus on German-Israeli relations.]

35791. SCHMITT, KARL/EDINGER, MICHAEL, eds.: *Israel in den neunziger Jahren und die deutsch-israelischen Beziehungen.* Jena: Univ.-Verl. Jena, 1996. 112 pp., footnotes. [Incl.: Zwischen Lobpreisung und Verteufelung. Die Haltung der deutschen Linken gegenüber Israel (Martin Kloke, 55–68). Antizionismus als Politik: Offiziöses Israelbild und Israelpolitik der DDR (Lothar Mertens, 69–88). Widerspruch und Wende: Alternativen der Israelpolitik der SED (Konrad Weiß, 89–98). Normalisierung des Nicht-Normalisierbaren? Podiumsgespräch mit Alex Carmel, Daniel Dagan (et al., 99–112).]

35792. SCHNEIDER, PETER: *Hitler in Tel Aviv.* [In]: Mittelweg 36, Jg. H. 4, Hamburg, 1997. Pp. 84–89, footnotes. [On an incident in Israel involving a member of a Berlin orchestra and on the obsession of Germans with indulging in self-reproach.]

35793. TIMM, ANGELIKA: *Hammer, Zirkel, Davidstern. Das gestörte Verhältnis der DDR zu Zionismus und Staat Israel.* Bonn: Bouvier, 1997. 614 pp., notes (401–452), docs., bibl. (596–609), index. [Cf.: "Deutscher Schatten über Israel" ignoriert (interview with A.Timm by Jürgen Elsässer) [in]: Israelitisches Wochenblatt, Jg. 97, Nr. 43, Zürich, 24. Okt. 1997. Pp. 4–7.] [Cf.: Besprechung (Arno Herzig) [in]: Aschkenas, Jg. 8, H. 1, Wien, 1998, pp. 255–257.]

35794. WEINGARDT, MARKUS A.: *Deutsch-iraelische Beziehungen. Zur Genese bilateraler Verträge 1949–1996.* Konstanz: Hartung-Gorre, 1997. 196 pp.

35795. ZIMMERMANN, MOSHE: *Chameleon and Phoenix – Israel's German image.* [In]: Tel Aviver Jahrbuch für deutsche Geschichte, Bd. 26, 1997, Gerlingen, 1997. Pp. 265–280, notes.

C. Church and Synagogue

35796. BURMEISTER, KARL HEINZ: *Der Arzt Meister David von Schaffhausen (ca. 1490–1562) und der gegen ihn erhobene Ritualmordvorwurf.* [In]: Schaffhauser Beiträge zur Geschichte, Bd. 73, Schaffhausen, 1996. Pp. 195–206, footnotes.

35797. CZERMAK, GERHARD: *Christen gegen Juden. Geschichte einer Verfolgung.* Von der Antike bis zum Holocaust, von 1945 bis heute. Reinbek: Rowohlt, 1997. 575 pp., bibl. (513–558), index (persons, subjects, 559–575). [Deals with Christian anti-Judaism/antisemitism; enlarged and updated edn.; for first edn. see No. 26873/YB XXXV.]

35798. FAENSEN, HUBERT: *Zur Synthese von Bluthostien- und Heiliggrab-Kult.* Überlegungen zu dem Vorgängerbau der Gnadenkapelle des märkischen Klosters Heiliggrabe. [In]: Sachsen und Anhalt. Jahrbuch der Historischen Kommission für Sachsen-Anhalt, Bd. 19, 1997. Festschrift für Ernst Schubert. Weimar, 1997. Pp. 237–255, illus., footnotes. [On the former Cistercian convent near Pritzwalk (Brandenburg) and its beginnings involved with blood libel accusations of the early 16th cent.]

35799. FUHRMANN, HORST: *Überall ist Mittelalter.* Von der Gegenwart einer vergangenen Zeit. München: Beck, 1996. 328 pp., annot. bibl. (273–303), index (306–328).] [Deals also with money lending, interest, usury and the Jews; the destruction of the Nuremberg community (137–146). Incl. an essay on Ernst H. Kantorowicz; see No. 35592.]

35800. LANDOLT, OLIVER: *"Wie die juden zu Diessenhofen ein armen knaben ermurtend, und wie es inen gieng". Ritualmordvorwürfe und die Judenverfolgungen von 1401.* [In]: Schaffhauser Beiträge zur Geschichte, Bd. 73, Schaffhausen, 1996. Pp. 161–206, footnotes.

35801. MÜNZ, CHRISTOPH: *". . . daß wir Christen sind. Über die Geburt des Antisemitismus aus dem Geist des Christentums.* [In]: Tribüne, Jg. 36, H. 141, Frankfurt am Main, 1997. Pp. 141–156.

35802. OSTEN-SACKEN, PETER VON DER: *Gründe und Ziele für eine Auseinandersetzung mit der antijüdischen Geschichte des Christentums.* [In]: Zeitschrift für Religions- und Geistesgeschichte, Jg. 49, H. 4, Leiden, 1997. Pp. 364–373, footnotes. [Refers also to the founding of the monastery Stift zum Heiliggrabe (Brandenburg), on the basis of a blood libel myth.]

35803. PETUCHOWSKI, JAKOB J./THOMA, CLEMENS: *Lexikon der jüdisch-christlichen Begegnung*. Hintergründe – Klärungen – Perspektiven. Neu bearb. von Clemens Thoma. Freiburg: Herder, 1997. 242 pp. [For previous edn. see No. 26880/YB XXXV.]

35804. HSIA, RONNIE PO-CHIA: *Trient 1475. Geschichte eines Ritualmordprozesses*. Aus dem Amerik. von Robin Cackett. Frankfurt am Main: S. Fischer, 1997. 223 pp., frontis., illus., notes (184–216), index (218–223). [Orig. edn. publ. in 1992 with the title 'Trent 1475. Stories of a ritual murder trial'.] [Cf.: Der inszenierte Wahn (Volker Reinhardt) [in]: Die Zeit, Nr. 41, Hamburg, 3.Okt. 1997, p. 21. Besprechung (Rainer Erb) [in]: Zeitschrift für Geschichtswissenschaft, Jg. 45, H. 6, Berlin, 1997, pp. 552–554.]

35805. RAGACS, URSULA: *"Mit Zaum und Zügel muß man ihr Ungestüm bändigen" – Ps 32,9. Ein Beitrag zur christlichen Hebraistik und antijüdischen Polemik im Mittelalter*. Frankfurt am Main; New York: Lang, 1997. 202 pp. Zugl.: Wien, Univ., Diss., 1995. (Judentum und Umwelt, Bd. 65.) [Deals with the 'Capistrum Iudaeorum' of the Dominican monk Raimund Martini, 13th cent.]

35806. RONIG, FRANZ: *Die Wernerkapelle in Bacharach*. Ein Denkmal rheinischer Kunstgeschichte und ein Mahnmal gegen Judenhaß. [In]: Rheinische Heimatpflege, Jg. 34, H. 4, Pulheim, 1997. Pp. 260–266.

35807. TREUE, WOLFGANG: *Der Trienter Judenprozeß*. Voraussetzungen – Abläufe – Auswirkungen (1475–1588). Hannover: Hahn, 1996. IX, 603 pp., illus., facsims., footnotes, bibl. (537–580), index (581–603), tabs., maps (8 pp.). (Forschungen zur Geschichte der Juden, Abt. A: Abhandlungen, Bd. 4.) [In Part I (Einleitung, 1–27) a.o. recent studies on the topic are critically examined. Incl. a chapt. (384–392, with 20 illus.) on the iconography of Simon of Trent. Book deals also extensively with the effects and repercussions of the 'ritual murder' trial and the resulting cult of Simon of Trent in German lands.]

D. Antisemitism

35808. ABRAMSON, HENRY: *A ready hatred: depictions of the Jewish woman in medieval antisemitic art and caricature*. [In]: Proceedings of the American Academy for Jewish Research, Vol. 62, New York, Jerusalem, 1996. Pp.1–18, illus., notes. [Draws heavily on German caricatures and woodcuts.]

35809. *Antisemitismus in Medien*. Arbeitshilfen für die politische Bildung. Hrsg.: Horst Dichanz [et al.]. Bonn: Bundeszentrale für politische Bildung, 1997. 98 pp., illus., bibl. [Brochure designed for adult education and for schools. Incl.: Teil A: Arbeitsmaterial, Teil B: Reader. Texte zur Geschichte des Antisemitismus und zur Bedeutung von Vorurteilen.]

35810. AUSTRIA. SOTTOPIETRA, DORIS: *Variationen eines Vorurteils: eine Entwicklungsgeschichte des Antisemitismus in Österreich*. Wien: Passagen-Verlag, 1997. 264 pp., bibl. (231–264). (Passagen Zeitgeschehen.)

35811. BEN-CHANAN, YAAKOV: *Juden und Deutsche. Deutsche Traditionen judenfeindlichen Denkens*. Wiesbaden: Hessische Landeszentrale für politische Bildung, 1997. 28 pp., bibl.

35812. BENZ, WOLFGANG/BERGMANN, WERNER: *Vorurteil und Völkermord: Entwicklungslinien des Antisemitismus*. Freiburg i. Br.: Herder, 1997. 439 pp. (Herder-Spektrum, Bd. 4577.) Orig.-Ausg.

35813. BERGGREN, LENA: *Race and religion: the worldview of Houston Stewart Chamberlain as presented in 'Die Grundlagen des neunzehnten Jahrhunderts'*. [In Swedish, with Engl. summary, pp. 118–119]. [In]: Historisk tidskrift, Stockholm, 1996. Pp. 92–119.

35814. BLASCHKE, OLAF: *Katholizismus und Antisemitismus im deutschen Kaiserreich*. Göttingen: Vandenhoeck & Ruprecht, 1997. 443 pp., (Kritische Studien zur Geschichtswissenschaft, 122.) Zugl.: Bielefeld, Univ., Diss., 1995. [Cf.: Der antisemitische Konsens. Katholiken im Kaiserreich: Olaf Blaschke zerstört eine Legende (Heinrich August Winkler) [in]: Die Zeit, Hamburg, 17. Okt. 1997, p. 36.]

35815. BRAUN, CHRISTINA VON: *"Le juif" et "la femme"*. *Deux stéréotypes de "l'autre" dans l'antisémitisme du XIXe siècle*. [In]: Revue germanique internationale 5, Evry Cedex, 1996. Pp. 123–139.

35816. BRECHTKEN, MAGNUS: *"Madagaskar für die Juden"*. Antisemitische Idee und politische Praxis 1885–1945. München: Oldenbourg, 1997. X, 336 pp., footnotes, illus., bibl. (303–328), index (331–336). [Cf.: Absurde Irrealität und Inhumanität. Madagaskar für die Juden: ein antisemitisches Projekt (Hans Fenske) [in]: 'FAZ', Nr. 231, Frankfurt am Main, 6. Okt. 1997, p. 12.]

35817. BRUMLIK, MICHA: *Motive christlicher Judenfeindschaft und Strategien ihrer Überwindung.* [In]: Für ein neues Miteinander von Christen und Juden [see No. 34707]. Pp. 114–128.

35818. CHAZAN, ROBERT: *Medieval stereotypes and modern antisemitism.* Berkeley: Univ. of California Press, 1997. XIII, 189 pp., notes. [Incl. Blood Libel allegations and antisemitism in Jewish settlements in Germany.]

—— DEFENCE. BORUT, JACOB: *Die jüdischen Abwehrvereine zu Beginn der neunziger Jahre des 19. Jahrhunderts.* [See No. 34679.]

35819. FRANKEL, JONATHAN: *The Damascus affair: "Ritual Murder," politics, and the Jews in 1840.* Cambridge; New York: Cambridge Univ. Press, 1997. XIV, 491 pp., illus., map, footnotes, bibl. (499–470). [Deals also with the controversial political reactions to this notorious blood libel case in Germany and its Jewish communities.]

35820. FULLER, STEVEN NYOLE: *The Nazi's literary grandfather. Adolf Bartels and cultural extremism, 1871–1945.* Frankfurt am Main; New York: Lang, 1996. 261 pp. (Studies in Modern German Literature, Vol. 62.) [A.B., racist, antisemite, literary critic.] [Besprechung (Hans Otto Horch) [in]: Aschkenas, Jg. 8, H. 1, Wien, 1998, pp. 252–254.]

35821. GASSERT, PHILIPP: *Amerika im Dritten Reich. Ideologie, Propaganda und Volksmeinung 1933–1945.* Stuttgart: Steiner, 1997. 415 pp., footnotes, bibl. (408–413). (Transatlantische Historische Studien, Bd. 7.) [Incl. chap. entitled 'Antisemitismus im deutschen Amerikabild'.]

35822. HAIBL, MICHAELA: *Vom "Ostjuden" zum "Bankier". Zur visuellen Genese zweier Judenstereotypen in populären Witzblättern.* [In]: Jahrbuch für Antisemitismusforschung 6, Frankfurt am Main; New York, 1997. Pp. 44–91, illus., notes. [Deals with 'Fliegende Blätter' and Austrian papers such as 'Figaro' and 'Kikeriki'.]

35823. *Handbuch zur "Völkischen Bewegung" 1871–1918.* Hrsg. von Uwe Puschner, Walter Schmitz und Justus H. Ulbricht. München; New Providence, 1996. XXVII, 978 pp., illus., footnotes, indexes (persons, 953–967; organis. and institutions, 968–975). [Cont. 45 essays, most of them dealing also with antisemitic aspects of the "völkisch" movement. Selected essays: Völkischer Antisemitismus im Kaiserreich (Werner Bergmann, 449–464). Der Fall Dreyfus in Deutschland (Benita Storch, 464–481). Völkische Kapitalismus-Kritik: Das Beispiel Warenhaus (Heike Hoffmann, 558–574). Incl. also short biographies of the "völkisch" protagonisten (897–934).]

35824. HEIL, JOHANNES: *"Antijudaismus" und Antisemitismus" – Begriffe als Bedeutungsträger.* [In]: Jahrbuch für Antisemitismusforschung 6, Frankfurt am Main; New York, 1997. Pp. 92–114, notes.

35825. HERZOG, ANDREAS: *"Wider den jüdischen Geist". Christlich argumentierender Antisemitismus 1871–1933.* [In]: Das jüdische Echo, Vol. 46, Wien, 1997. Pp. 58–67, illus., notes.

35826. HEUER, RENATE/WUTHENOW, RALPH-RAINER, eds.: *Antisemitismus – Zionismus – Antisemitismus 1850–1940.* Frankfurt am Main; New York: Campus, 1997. 296 pp., footnotes. [Cont. (titles partly abbr.): Die Schriften von Rühs und Fries zur Judenfrage (Gerald Hubmann,

9–34). Antisemitische Literaturkritik: Adolf Bartels (Rainer Brändle, 35–53). Über den Antisemitismus in Gustav Freytags Roman "Soll und Haben" (Dieter Brockmeyer, 54–65). Robert Jaffé: "Ahasver" (Pamela Wolf, 66–73). Gustav Landauers Judentum und seine Freundschaft mit Martin Buber (Birgit Seemann, 74–91). Zum Bildungsstreben der Galizischen Haskala in deutschsprachiger Literatur (Maria Klanska, 92–107). Das tausendjährige Dasein der böhmischen Juden (Alois Hofman, 108–128). Paradigmen eines "grenzenlosen" Antisemitismus. Dühring und Drumont im Vergleich (Egon Schwarz, 129–149). Samuel Lublinskis "Philozionismus" (Renate Heuer, 150–168). Briefe Samuel Lublinskis an Theodor Herzl (169–197). Zionismus als Utopie. Moritz Güdemanns Stellung zum "Nationaljudentum" (Frank Kind, 198–209). Gustav Landauers Wirkung auf den deutschsprachigen Zionismus (Siegbert Wolf, 210–226). Feuchtwangers Josephus Flavius und seine Idee des Judentums (Karl Kröhnke, 227–250). Eine Auswahlbibliographie zum Thema: Antisemitismus, Zionismus, Antizionismus (Holger Kiehnel, 251–296).]

35827. HÖDL, KLAUS: *Die Pathologisierung des jüdischen Körpers. Antisemitismus, Geschlecht und Medizin im Fin de Siècle*. Wien: Picus, 1997. 415 pp., illus., tabs., bibl. (372–409).

35828. HOLZ, KLAUS: *Immer noch auf dem Weg zu einer Theorie des Antisemitismus*. [In]: Soziologische Revue, Jg. 19, München, 1996. Pp. 173–180. [Review essay on recent books on antisemitism.]

35829. KASISCHKE-WURM, DANIELA: *Antisemitismus im Spiegel der Hamburger Presse während des Kaiserreichs (1884–1914)*. Hamburg: Lit, 1997. 457 pp. (Sozial- und Wirtschaftsgeschichte, Bd. 6.) Zugl.: Hamburg, Univ., Diss., 1997.

35830. KIEVAL, HILLEL J.: *Death and the nation: ritual murder as political discourse in the Czech lands*. [In]: Jewish History, Vol. 10, No. 1, Haifa, Spring 1996. Pp. 75–91, notes.

35831. LEIB, LADISLAUS: *Graven images: antisemitism and Jewish identity in Max Frisch and Arthur Miller*. [In]: The Jewish Quarterly, Vol. 44, No. 1, London, Spring 1997. Pp. 24–27.

35832. LINDEMANN, ALBERT S.: *Esau's tears: modern anti-semitism and the rise of the Jews*. Cambridge; New York: Cambridge Univ. Press, 1997. XXI, 568 pp., notes.

—— LOHRMANN, KLAUS: *Sind traditioneller Antijudaismus und Rassenantisemitismus wirklich zwei verschiedene Phänomene der Judenfeindschaft?* [See in No. 34939.]

35833. MCCULLOH, JOHN M.: *Jewish Ritual Murder: William of Norwich, Thomas of Monmouth, and the early dissemination of the myth*. [In]: Speculum: A Journal of Medieval Studies, Vol. 72, Cambridge, MA, 1997. Pp. 698–740, footnotes. [Incl. the expulsions after the crusades, 11th- and 12th-century-pogroms and blood libel accusations in the Rhineland.]

35834. MOJEM, HELMUTH: *Die Vertreibung aus dem Paradies*. Antisemitismus und Sexualität in Franz Fühmanns Erzählung 'Das Judenauto'. [In]: Jahrbuch der deutschen Schillergesellschaft, Jg. 41, Stuttgart, 1997. Pp.460–480, footnotes.

35835. NIRENBERG, DAVID: *Communities of violence: persecution of minorities in the Middle Ages*. Princeton, NJ: Princeton Univ. Press, 1996. 301 pp., notes, bibl. [Deals extensively with Jews, incl. Germany; also chap. on the persecution of European Jewry during the Black Death.]

35836. PICARD, JACQUES: *"Antisemitismus" erforschen?* Über Begriff und Funktion der Judenfeindschaft und die Problematik ihrer Erforschung. [In]: Schweizerische Zeitschrift für Geschichte, Vol. 47, Nr. 4, Basel, 1997. Pp. 580–607. [With French abstract.]

35837. POST WORLD WAR II. *Antisemitism and xenophobia in Germany after unification*. Ed. by Hermann Kurthen, Werner Bergmann, Rainer Erb. New York: Oxford Univ. Press, 1997. XV, 318 pp., tabs., notes, appendix (chronol.), bibl. (287–310).

35838. POST WORLD WAR II. BENZ, WOLFGANG: *Antisemitismus nach Hitler. Beobachtungen der amerikanischen Militärregierung aus dem Jahr 1947*. [In]: Jahrbuch für Antisemitismusforschung

6, Frankfurt am Main; New York, 1997. Pp. 349–362, notes. [Incl. hitherto unpubl. document.]

35839. POST WORLD WAR II. BERGMANN, WERNER: *Antisemitismus in öffentlichen Konflikten. Kollektives Lernen in der politischen Kultur der Bundesrepublik 1949–1989*. Frankfurt am Main: Campus, 1997. 535 pp., footnotes, bibl. (513–535). [Cf.: Besprechung (Helmut König) [in]: Zeitschrift für Geschichtswissenschaft, Jg. 45, H. 12, Berlin, 1997, pp. 1129–1130.]

35840. POST WORLD WAR II. BUTTERWEGGE, CHRISTOPH, ed.: *NS-Vergangenheit, Antisemitismus und Nationalismus in Deutschland*. Beiträge zur politischen Kultur der Bundesrepublik und zur politischen Bildung. Mit einem Vorwort von Ignatz Bubis, sowie Beiträgen von Christoph Butterwegge [et al.]. Baden-Baden: Nomos, 1997. 239 pp., footnotes. [Cont. 12 essays dealing with various aspects of "Vergangenheitsbewältigung", xenophobia and the New Right; section II incl.: "Wie die Zigeuner" – "wie die Juden". Antisemitismus und Antiziganismus im Vergleich (Wolfgang Wippermann, 69–84; see also No. 35849). Der deutsche Umgang mit dem Antisemitismus: Erinnerung und Verdrängung (Birgit Rommelspacher, 85–97).]

35841. POST WORLD WAR II. ERB, RAINER: *Antisemitische Straftäter der Jahre 1993 bis 1995*. [In]: Jahrbuch für Antisemitismusforschung 6, Frankfurt am Main; New York, 1997. Pp. 160–180, notes, tabs.

35842. RÖCKE, WERNER: *"So sein sie schedlicher den Kristen/dan der teufel mit all seinen listen." Christlicher Antijudaismus und Dämonisierung des Fremden in der städtischen Literatur des späten Mittelalters*. [In]: "Nicht allein mit den Worten. Festschrift für Joachim Dyck zum 60. Geburtstag. Hrsg. von Thomas Müller [et al.]. Stuttgart: Frommann-Holzboog, 1995. Pp. 124–134, footnotes. [Analyses two texts of Hans Folz.]

35843. SCHWANITZ, DIETRICH: *Der Antisemitismus oder die Paradoxierung der Außengrenze*. [In]: Soziale Systeme, Jg. 3, H. 2, Opladen, 1997. Pp. 237–256. [Incl. summary.]

35844. *Shylock: Zinsverbot und Geldverleih in jüdischer und christlicher Tradition*. Hrsg. von Johannes Heil und Bernd Wacker. München: Fink, 1997. 304 pp., illus., footnotes. [Selected essays: Antikapitalismus und Antisemitismus. Die Wirtschaftsmentalität der Katholiken im Wilhelminischen Deutschland (Olaf Blaschke, 133–146). Die Rothschilds und das Geld. Bilder und Legenden (Fritz Backhaus, 147–170). Hinter den Spiegeln: Mergels Uhr und Aarons Risiko. Aufsatz ohne Untertitel (Michael Schmidt, 171–192; on usury and Jews, as reflected in historiography, literature and other documents; incl. Annette v. Droste-Hülshoff, Johann Nepomuk von Schwerz). Weltherrschaft und Weltwirtschaft. Eine Skizze aus den Quellen zu einem Aspekt des Antisemitismus in der NSDAP-Propaganda (Wolfram Meyer zu Uptrup, 219–234). Über das Fortwuchern von Stereotypvorstellungen in der Geschichtswissenschaft (Stefan Rohrbacher, 235–252). Further essays are listed according to subject.]

35845. SPÖTTEL, MICHAEL: *Hamiten. Völkerkunde und Antisemitismus*. Frankfurt am Main; New York: Lang, 1997. 150 pp., footnotes, bibl. [Deals with Leo Frobenius, (Pater) Wilhelm Schmidt, Siegfried Passarge, Wilhelm E. Mühlmann and, in general, with German ethnology and its underlying antisemitism during the first half of the 20th century.]

35846. VIAENE, VINCENT: *Paul de Lagarde; a nineteenth-century 'radical' conservative and precursor of National Socialism?* [In]: European History Quarterly, Vol. 26, No. 4, London, 1996. Pp. 527–548, notes.

35847. VISSER, ELLEN DE: *Frau und Krieg. Weibliche Kriegsästhetik, weiblicher Rassismus und Antisemitismus*. Eine psychoanalytisch-tiefenhermeneutische Literaturanalyse. Münster: Westfäl. Dampfboot, 1997. 335 pp. Zugl.: Frankfurt am Main, Univ., Diss., 1995.

35848. WEISS, JOHN: *Der lange Weg zum Holocaust. Die Geschichte der Judenfeindschaft in Deutschland und Österreich*. Aus dem Amerikan. von Helmut Dierlamm [et al.]. Hoffmann u. Campe, 1997. 543 pp., notes (521–537), index (538–542). [For orig. edn. see No. 34065/YB XLII.]

35849. WIPPERMANN, WOLFGANG: *"Wie die Zigeuner". Antisemitismus und Antiziganismus im Vergleich.* Berlin: Elefanten, 1997. 272 pp. [Cf.: Besprechung (Peter Widmann) [in]: Zeitschrift für Geschichtswissenschaft, Jg. 45, H. 7, Berlin, 1997, pp. 645–647.]

35850. WOLLENBERG, JÖRG: *"Juden raus! Lessing raus!" Wie "in Deutschland die Tötung eines geistigen Menschen abrollt" (A. Zweig).* [In]: Mittelweg 36, Jg. 6, H. 1., Hamburg, 1997. Pp. 22–39, footnotes. [On the campaign of hatred against Theodor Lessing and the events culminating in his assassination in May 1933.]

E. Noted Germans and Jews

35851. BACHMANN, INGEBORG. WEIGEL, SIGRID: *Gershom Scholem und Ingeborg Bachmann. Ein Dialog über Messianismus und Ghetto.* [In]: Zeitschrift für deutsche Philologie, Bd. 115, Berlin, 1996. Pp. 608–616, footnotes. [With German and English abstract, p. 608.]

35852. BRENTANO, CLEMENS. OCH, GUNNAR: *Spuren jüdischer Mystik in Brentanos 'Romanzen vom Rosenkranz'.* [In]: Aurora, Jg. 57, Sigmaringen, 1997. Pp. 25–43, illus., footnotes. [Cf.: Clemens Brentano im Irrgarten der Antisemitismusforschung. Anmerkungen zu Gunnar Ochs Aufsatz "Spuren jüdischer Mystik in Brentanos 'Romanzen vom Rosenkranz' " (Martina Vordermayer, 233–236) [in]: Int. Jahrbuch der Bettina-von-Arnim-Gesellschaft, Bd.8/9, Berlin, 1997.]

35853. DROSTE-HÜLSHOFF, ANNETTE. CHASE, JEFFERSON S.: *Part of the story. The significance of Jews in Annette von Droste-Hülshoff's 'Die Judenbuche'.* [In]: Deutsche Vierteljahrsschrift für Literaturwissenschaft und Geistesgeschichte, Jg. 71, Bd. 71, Stuttgart, 1997. Pp. 127–145, footnotes. [Incl. Engl. and German abstracts.]

35854. DROSTE-HÜLSHOFF, ANNETTE. HUSZAI, VILLÖ DOROTHEA: *Denken Sie sich, der Mergel ist unschuldig an dem Morde. Zu Droste-Hülshoffs Novelle "Die Judenbuche".* [In]: Zeitschrift für deutsche Philologie, Bd. 116, Berlin, 1997. Pp. 481–499, footnotes. [With German and English abstract.]

35855. DROSTE-HÜLSHOFF, ANNETTE. LINDER, JUTTA: *Strafe oder Gnade? Zur 'Judenbuche' der Droste.* [In]: Droste-Jahrbuch 3, 1991–1996, Paderborn, 1997. Pp. 83–114, footnotes.

35856. GOETHE, JOHANN WOLFGANG VON. REGENSTEINER, HENRY: *Goethe and Yiddish.* [In]: Midstream, Vol. 43, No. 2, New York, Feb./March 1997. Pp. 32–33, notes. [Discusses Jewish influences on Goethe and his Yiddish classes.]

35857. HAUPTMANN, GERHART. TSCHÖRTNER, HEINZ DIETER: *Gerhart Hauptmann und Heinrich Heine.* Mit einem unbekannten Brief. [In]: Heine-Jahrbuch 1997, Jg. 36, Stuttgart, 1997. Pp. 169–172, notes.

35858. HEGEL, GEORG FRIEDRICH. O'REGAN, CYRIL: *Hegel and Anti-Judaism. Narrative and the inner circulation of the Kabbalah.* [In]: The Owl of Minerva, Vol. 28, No. 2, Bowling Green, OH, Spring 1997. Pp. 141–182, notes.

—— HEIDEGGER, MARTIN. ETTINGER, ELZBIETA: *Hannah Arendt – Martin Heidegger. Eine Geschichte.* [See No. 35475.]

35859. HEIDEGGER, MARTIN. YOUNG, JULIAN: *Heidegger, philosophy, Nazism.* Cambridge; New York: Cambridge Univ. Press, 1997. XV, 232 pp. [Cf.: An almost inebriate bewitchment (George Steiner) [in]: TLS, London, August 1997, p. 11.]

35860. HIPPEL, THEODOR GOTTLIEB VON. BECK, HAMILTON H.H.: *Neither Goshen nor Botany Bay. Hippel and the debate on improving the civic status of the Jews.* [In]: Lessing Year Book, Vol. 27, Detroit, MI, 1996. Pp. 63–101. [For data on Hippel see No. 28959/YB XXXVII.]

35861. HUMBOLDT, WILHELM VON. GROSSMAN, JEFFREY: *Wilhelm von Humboldt's linguistic ideology: the problem of pluralism and the absolute difference of national character – or, where do the Jews fit in?* [In]: German Studies Review, Vol. 20, No. 1, Tempe, AZ, Feb. 1997. Pp. 23–47. [Discusses H.'s attitude to Jews and the "Jewish Question".]

35862. LICHTENBERG, GEORG CHRISTOPH. SCHUBART, JULIA: *"Die Religion eine Sonntags-Affaire". Georg Christoph Lichtenberg zwischen aufklärerischer Toleranz und Antisemitismus.* [In]: Kleine Lauben, Arcadien und Schnabelewopski. Festschrift für Klaus Jeziorkowski. Hrsg. von Ingo Wintermeyer. Würzburg: Königshausen und Neumann, 1995. Pp. 40–48.

35863. LUTHER, MARTIN. *Luther und die Juden.* [Hrsg.: Evang. Kirche der Pfalz (Protestantische Landeskirche), Landeskirchenrat]. Speyer: Evang. Kirche der Pfalz, Landeskirchenrat, 1997. 55 pp., bibl. (Religionspädagogische Hefte: Ausg. B, Berufsbildende Schulen; 1997, Nr. 3.)

35864. LUTHER, MARTIN. MÜLLER, CHRISTIANE: *Martin Luther und die Juden.* [In]: Freiburger Rundbrief, N.F., Jg. 4, H. 1, Freiburg, 1997. Pp. 14–25, illus., footnotes.

35865. MANN, THOMAS. LEVESQUE, PAUL: *The double-edged sword: anti-semitism and anti-Wagnerism in Thomas Mann's 'Wälsungsblut'.* [In]: German Studies Review, Vol. 20, No. 1, Tempe, AZ, Feb. 1997. Pp. 9–21, notes.

35866. MANN, THOMAS. MARTIN, ARIANE: *Der europäische Publizist. Thomas Manns unbekannter Kriegs-Essay über Maximilian Harden: neue Quellen zu den 'Betrachtungen eines Unpolitischen'.* [In]: Heinrich Mann-Jahrbuch, Jg. 14, Lübeck, 1996. Pp. 185–209, footnotes.

35867. NIETZSCHE, FRIEDRICH. BRINKER, MENACHEM: *Nietzsche und die hebräischen Schriftsteller um die Jahrhundertwende.* [In]: Krisenwahrnehmungen im Fin de siècle. Jüdische und katholische Bildungseliten in Deutschland und der Schweiz [see No. 34914]. Pp. 101–118, footnotes.

35868. NIETZSCHE, FRIEDRICH. SANTANIELLO, WEAVER: *Nietzsche's 'Antichrist': 19th-century Christian Jews and the real "big lie."* [In]: Modern Judaism, Vol. 17, No. 2, Baltimore, May 1997. Pp. 163–177, notes. [On Nietzsche's opposition to antisemitism as expressed in his 'Antichrist'.]

35869. NIETZSCHE, FRIEDRICH. STEGMAIER, WERNER/KROCHMALNIK, DANIEL, eds.: *Jüdischer Nietzscheanismus.* Berlin; New York: de Gruyter, 1997. XXVI, 476 pp., footnotes, bibl.(431–455), indexes (names; subjects, 456–476). (Monographien und Texte zur Nietzsche-Forschung, Bd. 36.) [Based on a conference held in Greifswald Sept.3–6, 1995. Cont. (titles partly abbr.): Volk und Judentum bei Nietzsche (Josef Simon, 3–16). Jüdischer Nietzscheanismus seit 1988 – Ursprünge und Begriff (Friedrich Niewöhner, 17–34). Nietzsches Einfluß auf hebräische Schriftsteller des russischen Zarenreiches (Menachem Brinker, 35–52). Nietzsche und die jüdische Counter-History (Daniel Krochmalnik, 53–81). Nietzsche in der Philosophie Franz Rosenzweigs (Cordula Hufnagel, 82–89). Ein Kapitel aus der intellektuellen Frühgeschichte Gershom Scholems (Herbert Kopp-Oberstebrink, 90–105). Nietzsches Antike und die jüdische Kritik (Hubert Cancik, 106–126). Jüdischer Nietzscheanismus oder Nietzscheanischer Antisemitismus (Brandes, Nietzsche und Kierkegaard) (Gerd-Günter Grau, 127–150). Max Nordau als früher Nietzsche-Kritiker (Christoph Schulte, 151–167). Oskar Goldberg und Erich Unger im Zeichen Friedrich Nietzsches (Manfred Voigt, 168–187). Oscar Levys Nietzeanische Visionen (Uschi Nussbaumer-Benz, 188–208). Zu Gustav Landauers früher Nietzsche-Lektüre (Hanna Delf, 209–227). Nietzsche und die "Grenzjuden" (Jacob Golomb, 228–246). Egon Friedells eigenwillige Nähe zu Friedrich Nietzsche (Renate Reschke, 247–266). Freud in seinem Verhältnis zu Nietzsche (Peter Heller, 267–287). Judentum als "Rasse" bei Nietzsche und Freud (Wolf-Daniel Hartwich, 288–302). Levinas' Humanismus des anderen Menschen – ein Anti-Nietzscheanismus oder ein Nietzscheanismus (Werner Stegmaier, 303–325). Nietzsches "Zarathustra" und die Bibel (Maurice-Ruben Hayoun, 326–344). Friedrich Nietzsches Religionskritik und die Auslegung rabbinischer Quellen (Aharon R.E. Agus, 345–362).

Nietzsche aus der Sicht des Thora-Judentums (Aharon Shear-Yashuv, 363–383). Nietzsche, Antisemitismus und Massenmord (Steven E. Aschheim, 384–404). Nietzsche in Israel (Moshe Zimmermann, 405–424).]

35870. NIETZSCHE, FRIEDRICH WILHELM. *Nietzsche and Jewish culture*. Ed. by Jacob Golomb. New York: Routledge, 1997. XII, 282 pp., bibl. (263–266).

35871. RAPHAEL, FREDDY: *Die Juden zwischen der Wüste und der Stadt. Vergleichende Lektüre von Max Weber, Werner Sombart und Georg Simmel*. [In]: Schweizerisches Archiv für Volkskunde, Bd. 91, Basel, 1995. Pp. 21–32, notes.

35872. SACHER-MASOCH, LEOPOLD VON. MASSEY, IRVING: *Sacher-Masoch, Talmudist* [In]: Aschkenas, Jg. 7, H. 2, Wien, 1997. Pp. 341–388, footnotes. [On Leopold von Sacher-Masoch and the phenomenon of philosemitism in the nineteenth cent. against the background of today's philosemitism; deals mainly with his novel 'Pintschew und Mintschew'.]

35873. SCHMITT, CARL. GROSS, RAPHAEL: *"Jüdisches Gesetz und christliche Gnade". Carl Schmitts Kritik an Kelsen*. [In]: Mittelweg 36, Jg. 6, H. 3, Hamburg, 1997. Pp. 79–92, footnotes.

35874. SCHWEITZER, ALBERT. BERGEL, ALICE R. & KURT, eds.: *"Liebes Cembalinchen . . .". Albert Schweitzer – Alice Ehlers. Eine Freundschaft in Briefen*. Hrsg. von Alice R. und Kurt Bergel. Bodenheim b. Mainz: Philo, 1997. 120 pp., notes (105–119). [Alice Ehlers, 1887 Vienna – 1981 Los Angeles, harpsichordist, emigr. 1935 via UK to US. A friend since 1928, A.E. also helped Schweitzer with his humanitarian work through many charity concerts.]

35875. WEBER, MAX. SPÖTTEL, MICHAEL: *Max Weber und die jüdische Ethik*. Die Beziehung zwischen politischer Philosophie und Interpretation der jüdischen Kultur. Frankfurt am Main; New York: Lang, 1997. 151 pp., footnotes, bibl. (146–151). [Incl. chap. 'Weber und die Juden', dealing also with Weber's antisemitism.]

35876. YOVEL, YIRMIYAHA: *Sublimity and ressentiments: Hegel, Nietzsche and the Jews*. [In]: Jewish Social Studies, Vol. 3, No. 3, Bloomington, IN, Spring/Summer 1997. Pp. 1–25, notes.

X. FICTION AND POETRY

35877. ARNHEIM, RUDOLF: *Eine verkehrte Welt*. Phantastischer Roman. Hrsg. von Thomas B. Schumann. Hürth b. Köln: Ed. Memoria, 1997. 299 pp., illus. [Hitherto unpubl. novel, written in 1948.] [R.A., b. 1904 in Berlin, art psychologist, emigr. 1933 to Italy, 1939 to England, 1940 to the US. Lives in Ann Arbor.]

35878. CELAN, PAUL: *Die Gedichte aus dem Nachlass*. Hrsg. von Bertrand Badiou [et al.]. Anmerkungen von Barbara Wiedemann und Bertrand Badiou. Frankfurt am Main: Suhrkamp, 1997. 548 pp., illus., index. [Cont. ca. 500 poems.] [Cf.: Messerscharf und nah (Beatrice von Matt) [in]: 'NZZ', Nr. 176, Zürich, 2./3. Aug. 1997, p. 58.]

35879. FEINBERG, ANAT: *Das Leben und andere Irrtümer*. Aus dem Hebräischen von Barbara Linner. Gerlingen: Bleicher, 1997. 246 pp. [Autobiographical novel about an Israeli woman and a German Jew.]

35880. *Feuerharfe. Deutsche Gedichte jüdischer Autoren des 20. Jahrhunderts*. Hrsg. von Josef Billen. Leipzig: Reclam, 1997. 281 pp., bibl. (253–255). [Incl. Nachwort (ed. 226–252, notes).] [Cf.: Besprechung (Hans Otto Horch) [in]: Aschkenas, Jg. 8, H. 1, Wien, 1998, pp. 219–220.]

35881. HERSH, RENATE: *Die drei Ohren Gottes*. Roman. Eine jüdische Emigrantin erinnert sich an ihre Jugend im Isartal. Aus dem Engl. von Josef Bader. Hohenschäftlarn (Matthias-Bauer-Ring 11): G. Blomeyer; Ebenhausen b. München: Langewiesche-Brandt, 1995. 269 pp. [Autobiographical novel, depicting a pediatrician's familiy life in Bavaria between 1933 and 1939.]

35882. HILSENRATH, EDGAR: *Die Abenteuer des Ruben Jablonski*. Ein autobiographischer Roman. München: Piper, 1997. 326 pp. [E.H., data see No. 32454/YB XL.]

35883. ISLER, ALAN: *Der Prinz der West End Avenue*. Roman. Aus dem Amerik. von Karin Kersten. Berlin: Berlin Verlag, 1996. 315 pp. [Novel set in an old-people's home in New York, dealing with its Jewish émigré occupants, their survival stories and present involvement with their lay theatre 'Emma Lazarus Old Vic'. First publ. in Great Britain with the title 'The prince of West End Avenue' in 1995.] [Cf.: Hommage an das Leben (Jim G. Tobias) [in]: Aufbau, Vol. 63, New York, Aug. 1, 1997, p. 7.

35884. JOSEPH, ALBRECHT: *Der letzte Vorhang*. Roman. Aus dem Amerik. übers. und mit einem Nachwort von Rüdiger Völckers. Bonn: Weidle, 1997. 262 pp. [Roman à clef, depicting theatre life in Berlin shortly before the Nazi era, with Carl Zuckmayer, Alexander Granach, Erwin Piscator as some of its figures. Orig. title: 'Those years'.] [A.J. (1901–1991), theatre director, writer, translator, emigr. to the US, where he worked as a film cutter.]

35885. KÖRBER, LILI: *Die Ehe der Ruth Gompertz*. Roman Mannheim: Persona Verlag, 1997. 273 pp. [Autobiographical novel; first publ. in Vienna (Lanyi-Verlag) with the title 'Eine Jüdin erlebt das neue Deutschland', in 1934. Depicts life of a Jewish woman married to a non-Jew between summer 1932 and April 1933,] [L.K., 1897 Moscow – 1982 US, journalist, writer, emigr. in 1938 via France to the US.]

35886. MARIENTHAL, HAL: *Schumanns Reise*. Aus dem Amerikan. von Stefan Weidle. Bonn: Weidle, 1996. 329 pp., illus. [Autobiographical novel on the author's childhood years until emigration in 1936. Orig. title: 'Schumann's journey'.] [H.M., b. 1923 in Frankfurt am Main, scriptwriter, lives in New Mexico.]

35887. MARSHALL, LISELOTTE: *Die verlorene Sprache*. Roman. Mit einem Nachwort von Ruth Klüger. Aus dem Engl. von Ingrid Lebe. Frankfurt am Main: Fischer Taschenbuch-Verl., 1997. 303 pp. (Die Frau in der Gesellschaft.) [Autobiographical novel. Orig. title 'Tongue tied'. Author, b. 1923 in Usingen, survived the Nazi period in Switzerland, emigr. 1946 to the US. Lives in England.]

35888. MORGENSTERN, SOMA: *Die Blutsäule. Zeichen und Wunder am Sereth*. Hrsg. und mit einem Nachwort von Ingolf Schulte. Lüneburg: Dietrich zu Klampen Verlag, 1997. 199 pp. (Werkausgabe, Bd. 7.)

35889. NERY, JÚLIA: *Der Konsul*. Roman. Aus dem Portug. von Verena Grubenmann Schmid. Mit einem Vorwort von Patrik von zur Mühlen und einem Nachwort von Ilse Pollack. Zürich: Ed. Epoca, 1997. 204 pp. [Orig. Portug. edn. publ. in 1992 with the title 'O Cônsul'. For further details see No. 35161.]

35890. REINEROVÁ, LENKA: *Das Traumcafé einer Pragerin*. Erzählungen. Berlin: Aufbau Taschenbuch Verlag, 1996. 270 pp. [Autobiographical stories written by the last German-writing author of Prague. Dealing with her life as a journalist in Prague, exile in Paris, Marseille, Casablanca, Mexico, and also with the continued persecution and political pressure she endured in Czechoslovakia during the 1950s, the 1970s and 1980s.]

35891. SCHÖNE, LOTHAR: *Das jüdische Begräbnis*. Erzählung. Frankfurt am Main: Kiepenheuer und Witsch, 1997. 168 pp. [On the attempt, after his mother's death, of a son from a "mixed marriage", to reconstruct his parent's fate during the Nazi period.]

35892. SELIGMANN, RAFAEL: *Der Musterjude*. Roman. Hildesheim: Claassen, 1997. 355 pp. [Satirical novel about a Jew in present-day Germany.]

35893. SINGER, ISRAEL JOSHUA: *Die Familie Karnovski*. Roman. Aus dem Amerik. von Dora Winkler. Wien: Zsolnay, 1997. 501 pp., glossary. [On the life of a family, orig. from Poland, spanning three generations (1890–1938); set in Berlin (until 1933), later in New York. This novel by the brother of Isaac Bashevi Singer was first publ. in the US in 1943 in Yiddish, one year before he died. American transl. first publ. in 1969.] [Cf.: Ein Gleichnis vom verlorenen Sohn (Frauke Hamann) [in]: Das Parlament, Nr. 22–23, Bonn, 22./29. Mai 1998, p. 19.]

35894. SPIES, GERTY: *Bittere Jugend*. Ein Roman von Verfolgung und Überleben im Nationalsozialismus. Hrsg. von Hans-Georg Meyer. Mit einem Nachwort von Sigfrid Gauch und autobiographischen Notizen von Gerty Spies. Frankfurt am Main: Brandes & Apsel, 1997. 190 pp., port., illus. (Literarisches Programm, 56.) [Author, b. 1897 in Trier, married to a non-Jew, deported 1942 to Theresienstadt.]

35895. TSALKA, DAN: *Der Sohn des Rabbi Abraham*. Ein Roman aus dem Mittelalter. Aus dem Hebr. von Vera Loos und Naomi Nir-Bleiming. Bleicher: Gerlingen, 1997. 171 pp. [Novel set in late-medieval Germany dealing with political intrigue, religious struggles, love and revenge.]

35896. WEIL, GRETE. *Last trolley from Beethoven Straat*. Transl. from the German by John Barrett. Boston: Godine, 1997. 160 pp. [Autobiogr. novel on persecution of Jews in Nazi-occupied Amsterdam, first publ. in German in 1963, republ. in 1992.]

Index to Bibliography

Aachen, 34718
Abels, Heinz, 35429
Abels, Norbert, 35429
Abosch, Heinz, 35231
Abramson, Henry, 35808
Abulafia, David, 35591
Achern, 34719
Ackermann, Volker, 35277
'Acta Leopoldina', 35339
Adamczyk, Mieczyslaw Jerzy, 34886
Adamska, Janina, 35684
Adelsdorf, 34720
Adler, Alfred, 35578
Adler, Jankel, 35464
Adler, Joseph, 35413, 35617
Adler, Renate Karoline, 34847
Adler, Shimon, 34963
Adler, Victor, 35465
Adorno, Theodor W., 35429, 35456, 35459, 35466
Adorno, Theodor W. (*Briefe und Briefwechsel*), 35703
Adunka, Evelyn, 34896, 35537
Agus, Aharon R.E., 35869
Aharoni, Zvi, 35005
Ahren, Yizhak, 35415
Ahrens, Birgit, 35649
Albanis, Elisabeth, 35364
Albert, Samuel S., 35632
Albrich, Thomas, 35276
Aldenhoven, 35102
Aldingen, 35388
'Allgemeine' Jüd. Wochenzeitung, 35487, 35789
'Alma Mater Philippina', 35485
Almog, Shmuel, 35408
Alsace, 34703, 34878–34884, 35403
Alsfeld, 34780, 34960
Altenberg, Peter, 35467, 35468
Altona, 34788, 34789
Alvarez, Alexander, 35089
Aly, Götz, 35021, 35755
Ambronn, Karl-Otto, 34729
Améry, Jean, 35469–35472
'American Jewish Year Book', 35243, 35256
'American Scholar', 35349, 35653
'American Spectator' (The), 35193
Amir, Yehoyada, 35350
Ammon, Herbert, 35531
Amsterdam, 35370
Anderl, Gabriele, 34961
Anders, Günther, 35429, 35432, 35459

Angress, Werner T., 35241
Angster, Julia, 35274
Anklam, 34721
Anschluß, 34911
Anti-Judaism, 34939, 35769, 35771, 35797, 35798, 35802, 35804, 35805, 35807, 35824, 35858, 35863
Anti-Zionism, 35265, 35826
Antisemitism, 34763, 34821, 34828, 34872, 34897, 34939, 34948, 35112, 35212, 35221, 35375, 35389, 35411, 35466, 35623, 35761, 35808–35850, 35868, 35869, 35873, 35875
Antisemitism, Austria, 34896, 35810
Antisemitism, Christian, 35797, 35801, 35817, 35825
Antisemitism, Defence, 34679, 35111, 35373, 35419
Antisemitism, Imperial Germany, 34725, 35814, 35829, 35844
Antisemitism, in Teaching, 35809, 35863
Antisemitism, Medieval, 35818
Antisemitism, Middle Ages, 34688, 34767, 35796, 35800, 35804, 35808, 35842
Antisemitism, Nazi, 34767, 34949, 35111, 35226, 35844
Antisemitism, Post War, 35242, 35256, 35272, 35837–35841
Antisemitism, Switzerland, 34914, 34915
Antisemitism, Weimar, 35521
Antmann, S. Michal, 34728
Appel, Friedmar, 35731
Appelfeld, Aharon, 35473
Apsler, Alfred, 35484
Arad, Gulie Ne'eman, 35167
Arbeit an der Geschichte, 34705, 35480
Architecture, Jews in, 35422, 35526, 35632
'Archiv für Hessische Geschichte und Altertumskunde', 34795, 34798
'Archiv für Elektronik und Übertragunsgtechnik', 35501
'Archiv für Kulturgeschichte', 35660
'Archiv für Sozialgeschichte', 34692, 35065
'Archivalische Zeitschrift', 34729
'Der Archivar', 34946
Arendt, Hannah, 35342, 35429, 35432, 35455, 35474–35483, 35695, 35756, 35774
Argentina, 34916, 34917
'Ariadne', 35430
Armbrüster, Georg, 34924
Armed Forces, Jews in the, 34682, 34779, 34868, 34888, 35747

469

Arnheim, Rudolf, 35877
Arnold, Armin, 35509
Arnoldi, Udo, 34747
Arnoldsweiler, 34722
Arnstadt, 34723
Arnstein, George E., 35390
Aroneanu, Eugène, 35099
Aronsfeld, C.C., 35704
'(The) Art Bulletin', 35101
Art Dealers, 34818, 35667
Art Historians, 35457, 35697
Art, Jewish, 35393, 35394, 35397
Art, Jews and Judaism Depicted in, 35807
Art, Jews in, 34932, 35620, 35621, 35623, 35689
Aryanisation, 34747, 34916, 34971, 35002, 35043, 35075, 35217, 35448, 35449, 35463
Aschaffenburg, 34812
Aschenbrenner, Susanne, 35455
Aschheim, Steven E., 35046, 35087, 35756, 35774, 35869
'Aschkenas', 34938; 34679, 34700, 34708, 34781, 34871, 35314, 35345, 35356, 35364, 35417, 35418, 35526, 35611, 35679, 35763, 35781, 35793, 35820, 35872, 35880
'Aschkenas' (*Beiheft*), 35384
Aschoff, Diethard, 34962
Assimilation, Acculturation, 34681, 34699, 35374
35389
Assor, Reuven, 34899
Auerbach, Elias, 35398
Auerbach, Erich, 35485, 35705
'Aufbau', New York, 34793, 35581, 35883
Aufseß, 34769
'Augenblick', 35002
Augsburg, 34724
Augspurg, Anita, 35430
'Aurora', 35852
'Aus dem Antiquariat', 34916, 34940, 35577
'Aus Politik und Zeitgeschichte', 35294, 35304, 35306
Auschwitz, 34962–34965, 34995, 35006, 35041, 35108, 35113, 35123, 35175, 35279
Auschwitz Trial, 35148, 35779
Australia, Refugees, 34918
'Australian Jewish Historical Society Journal', 34918
Austria, 34692, 34885–34896, 35453, 35675, 35700, 35740
Austria, Antisemitism, 35810
Austria, Nazi Period, 34966, 34967, 34970
Austria, Post War, 34896
Austria, Post War Jewish Community, 35243
Austria, Refugees, 34911
Austrian-Hungarian Empire (see also Galicia, Hungary, Bohemia), 34886
Autobiographies, Memoirs, Diaries, Letters, 35487, 35702–35757
Autobiographies, Memoirs, Nazi Period, 34974,
34980, 35004, 35071, 35097, 35104, 35109, 35113, 35118, 35120, 35172, 35176, 35214, 35230, 35231, 35713, 35735
Autobiographies, Memoirs, Post-War Germany, 35749
Avidar-Tchernovitz, Yemima, 34789
Avisar, Ilan, 35167
Awes, Mosche, 34758

Babenhausen, 34812
Bach, Johann Sebastian, 35454
Bacher, Barbara, 34785
Bachmann, Felix, 35206
Bachmann, Ingeborg, 35506, 35851
Bachur, Yona, 34941
Backhaus, Fritz, 35844
Bad Homburg, 34857
Bad Kreuznach, 34810
Baden, 34703, 34725–34727, 34833, 34835, 35403
Baden-Württemberg, 34728, 34971
Badiou, Bertrand, 35878
Baeck, Leo, 34982, 35310–35313, 35320, 35325, 35429
Baeck, Leo (*Werke*), 35309
Bästlein, Klaus, 35142
Baiersdorf, 34769
Bajohr, Frank, 35075
Bala, Heike Catrin, 35757
Ballin, Albert, 35486
'Baltische Studien', 34721, 34755
Balzli, Beat, 35192
Bambauer, Klaus, 34874
Bandmann, Martin, 35406
Bank, Richard D., 34972
Banking, Jews in, 34791, 35463
Bar-Giora-Bamberger, Naftali, 34790, 34878
Bar-On, Dan, 34929, 35147, 35280, 35784
Barkai, Avraham, 34683, 34703
Barker, Andrew, 35467
Barkow, Ben, 34945
Barmen, 34850
Barondess, Jeremiah A., 34973
Barrett, John, 35896
Barron, Stephanie, 35440
Bartels, Adolf, 35820, 35826
Barthes, Roland, 35336
Bartolosch, Thomas A., 35179
Bartsch, Karl-Heinz, 34820
Barzel, Amnon, 34924
Barzel, Neima, 35785
Basle, 35403, 35414, 35415
Batnitzky, Leora, 35774
Battenberg, Friedrich, 34677, 34678, 34703, 34795, 34938
Batts, Michael S., 34717
Bauckmeier, Jochen, 34755
Bauer, Barbara, 35286
Bauer, Johanan E., 35323

Index to Bibliography

Bauer, Markus, 35485
Bauer, Yehuda, 34964, 35060
Baumel, Judith Tydor, 35244, 35245, 35399
Baumgartner, Andreas, 35126
Bavaria, 34729, 34803, 35445, 35881
Bayerdörfer, Hans-Peter, 35370, 35758
'Bayerisches Jahrbuch für Volkskunde', 34681, 35771
Bechtel, Delphine, 35379
Bechtoldt, Hans-Joachim, 34871
Beck, Hamilton H.H., 35860
Beck-Klein, Grete, 34974
Becker, Erna, 34980
Becker, Gerhard, 34721
Becker, Jurek, 35487 (*Obits.*), 35488
Becker, Waldemar, 34760
Becker, Werner, 34829
Becker-Cantarino, Barbara, 34734
Becker-Hammerstein, Waltraud, 34829
Beckschulte, Klaus, 35589
Beer, Mathias, 34677
Beethoven, Ludwig van, 35454
Behler, Diana I., 35547
Behmer, Markus, 35678
Behr, Shulamith, 35426
Beine, Manfred, 34852
Beiner, Friedhelm, 35280
'Beiträge zur Gesch. der Arbeiterbewegung', 35174, 35748
'Beiträge zur Oberbergischen Geschichte', 34849
Bejski, Moshe, 35160
Belgium, Nazi Period, 35122, 35133
Belting, Hans, 35591
Ben Gurion, David, 35203
Ben Natan, Asher, 34896
Ben-Chanan, Yaacov, 34814, 35811
Ben-Shlomo, Zev, 34945
Benario, Aron, 34767
Benda, Ernst, 35779
Bendavid, Lazarus, 34734
Bendix Family, 34761
Bendix, Paul, 34761
Bendremer, Jutta T., 34986
Benhabib, Seyla, 35483
Benjamin, Walter, 35334, 35429, 35432, 35456, 35459, 35489, 35490, 35491, 35774
Benjamin, Walter, *Gesammelte Briefe*, 35706
Benn, Gottfried, 35613, 35738
Benöhr, Hans-Peter, 35429
Benson, Robert L., 35591
Bentheim, 34730
'Bentheimer Jahrbuch', 34730
Benussan, G Rard, 35759
Benz, Wolfgang, 34947, 34949, 34975, 34976, 35006, 35028, 35204, 35220, 35264, 35714, 35779, 35812, 35838
Berding, Helmut, 34683, 34686 (*Festschrift*), 34780

Berenbaum, Michael, 34982
Berent, Margarete, 35429, 35445
Berg, Alban, 35703
Berg, Jimmy, 35492
Bergel, Alice R., 35874
Bergel, Kurt, 35874
Bergen-Belsen, 34977-34979, 35073, 35113, 35117, 35264
Berger, Natalie, 35383
Bergerson, Andrew Stuart, 35773
Berggren, Lena, 35813
Berghaus, Günther, 35010
Bergheim, 34731, 34732
Bergmann, Werner, 34947, 35242, 35812, 35823, 35837, 35839
'Berichte zur Wissenschaftsgeschichte', 35516, 35539
Bering, Dietz, 34682
Berkowitz, Michael, 35373, 35400, 35401
Berleburg, 34733
Berlin, 34692, 34734-34740, 34980, 34981, 35246, 35247, 35274, 35276, 35282-35284, 35322, 35385, 35425, 35428, 35448, 35594, 35643, 35745, 35746, 35748, 35884, 35893
Berlin-Kreuzberg, 35238
Berlin-Prenzlauer Berg, 34742
Berlin-Tempelhof, 34743
Berlin, Centrum Judaicum, 34726
Berlin, Holocaust Memorial, 35281, 35294, 35755, 35778
Berlin, Jüdisches Museum, 34741, 35623
Berlin, Jüdisches Museum, Oranienburger Straße, 35623
'Berliner Journal für Soziologie', 35522
Berlinger, Simon, 34767
Bernard, Birgit, 34983, 35620
Bernhard, Georg, 35739
Bernhard, Julia, 35701
Bernstein, Aron, 35365
Bernstein, Eduard, 35429, 35462
Bernstein, Michael André, 35167
Bers, Günter, 35103
Berthold, Werner, 35441, 35748
Bertz, Inka, 34736
Besser, Aliza, 34978
Best, Werner, 34994
Bethge, Eberhard, 35325
Bettelheim, Bruno, 35493
Bettingen, 35191
Betz, Albrecht, 35541
Bibliographies, Catalogues, Inventories, 34948, 34952, 34954, 34955, 34956, 35439
Bibliographies, Personal, 34709, 35472, 35671, 35678
Bielefeld, 34744, 34745
Biemann, Erwin, 34958
Biemann, Gabriel, 34967
Biermann, Gerd, 35429
Billen, Josef, 35880

Biller, Gerhard, 35370
Biller, Marita, 35274
Bilstein, Jochen, 34850
Bilz, Fritz, 35277
Binder, Otto, 35707
Biographia Judaica Bohemiae, 34899
Biographical Dictionaries, 34899
Birkenhauer, Anne, 34997
Birkmeyer, Regine, 34687
Birn, Ruth Bettina, 35047
Birnbaum, Hermann, 34778
Birnbaum, Nathan, 35415
Birstein, Jossel, 34941
Bischof, H.H., 35271
Biser, Eugen, 35627
Blaschke, Olaf, 35814, 35844
Blaschke, Wolfgang, 35277
Blau, Marietta, 35494
Blau-Weiß (Org.), 35401, 35406
Bleibtreu-Ehrenberg, Gisela, 35429
Bleier, Suzanne M., 35048
Bloch, Anny, 34878, 34884
Bloch, Ernst, 35334, 35350, 35429, 35456, 35495, 35496
Bloch, Iwan, 35429
Bloch, Jan Robert, 35429
Bloch, Joseph, 35370
'Bloch-Almanach', 35495
Blom, Philipp, 35507
Blomert, Reinhard, 35522
Blood Libel, 34767, 35796, 35798, 35800, 35802, 35804, 35806, 35807, 35819, 35830, 35833
Bloom, Cecil, 35498
Blue, Lionel, 35768
Blum, Karl, 34800
Blume, Gisela, 35040
Blume, Thomas, 35602
Blumenfeld, Erwin, 35497
Blumenfeld, Kurt, 35406
Blumenthal, W. Michael, 35006
Boberach, Heinz, 35268
Boccaccio, Giovanni, 35781
Bocholt, 34746
Bochum, 34704, 34747
Bodek, Andrzej, 35121
Bodemann, Y. Michal (Michael), 35243, 35258, 35285
Bodenfelde, 34814
Bodenheimer, Alfred, 34941, 35402, 35415, 35610, 35611
Bodenschatz, Johann Christoph Georg, 34769
Bodoff, Lippman, 35427
Bodsch, Ingrid, 35545
Böckh, Katrin, 34897
Böhm, Günter, 34789
Bölke-Fabian, Andrea, 34953
Boer, Harm den, 34789
Börnstein, Heinrich, 35708

'Börsenblatt für den Deutschen Buchhandel', 34715, 35436
Böschenstein, Bernhard, 35506
Bötticher, Walther, 35615
Böttiger, Paul, 35502
Bohemia, 34898–34902, 34905, 34908, 35826
'Bohemia', 34905
Bohrisch, Hans-Wilhelm, 34758
Bolgar, Marianne, 35094
Bolius, Gisela, 35690
Bolkosky, Sidney, 34984
Boll, Günter, 34878, 34883, 34884
Bollacher, Martin, 35500
Bollack, Jean, 35504
Bollag, David, 35507
Bollendorf, 34748
Bollgöhn, Sibylle, 34817
Bonhoeffer, Dietrich, 34991, 35312
Bonn, 34782, 34985, 35248, 35277, 35384, 35545
'Bonner Geschichtsblätter', 34985, 35248
Book Illustration, 35397
Book Trade, Jews in, 34909
Book-Burning, 35038
Borchard, Beatrix, 35733
Borchardt, Lucy, 35076
Borggraefe, Peter, 34844
Borut, Jacob, 34679, 34692, 34703
Bosold, Birgit, 35729
Bourel, Dominique, 34734
Bower, Tom, 35170, 35193
Bradley, Ernestine Schlant, 35782
Brämer, Andreas, 35251
Brändle, Rainer, 35826
Bräutigam, Petra, 34971
Braham, Randolph L., 35095
Brake, Helmut, 34780
Brake, Ludwig, 34780
Brakelmann, Günter, 35512
Bramann, Wilhelm, 34850
Brand, Gregor, 35330
Brandes, Georg, 35869
Bratislava (Pressburg), 34909
Braun, Bernhard, 35605
Braun, Christina von, 35815
Braun, Joachim, 34767, 35533
Braun, Michael, 35511
Braun, Serge, 34878
Brecht, Berthold, 35555, 35699
Brechtken, Magnus, 35816
Breidecker, Volker, 35601, 35726
Breitenstein, Andreas, 35502
Brendler, Konrad, 35280
Brenner, David A., 35380
Brenner, Michael, 34683, 35249
Brenner, Rachel F., 34987, 35684
Brentano, Clemens, 35852
Breslau, 34988, 35074, 35113
'Breslauer Zeitung', 35594
Bresslau, Harry, 35444

Index to Bibliography

Breuer, Dieter, 34821
Breuer, Isaac, 35415
Breuer, Mordechai, 34683, 34703, 35370
Brickner, Richard M., 35061
Briegleb, Klaus, 35542
Brieskorn, Egbert, 35605
Brinck, Christine, 35768
Brinker, Menachem, 35867, 35869
Brinkmann, Heinrich, 34780
Brinkmüller, Karl, 34760
Brix, Barbara, 34785
Brocke, Edna, 35429, 35483
Brocke, Michael, 34852
Brockmeyer, Dieter, 35826
Brockschmidt, Jens, 34704
Brod, Max, 35450, 35498
Brod, Toman, 35208
Broder, Henryk M., 35768
Broggini, Barbara, 35685
Broszat, Martin, 35087
Brown, Kenneth, 34789
Bruch, Rüdiger vom, 35779
'Brücken', 35450, 35452
Brumlik, Micha, 35260, 35350, 35429, 35432, 35817
Brummack, Jürgen, 35547
Brunkhorst, Hauke, 35429
Brunner, José, 35087
Brunngraber-Malottke, Ruth, 34791
Bruns-Wüstefeld, Alex, 35043
Brusten, Manfred, 35280
Brzosa, Ulrich, 34763
Buber, Martin, 34982, 35315–35318, 35320, 35334, 35429, 35442, 35774, 35826
Bubis, Ignatz, 34850, 35165, 35173, 35260, 35757
Bubis, Naomi, 35250
Buchenwald, 34965, 35041, 35117
'Buchhandelsgeschichte', 35626
Buck, Kurt, 35269
Budapest, Nazi Period, 35094
Budde, Gerda, 35310
Bühler, Karl, 35432
Büning, Eleonore, 35642
Büttner, Ursula, 34990, 35264
Bugaiski, Baerbel, 34853
Bukowina, 35210
Bulz, Emmanuel, 35370
Burgard, Friedhelm, 34688, 34697, 34827, 34869
Burgenland, 34885
Burger, Adolf, 35171
Burgmair, Wolfgang, 35625
Burkhardsfelden, 34796
Burmeister, Karl Heinz, 35796
Burrin, Philippe, 35087
Buruma, Ian, 35033
Bus, E., 34857
Buttenhausen, 34749

Buttenwiesen, 34750
Butterwegge, Christoph, 35840
Byron, George, 35454
Bögler, Helmut, 35005

Cage, John, 35667
Cahn, Albert, 34782
Calaprice, Alice, 35513
Calimani, Riccardo, 35428
Campbell, Sara, 35667
'Canadian Journal of History', 34754
Cancik, Hubert, 35869
Canetti, Elias, 35499, 35500
Canovan, Margaret, 35476, 35483
Capesius, Victor, 35148
Capogrossi Colognesi, Luigi, 35045
Caputh, 35711
Cargas, Harry James, 35224
Caricatures, Jews Depicted in, 35807, 35822
Carlebach, Julius, 34943, 35251, 35319, 35331
Carmel, Alex, 35791
Carr, Jonathan, 35631
Carrdus, Anna, 34943
Caspari, Volker, 35648
Cassirer, Ernst, 35432, 35457
Cassuto, Alfonso, 34789
Castelmur, Linus, 35194
Castrop, 34751
Cauer, Emil, 35501
Cauer, Wilhelm, 35501
Celan, Paul, 35358, 35432, 35442, 35502–35506, 35878
Celle, 34752
Cemeteries, 34718, 34720, 34728, 34744, 34747, 34750, 34752, 34759, 34763, 34769, 34781, 34787, 34789, 34790, 34797, 34800, 34807, 34810, 34811, 34835, 34839, 34844, 34847, 34852, 34859, 34865, 34868, 34873, 34890, 34901, 35386
'Central European History', 35052, 35521
Centralverein deutscher Staatsbürger jüd. Glaubens (C.V.), 35381
Cepl-Kaufmann, Gertrude, 35605
Cesarani, David, 34977, 35096, 35188, 35218
Chaitin, Julia, 35280
Chamberlain, Houston Stewart, 35813
Charpa, Ulrich, 35429
Chase, Jefferson S., 35853
Chazan, Robert, 35818
Chemnitz, 34854
Children, 34963, 35041, 35105, 35152, 35382
China, 34923, 34924
Chlada, Marvin, 35688
'(The) Chronicle of Higher Education', 35284
Church, Christians and Jews, 34763, 35318
Church, Christians and Jews, Nazi Period, 34990–34992, 35295
Church, Christians and Jews, Post War, 35252, 35325

Clark, Christopher, 34701
Claussen, Detlev, 35757
Cohen, Cosman David, 34746
Cohen, Daniel J., 34680
Cohen, Edmund D., 35050
Cohen, Frederick E., 34989
Cohen, Hermann, 35320, 35350, 35370, 35429, 35507, 35508
Cohen, Richard A., 35323
Cohen, Robert, 35659
Cohen, Susan Sarah, 34948
Cohen, Theodore, 34926
Cohn, Chaim, 35405
Cohn, Dorrit, 35586
Cohn, Gordon, 35721
Cohn, Haim, 34789
Cohn-Sherbok, Dan, 35320
Colijn, G. Jan, 35060
Colljung, Paul, 34748
Cologne, 34679, 34753, 34754, 34983, 34993, 35277
Comité zur Abwehr Antisemitischer Angriffe, 34679
Commemorations, 35167, 35285, 35294, 35303, 35304, 35306
'Commentary', 35037, 35203
Commichau, Gerhard, 34786
Communists, 35174, 35685, 35748
Concentration and Internment Camps, Ghettos, 34900, 35099, 35184, 35218
Conversion from Judaism, Baptism, 34701, 34799, 34846, 35110, 35338, 35510, 35551, 35557, 35684, 35763, 35764, 35769
Conversion to Judaism, 35768
'Convivium', 35365, 35375, 35376, 35488
Conze, Werner, 35755
Conzen, Peter, 35429
Cooper, John Michael, 35454
Coppenhagen, Isaac, 35545
Corbach, Dieter, 34849, 34993
Corbin-Schuffels, Anne-Marie, 34917, 35683
Corino, Karl, 35575
Coudert, Allison P., 35760
Court Jews, 35397, 35427
Cowell, Alan, 35051
Cramer, Robert (Ezriel), 34776
Crawford, Elisabeth, 35638
Crecelius, Wilhelm, 34850
'Critical Inquiry', 35056
Crusades, 34687, 34689, 34700, 34706
Czech Republic, 35243
Czechoslovakia, 34898, 34900, 34902, 34905, 35830
Czechoslovakia, Nazi Period, 34900, 34996, 35006, 35709
Czer, Andreas, 34836
Czermak, Gerhard, 35797
Czernowitz, 34903, 35176, 35220

Dachau, 34965, 35123
'Dachauer Hefte', 35082, 35270
Dämmig, Larissa, 34742
Däschler-Seiler, Siegfried, 34876
Dagan, Daniel, 35791
Daltroff, Jean, 34878
'Damals', 35410
Dammann, Richard, 34791
Dan, Joseph, 35342
Dannecker, Theodor, 35019
Danzig, 35721, 35722
Darmstadt, 34797, 35107
'David', 34909, 34961, 35394
David, Ferdinand, 35454
David, Moritz, 34747
Davidowicz, Klaus S., 35321
Davidson, Eugene, 35139
Davis, Charles, 35591
Davis, Hadassah, 35768
Davringhausen-Heinrich Maria, 35614
Daxelmüller, Christoph, 34681
Déak, Istvan, 35045, 35052
Debler, Ulrich, 34823
Debrunner, Albert M., 34914
Decker, Shoshana, 35487
Deggendorf, 34767
Del Caro, Adrian, 35503
Delf, Hanna, 35605, 35607, 35869
Demel, Katharina, 34896
Demetz, Peter, 34907
Demmin, 34755
Denes, Magda, 35097
'Denkmalpflege in Baden-Württemberg', 34728
Denmark, Nazi Period, 34994
Denunciation, 35138
Department Stores, 35448, 35449, 35823
Deportations, 34988, 34993, 35027, 35208
Deselaers, Manfred, 34995
Deshmukh, Marion F., 35687
Dessau, 34756, 35525
Dettling, Warnfried, 35582
Deutsch, Helene, 35429
Deutsch, Werner, 35432
Deutsch-Jüdische Geschichte in der Neuzeit, 34683
'Deutsche Studien', 35066
'Deutsche Vierteljahrsschrift für Literatur und Geistesgesch.', 35583, 35853
Deutsches Exilarchiv 1933 – 1945, 34934
Deutschkreutz, 34885
'(Der) Deutschunterricht', 35286
'Diagonal', 35179
Dichanz, Horst, 35809
Dick, Jutta, 35744, 35757
Dickinson, John K., 35495
Dictionary of the Holocaust, 34950
Dieburg, 34797
Diehl, Katrin, 34998, 35090
Diekmann, Irene, 34816
Diekmann, Silvia, 35623

Index to Bibliography

Diercks, Herbert, 35269
Diersburg, 34835
Diessenhofen, 35800
Dietermann, Klaus, 35180, 35302
Dietl, Wilhelm, 35005
Diez, 34757
'Dimensions', 35031, 35188, 35447
Diner, Dan, 34709, 35021, 35087, 35276, 35429, 35474, 35483
Dinglinger, Wolfgang, 35454
Dippel, John V.H., 34999
Dirschauer, Johannes, 35596
Dischereit, Esther, 35253
Dispeker, Thea, 34930
Displaced Persons, 34977, 35244, 35264, 35267, 35276, 35749
Döblin, Alfred, 35376, 35431, 35509, 35510
Dölemeyer, Barbara, 34678
Dönhoff, Marion, 35591
Döpmann, Hans Dieter, 34897
Döpp, Suska, 34753
'DÖW Jahrbuch', 35127
Doherty, Muriel, 34978
'Doitsu Bungaku', 34712
Domansky, Elisabeth, 35167
Domin, Hilde, 35511
Donat, Helmut, 35618
Donnert, Erich, 34894
Dora-Mittelbau, 35000
Dorsten, Jüd. Museum Westfalen, 35287
Dortmund, 34758
Dovern, Willi, 34762
Dowe, Dieter, 35053, 35065
Dowe, Ludger, 34762
Drensteinfurt, 34759
Dresden, 34854, 35001
Dresden, Sem, 35090
Dressen, Willi, 35144
Drewek, Peter, 35223
Drews, Jörg, 35136, 35602, 35727
Dreyfus Affair, 35370
Dreyfus, Jean-Marc, 34878
(Bad) Driburg, 34760
Droste-Hülshoff, Annette, 35844, 35853–35855
'Droste-Jahrbuch', 35855
Drumont, Edouard Adolphe, 35826
Dubnow, Simon, 35352, 35536
Dubrowska, Malgorzata, 35488
Duchen, Jessica, 35600
Dühring, Eugen, 35826
Dülmen, 34761
Düren, 34762
'Dürener Geschichtsblätter', 34722
Düsseldorf, 34763, 34764, 35003, 35230, 35277, 35766
Dyck, Joachim (*Festschrift*), 35842
Dyson, Freeman, 35513
Dytman, Miriam A., 35623

Early Modern Period (Pre-Enlightenment), 34677, 34681, 35781
'East European Jewish Affairs', 35275
Eastern Jewry, 34692, 34704, 34831, 34914, 34942, 35370, 35376, 35379, 35380, 35385, 35415, 35822
Ebbinghaus, Angelika, 35077, 35079
Eberstaller, Gerhard, 35650
Eckert, Brita, 35417
Eckert, Toni, 34769
Eckmann, Sabine, 35440
Eckstein-Diner, Bertha, 35443
Economists, 35582
Edelheit, Abraham J., 35203
Eder, Angelika, 35276
Eder, Manfred, 34767
Edinger, Michael, 35791
Edinger, Tilly, 34774
'Edith Stein Jahrbuch', 34691, 34975, 35123, 35240, 35318, 35321, 35458, 35461, 35518, 35557, 35668
Education, 34684, 34703, 34876, 34886, 35152, 35223, 35316, 35382, 35711, 35724
Edvardson, Cordelia, 35004
Egloffstein, 34769
Ehlers, Alice, 35874
Ehlert, Holger, 34763
Ehrenberg, Hans, 35512
Ehrenstein, Albert, 35367
Ehrlich, Ernst Ludwig, 35191, 35429
Eiber, Ludwig, 34949, 35232
Eichendorff, Joseph von, 35551
Eichholz, Max, 35079, 35080
Eichmann, Adolf, 34961, 35005, 35477
Eichmann, Johanna S., 35287
Einstein, Albert, 35401, 35429, 35432, 35513–35519
Eisenstadt, Jüd. Museum, 34885
Eisfelder, Horst, 34924
Eisner, Freya, 35520
Eisner, Kurt, 35520, 35521
Eladan, Jacques, 35370
Elb, Norbert, 35177
Eley, Geoff, 35773
Elias, Norbert, 35406, 35429, 35522, 35523, 35524
Eliav, Mordechai, 35322
Elkana, Eli see Michelsohn, Georg, 35525
Elon, Amos, 35664
Elsässer, Jürgen, 35793
Eltzbacher, Jakob Löb, 34852
Elvers, Rudolf, 35454
Emancipation, 34686, 34696, 34702, 34703, 34709, 34754, 34795, 34894, 34896, 35524, 35533, 35761, 35860
Emden, 34781
Emigration (see also country of emigration), 34703, 34843, 34931, 35222, 35430
Emter, Elisabeth, 35763

Enders, Hermann, 34858
Endicott Barnett, Vivian, 35667
Engel, Nils-Christian, 34847
Engel, Ulrich, 34711
Engelmann, Paul, 35526
Engler, Steffani, 35719
Engler, Wolfgang, 35476
Enlightenment, 34892, 34896
(Die) Enzyklopädie des Nationalsozialismus, 34949
Epple, Angelika, 35532
Epstein, Francis and Helen, 35725
Epstein, Helen, 35709
Erb, Rainer, 35242, 35804, 35837, 35841
Erbach, 34795
Erenz, Benedikt, 35546
Erfurt, 34765
Erikson, Erik H., 35429
Erler, Hans, 35429
Ermreuth, 34769
Errery, Roger, 35144
Erspamer, Peter R., 35761
(Der) Erste Zionistenkongreß von 1897, 35403
Esch, M.G., 35003
Eschebach, Insa, 35155, 35269
Esens, 35288
Espelage, Gregor, 35269
Essen, 35620
Esslingen, 34876
Esslingen Mahzor, 35396
Esslinger, Hans Ulrich, 35429
Ettinger, Elzbieta, 35475
Ettlinger, Karl, 35527
Eugster-Ulmer, Roger, 35510
'Europäische Ideen', 35431, 35487, 35575
'Europäische Rundschau', 35064
'European History Quarterly, 35846
'European Judaism', 35312, 35335, 35344, 35665
Euthanasia, 35036, 35042
Evetts, Deborah, 35396
Ewers, Hans-Heino, 35382
Ewing, William A., 35497
Exenberger, Herbert, 35484
'Exil', 35431
Exile, 34928, 35006, 35008, 35232, 35430, 35435
Exile, Journalism, 35438
Exile, Literature and Arts, 34912, 35007, 35433, 35436, 35437, 35440, 35441, 35510, 35530, 35577, 35700,
Exile, Social Sciences and Humanities, 35439, 35495, 34919
Exile, Theatre, Film, 35437
'Exilforschung, Int. Jahrbuch', 35232
(Der) Exodus aus Nazideutschland und die Folgen, 35432
Ezra, Abraham Ibn, 35323
Ezrahi, Sidra Dekoven, 35087

Faassen, Dina van, 34801
Fabry, Joseph and Judith, 35710
Fabréguet, Michel, 35218
Fackenheim, Emil L., 35320, 35323
Fänsen, Hubert Ae, 35798
Falke, Hermann, 35151
Fasse, Norbert, 35216
Faure, Ulrich, 35577
Faust, Jürgen, 34787
Federn, Etta, 35430
Feidel-Mertz, Hildegard, 35429, 35430, 35724
Feinberg, Anat, 35774, 35879
Feingold, Henry L., 35011, 35012
Feininger, Lyonel, 35667
Felstiner, John, 35504
Fenske, Hans, 35816
Ferris, David S., 35490
Ferris, Paul, 35529
Festschrift see Berding, Helmut; Dyck, Joachim; Friedlander Albert H.; Guggisberg, Hans R.; Heit, Alfred; Jaroschka, Walter; Jeziorkowski, Klaus; Loose, Hans-Dieter; Mieck, Ilja; Mühlpfordt, Günter; Schubert, Ernst; Wangermann, Ernst; Wellmann, Hans
Fetterman, Bonny V., 35224
Feuchte, Andreas, 35454
Feuchtwanger, Lion, 35367, 35528, 35826
Feuser-Weyrich, Alice, 34763
Fiedler, Jiri, 34901
Fiero, Petra S., 35469
Fiesel, Eva, 35445
Filehne, 34766
Final Solution (see also Holocaust), 34949, 34982, 35016–35021, 35036, 35091, 35169, 35816
Fings, Karola, 35277
Finkelgrün, Peter, 35022
Finkelstein, Norman G., 35070
Fisahn, Andreas, 35429
Fischer, Ernst Peter, 35514
Fischer, Gerhard, 35425
Fischer, Ralph, 35647
Fischer, Rosy, 35426
Fischer-Defoy, Christine, 34924
Fishbane, Michael, 35715
Fitzgerald, Gerald, 35183
Flacht, 34839
Flade, Roland, 34767
Flechtmann, Frank, 35585
Fleg, Edmond, 35370
Fleischmann, Johann, 34720
Flemming, Jans, 35389
Flensburg, 35765
Fleury, Jean, 34879
Flicker, Ted, 34927
Fliedl, Konstanze, 35670
Fliedner, Hans Joachim, 34835
Florek, Zdzislaw, 35684
Flores d'Arcais, Paolo, 35483
Föhse, Ulrich, 34850
Foitzik, Jan, 35274

Index to Bibliography

Folkers, Horst, 35350
Folz, Hans, 35842
Forced Labour, 35023–35026, 35175
Forchheim, 34769
'Forschungsstelle Judentum, Mitt. und Beiträge', 34935; 35313, 35658
Foschepoth, Josef, 35252
Fraenkel, André Aaron, 34878, 34881
Fraenkel, Ernst, 35429
Fränkel, Hirsch, 34805
Fränkel, Marta, 35455
Fränkische Lebensbilder, 35676
France, Nazi Period, 35104, 35218, 35239
France, Refugees, 35027, 35028, 35159, 35161, 35231, 35232
'Francia', 34917
Franck, Eduard, 35454
Franck, James, 35432
Franconia, 34703, 34720, 34768, 34769, 34808, 35351
Frank, Abraham, 34839, 35397
Frank, Anne, 34987, 35029, 35031, 35032, 35033, 35034, 35289
Frank, Jakob, 34904
Frank, Klaus D., 35442
Frank, Ludwig, 34835
Frank, Rudolf, 35375
Franke, Almut, 35516
Franke, Fabian, 35516
Franke, Manfred, 35136
Frankel, Jonathan, 35819
Frankel, Zacharias, 35314
Frankfurt am Main, 34770–34776, 35035, 35251, 35255, 35290, 35446, 35591, 35648, 35716
Frankfurt am Main, Jüdisches Museum, 34772
Frankfurt School, 34692, 35432
'Frankfurter Allg. Zeitung' ('FAZ'), 35020, 35343, 35397, 35487, 35504, 35512, 35575, 35594, 35601, 35612, 35642, 35657, 35677, 35698, 35701, 35703, 35731, 35732, 35816
'Frankfurter Judaistische Beiträge', 35326, 35327, 35351
'Frankfurter Zeitung', 35459, 35496, 35601, 35662
Frankl, Viktor Emil, 35710
Franz, Eckhart G., 34797
Frauenkirchen, 34885
'Free Inquiry', 35050
Freeman, Thomas, 35359
Frei, Dieter, 35415
Frei, Norbert, 35087
'Freiburger Rundbrief', 35054, 35252, 35864
Frenssen, Birte, 35621
Freud, Sigmund, 35350, 35372, 35429, 35529, 35579, 35684, 35710, 35869
Freudenthal, Joseph, 34816
Freudenthal, Max Michel, 34865
Freund, Florian, 34967

Freund, René, 35443
Freund, Susanne, 34684
Freundlich, Elisabeth, 35530
Freytag, Gustav, 35826
Fricke, Dieter, 35735
Fried, Johannes, 35591
Friedeburg, Robert von, 34703, 34821
Friedell, Egon, 35869
Friedländer, Henri, 35433, 35436 (*Obit.*)
Friedländer, Saul, 35037, 35087, 35167
Friedländer, Sophie, 35711
Friedlander, Albert H., 35309, 35335, 35768
Friedlander, Albert H. (*Festschrift*), 35324, 35325
Friedlander, Eli, 35087
Friedlander, Evelyn, 35387
Friedlander, Henry, 35036
Friedler, Egon, 35762
Friedman, Maurice, 35315
Friedman, Philip, 35038
Friedmann, Friedrich G., 35531
Friedrich, Thomas, 35623
Friedt, Heinz Gerd, 34731
Fries, Jakob Friedrich, 35826
Friesel, Evyatar, 35167, 35712
Frisch, Max, 35831
Fritz Bauer Institut, 34936
Frobenius, Leo, 35845
Fröndenberg, 35039
Fromer, Dafna, 35280
Fromm, Erich, 35061, 35334, 35406, 35429
Frühauf, Matthias, 34742
(*Die*) *frühen Nachkriegsprozesse*, 35269; 34979
Frühwald, Wolfgang, 35441
Fry, Varian, 35159
Fuchs, Konrad, 35070
Fühmann, Franz, 35834
Füllner, Bernd, 35540
Füllner, Karin, 35540
Für ein neues Miteinander von Juden und Christen, 34707; 34794, 35260, 35303, 35316, 35319, 35817
Fürth, 34777, 35040
Fürth, Henriette, 35532
Fuhrich-Grubert, Ursula, 34783
Fuhrmann, Horst, 35444, 35592, 35799
Fuller, Steven Nyole, 35820
Funk, Rainer, 35429
Furst, Peter, 35713
Fösing, Albrecht, 35515

Galicia, 34886, 34887, 35228, 35826
Galison, Peter L., 35494
Ganor, Solly, 35071
Gans, Eduard, 35377, 35533, 35534
Ganzfried, Daniel, 35476
Garber, Klaus, 34734
Gassert, Philipp, 35821
Gast, Uriel, 34913

Gauch, Sigfrid, 35894
Gauersheim, 34807
Gay, Peter, 35447
'Gedenkstätten-Rundbrief', 35026, 35301
Geier, Manfred, 35429
Geiger, Abraham, 35320
Gekle, Hanna, 35429
Gelbin, Cathy, 35774
Gelblum, Amira, 35430
Geldbach, Erich, 35060
Geldern, van, Family, 35397
Geller, Eva, 34711
Geller, Jay, 35360
Gellhaus, Axel, 35505
Gelsenkirchen, 35233
'(Der) Gemeinsame Weg', 35182
Genealogy, 34808, 34878, 34879, 35386, 35388, 35390
Genet, Jean-Philippe, 35591
Genger, Angela, 34763, 35002
Genin, Salomea, 35714
Genisa, 34703
Gentile, Carlo, 35297
Gera, 34778
Gerlach, Wolfgang, 35060
German Democratic Republic, 35259, 35265, 35272, 35624, 35718, 35753, 35791, 35793
'German History', 34701, 35008, 35046, 35067, 35146
'German Life and Letters', 35694
'German Quarterly', 35062
'German Studies Review', 35861, 35865
German-Jewish Relations, Post War, 35167
Germanic Review' (The), 35342
'Germanistische Mitteilungen', 35673
'Germanistisches Jahrbuch Polen', 35488
Germany, Immigration, 35247
Gerstenberger, Heide, 35597
'Geschichte im Westen', 34983, 35268, 35620
'Geschichte in Wissenschaft und Unterricht', 35290, 35770
'Geschichte und Gegenwart', 35683
'Geschichte und Gesellschaft', 34969, 35212, 35457, 35463
'Geschichte, Erziehung, Politik', 35048, 35070, 35091, 35135, 35209, 35282
Geseke, 34779
'Geseker Heimatblätter', 34779
Geve, Thomas, 35041
Geyer, Michael, 35773
Giere, Jacqueline D., 35264, 35276
Giersch, Robert, 34777
Gies, Miep, 35031
Giesey, Ralph E., 35591
Gießen, 34780
Gilbert, Martin, 35291
Gill, Manfred, 34756
Gillman, Abigail E., 35583
Gilman, Sander L., 35361, 35362, 35363

Ginzburg, Carlo, 35087
Giovannini, Norbert, 34794
Glas, Reinhold, 34769
Glass, James M., 35042
Glatter, 34752
Glatz, Joachim, 34839
Glatzer, Albert, 35633
Glatzer, Nahum N., 35715
Glotz, Peter, 35605
Glückel von Hameln, 34695, 35535
Glückstadt, 34781, 34787
Gobitz, Gérard, 35027
Goch, Stefan, 35233
Godesberg (Bad), 34782
'Godesberger Heimatblätter', 34782
Gödde, Christoph, 35706
Göhler, Gerhard, 35429
Görner, Rüdiger, 35543
Gössmann, Wilhelm, 35551
Goethe, Johann Wolfgang, 35536, 35856
Götschel, Willi, 35342, 35536
Göttingen, 34783, 35043, 35044
Gohl, Beate, 35035
Golczewski, Frank, 34861, 35277
Goldberg, Leonid, 34850
Goldberg, Oskar, 35869
Goldenbogen, Nora, 35001
Goldhagen Debate, 35045–35068, 35482
Goldhagen, Daniel J., 35045, 35049, 35059, 35061, 35069, 35070, 35755, 35756, 35778
Goldlust-Gingrich, Ellen D., 35157
Goldman, Robert N., 35517
Goldmann, Christina, 35381
Goldmann, Erwin, 34976
Goldschmidt, Hermann Levin, 35536 (*Obit.*), 35537
Goldschmidt, Meier Selig, 34776
Goldschmidt, Selig, 34776
Goldstein, Brigitte, 35599, 35714
Goldstein, Moritz, 35364
Goldstein, Sandra, 35404
Golec, Janusz, 35365
Golomb, Jacob, 35869, 35870
Gómez García, Monserrat, 34789
Gomperz, Marie von, 35651
Goodman-Thau, Eveline, 35350, 35405
Gottwald, Astrid, 35786
Gotzmann, Andreas, 34685, 34942
Grab, Walter, 35370, 35618
Grabherr, Eva, 34889
Gradwohl, Roland, 35415
Gräbe, Fritz, 35162
Graetz, Heinrich, 35320, 35326, 35327
Graetz, Michael, 34683, 34914, 35054
Graf, Friedrich Wilhelm, 35512
Graf, Johannes, 35763, 35764
Graml, Hermann, 34949
Grashof, Karl Theodor, 34767
Grau, Gerd-Günther, 35869

Index to Bibliography

'Grauzone', 35263
Graz, 34888
Great Britain, 34687, 35711
Great Britain, Antisemitism, 34921
Great Britain, Immigration, 34921
Great Britain, Nazi Period, 35218
Great Britain, Refugees, 34920, 35183, 35232, 35437
Grebing, Helga, 34692, 35429
Green, Kenneth Hart, 35346
Gregor, Neil, 35037
Greiner, Bernd, 35597
Grenville, John A.S., 34943
Griese, Kerstin, 34763
Griffioen, Pim, 35133
Grillparzer, Franz, 35772
Gronau, Dietrich, 35544
Gross, Raphael, 35873
Groß-Rosen, 35041
Grosser, Alfred, 34999, 35716
Grossert, Werner, 35525
Grossman, Jeffrey, 35861
Grossmann, Atina, 35773
Grossmann, Kurt R., 34704, 35538
Grubel, Fred, 34942, 35115
Gruber, Hans, 34889
Gruber, Ruth Ellen, 35765
Grünewald, Eckhart, 35591
Grünstadt, 34837
Grunenberg, Antonia, 35483
Gruner, Wolf, 35023–35026, 35072
Grynberg, Anne, 35218
Grynszpan, Herschel, 35124
Grözinger, Elvira, 35256
Guang, Pan, 34923
'(The) Guardian', 35005, 35170
Güdemann, Moritz, 35826
Guggenheim Family, 35388
Guggisberg, Hans R. (*Festschrift*), 34904
Gumbrecht, Moses, 34783
'Gutenberg-Jahrbuch', 35436
Gutman, Dawid, 35073
Gutmann, Thomas, 35766
Guttmann, Alexander, 35357
Gutzkow, Karl, 35377
Gypsies, 35849

Ha-Am, Achad, 35320, 35352
Haarscher, André-Marc, 34878, 34882, 34884
Haas, Norbert J., 34808
Haber, Fritz, 35539
Haber, Peter, 35403
Habermas, Jürgen, 35055
Habsburg-Hungary,
Hachshara, 35076
Hackeschmidt, Jörg, 35406, 35522, 35645
Hacohen, Ran, 35382
Hadda, Wolfgang, 35074
Haeberle, Erwin J., 35429

Häberlin, Heinrich, 34913
Hähn, Ulrike, 35282
Häntzschel, Hiltrud, 35429, 35445
Hafner, Katie, 35257
Hagemann, Harald, 35429
Hagenbach, 34769
Haggadah, 35397
Hahn, Barbara, 35729
Hahn, Hans Henning, 35371
Hahn, Hans-Werner, 34686
Hahn, Joachim, 35331
Hahne, Bernd, 34762
Hahnstetten, 34839
Haibl, Michaela, 35822
Haindorf, Alexander, 34684
Hakel, Hermann, 34896
Halakha, 34685
Halbmayr, Brigitte, 34896
Halkin, Hillel, 35203
Haller-Nevermann, Marie, 35679
Hamann, Christoph, 35425
Hamann, Frauke, 35893
Hamburg, 34785–34789, 35075, 35076–35080, 35264, 35829
Hamburg-Altona, 34787
Hamburg-Bahrenfeld, 34787
Hamburg-Wandsbek, 34790
Hameiri, Ilan, 35768
Hameln, Jente, 35390
Hammerstein, Notker, 35446
Hanau-Lichtenberg (Alsace), 34882, 34884
Handbuch zur "Völkischen Bewegung" 1871–1918, 35823
Handler, Andrew, 34910
Hanover, 34703, 34791, 34792, 35122, 35264
Hanschmidt, Elisabeth, 34852
Hansen, Nikoline, 35117
Hansen, Peter, 35618
Hansen, Ursula, 35618
Harden, Maximilian, 35779, 35866
Hardenberg, Henriette, 34695
Hardt, Ursula, 35652
Hare, A. Paul, 35280
Harlan, Veit, 35015
Harpprecht, Klaus, 35113
Harries-Schumann, Elisabeth (Lisa), 34803
Hartog, L.J., 35016
Hartwich, Wolf-Daniel, 35565, 35869
Haselbach, Dieter, 35429
Hasenjürgen, Brigitte, 35719
Hashomer Hazair, 34902
Haskalah, 35826
Hassler, Marianne, 35432
Hassler, Silke, 34896
Haumann, Heiko, 34904, 35403, 35407, 35415
Hauptmann, Gerhart, 35857
Hauschild, Jan-Christoph, 35546, 35551
Hausdorff, Felix, 35605
Hauser, Franz, 35454

Hauser, Martin, 35717
Haverkamp, Alfred, 34687, 34688
Hawrylchak, Sandra H., 34957
Hayoun, Maurice-Ruben, 35869
Hebard, Andrew, 35773
Hebbel, Friedrich, 35604
Hebrew Literature, 34689, 34700, 34724, 35276, 35382, 35396
Hechingen, 34793
Heer, Hannes, 35597
Heft, Sebastian, 35476
Hegel, Georg W. Friedrich, 35858, 35876
Hegewisch, Helga, 35768
Hehl, Ulrich von, 35085
Heid, Ludger, 34692, 34758, 35409, 35410, 35429
Heidegger, Martin, 35323, 35456, 35475, 35859
Heidelberg, 34794
'Heidelberger Jahrbücher', 35627
Heidelberger-Leonard, Irene, 35470
Heil, Johannes, 34947, 35049, 35824, 35844
Heilbut, Anthony, 34928
Heilbut, Ferdinand, 35386
Heilbut, Helga, 35386
Heiligenstadt, 34769
Heim, Susanne, 35021
Heimann, Dietrich, 35618
Heimann, Siegfried, 35274
'Heimat Dortmund', 34758
'Heimatbuch Hagen und Mark', 34784
'Heimatkalender, Landkreis Bitburg-Prüm', 34748, 34862
Heimböckel, Dieter, 35654
Heine, Heinrich, 34763, 35377, 35397, 35438, 35466, 35533, 35541–35572, 35708, 35766, 35857
Heine, Heinrich, *Düsseldorfer Heine-Ausgabe (DHA)*, 35540
'Heine-Jahrbuch', 35553, 35559, 35857
Heinemann, Hartmut, 34797, 34937
'Heinrich Mann-Jahrbuch', 35866
Heinrich, Christa, 34742
Heinz, Rudolf, 35350
Heit, Alfred (*Festschrift*), 34697
Heitmann, Margret, 35429
Helfenstein, Josef, 35667
Heller, Hermann, 35429
Heller, Peter, 35869
Hellman, Lillian, 35033
Hellweg, Martin, 35705
Hellwig-Unruh, Renate, 35454
Helmig, Martina, 35573
Helmont, Franciscus Mercurius von, 35760
Hempel-Küter, Christa, 35691
Hemstege, Andreas, 34852
Hennemann, Monika, 35454
Hennweiler, 34839
Henschel Family, 34916
Henschel, Gerhard, 35045

Hensel, Fanny (née Mendelssohn), 35454, 35573, 35574, 35642, 34695, 35732
Hensel, Wilhelm, 35454, 35573
Herberich-Marx, Geneviève, 34878
Herbert, Ulrich, 35021
Herbst, Detlev, 34814
Herbstrith, Waltraud, 35684
Herf, Jeffrey, 35258
Hering, Sabine, 35430
Hermann, Armin, 35432, 35518
Hermes, Claudia, 35477
Hermlin, Stephan, 35575 (*Obits.*)
Herms, Michael, 35624
Hermstrüwer, Inge, 35545
Herrlingen, 35081
Herrmann, Margit, 35082
Herrn, Rainer, 35429
Hersch, Jeanne, 35429
Hersh, Renate, 35881
Hertling, Viktoria, 35530
Hertz, Deborah, 35083
Hertz, Henriette, 35576
Hertzka, Theodor, 35415
Herwig, Rachel Monika, 35429
Herz, Henriette, 34734
Herz, Marcus, 34734
Herz, Thomas, 35767
Herzberg, Arno, 34766
Herzberg, Ruben, 34785
Herzberg, Tusia, 35234
Herzfelde, Wieland, 35495, 35577
Herzig, Arno, 34684, 34690, 34703, 34861, 35418, 35793
Herzka, Else Freistadt, 35578
Herzka, Heinz Stefan, 35578
Herzl, Theodor, 34896, 35320, 35408–35415, 35424, 35563, 35579, 35826
Herzog, Andreas, 35366, 35367, 35825
Heschel, Abraham Joshua, 35320, 35328
Heschel, Susannah, 35328
Hess, Moses, 35320
Hesse, 34680, 34703, 34795–34799, 34806, 34811, 34812, 34821, 34829, 34858, 34860, 34864, 34937, 35251
Hessing, Jakob, 34941, 35397, 35549
Hettenleidelheim, 34800
Hetzel, Marius, 35084
Heuberger, Georg, 34772, 34942
Heuberger, Rachel, 34691, 34707
Heuer, Renate, 34953, 35446, 35826
Heuer, Wolfgang, 35429, 35476
Heumann, Pierre, 35414, 35415
Heuser, Magdalene, 35535
Heutger, Nicolaus, 34815, 35235
Heuvel, William Vanden, 35011
Heydrich, Reinhard, 34996
Heym, Stefan, 35718, 35775
Heymann, Carl, 35626
Heymann, Fritz, 34763

Index to Bibliography 481

Heymann, Lida Gustava, 35430, 35580
Hieber, Jochen, 35487
Hiestand, Rudolf, 34687
Hilberg, Raul, 35056
Hild-Berg, Anette, 35429
Hildebrandt, Dieter, 35499
Hilden, 35136
Hildesheimer Seminary, 35322
Hildesheimer, Esriel (Historian), 34997, 35322
Hildesheimer, Meir, 35329
Hilferding, Rudolf, 35429
Hilfrich-Kunjappu, Carola, 35336
Hilsenrath, Edgar, 35116, 35882
Himmel, Barbara, 34768
Himmelsbach, Christiane, 35580
Hinz, Manfred, 35531
Hinze, Sibylle, 34742
Hippel, Theodor Gottlieb von, 35860
Hirsch, Heinz, 34819
Hirsch, Helmut, 35581
Hirsch, Herbert, 35060
Hirsch, Samson Raphael, 35320, 35321
Hirsch, Samuel, 35330
Hirsch, Waltraud, 35368
Hirschfeld, Gerhard, 34951
Hirschfeld, Magnus, 35429
Hirschfelder, Ulrike, 35343
Hirschman, Albert O., 35582
Historians, 35044, 35444, 35592, 35593, 35663
Historians' Debate, 35068, 35087, 35767
'Historical Journal of Film, Radio and Television', 35015
'Historical Journal', 35047
'Historical Social Research', 34727
Historiography, 34697, 34705, 35480
Historiography, Nazi Period, 35021, 35085, 35477
'Historische Mitteilungen', 35266
'Historische Zeitschrift', 34710, 35070
'Historisches Jahrbuch', 35085
'Historisk Tidskrift', 35187, 35813
'History and Memory', 35087
'History of European Ideas', 35420
Hitler, Adolf, 35088
Hochschule für die Wissenschaft des Judentums, 35357, 35745
Hock, Sabine, 35527
Hödl, Klaus, 35827
Höhn, Gerhard, 35550
Höltken, Th., 34757
Höpfner, Hans-Paul, 34985
Höppner, Solvejg, 34854
Hörner, Horst, 35316
Hörschelmann, Claudia, 34911, 34912
Hörtner, Werner, 35590
Höss, Rudolph, 34995, 35020
Hoffmann, Christhard, 34703
Hoffmann, Heike, 35823
Hoffmann, Johannes, 34861

Hoffmann, Peter, 35060
Hoffmeister, Gerhart, 35547
Hofheim A. Ts., 34811
Hofman, Alois, 35826
Hofmann, Andreas, 35276
Hofmann, Elias, 34942
Hofmann, Fritz, 34758
Hofmann, Michael, 35286
Hofmannsthal, Hugo von, 35583, 35586
Hofmeester, Karin, 35370
Hohenems, 34889, 35390
Hohmann, Joachim S., 34865
Hollender, Martin, 35551, 35581
Hollywood, 35667
Holocaust (see also Final Solution), 34950, 34956, 34982, 35012, 35036, 35089, 35091, 35092, 35128, 35157, 35167
Holocaust, Art, 35041
Holocaust, Cult of, 35778
Holocaust, Denial, 35112
Holocaust, Fiction, 35896
Holocaust, in Film, 35093, 35186
Holocaust, Historiography, 34936, 35063, 35086, 35095, 35167, 35477
Holocaust, Knowledge, 34964,
Holocaust, in Literature, 35090, 35158, 35219, 35777, 35782
35011, 35181, 35203, 35229
Holocaust, Teaching, 34936, 34984, 35280, 35286, 35295, 35299, 35300, 35305
Holocaust, Trauma, 35423
Holt, Linda, 35170, 35258
Holub, Robert C., 35547, 35551
Holz, Klaus, 35828
Holzinger, Hans, 35429
Homolka, Walter, 35324, 35768
Honigmann, Peter, 34946, 35276
Honnef, Klaus, 35434
Hoos, H.-H., 34872
Hopp, Andrea, 34771
Horb, 34847
Horch, Hans Otto, 34938, 35370, 35417, 35424, 35679, 35820, 35880
Horkheimer, Max, 35429, 35456, 35584
Horn, 34801
Horn, Gerd-Rainer, 35008
Horn, Gisela, 35668
Horn-Bad Meinberg, 34801
Hoss, Christiane, 34924
Houstian, Christina, 35667
Hrdlicka, Alfred, 35618
Hsia, Ronnie Po-Chia, 35804
Huber, Annegret, 35454
Hubmann, Gerald, 35826
Hüttenmeister, Frowald Gil, 34703
Hüttenmeister, Gil, 34847
Hufnagel, Cordula, 35869
Hug, Peter, 35195
Huhle, Rainer, 35147

Hull, Gordon, 35634
Humboldt, Wilhelm von, 35861
Hundt, Irina, 35696
Hungary, 35214, 35345, 35370
Hungary, Nazi Period, 35073, 35094–35098
Hungary, Post War, 34910, 35243
Hunsrück, 34802
'Hunsrücker Heimatblätter', 34802
Husserl, Edmund, 35323, 35429
Husson, Édouard, 35057
Huszai, Villoe Dorothea, 35854
Hyman, Paula E., 34703
Hysky-Dambmann, Henny, 34858
Hüppauf, Bernd, 35093

Ich Narr des Glücks, 35551
Ichenhausen, 34714, 34803
Identity, Jewish, 34692, 34896, 35359, 35360, 35361, 35365, 35366, 35372, 35374, 35488, 35583, 35831
Iggers, Wilma A., 34898
Ilbesheim, 34807
Ilisch, Peter, 34875
Illichmann, Jutta, 35259
'Illustrierte Neue Welt', 34896, 35526
Im Herzen der Finsternis, 35597; 35001
Im Schatten des Holocaust, 35264
Immermann, Carl, 35555
Immigration see Germany, Immigration
Imperial Germany, 34679, 34692, 34693, 34698, 34738, 35486, 35532
In Honorem: Albert H. Friedlander, 35324
Inama, Johannes, 34889
Inden, 35102
Industrialists, 34746, 34761, 34971
'Informationen. Studienkreis Deutscher Widerstand', 35236
Ingrisch, Doris, 35435
Inowlocki, Lena, 35276
'Int. Archiv. für Sozialgeschichte der Deutschen Literatur', 35691, 35764
'Int. Wiss. Korr. zur Gesch. der Arbeiterbewegung (IWK)', 35233, 35425, 35581
Integration (see also Assimilation, Acculturation), 34677
Internationales Alfred-Döblin-Kolloquium, 35510
'Internationales Jahrbuch der Bettina-von-Arnim-Gesellschaft', 35852
Internment Camps, 34918
Ishida, Motohiro, 34712
Isler, Alan, 35883
Israel, 34784, 35276, 35405, 35422, 35623, 35731, 35757, 35785, 35786–35789, 35794, 35795
'Israelitisches Wochenblatt', 34915, 35793
'Issues', 35426, 35666
Issum, 34804
Italy, 35804, 35807
Italy, Nazi Period, 35100

Jackson, Timothy R., 34716
Jacob, Benno, 35331
Jacob, Walter, 35768
Jacob, Werner, 35151
Jacobi, Hansres, 35649
Jacobs, Jack, 34692
Jacobsohn, Edith, 35585
Jäckel, Eberhard, 34997, 35060
Jäckel, Günter, 35723
Jäger, Achim, 35424
Jäger, Herbert, 35058, 35070
Jäger, Lorenz, 35504, 35605, 35731
Jaffé, Philipp, 35444
Jaffé, Robert, 35826
Jahn, Jürgen, 35495
Jahn, Manfred, 34854
Jahoda, Marie, 35719
'Jahrbuch Berliner Museen', 35622
'Jahrbuch der Deutschen Schillergesellschaft', 35699, 35834
'Jahrbuch der Grillparzer-Gesellschaft', 35772
'Jahrbuch des Bergheimer Geschichtsvereins', 34731, 34732
'Jahrbuch des Hist. Vereins Dillingen', 34750
'Jahrbuch des Kreises Düren', 34762
'Jahrbuch Extremismus & Demokratie', 35070
'Jahrbuch für Antisemitismusforschung', 34947; 35145, 35788, 35822, 35824, 35838, 35841
'Jahrbuch für den Kreis Limburg-Weilburg', 34872
'Jahrbuch Hochtaunuskreis', 34857
'Jahrbuch Westfalen', 35287
'Jahrbuch zur Geschichte und Wirkung des Holocaust', 35276; 35283, 35470
'Jahrbuch, Hist. Verein für Nördlingen', 34830
Jakobs, Hildegard, 34763
James, Kathleen, 35639
Jancke, G., 35535
Jankowski, Stanislaw M., 35229
Janowski, Bernd, 35331
Janssen, Karl-Heinz, 35229
Jaraczewsky, Adolph, 34765
Jarecki, Hilde, 35711
Jarka, Horst, 35492, 35682
Jaroschka, Walter (*Festschrift*), 34729
Jaskot, Paul B., 35101
Jasper, Willi, 35789
Jaspers, Karl, 35456
Jawlensky, Alexej von, 35667
Jawlensky, Angelica, 35667
Jeggle, Utz, 34703
Jehle, Manfred, 34942
Jeismann, Michael, 35020
Jelinek, Yeshayahu A., 35787
Jensch, Hugo, 34840
Jerke, Birgit, 34742
Jersch-Wenzel, Stefi, 34680, 34683, 34703
Jeschonnek, Bernd, 35053
Jestrabak, Heiner, 35688

Index to Bibliography

'Jewish Book Annual', 35357
'Jewish Book World', 35037, 35203
'Jewish Chronicle', 34945, 35033, 35037
'Jewish Frontier', 35012, 35237, 35273, 35617, 35272, 35273
'Jewish History', 35083, 35105, 35129, 35244, 35408, 35423, 35830,
Jewish Problem (see also Identity, Jewish), 35369, 35371, 35418, 35761
'(The) Jewish Quarterly Review', 35337
'(The) Jewish Quarterly', 34906, 35034, 35293, 35473, 35831
Jewish Question (see also Antisemitism), 35377, 35861
'Jewish Social Studies', 35298, 35876
Jewish Studies, Post-War Germany, 34944
Jews, in Medicine, 34926
Jeziorkowski, Klaus (*Festschrift*), 35862
Jiddistik-Mitteilungen', 34713
Job, Françoise, 34878
John, Heide, 35369
John, Michael, 34966
Johnson, Eric A., 35070
Jonas, Hans, 35332, 35406, 35429
Jonas, Regina, 35429
Jonca, Karol, 34988, 35182
Jones, Peter Ward, 35734
Jong, Rudolf De, 35605
Jordan, Ulrike, 35274
Joseph, Albrecht, 35884
Jospe, Raphael, 35323
'(The) Journal of the American Medical Association (JAMA)', 34973
'Journal of Contemporary History', 35421
'Journal of European Studies', 35777
'(The) Journal of Holocaust Education', 34984, 34989, 35205, 35295, 35299, 35300, 35305
Journalists, 35459, 35595, 35739
Judah, Walter Jonas, 34926
Judaism, Jewish History, in Teaching, 35290, 35303
Juden der Frankfurter Universität, 35446
Judt, Tony, 35045
('Das) Jüdische Echo', 35367, 35825
'Jüdischer Almanach', 34941; 35222, 35253, 35338, 35402, 35404, 35405, 35424, 35481, 35507, 35549, 35593
Jüdischer Frauenbund, 34773, 35430
Jüdischer Nietzscheanismus, 35869
Jüdisches Leben auf dem Lande, 34703
Jüdisches Leben in der Fränkischen Schweiz, 34769
Jülich, 35102, 35103
Jürgens, Arnold, 34979
Jürgens, Franz J., 35261
Jürgensen, Almuth, 35331
Jung, Andreas, 35485
Jung, Ulla, 34742
Jungbluth, Uli, 34839, 34860

Jungk, Robert, 35429
Justis, Diana Lynn, 35552

Kadelbach, Stefan, 35045
Kaden, Lalla, 35720
Kälter, Wolli, 35721
Kafka Family, 34908
Kafka, Franz, 34908, 35334, 35362, 35370, 35466, 35536, 35586–35588
Kahmen, Volker, 35602
Kahn, Robert Ludwig, 35589
Kaienburg, Hermann, 35134, 35269
Kaiser, Georg, 35605
Kaiser, Gert, 35397
Kaiser, Konstantin, 35742
Kaiser-Löffler, Hanneli, 35822
Kalchhauser, Martin, 34890
Kalisch, Judith, 34936
Kalmar, Fritz, 35590
Kalmbach, Peter, 35429
Kalter, Joachim, 35116
Kammler, Clemens, 35286
Kampe, Norbert, 35623
Kandinsky, Wassilly, 35667
Kanner, Mia Amalia, 35104
Kanovitch, Bernard, 35144
Kanter, Shauna, 35293
Kantorowicz, Ernst H., 35591, 35592
Kaplan, Laurence, 35337
Kaplan, Marion A., 34693, 35105, 35774
Karlsruhe, 34679
Kárná, Margita, 35208
Kárny, Miroslav, 34996, 35208
Karski, Jan, 35229
Kasischke-Wurm, Daniela, 35829
Kasper-Holtkotte, Cilli, 35384
Kassel, 34805
Kater, Michael H., 35106
Kattowitz, 34922
Katz, Jakob (Jacob), 35593
Katz, Pierre, 34878
Katz, Steven T., 35323
Kauffeldt, Rolf, 35605, 35606
Kaufman, Jonathan, 35262
Kaufmann, Andrea, 34848
Kaufmann, Uri R., 34703, 34707, 34726, 34797, 34836, 34884
Kawohl, Birgit, 35671
Kedar, Benjamin Ze'ev, 35593
Keilson, Hans, 35006, 35370
Keleman, Paul, 35416
Keller, Helga, 35107
Keller, Manfred, 34747
Kellermann, Henry J., 35140
Kelsen, Hans, 35429, 35873
Kemlein, Sophia, 34841
Kemp, Friedhelm, 35616
Kempner, Robert M.W., 35429
Kerr, Alfred, 35594

Kershaw, Ian, 35156
Kervégan, François, 35534
Kessler, Judith, 35247
Kestrich, 34806
Keuck, Thekla, 34804
Kibbutz Afikim, 35399
Kibbutz Buchenwald, 35245, 35399
Kiehnel, Holger, 35446, 35826
Kierkegaard, Soren, 35869
Kieval, Hillel J., 35333, 35830
Kimber, Robert and Rita, 35447
Kimmelman, Mira Ryczke, 35722
Kind, Frank, 35826
Kindertransport, 35114, 35183, 35230
King, Ian, 35694
Kippenheim, 34835
Kirchheimbolanden, 34807
Kirchheimer, Gloria Devidas, 34929
Kirchheimer, Manfred, 34929
Kirchhöfer, Birgit, 34742
Kirchhoff, Hans, 34994
Kirchschönbach, 34808
'Kiryat Sefer', 34952
Kisch, Egon Erwin, 35595
Kisker, K.P., 35271
Klamper, Elisabeth, 34968
Klanska, Maria, 35826
Klappert, Bertold, 35309, 35324
Klausmann, Christina, 34773
Klee, Ernst, 34965
Klee, Paul, 35667
Kleeberger, Peter, 35429
Kleger, Heinz, 35476
Klein, Anne, 35232
Klein, Dennis, 35188
Klein, Hans-Günter, 35454
Klein, Melanie, 35429
Klein, Wallace G., 35692
Klein-Rusteberg, Karl-Heinz, 35483
Kleinbongartz, Sigrid, 34763
Kleine, Anke, 34713
Klemp, Stefan, 35039
Klemperer, Victor, 35158, 35596–35598, 35723
Klerks, Annette, 34763
Klessmann, Eckart, 35732
Klezmer Music, 35765
Klier, Freya, 35431
Kliersfeld, Josef, 34747
Klittsee, 34885
Kloke, Martin, 35070, 35788, 35791
Kloocke, Kurt, 35547
Klüger, Ruth, 35158, 35553, 35887
Knigge, Volkhard, 35041
Knippschild, Dieter, 34758
Knoch-Mund, Gaby, 35769
Knörlein, Georg, 34769
Kobersdorf, 34885
Koblenz, 35384
Koch, Edita, 35431

Koch, Gertrud, 35087, 35429
Koch, Martin, 35091
Koch, Peter Ferdinand, 35196
Köhler, Gustav Ernst, 34796
Kölle, Lydia, 35358
'Kölner Zeitschrift für Soziologie und Sozialpsychologie', 35285
König, Helmut, 35839
König, Werner, 34714
Königseder, Angelika, 35276
Körber, Lili, 35885
Körner, Klaus, 35274
Körte, Mona, 35090
Körtels, Willi, 34832
Kössler, Gottfried, 35286
Köstler, Arthur, 35404
Kohl, Christiane, 35138
Kohlmannslehner, Dieter, 34797
Kohn, Jerome, 35483
Kohn, Werner, 34873
Kohring, Heinrich, 34859
Kohring, Rolf, 34774
Kolbet, Christiane, 34720
Koldehoff, Stefan, 35612
Kolks, Zeno, 34730
Koller, Guido, 34915
Kolling, Hubert, 35391
Kolmar, Gertrud, 34695, 35431, 35599
Kompert, Leopold, 35365
Konieczny, Alfred, 34988
Konopka, Gisela, 35429, 35724
Koopmann, Helmut, 35551
Kopf, Hedda Rosner, 35289
Kopp-Oberstebrink, Herbert, 35869
Koren, Chaja, 34695
Korn, Salomon, 35294
Korngold, Erich Wolfgang, 35600
Kornreich Gelissen, Rena, 35108
Korte, Hermann, 35523
Kortüm, Hans-Henning, 34694
'Kosmas', 35206
Kost, Gerhard, 34846
Kotzin, C.R., 35295
Kovaly, Heda M., 35725
Kracauer, Siegfried, 35429, 35459, 35601, 35726
Krafft, Fritz, 35432
Kraft, Werner, 35602, 35616, 35727
Kramer, Edith, 35603
Kramer, Edith (née Liebeck), 35109
Kraus, Elisabeth, 35643, 35644
Kraus, Karl, 35467
Kraus, Wolfgang, 35587
Kraushaar, Wolfgang, 35001
Krauss, Marita, 35274, 35431, 35445, 35770
Krefeld, 35384
Kreft, Gerald, 34774
Kreimeier, Klaus, 35447
'Kreis Bernkastel-Wittlich, Jahrbuch', 35330
Kreis, Georg, 35189

Krell, Robert M., 35128
Kresing-Wulf, Felix, 34951
Kreuter, Maria-Luise, 34949
Kreutzer, Leo, 35554
Kreutzer, Michael, 34742
Kreuzau, 34809
Kreuzberg see Berlin-Kreuzberg, 35237
(Bad) Kreuznach, 34810
Krisenwahrnehmungen im Fin de Siècle, 34914; 35354, 35646, 35867
Kristallnacht see November Pogrom
Kristan, Markus, 35632
Krochmalnik, Daniel, 34696, 35350, 35684, 35869
Kröger, Marianne, 35430
Kröhnke, Karl, 35826
Krohn, Claus-Dieter, 35232, 35274, 35432, 35628
Kroll, Frank-Lothar, 35676
Kronach, 34768
Kronauer, Ulrich, 35338
'Kronika Miasta Poznania', 34842
Kropat, Wolf-Arno, 35137
Kruse, Joseph A., 35547, 35551, 35555
Krusenotto, Wolfram, 35110
Krymalowski, Jeanette, 34695
Krzywinski, Ulrike, 34720
Kucher, Primus-Heinz, 35730
Künast, Hans-Jörg, 34724
Küntzel, Matthias, 35059
Kugler, Eve Rosenzweig, 35104
Kuh, Emil, 35604
Kuhlmann, Anne, 35431
Kuhls, Heike, 35296
Kuhn, Christoph, 35231
Kukatzki, Bernhard, 34807, 34837, 34838
Kulka, Otto Dov, 34997
Kunert, Günter, 35728
Kunreuth, 34769
Kurthen, Hermann, 35837
'Kurtrierisches Jahrbuch', 34870
Kury, Patrik, 35415
Kuschel, Andrea, 35263
Kushner, Tony, 34977
Kußmaul, Sibylle, 34831
Kuzmics, Helmut, 35660

Lacapra, Dominick, 35087
Ladwig-Winters, Simone, 35448, 35449
Lämke, Ortwin, 35556
Lagarde, Paul De, 35846
Lambert, Heribert, 35636
Lamberti, Marjorie, 35111, 35373
Lampe, Evelyn, 35371
Landauer, Carl, 35591
Landauer, Gustav, 35334, 35376, 35462, 3560–35607, 35826, 35869
Landauer, Karl, 35605
Landendörfer, Peter, 34769

Landesmann, Peter, 34893
(*Die*) *Landjudenschaften in Deutschland*, 34680
Landolt, Oliver, 35800
Landsberg am Lech, 35276
Landshoff, Fritz H., 35007
Landshut, Siegfried, 35608
Lang, Fritz, 35609
Lange, Thomas, 34797
Langenhain, 34811
Langer, Howard J., 35092
Langevin, Paul, 35516
Langewiesche, Dieter, 35212
Langgässer, Elisabeth, 35774
Langstadt, 34812
Lapide, Pinchas, 35557, 35768
Laqueur, Walter, 35112
Large, David Clay, 34828
Laska, Bernd A., 35429
Lasker-Schüler, Else, 35370, 35426, 35610–35616
Lasker-Schüler, Else, *Werke und Briefe, Kritische Ausgabe*, 35612
Lasker-Wallfisch, Anita, 35113
Lassalle, Ferdinand, 35617
Latin America, Refugees, 35590
Lauenförde, 34814
Laugwitz, Burkhard, 34930
Lausch, Hans, 34918, 35339
Lauterbach, 34780
Lazarus, Emma, 35551
Le Rider, Jacques, 35372
LeBor, Adam, 35197
Lederer, Emil, 35429
Lefort, Claude, 35476
Legal History (see also Emancipation), 34678, 34680, 34685, 34686, 34733
Legal Professions, Jews in, 34786, 35079, 35080, 35274, 35405
Lehmann, Hans Georg, 35274
Lehmann-Brune, Marlies, 35392
Lehnert, Herbert, 35062
Leib, Ladislaus, 35831
Leib, Moses, 35397
Leicht, Lisbeth Fischer, 35114
Leichter, Käthe, 35429
Leigh, Michael, 35335
Leinfellner, Elisabeth, 35637
Leipzig, 34813, 34854, 35104, 35115, 35116, 35661
Leist, Klaus, 35205
Lekebusch, Sigrid, 34763
Lensing, Leo A., 35467
Leo Baeck Institute, 34942, 35548
Leo Baeck Institute Lecture Series, 35782
Leo Baeck Institute, 'LBI Information. Nachrichten aus den Leo Baeck Instituten', 34942
Leo Baeck Institute, New York, 34940, 35390
Leo Baeck Institute, Occasional Papers, 35011

Leo Baeck Institute, Schriftenreihe, 34997
Leo Baeck Institute, 'Year Book', 34943; 34766, 34803, 34925, 34955, 35080, 35115, 35140, 35251, 35267, 35373, 35379, 35380, 35385, 35400, 35644, 35739
Leo, Gerhard, 35117
Lerchenmüller, Joachim, 35432
Lermen, Birgit, 35511
Lerner, Gerda, 35429
Lerner, Robert E., 35591
'Lessing Year Book', 35860
Lessing, Theodor, 35432, 35450, 35618, 35850
Lettow (Leo), Fritz, 35117
Leubauer, Ildiko, 34853
Levesque, Paul, 35865
Levi, Trude, 35118
Levin, Meyer, 35033
Levin, Rahel, see Varnhagen, Rahel
Levinas, Emmanuel, 35323, 35684, 35869
Levine, Glenn S., 35385
Levine, Paul A., 35187
Levinson, Nathan Peter, 34833, 3531, 35317
Levison, Wilhelm, 35444
Levy Picard, Yvonne, 34884
Levy, Oscar, 35869
Lewald, Fanny, 34695, 35619
Lewin, Kurt, 35432
Lewin, Miriam, 35432
Lewis, Hanna Ballin, 35619
Lewissohn, Cäcilie, 34980
Lewy, Fritz, 35620
Lexikon deutsch-jüdischer Autoren, 34953
Ley, Michael, 35017, 35119
Liber Amicorum Necnon et Amicarum für Alfred Heit, 34697; 34827, 34954
Liberalism (Rel.), 34684
Libeskind, Daniel, 34741
Libraries and Archives, 34726, 34743, 34937, 34958
Licharz, Werner, 35309
Lichtblau, Albert, 34692
Lichtblau, Klaus, 35680
Lichtenberg, Georg Christoph, 35862
Lichtigfeld, Isaac Emil, 35251
Liebermann Family, 35623
Liebermann, Max, 35621, 35622, 35623
Liebsch, Heike, 35001
Liedtke, Christian, 35558
Liepach, Martin, 34692, 34727, 34798, 35290
Liessmann, Konrad Paul, 35432
Lind, Jakov (Jacov), 34896, 35730
Linde, Hans, 35174
Lindemann, Albert S., 35832
Linder, Bert, 35120
Linder, Jutte, 35855
Lindner, Erik, 34698, 35626
Linhartová, Lenka, 35208
Linne, Karsten, 35077, 35079
Linnich, 35102

Linz, 34966
Lippe, 34801
Lippmann, Heinz, 35624
Lippoldsberg, 34814
Lissner, Cordula, 35277
'Literatur und Kritik', 35372
Literature, Jews depicted in, 34703, 35370, 35379, 35583, 35772, 35775, 35781, 35834, 35842, 35853, 35855
Literature, Jews in, 35366, 35458
'Literaturwissenschaftliches Jahrbuch', 35656
Littell, Franklin H., 35060
Littmann-Hotopp, Ingrid, 34735
Locke, Hubert C., 35060
Lodz (Ghetto), 35121
Loeb, James, 35625
Loeb, Kurt, 35433, 35436
Loeb, Ladislau, 35645
Löber, Petra, 34924
Löbl, Suzanna, 35122
Löffler, Hans F., 35655
Löhnert, Peter, 34756
Löwenbrück, Anna-Ruth, 34867
Löwenfeld, Heinrich, 35431
Löwenfeld, Raphael, 35431
Löwenstein, Otto, 35626
Löwental, Leo, 35406
Löwith, Karl, 35627
Löwy, Ernst, 35417
Löwy, Hanno, 35121, 35286
Löwy, Michael, 35334, 35605
Löwy, Ronny, 35276
Lohrbächer, Albrecht, 35303
Lohrmann, Klaus, 34939
Lokers, Jan, 35043
Lombardus, Marcus, 35769
London, 35370
Lonitz, Henri, 35703, 35706
Loose, Hans-Dieter (*Festschrift*), 34786, 35076, 35078
Lorber, Jakob, 35443
Lorenz, Dagmar C.G., 35451, 35772
Lorenz, Einhart, 35431
Lorenz, Ina S., 35076
Loring, Marianne (née Stampfer), 35028
Lorraine, 34878, 34884
Loshitzky, Yosefa, 35186
Lotter, Friedrich, 34767
Lowe, Adolph, 35429, 35432, 35628, 35648
Lowenfeld, Henry, 35629
Lowenstein, Steven M., 34683, 34703, 34929
Lowenthal-Hensel, Cécile, 35454
Lower Saxony, 34814, 34815, 35264
Lubell, Stephen, 35436
Lublinski, Samuel, 35826
Luckenwalde, 34816
Ludz, Ursula, 35478, 35483
Lübbe, Hermann, 35045
Lück, Helmut E., 35432

Index to Bibliography 487

Lüer, Edwin, 35452
Lüneburg, 34817
Lüth, Erich, 34789
Lukacs, John, 35088
Luther, Martin, 35863, 35864
'Lutherische Monatshefte', 35235
Lutz, Carl, 35098
Lutz, Edith, 35551, 35559
Lutz, Hannelore, 34764
Lutz, Karl, 35197
Lux, Rüdiger, 35658
Luxemburg, Rosa, 35442, 35630

'Maajan', 34883, 35386
Maarsen, Jaqueline, 35032
Mack, Michael, 35686
'Maclean's', 35284
Madagascar, 35816
'(Der) Märker', 34875
Magnus, Shulamit S., 34754
Magonet, Dorothea, 35768
Mahler, Gustav, 35466, 35631
'(Die) Mahnung', 35117, 35231
Maier, Joseph, 34876
Maier-Leibnitz, Heinz, 35432
Maierhof, Gudrun, 35430
'Mainfränkisches Jahrbuch für Geschichte und Kunst', 34812
Mainz, 35384
Makowski, Krzysztof, 34842, 34887
Mallmann, Klaus Michael, 35018, 35232
Manau, 34767
Manes, Philipp, 35205
Mankowitz, Ze'ev, 35323
Mann, Thomas, 35431, 35452, 35536, 35865, 35866
Mannheim, 34818
Mannheim, Karl, 35429, 35593
'Mannheimer Geschichtsblätter', 34818
Mannheimer, Max, 35123
Mappot, 35387
'Marbacher Magazin', 35007, 35602
Marcus, Ahron, 35415
Marcus, Marcel, 35325, 35415
Marcuse, Herbert, 35429
Mardi, Michael, 35473
Marek, Michaela, 34905
'Marginalien', 34743, 34932, 35577, 35585, 35614
Marienthal, Hal, 35886
Marino, Andy, 35124
Marks, Elias, 34684
Marmorek, Oskar, 35632
Marnheim, 34807
Marrus, Michael R., 35141
Marshall, Liselotte, 35887
Martens, Lorna, 35453
Marti, Urs, 35476
Martin, Angela, 34980

Martin, Ariane, 35866
Marx, Karl, 35371, 35418, 35633–35636
Marx, Reinhard, 34779
Marxism, 35418
Massey, Irving, 35872
Massie, Allan, 35777
Masters, Peter, 35125
Mathis, Wolfgang, 35501
Matt, Beatrice von, 35878
Mattenklott, Gert, 34736, 35605
Mattersburg, 34885
Mattioli, Aram, 34914
Matuschka, Michael E., 34720
Matzigkeit, Michael, 35605, 35606
Maurer, Trude, 34707, 34942
Mauthausen, 34966, 35126, 35127
Mauthner, Fritz, 35637
Mautner, Hella, 34933
Mautner, Willy, 34933
Maybaum, Ignaz, 35335
Mayer, Charles S., 35045
Mayer, Hans, 35731
Mayer, Shlomo, 35331
Mayrhofern, Fritz, 34966
'MB – Mitteilungsblatt des Irgun, Olei Merkas Europa', 35397
McCulloh, John M., 35833
McElvoy, Anne, 35753
McGilligan, Patrick, 35609
McGuiness, Brian, 35751
Mecklenburg, 34819
Mecklenburg, Frank, 35115
Mecklenburg-Vorpommern, 34721, 34755
Medek, Tilo, 35487
Medicine, Jews in, 34731, 35003, 35383, 35398, 35525, 35735
'Medien und Zeit', 35013
Meek, Harold A., 35393
Mehler, Sharon, 35250
Mehringer, Hartmut, 35274
Meinerzhagen, 34820
Meinetwegen ist die Welt erschaffen, 35429
'Meinhardus', 34820
Meitner, Lise, 35432, 35638
Melnick, Ralph, 35033
Memorials, 34839, 34851, 34888, 34889, 35040, 35134, 35279, 35283, 35284, 35294, 35296, 35307, 35308, 35778
Menczer, Aron, 34968
Mendelsohn, Erich, 35639, 35640
Mendelssohn Bartholdy, Carl, 35733
Mendelssohn Bartholdy, Paul, 35733
Mendelssohn Bartholdy Family, 35254, 35454,
Mendelssohn Studien, 35454
Mendelssohn, Cécile, 35734
Mendelssohn, Dorothea see Schlegel, Dorothea
Mendelssohn, Felix, 35454, 35641, 35642, 35732–35734

Mendelssohn, Moses, 34734, 35320, 35321, 35323, 35336–35340, 35350, 35377, 35536
Mendes, Aristides de Sousa, 35161
Mendes-Flohr, Paul, 34683, 35341, 35354, 35429
Mengele, Josef, 34965
Mennell, Stephen, 35524
Mentgen, Gerd, 34697, 34884
Mertens, Lothar, 34704, 35265, 35538, 35791
Merz-Benz, Peter-Ulrich, 35523
Merzhausen, 34821
Meschede, 34822
Meschel, Susan V., 34910
Messerschmidt, Manfred, 34682
Messianism, 34904
Mexico, Nazi Period, 35006
Mey, Eberhard, 34805
Meyer zu Uptrup, Wolfram, 35844
Meyer, Hans-Georg, 35894
Meyer, Michael A., 34683, 34942
Meyer, Selma, 35455
Meysels, Lucian O., 35465
Michaelis, Herbert, 35079, 35080
Michalak, Tim, 34758
Michelsohn, Georg (pseud. Eli Elkana), 35525
Michielin, Nina, 34847
Middle Ages, 34687, 34688, 34694, 34703, 34708, 34716, 34827, 34884, 34891, 35798, 35799, 35804, 35835, 35842, 35895
'Middle Eastern Studies', 35399
'Midstream', 34972, 35094, 35215, 35226, 35348, 35413, 35427, 35498, 35563, 35579, 35588, 35633, 35762, 35856
'(The) Midwest Quarterly', 35246
Mieck, Ilja (*Festschrift*), 34783
Miehlen, 34839
Mierendorff, Marta, 34980
Miesbeck, Peter, 35166
Milford, Karl, 35429
Miller, Arthur, 35831
Miller, Paul B., 35188
Miltenberg, 34823
Milton, Sybil, 35129
Mink, Andreas, 34793
Mirgel, Christiane, 35151
Mises, Ludwig von, 35429
Misrachi, 34909
'Mit der Ziehharmonika', 34912, 35161, 35484, 35487, 35537, 35553, 35590, 35686, 35730, 35742
'Mitt. der Hist. Vereinigung Wesel', 34874
Mittag, Susanne, 34737
'Mitteilungen des Oberhess. Geschichtsvereins Gießen', 34806
'Mitteilungen des Vereins für Gesch. der Stadt Nürnberg', 34831
'Mitteilungen HAR', 34788
'Mitteldeutsches Jahrbuch', 34737
Mittelmann, Hanni, 35370

'Mittelweg 36', 35058, 35070, 35086, 35158, 35199, 35258, 35471, 35472, 35792, 35850, 35873
Mittenzwei, Ingrid, 34894
Mittermaier, Carl Josef Anton, 35314
Mittlerweilersbach, 34769
Mixed Marriages, 34980, 35084, 35885
Mixed Marriages, Children of, 35004, 35177, 35728, 35891
'Modern Austrian Literature', 35359, 35468, 35530, 35586, 35659, 35692
'Modern Judaism', 35333, 35868
Moers, 34824
Mörs, Jürgen, 34844
Mohnhaupt, Heinz, 35534
Mojem, Helmuth, 35834
Mommsen, Hans, 35060, 35087, 35757
Mommsen, Wolfgang J., 35779
Moneta, Jakob, 35757
Money Lending, 34869, 34875, 35799
Monschau, 34825
'(Das) Monschauer Land. Jahrbuch', 34825
Montel, Angelika, 34896
Monz, Heinz, 34839, 34870, 35635
Moore, Bob, 35131
Moravia, 34901, 34906, 35123
Morawe, Bodo, 35560
Morgan, Michael L., 35167
'MorgenGlantz', 35760
Morgenstern, Matthias, 35351
Morgenstern, Soma, 35888
Morris, Nomi, 35284
Morsch, Günter, 35301
Moses, Erwin, 35735
Moses, Julius, 35735
Mosès, Stéphane, 35336, 35432
Mosse Family, 35643, 35644
Mosse, George L., 35006
Mosse, Marcus, 35644
Mosse, Werner E., 35370
Mühlen, 34826
Mühlmann, Eva-Maria, 34951
Mühlmann, Wilhelm E., 35845
Mühlpfordt, Günter (*Festschrift*), 34894
Müller, Albert, 34969
Müller, Andreas Uwe, 35684
Müller, Christiane, 35864
Müller, Christiane E., 34742
Müller, Christoph, 35429
Müller, Hanno, 34864
Müller, Hans-Harald, 35691
Müller, Ingo, 35429
Müller, Kurt, 34913
Müller, Maria, 35667
Müller, Reinhard, 35431
Müller, Thomas, 34954, 35431, 35629, 35842
Müller-Hill, Benno, 35144
Müller-Seidel, Walter, 35672
Münch, Peter L., 35266

Index to Bibliography

Münster, 34684
Münstermaifeld, 34827
Münz, Christoph, 35801
Muller, Jerry Z., 35687
Munich, 34828, 35521, 35625
Murakami, Junichi, 35045
Murnau, 35625
Muschg, Adolf, 35190
Museums, 35298, 35302
Music, Jewish, 35395, 35765
Musicians, Composers, 34920, 35574, 35600
Myers, Margarete L., 35267
Mysticism, 35852

Na'aman, Shlomo, 35418
Nachama, Andreas, 35353
'Nachrichten für den jüdischen Bürger Fürths', 34777
Nadler, Rajaa, 34769
Nägler, Frank, 34682
Nagata, Hiroaki, 34699
Nagel, Anne Chr., 35406
Names, 34837, 34878
Namyslo, Aleksandra, 34922
Naphtali, Fritz Perez, 35739
Nassau, 34829
'Nassauische Annalen', 34811, 34860, 35070
Nastätten, 34839
Nationalism, 34698, 34699, 34896, 35634
Natzweiler, 35117
Naujoks, Antje C., 35264
Nazi Crimes, 34956, 34965, 34973, 34995, 35042
Nazi Crimes, Prosecution of, 35005, 35142, 35146–35148, 35268–35270
Nazi Gold see Switzerland, Jewish Assets
Nazi Period, in Film, Radio and Theatre, 34951, 35014, 35015
Nazi Period, Jewish Life in Germany, 34710, 34981, 34998, 34999, 35105, 35138, 35152, 35370
Nazi Period, Jurisprudence, 35084
Nazi Period, Teaching, 35282, 35296
Nazi Politics, 35072, 35083, 35816
Ne'eman Arad, Gulie, 35087, 35130
Neander, Joachim, 35000
Necker, Gerold, 35343
Negt, Oskar, 35429
Neiss, Marion, 35006
Nekula, Marek, 35450
Nerlich, Michael, 35597
Nery, Júlia, 35889
Netherlands, Nazi Period, 35031, 35032, 35131–35133
Netherlands, Refugees, 35007, 35433, 35436
Neubach, Helmut, 34861
Neubauer, Adolphe, 34689
'Neue Beiträge zur Jülicher Geschichte', 35103
'Neue Deutsche Literatur' ('NdL'), 35569, 35575

'(Die) Neue Welt', 34896
Neuengamme, 35134
Neuenkirchen, 34852
Neugebauer, Wolfgang, 35663
Neumann, Bernd, 35483
Neumann, Franz L., 35429
Neumann, Michael, 35719
Neumann, Moritz, 34797
Neumarkt, 34729
Neuner, Franz Xaver, 34750
(Neunzehnhundertneunundneunzig) '1999, Zeitschrift für Sozialgesch. des 20. und 21. Jahrhunderts', 35133, 35169
Neunzig, Joseph, 35545
Neusner, Jacob, 35060
'New German Critique', 35093, 35474, 35773, 35774
'(The) New Leader', 35765
'New Left Review', 35070
New York, 34929, 35883
'(The) New York Review', 35033
'(The) New York Times', 35051
New, Mitya, 35198
Newhouse, E. Irene, 35390
Neyer, Maria Amata, 35684
Nickel, Gunther, 35699
Nicolai, Friedrich (orig. Lewinstein), 35432
Nicolaysen, Rainer, 35608
Nicosia, Francis R., 35373, 35419
Nieden, Susanne zur, 35001, 35597
'Niedersächsisches Jahrbuch für Landesgeschichte', 35043
Nief, Rosemary, 35299
Niehoff, Maren R., 35551
Niemöller-von Sell, Sibylle Sarah, 35768
Nietzsche, Friedrich, 35350, 35867–35870, 35876
Niewöhner, Friedrich, 35677, 35869
Niewyk, Donald L., 35373
Nirenberg, David, 35835
Nittenberg, Joanna, 34896
Nitzanshiftan, A., 35640
Nördlingen, 34830
Nolden, Nikolaus, 34809
Nolte, Ernst, 35070
"Non-Aryan" Christians, 34975, 35150
Nordau, Max, 35420, 35645, 35646, 35869
Nordhausen, 35135
Nordheim, Eckhard von, 35763
Nordhorn, 34730
Nordmann, Ingeborg, 35350, 35429, 35476
North-Rhine-Westphalia, 35297
Nosratian, Khosrow, 35429
Novak, David, 35347
November Pogrom, 34972, 35078, 35124, 35136, 35137, 35230
Nowack, Natalie, 35454
Nümbrecht, 34849, 34850
Nuhn, Heinrich, 34799

Nuremberg, 34831, 35138, 35799
Nuremberg Laws, 35119, 35138
Nuremberg Trials, 34982, 35139–35149, 35269, 35779
Nussbaum, Laureen, 35431
Nussbaumer-Benz, Uschi, 35869
'NZZ' ('Neue Zürcher Zeitung'), 34913, 35502, 35504, 35523, 35627, 35645, 35649, 35657, 35878

O'Doherty, Paul, 35775
O'Regan, Cyril, 35858
Obenaus, Herbert, 35264
Oberemmel, 34832
Oberländer, Franklin A., 35150
Obernbreit, 34767
'Oberschlesisches Jahrbuch', 34922
Oberweis, Michael, 34700
'(The) Observer', 35170, 35258
Och, Gunnar, 35852
Odenbach, 34972
Öllers, Norbert, 35370, 35612
Örtel, Wilfried, 34822
Östreich, Cornelia, 34843
Öxle, Otto Gerhard, 35591, 35776
Ofer, Dalia, 35210
Offe, Sabine, 35298
Offenbach, Jacques, 35647
Offenburg, 34833
Offermann, Toni, 34825
Offhaus, Ernst-Uwe, 34806
Ohm, Barbara, 34720
Okolica, Henry, 34865
Okroy, Michael, 34850
Olbrisch, Gabriele, 34867
Oldenburg, 34834
Olivier, Antje, 35574
Olpe, 35151
Olschewski, Boris, 35636
Omland, Sabine, 34759
Ophir, Baruch Zwi, 34788
Oppen, Asta von, 34991
Oppenheimer, Franz, 35429, 35648
Oppenheimer, Joseph Süß (Jud Süß), 35014, 35015, 35427,
Oppenheimer, Olga, 35426
Oppler, Edwin, 34782
'(Das) Orchester', 34930
Orfali, Stephanie Braun, 35736
Organisations, 34679, 34684, 34753, 34792, 35381, 35532
Organisations, Nazi Period, 35430
Organisations, Post War, 35265
Orland, Nahum (Nachum), 35698
Orlik, Emil, 35649, 35650, 35651
Ortenau, 34884
'(Die) Ortenau', 34835, 34882
Orth, Karin, 35020
Ortheil, Hanns-Josef, 35487

Orthodoxy, 34788, 34909, 35329, 35345, 35351, 35370
Ortmeyer, Benjamin, 35152
Osers, Ewald, 35515
Osiander, Andreas, 34769
'Ost und West', 35380
Osten-Sacken, Peter von der, 35802
Ostrowsky, Tal, 35280
Otto, Arnim, 34775
Otto, Eugen, 35649
Otto, Norbert, 35151
'Owl of Minerva', 35858

Paech, Norman, 35269
Painting, Jews depicted in, 35771
Palatinate, 34807, 34836, 34837, 34838
Palestine, 35398, 35417, 35422, 35735
Palestine, Immigration, 34961, 35737
Palestine, Refugees, 35701
Pangritz, Andreas, 35312, 35324
Panofsky, Erwin, 35726
Pappenheim, Bertha, 34695, 34773
Parge, Martina, 35061
Parik, Arno, 34901, 34905
Paris, 35370
'(Das) Parlament', 34999, 35893
Passarge, Siegfried, 35845
Passelecq, Georges, 34992
Patel, Christine, 35299
Patka, Marcus G., 35595
Patschovsky, Alexander, 34687
Paucker, Arnold, 34942, 35236, 35370, 35429
Paucker, Pauline, 35370
Paul, Gerhard, 35075, 35232, 35274
Pause, Barbara, 35010
Pavel, Ingrid von, 34732
Pawel, Ernst, 35561
Peck, Abraham J., 35276
Peck, Jeffrey M., 35062
Perels, Ernst, 35444
Perels, Joachim, 35269
Perutz, Leo, 35452
Perz, Bertrand, 34966
Peschel-Gutzeit, Lore Maria, 35142
Peter, Daniel, 34878
Peter, F., 34719
Peters, Dieter, 34718, 34744, 34810
Petropulos, Jonathan, 35188
Petuchowski, Jakob J., 35803
Pfabigan, Alfred, 35429
Pfaffenberger, Hans, 35429
Philanthropists, 35576, 35625, 35643
Philosemitism, 35757, 35872
'(Die) Philosophin', 35219
'Philosophy & Social Criticism', 35634
Philosophy and Learning, Jews in, 35637, 35752
Philosophy, Jewish, 35332
Photographers, 35434, 35497
'Physics Today', 35494, 35638

Picard, Jacques, 35836
Picard, Leo, 35737
Pick, Erika, 35577
Pick, Hella, 35698
Piel, Ingo, 34763
Pieper, Annemarie, 35429
Pierard, Richard V., 35060
Pierenkämper, Toni, 34761
Pietsch, Walter, 35345
Pinczower, Ephraim, 34743
Pine, Lisa, 35154
Pirna, 34840
Plaut, Elizabeth S., 35388
Plax, Martin J., 35348
Plener, Peter, 35673
Plessner, Elias, 34871
Plessner, Helmuth, 35429
Pörsch, Barbara, 34747
Poetry, 35525, 35880
Pohl, Dieter, 35063
Pohorelice, 34906
Pok, Attila, 35095
Polak, Wolfgang, 34758
Poland, 34704, 34841, 34904, 34941
Poland, Nazi Period, 35025, 35222
Political Sciences, Jews in, 35439
Politics, Jews in, 34692, 35274, 35669, 35681
'Politisches Denken', 35584
Pollack, Ilse, 35161, 35889
Pollak, Oliver B, 35206
Pollak, Richard, 35493
Pollfeyt, Didier, 35060
Pollock, Friedrich, 35429
Poma, Andrea, 35508
Pomerance, Aubrey, 34850
Pommer, Eric (Erich), 35652
Popper, Karl R., 35429, 35653
Popper, Richard, 34909
Porstmann, Gisbert, 35340
Portugal, Nazi Period, 35161, 35889
Posen, 34766, 34841–34843, 34887, 35644
Posen, Felix, 35006
Postel-Vinay, Anis, 35144
Pracht, Elfi, 34770, 34851
Prague, 34907, 34908, 35333, 35428, 35725, 35890
Prégardier, Elisabeth, 35110
Press, 35829
Press, Jewish, 34692, 34998, 35385, 35424, 35461
Pressburg (Bratislava), 34909, 35329
Prestel, Claudia, 34692
Pretzfeld, 34769
Preuss, Hugo, 35429
Preuss, Monika, 34725, 34728
Prieur, Jutta, 34763
Primor, Avi, 35789
Pringle, Annette, 34955
Printers, Hebrew, 34724

Prittie, Terence, 35747
'Proceedings of the American Academy for Jewish Research', 35808
Prosecution of Nazi Crimes see Nazi Crimes, Prosecution of
Proust, Marcel, 35370
Prussia, 34686, 34701, 34703, 35533
Psychoanalysts, Psychologists, 35432, 35578, 35629
Publishers, Printers, 34805, 35007, 35385, 35425, 35461, 35577, 35585, 35626
Pulzer, Peter, 34683, 34702, 34896
Puschner, Uwe, 35823

Quakers, 35164
Quandt, Helen, 34763
Quast, Anke, 35264
Querdenken, 34904

Raab Hansen, Jutta, 34920
Rabbis, 34747, 34788, 34876, 34893, 35251, 35330, 35345, 35688
Rabinbach, Anson, 35087, 35456
Rabinovici, Doron, 34896, 35263
Racism, 35042, 35083, 35813
Raczymow, Henri, 35370
Raddatz, Fritz J., 35487, 35562, 35575, 35718
Ragacs, Ursula, 35805
Rahe, Thomas, 34979
Randall, Marga L., 35173
Rapaport, Lynn, 35255
Raphael, Freddy, 34878, 35871
Rathenau, Walther, 35654–35656
Rau, Johannes, 35553
Rauch, Ralf, 34778
Raulet, Gérard, 35495
Raulff, Ulrich, 35457
Ravensbrück, 35155
Reach, Hilde, 35431
'Rechtshistorisches Journal', 35045, 35776
Recklinghausen, 34844, 34962
Reemtsma, Jan Philipp, 35001, 35158
Rees, Laurence, 35156
Reform Judaism (see also Liberalism (relig.), 34684, 34876, 35330
Refugee Policy, 34913, 34915, 35189, 35191
Refugees, Great Britain, 35125, 35164
Regehly, Thomas, 35605
Regensburg, 34846
Regensteiner, Henry, 35563, 35856
Regent, Carola, 35230
Regent, Karola (Hannele Zürndorfer), 34763
Regisheim, 34883
Rehrmann, Norbert, 35528
Reich, Wilhelm, 35429, 35443, 35657
Reich-Ranicki, Marcel, 35458, 35564
Reichmann, Eva G., 34942, 35429
Reichsbanner Schwarz-Rot-Gold, 34709

Reichsvertretung der Juden in Deutschland, 34997, 35111, 35381
Reilly, Jo, 34977
Reinerová, Lenka, 35006, 35890
Reinhardt, Volker, 35804
Reinharz, Jehuda, 35167
Reinhold, Josef, 34813
Reinhold-Postina, Eva, 34797
Reiss, Erich, 35738
Reiss, Johannes, 34885
Reisz, Matthew, 35034
Reiter, Margit, 35472
Remigration, 34833, 34896, 35231, 35261, 35274, 35277, 35431, 35770
Remscheid, 34850
Renda, Gerhard, 34745
Renz, Werner, 34956
Reschke, Renate, 35869
Reschwamm, Dorothea, 35135
Rescue for Jews, 35159, 35161, 35162, 35165
Resistance, Jewish, 35231–35240, 35373, 35748
Resistance, Non-Jewish, 34991, 35238
Resnais, Alain, 35773
Restitution, 35192, 35254, 35259, 35264, 35271, 35272, 35785
Reuter, Edzard, 35006
Reuter, Fritz, 34839
Reuter, Ulrike, 35551
Reuter, Ursula, 35681
'Reutlinger Geschichtsblätter', 34846
'Revue d'histoire de la Shoah', 35069, 35144
'Revue des Études Juives', 34886
'Revue Germanique Internationale', 35360, 35460, 35759, 35815
Rexingen, 34847
Rey, Manfred van, 35248
'Rhein-Lahnkreis: Heimatjahrbuch', 34757
Rheindahlen, 34848
'Rheindahlen Almanach', 34848
Rheinisch-Westfälische Wirtschaftsbiographien, 34746, 34761
'Rheinische Heimatpflege', 35806
Rheinische Lebensbilder, 35576, 35635
Rhineland, 34680, 34722, 34730, 34761–34763, 34804, 34809, 34824, 34849, 34851, 34877, 35136, 35384
Richarz, Monika, 34683, 34703, 35370
Richebächer, Sabine, 35657
Richmond, Colin, 34977
Richter, Brigitte, 35641
Richter, Erika, 34822
Ridder, Thomas, 35287
Rieber, A., 34857
Riebnig, 34988
Riedesel, Karl-Ernst, 34733
Riehen, 35191
Rieker, Yvonne, 35374, 35597
Riemer, Detlev, 34816
Riemer, Jehuda, 35739

Riemer, Shirley, 34931
Ries, Henry, 35279
Riesser, Gabriel, 34786
Rietberg, 34852
Rietz, Julius, 35733
Rietzschel, Thomas, 35612
Rihm, Wolfgang, 35703
Ring, Jennifer, 35479
Riordan, Colin, 35777
Ritchie, James M., 35437
Rites and Ceremonies, 34681, 34696, 34703, 34797, 34881, 34942, 35361, 35387
Ritter, Gerhard A., 35486
Ritual Bath, 34752, 34807
Roberts, Stephen, 35740
Rochelt, Hans, 35526
Rochlitz, Rainer, 35489
Rodden, John G., 35246
Roder, Bernt, 34742
Röck, Bernd, 35697
Röcke, Werner, 35842
Röll, Walter, 34716
Rölleke, Heinz, 35612
Römer, Nils, 35342
Rößling, Wilfried, 34725
Rohrbacher, Stefan, 34703, 35844
Rohrwasser, Michael, 35375
Rohwer, Jörn, 35600
Rokahr, Gerd, 35288
Romania, Nazi Period, 35210
'Romerike Berge', 34877, 35464, 35615
Roming, Gisela, 34703
Rommelspacher, Birgit, 35840
Ronig, Franz, 35806
Roosevelt, Franklin D., 35011
Roschewski, Heinz, 34915
Rosen, Judith, 35037
Rosen, Philip, 34950
Rosenberg, Erika, 35163
Rosenblüth, Felix, 35406
Rosenfeld, Alvin H., 35167
Rosenfeld, Dalia, 34967
Rosenfeld, Gavriel D., 35087, 35521
Rosenheim, 35166
Rosenthal, David, 35237, 35273
Rosenzweig, Franz, 35320, 35323, 35334, 35350, 35429, 35658, 35774, 35869
Rotenberg, Stella, 35168
Rotenburg an der Fulda, 34799
Roth, Joseph, 35367, 35376, 35659–35662
Roth, Karl Heinz, 35169
Roth, Ursula, 35551
Rothe, Hans-Joachim, 35605
Rother, Bernd, 35185
Rothfels, Hans, 35663
Rothmund, Heinrich, 34913, 34915
Rothschild Family, 35844
Rothschild, Mayer Amschel, 35427, 35664
Rottenbauer, 34767

Index to Bibliography

Rottweil, 35307
Rotwelsch (Thieves' Cant), 34712
Roviello, Anne-Marie, 35476
Rowan, Steven, 35708
Rubinstein, William D., 35170
Ruch, Martin, 34833
Rudder, Anneke de, 35145
Rudel, Josef Norbert, 34903
Rudnick, Ursula, 35665
Rübner, Tuvia, 35370
Rückkehr und Aufbau nach 1945, 35274
Rühle, Günther, 35594, 35701
Rühle-Gerstel, Alice, 35429
Rühs, Christian Friedrich, 35826
Rürup, Reinhard, 34703
Rüsen, Jörn, 35087
Runte-Wried, Bodo, 34960
Rural Jewry, 34680, 34703, 34727, 34749, 34762, 34769, 34797, 34798, 34803, 34811, 34820, 34821, 34826, 34834, 34860, 35844
Rusel, Jane, 35689
Russell, Judith, 35300
Russell, Steven, 35524
Rychlik, Otmar, 35650, 35651

Saarland, 35274
Sabelleck, Rainer, 34703
Sabler, Wolfgang, 35411
Sacher-Masoch, Leopold von, 35872
'Sachor. Beiträge zur jüd. Gesch. und zur Gedenkstättenarbeit', 34839
'Sachor. Ztschr. für Antisemitismusforschung', 34704
Sachs, Nelly, 35253, 35431, 35665
'Sachsen und Anhalt', 35798
Sachsen-Anhalt, 34853
Sachsenhausen, 35117, 35171, 35301
'Sächsische Heimatblätter', 34813
Safrian, Hans, 34967
Saint Sauveur-Henn, Anne, 34917
Salmon, Irit, 35041
Salomon, Charlotte, 34695, 35666
Salomon, Simon (Salter, Siegbert), 34862
Salons, 34734, 34737
Salter, Ronald, 34932
Salter, Siegbert, 34862
Sammons, Jeffrey L., 35547, 35551
Samosc, David, 35382
Sander, Gabriele, 35510
Sanders-Brahms, Helma, 35613
Sandvoß, Hans-Rainer, 35238
Saner, Hans, 35476
Santaniello, Weaver, 35868
Sarraga, Marian & Ramon F., 34789
Sarris, Viktor, 35432
Sarton-Saretzki, Edgar, 35172
Sassenberg, Marina, 35429, 35757
Sassin, Horst R., 34850, 35162
Sattler, Stephan, 35064

Sauerland, Karol, 35483
Sawelson-Gorse, Naomi, 35667
Saxony, 34840
Sayer, Adolf, 34847
Schäfer, Peter, 35343
Schäfer, Sigrid, 34758
Schäffer-Hegel, Barbara, 35429
Schäflich, Hermann, 35378
Schaffhausen, 35796
'Schaffhauser Beiträge zur Geschichte', 35796, 35800
Schaffner, Bertram, 35061
Schampel, Ingrid, 34782
Schapire, Rosa, 35426
Schaser, Angelika, 34783
Schaub, Lucia & Hans, 34720
Scheer, Regina, 34742
Scheffler, Karl, 35622
Schefold, Bertram, 35648
Schefold, Dian, 35429
Scheible, Hartmut, 35674
'Scheidewege', 35332, 35442
Scheit, Gerhard, 35471
Schenk, Hannelore, 34856
Scheps, Samuel, 35415
Schermbeck, 35173
Schettler, Katja, 34850, 35431
Scheyer, Galka (Emmy), 35667
Schicketanz, Till, 34938
Schieder, Theodor, 35755
Schild, Erwin, 34993
Schilde, Kurt, 34743, 35282, 35425
Schilp, Thomas, 34758
Schindel, Robert, 35263, 35359
Schindler, Anja, 35174
Schindler, Emilie, 35163
Schindler, Oskar, 35160, 35163
Schindler, Zdenek, 35208
Schine, Robert, 35313
Schinz, Marina, 35497
Schirrmacher, Frank, 35575
Schlegel, Dorothea, 35668
Schleichert, Hubert, 35637
Schlesinger, Arthur, 35011
Schlesinger, Mina, 34767
Schlesinger, Moritz, 35669
Schleswig-Holstein, 34787
Schlieben-Lange, Brigitte, 35432
Schlitz, 34855
Schlör, Joachim, 34692
Schlosser, Georges, 34884
Schloßmacher, Norbert, 35545
Schlüter, Margarete, 35326, 35327
Schmallenberg, 34856
'Schmallenberger Heimatblätter', 34856
Schmetterling, Astrid, 35666
Schmid Nörr, Gunzelin, 35432
Schmidt, Ernst-Erich, 34682
Schmidt, Michael, 34703, 35763, 35844

Schmidt, Ulf, 35146
Schmidt, Wilhelm, 35845
Schmidt, Willi, 34863
Schmidt, Wolfgang, 34682
Schmidt-Beste, Thomas, 35454
Schmidt-Glintzer, Helwig, 34724
Schmieheim, 34835
Schmierer, Wolfgang, 34958
Schmitt, Carl, 35873
Schmitt, Hans A., 35164
Schmitt, Karl, 34867, 35791
Schmitten, 34857
Schmitz, Walter, 35823
Schnabl, Hedi Argent, 34906
Schnaittach, 34769
Schneeberger, Michael, 34767
Schneider, Hubert, 34747
Schneider, Michael, 35065
Schneider, Peter, 35777, 35792
Schneider, Richard Chaim, 35196, 35778
Schneider, Ursula A., 35526
Schnitzler, Arthur, 35670–35675
Schnurmann, Siegfried, 34833
Schock, Ralph, 35662
Schönberg, Arnold, 35731
Schönbrunn, Gerhard, 34720
Schöne, Lothar, 35891
Schönfeld Family, 34722
Schoeps, Hans Joachim, 35676
Schoeps, Julius H., 34682, 34896, 34942, 34999, 35017, 35254, 35412, 35432, 35733, 35744
Schörken, Rudolf, 35230
Schöttler, Peter, 35591
Scholem, Gershom, 34789, 35334, 35342–35344, 35677, 35851, 35869
Scholz, Christian, 35757
Scholz, Dieter, 35622
Scholz, Dietmar, 34751
Schomacker, Tim, 35263
Schonig, Bruno, 35711
Schools (see also Education), 34684, 34763, 34865, 34876, 35711
Schopf, Wolfgang, 35438
Schoppmann, Claudia, 34980
Schorsch, Ismar, 34942
Schotten, 34858
Schrader, Hans-Jürgen, 35547
Schrader, Ulrike, 34850, 34877
Schrape, Joachim, 34834
Schrewe, Beate, 34852
'Schriften des Hist. Vereins Murnau am Staffelsee', 35625
Schrijver, Emile G.L., 35397
Schröder, Dieter, 35199
Schröder, Rainer, 35241
Schröter, Michael, 35429
Schroubek, Georg R., 34767
Schubart, Julia, 35862
Schubert, Elke, 35136, 35429

Schubert, Ernst (*Festschrift*), 35798
Schubert, Ursula, 35394
Schudt, Johann Jacob, 35760
Schüler-Springorum, Stefanie, 34981
Schütz, Chana C., 35623
Schütz, Erhard, 34738
Schuhmacher, Klaus, 35661
Schuhmann, Karl, 35429
Schulin, Ernst, 34705, 34710, 35355, 35480
Schulte, Christoph, 35343, 35356, 35645, 35869
Schulte, Ingolf, 35888
Schulte-Sasse, Linda, 35014
Schultz, Uwe, 35779
Schulz, Friedrich, 35519
Schulz-Jander, Eva M., 35790
Schulze, Peter, 34791, 34792
Schumann, Thomas B., 35877
Schuster, Walter, 34966
Schutzjuden, 34821
Schwab-Trapp, Michael, 35767
Schwabe, Günter, 35576
Schwabe, Ruth, 35618
Schwaben, 34703, 34826
Schwäbisch Hall, 34859
Schwalbach, 35351
Schwanitz, Dietrich, 35843
Schwarz, Angela, 35077
Schwarz, Eberhard, 35519
Schwarz, Egon, 35826
Schwarz, Fred, 35175
Schwarz, Howard, 35588
Schwarz, Peter, 34970
Schwarzmaier, Hansmartin, 34725
Schwarzmaier, Lore, 34725
Schwarzschild, Leopold, 35678
Schwarzwald, Eugenie, 35443
Schweickert, Alexander, 34836
Schweitzer, Albert, 35874
'Schweizer Monatshefte', 35543, 35654
'Schweizerische Zeitschrift für Geschichte', 35189, 35195, 35836
'Schweizerisches Archiv für Volkskunde', 35871
Schwerz, Johann Nepomuk von, 35844
Schwierz, Israel, 34868
Sciences and Mathematics, Jews in, 34692, 34756, 34918, 35432, 35494, 35501, 35737
Scott, Marilyn, 35468
Sebba, Anne, 35033
Second Generation Syndrome, 35250
Seeba, Hinrich C., 35432
Seeber, Ursula, 35590
Seemann, Birgit, 35826
Seemüller, Ulrich, 35081
(*Die*) *Sefarden in Hamburg*, 34789
Seghers, Anna, 35286, 35430, 35679, 35775
Seib, Barbara, 35446
Seidel, Esther, 35324, 35768
Seifert, Dorthe, 35481
Seiler, Lukrezia, 35191

Seitz, Josef, 34769
Seitz, Norbert, 35605
Selb, Günther, 35177
Selden, Camille, 35565
Self-Hatred see Jewish Problem
Selig, Friedrich Heinrich, 35763
Selig, Gottfried, 35763
Seligmann, Rafael, 35892
Sella, Dorothea, 35176
Selters, 34860
Sender, Toni, 35429
Senekowitsch, Martin, 34888
Senfft, Heinrich, 35482
Sennett, Richard, 35476
Sephardi Communities, 34781, 34787, 34789
Sevcenko, Ihor, 35591
Seyhan, Azade, 35547
Shalev, Avner, 35041
Shaltiel, David, 34789
Shanghai, 35006
Shanghai, Refugees, 34923, 34924, 34974, 35022, 35074
Shapira, Anita, 35167, 35276
Shapiro, Susan E., 35377
Shavit, David, 35178
Shear-Yashuv, Aharon, 35869
Shedletzky, Itta, 35612
Shephardson, Donald E., 35630
Sherman, Marc I., 35128
'Shofar', 34944
Shylock: Zinsverbot und Geldverleih, 35844; 34869, 35278, 35758
Siegen, 35302
'Siegener Beiträge. Beiträge für regionale Geschichte', 35302
Siegerland, 35179, 35180
Sielemann, Jürgen, 35078
Silberklang, David, 35181
Silbermann, Alphons, 35395
Silesia, 34703, 34861, 35182
Sillitoe, Alan, 35153
Sim, Dorrith M., 35183
Sime, Ruth Lewin, 35638
Simmel, Georg, 35680, 35871
Simon of Trent, 35807
Simon, Dieter, 35045
Simon, Heinrich, 35370
Simon, Helene, 35429
Simon, Hermann, 35353, 35621, 35623
Simon, Josef, 35869
Simons, Hans, 35274
Simsohn, Werner, 34778
Sinai, Amos, 34902
Singer, Israel Joshua, 35893
Singer, Paul, 35681
Sinzheimer, Hugo, 35429
Siodmak, Curt, 35741
Sippel, Heinrich, 34855
Skasa, Michael, 35594

Skrodzki, Karl Jürgen, 35612
Slovakia, Nazi Period, 34909
Smith, Gary, 35353
Smith, Gregory Bruce, 35349
Smith, Roger W., 35060
'Social Science History', 35089
Social Sciences, Jews in, 35523, 35608, 35628, 35648, 35680, 35686, 35719
Social Welfare, Social Reform, 34735, 35035, 35391, 35430
Socialists, Social Democrats, 34692, 35028, 35274, 35465, 35681, 35688, 35707, 35757
Söllner, Alfons, 35274, 35439
Sösemann, Bernd, 35754
Sofer, R. Moses, 35329
Sofsky, Wolfgang, 35184
Solingen, 34850
Solling, 34814
Somavilla, Ilse, 35752
Sombart, Werner, 35871
'Sommerakademie-News', 34939
Sonnen, Andrea, 34764
Sonnenfeld, Chaim Josef, 35345
Sottoppietra, Doris, 35810
Soviet Union, 35174, 35431, 35685
Soyfer, Jura, 35682
'Soziale Systeme', 35843
'Soziologische Revue', 35828
Spain, Nazi Period, 35185, 35748
Spalek, John M., 34957
Sparing, Frank, 34763
Sparr, Thomas, 35342, 35370, 35483
'Speculum', 35833
Speer, Albert, 35101, 35213
Speicher, 34862
Spelthahn, Gabriele, 35102
Sperber, Manès, 35683
Spevack, Edmund, 35274
Spielberg, Steven, 35186
Spies, Gerty, 35207, 35894
Spira, Bil, 35742
Spire, André, 35370
Spire, Marie-Brunette, 35370
Spirek, Christiane, 35431
Spitz, René A., 35429
Spitzer, Federica, 35204
Spitzer, Shlomo, 34891
Spöttel, Michael, 35845, 35875
Sprengel, Peter, 34739
St. Tönis, 34863
'St. Töniser Heimatbrief', 34863
Staar, Sonja, 35041
Stadler, Ulrich, 35547
Stamm, Rainer, 35464, 35614, 35615
'Stammbaum', 35390
Stampfer, Friedrich, 35028
Starke, Matthias, 35566
Stauf, Renate, 35567
Stavisky, Nellie, 35396

Steck, Manfred, 34826
Steffens, Gerd, 34797
Stegemann, Ekkehard W., 35324, 35325, 35344
Stegmaier, Werner, 35869
Stehle, Hansjakob, 34992
Steil, Dieter, 34780
Steinman, Lionel B., 34754
Stein, Edith, 34987, 35110
Steinbach (Kreis Gießen), 34864
Steinbach, Lothar, 35303
Steinbach, Peter, 34682, 35270, 35304
Steinberg, Jean-Louis, 35069
Steinberg, Madeleine, 35069
Steinberg, Michael P., 35491
Steinberger, Nathan, 35685
Steiner Family, 34909
Steiner, Franz Bärmann, 35686
Steiner, George, 35743
Steiner, Stephan, 35472
Steinhardt, Milton J., 35579
Steinheim, Johanna, 35744
Steinheim, Salomon Ludwig, 35320, 35744
Steinwender, Ulli, 34938
Stender, Wolfram, 35086
Stephan, Alexander, 35510
Stephan, Inge, 35429
Steppe, Hilde, 35391
Stern, Frank, 35167, 35264, 35757
Stern, Fritz, 35011, 35687
Stern, Hellmut, 35006
Stern, Jakob, 35688
Stern, Moritz, 34689
Stern, William, 35432
Sternheim, Carl, 35656
Steur, Claudia, 35019
Stevens, Michael E., 35157
Stevenson, Matthew, 35193
Stieg, Gerald, 35500
Stifter, Adalbert, 35772
Stone, Lilo, 35421
Stone, Norman, 35170
Storch, Benita, 35823
Storck, Joachim W., 34818
Storfer, Berthold, 34961
'Storia della Storiografia', 35355
Sträten, Herbert, 35165
Strasser, Christian, 35700
Strauss, Herbert A., 35745
Strauss, Léon, 34878
Strauss, Leo, 35346–35349, 35406
Strauss, Lotte, 35746
Strauss, Rahel, 35445
Strehlen, Martina, 34852
Streibel, Robert, 34890
Streit, Werner P., 34862
Stricker, Robert, 34896
Strobl, Ingrid, 35239
Strousberg, Bethel Henry, 35779
Struck, Hermann, 35689

Stude, Jürgen, 34884
Studemund-Halévy, Michael, 34781, 34787, 34789, 35386
'Studia Rosenthaliana', 35396
Sturm, Erdmann, 35605
Stuttgart, 34876, 34976, 35688
Suchecky, Bernard, 34992
Suchoff, David, 35342
Suchy, Barbara, 34763, 34955, 35002
'Südosteuropa-Jahrbuch', 34897
Sulzbach, Herbert, 35747
'(The) Sunday Times', 35170
Survival in Hiding, 34980, 35122, 35228, 35238, 35745, 35746
Survival Syndrome, 35128
Susman, Margarete, 34695, 35350, 35429
Sweden, Nazi Period, 35187
Switzerland, 34884, 34911–34915, 35194, 35196, 35202, 35403, 35414, 35415
Switzerland, Antisemitism, 34914
Switzerland, Jewish Assets, 35192-35202
Switzerland, Nazi Period, 35098, 35188, 35192, 35193, 35197, 35198, 35201
Switzerland, Refugees, 34911, 34913, 34915, 35189, 35191, 35746
Synagogues, 34703, 34725, 34730, 34732, 34752, 34759, 34763, 34768, 34777, 34797, 34807, 34850, 34851, 34852, 34901, 35393
Szöllösi-Janze, Margit, 35539
Szücs, Ladislaus, 35158

Taddey, Gerhard, 34958
Talheim, 34876
Tann (Rhön), 34865
Tannenbaum, Herbert, 34818
Tanner, Jakob, 34914
Tausenpfund, Walter, 34769
Taylor, Ronald, 34740
Teensma, Benjamin N., 34789
Tegel, Susan, 35015
'Tel Aviver Jahrbuch Für Deutsche Geschichte', 34921, 35018, 35221, 35598, 35756, 35784, 35786, 35795
Teller, Adam, 34941
Teppich, Fritz, 35748
Ternon, Yves, 35144
Terwey, Susanne, 34921
Tetzner, Lisa, 35690
Teufel, Helmut, 34892
Teuteberg, Hans-Jürgen, 34746, 34761
Teveth, Shabtai, 35203
Thalfang, 35330
Thalheimer, Siegfried, 34763
Theatre, Cabaret, Cinema, Jews in, 34739, 35010, 35370, 35447, 35652, 35741
Theatre, Film, Jews depicted in, 35380, 35758
Theel, Robert, 35656
Theresienstadt, 34902, 34972, 35123, 35178, 35204–35208

Thiel, Hans, 34811
Thiele, Martina, 35066
Thielking, Sigrid, 35286
Thierfelder, Jörg, 34707
Thörner, Klaus, 35059
Thoma, Clemens, 35803
Thoma, Dieter, 35752
Thürich, Ursula, 34942
Thürmer-Rohr, Christina, 35476
Thuringia, 34723, 34867, 34868, 35209
Tichy, Frank, 35693
Tiedemann, Rolf, 35466
Tiemann, Katharina, 34758
Tilch, Marianne, 35540, 35545
Tillich, Paul, 35605
'Times Literary Supplement', 35412
Timm, Angelika, 35272, 35757, 35793
Timm, Erika, 34717
Tittelbach-Helmrich, Wolfgang, 34723
Titz, 35102
Tobias, Jim G., 35883
Toch, Michael, 34703, 34708
Todd, Jane Marie, 35489
Todorow, Almut, 35459
Toller, Ernst, 35462, 35691
Torberg, Friedrich, 35692, 35693
Toury, Gideon, 34709
Toury, Jacob, 34703, 34709
Tragnitz, Jutta R., 35207
Trancík, Martin, 34909
Trapp, Frithjof, 35431
Traverso, Enzio, 35460, 35757
Traverso, Paola, 35598
Trent, 35804, 35807
Tress, Madeleine, 35275
Treue, Wolfgang, 35807
Treufuss-Schalenbeck, Bianca, 35378
'Tribüne', 34936, 35090, 35176, 35239, 35369, 35395, 35409, 35477, 35801
Trier, 34688, 34839, 34869, 34870, 35384, 35636
Triest, 35428
Trigano, Shmuel, 35167
Trilse-Finkelstein, Jochanan, 35559, 35568
Tröps, Dieter, 35151
'Trumah', 34696, 35310, 35341
Tsalka, Dan, 35895
Tschörtner, Heinz Dieter, 35857
Tschuy, Carl, 35098
Tucholsky, Kurt, 35694
Tübingen, 34871, 35212
Tüchersfeld, 34769
Tulln, 34970
Turk, Horst, 35411
Turkey, Refugees, 34919
Tweraser, Kurt, 35127

'Udim', 35311, 35317
Üding, Gert, 35496
Ühli Stauffer, Beatrice, 35578

Ulbricht, Justus H., 35823
Ullrich, Volker, 35020
Ullstein Family, 35425
Ulmer, Peter, 35627
'(Die) Umschau', 35683
Unger, Erich, 35869
Unger, Hartmut, 35669
United States Holocaust Memorial Museum, 35159
Universities and Jews, 34871, 34914, 34969, 34985, 35044, 35445, 35446, 35545, 35591, 35663
Unter Vorbehalt, 35277
Urbach, Nelly, 34933
Urbahn de Jauregui, Heidi, 35569
Urban, Paul, 35433, 35436
Urban-Fahr, Susanne, 35240, 35461
Uruguay, 34925
USA, 34929, 34930, 34932, 35157, 35667, 35708, 35821, 35893
USA, Holocaust, Reaction, 35011, 35167, 35181
USA, Immigration, 34703, 34843, 34884, 34927, 34931, 34933
USA, Nazi Period, 35130
USA, Refugees, 34928, 34931, 35104, 35510, 35721
USA, Refugees Policy, 35232
Usingen, 35887
Uslar, 34814

Valentin, Jean-Marie, 35500
Van der Vat, Dan, 35213
Varga, Péter, 35370
Varga, Susan, 35214
Varnhagen, Karl August, 35729
Varnhagen, Rahel, 35481, 35695, 35696, 35729
Varon, Benno Weiser, 35215
Vees, Adolf, 34793
Velbert, 34850
Velen-Ramsdorf, 35216
Verein für Cultur und Wissenschaft der Juden, 35533, 35559
Verein zur Abwehr des Antisemitismus, 34679
Vereinigung Badischer Israeliten, 34679
Vergangenheitsbewältigung, 35045, 35085, 35280, 35306, 35466, 35755, 35757, 35767, 35773, 35776, 35777, 35778, 35840
Verse-Herrmann, Angela, 35217
Vertlib, Vladimir, 34912, 35742
'Vestische Zeitschrift', 34751, 34962
'Vestischer Kalender', 34844
Viaene, Vincent, 35846
Vialon, Martin, 35705
Vienna, 34893, 34894, 34933, 34968, 34969, 35114, 35168, 35428, 35632, 35707, 35740,
Vierhaus, Rudolf, 34680
'Vierteljahrschrift für Sozial- und Wirtschaftsgeschichte', 35217

'Vierteljahrshefte für Zeitgeschichte', 34964, 35063
Vigé, Claude, 35370
Vincent, Isabel, 35201
'Vingtième Siècle', 35218
Visser, Ellende, 35847
Vital, David, 35412
Völckers, Rüdiger, 35884
Völker, Klaus, 35575
Vogelsberg, 34858
Voges, Dietmar-H., 34830
Vogt, Jochen, 35286
Voigt, Manfred, 35869
Voigts, Manfred, 35350
Volk, Andreas, 35601
Volkov, Shulamit, 34692, 35045, 35418
Vollrath, Hanna, 34687
Voolen, Edward van, 35397
Vorspohl, Elisabeth, 35429
Voswinckel, Peter, 35455
Vrba, Rudolf, 34964, 35006

Wachinger, Lorenz, 35318
Wachten, Johannes, 34772
Wacker, Bernd, 35844
Wacker, Jean-Claude, 35191
Waco, Laura, 35749
Waesche, Günter, 34853
Wagenseil, Johann Christoph, 35760
Wagner, Richard, 35555
Wagner, Ulrich, 34767
Wagnerová, Alena, 34908
Wahl Family, 34883
Wahrig-Schmidt, Bettina, 35455
Waldbröl, 34849
Waldviertel, 34890
'(Das) Waldviertel', 34890
Walk, Joseph, 35750
Walker, Mark, 35638
Wallau, 34811
Wallich Family, 35257
Wallner, Fritz, 35429
Walston, James, 35100
Walter, Hans-Albert, 35007
Walter, Robert, 35429
Wandlungen und Brüche, 34896
Wandres, Thomas, 35148
Wandsbek, 34790
Wangermann, Ernst (*Festschrift*), 34892
Wannbach, 34769
Wannsee-Conference, 35020
Warburg Institute, 35726
Warburg, Aby M., 35457, 35697
Wardi, Charlotte, 35370
Warhaftig, Myra, 35422
Wassermann, Jakob, 35536
Waszek, Norbert, 35534
Watkins, John, 35653
Weber, Annette, 34703, 35387

Weber, Britta, 34747
Weber, Hermann, 35624
Weber, Matthias M., 35625
Weber, Max, 35871, 35875
Wechsler, Hile, 35351
Wechsler, Judith Glatzer, 35715
Weckel, Ulrike, 35477
Wecker, Regina, 34914
Wedekind, Susanne, 35487
Wegeler, Cornelia, 35044
Wegner, Werner, 34925
Wehler, Hans-Ulrich, 35067
Wehowsky, Stephan, 35045
Weigand, Karlheinz, 35495
Weigel, Sigrid, 35219, 35476, 35506
Weil, Grete, 35896
Weil, Hans, 35429
Weilburg (Lahn), 34872
Weimar Republic, 34692, 34709, 34710, 35370, 35385, 35419, 35486, 35669
Weinberg, David H., 35352
Weinberg, Ulla, 34943
Weingardt, Markus A., 35794
Weininger, Otto, 35368
Weinke, Wilfried, 35079, 35080
Weinland, Martina, 34741
Weinstein, Rochelle, 34789
Weinzierl, Erika, 34896
Weinzierl, Ulrich, 35594, 35657
Weisberger, Adam M., 35462
Weiss, Ernst, 35452
Weiss, Hermann, 34949
Weiss, John, 35848
Weiss, Konrad, 35791
Weiss, Petra, 34769
Weiss, Yfaat, 34692, 35221, 35222
Weissberg, Liliane, 35695
Weissglas, Isak, 35220
Weissweiler, Eva, 35732
Weisz, Ruth, 35204
Wellmann, Hans (*Festschrift*), 34714
'(Die) Welt', 34896
Welzer, Harald, 35086
Wenck, Alexandra-Eileen, 35269
Wenk, Silke, 35283
Wenninger, Markus J., 34938
Wenzel, Uwe Justus, 35523, 35584, 35627
Werblowsky, R.J.Zwi, 35353
Werfel, Franz, 35536
'WerkstattGeschichte', 35020, 35477
Werl, 34873
'Werl. Gestern, heute, morgen', 34873
Werle, Gerhard, 35148
Werner, Michael, 35546, 35551
Werth, Nicolas, 35218
Wertheim Family, 35448, 35449
Wertheimer, Jürgen, 35432
Wertheimer, Max, 35432
Wertheimer, Michael, 35432

Index to Bibliography

Wesche, Markus, 35444
Wesel, 34874
West, Rebecca, 35149
Westerbork, 35175
Westerhoff, Eduard, 34746
Westphalia, 34684, 34703, 34746, 34820, 34861, 34873, 34875, 35039, 35216, 35223
Wetz, Franz Josef, 35429
Wetzel, Juliane, 34947, 35218, 35264, 35278
Wetzler, Simon, 34812
Weyers, Frank, 35434
Whissen, Thomas, 35099
White, Jim, 35005
Whiteside, Kerry H., 35476
Wichner, Ernest, 35220
Widmann, Peter, 35849
Wiedemann, Barbara, 35878
Wiehn, Erhard Roy, 34778, 34833, 34903, 34974, 35073, 35074, 35116, 35173, 35737
Wieland, Wolfgang, 35627
'Wiener Geschichtsblätter', 35435
Wiener Library, London, 34945
Wiener, Alfred, 34945
Wiesel, Elie, 35128, 35144, 35229, 35324
Wiesel, Pauline, 35729
Wiesemann, Falk, 35397
Wiesenthal, Simon, 35098, 35224, 35698, 35704
Wiesner, Herbert, 35220
Wieviorka, Annette, 35167, 35218
Wilbertz, Gisela, 34747
Wilcock, Evelyn, 35305
Wildt, Michael, 35020, 35597
Wilhelm II., 35486
'Wilhelm-Busch-Jahrbuch', 34791
Wilkomirski, Binjamin, 35225
Windfuhr, Manfred, 35540, 35570
Winkler, Heinrich August, 35814
Winkler, Kurt, 34741
Winkler, Markus, 35547
Winter, Mine, 34962
Wintermeyer, Ingo, 35862
Wintzenheim, 34884
Winz, Leo, 35380
Wippermann, Wolfgang, 35068, 35840, 35849
Wirsbitzki, Brigitta, 34824
Wisconsin, 35157
Wiseley, Andrew C., 35675
Wissenschaft des Judentums, 35314, 35326, 35327, 35343, 35354–35356, 35559
Wistrich, Robert S., 34896, 35037, 35226, 35413, 35423, 35646,
Witte, Bernd, 35397, 35605
Wittenberger, Georg, 34812
'Wittgenstein – Blätter des Wittgensteiner Heimatvereins', 34733
Wittgenstein, Ludwig, 35429, 35751, 35752
Wixforth, Harald, 35463
Wlaschek, Rudolf M., 34899, 34900
Wölfing, Willi, 34707

Wölk, Wolf, 35003
Wölk, Wolfgang, 34763
Wohlfahrt, Irving, 35774
Wolf, Frank, 35227
Wolf, Gerhard Philipp, 34769
Wolf, Kerstin, 35227
Wolf, Markus, 35753
Wolf, Pamela, 35826
Wolf, Siegbert, 35446, 35826
Wolf, Siegfried, 35209
Wolfen, 34756
Wolfenbüttel, 35746
Wolfenstein, Alfred, 35367
Wolff, Charlotte, 35429
Wolff, Jeanette, 35429
Wolff, Theodor, 35754
Wolffsohn, Michael, 35306, 35780
Wolffson, Isaac, 34786
Wolfsohn, Aron, 35382
Wolkowicz, Shlomo, 35228
Wollenberg, Jörg, 35618, 35850
Women, 34691–34693, 34707, 34734, 34737, 34774, 34980, 34986, 35126, 35155, 35219, 35238, 35363, 35370, 35415, 35426, 35430, 35435, 35445, 35452, 35455, 35494, 35532, 35535, 35574, 35638, 35668, 35757, 35847
Women's Int. League for Peace and Freedom, 35430
Women's Movement, 34773, 35580
Wood, E. Thomas, 35229
Worms, 35388
Wormser Family, 35388
Württemberg, 34703, 34749, 34826, 34876, 34958, 35307, 35388
Würzburg, 34767, 35745
Wunsch, Beate, 35424
Wuppertal, 34850
Wuppertal, 'Alte Synagoge', 34877
Wuthenow, Ralph-Rainer, 35826
Wyrsch, Rudolf A.H., 34722

Xhonneux, Renate, 34762
Xu, Pei, 35571

'Yad Vashem Studies', 34963, 34978, 34988, 35021, 35023, 35130, 35160, 35181, 35210, 35785
Yantian, Nicholas, 35264
Yiddish, 34680, 34711–34717, 35379, 35380, 35385, 35856
Young, James E., 35087, 35284, 35308
Young, Julian, 35859
Youth Aliyah, 35417
Youth Movement, 34753, 34763, 34792, 34902, 35370, 35401, 35406
Yovel, Yirmiyahu, 35876

Zabel, Hermann, 34784
Zacher, Eberhard, 34749
Zafren, Herbert C., 35357

Zak, Adam, 35531
Zappalà, Pietro, 35454
Zaugg, Karin, 35667
Zeckern, 34720
Zee, Nanda van der, 35132
'(Die) Zeit', 34683, 34992, 34999, 35020, 35022, 35055, 35075, 35136, 35190, 35229, 35409, 35487, 35499, 35546, 35575, 35582, 35594, 35598, 35600, 35612, 35718, 35752, 35789, 35804, 35814
'Zeitschrift des Vereins für Hamburgische Geschichte', 34786, 35076, 35078
'Zeitschrift des Vereins für Hess. Geschichte und Landeskunde', 34799, 34805
'Zeitschrift des Bergischen Geschichtsvereins', 35162
'Zeitschrift für die Gesch. des Oberrheins', 34726
'Zeitschrift für Deutsche Philologie', 35362, 35610, 35851, 35854
'Zeitschrift für Germanistik', 34738
'Zeitschrift für Geschichtswissenschaft', 34687, 34981, 34990, 35049, 35072, 35090, 35185, 35391, 35406, 35643, 35645, 35696, 35804, 35839, 35849
'Zeitschrift für Religions- und Geistesgeschichte', 35363, 35802
'Zeitschrift für Unternehmensgeschichte', 35486
'Zeitschrift zur Gesch. der Psychoanalyse', 35629
Zeliger, Barbie, 35218
Zeller, Ron, 35133
Zellwiller, 34884
Zelter, Carl Friedrich, 35454
Zentralarchiv zur Erforschung der Gesch. der Juden in Deutschland, 34946
Zentralrat der Juden in Deutschland, 35757
Zentrum für Antisemitismusforschung, Berlin, 34947
Zertal, Idith, 35276

Zetkin, Clara, 35688
Zeugin, Bettina, 35415
Zhitlowski, Haim, 35352
Ziege, Eva-Maria, 34999
Ziegler, Dieter, 35463
Ziegler, Edda, 35572
Ziegler, Jean, 35202
Zielke, Heiko, 34763
Ziemer, Hans-Werner, 34802, 34839
Zimmermann, Moshe, 34692, 34710, 35795, 35869
Zink, Wolfgang, 34866
Zion, Sidney, 35011
Zionism, 34763, 34896, 34909, 35012, 35167, 35402, 35764, 35370, 35400, 35402–35404, 35406, 35409, 35410, 35412, 35414, 35415, 35418, 35419, 35424, 35632, 35645, 35826
Zionism and Nazis, 35203
Zionism, Austria,
Zionism, Post War, 35264, 35793
Zionism, Weimar Germany, 35421
Zionist Congress, Post-War, 35273
Zitko, Hans, 34960
Ziwes, Franz-Josef, 34725
Zöller, Sonja, 35781
Zuckmayer, Carl, 35699, 35700
Zürndorfer, Adolf, 34763
Zürndorfer, Hannele, 35230
Zuntz (Zunz) Family, 35392
Zunz, Leopold, 35392
Zunzer, Daniela, 34742
Zur Mühlen, Bernt Ture von, 34715, 34940
Zur Mühlen, Patrik von, 35274, 35889
Zweig, Arnold, 35362, 35376, 35701, 35775
Zweig, Stefan, 35536
Zwiauer, Charlotte, 35603
'Zwischen Main und Taunus', 34866
Zymek, Bernd, 35223

List of Contributors

ALBANIS, Elisabeth, M.A., M. Phil., b. 1965 in Bremen, Germany. Tutor in Jewish History at Warwick University and doctoral student in Modern History at St. John's College, Oxford. Author of several articles on German-Jewish history, including 'Jakob Wasserman's Memorial to Walther Rathenau', in *German Life and Letters* (1997); 'Sir Ernest Cassel and Anglo-German Relations Before the Outbreak of the First World War, in *Cambridge Review of International Affairs* (1990); 'Moritz Goldstein. Texte zur jüdischen Selbstwahrnehmung aus dem Nachlaß', in *Aschkenas* (1997).

ASCHHEIM, Steven E., Ph.D., b. 1942 in Johannesburg, South Africa. Lecturer in European Cultural and Intellectual History at the Hebrew University of Jerusalem. Author of *Brothers and Strangers. The East European Jew in German and German-Jewish Consciousness, 1800–1923* (1982); *The Nietzsche Legacy in Germany, 1890–1990* (1982, German translation published 1996); *Culture and Catastrophe. German and Jewish Confrontations with National Socialism and Other Crises* (1996); and numerous articles on German-Jewish history. Editor of *Hannah Arendt in Jerusalem* (forthcoming). (Contributor to Year Books XXVIII and XXXVII.)

AYALON, Moshe, M.A., b. 1923 in Frankfurt am Main. Formerly an employee of the Israeli government, now a Research Fellow at the Strochlitz Institute of Holocaust Studies, University of Haifa. Author of articles on German-Jewish children in Frankfurt am Main. (Contributor to Year Book XLI.)

BAADER, Maria, M.A., M.Phil., b. 1959 in Giesen, Germany. Formerly a cabinet maker, now a graduate student at Columbia University, New York. Publications include 'Die Deborah', in *Jewish Women in America. An Historical Encyclopaedia* (1997) and 'Zweierlei Befreiung', in Jessica Jacoby, Claudia Schoppmann and Wendy Zena-Henry (eds.), *Nach der Shoa Geboren. Jüdische Frauen in Deutschland* (1994).

BERNSTEIN-NAHAR, Avi, Ph.D., b. 1963 in Orlando, Florida. Ray D. Wolfe Fellow in Jewish Studies at the University of Toronto.

CARSTEN, Francis Ludwig, D. Phil., D. Litt., b. 1911 in Berlin, d. 1998 in London. Formerly Professor of Central European History, University of London. Publications include *War against War. British and German Radical Movements in the First World War* (1982); *Britain and the Weimar Republic* (1984); *August Bebel* (1991); *Eduard Bernstein* (1993); *The German Workers and the Nazis* (1995). (Contributor to Year Book III.)

FRIESEL, Evyatar, Ph.D., b. 1930 in Germany. Professor Emeritus of Jewish History, Hebrew University of Jerusalem and Israel State Archivist. Author of *Zionist Policy after the Balfour Declaration* (1977, in Hebrew) and *Atlas of Modern Jewish History* (1990). (Contributor to Year Books XXXI, XXXIII, XXXVI and XLI.

GOTZMANN, Andreas, D. Phil., b. 1960 in Karlsruhe, Germany. Assistant Professor of Jewish History and Culture at the Seminary for Judaic Studies, University of Frankfurt. Publications include *Gold- und Silberschmück der Jüden in Marokko* (1989); *Jüdisches Recht im kulturellen Prozeß. Die Warnehmung der Halacha im Deutschand des 19. Jahrhunderts* (1997, Schriftenreihe wissenschaftlicher Abhandlungen des Leo Baeck Instituts); and several articles and essays on Jewish history and culture. Co-editor, with R. Bischoff and R. Hänke, *of Der jüdische Friedhof in Eppingen. Eine Dokumentation* (1989).

HABERMAN, Jacob, Ph.D., Dr. Jur., b. 1932 in Zürich. Formerly a business executive, now a rabbi. Publications include *Maimonides and Aquinas. A Contemporary Appraisal* (1979), and several articles with various Jewish themes.

KLEIN, Anne, b. 1958 in Cologne, Germany. Formerly an adult education specialist. Publications include "Manchmal will ich zu Hause die Bracha sprechen" in *Freitag*. Co-editor of *Die frumkeit der vrouwen. Frauen und Religion im Bielfeld des Späten Mittelalters und der Frühen Neuzeit* (1998) and articles on Jewish life in Berlin.

MATTHÄUS, Jürgen, Ph.D., b. 1958 in Dortmund, Germany. Historian at the U.S. Holocaust Memorial Museum, Washington. Publications include various articles on the Holocaust and German-Jewish history. Co-editor, with W. Benz and K. Kwiet, of *Einsatz im Ostland. Dokumente zum Völkermord im Baltikum und im Weißprußland, 1941–1944*, (1998). (Contributor to Year Book XXXIII.)

MURPHY, David T., Ph.D., b. 1960 in Rockford, Illinois. Associate Professor of History at Anderson University. Publications include *The Heroic Earth. Geopolitical Thought in Weimar Germany 1918–1933*; 'Space, Race and Geopolitical Necessity. Geopolitical Rhetoric in German Colonial Revanchism, 1919–1933', in Anne Godlewska and Neil Smith (eds.), *Geography and Empire* (1994).

NIEHOFF, Maren R., Ph.D., b. 1963 in Germany. Lecturer in the Department of Jewish Thought at the Hebrew University of Jerusalem. Publications include *The Figure of Joseph in Post-Biblical Jewish Literature* (1992); 'Jewish Hellenism in Nineteenth-Century *Wissenschaft des Judentums*. Between Modernity and Christianity', in *Schriften des Historischen Kollegs, Kolloquium 44* (forthcoming*); Identity and Culture in Philo of Alexandria* (forthcoming).(Contributor to Year Book XLI.)

REGNERI, Günter M., M.A., b. 1963 in Wuppertal, Germany. Former electronic engineer, now library assistant and freelance writer. Publications include 'Fremdenfeindlichkeit und Rassismus al ideologische Begriffe', in *"Fremde"*. *Zum*

Umgang mit in der Geschichte und Gegenwart. Dokumentationsreihe der Freien Universität Berlin (1993); *SJD – Die Falken in den FDJ-Akten. Reihe Archivhilfe*, No. 7, *Archiv der Arbeiterjugendbewegung* (1994).

SKOLNIK, Jonathan, M.A., M.Phil., b. 1967 in New York. Doctoral student at Columbia University. Publications include "Hier wuchsen die historischen Romane wild" Arnold Zweig's *De Vriendt kehrt heim* and the German-Jewish Historical Novel', in *Akten des IV. Internationalen Arnold-Zweig-Symposiums* (1998); 'Die seltsame Karriere der Familie Abarbanel', in Joseph Kruse and Bernd Witte (eds.), *Aufklärung in Skepsis. Heinrich Heine Zum 200. Geburtstag* (1997).

WILDT, Michael, Ph.D., b. 1954 in Essen, Germany. Scholar at the Hamburger Institut für Sozialforschung. Publications include *Am Beginn der "Konsumgesellschaft". Mangelfahrung, Lebenshaltung, Wohlstandshoffnung in Westdeutschland in den fünfziger Jahren* (1994); *Die Judenpolitik des SD 1935–1938. Eine Dokumentation* (1995); *Hans Reichmann, Deutsche Bürger und verfolgter Jude. Aufzeichnungen über Pogrom und Konzentrationslager 1937 bis 1939* (1998).

General Index to Year Book XLIII of the Leo Baeck Institute

Acculturation, *see* Assimilation
Adam, Uwe Dietrich, 250n
Adams, Arthur A. (Australian writer), 212n
Adler, Cyrus (US Jewish leader), 99
Adler, Liebman (Detroit cantor), 63
Adler, Samuel (rabbi), 85n
Aguilar, Grace (author), 62-63
Ahad Ha'Am (pseud. Asher Ginzberg) (Zionist leader, Hebrew author), 326
Akiba ben Joseph (1st-century rabbi), 86
Albany (NY) Jewish community, 56
Albo, Joseph (medieval religious philosopher), 108
Alexander II (Tsar of Russia), 151
Allemania (US German club), 56, 57, 60
Allen, Jay (US journalist), 303
Allen, William Sheridan, 175n
'Allgemeine Zeitung des Judenthums', 137, 227
Alliance Israélite Universelle, 134-135, 334: Archive, 131n
Alsatian Jewry, 55
Altmann, Alexander (rabbi, philosopher), 3n
Aly, Götz, 174n
American Federation of Labor, 288, 297
American Guild for German Cultural Freedom, 288n
'[The] American Israelite' (US journal, earlier 'The Israelite'), 47, 48, 50, 51, 52, 53-54, 55. 58, 60, 61, 62, 64-72
'American Jewess', 69-70
American Jewish Committee, 327
American Jewish Congress, 288
American Jewish Joint Distribution Committee (Joint), 168, 274, 279, 281, 287n
Amsterdam: emigrants to, 345
Angress, Werner T., 196n-197n
'[Der] Angriff', 246n
Antisemiten-Petition, 136, 146
Antisemitism, 81, 98, 163-164, 204, 225, 244, 317, 318, 321, 329, 340, 342: antisemitic legislation, 245, 247, 249-250, 253, 255, 262, 298n, 307: Austria, 263: Berliner Antisemitismusstreit, 129-153: G. Brand and, 199: H. S. Chamberlain, 182n: Communist, 342: and cooperative societies, 167: and Eastern European Jewry, 184: expulsion of Jews, 152, 155, 184, 264n: Finke, 319n: and geopolitics, 175-191: German, 175-191: 'Der Hammer', 207: Hobson, 186: "International Jewry", 246, 255: "Jewish dirtiness", 163-164: "Jewish hatred", 198, 207, 209-210, 223: Jung, 320: Lithuanian, 173: B. Long, 295n: Petition to Hitler against, 278: Radau-Antisemitismus, 241, 242, 263, 266, 268: Seraphim, 184n: stereotypes, 107, 110, 162-164, 168: Stoecker, 136, 145: Treitschke, 129-130, 135-138, 144-148, 152-153: United States, 310: Vichy France, 295-296: in WWI, 155, 162-164, 166-168, 173. *See also* Nazi Regime (Jews under), November Pogrom, Persecution
Antisemitism: defence, 129-153: Declaration of the Notables, 145: Virchow, 149-151
Antisemitism: Jewish defence, 230: Lissauer, 204
'Archiv für Rassen- und Gesellschaftsbiologie', 182
Arendt, Hannah (social historian), 269, 289, 293n, 298, 304n, 310n, 311
Armstrong, Hamilton Fish (US journalist), 287
Arnold, Matthew (poet), 84
Arnswalde Jewish community, 247
Aschheim, Steven E., 318n
Ascoli, Max (US refugee relief worker), 303
Ashton, Diane, 47n
Assimilation, 35, 48, 77, 104, 316, 334: assimilationism, 197, 198, 221, 222, 246, 259, 321: and dissimilation, 228-231, 236-237 Germany, 48, 49: in USA, 47, 50, 58-59
Aub, Josef (Reform rabbi), 122-123
Auerbach, Benjamin Hirsch (Chief Rabbi, Halberstadt), 105n, 108n, 113, 117, 124n
Auerbach, Berthold [Moses Baruch Auerbach] (author), 227
'Aufbau' (New York), 309
Aufklärung, *see* Enlightenment
Auschwitz concentration camp, 267
Australia: emigration to, 273, 280
Austria: Anschluß, 263, 287: National Socialists, 247, 251
Austrian Jewry: Israelitische Kultusgemeinde, 264: persecution, 263
Austro-Hungary: emigrants from, 142, 143, 147, 152
Auswärtiges Amt, 256, 261, 262
Avenarius, Ferdinand (writer, publisher), 217n
Avigur, Shaul (Haganah leader), 260

General Index

Azéma (mayor of Banyuls-sur-mer), 300, 301, 302

Bach, Johann Sebastian (composer), 203
Backer, George (of Joint), 281n
Bad Tölz Jewish community, 247
Baeck, Leo (rabbi, scholar, Reichsvertretung President), 135, 165, 277, 278
Baer, Seligmann [Isaak Dow] (rabbi, scholar), 77–78
Baer, Yitzak (Fritz) (historian), 226
Baerwald, Paul (Chairman, US Joint), 287n
Bakker, Geert, 177n
Balfour Declaration, 258
Baltic countries: German occupation (WWI), 156
Bamberger, Nathan Halevi (Würzburg rabbi), 124n
Bamberger, Seligmann Baer, *see* Baer, Seligmann
Bankers, Jewish, 340
Banse, Ewald (geopolitician), 188
Barkai, Avraham, 48n, 51n, 242n, 244
Barnes, Alan, 103n
Baron, Salo Wittmayer (historian), 325, 326, 328, 329
Bartels, Adolf (literary historian, antisemite), 199
Bauman, Zygmunt, 311
Baumgarten, Eduard (intellectual), 320n
Bavarian Jewry, 141
Baynes, Norman (historian, translator), 347
Bayrische Politische Polizei, 246
Beer, Peter (teacher), 105n, 108, 112n, 113, 115, 116, 124n
Beethoven, Ludwig van (composer), 203
Behr, Alexander (educational author), 105n, 124n
Beinfeld, Solon, 161n
Belke, Ingrid, 230
Bénédite, Daniel (refugee relief worker), 300, 302, 303
Benjamin, Walter (literary historian, philosopher), 300, 318n, 319, 322
Bergmann, Eugen von (demographer), 148, 153
Bergson, Henri (French philosopher), 83
Berkowitz, Henry (US rabbi), 66
Berlin Jewish community, 256, 275, 276, 339–344: anti-Jewish riots, 263: poverty and relief, 132: Reformgemeinde, 122, 198
Berlin, [Sir] Isaiah (philosopher), 93
Berliner Gesundheitspflegeverein, 131
Berliner Lokalkomitee der Alliance Israélite Universelle, 131n
'Berliner Post', 145, 146
Berliner Stadtverordnetenversammlung, 131, 134
'Berliner Tageblatt', 206, 207, 226
Bertram, Ernst (literary historian), 217

Best, [Karl Rudolf] Werner (Hessian Gauleiter, Heydrich's deputy), 257
Bialik, Chaim Nachmann (poet, Hebraist), 230n
Białystok-Grodno region (Poland): German occupation (WWI), 156
Bible criticism, 88, 92, 94–95
Bing, Abraham (Würzburg rabbi), 124n
Birnbaum, Arthur, 73n
Birobidjan, 184
Birshi Jewish community: German occupation (WWI), 164
Bismarck, Otto Fürst von (German statesman), 55, 151, 203, 207, 343
Black, J. Sutherland (editor), 94
Blau, Joseph L., 97–98
Bleichröder Archive, Harvard University, 131n
Bleichröder (bank), 343
Bloch, Ernst (philosopher), 318n
Block, Nora (Cassel judge), 294
Blücher, Gebhart Leberecht von (Prussian general), 202
Blücher, Heinrich (husband of H. Arendt), 304n
Blum, Léon (French Socialist politician), 295
Blunck, Hans Friedrich (Rector, University of Hamburg), 223n
Böckh, Richard (statistician), 134
Boehlich, Walter, 130n
Bohemian Jewry, 48, 55
Bohn, Frank (worker with refugees), 297
Bondy, Curt (educationalist), 277
Borchardt, Rudolf (Conservative author), 216
Borgman, F. W. (geopolitician), 184n
Bormann, Wilhelm (businessman, SD informer), 260, 261
Born & Busse (bank), 340
Born, Jennie (grandmother of F.L. Carsten), 339
Born, Julius (banker, convert), 340
Born, Ludwig (banker), 340
Born, Sigismund (grandfather of F.L. Carsten), 339
Borowitz, Eugen, 26n
Bowra, [Sir] [Cecil] Maurice (British classicist), 346
Boycotts, anti-Jewish, 245, 247–248
Brand, Guido (author), 196, 199
Braun, Frhr. Magnus von (of Deutsche Verwaltung), 159n
Braun, Wernher von (rocket scientist), 159n
Brecher, Frank W., 290n
Brecht, Bertolt (poet, playwright), 232n, 318
Breitscheid, Rudolf (SPD politician), 302
Brenner, Michael, 318n
Breslau Jewish community, 148, 281, 284
Breslau, Harry (historian), 147
Brickman, Seymour, 73n
Britain: emigrants to, 226, 344–345, 346–349: HICEM (HIAS/ICA Emigration Association) 297n: internment of refugees, 346–347:

General Index

and November Pogrom, 278: propaganda and re-education, 347–348
Broszat, Martin (historian), 175n
Browning, Christopher, 175
Bruce, [Sir] Michael (in attempt to avert November Pogrom), 278
Brunn, S. D., 177n
Bry, Gerhard (left-wing resister), 344
Buber, Martin (philosopher), 320, 322
Buchenwald concentration camp, 263
Buchheim, Hans, 269
Büdinger, Moses (teachers' seminary director), 105n, 107n, 121, 124n
Bülow, Bernhard Graf/Fürst von (Imperial German Chancellor), 200
Bülow, Hans Guido von (musician), 207
Bülow, Marie von (wife of Hans G, v, B), 207
Bürckel, Joseph (Gauleiter, Reichskommissar), 264
Buloff, Joseph (Jewish actor), 161
Bund (Jewish Socialist movement), 333
Bundesarchiv: Außenstelle Potsdam, 131: Zwischenarchiv Dahlwitz-Hoppegarten, 243
Bundesministerium des Innern, X
Burgdörfer, Friedrich (geopolitician), 179
Burleigh, Michael, 183n
Butler, Josephine (British feminist), 68

Cahana, Menahem, 3n
Carlyle, Thomas (historian), 339
Carmely, Klara Pomeranz, 221n
Carové, Friedrich Wilhelm (education official), 119n
Carrdus, Anna, 195n
Carsten family, 339, 340
Carsten, Francis Ludwig (historian), 339–349
Carsten, Frida (née Born, wife of Paul C.), 339
Carsten, Paul (ophthalmologist, father of F.L. Carsten), 339
Carsten, Ruth (wife of Francis L. C., née Moses), 347, 348, 349
Caspary, Helene (witness for possible US immigrants), 309
Cassel, [Selig] Paulus (theologian, convert)
Cassirer, Ernst (philosopher), 319
Censuses, 133, 138–139, 140, 142, 151, 162n
Central Archives for the History of the Jewish People (CAHJP), 131
Central Conference of American Rabbis (CCAR), 75, 93
Central Zionist Archives, 156n, 271n
Centralverein deutscher Staatsbürger jüdischen Glaubens (C.V.), 155, 197, 229, 230, 244, 256, 277, 327
Centre américain de secours, 297, 301
Centre d'Hébergement de Banyuls pour les Réfugiés, 301
Centre for Conservation and Restoration of Documents, Moscow (formerly Central State Archive), 131
Centre for the Preservation of Historical-Documentary Collections, Moscow (Special Archive), see Osobyi Archive
Chagall, Marc (artist), 289
Chamberlain, Houston Stewart (racist author), 182, 197, 212, 223
Chatham House, 348
Cheyne, T. K. (editor), 94
China: emigration to, 274
Christianity: Christian Romanticism, 4, 13: and Judaism, 43, 44: and Jewish education, 104, 105n, 108n, 110, 111, 119: "Non-Aryan" Christians, 280: and Zunz, 4, 6, 7, 8, 10, 11, 13
Christlich-soziale Bewegung, 136
Cincinnati Jewish community, 48, 50–51, 56, 57
Clark, George Norman (economic historian), 347
Clarke, Charles (translator), 212
Cohen, Arthur, 32
Cohen, Hermann (philosopher), 25–46, 73, 98, 132, 147
Cohen, Max (left-wing writer), 178n
Cohen, Naomi, 48n
Cohn, Willy (historian, Breslau diarist), 281n
Cole, David Henry (British geopolitician), 187–188
Cole, George D.H. (economist), 346
Colombia: forced emigration to, 258
Comité für die rumänischen Juden, 131n
Comité zur Abwehr antisemitischer Angriffe, 135
Committee for Catholic Refugees from Germany, 287n–288n
Communism, 345: and refugees in US, 291, 292, 293, 309, 310. See also Kommunistische Partei Deutschlands
Concentration camps, 266, 271–272, 273, 276, 279, 280, 281, 283, 287, 296, 310: "Konzentrationslager" (WWI), 171: in France, 294, 295, 296, 300, 304, See also individual camps
Conservative Judaism, 74, 94: religious education, 110, 112: in USA, 334
Conservatives, 145
Conversion, 20, 134, 198, 199
Conzen, Kathleen Neils, 57
Cooperative societies, 166–167
'Cornhill Magazine', 68
Crosland, C.A.R. (Anthony) (British politician), 346
Culture, Jewish, 5–6, 230–232, 323, 325–328. See also Literature, Jewish: Bildung, 34, 38, 48–61 passim, 64, 71
Culturverein, see Verein für Cultur und Wissenschaft der Juden
'C.V.-Zeitung', 226, 230
Czechoslovakia: emigration to, 273, 287

Daluege, Kurt (Nazi police chief), 254
Dannecker, Theodor (Eichmann's deputy), 251, 267
de Wette, Wilhelm Markus [Martin] Leberecht (orientalist, Protestant theologian), 4, 6, 7, 18, 24
'Deborah (Die Biene)' (Prague), 53
'[Die] Deborah' (US German-language journal, earlier 'Deborah'), 47, 48, 50–57, 58–72
Dehmel, Richard (poet, playwright), 217
Delmer, Sefton (journalist, propagandist), 347, 348
Demangeon, Albert (French geopolitician), 186, 187n
Democratic Socialist Club (Oxford), 346
Demography, 130, 132–133, 137–153
Derenbourg, Joseph (orientalist), 86n
Derrida, Jacques (literary philosopher), 83
Deutsch, William (founder of Western Hebrew College), 61
Deutsche Anthropologische Gesellschaft, 151
Deutsche Arbeitsfront, 252
Deutsche Fortschrittspartei, 150
'[Der] deutsche Jugendfreund', 53
'Deutsche Karpathenzeitung' (war newspaper), 218
Deutsche Verwaltung (German occupation authority, WWI), 157, 158–161, 165, 169, 170, 172
Deutsches Nachrichtenbüro (DNB), 259, 260
"Deutschtum", 319, 321, 322
Diaspora, 326, 329
DiCaprio, Lisa, 47n
Dickstein, Samuel (promoted investigation of Fascism), 292
"Dictionary of the Bible", 94
Dies, Martin (US Congressman), 292n
Dillen, J.G. van (Dutch historian), 345
Diner, Hasia, 47n, 48n, 55, 59
Dix, Otto (painter), 318, 341
Dohrn, Klaus (refugee in France), 309–310
Driver, Samuel Rolles (Hebraist), 83
Dubnow, Simon (historian), 324, 325, 327, 328, 330, 335–336
Durkheim, Emile (French sociologist), 83
'Dyhernfurther Priviligierte Zeitung', 52n

East Prussian Jewry, 148
Eastern European Jewry, 32, 34–35, 79, 198, 205, 221, 223, 229, 326, 333, 335. See also individual countries: expulsion from Germany, 152, 155: German reaction to (WWI) 162–164: immigration into Germany, 32, 129–130, 136–149, 151–152, 184: in USA, 50, 55: in WWI, 155–174
Eberhardt, Max (composer), 57
Ecuador: forced emigration to, 258
Education, Jewish: religious, 76, 78, 103–126: religious, in Germany, 103–126: religious, for girls, 108n: secular, 76–78, 340–341: statistics, 126n: in USA, 56–57, 59, 60–61, 64
Eger, Akiba (Akiwa, Akiva) (Halberstadt/Poznan rabbi), 118
Eichhorn, Johann Gottfried (historian, theologian), 4, 12, 13, 23
Eichmann, [Karl] Adolf (Nazi war criminal), 242, 251, 252, 253, 255–256, 257, 263, 266, 268: in Austria, 263–265: visit to Palestine, 260–261, 262
Einhorn, David (US leader of Jewish Reform, father-in-law of K. Kohler), 78
Einstein, Albert (physicist), 83
Eisen, Arnold, 25n
Elbogen, Ismar (historian, Judaist), 132
Elias, Norbert (sociologist), 345, 349
Eliasberg, Georg ("Org." member), 342, 343, 344
Eliezer ben Hyrcanus (1st/2nd-century rabbi), 86
Elkan, M. (educationalist), 121n
Elkin A. (of Philadelphia), 61
Ellenson, David, 73n
Emancipation, 82–83, 197, 317
Emergency Rescue Committee (ERC) (US body), 288–311 *passim*: clandestine rescue, 289–290, 297–303, 311
Emergency Visa Program (United States), 288, 290–291, 293, 294, 298, 305, 308, 309, 310–311
Emigration: to Britain, 226, 344–345, 346–349: forced, 241, 244, 247, 263, 264–265, 266–267, 271, 272, 273, 279, 280, 282, 283. See also Palestine (emigration): forced payment for, 267, 274, 275, 279–280, 284: to France, 287–311: from Nazi Germany, 241, 244, 246–247, 253, 258–267, 271–276, 277, 278–285, 344–346: Nazi attitudes, 241, 244, 246–247, 253, 258–263, 265, 271, 280–281: Reichsfluchtsteuer, 274: to Shanghai, 273–274, 276, 280–281, 283, 285: to USA, 50, 55, 141, 168, 265, 272, 277, 278, 280, 287–311, 327, 344. See also *other individual countries*
Emigration into Germany, 129–153: Eastern Europeans, 32, 129–130, 136–149, 151–152, 184: Grenzsperre, 155: statistics, 137, 141–143, 151–152. See also Demography
Encyclopaedia Biblica, 94
Endelman, Todd M., 326
Engels, Friedrich (Socialist theoretician), 343
Enlightenment, 3–24 *passim*, 103
Erler, Fritz (Socialist politician), 343
Ettinger, Shmuel (author), 325
Ettlinger, Jakob (rabbi, talmudist), 77
Evian Conference, 265, 272, 279, 287
Expressionism, 341

Fagan, Lena (helped refugees), 308
Fairgrieve, James (British geopolitician), 186, 187

General Index

Falk, Samuel (US rabbi), 56
Fassel, Hirsch Bär (Hungarian/Moravian rabbi), 73
Feuchtwanger, Edgar, 210n
Feuchtwanger, Lion (novelist), 225–226, 301
Feuchtwanger, Marta (wife of Lion F.), 301
Fiercks, A. Frhr. von, 143
Fimmen, Edo (of International Transport Workers' Federation), 345
Finke, Heinrich (Catholic historian), 319n
Finkelstein, Louis (US Jewish educationalist), 94
Fischach Jewish community: persecution, 247
Fischer, Aloys (racist writer), 182n
Fischer, K. (educational author), 108n
Fischer, Samuel (publisher), 217
Fittko, Hans (anti-Fascist), 300–301, 302
Fittko, Lisa (anti-Fascist), 300–301, 302
Flaischlen, Cäsar (dramatist), 217n
Fleischer, Heinrich Leberecht (orientalist), 84
Flesch, Reinhard (Gestapa-Referent), 254, 257
Flex, Walter (poet), 217n
Fontane, Theodor (novelist), 340
'Foreign Affairs' (US journal), 287
Foreign Policy Association, 295
Formstecher, Salomon (Offenbach rabbi, philosopher), 29n
Fraenkel, David (Dessau rabbi, co-founder 'Sulamith'), 50, 52
France: emigration to, 287–311: persecution in Vichy France, 290, 295–297, 300, 307: political dossiers, 244: Vichy regime, 287–311
Francolm, Isaac Ascher (novelist), 227
Frank, Hans (Nazi leader, Governor-General of Poland), 189
Frankel, Jonathan, 323–324
Frankel, Zacharias (rabbi, religious leader), 73, 74, 91
Frankfurt a.M. Jewish community: anti-Jewish riots, 263: Israelitische Religionsgesellschaft, 74: Philanthropin, 81, 112, 120n
Freemasons, 244, 245, 246, 251, 252
Freier, Bill (Willy Spira) (caricaturist, forger), 299
Freud, Sigmund (founder of psychoanalysis), 83, 320, 322
Freytag, Gustav (novelist), 340
Frick, Wilhelm (Nazi Interior Minister), 249
Friedländer, David (Berlin manufacturer, Jewish Reformer), 108
Friedmann, Wolfgang (jurist, in PWE), 348
Friedrich II (Frederick the Great, King of Prussia), 203, 215, 216
Friedrich Wilhelm I (King of Prussia), 349
Friedrich Wilhelm III (King of Prussia), 202
Fry, Eileen (wife of Varian F.), 307
Fry, Varian (refugee rescue worker), 289, 290, 294, 295, 297, 298–300, 302n, 303, 304, 307–308, 310, 311
Fuchs, Eugen (jurist, C.V. Chairman), 155n

Galician Jewry, 55, 136
Gallagher, Leo (brother-in-law of N. Block), 294
Gamaliel II of Yavneh (1st/2nd-century rabbi), 86
Gandhi, Mohandas Karamschand [Mahatma] (Indian statesman), 221
Garber, Marjorie, 235n
Gay, Peter, 229, 318
Geheimes Preußisches Staatsarchiv Berlin-Dahlem, 131
Geiger, Abraham (religious philosopher), 49, 76n, 77, 81, 84–85, 86n, 91, 94
Geiger, Ludwig (literary historian, editor), 199, 204, 209
Gemen (Westphalia) Jewish community: persecution, 247
Generalversammlung der Berliner Ärzte, 133
Gentz (of Deutsches Nachrichtenbüro), 260
'Geographische Zeitschrift', 182n
'Geopolitica', 186n
Geopolitics, 175–191: Arbeitsgemeinschaft für Geopolitik, 185, 190: individual geopoliticians and Jews, 177–188
George, Stefan (poet): Stefan George circle, 318
Gerard, James W. (US Ambassador, Berlin), 211
German Democratic Republic: archives, 243
German Jewry: citizenship, 103: communal tax, 41: community, 41–43: historiography, IX-X, 315–322, 323–336: honours, 196–197, 217: identity, 195–224, 229–230: military service, 204, 218, 276: patriotism, 16, 195–224, 340: political allegiances, 341–344: religious education, 103–126: rural, 48: symbiosis, see historiography
German language: in Jewish press, 51–53, 54, 56, 57, 58, 59; in sermons, 76
Germany: immigrants to, 129–153
Gesamtarchiv der deutschen Juden, 131
Gesellschaft für soziale Medizin, Hygiene und Medizinalstatistik, 135
Gesellschaft zur Förderung der Wissenschaft des Judentums, 95
Gestapa (Geheimes Staatspolizeiamt, Berlin), 245, 246–247, 249, 256, 257, 265
Gestapo (Geheime Staatspolizei), 273, 277, 279, 280–281, 282, 283, 305, 343, 344: and Sicherheitsdienst, 241–268 passim
Gesundheitspflegeverein des Berliner Bezirks der Arbeiterverbrüderung, 133
Gewerkskrankenverein, 133
Gilchrist, Sylvia, X
Gillis, John, 229
Ginzberg, Louis (talmudist), 92
Glanz, Rudolf (historian) 48n
Gluskinos, Willy (Jewish leader, Breslau), 281n
Goebbels, Joseph (Nazi leader), 246n, 263, 266
Göring, Hermann (Nazi leader), 266, 267, 274, 284

Goethe, Johann Wolfgang von (poet), 55, 203
Goldhagen, Daniel Jonah, 174n, 176
Goldman, Karla, 47n
[Die] Goldne Hundertzehn (clothing store), 340
Goldstein, Moritz (author, publishers' reader), 199, 201, 317
Gollwitzer, Heinz, 177n
'Good Housekeeping', 70
Gordon-Walker, Patrick (British Minister), 346
Goren, Arthur, 47n, 51n
Grabowsky, Adolf (geopolitician), 181n
Graetz, Heinrich (historian), 74, 135–137, 138, 145, 147, 325, 328, 330
Gratz, Rebecca (US Jewish author), 52
'[Die] Grenzboten', 152, 209
Grimm, Jacob Ludwig Karl (grammarian, philologist), 22, 321
Grimm, Wilhelm Karl (philologist, folklorist), 22, 321
Grodno: German occupation (WWI), 156
Grosz, George (Georg Ehrenfried) (satirical artist), 341
Groß-Breesen (Hachsharah training camp), 277
'[Der] Große Schauplatz', 52n
Gruchmann, Lothar (author), 190n
Grynberg, Anne, 299
Gürtner, Franz (Nazi Justice Minister), 249
Gundolf, Friedrich (literary historian), 318
Gurs concentration camp (France), 294, 304n
Gustloff, Wilhelm (Nazi politician), 260, 261

Haavara Agreement, 261n, 262
Haberman, Sinclair Curtis, 73n
Hacking, Ian, 130n
Haenisch, Konrad (Social Democratic politician), 206
Haganah, 259, 260–261
Hagen, Herbert (SD-Judenreferat head), 251–253, 257, 259, 263, 268: in Austria, 263–265: visit to Palestine, 260–262
Halifax, Edward Frederick Lindley Wood, first earl of (British statesman), 278
Halivni, David Weiss, 73n
'[Der] Hammer', 196n, 207
Hammerstein, Hans Frhr. von (general), 342
Hanover (rabbi, army chaplain), 165n
Harke, Hellmut, 183n
Hartshorne, Richard (American geographer), 188
'Haschiloah', 30n
Has[s]elbacher, Karl (head of Gestapa Jewish department), 254
Haskalah (Hebrew Enlightenment), 29, 83, 104, 108
Hastings (Biblical editor), 94
Hauptmann, Gerhart (dramatist, novelist), 217n
Haushofer, Karl (geopolitician), 177n, 179, 185, 190n

Haushofer, Martha (wife of Karl H.), 181n, 187n
Haushofer, Max (demographer, father of Karl H.), 183
Hebrew language, 83–84, 104, 107, 331
Hebrew Union College, 75, 80, 92, 95, 102
Hegel, Georg Wilhelm Friedrich (philosopher), Hegelianism, 8
Heidegger, Martin (philosopher), 318n, 319, 320n
Heim, Susanne, 174n
Heine, Heinrich, 21, 227
Heinemann, Isaac [Yishak] (author, religious philosopher), 81
Heinemann, Jeremias (educationalist), 53
Helbok, Adolf (racist writer)), 184n
Hennig, Richard (geopolitician), 179
Heppe, Theodor von (occupation administrator), 157n, 172
Herder, Johann Gottfried (philosopher), 4, 6, 7, 8, 10, 11, 12, 13, 15, 24
Herxheimer, Salomon (rabbi, teacher), 107n, 116, 124
Hess, Rudolf (Nazi leader), 179n, 181n
Hesse, Hermann (author), 318
Hettner, Alfred (geographer), 182n, 190n
Heydrich, Reinhard (Nazi leader), 241, 244, 245, 248, 249–250, 251, 254, 255, 256, 257, 260, 262, 264–265, 266
Heymann, Fritz (author), 226n
HICEM (HIAS/ICA Emigration Association), 297n
Hildesheimer Seminar, see Rabbinerseminar...
Hilferding, Rudolf (SPD politician), 302
Hilfsverein der deutschen Juden, 165, 168, 256, 277, 281
Hiller, Kurt (author, editor, pacifist), 226–227
Himmler, Heinrich (Nazi leader), 244, 245, 248, 253, 254, 266
Hinckeldey, Karl Ludwig Friedrich von (Police President of Berlin), 134
Hindenburg, Paul von Benneckendorff und von (fieldmarshal, German President), 156, 165, 196n
Hirsch, Emil (US Reform rabbi), 65
Hirsch, Otto (director of Reichsvertretung, lawyer), 277
Hirsch, Samson [ben] Raphael (rabbi, leader of Orthodoxy), 73–102, 104n, 113: linguistics, 83–84: and Reform, 76–82: and Wissenschaft des Judentums, 86–88, 90–91, 93n
Hirsch, Samuel (rabbi, religious philosopher), 29n
Hirschberg, Alfred (jurist, editor 'C.V.-Zeitung'), 230, 237
Hirschfeld (escapee from Vichy France), 302n
Hirschmann, Albert (Beamish, Albert Hermant) (political economist, worked for ERC), 301n
Historical Archive of Lithuania, 156n, 165n

Historiography, 315–322, 323–336: of antisemitism, 175–176: Gentile historians, 331–333: Historikerstreit, 332: and Israel, 331, 335: post-Holocaust, 328–330: revisionism, 316
Hitler, Adolf, 174, 179n, 189, 190, 227, 278, 342, 343, 347: and emigration, 262, 267: Jewish petition to, 277: and Jews, 322: "Mein Kampf", 241
Hitlerjugend (HJ), 247, 248, 249
Hobson, J. A. (British geopolitician, antisemite), 186
Hochschule für die Wissenschaft des Judentums, 134, 137
Hochstädter, Benjamin (Bad Ems rabbi), 105n, 106n, 116
Höcker, Oscar (author), 201
Hoffmann, Christhard, 316n, 331n
Hoffmann, David Zvi (Berlin rabbi), 81, 91
Hofmann (Breslau rabbi), 284
Hofmannsthal, Hugo von (poet, dramatist), 223n
Holdheim, Samuel (rabbi, leader of Reform), 105n, 112n, 121–122, 124n
Holländer, Ludwig (C.V. director, lawyer, publisher), 230
Homberg, Herz (educationalist), 108, 109n
'[The] Homemaker', 70
Homosexuality, 252
Horvitz, Rivka, 209
Horwitz, Hirsch (Chief Rabbi, Frankfurt a.M.), 112, 119, 120n
Hubbard, Evelyn, 73n
Hübner, Heinz-Werner, 190n
Hungarian Jewry, 48
Husserl, Edmund (phenomenologist, convert), 90n, 319n
Hyman, Joseph C. (of Joint), 281n
Hyman, Paula, 49, 232

Idel, Moshe, 3n
Identity, Jewish, 25–46, 134, 195–224, 227: German identity in USA, 48, 50, 54–59, 62, 64, 67, 71, 72: as nation, 76, 79–80: as religious community, 76, 78–80
Ilges, Walter (head of SD-Judenreferat), 246
Intergovernmental Committee for German Refugees (ICGR), 288n
Intermarriage, 249, 250
International Brigades, 345
International Catholic Help for Refugees (ICHR), 309
International Institute of Social History (Netherlands), 345
International Relief Association (IRA), 289n
International Rescue and Relief Committee (IRRC), 289n
International Transport Workers' Federation, 345

Internationaler Sozialistischer Kampfbund (ISK), 304n
Irving, David, 175n
Isenburg-Birstein, Fürst Franz Joseph (head of German occupation), 157, 159, 160, 168n, 172
Israel: and historiography, 331, 335
'[The] Israelite' *see* '[The] American Israelite'
'Isvestia'., 243

Jackson, Robert (US official), 293
Jacobi, Mary Putnam (physician), 69
Jacoby, Lucia (editor), 230n
Jaensch, Erich (Nazi philosopher), 320n
Jagendorf, Zvi, 319n
"Jahrbuch für Israeliten und Israelitinnen", 53
James, William (philosopher, psychologist), 95
Japan: and geopolitics, 176–177
Jellinek, Adolf (Chief Rabbi of Vienna), 22
Jenkins, Roy (British politician), 346
Jeremias, Alfred (orientalist), 79
'Jeschurun', 73, 74
Jewish Labor Committee, 288, 297
Jewish National and University Library, Jerusalem, 3
Jewish Theological Seminary (New York), 94
'Jewish Tribune' (US Jewish journal), 53n
Jochanan ben Sakai (1st-century rabbi), 86
Jochmann, Werner (historian), 250n
Johlson (Joelsohn), Josef (preacher, grammarian), 105n, 112, 119, 120n, 121, 124n
Johnson, Alvin (director of School for Social Research), 288n
'Jomsburg' (Nazi journal), 174
Joshua ben Hananiah (Chanaya) (1st/2nd-century rabbi), 86
Jost, Isaak Marcus (historian, editor), 124n
Judah (Jehuda) ha-Nasi (2nd-3rd century rabbi), 121
Judaism, 3–24: ceremonial wear, 76, 81, 99: choirs, 76: circumcision, 90: decorum, 76: dietary laws, 89, 90, 94, 99, 171, 339: Haggadah, 3–24: Halakhah, 13, 15, 17, 18, 20, 21, 115, 123–124: liturgy, 81: Midrash, 17, 18, 20–21, 22, 84: Mishnah, 42, 86: ritual, 110–115, 122: sermons, 3–24, 76: services under Nazi regime, 276, 284. *See also* Conservative, Liberal, Reform, Orthodox Judaism, Leopold Zunz
Judenzählung, 155
Jüdisch-Theologisches Seminar (Breslau), 73, 74
'Jüdische Rundschau', 226, 230
Jüdische Zeitschrift für Wissenschaft und Leben, 85
Jüdisches Comité vom 1. Dezember 1880, 135
Jünger, Ernst (author), 318n
Jung, Carl Gustav (psychologist), 320

Kabbalah, Jewish mysticism, 22
Kafka, Franz (Czech novelist), 230n

Kakies, Walter (would-be US immigrant), 309
Kallen, Horace M. (philosopher), 102n
Kampe, Norbert, 175
Kant, Immanuel (philosopher), 181, 182, 320
Kantorowicz, Ernst H. (historian)), 318
Kaplan, Marion, 47n
Kaplan, Simon, 39n
Karbe, Karl-Heinz, 131
Karpeles, Gustav (literary historian), 76
Katz, Jacob (historian), 317
Keller, Robert (refugee in France), 306
Kestner, Hans Schmidt (poet), 209
Kielmy Jewish community, 166: German occupation (WWI), 163
Kingdon, Frank (chairman of ERC), 304
Kirchner, Ernst Ludwig (painter, graphic artist), 318
Kiron, Arthur, 47n
Kjellen, Rudolf (geopolitician), 185, 188
Klausner, Joseph (Hebraist, historian), 86n
Kleeberg, Minna (feminist), 63
Klein, Dennis B., 229
Kleist, Heinrich von (poet, dramatist, novelist), 207
Klemperer, Victor (philologist)), 207n, 211–212
Knoeringen, Waldemar von (initiated Wilton Park POW camp), 348
Koellreutter, Otto (jurist), 189n
Königlich Preußisches Statistisches Bureau, 139, 143, 148
Koeppler, Heinz (ran Wilton Park POW camp), 348
Kohl, Louis von (geopolitician), 183n, 185n
Kohler, Kaufmann (rabbi, theologian in USA), 73–102; and Christianity, 92, 94, 95–96, 99, 100–101: and Orthodoxy, 75, 76, 92, 94
Komitee für den Osten, 157, 165
Kommunistische Partei Deutschlands (KPD), 243, 245, 341, 342, 343, 344, 345, 346
Kommunistischer Jugendverband Deutschlands (KJVD), 341
Korinman, Michel, 177n
Kovno (Kaunas): German occupation (WWI), 156
'Kownoer Zeitung', 161
Krause (of Interior Ministry), 254
Kravitz, Leonard S., 73n
Kriszhaber, Harry (trade unionist) and Maria, 296, 304
Krockow, Christian Graf von, 177n
Krutch, Joseph Wood (literary critic), 93
Küng, Hans, 82
Kuhn, Thomas Samuel, 82–83n
Kulturbund Deutscher Gelehrter und Künstler, 210n
Kulturbund deutscher Juden, 226, 282
Kundt-Kommission, 296
'[Der] Kunstwart', 199, 201
Kupischki Jewish community, 170

Kurland: German occupation (WWI), 157, 158
Kuttner, Erich (Socialist journalist), 345

Labour Club (Oxford), 346
Lachmann family, 340
'[The] Ladies' Home Journal', 70
Landauer, Gustav (anti-Marxist Socialist), 22, 209
Landesarchiv Berlin, 131
Landsberger, Franz (art historian), 231
Langmaid, Janet, X
Laqueur, Walter, 318, 319
Laurence, Frank, 103n
Lazarsfeld, Sofie (writer), 297
Lazarus, Moritz (philosopher), 85n, 135, 137–138, 145, 147
Le Vernet concentration camp (France), 293
League of Nations, 293n, 298: minorities protection, 255
Leeuw, G. van der, 79n
Lehmann, Emil (Dresden jurist), 54
Lehmann, Marcus (author), 227
Leimdörfer, David (Hamburg preacher), 124n
Leipzig Jewish community, 85n: Eastern European immigration, 147
Lenders, Lutz (Nazi propagandist), 229–230, 236
Lenin, Vladimir Ilyich (Soviet statesman), 343
Leo Baeck Institute: Archive, 131: bibliography, X: Jerusalem, 3n, 219: New York, 3n: Year Books, IX-X, 315, 332
Leopold [Maximilian Joseph Maria Arnulf Leopold], Prinz von Bayern (Prussian field-marshal), 165
Les Milles concentration camp (France), 295
Lessing, Gotthold Ephraim (poet, dramatist), 11
Leubuscher, Rudolf (physician, Liberal), 132, 133
Levi (rabbi, army chaplain), 165n
Levy, Barry (Orthodox rabbi), 84
Lewerenz, Lilli, 155n
Lewis, Clive Staples (author, Christian apologist), 97
Libau (Liepaja), Latvia: German occupation (WWI), 156
Liberal Judaism, 85, 321, 323, 325–328. *See also* Culture (Jewish)
Lichtenberger, Hermann, 3n
Lichtheim, George (writer), 349
Lieberkühn, Philip Julius (educational author), 108n
Liebermann family, 340
Liebermann, Felix (legal historian, brother of Max L.), 135
Liebermann, Max (artist), 135
Liebeschütz, Hans (medievalist, philosopher), 130n
Lilienthal, Max (US rabbi, editor), 51, 57, 60

Lindner, Erik, 196n
Lindner, Petra, 103n
Lissauer, Ernst (poet), 195–224: and Eastern Jewry, 198, 205, 221, 223: opposition to "Haßgesang", 207–210, 211–212, 218, 219: and Prussia, 198, 201–203, 205, 222: and racism, 201–202
Lister, Enrique (Spanish republican general), 301n
Literature, Jewish, 35–39, 195–224, 225–237: historical novels, 225–237: rabbinic literature, 4, 17–20, 35, 94: religious schoolbooks, 103–126: Sephardic themes, 226, 227–228
Lithuania: and refugees, 299
Lithuania, German occupation (WWI): Germanisation, 158–160: deportations, 171: forced labour, 169–171: resistance, 161–162, 169–170, 173
Lithuanian Academy of Science, 156n
Lithuanian Jewry, 55: emigration, 168: German occupation policy (WWI), 155–174: Russian policy (WWI), 160, 164, 165: statistics, 166
Lösener, Bernhard (civil servant), 250n
Loew, Rosalie (lawyer), 70
Loewe, Heinz-Dietrich, 331
Löwenheim, Walter (Kurt) ("Org." [later "Neu Beginnen"] leader), 342, 343
Löwenthal, Charlotte (wife of Richard L.), 341
Löwenthal, Richard (political scientist), 341, 342, 344
Long, Breckinridge (US Under-Secretary of State, antisemite), 292, 293, 294
Lowrie, Donald (president, Nîmes Committee), 300
Lowy, Adolf (New York rabbi), 61
Ludendorff, Erich (WWI general, nationalist politician), 156, 172, 174
Lussu (associate of M. Ascoli), 303
Luther, Martin (religious reformer), 203, 214

McCarthy, Mary (author), 310n
Macintyre, Alasdair, 25–26n
Mackinder, Halford (British geographer), 177, 185, 186, 187
Maclean, Pamela, 163n
Madagascar: forced emigration to, 184, 258
'Madame', 68
Magdeburg: anti-Jewish riots, 263
Mahan, Alfred Thayer (US geopolitician), 177
Maier, Joseph (Chief Rabbi, Württemberg), 105n, 109–110, 120, 124n
Maimonides, Moses [Rambam] (medieval codifier, philosopher), 31, 108, 114, 281
Mann, Erika (writer, daughter of Thomas M.), 288n
Mann, Golo (author), 216
Mann, Heinrich (novelist), 213, 289
Mann, Thomas (novelist, essayist), 198, 213, 216, 288n

Mannhardt, Johann Wilhelm (geopolitician), 178n
Mannheimer, Jenny (feminist), 65, 66
Mannheimer, Louise (feminist), 65n, 66
Marcu, Valeriu (historian), 226
Marrus, Michael R., 175n
Marshall, Louis (US Jewish politician), 99n
Marsland, Elizabeth, 212
Marthold, Jules de (French writer), 212
Martonne, Emanual de (geopolitician), 186n, 187n
Marx, Karl Heinrich (philosopher, political economist), 181
Massi, Ernesto (Italian geopolitician), 186n
Matuschka, Graf (German occupation official), 159, 163, 166
Maull, Otto (geopolitician), 179–180
Maximova, E., 243
Mayer, ?Nathan (US author), 58
Meckauer, Walter (writer, editor), 309
'Medicinische Reform', 133, 149
Medieval Jewry, 31, 35
Mehring, Walter (author, Dadaist), 305
Melville, Lewis (author), 212
Memorial Foundation for Jewish Culture, 3n
Mendelssohn, Moses (philosopher), 11–12, 59, 121, 123
'[Il] Messagero', 211
Messer, Ellen, 98n
Meyer (Breslau deputy), 146
Meyer, Michael A., 3n, 48n, 330n, 331n
Mildenstein, Leopold Itz Edler von (journalist, head of SD-Judenreferat), 246, 251
Miller, Arthur (playwright), 310n
Miller, Philip, 47n
Mingst, K. A., 177n
Moch, Julia (feminist), 69
Modernism, 318–319
Moïse, Penina (US Jewish author), 52
Mommsen, Hans, 269
Mommsen, Theodor (historian, jurist), 130, 145–146, 147
'Monatsschrift für Geschichte und Wissenschaft des Judent[h]ums', 27, 60
Moore, George Foot (theologian), 99
Moravian Jewry, 55
Moses, Adolph (Louisville rabbi), 65–66
Moses, Siegfried (international president of LBI), 277
Mosse, George L., 182n, 191
Mosse, Werner E., 200
Moyn, Samuel, 321
Mühlen, Patrik von zur, 299
Mühlestein, Hans (geopolitician), 182n

Nadel, Stanley, 47n, 48n
Napoleonic era, 201–203, 321
Nathan, Isaac S. (editor), 53n

National Council of Jewish Women (in USA) (NCJW), 65, 66, 68
'National-Zeitung', 145
Nationalism, German, 195–224
Nationalsozialistische Deutsche Arbeiterpartei, 242, 250, 251: Rassenpolitisches Amt, 254
Naturalisation, 152
Naumann, Friedrich (Liberal politician, theologian), 213
Nazi regime: Machtergreifung, 245, 343: police, 245: resistance, 293, 343–344, 345
Nazi regime, Jews under, 221–222, 225–237, 241–269, 271–285, 340, 343–344: antisemitic policies, 225, 241–269: census (proposed), 254: citizenship, 298n: control of anti-Jewish activity, 248–250: honours, 196–197: literary parallels, 226–227: Nazis and emigration, 258–263, 265, 280–281: public opinion, 248–249, 251
"Neu Beginnen", 343–344, 345
Neubach, Helmut, 152–153
Neue Reichsvertretung der Deutschen Juden, 277
Neumann family, 131
Neumann, Friedrich Julius (political economist), 148
Neumann, Heinz (Communist politician), 342
Neumann, Salomon (physician, statistician), 129–153
Neurath, Konstantin Frhr. von (German Foreign Minister), 261
'[The] New York Evening Post', 212
'[The] New York Times', 212, 301
'New York World', 67
Niedermayer, Oskar von (Soviet geopolitician), 186n
Nîmes Committee (relief organisations alliance), 299–300
Noakes, Jeremy, 175n
Nolde, Emil (painter), 318
Norling, Bernard, 175n
November Pogrom, 265–266, 267, 278, 280: attempt to avert, 278
Nuremberg Laws, 250

Oath "more judaico", 132
Oberbefehlshaber Ost (OberOst) (German military occupation authority, WWI), 156–158, 160, 165, 172, 174: Dezernat für Jüdische Angelegenheiten, 157
Obst, Erich (geopolitician), 178n
Ogilvie-Forbes, [Sir] George (British diplomatic adviser), 278
Oko, Adolph S. (librarian), 102
Olden, Rudolf (writer, editor), 346–347
Olita Jewish community, 173
Oppenheim family, 131
Oranienburg concentration camp, 277, 279
Oren, Susan, 47n

"Org" (secret revolutionary group, later "Neu Beginnen"), 342–343, 344
Orthodoxy, Jewish, 5n, 75, 77–78, 92, 321: in Eastern Europe, 79: Neo-Orthodoxy, 74, 75, 113: and religious education, 104n, 106–107, 108n, 109, 112–114, 116–120 *passim*, 123–126
OSE (Oeuvre de Secours aux Enfants), 299n
Osobyi Archive, 242–244
Ossietzky, Carl von (pacifist, editor), 318
'Ost und West', 209, 229
Otto, Franz (author), 201
Otto, Kerstin, 47n

Pacifists, 246
Palestine: Arabs, 260, 262: British Mandate, 258, 261, 262: emigration to, 258–262, 265, 273, 280, 282n: partition, 262
Paphnutius (pseudonym), 209
Passant, J. (writer), 348
Patriotism, Jewish, 57, 80–81: US Jewry, 57
Paucker, Arnold, X, 197n
Peck, Abraham, 47n
Peel Commission, 262
Perkins, Frances (US Labor Secretary), 293
Persecution in Third Reich, 241–269. *See also* Emigration (forced, France, Nazi regime (Jews under), November Pogrom: in 1935, 247–248: in summer 1938, 263: banning of services, 276: deportation, 267–268, 277, 278–279, 282: dismissals, 245, 253, 255–256, 343: economic persecution, 262–263, 267, 271, 274–275, 277, 279–280, 283–284: exclusion, 276, 277: forced labour, 267: Reichsfluchtsteuer, 274, 283–284: rescue attempts, 287–311: seizure of precious metals, etc., 274–275, 284
Pétain, Philippe (French field-marshal, head of Vichy Government), 288, 296
Petuchowski, Jacob J. (theologian), 104n
Peukert, Detlev J. K. (historian), 183
Pfeil, Elisabeth (geopolitician), 181n
Philippson, Ludwig (editor 'Allgemeine Zeitung des Judenthums'), 122, 124n, 227, 228, 231, 232, 234, 235, 236
Philippson, Phöbus (physician, author), 227
Philo Verlag, 230–231
Picard, Jakob (Jewish author), 230n
Pioneer Corps, 347
Piscator, Erwin (theatre and film director), 318
Plaut, Max (Jewish leader, Hamburg), 281, 282
Plessner, Salomon (Orthodox teacher, rabbi), 104n, 107, 113, 115, 118, 123, 125n
Ploetz, Alfred (racist author), 182
Plotho, von (German official), 343
Poland: and refugees, 298
Polish Jewry, 32–33, 34n, 55, 129, 136, 144–145: emigration to Shanghai, 280: in World War I, 155, 162n
Political Warfare Executive (PWE), 347–348

General Index

Polkes, Feivel [Feibl Folkes] (of Haganah), 259–261
Postan, Michael (economic historian), 347
Powicke, Maurice (historian),
Poznan Jewry, 48, 141, 142, 147, 148–149
Presber, Rudolf (author), 217n
President's Advisory Committee on Political Refugees (PACPR), 287–288, 289n, 294, 308, 309
Press, Jewish: in Germany, 52: in USA, 47–72
'Preußische Jahrbücher', 129, 130, 135, 136, 146, 147, 148
'Preußische Statistik', 143, 144, 149
Pridham, Geoffrey, 175n
Pringle, Annette, X
Prisoners of war: German, 348
Prussia: immigration to, 137, 141–143: Staatspolizei/Gestapo, 245: territorial acquisitions, 137, 139
Prussian Jewry: Emancipation, 132, 202, 204
Pulzer, Peter, 175n, 195n

Quatrefages de Bréau, Armand de (anthropologist), 150

Rabbinerseminar für das Orthodoxe Judentum, 91
Rabbinical Conferences, 50, 51
Racism, 178–183, 186–189, 201–202: stereotypes, 159–160. *See also* Antisemitism
Rahaman, Gabriele, X, 195n, 241n
Rahden, Till van, 229
Rang, Florenz Christian (author), 319n
Rapoport, Solomon Judah Leib [Salomon Jehudah, Shlomo Yehudah Löb], (rabbi, scholar), 16, 18–19, 20
"Rassenschande", 249, 250
Rath, Ernst vom (German diplomat), 278, 284
Rathjens, Karl (geographer), 178
Ratzel, Friedrich (journalist, German geopolitician), 177, 181, 182, 183, 184n, 185, 187
'Rebecka' (US Jewish journal), 53n
'Rebekka' (US Jewish journal), 53n
Rechter, David, 195n
Reform Judaism, 74, 75–82, 95, 98, 99, 101: Berliner Reformgemeinde, 121–122: and religious education, 109–126: in USA, 47–72, 327, 328, 334. *See also* K. Kohler, I.M. Wise: and women, 49–50, 52–53, 64, 65. *See also* I.M. Wise
Reichert, Franz (of Deutsches Nachrichtenbüro, Jerusalem), 259, 260, 261
Reichmann-[Jungmann], Eva G. (sociologist, historian), IX, 175n
Reichsbund jüdischer Frontsoldaten (RjF), 246, 277
Reichsfluchtsteuer, 274
Reichssicherheitshauptamt (RSHA), 131, 242–243, 244, 261, 267, 281, 307

Reichsstelle für Sippenforschung, 254
Reichsvereinigung der Juden in Deutschland, 135, 276, 279, 281–282, 306n
Reichsvertretung der Juden in Deutschland (der deutschen Juden), 256, 276, 277, 278. *See also* Neue Reichsvertretung
Rein, Mark (German Socialist), 345
Renan, Ernest (French historian), 93–94n
Resnick, Henry. 73n
Revolution: of 1848, 132
Rheinland Jewry, 142
Riedel (legal commentator), 345
Riesser, Gabriel (Liberal politician, judge, editor), 230
Rinderle, Walter, 175n
Ritschl, Albert (Christian theologian), 96
Rödelheim, Eleaser Susman (author), 108n
Rodellec du Porzic (head of Marseilles police), 307
Roeder, Frhr. von (German general), 170n
Roeseler, Hans (geopolitician), 184n
Roletto, Giorgio (Italian geopolitician), 186n
Romanticism, 5, 6, 7, 8–9, 14–15, 17, 19, 20–21, 23–24: Christian Romanticism, 4, 13
Römer, Nils, 47n
Roosevelt, Eleanor (wife of Franklin D.R.), 293n, 296, 307, 308
Roosevelt, Franklin Delano (US President), 265, 287, 288n, 293, 305, 308
Rose, Ernestine (feminist), 68
Rose, Paul Lawrence, 175
Rosenack (rabbi, army chaplain), 165n
Rosenberg, A. (? of Cincinnati), 57
Rosenberg, Alfred (Nazi ideologue), 262
Rosenbloom, Noah H., 76
Rosenfeld, Gavriel, 229
Rosenzweig, Franz (philosopher, translator), 229, 230, 318n, 322
Rosoff, Joann Abrams, 73n
Rossienie: German occupation (WWI), 159, 170n: Jewish community, 167
Rössler, Mechthild, 183n
Roth, Cecil (historian), 226n
Royce, Josiah (philosopher), 95
Rummel, Joseph F. (Archbishop, New Orleans), 287n
Rürup, Reinhard, 250n, 331n
Russian Jewry: emigration, 55, 136, 141, 143, 147, 152: geopolitical view, 180

Sachs, Michael (Berlin rabbi, scholar), 21, 22
Safrian, Hans, 242n
Saldogischki Jewish community, 171
Salomon-Neumann-Stiftung zur Pflege der Wissenschaft des Judentums, 131, 135
Samuel, Richard (of PWE), 348
Santayana, George (philosopher), 95
Sapir, Boris (of International Institute of Social History), 346

Sarner, Ferdinand (editor), 53n
Sartor, Lutz, 199n
Savigny, Friedrich Carl von (jurist, Prussian minister), 5–6, 15, 22
Savonarola (radical preacher), 203n
Schacht, Hjalmar Horace Greeley (Reichsbank president), 249, 340
Schadow Jewish community, 171
Schaulen (Schavli): German occupation (WWI), 156
Schechter, Solomon (religious philosopher), 94, 99
Schellenberg, Walter (of Sicherheitsdienst), 260
Schepers, Hans-Julius (geopolitician), 178n, 183n
Scherr, Johannes (author), 181n
Schiff, Jacob Henry (banker, philanthropist), 75
Schiller, Friedrich von (poet, dramatist), 55, 57, 58, 78, 203, 232
'Schlesische Presse', 136
Schleswig-Holstein Jewry, 142
Schleunes. Karl, 175n
Schmitt, Carl (jurist), 189n, 320
Scholem, Gershom (philosopher, authority on Jewish mysticism), 22, 87n, 318n
Schorr, Joshua Heschel (scholar, talmudist), 86n
Schorsch, Ismar, 3n, 86n, 227–228
Schröder, Kurt (SD-Judenreferat head), 251
Schröder, Rudolf Alexander (poet), 200, 214, 217
'[Der] Schulkampf', 341
Schutzstaffel (SS), 251. *See also* Sicherheitsdienst
Schwartz, Daniel, 3n
Schwartz, Shuly Rubin, 94
Schwarz, Israel (headmaster), 105n, 113–114, 118–119, 125n
Schwoerer, Viktor (Baden official), 320n
Seeckt, Hans von (German general), 218
Seeligman, Sigmund (historian), 226n, 236
Seghers, Anna, 291n
Seligsohn, Julius (jurist, of Reichsvereinigung), 276–285
Semjonow, Juri (Soviet geopolitician), 186n
Seraphim, Peter-Heinz (antisemitic writer), 184n
Seton-Watson, Robert William (historian), 347
Sforim, Mendele Mokher (author), 234
Shanghai: emigration to, 273–274, 276, 280–281, 283, 285
Sheppard, Eugene, 318n
Sicherheitsdienst (SD), 135, 241–269: compilation of data, 253–254, 257, 269: Judenreferat (Unterabteilung IV/2, Abteilung II 112), 242, 244, 246–247, 248–249, 251–252, 258, 259, 267: organisation of, 244–246, 251–253, 257: and Zionism, 246–247, 251, 259, 260–261
Silberstein, S. (author), 204
Silesian Jewry, 142, 147
Simion, Leonhard (publisher), 138

Simon, Ernst Akiba (educationalist), 219
'Simplicissimus', 226
Singer, Paul (Socialist politician), 134
Sinsheimer, Hermann (editor, theatre critic, writer), 225–237
Six, Franz Alfred (jurist, SS officer), 189, 253, 254, 255, 256, 257, 260
Skaudwile: German occupation (WWI), 159, 172: Jewish community, 167
Smith, Woodruff D., 177n
Sondheimer, H. (educational author), 105n, 108n
Sonneschein, Rose (feminist), 69n
Sonneschein, Solomon Hirsch (US rabbi, editor), 51, 53n, 69n
Sorkin, David, 48, 229, 316, 316, 327
South Africa: emigration to, 274, 281
Sozialdemokratische Partei Deutschlands (SPD), 243, 245, 341, 342, 343, 344, 345, 346
Sozialdemokratische Partei Deutschlands im Exil (Sopade), 343, 344, 345
Sozialistische Arbeiterjugend (SAJ), 343
Sozialistische Arbeiterpartei Deutschlands (SAP), 343
Sozialistischer Schülerbund (Socialist Pupils' League), 341
Spain: civil war, 345: and refugees, 296, 298, 300–303, 306, 307, 309
Spengler, Oswald (philosopher), 318n
Spielmann, Diane, 195n
Spielrein, Sabina (psychologists' patient), 320
Spykman, Nicholas John (geopolitician), 186, 187n
SS, *see* Schutzstaffel
Ständige Konferenz der Kultusminister der Länder in der BRD, X
Stahlecker, Walter (SD chief for Austria), 264
'Standarte', 178n
Statistics, *see* Demography, S. Neumann
Statistik der kontrollierten Wanderung, 139, 141, 142
Statistisches Bureau der Stadt Berlin, 133, 134n, 141
Statistisches Jahrbuch der Stadt Berlin, 134, 138
Statistisches Reichsamt, 179n, 254
Stein, Anna (witness for possible US immigrants), 309
Stein, Leopold (Chief Rabbi, Frankfurt a.M.), 105n, 116, 124n
Steinheim, Ludwig Salomon (religious philosopher, physician), 29n
Steinschneider, Moritz (M.S. Charbonah) (bibliographer, orientalist), 73–74, 88
Steinthal, Eduard (correspondent Hermann Cohen), 73n
Steinthal, Heymann [Hermann Chaim] (philologist), 85
Stern, Fritz, 131

Stern, Ludwig (headmaster), 105n, 112n, 113, 125n
Sternberg, Karel (refugee relief worker), 304n
Stettin Jewish community: persecution, 247
Stoecker, Adolf (antisemite, Court Chaplain, Berlin), 136, 145, 150
Stoll, Jakob (educational author), 107n
Stolp Jewish community, 152
Straßmann, Wolfgang (Chairman, Berlin city council), 145
Strauss, David Friedrich (Christian theologian), 96
Strauss, Herbert A., 290n, 292n
Strauss, Leo (philosopher), 318, 320
Streicher, Julius (Gauleiter of Franconia), 247
Struck, Hermann (graphic artist), 157
Stuckart, Wilhelm (state secretary, Interior Ministry), 254
Stupperich, Robert (Nazi author, later professor), 174
Sturm-Abteilung (SA), 245, 247, 249: "Röhm-Putsch", 245
'[Der] Stürmer', 244, 247, 248
Suchy, Barbara, X, 211
'Sulamith' (German-language Jewish journal, Dessau)), 50, 52
'Sulamith' (US German-language Jewish journal, St. Louis), 53n
Supan, Alexander (geography text-book writer), 178n
Suwalki-Vilna (WWI), 171
Switzerland: deportation to, 264n
Sybel, Heinrich (historian), 339
Syrkin, Nachman (Zionist author), 73n
Szajkowski, Zosa (historian), 155n

Tafel (German occupation official), 170
Takeuchi, Keiichi, 177n
Taylor, Alan John Percivale (historian), 348
Tec, Nechama, 155n, 290n
Thelen, Albert Vigoleis (Dutch poet), 231n
Thomas à Kempis [Hamerkin] (theologian), 93
Thomas, Edmund, 195n
Thompson, Dorothy (US writer), 287, 288n, 293n
Tiefenbrunner, Salomon (teacher), 106n
'Tijdschrift voor Geschiedenis', 345
Tiktin, Solomon (leader of Jewish Orthodoxy), 77
Tirpitz, Alfred von (German admiral), 177n
Toury, Jacob, 279
Treitschke, Heinrich von (historian), 129–130, 135–138, 144–148, 152–153
Trotsky, Leo (Russian revolutionary leader), 342
Tutenberg, Dr., 196n
Tyjn, Frau (of Amsterdam, ?Gertrude van Tijn), 274

Ulbricht, Walter (Communist leader), 345
United States Holocaust Memorial Museum, 289
United States of America: Alien Registration Law, 293, 305: Bloom-Van Nuys Bill, 305: emigration to, 50, 55, 141, 168, 265, 272, 278, 287–311, 327, 344: "hostage (close relatives) instruction", 305–307, 308, 309: Immigration and Naturalisation Service, 293: Interdepartmental Visa Review Committee (IVRC) (Interdepartmental Advisory Cttee), 294, 308: quota, 277, 280, 291, 294: refugees and politics, 290–294, 305, 309, 310: Special Committee to Investigate Un-American Activities, 292: Wagner-Rogers Bill, 310n: xenophobia, 291–293, 294, 310
United States of America, Jewry: education, 56–57, 59, 60–61, 64: East Europeans in, 50, 55: German Jews in, 47–64, 334, 335; See also K. Kohler: German identity, 48, 50, 54–59, 62, 64, 67, 71, 72: patriotism, 57: use of German language, 51–53, 54, 56, 57, 58, 59: press, 47–72: Turnvereine, 56, 58: women, 47–72 passim: Yiddish, 59

Verein für Cultur und Wissenschaft der Juden, 8, 17, 20
Verein für jüdische Geschichte und Literatur, 76
Verein für jüdische Statistik, 153
Verein zur Abwehr des Antisemitismus, 197, 211: 'Mitteilungen', 196n
Verzeanu, Maurice (refugee relief worker), 301, 302, 308
Vesper, Will (poet), 209
Victor, Walther (journalist, author), 297
Vidal de la Blache, Paul (French geopolitician), 186, 187n
Vilna: German occupation (WWI), 161, 171, 172
Virchow, Rudolf (pathologist, politician), 129, 132, 133, 134, 146, 149–151
Vitringa, Campegius (Dutch Hebraist), 18
Vochoc, Vladimir (Czech diplomat), 298
Vogel, Walther (geopolitician), 179, 181n
'Voice of Israel' (US Jewish journal), 53n
Völkisch ideas, 184, 189, 199, 320
'Völkischer Beobachter', 229
Volkov, Shulamit, 136, 229, 315, 321n, 323, 324, 325, 327, 328
Vortriede, Käthe (refugee in France), 306
'Vorwärts', 345
'Vossische Zeitung', 146
Vowinckel, Kurt (writer), 181n

Wagner, Adolf (political economist), 146, 147, 148, 153
Wagner, Paul (geography text-book writer), 178n

Wagner, Robert F. (US Senator, jurist), 309–310n
War Crimes Trials, 267, 268: Nuremberg, 243
Warren, Avra (US official), 310
Wassermann, Jakob (novelist), 321
Wassermann, Moses (novelist), 227
Wechsler, I. (of Portland, Oregon), 60–61
Weigert, Hans W. (author), 185
Weil, Jacob (educationalist), 9, 10, 21
Weimar Republic: Depression, 341–342; Jews in, 318–319, 340–343
Weinberg, Yeshayahu, 289
Weinrich, Otto (would-be US immigrant), 309
Weiss, R., 177n
Welles, Sumner (US diplomat), 296
Wessely, Hartwig [Naphtali Herz Weisel] (Hebrew author), 108
Wessely, Naphtali, see Wessely, Hartwig,
Whitehead, Alfred North (philosopher), 102
Whittlesey, Derwent (geopolitician), 186, 187n
Wiener, Max (historian, rabbi), 84n
Wiezajcie Jewish community, 171
Wilhelm II (German Emperor), 196, 202
Wilhelm, Kurt (Chief Rabbi of Stockholm), 81
Williams, Philip (British Socialist), 346
Willstätter, Elias (educationalist), 121n
Wilson, Duncan (British diplomat), 347
Wilton Park (camp for anti-Nazi POWs), 348
Winter (rabbi, army chaplain), 165n
Wippermann, Wolfgang, 183n
Wise, Isaac Mayer (rabbi, leader of US Reform Judaism), 47–72
Wisliceny, Dieter (SD-Judenreferat head), 251, 252–253, 254, 257, 259, 261, 267
Wissenschaft des Judentums, 3–4, 22, 28–32, 33–34, 46, 56, 86–88, 90–91, 93n, 95: Gesellschaft zur Förderung der Wissenschaft des Judentums, 95: 'Monatsschrift für Geschichte und Wissenschaft des Judent[h]ums', 27, 60
Wohlgemuth, Joseph (talmudist, religious philosopher), 210
Wolf, Abraham (talmudic scholar), 91n
Wolf, Joseph (preacher, co-founder 'Sulamith'), 52
Wolfenbüttel: Samsonsche Freischule, 3n
Wolfskehl, Karl (poet), 318
'Woman's Citizen', 70
'Woman's Journal', 70
'Women's Home Companion', 70
Women, Jewish: education, 60, 64, 67–68, 69, 70, 71, 72: emancipation, 63, 65, 66, 71, 72: "New Woman", 64–72: in USA, 47–72 *passim*
World War I: German occupation (Eastern Europe), 155–174: Jews in, 79, 81. 155–174, 195–224, 276: propaganda, 195–224; resistance to German occupation, 161–162, 170, 173
World War II: British propaganda, 347: German POWs, 348
Württemberg, Herzog von (chairman, ICHR), 309

Yerushalmi, Yosef H., 225n, 226
Yiddish, 59, 162–164
Yorck von Wartenburg, Johan David Ludewig, Graf (Prussian fieldmarshal), 203n
Young Men's Christian Association, 300
Youth organisations, Jewish, 246

Zechlin, Egmont (historian), 200, 211, 222n
'Zeitschrift für die gesammte Staatswissenschaft', 147
'Zeitschrift für die Wissenschaft des Judentums', 17
'Zeitschrift für Geopolitik', 179, 183–184
'Zeitschrift für Sozialismus', 344
'Zeitung der 10. Armee', 163
Zentralausschuß der deutschen Juden für Hilfe und Aufbau, 277
Zentrale Stelle der Landesjustizverwaltung zur Aufklärung von NS-Verbrechen, Ludwigsburg, 243
Zentralstelle für jüdische Auswanderung, 264–265, 266, 268
Zimmermann, Moshe, 331, 332
Zinner, Alfons (refugee in France), 306
Zionism, 79, 226, 227, 237, 251, 259, 260–261, 321, 323, 326, 327, 328, 329, 333
Zionistische Vereinigung für Deutschland (ZVfD), 229, 256, 277
Zionistisches Zentralbüro, 156n
Zuckermann, Hugo (singer, composer), 212
Zunz, Adelheid (wife of Leopold Z.), 4n
Zunz, Leopold (scholar, headmaster), 3–24, 88, 134. *See also* Christianity: Jewish nationality, 13–16, 29–21: and Moses, 8–11: and prophecy, 6–21: sermons, 3–4, 5, 6–24: Zunz-Stiftung, 134
Zweig, Arnold (novelist), 160n
Zweig, Stefan (author), 198, 201n, 211

Pauline Paucker
NEW BORDERS
The Working Life of Elizabeth Friedlander

Elizabeth Friedlander (1903–84) was one of the many German-Jewish graphic artists who made a striking contribution to British printing and publishing.

This monograph, lavishly illustrated from her own archive, records her career as a graphic designer and typographer in Germany, Italy, England & Ireland, setting her life and work in the context of exile. The illustrations range from calligraphy for *Die Dame,* Berlin, in the 'thirties, to designs for Kinsale Crafts in Ireland in the 'seventies; from Mondadori book work in Italy to designs for the Curwen Press and Penguin Books in England. And prints from the wood engravings made for these border ornaments issued by *Monotype*.

Issued in an edition of 350 copies signed by the author; slip-cased, 13 x 8 inches; 48 pages of text and 32 of illustrations, on *Zerkall* paper and in *Bembo* types. Priced £105 ($192), carriage paid from:

INCLINE PRESS
11 A Printer Street Oldham OL1 1PN
England

JSQ: A Journal on All Aspects of Jewish History and Culture

Jewish Studies Quarterly *JSQ*
Edited by Joseph Dan and Peter Schäfer

■ **Jewish Studies in the broadest possible terms** Jewish Studies Quarterly includes studies dedicated to all aspects of Jewish history and culture. Focusing on the whole spectrum of Jewish life and thought, JSQ wants to contribute to a better understanding of Judaism.

■ **A general journal of Jewish Studies** Jewish Studies Quarterly publishes both articles on specialised subjects and inter-disciplinary or general studies. Rather than having a book review section, JSQ will provide you with review-essays on central books, groups of books or projects on a particular subject.

■ **A platform for scholarly discussion** Jewish Studies Quarterly wants to increase the element of debate in Jewish Studies. Therefore, it publishes a selection of communications to the editors to central points raised in the articles. The authors of the articles are given the opportunity to respond to comments directed at their studies.

■ **Volume 5 (1998) No. 1 Survey of Contents:**
Peter Schäfer: Die Philologie der Kabbala ist nur eine Projektion auf eine Fläche: Gershom Sholem über die wahren Absichten seines Kabbalastudiums — *Yigael Schwartz:* In God's Imgage or Dust in Ashes. Literature and Religious Anguish — *Zmira H. Heizner:* Yizkhor. When *Memory Comes* becomes *Memory Fields.*

ISSN 0944-5706. Volume V (1998, 4 issues with approx. 90 pages per issue) DM 148.00 (plus postage)

■ *For the latest information turn to the Internet:*
http://www.mohr.de/zts-jsq.htm
Updated twice per month.

☐ Please send me a free sample copy of JSQ.

Name: _____

Adress: _____

_____
LBI

Mohr Siebeck Verlag
Postfach 2040
D-72010 Tübingen, Germany

Mohr Siebeck

NEW FROM MOHR: # Explorations of Jewish-German History

Andreas Gotzmann
Jüdisches Recht im kulturellen Prozeß
Die Wahrnehmung der Halacha im Deutschland des 19. Jahrhunderts

This study shows the redefinition of the position Jewish law held in nineteenth century Germany. It is based on an extensive study of sources from contemporary publications and periodicals but also from official and private archives.
1997. XI, 434 pages (Schriftenreihe wissenschaftlicher Abhandlungen des Leo Baeck Instituts 55). ISBN 3-16-146761-2 cloth DM 128.00

Deutsches Judentum unter dem Nationalsozialismus
Band 1: Dokumente zur Geschichte der Reichsvertretung der deutschen Juden 1933-1939
herausgegeben, eingeleitet und erläutert von Otto Dov Kulka unter Mitarbeit von Anne Birkenhauer und
Esriel Hildesheimer mit einem Vorwort von Eberhard Jäckel

Previous research on National Socialism and the Jews in the Third Reich has usually described the German Jews as passive victims of discrimination, persecution and extermination. The authors of this work attempt to set right this one-dimensional image by offering the first scientific presentation of primary sources on the history of the Jewish community in Nazi Germany and its central organization, the Reichsvertretung der deutschen Juden (1933-1939).
1997. XXIV, 614 pages (Schriftenreihe wissenschaftlicher Abhandlungen des Leo Baeck Instituts 54). ISBN 3-16-146413-3 cloth DM 178.00

Jüdisches Leben auf dem Lande
Studien zur deutsch-jüdischen Geschichte
Herausgegeben von Monika Richarz und Reinhard Rürup

The history of rural Jews was neglected for a long time, and it wasn't until the eighties that the interest of scholars in this subject began to grow. However the approaches made were mainly isolated and related to one certain place or the history of one particular family. The different research approaches made by the many disciplines involved have been brought together and the entire field has been covered for the first time in the present volume. The work presents an interim appraisal of the research developments and a variety of suggestions for further work in this field.
1997. XI, 444 pages (Schriftenreihe wissenschaftlicher Abhandlungen des Leo Baeck Instituts 56). ISBN 3-16-146842-2 cloth DM 98.00

**Jüdisches Leben
in der Weimarer Republik**
Jews in the Weimar Republic
Herausgegeben von Wolfgang Benz, Arnold Paucker und Peter Pulzer

In this collection of essays Wolfgang Benz introduces the latest research on the position of the Jewish minority in Germany between the collapse of the German Empire in 1918 and the rise of Nazism, raising questions about integration, toleration, group conflict and the role of minoritites.
1998. VI, 288 pages. (Schriftenreihe wissenschaftlicher Abhandlungen des Leo Baeck Instituts 57). ISBN 3-16-146873-2 cloth DM 98.00

Mohr Siebeck
http://www.mohr.de

NEU BEI MOHR: ## Stationen Deutsch-Jüdischer Geschichte und Kultur

Barbara von der Lühe
Die Musik war unsere Rettung
Die deutschsprachigen Gründungsmitglieder des Palestine Orchestra. Mit einem Geleitwort von Ignatz Bubis

Barbara von der Lühe untersucht die Lebenswege von 50 deutschsprachigen jüdischen Musikern, Dirigenten und Musikologen, die von 1933 bis 1939 aus Deutschland, aus Österreich und aus der ČSR nach Palästina emigrierten.
1998. XX, 356 Seiten (Schriftenreihe wissenschaftlicher Abhandlungen des Leo Baeck Instituts 58). ISBN 3-16-146975-5 Leinen DM 128,-/öS 934,-/sFR 109,-

Sechzig Jahre gegen den Strom
Ernst A. Simon – Briefe
Herausgegeben vom Leo Baeck Institute

Die gesammelten Briefe Ernst Simons zeigen seinen lebenslangen und unermüdlichen Versuch, Andersdenkende zu verstehen, Brücken zwischen Menschen aufzubauen und für menschliche Werte und Würde zu kämpfen.
1998. Ca. 340 Seiten (Schriftenreihe wissenschaftlicher Abhandlungen des Leo Baeck Insituts 59). ISBN 3-16-147000-1 Leinen ca. DM 140,-/ca. öS 1020,-/ca. sFR 120,- (November)

Jüdisches Leben auf dem Lande
Studien zur deutsch-jüdischen Geschichte
Herausgegeben von Monika Richarz und Reinhard Rürup

Historiker und andere Wissenschaftler beschäftigen sich mit der Geschichte des ländlichen Judentums in Deutschland von der Zeit des Mittelalters bis in die Gegenwart.
1997. XI, 444 Seiten (Schriftenreihe wissenschaftlicher Abhandlungen des Leo Baeck Instituts 56). ISBN 3-16-146842-2 Leinen DM 98,-/öS 715,-/sFR 89,-

Jüdisches Leben in der Weimarer Republik
Jews in the Weimar Republic
Herausgegeben von Wolfgang Benz, Arnold Paucker und Peter Pulzer

Die Autoren dieser Untersuchung bieten neue Forschungsergebnisse über Juden in der Gesellschaft, Politik, Wirtschaft und Kultur der Weimarer Republik, angereichert mit biographischem und statistischem Material.
1998. VI, 288 Seiten. (Schriftenreihe wissenschaftlicher Abhandlungen des Leo Baeck Instituts 57). ISBN 3-16-146873-2 Leinen DM 98,-/öS 715,-/sFR 89,-

Übersetzung des Talmud Yerushalmi
Herausgegeben von M. Hengel, P. Schäfer, H.-J. Becker, F.G. Hüttenmeister
Band III/2: Sota – Die des Ehebruchs verdächtige Frau
Übersetzt von F.G. Hüttenmeister unter Hinzuziehung eines Manuskripts von Leo Prijs
1998. XXIX, 284 Seiten. ISBN 3-16-147045-1 Leinen ca. DM 190,-/ca. öS 1390,-/ca. sFR 170,- (Oktober)

Mohr Siebeck
http://www.mohr.de

GERMAN HISTORY

Online in 1998

ARNOLD

The Journal of the German History Society

EDITORS: *Lynn Abrams,* University of Glasgow, UK and
Richard Bessel, The Open University, UK
REVIEW EDITOR: *Elizabeth Harvey,* University of Liverpool, UK

"The wide chronological range and emphasis on serious archival work make this journal of inestimable value even for non-specialists who are interested in German History."
The Times Higher Education Supplement

German History has won respect among German historians and scholars in related disciplines and in a short space of time has become a leader in its field. The journal is renowned for its breadth of coverage which encompasses all periods of German history and all German-speaking areas. It offers a unique combination of refereed research articles, conference reports, dissertation abstracts, and news of interest to German historians, as well as a substantial book review section.

SELECTED ARTICLES:
John Theibault, The Demography of the Thirty Years War Re-Visited: Gunther Franz and his Critics
Geoff Eley, Society and Politics in Bismarckian Germany
Raymond Stokes, In Search of the Socialist Artefact: Technology and Ideology in East Germany, 1945-1962

ISSN 0266-3554   3 issues per year   Approx 432 pages per volume   Volume 16 1998

ORDER BY E-MAIL! Send your subscription details or sample copy request to:
arnoldjournals@hodder.co.uk

[ ]   Please send me a **free sample copy** of *German History*
[ ]   Please enter my **1998** subscription to *German History*

	North America*	EC	Rest of World
Individual	US$59.00 [ ]	£37.00 [ ]	£39.00 [ ]
Institutional	US$104.00 [ ]	£65.00 [ ]	£69.00 [ ]
Privileged**	US$31.00 [ ]	£18.00 [ ]	
Privileged***	US$48.00 [ ]	£22.00 [ ]	

*Canadian customers, please add 7% GST
**German History Society   ***AHA and GSA Members (Please provide proof of membership)

[ ]   Please send me information about **Online** access
[ ]   I enclose a cheque payable to **Turpin Distribution Services Ltd**
[ ]   Please charge my credit card account: [ ] Mastercard [ ] Amex [ ] Barclaycard/Visa

Card no ....Expiry Date ....

Name ....Organisation ....

Address..

Please return this form to: Humanities, Marketing Dept, Arnold, 338 Euston Road, London, NW1 3BH.
Tel: +44 (0) 171 873 6000 Fax: +44 (0) 171 873 6325   LBIYB98

Diogenes Verlag

Leon de Winter
Serenade
Roman

176 Seiten
Leinen
32 DM/237 öS/32 sFr
ISBN 3-257-06108-0
Erscheint Februar 1996

Das Buch. Warum verschwindet eine kleine, alte Dame aus Amsterdam plötzlich aus ihrer Wohnung und läßt ihren zutiefst verunsicherten Sohn Ben, erfolgreicher Komponist schmalziger Werbespot-Musik, ratlos zurück? Zusammen mit ihrem betagten, aber feurigen Liebhaber Fred spürt er sie im kriegsgeschüttelten Jugoslawien auf, wo sie versucht, Waffen nach Sarajevo zu schmuggeln. Dafür hat sie gute Gründe; einer davon ist ein über fünfzig Jahre zurückliegendes, entsetzliches Geheimnis. Mit dieser Liebeserklärung eines Sohnes setzt Leon de Winter seiner Mutter ein Denkmal – warmherzig, komisch, traurig und wunderbar jüdisch. Startauflage: 100 000.

Der Autor. Leon de Winter, geboren 1954 in 's-H... Sohn niederländisch-orthodoxer J... freier Schrifts...

Jakob Arjouni
Magic Hoffmann
Roman

ca. 288 Seiten
Leinen
ca. 36 DM/267 öS/36 sFr
ISBN 3-257-06092-0
Erscheint März 1996

Das Buch. Vier Jahre sitzt Fred Hoffmann nach einem blödsinnigen Bankraub, weil er Annette und Nickel, seine Komplizen, nicht verpfeift. Doch als er herauskommt, wollen die beiden vom Aussteigen in Kanada nichts mehr wissen: Annette ist voll im Film-Business und Nickel auf dem Karrieretrip. Noch einmal bäumt sich Magic Hoffmann, der beste Tischfußballspieler im Knast, gegen das Schicksal auf... Boshaft-amüsante Zeitgeist-Lifestyle-Satire mit Seitenhieben auf Wohlstandsgejammer, Schicki-Micki-Szene und... tum, garniert mit vielen verbo... der beson...

Novitätenkatalog Herbst '96
für Sortiment und Verlag, Presse und Bibliotheken

Dick Francis
Zügellos
Roman

ca. 368 Seiten
Leinen
ca. 44 DM/326 öS/44 sFr
ISBN 3-257-06101-3
Erscheint März 1996

Das Buch. Als man die hübsche Frau eines Trainers erhängt im Stall findet, gibt es viele Verdächtige, aber keinen überführten Mörder. Ein Vierteljahrhundert später wird aus dem Verbrechen ein Drehbuch. Doch mit dem Film wird auch die Vergangenheit unerwartet lebendig, und auf einen alten Mord folgt ein neuer. Dick Francis' neuer Roman ist nicht nur für Pferdeliebhaber, sondern auch für Filmfans ein absoluter Pokaltip, der sein Tempo vom Start bis zum Finish durchhält. Startauflage: 50 000

Der Autor. Dick Francis, geboren 1920, war viele Jahre Englands erfolgreichster Jockey, bis ein mysteriöser Sturz 1956 seine Karriere beendete. Seit mehr als dreißig Jahren schreibt er Thriller, die alle das Pferderenn- und Wettmilieu als Hintergrund und die »längst die Grenzen des Krimis überschritten haben« (Süddeutsche Zeitung).

Donna Leon
Venezianische Scharade
Commissario Brunettis dritter Fall

384 Seiten
Leinen
39 DM/289 öS/39 sFr
ISBN 3-257-06103-X
Erscheint Februar 1996

Das Buch. Die Leiche mit den roten Schuhen und den ebenso roten Spitzenschlüpfern ist keine Frau, sondern ein Transvestit. Der aber genoß zu Lebzeiten den besten Ruf – ein ehrenwerter Bankdirektor und Vermögensverwalter eines achtbaren Sittlichkeitsvereins. Commissario Brunetti geht im brütendheißen Venedig der Sache nach und findet einen wahren Sumpf von Lastern aller Art. Vier Menschen sterben, bevor Brunetti mit Hilfe der roten Schuhe die Täter überführen kann. Donna Leons dritter Lagunen-Krimi, schwül wie die Hitze über den bröckelnden Palazzi und eiskalt wie die Keller der Bleikammern – ein Meisterstück des atmosphärischen Polizeiromans. Startauflage: 40 000

Die Autorin. Donna Leon wurde 1947 in New Jersey, USA, geboren und lebt seit über zehn Jahren in Venedig. Sie unterrichtet englische Literatur in Vicenza, einer Außenstelle der Universität Maryland.

Buchreport präsentiert Programme:
Der Novitätenkatalog ist Branchenstandard

Wer über die Programme der führenden deutschen Verlage informiert sein will, wird zuverlässig von **Buchreport** bedient. Bereits im Dezember und April erscheinen die **redaktionellen Vorschauen** mit ersten Übersichten. Jeweils im Januar und Juni folgen die großen Kompendien, die unter dem Titel »Buchreport-Novitätenkatalog« zu einem ausschlaggebenden Arbeitsmittel der Branche geworden sind.

Was wichtig ist,
steht zuerst im neuen Novitätenkatalog

Die klargegliederten Informationen ergeben seit jeher einen hohen Nachschlagewert.

Der Buchreport-Novitätenkatalog
ist zum Start der Vertreterreise präsent

Wenn die Vertreter zu ihrer Herbstreise starten, liegt der Buchreport-Novitätenkatalog bereits als erstes Arbeitsmittel des Herbstes vor. **(Erscheinungstermin: 4. Juni 1996)**

Der Buchreport-Novitätenkatalog
bietet Informationen zu Autor und Titel

Jeder Titel im Buchreport-Novitätenkatalog kann neben dem Kurztext zum Buch auch durch eine Information zum Autor ergänzt werden. So verlängert der Buchreport-Novitätenkatalog das Marketing der Verlage.

Der Buchreport-Novitätenkatalog
als aktuelles Adreßbuch des deutschsprachigen Buchhandels

Die Rückseite gibt detaillierte Auskunft über alle wichtigen Daten:

▶ Unter den Verlagsdaten finden Sie die Anschrift des Verlags, Postfach sowie Telefon- und Telefaxangaben.

▶ Die Rubrik »Ansprechpartner im Verlag« führt die zuständigen Personen für die Bereiche Verkauf, Vertrieb, Werbung, Presse sowie Autorenlesungen mit Telefondurchwahl-Nummern auf. (Alle Ansprechpartner werden im Personenregister aufgeführt.)

▶ Im Bereich »Vertreter« werden alle Verlagsvertreter im deutschsprachigen Raum mit Telefon- und Telefaxangaben aufgelistet. (Alle Vertreter finden Sie auch im Personenregister.)

▶ Der letzte Abschnitt dieser Seite gibt Auskunft über die Auslieferungen in Deutschland, Österreich und der Schweiz.

▶ Mit diesen Daten und Informationen wird der Buchreport-Novitätenkatalog wieder zum wichtigsten Arbeitsmittel der neuen Saison.

Sie sollten nicht zögern, Ihre wichtigen Herbst-Neuerscheinungen schon jetzt für den Buchreport-Novitätenkatalog anzumelden.

Auf Anfrage fertigen wir Ihnen auch gerne Fortdrucke in Farbe oder Schwarzweiß an.

Buchreport
Königswall 21, 44137 Dortmund
Postfach 10 18 52, 44018 Dortmund

Telefon Anzeigenabteilung:
02 31 / 90 56-205 Ingrid Conrad
02 31 / 90 56-401 Jutta Grünen
02 31 / 90 56-400 Sabine Müchler

We are delighted to announce that a fifty year cumulative index is now available for *German Life & Letters*. For *free* access, go to http://www.blackwellpublishers.co.uk/glal

German Life & Letters

Edited by G.P.G. Butler, Gerald Gillespie, Margaret Littler, J.M. Ritchie, John Sandford, R.C. Speirs and Helen Watanabe-O'Kelly

Long established as the leading journal in British German Studies, *German Life and Letters* offers a wide range of articles dealing with literary and non-literary concerns in the German-speaking world. It focuses on all major aspects of German culture, including: literature, art, language, politics and social history. Occasional special issues are published on topics such as women's studies, cinema and translation.

ORDER FORM
German Life & Letters

Subscription Rates, Volume 51/1998
ISSN 0016-8777

Published in: January, April, July, October

Institutional Rates, £127.00 (UK-Europe), $247.00 (N. America), £149.00 (Rest of World)

Personal Rates, £56.00 (UK-Europe), $111.00 (N. America), £67.00 (Rest of World)

☐ Please enter my subscription/send me a sample copy

☐ I enclose a cheque/money order payable to Blackwell Publishers

☐ Please charge my American Express/Diners Club/Mastercard/Visa account

Card Number..Expiry Date......................
Signature ....Date................................
Name ....
Address ....
....Postcode ....
email. ....

Payment must accompany orders

Please return this form to:
Journals Marketing, Blackwell Publishers, 108 Cowley Road, Oxford, OX4 1JF, UK.
Tel: +44 (0)1865 244083 Or to:
Journals Marketing, GLAL, Blackwell Publishers, 350 Main Street, Malden, MA 02148, USA.
Tel: +1 781 388 8200

SPECIAL OFFER for 1998
Electronic access is included in the institutional subscription to the print edition.

BLACKWELL *Publishers*

For more information, or to order a free sample copy, visit our website

http://www.blackwellpublishers.co.uk

Jüdischer Verlag
im Suhrkamp Verlag

Göran Rosenberg
Das verlorene Land
Israel – eine persönliche Geschichte
472 Seiten. Gebunden

S. J. Agnon
Schira
Roman. Aus dem Hebräischen von Tuvia Rübner
776 Seiten. Gebunden

Amos Oz
Das Schweigen des Himmels
Über S. J. Agnon
Aus dem Hebräischen von Ruth Achlama
264 Seiten. Gebunden

Jüdischer Almanach 1999
des Leo Baeck Instituts
Herausgegeben von Jakob Hessing und Alfred Bodenheimer
192 Seiten. Kartoniert

Der jüdische Kalender
Entstehung und Aufbau
Von Ludwig Basnizki
Mit zahlreichen Illustrationen
80 Seiten. Gebunden

conditio Judaica
Studien zur deutsch-jüdischen Literatur- und Kulturgeschichte

Dorothee Ostmeier
Sprache des Dramas – Drama der Sprache
Zur Poetik der Nelly Sachs

1997. VII, 156 Seiten. Kart. DM 82.–.
ISBN 3-484-65116-4 (Band 16)

In careful analyses of selected scenes from Nelly Sachs' dramas (1891–1970), the study pinpoints the Jewish, language-philosophical and aesthetic traditions central to the stage works of this author. The texts themselves represent an inherently complex process of artistic reflection on the limits between lyric and dramatic diction. By concentrating on individual texts by an author profoundly shaken by the shoah, the analysis situates her dramatic oeuvre in the context of the ongoing debate on obsessive memory in the face of the universal disappearance of idealist utopias.

Katrin Diehl
Die jüdische Presse im Dritten Reich
Zwischen Selbstbehauptung und Fremdbestimmung

1997. XIII, 362 Seiten. Kart. DM 142.–.
ISBN 3-484-65117-2 (Band 17)

Up to the pogrom of November 1938, German Jews were legally entitled to publish and there was a broad range of Jewish publications. Thereafter the National Socialists prohibited the over 100 Jewish periodicals hitherto available. With reference to content analyses of the four largest and most important newspapers and interviews with former journalists, the author inquires into the inherent potential for intellectual resistance and in so doing establishes a tentative ›typology of Jewish resistance behaviour‹. Brief monographs, a table of the titles of all traceable Jewish periodicals appearing during the Third Reich, an index of persons and a number of potted biographies also make the book a useful source of reference.

Gustav Landauer im Gespräch
Symposium zum 125. Geburtstag
Herausgegeben von Hanna Delf und Gert Mattenklott

1997. IX, 288 Seiten. Kart. DM 136.–.
ISBN 3-484-65118-0 (Band 18)

The writer Gustav Landauer (1870–1919) is one of the figures of political and literary life around the turn of the century whose importance for German-Jewish modernism has been largely neglected. Anarchist and reformer, writer and theatre critic, friend of Martin Buber and intellectual pioneer and mainstay of cultural Zionism, he left a body of work that has yet to be explored in all its variety and apparent contradictions. Hence the articles in this volume approach Landauer from a broad range of viewpoints.

Jüdische Selbstwahrnehmung – La prise de conscience de l'identité juïve
Herausgegeben von Hans Otto Horch und Charlotte Wardi

1997. XIII, 292 Seiten. Kart. DM 138.–.
ISBN 3-484-65119-9 (Band 19)

The articles in this volume originated from an international and interdisciplinary symposium organized in October 1994 by the Bibliothèque Nationale Luxembourg in collaboration with the Leo Baeck Institute (London), the Division of German-Jewish Literary History at the RWTH Technical University in Aachen and the Department of Hebrew and Comparative Literature of Haifa University. Common to all of them is the question of the various available modes of individual and collective Jewish self-awareness and self-definition existing in Central Europe in the period between 1870 and the Third Reich/Second World War.

Zwischen den Kulturen
Theorie und Praxis des interkulturellen Dialogs
Im Auftrag des Franz Rosenzweig-Forschungszentrums für deutsch-jüdische Literatur und Kulturgeschichte der Hebräischen Universität Jerusalem herausgegeben von Carola Hilfrich-Kunjappu und Stephane Mosès

1997. VI, 170 Seiten. Kart. DM 92.–.
ISBN 3-484-65120-2 (Band 20)

The articles in this volume originated from a symposium organized in 1994 by the Franz Rosenzweig Research Centre of the Hebrew University of Jerusalem. The aim was to elaborate a methodological framework for research into German-Jewish intercultural identity, centering on an attempt to define the ›intercultural space‹ between two cultures. This space proves to be the condition both of potential cultural renewal and of the real catastrophes occurring in the context of intercultural encounter. The problem of intercultural translation needs to be seen in terms of the theory and practice of dialogue across this space, inasfar as the locus of this problem is situated in the ›space‹ between translatability and untranslatability.

Unser aktuelles Verlagsprogramm im Internet: **http://www.niemeyer.de**

Max Niemeyer Verlag GmbH & Co. KG
Postfach 21 40 · D-72011 Tübingen

Niemeyer

Volumes I-XL of the Year Book are now available on CD-ROM

LEO BAECK INSTITUTE
YEAR BOOK
VOLUMES I - XL
1956 - 1995

LEO BAECK INSTITUTE
for the study of the history and culture
of German-speaking Jewry
NEW YORK, LONDON, JERUSALEM

Powered by Folio

For Windows 95

To order, contact the Leo Baeck Institute
129 East 73rd Street
New York, NY1002, USA
Tel. (212) 744 6400
Email: lbi1@lbi.com

IBTauris

Out of the Third Reich
Refugee Historians in Post-War Britain
Edited by Peter Alter

JULIUS CARLEBACH: Journey to the Centre of the Periphery FRANCIS L. CARSTEN: From Revolutionary Socialism to German History EDGAR J. FEUCHTWANGER: Recovering from Culture Shock JOHN GRENVILLE: From Gardener to Professor E.P. HENNOCK: Myself as Historian HELMUT G. KOENIGSBERGER: Fragments of an Unwritten Biography WOLF MENDL: A Slow Awakening

WERNER E. MOSSE: Self-Discovery: A European Historian HELMUT PAPPE: The Scholar as Businessman ARNOLD PAUCKER: Mommsenstrasse to Devonshire Street SIDNEY POLLARD: In Search of a Social Purpose PETER PULZER: From Danube to Isis: A Career in Two Cultures NICOLAI RUBINSTEIN: Germany, Italy and England WALTER ULLMANN: A Tale of Two Cultures.

I.B. Tauris/German Historical Institute
270pp. ISBN 18606 4189 X

"...a succession of colourful and often moving personal stories"
– History Today

To order contact:
Leo Baeck Institute, 4 Devonshire Street, London W1N 2BH
email: ap@lbilon.demon.co.uk

TRIBÜNE

Unabhängig Objektiv Kritisch

Zeitschrift zum Verständnis des Judentums

seit 1962

Geschichte & Gegenwart
Wirtschaft & Wissenschaft
Kunst & Kultur

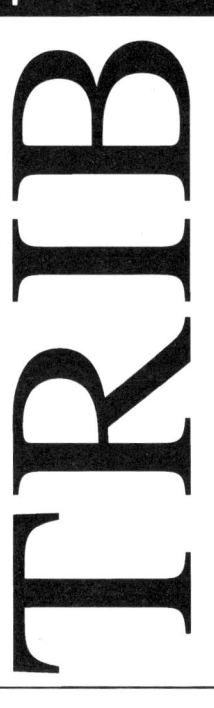

TRIBÜNE-Verlag
Habsburgerallee 72
D-60385 Frankfurt am Main
Tel.: +49 (0)69 943300-0
Fax: +49 (0)69 943300-23
e-mail: 0699433000-0001@t-online.de

böhlauWienneu

Fred Grubel
Schreib das auf eine Tafel die mit ihnen bleibt
Jüdisches Leben im 20. Jahrhundert
1998. 324 S. m. 26 SW-Abb. Br. ISBN 3-205-98871-X

Die Familie ist großbürgerlich-jüdisch und stammt aus der äußersten Provinz des Habsburgerreiches, Galizien. Sie läßt sich mit erfolgreicher Kürschnerei und Pelzhandel in Leipzig und Nürnberg nieder. Die Kindheit und Jugend des Autors Fred Grubel spannt sich zwischen Talmiglanz und der Kriegsnot des Wilhelminischen Zeitalters. Die täuschende Sicherheit der Weimarer Republik endet nach dem Jusstudium für den jungen Referendar mit seiner Entlassung aus dem sächsischen Justizdienst 1933. Während und nach dem Zweiten Weltkrieg ist Fred Grubel am Aufbau und an der Organisation von internationalen jüdischen Hilfseinrichtungen in New York beteiligt und wird schließlich Geschäftsführer, später internationaler Direktor der von Martin Buber zur Bewahrung und Erforschung neuer deutsch-jüdischer Geschichte gegründeten Leo Baeck-Institute New York – London – Jerusalem. Der 1908 in Leipzig geborene Chronist und Cousin des österreichischen Dichters und Schriftstellers Joseph Roth zeichnet zauberhafte Bilder eines innigen jüdischen Familienlebens in Deutschland vor dem Hintergrund der wechselvollen Geschichte unseres Jahrhunderts.

Erhältlich in Ihrer Buchhandlung!

Judaica

Desanka Schwara
Humor und Toleranz
Ostjüdische Anekdoten als historische Quelle
(Lebenswelten osteuropäischer Juden, Bd. 1) 1996. 268 S. 25 Abb. Br. DM 58,–
ISBN 3-412-03696-X

Viele Zeugnisse jüdischen Lebens sind vernichtet oder in aller Welt verstreut. Erhalten geblieben sind Textsammlungen jüdischen Humors. Die Autorin versucht, die Anekdoten und Witze der Vergessenheit zu entreißen und auf ihre Bedeutung und Aktualität hinzuweisen.

Monica Rüthers
Tewjes Töchter
Lebensentwürfe ostjüdischer Frauen im 19. Jahrhundert
(Lebenswelten osteuropäischer Juden, Bd. 2)
1996. 288 S. Br. DM 58,–
ISBN 3-412-03796-6

Die Töchter von Tewje, dem Milchmann, lösen sich in Scholem Alejchems Erzählungen Schritt für Schritt von der jüdischen Tradition und nehmen ihr Leben selbst in die Hand. Was hier in verdichteter Form dargestellt ist, war ein Zeitphänomen: Ostjüdische Frauen begannen, sich Gedanken zu machen über ihre Zukunft, über ihre Rolle in Gesellschaft und Ehe.

François Guesnet
Polnische Juden im 19. Jahrhundert
Lebensbedingungen, Rechtsnormen und Organisation im Wandel
(Lebenswelten osteuropäischer Juden, Bd. 3) 1998. Ca. 600 S. Br. Ca. DM 128,–
ISBN 3-412-03097-X

Jost Hermand
Judentum und deutsche Kultur
Beispiele einer schmerzhaften Symbiose
1996. VI, 266 Seiten. Gebunden mit Schutzumschlag.
DM 58,– ISBN 3-412-11395-6

Jost Hermand beleuchtet aus kulturgeschichtlichem Blickwinkel das widersprüchliche Verhältnis jüdischer Künstler und Intellektueller zu ihrer Heimat.

Manuel Köppen und Klaus Scherpe (Hg)
Bilder des Holocaust
Literatur - Film - Bildende Kunst
(Literatur - Kultur - Geschlecht. Kleine Reihe, Band 10)
1997. VI, 231 S. 24 Abb. Br. DM 35,– ISBN 3-412-05197-7

Gideon Greif
Wir weinten tränenlos...
Augenzeugenberichte der jüdischen Sonderkommandos in Auschwitz
1995. 358 S. zahlr. Abb. Br. DM 44,– ISBN 3-412-03794-X

Böhlau KÖLN WEIMAR

Theodor-Heuss-Str. 76, D-51149 Köln, Telefon (0 22 03) 30 70 21

YALE UNIVERSITY PRESS

My German Question
Growing Up in Nazi Berlin
Peter Gay

In this poignant book, a renowned historian tells of his youth as an assimilated, antireligious Jew in Nazi Germany from 1933 to 1939—"the story", says Peter Gay, "of a poisoning and how I dealt with it". With his customary eloquence and analytic acumen, Gay describes his family, the life they led, and the reasons they did not emigrate sooner, and he explores his own ambivalent feelings—then and now—towards Germany and the Germans. His account, marked by candour, modesty and insight—adds an important and curiously neglected perspective to the history of German Jewry.

November 240pp. 50 b/w illus. £15.50

The Renaissance of Jewish Culture in Weimar Germany

New in paper

Michael Brenner

In the first in-depth study of the Jewish population of Germany between the two world wars, Michael Brenner describes a people in the midst of redefining themselves. He shows how the Weimar Jews, participating but not assimilating in German society, created new forms of German-Jewish literature, music, fine art, education and scholarship by dressing Jewish traditions in the garb of modern forms of cultural expression.

"a fascinating and beautifully written book"—Julia Neuberger, *Jewish Chronicle*

320pp. 12 illus. Cloth £25.00 Paper £12.50

Yale University Press • 23 Pond Street • London NW3 2PN
Tel: 0171 431 4422 Fax: 0171 431 3755 e-mail: sales@yaleup.co.uk

We are delighted to announce that a fifty year cumulative index is now available for *German Life & Letters*. For *free* access, go to http://www.blackwellpublishers.co.uk/glal

German Life & Letters

Edited by G.P.G. Butler, Gerald Gillespie, Margaret Littler, J.M. Ritchie, John Sandford, R.C. Speirs and Helen Watanabe-O'Kelly

Long established as the leading journal in British German Studies, *German Life and Letters* offers a wide range of articles dealing with literary and non-literary concerns in the German-speaking world. It focuses on all major aspects of German culture, including: literature, art, language, politics and social history. Occasional special issues are published on topics such as women's studies, cinema and translation.

ORDER FORM   German Life & Letters

Subscription Rates, Volume 51/1998   ISSN 0016-8777

Published in: January, April, July, October

Institutional Rates, £127.00 (UK-Europe), $247.00 (N. America), £149.00 (Rest of World)

Personal Rates, £56.00 (UK-Europe), $111.00 (N. America), £67.00 (Rest of World)

☐ Please enter my subscription/send me a sample copy

☐ I enclose a cheque/money order payable to Blackwell Publishers

☐ Please charge my American Express/Diners Club/Mastercard/Visa account

Card Number..Expiry Date......................

Signature ....Date........................

Name ....

Address ....

....Postcode ....

email..

Payment must accompany orders

Please return this form to:
Journals Marketing, Blackwell Publishers, 108 Cowley Road, Oxford, OX4 1JF, UK.
Tel: +44 (0)1865 244083 Or to:
Journals Marketing, GLAL, Blackwell Publishers, 350 Main Street, Malden, MA 02148, USA.
Tel: +1 781 388 8200

SPECIAL OFFER for 1998
Electronic access is included in the institutional subscription to the print edition.

BLACKWELL *Publishers*

For more information, or to order a free sample copy, visit our website

http://www.blackwellpublishers.co.uk

ASCHKENAS
אשכנז

Journal for the history and culture of the Jews

Editors:
J. Friedrich Battenberg, Hans Otto Horch and Markus J. Wenninger
in connection to the Institute for the History of the Jews in Austria, St. Pölten
and the German Coordinating Advisory Board of the Society
for Christian-Jewish Cooperation.

Aschkenas will be published twice a year
Total volume approx. 500 pages,
DM 98.–
ISSN 1016 - 4987

All issues in soft cover

„Aschkenas" was originally the name for Germany, and denoted in a broader sense the Jews living in the areas from northern France to Poland, England to Hungary and upper Italy, as well as their culture, wich was strongly influenced by German traditions. This provides the centrale theme of this journal, although related aspects, such as the immigration of the sephardic Jews will also be included. Emphasis will be given to research undertaken up to the time of the emancipation of the Jews. „ASCHKENAS" will appear twice a year with essays, reports on research, book reviews and other references to problems and projects concerning the history and culture of the Jews up to the present time.

Exilforschung
Ein internationales Jahrbuch

Herausgegeben von
Claus-Dieter Krohn, Erwin
Rotermund, Lutz Winckler
und Wulf Koepke

Band 16
Exil und Avantgarden

etwa 280 Seiten, ca. DM 58,--
ca. öS 42,--/sfr 52,50
ISBN 3-88377-591-6

Der Band diskutiert und revidiert die Ergebnisse einer mehr als zwanzigjährigen Debatte um Bestand, Entwicklung oder Transformation der historischen Avantgarden unter den Bedingungen von Exil und Akkulturation. Die Beiträge thematisieren u. a. die Bereiche Literatur, bildende Kunst, Film und Musik.

Bisher sind u.a. erschienen:

Stalin und die Intellektuellen
391 Seiten

Erinnerungen ans Exil –
Autobiographien nach 1933
415 Seiten

Gedanken an Deutschland im Exil
400 Seiten

Das jüdische Exil
310 Seiten

Fluchtpunkte des Exils
260 Seiten

Vertreibung der Wissenschaften
243 Seiten

Publizistik im Exil
249 Seiten

Politische Aspekte des Exils
243 Seiten

Exil und Remigration
263 Seiten

Künste im Exil
212 Seiten, zahlr. Abb.

Frauen und Exil
Zwischen Anpassung und Selbstbehauptung
283 Seiten

Aspekte der künstlerischen Inneren Emigration 1933–1945
236 Seiten

Kulturtransfer im Exil
276 Seiten

Rückblick und Perspektiven
231 Seiten

Exil und Widerstand
282 Seiten

Mitglieder der Gesellschaft für Exilforschung erhalten die Jahrbücher im Rahmen ihrer Mitgliedschaft. Fordern Sie unseren Prospekt mit weiteren Informationen an.

Verlag
edition text + kritik
Levelingstraße 6a
81673 München
http://www.etk-muenchen.de

Zur Geschichte des Judentums in Deutschland

Dieter Lamping
Von Kafka bis Celan
Jüdischer Diskurs in der deutschen Literatur des 20. Jahrhunderts.
Sammlung Vandenhoeck. 1998.
Ca. 224 Seiten, Paperback
ca. DM 45,- / öS 329,- / SFr 41,50
ISBN 3-525-01221-7

In keinem Bereich deutscher Kultur haben Juden so viele und so tiefe Spuren hinterlassen wie in der Literatur. In ihrer großen Epoche, die etwa um 1820 mit Rahel Varnhagen, Ludwig Börne und Heinrich Heine beginnt und gut einhundert Jahre dauerte, haben jüdische Autoren wie Franz Kafka, Else Lasker-Schüler, Franz Werfel oder Joseph Roth deutsche Literatur geprägt.

Deutsch-jüdische Literatur des 20. Jahrhunderts ist aber nicht nur große deutsche, sondern auch große jüdische Literatur. Im Mittelpunkt des Buches steht deshalb die Frage, was denn das ‚Deutsche' und was das ‚Jüdische' an ihr sei. Jüdische Literatur in deutscher Sprache ist deutsch-jüdische Literatur vor allem durch die Darstellung jüdischer Erfahrungen - zumal der problematischen Assimilation, des Exils und des Holocaust.

Ursula Büttner / Martin Greschat
Die verlassenen Kinder der Kirche
Der Umgang mit Christen jüdischer Herkunft im „Dritten Reich".
Sammlung Vandenhoeck 1998.
151 Seiten, Paperback
ca. DM 28,- / öS 204,- / SFr 26,-
ISBN 3-525-01620-4

Nach den Nürnberger Gesetzen waren auch Christen jüdischer Herkunft der Diskriminierung und Verfolgung durch den nationalsozialistischen Staat ausgesetzt. Der Band gibt eine Einführung in die Situation und dokumentiert vor allem die Diskussion innerhalb der Bekennenden Kirche. Drei Einzelschicksale - Marga Meusel, Friedrich Weißler und Jochen Klepper - werden ausführlich vorgestellt.

Weitere Informationen:
Vandenhoeck & Ruprecht, Theologie / Germanistik,
D-37070 Göttingen. Fax: 0049-551-54782-14

V&R
Vandenhoeck & Ruprecht

JEWISH STUDIES FROM *Berghahn Books*

STUDIES IN PROGRESSIVE HALAKHAH
Published in Association with the Solomon B. Freehof Institute of Progressive Halakah
General Editor: Walter Jacob
This series brings a Jewish perspective to current social and religious problems, viewed through the lenses of tradition and the best modern scholarship, then recast into the framework of Liberal Judaism.

Volumes 1-7 edited by Walter Jacob and Moshe Zemer
Vol. 1: DYNAMIC JEWISH LAW
ISBN: 0 929699 03 3 £8.95 P/b
Vol. 2: RABBINIC-LAY RELATIONS IN JEWISH LAW ISBN: 0 929699 04 1 £7.95 P/b
Vol. 3: CONVERSION TO JUDAISM IN JEWISH LAW ISBN: 0 929699 05 X £8.50 P/b
Vol. 4: DEATH AND EUTHANASIA IN JEWISH LAW ISBN: 0 929699 06 5 £10.00 P/b
Vol. 5: THE FETUS AND FERTILITY IN JEWISH LAW ISBN: 0 929699 07 6 £10.00 P/b
Vol. 6: ISRAEL AND THE DIASPORA IN JEWISH LAW ISBN: 0 929699 09 2 £11.95 P/b

IN PREPARATION:
CRIME AND PUNISHMENT IN JEWISH LAW
GENDER ISSUES IN JEWISH LAW
THE ENVIRONMENT IN JEWISH LAW
GENETIC ENGINEERING IN JEWISH LAW

Berghahn Books now distribute the *Leo Baeck Institute Year Book* in the US. and Canada and the complete set on CD-ROM world-wide.
CLOTH *(US/Canada only)*
Published: October 1998
ISBN: 0 436 220784 $45.00
CD-ROM
Volumes 1-40   ISBN: 1 58181 183 4
£260.00/$399.00
Bibliography   ISBN: 1 57181 184 2
£200.00/$299.00

NEW SERIES
PROGRESSIVE JUDAISM TODAY
General Editor: David J. Goldberg, Rabbi, Liberal Jewish Synagogue, London
In this series, Progressive Jewish thinkers respond to up-to-date issues that affect not only Judaism but all religions as we prepare for the twenty-first century.

A JEWISH UNDERSTANDING OF THE WORLD - *John D. Rayner*
ISBN: 1 57181 973 8 £28.00 H/b
ISBN: 1 57181 974 6 £10.50 P/b
JEWISH RELIGIOUS LAW: A Progressive Perspective
John D. Rayner
ISBN: 1 57181 975 4 £28.00 H/b
ISBN: 1 57181 976 2 £10.50 P/b
AN UNDERSTANDING OF JUDAISM
John D. Rayner
ISBN: 1 57181 971 1 £35.00 H/b
ISBN: 1 57181 972 X £13.50 P/b

BERGHAHN JOURNALS
EUROPEAN JUDAISM: A Journal for the New Europe. *Editors: Jonathan Magonet, Leo Baeck College; Albert H. Friedlander, Rabbi, Westminster Synagogue. In association with the Leo Baeck College and the Michael Goulston Education Foundation*
"European Judaism makes an important contribution to the quest for global ethic. It explores the inner workings of the Jewish world, ... at the same time it is a medium for dialogue, examining in particular the relationship between Judaism, Christianity and Islam...a journal for the 'new' Europe." **Prof. Dr. H. K. Kueng, Tuebingen**
ISSN: 0014-3006 Published: twice yearly
Institutional Rate: **£60.00** / Individual Rate: **£18.00**

For further information contact:
Berghahn Books, 3 NewTec Place,
Magdalen Road, Oxford, OX4 1RE
Tel: 01865 250011 / Fax: 01865 250056
Email: BerghahnUK@aol.com
http://www.berghahnbooks.com

Hamburger Beiträge zur Sozial- und Zeitgeschichte (HBSZ)

Herausgegeben von der
Forschungsstelle für Zeitgeschichte in Hamburg (FZH)
vormals: Forschungsstelle für die Geschichte des Nationalsozialismus in Hamburg

In den »Hamburger Beiträgen zur Sozial- und Zeitgeschichte«
werden vornehmlich Darstellungen und Quellen zur deutschen Geschichte des
20. Jahrhunderts veröffentlicht. Besondere Berücksichtigung finden
Untersuchungen und Dokumentationen zu den Voraussetzungen und Strukturen,
Entwicklungen und Folgen der nationalsozialistischen Diktatur.

Bisher erschienen: Bände 1-35

Avraham Barkai

Hoffnung und Untergang

Studien zur deutsch-jüdischen
Geschichte des
19. und 20. Jahrhunderts
Darstellungen, Band 36

Linson mit Schutzumschlag
ca. 320 Seiten
ISBN 3-7672-1316-8
ca. DM 48,- / öS 350,- / Sfr 44,50
erscheint im November 1998

Die hier zumeist erstmals in deutscher Sprache veröffentlichten Aufsätze des international bekannten israelischen Historikers Avraham Barkai geben einen Überblick über wirtschaftliche und gesellschaftliche Aspekte jüdischen Lebens in Deutschland von der Mitte des 19. Jahrhunderts bis zur Vernichtung durch das nationalsozialistische Unrechtsregime.

Christians Verlag
Kleine Theaterstraße 10 · 20354 Hamburg
Tel.: 040/35 60 06-0 · Fax: 040/35 60 06-26

Hamburger Beiträge zur Sozial- und Zeitgeschichte (HBSZ)

Quellen

Christa Fladhammer, Michael Wildt (Hrsg.)
Max Brauer im Exil
Briefe und Reden aus den Jahren 1933-1946
»[...] an interesting contribution to a little-investigated chapter of German exile history«.
Oxford Journals
1994, geb., 360 S.   ISBN 3-7672-1219-6
DM 42,-/öS 307,-/Sfr 39,-

Ursula Büttner, Angelika Voß (Hrsg.)
Alfred Kantorowicz: Nachtbücher
Aufzeichnungen im französischen Exil
1935 bis 1939
»Die Herausgeberinnen [...] zeigen uns Kantorowicz ohne falsche Rücksicht. In ihrem mustergültigen Apparat steckt ein Handbuch der deutschen Emigration in Frankreich [...]«
Die Welt
1995, geb., 336 S.   ISBN 3-7672-1247-1
DM 48,-/öS 350,-/Sfr 44,50

Darstellungen

Bisher erschienen: Band 1 – 35
Lieferbare Titel (Auswahl):

Band 25
Yfaat Weiss
Schicksalsgemeinschaft im Wandel
Jüdische Erziehung im nationalsozialistischen Deutschland 1933-1938
»Vor 1933 [...] war ein eigentlich jüdisches Schulwesen nur wenig ausgeprägt [...] Wie und warum sich dies in der neuen Situation nach 1933 durchgreifend änderte, ist das mit beeindruckender Umsicht und ausgeprägter Sachkenntnis dargestellte Thema von Weiss.«
Aschkenas
1991, geb., 228 S.   ISBN 3-7672-1127-0
DM 29,80/öS 218,-/Sfr 27,50

Band 31
Axel Schildt
Moderne Zeiten
Freizeit, Massenmedien und »Zeitgeist« in der Bundesrepublik der 50er Jahre
» [...] ein spannendes, ungemein informatives Buch, nach dessen Lektüre der Leser ein präzises Verständnis gewonnen hat für die Ambivalenzen in der gesellschaftlichen Wirklichkeit und im geistigen Klima des Nachkriegsjahrzehnts.«
Frankfurter Allgemeine Zeitung
1995, geb., 736 S.   ISBN 3-7672-1218-8
DM 88,-/öS 642,-/Sfr 80,-

Band 32
Birthe Kundrus
Kriegerfrauen
Familienpolitik und Geschlechterverhältnisse im Ersten und Zweiten Weltkrieg
»Das Buch wird zum Standardwerk über die staatliche Versorgung der Soldatenfamilien in den beiden Weltkriegen werden.«
Frankfurter Allgemeine Zeitung
1995, geb., 592 S.   ISBN 3-7672-1246-3
DM 68,-/öS 496,-/Sfr 62,-

Band 33
Michael Zimmermann
Rassenutopie und Genozid
Die nationalsozialistische »Lösung der Zigeunerfrage«
»Mit Zimmermanns Buch liegt ein umfassender Überblick über die NS-Zigeunerverfolgung in Europa vor, das jetzt schon als wichtiges Standardwerk Geltung hat.«
Zeitschrift für Geschichtswissenschaft
1996, geb., 576 S.   ISBN 3-7672-1270-6
DM 68,-/öS 496,-/Sfr 62,-

Band 34
Patrick Wagner
Volksgemeinschaft ohne Verbrecher
Konzeptionen und Praxis der Kriminalpolizei in der Zeit der Weimarer Republik und des Nationalsozialismus
»Ein ungewöhnliches und ein ungewöhnlich gutes Buch, das ein wichtiges Thema auf einfallsreiche Weise bearbeitet und zudem auch noch vorzüglich geschrieben ist.«
Berliner Zeitung
1996, geb., 548 S.   ISBN 3-7672-1271-4
DM 68,-/öS 496,-/Sfr 62,-

Band 35
Frank Bajohr
»Arisierung« in Hamburg
Die Verdrängung der jüdischen Unternehmer 1933-1945
»Mit seiner exemplarischen Fallstudie [...] hat Frank Bajohr [...] Licht in das Dunkel dieses in der neueren deutschen Geschichte einzigartigen Besitzwechsels gebracht. Ihm ist es erstmals umfassend gelungen, die verschiedenen Gruppen zu beleuchten, die [...] materiellen Vorteil aus Vertreibung und Holocaust zogen.«
Die Zeit
1997, geb., 420 S.   ISBN 3-7672-1302-8
DM 54,-/öS 394,-/Sfr 49,-

Hamburger Beiträge
zur Sozial- und Zeitgeschichte (HBSZ)

Herausgegeben
von der Forschungsstelle für Zeitgeschichte
in Hamburg (FZH)

vormals: Forschungsstelle für die Geschichte des Nationalsozialismus in Hamburg

In den »Hamburger Beiträgen zur Sozial- und Zeitgeschichte« werden vornehmlich Darstellungen und Quellen zur deutschen Geschichte im 20. Jahrhundert veröffentlicht. Besondere Berücksichtigung finden Untersuchungen und Dokumentationen zu den Voraussetzungen und Strukturen, Entwicklungen und Folgen der nationalsozialistischen Diktatur.

Die FZH wurde 1960 unter der Bezeichnung »Forschungsstelle für die Geschichte des Nationalsozialismus in Hamburg« von der Freien und Hansestadt Hamburg gegründet, 1966 um die Hamburger Bibliothek für Sozialgeschichte und Arbeiterbewegung erweitert und 1997 in eine Stiftung überführt.

Christians Verlag · Kleine Theaterstraße 9-10 · 20354 Hamburg · Tel. 040/35 60 06-0 · Fax 040/35 60 06-26

Interested in history?
Then you need this book!

The first Zionist Congress of 1897
Background, significance and current impact

Published in 1997 on the occasion of the Herzl centenary in Basel.
By Prof. Dr. Heiko Haumann
and the staff of the Faculty of History at the University of Basel.
409 pages, 190 illustrations, bound.
ISBN 3-8055 6491-0

Special offer CHF 48 (instead of CHF 68) + PP
Dieses Buch ist auch auf deutsch erhältlich.

Available from
Basel Tourismus
Schifflände 5   CH-4001 Basel
Tel. ++41 61 268 68 21   Fax ++41 61 268 68 70
e-mail incoming.sales@baseltourismus.ch

NEU 1997
Tel Aviver Jahrbuch für
Deutsche Geschichte 1997
Band XXVI:
Deutschlandbilder
Herausgegeben im Auftrag
des Instituts für Deutsche
Geschichte von Dan Diner
544 Seiten. Broschiert
DM 78,- / öS 569,- / sFr 71,-
ISBN 3-88350-488-2
ISSN 0932-8408

Wie konstituiert sich das Bild
von Deutschland? Welche
Geschichtsbilder konstruieren
andere Nationen? Wie reflektiert sich darin das Selbstbewußtsein der betreffenden
Länder? – Diesen Fragen geht
die neue Ausgabe des Jahrbuchs über Deutschlandbilder
nach.
Zu den Autoren zählen Dan
Bar-On, Alon Confino,
Helmut Dubiel, Israel
Gershoni, Astrid Gottwald,
Oded Heilbronner, Lothar
Kettenacker, Richard Knight,
Jürgen Kocka, Karl Rudolf
Korte, Klaus-Michael
Mallmann, Gilad Margalit,
Fania Oz-Salzberger, Bruno
Schoch, Zohar Shavit, Hans
Süssmuth, Susanne Terwey,
Paola Traverso, Yfraat Weiss,
Moshe Zimmermann.

**Tel Aviver Jahrbuch für
Deutsche Geschichte**
Für vorhergehende Ausgaben
des Tel Aviver Jahrbuchs für
Deutsche Geschichte bitte
Sonderprospekt anfordern.

NEU 1997
Schriftenreihe des Instituts
für Deutsche Geschichte
der Universität Tel Aviv

**Zwischen Moral und
Realpolitik**
Deutsch-israelische Beziehungen 1945-1965. Eine Dokumentensammlung von Yeshayahu A. Jelinek, Band 16
688 Seiten. Broschiert
DM 78,- / öS 569,- / sFr 71,-
ISBN 3-88350-462-9

1995 jährte sich die Aufnahme der diplomatischen Beziehungen zwischen der Bundesrepublik Deutschland und
Israel zum dreißigsten Male.
Yeshayahu A. Jelinek hat eine
umfangreiche Archiv- und
Materialsammlung zusammengestellt, die einen plastischen und faszinierenden
Einblick in die Entwicklung
dieser Beziehungen bietet.

Shlomo Na'aman
Marxismus und Zionismus
Band 17
259 Seiten. Broschiert
DM 48,- / öS 350,- / sFr 45,-
ISBN 3-88350-463-7

Dieses Buch widmet sich der
Auffassung von Judentum und
»Judenfrage« von Marx und
dem frühen Marxismus bis
zum Leninismus und der Zeit
nach dem Ersten Weltkrieg.

NEU 1997
Jacob Toury
Deutschlands Stiefkinder
Ausgewählte Aufsätze
Band 18
232 Seiten. Broschiert
DM 48,- / öS 350,- / sFr 45,-
ISBN 3-88350-464-5

Aus dem Inhalt:
  Zur Gründungsgeschichte
  des Reichsbanners
  Schwarz-Rot-Gold
  Jüdische Aspekte der
  Reichsbannergründung
– Die Dynamik der Beziehungen zwischen Juden
  und Arbeiterbewegung
  im Deutschland des
  19. Jahrhunderts
– Der Prozeß der Lokal-
  Emanzipation - Herausbildung jüdischer Bürgerrechte in deutschen
  Ortschaften
– Zur Problematik der judischen Führungsschichten
  im deutschsprachigen
  Raum 1880-1933
  Gab es ein Krisenbewußtsein unter den Juden
  während der »Guten Jahre«
  der Weimarer Republik,
  1924-1929?

Bleicher Verlag

Weilimdorfer Straße 76 · 70839 Gerlingen